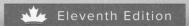
Eleventh Edition

Canadian
ORGANIZATIONAL
BEHAVIOUR

STEVEN L. McSHANE
UNIVERSITY OF NEWCASTLE (AUSTRALIA)

KEVIN TASA
YORK UNIVERSITY

SANDRA L. STEEN
UNIVERSITY OF REGINA

P9-DVN-118

Canadian Organizational Behaviour
Eleventh Edition

The Internet addresses listed in the text were accurate at the time of publication. The inclusion of a website does not indicate an endorsement by the authors or McGraw-Hill Ryerson, and McGraw-Hill Ryerson does not guarantee the accuracy of information presented at these sites.

ISBN-13: 978-1-26-032685-7
ISBN-10: 1-26-032685-3

2 3 4 5 6 7 TCP 23 22 21

Printed and bound in Canada.

Care has been taken to trace ownership of copyright material contained in this text; however, the publisher will welcome any information that enables it to rectify any reference or credit for subsequent editions.

Product Director: *Rhondda McNabb*
Portfolio Manager: *Amy Clarke-Spencley*
Marketing Manager: *Emily Park*
Content Developer: *Krisha Escobar*
Photo/Permission Editor: *Monika Schurmann*
Portfolio Associate: *Christine Albert*
Senior Supervising Editor: *Jessica Barnoski*
Copy Editor: *Sarah Fulton*
Plant Production Coordinator: *Jason Stubner*
Manufacturing Production Coordinator: *Jason Stubner*
Cover Designer: *Michelle Losier*
Cover Image: *© Abdelrahman Hassanein/Shutterstock*
Interior Design: *Michelle Losier*
Page Layout: *SPi Global*
Printer: *Transcontinental Printing Group*

About the Authors

STEVEN L. MCSHANE Steven L. McShane is conjoint professor at Newcastle Business School, University of Newcastle (Australia). He previously held the positions of professor at Simon Fraser University Business School in Canada, Winthrop Professor of Management at the University of Western Australia Graduate School of Management and Business School, and adjunct professor at Gustavson School of Business, University of Victoria (Canada). He also taught organizational behaviour in the IMBA program at the Antai College of Economics and Management at Shanghai Jiao Tong University. Early in his career, Steve taught in the business school at Queen's University in Canada. Steve has received awards for his teaching quality and innovation, and receives high ratings from students in Perth, Shanghai, Singapore, Manila, and other places where he has taught. He is also a popular visiting speaker, having given dozens of invited talks and seminars in recent years to faculty and students in the United States, China, Canada, Malaysia, India, and other countries.

Steve earned his PhD from Michigan State University, where he specialized in organizational behaviour and labour relations. He also holds a master's of industrial relations from the University of Toronto and an undergraduate degree from Queen's University. Steve is a past president of the Administrative Sciences Association of Canada and served as Director of Graduate Programs in Simon Fraser University's business faculty. He has conducted executive programs with Nokia, TÜV-SÜD, Wesfarmers Group, Main Roads WA, McGraw-Hill, ALCOA World Alumina Australia, and many other organizations.

Along with co-authoring *Canadian Organizational Behaviour,* Eleventh Edition, Steve is lead co-author of *Organizational Behavior,* Ninth Edition (2021) and *M: Organizational Behavior,* Fourth Edition (2019) in the United States, and *Organisational Behaviour: Asia Pacific,* Sixth Edition (2019) in that region. He is also co-author of editions or translations of his organizational behaviour book in China, India, Quebec, Taiwan, and Brazil. Steve has published several dozen articles and conference papers on workplace values, training transfer, organizational learning, exit-voice-loyalty, employee socialization, wrongful dismissal, media bias in business magazines, and other diverse topics.

Steve enjoys spending his leisure time hiking, swimming, body board surfing, canoeing, skiing, and travelling with his wife and two daughters.

KEVIN TASA Dr. Kevin Tasa is an associate professor of organizational behaviour at the Schulich School of Business, York University. He is also the program director for the school's master of management program. Prior to joining Schulich, he was an associate professor and director of the MBA program at the DeGroote School of Business, McMaster University. He is the recipient of the MBA Award for Teaching Excellence at both Schulich and McMaster. He is also an editorial board member of the *Journal of Organizational Behavior* and teaches courses in managerial negotiation and organizational behaviour at the masters and doctoral levels. With Roy Lewicki, Bruce Barry, and David Saunders, he co-authored *Essentials of Negotiation,* one of the most widely used negotiation textbooks in Canadian business schools.

Kevin received his doctorate in organizational behaviour from the Rotman School of Management at the University of Toronto. He also holds an MSc in health administration from the University of Toronto and a BComm from the University of Saskatchewan. His research has been published in top-tier journals such as *Academy of Management Journal, Journal of Applied Psychology, Organizational Behavior and Human Decision Processes,* and *Journal of Organizational Behavior.* Currently, his research focuses on team dynamics, such as boundary spanning and decision making under stress, as well as the situational and psychological determinants of unethical behaviour in negotiation.

Finally, Kevin frequently teaches seminars on negotiation skills and conflict management, serving as a faculty member with institutions such as the Physician Leadership Institute of the Canadian Medical Association, the Schulich Executive Education Centre, Linamar Corporation, the University of Alberta Executive Education, and the Hamilton Health Sciences Centre.

SANDRA L. STEEN Sandra L. Steen teaches in the Paul J. Hill School of Business and the Kenneth Levene Graduate School of Business at the University of Regina. Sandra also leads executive education and professional development sessions with the Centre for Management Development, Faculty of Business Administration. Sandra has an integrated education and background in both organizational behaviour and human resource management. She received her MBA from the University of Regina and has more than 25 years of leading, managing, teaching, and consulting across a wide range of organizations in the private, public, and not-for-profit sectors. Sandra teaches in the undergraduate, executive MBA, master of human resource management, master of administration in leadership, and Levene MBA - International business programs at the University of Regina. In addition to *Canadian Organizational Behaviour,* Eleventh Edition, Sandra is lead co-author with professors Raymond Noe (Ohio State University), John R. Hollenbeck (Michigan State University), Barry Gerhart (University of Wisconsin-Madison), and Patrick Wright (Cornell University) of *Human Resource Management,* Fourth Canadian Edition (2016).

Sandra is a Chartered Professional in Human Resources (CPHR) and a member of CPHR Saskatchewan. Sandra has received recognition for her teaching accomplishments, including "Inspiring Teacher Award— Business Administration." In her leisure time, Sandra enjoys time at the lake with her husband Aaron, and their children, Matt and Jess.

Brief Contents

Contents

CHAPTER 3

Perceiving Ourselves and Others in Organizations   58

CHAPTER 4

Workplace Emotions, Attitudes, and Stress   85

CHAPTER 8

Team Dynamics   199

CHAPTER 9

Communicating in Teams and Organizations   232

CHAPTER 10

Power and Influence in the Workplace 260

LEARNING OBJECTIVES 260

CHAPTER 11

Conflict and Negotiation in the Workplace 287

LEARNING OBJECTIVES 287

CHAPTER 12

Leadership in Organizational Settings 316

PART FOUR | **Organizational Processes**

CHAPTER 13

Designing Organizational Structures 340

CHAPTER 14

Organizational Culture   367

LEARNING OBJECTIVES   367

CHAPTER 15

Organizational Change   395

LEARNING OBJECTIVES   395

Preface

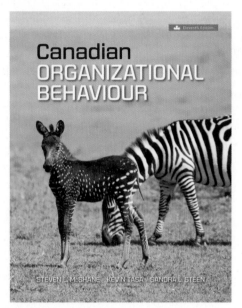

Welcome to the exciting world of organizational behaviour! Knowledge is replacing infrastructure. Social media and remote teams are transforming the way employees work together. Employees are guided more by values and self-leadership than by command-and-control management. Companies are looking for employees with emotional intelligence and effective teamwork skills, not just technical smarts.

Canadian Organizational Behaviour, Eleventh Edition, is written in the context of these emerging workplace realities. This edition explains how work–life integration is becoming an essential employee practice in the workplace; how social networks generate power and shape communication patterns; how emotions influence employee motivation, attitudes, and decisions; how self-concept is a significant determinant of individual behaviour, team cohesion, and leadership; and how adopting a global mindset has become an important employee characteristic in this increasingly interconnected world. This book also adopts the view that organizational behaviour is not just for managers; it is relevant and valuable to anyone who works in and around organizations.

Canadian and Global Focus

Canadian Organizational Behaviour, Eleventh Edition, is written by Canadians for Canadians. It includes several Canadian cases, is anchored by Canadian and global scholarship, and is filled with Canadian examples of organizational behaviour in practice. For example, you will read about how Verafin in St. John's, Newfoundland, thrives on a culture of teamwork; how Canadian financial services giant Manulife strives to be an inclusive workplace through nonconscious bias training; how Galvanize CEO Laurie Schultz has applied leadership practices to transform the Vancouver-headquartered organization into the global leader in cloud-based governance, risk management, and compliance software; how Canada Post generated feelings of inequity due to its different pay practices for urban versus rural/suburban mail carriers; and how Atlantic Lottery Corporation has become an award-winning hive of creativity by applying design thinking practices.

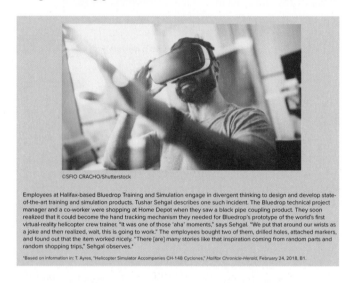

©SFIO CRACHO/Shutterstock

Employees at Halifax-based Bluedrop Training and Simulation engage in divergent thinking to design and develop state-of-the-art training and simulation products. Tushar Sehgal describes one such incident. The Bluedrop technical project manager and a co-worker were shopping at Home Depot when they saw a black pipe coupling product. They soon realized that it could become the hand tracking mechanism they needed for Bluedrop's prototype of the world's first virtual-reality helicopter crew trainer. "It was one of those 'aha' moments," says Sehgal. "We put that around our wrists as a joke and then realized, wait, this is going to work." The employees bought two of them, drilled holes, attached markers, and found out that the item worked nicely. "There [are] many stories like that inspiration coming from random parts and random shopping trips," Sehgal observes.

*Based on information in: T. Ayres, "Helicopter Simulator Accompanies CH-148 Cyclones," Halifax Chronicle-Herald, February 24, 2018, B1.

Along with its Canadian focus, this book has been written from the view that globalization has a profound influence on the workplace. We continue this global focus by discussing several international and cross-cultural issues throughout the book. Furthermore, every chapter includes truly global examples, not just how companies from North America operate in other parts of the world.

For example, we describe how smiling at customers tends to create more emotional labour in people from Russia than from Canada; how the witty "You People!" commercial produced by South African restaurant chain Nando's pokes fun at our tendency to stereotype others; how ING Bank and other European firms have introduced Obeya rooms to encourage more team-oriented decision making; how communication has been a key ingredient for successful organizational change at EE, the United Kingdom's largest mobile network; and how Emsisoft and Automattic succeed as distributed organizations with staff who work completely remotely around the world.

Linking Theory with Reality

Every chapter of *Canadian Organizational Behaviour,* Eleventh Edition, is filled with examples to make OB knowledge more meaningful and to illuminate the relevance and excitement of this field. These stories about real people and organizations translate academic theories into useful knowledge and real-life applications. For example, we describe how Canada's Jeremy Gutsche has built his expert power and personal brand as one of the world's leading trend spotters; how Uber executives are replacing the transportation network firm's dysfunctional culture with one that is more productive and ethical; how medical devices firm Stryker improves employee motivation and performance through strengths-based coaching; how a new organizational structure helped Sobeys (Canada's second-largest food retailer) recover and ultimately prosper following a disastrous acquisition; and how IKEA focuses on personal values when hiring job applicants around the world. This edition also relates the COVID-19 pandemic to several OB concepts and practices.

Galvanize CEO Laurie Schultz is recognized as one of Canada's best business leaders due to her vision, role modelling, transparent communication, and personalized support for employees at the Vancouver-based GRC software company.

Photo by Good Side Photo and provided by the Greater Vancouver Board of Trade

These case studies and anecdotes appear in many forms. Every chapter of *Canadian Organizational Behaviour,* Eleventh Edition, is filled with captioned photos and in-text examples about work life. Lengthier stories appear in Global Connections, which "connect" OB concepts with real organizational incidents and situations around the world. Case studies in each chapter as well as video case studies associated with this book connect OB concepts to emerging workplace realities. These anecdotes and detailed descriptions discuss large and small organizations in a wide range of industries across Canada and globally.

Contemporary Theory Foundation

Vivid real-world examples and practices are valuable only if they are connected to good theory. *Canadian Organizational Behaviour* has developed a reputation for its solid foundation of contemporary and classic research and writing. This evidence-based foundation is apparent from the amount and quality of literature cited in each chapter, including dozens of articles, books, and other sources. This results in what we believe is the most up-to-date organizational behaviour textbook available. These references also reveal that we reach out to marketing, information management, human resource management, and other business disciplines for new ideas. This book is rigorously focused on information that readers value, namely OB knowledge and practices. Consequently, with a few classic exceptions, we avoid writing a "who's-who" book; most scholars are named in the references, not in the main text.

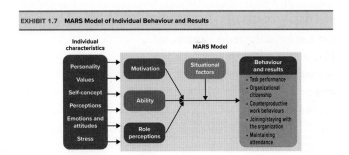
EXHIBIT 1.7   MARS Model of Individual Behaviour and Results

One of the driving forces for writing *Canadian Organizational Behaviour* was to provide a more responsive conduit for emerging OB knowledge to reach students, practitioners, and fellow scholars. To its credit, *Canadian Organizational Behaviour* is apparently the first major OB book to discuss the full self-concept model (not just core self-evaluation), workplace emotions, social identity theory, global mindset, four-drive theory, predictors of moral intensity, specific elements of social networks, appreciative inquiry, affective events theory (but without the jargon), somatic marker hypothesis (also without the jargon), remote teams, Schwartz's values model, employee engagement, learning orientation, social and information processing characteristics of job design, and several other groundbreaking topics. This edition continues this leadership by introducing the latest knowledge on design thinking, the shifting trends in digital communication in organizations, five strategies for regulating emotions, key cultural values of Indigenous Canadians, several caveats when applying the five-factor personality model, the ethic of care, psychological safety in team decision making and conflict management, four criteria for selecting the preferred communication channel, and reducing dysfunctional conflict through intergroup mirroring.

Organizational Behaviour Knowledge for Everyone

Another distinctive feature of *Canadian Organizational Behaviour,* Eleventh Edition is that it is written for everyone in organizations, not just managers. The philosophy of this book is that everyone who works in and around organizations needs to understand and make use of organizational behaviour knowledge. People throughout the organization—systems analysts, production employees, accounting professionals, and others—are taking on more responsibilities as companies remove layers of management and give the rest of us more autonomy and accountability for our work outcomes. This book helps everyone to make sense of organizational behaviour, and provides the conceptual tools to work more effectively in the workplace.

Active Learning and Critical Thinking Support

We teach organizational behaviour, so we understand how important it is to use a textbook that offers deep support for active learning and critical thinking. Business school accreditation associations also emphasize the importance of the learning experience, which further reinforces our attention on classroom activities. *Canadian Organizational Behaviour,* Eleventh Edition, includes more than two dozen case studies in various forms and levels of complexity. It offers four dozen self-assessments, most of which have been empirically tested and validated.

Student critical thinking is further aided with a Debating Point in each chapter. This feature demonstrates that seemingly obvious OB knowledge may be contested by contrary evidence and logical counterarguments. Debating Point boxes encourage students to continuously seek out divergent viewpoints and evidence rather than unquestioningly accept the validity of existing theories and practices.

Canadian Organizational Behaviour, Eleventh Edition, is also a rich resource for in-class activities, such as the Kumquat Conflict Role Play, Personal Values Exercise, Employee Involvement Cases, Deciphering the (Social) Network, World Café on the Emerging Workplace, Ethics Dilemma Vignettes, and the Cross-Cultural Communication Game.

Debating Point: CAN PEOPLE AVOID RELATIONSHIP CONFLICT DURING DISAGREEMENTS?

One of the core ideas in conflict theory is that people can disagree with each other regarding an issue (task conflict) without experiencing negative emotions toward each other (relationship conflict). The most popular book on negotiation makes this point by stating that the parties need to "separate the people from the problem." It advises that the participants need to view themselves as "working side by side, attacking the problem, not each other."

Scholars do recognize that separating task from relationship conflict isn't easy, but they claim it is possible. People with well-developed emotional intelligence can control negative emotional reactions (anger, frustration, hurt, etc.) and can reframe the conflict as a constructive event rather than as a personal attack. Research also suggests that relationship conflict is less likely to occur when the parties understand each other's views, such as in high-performing teams. Psychological safety norms have also been identified as a way to avoid relationship conflict while engaging in task conflict.

The ability to avoid relationship conflict during task conflict sounds promising in theory yet, in practice, it may be a bridge too far. Instead, some degree of relationship conflict may be inevitable. One of the most basic problems is that employees immediately and automatically experience negative emotions when they become aware that co-workers or supervisors disagree with their ideas or behaviour.

Negative emotions aren't just attributed to information in the opposing message; they are also attributed to the source of that message. This occurs because we naturally try to make sense of disruptive conditions, and this includes forming adverse interpretations about why a co-worker has disagreed with our proposal or behaviour. Consequently, relationship conflict seems to form as soon as we become aware that our ideas or actions are being challenged.

Relationship conflict may also be unavoidable because it disrupts the current or expected pattern of behaviour, which produces negative emotions toward those who caused that disruption. People have a natural desire to maintain the status quo. Even those who propose change want to see their ideas flow predictably through to the future without opposition. This effect occurs because people want to believe they control their situation, whereas disagreement reduces perceived control and predictability in the work environment.

Relationship conflict may also be inevitable in any disagreement because all communication has both a relational and substantive function. This means that when people interact with each other, they not only transmit and receive information (substantive), but also reinforce or strain the fabric of their relationship. Communication is important for one's relatedness needs, so a message that challenges another viewpoint (substantive) also seems to challenge the relationship.

* R. Fisher and W. Ury, *Getting to Yes: Negotiating an Agreement without Giving In* (Random House, 2012). Although few believe task and relationship conflict can be completely separated (Fisher and Ury included), several scholars have developed activities that emphasize the possibility of this separation. For example, see: L. Boyd, M. Gupta, and F. Kuzmits, "The Evaporating Cloud: A Tool for Resolving Workplace Conflict," *International Journal of Conflict Management* 22 (2011): 394–412; C.A. Blair and D.E. Desplaces, "Conflict Management through the Negotiations Canvas: Getting Participants to Understand," *Conflict Resolution Quarterly* 36 (2018): 39–51.
** "For a summary of these views, see: T.A. O'Neill et al., "The Structure and Function of Team Conflict State Profiles," *Journal of Management* 44 (2018): 811–36.
*** M.D. Seery et al., "Alone against the Group: A Unanimously Disagreeing Group Leads to Conformity, but Cardiovascular Threat Depends on One's Goals," *Psychophysiology* 53 (2016): 1263–71; A. Hagemeister and J. Volmer, "Do Social Conflicts at Work Affect Employees' Job Satisfaction? The Moderating Role of Emotion Regulation," *International Journal of Conflict Management* 29 (2017): 213–35.
**** W. Samuelson and R. Zeckhauser, "Status Quo Bias in Decision Making," *Journal of Risk and Uncertainty* 1 (1988): 7–59; D. Proudfoot and A.C. Kay, "System Justification in Organizational Contexts: How a Motivated Preference for the Status Quo Can Affect Organizational Attitudes and Behaviors," *Research in Organizational Behavior* 34 (2014): 173–87; D. De Clercq and I. Belausteguigoitia, "Overcoming the Dark Side of Task Conflict: Buffering Roles of Transformational Leadership, Tenacity, and Passion for Work," *European Management Journal* 35 (2017): 78–90.
***** A.C. Mooney, P.J. Holahan, and A.C. Amason, "Don't Take It Personally: Exploring Cognitive Conflict as a Mediator of Affective Conflict," *Journal of Management Studies* 44 (2007): 733–58; S.J. Beck and J. Keyton, "Perceiving Strategic Meeting Interaction," *Small Group Research* 40 (2009): 223–46; L.R. Weingart et al., "The Directness and Oppositional Intensity of Conflict Expression," *Academy of Management Review* 40 (2015): 235–62.

Critical Thinking Questions

1. Superb Consultants has submitted a proposal to analyze your organization's culture. The proposal states that Superb has developed a revolutionary new survey to tap the company's true culture. The survey takes just 10 minutes to complete, and the consultants say results can be based on a small sample of employees. Discuss the merits and limitations of this proposal.

2. All members of the executive team at Claybuild, a national manufacturer of bricks and related building materials, strongly believe that quality control and efficiency are the two cornerstones of the company's future success. Every Claybuild executive meeting begins by discussing ways to improve product quality and operate more efficiently in the manufacturing process, distribution system, and administrative processes. The company's website proudly describes its dedication to quality and efficiency. The CEO has given speeches to several retail client events on Claybuild's quality–efficiency culture. However, an industry expert suggests that quality and efficiency represent Claybuild's espoused culture, but not so much its enacted culture. What does the industry expert mean by this, and what evidence might suggest that their opinion is correct?

3. The CEO of a manufacturing firm wants everyone to support the organization's dominant culture of lean efficiency and hard work. The CEO has introduced a new reward system to reinforce this culture and personally interviews all professional and managerial applicants to ensure that they bring similar values to the organization. Some employees who criticized these values had their careers sidelined until they left. Two midlevel managers were fired for supporting contrary values, such as work–life integration. Based on your knowledge of organizational subcultures, what are the potential problems the CEO is creating?

Changes to the Eleventh Edition

Canadian Organizational Behaviour, Eleventh Edition, has received more updating and revision than any previous edition of this book. In fact, the word "renewal" comes to mind when viewing the changes in some chapters. These improvements have occurred thanks to reviews from organizational behaviour instructors across several countries, along with our regular practice of scanning the diverse literature for new evidence-based information. The most substantial changes have occurred in Chapter 1 (Introduction to the Field of Organizational Behaviour), Chapter 2 (Individual Differences: Personality and Values), Chapter 5 (Foundations of Employee Motivation), Chapter 8 (Team Dynamics), Chapter 9 (Communicating in Teams and Organizations), and Chapter 11 (Conflict and Negotiation in the Workplace).

Together with dozens of conceptual improvements, this edition replaces most examples with new real-world stories that satisfy our criteria of being relevant, recent, and interesting. Fourteen of the fifteen chapter-opening case studies are new. Most of the captioned photos and Global Connections features are new or updated. We have also added new content on Indigenous Canadians regarding cultural values, nonconscious bias, communication styles, and other OB topics. This edition has dozens of new in-text examples as well as several new case studies and class activities to support the active learning process. Most OB by the Numbers features have also been updated or replaced.

Here are the main conceptual improvements in *Canadian Organizational Behaviour,* Eleventh Edition:

- *Chapter 1: Introduction to the Field of Organizational Behaviour*—Almost every section of this chapter has been revised, updated, or replaced. This edition has a new section on the emerging workplace landscape, which includes new content on work–life integration, the inclusive workplace, and employment relationships. It also significantly updates the topic of remote work (the narrower topic of telecommuting was covered in previous editions). The section on the importance of organizational behaviour now more fully explains why OB is important for students. It also succinctly introduces key organizational effectiveness concepts to explain why OB is vital for organizations. The section on OB anchors now includes a fifth anchor on OB's practical orientation. This chapter also has a stronger micro-OB focus by including the MARS Model of individual behaviour and the five types of individual behaviour (previously in Chapter 2).

- *Chapter 2: Individual Differences: Personality and Values*—Along with its slightly revised title, this edition brings a number of noticeable updates and changes to the chapter. It now has a full discussion about the dark triad (Machiavellianism, narcissism, and psychopathy) and its relevance to organizational behaviour. This edition also has a new separate discussion regarding four caveats when applying the five-factor model of personality in organizations. Also included in this edition is a fourth ethical principle: the ethic of care. We have also moved the topics of MARS Model and types of individual behaviour from this chapter to Chapter 1.

- *Chapter 3: Perceiving Ourselves and Others in Organizations*—This book pioneered the full model of self-concept and its relevance to organizational behaviour. This edition further refines that discussion, particularly in explaining how people develop self-concept clarity and how self-concept characteristics affect behaviour and performance. This chapter also updates writing on perceptual organization and interpretation, intentional discrimination, and improving self-awareness of perceptual biases.

- *Chapter 4: Workplace Emotions, Attitudes, and Stress*—This was the first OB book to fully incorporate the concept of emotions in organizational behaviour across various topics (perceptions, attitudes, motivation, decisions, etc.). This edition further develops this topic by revising the section on managing emotions and adding recent knowledge about the five strategies that people use to regulate their emotions. This edition also updates the topic of organizational commitment, incorporates normative commitment, and has minor rewriting on managing workplace stress.

- *Chapter 5: Foundations of Employee Motivation*—This edition significantly revises and updates the topics of procedural and interactional justice, including a new exhibit listing the specific rules of these two forms of organizational justice. The characteristics of effective feedback are discussed more fully, including the addition of an exhibit that defines and illustrates each characteristic. The section on drive-based motivation theories has been reorganized to place more emphasis on the recent four-drive theory. This edition also revises the chapter's opening topic on the meaning of motivation and engagement.

- *Chapter 6: Applied Performance Practices*—Along with replacing most examples and updating references, this chapter has a number of subtle changes, notably on motivational job design practices, financial reward practices, and psychological empowerment. It also has a new Debating Point feature.

- *Chapter 7: Decision Making and Creativity*—This chapter has been substantially revised and updated in several ways. It presents the emerging topic of design thinking as a creative decision-making practice, including its associated principles and activities. Another area that has been substantially rewritten is the topic of problems with information processing when choosing alternatives. This edition has added a visual example illustrating how valences and probabilities are applied in rational choice decision making. Other noticeable revisions involve problems with maximization and evaluating decision outcomes more effectively.

- *Chapter 8: Team Dynamics*—We have revised, clarified, updated, and generally improved several sections of this chapter. The entire team effectiveness model has been streamlined and most of the team processes section has been reorganized and rewritten. That section now has a more complete and updated discussion of team mental models as well as updated content on team norms and team roles. This edition also has more complete discussion than in previous editions on psychological safety as a factor in effective team decision making. Other topics that benefited from minor rewriting and updating include how teams motivate employees, how to minimize social loafing, characteristics of remote (virtual) teams, and the three factors that distinguish types of teams.

- *Chapter 9: Communicating in Teams and Organizations*—This edition has substantially rewritten the section on choosing the best communication channel. This topic now fully discusses four key factors (synchronicity, social presence, social acceptance, and media richness), along with their associated contingencies to communication channel selection. We have also substantially updated the topic of digital communication, including a new exhibit on the rapidly changing popularity of various digital communication channels, along with associated discussion about why these changes are occurring. Social media communication is also more fully defined and discussed.

- *Chapter 10: Power and Influence in the Workplace*—The topic of nonsubstitutability as a contingency of power has been rewritten, and the associated topic of personal brand is discussed more fully. We more fully discuss the troubling issue of deference to power in organizations. The definition of organizational politics is explained in more detail, particularly with reference to recent writing about "positive politics." Other topics on organizational politics—individual differences and minimizing politics—have been rewritten.

- *Chapter 11: Conflict and Negotiation in the Workplace*—This edition significantly revises most sections of this chapter. The topic of task and relationship conflict has been revised for greater clarity. That section also significantly updates strategies to minimize relationship conflict during task conflict, including the role of psychological safety. A new Debating Point feature has also been added around that topic. The topic of conflict-handling contingencies has been revised, and now includes the factor of maintaining harmony. You will also find noticeable updates on structural ways to manage conflict, particularly on reducing differentiation and on improving communication and mutual understanding. The section on negotiation has also been significantly revised and streamlined. It now provides better clarity on the distributive versus integrative approach to negotiations, the importance of setting goals and understanding needs, and the process of information gathering. The negotiation setting also now includes information about settings and audiences as well as recent knowledge about gender and negotiation.

- *Chapter 12: Leadership in Organizational Settings*—The most significant change in this chapter is that it reorganizes and revises the managerial leadership section, including the removal of a couple of older topics. The discussion about transformational leadership and charisma has been rewritten. Other refinements and updates are found on the strategic vision of transformational leadership, servant leadership, and leadership substitutes theory (including a new exhibit).

- *Chapter 13: Designing Organizational Structures*—This edition updates discussion on span of control. The mechanistic-organic structures exhibit has been revised for better clarity and style. The types of divisional structure exhibit has also been revised with new company examples. This edition also includes a new Debating Point feature.

- *Chapter 14: Organizational Culture*—In this edition, several aspects of the organizational socialization section have been revised, such as discussion on the inherent conflicts in pre-employment socialization and the issue of whether socialization changes employee values or mostly communicates values-consistent behaviour. This chapter has minor revisions on the meaning of a strong organizational culture, organizational culture and business ethics, and merging organizational cultures.

- *Chapter 15: Organizational Change*—This chapter has relatively minor changes from the previous edition. It updates and revises some writing on appreciative inquiry and on the dynamics of unfreezing, changing, and refreezing change.

Supporting the OB Learning Experience

The changes described above refer only to the conceptual content in the main body of this book. *Canadian Organizational Behaviour,* Eleventh Edition, also has improved technology supplements, cases, Team Exercises, and Self-Assessments.

Team Exercise:
TEAM TOWER POWER

Purpose This exercise is designed to help you understand team roles, team development, and other issues in the development and maintenance of effective teams.

Materials The instructor will provide enough LEGO® pieces or similar materials for each team to complete the assigned task. All teams should have identical (or very similar) amounts and types of pieces. The instructor will need a measuring tape and stopwatch. Students may use writing materials during the design stage (see Instructions). The instructor will distribute a "Team Objectives Sheet" and "Tower Specifications Effectiveness Sheet" to all teams.

Instructions The instructor will divide the class into teams. Depending on class size and space availability, teams may have between four and seven members, but all should be approximately equal size.

Each team has 20 minutes to design a tower that uses only the materials provided, is freestanding, and provides an optimal return on investment. Team members may wish to draw their tower on paper or a flip chart to facilitate the tower's design. Teams are free to practise building their tower during this stage. Preferably, each team will have a secluded space so

CHAPTER CASES AND ADDITIONAL CASES

Every chapter includes at least one short case that challenges students to diagnose issues and apply ideas from that chapter. Eleven additional cases appear at the end of the book.

EXPERIENTIAL EXERCISES AND SELF-ASSESSMENTS

Experiential exercises and self-assessments represent an important part of active learning. *Canadian Organizational Behaviour,* Eleventh Edition, facilitates this important learning process by offering one or more team or class exercises in every chapter. Self-assessments personalize the meaning of several organizational behaviour concepts, and this edition features four dozen of them in Connect, with automated scoring and detailed feedback. Small call-out icons in every chapter help students locate text content most relevant to each of these excellent resources. In addition, the last page of each chapter has a convenient table that briefly describes the self-assessments in Connect associated with that chapter.

Case Study:
DOGGED BY THE WRONG PROBLEM

by Steven L. McShane, University of Newcastle (Australia)

More than 3 million dogs enter animal shelters each year in the United States, and almost one-third of these have been surrendered by their owners. Until recently, animal shelter employees assumed that the owners didn't want their pets anymore, so they focused their resources on ways to get the surrendered dogs re-adopted with new owners.

Now, animal shelters recognize that they were focused on the wrong problem to some extent. Most owners of surrendered dogs love their pets but believe they are unable to keep them due to financial or family difficulties. "Owner surrenders are not a people problem," explains Lori Weise, founder of Downtown Dog Rescue in Los Angeles. "By and large, they are a poverty problem. These families love their dogs as much as we do, but they are also exceptionally poor." Even when owners surrender their dog due to the pet's behaviour, animal shelter staff have learned that the problem is often the owners' lack of basic training to improve their pet's behaviour.

These discoveries have been a wake-up call for animal shelters. Along with finding new homes for surrendered dogs, shelters now also focus on strategies that enable own-

Inspired by the work of Downtown Dog Rescue in Los Angeles, ACC now takes a dramatically different approach to dog surrenders. Instead of answering a few questions asked by busy front desk staff, owners who intend to surrender their dogs are now greeted by trained ACC admission counsellors with impeccable people skills. In a private office, these counsellors listen to the owner's story about why they want or need to surrender their dog. These counsellors are trained by licensed social workers to maintain a nonjudgemental attitude toward the owners and to handle difficult situations. "Once that person (the pet owner) doesn't feel like they're going to be judged in that moment, they might open up and tell you the real situation," says Simpson.

Based on the information from these conversations, ACC counsellors direct some owners to support groups that can provide assistance, such as financial support or temporary lodging for the dog. In other situations, the owners are invited to attend brief training programs where they receive instruction on how to improve the pet's behaviour. The conversations also help counsellors determine which pets are better off with new owners. As new situations arise, ACC staff have found increasingly

Additional Cases

CASE 1   **ARCTIC MINING CONSULTANTS**
CASE 2   **BRIDGING THE TWO WORLDS: THE ORGANIZATIONAL DILEMMA**
CASE 3   **KEEPING SUZANNE CHALMERS**
CASE 4   **NORTHWEST CANADIAN FOREST PRODUCTS LIMITED (REVISED)**
CASE 5   **SIMMONS LABORATORIES**
CASE 6   **TAMARACK INDUSTRIES**
CASE 7   **THE OUTSTANDING FACULTY AWARD**
CASE 8   **THE REGENCY GRAND HOTEL**
CASE 9   **THE SHIPPING INDUSTRY ACCOUNTING TEAM**
CASE 10   **VERBERG KANSEN N.V.**
CASE 11   **VÊTEMENTS LTÉE**

KEY TERMS AND LEARNING OBJECTIVES

While minimizing unnecessary jargon, *Canadian Organizational Behaviour* assists the learning process by spotlighting key terms and providing brief definitions for them. Also look for the learning objectives presented at the beginning of each chapter and linked to chapter content by numbered icons. An excellent study tool!

Key Terms

affective organizational commitment	general adaptation syndrome
attitudes	job satisfaction
cognitive dissonance	norm of reciprocity
continuance commitment	service profit chain model
emotional intelligence (EI)	stress
emotional labour	stressors
emotions	trust
exit-voice-loyalty-neglect (EVLN) model	work–life integration

Class Exercise:
EMPLOYEE INVOLVEMENT INCIDENTS

Purpose This exercise is designed to help you understand the contingencies of employee involvement.

Instructions (Small or Large Class) Four scenarios are presented in this exercise. Assume you are the manager or person in charge. For each scenario, identify the preferred level of employee involvement from one of the five levels described below. For each scenario, identify and justify what factors led you to choose this level of employee involvement rather than the others. Also, be prepared to discuss what problems might occur with less or more involvement in this case (where possible).

1. *Decide alone.* Use your personal knowledge and insight to complete the entire decision process without conferring with anyone else.

department employs about 300 people who are responsible for constructing and maintaining water lines throughout the city. Although you have an engineering background, the work is complex and involves several professions and trades. Even the TD group's first line supervisors (one or two levels below you in the hierarchy) are not fully knowledgeable of all aspects of the business.

You believe that most employees support or at least accept the city's recent mandate to reduce costs (called the "productivity dividend initiative"). The city leaders have stated that this initiative will not result in any layoffs this year. However, the labour union representing most nonmanagement staff in the water agency (including most of your employees) is concerned that the productivity dividend initiative will reduce employment numbers over time and increase employee

Self-Assessments for Chapter 3

SELF-ASSESSMENT NAME	DESCRIPTION
How much does work define your self-concept?	Work is part of our lives. Some people view work as central to their identity as individuals, whereas others consider work to be secondary to other life interests. This self-assessment estimates the extent to which work is central to your self-concept.
How much general self-efficacy do you have?	Self-efficacy refers to a person's belief that they have the ability, motivation, and resources to complete a task successfully. Although self-efficacy is often situation-specific, people also develop a more general self-efficacy if they perform tasks in a variety of situations. This self-assessment estimates your general self-efficacy.
What is your locus of control?	Locus of control is one component of self-evaluation, which is part of an individual's self-concept. It is a person's general belief about the amount of control they have over life events. This self-assessment estimates the extent to which you have an internal or external locus-of-control.
How much perceptual structure do you need?	Some people have a greater need than do others to quickly or completely "make sense" of things around them. This personal need for perceptual structure relates to selective attention as well as perceptual organization and interpretation. This self-assessment estimates your personal need for perceptual structure.
How strong is your perspective taking (cognitive empathy)?	Empathy refers to a person's understanding of and sensitivity to the feelings, thoughts, and situation of others. The "understanding" part of empathy is called perspective taking or cognitive empathy. It refers to a rational understanding of another person's circumstances. This self-assessment estimates how well you cognitively understand another person's situational and individual circumstances.
How strong is your emotional empathy?	Empathy refers to a person's understanding of and sensitivity to the feelings, thoughts, and situation of others. The "sensitivity" part of empathy is called emotional empathy. It refers to experiencing the feelings of the other person. This self-assessment estimates how well you are able to experience the emotions or feelings of another person.

LEARNING OBJECTIVES

After reading this chapter, you should be able to:

LO1 Define employee motivation and engagement.

LO2 Explain how drives and emotions influence employee motivation.

LO3 Discuss the employee motivation implications of four-drive theory, Maslow's needs hierarchy, intrinsic and extrinsic motivation, and learned needs theory.

LO4 Discuss the expectancy theory model, including its practical implications.

LO5 Outline organizational behaviour modification (OB Mod) and social cognitive theory, and explain their relevance to employee motivation.

LO6 Describe the characteristics of effective goal setting and feedback.

LO7 Explain how equity theory, procedural justice, and interactional justice influence employee motivation.

Teaching and Learning Tools

AWARD-WINNING TECHNOLOGY

McGraw Hill Connect® is an award-winning digital teaching and learning solution that empowers students to achieve better outcomes and enables instructors to improve efficiency with course management. Within Connect, students have access to SmartBook®, McGraw Hill's adaptive learning and reading resource. SmartBook prompts students with questions based on the material they are studying. By assessing individual answers, SmartBook learns what each student knows and identifies which topics they need to practise, giving each student a personalized learning experience and path to success.

Connect's key features include analytics and reporting, simple assignment management, smart grading, the opportunity to post your own resources, and the Connect Instructor Library, a repository for additional resources to improve student engagement in and out of the classroom.

Instructor resources for *Canadian Organizational Behaviour,* Eleventh Edition:

- Instructor's Manual
- Test Bank
- Video Cases
- Microsoft® PowerPoint® Presentations
- Manager's Hot Seat Videos

INSTRUCTOR RESOURCES

McShane Connect is a one-stop shop for instructor resources, including:

Instructor's Manual: Written by the book's authors, the Instructor's Manual supports instructors' needs in many ways. Each chapter includes the learning objectives, glossary of key terms, a chapter synopsis, complete lecture outline, and solutions to the end-of-chapter discussion questions. It also includes teaching notes for the chapter case(s), team and class exercises, and self-assessments. The Instructor's Manual also includes teaching notes for the end-of-text cases.

Computerized Test Bank: Updated by Michael Halinski of Ryerson University, this flexible and easy-to-use electronic testing program allows instructors to create tests from book-specific items. The Test Bank contains a broad selection of multiple choice, true/false, and essay questions and instructors may add their own questions as well. Multiple versions of the test can be created and printed.

Video Cases: The accompanying video cases are available to instructors through video streaming in Connect. Teaching notes can be found in the Instructor's Resource section in Connect.

PowerPoint® Presentations: Written by the text authors, these robust presentations offer high-quality visuals to bring key OB concepts to life.

Manager's Hot Seat Videos: This resource allows students to watch real managers apply their years of experience to management and organizational behaviour issues. Students assume the role of the manager as they watch the video and then answer multiple-choice questions following the segment. The Manager's Hot Seat Videos are ideal for group or classroom discussions.

Writing Assignments: The Writing Assignment tool delivers a learning experience to help students improve their written communication skills and conceptual understanding. As an instructor you can assign, monitor, grade, and provide feedback on writing more efficiently and effectively.

Test Builder

Available within Connect, Test Builder is a cloud-based tool that enables instructors to format tests that can be printed or administered within a Learning Management System. Test Builder offers a modern, streamlined interface for easy content configuration that matches course needs, without requiring a download.

Test Builder allows you to:

- access all test bank content from a particular title
- easily pinpoint the most relevant content through robust filtering options
- manipulate the order of questions or scramble questions and/or answers

- pin questions to a specific location within a test
- choose the layout and spacing
- add instructions and configure default settings

Test Builder provides a secure interface for better protection of content and allows for just-in-time updates to flow directly into assessments.

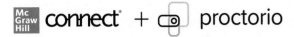

Remote Proctoring & Browser-Locking Capabilities
New remote proctoring and browser-locking capabilities, hosted by Proctorio within Connect, provide control of the assessment environment by enabling security options and verifying the identity of the student.

Seamlessly integrated within Connect, these services allow instructors to control students' assessment experience by restricting browser activity, recording students' activity, and verifying students are doing their own work.

Instant and detailed reporting gives instructors an at-a-glance view of potential academic integrity concerns, thereby avoiding personal bias and supporting evidence-based claims.

Acknowledgements

Organizational behaviour is a fascinating subject. It is also incredibly relevant and valuable, which becomes apparent while developing a world-class book such as *Canadian Organizational Behaviour,* Eleventh Edition. Throughout this project, we witnessed the power of teamwork, the excitement of creative thinking, and the motivational force of the vision that we collectively held as our aspiration. The tight coordination and innovative synergy was evident throughout this venture. Our teamwork is even more amazing when you consider that most of us in this project are scattered throughout Canada, and the lead co-author (Steve) spends most of his time on the other side of the planet!

Portfolio Manager Amy Clarke-Spencley led the development of *Canadian Organizational Behaviour* with unwavering enthusiasm and foresight. Content Developer Krisha Escobar orchestrated the daily process with superhuman skill and determination, which is particularly important given the magnitude of this revision, the multiple authors, the pressing deadlines, and the 24-hour time zones in which we operated. Photo researcher and permissions editor Monika Schurmann wowed us with her ability and persistence in tracking down the images and rights that we sought out. Michelle Losier created a refreshing book design that elegantly incorporated the writing, exhibits, examples, photos, and many other resources that we pack into this volume. We also extend our thanks to Sarah Fulton for superb copy editing, Supervising Editor, Jessica Barnoski, for leading the production process like a precision timepiece, and Emily Park, for her excellent marketing and sales development work. Thanks to you all. This has been a truly wonderful journey!

Several dozen instructors around the world reviewed parts or all of *Canadian Organizational Behaviour,* Eleventh Edition, or related editions in the United States, Asia Pacific region, and elsewhere since the previous Canadian edition. Their compliments were energizing, and their suggestions significantly improved the final product.

Steve is forever grateful to his students over the years at Simon Fraser University, University of Western Australia, the IMBA program at Shanghai Jiao Tong University, and elsewhere for sharing their learning and work experiences in his organizational behaviour classes. These interactions have helped the development of this textbook in Canada, the United States, and the Asia-Pacific region. Steve is honoured to work with Kevin Tasa and Sandra Steen on *Canadian Organizational Behaviour,* as well as with his other co-authors, including Mary Ann von Glinow (Florida International University) in the two editions in the United States, and Mara Olekalns (University of Melbourne), Alex Newman (Deakin University), and Angela Martin (University of Tasmania) on the Asia-Pacific edition. He also thanks the co-authors of other translations and adaptations. Most of all, Steve is forever indebted to his wife, Donna McClement, and to their wonderful daughters, Bryton and Madison. Their love and support give special meaning to Steve's life.

Effective. Efficient. Easy to Use.

McGraw Hill Connect is an award-winning digital teaching and learning solution that empowers students to achieve better outcomes and enables instructors to improve course-management efficiency.

Personalized & Adaptive Learning

Connect's integrated SmartBook helps students study more efficiently, highlighting where in the text to focus and asking review questions to give each student a personalized learning experience and path to success.

High-Quality Course Material

Our trusted solutions are designed to help students actively engage in course content and develop critical higher-level thinking skills, while offering you the flexibility to tailor your course to meet your needs.

Analytics & Reporting

Monitor progress and improve focus with Connect's visual and actionable dashboards. Reporting features empower instructors and students with real-time performance analytics.

Seamless Integration

Link your Learning Management System with Connect for single sign-on and gradebook synchronization, with all-in-one ease for you and your students.

Impact of Connect on Pass Rates

72.5%
Without Connect

85.2%
With Connect

SMARTBOOK®

NEW SmartBook 2.0 builds on our market-leading adaptive technology with enhanced capabilities and a streamlined interface that deliver a more usable, accessible, and mobile learning experience for both students and instructors.

Available on mobile smart devices – with both online and offline access – the ReadAnywhere app lets students study anywhere, anytime.

SUPPORT AT EVERY STEP

McGraw Hill ensures you are supported every step of the way. From course design and set up, to instructor training, LMS integration and ongoing support, your Digital Success Consultant is there to make your course as effective as possible.

Learn more about Connect at mheducation.ca

PART ONE | Introduction

CHAPTER 1

Introduction to the Field of Organizational Behaviour

LEARNING OBJECTIVES

After reading this chapter, you should be able to:

LO1 Define organizational behaviour and organizations.

LO2 Explain why organizational behaviour knowledge is important for you and for organizations.

LO3 Describe the anchors on which organizational behaviour knowledge is based.

LO4 Summarize the workplace trends of diversity and the inclusive workplace, work–life integration, remote work, and emerging employment relationships.

LO5 Describe the four factors that directly influence individual behaviour and performance.

LO6 Summarize the five types of individual behaviour in organizations.

BlueCat Networks has developed a global reputation for its innovative, security-focused network technology. It is recognized annually as one of the best places to work in Canada and recently won the Canadian HR award for having the best organizational culture.

With global headquarters nestled in a forested North York setting, BlueCat provides subsidized meals, town hall meetings with the executive team, work-life integration initiatives (such as its award-winning annual Wellness Week), ongoing training and development, a relatively flat organizational structure, and a strong culture. "Treating our employees well has been core to our business philosophy," says CEO Michael Harris. "Providing a nurturing workplace dates back to the very beginning of BlueCat."

Toronto-based BlueCat Networks has become a highly successful technology company by supporting teamwork and collaboration, a strong organizational culture, effective decision making and creativity, and many other organizational behaviour practices.
©BlueCat Networks

BlueCat's 400 employees participated in the process of identifying the tech firm's five core values. "Our winning culture is our secret sauce," says Cheryl Kerrigan, BlueCat's VP, People. "It differentiates us with our customers, it guides who we hire, who we promote and how we lead." She adds that these values are not just words on a wall. "We really hold each other to account by making sure that we are living the five values."

Effective decision making is central to BlueCat 's success. As one employee points out: "What we do is solve problems in some of the most cutting-edge parts of our technology space." Risk taking is an important part of creativity, so BlueCat supports people who try out new ideas, even if they don't always work. "I think it's important to recognize people for taking risks," says Harris. "And the most obvious way of doing that is not to punish people who take risks and make mistakes."

BlueCat employees also speak proudly about the company's emphasis on teamwork and inter-departmental collaboration. "There are very few silos at BlueCat," says chief financial officer Stephen Devito. "Everybody likes to work together, and I think together we' re much stronger than we are as an individual." Harris echoes this view. "[BlueCat] people are working together and going out of their way to work together," he observes.[1]

Welcome to the Field of Organizational Behaviour!

Teamwork and collaboration. Strong organizational culture. Effective decision making and creativity. These are just a few of the organizational behaviour topics and practices that have made BlueCat Networks a successful organization in a highly competitive and dynamic environment. In every sector of the economy, organizations need to employ skilled and motivated people who can be creative, work in teams, and maintain a healthy lifestyle. They need leaders with foresight and vision, who support innovative work practices, and who make decisions that consider the interests of multiple stakeholders. In other words, the best companies succeed through applying the concepts and practices that we discuss in this organizational behaviour book.

Our purpose is to help you understand what goes on in organizations. We examine the factors that make companies effective, improve employee well-being, and drive successful collaboration among co-workers. We look at organizations from numerous and diverse perspectives, from the deepest foundations of employee thoughts and behaviour (personality, self-concept, attitudes, etc.) to the macro-level interplay among the organization's structure, culture, and the external environment. Along this journey, we emphasize why things happen and what you can do to predict and guide organizational events.

We begin this chapter by introducing you to the field of organizational behaviour (OB) and its historical origins. This is followed by details about why OB is important for your career and why organizations depend on OB knowledge to survive and thrive. An integrative model of organizational behaviour is presented, which illustrates the interconnectedness of OB topics and serves as a road map to guide you through this book. We then describe the philosophical anchors that guide the development of organizational behaviour knowledge. This is followed by an overview of four emerging features of the workplace environment:

diversity and the inclusive workplace, work–life integration, remote work, and emerging employment relationships. The latter part of this chapter introduces the MARS model, which outlines the four direct drivers of individual behaviour and performance. The final section identifies the five main types of individual behaviour.

WHAT IS ORGANIZATIONAL BEHAVIOUR?

LO1

Organizational behaviour (OB) is the study of what people think, feel, and do in and around organizations. It looks at employee behaviours, decisions, perceptions, and emotional responses. It examines how individuals and teams in organizations relate to each other and to their counter-parts in other organizations. OB also encompasses the study of how organizations interact with their external environments, particularly in the context of employee behaviour and decisions. OB researchers systematically study these topics at multiple levels of analysis, namely, at the level of the individual, team (including interpersonal), and organization.[2]

> **organizational behaviour (OB)** The study of what people think, feel, and do in and around organizations.

The definition of organizational behaviour begs the question: What are organizations? **Organizations** are groups of people who work interdependently toward some purpose.[3] Notice that organizations are not buildings or government-registered entities. In fact, many organizations exist with neither physical walls nor government documentation to confer their legal status. Organizations have existed for as long as people have worked together. Massive temples dating back to 3500 BCE were constructed through the organized actions of multitudes of people.

> **organizations** Groups of people who work interdependently toward some purpose.

©Kepler Communications

Kepler Communications illustrates the power of organizations. Within its first four years in business, the Toronto-based start-up has designed and launched two bread-box sized satellites and secured venture capital to fund several more. These nano-satellites can transfer data much more quickly, cheaply, and efficiently than traditional satellites. "You can think of it like routers in space," says Mina Mitry, Kepler's co-founder and CEO (shown in this photo). Kepler is already competing successfully against two global juggernauts: Elon Musk's SpaceX and SoftBank's OneWeb. "Putting together the right team has made our company what it is today," says Mitry. He adds: "Innovation can only exist with a clear vision and a good underlying motivation—that is, to make a better version of the world."*

*T. Soper, "Startup Spotlight: Kepler Is Building Communications Infrastructure for the 'new Space Economy," *GeekWire,* May 12, 2016; J. Cowgill, "Bringing Connectivity to Space with Kepler Communications," *Medium,* October 15, 2018; A. Saltzman, "Companies Look to Cash in on Out-of-This-World Profits in New Space Economy," *CBC News,* July 17, 2019; M. Harris, "SpaceX, OneWeb, Or Kepler Communications: Who Really Launched The First Ku Band Satellite?" *IEEE Spectrum,* August 29, 2019; "Kepler Communications Inc.," accessed October 3, 2019, https://www.keplercommunications.com/company/team.

Craftspeople and merchants in ancient Rome formed guilds with elected managers. More than 1,000 years ago, Chinese factories were producing 125,000 tons of iron each year. Closer to home, the Hudson's Bay Company holds the distinction of being North America's oldest commercial enterprise. Founded in 1670, the company was granted exclusive control over one-quarter of North America, including most of western Canada, for almost 200 years.[4]

One key feature of organizations is that they are collective entities. They consist of human beings—typically, but not necessarily, employees—who interact with each other in an *organized* way. This organized relationship requires communication, coordination, and collaboration to achieve organizational objectives. As such, all organizational members have degrees of interdependence; they accomplish goals by sharing materials, information, or expertise with co-workers.

A second key feature of organizations is that their members have a collective sense of purpose. This collective purpose isn't always well defined or agreed upon. Companies typically have vision and mission statements, but these documents are sometimes out of date or don't describe what employees and leaders actually try to achieve. Still, imagine an organization without a collective sense of purpose. It would be an assemblage of people without direction or unifying force. So whether they are creating network technology at BlueCat or designing transportation infrastructure at Hatch Ltd., people working in organizations do have some sense of collective purpose. As Steve Jobs, the late co-founder of Apple Inc. and Pixar Animation Studios, once said: "A company is one of humanity's most amazing inventions. It's totally abstract. Sure, you have to build something with bricks and mortar to put the people in, but basically a company is this abstract construct we've invented, and it's incredibly powerful."[5]

HISTORICAL FOUNDATIONS OF ORGANIZATIONAL BEHAVIOUR

Organizational behaviour emerged as a distinct field sometime around the early 1940s.[6] During that decade, a few researchers began describing their research as organizational (rather than sociological or psychological). And by the late 1940s, Harvard University had changed the name of its MBA human relations course to "Organizational Behaviour."

Although the field of OB has relatively recent origins, experts in other fields have been studying organizations for many centuries. The Greek philosopher Plato (400 BCE) wrote about the essence of leadership, and the Chinese philosopher Confucius (500 BCE) extolled the virtues of ethics and leadership. Economist Adam Smith (1700s) discussed the benefits of job specialization and division of labour. German sociologist Max Weber (early 1900s) wrote about rational organizations, the work ethic, and charismatic leadership. Around the same time, industrial engineer Frederick Winslow Taylor proposed systematic ways to organize work processes and motivate employees through goal setting and rewards.[7]

Before becoming Canada's longest serving prime minister, William Lyon Mackenzie King was a pioneering consultant who wrote about the need for more worker involvement and organizational reward systems (1910s). Political scientist Mary Parker Follett (1920s) offered new ways of thinking about constructive conflict, team dynamics, power, and leadership. Harvard professor Elton Mayo and his colleagues (1930s and 1940s) established the "human relations" school of management, which pioneered research on employee attitudes, formal team dynamics, informal groups, and supervisor leadership style. Telephone executive and Harvard associate Chester Barnard (1930s) wrote insightful views regarding organizational communication, coordination, leadership and authority, organizations as open systems, and team dynamics.[8] This brief historical tour demonstrates that OB has been around for a long time; however, it wasn't organized into a unified discipline until around World War II.

Why Organizational Behaviour Is Important

LO2

In all likelihood, you are reading this book as part of a required course in organizational behaviour. Apart from degree or diploma requirements, why should you learn the ideas and practices discussed in this book? After all, who ever heard of a career path leading to a "vice-president of OB" or a "chief OB officer"? Our answer to this question comes in two parts: why OB is important for you personally and why OB is important for organizations generally.

WHY OB IS IMPORTANT FOR YOU

Throughout our careers teaching undergraduate, graduate, and executive programs, we noticed that the more work experience students have, the more they tend to consider organizational behaviour as one of their most valued courses. Why? Because they have learned over time that OB is important to them, whether as technical professionals or senior executives.[9] This observation is supported by numerous surveys that ask employers to identify the most important skills and knowledge they look for in new hires. Technical skills are important, of course, particularly for highly specialized jobs and professions. But the skills and knowledge that employers tend to rank above anything else are the topics found in this and other organizational behaviour books.

Exhibit 1.1 lists the most important skills for new employees identified by employers in four recent major surveys. Every list identifies problem solving (including analytic thinking and strategic thinking), which you will learn about along with creativity and employee involvement in Chapter 7. The ability to work effectively in teams (also listed as collaboration, interpersonal skills, and people management) is another top-ranked skill that employers look for in job applicants. The team dynamics theme is fully discussed in Chapter 8, but it also relates to several others topics, such as understanding and managing emotions (Chapter 4), influencing others (Chapter 10), and managing conflict (Chapter 11).

Communication, which is featured in Chapter 9, is a third skill that employers in all four surveys identify as important for new hires. Leadership appears in three lists (in the

EXHIBIT 1.1 Most Important Skills for New Employees

Business Council of Canada (entry-level hires list)	National Association of Colleges and Employers (United States)	Bloomberg Skills Report (United States)	Australian Institute of Management
• Collaboration, teamwork, interpersonal skills	• Problem solving	• Communication skills	• Communication
• Communication skills	• Ability to work in a team	• Analytical thinking	• Leadership
• Problem-solving skills	• Communication (written)	• Work collaboratively	• Emotional intelligence
• Analytical capabilities	• Leadership	• Strategic thinking	• People management
• Resiliency	• Strong work ethic	• Leadership skills	• Problem solving

Canadian survey, leadership is the second most important for mid-level hires, but not among the top five for entry-level hires). You will learn about the various perspectives and ways of leading others in Chapter 12, but it is also associated with several other topics, such as motivating people (Chapters 5 and 6) and leading organizational change (Chapter 15). Overall, these and other surveys suggest that OB offers a core foundation of knowledge and skill development for your success in organizations.[10]

Better Personal Theories to Predict and Influence

Along with providing the specific knowledge and skills identified in these surveys, this book serves a broader purpose: to help you adopt better personal theories to understand, predict, and influence organizational events. Every one of us has an inherent drive to comprehend what is going on around us.[11] This need is particularly strong in organizations because they are highly complex and ambiguous contexts that have a profound effect on us. Throughout our lives, we develop personal theories to make sense of what happens around us. Our personal models are sometimes accurate, sometimes too simplified to fit specific situations, and occasionally wrong. Even some ideas that look like "common sense" may be inaccurate or oversimplified.[12]

The field of organizational behaviour applies systematic research to develop evidence-based theories. These theories help you to refine your personal theories, so you are better able to get things done in the workplace by predicting and influencing organizational events.[13] Organizations are people who work together to accomplish things. Therefore, no matter what career path you choose, OB theories and practices are enormously valuable to help you perform your job and work more effectively within organizations.

Organizational Behaviour Is for Everyone

You may have noticed that we haven't mentioned "managers" in this discussion on why OB is important for you. Effective management (and leadership) does depend on OB concepts and practices, but this book pioneered the broader view that OB is valuable for everyone who works in and around organizations. Whether you are a software engineer, customer service representative, foreign exchange analyst, or chief executive officer, you need to understand and apply the many organizational behaviour topics that are discussed in this book. In fact, OB knowledge is probably more valuable than ever before because employees increasingly need to be proactive, self-motivated, and able to work effectively with co-workers without management intervention. As one forward-thinking OB writer wrote a half-century ago: Every employee is a manager.[14]

WHY OB IS IMPORTANT FOR ORGANIZATIONS

Along with benefiting you as an individual, the field of organizational behaviour is vital to the organization's survival and success.[15] For instance, the best companies to work for (i.e., companies with the highest levels of employee satisfaction) enjoy significantly higher financial performance than other businesses within the same industry. Companies with higher levels of employee engagement have higher sales and profitability. OB practices are also associated with various indicators of hospital performance, such as lower patient mortality rates and higher patient satisfaction. Other studies have consistently found a positive relationship between the quality of leadership and the company's financial performance.

Financial analysts also rely on several organizational behaviour variables—including leadership, performance-based rewards, employee development, and employee attitudes—as "positive screens" for selecting companies with the highest and most consistent long-term investment returns. For example, a leading Canadian investment analyst identified the top five factors to consider when deciding whether to invest in a company. First on his list was whether the company's "management team has great prior experience and a vested interest in their company."[16]

Almost all organizational behaviour theories have the implicit or explicit objective of making organizations more effective.[17] In fact, **organizational effectiveness** is considered the "ultimate dependent variable" in organizational behaviour.[18] Organizational performance, success, goodness, health, competitiveness, and excellence are alternative labels for organizational effectiveness. Organizations are effective when they have a good fit with their external environment, effectively transform inputs to outputs through human capital, and satisfy the needs of key stakeholders.[19] Let's look at these elements to understand how OB knowledge improves organizational effectiveness.

organizational effectiveness The extent to which an organization has a good fit with its external environment, effectively transforms inputs to outputs through human capital, and satisfies the needs of key stakeholders.

Organizations as Open Systems

One of the fundamental views in organizational behaviour is that organizations are **open systems**.[20] They are complex organisms that "live" within an

open systems The view that organizations depend on the external environment for resources, affect that environment through their output, and consist of internal subsystems that transform inputs to outputs.

EXHIBIT 1.2 **Organizations as Open Systems**

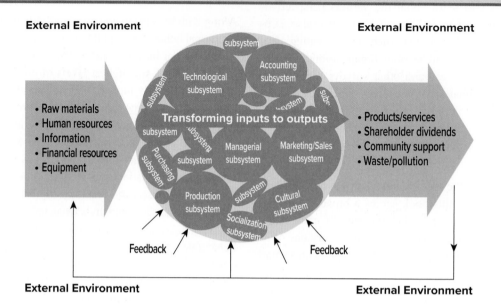

The open systems view, with external environments surrounding the transforming organization.

external environment, as Exhibit 1.2 illustrates. The word *open* describes this permeable relationship, whereas *closed systems* operate without dependence on or interaction with an external environment. Organizations depend on the external environment for resources, including raw materials, job applicants, financial resources, information, and equipment. The environment also consists of laws, cultural norms, and other expectations that place demands on how organizations should operate.

The open systems view recognizes that organizations have numerous subsystems (departments, teams, technological processes, etc.) that transform the incoming resources into outputs that are returned to the external environment. Some outputs, such as products and services, may be valued by the external environment; other outputs, such as employee layoffs and pollution, are undesirable by-products. Throughout this process, organizations receive feedback regarding the value of their outputs, the availability of future inputs, and the appropriateness of the transformation process.

As open systems, organizations are effective when they maintain a good "fit" with their external environment.[21] A good fit exists when the organization's inputs, processes, and outputs are aligned with the resources available in the external environment and with the needs and expectations of that environment. Organizational behaviour knowledge is highly relevant to the open systems view by identifying organizational characteristics that "fit" some external environments better than others. For example, the external environment is a key factor in choosing the best organizational structure (Chapter 13) and organizational culture (Chapter 14). This topic also relates to leadership (Chapter 12), organizational change (Chapter 15), and job design (Chapter 6).

OB theories also offer guidance regarding the transformation of inputs to outputs, including how internal subsystems coordinate with one another.[22] For instance, the opening case study noted that employees at BlueCat Networks rely on teamwork and interdepartmental collaboration to more effectively serve clients. We discuss how to create and support effective teams (Chapter 8) and how organizations rely on a variety of coordinating mechanisms (Chapter 13). The transformation process also relates to how employees influence each other (Chapter 10) and how successful companies improve coordination through a strong organizational culture (Chapter 14).

Human Capital as the Organization's Competitive Advantage

The most important ingredient in the organization's process of transforming inputs to outputs is human capital. **Human capital** refers to the knowledge, skills, abilities, creativity, and other valued resources that employees bring to the organization. It is a competitive advantage because employees are essential for the organization's survival and success. Furthermore, their talents are difficult to find, copy, and replace with technology.[23] Consequently, effective organizations introduce workplace practices that enhance human capital.[24] These practices are identified and discussed throughout this book. For example, some OB themes identify ways to strengthen employee motivation through enriched jobs, rewards, feedback, and fair work practices (Chapters 5 and 6). Other topics

> **human capital** The knowledge, skills, abilities, creative thinking, and other valued resources that employees bring to the organization.

discuss the value of employee involvement (Chapter 7) and the features of effective self-directed work teams (Chapter 8).

Organizations potentially boost their effectiveness through human capital development in three ways.[25] First, human capital development partly occurs by improving employee skills and knowledge. As we will explain toward the end of this chapter, as a person's ability improves, their performance tends to improve, which, in turn, improves the organization's success. Second, companies with superior human capital are better at adapting to rapidly changing environments. This adaptability occurs because highly skilled employees who have freedom to perform their work are better at performing diverse tasks in unfamiliar situations. Third, developing human capital means the company is investing in and rewarding its workforce, which motivates employees to reciprocate through greater effort in their jobs and assistance to co-workers.

Organizations and Their Stakeholders

As open systems, organizations need to adjust to the evolving needs and expectations of stakeholders. **Stakeholders** include customers, suppliers, the local community and national society, interest groups, shareholders, governments, and many other entities that affect, or are affected by, the company's objectives and actions.[26]

stakeholders Individuals, groups, and other entities that affect, or are affected by, the organization's objectives and actions.

Organizations are more effective when they understand, manage, and satisfy stakeholder needs and expectations. However, this is easier said than done because stakeholders have conflicting interests and organizations lack sufficient resources to satisfy everyone.

Several organizational behaviour topics give us a better understanding of stakeholder relations.[27] In particular, research has identified several factors that influence the prioritization of stakeholders, including stakeholder power (Chapter 10), how executives perceive the organization's environment (Chapters 3 and 13), the organization's culture (Chapter 14), and the personal values of the corporate board and executive team (Chapter 2).

Personal values play a key role in stakeholder relations. **Values** are relatively stable, evaluative beliefs that guide our preferences for outcomes or courses of action in a variety of situations.[28] They help us know what is right or wrong, or good or bad, in a particular situation. Chapter 2 explains how values anchor our thoughts and, to some extent, motivate our decisions and behaviour. With regard to stakeholders, the company's executive team and board of directors rely on their personal values to decide how the company should prioritize its investments for future growth and how its current earnings should be distributed (e.g., to shareholders, employees, community, etc.).

values Relatively stable evaluative beliefs that guide a person's preferences for outcomes or courses of action in a variety of situations.

Global Connections 1.1

21 DAYS OF Y'ELLO CARE*

MTN Group is the largest mobile telecommunications company in Africa and a leader in corporate social responsibility (CSR). Over the first three weeks in June, MTN's award-winning "21 Days of Y'ello Care" program involves many of the company's 19,000 employees in various CSR events, typically focused on technology, life skills, and community health. For example, MTN volunteers in Nigeria recently set up digital libraries in schools, conducted ICT and business skills training, and raised awareness of mental wellness issues among youth. "Our goal for this year's Y'ello Care [program] is to do our part to support young people and help tackle the various issues they face," said an executive at MTN Nigeria of that campaign.

©REUTERS/Alamy Stock Photo

* "MTN Employees Give Back for 21 Days of Y'ello Care," News release (Johannesburg, South Africa: MTN, May 31, 2018);"MTN Employees Empower Youth during 21 Days of Y'ello Care," *IOL Business Report (South Africa)*, June 4, 2019; "MTN Employees Empower Youth during 21 Days of Y'ello Care," *The Guardian (Lagos, Nigeria)*, June 20, 2019.

One topic that is closely aligned with personal values and stakeholders is corporate social responsibility. **Corporate social responsibility (CSR)** consists of organizational activities intended to benefit society and the environment beyond the firm's immediate financial interests or legal obligations.[29] It is the view that companies have a contract with society, in which they must serve stakeholders beyond shareholders and customers. This is known as the triple-bottom-line philosophy. Firms that adopt the triple bottom line aim to survive and be profitable in the marketplace (economic), but they also intend to maintain or improve conditions for society (social) as well as the physical environment. The emerging evidence is that companies with a positive CSR reputation tend to have better financial performance, more loyal employees, and better relations with customers, job applicants, and other stakeholders.[30]

> **corporate social responsibility (CSR)** Organizational activities intended to benefit society and the environment beyond the firm's immediate financial interests or legal obligations.

CONNECTING THE DOTS: AN INTEGRATIVE MODEL OF ORGANIZATIONAL BEHAVIOUR

Our discussion in the previous section not only highlights the importance of organizational behaviour for you as well as the organization. It also reveals that OB is a diverse and interconnected field of knowledge. Exhibit 1.3 provides an integrative road map to help you navigate the various organizational behaviour topics throughout this book. You might think of this diagram as a meta-model—a model that incorporates and connects specific OB concepts, each of which has its own explanatory models. In other words, Exhibit 1.3 gives you a bird's-eye view of the book and its various topics, so you can more easily see how they fit together.

EXHIBIT 1.3   An Integrative Model of Organizational Behaviour

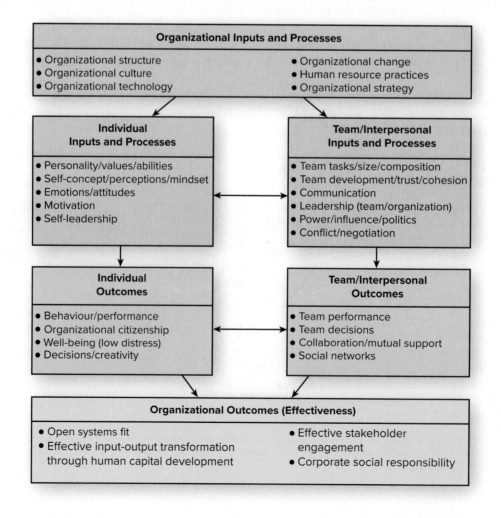

As Exhibit 1.3 illustrates, individual inputs and processes influence individual outcomes, which, in turn, have a direct effect on the organization's effectiveness. For example, how well organizations transform inputs to outputs and satisfy key stakeholders is dependent on how well employees perform their jobs and make logical and creative decisions. Individual inputs, processes, and outcomes are identified in the two left-side boxes of our integrative OB model and are the centre of attention in Part 2 of this book. We will learn about personality and values—two of the most important individual characteristics—and later examine self-concept, perceptions, emotions, attitudes, motivation, and self-leadership.

Part 3 of this book directs our attention to team and interpersonal inputs, processes, and outcomes. These topics are found in the two boxes on the right side of Exhibit 1.3. The chapter on team dynamics (Chapter 8) offers an integrative model for that specific topic, which shows how team inputs (e.g., team composition, size, and other team characteristics) influence team processes (team development, cohesion, and others), which then affect team performance and other outcomes. Later chapters in Part 3 examine specific interpersonal and team processes listed in Exhibit 1.3, including communication, power and influence, conflict, and leadership.

Exhibit 1.3 illustrates that team processes and outcomes affect individual processes and outcomes. As an example, an individual's personal well-being is partly affected by the mutual support received from team members and other co-workers. The opposite is also true: individual processes affect team and interpersonal dynamics in organizations. For instance, we will learn that self-concept among individual team members influences the team's cohesion.

The top area of Exhibit 1.3 highlights the macro-level influence of organizational inputs and processes on both teams and individuals. These organizational-level variables are mainly discussed in Part 4, including organizational structure, organizational culture, and organizational change. However, we will also refer to human resource practices, information systems, and additional organizational-level variables throughout this book where they have a known effect on individual, interpersonal, and team dynamics.

Anchors of Organizational Behaviour Knowledge

LO3

Earlier, we pointed out that the field of organizational behaviour benefits you because it offers carefully constructed and tested theories and practices. By offering relatively accurate models of reality, OB helps you to refine your personal theories, which makes it easier to understand, predict, and influence organizational events. The field of OB relies on a set of basic beliefs (see Exhibit 1.4). These conceptual anchors represent the principles on which OB knowledge is developed and refined.[31]

THE SYSTEMATIC RESEARCH ANCHOR

A key feature of OB knowledge is that it should be based on systematic research, which typically involves forming research questions, systematically collecting data, and

---

EXHIBIT 1.4   Anchors of Organizational Behaviour Knowledge

Anchor	Description
Systematic research anchor	Study organizations using systematic research methods
Practical orientation anchor	Ensure that OB theories are useful in organizations
Multidisciplinary anchor	Import knowledge from other disciplines, not just create its own knowledge
Contingency anchor	Recognize that the effectiveness of an action may depend on the situation
Multiple levels of analysis anchor	Understand OB events from three levels of analysis: individual, team, organization

testing hypotheses against those data.[32] The Appendix at the end of this book provides a brief overview of these research methods. Systematic research investigation supports **evidence-based management**, which involves mak-

> **evidence-based management** The practice of making decisions and taking actions based on research evidence.

ing decisions and taking actions guided by research evidence. It makes perfect sense that management practice should be founded on the best available systematic knowledge. Yet corporate leaders and others often embrace fads, untested consulting models, and their own pet beliefs without bothering to find out if they actually work![33]

One reason why corporate decision makers overlook evidence-based knowledge is that they are bombarded with ideas from consultant reports, popular business books, newspaper articles, and other sources, which makes it difficult to figure out which ones are based on solid evidence. In contrast, OB and other business school research receives limited attention in newspapers and other public sources.[34] A second reason is that good OB research is necessarily generic; it is rarely described in the context of a specific problem in a specific organization. Decision makers therefore have the difficult task of figuring out which theories are relevant to their unique situation.

A third reason is that popular management fads lacking research evidence gain popularity because the sources of these fads are rewarded for marketing their ideas, not for testing to see if they actually work. Fourth, human beings are affected by several perceptual errors and decision-making biases, as we will learn in Chapter 3 and Chapter 7. For instance, decision makers have a natural tendency to look for evidence that supports their pet beliefs and ignore evidence that opposes those beliefs.

OB experts have proposed a few simple suggestions to create a more evidence-based organization.[35] First, be skeptical of hype, which is apparent when so-called experts say the idea is "new," "revolutionary," and "proven." In reality, most management ideas are adaptations, evolutionary, and never "proven" (science can disprove, but never prove; it can only find evidence to support a practice). Second, the company should embrace collective expertise rather than rely on charismatic stars and management gurus. Third, stories provide useful illustrations and possibly preliminary evidence of a useful practice, but they should never become the main foundation to support management action. Instead, rely on more systematic investigation with a larger sample. Finally, take a neutral stance toward popular trends and ideologies. Executives tend to get caught up in what their counterparts at other companies are doing without determining the validity of those trendy practices or the relevance to their organizations.

Debating Point: IS THERE ENOUGH EVIDENCE TO SUPPORT EVIDENCE-BASED MANAGEMENT?

One of the core anchors of organizational behaviour is that knowledge must be built on a solid foundation of scientifically based research. This evidence-based management approach embraces scientific methods. It also advises corporate leaders to become more aware of evidence-based knowledge, and to use diagnostic tools (such as surveys and checklists) to apply those principles in the workplace.

It seems obvious that we should rely on good evidence rather than bad evidence (or no evidence at all) to make good decisions in the workplace. Yet there is another side to this debate. The question isn't whether good evidence is valuable; it is about the meaning of "good evidence." One concern is that scholars might be advocating an interpretation of good evidence that is far too narrow.* They typically limit evidence to empirical correlational research, whereas descriptive and qualitative information often provide additional evidence, and occasionally the only feasible evidence. A half-century ago, sociologist William Bruce Cameron warned against this empiricist bias with this memorable chiasmus: "Not everything that can be counted counts, and not everything that counts can be counted."**

Another concern is that managers don't view organizational research as particularly relevant to the issues they face.*** Much university research is derived from cross-sectional surveys that depend on uncontaminated, quantifiable measures. But managers say they need research that is closer to real-world variables and conditions. Unfortunately, only about 2 percent of organizational studies are real-world experiments, mainly because these field studies take more time and are usually empirically messy, which may make them more difficult to get published.****

A third concern is that systematic elements of organizational research studies (e.g., sample size, measurement reliability, advanced data analysis methods) can mask other potentially serious underlying faults. Cross-cultural studies, for instance, often use college student samples to represent an entire culture. Lab studies with students assume they replicate workplace conditions, yet ignore important differences with employee characteristics. These and many other faults may explain why replicated studies often produce different results from the original. And even if the published research is valid, the collective knowledge is still somewhat inaccurate because studies with nonsignificant results are much less likely to get published (partly because authors don't bother to submit papers with non-significant findings).*****

* M.A. Cronin and R. Klimoski, "Broadening the View of What Constitutes 'Evidence,'" *Industrial and Organizational Psychology* 4, no. 1 (2011): 57–61; P.E. Spector and L.L. Meier, "Methodologies for the Study of Organizational Behavior Processes: How to Find Your Keys in the Dark," *Journal of Organizational Behavior* 35, no. 8 (2014): 1109–19; K. Morrell and M. Learmonth, "Against Evidence-Based Management, for Management Learning," *Academy of Management Learning & Education* 14, no. 4 (2015): 520–33.

** W.B. Cameron, *Informal Sociology: A Casual Introduction to Sociological Thinking* (Random House, 1963), 13; "Not Everything That Counts Can Be Counted–Quote Investigator," May 26, 2010, https://quoteinvestigator.com/2010/05/26/everything-counts-einstein/.

*** J.M. Bartunek and S.L. Rynes, "Academics and Practitioners Are Alike and Unlike: The Paradoxes of Academic–Practitioner Relationships," *Journal of Management* 40, no. 5 (2014): 1181–1201, https://doi.org/10.1177/0149206314529160; S. Johnson and K. Orr, "What Is Business School Research for? Academic and Stakeholder Perspectives, Politics and Relationality," *Studies in Higher Education* 0, no. 0 (2019): 1–22, https://doi.org/10.1080/03075079.2018.1564901.

**** J. Greenberg and E.C. Tomlinson, "Situated Experiments in Organizations: Transplanting the Lab to the Field," *Journal of Management* 30, no. 5 (2004): 703–24;W. Zhang, A. Levenson, and C. Crossley, "Move Your Research from the Ivy Tower to the Board Room: A Primer on Action Research for Academics, Consultants, and Business Executives," *Human Resource Management* 54, no. 1 (2015): 151–74.

***** A. Franco, N. Malhotra, and G. Simonovits, "Publication Bias in the Social Sciences: Unlocking the File Drawer," *Science* 345, no. 6203 (2014): 1502–05; G.C. Banks, S. Kepes, and M.A. McDaniel, "Publication Bias: Understanding the Myths Concerning Threats to the Advancement of Science," in *More Statistical and Methodological Myths and Urban Legends,* ed. C.E. Lance and R.J. Vandenberg (New York: Routledge, 2015), 36–64. On the uneven replication of research, see: Open Science Collaboration, "Estimating the Reproducibility of Psychological Science," *Science* 349, no. 6251 (2015): 943, aac4716–1–aac16–8; C.J. Anderson et al., "Response to Comment on 'Estimating the Reproducibility of Psychological Science,'" *Science* 351, no. 6277 (2016): 1037c. Even meta-analyses might not be the magic solution to research bias and variability. See:J. Vrieze, "Meta-Analyses Were Supposed to End Scientific Debates. Often, They Only Cause More Controversy," *Science,* September 18, 2018, https://doi.org/10.1126/science.aav4617.

THE PRACTICAL ORIENTATION ANCHOR

Organizational behaviour doesn't just develop theories for the sake of being interesting. Most OB theories need to be useful in practice, whether for executive teams or for the rest of us in everyday work activities. This is consistent with our statement earlier in this chapter that almost all organizational behaviour theories have the implicit or explicit objective of making organizations more effective. OB experts have had a number of debates on this matter, particularly whether the high degree of methodological rigour demanded in some publications conflicts with, rather than supports, the relevance of that research.[36]

The true "impact" of an OB theory is how well it finds its way into organizational life and becomes a valuable asset for improving the organization's effectiveness. For instance, the MARS model (introduced later in this chapter) is a useful framework for coaching employees, a diagnostic tool for determining how a work issue occurred, and a guide for implementing some forms of organizational change. Other chapters offer specific advice on how to energize employees, improve customer service through employee attitudes, create more effective teams, determine the best communication channel for a specific situation, build a strong corporate culture, determine when to involve others in your decisions, handle conflict effectively, and so forth. After reading this book, you will have a toolkit of theories that are not only interesting, but are practical to use in organizations.

THE MULTIDISCIPLINARY ANCHOR

Another organizational behaviour anchor recommends that the field should welcome theories and knowledge from other disciplines, not just from its own isolated research base. For instance, psychological research has aided our understanding of individual and interpersonal behaviour. Sociologists have contributed to our knowledge of team dynamics, organizational socialization, organizational power, and other aspects of the social system. OB knowledge has also benefited from knowledge in emerging fields such as communications, marketing, and information systems.

This practice of borrowing theory from other disciplines is inevitable. Organizations have central roles in society, so they are studied in many social sciences.[37] Furthermore, organizations consist of people who interact with one another, so there is an inherent intersection between OB and most disciplines that study human beings. However, by relying too much on theories developed in other fields, OB faces the risk of lagging rather than leading in knowledge production. In contrast, OB-bred theories allow researchers to concentrate on the quality and usefulness of the theory, and be the first to understand and apply that knowledge.[38]

THE CONTINGENCY ANCHOR

People and their work environments are complex, and the field of organizational behaviour recognizes this by stating that the effect of one variable on another variable often depends on the characteristics of the situation or people involved. In practice, this means that a single outcome or solution rarely exists; a particular action may have different consequences under different conditions.[39] For example, later in this chapter we discuss how the success of remote work (e.g. telecommuting) depends on specific characteristics of the employee, job, and organization. Contingencies are identified in many OB theories, such as the best leadership style, the best conflict-handling style, and the best organizational structure. Of course, it would be so much simpler if we could rely on "one best way" theories, in which a particular concept or practice has the same results in every situation. OB experts do try to keep theories as simple as possible, but the contingency anchor is always on their minds.[40]

THE MULTIPLE LEVELS OF ANALYSIS ANCHOR

Organizational behaviour recognizes that what goes on in organizations can be placed into three levels of analysis: individual, team (including interpersonal), and organization.

In fact, advanced empirical research carefully identifies the appropriate level of analysis for each variable in the study and then measures at that level of analysis. For example, team norms and cohesion are measured as a team variable, not as a characteristic of individuals within each team.

Although OB research and writing pegs each variable within one of these levels of analysis, most variables are understood best by thinking of them from all three levels of analysis.[41] Communication is located in this book as a team (interpersonal) process, for example, but it also includes individual and organizational processes. Therefore, you should try to think about each OB topic at the individual, team, and organizational levels, not at just one of these levels.

The Emerging Workplace Landscape

LO4

Organizations are experiencing unprecedented change. Global competition, rapid and disruptive technological change, and many other factors have substantially altered

©i viewfinder/Shutterstock

Supporting workforce diversity and inclusiveness is a top priority at the Vancouver Airport Authority (YVR). "At YVR, we truly believe in inclusiveness—that everybody should be able to fly and enjoy the world and, in the same way, that everybody should be able to have a great career working at the airport," says a YVR executive. The organization holds regular diversity awareness courses, hosts career fairs for people with disabilities, and distributes information about job openings to dozens of outreach groups. YVR's executive team sets specific hiring targets for women, Indigenous peoples, persons with disabilities, and members of visible minorities. YVR also has a well-established women in management program. Women now represent more than 40 percent of YVR's managers and more than half of its executives and board members.*

***"Top Employer: Vancouver Airport Authority —Recognized as One of Canada's Best Diversity Employers (2019)," BC's Top Employers 2019, February 21, 2019, https://content.eluta.ca/top-employer-vancouver-airport; "Vancouver Airport Authority Selected as One of Canada's Best Diversity Employers and One of BC's Top Employers," News Release (Vancouver: Vancouver Airport Authority, March 1, 2019); C. Richmond, "Need Employees? Talk to Someone with a Disability," Vancouver Airport Authority, CEO's Corner (blog), September 25, 2019, http://www.yvr.ca/en/blog/2019/ceo-corner-september-2019; "Top Employer: Vancouver Airport Authority," accessed October 5, 2019, https://content.eluta.ca/top-employer-vancouver-airport.; "Diversity," Vancouver Airport Authority, 2019, http://www.yvr.ca/en/passengers/careers/diversity.

business strategy and everyday workplace activities. The field of organizational behaviour plays a vital role in guiding organizations through this continuous turbulence. In this section, we look at four emerging workplace developments: diversity/inclusive workplaces, work–life integration, remote work, and employment relationships.

DIVERSITY AND THE INCLUSIVE WORKPLACE

An important objective of successful Canadian organizations is to create an **inclusive workplace.** Organizations that support an inclusive workplace view diversity as a valued resource. They value people of all identities and allow them to be fully themselves while contributing to the organization.[42] At the individual level, an inclusive workplace enables people, irrespective of their backgrounds, to feel psychologically safe, engaged, valued, authentic, listened to, and respected. At a collective level, an inclusive workplace gives diverse groups voice through formal structures, such as diversity councils, and everyday processes, such as representation in teams and casual gatherings. It also continually assesses recruitment, rewards, social and information networks, and other organizational systems to ensure that they do not unfairly favour some groups over others.

inclusive workplace A workplace that values people of all identities and allows them to be fully themselves while contributing to the organization.

When diversity is mentioned, most people initially think about **surface-level diversity**, that is, the observable demographic and other overt differences among members of a group, such as their race, ethnicity, gender, age, and physical capabilities.[43] Surface-level diversity in Canada and many other countries has increased substantially over the past few decades. For instance, more than 22 percent of Canadians currently belong to a "visible minority" group, up from 19 percent in 2011, 16 percent in 2006, 13 percent in 2001, and just 5 percent in 1981. South Asian, Chinese, Black, and Filipino are the four largest visible minority groups in Canada.[44]

surface-level diversity The observable demographic or physiological differences in people, such as their race, ethnicity, gender, age, and physical disabilities.

Diversity also includes differences in personalities, beliefs, values, and attitudes.[45] We can't directly see this **deep-level diversity**, but it is evident in a person's words, decisions, and actions. Deep-level diversity is revealed when employees have conflicting perceptions

deep-level diversity Differences in the psychological characteristics of employees, including personalities, beliefs, values, and attitudes.

and attitudes about the same situation (see Chapter 11) and when they form like-minded informal social groups (see Chapter 8). Some deep-level diversity is associated with surface-level attributes. For example, studies report significant differences between men and women regarding their preference of conflict-handling styles, ethical principles, and approaches to communicating with other people in various situations.[46]

An example of diversity that has both surface-level and deep-level characteristics is the multigenerational workforce.[47] Exhibit 1.5 illustrates the distribution of the Canadian labour force by major generational cohorts: *Silents* (born earlier than 1946), *Baby Boomers* (born from 1946 to 1964), *Generation X* (born from 1965 to 1980), *Millennials* (born from 1981 to 1996), and *Generation Z* (born after 1996). Gen-Xers and Millennials each represent about one-third of the current labour force.

Generational deep-level diversity does exist to some extent, but it tends to be much more subtle than the popular press would suggest. Also, some generational differences are actually due to age, not cohort.[48] One analysis of German data over 25 years found that generational groups held similar attitudes (importance of job success, importance of self-actualization, confidence in the future, worry

EXHIBIT 1.5   Canada's Multigenerational Workforce

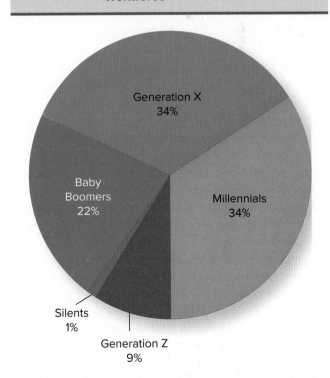

This exhibit shows the percentage of the Canadian labour force in each generational cohort. Source: Based on data in Statistics Canada, "Labour Force Characteristics by Sex and Detailed Age Group in 2018" (Ottawa: Statistics Canada, April 5, 2019).

about job security, etc.) when they were a particular age. An analysis of more than 100 studies also reported that generational cohorts have a similar degree of work ethic when they are a given age. Two studies of U.S federal government workers over time identified small generational differences in various job attitudes, but these were trivial compared to attitude differences within each generational cohort. The point here is that differences in needs, expectations, and attitudes do exist across age groups, but this deep-level diversity is due more to the person's stage in life and less to whether they were born into a specific cohort (Millennial, Baby Boomer, etc.).

Consequences of Diversity

Workforce diversity offers numerous benefits.[49] Teams with high informational diversity (where members have different knowledge and skills) tend to be more creative and make better decisions in complex situations compared to teams with less informational diversity. A workforce with surface- and deep-level diversity is also more representative of most communities, so companies are better able to recognize and address community needs. Overall, inclusive workplaces produce better decisions, employee attitudes, team performance, and a host of other favourable outcomes for employees and the organization. However, these benefits are contingent on a variety of factors, such as leadership, team structure, psychological safety perceptions, and employees' personal values.[50]

Diversity also poses challenges in the workplace.[51] One problem is that employees with diverse backgrounds usually take longer to perform effectively together because they experience numerous communication problems and create "faultlines" in informal group dynamics (see Chapter 8). One recent study found that research teams in the Formula 1 race car industry performed better as their diversity (range of experience) increased to a point, but performance was lower in highly diverse teams because they couldn't communicate or coordinate as well as less diverse teams. Some forms of diversity also increase the risk of dysfunctional conflict, which reduces information sharing and satisfaction with co-workers (see Chapter 11). These problems can offset the advantages of diversity in some situations.

But even with these challenges, companies need to make diversity a priority because surface-level diversity, as well as some forms of deep-level diversity, are moral and legal imperatives. Companies that offer an inclusive workplace are, in essence, fulfilling the ethical standard of fairness in their decisions regarding employment and the allocation of rewards. Inclusive workplace practices improve the quality of hiring and promotion, and increase employee satisfaction and loyalty. Companies that create an inclusive workplace also nurture a culture of respect that, in turn, improves cooperation and coordination among employees.

WORK–LIFE INTEGRATION

Before the digital age, most employees would finish work after eight or nine hours at the office or factory and could separate their personal time from their employment. Few people had complete separation of these roles, of course. Employees either brought paperwork home or thought about workplace issues long after their official work day had ended. Even so, the past is a stark contrast to the situation today in which information technology tethers a large percentage of employees to work on a 24/7 schedule. Globalization has contributed to this blending of work and nonwork because employees now need to be "on-call" with co-workers, suppliers, and clients who live in different time zones around the planet.

Little wonder that one feature employees value in a job is the ability to integrate work with nonwork activities.[52] **Work–life integration** refers to the extent to which people are effectively engaged in their various work and nonwork roles and have a low degree of role conflict across those life domains.[53] This phrase has replaced *work–life balance,* which incorrectly implies that work and nonwork roles are completely separate and opposing partitions (like a balance of a scale). "There is no such thing as work–life balance," says Lisa Sterling, executive vice president and Chief People & Culture Officer at human resource software company Ceridian in Minneapolis and Toronto. "You've got to get to a point at which work and life integrate, and you figure out organizationally and individually how to make those two things work together."[54]

> **work–life integration** The extent to which people are effectively engaged in their various work and nonwork roles and have a low degree of role conflict across those life domains.

To understand work–life integration, consider that each of us has multiple roles and associated self-concepts, such as accountant, parent, friend, manager, and sports fan (see Chapter 3). Work–life integration occurs by satisfying the demands and experiencing the positive emotions of our various segments of life. These roles are inherently integrated because the resources generated and consumed by one role enhance or starve other roles.[55] People with a fulfilling home life, for example, develop social support, positive moods, relaxation, and other resources that can enrich their work, as well as other roles. Similarly, the resources gained at work— new skills, financial rewards, feelings of success, and so forth—contribute to home and other nonwork roles.

Unfortunately, many people don't experience resource enrichment across roles. Instead, the heavy demands of one role deplete personal resources, which starve other roles. Employees who spend most waking hours performing or thinking about their job—whether at the workplace, at home, or on vacation—have insufficient time and energy remaining for other aspects of their lives. They experience what is widely known as work–life conflict. In summary, a person's work roles and nonwork roles are inherently integrated because the physical, cognitive, and emotional resources produced or consumed by one role potentially enrich or undermine the success and enjoyment of other roles.

Practising Work–Life Integration

How do individuals and organizations maximize work–life integration?[56] One strategy is to literally integrate two or more roles. An increasingly popular trend is to conduct meetings during an exercise walk. Some companies encourage staff to bring their dogs to work, which is both comforting and requires an occasional break to walk the four-legged friend. On-site child care is a form of integration because it allows employees to switch from work to parent roles throughout the day. These integration efforts are not always effective, but they illustrate that blending work and nonwork roles is more viable than we previously understood.

A second work–life integration strategy occurs through flexible work scheduling.[57] For instance, you might remotely attend a meeting from home in the evening with co-workers who live in other time zones, then arrive at work late the next morning after doing a few household chores. Organizations also have parental and other personal leave benefits to support higher demands at home in the short term. A third work–life integration strategy is to ensure that your various work and nonwork roles are aligned with your personal characteristics. In other words, your job, family life, sports activities, and so forth should roughly be consistent with your personality and values.

Although work is integrated with other life roles, a fourth strategy is to engage in some degree of "boundary management" across those roles.[58] Employees are more likely to set aside work-free times in their private lives when they observe this behaviour in managers. Several organizations adopt more structured boundary management through rules that prohibit work-related communication (except in extreme emergencies) after the regular work day. The French government has taken this one step further: It passed legislation giving employees the "right to disconnect," that is, they have a legal right to ignore company messages after hours.

REMOTE WORK

Blending work with other life roles is particularly noticeable when employees sometimes work from home rather than at the organization's physical work site. This activity is the most widely known variation of *remote work* (formerly called *telecommuting* or *teleworking*).[59] Remote work also occurs when employees are temporarily or indefinitely assigned to a client's workplace—an arrangement that we describe in the next section on employment relationships. Remote work is increasingly common because employees can connect relatively easily with co-workers, clients, and company data through various forms of information technology.

What percentage of Canadians work remotely? The number varies across surveys due to sampling problems and the complex issue of which occupations to include or exclude (farmers, travelling salespeople, independent contractors, etc.).[60] Statistics Canada estimates that, excluding farmers and contractors, only 7 percent of Canadians perform some of their paid work from home each week. In another study, however, almost two-thirds of Canadian employers say they allow some of their employees to work remotely, suggesting that the actual percentage of employees occasionally working from home or cafés may be higher.

Remote working increased dramatically when the recent COVID-19 pandemic forced businesses in Canada and elsewhere to apply social distancing and self-isolation practices. One very large panel survey reported that 61 percent of full-time American employees were working from home due to COVID-19 a few weeks after it became a serious health concern (but before it first peaked). In comparison, 33 percent of these employees were working at home two weeks earlier, just as the social distancing and self-isolation requirements were being introduced. Some companies, such as Optus (a large Australian telecommunications firm), say they will move some employee groups permanently to remote work arrangements, even after the pandemic is over.[61]

Some companies employed a fully remote workforce long before the COVID-19 pandemic motivated many employers to apply this work arrangement. Buffer, Automattic, Emsisoft, and Sonatype have no physical head office; every employee works at home, in cafés, or from other places of their choosing. Most fully remote companies (also called *distributed organizations*) have only a few dozen workers. But Automattic, which develops WordPress (powering one-quarter of the world's websites), employs more than 1,200 people across 77 countries. Approximately 50 of these "Automatticians" live and work in Canada (across seven provinces). Automattic did have a head office in San Francisco, but it was closed because very few employees showed up to work there.[62]

Remote Work Benefits and Risks

In spite of its popularity among employees, remote work is a controversial issue in the workplace because it has both benefits and risks for organizations as well as remote workers

Global Connections 1.2

EMSISOFT THRIVES AS A FULLY REMOTE ORGANIZATION*

When Christian Mairoll launched Emsisoft 15 years ago in Austria, he probably didn't imagine that the anti-malware company would now employ more than three dozen people scattered around the planet and that he would be leading them remotely from a sheep farm in New Zealand.

During the start-up, Mairoll shunned bank loans and venture capital funding, but didn't have enough money for a physical office. Instead, he contracted with software developers remotely—the first hire was from Siberia! As the business grew, more people were hired from different parts of the world. Today, Emsisoft is a completely remote company with no physical head office.

"When I started doing all-remote, it was a special thing," says Mairoll. "As we celebrate our 15th anniversary, I'm proud to say that Emsisoft is living proof that all-remote is a viable, effective, and sustainable business model."

A decade after leading the business from Europe, Mairoll decided to change his lifestyle by moving to New Zealand. He discovered that his new time zone overlapped nicely with the work hours of most of his staff. He typically convenes online meetings before 6:00 a.m., when the Eastern European crew are finishing and the North American staff are halfway through their day. By lunchtime in New Zealand, the Americans have logged off, which gives Mairoll a few hours of free time. During late afternoon in New Zealand, the Asian staff have begun to work, so Mairoll checks in with them before finishing his day.

There are numerous benefits of a fully remote company versus requiring staff to work in one physical location, says Mairoll. "Hiring from anywhere and everywhere allows us to access the best talent on the planet. It's also much easier for us to hire locals for roles that require native speakers. . . . In addition, having staff around the world means we can better serve our customers across different time zones."

However, Mairoll emphasizes that a completely remote organization requires staff who can manage themselves without supervision. "There's definitely the potential to lose focus and motivation when working from home," he says. "You need to be able to get things done, even if there is no immediate supervision or pressure from your team."

Language is also an issue, but Emsisoft mainly uses English text-based communication, which is easier for foreign language speakers to master than spoken conversations. Another issue is building strong team cohesion. "I think it takes slightly more effort in team building to establish strong team bonds over the Internet, but I don't see it as a major blocker at all," Mairoll suggests.

©Kostenko Maxim/Shutterstock

* J. Trigwell, "What I've Learned about Running an All-Remote Company during 15-Years as the CEO of the World's First All-Remote AV Company," *Emsisoft | Security Blog*(blog), November 20, 2018, https://blog.emsisoft.com/en/32308/what-ive-learned-about-running-an-all-remote-company-during-15-years-as-the-ceo-of-the-worlds-first-all-remote-av-company/; R. Chan, "How a Tech CEO Runs His 40-Employee Company from a Farm in New Zealand," *stuff.co.nz,* January 21, 2019.

(see Exhibit 1.6).[63] Several contingencies also enhance and undermine its effectiveness. One benefit is that remote workers usually experience better work–life integration because they have more time and somewhat more control to juggle work with family obligations. WestJet sales agent Carla Holub, who now works from her home north of Calgary a few days each week, praises this benefit. "It just freed up a good two hours of my personal time being able to work from my home office." Work–life integration is more difficult, however, when employees lack sufficient workspace and privacy at home and have increased family responsibilities on days when they work from home.

Job applicants—particularly Millennials—identify remote work as an attractive job feature, and turnover is usually lower among employees who are able to work from home. Research also indicates that remote workers have higher productivity than other employees, likely because they experience less stress and tend to convert some of the former commuting time

Are you a good remote worker? You can discover how well you would adjust to remote work by completing this self-assessment in Connect.

EXHIBIT 1.6 **Potential Benefits and Risks of Remote Working**

Potential Benefits	Potential Risks
• Better employee work–life integration	• More social isolation
• Attractive benefit for job applicants	• Lower team cohesion
• Low employee turnover	• Weaker organizational culture
• Higher employee productivity	• More stressful due to home space and roles
• Reduced greenhouse gas emissions	
• Reduced corporate real estate and office costs	

into work time. Working remotely also improves productivity by enabling employees to perform their jobs at times when natural disasters, such as the COVID-19 pandemic, block access to the office.

Due to less commuting, remote work offers considerable financial benefits for employees, including less unpaid time travelling, vehicle use, fuel costs, and other commuting expenses. One recent study of remote workers in southwestern Ontario estimated savings between $8,820 and $29,426 per year, depending on the number of days working from home each week.[64] With less commuting, remote work also benefits society in the form of lower greenhouse gas emissions and less need for taxpayer-funded transportation infrastructure. Companies also benefit from lower real estate costs.

Remote work also has several disadvantages or risks.[65] People who regularly or mostly work from home report higher levels of social isolation, including weaker relationships with co-workers. They also receive less word-of-mouth information, which may have implications for promotional opportunities and workplace relations. Teams potentially suffer from lower cohesion. Organizations risk having a weaker culture when most employees work from home for a significant part of their workweek.

The success of remote working depends on several characteristics of the employee, job, and organization.[66] Employees who work effectively from home typically have higher self-motivation, self-organization, need for autonomy, and information technology skills. They also fulfil their social needs more from sources outside the workplace.

Jobs are better suited to remote work when the tasks require few resources at the workplace, the work is performed independently from co-workers, and task performance is measurable.

Remote work tends to be more successful when organizations reward and promote employees based on their performance rather than their presence in the office (face time). These firms also help remote workers maintain sufficient cohesion with their team and psychological connectedness with the organization. This occurs through regular supportive communication with the supervisor and teammates. In some instances, companies may need to limit the number of days that employees work from home, such as by having special meetings or events where all employees assemble at the workplace. Visual communication channels, such as video conferences with cameras turned on, also improve personal relatedness.

EMPLOYMENT RELATIONSHIPS

Another rapidly evolving workplace characteristic is the individual's formal employment relationship with the organization.[67] Historically, most workers have been in full-time, permanent jobs (called *direct employment*). This relationship assumes continuous employment (lifetime employment, in rare cases), usually with expectations of career advancement and the organization's investment in the employee's skills. An increasing percentage of employees—currently about 13 percent in Canada—have more fragile forms of direct employment, such as part-time, on-call, casual, and seasonal employment.

Although direct employment still dominates the Canadian labour market, indirect employment and self-employed contract work are the fastest growing work relationships. Indirect employment occurs when people work for an employment agency and are temporarily assigned (temps) or indefinitely "leased" to client firms. The global organization representing temp agencies estimates that approximately 2.8 percent of the Canadian labour force works through temp agencies, compared to more than 9 percent of the U.S. labour force. A recent in-depth report estimated that there are almost 2,600 temp employment agencies in Ontario alone.[68]

The rapid growth of indirect employment has occurred as companies outsource noncore work activities, such as information technology and customer contact centres, to firms that specialize in these services. However, some companies have also outsourced core jobs to agencies because they believe it will increase workforce flexibility, reduce unionization, and shift employment law obligations.

Self-employed contract work, the third type of employment relationship, has recently dominated the public's attention because of the increasing number of freelancers in the "gig economy." Fifteen percent of the Canadian labour force is self-employed, but this number likely excludes people who do contract work as second jobs beyond their jobs as employees. One American survey reports that more than one-third of the workforce in that country performs self-employed contract work.[69]

Traditionally, a self-employed contractor represents an independent organization that provides services to a client organization. The emergence of Uber, Airbnb, Uber Eats, and other branded platforms has created a less independent form of this relationship. Some experts suggest that platform-based workers are closer to on-call direct employees rather than contractors because they are dependent on the platform, abide by its work standards, and in some instances provide transportation, food delivery, or accommodation services when required by the platform.[70]

Consequences of Emerging Employment Relationships

Indirect employment and self-employed contract work increase job performance under some circumstances, but direct employment relationships tend to produce higher work quality, innovation, and agility. This is because permanent employees tend to have lower turnover, higher commitment, and more involvement in the company. They also tend to receive more organizational investment in their training, rewards, and other high-performance work practices.

Teams that include both direct employment and agency workers tend to have weaker social networks, which results in less information sharing (see Chapter 10). Contract workers generally have similar levels of job satisfaction as direct employment workers, whereas agency workers tend to have lower job satisfaction. In fact, the presence of agency (outsourced) workers can adversely affect the satisfaction and commitment of permanent employees in the client organization. Direct employment anchors an individual's self-concept (see Chapter 3), whereas people working in outsourced/agency and contract relationships need to discover how to replicate this stability in their self-view and role. Finally, organizations have a myriad of structural controls to manage the performance of indirect and contract workers. However, managers in client firms seem to experience more ambiguity in their roles and less discretion in their daily attempts to guide the work of people who are technically not their own employees.[71]

MARS Model of Individual Behaviour and Performance

LO5

For most of the past century, experts have investigated the direct predictors of individual behaviour and performance.[72] One of the earliest formulas was *performance = person × situation,* where *person* includes individual characteristics and *situation* represents external influences on the individual's behaviour. Another frequently mentioned formula is *performance = ability × motivation.*[73] Sometimes known as the "skill-and-will" model, this formula elaborates two specific characteristics within the person that influence individual performance. Some organizational studies use the *ability–motivation–opportunity (AMO)* model, which refers to the three variables but with a limited interpretation of the situation. Along with ability, motivation, and situation, researchers have more recently identified a fourth direct predictor of individual behaviour and performance: role perceptions (the individual's expected role obligations).[74]

These four variables—motivation, ability, role perceptions, and situational factors—are represented in the **MARS model** of individual behaviour and results (see Exhibit 1.7). *MARS* is the acronym for these four concepts.[75] All four factors are essential influences on an individual's voluntary behaviour and performance; if any one of them is low in a given situation, the employee is less likely to engage in the behaviour or will perform the behaviour poorly. For example, motivated salespeople with clear role perceptions and sufficient resources (situational factors) will not perform their jobs as well if they lack sales skills and related knowledge (ability).

> **MARS model** A model depicting the four variables—motivation, ability, role perceptions, and situational factors—that directly influence an individual's voluntary behaviour and performance.

Motivation, ability, and role perceptions are clustered together in the model because they are located within the person. Situational factors are external to the individual but still affect their behaviour and performance.[76] The four MARS variables are the direct predictors of employee performance, customer service, co-worker collegiality, ethical behaviour, and all other forms of voluntary behaviour in the workplace. Let's look at each of the four factors in the MARS model.

EMPLOYEE MOTIVATION

Motivation represents the forces within a person that affect the direction,

> **motivation** The forces within a person that affect the direction, intensity, and persistence of effort for voluntary behaviour.

EXHIBIT 1.7   MARS Model of Individual Behaviour and Results

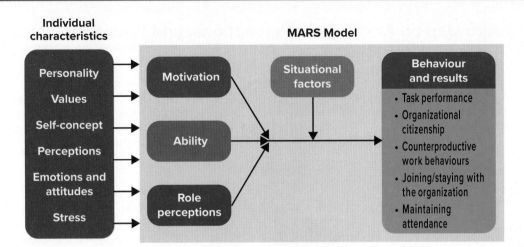

intensity, and persistence of effort for voluntary behaviour.[77] *Direction* refers to the path along which people steer their effort. In other words, motivation is goal-directed, not random. People have choices about what they are trying to achieve and at what level of quality, quantity, and so forth. They are motivated to arrive at work on time, finish a project a few hours early, or aim for many other targets.

The second element of motivation, called *intensity,* is the amount of effort allocated to the goal. Intensity is all about how much people push themselves to complete a task. Two employees might be motivated to finish their project within the next few hours (direction), but only one of them puts forth enough effort (intensity) to achieve this goal. The third element of motivation is *persistence,* which refers to the length of time that the individual continues to exert effort toward an objective. Employees sustain their effort until they reach their goal or give up beforehand.

To help remember these three elements of motivation, consider the metaphor of driving a car in which the thrust of the engine is your effort. Direction refers to where you steer the car, intensity is how much you put your foot down on the gas pedal, and persistence is for how long you drive toward your destination. Remember that motivation is a force that exists within individuals; it is not their actual behaviour. Thus, direction, intensity, and persistence are cognitive (thoughts) and emotional conditions that directly cause us to move.

ABILITY

Employee abilities have a well-known influence on behaviour and task performance. **Ability** includes both the learned capabilities and natural aptitudes required to successfully complete a task. *Learned capabilities* include the skills and knowledge that people acquire, such as through training, practice, and other forms of learning. Learned capabilities tend to wane over time if they are not regularly put to use. *Aptitudes* are the natural talents that help employees learn specific tasks more quickly and perform them better. For example, finger dexterity is an aptitude by which individuals learn more quickly and potentially achieve higher performance at picking up and handling small objects with their fingers. Employees with high finger dexterity are not necessarily better than others at first; rather, they usually learn the skill faster and potentially reach a higher level of performance.[78]

The challenge is to match a person's abilities with the job's requirements because a good match tends to increase employee performance and well-being. One matching strategy is to select applicants who already demonstrate the required abilities. For example, companies ask applicants to perform work samples, provide references for checking their past performance, and complete various selection tests. A second strategy is to train employees who lack specific knowledge or skills needed for the job.[79] The third person–job matching strategy is to redesign the job so that employees are given tasks only within their current abilities. For example, a complex task might be simplified—some aspects of the work are transferred to others—so a new employee is only assigned tasks that they are currently able to perform. As the employee becomes more competent at these tasks, other tasks are added back into the job.

ability The natural aptitudes and learned capabilities required to successfully complete a task.

OB by the NUMBERS

Mind the MARS Gap on Ability, Role Perceptions, and Situational Factors*

83% of 160,000 Canadian federal government employees strongly or somewhat agree that their job is a good fit with their skills.

81% of 1,001 Canadian employees surveyed say they are motivated by their job.

50% of 2.2 million employees worldwide agree that they know what is expected of them.

24% of 20,000 employees surveyed across 500 organizations say not having the tools needed to do the job has decreased their productivity.

40% of 25,000 employees worldwide strongly agree that their managers have clearly defined their roles and responsibilities.

*The TINYpulse 2015 Employee Engagement & Organizational Culture Report: The Era of Personal and Peer Accountability(Seattle: TINYpulse, February 2016); Gallup Inc.,State of the American Workplace(Washington, DC: Gallup, February 23, 2017; "2018 Public Service Employee Survey: Results for the Public Service" (Ottawa: Government of Canada, Treasury Board of Canada Secretariat, 2019); TINYpulse, "The 2019 Employee Engagement Report" (Seattle, February 22, 2019); "Personal Achievement and Interpersonal Relations Driving Canadian Workers," News Release (Montreal: Hamster, May 21, 2019). The sample of 20,000 in the TINYpulse 2016 report is inferred from the sample of its 2019 report. The 2016 survey only states the number of responses (400,000).

ROLE PERCEPTIONS

Along with motivation and ability, employees require accurate **role perceptions** to perform their jobs well. Role perceptions refer to how clearly people understand what is expected of them, such as their job duties. These perceptions range from role clarity to role ambiguity. When 7,000 employees in a global survey were asked what would most improve their performance, "greater clarity about what the organization needs from me" was identified as the most important factor.[80]

role perceptions The degree to which a person understands the job duties assigned to or expected of them.

Role clarity exists in three forms. First, employees have clear role perceptions when they understand the specific duties or consequences for which they are accountable. This may seem obvious, but employees are occasionally evaluated on job duties they were never told was within their zone of responsibility. This lack of role clarity may be an increasing concern as organizations move away from precisely defined job descriptions to broader work responsibilities.

Second, role clarity exists when employees understand the priority of their various tasks and performance expectations. This is illustrated in the classic dilemma of prioritizing quantity versus quality, such as how many customers to serve in an hour (quantity) versus how well the employee should serve each customer (quality). Role clarity in the form of task priorities also exists in the dilemma of allocating personal time and resources, such as how much time managers should devote to coaching employees versus meeting with clients. The third form of role perceptions involves understanding the preferred behaviours or procedures for accomplishing tasks. Role ambiguity exists when an employee knows two or three ways to perform a task, but misunderstands which of these the company prefers.

Role perceptions are important because they represent how well employees know where to direct their effort.[81] Employees with role clarity perform work more accurately and efficiently whereas those with role ambiguity waste considerable time and energy by performing the wrong tasks or the right tasks in the wrong way. Furthermore, role clarity is essential for coordination with co-workers and other stakeholders. For instance, performers at Canada's Cirque du Soleil depend on each other to perform precise behaviours at exact times, such as catching each other in midair. Role clarity ensures that these expectations are met and the performances are executed safely. Finally, role clarity motivates employees because they have a higher belief that their effort will produce the expected outcomes. In other words, people are more confident exerting the required effort when they know what is expected of them.

SITUATIONAL FACTORS

Individual behaviour and performance also depend on the situation, which is any context beyond the employee's immediate control.[82] The situation has two main influences on individual

©AP Photo/Julio Cortez

Virtual reality training is helping Walmart employees improve their knowledge, skills, and role perceptions. To experience the chaos of a virtual Black Friday workday, one employee slips on VR goggles and acts out the role. Meanwhile, other classmates view a projection of the same scene of long lines, confused shoppers, a toddler standing on a shopping cart seat, and a manager searching for lost keys. The instructor tests role perceptions by asking the goggled student and other classmates to prioritize what should be done, and to describe the preferred behaviours for each incident. For example, Walmart has a preferred way to correct the child's risky behaviour in the shopping cart (hint: don't tell the child directly). "Black Friday is a busy, hectic day for everyone," says Sandi Hughes, a Walmart employee in St. Petersburg, Florida. "With the VR, an associate can feel how it can play out."*

*L. Mirabella, "Walmart Employees Get Real Look at Retail World; Virtual Reality Technology Prepares Supervisors for Situations That Might Arise," *Baltimore Sun,* December 3, 2017; H. Shively, "Area Stores Training Employees Using Virtual Reality," *TCA Regional News,* November 12, 2018; S. DiNatale, "What's It Like to Train for Walmart's Black Friday? Local Stores Use Virtual Reality Goggles," *Tampa Bay Times,* November 13, 2018.

behaviour and performance.[83] One influence is that the work context constrains or facilitates behaviour and performance. Employees who are motivated, skilled, and know their role obligations will nevertheless perform poorly if they lack time, budget, physical work facilities, and other resources. The second influence is that the work environment provides cues to guide and motivate people. For example, companies install barriers and warning signs in dangerous areas. These workplace features are situational factors that cue employees to avoid the nearby hazards.

Types of Individual Behaviour

LO6

The four elements of the MARS model—motivation, ability, role perceptions, and situational factors—affect all voluntary workplace behaviours and performance. There are many varieties of individual behaviour, but most can be organized

into the five categories described in this section: task performance, organizational citizenship behaviours, counterproductive work behaviours, joining and staying with the organization, and maintaining work attendance (Exhibit 1.8).

TASK PERFORMANCE

Task performance refers to the individual's voluntary goal-directed behaviours that contribute to organizational objectives.[84] Most jobs require incumbents to complete several tasks. For example, foreign exchange traders at RBC Capital Markets in Toronto and elsewhere must be able to identify and execute profitable trades, work cooperatively with clients and co-workers, assist in training new staff, and work on special computer and other digital equipment without

task performance The individual's voluntary goal-directed behaviours that contribute to organizational objectives.

EXHIBIT 1.8   Five Types of Individual Behaviour in the Workplace

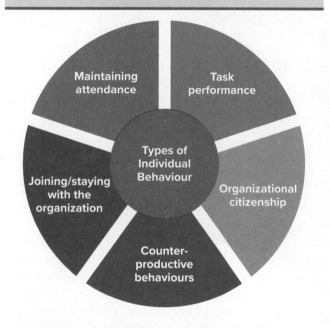

error. All tasks involve various degrees of working with people, data, things, and ideas.[85] Foreign exchange traders, for instance, mainly work with data (e.g., performing technical analysis of trends), but also with people (e.g., sharing information with co-workers and clients) and ideas (interpreting charts and economic reports).

There are three types of task performance: proficient, adaptive, and proactive.[86]

- *Proficient task performance* refers to performing the work efficiently and accurately. It involves accomplishing the assigned work at or above the expected standards of quality, quantity, and other indicators of effectiveness.
- *Adaptive task performance* refers to how well employees modify their thoughts and behaviour to align with and support a new or changing work process or work setting. Essentially, adaptive task performance is about how well employees respond to change in the workplace and in their job duties.
- *Proactive task performance* refers to how well employees take the initiative to anticipate and introduce new work

Global Connections 1.3

ADAPTIVE PERFORMANCE IN DAIMLER'S SWARM TEAMS*

Employees with high adaptive performance are increasingly important at Daimler AG. The German automobile giant is creating more fluid team-based structures to keep pace with rapidly changing consumer preferences and technological innovations. "The world we live and work in is undergoing unprecedented change," advises Daimler senior executive Wilfried Porth. "Creativity, flexibility and responsiveness are the top skills going forward into the future."

Daimler is shifting up to 20 percent of its employees out of its traditional rigid hierarchy into a more fluid and highly variable structure of temporary swarm teams. "Swarms work autonomously, are self-organized, set goals and roles, have complete end-to-end responsibility, and include a diverse range of people across functions and skill sets," explains Sabine Scheunert, vice president Digital and IT Marketing/Sales of Daimler's Mercedes-Benz Cars unit.

Some swarms have a dozen team members on short-term projects; others are large-scale projects (such as Daimler's next-generation procurement process) that bring together up to 80 experts from across the organization. No matter what size or duration, swarms require members who can comfortably and efficiently adapt their roles and membership in different swarm projects where their skills are needed.

©Sueddeutsche Zeitung Photo/Alamy Stock Photo

* J. Brecht, "How to Make Swarms Work.," LinkedIn, March 7, 2018, https://www.linkedin.com/pulse/how-make-swarms-work-jan-brecht; "Ready to Be Different," Diversity Report (Stuttgart: Daimler AG, May 24, 2018); R. Deiser, "Part 5: Agility in Practice: The Swarm Organization at Daimler," *The Digital Transformation People* (blog), May 7, 2019, https://www.thedigitaltransformationpeople.com/channels/people-and-change/agility-in-practice-the-swarm-organization-at-daimler/; Capgemini Research Institute, "Daimler: Accelerating Digital Innovation by Transforming Culture, Collaboration, and Talent: An Interview with Sabine Scheunert, Daimler AG," Digital Leadership (Paris: Capgemini, February 8, 2019).

patterns that benefit the organization. Proactive behaviours bring about change in oneself, co-workers, and the workplace to achieve what is perceived to be a better future for the organization.

Employees in almost every job are expected to perform their work proficiently. However, adaptive and proactive task performance are also important when the work is ambiguous or dynamic. These conditions exist when the client's expectations are unclear, resources to perform the work have uncertain availability, and the methods used to perform the work are rapidly evolving due to emerging technology.

ORGANIZATIONAL CITIZENSHIP BEHAVIOURS

Employee behaviour extends beyond performing specific tasks. It also includes **organizational citizenship behaviours (OCBs),** which are various forms of cooperation and helpfulness to others that support the organization's social and psychological context.[87] Some OCBs are directed toward individuals, such as assisting co-workers with their work problems, adjusting your work schedule to accommodate co-workers, showing genuine courtesy toward co-workers, and sharing your work resources (supplies, technology, staff) with co-workers. Other OCBs represent cooperation and helpfulness toward the organization, such as supporting the company's public image, offering ideas beyond those required for one's own job, attending events that support the organization, and keeping up with new developments in the organization. Some organizational citizenship behaviours are discretionary (employees don't have to perform them), whereas other OCBs are job requirements even if they aren't explicitly stated in job descriptions. In fact, research suggests that managers often evaluate performance by the employee's organizational citizenship behaviours as much as their task performance.[88]

OCBs can have a significant effect on individual, team, and organizational effectiveness.[89] High-OCB employees receive more support from co-workers which, in turn, supports their own task performance. OCBs also increase team performance because members depend on one another. However, engaging in OCBs can have negative consequences.[90] OCBs take time and energy away from performing tasks, so employees who give more attention to OCBs risk lower career success in companies that reward task performance. Also, employees who frequently perform OCBs

> **organizational citizenship behaviours (OCBs)** Various forms of cooperation and helpfulness to others that support the organization's social and psychological context.

tend to have higher work–family conflict because of the amount of time required for these activities.

COUNTERPRODUCTIVE WORK BEHAVIOURS

Organizational behaviour is interested in all workplace behaviours, including dysfunctional activities collectively known as **counterproductive work behaviours (CWBs)**. CWBs are voluntary behaviours that have the potential to directly or indirectly harm the organization or its stakeholders.[91] This concept includes a wide array of intentional and unintentional behaviours, such as harassing co-workers, creating unnecessary conflict, deviating from preferred work methods (e.g., shortcuts that undermine work quality), being untruthful, stealing, sabotaging work, and wasting resources. CWBs are not minor concerns; research suggests that they can substantially undermine the organization's effectiveness.

> **counterproductive work behaviours (CWBs)** Voluntary behaviours that have the potential to directly or indirectly harm the organization.

JOINING AND STAYING WITH THE ORGANIZATION

Companies suffer and potentially fail if they can't hire and retain enough people with the right skills and knowledge to perform the work.[92] This isn't a hypothetical statement. During times of economic growth, Canadian companies consistently identify the shortage of skilled labour as the number-one factor limiting their ability to increase sales or production.

The effects of staff shortages are even more dramatic during crises, such as the coronavirus (COVID-19) pandemic. Some hospitals in Toronto were so short-staffed due to the virus that employees who would normally enter two-week self-isolation periods after returning from overseas were asked to immediately report for work. Quebec found it so difficult to staff the province's long-term care homes during the pandemic that the federal government sent 1,000 soldiers and dozens of military staff with medical training to temporarily assist these facilities in caring for elderly Canadians.[93]

Even when companies are able to hire qualified staff in the face of shortages, they need to ensure that these employees stay with the company.[94] Earlier in this chapter, we explained that human capital is the organization's main source of competitive advantage. The importance of human capital is particularly apparent when employees quit. Those who leave remove valuable knowledge, skills, and relationships with co-workers and external stakeholders, all of which take time for new staff to acquire. Other problems with employee turnover are discussed in later chapters, such as its adverse effect on customer service, team development, and corporate culture strength. Employee turnover does offer some benefits, such as opening up positions so new employees with fresh ideas can be hired and removing people without counterproductive work behaviours. But overall, turnover usually has a negative effect on organizational effectiveness.

MAINTAINING WORK ATTENDANCE

Along with attracting and retaining employees, organizations need everyone to show up for work at scheduled times. Unscheduled absenteeism can lead to increased workloads or overtime among co-workers, lower performance by temporary staff filling the vacant positions, poorer coordination in the work process, poorer customer service, and potentially more workplace accidents.[95] Canadian employees are absent an average of 10 days of scheduled work each year, including eight days due to illness or injury and two days due to personal or family reasons. How absenteeism is calculated varies across countries, but an approximate comparison is that Americans are absent an average of four days per year (including 2.5 days due to illness or injury) and British employees are absent due to sickness (illness or injury) an average of 4.1 days per year.[96]

What are the main causes of absenteeism and lateness?[97] Much absenteeism is due to situational factors, such as personal illness, family demands (e.g., sick children), and bad weather. Other absenteeism occurs because employees need to get away from workplace bullying, difficult customers, boring work, and other stressful conditions. Absenteeism is also higher in organizations with generous sick leave because this benefit minimizes the financial loss of taking time away from work. Absenteeism also varies from one employee to the next due to personal values and personality. Finally, studies report that absenteeism is higher in teams with strong absence norms, meaning that team members tolerate and even expect co-workers to take time off.

Presenteeism

Although most companies focus on minimizing absenteeism, a potentially equally serious behaviour is *presenteeism*—showing up for work when unwell, injured, preoccupied by personal problems, or faced with dangerous conditions getting to work.[98] Employees who show up for work when they should be

---

 ## Global Connections 1.4

THE DOCTOR IS ILL. . .BUT WILL SEE YOU NOW*

Most physicians urge sick patients to stay home, yet few take their own advice. Three-quarters of New Zealand doctors working in hospitals say they went to work while unwell over the previous year. Approximately the same percentage of Swedish doctors recently surveyed admitted that over the previous year they had gone to work one or more times with an illness for which they would have advised patients to stay at home.

"Presenteeism is the elephant in the room that nobody wants to talk or do anything about," suggests Michael Edmond, an executive and physician at the University of Iowa Hospitals & Clinics. It is difficult for medical centres to find a replacement on short notice and many doctors feel guilty letting down their co-workers and patients.

"There is an unspoken understanding that you probably should be on your deathbed if you are calling in sick," says an attending physician at a Philadelphia hospital where 83 percent of doctors admitted working while sick within the past year. "It inconveniences my colleagues, is complicated to pay back shifts, and makes me look bad to do so."

©pathdoc/Shutterstock

* M.B. Edmond, "How Sick Is Too Sick to Work? Presenteeism in Healthcare," *Medscape,* September 23, 2015; C. Chambers, *Superheroes Don't Take Sick Leave,* Association of Salaried Medical Specialists (New Zealand), November 2015; J.E. Szymczak et al., "Reasons Why Physicians and Advanced Practice Clinicians Work While Sick: A Mixed-Methods Analysis," *JAMA Pediatrics* 169, no. 9 (2015): 815–21; S. Marie Gustafsson, K. Schenck-Gustafsson, and A. Fridner, "Gender Differences in Reasons for Sickness Presenteeism - a Study among GPs in a Swedish Health Care Organization," *Annals of Occupational and Environmental Medicine* 28, no. 50 (2016).

absent tend to be less productive and may reduce the productivity of co-workers. They may also worsen their own health and spread disease to co-workers. This latter risk of presenteeism had particularly serious consequences during the COVID-19 pandemic. Entire offices and production facilities shut down after just one employee went to work while ill, which quickly spread the virus to dozens or hundreds of other people.

Presenteeism is more common among employees with low job security (such as new and temporary staff), employees who lack sick leave pay or similar financial buffers, and those whose absence would immediately affect many people. Personality, which we discuss in Chapter 2, also motivates some people to show up for work when others would gladly recover at home.[99]

The Journey Begins

This chapter gives you some background about the field of organizational behaviour, the emerging landscape of organizations, and why OB is important for you and for organizations. It also introduces the foundations of individual behaviour and performance as well as the main types of individual behaviour. But this is only the beginning of our journey. Throughout this book, we will challenge you to learn new ways of thinking about how people work in and around organizations. We begin this process in Chapter 2 through to Chapter 7 by looking at personality, values, and other individual differences that indirectly predict individual behaviour through the MARS model. Next, this book moves to the team level of analysis. We examine a model of team effectiveness and specific features of high-performance teams. We also look at communication, power and influence, conflict, and leadership. Finally, we shift our focus to the organizational level of analysis, where the topics of organizational structure, organizational culture, and organizational change are examined in detail.

Chapter Summary

LO1

Define organizational behaviour and organizations.

Organizational behaviour is the study of what people think, feel, and do in and around organizations. It examines how individuals and teams in organizations relate to one another, and how organizations interact with their external environments. This field of knowledge emerged around the early 1940s, but organizations have been studied by other disciplines for more than two thousand years. Organizations are groups of people who work interdependently toward some purpose. They consist of people who interact with one another in an organized way and have a collective sense of purpose.

LO2

Explain why organizational behaviour knowledge is important for you and for organizations.

Organizational behaviour is important for you because it offers a core foundation of knowledge and skill development for your success in organizations. The skills and knowledge that employers look for in new hires, above anything else, are the topics found in organizational behaviour, including problem solving, working effectively in teams, communication, and leadership. More broadly, OB helps you adopt better personal theories to understand, predict, and influence organizational events. OB knowledge is for everyone, not just managers.

OB theories and practices are vital to the organization's survival and success. In fact, most OB theories implicitly or explicitly try to improve organizational effectiveness—an ideal state in which an organization has a good fit with its external environment, effectively transforms inputs to outputs through human capital, and satisfies the needs of key stakeholders. Organizational behaviour knowledge is highly relevant to the open systems view of organizations by identifying organizational characteristics that "fit" some external environments better than others. OB theories offer guidance on how to effectively transform inputs to outputs.

OB is also important for organizations because it identifies ways for organizations to develop and leverage the potential of human capital—the knowledge, skills, abilities, creativity, and other valued resources that employees bring to the organization. Several organizational behaviour topics also give us a better understanding of relations with stakeholders—individuals, groups, and other entities that affect, or are affected by, the organization's objectives and actions. This latter focus includes the role of personal values (the relatively stable, evaluative beliefs that guide a person's preferences for outcomes or courses of action in a variety of situations) and corporate social responsibility (organizational activities intended to benefit society and the environment beyond the firm's immediate financial interests or legal obligations).

LO3

Describe the anchors on which organizational behaviour knowledge is based.

The systematic research anchor states that OB knowledge should be based on systematic research, consistent with evidence-based management. The practical orientation anchor states that OB theories need to be useful in practice, such as by helping organizations become more effective. The multidisciplinary anchor states that the field should develop from knowledge in other disciplines (e.g., psychology, sociology, economics), not just from its own isolated research base. The contingency anchor states that OB theories generally need to consider that there will be different consequences in different situations. The multiple levels of analysis anchor states that OB topics may be viewed from the individual, team, and organization levels of analysis.

LO4

Summarize the workplace trends of diversity and the inclusive workplace, work–life integration, remote work, and emerging employment relationships.

An inclusive workplace values people of all identities and allows them to be fully themselves while contributing to the organization. It views diversity as a valued resource. An organization's workforce has both surface-level diversity (observable demographic and other overt differences in people) and deep-level diversity (differences in personalities, beliefs, values, and attitudes). Inclusive workplaces produce better decisions, employee attitudes, team performance, and a host of other favourable outcomes for employees and the organization. However, diversity also poses challenges, such as dysfunctional conflict and slower team development.

Work–life integration refers to the degree that people are effectively engaged in their various work and nonwork roles and have a low degree of role conflict across those life domains. Various work and nonwork roles are inherently integrated because the physical, cognitive, and emotional resources produced or consumed by one role potentially enrich or undermine the success and enjoyment of other roles. There are several ways to maximize work–life integration, such as by doing things that mix two roles, engaging in flexible work scheduling, ensuring that work and nonwork roles are aligned with your personal characteristics, and engaging in some degree of "boundary management" across roles.

An increasing percentage of the workforce performs their jobs remotely some or all of the time rather than at the organization's physical work site. Some organizations are completely remote—everyone works at home and at cafés and the company has no physical head office. Working remotely potentially benefits employees and employers, but there are also disadvantages. The effectiveness of remote work depends on the employee, job, and organization.

Most of the workforce has a direct employment relationship—working as an employee for an organization—but an increasing percentage has more fragile direct employment relationships (part-time, on-call, etc.). The largest labour market growth has been indirect (outsourced/agency) and contract work. Some contractors negotiate their own contracts with the client, whereas others work through branded platform companies (e.g., Uber). These emerging employment relationships have both positive and negative consequences for job performance, job satisfaction, team dynamics, self-concept stability and clarity, and the ambiguity of managerial roles.

LO5

Describe the four factors that directly influence individual behaviour and performance.

Four variables—motivation, ability, role perceptions, and situational factors—which are represented by the acronym MARS, directly influence individual behaviour and performance. Motivation represents the forces within a person that affect their direction, intensity, and persistence of voluntary behaviour; ability includes both the natural aptitudes and the learned capabilities required to successfully complete a task; role perceptions are the extent to which people understand the job duties (roles) assigned to them or expected of them; and situational factors include conditions beyond the employee's immediate control that constrain or facilitate behaviour and performance.

LO6

Summarize the five types of individual behaviour in organizations.

There are five main types of workplace behaviour. Task performance refers to goal-directed behaviours under the individual's control that support organizational objectives. It includes proficiency, adaptivity, and proactivity. Organizational citizenship behaviours consist of various forms of cooperation and helpfulness to others that support the organization's social and psychological context. Counterproductive work behaviours are voluntary behaviours that have the potential to directly or indirectly harm the organization. Joining and staying with the organization refers to agreeing to become an organizational member and remaining with the organization. Maintaining work attendance includes minimizing absenteeism when capable of working and avoiding scheduled work when not fit (i.e., low presenteeism).

Key Terms

ability

corporate social responsibility (CSR)

counterproductive work behaviours (CWBs)

deep-level diversity

evidence-based management

human capital

inclusive workplace

MARS model

motivation

open systems

organizational behaviour (OB)

organizational citizenship behaviours (OCBs)

organizational effectiveness

organizations

role perceptions

stakeholders

surface-level diversity

task performance

values

work–life integration

Critical Thinking Questions

1. A friend suggests that organizational behaviour courses are useful only to people in management careers. Discuss the accuracy of your friend's statement.

2. Problem solving, teamwork, communication, and leadership are four of the top skills identified by employers as most important when hiring (see Exhibit 1.1). How have these skills been important (or unimportant) for you in jobs that you have held or as a student? Identify one other skill that you would place at or near the top of the list for working effectively in organizations.

3. A young college or university student from Canada is interested in doing international business across China, India, Brazil, and Russia. Discuss how the knowledge of OB can be useful to the student.

4. A common refrain among executives is "People are our most important asset." Relate this statement to how organizational behaviour theories and practices improve organizational effectiveness through human capital.

5. Corporate social responsibility is one of the hottest issues in corporate boardrooms these days, partly because it is becoming increasingly important to employees and other stakeholders. In your opinion, why have stakeholders given CSR more attention recently? Does abiding by CSR standards potentially cause companies to have conflicting objectives with some stakeholders in some situations?

6. What does *evidence-based management* mean? Describe situations you have heard about in which companies have practised evidence-based management, as well as situations in which companies have relied on fads that lacked sufficient evidence of their worth.

7. Work–life integration is one of the most important issues that job applicants consider when choosing where to work. Think about the variety of specific benefits, working conditions, or resources that employers offer to support work–life integration. Which of these is most valuable to you personally at this stage in your life and career? Why? In what ways have you personally been able to minimize conflict between your work (including school) and nonwork roles?

8. Emsisoft and Automattic are completely remote (distributed) companies. Everyone who works for these firms performs their jobs from home or cafés. In your opinion, will distributed companies become more common in the future? Why or why not? Would you prefer working in a remote company—one that has no physical location, just (maybe) an occasional gathering of staff at a conference setting or resort? Or do you prefer working face-to-face with co-workers most days at a company work site? Why?

9. A federal government department has high levels of absenteeism among the office staff. The head of office administration argues that employees are misusing the company's sick leave benefits. However, some of the mostly female staff members have explained that family responsibilities interfere with work. Using the MARS model, as well as your knowledge of absenteeism behaviour, discuss some of the possible reasons for absenteeism here and how it might be reduced.

10. Why might employees display presenteeism? What can organizations do to reduce presenteeism and how ethical are these strategies?

 Case Study:

PROMOTING SAFE BEHAVIOUR AT MOTHER PARKERS

by Steven L. McShane, University of Newcastle (Australia)

Most companies try to create a safe work environment, but few are as dedicated as Mother Parkers Tea & Coffee Inc. As North America's largest private-label coffee producer, the Canadian company infuses safety knowledge, awareness, and engagement in every employee and contractor. "One of our priorities here has been to provide a safe workplace to our employees," says Adrian Khan, Mother Parkers's Senior Manager of Environmental, Health, Safety, and Security for North America. "They make a commitment to us to help produce great quality products; we make a commitment to them to provide them with a safe working environment."

To begin with, Mother Parkers creates a physically safe work environment through well-designed barriers and cues at its award-winning automated production facilities in

Mississauga, Ontario, and Fort Worth, Texas. The production floor includes physical barriers to separate people from moving equipment. Safe walking areas are brightly marked, including specific spots where people must stop and look both ways before crossing forklift travel areas. At eye level next to doors are signs specifying what equipment (shoes, eyewear, etc.) must be worn before entering the next area. Updated lighting systems provide superior visibility and eye comfort.

Another way that Mother Parkers supports safe behaviour is by investing in employee training. Staff learn safety procedures before they are allowed to enter the production floor. They also learn about new safety technology and practices from community experts at special health-and-safety-day events.

Employee involvement is an important part of safety improvement at Mother Parkers. Employees participate in safety issues so decisions are based on a full complement of knowledge from employees, not just from management and outside experts. "We wanted to empower the operators to recognize hazards in their work area, voice those concerns, and to be a part of the solutions," says Khan, who recently won a national safety leadership award. "When it comes down to it, they are the experts running the machines who know exactly what the hazards are in the workplace." For example, when the company decided to buy an ergonomic roll lifter (a machine that holds and transports heavy rolls of metal), employees on the ergonomics team tested many of the roll lifters on the market to determine which one was the best fit for their application.

Mother Parkers has held numerous "ergonomic blitzes," whereby an external consultant and production staff conduct an intensive review of health and safety concerns in each specific work area. "We jump-started our program by having ergonomics blitz events so that the team could 'Find It' (hazards), 'Fix It' (countermeasures), and 'Check It' (happy operators)," says Khan. "From there, the team would have a number of short-term solutions that could be implemented immediately, and also a list of longer-term improvements that could be planned for."

A special cross-functional team developed from these "ergo blitzes," whose members now serve as role models for safety behaviour and as valuable sources of safety knowledge. "This creates a go-to group of operators on the floor that their peers feel comfortable with and can go to if they want to report an issue," Khan observes.

Employee involvement also generates employee commitment to safety. "There's a high level of engagement here," says a Mother Parkers production manager. "The operators have been developing most of the procedures for equipment operation, cleaning, quality checks, and troubleshooting. The operators take ownership of their positions." Mike Bate, Mother Parkers's vice-president of human resources, notes that employees are more motivated to act safely because the company pays attention to their ideas. "Our health and safety committees are now engaged, they have plans, they have ideas, people's voices get heard. And when they bring issues on the table, those issues get dealt with and they get addressed and they are part of the planning process."

Another way that Mother Parkers promotes workplace safety is by continuously reminding everyone that safety is an important part of everyone's job. This message occurs through ongoing safety training, employee involvement in ergonomic risk prevention, and the presence of numerous workplace safety cues. Reminding everyone about safety is even a daily event. "Safety is the core of everything we do here," explains the production manager of Mother Parkers's award-winning RealCup operations. "We begin our production meetings and shift handovers by talking about safety."

Safety-focused expectations also extend to contractors, all of whom complete a safety training program before their projects begin. "We set expectations and standards with contractors before they come on site on what it means to be on site at Mother Parkers from a health and safety perspective," says Mike Bate. "Before they even get approved to come on site and work with us as a contractor [they have to] register themselves to say they have gone through this education. So by the time they arrive, [contractors] understand the risks, they bring the proper protective equipment that may be required, or they understand what they need from us to make the workplace safe for them to work in."

Discussion Questions

1. Apply the MARS model to explain how Mother Parkers improves safety in the workplace.

2. What other organizational behaviour topics are generally apparent in this description of how Mother Parkers creates a safe workplace?

Class Exercise:
WORLD CAFÉ ON THE EMERGING WORKPLACE

by Steven L. McShane, University of Newcastle (Australia)

Purpose This exercise is designed to help you understand organizational behaviour issues that arise in the emerging workplace landscape, particularly regarding inclusive workplace, remote work, and emerging employment relationships (agency and contract workers).

Materials The learning space should allow for one large table or other dedicated area for every 10 or so students in the class. One person at each table (the "scribe") should have some means (e.g., paper/pencil, computer/tablet) of documenting ideas presented.

Instructions

Step 1: Students are organized into teams of approximately 10 people. Each team is initially assigned to a large table or dedicated space for the team. The instructor will assign one of the three themes (see below) to each table. For example, if the class has 60 students, there would be six tables of 10 students. Two tables would be assigned the theme of inclusive workplace, two tables would look at remote work, and two tables would look at employment relationships (agency/contract work).

Step 2: One person on each team volunteers to be the "scribe" for that table. Throughout the exercise, the scribe documents the main ideas presented by students who attend that table. The scribe remains at that table for the entire exercise (other team members will move to other tables during the exercise). All scribes will later debrief the class on the key points they documented on the theme assigned to their table.

Step 3: Teams will read the questions assigned to the theme of their initial table (see below). They have a fixed time (usually between 10 and 15 minutes) to discuss their views and offer answers to those questions.

Step 4: After the preset discussion time has ended, the instructor will direct students at each table (except the scribe, who remains at the table) to another table that has a different theme. For example, students at a "remote work" table would move to a table assigned the "agency/contract work" or "inclusive workplace" theme. Students will read the questions assigned to the theme of this second table. The instructor again assigns a fixed time (10–15 minutes) for students to discuss their new theme.

Step 5: The scribe will add the ideas presented by the second group to those provided by the first group. The scribe should *not* tell the second group what the first group discussed about this theme. The scribe should remain quiet, except for asking for clarification.

Step 6: After the preset discussion time has ended, the instructor will direct students at each table (except the scribe

who remains at the table) to the third table that has a different theme from the previous two tables. Scribes document ideas from their third group without informing them of what the previous teams discussed on that theme.

Step 7: After the third round of discussion has ended, the whole class will gather and listen to the main ideas documented by the scribes. This is usually 3 to 5 minutes per scribe. If two or more tables have the same theme, the scribes of those tables should present at the same time or consecutively (e.g., if two scribes have the remote work theme, they should speak to the class together or one after the other).

WORLD CAFÉ DISCUSSION THEMES

Table 1: Inclusive Workplace

An inclusive workplace values people of all identities (i.e., surface- and deep-level diversity) and allows them to be fully themselves while contributing to the organization.

1. What challenges do organizations and their employees experience on their journey toward an inclusive workplace? Provide specific examples.

2. How can leaders (supervisors to executives) support and maintain workplace diversity? Provide specific examples from your experience in an organization that emphasizes and leverages (or undermines) the value of diversity.

3. What personal characteristics of leaders (supervisors to executives) make them better (or worse) equipped to support and lead people in an inclusive workplace? Why are those attributes important?

Table 2: Remote Workers

Remote workers are people who work from home or other off-site locations (not at client sites) some or all of the time.

1. What are the challenges for the organization and for employees who work remotely in terms of their effectiveness and well-being in this work arrangement? Provide specific examples. Several firms (Yahoo, IBM, etc.) have recently reduced the level of remote work. What problems do you think they experienced?

2. What personal characteristics enable some people to work remotely better (or worse) than other people? Why are those attributes important?

3. How can leaders (supervisors to executives) support and maintain the performance of remote workers? Provide specific examples from your experience as a remote worker, a supervisor of remote workers, or knowledge of others in those situations.

Table 3: Agency and Contract Workers

Agency workers work regularly at a client site but are employed by another firm (outsource company). Contractors are self-employed. This table will refer only to contractors who work at client sites.

1. What are the challenges for the organization and for employees who work as agency employees or contractors in terms of their effectiveness and well-being in this work arrangement? Provide specific examples.

2. What personal characteristics enable some people to work as agency/contract workers better (or worse) than other people? Why are those attributes important?

3. How can leaders (supervisors to executives) support and maintain the performance of agency and contract workers who are not their own employees? Provide specific examples from your experience as an agency/contract worker, a manager of agency/contract workers, or knowledge of others in those situations.

 Class Exercise:
IT ALL MAKES SENSE?

Purpose This exercise is designed to help you understand how organizational behaviour knowledge can help you refine and improve your personal theories about what goes on in organizations.

Instructions Read each of the statements below and determine whether each statement is true or false, in your opinion. The class will consider the answers to each question and discuss the implications for studying organizational behaviour.

This exercise may also be conducted as a team activity, whereby students answer these questions in teams rather than alone.

1.	True	False	A happy worker is a productive worker.
2.	True	False	A decision maker's effectiveness increases with the number of choices or alternatives available to them.
3.	True	False	Organizations are more effective when they minimize conflict among employees.
4.	True	False	Employees have more power with many close friends than with many acquaintances.
5.	True	False	Companies are more successful when they have strong corporate cultures.
6.	True	False	Employees perform better without stress.
7.	True	False	The best way to change people and organizations is by pinpointing the source of their current problems.
8.	True	False	Female leaders involve employees in decisions to a greater degree than do male leaders.
9.	True	False	The best decisions are made without emotion.
10.	True	False	If employees feel they are paid unfairly, nothing other than changing their pay will reduce their feelings of injustice.

Self-Assessment for Chapter 1

SELF-ASSESSMENT NAME	DESCRIPTION
Are you a good remote worker?	Remote work is an increasingly popular workplace activity, and it potentially offers benefits for both companies and employees. However, some people are better suited than others to remote work. This self-assessment estimates personal characteristics that relate to employee success at working remotely, thereby providing a rough indication of how well you might adjust to this work arrangement.

CHAPTER 2

Individual Differences: Personality and Values

LEARNING OBJECTIVES

After reading this chapter, you should be able to:

LO1 Define personality and discuss how the Big Five personality factors relate to workplace behaviour and performance.

LO2 Describe the dark triad of personality and the MBTI types and discuss their implications for organizational behaviour.

LO3 Summarize Schwartz's model of individual values and discuss the conditions where values influence behaviour.

LO4 Describe four ethical principles and discuss three factors that influence ethical behaviour.

LO5 Describe five values commonly studied across cultures, and discuss the diverse cultures within Canada.

Getting hired at Bridgewater Associates—the world's largest hedge fund—is not a cakewalk. Job applicants first watch online videos depicting the culture and daily office life at the American investment firm. Next, they spend a few hours completing four online assessments of their personality and values. Applicants who pass the online selection process engage in a structured interview over the phone with consultants, who further assess the individual's character. Even after accepting Bridgewater's job offer, new recruits take a final two-hour personality and personal values assessment developed by the company.

Bridgewater Associates founder Ray Dalio says assessing an individual's personality and values helps the investment firm assign people to jobs that fit their personal attributes. "I needed a systematic approach to capturing and recording our differences so that we could actively take them into consideration when putting people into different roles at Bridgewater," he wrote in his book *Principles: Life and Work.* The information is also used to diagnose why conflicts occur and why problems arise.

Bridgewater Associates places considerable weight on the personality, values, and other individual differences of its job applicants and employees.

©Monkey Business Images/Shutterstock

Each employee's personality, values, and other attributes are displayed on baseball cards available through a digital app to everyone in the company. Each attribute has a score based on the personality test results as well as subsequent ongoing instant evaluations by co-workers. "I found that we needed to have these [baseball cards] and refer to them regularly because without them, people tended to interact with each other without any regard to who was good or bad at what," says Dalio.[1]

Bridgewater Associates places considerable weight on the personality, values, and other individual differences of its job applicants and employees. It views personality and values as strong predictors of a person's decisions and behaviour, which then relate to how well they fit into particular roles and how well they work with others at Bridgewater.

Part 2 of this book discusses individual differences and begins in this chapter by presenting current knowledge about personality and values in organizations. We describe the meaning and origins of personality, introduce the five-factor personality model, and identify how each dimension of this highly regarded model relates to job performance and related behaviours. Two other personality models are then introduced: the dark triad (Machiavellianism, narcissism, and psychopathy) and the Jungian personality theory applied by the Myers-Briggs Type Indicator (MBTI). Next, our attention turns to personal values. We describe Schwartz's values circumplex model, explain how personal values influence workplace decisions and behaviour, and introduce the concept of values congruence. Later, we examine ethical values and the mechanisms through which they influence a person's decisions and behaviour. The final section of this chapter describes the best known cross-cultural values, explains their relevance to organizational behaviour, and examines similarities and differences in personal values across Canada and with people in the United States.

Personality and the Five-Factor Model in Organizations

LO1

personality The relatively enduring pattern of thoughts, emotions, and behaviours that characterize a person, along with the psychological processes behind those characteristics.

On any given day in almost every workplace, employees will invariably mention either their own or someone else's personality. **Personality** refers to the relatively enduring pattern of thoughts, emotions, and behaviours that characterize a person, along with the psychological processes behind those characteristics.[2] In essence, personality is the bundle of characteristics that makes us similar to or different from other

people. We estimate an individual's personality by what they say or do, and we infer the person's internal states—including thoughts and emotions—from these observable behaviours.

People engage in a wide range of behaviours in their daily lives, yet close inspection of those actions reveals discernible patterns called *personality traits*.[3] Traits are broad concepts that allow us to label and understand individual differences. For example, some of your friends are likely quite talkative whereas others are quieter. Some people like to take risks whereas others are risk-averse. Each trait implies that there is something within the person, rather than environmental influences alone, that predicts this behavioural tendency. In fact, studies report that an individual's personality traits measured in childhood predict various behaviours and outcomes in adulthood, including educational attainment, employment success, marital relationships, illegal activities, and health-risk behaviours.[4]

Although people have behavioural tendencies, they do not act the same way in all situations. Such consistency would be considered abnormal because it indicates a person's insensitivity to social norms, reward systems, and other external conditions.[5] People vary their behaviour to suit the situation, even if the behaviour is at odds with their personality. For example, talkative people remain relatively quiet in a library where "no talking" rules are explicit and strictly enforced. Even there, however, personality differences are apparent, because talkative people tend to do more chatting in libraries relative to how much other people talk in that setting.

WHAT CAUSES PERSONALITY: NATURE VERSUS NURTURE

Personality is shaped by both nature and nurture, although the relative importance of each continues to be debated and studied.[6] *Nature* refers to our genetic or hereditary origins—the genes that we inherit from our parents. Studies of identical twins reveal that heredity has a very large effect on personality; up to 50 percent of variation in behaviour and 30 percent of temperament preferences can be attributed to a person's genetic characteristics. In other words, genetic code not only determines our eye colour, skin tone, and physical shape; it also significantly affects our attitudes, decisions, and behaviour.

Personality is also shaped by *nurture*—our socialization, life experiences, and other forms of interaction with

©David Cooper/Toronto Star/Getty Images

Paladin Security Group Ltd. is Canada's largest independent security provider. One reason for this success is the Burnaby, B.C.-based firm's careful assessment of each job applicant's personality, skills, and other strengths. Through detailed interviews and psychological profiling, the company determines to what degree each job applicant's personality traits are similar to successful employees in that role. "We took our best and highest-performing people in every vertical and profiled them to find out exactly what traits and tendencies they have that make them so successful," says Paladin executive Chad Kalyk. Paladin CEO, Ashley Cooper, explains that different security jobs require people with different personality traits. "In health-care security, for example, we're looking for a high level of empathy. At an industrial site, we're looking for high scores in task orientation and attention to detail."*

* "How to Prepare for a Security Guard Interview," *Paladin Security* (blog), June 27, 2019, https://paladinsecurity.com/security-careers/how-to-prepare-for-a-security-guard-interview/; R. Counter, "How Paladin Security Group Became Canada's Largest Full-Service Security Firm," *Canadian Business*, October 31, 2019.

the environment. Personality develops and changes mainly from childhood to young adulthood, typically stabilizing by around age 30. However, some personality changes continue to occur later in life. For instance, a few traits (openness to experience, social vitality) increase through to young adulthood, then decline in later years, whereas other traits (agreeableness, conscientiousness) tend to increase through to late life. Our personality can also change somewhat due to the job we work in over a long time period. Even migrating to another culture can change our personality to some extent.[7]

The main explanation for why personality becomes more stable by adulthood is that we form a clearer and more rigid self-concept. This increasing clarity of "who we are" anchors our behaviour with the help of the *executive function*. This is the part of the brain that monitors and regulates goal-directed behaviour to keep it consistent with our self-concept. Our self-view becomes clearer and more stable with age, which increases the stability and consistency of our

personality and behaviour.[8] We discuss self-concept in more detail in Chapter 3. The main point here is that personality is not completely determined by heredity; it is also shaped by life experiences, particularly early in a person's life.

FIVE-FACTOR MODEL OF PERSONALITY

Sociable, anxious, curious, dependable, suspicious, talkative, adventurous, and hundreds of other personality traits have been described over the years, so experts have tried to organize them into smaller clusters. The most researched and respected clustering of personality traits is the **five-factor model**, also known as the

five-factor (Big Five) model The five broad dimensions representing most personality traits: conscientiousness, neuroticism, openness to experience, agreeableness, and extraversion.

EXHIBIT 2.1   Five-Factor Model of Personality

Personality factor	People with higher scores on this factor tend to be more:
Conscientiousness	Organized, dependable, goal-focused, thorough, disciplined, methodical, industrious
Agreeableness	Trusting, helpful, good-natured, considerate, tolerant, selfless, generous, flexible
Neuroticism	Anxious, insecure, self-conscious, depressed, temperamental
Openness to experience	Imaginative, creative, unconventional, curious, nonconforming, autonomous, perceptive
Extraversion	Outgoing, talkative, energetic, sociable, assertive

Big Five.[9] Several decades ago, personality experts identified more than 17,000 words that describe an individual's personality. These words were distilled down to five broad personality dimensions, each with a cluster of specific traits. Similar results were found in studies of different languages, suggesting that the five-factor model is fairly robust across cultures. These Big Five factors, represented by the handy acronym *CANOE,* are outlined in Exhibit 2.1 and described below.

- **Conscientiousness.** Characterizes people who are organized, dependable, goal-focused, thorough, disciplined, methodical, and industrious. People with low conscientiousness tend to be careless, disorganized, and less thorough.

- **Agreeableness.** Describes people who are trusting, helpful, good-natured, considerate, tolerant, selfless, generous, and flexible. People with low agreeableness tend to be uncooperative and intolerant of others' needs as well as more suspicious and self-focused.

- **Neuroticism.** Refers to people who tend to be anxious, insecure, self-conscious, depressed, and temperamental. In contrast, people with low neuroticism (high emotional stability) are poised, secure, and calm.

- **Openness to experience.** Characterizes people who are imaginative, creative, unconventional, curious, nonconforming, autonomous, and aesthetically perceptive. Those with low scores on this factor tend to be more resistant to change, less open to new ideas, and more conventional and fixed in their ways.

- **Extraversion.** Describes people who are outgoing, talkative, energetic, sociable, and assertive. The opposite is *introversion,* which characterizes those who are quiet, cautious, and less interactive with others. Extraverts get their energy from the outer world (people and things around them), whereas introverts get their energy from the internal world, such as personal reflection on concepts and ideas. Introverts do not necessarily lack social skills. Instead, they are more inclined to direct their interests to ideas than to social events. Introverts feel more comfortable being alone than do extraverts.

conscientiousness A personality dimension describing people who are organized, dependable, goal-focused, thorough, disciplined, methodical, and industrious.

agreeableness A personality dimension describing people who are trusting, helpful, good-natured, considerate, tolerant, selfless, generous, and flexible.

neuroticism A personality dimension describing people who tend to be anxious, insecure, self-conscious, depressed, and temperamental.

openness to experience A personality dimension describing people who are imaginative, creative, unconventional, curious, nonconforming, autonomous, and aesthetically perceptive.

extraversion A personality dimension describing people who are outgoing, talkative, sociable, and assertive.

What is your Big Five personality? You can discover your Big Five personality by completing this self-assessment in Connect.

 Are you introverted or extraverted? You can discover your level of introversion or extraversion by completing this self-assessment in Connect.

Five-Factor Model and Work Performance

Personality mainly affects behaviour and performance through motivation, specifically by influencing the individual's choice of goals (direction) as well as intensity and persistence of effort toward those goals. Consequently, all of the Big Five factors predict one or more types of employee behaviour and performance to some extent.

Exhibit 2.2 highlights which Big Five personality factors best predict the three types of task performance as well as organizational citizenship and counterproductive work behaviours (see Chapter 1).[10] Conscientiousness stands out as the best overall personality predictor of proficient task performance for most jobs. The specific conscientiousness traits of industriousness (achievement, self-discipline, purposefulness) and

dutifulness are the best predictors of proficient task performance. Conscientious employees set higher personal goals for themselves and are more persistent. They also engage in more organizational citizenship and in less counterproductive work behaviour. Conscientiousness is a weak predictor of adaptive performance (responding to change) and proactive performance (taking initiative toward new work patterns). In fact, two specific conscientiousness traits—orderliness and dependability—tend to suppress adaptivity.

Extraversion is the second best overall personality predictor of proficient task performance, but it is a much weaker predictor than is conscientiousness. Among the specific traits within the extraversion factor, assertiveness and positive emotionality are the strongest predictors of proficient task performance. Assertiveness is also a strong predictor of

---

EXHIBIT 2.2   Five-Factor Personality and Work Performance

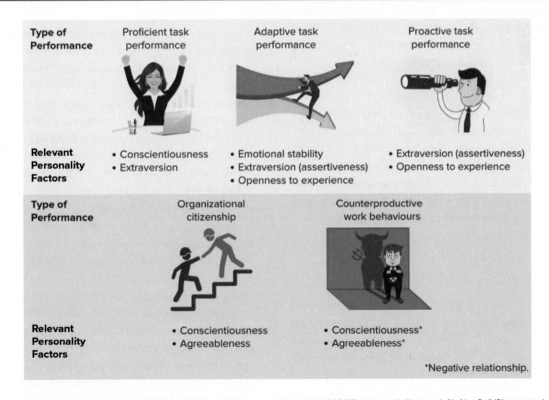

(top-left): Ildar Galeev/Shutterstock; (top-centre): Ho Yeow Hui/Shutterstock; (top-right): malika.1028/Shutterstock; (bottom-left): Aha-Soft/Shutterstock; (bottom-right): Sign N Symbol Production/Shutterstock

Can you identify personality traits from blogging words? You can discover how well you interpret someone's personality in blogs and other writing by completing this self-assessment in Connect.

adaptive and proactive performance. Assertive employees tend to have a "take charge" approach to situations, which is consistent with adapting to change and proactively initiating change. Extraversion is associated with influencing others and being comfortable in social settings, which (along with being assertive) explains why effective leaders and salespeople tend to be somewhat more extraverted than the general population.

Agreeableness is positively associated with organizational citizenship and negatively associated with counterproductive work behaviours.[11] The reason for this is that employees with high agreeableness are motivated to be cooperative, sensitive, flexible, and supportive. Agreeableness does not predict proficient or proactive task performance very well, mainly because it is associated with lower motivation to set goals and achieve results. However, employees with higher (but not too high) agreeableness tend to improve team performance through better knowledge sharing and motivation to help the team. Agreeableness also has a positive effect on friendliness behaviour in customer service jobs.[12]

Openness to experience is a weak predictor of proficient task performance, but it is one of the best personality predictors of adaptive and proactive performance. The main reason is that employees with higher openness scores have more curiosity, imagination, and tolerance of change.[13] These traits also explain why openness to experience is associated with successful performance in creative work.

Emotional stability (low neuroticism) is one of the best personality predictors of adaptive performance.[14] The main explanation is that employees with higher emotional stability cope better with the ambiguity and uncertainty of change. In contrast, those with higher neuroticism view change as a threat, so they tend to avoid change and experience more stress when faced with workplace adjustments. These characteristics would suggest that emotional stability also predicts proactive performance, but the limited research has reported mixed results.

CAVEATS WHEN APPLYING THE FIVE-FACTOR MODEL

The five-factor model of personality is widely accepted among scholars and has a deep research foundation to support its structure and usefulness at predicting workplace behaviour. However, we need to alert you to several issues to better understand and apply this theory to the workplace.

- *Higher isn't always better.* A common assumption is that the "perfect employee" has the highest scores on all of the Big Five personality factors (where emotional stability is high and neuroticism is low). Part of the problem may be that the labels and structure of the Big Five factors have a strong linear bias (high is good, low is bad).[15] But several studies have reported that the best employees don't have the highest scores on some personality factors. In other words, the relationship between personality and performance is often nonlinear. Employees with moderate extraversion perform better in sales jobs than those with high or low extraversion.[16] One recent study found that students with the best peer-rated contributions to teamwork have relatively high extraversion but moderately high conscientiousness, and rate only around the mid-point on agreeableness.

- *Specific traits sometimes predict better than the Big Five factors.* We pay so much attention to the Big Five factors that the specific personality traits within each factor are often forgotten. Yet, specific traits are sometimes better than the broader factor at predicting behaviour and performance. This was noted earlier in this section when we pointed out that the specific extraversion traits of assertiveness and positive emotionality predict proficient task performance better than the overall extraversion factor.

- *Personality isn't static.* There is an unfortunate tendency to think an adult's personality is frozen for a lifetime. Labelling people ("She's an introvert") reinforces this fallacy that personality is static. Personality does stabilize around age 30, but that doesn't mean it is static. As we noted at the beginning of this topic, some Big Five factors tend to increase or decrease as we age. Personality can also shift when the individual's environment changes significantly over a long time, such as when moving to a different culture or working in a job for many years.

- *The five-factor model doesn't cover all personality.* A common mistake is to assume that the five-factor model measures all aspects of personality.[17] The five-factor model does capture a large portion of the domain we call *personality,* but not all of it. There are several perspectives or approaches to personality, each of which has a somewhat different view or emphasis. For example, needs and motives, which we discuss in Chapter 5, are discussed as components of some personality models, but not others. The existence of personality concepts beyond the five-factor model is apparent in the next section of this chapter, which introduces two other models of personality that only partially overlap with the Big Five factors.

Other Personality Concepts: The Dark Triad and MBTI Types

LO2

THE DARK TRIAD

Several decades ago when personality experts distilled thousands of dictionary words down to the five-factor model, they deliberately excluded words with explicitly positive or negative valence, such as *humble* (positive) or *sinister* (negative). They initially even excluded words such as *agreeable* and *ambitious* that were later added to the Big Five analysis. The process of reducing words into categories also chopped off weaker clusters that coincidentally had positive or negative orientations. Yet, some of these excluded traits (such as *impulsive*) appeared in earlier personality models and were widely known in clinical work.[18]

Personality researchers eventually re-examined traits with positive and negative valences. From that work, two scholars in Canada identified a new cluster, which they called the **dark triad**.[19] The dark triad includes three socially undesirable personality traits—Machiavellianism, narcissism, and psychopathy. Each of these three traits has distinct characteristics, but collectively they have a common "dark core" consisting of either low humility/honesty or a tendency to malevolently undermine others to maximize one's own gains.[20]

dark triad A cluster of three socially undesirable (dark) personality traits: Machiavellianism, narcissism, and psychopathy.

- **Machiavellianism.** This personality trait is named after Niccolò Machiavelli, the 16th-century Italian philosopher who wrote *The Prince,* a famous treatise about political behaviour. People with high Machiavellianism (*high-Machs*) demonstrate a strong motivation to get what they want at the expense of others. They believe that deceit is a natural and acceptable way to achieve their goals; indeed, they take pleasure in misleading, outwitting, and otherwise controlling others. High-Machs routinely use lies, manipulation, exploitation, and other undesirable influence tactics. They have a cynical disregard for moral principles, believe that getting more than one deserves is acceptable, and seldom empathize with or trust co-workers.[21]

Machiavellianism A personality trait of people who demonstrate a strong motivation to achieve their own goals at the expense of others, who believe that deceit is a natural and acceptable way to achieve their goals, who take pleasure in outwitting and misleading others using crude influence tactics, and who have a cynical disregard for morality.

- **Narcissism.** This personality trait is named after Narcissus, the young male hunter in Greek mythology who was so obsessed with his beauty that he could not stop admiring his reflection in a pool of water (he died of thirst because he didn't want to stop looking at himself). This trait is evident in people who have an obsessive belief in their superiority and entitlement. Along with their grandiose, inflated self-view, narcissists have an excessive need for attention, so they aggressively engage in self-promotion, exhibitionism, and other attention-seeking behaviours. Although known to be initially charming, narcissists are intensely envious of others, which is eventually apparent in their arrogance, schadenfreude (deriving pleasure from another person's misfortune), callous disregard for others' feelings (i.e., low empathy), and exploitation of others for personal aggrandizement.[22]

narcissism A personality trait of people with a grandiose, obsessive belief in their superiority and entitlement, a propensity to aggressively engage in attention-seeking behaviours, an intense envy of others, and tendency to exhibit arrogance, callousness, and exploitation of others for personal aggrandizement.

psychopathy A personality trait of people who ruthlessly dominate and manipulate others without empathy or any feelings of remorse or anxiety, use superficial charm, yet are social predators who engage in antisocial, impulsive, and often fraudulent thrill-seeking behaviour.

- **Psychopathy.** This personality trait is often considered the most sinister of the triad. It refers to social predators who ruthlessly dominate and manipulate others, yet without empathy or any feelings of remorse or anxiety. They are selfish self-promoters who use superficial charm (called the "mask" of psychopathy), yet engage in antisocial, impulsive, and often fraudulent thrill-seeking behaviour. These people callously do as they please and take what they want.[23]

The Dark Triad in the Workplace

Machiavellianism, narcissism, and psychopathy may seem like they belong in textbooks on criminology or medieval politics, not organizational behaviour. Yet, these traits are gaining attention because they are prevalent throughout the workplace. As one personality researcher warned in his keynote address to the Canadian Police Association: "Not all psychopaths are in prison. Some are in the boardroom."[24]

Dishonesty is a core characteristic of the dark triad, so people with these traits are more likely to lie and deceive others at work. Similarly, they malevolently undermine others to maximize their own gains. This is the essence of

Global Connections 2.1

IS YOUR CEO NARCISSISTIC? COUNT THE TWEETS*

Elon Musk has never been shy about saying what he thinks. The Canadian-South African entrepreneur and CEO of Tesla, SpaceX, and the Boring Company tweets an average of 88 messages per month to his 35 million followers. His twitter mania has occasionally reached 400 messages in one month alone. To put this in perspective, only 7 percent of Canada's top 100 CEOs are on Twitter at all, and most of them have an average of only 316 followers!

Public relations experts suggest that Musk's tweet mania and his flair for crafting casual messages makes him a good communicator. But the volume of tweets might also reveal narcissistic tendencies. A recent meta-analysis reported that individuals with high scores on grandiose narcissism produce a significantly higher number of tweets and Facebook updates, have more friends (or followers), and post more selfies. To a lesser extent, they also spend more time on social media.

Grandiose narcissism refers to people who are interpersonally dominant, self-absorbed, overconfident, and have an inflated sense of superiority and entitlement. As part of the dark triad, narcissists also tend to be more disagreeable and antagonistic toward others compared to the average person. Twitter tweets and Facebook updates fit nicely with grandiose narcissism because these people prefer emotionally shallow social relationships and rely on mass communication to fulfil their need for attention and self-promotion.

Elon Musk's tweet output doesn't necessarily mean that he is narcissistic, although more than a dozen leading newspapers, magazines, and business-school blogs have recently made that assertion. Also, the aggressive and antagonistic content of Musk's tweets are consistent with grandiose narcissism.

Tesla's legal tussles with the U.S. Securities and Exchange Commission and other government agencies (arising from Musk's tweets) are also consistent with studies on narcissistic executives. One recent study concluded that "narcissistic CEOs subject their organizations to undue legal risk because they are overconfident about their ability to win and less sensitive to the costs to their organizations of such litigation."

But Elon Musk might have the last word on this matter: "If I am a narcissist (which might be true), at least I am a useful one," he has tweeted.

©John Raoux/AP Photo

* "New Study: Only Half of Canada's Top 100 CEOs Are on Social Media," News Release (Toronto: Signal Leadership Communication Inc, September 29, 2016); M.J. Coren and Y. Zhou, "We've Tracked All of Musk's Tweets since 2015. It's Never Been like This," *Quartz,* June 1, 2018; D. Lovric and T. Chamorro-Premuzic, "Why Great Success Can Bring Out the Worst Parts of Our Personalities," *Harvard Business Review (Online),* August 9, 2018; S. Singh, S.D. Farley, and J.J. Donahue, "Grandiosity on Display: Social Media Behaviors and Dimensions of Narcissism," *Personality and Individual Differences* 134 (2018): 308–13, https://doi.org/10.1016/j.paid.2018.06.039; J.L. McCain and W.K. Campbell, "Narcissism and Social Media Use: A Meta-Analytic Review," *Psychology of Popular Media Culture* 7, no. 3 (2018): 308–27, https://doi.org/10.1037/ppm0000137; C.A. O'Reilly, B. Doerr, and J.A. Chatman, "'See You in Court': How CEO Narcissism Increases Firms' Vulnerability to Lawsuits," *The Leadership Quarterly* 29, no. 3 (2018): 365–78, https://doi.org/10.1016/j.leaqua.2017.08.001; P. Marx, "Opinion | Elon Musk's Twitter Meltdowns Are Just the Beginning," *NBC News,* October 24, 2018; S. Ben-Hur, "Will Elon Musk's Narcissism Be His Downfall?," Research & Knowledge, *IMD Business School*(blog), October 2018, https://www.imd.org/research-knowledge/articles/Will-Elon-Musks-narcissism-be-his-downfall/; A. Ohnsman, "Elon Musk's Tesla Tweet Puts CEO Role At Risk Again," *Forbes,* February 25, 2019; M.J. Coren, "Elon Musk May Not Be the Narcissist Tesla Needs Right Now," *Quartz,* March 4, 2019.

organizational politics The use of influence tactics for personal gain at the perceived expense of others and the organization.

organizational politics (see Chapter 10), which is about using influence tactics for personal gain at the expense of others and the interests of the entire organization. Political tactics produce a host of dysfunctional outcomes, ranging from employee stress and dissatisfaction to unproductive use of organizational resources. People with dark triad personality traits are dysfunctional team members in the long term because, by definition, they don't trust co-workers and focus on their own goals at the expense of team goals.[25] At the same time, they are known to help others in the short run when it serves their self-interest.

How Machiavellian are you? You can discover how much you value the political tactics emphasized by Machiavelli by locating this self-assessment in Connect.

The dark triad traits are strongly associated with serious white-collar crime behaviour. For instance, one study reported that a dark triad measure from video analysis was highly effective at identifying chief executive officers who were implicated in unethical misconduct and fraud.[26] People with dark triad personality traits are more likely to engage in bullying and other forms of workplace aggression.[27] They also tend to make decisions that produce poorer absolute and risk-adjusted investment returns. In particular, those with high psychopathy take excessive risks due to their overconfidence and disregard for consequences.[28] The dark triad predicts **counterproductive work behaviours**, but not as well as do the specific Big Five factors of low agreeableness and low conscientiousness.

> **counterproductive work behaviours (CWBs)** Voluntary behaviours that have the potential to directly or indirectly harm the organization.

People who possess dark triad personality traits aren't always worse off. They have a manipulative political skill, which some supervisors rate favourably in employee performance. Being manipulative also occasionally helps employees move into more powerful positions in informal employee networks. Narcissistic CEOs tend to have higher direct pay as well as a higher gap in pay from other members of the executive team.[29]

JUNGIAN PERSONALITY THEORY AND THE MYERS-BRIGGS TYPE INDICATOR

> **Myers-Briggs Type Indicator (MBTI)** An instrument designed to measure the elements of Jungian personality theory, particularly preferences regarding perceiving and judging information.

The five-factor model of personality has the most research support, but it is not the most popular personality test in organizations. That distinction goes to Jungian personality theory, which is measured through the Myers-Briggs Type Indicator (MBTI) (see Exhibit 2.3).

Nearly a century ago, Swiss psychiatrist Carl Jung proposed that personality is mainly represented by the individual's preferences regarding perceiving and judging information.[30] Jung explained that the perceiving function—how people prefer to gather information—occurs through two competing orientations: *sensing (S)* and *intuition (N)*. Sensing involves perceiving information directly through the five senses; it relies on an organized structure to acquire factual and preferably quantitative details. In contrast, intuition relies more on insight and subjective experience to see relationships among variables. Sensing types focus on the here and now, whereas intuitive types focus more on future possibilities.

Jung also proposed that the judging function—how people prefer making decisions based on what they have perceived—consists of two competing processes: *thinking (T)* and *feeling (F)*. People with a thinking orientation rely on rational cause–effect logic and systematic data collection to make decisions. Those with a strong feeling orientation, on the other hand, give more weight to their emotional responses to the options presented, as well as to how those choices affect others. Jung noted that in addition to the four core processes of sensing, intuition, thinking, and feeling, people differ in their level of extraversion–introversion, which was introduced earlier as one of the Big Five personality factors.

The MBTI extends Jung's list of personality traits described above by also measuring Jung's broader categories of *perceiving* and *judging,* which represent a person's attitude toward the external world. People with a perceiving orientation are open, curious, and flexible. They like to keep their options open and to adapt spontaneously to events as they unfold. Judging types prefer order and structure and want to resolve problems quickly.

MBTI has a number of benefits, but it is usually a poor predictor of job performance and is generally not recommended for employment selection or promotion decisions.[31] There are also issues with its measurement. MBTI can potentially identify employees who prefer face-to-face versus remote teamwork, but it does not predict how well a team develops. It also has questionable value in predicting leadership effectiveness.

In spite of these limitations, the MBTI is the most widely studied measure of cognitive style in management research and is the most popular personality test for career counselling and executive coaching.[32] It is even being used by artificial intelligence engineers to adapt the behaviour of robots to user preferences. MBTI takes a neutral or balanced approach by recognizing both the strengths and limitations of each personality type in different situations. In contrast, the five-factor model views people with higher scores as better than those with lower scores on each dimension. As such, the Big Five model may have adopted a restrictive view of personality that is more difficult to apply in coaching and development settings.[33]

EXHIBIT 2.3   Jungian and Myers-Briggs Type Indicator Types

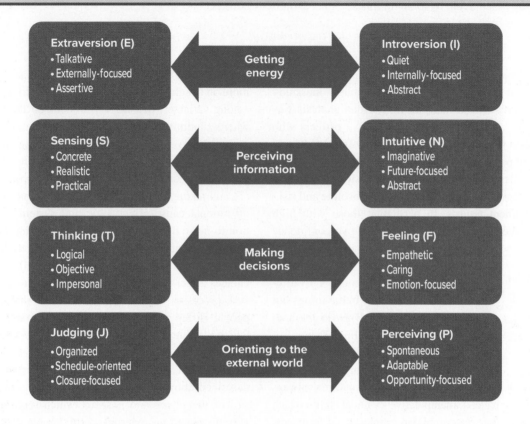

 Are you a sensing or intuitive type? You can discover the extent to which you are a sensing or intuitive type by completing this self-assessment in Connect.

Debating Point: SHOULD COMPANIES USE PERSONALITY TESTS TO SELECT JOB APPLICANTS?

Personality theory has made significant strides over the past two decades, particularly in demonstrating that specific traits are associated with specific workplace behaviours and outcomes. Various studies have reported that the Big Five dimensions predict overall job performance, organizational citizenship, leadership, counterproductive work behaviours, training performance, team performance, and a host of other important outcomes. These findings cast a strong vote in favour of personality testing in the workplace.

A few prominent personality experts urge caution, however.* They point out that, although traits are associated with workplace behaviour to some extent, there are better predictors of work performance, such as work samples and past performance. Furthermore, selection procedures typically assume that more of a personality trait is better, whereas an increasing number of studies indicate that the best candidates might be closer to the middle than the extremes of the range. For instance, job performance apparently increases with conscientiousness, yet employees with high conscientiousness might be so thorough that they become perfectionists, which can stifle rather than enhance job performance.** A third concern is that, depending on how the selection decision applies the test results, personality instruments may unfairly discriminate against specific groups of people.***

A fourth worry is that most personality tests are self-report scales, so applicants might try to fake their answers.**** Worse, the test scores might not represent the individual's personality or anything else meaningful because test takers often don't know what personality traits the company is looking for. Studies show that candidates who try to fake "good" personality scores change the selection results. Supporters of personality testing offer the counter-argument that few job applicants try to fake their scores. One major study found that most personality dimensions are estimated better by observers than by self-ratings. However, few companies rely on ratings from other people.*****

* K. Murphy and J.L. Dzieweczynski, "Why Don't Measures of Broad Dimensions of Personality Perform Better as Predictors of Job Performance?," *Human Performance* 18, no. 4 (2005): 343–57; F.P. Morgeson et al., "Reconsidering the Use of Personality Tests in Personnel Selection Contexts," *Personnel Psychology* 60, no. 3 (2007): 683–729; N. Schmitt, "Personality and Cognitive Ability as Predictors of Effective Performance at Work," *Annual Review of Organizational Psychology and Organizational Behavior* 1, no. 1 (2014): 45–65.

** J. Stoeber, K. Otto, and C. Dalbert, "Perfectionism and the Big Five: Conscientiousness Predicts Longitudinal Increases in Self-Oriented Perfectionism," *Personality and Individual Differences* 47, no. 4 (2009): 363–68; C.J. Boyce, A.M. Wood, and G.D.A. Brown, "The Dark Side of Conscientiousness: Conscientious People Experience Greater Drops in Life Satisfaction Following Unemployment," *Journal of Research in Personality* 44, no. 4 (2010): 535–39.

*** S.D. Risavy and P.A. Hausdorf, "Personality Testing in Personnel Selection: Adverse Impact and Differential Hiring Rates," *International Journal of Selection and Assessment* 19, no. 1 (2011): 18–30.

**** N.S. Hartman and W.L. Grubb, "Deliberate Faking on Personality and Emotional Intelligence Measures," *Psychological Reports* 108, no. 1 (2011): 120–38; J.J. Donovan, S.A. Dwight, and D. Schneider, "The Impact of Applicant Faking on Selection Measures, Hiring Decisions, and Employee Performance," *Journal of Business and Psychology* 29, no. 3 (2014): 479–93.

***** B.S. Connelly and D.S. Ones, "An Other Perspective on Personality: Meta-Analytic Integration of Observers' Accuracy and Predictive Validity," *Psychological Bulletin* 136, no. 6 (2010): 1092–122; J.J. Jackson et al., "Your Friends Know How Long You Will Live: A 75-Year Study of Peer-Rated Personality Traits," *Psychological Science* 26, no. 3 (2015): 335–40.

Values in the Workplace

LO3

Assiniboine Credit Union has developed an enviable reputation as a values-driven organization that supports financial literacy training, community hiring, social purchasing, social-impact financial services, and other corporate social responsibility initiatives. By demonstrating its values orientation, the Winnipeg-based financial institution has become a magnet for job applicants with like-minded personal values. "When you can align your personal values with the company you're working for, it takes being a great place to work to a whole new level," advises an Assiniboine Credit Union executive.[34]

> **values** Relatively stable evaluative beliefs that guide a person's preferences for outcomes or courses of action in a variety of situations.

Most of us think about our personal values when deciding where to work and what choices we make every day on the job. **Values**, a concept that we introduced in Chapter 1, are stable, evaluative beliefs that guide our preferences for outcomes or courses of action in a variety of situations.[35] They are perceptions about what is good or bad, right or wrong. They tell us what we "ought" to do. Personal values serve as a moral compass; they influence our motivation and potentially our decisions and actions in various situations. They also provide justification for past decisions and behaviour.

People arrange values into a hierarchy of preferences, called a *value system*(or, more correctly, a *values system*). Some individuals value new challenges more than they value conformity. Others value generosity more than frugality. Each person's unique values system is developed and reinforced through socialization from parents, religious institutions, friends, personal experiences, and the society in which they live. As such, a person's hierarchy of values is stable and long-lasting. For example, one study found that a sample of adolescents had values systems that were remarkably similar 20 years later as adults.[36]

Our description of values has focused on individuals, whereas Assiniboine Credit Union is described as a values-driven organization. In reality, values exist only within individuals—we call them *personal values*. However, groups of people might hold the same or similar values, so we tend to ascribe these *shared values* to the team, department, organization, profession, or entire society. The values shared by people throughout an organization (*organizational values*) receive fuller discussion in Chapter 14 because they are a central component of organizational culture. The values shared across a society (*cultural values*) receive attention in the last section of this chapter.

Values and personality traits are related to each other, but the two concepts differ in a few ways.[37] The most noticeable distinction is that values are evaluative (they tell us what we *ought* to do), whereas personality traits are descriptive (they refer to what we naturally *tend* to do). A second distinction is that personality traits have minimal conflict with each other—you can have high agreeableness as well as high introversion, for example—whereas some values are opposed to other values. This opposing effect means that someone who values excitement and challenge would have difficulty also valuing stability and moderation. Third, although personality and values are both partly determined by heredity, values are influenced more by socialization whereas heredity has a stronger influence on an individual's personality traits.

©Stuart C. Wilson/Stringer/Getty Images

Julie Averill's decision to join Vancouver-based Lululemon was partly motivated by the opportunity to guide the athletic apparel firm's digital transformation. But the veteran information technology executive also considered the fit between her personal values and Lululemon's culture. "I choose to work with companies that have values that align with my own, and who care about important things in the world," says Averill, who is remotely located in Seattle with Lululemon's technology team. "I get inspired every day by people who live their lives to their values and find their passion along the way."*

*"Reign FC Legend: Julie Averill," *Medium,* May 12, 2017; S.A. Schwartz, "Lululemon CTO Aligns Personal Values with the Company's Mission through Tech," *CIO Dive,* December 5, 2018; R. Torres, "CTO of the Year: Julie Averill, Lululemon," *CIO Dive,* December 12, 2019.

TYPES OF VALUES

Values come in many forms, and experts on this topic have devoted considerable attention to organizing them into clusters. By far, the most widely accepted model of personal values is Schwartz's values circumplex, developed and tested by social psychologist Shalom Schwartz and his colleagues.[38] This model clusters 57 values into 10 broad values categories that are organized into the circular model (circumplex) shown in Exhibit 2.4. The 10 categories include universalism, benevolence, tradition, conformity, security, power, achievement, hedonism, stimulation, and self-direction. Each category is a cluster of several specific values (not shown in the exhibit). For example, conformity includes the values of politeness, honouring parents, self-discipline, and obedience.

The 10 broad values categories are further clustered into four quadrants. One quadrant, called *openness to change,* refers to the extent to which a person is motivated to pursue innovative ways. It includes the values categories of self-direction (creativity, independent thought), stimulation (excitement and challenge), and hedonism (pursuit of pleasure, enjoyment, gratification of desires). The opposing quadrant is *conservation,* which is the extent to which a person is motivated to preserve the status quo. The conservation quadrant includes the values categories of conformity (adherence to social norms and expectations), security (safety and stability), and tradition (moderation and preservation of the status quo).

The third quadrant in Schwartz's circumplex model, called *self-enhancement,* refers to how much a person is motivated by self-interest. It includes the values categories of achievement (pursuit of personal success), power (dominance over others), and hedonism (a values category shared with openness to change). The opposite of self-enhancement is *self-transcendence,* which refers to motivation to promote the welfare of others and nature. Self-transcendence includes the values categories of benevolence (concern for others in one's life) and universalism (concern for the welfare of all people and nature).

VALUES AND INDIVIDUAL BEHAVIOUR

Personal values motivate our decisions and behaviour in three ways:[39]

- *Values influence the attractiveness of choices.* Our decisions are guided by personal values because those values generate positive or negative feelings (valences) toward the available choices. We experience more positive

EXHIBIT 2.4 Schwartz's Values Circumplex

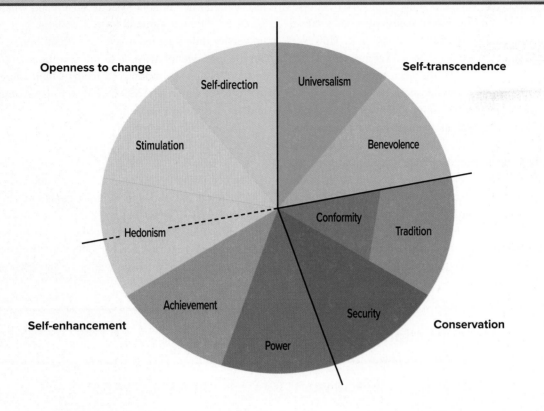

 What are your dominant values? You can discover your values system hierarchy in Schwartz's model by completing this self-assessment in Connect.

feelings toward choices that are aligned with our values and negative feelings toward alternatives that are contrary to our values. If stimulation is at the top of your values hierarchy, for instance, then jobs that offer new experiences will appeal to you more than jobs that have predictable and stable tasks.

- *Values frame our perceptions of reality.* We are constantly bombarded with stimuli from our surroundings. Personal values influence whether we notice something as well as how we interpret it (see Chapter 3). Our decisions and actions are affected by how we perceive those situations.

- *Values help regulate the consistency of behaviour.* People are motivated to act consistently with their personal values and other aspects of their self-concept. If achievement is a key feature of your self-view and public image, then you are motivated to act in ways that are consistent with that value. The more clearly a behaviour is aligned with a specific value that identifies us, the more motivated we are to engage in that behaviour.

Personal values motivate behaviour to some extent, but this connection isn't as strong as we might like to believe.[40] One reason for this "disconnect" between personal values and individual behaviour is the situation. Personal values motivate us to engage in specific behaviour, but the MARS model points out that the situation can prevent us from engaging in values-consistent behaviour. For example, individuals with strong self-transcendent values are motivated to engage in recycling and other environmentally friendly behaviours, but lack of recycling facilities prevents or severely limits this behaviour. A second reason why an individual's behaviour deviates from their personal values is the presence of strong counter-motivational forces. As an example, employees caught in illegal business dealings sometimes attribute their unethical activities to pressure from management to achieve their performance targets at any cost.

A third reason why decisions and behaviour are inconsistent with our personal values is that we don't actively think about them much of the time.[41] Values are abstract concepts, so their relevance is not obvious in many situations. Furthermore, many decisions and actions occur routinely, so we don't actively evaluate their consistency with our values. We do consciously consider our values in some situations, of course. For example, the importance to us of security becomes salient when deciding whether to perform a risky task. However, many daily events do not trigger values awareness, so we act without their guidance. We literally need to be reminded of our values so they can guide our decisions and actions.

The effect of values awareness on behaviour was apparent in a study in which students were given a math test and received a payment for each correct answer.[42] One group couldn't lie about their results because they submitted their results to the experimenter for scoring. A second group could lie because they scored the test themselves and told the experimenter their test score. A third group was similar to the second (they scored their own test), but that test included the following statement, and students were required to sign their name below that statement: "I understand that this short survey falls

under (the university's) honour system." The researchers estimated that some students cheated when they scored their own test without the "honour system" statement, whereas no one given the "honour system" form lied about their results. The university didn't actually have an official honour statement, but the message made students pay attention to their honesty. In short, people are more likely to apply their values (honesty, in this case) when they are explicitly reminded of those values and see their relevance to the situation.

VALUES CONGRUENCE

At the beginning of this section, an executive at Assiniboine Credit Union counselled that employees are much more satisfied and effective when they work for a company that fits their personal values. The key concept here is *values congruence,* which refers to how similar a person's values hierarchy is to the values hierarchy of the organization or any other entity (such

---

 ## Global Connections 2.2

"YOUR VALUES ARE MORE IMPORTANT THAN YOUR CV" AT IKEA*

When IKEA Canada recently advertised a job opening for a "Goods Flow Co-worker" in Ottawa, the job description identified experience in material handling equipment, computer aptitude, ability to lift up to 50 pounds (23 kg), and other traditional criteria. But it also requested something that isn't found in most job ads: "The IKEA values really reflect my own values."

IKEA describes itself as a values-driven company, so job applicants need to assess whether their personal values are congruent with the global retailer's organizational values. "We recruit by values," explains Anna Carin Månsson, Country HR Manager, IKEA India. "We like to understand personal values of a candidate and how these come out in typical behaviour in everyday life."

Månsson's team pays attention to whether job applicants have really considered values congruence. "When recruiting for IKEA, it is attractive to recognize that the applicant has read up about the company and managed to describe the connection—i.e., what are the values they have as a person which makes them the perfect fit for working with the organization."

"Your values are more important than your CV" at IKEA, says D'neale Prosser, the national talent manager at IKEA Australia. Prosser adds that values congruence isn't just useful for getting hired at IKEA. It is central to a person's success and happiness in life. "Find an organization that connects with your personal values and allows you to be yourself at work," advises Prosser. "This will add value and meaning to your everyday life."

©UPI/Alamy Stock Photo

* "'We Believe That Your Values Are More Important than Your CV,'"*Human Resources Director Australia,* April 11, 2018; V. Sawhney, "What I Look for in Candidates: An Interview with Anna-Carin Månsson," *HBR Ascend*(blog), August 2018, https://hbrascend.org/topics/look-candidate-interview-an-na-carin-mansson/; N. Yazxhi, "BM Expert: How to Future Proof Your Career," *Bellamumma*(blog), October 17, 2018, http://bellamumma.com/2018/10/17/bm-expert-how-to-future-proof-your-career/; C. Lamba, "Understanding the HR Policies of IKEA," *India Retailing,* December 17, 2018. The job advertisement for a Goodsflow Co-worker in Ottawa was retrieved from IKEA Canada's jobs website on December 14, 2019.

as a team or society). When personal values are congruent with the organization's values, employees tend to experience higher job satisfaction, loyalty, and organizational citizenship. They also have less stress and turnover. Furthermore, employees are more likely to make decisions that are compatible with organizational expectations when their personal values are congruent with the organization's shared values.[43]

Are organizations the most successful when every employee's personal values align with the company's values? Not at all! While a large degree of values congruence is necessary for the reasons just noted, organizations also benefit from some level of incongruence. Employees with diverse values offer different perspectives, which potentially lead to better decision making. Also, too much congruence can create a "corporate cult" that potentially undermines creativity, organizational flexibility, and business ethics (see Chapter 14).

Ethical Values and Behaviour

LO4

When 1,000 Canadians were asked to identify the most important qualities of an ideal leader, 95 percent chose "honesty." In another survey, both Canadian employees and executives placed "integrity" at the top of the list of attributes of an effective corporate leader. And when 195 business leaders across 15 countries were asked to identify the most important leader competencies, "high ethics and moral standards" was the top-rated item from the list of 74 characteristics.[44] These surveys reveal the importance of ethics in the workplace. *Ethics* refers to the study of moral principles or values that determine whether actions are right or wrong and outcomes are good or bad. People rely on their ethical values to determine "the right thing to do."

FOUR ETHICAL PRINCIPLES

Most ethical issues are associated with four ethical principles: utilitarianism, individual rights, distributive justice, and the ethic of care.[45] Your personal values might sway you more toward one principle than the others, but all four should be actively considered when making decisions that have ethical implications.

- *Utilitarianism.* This principle says the only moral obligation is to seek the greatest good for the greatest number of people. We should choose the option that provides the highest degree of satisfaction to those affected. One problem is that utilitarianism requires a cost–benefit analysis, yet many outcomes aren't measurable. Another problem is that utilitarianism focuses only on outcomes, whereas the means of achieving those outcomes may be considered unethical by other principles.

- *Individual rights.* This principle says that everyone has the same set of natural rights, such as freedom of speech, freedom of movement, the right to physical security, and the right to fair trial. The individual rights principle extends beyond legal rights to human rights that everyone is granted as a moral norm of society. One problem with this principle is that some individual rights may conflict with others. The shareholders' right to be informed about corporate activities may ultimately conflict with an executive's right to privacy, for example.

- *Distributive justice.* This principle says that the benefits and burdens of similar individuals should be the same; otherwise they should be proportional. For example, employees who contribute equally in their work should receive similar rewards, whereas those who make a lesser contribution should receive less. A variation of this principle says that inequalities are acceptable when they benefit the least well off in society. The main problem with the distributive justice principle is that it is difficult to agree on who is "similar" and what factors are relevant. We discuss distributive justice further in Chapter 5.

- *Ethic of care.* This principle states that everyone has a moral obligation to help others within their relational sphere to grow and self-actualize.[46] Thus, caring for others is a fundamental characteristic of humanity and an ethical virtue. Ethic of care includes being attentive to others' needs, using one's abilities to give care to others, and being responsive to (having empathy for) the person receiving care. This principle is found in writing about how organizations should serve stakeholders and how leaders should serve employees (see servant leadership in Chapter 12).[47]

MORAL INTENSITY, MORAL SENSITIVITY, AND SITUATIONAL INFLUENCES

Along with ethical principles and their underlying values, three other factors also influence ethical conduct in the workplace: the moral intensity of the issue, the individual's moral sensitivity, and situational factors.[48]

Moral Intensity

Moral intensity is the degree to which an issue demands the application of ethical principles. The higher the moral intensity of an issue, the more the decision maker needs to carefully apply ethical principles to make the best choice. The moral intensity of an issue is essentially about (a) how seriously (good or bad) people will be affected by the decision, (b) the

moral intensity The degree to which an issue demands the application of ethical principles.

Global Connections 2.3

ALCOA EXECUTIVE SETS ETHICAL STANDARD IN RUSSIA*

When William O'Rourke became Alcoa Russia's first CEO, he knew that bribery was a serious problem in that country, so he made his position clear to staff: "We don't condone it. We don't participate in it. We are not going to do it. Period." This ethical mandate was soon tested when local police stopped delivery of an $18 million furnace and declared that delivery would resume only after Alcoa paid $25,000 to a local government official (all figures are in U.S. dollars).

"My bonus was based in large part on making the planned investments happen on time," says O'Rourke. A few Alcoa executives in the United States advised that he should do whatever it takes to keep the work on schedule, implying that perhaps it would be better to pay the bribe. "Nonetheless," he recalls, "I stood my ground." The new furnace arrived three days later

without any bribery payment. It took another 18 months before the bribery attempts stopped.

©Ozgur Donmaz/Getty Images

* J.T. Kennedy, "Alcoa's William O'Rourke: Ethical Business Practices, from Russia to Sustainability," *Carnegie Council,* 27 April 2011; A. Graham, "The Thought Leader Interview: William J. O'Rourke," *strategy+business,* Winter 2012, 1–7; The Wheatley Institution, "Seek True North: Stories on Leadership and Ethics — Bill O'Rourke," (YouTube, 2 August 2016), https://www.youtube.com/watch?v=bmFDXecIqJM, Video (accessed 24 January 2017).

probability that those good or bad outcomes will occur, and (c) how many people will be affected.[49] This is a variation of the classic expectancy-valence decision model that is applied in many organizational behaviour concepts, including attitudes (Chapter 4), employee motivation (Chapter 5), and rational choice decision making (Chapter 7).

Moral Sensitivity

Moral sensitivity (also called *ethical sensitivity*) is a person's ability to detect a moral dilemma and estimate its relative importance.[50] It is a characteristic of the decision maker, not of the situation. People with high moral sensitivity can more quickly and accurately estimate the moral intensity of the issue. This awareness does not necessarily translate into more ethical behaviour; it just means they are more likely to be aware when unethical decisions and behaviour occur.

Several factors are associated with a person's moral sensitivity.[51]

- *Expertise or knowledge of prescriptive norms and rules.* Some people are more aware of illegal or unethical

> **moral sensitivity** A person's ability to recognize the presence of an ethical issue and determine its relative importance.

conduct due to their professional training. For example, accountants are more morally sensitive regarding specific accounting procedures than are people who lack experience in this profession.

- *Previous experience with specific moral dilemmas.* Past incidents generate internal cues that trigger awareness of future ethical dilemmas with similar characteristics.

- *Ability to empathize with those affected by the decision.* People with higher empathy for those affected by the decision would have greater moral sensitivity regarding the moral intensity of the issue. On average, women have higher moral sensitivity compared to men, partly because women tend to have higher empathy.

- *A strong self-view of being a morally sensitive person.*[52] Employees who strongly define themselves by their moral character (called their *moral identity*) are more sensitive to moral dilemmas because they put more energy into maintaining ethical conduct.

- *A high degree of situational mindfulness.*[53] **Mindfulness** refers to a person's receptive and impartial attention to and

> **mindfulness** A person's receptive and impartial attention to and awareness of the present situation as well as to one's own thoughts and emotions in that moment.

Ethical Behaviour in the Workplace*

63% of 300 companies across several countries that are adopting artificial intelligence (AI) have an ethics committee to review its use (73% of Canadian firms in the sample have a committee).

59% of 161,481 Canadian government employees strongly or somewhat agree that senior managers in their department or agency lead by example in ethical behaviour.

32% of 1,000 Canadians surveyed believe there is widespread corruption within businesses in this country (60% of Americans say this about U.S. businesses).

11% of 766 Canadian employees surveyed say they have felt pressured to compromise ethical standards (time and bosses are the two most common pressures).

19% of more than 18,000 employees surveyed worldwide say they observed corruption in their organization within the previous 12 months (ranging from 14% in Europe to 27% in Africa/Middle East).

©3D_creation/Shutterstock

*K. Neuman, "Canadians' Confidence in National Institutions Steady," *Policy Options,* August 2, 2018; L. Greiner, "Canadian Firms Care More about AI Ethics than U.S.: SAS Survey," *IT World Canada,* September 24, 2018; "2018 Public Service Employee Survey: Results for the Public Service" (Ottawa: Government of Canada, Treasury Board of Canada Secretariat, 2019); G. Donde, K. Somasundaram, and L. Frank, "Ethics at Work: 2018 Survey of Employees: Canada" (London: Institute of Business Ethics, June 26, 2019); Ethics & Compliance Initiative, "2019 Global Business Ethics Survey -- Workplace Misconduct and Reporting: A Global Look" (Vienna, VA: Ethics & Compliance Initiative, November 27, 2019).

awareness of the present situation as well as to one's own thoughts and emotions in that moment. Mindfulness increases moral sensitivity because it involves actively monitoring the environment as well as being sensitive to our responses to that environment. This vigilance requires effort as well as skill to receptively evaluate our thoughts and emotions. Unfortunately, we have a natural tendency to minimize effort, which leads to less mindfulness. For instance, employees often assume that highly-regarded professionals and executives are being ethical by virtue of their expertise and reputation, so they don't pay attention to possible illegal activity by these people.

Situational Factors

Along with moral intensity and moral sensitivity, ethical conduct is influenced by the situation in which the conduct occurs.[54] One of the most frequently identified situational influences for unethical behaviour is pressure from top management. A recent survey of more than 13,000 employees across 13 countries reported that fully one-third had observed misconduct and 22 percent had experienced pressure to compromise organizational standards. Canada was not included

in that study, but in another survey one-third of Canadians strongly or somewhat agreed with this statement: "In my workplace, delivering results is more important than doing the right thing." Twenty-two percent agreed with the statement: "I feel that I have to compromise my own personal ethics or values to keep my job."[55] Situational factors such as pressure from management do not justify unethical conduct. Rather, we need to be aware of these factors so organizations can reduce their prevalence.

SUPPORTING ETHICAL BEHAVIOUR

Most large and medium-sized organizations in Canada and other developed countries apply one or more strategies to improve ethical conduct. The most common ethics initiative is a code of ethical conduct—a statement about desired practices, rules of conduct, and philosophy about the organization's relationship to its stakeholders and the environment.[56] These codes are supposed to motivate and guide employee behaviour, signal the importance of ethical conduct, and build the firm's trustworthiness to stakeholders. However, critics suggest that they do little to reduce unethical conduct.

Another strategy to improve ethical conduct is to train and regularly evaluate employees about their knowledge of proper ethical conduct. Many large firms have annual quizzes to test employee awareness of company rules and practices on important ethical issues such as giving gifts and receiving sensitive information about competitors or governments. In some firms, employees participate in elaborate games that present increasingly challenging and complex moral dilemmas.

A growing ethics practice is a confidential telephone hotline and website, typically operated by an independent organization, whereby employees can anonymously report suspicious behaviour. For instance, Halifax-based conglomerate IMP Group has such a hotline for all employees, suppliers, customers, and other stakeholders. A few very large businesses also employ ombudspersons who receive information confidentially from employees and proactively investigate possible wrongdoing.

Training, hotlines, and related activities improve ethical conduct to some extent, but the most powerful foundation is a set of shared values that reinforces ethical conduct. "A good, ethical system requires more than just signposts pointing employees in the right direction," advises the Canadian Centre for Ethics and Corporate Policy. Instead, ethical conduct occurs through "a set of beliefs, values, norms and practices that comprise an ethical culture." As we describe in Chapter 14 (organizational culture), an ethical culture is supported by the conduct and vigilance of corporate leaders. By acting with the highest moral standards, leaders not only gain support and trust from followers; they role-model the ethical standards that employees are more likely to follow.[57]

Values across Cultures

LO5

Values differ not only among individuals and across organizations. They also vary across entire societies. In this section, we introduce five values that have cross-cultural significance: individualism, collectivism, power distance, uncertainty avoidance, and achievement-nurturing orientation. Exhibit 2.5 summarizes these concepts and lists a sample of countries that have high, medium, or low scores on these values.

INDIVIDUALISM AND COLLECTIVISM

Two seemingly inseparable cross-cultural values are individualism and collectivism. **Individualism** is the extent to which we value independence and

individualism A cross-cultural value describing the degree to which people in a culture emphasize independence and personal uniqueness.

EXHIBIT 2.5 Five Cross-Cultural Values

Value	Sample Countries	Representative Beliefs/Behaviours in "High" Cultures
Individualism	High: Canada, United States, Chile, South Africa Medium: Japan, Denmark Low: Taiwan, Venezuela	Defines self more by one's uniqueness; personal goals have priority; decisions have low consideration of effect on others; relationships are viewed as more instrumental and fluid.
Collectivism	High: Israel, Taiwan Medium: India, Denmark Low: Canada, United States, Germany, Japan	Defines self more by one's in-group membership; goals of self-sacrifice and harmony have priority; behaviour regulated by in-group norms; in-group memberships are viewed as stable with a strong differentiation with out-groups.
Power Distance	High: India, Malaysia Medium: Canada, United States, Japan Low: Denmark, Israel	Reluctant to disagree with or contradict the boss; managers are expected and preferred decision makers; perception of dependence (versus interdependence) with the boss.
Uncertainty Avoidance	High: Belgium, Greece Medium: Canada, United States, Norway Low: Denmark, Singapore	Prefer predictable situations; value stable employment, strict laws, and low conflict; dislike deviations from normal behaviour.
Achievement-Nurturing Orientation	High: Austria, Japan Medium: Canada, United States, Brazil Low: Sweden, Netherlands	Focus on outcomes (versus relationships); decisions based on contribution (equity versus equality); low empathy or showing emotions (versus strong empathy and caring).

How much do you value individualism and collectivism? You can discover your level of individualism and collectivism by completing this self-assessment in Connect.

What is your level of power distance? You can discover your power distance orientation by completing this self-assessment in Connect.

personal uniqueness. Highly individualist people value personal freedom, self-sufficiency, control over their own lives, and appreciation of the unique qualities that distinguish them from others. Canadians, Americans, Chileans, and South Africans generally exhibit high individualism, whereas Taiwan and Venezuela are countries with low individualism.[58] **Collectivism** is the extent to which we value our duty to groups to which we belong and to group harmony. Highly collectivist people define themselves by their group memberships, emphasize their personal connection to others in their in-groups, and value the goals and well-being of people within those groups.[59] Low collectivism countries include Canada, Japan, and Germany, whereas Israelis and Taiwanese have relatively high collectivism.

> **collectivism** A cross-cultural value describing the degree to which people in a culture emphasize duty to groups to which they belong and to group harmony.

Contrary to popular belief, individualism is not the opposite of collectivism. In fact, the two concepts are typically uncorrelated.[60] For example, cultures that highly value duty to one's group do not necessarily give a low priority to personal freedom and uniqueness. Generally, people across all cultures define themselves by both their uniqueness and their relationship to others. It is an inherent characteristic of everyone's self-concept, which we discuss in the next chapter. Some cultures emphasize uniqueness over group obligations or vice versa, but both have a place in a person's values and self-concept.

Also note that people in Japan have relatively low collectivism. This is contrary to the view stated in many cross-cultural books, which claim that Japan is one of the most collectivist countries on the planet! There are several explanations for the historical misinterpretation, ranging from problems defining and measuring collectivism to erroneous reporting of early cross-cultural research. Whatever the reasons, studies consistently report that people in Japan tend to have relatively low collectivism and moderate individualism (as indicated in Exhibit 2.5).[61]

POWER DISTANCE

Power distance refers to the extent to which people accept unequal distribution of power in a society.[62] Individuals with high power distance accept and value unequal power. Those in higher positions expect obedience to authority; those in lower positions are comfortable receiving commands from their superiors without consultation or debate. People with high power distance also prefer to resolve differences through formal procedures rather than direct informal discussion. In contrast, people with low power distance expect relatively equal power sharing. They view the relationship with their boss as one of interdependence, not dependence; that is, they believe their boss is also dependent on them, so they expect power sharing and consultation before decisions affecting them are made. People in India and Malaysia tend to have high power distance, whereas people in Denmark and Israel generally have low power distance. Canadians collectively have medium-low power distance.

> **power distance** A cross-cultural value describing the degree to which people in a culture accept unequal distribution of power in a society.

UNCERTAINTY AVOIDANCE

Uncertainty avoidance is the degree to which people tolerate ambiguity (low uncertainty avoidance) or feel threatened by ambiguity and uncertainty (high uncertainty avoidance). Employees with high uncertainty avoidance value structured situations in which rules of conduct and decision making are clearly documented. They usually prefer direct rather than indirect or ambiguous communications. Uncertainty avoidance tends to be high in Belgium and Greece and very high in Japan. It is generally low in Denmark and Singapore. Canadians collectively have medium-low uncertainty avoidance.

> **uncertainty avoidance** A cross-cultural value describing the degree to which people in a culture tolerate ambiguity (low uncertainty avoidance) or feel threatened by ambiguity and uncertainty (high uncertainty avoidance).

ACHIEVEMENT-NURTURING ORIENTATION

achievement-nurturing orientation A cross-cultural value describing the degree to which people in a culture emphasize competitive versus cooperative relations with other people.

Achievement-nurturing orientation reflects a competitive versus cooperative view of relations with other people.[63] People with a high achievement orientation value assertiveness, competitiveness, and materialism. They appreciate people who are tough, and they favour the acquisition of money and material goods. In contrast, people in cultures with low achievement orientation (i.e., high nurturing orientation) emphasize relationships and the well-being of others. They focus on human interaction and caring rather than competition and personal success. People in Sweden, Norway, and the Netherlands score very low on achievement orientation (i.e., high nurturing orientation). In contrast, very high achievement orientation scores have been reported in Japan and Austria. Canada and the United States place a little above the middle of the range on achievement-nurturing orientation.

CAVEATS ABOUT CROSS-CULTURAL KNOWLEDGE

Cross-cultural organizational research has gained considerable attention over the past two decades, likely due to increased globalization and cultural diversity within organizations. Our knowledge of cross-cultural dynamics has blossomed, and many of these findings will be discussed in other chapters, such as leadership, conflict, and influence. However, we also need to raise a few warning flags about cross-cultural knowledge. One problem is that too many studies have relied on small, convenient samples (such as students attending one university) to represent an entire culture.[64] The result is that many cross-cultural studies draw conclusions that might not generalize to the cultures they intended to represent.

A second problem is that cross-cultural studies often assume that each country has one culture.[65] In reality, many countries (including Canada) have become culturally diverse. As more countries embrace globalization and multiculturalism, it becomes even less appropriate to assume that an entire country has one unified culture. A third concern is that cross-cultural research and writing continues to rely on a major study conducted almost four decades ago of 116,000 IBM employees across dozens of countries. That study helped to ignite subsequent cross-cultural research, but its findings are becoming out of date as values in some cultures have shifted over the years.[66]

CULTURAL DIVERSITY WITHIN CANADA

Some cross-cultural studies give the impression that Canada is a homogeneous country where people hold identical or very similar values. Of course, anyone who lives here knows otherwise. Canada is the first country in the world to officially embrace multiculturalism.[67] But in addition to the surface-level diversity reflected in multiculturalism, most

 Global Connections 2.4

CROSS-CULTURAL HICCUPS AT BEAM SUNTORY*

Japanese alcoholic beverage company Suntory Holdings Ltd. has a few cross-cultural hiccups to go through after acquiring Jim Beam, a bourbon producer in Kentucky. "We have to overcome the huge differences in the Japanese mentality and the American mentality," Suntory CEO Takeshi Niinami advised soon after the acquisition. "It creates misunderstandings."

Niinami (in photo) says he prefers the "blunt but honest" American approach, but that style may conflict with the Japanese preference for modesty, detail, and consensus. Compared to Americans, Japanese employees are also more likely to have expectations of lifetime employment and less incentivized reward systems. "Beam and Suntory definitely have differences," Niinami acknowledges. "This is not an easy task. But I'm ready for it."

©Bloomberg/Getty Images

* T. Mickle and E. Pfanner, "Jim Beam's New Owner Mixes Global Cocktail," *Wall Street Journal*, May 4, 2015, A1; K. Moritsugu, "Merging US, Japan Work Cultures a Challenge for Beam Suntory," *Associated Press*, January 15, 2016.

Canadians may be surprised at how much deep-level diversity also exists within this country.

The best-known deep-level cultural differences are between Canadian anglophones and francophones. At one time, francophones were more religious, traditional, and deferential to authority, compared with anglophones. Now, the situation is almost reversed. Relative to anglophones, francophones have significantly less deference to authority, less acceptance of Canada's military activities abroad, and more tolerance and morally permissive views regarding marriage, sexual activity, and nonmarried parenthood.[68] At the same time, anglophone and francophone Canadians seem to be converging on several values associated with the workplace, secularism, and environmentalism.[69]

Canada's cultural diversity is further evident in the values of its Indigenous communities and their businesses. Indigenous people in Canada are far from homogeneous; there are hundreds of such communities, most of which have unique histories and experiences. Yet, several studies reveal that Indigenous Canadians share some common cultural values. Four values mentioned most often are:[70]

- *High collectivism.* Relationships represent one of the most frequently mentioned cultural values in Indigenous communities. Interconnectedness of community members, including employees within organizations, is highly valued. This is also part of holistic thinking about the community's connection with nature.

- *Low power distance.* Indigenous communities place a high priority on consensus and thereby reduce the leader's control over group decisions. Indigenous organizations are also noted for decentralized (rather than hierarchical) leadership, in which the many dimensions and duties of this role are shared among several people. Although Indigenous cultures value respect for elders, those in power are more likely to defer to the group's wishes than we usually find in European-based cultures.

- *Non-interference.* Most Indigenous cultures in Canada emphasize trust and forgiveness, which includes avoiding the temptation to direct others down a particular path. This is associated with low power distance, because attempting to influence people involves applying your power over them. Non-interference is also associated with the tendency to avoid conflict (at least within the community). One expert observes that in Indigenous communities "displeasure is not typically displayed by explicit and open disapproval of another's actions."

- *Natural time orientation.* Indigenous cultures tend to view time as less structured than in European cultures. This difference may be due to historic dependence on nature for survival. Natural time orientation places greater emphasis on patience to act when conditions are right according to the situation or to act when it is necessary. This orientation also implies that forcing things to happen according to a schedule is less successful (and less natural).

Cultural geographers have also reported differences in personal values and personality traits across Canadian regions. Rigorous analysis has been limited, but a few studies have recently found that egalitarianism (preference for minimal income differences) is significantly higher throughout Atlantic Canada and Quebec than in Alberta, and that personal responsibility and market liberalism (free market capitalism) are stronger in all three prairie provinces than elsewhere in Canada.[71] Significant differences in the Big Five personality traits have been reported across regions of the United States and United Kingdom. There is no comparable research in Canada, but one study suggests that openness to experience and emotional stability are highest in British Columbia and lowest in Quebec.[72] Personal values differ across regions because regional institutions—such as local governments, educational systems, and dominant religious groups—have a greater influence than do national institutions on socialization practices. Studies also suggests that people migrate to places that are more compatible with their values and self-views.[73]

Canadian versus American Values

Canadians increasingly shop at American-owned stores and have close associations with friends and co-workers in the United States. Yet, the values held by people in these two countries are more divergent today than a few decades ago. "Canadians may like Americans, speak the same language, and consume more of their fast food and popular culture, but we embrace a different hierarchy of values," writes social policy researcher Michael Adams.[74] Another Canadian cultural expert suggests that the 49th parallel border is more than just an imaginary geographic division; it is a symbol of the widening ideological divide in North America.[75]

Canadians and Americans are similar in many ways, but they have also consistently differed over the years on several key values. One difference, reported in several studies, is that Canadians have significantly higher tolerance or moral permissiveness than do Americans. This is reflected in greater acceptance of nontraditional families and of multicultural immigration. Canadians are also more willing to allow collective rights over individual rights and are less accepting of large wealth differences within society. Another cultural difference is that Canadians are much less likely than Americans to be associated with a religious institution and to believe that these institutions should influence public policy. Canadians are also much more likely to believe that organizations work better without a single leader. Perhaps the most significant difference in values between the two countries is in beliefs about patriarchal authority. In the early 1980s, more than 40 percent of Canadians and Americans agreed that the father should be the master of the home. Today, 24 percent of Canadians hold this view, compared to 41 percent of Americans.[76]

Chapter Summary

LO1

Define personality and discuss how the Big Five personality factors relate to workplace behaviour and performance.

Personality refers to the relatively enduring pattern of thoughts, emotions, and behaviours that characterizes a person, along with the psychological processes behind those characteristics. Personality is formed through heredity (nature) as well as socialization (nurture).

The Big Five personality factors include conscientiousness, agreeableness, neuroticism, openness to experience, and extraversion. Conscientiousness and extraversion are the best overall predictors of job performance in most job groups. Extraversion and openness to experience are the best predictors of adaptive and proactive performance. Emotional stability (low neuroticism) is also associated with better adaptivity. Conscientiousness and agreeableness are the two best personality predictors of organizational citizenship and (negatively) counterproductive work behaviours.

Four issues to consider about the Big Five personality factors is that (a) people with higher personality levels aren't necessarily the best performers, (b) specific personality traits are sometimes better predictors of behaviour than are the broader Big Five factors, (c) personality changes to some extent over a person's lifetime, and (d) the five-factor model doesn't cover all of an individual's personality.

LO2

Describe the dark triad of personality and the MBTI types and discuss their implications for organizational behaviour.

The dark triad is a cluster of three socially undesirable personality traits: Machiavellianism, narcissism, and psychopathy. They have a common core of low humility/honesty or a tendency to malevolently undermine others to maximize one's own gains. Machiavellianism refers to people who demonstrate a strong motivation to achieve their own goals at the expense of others, who believe that deceit is a natural and acceptable way to achieve their goals, who take pleasure in outwitting and misleading others using crude influence tactics, and who have a cynical disregard for morality. Narcissism is a personality trait of people with a grandiose, obsessive belief in their superiority and entitlement, a propensity to aggressively engage in attention-seeking behaviours, an intensive envy of others, and tendency to exhibit arrogance, callousness, and exploitation of others for personal aggrandizement. Psychopathy refers to people who ruthlessly dominate and manipulate others without empathy or any feelings of remorse or anxiety, use superficial charm, yet are social predators who engage in antisocial, impulsive, and often fraudulent thrill-seeking behaviour. People with the dark triad personality engage in more organizational politics, white-collar crime, workplace aggression, and (to some degree) counterproductive work behaviours and poor team behaviour. They also make riskier decisions, resulting in poorer investment returns. However, the dark triad personality is also associated with manipulative political skill that can lead to higher performance reviews, more central positions in employee networks, and better pay.

Based on Jungian personality theory, the Myers-Briggs Type Indicator (MBTI) identifies competing orientations for getting energy (extraversion versus introversion), perceiving information (sensing versus intuiting), processing information and making decisions (thinking versus feeling), and orienting to the external world (judging versus perceiving). The MBTI improves self-awareness for career development and mutual understanding but is more popular than valid.

LO3

Summarize Schwartz's model of individual values and discuss the conditions where values influence behaviour.

Values are stable, evaluative beliefs that guide our preferences for outcomes or courses of action in a variety of situations. Compared to personality traits, values are evaluative (rather than descriptive), more likely to conflict, and formed more from socialization than heredity. Schwartz's model organizes 57 values into a circumplex of 10 dimensions along two bipolar dimensions: openness to change to conservation and self-enhancement to self-transcendence. Values influence behaviour in three ways: (1) shaping the attractiveness of choices, (2) framing perceptions of reality, and (3) aligning behaviour with self-concept and self-presentation. However, the effect of values on behaviour also depends on whether the situation supports or prevents that behaviour and on how actively we think about them and understand their relevance to the situation. Values congruence refers to how similar a person's values hierarchy is to the values hierarchy of another source (organization, team, etc.).

LO4

Describe four ethical principles and discuss three factors that influence ethical behaviour.

Ethics refers to the study of moral principles or values that determine whether actions are right or wrong and outcomes are good or bad. Four ethical principles are utilitarianism (greatest good for the greatest number), individual rights (upholding natural rights), distributive justice (same or proportional benefits and burdens), and ethic of care (the moral obligation to help others). Ethical behaviour is influenced by the degree to which an issue demands the application of ethical principles (moral intensity), the individual's ability to recognize the presence and relative importance of an ethical issue (moral sensitivity), and situational forces. Ethical conduct at work is supported by codes of ethical conduct, mechanisms for communicating ethical violations, the organization's culture, and the leader's behaviour.

LO5

Describe five values commonly studied across cultures and discuss the diverse cultures within Canada.

Five values commonly studied across cultures are individualism (valuing independence and personal uniqueness); collectivism (valuing duty to in-groups and to group harmony); power distance (valuing unequal distribution of power); uncertainty avoidance (tolerating or feeling threatened by ambiguity and uncertainty); and achievement-nurturing orientation (valuing competition versus cooperation).

Canada is a multicultural society, which includes both surface-level and deep-level diversity. Anglophones and francophones differ with respect to several values (deference to authority, moral permissiveness, etc.), but they converge on others. Canada's many Indigenous communities are quite diverse but have some degree of common values regarding high collectivism, low power distance, non-interference, and natural time orientation. All regions in Canada differ from one another on some values (e.g., egalitarianism and personal responsibility) and personality traits (e.g., openness to experience). Canadians and Americans are similar in many ways, but they also have long-standing cultural differences, particularly regarding the values of tolerance, collective rights, secularism, and patriarchal authority.

Key Terms

achievement-nurturing orientation	moral sensitivity
agreeableness	Myers-Briggs Type Indicator (MBTI)
collectivism	narcissism
conscientiousness	neuroticism
counterproductive work behaviours (CWBs)	openness to experience
dark triad	organizational politics
extraversion	personality
five-factor (Big Five) model	power distance
individualism	psychopathy
Machiavellianism	uncertainty avoidance
mindfulness	values
moral intensity	

Critical Thinking Questions

1. Studies report that heredity has a strong influence on an individual's personality. What are the implications of this in organizational settings?

2. All candidates applying for a management trainee position are given a personality test that measures the five dimensions in the five-factor model. Which personality traits would you consider to be the most important for this type of job? Explain your answer.

3. As head of product development for mobile telephones, you are about to hire someone to assist in the human interface features of product design. The nature of this work calls for a creative, "break out of the box" thinker who works well in a team setting. Five short-listed applicants have completed a valid measure of the Big Five personality factors. If these applicants all have similar intelligence and work experience, which Big Five personality factors would best predict job performance (you may select one or more factors). Which Big Five factor would be least relevant? Justify your answer.

4. The dark triad is understandably a personality cluster of great concern in organizations. Yet, even though it consists of three socially undesirable personality traits, there is evidence that senior executives are more likely than the rest of us to possess some of these traits. Why would this occur? Does this mean that the dark triad isn't so bad after all?

5. This chapter discussed values congruence mostly in the context of an employee's personal values versus the organization's values. But values congruence also relates to the juxtaposition of other pairs of value systems. Explain how values congruence is relevant with respect to organizational versus professional values (i.e., values of a professional occupation, such as physician, accountant, pharmacist).

6. The CEO and two other executives at an automotive parts manufacturer were recently fired after being charged with fixing prices on several key automotive parts sold to the auto industry. Executives at competing manufacturers face the same charges for also participating in this collusion. Profit margins have come under intense pressure in the industry, which could cause one or more auto parts firms (possibly this company) to go bankrupt. When the wrongdoing was discovered, most employees involved in product pricing (but not implicated in price fixing) were surprised. The executives were highly respected in their fields of expertise, so many staff members interpreted the unusual pricing decisions as a new strategy, not an illegal activity. Apply your knowledge of personal and ethical values and behaviour to explain why the unethical activity may have occurred.

7. "All decisions are ethical decisions." Comment on this statement, particularly by referring to the concepts of moral intensity and moral sensitivity.

8. People in a particular South American country have high power distance and high collectivism. What does this mean, and what are the implications of this information when you (a senior executive) visit employees working for your company in that country?

📖 Case Study:
SNC-LAVALIN GROUP INC.

by Steven L. McShane, University of Newcastle (Australia)

Bribery of foreign public officials, conspiracy to commit fraud and forgery, money laundering, possessing property obtained by crime, and attempts to secretly smuggle the son of a former dictator into safer countries. Sounds like the plot of a twisted crime novel. Yet these are the charges laid against former executives at SNC-Lavalin (SNCL), one of Canada's largest engineering and construction firms.

The Royal Canadian Mounted Police allege that over the past decade SNCL funnelled $118 million through offshore bank accounts as bribes to secure contracts in Libya. Separately, the World Bank, the African Development Bank, Swiss police, and other entities uncovered evidence that SNCL bribed or attempted to bribe government staff and leaders to win contracts in Africa and Asia. SNCL is also being investigated for unethical activities in contract bidding on a major Canadian project involving a Montreal superhospital. Almost a dozen former SNCL executives, most of whom held senior positions, either face charges of criminal activity or are under investigation. The company and its 100 subsidiaries have been banned for a decade from bidding on World Bank–funded contracts.

The World Bank and other investigators report that in several contracts SNCL processed bribes through an expense line called "project consultancy cost" or PCC. For example, SNCL settled a corruption case filed by the African Development Bank, which had discovered project consultancy cost items representing 7.5 percent of the total contract value of two SNCL road projects in Uganda and Mozambique. The engineering firm has acknowledged that none of these expenses were legitimate. "Everybody used this term, and all know what that means," admits SNCL's former director of international projects. "Sometimes it was 'project consultancy cost,' sometimes 'project commercial cost,' but [the] real fact is the intention is [a] bribe."

SNCL paid many of the PCC bribes indirectly through employees. One SNCL engineer in Nigeria said he was told to use his personal funds to pay a Nigerian official for a "soils investigation." The official had selected the engineering firm for a contract. The engineer was subsequently reimbursed by SNCL through a fictitious company. When asked why he participated in the kickback scheme, the engineer (who now works in India for another company) replied: "When the boss asks, in that part of the world. . .what would you do if you were put in my shoes if you were in a remote area of Nigeria?"

Another way that SNCL executives apparently bribed officials was through "agent fees." Retaining a local agent is common and sometimes required for foreign contracts bids

to arrange permits, imports, and other activities. However, investigators uncovered numerous questionable transfers of large funds from SNCL to banks in Switzerland, the Bahamas, and other countries, allegedly for agent fees.

The largest corruption of the "agent fee" process involved SNCL transferring more than $120 million over 10 years to a Swiss bank account controlled by an SNCL executive vice-president working in North Africa and later at headquarters in Montreal. The executive was subsequently convicted and served jail time in Switzerland for corruption and money laundering regarding these funds, $47 million of which he handed over to Swiss authorities as part of that conviction. During the Swiss trial, the executive admitted that he bribed Saadi Gaddafi, a son of Libya's dictator at that time, for the purpose of having SNCL win five major contracts in Libya. In separate charges, an RCMP affidavit claims that the same executive masterminded a failed attempt to smuggle Saadi Gaddafi and his family into Mexico. A former SNCL contractor in Canada spent 18 months in a Mexican prison in relation to that mission.

SNCL is suing the executive convicted in Switzerland and others for recovery of the transferred funds, claiming that they were intended as legitimate agent fees. The executive counterclaims that the top brass (below the board level) had arranged or knew these funds were being used for bribery payments and that the executive was following orders. Separate actions by SNCL's CEO at the time lend support to the jailed executive's claims. Specifically, in spite of opposition from the chief financial officer and head of international operations, the CEO authorized undocumented payments totalling $56 million to unknown "agents" in Libya and the Bahamas. Quebec's anti-corruption police say the CEO's largest undocumented payment ($22.5 million sent to the Bahamas) was a bribe to win a major Montreal superhospital contract. The CEO resigned when an internal review informed SNCL's board of the CEO's actions. The board granted the CEO a severance payout, but those payments were later stopped when Quebec's anti-corruption police charged the former CEO with fraud.

Another SNCL vice-president now facing several charges also admits to engaging in bribery and related crimes. He explained that SNC-Lavalin had "a corporate culture where it was common practice to do all that was necessary, including the payment of 'commissions' and other benefits to obtain contracts, including in Libya." The second executive also argued that he was under pressure to engage in these illegal activities because the executive above him said "that he had to follow their orders to satisfy their expectations." In fact, a few former SNCL executives have since tried to sue the company for wrongful dismissal on the grounds that their illegal activities were required by the company to keep their jobs.

SNCL's board of directors seems to have downplayed personal responsibility for these events. Very early in the RCMP investigation, SNCL's board received an anonymous internal letter describing the bribery activities, yet the board later admitted that it only "took note" of the allegations, pointing out that they have "received anonymous letters before that have no credibility." And when the extent of wrongdoing at SNCL eventually became public, the board chair said: "Clearly, our board of directors can't govern something that they don't know about, or prevent something they are not aware of."

Discussion Questions

1. Explain how moral sensitivity and moral intensity apply to the unethical behaviour among several SNC-Lavalin executives and other staff.

2. This case describes several incidents of unethical and illegal behaviour at SNC-Lavalin. To what extent did motivation, ability, role perceptions, and situation (i.e., MARS model from Chapter 1) influence this behaviour among executives and employees? How did the personal values of these people affect their actions?

3. What steps should SNC-Lavalin and other companies in this situation take to minimize these types of corporate wrongdoing?

Team Exercise:
ETHICS DILEMMA VIGNETTES

by Steven L. McShane, University of Newcastle (Australia)

Purpose This exercise is designed to make you aware of the ethical dilemmas people face in various business situations, as well as the competing principles and values that operate in these situations.

Instructions (Small Class) The instructor will form teams of four or five students. Team members will read each case below and discuss the extent to which the company's action in each case was ethical. Teams should be prepared to justify their evaluation using ethics principles and the perceived moral intensity of each incident.

Instructions (Large Class) Working alone, read each case below and determine the extent to which the company's action in each case was ethical. The instructor will use a show of hands to determine the extent to which students believe the case represents an ethical dilemma (high or low moral intensity) and the extent to which the main people or company in each incident acted ethically.

CASE ONE

A large multinational grocery chain that emphasizes healthy lifestyles is recognized as one of the nation's "greenest" companies, has generous employee benefits, and is perennially rated as one of the best places to work. Employees receive a 20 percent discount on company products. However, those who participate in the company's voluntary "Healthy Discount Incentive Program" receive up to an additional 10 percent discount on their purchases (i.e., up to a total 30 percent discount). These additional discounts are calculated from employees' blood pressure, total cholesterol (or LDL) levels, Body Mass Index (BMI), and nicotine-free

lifestyle. For example, the full additional 10 percent discount is awarded to those who do not use nicotine products, have 110/70 or lower blood pressure, have cholesterol levels under 150, and have a BMI of less than 24. Employees do not receive the additional discount if they use nicotine products, or have any one of the following: blood pressure above 140/90, cholesterol of 195 or higher, or BMI of 30 or higher. In his letter to employees when announcing the plan, the CEO explained that these incentives "encourage our Team Members to be healthier and to lower our healthcare costs."

CASE TWO

A 16-year-old hired as an office administrator at a small import services company started posting her thoughts about the job on her Facebook site. After her first day, she wrote: "first day at work. omg!! So dull!!" Two days later, she complained "all i do is shred holepunch n scan paper!!! omg!" Two weeks later she added "im so totally bord!!!" These comments were intermixed with the other usual banter about her life. Her Facebook site did not mention the name of the company where she worked. Three weeks after being hired, the employee was called into the owner's office, where he fired her for the comments on Facebook, then had her escorted from the building. The owner argues that these comments put the company in a bad light, and her "display of disrespect and dissatisfaction undermined the relationship and made it untenable."

CASE THREE

The waiter at a café in a large city mixed up Heidi Clarke's meal order with the meal that a male customer at a nearby table had requested. The two strangers discovered the mistake and briefly enjoyed a friendly chat while swapping plates. The male patron departed soon after but accidentally left his new tuxedo jacket behind on his chair. Clarke wanted to meet him again, so she took the jacket home. Following a friend's suggestion, Heidi launched a YouTube video and website, in which she shyly told her story, detailed the jacket's features, and prominently displayed a label with the name of a popular fashion retailer. The website even included photos of Heidi posing in the jacket. The next day, she gave the café staff the jacket and a note with her name and phone number. Heidi's YouTube video soon went viral, her website crashed from so many visitors, and a major newspaper and television station featured Heidi's quest to find the man with the missing jacket. The incident is a romantic reversal of the Cinderella story . . . except it was a fake event staged by a marketing company. "Heidi" is an actress and model hired by the marketer to promote the fashion retailer's new line of jackets for men. A partner at the marketing firm justified the hoax by saying that "when you've got a very well-established brand you need to do something that's got talkability and intrigue to reassess what that brand is about." The marketing executive argued that this was an acceptable marketing event because "nobody's been harmed" and the firm intended to eventually reveal the truth. Indeed, the actress (whose real name is Lily, not Heidi) released a second video acknowledging that the incident was fake and explaining that she's a hopeless romantic who loves a good love story.

CASE FOUR

Computer printer manufacturers usually sell printers at a low margin over cost and generate much more income from subsequent sales of the high-margin ink cartridges required for each printer. One global printer manufacturer now designs its printers so that they work only with ink cartridges made in the same region. Ink cartridges purchased in Canada will not work with the same printer model sold in Europe, for example. This "region coding" of ink cartridges does not improve performance. Rather, it prevents consumers and grey marketers from buying the product at a lower price in another region. The company says this policy allows it to maintain stable prices within a region rather than continually changing prices due to currency fluctuations.

CASE FIVE

A large European bank requires all employees to open a bank account with that bank. The bank deposits employee paycheques to those accounts. The bank explains that this is a formal policy which all employees agree to at the time of hire. Furthermore, failure to have an account with the bank shows disloyalty, which could limit the employee's career advancement opportunities with the bank. Until recently, the bank has reluctantly agreed to deposit paycheques to accounts at other banks for a small percentage of employees. Now, bank executives want to reinforce the policy. They announce that employees have three months to open an account with the bank or face disciplinary action.

 ## Class Exercise:
PERSONAL VALUES EXERCISE

by Steven L. McShane, University of Newcastle (Australia)

Purpose This exercise is designed to help you understand Schwartz's values model and relate its elements to your personal values and the values held by others in your class.

Instructions Your instructor will distribute a sheet with 44 words and phrases representing different personal values. Read these words and phrases carefully, then follow these steps:

1. Pick THREE (3) of these words/phrases that represent the MOST important values to you personally. Print each of the three values on the three yellow-coloured sticky (Post-It) notes provided by your instructor (i.e., print one value on each note). Do not put your name on any sticky notes.

2. From the remaining 41 values on the sheet provided by your instructor, pick THREE (3) of these that represent the LEAST important values to you personally. Print each of the three values on three sticky notes of the second colour provided by your instructor (i.e., print one value on each note).

3. The instructor will advise you what to do with the six sticky notes on which you wrote your most and least important values.

4. The class will engage in a debriefing, using the information created in the third step of this activity.

Self-Assessments for Chapter 2

SELF-ASSESSMENT NAME	DESCRIPTION
What is your Big Five personality?	Personality experts have organized the dozens of personality traits into five main dimensions, known as the five-factor or "Big Five" model. Each dimension consists of several specific personality traits that cluster together. Most scholarly research on personality relies on this model, but it is also useful in everyday life as a relatively easy categorization of personalities. This self-assessment estimates your personality on the Big Five dimensions.
Are you introverted or extraverted?	One of the most widely studied and discussed personality dimensions is introversion–extraversion. Introversion characterizes people who tend to be quiet, shy, and cautious. Extraversion characterizes people who tend to be outgoing, talkative, sociable, and assertive. This self-assessment estimates the extent to which you have an introverted or extraverted personality.
Can you identify personality traits from blogging words?	Personality influences all aspects of our lives, including the words we use when writing blogs. In fact, some companies now use sophisticated software to estimate the personality traits of job applicants from the words they use in blogs and other online writing. This self-assessment estimates how well you interpret someone's personality in blogs and other writing.
How Machiavellian are you?	Machiavellianisn is a personality trait characteristic of people who demonstrate a strong motivation to achieve their own goals at the expense of others, who believe that deceit is a natural and acceptable way to achieve their goals, who take pleasure in outwitting and misleading others using crude influence tactics, and who have a cynical disregard for morality. Few people want to be viewed as Machiavellian, yet many of us exhibit aspects of this trait to some extent. This self-assessment estimates the extent to which you believe that you have Machiavellian tendencies.
Are you a sensing or intuitive type?	Nearly a century ago, Swiss psychiatrist Carl Jung proposed that personality is primarily represented by the individual's preferences regarding perceiving and judging information. Jung explained that perceiving, which involves how people prefer to gather information or perceive the world around them, occurs through two competing orientations: sensing (S) and intuition (N). This self-assessment estimates your score on this Jungian personality type (S/N).
What are your dominant values?	Values are stable, evaluative beliefs that guide our preferences for outcomes or courses of action in a variety of situations. They are perceptions about what is good or bad, right or wrong. We arrange our personal values into a hierarchy of preferences, called a value system. Schwartz's values circumplex organizes the dozens of personal values into 10 categories placed in a circle (circumplex). This self-assessment assesses the relative importance to you of the 10 categories of values in Schwartz's circumplex model.
How much do you value individualism and collectivism?	Cross-cultural values have become an important part of organizational life due to globalization and an increasingly multicultural workforce. Two of the most commonly studied cross-cultural values are individualism and collectivism. This self-assessment estimates your score on these two cross-cultural values.
What is your level of power distance?	Some employees value obedience to authority and are comfortable receiving commands from their superiors without consultation or debate. Others expect equal status and authority with their manager. This power distance orientation varies from one person to the next; it also varies across cultures. This self-assessment estimates your score on this cross-cultural value.

CHAPTER 3

Perceiving Ourselves and Others in Organizations

LEARNING OBJECTIVES

After reading this chapter, you should be able to:

LO1 Describe the elements of self-concept and explain how each affects an individual's behaviour and well-being.

LO2 Outline the perceptual process and discuss the effects of categorical thinking and mental models in that process.

LO3 Discuss how stereotyping, attribution, self-fulfilling prophecy, halo, false-consensus, primacy, and recency effects influence the perceptual process.

LO4 Discuss three ways to improve perceptions, with specific application to organizational situations.

LO5 Outline the main features of a global mindset and justify its usefulness to employees and organizations.

Heidi Cossey excelled in math and science throughout high school in Alberta, but nobody suggested that she might enjoy a career in engineering. "All I knew is that I wanted to help people," recalls the geo-environmental engineer. "I didn't know you could actually do that in engineering." And when Cossey began her engineering studies, some of her acquaintances either showed surprise or expressed doubt about her success. "I can't tell you how many people have told me I should be a hairdresser instead of an engineer," she says. "Unfortunately, I think women will still have to prove themselves for a while yet."

Engineering is considered one of the most fulfilling and well-paying careers. Yet, women represent less than 15 percent of the engineering workforce in Canada (similar to several other countries) and little more than 20 percent of students enrolled in Canadian engineering programs.

One reason for the alarming under-representation of women is the misguided stereotype of engineering as a traditional male job involving work in physically difficult terrain. One recent survey found that stereotypes dissuaded 74 percent of Canadian girls from considering a career in engineering and other STEM occupations. "We need to urgently change the image of women in engineering," urges

Stereotypes, discrimination, and other misperceptions are a few of the reasons why women are under-represented in the engineering profession.

©Monkey Business Images/Shutterstock

Michelle Unger, a civil engineer specializing in subsea and pipeline technology. "I do not wear a hard hat, or work in a muddy field. Very few of us will ever do that."

Female engineers also face various forms of discrimination and prejudice. For example, a Google engineer in California and the CEO of a South African engineering association recently espoused long-refuted ideas that women aren't suited biologically or personality-wise to engineering. "I think a lot of men don't realize their own bias to hiring or working with women," says Bruce Matthews, chief executive of the Consulting Engineers of Ontario.

Kathy Tarnai-Lokhorst, president of Engineers and Geoscientists of British Columbia, believes that these perceptual biases and distorted stereotypes will evaporate as the profession develops more female engineer role models. "Seeing oneself represented in the industry where they work can change a person's ideas about what they are capable of, and instil a sense of belonging," she explains. Elly Williams, an engineering student in Australia, agrees. "I believe that what we need to show young women is that they don't have to fit one of society's constructed stereotypes to be a successful engineer; they just have to be passionate about creating things to help people."[1]

Companies that employ engineers face two challenges in attracting and keeping women in this profession: (1) the concept women have about themselves as engineers; and (2) the perceptions they and others have about engineers and about women in these roles. We discuss both of these related topics in this chapter. First, we examine how people perceive themselves—their self-concept—and how that self-perception affects their decisions and behaviour. Next, we focus on perceptions in organizational settings, beginning with how we select, organize, and interpret information. We also review several specific perceptual processes, such as stereotyping, attribution, and self-fulfilling prophecy. This is followed by discussion of potentially effective ways to improve perceptions. The final section of this chapter reviews the main elements of global mindset, a largely perceptual process valued in this increasingly globalized world.

Self-Concept: How We Perceive Ourselves

LO1

Why are there so few female engineers in Canada and many other countries? As the opening case study to this chapter suggests, many people have inaccurate perceptions about this profession—associating it with an image that is incompatible with the ideal self-concept for many women. In addition, as Heidi Cossey observed, young women receive low-expectation signals from people around them, which affects their self-evaluation as an engineer. This amplifies their existing self-doubts regarding performance in engineering-related courses. For instance, one recent study found that 14-year-old girls significantly underestimated their performance on science and technology tests, whereas boys slightly overrated themselves, even though average scores are about the same for both genders.[2]

These barriers to women entering engineering are core elements of self-concept. **Self-concept** refers to an individual's self-beliefs and self-evaluations.[3] It is the, Who am I? and How do I feel about myself? that people ask themselves and that guide their decisions and actions. Whether contemplating a career in engineering or

> **self-concept** An individual's self-beliefs and self-evaluations.

any other occupation, we compare our mental images of that job with our current perceived self and desired ideal self. We also evaluate our current and desired abilities to determine whether they make a good fit with that type of work. Our self-concept is defined at three levels: individual, relational, and collective. Specifically, we view ourselves in terms of our personal traits (individual self), connections to friends and co-workers (relational self), and roles in teams, organizations, social groups, and other entities (collective self).[4]

SELF-CONCEPT COMPLEXITY, CONSISTENCY, AND CLARITY

An individual's self-concept can be described by three characteristics: complexity, consistency, and clarity (see Exhibit 3.1). *Complexity* refers to the number of distinct and important roles or identities that people perceive about themselves.[5] Everyone has some degree of complexity because they see themselves in different roles at various times (student, friend, daughter, sports fan, etc.). People are generally motivated to increase their complexity (called *self-expansion*) as they seek out new opportunities and social connections. Your self-concept becomes more complex, for

---

EXHIBIT 3.1 **Self-Concept Characteristics and Processes**

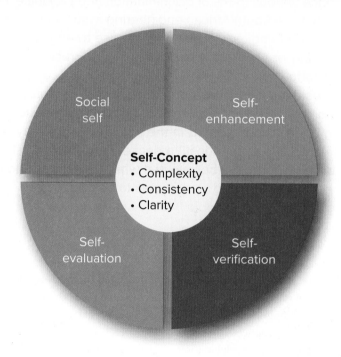

example, as you move from being an accountant to a manager because you have acquired additional roles.

Self-concept complexity is defined by more than just the number of identities a person has; it is also defined by the separation of those identities. An individual with several identities might still have low self-concept complexity when those identities are highly interconnected, such as when they are all work-related (manager, engineer, family income earner). Complexity is higher when the multiple identities have a low correlation with each other, such as when they apply to fairly distinct spheres of life.

Although everyone has multiple selves, only some of those identities dominate their attention at any one time.[6] A particular self-view (parent, manager, etc.) is usually domain specific; it is more likely to be activated in some settings than in others. People shift their self-concept more easily when the activated self-view is important and compatible with the situation. For instance, as people travel from home to work, they can usually shift their self-view from being a parent to being an executive because each role is important and fits into the home and work contexts, respectively. In contrast, some employees struggle to focus on their occupational self-concept when working from home (remote work).

Consistency, the second self-concept characteristic, is the degree to which a person's identities require similar personal attributes. High consistency exists when the individual's

personal attributes are compatible with their various self-views, and when those self-views are compatible with each other. Low consistency occurs when some self-views require personal attributes that conflict with attributes required for other self-views, such as when a safety-conscious engineer also identifies as a risk-oriented snowboarder. Low consistency also occurs when an individual's dominant self-views are incompatible with their actual personal attributes. This would occur when someone has a self-concept as a highly creative individual yet has moderately low openness-to-experience personality and values.

The third self-concept characteristic is *clarity,* which refers to the degree to which a person's self-concept is clear, confidently defined, and stable.[7] Clarity occurs when someone is confident about "who I am" and can describe their identities to others and provide the same description over time. Self-concept clarity increases with age because personality and values become relatively stable by adulthood and people develop better self-awareness through life experiences. Self-concept is also clearer when a person's multiple selves have higher consistency. This makes sense because low consistency produces ambiguity about a person's underlying characteristics. For example, someone whose self-view includes the contrasting identities of cautious engineer and risk-oriented snowboarder would have difficulty defining himself or herself clearly or with much confidence.[8]

Global Connections 3.1

CAREER ALIGNMENT THROUGH SELF-CONCEPT CLARITY*

Richard Alderson was developing an enviable career as a business consultant in London after graduating from university. "On the surface, I had a good job in a big company," Anderson recalls. "I'd done what was expected of me post-university."

But Alderson eventually realized that this career path was incompatible with his self-concept. In social gatherings, he would "feel embarrassed about talking about my work because it wasn't something that felt aligned with me. There was nothing wrong with the job or the company; they simply weren't right for me," recalls Alderson, who has since formed a company offering coaching and workshops for people who face similar career incompatibility issues.

Alderson's experience isn't unusual. Many people complete an educational program and enter a career before their self-concept is clear and confidently defined. "Your twenties are a time of considerable personality development and growth—and only at 30 do you start

©Jose Luis Pelaez Inc/Blend Images LLC

to discover who you really are," suggests Kedge Martin, the founder of a career development and life-skills agency in London.

* R. Alderson, "I Felt Numb, Uninspired by My Work and Stuck in Groundhog Day," *The Guardian,* October 7, 2015; S. Inge, "New Decade, New Job: How to Change Career in Your Thirties," *The Telegraph,* August 6, 2018.

Effects of Self-Concept Characteristics on Well-Being and Behaviour

Psychological well-being tends to be higher among people with fairly distinct multiple selves (complexity) that are well established (clarity) and require similar personal attributes that are compatible with the individual's character (consistency).[9] Self-concept complexity protects our self-esteem when some roles are threatened or damaged. A complex self is similar to a ship with several compartments that can be sealed off from one another. If one compartment is damaged, the other compartments remain intact, so the ship remains afloat. A complex self offers the same benefits: if one identity is damaged by events—job loss, for example—the person's mental health stays afloat because the other selves remain intact. In contrast, people with low complexity, including those whose multiple selves are highly interconnected, suffer severe loss when they experience failure because these events affect a large part of themselves.

People also tend to have better well-being when their multiple selves are in harmony with one another and with their personality and values (consistency).[10] Self-concept complexity helps people adapt, but too much variation causes internal tension and conflict. Well-being also tends to

increase with self-concept clarity. People who are unsure of their self-views are more easily influenced by others, experience more stress when making decisions, and feel more threatened by social forces that undermine their self-confidence and self-esteem.[11]

Self-concept complexity, consistency, and clarity have both positive and negative influences on individual behaviour and performance.[12] Employees with complex identities tend to have more adaptive decision-making and performance. This likely occurs because multiple selves generate more diverse experiences and role patterns, so these employees can more easily alter their thinking and behaviour to suit new tasks and work environments. A second benefit is that self-concept complexity often produces more diverse social networks, which gives employees access to more resources and social support to perform their jobs.

Against these benefits is the problem that highly complex self-concepts require more effort to maintain and juggle, which can be stressful. Low complexity self-concepts, on the other hand, require less effort and resources to develop. For example, people who define themselves mainly by their work (low complexity) tend to have better job performance due to their longer work hours, more investment in skill

How much does work define your self-concept? You can discover the extent to which work is central to your self-concept by completing this self-assessment in Connect.

development, and more concentration on work. They also have lower absenteeism and turnover.

Self-concept clarity tends to improve performance and is considered vital for leadership roles.[13] Clarity also provides a more lucid career path, which enables people to direct their effort more efficiently toward career success. Another benefit is that people with high self-concept clarity feel less threatened by interpersonal conflict, which increases their ability to resolve conflicts through constructive problem-solving behaviours. However, those with very high clarity may have role inflexibility, with the result that they cannot adapt to changing job duties or environmental conditions.

Along with the three self-concept characteristics, Exhibit 3.1 identifies four processes that shape self-concept and motivate a person's decisions and behaviour. Let's look at each of these four "selves": self-enhancement, self-verification, self-evaluation, and social self (social identity).

SELF-ENHANCEMENT

A century ago, educational philosopher John Dewey said that "the deepest urge in human nature is the desire to be important."[14] Dewey recognized that people are inherently motivated to perceive themselves (and to be perceived by others) as competent, attractive, lucky, ethical, and important.[15] This phenomenon, called **self-enhancement**, is observed in many ways. Individuals tend to rate themselves above average, believe that they have a better than average probability of success, and attribute their successes to personal motivation or ability while blaming the situation for their mistakes. For instance, one study reported that 70 percent of students believe their academic performance is above average; 62 percent say they have above-average leadership ability compared to other students. People don't believe they are above average in all circumstances, only for things that are important to them and are relatively common rather than rare.[16]

> **self-enhancement** A person's inherent motivation to have a positive self-concept (and to have others perceive them favourably), such as being competent, attractive, lucky, ethical, and important.

Self-enhancement has both positive and negative consequences in organizational settings.[17] On the positive side, individuals tend to experience better mental and physical health when they amplify their self-concept. Overconfidence also generates a "can do" attitude (which we discuss later) that motivates persistence in difficult or risky tasks. On the negative side, self-enhancement causes people to overestimate future returns in investment decisions and to engage in unsafe behaviour (such as dangerous driving). It also motivates executives to repeat ineffective decisions (because they ignore negative feedback), launch misguided corporate diversification strategies, and acquire excessive corporate debt. Generally, though, successful companies strive to help employees feel valued, which generates some degree of self-enhancement.

SELF-VERIFICATION

Individuals try to confirm and maintain their existing self-concept.[18] This process, called **self-verification**, stabilizes an individual's self-view, which, in turn, guides their thoughts and actions. Employees actively communicate their self-concept so co-workers understand it and provide verifying feedback when observed. For example, you might let co-workers know that you are a very organized person; later, they compliment you on occasions where you have indeed been very organized. One recent study reported that when a person's identity as a leader is questioned by others, the leader applies self-verification strategies, such as making their role performance more visible (e.g., working longer hours), adopting a less threatening style of that self-view, and directly confronting those who doubt or disagree with their self-view as a leader.[19]

> **self-verification** A person's inherent motivation to confirm and maintain their existing self-concept.

Unlike self-enhancement, self-verification includes seeking feedback that is not necessarily flattering (e.g., I'm a numbers person, not a people person). Experts continue to debate whether and under what conditions people prefer information that supports self-enhancement or self-verification.[20] In other words, do we prefer compliments rather than accurate critiques about weaknesses that we readily acknowledge? The answer is likely an internal tug-of-war; we enjoy compliments, but less so if they are significantly contrary to our self-view.

Self-verification is associated with several OB topics.[21] First, it affects the perceptual process because employees are more likely to remember information that verifies their self-concept and nonconsciously screen out information (particularly negative information) that is contrary to their self-view. Second, people with high self-concept clarity will consciously dismiss feedback that contradicts their self-view.

Third, employees are motivated to interact with others who affirm their self-views, and this affects how well they get along with their boss and team members.

SELF-EVALUATION

Almost everyone strives to have a positive self-concept, but some people have a more positive evaluation of themselves than do others. This *self-evaluation* is mostly defined by three elements: self-esteem, self-efficacy, and locus of control.[22]

Self-Esteem

Self-esteem—the extent to which people like, respect, and are satisfied with themselves—represents a comprehensive self-evaluation. People have degrees of self-esteem for each of their various roles, such as believing themselves to be a good student, a good driver, and a good parent. From these multiple self-appraisals, people form an overall evaluation of themselves, known as their global self-esteem. People with high self-esteem are less influenced by others, tend to persist in spite of failure, and have a higher propensity to think logically.[23]

Self-Efficacy

Self-efficacy refers to a person's belief that they can successfully complete a task.[24] Those with high self-efficacy have a "can do" attitude. They believe they possess the energy (motivation), ability, clear expectations (role perceptions), and resources (situational factors) to perform the task. In other words, self-efficacy is an individual's perception regarding the MARS model in a specific situation. Self-efficacy is often task-specific, but it can also be more generalized. People have a general self-efficacy when they believe they can be successful across a variety of situations.[25] People with higher general self-efficacy have a more positive overall self-evaluation.

> **self-efficacy** A person's belief that they have the ability, motivation, correct role perceptions, and favourable situation to complete a task successfully.

Locus of Control

Locus of control is defined as a person's general beliefs about the amount of control they have over personal life events.[26] Individuals with an internal locus of control believe that life events are caused mainly by their personal characteristics (i.e., motivation and abilities). Those with an external locus of control believe events are due mainly to fate, luck, or conditions in the external environment. Locus of control is a generalized belief that varies to some extent with the situation. People with an external locus of control generally believe that life's outcomes are beyond their control, but they also believe they have control over the results of tasks they perform often. An individual's locus of control tendency is most apparent in new situations, where their ability to control events is uncertain.

> **locus of control** A person's general belief about the amount of control they have over personal life events.

People with an internal locus of control have a more positive self-evaluation. They also tend to perform better in most employment situations, are more successful in their careers, earn more money, and are better suited for leadership positions. Internals are also more satisfied with their jobs, cope better in stressful situations, and are more motivated by performance-based reward systems.[27]

THE SOCIAL SELF

We began this topic by stating that an individual's self-concept exists at three levels: individual, relational, and collective. These three levels recognize two opposing human motivations that influence how people view themselves.[28]

- *Motivation to be distinctive and different from other people.* The individual self, called *personal identity* or *internal self-concept,* fulfils the need for distinctiveness because it involves defining ourselves by our personality, values, abilities, qualifications, achievements, and other personal attributes. Everyone has a unique combination of personal characteristics, and we embrace this uniqueness to some degree. For instance, an unusual

 How much general self-efficacy do you have? You can discover your level of general self-efficacy by completing this self-assessment in Connect.

 What is your locus of control? You can discover your general locus of control orientation by completing this self-assessment in Connect.

skill or accomplishment that distinguishes you from your co-workers is part of your personal identity.

- *Motivation for inclusion and assimilation with other people.* The relational and collective self-concepts fulfil the fundamental drive for affiliation because they involve both interaction and interdependence with others.[29] Human beings are social animals; we have an inherent drive to be associated with others and to be recognized as part of social communities. This drive to belong motivates all individuals to define themselves to some degree by their interpersonal and collective relationships, a definition known as their *social identity* or *external self-concept.*

Social identity is the foundation of **social identity theory**, which says that people define themselves by the groups to which they belong or have an emotional attachment.[30]

> **social identity theory** A theory stating that people define themselves by the groups to which they belong or have an emotional attachment.

For instance, someone might have a social identity as a Canadian, a graduate of Université Laval, and an employee at Desjardins Group (see Exhibit 3.2).

Social identity is a complex combination of many memberships arranged in a hierarchy of importance. One factor determining importance is how easily you are identified as a member of the reference group, such as by your gender, age, and ethnicity. A second factor is your minority status in a group. It is difficult to ignore your gender in a class where most other students are another gender, for example. In that context, gender tends to become a stronger defining feature of your social identity than it is in social settings where there are many people of your gender.

The group's status is another important social identity factor because association with the group makes us feel better about ourselves (i.e., self-enhancement). Medical doctors usually define themselves by their profession because of its high status. Some people describe themselves by where they work ("I work at Shopify") because their employer has a good reputation. Others never mention where they work because their employer is noted for poor relations with employees or has a poor reputation in the community.[31]

Everyone tries to balance personal and social identities to some degree, but the priority for uniqueness (personal identities) versus belongingness (social identities) differs from one person to the next. People whose self-concepts are heavily defined by social rather than personal identities are more motivated to abide by team norms and are more easily influenced by peer pressure. Those who place more emphasis on personal identities, on the other hand, speak out more frequently against the majority and are less motivated to follow the team's wishes. Furthermore, expressing disagreement with others is a sign of distinctiveness and can help employees form a clearer self-concept, particularly when that disagreement is based on differences in personal values.[32]

SELF-CONCEPT AND ORGANIZATIONAL BEHAVIOUR

Self-concept become a hot topic in the social sciences and is starting to bloom in organizational behaviour research.[33] This section briefly noted that self-concept influences human perceptions, decision making, motivation, stress, team dynamics, leadership

---

EXHIBIT 3.2   Social Identity Theory Example

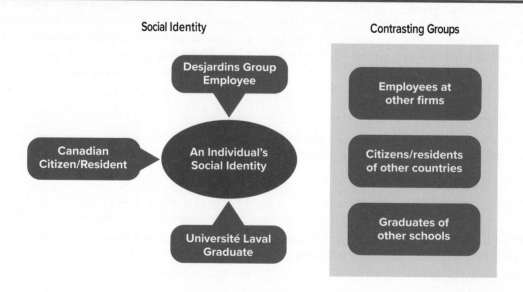

Global Connections 3.2

STARBUCKS NURTURES EMPLOYEES' SOCIAL IDENTITY IN CHINA*

Starbucks Coffee Company has become a success story in China by making the American coffee-house chain an integral part of employees' social identity. It does this in several ways. First, employees (who are called "partners") easily connect with Starbucks' core values of performance, innovation, respect, and belonging.

Second, Starbucks has positioned itself as a premium brand, which further elevates employee pride. The company offers competitive pay, comprehensive health insurance, an employee ownership plan, a housing allowance for full-time staff, and ongoing training and career development.

Starbucks staff also proudly identify with their employer because of its well-known emphasis on families—an important value in Chinese culture. The company holds an annual "Partner Family Forum," where employees and their parents learn about Starbucks and its future in China. The chain also recently introduced special critical-illness insurance for employees' elderly

©humphery/Shutterstock

parents. "We have always aspired to create a culture that our employees are proud to belong to," says an executive at Starbucks Asia Pacific.

* Starbucks, "Starbucks Strengthens Commitment in China," news release (Chengdu, China, January 12, 2016); M. Zakkour, "Why Starbucks Succeeded in China: A Lesson for All Retailers," *Forbes,* August 24, 2017; Starbucks, "Starbucks Redefines Partner Benefits in China," news release (Beijing, China, April 11, 2017); O. Farry, "Harnessing the Power," *South China Morning Post (Hong Kong),* November 17, 2017, 1.

development, and several other OB topics. Consequently, we will refer to self-concept later in this chapter and in many other topics throughout this book.

Perceiving the World around Us

LO2

We spend considerable time perceiving ourselves, but most of our perceptual energy is directed toward the outer world. Whether as a chemical engineer, forensic accountant, or senior executive, we need to make sense of the world around us, including the conditions that challenge the accuracy of those perceptions. **Perception** is the process of receiving information about and making sense of our surrounding environment. It includes determining which information to notice, how to categorize this information, and how to interpret it within the framework of our existing knowledge.

perception The process of receiving information about and making sense of our surrounding environment.

The perceptual process generally follows the steps shown in Exhibit 3.3. Perception begins when environmental stimuli are received through our senses. We are continually bombarded by external stimuli. Most are screened out; the rest are organized and interpreted. The process of attending to some information received by our senses and ignoring other information is called **selective attention**. Selective attention is influenced by characteristics of the person or object being perceived, particularly size, intensity, motion, repetition, and novelty. For example, a small, flashing red light on a nurses' workstation console is immediately noticed because it is bright (intensity), flashing (motion), a rare event (novelty), and has symbolic meaning that a patient's vital signs are failing. Notice that selective attention is also influenced by the context in which the target is perceived. For instance, selective attention is triggered by things or people who are out of context, such as someone with a foreign accent in a setting where most people have a local accent.

selective attention The process of attending to some information received by our senses and ignoring other information.

Characteristics of the perceiver also influence selective attention, usually without the perceiver's awareness.[34] When information is received through the senses, our brain quickly and nonconsciously assesses whether it is relevant or irrelevant to us and then attaches emotional markers (worry, happiness, boredom) to the retained information.[35] Emotional

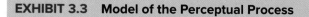

EXHIBIT 3.3   Model of the Perceptual Process

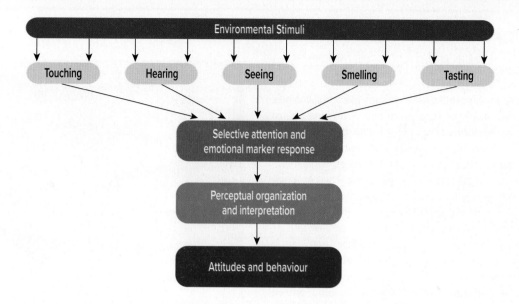

markers play a vital role in storing and retaining information in memory; those emotions are later reproduced when recalling the information. The selective attention process is far from perfect, however. The Greek philosopher Plato acknowledged this imperfection long ago when he wrote that we see reality only as shadows reflecting against the rough wall of a cave.[36]

One selective attention bias is the effect of our assumptions and expectations about future events. You are more likely to notice a particular co-worker's email among the daily avalanche of messages when you are expecting to receive that email (even more so if it is important). Unfortunately, expectations and assumptions also cause us to screen out potentially important information. In one study, students were asked to watch a 30-second video clip in which several people passed around two basketballs. Students in one group were instructed simply to watch the video clip. Most of them readily noticed a person dressed in a gorilla suit walking among the players for nine seconds and stopping to thump his or her chest. Students in a second group were asked to count the number of times one of the two basketballs was passed around. Only half of the people in this latter group noticed the intruding gorilla.[37]

Another selective attention problem, called **confirmation bias**, is the nonconscious tendency for people to screen out information that is contrary to their decisions, beliefs, values, and assumptions, while more readily accepting information that confirms those elements.[38] When making an important decision, such as investing in a costly project, we tend to pay attention to information that supports that decision, ignore information that questions the wisdom of the decision, and more easily recall the supportive than the opposing information. Confirmation bias is a well-known perceptual problem in law enforcement when law enforcement professionals form a theory too early in an investigation. A recent report on wrongful convictions by Canadian federal, provincial, and territorial departments of justice devoted an entire chapter to this "tunnel vision," which occurs when prosecutors or police "focus on a particular theory of a case and . . . dismiss or undervalue evidence which contradicts that theory."[39]

PERCEPTUAL ORGANIZATION AND INTERPRETATION

We pay attention to a tiny fraction of the stimuli received by the senses. Even so, human beings further reduce the huge volume and complexity of the information received through various perceptual grouping strategies. Perceptual grouping occurs mostly without our awareness, yet it is the foundation for making sense of things and fulfilling our need for cognitive closure.

The most common and far-reaching perceptual grouping process is **categorical thinking**—the mostly nonconscious process of organizing people and objects into preconceived categories that are stored in our long-term memory.[40] People are usually grouped together based on their observable similarity, such as gender, age, race, or clothing style. This

confirmation bias The process of screening out information that is contrary to our values and assumptions, and to more readily accept confirming information.

categorical thinking Organizing people and objects into preconceived categories that are stored in our long-term memory.

©Bill Graveland/The Canadian Press

"It is a capital mistake to theorize before you have all the evidence," warned the mythical detective Sherlock Holmes in *A Study in Scarlet.* "It biases the judgment." Law enforcement agencies try to follow this advice, but many flawed investigations are caused by confirmation bias. An Alberta judge recently identified this "tunnel vision" in the behaviour of the lead detective of a re-opened sexual harassment investigation. According to court records, the detective told two people during an interview that some witnesses were already "on board" and that the "investigation will end with a positive result." He also told a colleague that the accused was guilty beyond a reasonable doubt. The detective stated in court that the accused was "still providing false information" to the community, which he later admitted was how he interpreted the accused's claim to others that he was innocent. The court also felt that the detective had withheld, lost, and failed to recreate evidence that did not support the guilty verdict. The judge stayed (suspended) all charges due to the detective's confirmation bias and other errors.*

* The Sherlock Holmes quotation is from A. Conan Doyle, "A Study in Scarlet," in *The Complete Sherlock Holmes* (New York: Fine Creative Media, 2003), 3–96. Sherlock Holmes offers similar advice in "A Scandal in Bohemia," p. 189. The Alberta case is: *R. v. Iskander,* 2017 ABPC 191 (CanLII).

categorization process also groups people together by their proximity to one another. If you notice a group of employees working in the same area and know that some of them are marketing staff, you will likely assume that the others in that group are also marketing staff.

A second perceptual grouping process organizes incoming information by filling in the missing pieces of the puzzle. Everyone wants to make sense of what goes on around them, so they make assumptions about missing information by relying on past images and experiences in those situations. For instance, people engage in this cognitive closure by assuming what happened at a meeting that they didn't attend (e.g., who was there, where it was held). A related process is one in which people tend to see patterns that, in fact, are random events. For example,

people incorrectly believe that a sports player or gambler with a string of wins is more likely to win next time as well.[41]

The process of "making sense" of the external environment involves interpreting incoming information, not just organizing it. This happens as quickly as selecting and organizing because the previously mentioned emotional markers are tagged to incoming stimuli; these markers are essentially quick judgments about whether that information is good or bad for us. How much time does it take to make these quick judgments? Recent studies estimate that we make reliable judgments about another individual's trustworthiness based on viewing a facial image for as little as 50 milliseconds (one-twentieth of a second). In fact, our opinion regarding whether we like or trust a person is about the same whether

How much perceptual structure do you need? You can discover your need for perceptual structure by locating this self-assessment in Connect.

we see the person's face for a minute or a fraction of a second.[42] Collectively, these studies reveal that selective attention, perceptual organization, and interpretation operate very quickly and to a large extent without our awareness.

Mental Models

To achieve our goals with some degree of predictability and sanity, we need road maps of the environments in which we live. These road maps, called **mental models**, are knowledge structures that we develop to describe, explain, and predict the world around us.[43] They consist of visual or relational images in our mind, such as what the classroom looks like or what happens when we submit an assignment late. Mental models partly rely on the process of perceptual grouping because they fill in the missing pieces, including the causal connection among events. For example, you have a mental model about attending a class lecture or seminar, including assumptions or expectations about where the instructor and students arrange themselves in the room, how they ask and answer questions, and so forth. In other words, you create a mental image of a class in progress.

> **mental models** Knowledge structures that we develop to describe, explain, and predict the world around us.

Mental models are important for sense making, yet they also make it difficult to see the world in different ways. For example, accounting professionals tend to see corporate problems from an accounting perspective, whereas marketing professionals see the same problems from a marketing perspective. Mental models also block our recognition of new opportunities.

How do we change mental models? That's a tough challenge. After all, we develop these knowledge structures from several years of experience and reinforcement. The most important strategy is to be aware of and frequently question our mental models. We also need to be more aware of our assumptions, which are often based on mental models. Working with people from diverse backgrounds is another way to break out of existing mental models. Colleagues from different cultures and areas of expertise tend to have different mental models, so working with them makes our own assumptions more obvious.

Specific Perceptual Processes and Problems

LO3

Within the general perceptual process are specific subprocesses and associated perceptual errors. In this section of the chapter, we discuss several of these perceptual processes and biases as well as their implications for organizational behaviour, beginning with the most widely known one: stereotyping.

STEREOTYPING IN ORGANIZATIONS

Stereotyping is the perceptual process in which we assign characteristics to an identifiable group and then automatically transfer those features to anyone we believe is a member of that group.[44] The assigned characteristics tend to be difficult to observe, such as personality traits and abilities, but they can also include physical characteristics and a host of other qualities. If we learn that someone is a professor, for example, we implicitly assume the person is probably also intelligent, absent-minded, and socially challenged.

> **stereotyping** The process of assigning traits to people based on their membership in a social category.

Stereotypes are formed to some extent from personal experience, but they are mainly provided to us through media images (e.g., movie characters) and other cultural prototypes. Consequently, stereotypes are shared beliefs across an entire society and often across several cultures, rather than beliefs that differ from one person to the next. Most stereotypes have a few kernels of truth; they are more likely to characterize people within the group than the rest of us.[45] Still, as the opening case study to this chapter pointed out, stereotypes embellish or distort the kernels of truth and include other features that are not representative of people in that group. In spite of their inaccuracy, stereotypes about engineers, for example, remain persistent enough to discourage many women from pursuing this profession.

Why People Stereotype

People engage in stereotyping because, as a form of categorical thinking, it is usually a nonconscious "energy-saving" process that simplifies our understanding of the world. It is easier to remember features of a stereotype than the constellation of characteristics unique to each person we meet. A second reason is that we have an innate need to understand and anticipate how others will behave. We don't have much information about people initially or when we seldom interact with them, so we rely on stereotypes to fill in the missing pieces. The higher the perceiver's need for cognitive closure, the higher their reliance on stereotypes.[46]

A third explanation for stereotyping is that it is motivated by the observer's own need for social identity and self-enhancement. Earlier in this chapter we explained that people define themselves by the groups to which they belong or have an emotional attachment. They are also motivated to maintain a positive self-concept. This combination of social identity and self-enhancement leads to the process of categorization, homogenization, and differentiation, all of which are the foundations of stereotyping:[47]

- *Categorization.* Social identity is a comparative process, and the comparison begins by categorizing people into

Global Connections 3.3

YOU PEOPLE! EXPOSING STEREOTYPING IN SOUTH AFRICA*

South African restaurant chain Nando's recently launched a witty advertisement that pokes fun at our tendency to stereotype people who are different from us. The "You People" video has several brief scenes where viewers easily misperceive the actors' role in the scene (upscale customer versus employee) or the meaning of their actions (running for exercise versus running away from police). It also shows that those who stereotype "you people" fail to recognize similar behaviour in themselves.

"'You people' is a phrase often used by South Africans when describing people who are different to them," says Doug Place, Nando's chief marketing officer in Johannesburg. "It's a phrase that goes hand in hand with an unconscious bias."

Place explains that Nando's created the ad to encourage discussion about stereotyping and to promote

©Aaron Amat/Shutterstock

greater harmony in society. "If you're watching our ad and say 'I've done that' (hopefully with a guilty smile), then we've been successful at starting a crucial conversation—hopefully one that starts with 'us people'."

* J. Richardson, "Nando's Takes on Stereotypes with Their Hilarious New Ad: #YouPeople [Video]," *The South African,* November 26, 2018; J. Tennant, "#NewCampaign: All You People, This Ad's for You," *Advertising News,* November 26, 2018.

distinct groups. By viewing someone (including yourself) as a Nova Scotian, for example, you remove that person's individuality and, instead, see them as a prototypical representative of the group called Nova Scotians. This categorization then allows you to distinguish Nova Scotians from people who live in, say, Ontario or Alberta.

- *Homogenization.* To simplify the comparison process, we tend to think that people within each group are very similar to one another. For instance, we think Nova Scotians collectively have similar attitudes and characteristics, whereas Ontarians collectively have their own set of characteristics. Of course, every individual is unique, but we often lose sight of this fact when thinking about our social identity and how we compare to people in other social groups.

- *Differentiation.* Along with categorizing and homogenizing people, we tend to assign more favourable characteristics to people in our social identity groups than to people in other groups.[48] This differentiation is motivated by self-enhancement because being in a "better" group produces higher self-esteem. Differentiation is often subtle, but it can escalate into a "good guy versus bad guy" contrast when groups engage in overt conflict with each other. In other words, when out-group members threaten our self-concept, we are particularly motivated (often without our awareness) to assign negative stereotypes

to them. Some research suggests that men have stronger differentiation biases than do women, but we all differentiate to some extent.

Problems with Stereotyping

Everyone engages in stereotyping, but this process leads to perceptual biases as well as flawed decisions and behaviours in the workplace. One problem with stereotypes is that they are inaccurate. A stereotype does not describe everyone because members of the stereotyped group are not identical. Furthermore, although a stereotype typically has kernels of truth, most characteristics are distorted and embellished to such an extent that they describe very few people in the group. The traditional accountant stereotype (boring, cautious, calculating) perhaps describes a few accountants, but it is certainly not characteristic of all, or even most, people in this profession. Nevertheless, once we categorize someone as an accountant, the nonobservable stereotypical features of accountants are transferred to that individual, even though we have no evidence that they actually have those characteristics.

A second problem with stereotypes is that they produce **stereotype threat**. This is a condition whereby members of a group are so concerned about the negative stereotype assigned to their group that

stereotype threat An individual's concern about confirming a negative stereotype about their group.

they end up displaying the stereotype trait they are trying to avoid.[49] Stereotype threat occurs because people anxiously try to avoid confirming the undesirable stereotype traits of their group and try to push the negative image from their mind. These two cognitive activities divert energy and attention, which makes it more difficult to perform the task well. The negative stereotype also can weaken self-efficacy; it is difficult to be confident in your ability when your group's stereotype suggests otherwise.

For example, women perform worse on math and science tests when sensitized to the generally false but widely held belief that women underperform men in these subjects. They also tend to have lower scores when there are few women in the group being tested. Women achieve much higher scores when the gender stereotype is not salient, such as when taking the test with many women in the class. Almost anyone can be affected by stereotype threat, but studies have particularly observed it for women, some minority groups, and older people.

A third problem with stereotyping is that it lays the foundation for unfair discrimination. Most of this perceptual bias occurs as *unintentional (systemic) discrimination,* whereby decision makers rely on stereotypes to establish notions of the "ideal" person in specific roles. Those who don't fit the ideal tend to receive a less favourable evaluation than someone who is compatible with the occupational stereotype.

Unintentional systemic discrimination also affects employment opportunities and salaries. For example, science faculty from several research intensive universities were given the application materials of either a (fictitious) male or female undergraduate student who was purportedly applying for a science laboratory manager job. The applications were identical other than the name and gender of the applicant, yet the male applicant received significantly higher ratings than the female applicant on competence and hireability. The male applicant also received a 15 percent higher recommended salary than did the female applicant. Female faculty exhibited as much gender bias as the male faculty.[50]

©Jacob Lund/Shutterstock

Women represent about 45 percent of the Canadian workforce and almost one-third of middle managers. Yet just a decade ago (2010) they comprised only 12 percent of board members on Canadian publicly-traded (TSX) companies. Fortunately, widespread attention and government initiatives have pushed against systemic discrimination. Women now represent 30 percent of board members of TSX companies. The percentages of women on corporate boards are highest in France (44 percent), Norway (41 percent), Belgium (36 percent), and Sweden (35 percent). The lowest female representation on corporate boards occurs in South Korea (3 percent), the Middle East (less than 5 percent), and Japan (6 percent).*

* M. Ellis and M.T. Eastman, "Women on Boards: Progress Report 2018" (New York: MSCI, December 2018); R. Kersley et al., "The CS Gender 3000 in 2019: The Changing Face of Companies" (Zurich: Credit Suisse Research Institute, October 10, 2019). Data on female workforce and middle management representation in Canada are summarized at: Catalyst, "Statistical Overview of Women in the Workforce: Canada," *Knowledge Center* (New York: Catalyst, 6 April 2016), http://www.catalyst.org/knowledge/statistical-overview-women-workforce (accessed 10 January 2017).

Worse than systemic discrimination is *intentional discrimination* or *prejudice,* in which people hold unfounded negative attitudes toward people belonging to a particular stereotyped group.[51] Intentional discrimination deliberately puts the target person at an unfair disadvantage, which is unfortunately still common in organizations. One recent meta-analysis estimated that minority applicants in OECD countries need to submit almost 50 percent more job applications to receive the same number of interviews as majority applicants. For instance, some French firms have used the code BBR as a signal that they want recruiters to hire someone who is Caucasian. "Some people asked for what in French is called a BBR; it's a code to say a 'Bleu-Blanc-Rouge'—the colours of our national flag," explains one French recruiter. "It was to tell the recruitment agency I am a racist company but I do not want it to appear as such so I use an external supplier to bypass the law."[52]

If stereotyping is such a problem, shouldn't we try to avoid this process altogether? Unfortunately, it's not that simple. Most experts agree that categorical thinking (including stereotyping) is an automatic and nonconscious process. Specialized training programs can minimize stereotype activation to some extent, but for the most part the process is hardwired in our brain cells.[53] Also remember that stereotyping helps us in several valuable (although fallible) ways described earlier: minimizing mental effort, filling in missing information, and supporting our social identity.

The good news is that while it is very difficult to prevent the *activation* of stereotypes, we can minimize the *application* of stereotypic information. In other words, although we automatically categorize people and assign stereotypic traits to them, we can consciously minimize the extent that we rely on that stereotypic information.[54] Later in this chapter, we identify ways to minimize stereotyping and other perceptual biases.

ATTRIBUTION THEORY

Another widely discussed perceptual phenomenon in organizational settings is the **attribution process**.[55] Attribution involves forming beliefs about the causes of behaviour or events. Generally, we perceive whether an observed behaviour or event is caused mainly by characteristics of the person (internal factors) or by the environment (external factors). Internal factors include the person's ability or motivation, whereas external factors include resources, co-worker support, or luck.

attribution process The perceptual process of deciding whether an observed behaviour or event is caused largely by internal or external factors.

If someone doesn't show up for an important meeting, for instance, we infer either internal attributions (the co-worker is forgetful, lacks motivation, etc.) or external attributions (traffic, a family emergency, etc.) to make sense of the person's absence.

People rely on the three attribution rules—consistency, distinctiveness, and consensus—to decide whether another individual's behaviour and performance are caused mainly by personal characteristics or by situational influences (see Exhibit 3.4).[56] To help explain how these three attribution rules operate, imagine a situation in which an employee is making poor-quality products on a particular machine. We would probably conclude that the employee lacks skill or motivation (an internal attribution) if the employee consistently makes poor-quality products on this machine (high consistency), the employee makes poor-quality products on other machines (low distinctiveness), and other employees make good-quality products on this machine (low consensus). In contrast, we would believe something is wrong with the machine (an external attribution) if the employee consistently makes poor-quality products on this machine (high consistency), the employee makes good-quality products on other machines (high distinctiveness), and other employees make poor-quality products on this machine (high consensus).

Notice that *consistency is high for both internal and external attributions.* This occurs because low consistency (the person's output quality on this machine is sometimes good and sometimes poor) weakens our confidence about whether the source of the problem is the person or the machine. In other words, distinctiveness and consensus determine whether the attribution should be internal or external, whereas consistency determines how confident we should be in that attribution.

The attribution process is important because understanding cause–effect relationships enables us to work effectively with others and to assign praise or blame to them.[57] Suppose a co-worker didn't complete their task on a team project. You would approach this situation differently if you believed the co-worker was lazy or lacked sufficient skill (an internal attribution) than if you believed the poor performance was due to lack of time or resources available to the co-worker (an external attribution). We also react differently to attributions of our own behaviour and performance. Students who make internal attributions about their poor grades, for instance, are more likely to drop out of their programs than if they make external attributions about those grades.[58]

Attribution Errors

The attribution process is susceptible to errors. One such error is **self-serving bias**—the tendency to attribute our failures to external causes more than internal causes, while successes are due more to internal than external factors.[59] Simply

self-serving bias The tendency to attribute our favourable outcomes to internal factors and our failures to external factors.

EXHIBIT 3.4 Attribution Theory Rules

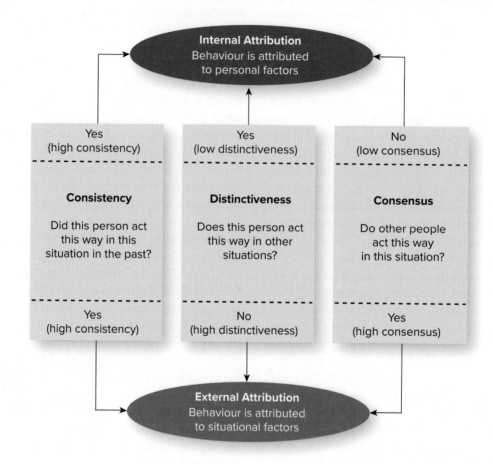

put, we take credit for our successes and blame others or the situation for our mistakes. In annual reports, for example, executives mainly refer to their personal qualities as reasons for the company's successes and to external factors (competitors, economic problems, skill shortages) as reasons for the company's failures.[60] Self-serving bias occurs mainly because of the self-enhancement process described earlier in this chapter. By pointing to external causes of their own failures and internal causes of their successes, people generate a more positive self-concept.

Another widely studied attribution error, **fundamental attribution error** (also called *correspondence bias),* is the tendency to overemphasize internal causes of another person's behaviour and to discount or ignore external causes of their behaviour.[61] We are more likely to attribute a co-worker's late arrival for work to lack of motivation rather than to situational constraints (such as traffic congestion). This phenomenon occurs because observers can't easily see the

external factors that constrain another person's behaviour. Also, people like to think that human beings (not the situation) are the prime causes of their behaviour, so internal attributions receive preference in ambiguous situations. However, fundamental attribution error might not be as common or severe as was previously thought, particularly in cultures that emphasize the context of behaviour and where co-workers have high mutual understanding of each other's work environment.[62]

SELF-FULFILLING PROPHECY

Self-fulfilling prophecy occurs when our expectations about another person cause that individual to act in a way that is consistent with those expectations. In other words, our perceptions can influence reality. Exhibit 3.5 illustrates the four steps in the self-fulfilling prophecy process using the example of a supervisor

fundamental attribution error The tendency to see the person rather than the situation as the main cause of that person's behaviour.

self-fulfilling prophecy The perceptual process in which our expectations about another person cause that person to act more consistently with those expectations.

EXHIBIT 3.5   The Self-Fulfilling Prophecy Cycle

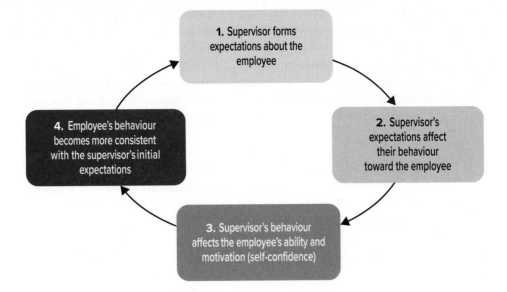

and a subordinate.[63] First, the supervisor forms expectations about the employee's future behaviour and performance. These expectations are sometimes inaccurate because first impressions are usually formed from limited information. Second, the supervisor's expectations influence their behaviour toward employees. In particular, high-expectancy employees (those expected to do well) receive more emotional support through nonverbal cues (e.g., more smiling and eye contact from the boss), more frequent and valuable feedback and reinforcement, more challenging goals, better training, and more opportunities to demonstrate good performance.[64]

The third step in self-fulfilling prophecy includes two effects of the supervisor's behaviour on the employee. One effect is that a high-expectancy employee learns more skills and knowledge than does a low-expectancy employee because of better training and more practice opportunities. The other effect is that the high-expectancy employee becomes more self-confident, which results in stronger motivation and willingness to set challenging goals.[65] In the final step, high-expectancy employees have higher motivation and better skills, resulting in better performance, while the opposite is true of low-expectancy employees.

Self-fulfilling prophecy has been observed in many contexts. In one study, four Israeli Defence Force combat command course instructors were told that one-third of the incoming trainees had high command potential, one-third had normal potential, and the rest had unknown potential. The trainees had been randomly placed into these categories by the researchers, but the instructors were led to believe that the information they received was accurate. Consistent with self-fulfilling prophecy, the high-expectancy soldiers performed significantly better by the end of the course than did the trainees in the other groups. They also had more favourable attitudes toward the course and the instructor's leadership effectiveness. An analysis of dozens of leader intervention studies over the years found that self-fulfilling prophecy is one of the most powerful leadership effects on follower behaviour and performance.[66]

Contingencies of Self-Fulfilling Prophecy

Self-fulfilling prophecy has a stronger effect at the beginning of a relationship, such as when employees are first hired. It is also stronger when several people (rather than just one person) hold the same expectations of the individual. In other words, we might be able to ignore one person's doubts about our potential but not the collective doubts of several people. The self-fulfilling prophecy effect is also stronger among people with a history of low achievement. These people tend to have lower self-esteem, so they are more easily influenced by others' opinions of them.[67]

The main lesson from the self-fulfilling prophecy literature is that leaders need to develop and maintain a positive, yet realistic, expectation toward all employees. This recommendation is consistent with the emerging philosophy of **positive organizational behaviour**, which suggests that focusing on the positive rather than negative aspects of life will improve organizational success and individual

positive organizational behaviour A perspective of organizational behaviour that focuses on building positive qualities and traits within individuals or institutions as opposed to focusing on what is wrong with them.

well-being. Communicating realistic hope and optimism is so important that a recent Canadian study as well as earlier international research identified it as one of the critical success factors for physicians and surgeons. Training programs that make leaders aware of the power of positive expectations seem to have minimal effect, however. Instead, generating positive expectations and hope depend on a corporate culture of support and learning. Hiring supervisors who are inherently optimistic toward their staff is another way of increasing the incidence of positive self-fulfilling prophecies.[68]

OTHER PERCEPTUAL EFFECTS

Self-fulfilling prophecy, attribution, and stereotyping are among the most common perceptual processes and biases in organizational settings, but there are many others. Four additional biases that have received attention in organizational settings are briefly described below.

Halo Effect

The **halo effect** occurs when our general impression of a person, usually based on one prominent characteristic, distorts our perception of other characteristics of that person.[69]

> **halo effect** A perceptual error whereby our general impression of a person, usually based on one prominent characteristic, colours our perception of other characteristics of that person.

If a supervisor who values punctuality notices that an employee is sometimes late for work, the supervisor might form a negative overall opinion of the employee and evaluate that person's other performance dimensions unfavourably as well. The halo effect is most likely to occur when important information about the perceived target is missing or we are not sufficiently motivated to search for it. Instead, we use our general impression of the person to fill in the missing information.

False-Consensus Effect

The **false-consensus effect** (also called *similar-to-me effect*) occurs when people overestimate the extent to which others have similar beliefs or behaviours to their own.[70] Employees who are thinking of quitting their jobs overestimate the percentage of their co-workers who are also thinking about quitting, for example. The false-consensus effect occurs partly because we are comforted by the belief that others are

> **false-consensus effect** A perceptual error in which we overestimate the extent to which others have beliefs and characteristics similar to our own.

similar to us, particularly regarding less acceptable or divisive behaviour. A second explanation is that we interact more with people who have similar views and behaviours. This frequent interaction causes us to overestimate how common those views and behaviours are in the entire organization or society.

A third explanation for false-consensus effect is confirmation bias. We are more likely to remember information that is consistent with our own views and selectively screen out information that is contrary to our beliefs. A fourth explanation is that our social identity process homogenizes people within groups, so we tend to think that everyone in that group has similar opinions and behaviour, including the false-consensus attitude or behaviour.

Recency Effect

The **recency effect** occurs when the most recent information dominates our perceptions.[71] This perceptual bias is most common when people (especially those with limited experience) make a decision involving complex information. For instance, auditors digest large volumes of information in forming a judgment about financial documents. They are susceptible to recency effect because the most recent information received prior to rendering their decision may receive more weight than information received at the beginning of the audit. Similarly, when supervisors evaluate the performance of employees over the previous year, the most recent performance information dominates the evaluation because it is the most easily recalled.

> **recency effect** A perceptual error in which the most recent information dominates our perception of others.

Primacy Effect

The **primacy effect** is our tendency to rely on the first information we receive about people to quickly form an opinion of them.[72] It is the notion that first impressions are lasting impressions. This rapid perceptual organization and interpretation occurs because we need to make sense of the situation and, in particular, to trust others. The problem is that first impressions—particularly negative first impressions—are difficult to change. After categorizing someone, we tend to select subsequent information that supports our first impression and screen out information that opposes that impression. A faulty first impression can be corrected more easily within a very short time after it is formed.

> **primacy effect** A perceptual error in which we quickly form an opinion of people based on the first information we receive about them.

OB by the NUMBERS

First Impressions Count for Job Applicants*

67% of 1,014 employers **say they would not hire an applicant who sends text messages or uses their phone during the job interview.**

77% of 1,138 employers **say they instantly reject resumé with typos or bad grammar.**

48% of 1,014 employers **say they would not hire an applicant who talks negatively during the job interview about current or previous employers.**

23% of 1,138 employers **say they spend less than 30 seconds looking at a resumé.**

32% of 2,076 employers **say they automatically dismiss a job applicant whose resumé includes a large amount of wording from the job posting.**

©baranq/Shutterstock

*"Careerbuilder Releases Study of Common and Not-So-Common Resume Mistakes That Can Cost You the Job," News Release (Chicago: Careerbuilder, September 11, 2013); "The Most Unusual Interview Mistakes and Biggest Body Language Mishaps, According to Annual CareerBuilder Survey," News Release (Chicago and Atlanta: CareerBuilder, February 22, 2018); "Employers Share Their Most Outrageous Resume Mistakes and Instant Deal Breakers in a New CareerBuilder Study," News Release (Chicago and Atlanta: CareerBuilder, August 24, 2018).

Improving Perceptions

LO4

We can't bypass the perceptual process, but we should try to minimize perceptual biases and distortions. Three potentially effective ways to improve perceptions include awareness of perceptual biases, self-awareness, and meaningful interaction.

AWARENESS OF PERCEPTUAL BIASES

One of the most obvious and widely practised ways to reduce perceptual biases is by knowing that they exist. For example, diversity awareness training tries to minimize discrimination by making people aware of systemic discrimination as well as prejudices that occur through stereotyping. This training also attempts to dispel myths about people from various cultural and demographic groups. Awareness of perceptual biases can reduce these biases to some extent by making people more mindful of their thoughts and actions. However, awareness training has only a limited effect.[73] One problem is that teaching people to reject incorrect stereotypes has the

unintended effect of reinforcing rather than reducing reliance on those stereotypes. Another problem is that diversity training is ineffective for people with deeply held prejudices against those groups.

IMPROVING SELF-AWARENESS

A more successful way to minimize perceptual biases is by increasing self-awareness.[74] By discovering our own perceptual biases, we begin to reduce those biases through increased open-mindedness toward others. Self-awareness is also the first step to take in becoming an authentic leader (see Chapter 12). Essentially, leaders need to understand their own values, strengths, and biases as a foundation for building a vision and leading others toward that vision.[75]

But how do we become more self-aware? One approach is to complete formal tests that indicate any implicit biases we might have toward others. One such instrument is the Implicit Association Test (IAT), which attempts to detect subtle racial, age, gender, disability, and other forms of bias by associating positive and negative words with specific groups of people.[76] Although the reliability and accuracy

Debating Point: DO DIVERSITY PROGRAMS REDUCE PERCEPTUAL BIASES?*

Diversity training programs are well-entrenched bastions in the battle against workplace discrimination. In most programs, participants are reminded to respect cultural and gender differences. They also learn about common assumptions and biases that people make about other demographic groups. When companies lose discrimination cases, one of their first requirements is to introduce diversity training to remedy the problem.

Despite its good intentions, diversity training might not be as useful as one would hope. One concern is that most sessions are mandatory, so employees aren't really committed to their content. Biases and prejudices are deeply anchored, so a half-day lecture and group chat on diversity likely won't change employee perceptions and behaviour. Even if they motivate employees to be more tolerant of others and to avoid stereotypes, the good intentions of these programs evaporate quickly in organizations that lack an inclusive culture.

Perversely, the mere presence of diversity training may undermine its beneficial objectives. There is some evidence that discussing demographic and cultural differences increases rather than decreases stereotyping. Students in one study showed more bias against elderly people after watching a video encouraging them to be less biased against older people! Participants at some diversity training programs felt defensive and stressed because the diversity session made them feel unfairly prejudiced or the focus of unwanted attention.

Studies also report that diversity awareness programs create an illusion of fairness. Disadvantaged employees in companies with these programs are more likely to believe their employer doesn't engage in unfair discrimination. However, this perception of fairness makes employees less aware of incidents where the company does engage in unfair discrimination.

* J. Watson, "When Diversity Training Goes Awry," *Black Issues in Higher Education,* January 24, 2008, 11; E.L. Paluck and D.P. Green, "Prejudice Reduction: What Works? A Review and Assessment of Research and Practice," *Annual Review of Psychology* 60, no. 1 (2009): 339–67; M.M. Duguid and M.C. Thomas-Hunt, "Condoning Stereotyping? How Awareness of Stereotyping Prevalence Impacts Expression of Stereotypes," *Journal of Applied Psychology* 100, no. 2 (2015): 343–59; L.M. Brady et al., "It's Fair for Us: Diversity Structures Cause Women to Legitimize Discrimination," *Journal of Experimental Social Psychology* 57 (2015): 100–10; F. Dobbin and A. Kalev, "Why Diversity Programs Fail," *Harvard Business Review* 94, no. 7/8 (2016): 52–60; J. Jargon and R. Feintzeig, "Starbucks Racial Bias Training 'Uncomfortable' and 'Enlightening': Employees React," *Wall Street Journal,* May 31, 2018.

of the IAT is still being debated by scholars, the test does seem to provide some evidence of specific biases. Manulife Financial, Canadian Broadcasting Corporation, Accenture Canada, the City of Edmonton, and many other organizations have introduced the IAT or similar tests to help managers and other employees discover their implicit biases.[77]

Another way to reduce perceptual biases through increased self-awareness is by applying the **Johari Window**.[78] Developed by psychologists Joseph Luft and Harry Ingram (hence the name "Johari"), this model of self-awareness and mutual understanding divides information about you into four "windows"—open, blind, hidden, and unknown—based on whether your own values, beliefs, and experiences are known to you and to others (see Exhibit 3.6). The *open area* includes information about you that is known both to you and to others. The *blind area* refers to information that is known to others but not to you. For example, your colleagues might notice that you are self-conscious and awkward when meeting the company chief executive,

Johari Window A model of self-awareness and mutual understanding with others that advocates disclosure and feedback to increase our open area and reduce the blind, hidden, and unknown areas.

but you are unaware of this fact. Information known to you but unknown to others is found in the *hidden area.* Finally, the *unknown area* includes your values, beliefs, talents, and behaviours that aren't known to you or others.

The main objective of the Johari Window is to increase the size of the open area so that both you and your colleagues are more aware of your underlying beliefs, values, and perceptual biases. This is partly accomplished by reducing the hidden area through *disclosure*—informing others of your personal characteristics that may influence the work relationship. The open area also increases through *feedback* from others about your behaviour. Feedback reduces your blind area because, according to recent studies, people near you are good sources of information about many (but not all) of your traits and behaviours.[79] Finally, the combination of disclosure and feedback occasionally produces revelations about you in the unknown area.

The Johari Window and Implicit Association Test improve self-awareness, which potentially minimizes biases by making us more open-minded and nonjudgmental. However, two problems may limit these benefits. First, implicit biases are similar to stereotypes—they are automatically activated and, consequently, difficult to prevent. However, as with

©Robert Kneschke/Shutterstock

Manulife strives to be an inclusive workplace in which everyone can bring their authentic and whole self to work. To achieve this, the Canadian financial services company's entire global senior executive group and more than 26,000 of its managers and employees have completed a nonconscious bias training program. The program gives each participant confidential feedback on their personal biases (through the IAT or similar test) and provides guidance on how to manage those perceptions and attitudes. "There needs to be a focus on inclusion, and unconscious bias training is one way that we're working to shift our culture," explains Sandeep Tatla, Manulife's Global Head of Diversity & Inclusion.*

*S. Tatla, "A Great Start to 2019 - Manulife Named to Bloomberg's 2019 Gender-Equality Index," LinkedIn, *Pulse* (blog), January 16, 2019, https://www.linke-din.com/pulse/great-start-2019-manulife-named-bloombergs-index-sandeep-tatla; "2018 Sustainability Report" (Toronto: Manulife Financial Corporation, June 4, 2019).

EXHIBIT 3.6   **Johari Window Model of Self-Awareness and Mutual Understanding**

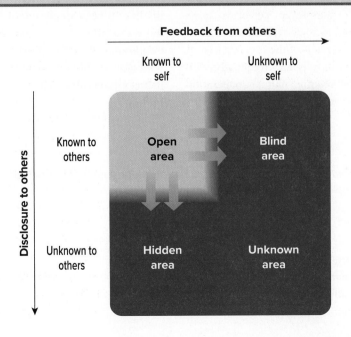

stereotypes, even though implicit biases are still activated, we can potentially minimize the application of those biases in our decisions and behaviour.

The second problem is that perceptual bias self-awareness can cause people to become more sensitized and self-conscious when interacting with people who are the target of that bias. In one Canadian study, one group of White (Caucasian) participants completed an IAT that examined their implicit bias against Indigenous Canadians, whereas a second group of White participants did not take the IAT. All White participants were then paired with Indigenous peers, and for 15 minutes they discussed career goals, academic experiences, or other assigned topics. Everyone then confidentially completed an evaluation of their discussion partner. The study found that the White participants who completed the IAT were more cautious and demonstrated less positive regard toward their Indigenous discussion partners than were the White participants who did not complete the IAT. In other words, increased self-awareness of implicit bias can lead to less favourable interaction with the targets of that bias.[80]

MEANINGFUL INTERACTION

Meaningful interaction is any activity in which people engage in valued (meaningful, not trivial) activities.[81] This process is founded on the **contact hypothesis**, which states that, under specific conditions, people who interact with each other will be less perceptually biased because they have a more personal understanding of the other person and their group.[82] Meaningful interaction occurs when executives work beside front-line staff or when any employee performs tasks with co-workers from other parts of the organization. It is strongest when people work closely and frequently with each other on a shared goal that requires mutual cooperation and reliance. Furthermore, everyone should have equal status

contact hypothesis A theory stating that the more we interact with someone, the less prejudiced or perceptually biased we will be against that person.

in that context, should be engaged in a meaningful task, and should have positive experiences with each other in those interactions.

Meaningful interaction occurred as a well-timed coincidence several years ago, when executives at Mercer Peace River Pulp Ltd. in Alberta were working through difficult discussions with environmentalists. During those meetings, the river threatened to flood, so everyone got involved sandbagging the dyke. One Peace River Pulp executive vividly recalls the occasion because he was sandbagging alongside one of the most active environmental critics. "We both looked at one another and I think we both realized we had more in common than we may have thought," he says.[83]

Meaningful interaction reduces dependence on stereotypes because it diminishes psychological distance, improves our knowledge about individuals, and helps us to observe their unique attributes in action.[84] Meaningful interaction also potentially improves empathy toward others. **Empathy** refers to understanding and being sensitive to the feelings, thoughts, and situations of others.[85] People empathize when they visualize themselves in the other person's place as if they are the other person. This perceptual experience is cognitive, emotional, and experiential. In other words, empathy occurs when we understand the other person's situation, feel their emotions in that context, and to some degree react to those thoughts and feelings as the other person does.

empathy A person's understanding of and sensitivity to the feelings, thoughts, and situations of others.

Empathizing reduces attribution errors by improving our sensitivity to the external causes of another person's performance and behaviour. A supervisor who imagines what it's like to be a single mother, for example, would become more sensitive to the external causes of lateness and other events among such employees. However, trying to empathize with others without spending time with them might actually increase rather than reduce stereotyping and other perceptual biases.[86]

How strong is your perspective taking? You can discover your level of perspective taking (cognitive empathy) by completing this self-assessment in Connect.

How strong is your emotional empathy? You can discover your level of emotional empathy by completing this self-assessment in Connect.

Global Mindset: Developing Perceptions across Borders

LO5

Shiseido is changing the way it views itself as a global organization. "It's no longer about Japan and the rest of the world," explains Shiseido executive Roselin Lee. The Japanese personal care company has acquired Western brands and decentralized decisions to regional headquarters beyond Japan. Most of all, Shiseido is training employees so they are ready for this globalized future. "The structure of the program ties back closely to the attributes and behaviours that we want our future-ready leaders to have—agile, inclusive, digitally savvy, innovative, and most importantly, have a global mindset," says Lee, who is Shiseido's Singapore-based HR executive in the Asia Pacific region.[87]

Global mindset refers to an individual's ability to perceive, know about, and process information across cultures. It includes the following four specific elements.[88]

- *Adopting a global perspective.* A global mindset increases as the individual acquires more of a global than a local/parochial frame of reference about their business and its environment. This frame of reference includes accumulating knowledge and appreciation of many cultures without judging the competence of others by their national or ethnic origins.

global mindset An individual's ability to perceive, appreciate, and empathize with people from other cultures, and to process complex cross-cultural information.

- *Empathizing and acting effectively across cultures.* A global mindset includes understanding the perceptions and emotions of co-workers from other cultures in various situations. Furthermore, this empathy translates into effective use of words and behaviours that are compatible with the local culture.

- *Processing complex information about novel environments.* People who work across cultures are frequently

Global Connections 3.4

EY CULTIVATES A GLOBAL MINDSET THROUGH INTERNATIONAL SECONDMENTS*

Cathy Ng usually works in EY's (formerly Ernst & Young's) offices in Hong Kong, but she jumped at the offer of a temporary transfer to London. "My secondment to EY London has allowed me to develop a global mindset by working with individuals from different backgrounds and cultures. It is interesting to know that there are different ways of looking at the same thing and therefore bringing different insights and ways of improving our work."

Jessica Lönnqvist, an EY transactions diligence manager from Helsinki, Finland, also benefited from her temporary transfer to EY's offices in Milan, Italy. "My three-month secondment in Milan with EY was an invaluable experience. It exposed me to new, bigger clients and stretched my technical knowledge," says Lönnqvist. She particularly noted how working with people from around the world improves a person's perceptions and abilities. "The global mindset of EY people is really inspiring. The open, international, and collaborative environment is so valuable."

Along with developing a global mindset in its employees, EY actively looks for this competency in job

©Willy Barton/Shutterstock

applicants. "We need candidates who can work effectively in teams, analyze, innovate and think with a global mindset, regardless of their domain expertise or background," says Larry Nash, EY's director of recruiting for North, Central, and South America.

* "The EY Global Mindset: Cathy Ng," EY-Financial Services, FSCareers:Top Stories, accessed March 9, 2019, https://www.fscareers.ey.com/top-stories/apac_cathy-ng/; J. Lönnqvist, "EY - Jessica Lönnqvist," EY Global-Careers- Inspiring Women, *My Journey* (blog), 2018, https://www.ey.com/gl/en/careers/ey-jessica-lonnqvist; S. McCabe, "EY Eyes over 15,000 New Hires in 2019," *Accounting Today,* October 10, 2018; C. Ng. "How has working in EY help to expand your understanding of the different cultures globally?" 2019.

placed in new situations that require quick understanding and decision making. This calls for a capacity to cognitively receive and analyze large volumes of information in these new and diverse situations.

- *Developing new multilevel mental models.* A global mindset involves the capacity to quickly develop useful mental models of situations, particularly at both a local and global level of analysis. Ultimately, those with a strong global mindset apply multiple levels of understanding to workplace issues in multicultural settings.

A global mindset offers tremendous value to organizations as well as to the employee's career opportunities.[89] Employees form better relationships across cultures by understanding and showing respect to distant colleagues and partners. They can sift through huge volumes of ambiguous and novel information transmitted in multinational relationships. They have a capacity to form networks and to exchange resources more rapidly across borders. They also develop greater sensitivity and respond more quickly to emerging global opportunities.

DEVELOPING A GLOBAL MINDSET

Developing a global mindset involves improving one's perceptions, so the practices described earlier regarding awareness, self-awareness, and meaningful interaction are relevant.

As with most perceptual capabilities, a global mindset begins with awareness of the concept, followed by self-awareness of one's current level of development. By understanding their own beliefs, values, and attitudes, employees become more open-minded and nonjudgmental when receiving and processing complex information for decision making. In addition, companies develop a global mindset by providing opportunities for employees to compare their own mental models with those of co-workers or partners from other regions of the world. For example, employees might participate in online forums about how well a product's design or marketing strategy is received in Canada versus India or Chile. When companies engage in regular discussions about global competitors, suppliers, and other stakeholders, they eventually move the employee's sphere of awareness toward that global level.

A global mindset develops through better knowledge of people and cultures. Some of that knowledge is acquired through formal programs, such as diversity training, but deeper absorption results from immersion in those cultures.[90] Just as executives need to experience front-line jobs to better understand their customers and employees, employees also need to have meaningful interaction with colleagues from other cultures in those cultural settings. The deeper the immersion in the local environment (such as following local practices, eating local food, and using the local language), the greater the potential to understand the perspectives and attitudes of colleagues in those cultures.

Chapter Summary

LO1

Describe the elements of self-concept and explain how each affects an individual's behaviour and well-being.

Self-concept includes an individual's self-beliefs and self-evaluations. It has three structural characteristics—complexity, consistency, and clarity—all of which influence employee well-being, behaviour, and performance. People are inherently motivated to promote and protect their self-concept (self-enhancement) and to verify and maintain their existing self-concept (self-verification). Self-evaluation consists of self-esteem, self-efficacy, and locus of control. Self-concept also consists of both personal identity and social identity. Social identity theory explains how people define themselves by the groups to which they belong or have an emotional attachment.

LO2

Outline the perceptual process and discuss the effects of categorical thinking and mental models in that process.

Perception involves selecting, organizing, and interpreting information to make sense of the world around us. Perceptual organization

applies categorical thinking—the mostly nonconscious process of organizing people and objects into preconceived categories that are stored in our long-term memory. Mental models—knowledge structures that we develop to describe, explain, and predict the world around us—also help us make sense of incoming stimuli.

LO3

Discuss how stereotyping, attribution, self-fulfilling prophecy, halo, false-consensus, recency, and primacy effects influence the perceptual process.

Stereotyping occurs when people assign traits to others based on their membership in a social category. This assignment economizes mental effort, fills in missing information, and enhances our self-concept, but it also lays the foundation for stereotype threat as well as systemic and intentional discrimination. The attribution process involves deciding whether an observed behaviour or event is caused mainly by the person (internal factors) or the environment (external factors). Attributions are decided by perceived consistency, distinctiveness, and consensus of the behaviour. This process is subject to self-serving bias and fundamental attribution error. A self-fulfilling prophecy occurs when our expectations about another person cause that person to act in a way that is consistent with those expectations. This effect is stronger when employees first join the work unit, when several people hold these expectations, and when the employee has a history of low achievement. Four other perceptual errors commonly observed in organizations are the halo effect, false-consensus effect, recency effect, and primacy effect.

LO4

Discuss three ways to improve perceptions, with specific application to organizational situations.

One way to minimize perceptual biases is to become more aware of their existence. Awareness of these biases makes people more mindful of their thoughts and actions, but this training sometimes reinforces rather than reduces reliance on stereotypes and tends to be ineffective for people with deeply held prejudices. A second strategy is to become more aware of biases in our own decisions and behaviour. Self-awareness increases through formal tests such as the IAT and by applying the Johari Window, which is a process in which others provide feedback to you about your behaviour, and you offer disclosure to them about yourself. The third strategy is meaningful interaction, which applies the contact hypothesis that people who interact will be less prejudiced or perceptually biased toward one another. Meaningful interaction is strongest when people work closely and frequently with relatively equal status on a shared meaningful task that requires cooperation and reliance on one another. Meaningful interaction tends to improve empathy, which is a person's understanding and sensitivity to the feelings, thoughts, and situations of others.

LO5

Outline the main features of a global mindset and justify its usefulness to employees and organizations.

A global mindset refers to an individual's ability to perceive, know about, and process information across cultures. This includes (1) an awareness of, openness to, and respect for other views and practices in the world; (2) the capacity to empathize and act effectively across cultures; (3) an ability to process complex information about novel environments; and (4) the ability to comprehend and reconcile intercultural matters with multiple levels of thinking. A global mindset enables people to develop better cross-cultural relationships, to digest huge volumes of cross-cultural information, and to identify and respond more quickly to emerging global opportunities. Employees develop a global mindset through self-awareness, opportunities to compare their own mental models with people from other cultures, formal cross-cultural training, and immersion in other cultures.

Key Terms

attribution process

categorical thinking

confirmation bias

contact hypothesis

empathy

false-consensus effect

fundamental attribution error

global mindset

halo effect

Johari Window

locus of control

mental models

perception

positive organizational behaviour

primacy effect

recency effect

selective attention

self-concept

self-efficacy

self-enhancement

self-fulfilling prophecy

self-serving bias

self-verification

social identity theory

stereotype threat

stereotyping

Critical Thinking Questions

1. You are manager of a district that has just hired several recent university and college graduates. Most of these people are starting their first full-time job, although most or all have held part-time and summer positions in the past. They have general knowledge of their particular skill area (accounting, engineering, marketing, etc.) but know relatively little about specific business practices and developments. Explain how you would nurture the self-concepts of these new hires to strengthen their performance and maintain their psychological well-being. Also explain how you might reconcile the tendency for self-enhancement while preventing the new employees from forming a negative self-evaluation.

2. Do you define yourself in terms of the school you attend? Why or why not? What are the implications of your answer for your university or college?

3. A high-performance company has launched a "total focus" initiative that requires all employees to give complete attention and dedication to the company's growth and success. In an email to all staff members, the CEO wrote: "We live in a competitive world, and only those businesses whose employees give their total focus to the business will survive. As such, we are offering a generous severance to employees leaving because they can't devote 110 percent to this firm." The company announced that it will invest heavily in employee training and career development, but employees who hold second jobs or have side businesses will be asked to leave. Discuss the company's "total focus" initiative and its consequences from the perspective of employee self-concept complexity, consistency, and clarity.

4. Several years ago, senior executives at Canadian energy company CanOil wanted to acquire an exploration company (HBOG) that was owned by an American energy company, AmOil. Rather than face a hostile takeover and unfavourable tax implications, CanOil's two top executives met with the CEO of AmOil to discuss a friendly exchange of stock to carry out the transaction. AmOil's chief executive was unaware of CanOil's plans, and as the meeting began, the AmOil executive warned that he was there merely to listen. The CanOil executives were confident that AmOil wanted to sell HBOG because energy legislation at the time made HBOG a poor investment for AmOil. AmOil's CEO remained silent for most of the meeting, which CanOil executives interpreted as an implied agreement to proceed to buy AmOil stock on the market. But when CanOil launched the stock purchase a month later, AmOil's CEO was both surprised and outraged. He thought he had given the CanOil executives the cold shoulder, remaining silent to show his lack of interest in the deal. The misunderstanding nearly bankrupted CanOil because AmOil reacted by protecting its stock. What perceptual problem(s) likely occurred that led to this misunderstanding?

5. Before joining an organization or beginning education at a new school, we form mental models of what the work setting and activities will be like. How did your pre-employment or pre-enrollment mental models differ from the actual situation? Why did your mental models differ from reality, and what effect did those differences have on your adjustment to the new work or school?

6. During a diversity management session, a manager suggests that stereotypes are a necessary part of working with others. "I have to make assumptions about what's in the other person's head, and stereotypes help me do that," she explains. "It's better to rely on stereotypes than to enter a working relationship with someone from another culture without any idea of what they believe in!" Discuss the merits of and problems with the manager's statement.

7. Describe how a manager or coach could use the process of self-fulfilling prophecy to enhance an individual's performance.

8. Self-awareness is increasingly recognized as an important ingredient for effective leadership. Suppose that you are responsible for creating a leadership development program in a government organization. What activities or processes would you introduce to help participants in this program constructively develop better self-awareness of their personality, values, and personal biases?

9. Almost everyone in a college or university business program has developed some degree of global mindset. What events or activities in your life have helped to nurture the global mindset you have developed so far? What actions can you take now, while still attending school, to further develop your global mindset?

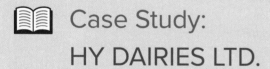 Case Study:
HY DAIRIES LTD.

by Steven L. McShane, University of Newcastle (Australia)

Syd Gilman read the latest sales figures with a great deal of satisfaction. The vice-president of marketing at Hy Dairies Ltd., a large Canadian milk products manufacturer, was pleased to see that the marketing campaign to improve sagging sales of Hy's gourmet ice cream brand was working. Sales volume and market share of the product had increased significantly over the past two quarters compared with the previous year.

The improved sales of Hy's gourmet ice cream could be credited to Rochelle Beauport, who was assigned to the gourmet ice cream brand last year. Beauport had joined Hy less than two years ago as an assistant brand manager after leaving a similar job at a food products firm. She was one of the few women of colour in marketing management at Hy Dairies and had a promising career with the company. Gilman was pleased with Beauport's work and tried to let her know this in the annual performance reviews. He now had an excellent opportunity to reward her by offering her the recently vacated position of marketing research coordinator. Although technically only a lateral transfer with a modest salary increase, the marketing research coordinator job would give Beauport broader experience in some high-profile work, which would enhance her career with Hy Dairies. Few people were aware that Gilman's own career had been boosted by working as marketing research coordinator at Hy several years earlier.

Rochelle Beauport had also seen the latest sales figures on Hy's gourmet ice cream and was expecting Gilman's call to set up a meeting that morning. Gilman began the conversation by briefly mentioning the favourable sales figures, and then explained that he wanted Beauport to take the marketing research coordinator job. Beauport was shocked by the news. She enjoyed brand management and particularly the challenge involved with controlling a product that directly affected the company's profitability. Marketing research coordinator was a technical support position—a "backroom" job—far removed from the company's bottom-line activities. Marketing research was not the route to top management in most organizations, thought Beauport. She had been sidelined.

After a long silence, Beauport managed a weak "Thank you, Mr. Gilman." She was too bewildered to protest. She wanted to collect her thoughts and reflect on what she had done wrong. Also, she did not know her boss well enough to be openly critical.

Gilman recognized Beauport's surprise, which he naturally assumed was her positive response to hearing of this wonderful career opportunity. He, too, had been delighted several years earlier about his temporary transfer to marketing research to round out his marketing experience. "This move will be good for both you and Hy Dairies," said Gilman, as he escorted Beauport from his office.

Beauport was preoccupied with several tasks that afternoon, but was able to consider the day's events that evening. She was one of the top women and few minorities in brand management at Hy Dairies and feared that she was being sidelined because the company didn't want women or people of colour in top management. Her previous employer had made it quite clear that women "couldn't take the heat" in marketing management and tended to place them in technical support positions after a brief term in lower brand-management jobs. Obviously, Syd Gilman and Hy Dairies were following the same game plan. Gilman's comments that the coordinator job would be good for her was just a nice way of saying that Beauport couldn't go any further in brand management at Hy Dairies.

Beauport now faced the difficult decision of whether to confront Gilman and try to change Hy Dairies' sexist and possibly racist practices or to leave the company.

Discussion Questions

1. Apply your knowledge of stereotyping and self-concept to explain what went wrong here.

2. What other perceptual error is apparent in this case study?

3. What can organizations do to minimize misperceptions in these types of situations?

 Team Exercise:

PERSONAL AND ORGANIZATIONAL STRATEGIES FOR DEVELOPING A GLOBAL MINDSET

Purpose This exercise is designed to help you understand and discover ways to improve your global mindset.

Materials None.

Instructions

Step 1: Students are organized into teams, in which the following questions will be discussed. Teams will prepare a list of global mindset–enhancing activities organized around two categories: (1) organizationally generated activities and (2) personal development activities.

- Organizationally generated activities: What organizational practices—interventions or conditions created deliberately by the organization—have you experienced or know that others have experienced that develop a person's global mindset? Be specific in your description of each activity and, where possible, identify the element (elements) of global mindset that improves through that activity.

- Personal development activities: Suppose someone asked you what personal steps they could take to develop a global mindset. What would you recommend? Think about ways that you have personally developed your (or have good knowledge of someone else who has developed their) global mindset. Your suggestions should say what specific elements of global mindset are improved through each activity.

Step 2: The class debriefs, where teams are asked to describe specific personal or organizational activities to others in the class. Look for common themes, as well as challenges people might face while trying to develop a global mindset.

Self-Assessments for Chapter 3

SELF-ASSESSMENT NAME	DESCRIPTION
How much does work define your self-concept?	Work is part of our lives. Some people view work as central to their identity as individuals, whereas others consider work to be secondary to other life interests. This self-assessment estimates the extent to which work is central to your self-concept.
How much general self-efficacy do you have?	Self-efficacy refers to a person's belief that they have the ability, motivation, and resources to complete a task successfully. Although self-efficacy is often situation-specific, people also develop a more general self-efficacy if they perform tasks in a variety of situations. This self-assessment estimates your general self-efficacy.
What is your locus of control?	Locus of control is one component of self-evaluation, which is part of an individual's self-concept. It is a person's general belief about the amount of control they have over life events. This self-assessment estimates the extent to which you have an internal or external locus-of-control.
How much perceptual structure do you need?	Some people have a greater need than do others to quickly or completely "make sense" of things around them. This personal need for perceptual structure relates to selective attention as well as perceptual organization and interpretation. This self-assessment estimates your personal need for perceptual structure.
How strong is your perspective taking (cognitive empathy)?	Empathy refers to a person's understanding of and sensitivity to the feelings, thoughts, and situation of others. The "understanding" part of empathy is called perspective taking or cognitive empathy. It refers to a rational understanding of another person's circumstances. This self-assessment estimates how well you cognitively understand another person's situational and individual circumstances.
How strong is your emotional empathy?	Empathy refers to a person's understanding of and sensitivity to the feelings, thoughts, and situation of others. The "sensitivity" part of empathy is called emotional empathy. It refers to experiencing the feelings of the other person. This self-assessment estimates how well you are able to experience the emotions or feelings of another person.

CHAPTER 4
Workplace Emotions, Attitudes, and Stress

LEARNING OBJECTIVES

After reading this chapter, you should be able to:

LO1 Explain how emotions and cognition (conscious reasoning) influence attitudes and behaviour.

LO2 Discuss the dynamics of emotional labour and the role of emotional intelligence in the workplace.

LO3 Summarize the consequences of job dissatisfaction as well as strategies to increase organizational (affective) commitment.

LO4 Describe the stress experience and review four major stressors.

LO5 Identify five ways to manage workplace stress.

Employee emotions and attitudes are important at Quebec City, so much so that the municipality conducts a weekly digital pulse survey consisting of a few questions to check in on how staff are feeling. Quebec City's leaders keep track of the results on a chart called "Moral des Troupes" (Morale of the Troops). The chart is currently filled with green dots, indicating that employee emotions and attitudes have been consistently at the positive end of the range.

Frequent pulse surveys give employees the opportunity to more accurately communicate their current emotions, rather than a vague recollection of how they felt over the previous year. They also give organizational leaders real-time awareness of emerging morale issues. "We listen to our employees' feedback through biweekly pulse surveys, and we react quickly," says Marc Parent, CEO of CAE, the Montreal-based world leader in simulation technologies.

Employee emotions and attitudes are so important at Quebec City, CAE Inc., and other Canadian organizations that they rely on pulse surveys to regularly check in on employee feelings.
©PHOVOIR/Alamy Stock Photo

Companies also create special pulse surveys to quickly gauge employee feelings about specific, timely issues such as the devastating COVID-19 pandemic. "In normal times, we conduct a quarterly pulse survey to keep on top of employee satisfaction," explains an executive at an American e-commerce platform. "This week, we conducted a quick COVID-related version to check in on employees and understand their feelings regarding a variety of topics." The pulse check discovered that employees' top concerns were about working from home, health risks of the virus, and how the virus might affect the company's financial situation.

"Pulse surveys can be an extremely effective platform for capturing employee input, especially when using an anonymous and easy-to-use interface, such as single-click surveys," says Natalie Baumgartner, chief workforce scientist at Achievers, a Toronto-based company that develops a popular digital platform for employee recognition and rewards. "Offering a fast and secure way for employees to voice their opinion can give businesses a clear understanding of the engagement of their people and insight into their views on particular issues."[1]

Quebec City, CAE, and other Canadian organizations recognize that emotions and attitudes influence employee behaviour and well-being, and ultimately affect the organization's performance and customer service. The field of organizational behaviour has experienced a major shift in thinking about workplace emotions. This chapter begins by introducing the concept and explaining its relationship to attitudes and behaviour. Next, we consider the dynamics of emotional labour, followed by the popular topic of emotional intelligence. The specific work attitudes of job satisfaction and organizational commitment are then discussed, including their association with various employee behaviours and work performance. The final section looks at work-related stress, including the stress experience, four prominent stressors, individual differences in stress, and ways to combat excessive stress.

Emotions in the Workplace

LO1

Emotions influence almost everything we do in the workplace. This is a strong statement, and one that would have rarely been expressed by organizational behaviour experts two decades ago. Most OB theories still assume that a person's thoughts and actions are governed primarily or exclusively by logical thinking (called *cognition*).[2] Yet groundbreaking neuroscience discoveries have revealed that our perceptions, attitudes, decisions, and behaviour are influenced by emotions as well as cognition.[3] In fact, emotions may have the greater influence because they often occur before cognitive processes and, consequently, influence the latter. By ignoring emotionality, many theories have overlooked a large piece of the puzzle concerning human behaviour in the workplace.

Emotions are physiological, behavioural, and psychological episodes experienced toward an object, person, or event that create a state of readiness.[4] These "episodes" are very brief events, some lasting less than a second. However, we usually experience emotions over

emotions Physiological, behavioural, and psychological episodes experienced toward an object, person, or event that create a state of readiness.

several minutes or longer because they occur in waves as we continue to think about the source of the emotion. Emotions are directed toward someone or something. For example, we experience joy, fear, anger, and other emotional episodes toward tasks, customers, or a mobile phone app we are using. This differs from *moods,* which are not directed toward anything in particular and tend to be longer-term background emotional states.

Emotions are experiences. They represent changes in our physiological state (e.g., blood pressure, heart rate), psychological state (e.g., thought process), and behaviour (e.g., facial expression).[5] Most emotional reactions are subtle; they occur without our awareness. This is an important point because the topic of emotions often conjures up images of people "getting emotional." In reality, most emotions are fleeting, nonconscious events that influence our conscious thinking and behaviour.[6] Finally, emotions put us in a state of readiness. When we get worried, for example, our heart rate and blood pressure increase to make our body better prepared to engage in fight or flight. Strong emotions trigger our conscious awareness of a threat or opportunity in the external environment. The "state of readiness" generated by emotions is the engine of our motivation, which we discuss more fully in Chapter 5.[7]

TYPES OF EMOTIONS

People experience many emotions and various combinations of emotions, but all of them have two common features, illustrated in Exhibit 4.1.[8] One feature is that emotions vary in their level of activation. By definition, emotions put us in a state of readiness and, as we discuss in the next chapter, they are the primary source of a person's motivation. Some emotional experiences, such as when we are suddenly surprised, are strong enough to consciously motivate us to act without careful thought. Most emotional experiences are more subtle, but even they activate enough to make us more aware of our environment.

The second feature is that all emotions evaluate the situation as positive or negative, good or bad, helpful or harmful, and so forth. In other words, all emotions have an associated valence (called *core affect*), signalling that the perceived object or event should be approached or avoided. Negative

If employees are experiencing the wrong emotions or moods, it may be time to change the lighting. Almost a century ago, MIT and Harvard researchers dismissed the effects of lighting on human thoughts and behaviour, whereas numerous recent studies report that lighting intensity and warmth can influence emotions and moods. Bright white lighting tends to increase employee alertness and vitality, resulting in faster reaction times on tasks. Moderate intensity warm lighting seems to improve interpersonal relations, whereas low-intensity cool lighting reduces socially oriented emotions and motivation. The combination of light intensity and warmth also influences how much employees regulate their emotions in that setting.*

* K.C.H.J. Smolders and Y.A.W. de Kort, "Bright Light and Mental Fatigue: Effects on Alertness, Vitality, Performance and Physiological Arousal," *Journal of Environmental Psychology, Light, Lighting, and Human Behaviour,* 39 (2014): 77–91, https://doi.org/10.1016/j.jenvp.2013.12.010.; M.G. Figueiro et al., "The Impact of Daytime Light Exposures on Sleep and Mood in Office Workers," *Sleep Health* 3, no. 3 (2017): 204–15, https://doi.org/10.1016/j.sleh.2017.03.005; X. (Irene) Huang, P. Dong, and A.A. Labroo, "Feeling Disconnected from Others: The Effects of Ambient Darkness on Hedonic Choice," *International Journal of Research in Marketing* 35, no. 1 (2018): 144–53, https://doi.org/10.1016/j.ijresmar.2017.12.005; L. Veenstra and S.L. Koole, "Disarming Darkness: Effects of Ambient Lighting on Approach Motivation and State Anger among People with Varying Trait Anger," *Journal of Environmental Psychology* 60 (2018): 34–40, https://doi.org/10.1016/j.jenvp.2018.07.005; S.Y. Kang, N. Youn, and H.C. Yoon, "The Self-Regulatory Power of Environmental Lighting: The Effect of Illuminance and Correlated Color Temperature," *Journal of Environmental Psychology* 62 (2019): 30–41, https://doi.org/10.1016/j.jenvp.2019.02.006.

©oversnap/Getty Images

EXHIBIT 4.1   Circumplex Model of Emotions

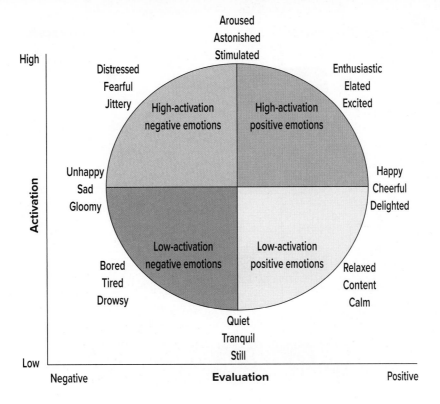

emotions tend to generate stronger levels of activation than do positive emotions.[9] Fear and anger, for instance, are more intense experiences than are joy and delight, so they have a stronger influence on our actions. This valence asymmetry likely occurs because negative emotions protect us from harm and are therefore more critical for our survival.

EMOTIONS, ATTITUDES, AND BEHAVIOUR

To understand how emotions influence our thoughts and behaviour in the workplace, we first need to know about attitudes. **Attitudes** represent the cluster of beliefs, assessed feelings, and behavioural intentions toward a person, object, or event (called an *attitude object*).[10] Attitudes are *judgments,* whereas emotions are *experiences.* In other words, attitudes involve evaluations of an attitude object, whereas emotions operate as events, usually without our awareness. Attitudes sometimes operate nonconsciously, but most of the time we are aware of

attitudes The cluster of beliefs, assessed feelings, and behavioural intentions towards a person, object, or event (called an *attitude object*).

and consciously think about our attitudes. Another distinction is that we experience most emotions very briefly, whereas our attitude toward someone or something is more stable over time.[11]

Until recently, experts believed that attitudes could be understood just by the three cognitive components illustrated on the left side of Exhibit 4.2: beliefs, feelings, and behavioural intentions. Now evidence suggests that a parallel emotional process is also at work, shown on the right side of the exhibit.[12] Using attitude toward mergers as an example, let's look more closely at this model, beginning with the traditional cognitive perspective of attitudes.

- *Beliefs.* Beliefs are your established perceptions about the attitude object—what you believe to be true.[13] For example, you might believe that mergers reduce job security for employees in the merged firms, or that mergers increase the company's competitiveness in this era of globalization. These beliefs are perceived facts that you acquire from experience and other forms of learning. Each of these beliefs also has a valence; that is, we have a positive or negative feeling about each belief (e.g., less job security is bad).

EXHIBIT 4.2   Model of Emotions, Attitudes, and Behaviour

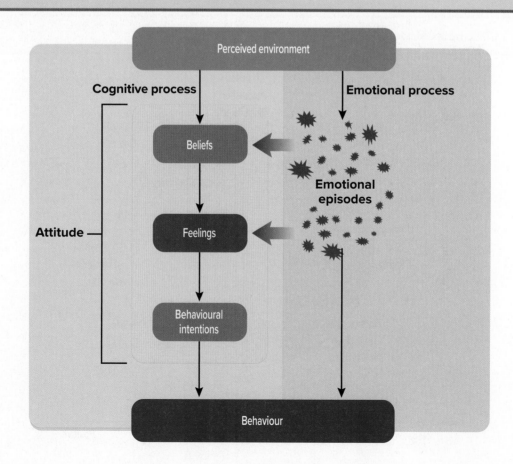

- *Feelings.* This element represents your conscious positive or negative evaluations of the attitude object. Some people think mergers are good; others think they are bad. Your positive or negative opinion of mergers represents your assessed feelings. According to the traditional cognitive perspective of attitudes (the left side of the model), feelings are calculated from your beliefs about mergers and the associated feelings about those beliefs. Consider the example of your attitude toward mergers. If you believe that mergers typically have negative consequences such as layoffs and organizational politics, then you will form negative feelings toward mergers in general or about a specific planned merger in your organization.

- *Behavioural intentions.* Behavioural intentions represent your motivation to engage in a particular behaviour regarding the attitude object.[14] Upon hearing that the company will merge with another organization, you might become motivated to look for a job elsewhere or possibly to complain to management about the merger decision. Your feelings toward mergers motivate your behavioural intentions, and which actions you choose depends on your past experiences, personality, and social norms of appropriate behaviour.

Attitude–Behaviour Contingencies

The cognitive model of attitudes (beliefs–feelings–intentions) gives the impression that we can predict behaviour from each element of an individual's attitude. This is potentially true, but contingencies at each stage in the model can weaken that predictability. Let's begin with the beliefs–feelings link. People with the same beliefs might form quite different feelings toward the attitude object because they have different valences for those beliefs. Two employees who work for the same boss share the belief that their boss makes them work hard. Yet one employee dislikes the boss because of a negative valence toward hard work whereas the other employee likes the boss because of a positive valence toward hard work.

The effect of feelings on behavioural intentions also depends on contingencies, particularly an individual's personality, values, self-concept, experiences, and other personal characteristics. For instance, two employees might equally dislike their boss, but one employee intends to complain to the union or upper management whereas the other employee intends to find a job elsewhere. Later in this chapter, we describe the four main responses to dissatisfaction and other negative attitudes.

Finally, the model indicates that behavioural intentions are the best predictors of a person's behaviour. However, the strength of this link also depends on situational factors as well as the person's ability and role perceptions (see the MARS model in Chapter 1). For example, two people might intend to quit because they dislike their boss, but only one does so because the other employee can't find another job.

HOW EMOTIONS INFLUENCE ATTITUDES AND BEHAVIOUR

The cognitive model describes attitude formation and dynamics to some extent, but emotions also have a central role in this process.[15] The right side of Exhibit 4.2 illustrates this process, which (like the cognitive process) also begins with perceptions of the world around us. Our brain tags incoming sensory information with emotional markers based on a quick and imprecise evaluation of whether that information supports or threatens our innate drives. These markers are not calculated feelings; they are automatic and nonconscious emotional responses based on very thin slices of sensory information.[16] The experienced emotions then influence our feelings about the attitude object.

Consider once again your attitude toward mergers. You might experience worry, nervousness, or relief upon learning that your company intends to merge with a competitor. The fuzzy dots on the right side of Exhibit 4.2 illustrate the numerous emotional episodes you experience upon hearing the merger announcement, subsequently thinking about the merger, discussing the merger with co-workers, and so on. These emotions are transmitted to your brain's cognitive centres, where they are logically analyzed along with other information about the attitude object.[17] So, while you are consciously evaluating whether the merger is good or bad, your emotions are already sending core affect (good–bad) signals, and those emotional signals sway your conscious evaluation. In fact, we often deliberately "listen in" on our emotions to help us consciously decide whether to support or oppose something.[18]

The influence of both cognitive reasoning and emotions on attitudes is most apparent when they disagree with each other. People occasionally experience this mental tug-of-war, sensing that something isn't right even though they can't think of any logical reason to be concerned. This internal conflict or ambivalence indicates that the person's logical analysis of the situation (left side of Exhibit 4.2) generates feelings that differ from the emotional response (right side of Exhibit 4.2).[19] Should we pay attention to our emotions or our logical analysis? This question is not easy to answer, but some studies indicate that logical analysis should play a central role in most decisions. Although executives are known to make quick decisions based on their gut feelings (emotional response), their best decisions tend to occur after logically working through the alternatives.[20]

©Wayne Glowacki/Winnipeg Free Press

Canadian companies have long recognized the benefits of instilling fun into the workplace. At Toronto advertising firm Grip Ltd., employees collaborate in funky spaces and descend to the main entrance via a bright orange slide. The three dozen employees at Woodcock Cycle Works, Winnipeg's largest cycling retailer (shown in this photo), enjoy after-hours bike rides, bonfires, and pizza dinners. Toronto-based Lift & Co. generates positive emotions through quirky meeting-room names, such as Back of a U-Haul, University Dorm, and (for large meetings) the Banff National Park room. "It's part of the culture to make our spaces creative and fun," explains Sara McMillen, director of communications at the cannabis technology and events firm."*

* F. McInnis, "Great Offices: An Ad Agency's Quirky John Street Headquarters, Complete with Slide," *Toronto Life*, 4 April 2013; J. Botelho-Urbanski, "Good Job!," *Winnipeg Free Press*, November 25, 2017; T. Deschamps, "Meet You in 'Back of a U-Haul'":Boardroom Names Get Weird as Firms Welcome More Fun at Work,'"*Toronto Star*, August 12, 2019; "Grip Ltd.'s Creative Playground," Apartment Therapy, accessed October 15, 2019, https://www.apartmenttherapy.com/grip-ltd2-creative-workspace-tour-196741.

GENERATING POSITIVE EMOTIONS AT WORK

Many organizational leaders seem to be well aware of the dual cognitive–emotional attitude process because they try to craft a workplace that will generate more positive emotional experiences.[21] Google Inc. is famous for its superb perks, including in-house coffee bars, gourmet cafeterias, conversation areas that look like vintage subway cars, personal development courses, game rooms, free haircuts, and slides to descend to the floor below. Admiral Group, the U.K.'s top-rated employer and one of the best places to work in Canada, has a "Ministry of Fun" committee that introduces plenty of positive emotions through Nintendo Wii competitions, interdepartmental Olympics, and other fun activities. One of the best places to work in the United States is Zoom Video Communications, which also has an entire team—called the happiness crew—at each location dedicated to maintaining a positive and engaging workplace. "If you get an offer to work at Zoom, take it," advises a Zoom employee. "Zoom takes employee happiness seriously and people genuinely love the company."[22]

Some critics might argue that the organization's main focus should be to create positive emotions through the job itself as well as through natural everyday occurrences, such as polite customers and supportive co-workers. Still, most people perform work that produces some negative emotions, and research has found that humour and fun at work—whether natural or contrived—can potentially offset some of the negative experiences.[23] Overall, corporate leaders need to keep in mind that emotions shape employee attitudes and, as we will discuss later, attitudes influence various forms of work-related behaviour.

One last comment about Exhibit 4.2: Notice the arrow from the emotional episodes to behaviour. It indicates that emotions can directly (without conscious thinking) influence a person's behaviour. This occurs when we jump suddenly if someone sneaks up on us. It also occurs in everyday situations because even low-intensity emotions automatically change our facial expressions. These actions are not carefully thought out. They are automatic emotional responses that are learned or hardwired by heredity for particular situations.[24]

COGNITIVE DISSONANCE

Imagine that you have just signed a contract for new digital whiteboards to be installed throughout the company's meeting rooms. The deal was expensive but, after consulting with several staff, you felt that the technology would be valuable in this technological age. Yet you felt a twinge of regret soon after signing the contract. This emotional experience is **cognitive dissonance**, which occurs when people perceive that their beliefs, feelings, and behaviour are incongruent with each other.[25] The inconsistency among these three attitude components generates emotions (such as feeling hypocritical) that motivate the person to create more consistency by changing one or more of them.

cognitive dissonance An emotional experience caused by a perception that our beliefs, feelings, and behaviour are incongruent with one another.

Why did you experience cognitive dissonance after purchasing the digital whiteboards? Perhaps you remembered that some staff wanted flexibility, whereas the whiteboards require special markers and computer software. Or maybe you had a fleeting realization that buying digital whiteboards costing several times more than traditional whiteboards is inconsistent with your personal values and your company's culture of thriftiness. Whatever the reason, the dissonance occurs because your attitude (it's good to be cost conscious) is inconsistent with your behaviour (buying expensive whiteboards). Most people like to think of themselves—and be viewed by others—as rational and logical. Cognitive dissonance occurs when our behaviour and beliefs conflict, which is not so rational.

How do we reduce cognitive dissonance?[26] Most behaviours can't be undone or are too expensive to reverse. Also, reversing the behaviour rarely reduces dissonance because the event is publicly known—you and your co-workers already know that you bought the digital whiteboards and did so willingly.

People typically reduce cognitive dissonance by changing their beliefs and feelings. One dissonance-reducing strategy is to amplify or discover additional positive features of their selected alternative (e.g., the boards can change handwriting into typed text). A second strategy is to amplify or discover additional problems or weaknesses with the alternatives they didn't choose (e.g., traditional boards are poor projection screens).

A third strategy is more indirect; rather than trying to ignore the high price of the digital whiteboards, you reduce dissonance by emphasizing how your other decisions have been frugal. This framing compensates for your expensive

---

Debating Point: IS HAVING FUN AT WORK REALLY A GOOD IDEA?

"Fun at work" has become such a hot business fad that companies without a "fun" committee are considered insensitive taskmasters. Having fun at work can improve employee attitudes in many situations, but are special fun events really necessary or beneficial?

Some critics vote No! They argue that contrived fun events at work can backfire.* Some types of fun aren't fun at all to some people. In fact, many employees might be offended by the silliness of some activities contrived by management or a few staff. Others resent having fun forced on them. One expert warned, "Once the idea of fun is formally institutionalized from above, it can lead to employees becoming resentful. They feel patronized and condescended, and it breeds anger and frustration."**

The meaning and value of fun at work might also vary across generations; what works for Millennials could backfire for Baby Boomers and vice versa. Another concern is that fun-focused companies might take their eye off the bottom line. "At the end of the day, you have to make money to stay here," says Mike Pitcher, former CEO of LeasePlan USA (which does have a "fun" committee). "If work was [all] fun, they'd call it fun."***

* D.L. Collinson, "Managing Humour," *Journal of Management Studies* 39, no. 3 (2002): 269–88; K. Owler, R. Morrison, and B. Plester, "Does Fun Work? The Complexity of Promoting Fun at Work," *Journal of Management and Organization* 16, no. 3 (2010): 338–52; B. Plester, H. Cooper-Thomas, and J. Winquist, "The Fun Paradox," *Employee Relations* 37, no. 3 (2015): 380–98.

** M. McLaughlin. "Bosses Blind to Horrors of 'Fun Days'." *Scotland on Sunday,* 3 January 2010, 10.

*** M. Tierney. "They're All in It Together" *Atlanta Journal-Constitution,* 16 April 2011, G7. This view was also emphasized by a German business leader: "Schumpeter: Down with Fun," *Economist Intelligence Unit, Executive Briefing* (London), September 22, 2010.

What is your emotional personality? You can discover your emotional trait tendencies by completing this self-assessment in Connect.

whiteboard fling and thereby maintains your self-concept and public image as a thrifty decision maker. Each of these mental acrobatics maintains some degree of consistency between the person's behaviour (buying expensive white-boards) and attitudes (being thrifty).

EMOTIONS AND PERSONALITY

Throughout this section, we have implied that emotional experiences are triggered by workplace experiences. This is mostly true, but emotions are also partly determined by an individual's personality.[27] Individuals with higher emotional stability and extraverted personalities (see Chapter 2) tend to experience more positive emotions. Those with higher neuroticism (lower emotional stability) and introverted personalities tend to experience more negative emotions. Although positive and negative emotional traits have some effect, studies have found that the actual situation in which people work has a noticeably stronger influence on their attitudes and behaviour.[28]

Managing Emotions at Work

LO2

Employees are expected to manage their emotions in the workplace. They must conceal their frustration when serving an irritating customer, display compassion to an ill patient, and hide their boredom in a long meeting with other executives. These are all forms of **emotional labour**—the effort, planning, and control needed to express organizationally desired emotions during interpersonal transactions.[29]

emotional labour The effort, planning, and control needed to express organizationally desired emotions during interpersonal transactions.

Almost everyone is required to abide by *display rules*. These norms or explicit rules require employees to display behaviours representing specific emotions and to hide observable evidence of other emotions. Emotional labour demands are higher in jobs requiring a variety of emotions (e.g., anger as well as joy) and more intense emotions (e.g., showing delight rather than smiling weakly), as well as in jobs where interaction with clients is frequent and longer. Emotional labour also increases when employees must precisely rather than casually abide by the display rules.[30] This work requirement is most common in service industries, where employees have frequent face-to-face interaction with clients.

Employees sometimes need to show emotions that are quite different from---sometimes opposite to---the emotions they actually experience at that moment. For instance, they must display patience and positive feelings toward an irate customer who they actually dislike. This incongruence produces a stressful emotional tension and requires considerably more mental effort than when the emotional display rules are similar to the employee's actual emotions at that moment. Emotional labour may also require employees to act contrary to their self-concept, which can lead to psychological separation from self as well as job dissatisfaction.[31]

EMOTIONAL DISPLAY NORMS ACROSS CULTURES

The extent to which employees are expected to hide their true emotions varies considerably across cultures.[32] One large global study reports that several countries in Asia and Africa strongly discourage emotional expression. Instead, people are expected to be subdued, have relatively monotonic voice intonation, and avoid physical movement and touching that display emotions. In contrast, several Latin and Middle Eastern cultures allow or encourage more vivid display of emotions and expect people to act more consistently with their true emotions. In these cultures, people are expected to reveal their thoughts and feelings, be dramatic in their conversational tones, and be animated in their use of nonverbal behaviours. For example, 81 percent of Ethiopians and 74 percent of Japanese in the study agreed that it is considered unprofessional to overtly express emotions in their culture, whereas 43 percent of Americans, 33 percent of Italians, and only 19 percent of Spaniards, Cubans, and Egyptians agreed with that statement.[33]

Many Asian countries have cultural norms that discourage public display of intense emotions (anger, delight, etc.), whereas these emotion display norms are weaker in North America, Europe, and many other cultures. Furthermore, when required to suppress their true emotions at work, employees from cultures that tolerate or encourage emotional expression experience more stress and lower life satisfaction compared to co-workers from cultures that discourage emotional expression. One Chinese company even tried to reduce employee stress by holding a "no-face" day, in which employees wore masks so they didn't need to worry about the emotions their faces displayed![34]

Global Connections 4.1

SMILING IN RUSSIA: MORE EMOTIONAL LABOUR THAN IN CANADA*

When Russia prepared to host the 21st World Cup, it taught train conductors and other customer-facing employees how to smile at foreigners. "Russian people usually don't smile," explains a trainer involved in the smile program. "That's why when other people come to Russia, they think Russians are not friendly."

Even in customer service roles, Russians have a reputation of being more forthright and dour than Canadians. However, the low prospect of a smile from Russian employees doesn't mean that they are unhappy or dislike you. Russians just have a different interpretation of smiling than do people in Canada and most other Western societies. Consequently, Russians likely experience more emotional labour when forced to smile at customers.

One recent study found that people in Russia and several other cultures (Japan, Korea, Iran, France, etc.) tend to view strangers who smile often as less intelligent. This is reflected in the well-known Russian proverb: "Smiling for no reason is a sign of stupidity." In contrast, frequent smiling is interpreted as a sign of higher intelligence in several other cultures, particularly Germany, Switzerland, Malaysia, China, and Austria.

According to the recent cross-cultural study on smiling, societies with high levels of corruption view people (particularly men) who smile fairly often as less honest than nonsmiling strangers. Russia has a high corruption score, so Russians have less trust in people who smile.

Russian film director Yulia Melamed recently experienced this when she was stopped by a police officer in Moscow and asked to show her identification. After doing so, she asked why the officer stopped her. "Because you were smiling," he replied. Melamed explains that in Russia "it is strange for a person to walk on the street and smile. It looked alien and suspicious."

©ZUMA Press, Inc./Alamy Stock Photo

* K. Krys et al., "Be Careful Where You Smile: Culture Shapes Judgments of Intelligence and Honesty of Smiling Individuals," *Journal of Nonverbal Behavior* 40, no. 2 (2016): 101–16, https://doi.org/10.1007/s10919-015-0226-4; S. Rosenberg, "Why Russians Are Being Taught to Smile," *BBC News* (London: BBC, June 9, 2018); C. Baker, "What a Russian Smile Means," *Nautilus,* June 21, 2018.

STRATEGIES FOR DISPLAYING EXPECTED EMOTIONS

Emotional labour is ultimately about displaying expected emotions through facial expressions and other behaviour. Two general approaches to emotional labour are (a) pretending to have the expected emotions by consciously trying to display behaviours depicting those emotions, and (b) actively changing our perceptions and situation so they naturally produce the expected emotions and associated behaviours.

The first approach—consciously pretending to display the expected emotions—is known as *surface acting*. For example, we try to show interest in a client's lengthy explanation even though we are actually weary from hearing it. We act out the verbal and nonverbal behaviours that symbolize the expected emotions, even though our actual emotions are quite different.[35]

Surface acting is usually (but not always) a poor strategy for emotional labour. It requires considerable mental effort that is often stressful and alienating from the role.[36]

Pretending to feel particular emotions is also challenging. A genuine emotion automatically activates a complex set of facial muscles and body positions, all of which are difficult to replicate when pretending to have this emotion. Meanwhile, our true emotions tend to reveal themselves as subtle gestures, usually without our awareness. More often than not, observers recognize fake emotions, which undermines the social exchange.[37]

Regulating Emotions

The second approach to displaying the expected emotions is to actually experience those emotions (rather than faking them). In other words, we consciously alter our perceptions or situation to naturally generate the desired emotions and the behaviours that display those emotions. There are five main strategies for regulating our emotions.[38]

- *Change the situation.* This approach involves moving out of or into work settings that produce or avoid specific emotions. One example would be temporarily leaving a work area that makes us feel lethargic. At the same time, we might have a short walking break outside to regain our vigour. Another example is keeping away from a particular client who is deeply irritating.

- *Modify the situation.* Within the same physical location, people modify that setting to create or avoid specific emotions. For instance, we might stop working on a task that is aggravating and move to a more enjoyable task so that we don't experience (and display) a sour demeanour. Or, if a discussion with co-workers becomes awkward or sensitive (such as discussing national politics), we might shift the conversation to a less emotionally laden topic.

- *Suppress or amplify emotions.* This strategy involves consciously trying to block out thoughts that produce dysfunctional emotions or more actively think about things that produce expected emotions.[39] For instance, some medical staff suppress their emotional responses to patient suffering by maintaining an impersonal relationship with patients.

- *Shift attention.* This strategy involves changing the focus of our attention. Suppose that earlier today you led a client presentation that didn't go well. To minimize the negative emotions of that event, you might engage in work (such as another project with co-workers) that takes your mind off the flawed presentation.

- *Reframe the situation.* Reframing is a cognitive re-evaluation of a particular event that generates more desirable emotions. Rather than viewing a client presentation as a failure, you might reframe the event as a learning moment that had a low probability of success. Flight attendants apply reframing when they define an incident with an unruly passenger as a test of their customer service skill. These interactions are challenging accomplishments rather than dreaded chores.[40]

Employees who actually produce the emotions that are expected in a particular situation are engaging in *deep acting,* whereas surface acting pretends to have a desired emotion by acting out the behaviour associated with that emotion.[41] All five emotion-regulation strategies generate deep acting, but reframing the situation and shifting attention are likely the most common. Changing and modifying the situation can be applied when employees work alone, but seldom when attending a client meeting, interacting with an upset passenger, or in most other work-related social interactions. Suppressing or amplifying emotions produces deep acting, but these cognitive activities may actually involve reframing the situation and shifting attention. But no matter which strategy is applied to manage emotions, emotion regulation requires emotional intelligence, which we discuss next.

Emotional Intelligence

The University of South Florida (USF) College of Medicine discovered from surveys that its graduates required emotional intelligence training to perform their jobs better. Now, some of its students enrol in a special program that "focuses on values-based care, leadership, health care systems and emotional intelligence." The program includes coaching and role-modeling by hospital staff at Lehigh Valley Health Network, which helps medical students to develop their ability to understand and manage emotions. "I use the emotional intelligence concepts nearly every minute of my day," says a physician who graduated from USF's medical program.[42]

The University of South Florida Health and many other organizations have embraced the idea that **emotional intelligence (EI)** improves performance in many types of jobs. Emotional intelligence includes a set of *abilities* that enable us to recognize and regulate our own emotions as well as the emotions of other people. This definition refers to the four main dimensions shown in Exhibit 4.3.[43]

> **emotional intelligence (EI)** A set of abilities to perceive and express emotion, assimilate emotion in thought, understand and reason with emotion, and regulate emotion in oneself and others.

- *Awareness of our own emotions.* This is the ability to perceive and understand the meaning of our own emotions. People with higher emotional intelligence have better awareness of their emotions and are better able to make sense of them. They can eavesdrop on their emotional responses to specific situations and use this awareness as conscious information.[44]

- *Management of our own emotions.* Everyone manages their own emotions to some extent. We suppress disruptive impulses and try not to feel angry or frustrated when events go against us. We try to feel joy and happiness toward others on such occasions. We re-energize ourselves to break out of midday lethargy. More generally, management of our own emotions involves deep acting and the associated emotion regulation practices described earlier.

- *Awareness of others' emotions.* This dimension refers to the ability to perceive and understand the emotions of other people.[45] It relates to *empathy*—having an understanding of and sensitivity to the feelings, thoughts, and situations of others (see Chapter 3). This ability includes understanding the other person's situation, experiencing their emotions, and knowing their needs even when unstated. Awareness of others' emotions also includes being organizationally aware, such as sensing office politics and the presence of informal social networks.

How well do you recognize and regulate emotions? You can discover your perceived level of emotional intelligence by completing this self-assessment in Connect.

EXHIBIT 4.3   Dimensions of Emotional Intelligence

	Yourself	Others
Recognition of Emotions	Awareness of our own emotions	Awareness of others' emotions
Regulation of Emotions	Management of our own emotions	Management of others' emotions

Abilities

- *Management of others' emotions.* This dimension of EI refers to managing other people's emotions. It includes consoling people who feel sad, emotionally inspiring team members to complete a class project on time, getting strangers to feel comfortable working with you, and dissipating co-worker stress and other dysfunctional emotions that they experience.

The four dimensions of emotional intelligence form a foundational hierarchy.[46] Awareness of your own emotions is the lowest foundation in that hierarchy because you need awareness to engage in the higher levels of emotional intelligence. You can't manage your own emotions if you don't know what they are. Managing other people's emotions is the highest level of EI because this ability requires awareness of your own and others' emotions. To diffuse an angry conflict between two employees, for example, you need to understand the emotions they are experiencing and manage your emotions (and display of emotions). To manage your own emotions, you also need to be aware of your current emotions.

EMOTIONAL INTELLIGENCE OUTCOMES AND DEVELOPMENT

Most jobs involve social interaction with co-workers or external stakeholders, so employees need emotional intelligence to work effectively.[47] Studies suggest that people with high EI are more effective team members, perform better in jobs requiring emotional labour, make better decisions involving other people, and maintain a more positive mindset for creative work. EI is also associated with effective leadership because leaders engage in emotional labour (e.g., showing patience to employees even when they might feel frustrated) and actively regulate the emotions of others (e.g., generating staff optimism after they lost an important contract). However, emotional intelligence does not improve some forms of performance, such as tasks with minimal social interaction.[48]

Given the potential value of emotional intelligence, it's not surprising that organizations try to measure this ability in job applicants. Slightly more than half of Australian and U.K. managers recently surveyed say they actively consider the emotional intelligence of job applicants during the hiring process.[49] Several organizations have also introduced training programs to improve employees' emotional intelligence.[50] For instance, new hires at Fidelity Canada take emotional intelligence training along with other soft skills and technical education. The San Diego Police Department conducts a course in which officers develop emotional intelligence and effective communication skills, including de-escalation role-playing scenarios. Emotional intelligence also increases with age; it is part of the process called maturity.

So far, this chapter has introduced the model of emotions and attitudes, as well as emotional intelligence, as the means by which we manage emotions in the workplace. The next two sections look at two specific attitudes: job satisfaction and organizational commitment. These two attitudes are so important in our understanding of workplace behaviour that some experts suggest the two combined should be called "overall job attitude."[51]

Global Connections 4.2

DEVELOPING EMOTIONAL INTELLIGENCE AT INDIAN RAILWAYS*

Indian Railways, the largest employer in India, is experiencing rapid change, and it requires managers with high emotional intelligence to effectively lead that change. "Indian Railways is right now going through substantial transformation," explains a senior trainer at the company's management development centre. "There was thus a need to build capabilities that complement transformation efforts. The change champion has to be emotionally intelligent."

Thousands of managers are attending workshops to help them understand emotional intelligence and its relevance to their leadership roles every day. They complete a well-known emotional intelligence test developed by a Canadian company. This is followed by feedback and coaching to help the managers improve weaker aspects of their emotional intelligence.

Indian Railways managers who have completed the workshops say that having higher emotional intelligence will result in better management—labour union relations, leadership of employees, decision making, and customer service. "Coping with stressful or difficult situations and believing that one can manage or influence situations in a positive manner is the main aim of the EI module," says one divisional railway manager.

Indian Railways Board chairman Ashwani Lohani, who initiated the massive program, suggests that it is part of a larger strategy toward executive development. "Emotional intelligence is just one component of a larger canvas of better training for railway officers. My emphasis across the organization is 'satyanishtha'—a mission for inculcating ethics and integrity among our employees. EI is an input in that direction."

©Kumar Sriskandan/Alamy Stock Photo

* "Railways Plans to Improve Senior Leaders' EQ," *Mint (India),* November 16, 2018; "To Improve Service, Railways to Give Emotional Intelligence Training to Its Officers," *India Today,* December 17, 2018; S.N. Sharma, "Can Emotional Intelligence Training for Staff Make Indian Railways Safer? [Railways]," *The Economic Times (India),* December 23, 2018.

Job Satisfaction

LO3

When people mention work attitudes, they are typically referring to **job satisfaction**, a person's evaluation of their job and work context.[52] It is an *appraisal* of the perceived job characteristics, work environment, and emotional experiences at work. Satisfied employees have a favourable evaluation of their jobs, based on their observations and emotional experiences. Job satisfaction is best viewed as a collection of attitudes about different aspects of the job and work context. You might like your co-workers but be less satisfied with your workload, for instance.

job satisfaction A person's evaluation of their job and work context.

How satisfied are employees at work? The answer depends on the person, the workplace, and the country. Global surveys, such as the one shown in Exhibit 4.4, estimate that job satisfaction tends to be highest in India, Mexico, and some Nordic countries (such as Denmark and Norway). In this and several other surveys, job satisfaction among Canadians is around the global average or above average. The lowest levels of overall job satisfaction are typically reported in some Asian countries (such as Japan, Hong Kong, and Singapore).[53]

Can we conclude from these surveys that most employees in India and Mexico are happy at work? Possibly, but their overall job satisfaction probably isn't as high as these statistics suggest. One problem is that surveys often ask a single direct question, such as: "How satisfied are you with your job?" Many dissatisfied employees are reluctant to

EXHIBIT 4.4   Job Satisfaction in Selected Countries*

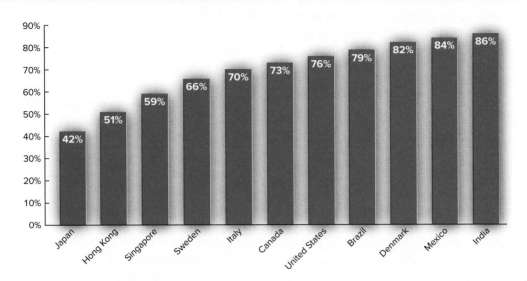

Note: Percentage of employees in each country who said they are, in general, satisfied or very satisfied working for their current employer. Survey data were collected in 2019 for Randstad Holdings nv, with a minimum of 400 employees in each country. This exhibit shows results from selected countries across the full range of 34 countries studied.

* "Randstad Workmonitor Q3 2019" (Amsterdam: Randstad Holding nv, September 5, 2019). Survey data were collected from 34 countries with a minimum of 400 interviews per country of adults working 24 or more hours per week. Respondents were asked: "How satisfied are you in general about working with your current employer?"

reveal their feelings to such a direct question because this is tantamount to admitting that they made a poor job choice and are not enjoying a large part of their life. The inflated results are evident in the fact that employees tend to report less satisfaction when asked about specific aspects of their work. For instance, 79 percent of Canadian federal government employees agree or strongly agree that they like their job overall, yet only 53 percent are satisfied with how interpersonal issues are resolved in their work unit, and only 67 percent would recommend their department or agency as a great place to work.[54]

A second problem is that cultural values make it difficult to compare job satisfaction across countries. People in Japan tend to subdue their emotions in public, and there is evidence that they also avoid extreme survey ratings such as "very satisfied." A third problem with job satisfaction ratings is that job satisfaction changes with economic conditions. Employees with the highest job satisfaction in current surveys tend to be in countries where the economies are chugging along quite well.[55]

JOB SATISFACTION AND WORK BEHAVIOUR

Does job satisfaction influence workplace behaviour? In general, yes! Job satisfaction affects many of the individual behaviours introduced in Chapter 1 (task performance,

organizational citizenship, quitting, absenteeism, etc.).[56] However, a more precise answer is that the effect of job satisfaction and dissatisfaction on individual behaviour depends on the person and the situation. A useful template for organizing and understanding the consequences of job dissatisfaction is the **exit-voice-loyalty-neglect (EVLN) model**. As the name suggests, the EVLN model identifies four ways that employees respond to dissatisfaction:[57]

- *Exit*. Exit includes leaving the organization, transferring to another work unit, or at least trying to get away from the dissatisfying situation. The traditional theory is that job dissatisfaction builds over time and eventually becomes strong enough to motivate employees to search for better work opportunities elsewhere. This is likely true to some extent, but it is more likely that specific "shock events" quickly energize employees to think about and engage in exit behaviour. For example, the emotional reaction you experience to an unfair management decision or a conflict episode with a co-worker motivates you to look at job ads and speak to friends about job opportunities where they work. This begins the process of visualizing yourself working at another company and psychologically withdrawing from your current employer.[58]

> **exit-voice-loyalty-neglect (EVLN) model** The four ways, as indicated in the name, that employees respond to job dissatisfaction.

- *Voice.* Voice is any attempt to change, rather than escape from, the dissatisfying situation. Voice can be a constructive response, such as recommending ways for management to improve the situation, or it can be more confrontational, such as filing formal grievances or forming a coalition to oppose a decision.[59] In the extreme, some employees might engage in counterproductive behaviours to get attention and force changes in the organization.

- *Loyalty.* In the original version of this model, loyalty was only briefly mentioned as an outcome of dissatisfaction. Instead, the original model stated that loyalty predicted whether people chose exit or voice (i.e., high loyalty resulted in voice; low loyalty produced exit).[60] More recent writers describe loyalty as an outcome, but in various and somewhat unclear ways. Generally, they suggest that "loyalists" are employees who respond to dissatisfaction by patiently waiting— some say they "suffer in silence"—for the problem to work itself out or be resolved by others.[61]

- *Neglect.* Neglect includes reducing work effort, paying less attention to quality, and increasing absenteeism and lateness. It is a passive activity with negative consequences for the organization.

Which of the four EVLN alternatives do employees use? It depends on the person and the situation.[62] Voice is more common or frequent among employees with higher extraversion and conscientiousness, likely because these personality factors relate to a person's assertiveness, dutifulness, and outgoing nature. Past experience also influences which EVLN action is applied. Employees who were unsuccessful with voice in the past are more likely to engage in exit or neglect when experiencing job dissatisfaction in the future. Loyalty, as it was intended in the original exit–voice–loyalty model, is another important factor. Specifically, employees are more likely to quit when they have low loyalty to the company, and they are more likely to engage in voice when they have high loyalty. An employee's response to dissatisfaction also depends on the situation. Employees are less likely to use the exit option when there are few alternative job prospects, for example. Dissatisfied employees are more likely to use voice than the other options when they are aware that other employees are dependent on them and when organizational leaders encourage employees to discuss their concerns.[63]

JOB SATISFACTION AND PERFORMANCE

What about job satisfaction and job performance? Is it true or false that "a happy worker is a productive worker?" This is one of the oldest debates in workplace attitudes, and one that has flip-flopped over the years.[64] In recent years, studies have fairly consistently concluded that the "happy worker" hypothesis is true, but only to some extent. In other words, there is a moderately positive relationship between job satisfaction and performance.[65]

Why does job satisfaction affect employee performance only "to some extent"? One reason is that general attitudes (such as job satisfaction) don't predict specific behaviours very well. The EVLN model reveals that reduced performance (a form of neglect) is only one of four possible responses to dissatisfaction. A second reason is that some employees have little control over their performance because their work effort is paced by work technology or interdependence with co-workers in the production process. An assembly-line worker, for instance, installs a fixed number of windshields each hour with about the same quality of installation whether they have high or low job satisfaction.

A third consideration is that job performance might cause job satisfaction, rather than vice versa.[66] Higher performers tend to have higher satisfaction because they receive more rewards and recognition than do low-performing employees. The connection between job satisfaction and performance isn't stronger because many organizations do not reward good performance very well.

JOB SATISFACTION AND CUSTOMER SATISFACTION

Earls Restaurants Ltd. has survived and thrived for over 30 years in a highly competitive business. A key ingredient in the Vancouver-based company's success is stated in its motto: "Great guest experiences begin with great partner experiences." Throughout the years, Earls' founders and leaders have embraced the idea that customers are more satisfied with their dining experience when the cooks, servers, and other staff (all of whom are called partners at Earls) have positive emotions and attitudes regarding their jobs and employer.[67]

Earls Restaurants maintains strong customer service by applying the **service profit chain model.** This model, which is diagrammed in Exhibit 4.5, proposes that job satisfaction has a positive effect on customer service, which flows on to shareholder financial returns. The process begins with workplace practices that increase or decrease job satisfaction. Job satisfaction then influences whether employees stay (employee retention) as well as their motivation and behaviour on the job. Retention, motivation, and behaviour affect service quality, which influences

> **service profit chain model** A theory explaining how employees' job satisfaction influences company profitability indirectly through service quality, customer loyalty, and related factors.

©Cathy Yeulet/iStockphoto/Getty Images

The Co-operators has the highest satisfaction ratings among automobile insurance customers in Ontario, Alberta, and the Atlantic region. The Guelph, Ontario, company also has the most satisfied home insurance customers in Atlantic Canada and Ontario, and second-most satisfied customers (after BCAA) in Western Canada. One key reason why The Co-operators achieves such consistently favourable customer results is the service profit chain model; the company has more satisfied customers by having more satisfied employees. In fact, over the past 16 years the firm has been named annually as one of Canada's Best Employers. "We believe an engaged team leads to happy employees, and happy employees lead to happy customers," says Co-operators CEO Rob Wesseling.*

* M. Nguyen, "Why People Still Matter to Canada's Best Employers," *Canadian Business,* November 8, 2018; "2019 Canada Auto Insurance Satisfaction Study," News Release (Toronto: J.D. Power Canada, February 14, 2019); "2019 Canada Home Insurance Satisfaction Study," News Release (Toronto: J.D. Power Canada, March 28, 2019).

the customer's satisfaction, perceived value of the service, and tendency to recommend the service to others (referrals). These customer activities influence the company's profitability and growth. The service profit chain model has strong research support. However, the benefits of job satisfaction do take considerable time to flow through to the organization's bottom line.[68]

Within the service profit chain model are two key explanations for why satisfied employees tend to produce happier and more loyal customers.[69] One explanation is that job satisfaction tends to put employees in a more positive mood, and people in a good mood more naturally and frequently display friendliness and positive emotions. When employees have good feelings, their display of positive emotions

EXHIBIT 4.5   Service Profit Chain Model

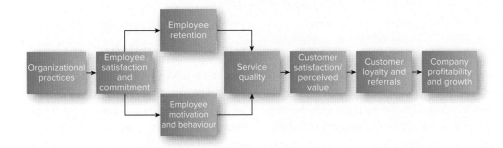

How committed are you to your school? You can discover your affective commitment as a student at your school by completing this self-assessment in Connect.

"rubs off" on most (but not all) customers, so customers feel happier and consequently form a positive evaluation of the service experience (i.e., higher service quality). The effect is also mutual; happy customers make employees happier, which can lead to a virtuous cycle of positive emotions in the service experience.

The second explanation is that satisfied employees are less likely to quit their jobs, so they have more work experience (i.e., better knowledge and skills) to serve clients. Lower turnover also enables customers to have the same employees serve them on different occasions, providing more consistent service. Some evidence indicates that customers build their loyalty to specific employees, not to the organization, so keeping employee turnover low tends to build customer loyalty.

JOB SATISFACTION AND BUSINESS ETHICS

Along with its significant effect on employee behaviour, job satisfaction is an ethical issue that influences the organization's reputation in the community. People spend a large portion of their time working in organizations, and many societies now expect companies to provide work environments that are safe and enjoyable. Indeed, employees in several countries closely monitor ratings of the best companies to work for, an indication that employee satisfaction is a virtue worth considerable goodwill to employers. The importance of this reputation is apparent when an organization has low job satisfaction. The company typically tries to hide this fact, and when morale problems become public, corporate leaders are usually quick to take steps to improve the situation.

Organizational Commitment

Organizational commitment—specifically **affective organizational commitment**—represents the other half (with job satisfaction) of what some experts call "overall job attitude." Affective commitment is the employee's emotional attachment to, involvement in, and identification with an organization. It is a psychological bond whereby one chooses to be dedicated to and responsible for the organization. Furthermore, affective commitment is an autonomous form

> **affective organizational commitment** An individual's emotional attachment to, involvement in, and identification with an organization.

of commitment; that is, the employee is motivated by internal strivings of self-concept and values alignment rather than by external forces.[70]

Affective commitment differs from **continuance commitment**, which is a calculative attachment to the organization. Continuance commitment occurs when the employee faces significant social or economic sacrifice if they were to leave the company (e.g., "I hate this place but can't afford to quit!").[71] This happens when quitting forfeits a large deferred financial bonus or risks weakening social bonds with friends at work. Continuance commitment also occurs when people have limited alternative employment opportunities (e.g., "I dislike working here but there are no other jobs available"). In each situation, continuance commitment is motivation to remain with and participate in the organization due to external factors, whereas the motivation of affective commitment originates internally from the person's identity, bond, and psychological attachment to the organization.

> **continuance commitment** An individual's calculative attachment to an organization.

Affective and continuance commitment have a third sibling, called *normative commitment,* which refers to a felt obligation or moral duty to the organization.[72] Felt obligation applies the **norm of reciprocity**—a natural human motivation to support, contribute, and otherwise "pay back" the organization because it has invested in and supported the employee (see Chapter 10). The sense of moral duty is the motivation to remain with and contribute to the organization because it is the right thing to do as a member of the organization. Normative commitment receives less attention because it overlaps somewhat with affective commitment and its meaning is somewhat ambiguous.

> **norm of reciprocity** A felt obligation and social expectation of helping or otherwise giving something of value to someone who has already helped or given something of value to you.

CONSEQUENCES OF AFFECTIVE AND CONTINUANCE COMMITMENT

Affective commitment can be a significant competitive advantage.[73] Employees with a strong psychological bond to the organization are less likely to quit their jobs and be absent from work. They also have higher work motivation and organizational citizenship, as well as somewhat higher job performance. Affective commitment also improves customer satisfaction because long-tenure employees have better knowledge of work practices and clients like to do business with the same employees. One concern is that employees with very high loyalty tend to have high conformity, which results in lower creativity. Another problem is that employees with very high commitment are more motivated to engage in illegal activity in defence of the organization. However, most companies suffer from too little rather than too much affective commitment.

In contrast to the benefits of affective commitment, employees with high levels of continuance commitment tend to have *lower* performance and are *less* likely to engage in organizational citizenship behaviours. Furthermore, unionized employees with high continuance commitment are more likely to use formal grievances, whereas employees with high affective commitment engage in more cooperative problem solving when employee–employer relations sour.[74] Although some level of financial connection may be necessary, employers should not rely on continuance commitment to retain staff. Instead, they should focus on winning employees' hearts through affective commitment.

BUILDING AFFECTIVE COMMITMENT

There are almost as many ways to build and maintain affective commitment as there are topics in this textbook, but here are the most frequently mentioned strategies in the literature:

- *Justice and support.* Affective commitment is higher in organizations that support organizational justice, which we discuss in the next chapter. Similarly, organizations that support employee well-being tend to cultivate higher levels of loyalty in return.[75]
- *Shared values.* The definition of affective commitment refers to a person's identification with the organization, and that identification is highest when employees believe their values are congruent with the organization's dominant values. Employees also experience more positive emotions when their personal values are aligned with corporate values and actions, and these positive emotions increase their motivation to stay with the organization.[76]
- *Trust.* **Trust** refers to positive expectations one person has toward another person or group in situations involving risk.[77] Trust means putting faith in others. It is also a reciprocal activity: To receive trust, you must demonstrate trust. Employees identify with and feel obliged to work for an organization only when they trust its leaders. This explains why layoffs are one of the greatest blows to affective

trust Positive expectations one person has toward another person or group in situations involving risk.

commitment. By reducing job security, companies reduce the trust employees have in their employer and the employment relationship.[78]

- *Organizational comprehension.* Organizational comprehension refers to how well employees understand the organization, including its strategic direction, social dynamics, and physical layout.[79] This awareness is a necessary prerequisite to affective commitment because it is difficult to identify with or feel loyal to something that you don't know very well. Furthermore, lack of information produces uncertainty, and the resulting stress can distance employees from that source of uncertainty (i.e., the organization). The practical implication here is to ensure that employees develop a reasonably clear and complete mental model of the organization. This occurs by giving staff information and opportunities to keep up-to-date about organizational events, to interact with co-workers, to discover what goes on in different parts of the organization, and to learn about the organization's history and future plans.[80]
- *Employee involvement.* Employee involvement increases affective commitment by strengthening the employee's psychological ownership and social identity with the organization.[81] Employees feel that they are an integral part of the organization when they participate in decisions that guide the organization's future (see Chapter 7). Employee involvement also builds loyalty because giving this power is a demonstration of the company's trust in its employees.

Organizational commitment and job satisfaction represent two of the most often studied and discussed attitudes in the workplace. Each is linked to emotional episodes and cognitive judgments about the workplace and one's relationship with the company. Emotions also play an important role in another concept that is on everyone's mind these days: stress. The final section of this chapter provides an overview of work-related stress and how it can be managed.

Work-Related Stress and Its Management

LO4

When asked if they often feel stressed by their work, most employees these days will answer with an emphatic Yes! Not only do most people understand the concept; they feel they have plenty of personal experience with it. **Stress** is most often described as an adaptive response to a situation that is perceived

stress An adaptive response to a situation that is perceived as challenging or threatening to the person's well-being.

How stressed are you? You can discover your perceived general level of stress over the past month by completing this self-assessment in Connect.

by the NUMBERS

Stressed Out, Burnt-Out!*

40% of National Health Service employees in the U.K. report feeling unwell as a result of work-related stress over the previous year.

35% of 1,005 Canadian employees surveyed say they are more stressed now from work than they were five years ago.

35% of 151,000 adults interviewed across 142 countries said they had experienced significant stress the previous day.

12% of 13,200 adults representative of the population in 22 countries (including Canada) say their work-related stress is unmanageable.

24% of more than 100,000 Canadian adults (18-64 years) surveyed say that most days in their life are quite a bit or extremely stressful.

©donskarpo/Getty Images

* Statistics Canada, "Perceived Life Stress, by Age Group," Health Characteristics, Annual Estimates (Ottawa: Statistics Canada, June 26, 2018), https://doi.org/10.25318/1310009601-eng.; "Morneau Shepell Finds Increase in Workplace and Personal Stress, While Sense of Stigma Declines," News Release (Toronto: Morneau Shepell, January 29, 2019); "NHS Staff Survey 2018: National Results Briefing" (London: National Health Service, February 26, 2019); "2019 CIGNA 360 Well-Being Survey: Well and Beyond" (Bloomfield, CT: CIGNA, March 26, 2019); "2019 Global Emotions Report" (Washington, D.C.: Gallup, April 18, 2019).

as challenging or threatening to a person's well-being.[82] It is a physiological and psychological condition that prepares us to adapt to hostile or noxious environmental conditions. Our heart rate increases, muscles tighten, breathing speeds up, and perspiration increases. Our body also moves more blood to the brain, releases adrenaline and other hormones, fuels the system by releasing more glucose and fatty acids, activates systems that sharpen our senses, and conserves resources by suppressing our immune response. One school of thought suggests that stress is a negative evaluation of the external environment. However, critics of this *cognitive appraisal* perspective point out that stress is more accurately described as an emotional experience, which may occur before or after a conscious evaluation of the situation.[83]

Whether stress is a complex emotion or a cognitive evaluation of the environment, it has become a pervasive experience in the daily lives of most people. Stress is typically described as a negative experience. This is known as *distress*—the degree of physiological, psychological, and behavioural deviation from healthy functioning. However, some level of stress—called *eustress*—is a necessary part of life because it activates and motivates people to achieve goals, change their environments, and succeed in life's challenges.[84] Our focus is on the causes and management of distress, because it has become a chronic problem in many societies.

GENERAL ADAPTATION SYNDROME

The word *stress* was first used more than 500 years ago to describe the human response to harsh environmental conditions. However, it wasn't until the 1930s that Canadian researcher Hans Selye (often described as the father of stress research) first documented the stress experience, called **general adaptation syndrome**. Selye determined (initially by studying rats) that people have a fairly consistent and automatic physiological response to stressful situations, which helps them to cope with environmental demands.[85]

> **general adaptation syndrome** A model of the stress experience, consisting of three stages: alarm reaction, resistance, and exhaustion.

EXHIBIT 4.6   General Adaptation Syndrome

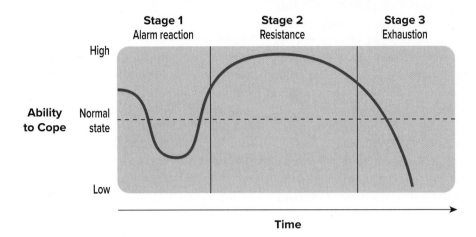

The general adaptation syndrome consists of the three stages shown in Exhibit 4.6. The *alarm reaction* stage occurs when a threat or challenge activates the physiological stress responses that we described a few paragraphs ago. The individual's energy level and coping effectiveness decrease in response to the initial shock. The second stage, *resistance,* activates various biochemical, psychological, and behavioural mechanisms that give the individual more energy and engage coping mechanisms to overcome or remove the source of stress. To focus energy on the source of the stress, the body reduces resources to the immune system during this stage. This explains why people are more likely to catch a cold or some other illness when they experience prolonged stress. People have a limited resistance capacity, and if the source of stress persists, the individual will eventually move into the third stage, *exhaustion.* Most of us are able to remove the source of stress or remove ourselves from that source before becoming too exhausted. However, people who frequently reach exhaustion have increased risk of long-term physiological (notably, brain) and psychological (mental health) damage.[86]

CONSEQUENCES OF DISTRESS

Stress takes its toll on the human body.[87] Many people experience tension headaches, muscle pain, and related problems mainly due to muscle contractions from the stress response. High stress levels also contribute to cardiovascular disease, including heart attacks and strokes, and may be associated with some forms of cancer. One major review estimated that more than 100,000 deaths annually and as much as 8 percent of health care costs in the United States are due to the consequences of work-related stress. Stress also produces various psychological consequences, such as job dissatisfaction, moodiness, depression, and lower organizational commitment. Furthermore, various behavioural outcomes have been linked to high or persistent stress, including lower job performance, poor decision making, and increased workplace accidents and aggressive behaviour. Most people react to stress through "fight or flight," so, as a form of flight, increased absenteeism is another outcome of stress.[88]

One particular stress consequence, called *job burnout,* occurs when people experience emotional exhaustion, cynicism, and reduced feelings of personal accomplishment.[89] *Emotional exhaustion,* the first stage, is characterized by tiredness, a lack of energy, and a feeling that one's emotional resources are depleted. This is followed by *cynicism* (also called *depersonalization),* which is an indifferent attitude toward work, emotional detachment from clients, a cynical view of the organization, and a tendency to strictly follow rules and regulations rather than adapt to the needs of others. The final stage of burnout, called *reduced personal accomplishment,* entails feelings of diminished confidence in one's ability to perform the job well. In such situations, employees develop a sense of learned helplessness as they no longer believe that their efforts make a difference.

STRESSORS: THE CAUSES OF STRESS

Before identifying ways to manage work-related stress, we must first understand its causes, known as stressors. **Stressors** include any environmental conditions that place a physical or emotional demand on a person.[90] There are numerous stressors in the workplace and in life in general. We will briefly describe four of the most common work-related stressors: organizational constraints, interpersonal conflict, work overload, and low task control.[91]

> **stressors** Environmental conditions that place a physical or emotional demand on the person.

Organizational Constraints

Stress research has identified organizational constraints as one of the most pervasive causes of workplace stress.[92] This stressor includes lack of equipment, supplies, budget funding, co-worker support, information, and other resources necessary to complete the required work. Most employees experience stress because these constraints interfere with task performance, which indirectly threatens their rewards, status, and job security. Organizational constraints refer to situational factors, which comprise one of the four direct predictors of individual behaviour and performance (see the MARS model in Chapter 1. It is the only direct influence on individual performance that is beyond the employee's immediate control. This lack of control is a powerful stressor because it threatens the individual's fundamental drive to influence their external environment.

Interpersonal Conflict

Organizations consist of groups of people working interdependently toward some purpose. But even though they share common organizational goals, employees experience conflict because they frequently disagree with each other regarding how to achieve those goals as well as how the work and resources should be distributed along that journey. As we will learn in Chapter 11, dysfunctional conflict can easily flare up and, left unchecked, escalate to a level that produces considerable stress and counterproductive work behaviours. In organizational settings, most interpersonal conflict is

©Rstelmach | Dreamstime.com

Harassment is much too common in the workplace, and the City of Edmonton is no exception. Almost one-quarter (23.8 percent) of the municipality's employees say they have been harassed at work within the previous year. For example, staff in the accounts payable office complained that their manager harassed and bullied them for years. When they tried in vain to warn about serious flaws in Edmonton's new invoice payment system, the manager blamed the eight employees for not adequately performing their jobs. He accused them of lacking the experience and credentials to judge the new system.

An external audit eventually confirmed the employees' worries: the new payment system had systemic errors. The accounts payable office employees filed a harassment complaint against their manager, who was eventually fired. Unfortunately, the staff members had suffered severe stress; several had taken sick leave to recover. "There are eight members that are very hurt," said accounts payable office co-ordinator Darlene Woodham in a presentation to Edmonton City council. "There are people who are seriously sick because of being harassed. They can't function."*

* E. Stolte, "'Very Hurt': Years of Harassment Finally Led to Managerial Change I Edmonton Journal," *Edmonton Journal,* July 5, 2018; "2018 Employee Engagement & Diversity Survey Results" (City of Edmonton, January 15, 2019); E. Stolte, "Audit into City Payment System Illustrates How Workplace Culture Can Hit Bottom Line," *Edmonton Journal,* January 25, 2019.

Are you a workaholic? You can discover the extent to which you are a workaholic by completing this self-assessment in Connect.

caused by structural sources, such as ambiguous rules, lack of resources, and conflicting goals between employees or departments. However, one form of interpersonal conflict that has become an increasing concern is workplace harassment, including workplace bullying, sexual harassment, and other forms of incivility and mistreatment by co-workers, managers, or customers.[93]

Work Overload

"We just keep rushing along in a confused state of never having time to do the things that seem to be pressing upon us." Sound familiar? Most Canadians have probably had a similar thought in the past year. But although this comment comes from Canada, it wasn't written in the past year or even in the past decade. It appeared in an article called "Let's Slow Down!" in a Royal Bank of Canada newsletter in 1949![94] The fact is, people have been struggling for more than half a century with work overload. Employees are expected (or believe they are expected) to complete more work with more effort than they can provide within the allotted time.[95]

Work overload is evident when employees consume more of their personal time to get the job done. Technology and globalization also contribute to work overload because they tether employees to work for more hours of the day. People increasingly work with co-workers in distant time zones, and their communication habits of being constantly "on" make it difficult to separate work from personal life. Some employees contribute to work overload by adopting an "ideal worker norm" in which they expect themselves and others to work longer hours. For many, toiling away far beyond the normal workweek is a badge of honour, a symbol of their superhuman capacity to perform above others. For example, 39 percent of Millennial employees in one recent large-scale survey admitted that they work long hours and have a 24/7 schedule so they look like a "work martyr" to their boss.[96]

Low Task Control

Workplace stress is higher when employees lack control over how and when they perform their tasks as well as over the pace of work activity. Work is potentially more stressful when it is paced by a machine, involves monitoring equipment, or when the work schedule is controlled by someone else. Low task control is a stressor because employees face high workloads without the ability to adjust the pace of the load to their own energy, attention span, and other resources. Furthermore, the degree to which low task control is a stressor increases with the burden of responsibility

the employee must carry.[97] Assembly-line workers have low task control, but their stress can be fairly low if their level of responsibility is also low. In contrast, sports coaches are under immense pressure to win games (high responsibility), yet they have little control over what happens on the playing field (low task control).

INDIVIDUAL DIFFERENCES IN STRESS

Two employees exposed to the same stressor often experience different levels of stress. One reason is that a person's response to stressors varies with their physical health. Regular exercise and a healthy lifestyle produce a larger store of energy to cope with stress. A second reason is that people use different strategies to cope with the stressor.[98] Some try to remove the stressor or to minimize its presence. Others seek out support from co-workers and friends or try to reframe the stressor in a more positive light. Some coping strategies work better for specific stressors and some are better across all stressors.[99] Those who prefer a less effective coping mechanism in a particular situation would experience more stress in response to that situation.

Personality is a third reason why people experience different levels of stress when faced with the same stressor.[100] Individuals with low neuroticism (high emotional stability) usually experience lower stress levels because, by definition, they are less prone to anxiety, depression, and other negative emotions. Extraverts also tend to experience lower stress than do introverts, likely because extraversion includes a degree of positive thinking and extraverts interact with others, which helps buffer the effect of stressors. Those with a positive self-concept—high self-esteem, self-efficacy, and internal locus of control (see Chapter 3)—feel more confident and in control when faced with a stressor. In other words, they tend to have a stronger sense of optimism.[101] Stress also tends to be higher among those who suffer from *workaholism*. Workaholics have an uncontrollable work motivation, constantly think about work, and have low work enjoyment.[102]

MANAGING WORK-RELATED STRESS

LO5

Many people deny the existence of their stress until it has serious outcomes. This avoidance strategy amplifies the stress, because the failure to cope with stress becomes another stressor on top of the one that created the stress in the first place. To prevent this vicious cycle, employers and

Global Connections 4.3

REDUCING STRESS BY REWARDING LONGER SLEEPS*

Japanese employees are chronically overworked and sleep deprived. Using fitness trackers, one study found that Japanese men and women sleep only 6 hours and 35 minutes each day, on average, which is the lowest among 28 countries studied.

Crazy Inc. hopes to reduce the Japanese penchant for overwork by motivating people to sleep longer. The Tokyo-based upscale wedding organizer awards points to employees who sleep at least six hours every night for at least five days each week. Employee sleep patterns are tracked by an app developed by a mattress manufacturer. The points, which are exchanged for food in the company cafeteria, can add up to more than $500 per year.

©david pearson/Alamy Stock Photo

* M. Katanuma, "The Company That Pays Its Employees to Get a Full Night's Sleep," *Bloomberg,* October 21, 2018; L. Lewis, "Japan Wakes up to Sleep Shortage Problems," *Financial Times,* November 20, 2018; J. McCurry, "Snoozing on the Job: Japanese Firms Tackle Epidemic of Sleeplessness," *The Guardian,* January 8, 2019.

employees need to apply one or more of the stress management strategies described next: remove the stressor, withdraw from the stressor, change stress perceptions, control stress consequences, and receive social support.[103]

Remove the Stressor

There are many ways to remove the stressor, but some of the more common actions involve assigning employees to jobs that match their skills and preferences, reducing excessive workplace noise, having a complaint system and taking corrective action against harassment, and giving employees more control over the work process. Another important way that companies can remove stressors is through **work–life integration** initiatives (see Chapter 1). For example, personal leave benefits, such as maternity and paternity leave, temporarily offer employees paid nonwork time to manage special circumstances. Remote work potentially improves work–life integration by reducing or eliminating commuting time and increasing flexibility to perform nonwork obligations (such as picking up the kids from school). Some companies and at least one government (France) have

work–life integration The extent to which people are effectively engaged in their various work and nonwork roles and have a low degree of role conflict across those life domains.

introduced policies that prohibit managers and employees from communicating work-related issues during nonwork hours.[104]

Withdraw from the Stressor

Removing the stressor may be the ideal solution, but it isn't feasible in every situation. Another strategy is to permanently or temporarily remove employees from the stressor. Permanent withdrawal occurs when employees are transferred to jobs that are more compatible with their abilities and values. Temporarily withdrawing from stressors is the most frequent way that employees manage stress. Vacations and holidays are important opportunities for employees to recover from stress and re-energize for future challenges. A small number of companies offer paid or unpaid sabbaticals.[105] Many firms also provide innovative ways for employees to withdraw from stressful work throughout the day, such as games rooms, ice cream cart breaks, nap rooms, and cafeterias that include live piano recitals.

Change Stress Perceptions

How much stress employees experience depends on how they perceive the stressor.[106] Consequently, another way to manage stress is by coaching employees to improve their self-concept, personal goal setting, and self-reinforcement practices. Job challenges are perceived as less threatening when

How do you cope with stressful situations? You can discover your preferences among four coping strategies by completing this self-assessment in Connect.

employees develop these self-views and self-management activities. In addition, research suggests that some (but not all) forms of humour can improve optimism and create positive emotions by taking some psychological weight off a stressful situation.[107]

Control Stress Consequences

Keeping physically fit and maintaining a healthy lifestyle are effective stress management strategies because they control stress consequences. Good physical fitness reduces the adverse physiological consequences of stress by helping employees moderate their breathing and heart rate, muscle tension, and stomach acidity. The key variable here is physical fitness, not exercise. Exercise leads to physical fitness, but research suggests that exercise does not reduce stress symptoms among people who are not yet physically fit.[108] Various forms of meditation can potentially reduce anxiety and other symptoms of stress, but their effect on blood pressure and other physiological symptoms is minimal.[109] Wellness programs can help control the consequences of stress. These programs inform employees about the benefits of better nutrition and fitness, regular sleep, and other good health habits. Finally, many large employers offer *employee assistance programs (EAPs)*—counselling services that help employees resolve marital, financial, or work-related troubles.

Receive Social Support

Social support occurs when co-workers, supervisors, family members, friends, and others provide emotional and/or informational support to buffer an individual's stress experience. Social support potentially improves the person's optimism and self-confidence, because support makes people feel valued and worthy. Social support also provides information to help the person interpret, comprehend, and possibly remove the stressor. For instance, to reduce a new employee's stress, co-workers could describe ways to handle difficult customers. Seeking social support is called a "tend and befriend" response to stress, and research suggests that women often take this route rather than the "fight or flight" response mentioned earlier.[110]

Chapter Summary

LO1

Explain how emotions and cognition (conscious reasoning) influence attitudes and behaviour.

Emotions are physiological, behavioural, and psychological episodes experienced toward an object, person, or event that create a state of readiness. Emotions differ from attitudes, which represent a cluster of beliefs, feelings, and behavioural intentions toward a person, object, or event. Beliefs are a person's established perceptions about the attitude object. Feelings are positive or negative evaluations of the attitude object. Behavioural intentions represent a motivation to engage in a particular behaviour toward the target.

Attitudes have traditionally been described as a purely rational process in which beliefs predict feelings, which predict behavioural intentions, which predict behaviour. We now know that emotions have an influence on behaviour that is equal to or greater than that of cognition. This dual process is apparent when we internally experience a conflict between what logically seems good or bad and what we emotionally feel is good or bad in a situation. Emotions also affect behaviour directly. Behaviour sometimes influences our subsequent attitudes through cognitive dissonance.

LO2

Discuss the dynamics of emotional labour and the role of emotional intelligence in the workplace.

Emotional labour consists of the effort, planning, and control needed to express organizationally desired emotions during interpersonal transactions. It is more common in jobs requiring a variety of emotions and more intense emotions, as well as in jobs in which interactions with clients are frequent and long in duration. Employees experience stress, job dissatisfaction, and low job performance when the emotions they are required to display differ markedly from the emotions they actually experience at that time. The extent to which employees are expected to hide their true emotions varies considerably across cultures.

Employees sometimes fulfil their emotional labour obligations through surface acting—they consciously display behaviours that represent the expected emotions even though their actual emotions are different. A second strategy is deep acting, whereby employees actively change their true emotions so they are similar to the required emotions. The five ways to regulate emotions are to: (a) change the situation, (b) modify the situation, (c) suppress or amplify emotions, (d) shift attention, and (e) reframe the situation.

Emotional intelligence is the ability to perceive and express emotion, assimilate emotion in thought, understand and reason with emotion, and regulate emotion in oneself and others. This concept includes four components arranged in a hierarchy (from lowest to highest): awareness of one's own emotions, management of one's own emotions, awareness of others' emotions, and management of others' emotions. Emotional intelligence can be learned to some extent.

LO3

Summarize the consequences of job dissatisfaction, as well as strategies to increase organizational (affective) commitment.

Job satisfaction represents a person's evaluation of their job and work context. Four types of job dissatisfaction consequences are quitting or otherwise getting away from the dissatisfying situation (exit), attempting to change the dissatisfying situation (voice), patiently waiting for the problem to sort itself out (loyalty), and reducing work effort and performance (neglect). Job satisfaction has a moderate relationship with job performance and with customer satisfaction. Affective organizational commitment (loyalty) is the employee's emotional attachment to, identification with, and involvement in a particular organization. This contrasts with continuance commitment, which is a calculative bond with the organization. Normative commitment—a felt obligation or moral duty to the organization—is a third form of organizational commitment. Companies build loyalty through justice and support, shared values, trust, organizational comprehension, and employee involvement.

LO4

Describe the stress experience and review four major stressors.

Stress is an adaptive response to a situation that is perceived as challenging or threatening to a person's well-being. The stress experience, called general adaptation syndrome, involves moving through three stages: alarm, resistance, and exhaustion. Stressors are the causes of stress and include any environmental conditions that place a physical or emotional demand on a person. Four of the most common workplace stressors are organizational constraints, interpersonal conflict, work overload, and low task control.

LO5

Identify five ways to manage workplace stress.

Many interventions are available to manage work-related stress, including removing the stressor, withdrawing from the stressor, changing stress perceptions, controlling stress consequences, and receiving social support.

Key Terms

affective organizational commitment
attitudes
cognitive dissonance
continuance commitment
emotional intelligence (EI)
emotional labour
emotions
exit-voice-loyalty-neglect (EVLN) model

general adaptation syndrome
job satisfaction
norm of reciprocity
service profit chain model
stress
stressors
trust
work–life integration

Critical Thinking Questions

1. It has almost become a mandatory practice for companies to ensure that employees have fun at work. Many workplaces now have fully-stocked lounges, games rooms, funky painted walls, and regular social events. A few even have a slide to travel down to the next floor. However, some experts warn that imposing fun at work can have negative consequences. "Once the idea of fun is formally institutionalized from above, it can lead to employees becoming resentful," warns one critic. "They feel patronized and condescended, and it breeds anger and frustration." Apply the model of emotions, attitudes, and behaviour to explain how fun activities might improve customer satisfaction, as well as how they might result in poorer customer satisfaction.

2. Studies suggest that university and college instructors are frequently required to engage in emotional labour. Identify the situations in which emotional labour is required for this job. In your opinion, is emotional labour more troublesome for college instructors or for call centre staff working at an emergency service?

3. Recall situations where you had to regulate your emotions. For example, think of times when you wanted to feel more serious than you would otherwise, or experience more happiness for someone at a time when events caused your emotions to be less positive. Which of the five emotion regulation strategies did you apply? Why were those strategies chosen? How difficult was it to actually change your emotions?

4. "Emotional intelligence is more important than cognitive intelligence in influencing an individual's success." Do you agree or disagree with this statement? Support your perspective.

5. "Happy employees lead to happy customers." Explain why this statement tends to be true and identify conditions in which it might not be true.

6. In this chapter, we highlighted work-related stressors, including organizational constraints (e.g., lack of resources), interpersonal conflict (including harassment), work overload, and low task control. Of course, there are many nonwork-related stressors that increasingly come into play. Discuss these and their impact on the work environment.

7. Two college graduates recently joined the same major newspaper as journalists. Both work long hours and have tight deadlines for completing their stories. They are under constant pressure to scout out new leads and be the first to report new controversies. One journalist is increasingly fatigued and despondent and has taken several days of sick leave. The other is getting the work done and seems to enjoy the challenges. Use your knowledge of stress to explain why these two journalists are reacting differently to their jobs.

8. A senior official of a labour union stated: "All stress management does is help people cope with poor management. [Employers] should really be into stress reduction." Discuss the validity of this statement.

 ## Case Study:

DIANA'S DISAPPOINTMENT: THE PROMOTION STUMBLING BLOCK

by Rosemary Maellaro, University of Dallas

Diana Gillen had an uneasy feeling of apprehension as she arrived at the Cobb Street Grille corporate offices. Today she was meeting with her supervisor, Julie Spencer, and regional director, Tom Miner, to learn the outcome of her promotion interview for the district manager position. Diana had been employed by this casual dining restaurant chain for 12 years and had worked her way up from server to general manager. Based on her track record, she was the obvious choice for the promotion; and her friends assured her that the interview process was merely a formality. Diana was still anxious, though, and feared that the news might not be positive. She knew she was more than qualified for the job, but that didn't guarantee anything these days.

Nine months ago, when Diana interviewed for the last district manager opening, she thought her selection for the job was inevitable. She was shocked when that didn't happen. Diana was so upset about not getting promoted then that she initially decided not to apply for the current opening. She eventually changed her mind—after all, the company had just named her Restaurant Manager of the Year and entrusted her with managing its flagship location. Diana thought her chances had to be really good this time.

A multi-unit management position was a desirable move up for any general manager and was a goal to which Diana had aspired since she began working in the industry. When she had not been promoted the last time, Julie explained that her people skills needed to improve. But Diana knew that explanation had little to do with why she hadn't gotten

the job—the real reason was corporate politics. She heard that the person they hired was some superstar from the outside—a district manager from another restaurant company who supposedly had strong multi-unit management experience and a proven track record of developing restaurant managers. Despite what she was told, she was convinced that Tom, her regional manager, had been unduly pressured to hire this person, who had been referred by the CEO.

The decision to hire the outsider may have impressed the CEO, but it enraged Diana. With her successful track record as a restaurant manager for the Cobb Street Grille, she was much more capable, in her opinion, of overseeing multiple units than someone who was new to the operation. Besides, district managers had always been promoted internally among the restaurant managers and she was unofficially designated as the next person to move up to a district position. Tom had hired the outside candidate as a political manoeuvre to put himself in a good light with management, even though it meant overlooking a loyal employee like her in the process. Diana had no patience with people who made business decisions for the wrong reasons. She worked very hard to avoid politics—and it especially irritated her when the political actions of others negatively impacted on her.

Diana was ready to be a district manager nine months ago, and thought she was even more qualified today—provided the decision was based on performance. She ran a tight ship, managing her restaurant completely by the book. She meticulously adhered to policies and procedures and rigorously controlled expenses. Her sales were growing, in spite of new competition in the market, and she received relatively few customer complaints. The only number that was a little out of line was the higher turnover among her staff.

Diana was not too concerned about the increasing number of terminations, however; there was a perfectly logical explanation for this. It was because she had high standards—for herself and her employees. Any employee who delivered less than 110 percent at all times would be better off finding a job somewhere else. Diana didn't think she should bend the rules for anyone, for whatever reason. A few months ago, for example, she had to fire three otherwise good employees who decided to try a new customer service tactic—a so-called innovation they dreamed up—rather than complying with the established process. As the general manager, it was her responsibility to make sure that the restaurant was managed strictly in accordance with the operations manual and she could not allow deviations. This by-the-book approach to managing had served her well for many years. It had got her promoted in the past and she was not about to jinx that now. Losing a few employees now and then— particularly those who had difficulty following the rules—was simply the cost of doing business.

During a recent visit, Julie suggested that Diana might try creating a friendlier work environment because she seemed aloof and interacted with employees somewhat mechanically. Julie even told her that she overheard employees refer to Diana as the "Ice Maiden" behind her back. Diana was surprised that Julie brought this up because her boss rarely criticized her. They had an unspoken agreement: since Diana was so technically competent and always met her financial targets, Julie didn't need to give her much input. Diana was happy to be left alone to run her restaurant without needless advice.

At any rate, Diana rarely paid attention to what employees said about her. She wasn't about to let something as childish as a silly name cause her to modify a successful management strategy. What's more, even though she had recently lost more than the average number of employees due to "personality differences" or "miscommunications" over her directives, her superiors did not seem to mind when she consistently delivered strong bottom-line results every month.

As she waited in the conference room for the others, Diana worried that she was not going to get the promotion. Julie had sounded different in the voicemail message she left to inform her about this meeting, but Diana couldn't put her finger on exactly what it was. She would be very angry if she was passed over again and wondered what excuse they would have this time. Then her mind wandered to how her employees would respond to her if she did not get the promotion. They all knew how much she wanted the job and she cringed to think how embarrassed she would be if she didn't get it. Her eyes began to mist over at the sheer thought of having to face them if she was not promoted today.

Julie and Tom entered the room and the meeting was underway. They told Diana, as kindly as they could, that she would not be promoted at this time; one of her colleagues would become the new district manager. She was incredulous. The individual who got promoted had been with the company only three years—and Diana had trained her! She tried to comprehend how this happened, but it did not make sense. Before any further explanation could be offered, she burst into tears and left the room. As she tried in vain to regain her composure, Diana was overcome with crushing disappointment.

Discussion Questions

1. Apply your knowledge of the four emotional intelligence dimensions to discuss the likely reasons why Diana wasn't offered a promotion.

2. What skills does Diana need to develop to be promotable in the future? What can the company do to support her developmental efforts?

©Rosemary Maellaro

 # Case Study:
ROUGH SEAS ON THE LINK650

by Steven L. McShane, University of Newcastle (Australia)

Professor Suzanne Baxter was preparing for her first class of the semester when Shaun O'Neill knocked lightly on the open door and announced himself: "Hi, Professor, I don't suppose you remember me?" Professor Baxter had large classes, but she did remember that Shaun had been a student in her organizational behaviour class a few years earlier. Shaun had decided to work in the oil industry for a couple of years before returning to school to complete his diploma.

"Welcome back!" Baxter said as she beckoned him into the office. "I heard you were working on an oil rig in the United Kingdom. How was it?"

"Well, professor," Shaun began, "I had worked two summers in the Texan oil fields and my family's from Ireland, so I hoped to get a job on the LINK650. It's that new WestOil drilling rig that arrived with so much fanfare in the North Sea fields a few years ago. The LINK650 was built by LINK Inc. in Texas. A standard practice in this industry is for the rig manufacturer to manage day-to-day rig operations, so employees on the LINK650 are managed completely by LINK managers with no involvement from WestOil. We all know that drilling rig jobs are dangerous, but they pay well and offer generous time off. A local newspaper there said that nearly one thousand people lined up to complete job applications for the 50 nontechnical positions available. I was lucky enough to get one of those jobs.

"Everyone hired on the LINK650 was enthusiastic and proud. We were among the chosen few and were really pumped up about working on a new rig that had received so much media attention. I was quite impressed with the recruiters—so were several other hires—because they really seemed to be concerned about our welfare out on the platform. I later discovered that the recruiters came from a consulting firm that specializes in hiring people. Come to think of it, we didn't meet a single LINK manager during that process. Maybe things would have been different if some of those LINK supervisors had interviewed us.

"Working on LINK650 was a real shock, even though most of us had some experience working in the oil fields. I'd say that not one of the 50 nontechnical people hired was quite prepared for the brutal jobs on the oil rig. We did the dirtiest jobs in the biting cold winds of the North Sea. Still, during the first few months, most of us wanted to show the company that we were dedicated to getting the job done. A couple of the new hires quit within a few weeks, but most of the people hired with me really got along well—you know, just like the ideas you mentioned in class. We formed a special bond that helped us through the bad weather and gruelling work.

"The LINK650 supervisors were another matter. They were mean taskmasters who had worked for many years on oil rigs in the Gulf of Mexico or North Sea. They seemed to relish the idea of treating their employees the same way they had been treated before becoming managers. We put up with their abuse for the first few months, but things got worse when the LINK650 was shut down twice to correct mechanical problems. These setbacks embarrassed LINK's management and they put more pressure on the supervisors to get us back on schedule.

"The supervisors started to ignore equipment problems and pushed us to get jobs done more quickly without regard to safety procedures. They routinely shouted obscenities at employees in front of others. A couple of my workmates were fired and a couple of others quit their jobs. I almost lost my job one day just because my boss thought I was deliberately working slowly. He didn't realize—or care—that the fittings I was connecting were damaged. Several people started finding ways to avoid the supervisors and get as little work done as possible. Many of my co-workers developed back problems. We jokingly called it the 'rigger's backache' because some employees faked their ailment to leave the rig with paid sick leave.

"Along with having lousy supervisors, we were always kept in the dark about the problems on the rig. Supervisors said that they didn't know anything, which was partly true, but they said we shouldn't be so interested in things that didn't concern us. But the rig's problems, as well as its future contract work, were a major concern to crew members who weren't ready to quit. Their job security depended on the rig's production levels and whether WestOil would sign contracts to drill new holes. Given the rig's problems, most of us were concerned that we would be laid off at any time.

"Everything came to a head when Bob MacKenzie was killed because someone secured a hoist improperly. Not sure if it was mentioned in the papers here, but it was big news around this time last year. A government inquiry concluded that the person responsible wasn't properly trained and that employees were being pushed to finish jobs without safety precautions. Anyway, while the inquiry was going on, several employees decided to unionize the rig. It wasn't long before most employees on LINK650 had signed union cards. That really shocked LINK's management and the entire oil industry because it was, I think, just the second time that a rig had ever been unionized there.

"Since then, management has been doing everything in its power to get rid of the union. It sent a 'safety officer' to the rig, although we eventually realized that he was a consultant the company hired to undermine union support. Several managers were sent to special seminars on how to manage a unionized workforce, although one of the topics was how to break the union.

"So you see, professor, I joined LINK as an enthusiastic employee and quit last month with no desire to lift a finger for them. It really bothers me, because I was always told to do your best, no matter how tough the situation. It's been quite an experience."

Discussion Questions

1. Identify the various ways that employees expressed their job dissatisfaction on the LINK650.

2. Shaun O'Neill's commitment to the LINK organization dwindled over his two years of employment. Discuss the factors that affected his organizational commitment.

Team Exercise:
RANKING JOBS ON THEIR EMOTIONAL LABOUR

Purpose This exercise is designed to help you understand the jobs in which people tend to experience higher or lower degrees of emotional labour.

Instructions

Step 1: Individually rank-order the extent that the jobs listed below require emotional labour. In other words, assign a "1" to the job you believe requires the most effort, planning, and control to express organizationally desired emotions during interpersonal transactions. Assign a "10" to the job you believe requires the least amount of emotional labour. Mark your rankings in column 1.

Step 2: The instructor will form teams of four or five members and each team will rank-order the items on the basis of consensus (not simply averaging the individual rankings). These results are placed in column 2.

Step 3: The instructor will provide expert ranking information. This information should be written in column 3. Then students calculate the differences in columns 4 and 5.

Step 4: The class will compare the results and discuss the features of jobs with high emotional labour.

Occupational Emotional Labour Scoring Sheet

Occupation	(1) Individual ranking	(2) Team ranking	(3) Expert ranking	(4) Absolute difference of 1 and 3	(5) Absolute difference of 2 and 3
Bartender					
Cashier					
Dental hygienist					
Insurance adjuster					
Lawyer					
Librarian					
Postal clerk					
Registered nurse					
Social worker					
Television announcer					
			TOTAL		
				Your score	Team score

(The lower the score, the better.)

Self-Assessments for Chapter 4

SELF-ASSESSMENT NAME	DESCRIPTION
What is your emotional personality?	Emotions are influenced by the situation, but also by the individual's own personality. In particular, people tend to have a dispositional mood, that is, the level and valence of emotion that they naturally experience due to their personality. This self-assessment estimates your emotional trait tendencies.
How well do you recognize and regulate emotions?	Emotional intelligence is an important concept that potentially enables us to be more effective with others in the workplace and other social settings. Emotional intelligence is best measured as an ability test. However, you can estimate your level of emotional intelligence to some extent by reflecting on events that required your awareness and management of emotions. This instrument assesses your self-perceived emotional intelligence on the four dimensions.
How committed are you to your school?	Organizational (affective) commitment refers to an individual's emotional attachment to, involvement in, and identification with an organization. It is mostly discussed in this book as an employee's attitude toward the company where he or she works. But affective commitment is also relevant to a student's attitude toward the college or university where he or she is taking courses. This self-assessment estimates your affective organizational commitment to your school.
How stressed are you?	Stress is an adaptive response to a situation that is perceived as challenging or threatening to the person's well-being. It is an increasing concern in today's society. This self-assessment estimates your perceived general level of stress.
Are you a workaholic?	Some people have an uncontrollable work motivation, constantly think about work, and have low work enjoyment. People with these personal characteristics are called workaholics, and they tend to experience high levels of (dis)stress, which can produce long-term health problems. This self-assessment estimates the degree to which you have this stress-related personal characteristic.
How do you cope with stressful situations?	People cope with stress in several ways. The best coping strategy usually depends on the source of stress and other circumstances. However, people also have a natural preference for some types of coping strategies over others. This self-assessment identifies the type of coping strategy you prefer to use in stressful situations.

CHAPTER 5
Foundations of Employee Motivation

Accenture in Canada and globally has launched a radically different way to motivate employees. The consulting firm ditched its traditional performance appraisal system in which managers annually evaluated employees, ranked their performance against peers on a forced distribution scale, and held a formal meeting to discuss the results for that time period. Accenture now takes a coaching approach to employee motivation and performance. Managers have regular informal, constructive, forward-looking discussions that focus on employee achievements and career development. Employee performance is no longer numerically scored or ranked.

"We realized that investing significant time in backward-looking performance appraisals—and figuring out the Holy Grail of forced rankings—simply does not yield the best outcomes for our company or our people," observes Nicholas Greschner, global HR business partner at Accenture's Canadian operations. "Millennials

To improve employee motivation, many Canadian organizations have replaced their traditional formal performance appraisal systems with more frequent, forward-looking coaching and developmental conversations.
©Chris Ryan/OJO Images/age fotostock

and Gen Z-ers don't want hierarchy, formal feedback processes, and appraisals. They demand real-time, in-person feedback, forward-looking conversations and support to grow their careers."

Adobe Systems Canada in Ottawa also replaced traditional performance reviews with much more frequent, constructive, and future-focused "Check-Ins" about employees' personal development. "In a time when agility, teamwork and innovation matter most, you can't afford to breed competition, wait a year to tell people how they are doing, and then have them leave because they were disillusioned with how they ranked against their peers," explains Donna Morris, global chief human resource officer of the software firm.

Accenture and Adobe aren't the only businesses in Canada that are improving employee motivation by ditching the traditional performance appraisal system. One recent survey reports that more than half of Canadian organizations have updated their performance review process over the past two years. The most common changes include making the process shorter, providing feedback more often, and eliminating performance rating scales.[1]

Accenture, Adobe Systems, and several other organizations in Canada are discovering that their traditional performance appraisal systems might not be motivating employees as much as they thought. Some traditional performance reviews even have the opposite effect; they disengage employees and motivate behaviour that undermines the organization's success.

The theme of this chapter is employee motivation. We begin by introducing the definition of motivation and the often-stated associated phrase, employee engagement. Next, we explain how drives and emotions are the prime movers of employee motivation. The prominent drive-based theories of motivation are then described. Next, expectancy theory is described, including the practical implications of this popular cognitive decision model of employee motivation. Organizational behaviour modification and social cognitive theory are then introduced and linked to expectancy theory. The latter sections of this chapter outline the key components of goal setting and feedback, and three types of organizational justice: distributive, procedural, and interactional.

Employee Motivation, Drives, and Needs

LO1

Employee motivation should be on anyone's short list of the most important topics in organizational behaviour. Why? Because motivation is one of the four elements of the MARS model, meaning that it is critical to understanding human behaviour and performance (see Chapter 1). Even when people are able to perform the work (A), understand their role responsibilities (R), and work in a setting that supports their work objectives (S), they won't get the job done without sufficient motivation (M) to achieve those tasks.

Motivation is defined as the forces within a person that affect the direction, intensity, and persistence of their effort for voluntary behaviour.[2] *Direction* refers to what people are focused on achieving; in other words, the goal or outcome toward which they steer their effort. *Intensity* is the amount of physical, cognitive, and emotional energy expended at a given moment to achieve a task or other objective. *Persistence,* the third element of motivation, refers to how long people sustain their effort as they move toward their goal. In short, motivated employees exert varying levels of effort (intensity), for varying lengths of time (persistence), toward various goals (direction).

When executives discuss employee motivation these days, they are just as likely to use the phrase **employee engagement**. Employee engagement is an individual's emotional and cognitive (logical) motivation, particularly a focused, intense, persistent, and purposive effort toward work-related goals.[3] It is associated with self-efficacy—the belief that you have the ability, role clarity, and resources to get the job done (see Chapter 3). Employee engagement also includes a high level of absorption in the work—the experience of focusing intensely on the task with limited awareness of events beyond that work.

Employee engagement predicts employee and work unit performance.[4] Unfortunately, surveys consistently report that few Canadian employees are fully engaged at work. The numbers vary across studies, but recent results from a widely recognized survey estimate that only 34 percent of employees in Canada are engaged, and 13 percent are actively disengaged. Actively disengaged employees tend to be disruptive at work, not just disconnected from work. The lowest levels of employee engagement are recorded in several Asian countries (Japan, China, South Korea, and Taiwan) and a few European countries (notably Italy, Netherlands, and France). The highest levels of employee engagement are reported in the United States, Brazil, and India.[5]

> **motivation** The forces within a person that affect the direction, intensity, and persistence of effort for voluntary behaviour.

> **employee engagement** A person's emotional and cognitive motivation, particularly a focused, intense, persistent, and purposive effort toward work-related goals.

©Accent Inns

Employee engagement is important at Accent Inns. The Victoria, B.C.-based hotel group provides an onboarding program for new hires, comprehensive training programs, two-way feedback, and active involvement in community support projects. Ninety-eight percent of employees say they are happy working at Accent Inns. For the top three words that describe working there, employees chose Family, Fun, and Encouraging. "I want our hotels to be little communities," says Accent Inns CEO Mandy Farmer. "Little families where people take care of each other and where they feel like they are well taken care of." Accent Inns was recently recognized at the North American Employee Engagement Awards. It also received the Employees First Award for its employment practices in the the B.C. Tourism industry.*

* "Case Study: Accent Inns: Looking After Your Staff Lets Your Business Look After Itself," *Go2HR* (blog), May 13, 2016; "Hotel Zed Wins Award for Going the Extra Mile for Employees," *Kelowna Capital News,* March 2, 2019; "Accent Inns Recognized at Employee Engagement Awards," *Hotelier Magazine,* June 28, 2019.The quotation and recent survey results were provided by Accent Inns in March 2020.

EMPLOYEE DRIVES AND NEEDS

LO2

To build a more engaged and motivated workforce, we first need to understand where motivation begins, that is, the motivational "forces" or "prime movers" of employee behaviour.[6]

Our starting point is **drives** (also called *primary needs*), which we define as hardwired characteristics of the brain that attempt to keep us in balance by correcting deficiencies.

drives Hardwired characteristics of the brain that correct deficiencies or maintain an internal equilibrium by producing emotions to energize individuals.

Neuroscience (brain) research has highlighted the central role of emotions in this process. Specifically, drives produce emotions that energize us to act on our environment.[7] There is no agreed-upon list of human drives, but research has consistently identified several, such as the drive to have social interaction and bonding, to develop our competence, to make sense of our surroundings, and to defend ourselves against physical and psychological harm.[8]

Drives are universal and innate, which means that everyone has them and they exist from birth. Drives are the starting point of motivation because they generate emotions that, as we learned in Chapter 4, put people in a state of readiness to act on their environment. Cognition (logical thinking) also plays an important role in motivation, but emotions are the real sources of energy in human behaviour.[9] In fact, both *emotion* and *motivation* originate from the same Latin word, *movere,* which means "to move."

Exhibit 5.1 illustrates how drives and emotions translate into felt needs and behaviour. Drives, and the emotions produced by these drives, generate human needs. We define **needs** as goal-directed forces that people experience. They are the motivational forces of emotions channelled toward specific goals and associated behaviours to correct deficiencies or imbalances. For example, you sense a need to interact with people after being alone for a while, or to do something challenging after performing tedious activities. As one leading neuroscientist explains: "drives express themselves directly in background emotions and we eventually become aware of their existence by means of background feelings."[10] In other words, needs are the emotions that we eventually become consciously aware of.

Consider the following example: You arrive at work to discover a stranger sitting at your desk. This situation produces emotions (worry, curiosity) that motivate you to act. These emotions are generated from drives, such as the drive to defend and drive to comprehend. When strong enough, these emotions motivate you to do something about this situation, such as finding out who that person is and possibly seeking reassurance from co-workers that your job is still safe. In this case, you have a need to make sense of what is going on (comprehend), to feel secure, and possibly to correct a sense of personal violation (defend). Notice that your emotional reactions to seeing the stranger sitting at your desk represent the forces that move you, and that your logical thinking plays an active role in channelling those emotions toward specific goals and behaviours.

> **needs** Goal-directed forces that people experience.

INDIVIDUAL DIFFERENCES IN NEEDS

Everyone has the same drives; they are hardwired in us through evolution. However, people develop different intensities of needs in a particular situation. Exhibit 5.1 explains why this difference occurs. The left side of the model shows that the individual's self-concept (as well as personality and values), social norms, and past experience amplify or suppress emotions, thereby resulting in stronger or weaker needs.[11] For example, people who define themselves as very sociable typically experience a need for social interaction after being alone for a while, whereas people who view themselves as less sociable would experience a less intense need to be with others over that time. These individual differences also explain why needs can be "learned" to some extent. Socialization and reinforcement may increase or decrease a person's need for social interaction, achievement, and so forth. We will discuss learned needs in the next section of this chapter.

Individual differences—including self-concept, social norms, and past experience—regulate the motivation process in a second way. They influence what goals and behaviours are motivated by the felt emotions, as the right side of Exhibit 5.1 illustrates. Consider the earlier example of the stranger sitting at your desk. You probably wouldn't walk up to the person and demand that they leave; such blunt behaviour is contrary to social norms in most cultures. Employees who view themselves as forthright might approach the stranger directly, whereas those who have a different personality and self-view are more likely to first gather information from co-workers before approaching the individual. In short, your drives (to comprehend, to defend, to bond, etc.) and resulting emotions energize you to act, and your self-concept, social norms, and past experience direct that energy toward goal-directed behaviour.

Exhibit 5.1 provides a useful template for understanding how drives and emotions are the prime sources of employee motivation and how individual characteristics (self-concept, experience, social norms) influence goal-directed behaviour. We will refer to elements of this drive theory of motivation when we discuss four-drive theory, expectancy theory, equity theory, and other concepts in this chapter. The next section describes theories that explain the dynamics of drives and needs.

EXHIBIT 5.1   Drives, Needs, and Behaviour

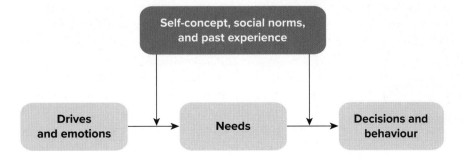

Drive-Based Motivation Theories

LO3

FOUR-DRIVE THEORY

The process through which drives, emotions, and needs influence motivation is most effectively explained by **four-drive theory.** This theory states that emotions are the source of human motivation and that these emotions are generated through four drives (all of which have been identified from earlier psychological, sociological, and anthropological research):[12]

> **four-drive theory** A motivation theory based on the innate drives to acquire, bond, comprehend, and defend that incorporates both emotions and rationality.

- *Drive to acquire.* This is the drive to seek, take, control, and retain objects and personal experiences. It produces various needs, including achievement, competence, status, and self-esteem.[13] The drive to acquire also motivates competition.
- *Drive to bond.* This drive produces the need for belonging and affiliation.[14] It explains why our self-concept is partly defined by associations with social groups (see Chapter 3). The drive to bond motivates people to cooperate and, consequently, is essential for organizations and societies.
- *Drive to comprehend.* We are inherently curious and need to make sense of our environment and ourselves.[15] When observing something that is inconsistent with or beyond our current knowledge, we experience a tension that motivates us to close that information gap. The drive to comprehend motivates curiosity as well as the broader need to reach our knowledge potential.

- *Drive to defend.* This is the drive to protect ourselves physically, psychologically, and socially. Probably the first drive to develop in human beings, it creates a fight-or-flight response when we are confronted with threats to our physical safety, our possessions, our self-concept, our values, and the well-being of people around us.[16]

All drives are hardwired in our brains and exist in all human beings. They are also independent of one another; there is no hierarchy of drives. Four-drive theory also claims that no fundamental drives are excluded from the model. Another key feature is that three of the four drives are proactive—we regularly try to fulfil them. Therefore, need "fulfillment" is brief and ongoing. Only the drive to defend is reactive—it is triggered by threat.

How Drives Influence Motivation and Behaviour

Recall from Chapter 3 that the stimuli received through our senses are quickly and nonconsciously tagged with emotional markers.[17] Four-drive theory proposes that the four drives determine which emotions are tagged to incoming stimuli. Most of the time, we aren't aware of these tagged emotions because they are subtle and fleeting. However, emotions do become conscious experiences when they are sufficiently strong or when they significantly conflict with one another.

Four-drive theory also recognizes that our social norms, personal values, and past experience—which the theory calls our "mental skill set"—guide our motivational energy and reduce the felt need (see Exhibit 5.2). In other words, our mental skill set chooses courses of action that are acceptable to society, consistent with our own moral compass, and have a high probability of achieving the goal of fulfilling our felt needs.[18]

EXHIBIT 5.2   Four-Drive Theory of Motivation

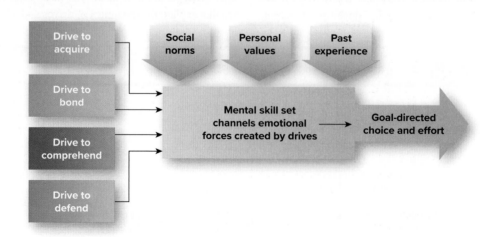

Practical Implications of Four-Drive Theory

Four-drive theory recommends that jobs and workplaces should provide a balanced opportunity for employees to fulfil the four drives.[19] There are really two recommendations here. The first is that the best workplaces help employees fulfil all four drives. Employees continually seek fulfilment of their innate drives, so successful companies provide sufficient rewards, learning opportunities, social interaction, and so forth for all employees.

The second recommendation is that fulfilment of the four drives must be kept in balance, that is, organizations shouldn't give employees too much or too little opportunity to fulfil each drive. The reason for this advice is that the four drives counterbalance each other. The drive to bond, which motivates mutual support and cohesion, counterbalances the drive to acquire, which motivates competitiveness. An organization that fuels the drive to acquire without encouraging the drive to bond may eventually suffer from organizational politics, dysfunctional conflict, and insufficient collaboration.[20] The drive to comprehend, which motivates investigation of the unknown, counterbalances the drive to defend, which motivates avoidance of the unknown. Change and novelty in the workplace will feed the drive to comprehend, but too much of it will trigger the drive to defend to such an extent that employees become territorial and resistant to change.

Four-drive theory is based on a deep foundation of neuroscientific, psychological, sociological, and anthropological research. The theory explains why needs vary from one person to the next and recognizes that motivation is influenced by human thought and social influences (not just instinct).[21] Even so, the theory is more recent than other motivation models and is far from complete. Most experts would argue that one or two other drives should be included. Furthermore, social norms, personal values, and past experience probably don't represent the full set of individual characteristics that translate emotions into goal-directed effort. For example, personality and self-concept probably also moderate the effect of drives and needs on decisions and behaviour.

MASLOW'S NEEDS HIERARCHY THEORY

Mention needs and drives to most people and they will probably refer to **Maslow's needs hierarchy theory**, which was developed by psychologist Abraham Maslow in the 1940s.[22] Maslow condensed and

> **Maslow's needs hierarchy theory** A motivation theory of needs arranged in a hierarchy, whereby people are motivated to fulfill a higher need as a lower one becomes gratified.

 Global Connections 5.1

PETRONAS BALANCES FULFILMENT OF EMPLOYEES' DRIVES*

Petroliam Nasional Bhd (Petronas) is rated as the best company to work for in Malaysia, partly because it actively tries to balance employees' fulfilment of their four drives. The energy giant challenges employees to step out of their comfort zone by acquiring new skills, but this is counteracted with work–life integration and supportive management.

Some employees say promotions and performance standards are competitive, but this is balanced by Petronas' strong culture of teamwork. "Good place for work–life balance," says a Petronas application developer, who also points out that the company "greatly challenge[s] your skill to the limit."

A Petronas manager in Kuala Lumpur advises that employees get "lots of new projects, which require moving out of [their] comfort zone," but adds that the company also fosters "good camaraderie with colleagues." Another

Petronas technical employee observes: "The staff here are team players. They are welcoming and helpful."

©MARCO BERTORELLO/Getty Images

* "PETRONAS Ranked the Most Attractive Company to Work for in 2019," News Release (Kuala Lumpur: Randstad Malaysia, August 22, 2019). Employee quotations are comments on Malaysia's most popular job advertising site, jobstreet.com.my between December 2016 and January 2018.

How strong are your growth needs? You can discover your growth need strength by completing this self-assessment in Connect.

EXHIBIT 5.3 **Maslow's Needs Hierarchy**

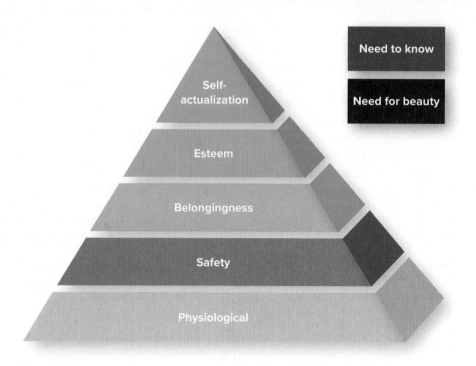

organized the dozens of previously studied drives (which he called *primary needs*) into five basic categories, organized in a hierarchy from lowest to highest (see Exhibit 5.3):[23] *physiological* (need for food, air, water, shelter, etc.), *safety* (need for security and stability), *belongingness/love* (need for interaction with and affection from others), *esteem* (need for self-esteem and social esteem/status), and *self-actualization* (need for self-fulfilment, realization of one's potential). Maslow also identified two sets of needs outside the hierarchy. The *need to know* recognizes that human beings are inherently curious about the unknown and unexplained in their surroundings. In addition, Maslow suggested that everyone has a *need for beauty* (aesthetic needs)—an inherent attraction "to beauty, symmetry, and possibly to simplicity, completion, and order."[24]

Maslow proposed that we are motivated simultaneously by several needs, but the strongest motivation comes from the lowest unsatisfied need. When satisfied, the next higher need in the hierarchy becomes the strongest motivator and remains so even if never satisfied. The exception to this need fulfilment process is self-actualization. Human beings have an ongoing need for self-actualization; it is never really

fulfilled. Thus, while the bottom four groups are *deficiency needs* because they become activated when unfulfilled, self-actualization is known as a *growth need* because it continues to develop even when temporarily satiated.

Even though it is widely known, Maslow's needs hierarchy theory was rejected long ago by motivation experts.[25] The main flaw is that not everyone has the same needs hierarchy. Some people place social status at the top of their personal hierarchy, whereas others view personal development and growth above social relations or status. This variation occurs because employee needs are strongly influenced by self-concept, personal values, and personality.[26] People have different hierarchies of values (see Chapter 2), so they also have parallel differences in their needs hierarchies. If your most important values lean toward power and achievement, for example, status needs will likely be at the top of your needs hierarchy. Furthermore, a person's values hierarchy can change over time, so their needs hierarchy also changes over time.[27]

Why have we introduced Maslow's needs hierarchy model? One reason is that the theory is widely known and incorrectly assumed to be valid; therefore, organizational behaviour students need to be aware of its true status. The other reason is that through this theory, Maslow transformed how we now think about human motivation.[28] First, he emphasized that needs should be studied together (holistically) because human behaviour is typically initiated by more than one need at the same time (previously, needs were studied separately from one another).[29] Second, he recognized that motivation can be shaped by human thoughts (such as personal values), whereas earlier motivation experts focused mainly on how instincts motivate behaviour.[30] Third, Maslow adopted a positive view of motivation, whereas previous motivation theories focused on need deficiencies such as hunger. Maslow's positive perspective is revealed in his emphasis on growth needs and *self-actualization,* suggesting that people are naturally motivated to reach their potential.[31]

INTRINSIC AND EXTRINSIC MOTIVATION

By extolling the importance of self-actualization, Maslow launched an entirely new way of thinking about human motivation. People experience self-actualization by applying their skills and knowledge, observing how their talents achieve meaningful results, and experiencing personal growth through learning.

These are the conditions for **intrinsic motivation,** which is motivation that occurs when people are fulfilling their needs for competence and autonomy by engaging in the activity itself, rather than from an externally controlled outcome of that activity.[32] Intrinsically motivated employees apply their talents toward a meaningful task and experience progress or success in that task.[33] They feel competent when applying their skills and observing positive, meaningful outcomes from that effort. They feel autonomous when their motivation is self-initiated rather than controlled from an external source.

Intrinsic motivation contrasts with **extrinsic motivation,** which is motivation that occurs when people want to engage in an activity for instrumental reasons, that is, to receive something that is beyond their personal control. This involves

> **intrinsic motivation** Motivation that occurs when people are fulfilling their needs for competence and autonomy by engaging in the activity itself, rather than from an externally controlled outcome of that activity.

Airbnb, San Francisco. USA. The/ZUMA Press/Newscom

Employees at Airbnb, the online vacation accommodation company, say they feel intrinsically motivated through autonomy and personal growth. "I feel realized, motivated, welcomed every single day," declares an Airbnb employee in Sao Paulo, Brazil. "Lot of autonomy and a great company to work for," reports an employee in the Netherlands. "Fundamentally we believe that [employees] having more control over what they work on is more motivating and leads to higher-quality results," explains an Airbnb executive.*

* O. Thomas, "How Airbnb Manages Not to Manage Engineers," *readwrite,* June 5, 2014; M. Curtis, "The Antidote to Bureaucracy Is Good Judgment," *Airbnb News,* Airbnb, May 15, 2015, http://nerds.airbnb.com/the-antidote-to-bureaucracy-is-good-judgement/. Employee quotations are from Glassdoor in 2015 and 2016.

extrinsic motivation Motivation that occurs when people want to engage in an activity for instrumental reasons, that is, to receive something that is beyond their personal control.

directing one's effort toward a reward controlled by others that indirectly fulfils a need. Extrinsic motivators exist throughout organizations, such as pay incentives, recognition awards, and frequent reminders from the boss about work deadlines. Extrinsic motivation also occurs indirectly, such as when we are motivated to complete our part of a team project partly due to our concerns about how team members will react if we submit it late or with inferior quality.

Does Extrinsic Motivation Undermine Intrinsic Motivation?

There are two contrasting hypotheses about how extrinsic and intrinsic motivation work together.[34] The additive hypothesis is that someone performing an intrinsically motivating job becomes even more motivated by also receiving an extrinsic source of motivation for that work. The extrinsic motivator energizes the employee more than the intrinsic motivator alone. The contrasting hypothesis is that introducing extrinsic sources of motivation will reduce intrinsic motivation. For example, employees who were energized by the work itself will experience less of that intrinsic motivation when they receive extrinsic rewards, such as a performance bonus. The explanation is that introducing extrinsic motivators diminishes the employee's feeling of autonomy, which is a key source of intrinsic motivation.

Which hypothesis is correct? So far, the research evidence is mixed. Extrinsic motivators may reduce existing intrinsic motivation to some extent and under some conditions, but the effect is often minimal. Extrinsic rewards do not undermine intrinsic motivation when they are unexpected (e.g., a surprise bonus), when they have low value relative to the intrinsic motivator, and when they are not contingent on specific behaviour (such as receiving a fixed salary). Even so, when employees are engaged in intrinsically motivating work, employers should be careful about the potential unintended effect of undermining that motivation with performance bonuses and other sources of extrinsic motivation.[35]

LEARNED NEEDS THEORY

In the previous section of this chapter, we explained that needs are shaped, amplified, or suppressed through self-concept, social norms, and past experience. Maslow noted this when he observed that individual differences influence the strength of higher-order needs, such as the need to belong. Psychologist David McClelland further investigated the idea that a person's needs can be strengthened or

weakened through reinforcement, learning, and social conditions. He examined three "learned" needs: achievement, power, and affiliation.[36]

- People with a high **need for achievement (nAch)** choose moderately challenging tasks, desire unambiguous feedback and recognition for their success, and prefer working alone rather than in teams. Except as a source of feedback, money is a weak motivator for people with high nAch, whereas it can be a strong motivator for those with low nAch.[37] Successful entrepreneurs tend to have a high nAch, possibly because they establish challenging goals for themselves and thrive on competition.[38]

  need for achievement (nAch) A learned need in which people want to accomplish reasonably challenging goals and desire unambiguous feedback and recognition for their success.

- People with a high **need for affiliation (nAff)** seek approval from others, want to conform to others' wishes and expectations, and avoid conflict and confrontation. High nAff employees generally work well in jobs responsible for cultivating long-term relations. However, with a strong need for approval, high nAff employees tend to be less effective at allocating scarce resources and making other decisions that potentially generate conflict. This suggests that leaders should have low nAff, but a few studies have found that leaders should have at least moderate levels of nAff to be supportive of employee needs.[39]

  need for affiliation (nAff) A learned need in which people seek approval from others, conform to their wishes and expectations, and avoid conflict and confrontation.

- People with a high **need for power (nPow)** want to exercise control over others, are highly involved in team decisions, rely on persuasion, and are concerned about maintaining their leadership position. There are two types of nPow.[40] The need for *personalized power* occurs when individuals enjoy their power for its own sake, use it to advance personal interests, and wear their power as a status symbol. The need for *socialized power* exists when individuals desire power as a means to help others. Effective leaders have a high need for socialized rather than personalized power. They demonstrate altruism and

  need for power (nPow) A learned need in which people want to control their environment, including people and material resources, to benefit either themselves (personalized power) or others (socialized power).

How strong are your learned needs? You can discover the strength of these learned needs in you by completing this self-assessment in Connect.

social responsibility and are concerned about the consequences of their own actions on others.

Changing (Learning) Need Strength

McClelland developed training programs to test the idea that needs can be learned (amplified or suppressed) through reinforcement, learning, and social conditions. One program increased achievement motivation by having participants write achievement-oriented stories, practise achievement-oriented behaviours in business games, and meet frequently with other trainees to maintain their new-found achievement motivation.[41] These training programs changed how people viewed themselves (their self-concept), which amplified their need for achievement, affiliation, or power.

Expectancy Theory of Motivation

LO4

The theories described so far mainly explain *what motivates us*—the prime movers of employee motivation—but they don't tell us *what we are motivated to do.* Four-drive theory recognizes that social norms, personal values, and past experience direct our effort, but it doesn't offer any detail about what goals we choose or where our effort is directed under various circumstances.

Expectancy theory offers a more detailed understanding of the logical decisions employees make when directing their effort toward specific behaviour. Essentially, the theory states that work effort is directed toward behaviours that people believe will produce the most favourable outcomes. It assumes that people are rational decision makers who choose a target that will best fulfil their needs. This choice is based on the probability that specific events will occur and the positive or negative valences (expected satisfaction) resulting from those events.[42] As illustrated in Exhibit 5.4, an individual's level of effort depends on three factors: effort-to-performance (E-to-P) expectancy, performance-to-outcome (P-to-O) expectancy, and outcome valences. Employee motivation is influenced by all three components of the expectancy theory model.[43] If any component weakens, motivation weakens.

> **expectancy theory** A motivation theory based on the idea that work effort is directed toward behaviours that people believe will lead to desired outcomes.

- *E-to-P expectancy.* This is the individual's perception that their effort will result in a specific level of performance. In some situations, employees may believe that they can unquestionably accomplish the task (a probability of 1.0). In other situations, they expect that even their highest level of effort will not result in the desired performance level (a probability of 0.0). In most cases, the

EXHIBIT 5.4   Expectancy Theory of Motivation

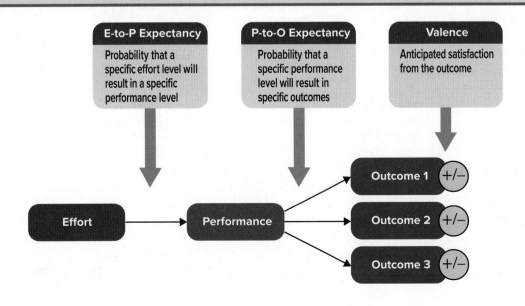

E-to-P expectancy falls somewhere between these two extremes.

- *P-to-O expectancy.* This is the perceived probability that a specific behaviour or performance level will lead to a specific outcome. In extreme cases, employees may believe that accomplishing a specific task (performance) will definitely result in a specific outcome (a probability of 1.0), or they may believe that successful performance will have no effect on this outcome (a probability of 0.0). More often, the P-to-O expectancy falls somewhere between these two extremes.

- *Outcome valences.* A *valence* is the anticipated satisfaction or dissatisfaction that an individual feels toward an outcome.[44] It ranges from negative to positive. (The actual range doesn't matter; it may be from -1 to $+1$ or from -100 to $+100$.) Outcomes have a positive valence when they are consistent with our values and satisfy our needs; they have a negative valence when they oppose our values and inhibit need fulfilment.

EXPECTANCY THEORY IN PRACTICE

One of the appealing characteristics of expectancy theory is that it provides clear guidelines for increasing employee motivation.[45] Several practical applications of expectancy theory are listed in Exhibit 5.5 and described below.

Increasing E-to-P Expectancies

E-to-P expectancies are influenced by the individual's belief that they can successfully complete the task. In other words, people with higher E-to-P expectancies have higher self-efficacy (see Chapter 3). Some companies increase this can-do attitude by assuring employees that they have the required abilities and resources as well as clear role perceptions to reach the desired levels of performance. An important part of this process involves matching employee abilities to job requirements and clearly communicating the tasks required for the job. Similarly, E-to-P expectancies are learned, so behaviour modelling and supportive feedback typically strengthen the individual's belief that they are able to perform the task.

Increasing P-to-O Expectancies

The most obvious ways to improve P-to-O expectancies are to measure employee performance accurately and distribute more valued rewards to those with higher job performance. P-to-O expectancies are perceptions, so employees also need to believe that higher performance will result in higher rewards. Furthermore, they need to know how that connection occurs, so leaders should use examples, anecdotes, and public ceremonies to illustrate when behaviour has been rewarded.

EXHIBIT 5.5   Practical Applications of Expectancy Theory

Expectancy theory component	Objective	Applications
E → P expectancies	To increase the employee's belief they are capable of performing the job successfully	• Select people with the required skills and knowledge. • Provide required training and clarify job requirements. • Provide sufficient time and resources. • Assign simpler or fewer tasks until employees can master them. • Provide examples of similar employees who have successfully performed the task. • Provide coaching to employees who lack self-confidence.
P → O expectancies	To increase the employee's belief that their good performance will result in specific valued outcomes	• Measure job performance accurately. • Clearly explain the outcomes that will result from successful performance. • Describe how the employee's rewards were based on past performance. • Provide examples of other employees whose good performance has resulted in higher rewards.
Outcome valences	To increase the employee's expected value of outcomes resulting from desired performance	• Distribute rewards that employees value. • Individualize rewards. • Minimize the presence of countervalent outcomes.

OB by the NUMBERS

Performance-to-Outcome Expectancy: Motivation's Weak Link*

56% of 8,254 employees surveyed in seven countries (including Canada) say they have a good understanding of how employees in their company are compensated (36% say they don't have a good understanding).

39% of 615,395 U.S. federal government employees believe that differences in performance are recognized in a meaningful way in their work unit.

41% of 160,747 Canadian government employees say that unsatisfactory employee performance is managed effectively in their department.

45% of 31,000 employees globally believe there is a clear link between their performance and their pay.

©Oxford/Getty Images

* Glassdoor, Global Salary Transparency Survey: Employee Perceptions of Talking Pay (Mill Valley, CA: Glassdoor, April 2016); "Global Workforce Study" (London: Willis Towers Watson, 2017); "2018 Public Service Employee Survey: Results for the Public Service" (Ottawa: Government of Canada, Treasury Board of Canada Secretariat, 2019); Office of Personnel Management, "2019 Federal Employee Viewpoint Survey" (Washington, DC: United States Government, October 2019).

Increasing Outcome Valences

One size does not fit all when motivating and rewarding people. The valence of a reward varies from one person to the next because each person has different need priorities. One solution is to individualize rewards by allowing employees to choose the rewards of greatest value to them. When this isn't possible, companies should find a reward that everyone values to some degree. Consider the following Canadian story: Top-performing employees in one organization were rewarded with a one-week Caribbean cruise with the company's executive team. Many were likely delighted, but at least one top performer was aghast at the thought of going on a cruise with senior management. "I don't like schmoozing, I don't like feeling trapped. Why couldn't they just give me the money?" she complained. In the end, the employee went on the cruise, but spent most of her time working in her stateroom.[46] Finally, we need to watch out for countervalent outcomes. If a company offers individual performance bonuses, for example, it should beware of team norms that discourage employees from working above a minimum standard. These norms and associated peer pressure are countervalent outcomes to the bonus.

Overall, expectancy theory is a useful model that explains how people rationally figure out the best direction, intensity, and persistence of effort. Early studies had difficulty empirically researching expectancy theory, but the theory seems to predict employee motivation in a variety of situations and cultures.[47] Expectancy theory does have limitations, however.[48] First, it assumes that people are perfectly rational decision makers; in reality, human decisions are not perfectly rational (see Chapter 7). A second concern is that the theory mainly explains extrinsic motivation, whereas applying the model's features to intrinsic motivation is more difficult (although not impossible). Third, expectancy theory ignores emotions as a source of motivation. The valence element of expectancy theory captures some of this emotional process, but only peripherally.[49] Fourth, E-to-P and P-to-O expectancies are critical components of expectancy theory, yet the theory doesn't explain how employees develop these expectancies. Two theories that do explain how expectancies are developed are organizational behaviour modification and social cognitive theory, which we describe next.

Organizational Behaviour Modification and Social Cognitive Theory

LO5

Expectancy theory states that motivation is determined by employee beliefs about expected performance and outcomes. But how do employees learn these expectancy beliefs? For example, how do they form the impression that one level of task performance is more likely than another performance level to produce a pay increase, promotion, or other outcomes? Two theories—organizational behaviour modification (OB Mod) and social cognitive theory—complement expectancy theory by explaining how people *learn* what to expect from their actions, which is how people develop the expectancies that affect motivation.

ORGANIZATIONAL BEHAVIOUR MODIFICATION

For most of the first half of the 1900s, the dominant paradigm about managing individual behaviour was *behaviourism,* which argues that a good theory should rely exclusively on behaviour and the environment and ignore nonobservable cognitions and emotions.[50] Although behaviourists don't deny the existence of human thoughts and attitudes, they view them as unobservable and, therefore, irrelevant to scientific study. A variation of this paradigm, called **organizational behaviour modification (OB Mod),** eventually entered organizational studies of motivation and learning.[51]

> **organizational behaviour modification (OB Mod)** A theory that explains employee behaviour in terms of the antecedent conditions and consequences of that behaviour.

A-B-Cs of OB Mod

The core elements of OB Mod are depicted in the A-B-C model shown in Exhibit 5.6. Essentially, OB Mod attempts to change behaviour (B) by managing its antecedents (A) and consequences (C).[52] *Consequences* are events following a particular behaviour that influence its future occurrence. Consequences include receiving words of thanks from co-workers after assisting them, enjoying preferred work schedules after being with the company longer than the average employee, and finding useful information on your smartphone after checking for new messages. Consequences also include no outcome at all, such as when no one says anything about how well you have been serving customers.

Antecedents are events preceding the behaviour, informing employees that a particular action will produce specific consequences. An antecedent could be a sound from your smartphone signalling that a text message has arrived. Or it could be your supervisor's request to complete a specific task by tomorrow. Notice that antecedents do not cause behaviour. The sound from your smartphone doesn't cause you to open the text message. Rather, the sound (antecedent) is a cue signalling that if you look at your phone messages (behaviour), you will find a new message with potentially useful information (consequence).

Contingencies and Schedules of Reinforcement

OB Mod identifies four types of consequences, called the *contingencies of reinforcement.*[53] *Positive reinforcement* refers to any consequence that, when introduced, increases or maintains the frequency or future probability of a specific behaviour. Receiving praise from co-workers is an example of positive reinforcement because the praise usually maintains or increases your likelihood of helping them in future. *Punishment* refers to any consequence that decreases the frequency or future probability of a specific behaviour occurring. Most of us would consider being demoted or criticized by our co-workers as forms of punishment. A third type of consequence is *extinction.* Extinction occurs when the target behaviour decreases because no consequence follows it. For instance, research suggests that performance tends to decline when managers stop congratulating employees for their good work.[54]

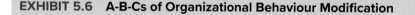

EXHIBIT 5.6   A-B-Cs of Organizational Behaviour Modification

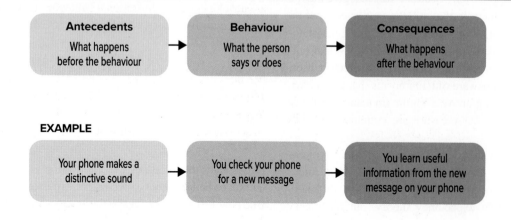

The fourth consequence in OB Mod, called *negative reinforcement,* is often confused with the application of punishment. It's actually the opposite—the removal of punishment. Negative reinforcement occurs when the removal or avoidance of a consequence increases or maintains the frequency or future probability of a specific behaviour. For example, managers apply negative reinforcement when they *stop* criticizing employees whose substandard performance has improved.

Which of these four consequences works best? In most situations, positive reinforcement should follow desired behaviours and extinction (do nothing) should follow undesirable behaviours. Positive reinforcement is preferred because focusing on the positive rather than negative aspects of life tends to improve organizational success and individual well-being.[55] In contrast, punishment and negative reinforcement generate negative emotions and attitudes toward the person (e.g., supervisor) and organization who initiated and later removed the punishment. However, punishment (dismissal, suspension, demotion, etc.) may be necessary consequences for extreme behaviours, such as deliberately hurting a co-worker or stealing inventory. Indeed, research suggests that, under some conditions, punishment maintains a sense of fairness among those affected by or aware of the employee's indiscretion.[56]

Along with the four consequences, OB Mod considers the frequency and timing of these reinforcers (called the *schedules of reinforcement*).[57] The most effective reinforcement schedule for learning new tasks is *continuous reinforcement*— providing positive reinforcement after every occurrence of the desired behaviour. For motivating behaviour, the most effective reinforcement schedule tends to be the *variable ratio schedule*---providing positive reinforcement after a varying number of times. Salespeople experience variable ratio reinforcement because they make a successful sale (positive reinforcement) after a varying number of client calls. The variable ratio schedule makes behaviour highly resistant to extinction because the reinforcer is never expected after a fixed period of time or after a fixed number of behaviours.

Evaluating OB Mod

Everyone uses organizational behaviour modification principles in one form or another to motivate people. We thank co-workers for a job well done, are silent when displeased, and sometimes try to punish those who go against our wishes. OB Mod also occurs in various formal programs to reduce absenteeism, improve task performance, encourage safe work behaviours, and promote a healthier lifestyle. An innovative and increasingly popular workplace behaviour modification strategy relies on "gamification"—reinforcing behaviour through digital games in which employees earn points and "badges" and compete for top positions on leader boards. Research indicates that gamification potentially reinforces learning and desired behaviours through positive reinforcement and extinction. However, it can also produce negative outcomes (lower performance, higher employee turnover, etc.) when the intervention electronically monitors employee behaviour or is linked to financial rewards.[58]

In spite of its widespread use, organizational behaviour modification has a number of limitations. One limitation is "reward inflation," in which the reinforcer is eventually considered an entitlement. For this reason, most OB Mod programs must run infrequently and for a short duration. Another concern is that the variable ratio schedule of reinforcement tends to create a lottery-style reward system, which might be viewed as too erratic for formal rewards and is unpopular to people who dislike gambling. Probably the most significant problem is OB Mod's radical view that behaviour is learned only through personal interaction with the environment.[59] This view is no longer accepted; instead, experts recognize that people also learn and are motivated by observing others and inferring possible consequences of their actions. This learning process is explained by social cognitive theory.

SOCIAL COGNITIVE THEORY

Social cognitive theory states that much learning occurs by observing and modelling others as well as by anticipating the consequences of our behaviour.[60] Observation and modelling (imitation) had been studied for many years, but Canadian social scientist Albert Bandura reframed these ideas within a cognitive (internal thoughts) perspective as an alternative to the behaviourist approach. There are several pieces to social cognitive theory, but the three most relevant to employee motivation are learning behaviour consequences, behaviour modelling, and self-regulation.

> **social cognitive theory**
> A theory that explains how learning and motivation occur by observing and modelling others as well as by anticipating the consequences of our behaviour.

Learning Behaviour Consequences

People learn the consequences of behaviour by observing or hearing about what happened to other people, not just by directly experiencing the consequences.[61] Hearing that a co-worker was fired for being rude to a client increases your belief that rude behaviour will result in being fired. In the language of expectancy theory, learning behaviour consequences changes a person's perceived P-to-O expectancy. Furthermore, people logically anticipate consequences in

Global Connections 5.2

KPMG MOTIVATES EMPLOYEE LEARNING WITH GAMIFICATION*

To improve employee knowledge about its global capabilities (audit, tax, advisory, etc.), KPMG developed an app that applies OB Mod principles through gamification. "We needed to do something different and fun and used game elements like time pressure, rapid feedback, and scores to engage our people," explains an executive at the professional services firm.

Through the app, called Globerunner, players race around the world answering questions about the firm's service capabilities in various global operations, such as, "A CFO needs help with X—which offering can help?" They acquire points for correct answers, earn badges for completed missions, and gain access to questions in other locations. They can also compare their success against co-workers on a global leaderboard and challenge others in tournaments.

KPMG estimates that Globerunner has improved employee knowledge by 24 percent. More than

80 percent of employees (including those who don't play online games) enjoyed the learning experience.

©Jose Luis Pelaez Inc/Blend Images LLC

* C. Mazy, "How Companies Can Raise Their Game," *Financial Times—IE Corporate Learning Alliance,* February 19, 2018;KPMG International, "Playing for Success" (Amstelveen, The Netherlands, June 28, 2018).

---

related situations. For instance, the story about the fired employee might also strengthen your P-to-O expectancy that being rude toward co-workers and suppliers (not just clients) will get you fired.

Behaviour Modelling

Along with observing others, people learn by imitating and practising their behaviours.[62] Modelling the behaviour of others gives learners direct sensory experience, which helps them to acquire knowledge and skills, such as the subtle person–machine interaction while driving a vehicle. Behaviour modelling also increases E-to-P expectancy because people develop a stronger self-efficacy (see Chapter 3) after observing others and performing the task successfully themselves. Self-efficacy particularly improves when observers are similar to the model in age, experience, gender, and related characteristics.

Self-Regulation

An important feature of social cognitive theory is that human beings set goals and engage in other forms of intentional, purposive action.[63] They establish their own short- and long-term objectives, choose their own standards of

achievement, work out a plan of action, consider back-up alternatives, and have the forethought to anticipate the consequences of their goal-directed behaviour.

Furthermore, people self-regulate by engaging in **self-reinforcement**; they reward and punish themselves for exceeding or falling short of their self-set goals. For example, you might have a goal of completing the rest of this chapter, after which you reward yourself by having a snack. Raiding the refrigerator is a form of self-induced positive reinforcement for completing this reading assignment.

> **self-reinforcement** Reinforcement that occurs when an employee has control over a reinforcer but doesn't 'take' it until completing a self-set goal.

OB Mod and social cognitive theory explain how people learn probabilities of successful performance (E-to-P expectancies) as well as probabilities of various outcomes from that performance (P-to-O expectancies). As such, these theories explain motivation through their relationship with expectancy theory of motivation, described earlier. Elements of these theories also help us to understand other motivation processes. For instance, self-regulation is the cornerstone of motivation through goal setting and feedback, which we discuss next.

Goal Setting and Feedback

LO6

Key performance indicators, task objectives, stretch targets, job duties. No matter what they are called, goals figure prominently in everyone's job. A **goal** is a cognitive representation of a desired end state that a person is committed to attain.[64] Goals motivate people by clarifying role perceptions and, consequently, the direction of effort. Goals also amplify the intensity and persistence of effort because they make it easier to judge how much energy is required to reach them. However, the motivational potential of goals depends on how well they are stated.[65] Rather than just trying to "do your best," effective goals have several characteristics identified in the popular acronym SMARTER.[66]

> **goal** A cognitive representation of a desired end state that a person is committed to attain.

- *Specific.* Goals lead to better performance when they are specific. Specific goals state what needs to be accomplished, how it should be accomplished, and where, when, and with whom it should be accomplished. Specific goals clarify performance expectations so employees can direct their effort more efficiently and reliably.

- *Measurable.* Goals need to be measurable because motivation occurs when people have some indication of their progress and achievement of those goals. This measurement ideally includes how much (quantity), how well (quality), and at what cost the goal was achieved. However, some types of employee performance are difficult to measure, and they risk being neglected in companies preoccupied with quantifiable outcomes.[67]

- *Achievable.* One of the trickiest aspects of goal setting is developing goals that are sufficiently but not overly challenging.[68] Easy goals motivate employees to perform well below their potential. Yet goals that are too challenging may also lead to substandard effort if employees

©Bojan Milinkov/Shutterstock

The City of Toronto's call centre—311 Toronto—operates 24 hours per day, 7 days per week, and answers 3.6 million non-emergency customer calls in 180 languages each year. As the largest call centre of its kind in North America, 311 Toronto motivates its employees with SMARTER goals. One goal is to answer 80 percent of the calls within 75 seconds. Another objective is that conversations have an average talk time of 270 seconds. A third goal is to resolve 70 percent of calls at the first point of contact (i.e., not forwarding the caller elsewhere or calling back later). The 311 Toronto operations centre also strengthens employee motivation through visual feedback. On one wall is a massive screen that displays current statistics associated with these and other key performance indicators.*

* M. Warren, "Toronto Is Known for Dead Raccoons and Potholes. The City's 311 Nerve Centre Knows This Reputation Is Well-Earned," *Toronto Star,* November 18, 2018; "311 Toronto Budget Notes," Budget TO 2019 (Toronto: City of Toronto, January 25, 2019).

believe there is a low probability of accomplishing them (i.e., low E-to-P expectancy). Recent studies have also found that very difficult goals increase the probability that employees will engage in unethical behaviour to achieve them.[69]

- *Relevant.* Goals need to be relevant to the job and within the employee's control. For example, a goal to reduce waste materials won't motivate employees who have negligible control over waste in the production process.

- *Time-framed.* Goals need a due date. They should specify when the objective should be completed or when it will be assessed for comparison against a standard.

- *Exciting.* Goals tend to be more effective when employees are committed to them, not just compliant. Challenging goals tend to be more exciting for most (but not all) employees because growth need fulfilment is stronger when difficult goals are achieved. Goal commitment also increases when employees are involved in goal setting.[70]

- *Reviewed.* The motivational value of goals depends on employees receiving feedback about reaching those goals.[71] Effective feedback requires measurement, which we discussed earlier in this list, but it also includes reflecting on or discussing with others your goal progress and accomplishment. Reviewing goal progress and accomplishment helps employees to redirect their effort. It is also a potential source of recognition that fulfils growth needs.

CHARACTERISTICS OF EFFECTIVE FEEDBACK

The opening case study for this chapter described why Accenture and Adobe Systems in Canada and elsewhere have replaced their traditional performance appraisal systems with real-time, coaching-oriented feedback. This dramatic shift has occurred mainly because traditional performance reviews do not satisfy some of the critical features of effective feedback. Feedback—information that lets us know whether we have achieved the goal or are properly directing our effort toward it—is an essential partner with goal setting. Feedback contributes to motivation and performance by clarifying role perceptions, improving employee skills and knowledge, and strengthening self-efficacy.[72]

Effective feedback has many of the same characteristics as effective goal setting (see Exhibit 5.7).[73] It should be *specific,*

EXHIBIT 5.7   Characteristics of Effective Feedback

Feedback characteristic	Description	Example
Specific	Information refers to identifiable behaviours and (when possible) measurable outcomes	"Inventory shrinkage (theft, damage) fell to 1 percent of inventory over the previous three months."
Relevant	Information should relate to behaviours and outcomes within the individual's or team's control	"You have submitted the monthly budget reports without error and on time every month over the past year, one of the few district managers to do so." (Where district managers have few situational barriers to submitting the reports accurately or on schedule).
Timely	Information should be available soon after the behaviour or results occur	"Two of our customers noted this week that you were unable to answer their questions about how the new widget model differs from the previous model."
Credible	Information source should: • have complete and accurate information • recall information reliably • be unbiased in communicating and applying the feedback • describe the feedback in a supportive and empathetic manner	Supervisor has good knowledge of the employee's job duties, regularly observes them performing the work, and offers constructive feedback with optimism and sensitivity on how the employee can perform specific tasks better.
Sufficiently frequent	Information is provided: • more often for those learning new tasks • according to the job cycle's frequency	Supervisor meets twice monthly with every experienced production employee and checks in at least twice weekly with every new employee to discuss their individual safety behaviour and output (where task cycle times are usually less than one hour).

meaning that the information should refer to identifiable behaviours and, when possible, measurable outcomes (e.g., sales increased by 5 percent last month). Feedback should also be *relevant;* it should relate to behaviours and outcomes within the individual's or team's control. Effective feedback is also *timely,* that is, the information is available soon after the behaviour or results occur—not six months later in a performance review meeting. Timely feedback gives employees a clearer association between their actions and the consequences.

A fourth characteristic of effective feedback is that it is *credible.* A feedback source is credible when employees believe that person has complete and accurate information about the employee's performance, is reliable at recalling that information, is unbiased in communicating and applying the feedback to decisions (such as performance ratings), and describes the feedback in a supportive and empathetic manner. These conditions explain why performance feedback is typically less credible during traditional performance appraisals than during real-time coaching-style feedback.[74] Supervisors have difficulty completely and reliably recalling performance information over such a long time. In addition, supervisors have two roles—coach and judge—in traditional performance reviews.

The latter can undermine the supervisor's perceived neutrality as well as supportiveness during the feedback session.

One other important characteristic of effective feedback is that it should be *sufficiently frequent.* How frequent is "sufficiently"? The answer depends on at least two things. One consideration is the employee's knowledge and experience with the task. Employees working on new tasks should receive more frequent feedback because they require more behaviour guidance and reinforcement. Experienced employees can receive less frequent feedback when performing familiar tasks. The second factor is how long it takes to complete the task (i.e., its cycle time). Less frequent feedback usually occurs in jobs with a long cycle time (e.g., executives and scientists) because indicators of goal progress and accomplishment in these jobs are less frequent than in jobs with a short cycle time (e.g., grocery store cashiers).

Feedback through Strengths-Based Coaching

As the co-founder of Vancouver-based WealthBar, Tea Nicola is nurturing a "culture of healthy management," which includes plenty of strengths-based coaching to

---

Global Connections 5.3

STRENGTHS-BASED COACHING AT STRYKER*

Stryker is rated as one of the top places to work in Canada, the United States, Australia, and in most other regions where the medical devices firm does business. These accolades are partly due to Stryker's deeply embedded practice of strengths-based coaching. Employees discover their strengths through a commercial assessment, and the company encourages them to let co-workers know their top five strengths.

"Stryker has an amazing culture, built by amazing people," says one of the company's inventory managers at its Canadian headquarters in Hamilton, Ontario. "I get to use my unique combination of strengths to solve problems and deliver results for our customers. I am my authentic self at work and am grateful to be able to work at a place that celebrates my achievements."

"We work with people to understand how to use their strengths in a positive way, and encourage them to own their career using those strengths," says Erin Cramlet, Stryker South Pacific HR director. Ryan McCarthy, managing director at Stryker-Medical Asia Pacific, explains

further: "What strengths has allowed me to do as a leader is to truly treat people as individuals and find the best in each person." McCarthy says his role as a leader is "to ensure the individual has the opportunity to use those strengths every day in an engaging environment."

©ProStockStudio/Shutterstock

* Gallup Strengths Center, 'Gallup Called to Coach with Ryan Mccarthy–Australia Singapore Edition', Podcast in *Called to Coach,* (YouTube, 5 October 2016); C. Scobie, 'Fighting the Good Fight, for the People', *Acuity,* Feb/March 2017; '5 Keys to Strengths-Based Talent Success at Australia's Best Place to Work', *Inside HR,* 29 January 2018.

employees. "Focusing people on what they're bad at is what creates anxiety, and that leads to negativity toward the workplace," Nicola warns. Kyron Keogh agrees. "It's important to reward and encourage strengths. Instead of looking at weakness, look at areas for development," says the co-founder of Rox, the award-winning luxury retail jewellery chain headquartered in Glasgow, Scotland. "It's vital to ensure that staff stay motivated and upbeat in a sales environment."[75]

Strengths-based coaching (also known as *appreciative coaching*) is a positive approach to feedback that maximizes employees' potential by focusing on their strengths rather than weaknesses.[76] In strengths-based coaching, employees describe areas of work where they excel or demonstrate potential. The coach directs this discussion by asking exploratory questions that help employees discover ways to build these strengths. Situational barriers, as well as strategies to overcome those barriers, are identified to further support the employee's potential.

> **strengths-based coaching** An approach to coaching and feedback that focuses on building and leveraging the employee's strengths rather than trying to correct their weaknesses.

Strengths-based coaching might not be best in all situations, but it is associated with higher employee motivation, satisfaction, self-efficacy, and relations with management.[77] One reason is that people are more receptive to information about their strengths than they are to information about their flaws. In fact, for more than three decades scholars have warned that traditional problem-focused feedback leads to employee defensiveness and potentially lower self-efficacy, which can result in reduced (rather than increased) employee performance.[78] Strengths-based coaching also makes sense because personality becomes quite stable in the early stages of an individual's career, which limits their flexibility regarding interests, preferences, and abilities.[79] Consequently, employees become less motivated and less able to improve themselves in areas where they previously lacked interest or skill.

SOURCES OF FEEDBACK

Feedback can originate from nonsocial or social sources. Nonsocial sources provide feedback without someone communicating that information. Corporate intranets allow many executives to receive feedback instantaneously on their computer or other digital device, usually in the form of graphic output on an executive dashboard. Employees at contact centres view electronic displays showing how many callers are waiting and the average time they have been waiting.

Some companies set up *multisource (360-degree) feedback* which, as the name implies, is information about an employee's performance collected from a full circle of people, including subordinates, peers, supervisors, and customers. Multisource feedback tends to provide more complete and accurate information than feedback from a supervisor alone. It is particularly useful when the supervisor is unable to observe the employee's behaviour or performance in every situation. Lower-level employees also feel a greater sense of fairness when they are able to provide upward feedback about their boss's performance.[80]

However, multisource feedback can be expensive and time-consuming. Furthermore, people have markedly different opinions about an employee, so multisource feedback can be more confusing than meaningful. A third concern is that peers tend to minimize interpersonal conflict by providing inflated rather than accurate feedback. A fourth issue is that employees experience a stronger emotional reaction when they receive critical feedback from many people rather than from just one person (such as the boss).

The preferred feedback source depends on the purpose of the information. Feedback from nonsocial sources, such as digital images or feedback directly from the job, is better when employees need to learn about goal progress and accomplishment. This is because information from nonsocial sources is considered more accurate than information from social sources. Negative feedback from nonsocial sources is also less damaging to self-esteem. In contrast, social sources tend to delay or exclude some negative information as well as distort the bad news in a positive way.[81] Employees should receive some positive feedback from social sources. It feels better to have co-workers say that you are performing the job well than to discover this from data on an impersonal digital dashboard.

EVALUATING GOAL SETTING AND FEEDBACK

Goal setting (in partnership with feedback) is generally a highly effective practice for employee motivation and performance.[82] Putting goal setting into practice can be challenging, however.[83] It tends to focus employees on a narrow subset of measurable performance indicators while ignoring aspects of job performance that are difficult to measure. This problem is captured in the saying: "What gets measured, gets done." Another concern is that very difficult goals may motivate some people to engage in unethical behaviour to achieve those targets. Difficult goals are also stressful, which can undermine overall job performance.

Yet another problem is that goal setting tends to interfere with the learning process in new, complex jobs. Therefore, setting performance goals may be effective for employees who are already experienced in a job but should be avoided where they are in the middle of an intense learning process. A final issue is that when goal achievement is tied to

What is your goal orientation? You can discover your dominant goal orientation by completing this self-assessment in Connect.

financial rewards, many employees are motivated to set easy goals (while making the boss think they are difficult) so that they have a higher probability of receiving the bonus or pay increase. As a former Ford Motor Company CEO once quipped: "At Ford, we hire very smart people. They quickly learn how to make relatively easy goals look difficult!"[84]

Organizational Justice

LO7

Treating employees fairly is both morally correct and good for employee motivation, loyalty, and well-being. Yet feelings of injustice occur regularly in the workplace. Almost half of Canadians in accounting, finance, technology, and related jobs believe they are underpaid, whereas only 1 percent say they are overpaid. The other 50 percent of those surveyed say they are adequately paid. Two surveys of American employees report almost identical results. Half believe their pay is fair, a little under half think they are underpaid, and 5 percent say they are overpaid.[85] These examples are about fair pay, but there are many other types of perceived workplace injustices, such as who gets promoted, how employees are treated by management, and whether resource allocation decisions are transparent and unbiased.

How can we improve workplace justice? Our answer begins by explaining that there are several types of organizational justice, each of which has some degree of unique influence on whether people believe the situation is fair or unfair.[86] We will discuss the three most common varieties (there are others): distributive, procedural, and interactional justice. All three types of justice refer to the perception that appropriate formal or informal rules have been applied to the situation. People have a sense of fairness when they believe those rules are being followed.[87]

- **Distributive justice** refers to the perception that appropriate decision criteria (rules) have been applied to calculate how various benefits and burdens are distributed. These criteria—such as effort, need, or membership—determine how much each person should receive, such as higher pay, more tedious tasks, better workspace, and so on.

distributive justice The perception that appropriate decision criteria (rules) have been applied to calculate how various benefits and burdens are distributed.

- **Procedural justice** is the perception that appropriate procedural rules have been applied throughout the decision process. Procedural justice tends to be higher, for example, when the decision maker demonstrates neutrality (no favouritism), allows everyone involved to have their say, and allows an appeal of the decision.

procedural justice The perception that appropriate procedural rules have been applied throughout the decision process.

- **Interactional justice** is the perception that appropriate rules have been applied in the way employees are treated throughout the decision process. For example, we believe there is interactional justice when the decision maker is polite toward the potential beneficiaries and is honest and candid in providing information about the decision.

interactional justice The perception that appropriate rules have been applied in the way the people involved are treated throughout the decision process.

DISTRIBUTIVE JUSTICE AND EQUITY THEORY

At its most basic level, employment in any organization is an exchange relationship; we provide our time, skills, and behaviour in exchange for pay, fulfilling work, skill development opportunities, and so forth. What is considered "fair" in this exchange relationship depends on what criteria we use to determine distributive justice in various situations.[88] In some situations, we might believe that everyone should receive the same benefits. This *equality principle* is applied, for instance, when everyone gets subsidized meals in the company cafeteria. In other situations, we believe that those with the greatest need should receive more outcomes than those with less need (called the *need principle*). An example of this principle is the practice of giving employees who are ill paid time off to recover. The *equity principle* states that the benefits people receive should be in proportion to what they contribute to the organization. The equity principle relates to the most common set of distributive justice rules in organizational settings, so let's look at equity-based distributive justice in more detail.

Feelings of equity are explained by **equity theory**, which says that employees determine whether a decision is equitable by comparing their own outcome/

equity theory A theory explaining how people develop perceptions of fairness in the distribution and exchange of resources.

Debating Point: DOES EQUITY MOTIVATE MORE THAN EQUALITY?*

It seems obvious that employees with higher performance, skills, or other contributions to the organization should receive more generous pay and other rewards. Increasing the pay differential (wage dispersion) between high and low contributors should boost employee motivation to achieve a higher standard of performance. It should also increase company performance by motivating the top performers to stay and the bottom performers to leave. A large wage dispersion is also consistent with justice and fairness. Differentiating rewards based on employee performance, skills, and other forms of contribution is consistent with the principle of meritocracy. It is also consistent with the ethical principle of justice, which states that those who contribute more should receive more in return (Chapter 2). Furthermore, performance-based pay is one of the pillars of human capital (see Chapter 1).

But workplaces that have large wage dispersions might not be receiving the performance dividends they expect. Several (but not all) studies have found that sports teams with relatively small pay differences among team members perform better than sport teams with relatively high pay differences. Teams that pay huge salaries or bonuses to stars do not score more points or win more games. Also, turnover among players and managers tends to increase

with the size of the wage dispersion. One study extended these observations to all industries. Companies that have a higher dispersion of wage increases (larger increases to higher-paid staff) perform worse than companies with an equal dispersion of wage increases. Another study reported that information technology companies with larger salary differences among top management teams had worse shareholder returns and market-to-book value compared to IT companies with less pay inequality.

Why would larger pay ranges undermine rather than enhance employee and organizational performance? One reason is that pay differences produce status differences, which can undermine cooperation among employees. A second reason is that large pay differences might increase (rather than decrease) feelings of injustice. Most people think they are above average, so large pay differences clearly place many employees below their self-evaluations. Also, employees tend to underestimate the contribution of higher-paid co-workers and assume those higher-paid co-workers also receive other rewards (such as preferential treatment). In short, lower-paid employees often believe higher-paid employees are overpaid, which reduces the lower-paid workers' motivation and performance.

* C. Grund and N. Westergaard-Nielsen, "The Dispersion of Employees' Wage Increases and Firm Performance," *Industrial & Labor Relations Review* 61, no. 4 (2008): 485–501; H. Katayama and H. Nuch, "A Game-Level Analysis of Salary Dispersion and Team Performance in the National Basketball Association," *Applied Economics* 43, no. 10 (2011): 1193–207; P.E. Downes and D. Choi, "Employee Reactions to Pay Dispersion: A Typology of Existing Research," *Human Resource Management Review* 24, no. 1 (2014): 53–66; S.A. Conroy et al., "A Multilevel Approach to the Effects of Pay Variation," *Research in Personnel and Human Resources Management* 32 (2014): 1–64.

input ratio to the outcome/input ratio of another person or group.[89] As Exhibit 5.8 illustrates, the *outcome/input ratio* is the value of the outcomes you receive divided by the value of the inputs you provide in the exchange relationship. Inputs include such things as skill, effort, reputation, performance, experience, and hours worked. Outcomes are what employees receive from the organization, such as pay, promotions, recognition, interesting jobs, and opportunities to improve one's skills and knowledge.

A central feature of equity theory is that individuals determine fairness in terms of a *comparison other*.[90] The comparison other might be another person or group of people in other jobs (e.g., comparing your pay with the CEO's pay) or another organization. Some research suggests that employees frequently collect information on several referents to form a "generalized" comparison other.[91] For the most part, however, the comparison other varies

from one person and situation to the next and is not easily identifiable.

The comparison of our own outcome/input ratio with the ratio of someone else results in perceptions of equity, under-reward inequity, or overreward inequity. In the equity condition, people believe that their outcome/input ratio is similar to the ratio of the comparison other. In the underreward inequity situation, people believe their outcome/input ratio is lower than the comparison other's ratio. In the overreward inequity condition, people believe their outcome/input ratio is higher than the comparison other's ratio.

Inequity and Employee Motivation

How do perceptions of equity or inequity affect employee motivation? The answer is illustrated in Exhibit 5.9. When people believe they are under- or overrewarded, they experience negative emotions (called *inequity tension*).[92] As we

EXHIBIT 5.8   Equity Theory Model

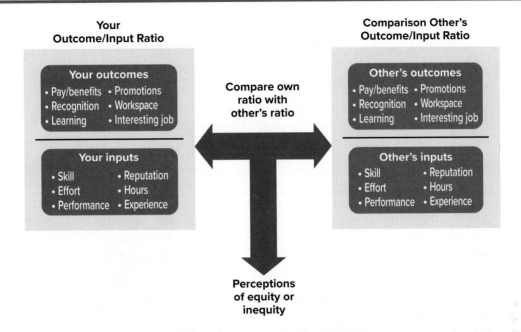

EXHIBIT 5.9   Motivational Effects of Inequity Perceptions

have pointed out throughout this chapter, emotions are the engines of motivation. In the case of inequity, people are motivated to reduce the emotional tension. Most people have a strong emotional response when they believe a situation is unfair, and this emotion nags them until they take steps to correct the perceived inequity.

There are several ways to try to reduce the inequity tension.[93] Let's consider each of these in the context of under-reward inequity. One action is to reduce our inputs so the outcome/ input ratio is similar to that of the higher-paid co-worker. Some employees do this by working more slowly, offering fewer suggestions, and engaging in less organizational citizenship behaviour. A second action is to increase our outcomes. Some people who think they are underpaid ask for a pay raise. Others make unauthorized

use of company resources. A third behavioural response is to increase the comparison other's inputs. We might subtly ask the better-paid co-worker to do a larger share of the work, for instance. A fourth action is to reduce the comparison other's outcomes. This might occur by ensuring that the co-worker gets less desirable jobs or working conditions. Another action, although uncommon, is to ask the company to reduce the co-worker's pay so it is the same as ours.

A fifth action involves changing our beliefs about the situation rather than changing our behaviour. For example, we might believe that the co-worker really is providing more inputs (e.g., working longer hours) for that higher pay. Alternatively, we might change our perceived valence of some outcomes. Rather than thinking that a co-worker's work-related travel is

How sensitive are you to inequities? You can discover your level of equity sensitivity by completing this self-assessment in Connect.

©John Lehmann/Globe and Mail/The Canadian Press

Melissa Leverrier earns a fixed hourly rate along with overtime pay as a Canada Post urban mail carrier in Chilliwack, B.C. Sandee Saamanen does similar work as a Canada Post rural suburban mail carrier (RSMC) in nearby Agassiz. But Saamanen does not receive overtime pay and her paycheque is determined by how many parcels she delivers, distance travelled, and other performance criteria. An arbitrator recently concluded that this dual compensation system is unfair. RSMCs receive significantly lower earnings than their urban counterparts for performing essentially the same work. "She [Sandee Saamanen] has a different uniform than I, but honestly we're all doing the same thing," Leverrier complains. Canada Post is now adjusting the RSMC pay rates. "It's just another small step towards equality," says Leverrier.*

*"Arbitrator Rules Wage Gap Exists between Rural, Urban Mail Carriers," *CBC News,* June 1, 2018; N. Grossman, "Agassiz Postal Workers Join Canada Post Strike, Push for Equality to Urban Carriers," *The Agassiz - Harrison Observer,* October 29, 2018; "Retroactive Payments, Collection of Premiums to Appear on Your October 17 Pay Statement" (Canada Post letter to RSMC employees, October 2019).

a desirable perk, we instead perceive most of that travel as an undesirable nuisance. A sixth action to reduce the inequity tension is to change the comparison other. Instead of comparing ourselves with the higher-paid co-worker, we might increasingly compare with a friend or neighbour who works in a similar job. Finally, if the inequity tension is strong enough and can't be reduced through other actions, we might leave the field. This occurs by moving to another department, joining another company, or keeping away from the work site where the higher paid co-worker is located.

People who feel overreward inequity would reverse these actions. Some overrewarded employees reduce their feelings of inequity by working harder; others encourage the underrewarded co-worker to work at a more leisurely pace. A common reaction, however, is that the overrewarded employee changes their perceptions to justify the more favourable outcomes, such as believing the assigned work is more difficult or their skills are more valuable than the lower-paid co-worker's skills. As Pierre Berton, the popular late Canadian journalist, author, and historian once said: "I was underpaid for the first half of my life. I don't mind being overpaid for the second half."[94]

Evaluating Equity Theory

Equity theory is quite successful at understanding (usually in hindsight) why people feel unfairly rewarded.[95] However, it is more difficult to use as a practical tool for predicting and preventing inequity in the future. The main problem is that people vary in their choice of comparison other and which inputs or outcomes are most valuable. Therefore, leaders need to minimize the risk of inequity feelings by knowing their employees well enough to understand their priority of outcomes and inputs. Open communication is also important because it lets decision makers know from the employees affected whether they believe decisions are unfair. A second problem is that equity theory accounts for only some of our feelings of fairness in the workplace. Procedural and interactional justice can be just as important as distributive justice.

PROCEDURAL AND INTERACTIONAL JUSTICE

Procedural justice is the perception that appropriate rules are applied in the procedures used throughout the course of deciding the distribution of workplace benefits and burdens. *Interactional justice* is the perception that appropriate rules are applied in the way the people involved are treated throughout that decision process.[96] Exhibit 5.10 lists the main rules that people consider when determining procedural and interactional justice.

There are several ways to maintain procedural justice.[97] Decision makers must be perceived as unbiased, without self-interest in the results, and not blinded by narrow doctrines. Their allocation decisions need to be based on as much relevant and accurate information as possible. Those decisions also need to take into account the positions and circumstances of the diverse groups affected by the outcomes. Another factor to consider in procedural justice is whether the decision criteria and decision procedures are compatible with ethical principles. For example, gathering accurate information might not be fair if it involves closely monitoring employees or violating their individual privacy. The decision criteria used to allocate benefits as well as

the procedural justice rules need to be applied consistently to everyone (equality) and over time (stability).

Another important condition for procedural justice is that employees are given "voice" in the process—they have the opportunity to present their evidence and opinions to decision makers. Voice improves the quality of information applied to the decision. It also provides a value-expressive function; employees tend to feel better after having an opportunity to speak their mind. Lastly, employees should have a right to appeal the decision (so it is reviewed and possibly overturned) if they believe there were errors in how resources were distributed or flaws in the procedures leading to that decision.

Interactional justice also depends on a set of rules that people believe are being applied to the situation.[98] Two of these rules—treating people with politeness and with respect—support the feeling of fairness in the interpersonal relationship. Abusive supervision is a clear example of violation of these interactional justice rules because employees are treated rudely and their self-worth is attacked.[99] To generate a sense of fairness regarding the information provided, employees should receive thorough and well-justified explanations about the decision, and honest, candid, and timely information about the decision. For instance, people are more likely to feel that a decision is unfair if decision makers refuse to explain how the decision was made, or if they seem evasive in their explanation.

Consequences of Procedural and Interactional Injustice

Employees who believe procedural or interactional justice rules have been violated experience negative emotions, such as anger, frustration, insult, resentment, and shame.[100] How employees direct the energy from these emotions depends

---

EXHIBIT 5.10   Procedural and interactional Justice Rules

Procedural justice rules	Interactional justice rules
• Decision makers are not biased by self-interest or restrictive doctrines.	• Employees are treated in a polite manner.
• Allocation decisions are based on a full complement of accurate information.	• Employees are treated with respect.
• Decision makers consider the interests of all groups affected by the outcomes.	• Employees receive thorough and well-justified explanations about the decision.
• Decisions and procedures are compatible with ethical principles.	• Employees receive honest, candid, and timely information about the decision.
• Decision criteria and procedures are applied consistently across persons and over time.	
• Employees have the opportunity to present their evidence and opinions to decision makers (voice).	
• Questionable decisions and procedures can be appealed and overturned.	

on their personal characteristics and experiences. Generally, research has found that procedural or interactional injustice often results in less work effort (and performance), fewer organizational citizenship behaviours, less cooperation with co-workers, increased involvement in union activities, and increased turnover.

Victims of procedural and interactional injustice sometimes retaliate to restore their self-esteem, reinstate their status and power in the relationship, and educate the perpetrator of the injustice.[101] A related outcome is increased aggression toward the decision maker (e.g., supervisor) and sometimes toward co-workers who are seemingly treated more favourably. Procedural or interactional injustice can also lead to more extreme dysfunctional behaviours, such as theft, sabotage, and violence.

Chapter Summary

LO1

Define employee motivation and engagement.

Motivation is defined as the forces within a person that affect the direction, intensity, and persistence of voluntary behaviour. Employee engagement is defined as an individual's emotional and cognitive (rational) motivation, particularly a focused, intense, persistent, and purposive effort toward work-related goals. Supporting employee motivation and engagement is challenging because the workforce is more diverse than ever before, and because organizations have reduced supervision and other traditional control systems.

LO2

Explain how drives and emotions influence employee motivation.

Drives (also called primary needs) are neural states that energize individuals to correct deficiencies or maintain an internal equilibrium. They generate emotions, which put us in a state of readiness to act. Needs—goal-directed forces that people experience—are shaped by the individual's self-concept (including personality and values), social norms, and past experience.

LO3

Discuss the employee motivation implications of four-drive theory, Maslow's needs hierarchy, intrinsic and extrinsic motivation, and learned needs theory.

Four-drive theory states that emotions are the source of human motivation. The drives to acquire, bond, comprehend, and defend produce emotions, which become conscious needs. The employee's personal characteristics and experiences (mental skill set) direct emotional energy to goals perceived to have a high probability of fulfilling those felt needs. Four-drive theory's two recommendations are that organizations should help employees fulfil all four drives and that fulfilment of the four drives must be kept in balance.

Maslow's needs hierarchy groups needs into a hierarchy of five levels and states that the lowest needs are initially most important but higher needs become more important as the lower ones are satisfied. Although very popular, the theory's assumption that everyone has the same needs hierarchy lacks research support. Needs hierarchies vary from one person to the next according to their personal values. However, Maslow proposed more useful ways to think about human motivation, specifically that motivation theories need to be holistic, humanistic, and positive-oriented.

Intrinsic motivation refers to motivation controlled by the individual and experienced from the activity itself, whereas extrinsic motivation occurs when people are motivated to receive something that is beyond their personal control for instrumental reasons. Intrinsic motivation is anchored in the innate drives for competence and autonomy. Some research suggests that extrinsic motivators may reduce existing intrinsic motivation to some extent and under some conditions, but the effect is often minimal.

McClelland's learned needs theory argues that needs can be strengthened through learning. The three needs studied in this respect are need for achievement, need for power, and need for affiliation.

LO4

Discuss the expectancy theory model, including its practical implications.

Expectancy theory states that work effort is determined by the perceived probability that a specific level of effort will produce a specific level of performance (E-to-P expectancy), the perceived probability that a specific behaviour or performance level will lead to specific outcomes (P-to-O expectancy), and the valences the person ascribes to those outcomes. The E-to-P expectancy increases by improving the employee's ability and confidence to perform the job. The P-to-O expectancy increases by measuring performance accurately, distributing higher rewards to better performers, and showing employees that rewards are performance-based. Outcome valences increase by finding out what employees want and using these resources as rewards.

LO5

Outline organizational behaviour modification (OB Mod) and social cognitive theory, and explain their relevance to employee motivation.

Organizational behaviour modification takes the behaviourist view that the environment teaches people to alter their behaviour so they maximize positive consequences and minimize adverse consequences. Antecedents are environmental stimuli that provoke (not necessarily cause) behaviour. Consequences are events following behaviour that influence its future occurrence. Consequences include positive reinforcement, punishment, negative reinforcement, and extinction. The schedules of reinforcement also influence behaviour.

Social cognitive theory states that much learning and motivation occurs by observing and modelling others as well as by anticipating the consequences of our behaviour. It suggests that people typically infer (rather than only directly experience) cause–effect relationships, anticipate the consequences of their actions, develop self-efficacy in performing behaviour, exercise personal control over their behaviour, and reflect on their direct experiences. The theory emphasizes self-regulation of individual behaviour, including self-reinforcement, which is the tendency of people to reward and punish themselves as a consequence of their actions.

LO6

Describe the characteristics of effective goal setting and feedback.

A goal is a cognitive representation of a desired end state that a person is committed to attain, and goal setting is the process of motivating employees and clarifying their role perceptions by establishing performance objectives. Goals are more effective when they are SMARTER (specific, measurable, achievable, relevant, time-framed, exciting, and reviewed). Effective feedback is specific, relevant, timely, credible, and sufficiently frequent. Strengths-based coaching maximizes employees' potential by focusing on their strengths rather than weaknesses. Strengths-based coaching tends to be effective because people are more receptive to information about their strengths rather than flaws, and because a person's motivation and ability becomes more stable over time. Employees usually prefer nonsocial feedback sources to learn about their progress toward goal accomplishment.

LO7

Explain how equity theory, procedural justice, and interactional justice influence employee motivation.

Organizational justice exists in several forms, the main three of which are distributive, procedural, and interactional. Distributive justice refers to the perception that appropriate decision criteria (rules) have been applied to calculate how various benefits and burdens are distributed. These rules relate to equality, need, or equity. Equity theory has four elements: outcome–input ratio, comparison other, equity evaluation, and consequences of inequity. The theory also explains what people are motivated to do when they feel inequitably treated.

Procedural justice is the perception that appropriate procedural rules have been applied throughout the decision process. These rules include that the decision maker is unbiased, considers the full complement of accurate information, considers the interests of all groups affected, applies ethical principles, applies decision criteria and procedural rules consistently, allows employees to present their views, and allows appeal of decisions. Interactional justice is the perception that appropriate rules have been applied in the way employees are treated throughout the decision process. These rules include that employees are treated with respect and politely, that employees receive explanations that are thorough and logical, and that they receive honest and timely information about the decision. Lack of procedural and interactional justice results in negative emotions (ranging from anger to shame) as well as a variety of behaviours that harm the organization (such as lower performance and higher incidence of turnover, aggression, and theft).

Key Terms

distributive justice

drives

employee engagement

equity theory

expectancy theory

extrinsic motivation

four-drive theory

goal

interactional justice

intrinsic motivation

Maslow's needs hierarchy theory

motivation

need for achievement (nAch)

need for affiliation (nAff)

need for power (nPow)

needs

organizational behaviour modification (OB Mod)

procedural justice

self-reinforcement

social cognitive theory

strengths-based coaching

Critical Thinking Questions

1. Four-drive theory recommends that companies must keep fulfilment of the four drives in balance. What is this "balance" and why is it important? Give an example (real or hypothetical) of how a company maintains balanced drive fulfilment. Also describe a company that does not provide this balance, including the consequences of this imbalance on employees' attitudes and behaviour.

2. Learned needs theory states that needs can be strengthened or weakened. How might a company strengthen the achievement needs of its management team?

3. Everyone who works as an electronic game developer has extrinsic sources of motivation, and most also experience some degree of intrinsic motivation. Considering the dynamics of extrinsic and intrinsic motivation, what should companies in this industry do to ensure that their game developers are highly motivated at work?

4. The opening case study for this chapter describes how many companies have shifted from traditional annual performance appraisals to frequent, constructive, and future-focused development reviews. Apply expectancy theory to explain why the more frequent feedback and more strengths-based future focus of the new performance review process might motivate employees more than the traditional judgment-oriented, problem-focused, annual performance appraisal process.

5. Describe a situation in which you used organizational behaviour modification to increase or decrease someone's motivation regarding a specific behaviour. What specifically did you do? What was the result?

6. Using your knowledge of the characteristics of effective goals, establish two meaningful goals related to your performance in this class.

7. Most people think they are "worth more" than they are paid. Furthermore, most employees seem to feel that they exhibit better leadership skills and interpersonal skills than others. Please comment on this human tendency.

8. You are an external consultant hired by a large organization to investigate possible causes of employee perceptions of procedural and interactional injustice regarding various management decisions (promotions, vacation rostering, assigned tasks, office location, and so forth). Many employees have complained that management is unfair in how it makes these decisions. Even those who say they get a fair deal in these decisions agree that the process is suspicious and therefore subject to doubt by those who receive less than they expected. In a few instances, employees have also complained about the information (or lack of information) they receive about how the decision was justified, as well as how they have been treated when trying to discuss the decision with management. As an external consultant, identify specific activities and issues you would investigate to pinpoint the ways in which management can improve employee perceptions of procedural and interactional justice.

Case Study:
PREDICTING HARRY'S WORK EFFORT

by **Robert J. Oppenheimer, Concordia University**

Purpose This exercise is designed to help you to understand expectancy theory and how its elements affect a person's level of effort toward job performance.

Instructions This exercise may be completed either individually or in small teams of 4 or 5 people. When the individuals (or teams) have completed the exercise, the results will be discussed and compared with others in the class.

Read the following interview case. Then calculate whether Harry will engage in high or "just acceptable" performance effort under the conditions described. Valence scores range from −1.0 to + 1.0. All expectancies are probabilities ranging from 0 (no chance) to 1.0 (definitely will occur). The effort level scores are calculated by multiplying each valence by the appropriate P-to-O expectancy, summing these results, then multiplying the sum by the E-to-P expectancy.

INTERVIEW WITH HARRY

Interviewer: Hi, Harry. I have been asked to talk to you about your job. Do you mind if I ask you a few questions?

Harry: No, not at all.

Interviewer: Thanks, Harry. What are the things that you would anticipate getting satisfaction from as a result of your job?

Harry: What do you mean?

Interviewer: Well, what is important to you with regard to your job here?

Harry: I guess most important is job security. As a matter of fact, I can't think of anything that is more important to me. I think getting a raise would be nice, and a promotion would be even better.

Interviewer: Anything else that you think would be nice to get, or for that matter, that you would want to avoid?

Harry: I certainly would not want my buddies to make fun of me. We're pretty friendly, and this is really important to me.

Interviewer: Anything else?

Harry: No, not really. That seems to be it.

Interviewer: How satisfied do you think you would be with each of these?

Harry: What do you mean?

Interviewer: Well, assume that something that you would really like has a value of + 1.0 and something you would really not like, that is you would want to avoid, has a value of − 1.0, and something you are indifferent about has a value of 0.

Harry: OK. Getting a raise would have a value of .5; a promotion is more important, so I'd say .7; and having my buddies make fun of me, .9.

Interviewer: But, I thought you didn't want your buddies to make fun of you.

Harry: I don't.

Interviewer: But you gave it a value of .9.

Harry: Oh, I guess it should be −.9.

Interviewer: OK, I just want to be sure I understand what you're saying. Harry, what do you think the chances are of these things happening?

Harry: That depends.

Interviewer: On what?

Harry: On whether my performance is high or just acceptable.

Interviewer: What if it is high?

Harry: I figure I stand about a 50–50 chance of getting a raise and/or a promotion, but I also think that there is a 90 percent chance that my buddies will make fun of me.

Interviewer: What about job security?

Harry: I am certain my job is secure here, whether my performance is high or just acceptable. I can't remember the last guy who was doing his job and got fired. But if my performance is just acceptable, my chances of a raise or promotion are about 10 percent. However, then the guys will not make fun of me. That I am certain about.

Interviewer: What is the likelihood of your performance level being high?

Harry: That depends. If I work very hard and put out a high degree of effort, I'd say that my chance of my performance being high is about 90 percent. But if I put out a low level of effort, you know—if I just take it easy—then I figure that the chances of my doing an acceptable job is about 80 percent.

Interviewer: Well, which would you do: put out a low level or a high level of effort?

Harry: With all the questions you asked me, you should be able to tell me.

Interviewer: You may be right!

Harry: Yeah? That's nice. Hey, if you don't have any other questions, I'd like to join the guys for coffee.

Interviewer: OK, thanks for your time.

Harry: You're welcome.

Discussion Question

1. Use the expectancy theory model to predict Harry's motivation to achieve high or "just acceptable" performance in his job. Identify and discuss the factors that influence this motivation.

Developed by Robert J. Oppenheimer, Ph.D. Professor of Management, Concordia University, Montreal, Canada.

 Case Study:
BARRIE SUPER SUBS

By Steven L. McShane, University of Newcastle (Australia)

Barrie Super Subs is one of the larger takeout restaurants in the Super Subs chain, which includes 300 locations across Canada. This outlet has a restaurant manager, an assistant manager, and several part-time team leaders. The restaurant manager rarely has time to serve customers, and head office discourages them from performing front-line work. The assistant manager serves customers for a couple of hours during the busy lunchtime but otherwise assists the restaurant manager with purchasing, accounts, hiring, and other operations. Most team leaders are college students and serve customers alongside other employees, particularly from late afternoon to night closing. Most employees are also students who work part-time; a few are in high school. All regular staff earn minimum pay rates.

Barrie Super Subs has experienced below average profitability over the past 18 months, which has reduced the monthly bonus paid to the restaurant manager and assistant manager. This bonus is calculated by percentage of "wastage" (unsold, damaged, or unaccounted for food and drinks) relative to sales; the lower the percentage of wastage, the higher the bonus. Wastage occurs when employees drop or spill food, cut up more toppings than are sold, burn heated subs, prepare an order incorrectly, and eat or give away food without permission. When employees make mistakes, the expense is supposed to come out of their paycheque. Unauthorized eating and giving away food are grounds for immediate dismissal. However, team leaders are reluctant to report any accidental or deliberate wastage, even when confronted by the restaurant manager about the store's high wastage over the previous week and month. One team leader who reported several accidental wastage incidents eventually quit after being snubbed by co-workers who attended the same college classes.

Barrie Super Subs gives employees a food allowance if they work continuously for at least four and a half hours. Staff complain that the allowance is meagre and that they are often ineligible for the food allowance because many shifts are only three or four hours. Employees who work these shorter shifts sometimes help themselves to food and drinks when the managers aren't around, claiming that their hard work justifies the free meal. Some also claim the food is a low company expense and makes up for their small paycheque, relative to what many of their friends earn elsewhere. Several (but not most) employees give some of their friends generous helpings as well as occasional free soft drinks and chips. Employees say handing out free food to friends makes them more popular with their peers.

Five months ago, the Barrie restaurant's wastage (mainly deliberate wastage) had risen to the point where the two managers no longer received a bonus. The restaurant manager reacted by giving the food allowance only to those who work for six or more hours in a single shift. This action excluded even more staff from receiving the food allowance, but it did not discourage employees from eating or giving away food. However, almost 20 percent of the experienced college staff left for other jobs over the following two months. Many of those who stayed discouraged friends from considering jobs at Super Subs. Morale declined, which dampened the fun atmosphere that had existed to some extent in the past. Relations between employees and managers soured further.

With relatively low unemployment, the restaurant manager found it difficult to hire replacements, particularly people with previous work experience of any kind. Temporary staff shortages required the two managers to spend more time working in food preparation and training new staff. Their increased presence in the restaurant significantly reduced deliberate wastage, but accidental wastage increased somewhat as the greater number of inexperienced staff made more mistakes.

After three months, Barrie Super Subs' manager and assistant manager were confident that the situation had improved, so they spent less time training staff and serving customers. Indeed, they received a moderate bonus after the third month in the store. However, wastage increased again soon after the managers withdrew from daily operations. The experienced employees started eating more food, and the new staff soon joined in this practice. Exasperated, the restaurant manager took bolder steps. He completely removed the food allowance and threatened to fire any employee caught consuming or giving away food.

Wastage dropped somewhat over the next month but is now creeping upward again.

Discussion Questions

1. What symptoms in this case suggest that something has gone wrong?

2. What are the main causes of these symptoms?

3. What actions should Barrie Super Subs' managers take to correct these problems?

© 2011 Steven L. McShane. Inspired by an early case written by J.E. Dittrich and R.A. Zawacki.

 Class Exercise:
NEEDS PRIORITY EXERCISE

Purpose This class exercise is designed to help you understand employee needs in the workplace.

Instructions (Small Class)

Step 1: The table below lists in alphabetical order 16 characteristics of the job or work environment. Working alone, use the far-left column to rank-order the importance of these characteristics to you personally. Write in "1" beside the most important characteristic, "2" for the second most important, and so on through to "16" for the least important characteristic on this list.

Step 2: Students are assigned to teams, where they compare each other's rank-order results. Note reasons for the largest variations in rankings and be prepared to discuss these reasons with the entire class. Students should pay close attention to different needs, self-concepts, and various forms of diversity (ethnicity, profession, age, etc.) within the class

to identify possible explanations for any variation of results across students.

Step 3: The instructor will provide results of a recent large-scale survey of younger Canadian postsecondary students (i.e., born in 1980 or since). When these results are presented, discuss the reasons for any noticeable differences between the survey and class rankings. Relate the differences to your understanding of the emerging view of employee needs and drives in work settings.

Instructions (Large Class)

Step 1: Same as above.

Step 2: The instructor will ask students, by a show of hands (or use of classroom technology), to identify their top-ranked attributes.

Step 3: Same as above.

Personal Ranking of Work-Related Attributes

Attributes of Work (Listed Alphabetically)	Your Ranking (1 = most important)
Challenging work	
Commitment to social responsibility	
Good health and benefits plan	
Good initial salary level	
Good people to report to	
Good people to work with	
Good training opportunities/developing new skills	
Good variety of work	
Job security	
Opportunities for advancement in position	
Opportunities to have a personal impact	
Opportunities to have a social impact	
Opportunity to travel	
Organization is a leader in its field	
Strong commitment to employee diversity	
Work–life integration	

Self-Assessments for Chapter 5

SELF-ASSESSMENT NAME	DESCRIPTION
How strong are your growth needs?	Many human needs are called "deficiency" needs because they become active only when unfulfilled. However, Abraham Maslow popularized the idea that people also have "growth needs," which continue to motivate even when temporarily satiated. Growth needs are associated with self-actualization and intrinsic motivation. People vary in their growth need strength, which is evident from the type of work they prefer. This self-assessment estimates your growth need strength.
How strong are your learned needs?	Everyone has the same innate drives, but these drives produce different need strengths due to each person's socialization and personality. David McClelland particularly examined three learned needs, two of which are measured in this self-assessment. This self-assessment estimates the strength of these learned needs in you.
What is your goal orientation?	Everyone sets goals for themselves, but people differ in the nature of those goals. Some view goals as challenges that assist learning. Others see goals as demonstrations of one's competence. Still others view goals as threatening one's image if they are not achieved. This self-assessment estimates your dominant goal orientation.
How sensitive are you to inequities?	Correcting feelings of inequity is one of the most powerful motivating forces in the workplace. But people react differently to equitable and inequitable situations based on their equity sensitivity. Equity sensitivity refers to a person's outcome/input preferences and reaction to various outcome/input ratios when compared to other people. This self-assessment estimates your level of equity sensitivity.

CHAPTER 6
Applied Performance Practices

LEARNING OBJECTIVES

After reading this chapter, you should be able to:

LO1 Discuss the meaning of money and identify several individual, team, and organizational-level performance-based rewards.

LO2 Describe five ways to improve reward effectiveness.

LO3 List the advantages and disadvantages of job specialization.

LO4 Diagram the job characteristics model and describe three ways to improve employee motivation through job design.

LO5 Define psychological empowerment and identify strategies that support empowerment.

LO6 Describe the five elements of self-leadership and identify specific personal and work environment influences on self-leadership.

When Cathy Thorpe became the first externally hired CEO of Nurse Next Door, she discovered how to further empower its franchisees and their employees. By removing middle management, performance reviews, and other forms of centralized control, the Vancouver-based home care services company enriched franchise-level jobs with more autonomy and felt responsibility.

"We don't need middle managers to manage people," Thorpe explains. "It was starting to affect [franchisee and employee] performance because they were complacent with waiting for direction from us instead of being proactive."

Accountability accompanies autonomy. So, with further training of franchisees and their employ-

Vancouver-based Nurse Next Door has thrived through a period of hyper growth by applying job enrichment, empowerment, and self-leadership practices.
©AP Photo/Chris Carlson/The Canadian Press

ees, Nurse Next Door made self-leadership a central element of its culture. "We set our people up for success and also encourage a culture of self-leadership," says Tiffany Rubin, owner of one of Nurse Next Door's largest franchises in the United States.

Cathy Thorpe emphasizes that everyone needs to be able to manage themselves to support Nurse Next Door's hyper growth (it is currently among Canada's fastest growing companies). "We introduced a concept of self-leadership to help everyone slow down by empowering our people to make decisions, to be passionate, purposeful and mindful — to be self-led," she says. "We need everyone in our organization to hone these skills and take personal and professional accountability."

Nurse Next Door has thrived through a culture of autonomy and self-leadership, but franchise owner Tiffany Rubin warns that "if you require complete structure, this may not be the best environment for you." Cathy Thorpe agrees that self-leadership isn't suitable in situations where "people feel comfortable being told what to do and some leaders don't feel comfortable leading less." She sums up the company's model of success: "At Nurse Next Door, we are empowering our people to own their role and to have the space they need to do their job. No micromanaging, no tiered hierarchies."[1]

Nurse Next Door is one of Canada's fastest growing companies because its employees are motivated by enriched jobs, an empowering work environment, and a culture that encourages self-leadership practices. All three topics are discussed in this chapter, along with financial rewards.

The chapter begins by examining the meaning of money. This is followed by an overview of financial reward practices, including the different types of rewards and how to implement rewards effectively. Next, we look at the conceptual foundations of job design, followed by specific job design strategies for motivating employees. We then consider the elements of empowerment, as well as conditions that support empowerment. The final part of the chapter explains how employees manage their own performance through self-leadership.

The Meaning of Money in the Workplace

LO1

Rewarding people with money is one of the oldest applied performance practices, and is certainly the most widespread. At the most basic level, money and other financial rewards represent a form of exchange; employees provide their labour, skill, and knowledge in return for money and benefits from the organization. From this perspective, money and related rewards align employee goals with organizational goals. This concept of economic exchange can be found across most societies. The word for *pay* in Malaysian and Slovak means "to replace a loss"; in Hebrew and Swedish it means "making equal."[2]

However, money is much more than a form of compensation for an employee's contribution to organizational objectives. Money relates to our needs, our emotions, and our self-concept. It is a symbol of achievement and status, a motivator, a source of enhanced or reduced anxiety, and an influence on our propensity to make ethical or risky decisions. It also generates a variety of emotions, some of which are negative (anxiety, depression, anger, helplessness, etc.).[3] Furthermore, money influences human thoughts and behaviour nonconsciously to some extent.[4] According to one expert, "Money is probably the most emotionally meaningful object in contemporary life."[5]

The meaning of money varies considerably from one person to the next. Some people value it as an instrument for acquiring other things of value; others value money for its own sake. A widely studied model of money attitudes suggests that people have a strong "money ethic" or "monetary intelligence" when they believe that money is not evil, that it is a symbol of achievement, respect, and power, and that it should be budgeted carefully. These attitudes toward money influence an individual's ethical conduct, organizational citizenship, and many other behaviours and attitudes.[6]

Do men and women have different perceptions and attitudes toward money? Apparently so, according to several studies.[7] In almost all societies, men attach more importance or value to money than do women. Men are more likely than women to view money as a symbol of power and status as well as the means to autonomy. Women are more likely to view money in terms of things for which it can be exchanged and particularly as a symbol of generosity and caring by using it to buy things for others.

The meaning of money also varies across cultures.[8] People in China, Japan, and other countries with high power distance (acceptance of unequal distribution of power in a society—see Chapter 2) tend to have a high respect and priority for money, whereas people in countries with a strong egalitarian culture (such as Denmark, Austria, and Israel) are discouraged from openly talking about money or displaying their personal wealth. One study suggests that Swiss culture values saving money whereas Italian culture places more value on spending it.

The motivational effect of money is much greater than was previously believed, and this effect is due more to its symbolic value than to what it can buy.[9] Philosopher John Stuart Mill made this observation almost 150 years ago when he wrote: "The love of money is not only one of the strongest

 What is your attitude toward money? You can discover your attitude toward money by completing this self-assessment in Connect.

moving forces of human life, but money is, in many cases, desired in and for itself."[10] People who earn higher pay tend to have higher job performance because the higher paycheque enhances their self-concept evaluation. Others have noted that the symbolic value of money depends on how it is distributed in the organization and how many people receive that financial reward.

Overall, current organizational behaviour thinking indicates that money is much more than a means of exchange between employer and employee. It fulfils a variety of needs, influences emotions, and shapes or represents a person's self-concept. These findings are important to remember when the employer is distributing financial rewards in the workplace. Over the next few pages, we look at various reward practices and how to improve the implementation of performance-based rewards.

Financial Reward Practices

Financial rewards come in many forms, which can be organized into the four specific objectives identified in Exhibit 6.1: membership and seniority, job status, competencies, and performance.

MEMBERSHIP- AND SENIORITY-BASED REWARDS

Membership-based and seniority-based rewards (sometimes called "pay for pulse") represent the largest part of most paycheques. Some employee benefits are provided equally to everyone, such as free or subsidized meals during work. Other rewards increase with seniority. For example, employees with 10 or more years of service at the Paul Scherrer Institute near Zurich, Switzerland, receive an annual loyalty bonus equal to half a month's salary; those with 20 or more years of service at the natural and engineering sciences research centre receive a bonus equal to a full month's salary.[11]

These membership- and seniority-based rewards potentially reduce turnover and attract job applicants, particularly those who desire predictable income. However, they do not directly motivate job performance; on the contrary, they discourage poor performers from seeking work better suited to

EXHIBIT 6.1   Reward Objectives, Advantages, and Disadvantages

Reward objective	Sample rewards	Advantages	Disadvantages
Membership/ seniority	• Fixed pay • Most employee benefits • Paid time off	• May attract applicants • Minimizes stress of insecurity • Reduces turnover	• Doesn't directly motivate performance • May discourage poor performers from leaving • "Golden handcuffs" may undermine performance
Job status	• Promotion-based pay increase • Status-based benefits	• Tries to maintain internal equity • Minimizes pay discrimination • Motivates employees to compete for promotions	• Encourages hierarchy, which may increase costs and reduce responsiveness • Reinforces status differences • Motivates job competition and exaggerated job worth
Competencies	• Pay increase based on competency • Skill-based pay	• Improves workforce flexibility • Tends to improve quality • Motivates career development	• Relies on subjective measurement of competencies • Skill-based pay plans are expensive
Task performance	• Commissions • Merit pay • Gainsharing • Profit sharing • Share options	• Motivates task performance • Attracts performance-oriented applicants • Organizational rewards create an ownership culture • Pay variability may avoid layoffs during downturns	• May weaken intrinsic motivation • May distance reward giver from receiver • May discourage creativity • Tends to address symptoms, not underlying causes of behaviour

their abilities. Instead, the good performers are more easily lured to better-paying jobs. Some of these rewards are also "golden handcuffs"—they discourage employees from quitting because of deferred bonuses or generous benefits that are not available elsewhere. The problem is that golden handcuffs potentially weaken job performance because they generate continuance rather than affective commitment (see Chapter 4).

JOB STATUS–BASED REWARDS

Almost every organization rewards employees to some extent on the basis of the status or worth of the jobs they occupy. In some parts of the world, companies measure job worth through **job evaluation**. Most job evaluation methods give higher value to jobs that require more skill and effort, have more responsibility, and have more difficult working conditions.[12] The higher worth assigned to a job, the higher the minimum and maximum pay for people in that job. Along with receiving higher pay, employees with more valued jobs sometimes receive larger offices, company-paid vehicles, and other perks.

job evaluation Systematically rating the worth of jobs within an organization by measuring their required skill, effort, responsibility, and working conditions.

Job status-based rewards try to improve feelings of fairness by distributing more pay to people in higher-valued jobs. These rewards also motivate employees to compete for promotions. However, at a time when companies are trying to be more cost-efficient and responsive to the external environment, job status-based rewards potentially do the opposite by encouraging a bureaucratic hierarchy. These rewards also reinforce a status mentality, whereas Millennial employees expect a more egalitarian workplace. Furthermore, status-based pay potentially motivates employees to compete with each other for higher-status jobs, to exaggerate their job duties, and to hoard resources as ways to increase the worth of their current job.[13]

COMPETENCY-BASED REWARDS

In recent years, many companies have shifted reward priorities to skills, knowledge, and other personal characteristics that lead to superior performance. The two main reward practices in this category are competency-based pay structures and skill-based pay structures.

Competency-based pay structures identify clusters of skills, knowledge, and experience specific to each broad job group as well as clusters relevant across all job groups. Employees progress through the pay range within their job group as they demonstrate higher levels of those competencies.[14] For example, the pay system at one mid-sized power company lists accountability, technical competency, and a few other skills relevant to everyone in the organization. Each of the company's four broad organizational levels also has a specific set of competencies. For instance, technical acumen and team skills are two skill sets that influence pay among employees in the technical/professional job group, whereas strategic thinking and managing stakeholders are two competencies specific to the executive group. Employees within each job group receive higher pay as they demonstrate better skills, knowledge, and experience for the organization-wide and job group–specific competencies.[15]

Skill-based pay structures are more measurable competency-based reward systems in which employees receive higher pay based on how quickly or accurately they perform specific tasks and operate equipment.[16] High Liner Foods, the Nova Scotia–based frozen seafood company, assigns pay rates to employees based on the number and difficulty of skills they have mastered. "We're setting our sites up for a skill-based pay system, so as employees learn and demonstrate certain skills, they move into a different pay bracket," explains a High Liner executive.

Competency-based rewards motivate employees to learn new skills.[17] This tends to support a more flexible workforce, increase employee creativity, and allow employees to be more adaptive to new practices in a dynamic environment. Product or service quality also tends to improve because employees with multiple skills are more likely to understand the work process and know how to improve it.

However, competency-based pay plans have not always worked out as well as promised by their advocates. They are often over-designed, making it difficult to communicate these pay systems to employees. Competency definitions tend to be abstract, which raises questions about fairness when employers are relying on these definitions to award pay increases. Skill-based pay systems measure specific skills, so they are usually more objective. However, they are expensive because employees spend more time learning new tasks.[18]

PERFORMANCE-BASED REWARDS

Performance-based rewards have existed for more than 4,000 years, since shepherds and other workers during the Third Dynasty of Ur (located in modern-day Iraq) had strict performance standards and received harsh penalties if their output (number of sheep delivered) fell short of those standards. Hundreds of years later, the most productive weavers in ancient Babylon received higher payment (in food) than co-workers with lower productivity.[19] Today, performance-based rewards exist in many forms across most cultures. Here is an overview of some of the most popular individual, team, and organizational performance-based rewards.

Global Connections 6.1

SKILL-BASED PAY AT WONDERFUL COMPANY*

Wonderful Company is the parent company of the world's largest flower delivery service (Teleflora), the world's largest grower of tree nuts, the largest citrus grower in North America, and other diversified businesses. These operations require employees who are motivated and rewarded for developing valuable skills, so Wonderful Co. has introduced a skill-based reward system for production staff.

Employees are assigned to skill blocks, such as Operator 5 and Mechanical 1. These pay groups have clearly defined skills as well as pathways to higher skill blocks. As an example, an employee in the Mechanical 1 block needs to know how to operate the correction tensioning tool, calculate chain deflection for each system, demonstrate the correct use of an Accu-Glide conveyor service, and so forth.

Higher pay rates are earned as the employee demonstrates mastery of skills in the next skill block. If someone in a general operator job wants to enter the refrigeration technician skill group, they would begin by learning the specific skills in the Mechanical 1 skill block. The employee would receive a higher pay rate after measurable demonstration of those skills.

©imageBROKER/Alamy Stock Photo

The employee would next learn skills associated with Mechanical 2 skill block and receive a higher pay rate when these are mastered. Electrical 1 and other skill blocks are also part of the refrigeration technician skill group, which the employee could also learn over time.

* Based on information in: G. Simonoff and B. Kazar, "Build and Benefit from a Skill-Based Pay System," *Plant Services,* August 16, 2018.

Individual Rewards

Many employees receive individual bonuses or other rewards for accomplishing a specific task or exceeding annual performance goals. The referral bonus—which is paid when a friend is hired by the company —is one of the most common individual bonuses for non-executive staff in Canada. Housekeeping staff in many hotels are paid a piece rate—a specific amount earned for each room cleaned.[20] Other hotels pay an hourly rate plus a per-room bonus. Real estate agents and other salespeople typically earn *commissions,* in which their pay depends on the sales volume they generate.

Team Rewards

Organizations have shifted their focus from individuals to teams, and accompanying this transition has been the introduction of more team-based rewards. Nucor Corp. relies heavily on team-based rewards. The American steelmaker's employees earn bonuses that can exceed half their total pay, determined by how much steel is produced by the team.

This team-based bonus system also includes penalties. If employees catch a bad batch of steel before it leaves the mini-mill, they lose their bonus for that shipment. But if a bad batch makes its way to the customer, the team loses three times its usual bonus.[21]

Another form of team-based performance reward is the **gainsharing plan**, which calculates bonuses from the department's or business unit's cost savings and productivity improvement. Gainsharing plans tend to improve team dynamics, knowledge sharing, and pay satisfaction. They also create a reasonably strong link between effort and performance because much of the cost reduction and labour efficiency is within the team's control.[22]

> **gainsharing plan** A team-based reward that calculates bonuses from the work unit's cost savings and productivity improvement.

One division of BC Hydro has a gainsharing arrangement in which employees can earn up to 5 percent beyond their base pay when they collectively achieve or exceed a combination of company, business unit, and departmental target goals. Canadian mining and forestry companies have had

OB by the NUMBERS

Global Variations in Performance-Based Pay*

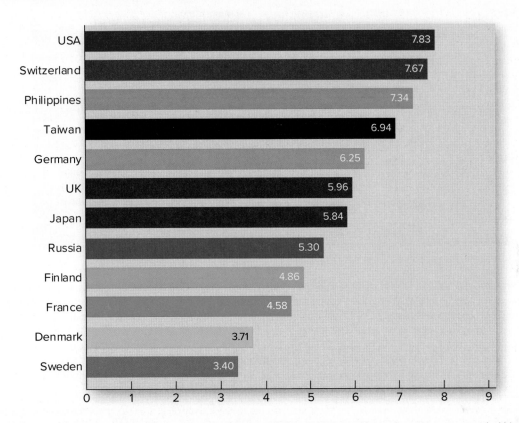

Scores represent the average number of individual pay-for-performance (I-PFP) practices used by each company surveyed within the specified country. The I-PFP include such practices as using performance-based rewards, using performance appraisals to make pay decisions, etc. The study surveyed 4,207 companies (minimum 100 employees) in 27 countries. This exhibit displays a sample across the range of the countries studied.

* Based on data reported in: P. Gooderham et al., "A Multilevel Analysis of the Use of Individual Pay-for-Performance Systems," *Journal of Management* 44, no. 4 (2018): 1479–1504, https://doi.org/10.1177/0149206315610634. Data were collected in 2009–2010. These results are moderately similar to a 2013 global survey sponsored by Kelly Services.

gainsharing plans over the years, but the number that are still active is unknown. Some hospitals in the United States have cautiously introduced a form of gainsharing, whereby physicians and medical staff in a medical unit (cardiology, orthopedics, etc.) are collectively rewarded for cost reductions in surgery and patient care. A recent Canadian report suggests that hospitals in this country are unlikely to introduce gainsharing incentives due to the way that hospitals are funded.[23]

Organizational Rewards

Along with individual and team-based rewards, many firms motivate employees with organizational-level rewards. Many businesses distribute bonuses to all employees for achieving preset organizational goals or as a companywide (rather than team-based) variation of a gainsharing plan.

Hilcorp Energy Company is one example. The U.S. oil and gas firm pays annual bonuses determined by the company's production rate, midstream income, reserves, and operating costs. "The annual bonus payout is up to 60 percent of salary and is the same number for every employee—no team component, no individual component—one number for the entire organization," explains CEO Greg Lalicker. Another unique organizational reward is the "economic stability dividend" negotiated by the British Columbia provincial government. B.C. government employees receive a negotiated pay increase, but a further increase will occur if the province's economic growth exceeds the rate projected by an independent panel. In a recent four-year period, this organization-wide reward has given B.C. government employees pay increases totalling almost 2 percent beyond their fixed 5.5 percent wage increases.[24]

©Helen H. Richardson/Getty Images

As Canada's largest contractor (and eighth largest in the United States), PCL Construction motivates employees through their involvement in amazing projects and the associated learning opportunities. But the Edmonton-based company is also owned by 90 percent of its salaried employees, creating a further incentive to contribute to the organization's success. "I've seen in other places where people will do their job and leave," says Amrit Virk, a PCL engineer in Richmond, B.C. "Here [at PCL], everyone has a stake in my performance, as well as their own." Another PCL employee explains that "being an employee at PCL as well as being a partial owner of PCL has a compounding effect on the bottom line. Overall PCL success results in a higher dividend for partial owners like me and the people working here."*

* J. Goodman, "Top Construction Execs Reveal Challenges, Opportunities," *Construction Dive,* May 30, 2019; R. Yerema and K. Leung, "Top Employer: PCL Construction," *Canada's Top 100 (2020)* (blog), November 21, 2019, https://reviews.canadastop100.com/top-employer-pcl; The quotation from the anonymous employee is from Glassdoor site for PCL Construction, accessed January 5, 2020.

Employee share ownership plans (ESOPs) are organizational rewards that encourage employees to buy company stock, usually at a discounted price. Some companies, such as PCL Construction, are owned entirely by employees. But motivation exists even where employees own only some shares in the company because the financial reward of ESOPs occurs in the form of dividends and market appreciation of the shares.

While ESOPs involve purchasing company shares, **share options** give employees the right to purchase company shares at a predetermined price up to a fixed expiration date. Here's how share options work: The company might offer its employees the right to purchase 100 shares at $50 per share at any time between two and six years from now. If the share price is, say, $60 two years later, employees could earn $10 from these options, or they could wait up to six years for the share price to rise further. If the share price never rises above $50 during that time, employees are "out of the money," so they would just let the options expire. The intention of share options is to motivate employees to make the company more profitable, thereby raising the company's share price and enabling them to reap the value above the predetermined price of the share options.

Another type of organizational-level reward is the **profit-sharing plan**, in which employees receive a percentage of the previous year's company profits. Lee Valley Tools, the iconic Ottawa-based

employee share ownership plans (ESOPs) A reward system that encourages employees to buy company shares.

share options A reward system that gives employees the right to purchase company shares at a future date at a predetermined price.

profit-sharing plan A reward system that pays bonuses to employees on the basis of the previous year's level of corporate profits.

manufacturer and retailer of quality woodworking and gardening tools, distributes 25 percent of its annual profits to its 850 employees, with the CEO receiving the same amount of profit-sharing bonus as the lowest-paid employee. Hydro Quebec distributes approximately 1 percent of its net profits to a large percentage of its employees. Most goes to 1,500 managers and executives, but engineers and other professionals also receive some of the bonus, calculated as a percentage of their base salary.[25]

Evaluating Organizational-Level Rewards

How effective are organizational-level rewards? Research indicates that ESOPs and share options tend to create an ownership culture in which employees feel aligned with the organization's success.[26] They may also increase firm performance under some circumstances, but the effects are modest.[27] Profit sharing and organization-wide productivity bonuses are also associated with improved productivity, but their effectiveness depends on industry, bonus complexity, and other factors.[28] Profit sharing also has the advantage of automatically adjusting employee compensation with the firm's prosperity, thereby reducing the need for layoffs or negotiated pay reductions during recessions.

One reason why organizational rewards don't improve motivation or performance very much is that employees perceive a weak connection between their individual effort and the determinants of those rewards (i.e., corporate profits or share price). Even in small firms, the company's share price or profitability are influenced by economic conditions, competition, and other factors beyond the employee's immediate control. This low individual performance-to-outcome expectancy suppresses the incentive's motivational effect. However, a few studies have found that ESOPs and other organizational rewards have a more robust influence on motivation and firm performance when employees are also involved in organizational decisions.[29] We discuss employee involvement in the next chapter (Chapter 7).

Improving Reward Effectiveness

LO2

Performance-based rewards have come under attack for discouraging creativity, distancing management from employees, distracting employees from the meaningfulness of the work itself, and being quick fixes that ignore the true causes of poor performance. Studies have even reported that the heightened stress created by very large rewards can reduce, rather than increase, performance.[30] Although these issues have kernels of truth under specific circumstances, they do not necessarily mean that we should abandon performance-based pay. On the contrary, top-performing

companies are more likely to have performance-based (or competency-based) rewards, which is consistent with evidence that these rewards are an important factor in human capital development (see Chapter 1).[31] Reward systems do motivate most employees, but only under the right conditions. Here are some of the more important strategies for improving reward effectiveness.

LINK REWARDS TO PERFORMANCE

Organizational behaviour modification theory and expectancy theory (Chapter 5) both recommend that employees with better performance should be rewarded more than those with poorer performance. Unfortunately, this simple principle seems to be unusually difficult to apply. Few employees see a relationship between job performance and the amount of pay they and their co-workers receive. One survey reported that only 42 percent of employees globally say they think there is a clear link between their job performance and pay. Only 25 percent of Swedish employees and 36 percent of American employees see a pay–performance link. Even employers are doubtful that their pay systems work: only 32 percent of mid-sized Canadian and American employers believe their formal performance pay system actually differentiates pay based on employee performance.[32]

How can companies improve the pay–performance linkage? Inconsistencies and bias can be minimized through gainsharing, ESOPs, and other plans that use objective performance measures. Where subjective measures of performance are necessary, companies should rely on multiple sources of information. Companies also need to apply rewards soon after the performance occurs, and in a large-enough dose (such as a bonus rather than a pay increase), so employees experience positive emotions when they receive the reward.[33]

ENSURE THAT REWARDS ARE RELEVANT

Companies need to align rewards with performance within the employee's control. The more employees see a "line of sight" between their daily actions and the reward, the more they are motivated to improve performance. "We call it return on controllable assets," explains Michael Kneeland, chairman and former CEO of United Rentals. Bonuses at the world's largest equipment rental company are determined by how profitably United managers take care of assets within their control. Higher-level managers earn bonuses based more on overall fleet performance, whereas branch managers are rewarded more for parts and inventory efficiencies at their local operations. "These are things within their control that they are assessed on," says Kneeland.[34] Reward systems

Global Connections 6.2

WHEN REWARDS GO WRONG*

For many years, the paycheques of almost all public transit bus drivers in Santiago, Chile, were determined by the number of fare-paying passengers. This incentive motivated the drivers to begin their route on time, take shorter breaks, drive efficiently, and ensure that passengers paid their fare.

But the drivers' reward system also had horrendous unintended consequences. To take on more passengers, bus drivers aggressively raced with competing buses to the next passenger waiting area, sometimes cutting off each other and risking the safety of people in nearby vehicles. Drivers reduced time at each stop by speeding off before passengers were safely on board. They also left the bus doors open, resulting in many passenger injuries and fatalities. Some drivers drove past waiting areas if there was only one person waiting and completely skipped stops with schoolchildren because those passengers paid only one-third of the regular fare. Studies reported that Santiago's transit buses caused one fatal accident every three days, and that drivers paid per passenger caused twice as many traffic accidents as drivers paid per hour.

Santiago later integrated its public transit system and drivers afterwards earned only hourly pay. Unfortunately,

©David R. Frazier Photolibrary, Inc./Alamy Stock Photo

under this reward system drivers were no longer motivated to ensure that passengers pay the fare (about one-third are freeloaders), and some skipped passenger stops altogether when they were behind schedule or at the end of their workday. Santiago recently changed driver pay once again, instituting a combination of fixed pay and bonuses determined by several performance indicators and reduced fare evasion.

* I. Tiznado et al., "Incentive Schemes for Bus Drivers: The Case of the Public Transit System in Santiago, Chile," *Research in Transportation Economics* 48 (2014): 77–83; R.M. Johnson, D.H. Reiley, and J.C. Muñoz, "'The War for the Fare': How Driver Compensation Affects Bus System Performance," *Economic Inquiry* 53, no. 3 (2015): 1401–19.

also need to correct for situational factors. Salespeople in one region may have higher sales because the economy is stronger there than elsewhere, so sales bonuses need to be adjusted for such economic factors.

USE TEAM REWARDS FOR INTERDEPENDENT JOBS

Team rewards are better than individual rewards when employees work in highly interdependent jobs because it is difficult to measure individual performance in these situations. Nucor Corp. relies on team-based bonuses for this reason; producing steel is a team effort, so employees earn bonuses based on team performance. Team rewards also encourage cooperation, which is more important when work is highly interdependent. Employees also favour team-based work when rewards are determined by team performance. One concern, however, is that employees (particularly the

most productive employees) in Canada and many other low-collectivism cultures prefer rewards based on their individual performance rather than team performance.[35]

ENSURE THAT REWARDS ARE VALUED

It seems obvious that rewards work best when they are valued. Yet companies sometimes make false assumptions about what employees want, with unfortunate consequences. For instance, a manager at one Canadian firm honoured an employee's 25th year of service by buying her a box of Timbits to be shared with other staff. The employee was insulted. She privately complained later to co-workers that she would rather receive nothing than "a piddling box of doughnuts."[36] The solution, of course, is to ask employees what they value. Campbell Soup did this several years ago at its Canadian distribution centres. Executives thought the employees would ask for more money in a special team reward program. Instead, distribution staff said the most valued reward was a leather jacket with the Campbell Soup logo on the back. The leather jackets cost much less, yet were worth much more than the financial bonus the company had intended to distribute.[37]

WATCH OUT FOR UNINTENDED CONSEQUENCES

Performance-based reward systems sometimes have an unexpected—and undesirable—effect on employee behaviours.[38] Many companies have discovered that rewarding employees for how much they produce results in lower quality and more product defects. Employees who work mainly on piece-rate pay experience worse physical and emotional health than employees in similar jobs who earn hourly pay.

Unusual reward systems can sometimes have equally unusual unintended consequences. Consider the following example: A food processing plant discovered that insect parts were somehow getting into the frozen peas during processing. To solve this serious problem, management decided to reward production staff for any insect parts they found in the peas. The incentive worked! Employees found hundreds of insect parts that they dutifully turned in for the bonus. The problem was that many of these insect pieces came from the employees' backyards, not from the production line.[39] Avoiding unintended consequences of rewards isn't easy, but these risks can be minimized by carefully thinking through what the rewards will actually motivate people to do and, where possible, testing the incentives in a pilot project before applying them across the organization.

Financial rewards come in many forms and, as mentioned at the outset of this section, they influence employees in complex ways. But money isn't the only thing that motivates people to join an organization and perform effectively. Employees are usually much more engaged in their work through intrinsic rather than extrinsic sources of motivation. As we discussed in Chapter 5, intrinsic motivation is controlled by the individual and experienced from the activity itself. In other words, companies motivate employees mainly by designing interesting and challenging jobs, which is the topic we discuss next.

Job Design Practices

LO3

How do you build a better job? That question has challenged organizational behaviour experts, psychologists, engineers, and economists for a few centuries. Some jobs have very few tasks and usually require very little skill. Other jobs are immensely complex and require years of experience and

learning to master them. From one extreme to the other, jobs have different effects on work efficiency and employee motivation. The ideal, at least from the organization's perspective, is to find the right combination so that work is performed efficiently but employees are engaged and satisfied.[40] Job design—the process of assigning tasks to a job, including the interdependency of those tasks with other jobs—tries to balance these potentially competing effects of efficiency and motivation. To understand this issue more fully, we'll begin by describing early job design efforts aimed at increasing work efficiency through job specialization.

JOB DESIGN AND WORK EFFICIENCY

By any measure, supermarket cashiers have highly repetitive work. One consulting firm estimated that cashiers should be able to scan each item in an average of 4.6 seconds. Cashiers at five British supermarket chains took between 1.75 and 3.25 seconds to scan each item from a standardized list of 20 products. Along with scanning, cashiers process the payment, move the divider stick, and (in some stores) bag the checked groceries.[41]

Supermarket cashiers perform jobs with a high degree of **job specialization**. Job specialization occurs when the work required to serve a customer—or provide any other product or service—is subdivided into separate jobs assigned to different people. For instance, supermarkets have separate

> **job specialization** The result of division of labour in which work is subdivided into separate jobs assigned to different people.

jobs for checking out customers, stocking shelves, preparing fresh foods, and so forth. Except in the smallest family grocery stores, one person would not perform all of these tasks as part of one job. Each resulting job includes a narrow subset of tasks, usually completed in a short cycle time. *Cycle time* is the time required to complete the task before starting over with another item or client. Supermarket cashiers have a cycle time of about 4 seconds to scan each item before they repeat the activity with the next item. They also have a cycle time for serving each customer, which works out to somewhere between 20 and 40 times per hour in busy stores.

Why would companies divide work into such tiny bits? The simple answer is that job specialization potentially improves work efficiency. It does so in four ways:

- *Fewer skills and less knowledge to learn.* Employees can master specialized jobs more quickly because there are fewer physical and mental skills and knowledge to learn and therefore less time required to become proficient in the job.

- *More frequent practice.* More specialized jobs typically have shorter cycle times. Shorter task cycles give

Global Connections 6.3

JOB SPECIALIZATION AT THE ARSENAL OF VENICE*

The Arsenal of Venice introduced job specialization in the sixteenth century—200 years before economist Adam Smith famously praised this form of job design. Founded in 1104 CE, the state-owned shipbuilder in Italy eventually employed up to 4,000 people in specialized jobs (carpenters, iron workers, warehouse supervisors, etc.) to build ships and accessories (e.g., ropes).

In 1570, the Arsenal had become so efficient through specialization that it built and outfitted 100 ships in two months. The organization even had an assembly line along the waterway where workers apportioned food, ammunition, and other supplies from specially designed warehouses to the newly-built vessels as they travelled past.

©PAINTING/Alamy Stock Photo

* R.C. Davis, "Arsenal and *Arsenalotti:* Workplace and Community in Seventeenth-Century Venice," in *The Workplace before the Factory,* ed. T.M. Safley and L.N. Rosenband (Ithaca, NY: Cornell University Press, 1993), 180–203; R. Crowley, "Arsenal of Venice: World's First Weapons Factory," *Military History,* March 2011, 62–70.

employees more frequent practice with the task, so jobs are mastered more quickly.

- *Less attention residue from changing tasks.* Employees experience "attention residue" after they change from one type of task to another. Specifically, their mental attention lingers on the previous type of work, which slows down performance on the new task. Specialized jobs have fewer and less varied tasks, so there is less changeover and, consequently, less attention residue and productivity loss.[42]

- *Better person–job matching.* Job specialization tends to increase work efficiency by enabling employers to more precisely match employees with specific aptitudes, skills, knowledge, interests, and other characteristics to the jobs for which these talents are best suited.[43]

The benefits of job specialization were noted more than 2,300 years ago by the Chinese philosopher Mencius and the Greek philosopher Plato. Scottish economist Adam Smith wrote 250 years ago about the advantages of job specialization. Smith described a small factory where 10 pin makers collectively produced as many as 48,000 pins per day because they performed specialized tasks. One person straightened the metal, another cut it, another sharpened one end of the cut piece, yet another added a white tip to the other end, and so forth. By comparison, Smith suggested that if each of these 10 people was individually expected to produce complete pins, the group would collectively manufacture no more than 20 pins per day.[44]

SCIENTIFIC MANAGEMENT

One of the strongest advocates of job specialization was Frederick Winslow Taylor, an American industrial engineer who introduced the principles of **scientific management** in the early 1900s.[45] Scientific management consists of a toolkit of activities. Some of these interventions— employee selection, training, goal setting, and work incentives—are common today but

> **scientific management** The practice of systematically partitioning work into its smallest elements and standardizing tasks to achieve maximum efficiency.

were rare until Taylor popularized them. However, scientific management is mainly associated with high levels of job specialization and standardization of tasks to achieve maximum efficiency.

Taylor recommended that the most effective companies should have detailed procedures and work practices developed by engineers, enforced by supervisors, and executed by employees. Even supervisory tasks should be divided among different people (operations, inspection, discipline). Although the accuracy of Taylor's evidence is suspect, scientific management practices do improve work efficiency in many situations. These productivity gains are partly due to training, goal setting, and work incentives, but job specialization quickly became popular in its own right.

PROBLEMS WITH JOB SPECIALIZATION

Frederick Winslow Taylor and his contemporaries focused on how job specialization reduces labour "waste" by improving the mechanical efficiency of work (i.e., matching skills, faster learning, less switchover time). Yet they didn't seem to notice how this extreme job specialization negatively affects employee attitudes and motivation. Some jobs—such as scanning grocery items—are so specialized and repetitive that they become tedious, socially isolating, and cognitively dysfunctional. Specialized jobs with very short cycle times often produce higher employee turnover and absenteeism. Companies sometimes have to pay higher wages to attract job applicants to this dissatisfying, narrowly defined work.[46]

Job specialization affects output quality, but in two opposing ways. On the positive side, employees in specialized jobs tend to produce higher quality output because, as we mentioned earlier, they master their work faster compared to people in jobs with a wide variety of tasks. This higher proficiency explains why specialist lawyers tend to provide better quality service than do generalist lawyers.[47]

However, job specialization also has two negative effects on work quality. First, many jobs (such as supermarket cashiers) are specialized to the point that they are highly repetitive and tedious. Tedious work tends to reduce work attentiveness and motivation, both of which undermine the quality of output. Second, by performing a tiny piece of the overall product or service, employees in specialized jobs have difficulty striving for better quality or even noticing flaws with the work unit's overall output.

Job Design and Work Motivation

LO4

Frederick Winslow Taylor may have overlooked the motivational potential of job characteristics, but it is now the central focus of many job design initiatives.

JOB CHARACTERISTICS MODEL

The motivational potential of the job itself is depicted in the **job characteristics model**, shown in Exhibit 6.2. The model identifies five core job dimensions that produce three psychological states. Employees who experience these psychological states tend to have higher levels of intrinsic motivation, work performance (quality and efficiency), and job satisfaction with the work itself.[48]

> **job characteristics model**
> A job design model that relates the motivational properties of jobs to specific personal and organizational consequences of those properties.

EXHIBIT 6.2 The Job Characteristics Model

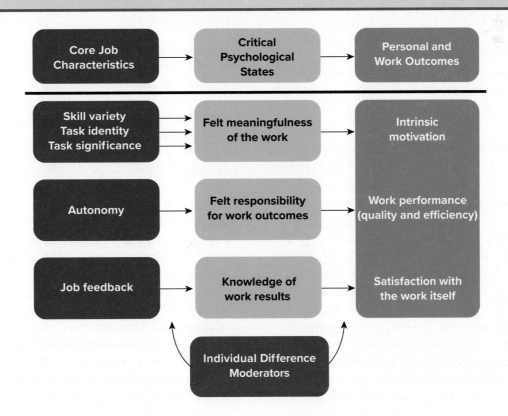

Global Connections 6.4

THRIVING ON ENRICHED JOBS AT SOFTCOM NIGERIA*

Softcom Ltd. is a shining star in Nigeria's emerging technology industry. This success is partly due to the software company's capacity to motivate its 165 employees through highly enriched jobs. Softcom staff are energized by the high task significance of their work, such as a Patient Adherence Program for pharmaceutical company GSK, a digital wallet payment and financial services product (Eyowo), and a nationwide program with digital foundations (called N-Power) to reintroduce 500,000 Nigerians to the labour market.

"The sheer scale, size and audacity of what we're doing here is one of the motivating factors for me to come to work," enthuses Abiola Fajimi, who leads one of Softcom's engineering development teams. "At Softcom, there is always a sense of purpose," adds another Softcom employee. "We are all committed to the goal of solving some of Africa's biggest challenges, and that in itself is what connects everything and everyone."

Along with meaningful work, Softcom employees say they are motivated by the high degree of autonomy in their jobs. "I've realized that maybe just the freedom

©10'000 Hours/Getty Images

is what comforts people. Nobody is ringing the bell for opening time and closing time," says Abiola Fajimi. "There's just that expectation for you to take ownership of your time and ideas. That level of expectation will drive you to find the most productive ways to work."

* "Toluyemi Nathaniel Talks about Being a Woman in the Tech Space with Softcom," BellaNaija (blog), July 2, 2018; Y. Ogunlami, "Nigerian Engineers in Hijabs," *Pulse Nigeria*, August 3, 2018; "75 Softcomers Were Broken into 7 Hackathon Teams," Twitter (Lagos, Nigeria: Softcom, January 24, 2019), https://twitter.com/SoftcomNG/status/1088474546041208832; D.I. Adeleke, "I Visited a Young Nigerian Tech Company Generating Millions in Revenue and This Is What I Learned," *Pulse Nigeria*, January 29, 2019. Some information and quotations are also from Softcom's website: https://softcom.ng/.

Core Job Characteristics

The job characteristics model identifies five core job characteristics. Under the right conditions, employees are more motivated and satisfied when jobs have higher levels of these characteristics:

- *Skill variety.* **Skill variety** refers to the use of different skills and talents to perform tasks within a job. For example, sales clerks who normally only serve customers might be assigned the additional duties of stocking inventory and changing storefront displays.

skill variety The extent to which employees must use different skills and talents to perform tasks within their jobs.

task identity The degree to which a job requires completion of a whole or an identifiable piece of work.

- *Task identity.* **Task identity** is the degree to which a job requires completion of a whole or identifiable piece of work, such as assembling an entire broadband modem rather than just soldering in the circuitry.

- *Task significance.* **Task significance** is the degree to which the job affects the organization and/or larger society. This job characteristic is most strongly felt when employees regularly and directly see how their work affects customers

task significance The degree to which a job has a substantial impact on the organization and/or larger society.

or others in society. As an example, when chefs in one study were able to directly observe the customers who ordered food (and vice versa), they felt more appreciated and, consequently, exerted more effort and felt more satisfied with their job. "When [the customers] can see us [make their food], they appreciate it, and I appreciate that. It makes me want to improve," says a cook who participated in the study.[49] Task significance is often difficult to perceive, however, for employees who work in labs, factories, and offices away from end users. To boost their task significance, some companies arrange occasional meetings in which customers describe how they value products these employees create. This recently occurred at Microsoft Austria, when employees tagged along with their clients (police officers, hospital employees) at the client sites for several days. The purpose of these immersion visits was to gather information about client needs for product development. Yet, Microsoft management also noticed that employees were noticeably "lit up" after these visits because they had become more aware of how their work was important for those clients.[50]

- *Autonomy.* As we learned in Chapter 5, autonomy is a key ingredient for intrinsic motivation.[51] In jobs with high levels of autonomy, employees make their own decisions rather than rely on detailed instructions from supervisors or procedure manuals. These jobs provide freedom, independence, and discretion in scheduling the work and determining the procedures to be used to complete the work.

- *Job feedback.* Job feedback is the degree to which employees can tell how well they are doing from direct sensory information from the job itself. Airline pilots can tell how well they land their aircraft, and road crews can see how well they have prepared the roadbed and laid the asphalt.

Critical Psychological States

The five core job characteristics affect employee motivation and satisfaction through three critical psychological states, shown in Exhibit 6.2. Skill variety, task identity, and task significance directly contribute to the job's *felt meaningfulness of the work*—the belief that one's work is worthwhile or important. Autonomy directly contributes to *felt responsibility for work outcomes*—a sense of being personally accountable for the work outcomes. The third critical psychological state is *knowledge of work results*—an awareness of the work outcomes based on information from the job itself.

Individual Differences

Job design doesn't increase work motivation for everyone in every situation. Employees must have the required skills and knowledge to master the more challenging work. Otherwise, job design tends to increase stress and reduce job performance. The original model also states that employees will be motivated only when they have a high *growth need strength* (the need for personal growth and development— similar to self-actualization).[52] However, research findings have been mixed, suggesting that employees might be motivated by the job no matter how they score on growth needs.[53]

SOCIAL AND INFORMATION PROCESSING JOB CHARACTERISTICS

The job characteristics model overlooks two other types of job features: social characteristics and information processing demands.[54] Two social job characteristics are:

- *Social interaction requirements.* This is the extent to which the job requires employees to interact with co-workers, clients, suppliers, and other stakeholders. Jobs with high social interaction requirements tend to be more motivating because employees need greater use of emotional labour and regulation (see Chapter 4). Social interaction also increases the complexity of the work due to the person's interdependence with these other people (see *task interdependence* in Chapter 8).

- *Social feedback.* A second social characteristic of the job is feedback from others. Jobs that include feedback from people may be just as motivating as jobs that provide feedback from the task itself. Feedback from others may be communicated explicitly through conversation or more implicitly through subtle nonverbal cues.

The other category of job characteristics missing from the job characteristics model is *information processing demands* of the job.[55] Two key information processing demands are:

- **Task variability**. This information processing demand refers to how predictable the job duties are from one day to the next. Task variability increases employee motivation because employees in these jobs have non-routine work patterns; they perform different types of tasks from one day to the next, and don't know which tasks are required until that time. Jobs with low task variability, on the other hand, are less motivating because the work is repetitive; employees perform similar tasks using similar skills in the same way every day.

> **task variability** The degree to which job duties are nonroutine and unpredictable; employees perform diverse tasks from one day to the next because they are faced with unfamiliar and unexpected issues.

- **Task analyzability**. This information processing demand refers to how much the job can be performed using known procedures and rules. Jobs with high task analyzability have low information processing demand because job incumbents rely on established guidelines for most decisions and actions. Consequently, employees are less motivated when performing jobs with high task analyzability. Jobs with low task analyzability, on the other hand, have higher motivational potential because employees need to rely on their creativity and judgment to determine the best courses of action for most

> **task analyzability** The degree to which job duties allow the application of established procedures and rules to guide decisions and behaviour (high analyzability); employee creativity and judgment are necessary to perform jobs with low task analyzability.

tasks. The novel or complex work activities in low task analyzability jobs make it difficult to create fixed procedures and rules.

Task variability and task analyzability will be discussed again in Chapter 8 in the context of task structures for teams and in Chapter 13 when we look at contingencies for designing organizational structures.

JOB DESIGN PRACTICES THAT MOTIVATE

Three main strategies can increase the motivational potential of jobs: frequent job rotation, job enlargement, and job enrichment.

Frequent Job Rotation

One common job design practice is to rotate production employees through two or more jobs each day for the purpose of improving the motivational and physiological conditions of the work. This frequent job rotation is often confused with career development transfers, in which professional and managerial employees move once or twice each year to different jobs.

Canadian companies typically have frequent job rotation to reduce the risk of repetitive strain and heavy lifting injuries. Machine operators at Mauser Packaging Solutions in Aldergrove, B.C., rotate work stations every one to two hours to minimize aches and sprains that occur when working on one machine all day. The packaging firm has achieved one of the province's highest safety designations.[56]

A second benefit of frequent job rotation is that employees learn how to perform multiple jobs. This multiskilling makes it easier for companies to fill positions that are vacant due to vacations and other absences. A third benefit is that employees develop a clearer picture of the production or service process and ways to improve output

quality. In other words, job rotation seems to reverse the performance quality problem that we discussed earlier for job specialization. The fourth potential benefit of frequent job rotation is that employees use a wider variety of skills throughout the workday— their daily work has more skill variety—which potentially improves their motivation and satisfaction.

EYE Lighting International practises frequent job rotation because of these benefits. "Every employee on the factory floor changes positions at least once a day," says an executive at the American subsidiary of Iwasaki Electric of Japan. "The employees love it because they don't get bored in their daily job. Ergonomically, it's good for them because they're not doing the same repetitive task day-in and day-out." The EYE Lighting executive also notes that job rotation gives the company "a tremendous amount of flexibility" when assigning work.[57]

Job Enlargement

Job enlargement is the practice of increasing the number and variety of related tasks assigned to a job held by an employee. This might involve combining two or more complete jobs into one or just adding one or two more tasks to an existing job.[58] Either way, skill variety increases because there are more tasks to perform. Video journalist is an example of an enlarged job. As Exhibit 6.3 illustrates, a traditional news team consists of a camera operator, a sound and lighting specialist, and the journalist who writes and presents or narrates the story. One video journalist performs the tasks of all of these jobs.

Job enlargement offers the same benefits as job rotation because adding more and varied tasks gives employees more skill variety and reduces the risk of repetitive strain injuries. Early research concluded that job enlargement often

> **job enlargement** The practice of increasing the number and variety of related tasks assigned to a job.

EXHIBIT 6.3 Job Enlargement of Video Journalists

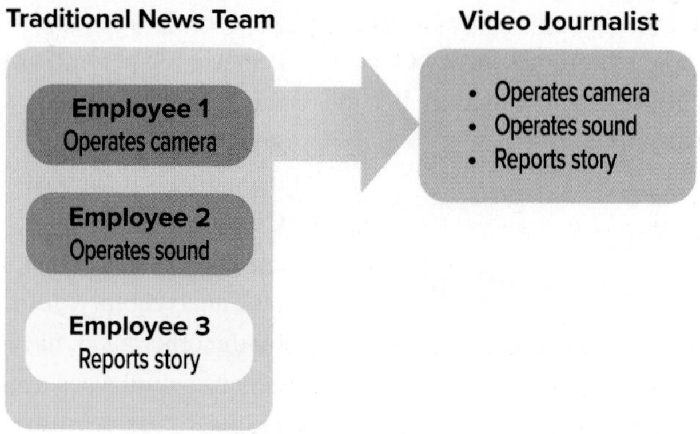

Traditional News Team

Employee 1
Operates camera

Employee 2
Operates sound

Employee 3
Reports story

Video Journalist

- Operates camera
- Operates sound
- Reports story

Debating Point: JOB ROTATION HAS COSTS, NOT JUST BENEFITS

Frequent job rotation—in which employees switch jobs with co-workers one or more times each day—is considered a valuable practice in many production and service job groups. It minimizes health risks from repetitive strain and heavy lifting by relieving employees of that strain for part of the day or, at least, allows them to use different muscle groups in the rotated jobs. Employees in the rotation cycle see a larger part of the production process, so they can more easily identify quality problems and their solutions. Job rotation also increases workforce flexibility by training employees in multiple jobs. Finally, job rotation increases skill variety throughout the workday, which supports at least one motivational component of job design.

These job design benefits are widely recognized and applauded, but less attention seems to be given to the potential problems and limitations of this practice. One concern is that employee task performance may be lower when performing two or more jobs each day, even when each job has a narrow range of tasks.* This performance deficit occurs because employees who perform several jobs have less time to practise and perfect their performance within each job. A related concern is that job rotation produces higher training costs because employees need to learn the procedures for each job in the rotation cluster. Task performance also suffers because the various jobs likely require somewhat different aptitudes, such as finger dexterity or emotional intelligence. Consequently, job rotation does not assign employees as precisely to tasks that fit their natural aptitudes.

Frequent job rotation also likely undermines task performance due to the problem of attention residue.** Attention residue occurs when we continue to think about a previous task after switching over to another task. An employee who worked on inventory at the beginning of a shift might continue to think about inventory decisions and problems after rotating into a cashier position. Consequently, the employee is less mindful of their checkout duties and is more susceptible to errors in that role. The more frequent the job rotation, the more risk that attention residue will undermine performance in the current position.

Job rotation also overlooks the idea that people are more motivated to perform some types of work than others.*** Some enjoy physical work whereas others prefer work that involves social interaction, for example. In fact, people often define themselves by specific jobs, such as being a customer-focused person rather than a number-cruncher. Job rotation might undermine employee motivation because employees are required to perform tasks they don't like and that are misaligned with their self-concept.

A fourth concern is that job rotation might make it more difficult to identify individual performance or accountability for job site maintenance. If several employees switch jobs every two hours, then each job will have three or more job incumbents within one work shift. Nine or more employees would have been in that position over 24 hours in a continuous production system. Unless work output is tagged or time stamped, it becomes difficult to know which of these employees made mistakes, didn't sufficiently prepare the work area for others, and so forth. Aware of their performance anonymity, some employees in job rotation clusters will engage in social loafing—they exert less effort and produce lower quality or quantity output because their work output is less identifiable.****

* S.G.H. Meyerding, "Job Characteristics and Job Satisfaction: A Test of Warr's Vitamin Model in German Horticulture.," *The Psychologist-Manager Journal* 18, no. 2 (2015): 86–107, https://doi.org/10.1037/mgr0000029; R. Su, C. Murdock, and J. Rounds, "Person-Environment Fit.," in *APA Handbook of Career Intervention, Volume 1: Foundations.,* ed. P.J. Hartung, M.L. Savickas, and W.B. Walsh (Washington: American Psychological Association, 2015), 81–98, https://doi.org/10.1037/14438-005.

** S. Leroy and T.M. Glomb, "Tasks Interrupted: How Anticipating Time Pressure on Resumption of an Interrupted Task Causes Attention Residue and Low Performance on Interrupting Tasks and How a 'Ready-to-Resume' Plan Mitigates the Effects," *Organization Science* 29, no. 3 (2018): 380–97, https://doi.org/10.1287/orsc.2017.1184.

*** E.H. Schein and J. Van Maanen, "Career Anchors and Job/Role Planning: Tools for Career and Talent Management," *Organizational Dynamics* 45, no. 3 (2016): 165–73, https://doi.org/10.1016/j.orgdyn.2016.07.002; M. Abessolo, J. Rossier, and A. Hirschi, "Basic Values, Career Orientations, and Career Anchors: Empirical Investigation of Relationships," *Frontiers in Psychology* 8 (2017), https://doi.org/10.3389/fpsyg.2017.01556.

**** B. Latane, K. Williams, and S. Harkins, "Many Hands Make Light the Work: The Causes and Consequences of Social Loafing," *Journal of Personality* 37, no. 6 (1979): 822–32; R.B. Lount and S.L. Wilk, "Working Harder or Hardly Working? Posting Performance Eliminates Social Loafing and Promotes Social Laboring in Workgroups," *Management Science* 60, no. 5 (2014): 1098–1106, https://doi.org/10.1287/mnsc.2013.1820; F. Chen, L. Zhang, and J. Latimer, "How Much Has My Co-Worker Contributed? The Impact of Anonymity and Feedback on Social Loafing in Asynchronous Virtual Collaboration," *International Journal of Information Management* 34, no. 5 (2014): 652–59, https://doi.org/10.1016/j.ijinfomgt.2014.05.001.

produced higher employee motivation, job satisfaction, and work efficiency.[59] However, simply giving employees more tasks falls significantly short of the motivational potential of jobs as defined by the job characteristics model. Instead, a job's full motivational potential occurs when skill variety is combined with more autonomy and job knowledge.[60] In other words, employees are motivated when they perform a variety of tasks *and* have the freedom and knowledge to structure their work to achieve the highest satisfaction and performance. These job characteristics are at the heart of job enrichment.

Job Enrichment

Job enrichment occurs when employees are given more responsibility for scheduling, coordinating, and planning their own work.[61] For example, rather than reading a prepared script for each client interaction, customer service employees are given both training and discretion regarding how long they should engage in conversation with a client and what to say to them. Some call centre agents even have budgets to send small gifts to customers following special conversations. "You never know what they're going to type," says an employee who provides online chat-based

> **job enrichment** The practice of giving employees more responsibility for scheduling, coordinating, and planning their own work.

customer service at Dollar Shave Club. "I have to listen and respond. That's all improv is."[62]

People who perform enriched jobs tend to have higher job satisfaction and work motivation, along with lower absenteeism and turnover. Productivity is also higher when task identity and job feedback are improved. Product and service quality tend to improve because job enrichment increases the jobholder's perceived responsibility and sense of ownership over the product or service.[63]

One way to increase job enrichment is by combining highly interdependent tasks into one job. This *natural grouping* approach occurs in the video journalist job because it naturally groups tasks together to complete an entire product (i.e., a news story). By forming natural work units, jobholders have stronger feelings of responsibility for an identifiable body of work. They feel a sense of ownership and, therefore, tend to deliver higher quality work output. Forming natural work units increases task identity and task significance because employees perform a complete product or service and can more readily see how their work affects others.

©DayOwl/Shutterstock

Telus Communications increased job enrichment among its service technicians by establishing direct client relationships. Previously, clients communicated only with customer service staff at the Canadian telecommunications company; service technicians performed the technical tasks with minimal customer interaction or responsibilities. Now, service technicians are responsible for both technical and customer service activities for their respective assignments. Telus job ads for technicians clearly emphasize these multiple roles: "You will be responsible for installing, maintaining and supporting [Telus products] while driving future growth for TELUS by [providing] exemplary customer service and education to our customers face to face on both new and existing products in the customer's home." As one Telus technician commented: "It's great for me personally, because I have a lot more ownership of the customer relationship."*

* "Putting Customers First Is Critical to Success: Telus," *National Post,* February 4, 2013. The job description is for Digital Home Technician-Greater Vancouver on Telus' job vacancies website (Taleo) on April 7, 2019.

A second job enrichment strategy, called *establishing client relationships,* involves putting employees in direct contact with their clients rather than using another job group or the supervisor as the liaison between the employee and the customer. Establishing client relationships increases task significance because employees see a line-of-sight connection between their work and consequences for customers. By being directly responsible for specific clients, employees also have more information and can make better decisions affecting those clients.[64]

Grouping a natural cluster of tasks and establishing client relationships are common ways to enrich jobs, but the heart of the job enrichment philosophy is to give employees more autonomy over their work. This basic idea is at the heart of psychological empowerment, which we discuss next.

Psychological Empowerment Practices

LO5

Psychological empowerment is a well-known outcome of job enrichment, although it is also influenced by other work conditions as well as employee characteristics. **Psychological empowerment** refers to a perceptual and emotional state in which people experience more self-determination, meaning, competence, and impact regarding their role in the organization.[65]

> **psychological empowerment** A perceptual and emotional state in which people experience more self-determination, meaning, competence, and impact regarding their role in the organization.

- *Self-determination.* Employees feel that they have freedom, independence, and discretion over their work activities.
- *Meaning.* Employees who feel empowered care about their work and believe that what they do is important.
- *Competence.* Employees are confident about their ability to perform the work well and have a capacity to grow with new challenges.
- *Impact.* Employees view themselves as active participants in the organization; that is, their decisions and actions have an influence on the company's success.

SUPPORTING PSYCHOLOGICAL EMPOWERMENT

When leaders say they are "empowering" the workforce, they really mean that they are changing the work environment to support psychological empowerment.[66] A wide variety of workplace conditions—often called *structural empowerment* practices—potentially enhance or support psychological empowerment.[67]

Job characteristics clearly influence the degree to which people feel empowered.[68] Employees are much more likely to experience self-determination when working in jobs with a high degree of autonomy and minimal bureaucratic control. They experience more meaningfulness when working in jobs with high levels of task identity and task significance. Employees experience more self-confidence when working in jobs that allow them to receive feedback about their performance and accomplishments.

Several organizational and work-context factors also influence empowerment.[69] People experience more empowerment in organizations in which information and other resources are easily accessible, and in which employees receive formal training and are encouraged to learn through informal experimentation. Empowerment also requires corporate leaders to trust employees and be willing to take the risks that empowerment creates.

Along with job and workplace conditions, psychological empowerment depends on personal characteristics. In particular, employees must possess the skills and knowledge necessary to perform the work and to handle the additional decision-making requirements.

Psychological empowerment can substantially improve motivation and performance. For instance, restaurant servers with higher empowerment provide better customer service and engage in more organizational citizenship behaviours (specifically, helping other busy servers with their workload).[70] However, organizational and cultural circumstances can limit the extent to which the conditions for empowerment produce feelings of empowerment. A few studies have observed, for example, that increased autonomy and discretion do not result in higher feelings of empowerment in high power distance cultures because this self-determination conflicts with the norms of high power distance (deferring to the boss's power). Whether employees feel empowered when structural conditions for empowerment are present also depends on how much they trust the company's leaders.[71]

Self-Leadership Practices

LO6

The opening case study for this chapter described how Nurse Next Door delegates responsibility and expects everyone

---

Are you empowered as a student? You can discover your level of empowerment as a student by completing this self-assessment in Connect.

to manage themselves—as CEO Cathy Thorpe says: "to be self-led." Dave Burke, Google's vice-president of engineering for the Android operating system, says that Google takes the same approach. "Being laid back is one part of [Google's] culture," says Burke. "The flip side is that we are a very driven company that gets things done. The key to this is employing highly self-motivated people."[72]

Nurse Next Door, Google, and many other firms seek out job applicants who are self-starters, self-motivated, and proactive. These are people who engage in **self-leadership**. They establish the self-direction and self-motivation needed to perform a task without their managers generating that motivation or initiative.[73] Self-leadership includes a toolkit of behavioural activities borrowed from social cognitive theory and goal setting (see Chapter 5). It also includes constructive thought processes that have been extensively studied in sports psychology.

> **self-leadership** Specific cognitive and behavioural strategies to achieve personal goals and standards through self-direction and self-motivation.

Self-leadership consists of several activities, particularly the five identified in Exhibit 6.4. These elements generally follow each other in a sequence: personal goal setting, constructive thought patterns, designing natural rewards, self-monitoring, and self-reinforcement.[74]

PERSONAL GOAL SETTING

Self-leadership refers to leading oneself toward objectives, so the process necessarily begins by setting goals. These goals are self-determined, rather than assigned by or jointly decided with a supervisor. Research suggests that employees are more motivated and perform better when they set their own goals, particularly in combination with other self-leadership practices.[75] Personal goal setting also requires a high degree of self-awareness, because people need to understand their current behaviour and performance before establishing meaningful goals for personal development.

CONSTRUCTIVE THOUGHT PATTERNS

Before beginning a task and while performing it, employees engage in two positive (constructive) thought strategies about that work and its accomplishment: positive self-talk and mental imagery.

Positive Self-Talk

Do you ever talk to yourself? Most of us do, according to a major study of Canadian college students.[76] **Self-talk** refers to any situation in which we talk to ourselves about our own thoughts or actions. The problem is that most self-talk is negative; we criticize much more than encourage or congratulate ourselves. Negative self-talk undermines our confidence and potential to perform a particular task. In contrast, positive self-talk creates a "can-do" belief and thereby increases motivation by raising our self-efficacy and reducing anxiety about challenging tasks.[77] We often hear that professional athletes "psyche" themselves up before an important event. They tell themselves that they can achieve their goal and that they have practised enough to reach that goal. They are motivating themselves through self-talk.

> **self-talk** The process of talking to ourselves about our own thoughts or actions.

Mental Imagery

You've probably heard the phrase "I'll cross that bridge when I come to it!" Self-leadership takes the opposite view. It suggests that we need to mentally visualize specific future behaviours as well as the successful outcomes of those behaviours. In our mind's eye, we practise a task, successfully perform that task, and receive the rewards of that successful performance. This process is known as **mental imagery**.[78]

> **mental imagery** The process of mentally practising a task and visualizing its successful completion.

From our description, you can see that mental imagery has two components. One component involves mentally practising the task, anticipating obstacles to goal accomplishment, and working out solutions to those obstacles before they occur. By mentally walking through the activities required to accomplish the task, we begin to see problems that may occur. We can then imagine what responses would be best for each contingency.[79]

The other part of mental imagery involves visualizing successful completion of the task. You might imagine the

---

EXHIBIT 6.4 Elements of Self-Leadership

Personal goal setting → Constructive thought patterns → Designing natural rewards → Self-monitoring → Self-reinforcement

Global Connections 6.5

OVERCOMING NEGATIVE SELF-TALK*

Sarah Coll is a successful orthopedic surgeon in a country (Australia) where only 4 percent of people in this field are women. She is adept at brushing off the occasional sexist comment about women in this profession. But more difficult to ignore is her own negative self-talk. "When it's your internal monologue, that's much more challenging," she says. "It's so quiet, and so subversive."

Everyone—including world-class athletes, high-performance executives, and successful surgeons—has a natural tendency to engage in negative self-talk more than constructive self-talk. It is one of the great challenges people need to tackle along their journey toward self-leadership.

Coll applies two strategies to minimize negative self-talk. The first is to face the inner voice of self-doubt head-on. "I've made myself accept that that negative self-talk is there, and I've gone to lengths to notice it, which is extremely unpleasant," she admits. "I think that's always the first step to stopping it is to stare it in the eye."

Coll's second strategy is to engage in constructive mental imagery. She thinks about her objective for each surgical procedure, and visualizes performing

©ERproductions Ltd/Blend Images LLC

a technically perfect operation that her entire theatre team enjoys. Coll also consciously praises herself about her success. "Ten years [into my career] I can tell myself I'm offering the patient a world-class procedure," she says. "I'm offering the patient the best they could get in the world."

* Based on information in: M. Dulaney, "Impostor Syndrome can be Your Loudest Critic — Here's How to Silence It," *ABC News (Australia)*, February 27, 2019.

experience of completing the task and the positive results that follow, such as being promoted, receiving a prestigious award, or taking time off work. Visualizing successful performance and its rewards activates energizing emotions, which increases the individual's goal commitment and motivation to complete the task effectively.[80] This is the strategy that Tony Wang applies to motivate himself. "Since I am in sales, I think about the reward I get for closing new business—the commission cheque—and the things it will allow me to do that I really enjoy," explains the sales employee. "Or I think about the feeling I get when I am successful at something and how it makes me feel good, and use that to get me going."[81]

DESIGNING NATURAL REWARDS

Self-leadership recognizes that employees actively "craft" their jobs. To varying degrees, people often have enough discretion in their jobs to make changes that match their needs and preferences, which makes them more satisfying and motivating.[82] Employees develop natural rewards within

their job by expanding tasks that they inherently enjoy, offloading to others tasks they do not enjoy or that exceed their reasonable workload, and changing how tasks are accomplished in ways that make them more developmental and interesting. Employees also produce natural rewards by cognitively reframing the activity, such as by being more vigilant regarding the importance of the work for clients or by more positively viewing difficult tasks as interesting challenges (see Chapter 4 on regulating emotions).

SELF-MONITORING

Self-monitoring is the process of keeping track at regular intervals of one's progress toward a goal by using naturally occurring feedback. Self-monitoring significantly improves employee performance.[83] However, some types of self-monitoring are better than others. Some people can receive feedback from the job itself, such as members of a lawn maintenance crew who can see how they are improving the appearance of their client's property. But many of us are unable to observe our work output so quickly or easily. Instead, feedback mechanisms need to be designed. Salespeople might arrange to receive monthly reports on sales levels in their territory. Production staff might have gauges or computer feedback systems installed so they can see how many errors are made on the production line. Research suggests that people who have control over the timing of performance feedback perform their tasks better than do those with feedback assigned by others.[84]

SELF-REINFORCEMENT

Self-leadership includes *self-reinforcement,* which is part of social cognitive theory described in Chapter 5. Self-reinforcement occurs whenever an employee has control over a reinforcer but doesn't "take" the reinforcer until completing a self-set goal. A common example is taking a break after reaching a predetermined stage of your work. The work break is a self-induced form of positive reinforcement. Self-reinforcement also occurs when you decide to do a more enjoyable task after completing a task that you dislike. For example, after slogging through a difficult report, you might decide to spend time doing a more pleasant task, such as catching up on industry news by scanning websites. One of the challenges with self-reinforcement is the temptation to take the reward before you should. Recent writing has explored situational and emotional strategies to manage these temptations so self-reinforcement remains true to one's original intentions.[85]

EFFECTIVENESS OF SELF-LEADERSHIP

Self-leadership is shaping up to be a valuable applied performance practice in organizational settings. A respectable body of research shows consistent support for most elements of self-leadership.[86] Furthermore, self-leadership strategies seem to work just as well across cultures.[87] Austrian army soldiers who completed a self-leadership training course performed better on physical tests (such as time taken to complete an obstacle course) and educational tests on subjects they were studying at the time, compared to soldiers who didn't take the course. Employees in a mining operation wore safety equipment more frequently after engaging in self-set goals and self-monitoring activities.

By applying mental imagery, supervisors and process engineers in a pulp and paper mill more effectively transferred what they learned in an interpersonal communication skills class back to the job. Studies also indicate that constructive thought processes improve individual performance in various sports activities. Indeed, almost all Olympic athletes rely on mental rehearsal and positive self-talk to achieve their performance goals.[88]

PERSONAL AND SITUATIONAL PREDICTORS OF SELF-LEADERSHIP

Some research suggests that self-leadership behaviours are more frequently found in people with higher levels of conscientiousness and extraversion. People with a positive self-concept evaluation (i.e., self-esteem, self-efficacy, and internal locus of control) are also more likely to apply self-leadership strategies.[89]

The work environment influences the extent to which employees engage in self-leadership. Specifically, self-leadership activities flourish when employees have some degree of autonomy, when they believe their boss is empowering rather than controlling, and when there is a high degree of trust between them. Employees are also more likely to engage in self-monitoring in companies that emphasize continuous measurement of performance.[90] Overall, self-leadership promises to be an important concept and practice for improving employee motivation and performance.

 How well do you practise self-leadership? You can discover how well you practise various self-leadership activities by completing this self-assessment in Connect.

 Do you have a proactive personality? You can discover the extent to which you have a proactive personality by completing this self-assessment in Connect.

Chapter Summary

LO1

Discuss the meaning of money and identify several individual, team, and organizational-level performance-based rewards.

Money (and other financial rewards) is a fundamental part of the employment relationship, but it also relates to our needs, our emotions, and our self-concept. It is viewed as a symbol of status and prestige, as a source of security, as a source of evil, or as a source of anxiety or feelings of inadequacy.

Organizations reward employees for their membership and seniority, job status, competencies, and performance. Membership-based rewards may attract job applicants and seniority-based rewards reduce turnover, but they may discourage poor performers from quitting. Job status–based rewards try to maintain internal equity and motivate employees to compete for promotions. However, they tend to encourage a bureaucratic hierarchy, support status differences, and motivate employees to compete and hoard resources. Competency-based rewards are becoming increasingly popular because they encourage skill development. However, some of these pay systems measure competence subjectively and most increase the costs of learning new skills.

Awards and bonuses, commissions, and other individual performance-based rewards have existed for centuries and are widely used. Many companies are shifting to team-based rewards such as gainsharing plans and to organizational rewards such as employee share ownership plans (ESOPs), share options, and profit sharing. ESOPs and share options create an ownership culture, but employees often perceive a weak connection between individual performance and the organizational reward.

LO2

Describe five ways to improve reward effectiveness.

Financial rewards have a number of limitations, but reward effectiveness can be improved in several ways. Organizational leaders should ensure that rewards are linked to work performance, rewards are aligned with performance within the employee's control, team rewards are used where jobs are interdependent, rewards are valued by employees, and rewards have no unintended consequences.

LO3

List the advantages and disadvantages of job specialization.

Job design is the process of assigning tasks to a job, including the interdependency of those tasks with other jobs. Job specialization subdivides work into separate jobs for different people. This increases work efficiency because employees master the tasks quickly, spend less time changing tasks, require less training, and can be matched more closely with the jobs best suited to their skills. However, job specialization may reduce work motivation, create mental health problems, lower product or service quality, and increase costs through discontentment, absenteeism, and turnover.

LO4

Diagram the job characteristics model and describe three ways to improve employee motivation through job design.

The job characteristics model is a template for job redesign that specifies core job dimensions, psychological states, and individual differences. The five core job dimensions are skill variety, task identity, task significance, autonomy, and job feedback. Jobs also vary in their required social interaction (task interdependence), predictability of work activities (task variability), and procedural clarity (task analyzability). Contemporary job design strategies try to motivate employees through job rotation, job enlargement, and job enrichment. Organizations introduce job rotation to reduce job boredom, develop a more flexible workforce, and reduce the incidence of repetitive strain injuries. Job enlargement involves increasing the number of tasks within the job. Two ways to enrich jobs are clustering tasks into natural groups and establishing client relationships.

LO5

Define psychological empowerment and identify strategies that support empowerment.

Psychological empowerment is a perceptual and emotional state in which people experience more self-determination, meaning, competence, and impact regarding their role in the organization. Individual characteristics seem to have a minor influence on empowerment. Job design is a major influence, particularly autonomy, task identity, task significance, and job feedback. Empowerment is also supported at the organizational level through information, communication, resources, encouraging experimentation, and trust by corporate leaders in their employees.

LO6

Describe the five elements of self-leadership and identify specific personal and work environment influences on self-leadership.

Self-leadership refers to specific cognitive and behavioural strategies to achieve personal goals and standards through self-direction and self-motivation. These strategies include personal goal setting, constructive thought patterns, designing natural rewards, self-monitoring, and self-reinforcement. Constructive thought patterns include self-talk and mental imagery. Self-talk occurs in any situation in which a person talks internally about their own thoughts or actions. Mental imagery involves mentally practising a task and imagining successfully performing it. People with higher levels of conscientiousness, extraversion, and a positive self-concept are more likely to apply self-leadership strategies. Self-leadership also increases in workplaces that support empowerment and have high trust between employees and management.

Key Terms

employee share ownership plans (ESOPs)
gainsharing plan
job characteristics model
job enlargement
job enrichment
job evaluation
job specialization
mental imagery
profit-sharing plan
psychological empowerment

scientific management
self-leadership
self-talk
share options
skill variety
task analyzability
task identity
task significance
task variability

Critical Thinking Questions

1. As a consultant, you have been asked to recommend either a gainsharing plan or a profit-sharing plan for employees who work in the four regional distribution and warehousing facilities of a large retail organization. Which reward system would you recommend? Explain your answer.

2. Which of the performance reward practices—individual, team, or organizational—would work better in improving organizational goals? Please comment with reference to an organization of your choice.

3. Kelowna Tire Corporation redesigned its production facilities around a team-based system. However, the company president believes that employees will not be motivated unless they receive incentives based on their individual performance. Give three reasons why Kelowna Tire should introduce team-based rather than individual rewards in this setting.

4. What can organizations do to increase the effectiveness of financial rewards?

5. Most of us have watched pizzas being made while waiting in a pizzeria. What level of job specialization do you usually notice in these operations? Why does this high or low level of specialization exist? If some pizzerias have different levels of specialization than others, identify the contingencies that might explain these differences.

6. Can a manager or supervisor "empower" an employee? Discuss fully.

7. Describe a time when you practised self-leadership to successfully perform a task. With reference to each step in the self-leadership process, describe what you did to achieve this success.

8. The city manager of a large Canadian municipality wants to reduce supervisory costs by encouraging employees to motivate and manage themselves much of the time. The manager has heard of self-leadership and believes that it may be a key strategy to reduce the number of supervisors in the organization. Discuss the extent to which self-leadership practices among employees would support the city manager's objectives. Also, summarize the content of a training module that would improve any one of the self-leadership practices.

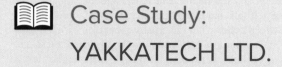 Case Study:
YAKKATECH LTD.

by Steven L. McShane, University of Newcastle (Australia)

YakkaTech Ltd. is an information technology services firm employing 1,500 people across Canada. YakkaTech has a consulting division, which mainly installs and upgrades enterprise software systems and related hardware on the client's site. YakkaTech also has a customer service division, which consists of four customer contact centres serving clients within each region.

Each customer contact centre consists of a half-dozen departments representing functional specializations (computer systems, intranet infrastructure, storage systems, enterprise software systems, customer billing, etc.). These centres typically have more than two dozen employees in each department. When a client submits a problem to the centre using the online form, the message or call is directed to the department where the issue best applies. The query is given a "ticket" number and is assigned to the next available employee in that department. Individual employees are solely responsible for the tickets assigned to them. The employee investigates and corrects the issue, and the ticket is "closed" when the client agrees that the problem has been resolved.

If the client experiences the same problem again, even a few days later, a new ticket is issued and sent to whichever employee is available to receive the ticket. A client's problems are almost always handled by different employees each time, even when the issue is sent to the same department. Furthermore, when a customer centre department is heavily backlogged, clients are redirected to the same department at another regional centre where their problem can be addressed more quickly.

At one time, YakkaTech operated more than a dozen small customer contact centres in each city because client problems had to be diagnosed and resolved on-site. Today, employees can investigate most software and hardware system faults from the centre through remote monitoring systems, rather than personally visiting the client. Consequently, eight years ago YakkaTech amalgamated its customer service operations into four large regional centres. Customer service staff work entirely within the centre. When a client visit is required, the ticket is transferred to an individual or team in the consulting business, who then visits the client.

YakkaTech's customer service business has nearly doubled over the past five years, but with this growth has come increasing numbers of customer complaints regarding poor quality service. Many say that employees seem indifferent to the client's problems. Others have commented on the slow response to their problems where the issue requires involvement of more than one department. Several clients have also complained that they are continually educating YakkaTech's customer service employees about details of their unique IT systems infrastructure.

Another concern is that, until 18 months ago, YakkaTech's voluntary employee turnover rates in the contact centres had risen above the industry average. This increased labour costs due to the expense of recruiting new technical staff as well as lower productivity of new employees. According to results of an employee survey two years ago (as well as informal comments since then), many employees feel that their work is monotonous. Some also said that they feel disconnected from the consequences of their work. A few also complained about ongoing conflicts with people in other departments and the stress of serving dissatisfied clients.

Eighteen months ago, YakkaTech's executive team decided to raise pay rates for its customer service staff to become among the highest in the industry. The assumption was that the high pay rates would improve morale and reduce turnover, thereby reducing hiring costs and improving productivity. In addition, YakkaTech introduced a vested profit-sharing plan, in which employees received the profit-sharing bonus only if they remained with the company for two years after the bonus was awarded. Employees who quit or were fired for just cause before the vesting period forfeited the bonus.

Employee turnover rates dropped dramatically, so the executive team concluded that customer service quality and productivity would improve. Instead, customer complaints and productivity remain below expectations and, in some cases, have worsened. Experienced employees continue to complain about the work. There are a few disturbing incidents where employees are careless at solving client problems or do not bother to forward tickets that should have been assigned to another department. Employee referrals (where staff recommend friends to join the company) have become rare events, whereas at one time they represented a significant source of qualified job applicants. Furthermore, a few executives have recently overheard employees say that they would like to work elsewhere but can't afford to leave YakkaTech.

Discussion Questions

1. What symptom(s) in this case suggest that something has gone wrong?

2. What are the main causes of these symptoms?

3. What actions should YakkaTech executives take to correct these problems?

© 2009 Steven L. McShane

Team Exercise:

IS STUDENT WORK ENRICHED?

Purpose This exercise is designed to help you learn how to measure the motivational potential of jobs and evaluate the extent that jobs should be further enriched.

Instructions (Small Class) Being a student is like a job in several ways. You have tasks to perform, and someone (such as your instructor) oversees your work. Although few people want to be students most of their lives (the pay rate is too low!), it may be interesting to determine how enriched your job is as a student.

1. Students are placed into teams (preferably four or five people).

2. Working alone, each student completes both sets of measures in this exercise. Then, using the guidelines below, they individually calculate the score for the five core job characteristics as well as the overall motivating-potential score for the job.

3. Members of each team compare their individual results. The group should identify differences of opinion for each core job characteristic. They should also note which core job characteristics have the lowest scores and recommend how these scores could be increased.

4. The entire class will then meet to discuss the results of the exercise. The instructor may ask some teams to present their comparisons and recommendations for a particular core job characteristic.

Instructions (Large Class)

1. Working alone, each student completes both sets of measures in this exercise. Then, using the guidelines below, each student individually calculates the score for the five core job characteristics as well as the overall motivating-potential score for the job.

2. Using a show of hands or classroom technology, students indicate their results for each core job characteristic. The instructor will ask for results for several ranges across the scales. Alternatively, students can complete this activity prior to class and submit their results through online classroom technology. Later, the instructor will provide feedback to the class showing the collective results (i.e., distribution of results across the range of scores).

3. Where possible, the instructor might ask students with very high or very low results to discuss their views with the class.

Job Diagnostic Survey							
Circle the number on the right that best describes student work.	Very little		Moderately				Very much
1. To what extent does student work permit you to decide on your own how to go about doing the work?	1	2	3	4	5	6	7
2. To what extent does student work involve doing a whole or identifiable piece of work, rather than a small portion of the overall work process?	1	2	3	4	5	6	7
3. To what extent does student work require you to do many different things, using a variety of your skills and talents?	1	2	3	4	5	6	7
4. To what extent are the results of your work as a student likely to significantly affect the lives and well-being of other people (e.g., within your school, your family, society)?	1	2	3	4	5	6	7
5. To what extent does working on student activities provide information about your performance?	1	2	3	4	5	6	7

Circle the number on the right that best describes student work.	Very inaccurate		Uncertain			Very accurate	
6. Being a student requires me to use a number of complex and high-level skills.	1	2	3	4	5	6	7
7. Student work is arranged so that I do not have the chance to do an entire piece of work from beginning to end.	7	6	5	4	3	2	1
8. Doing the work required of students provides many chances for me to figure out how well I am doing.	1	2	3	4	5	6	7
9. The work students must do is quite simple and repetitive.	7	6	5	4	3	2	1
10. The work of a student is the type where a lot of other people can be affected by how well the work gets done.	1	2	3	4	5	6	7
11. Student work denies me any chance to use my personal initiative or judgment in carrying out the work.	7	6	5	4	3	2	1
12. Student work provides me the chance to completely finish the pieces of work I begin.	1	2	3	4	5	6	7
13. Doing student work by itself provides very few clues about whether I am performing well.	7	6	5	4	3	2	1
14. As a student, I have considerable opportunity for independence and freedom in how I do the work.	1	2	3	4	5	6	7
15. The work I perform as a student is not very significant or important in the broader scheme of things.	7	6	5	4	3	2	1

Scoring Core Job Characteristics: Use the following set of calculations to estimate the motivating-potential score for the job of being a student. Use your answers from the Job Diagnostic Survey that you completed above.

Core Job Characteristics	Calculation	Core Job Characteristics	Calculation
Skill variety (SV)	$\dfrac{\text{Question } 3 + 6 + 9}{3} = $ _____	**Autonomy**	$\dfrac{\text{Question } 1 + 11 + 14}{3} = $ _____
Task identity (TI)	$\dfrac{\text{Question } 2 + 7 + 12}{3} = $ _____	**Job feedback**	$\dfrac{\text{Question } 5 + 8 + 13}{3} = $ _____
Task significance (TS)	$\dfrac{\text{Question } 4 + 10 + 15}{3} = $ _____		

Calculating Motivating-Potential Score (MPS): Use the following formula and the earlier results to calculate the motivating-potential score. Notice that skill variety, task identity, and task significance are averaged before being multiplied by the score for autonomy and job feedback.

$$\left(\frac{SV + TI + TS}{3}\right) \times \text{Autonomy} \times \text{Job Feedback}$$

$$\left(\frac{\underline{} + \underline{} + \underline{}}{3}\right) \times \underline{} \times \underline{} = \underline{}$$

Self-Assessments for Chapter 6

SELF-ASSESSMENT NAME	DESCRIPTION
What is your attitude toward money?	Money is a fundamental part of the employment relationship, but it is more than just an economic medium of exchange. Money affects our needs, our emotions, and our self-concept. People hold a variety of attitudes toward money. One widely studied set of attitudes is known as the "money ethic." This self-assessment estimates how much you budget, respect, and worry about money.
Are you empowered as a student?	Empowerment is a psychological concept represented by feelings of self-determination, meaning, competence, and impact. The empowerment concept applies to people in a variety of situations, not just the workplace. This self-assessment, which specifically refers to your position as a student at your college or university, estimates your level of empowerment overall and on each of its four dimensions.
How well do you practise self-leadership?	Self-leadership refers to specific cognitive and behavioural strategies that people apply to themselves to support the self-direction and self-motivation needed to perform a task. It recognizes that successful employees mostly regulate their own actions rather than rely on others to motivate them. This self-assessment estimates how much you engage in several self-leadership activities.
Do you have a proactive personality?	People differ in how much they try to influence the environments in which they live. Those with a proactive personality take action to change things while less proactive people adapt to the existing situation. Proactive personality is a stable personality characteristic, and is associated with self-leadership. This self-assessment estimates the extent to which your disposition includes the tendency to take personal initiative.

CHAPTER 7

Decision Making and Creativity

LEARNING OBJECTIVES

After reading this chapter, you should be able to:

LO1 Describe the elements of rational choice decision making.

LO2 Explain why people don't apply rational choice decision making when identifying problems/opportunities, evaluating/choosing alternatives, and evaluating decision outcomes.

LO3 Discuss the roles of emotions and intuition in decision making.

LO4 Describe employee characteristics, workplace conditions, and specific activities that support creativity.

LO5 Describe the benefits of employee involvement and identify four contingencies that affect the optimal level of employee involvement.

Atlantic Lottery Corporation (ALC) has become a lightning rod of creativity and responsive decision making. In fact, the Crown corporation was recently recognized as one of the most innovative lottery organizations in North America. ALC has accelerated its creative output by adapting design thinking as its template for decision making. Design thinking is a holistic process that involves multiple stakeholders, embraces ambiguity rather than static solutions, and relies on low-cost prototypes with rapid customer feedback to test ideas.

ALC's product development team discovers problems and opportunities by conducting non-directive immersion interviews to understand the customer experience. "Sometimes we just go to a coffee shop and offer people a gift certificate to sit and give us their ideas and opinions," says

Atlantic Lottery Corporation is one of North America's most innovative businesses in its industry because it applies the design thinking principles of decision making.
©wavebreakmedia/Shutterstock

Jean Marc Landry, Atlantic Lottery vice president of player experience & innovation. "What they tend to give us is rich, deep insight." Great ideas also occur when customers describe their delight with completely different products and services. "Customers will talk about how a company like Uber enriches their lives and we look for ways to apply that thinking to our own products," says Landry.

Rather than hiding unfinished products from public view, ALC takes the "risky" approach by enlisting customers to test prototypes—rough early versions of the product—and quickly seeks their feedback to make further refinements. "Now we start showing products to customers immediately in the design stage. . .we often develop four or five iterations of a product before we produce a final version," says Landry. "We get really quick output from these events because really quickly you can design an idea and have it prototyped within a couple days."

Decision making through design thinking may have sprouted from ALC's product development group, but employees throughout the organization are now learning to apply these principles in their decisions. "Whatever the problem, you can use this approach [design thinking]. It's become a part of our culture," Landry explains. "Those little tests, and those little risks, and those experiences have developed a new mindset in the organization," says Julie LeBlanc Steeves, ALC's manager of player experience.[1]

The executive team at Atlantic Lottery Corporation invested heavily in an emerging model of decision making because the company's future depends on employee decisions that are more responsive and creative. All organizations depend on employees to foresee and correctly identify problems or opportunities, to consider the full range of alternatives, to pick the best alternative based on several relevant factors, and to execute and evaluate those decisions effectively and objectively.

This chapter examines each of these themes. It begins by describing the rational choice view of decision making. Next, the human limitations of rational choice—we call it imperfect rationality—are discussed in the context of how human beings actually make decisions. We also examine the emerging view that decisions consist of a complex interaction of logic and emotion. The latter part of this chapter focuses on two topics that intertwine with decision making: creativity and employee involvement.

Rational Choice Decision Making

LO1

Decision making is the process of making choices among alternatives with the intention of moving toward some desired state of affairs.[2] How can we make effective decisions in organizations? This chapter answers this question by describing different ways of thinking about decision making and by examining several issues at each stage of the decision-making process. We begin this journey by discussing the earliest perspective—**rational choice decision making**—which is the process of using pure

decision making The conscious process of making choices among alternatives with the intention of moving toward some desired state of affairs.

rational choice decision making The process of using pure logic and all available information about all alternatives to choose the alternative with the highest value.

logic and all available information about all alternatives to choose the alternative with the highest value. Choices with the highest value might have the highest expected profitability, customer satisfaction, employee well-being, or some combination of these outcomes.

For most of written history, Western societies have characterized rational choice as an ideal state of decision making. The rational choice view was established 2,500 years ago when Plato and his contemporaries in ancient Greece raised logical debate and reasoning to a fine art.[3] About 400 years ago, Descartes and other European philosophers emphasized that the ability to make logical decisions is one of the most important accomplishments of human beings. In the 1700s, Scottish philosophers refined the notion that the best choice is the one that offers the greatest satisfaction. As we shall discover, these views of rational choice decision making are flawed, but this approach provides a useful foundation to understand this topic.

Rational choice decisions often involve complex calculations of data to produce a formula that points to the best choice. Basically, this formula determines the best alternative by calculating the probability that various outcomes will occur from the choices and the expected satisfaction (valences) from each of those outcomes.[4] We have already described similar calculations of probability and valences in organizational behaviour theories presented earlier in this book, notably the attitude model in Chapter 4 and expectancy theory of motivation in Chapter 5.

The example shown in Exhibit 7.1 will help to explain how the rational choice calculation works.[5] Suppose that you are given the task of choosing a new supplier of a specific raw material used in the company's products. From experience, you estimate that the preferred supplier should provide a high-quality product (+9) with low prices (+6) and on-time delivery (+4).[6] The numbers, which are on a plus or minus 10-point scale in this example, indicate the valence of each outcome, that is, its expected satisfaction or importance. You

---

EXHIBIT 7.1	Rational Choice Decision-Making Example

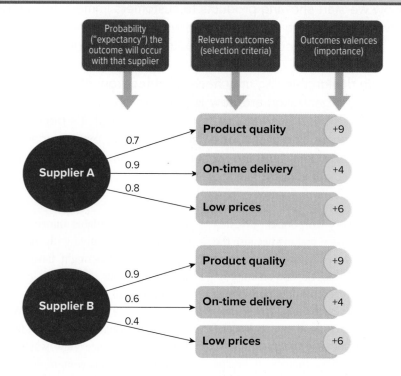

estimate that supplier A has excellent on-time delivery (about 90 percent probability of exceeding the company's expectations), an 80 percent likelihood of offering low prices, and a 70 percent probability of reliably providing a product with exceptional quality. Supplier B has a 90 percent chance of providing very high product quality but a lower likelihood of on-time delivery (60 percent) and of offering the low prices (40 percent).

Which of these two suppliers should be selected? A rational choice decision maker would choose Supplier A because that company would produce the highest expected satisfaction. This composite valence is calculated by multiplying the valence of each outcome by the probability of that outcome occurring, then adding those results across all three outcomes. The supplier with the higher score is the better choice, given available information. The key point from this example is that all rational decisions rely primarily on two pieces of information: (a) the probability that each outcome will occur and (b) the valence or expected satisfaction of each outcome.

RATIONAL CHOICE DECISION PROCESS

Calculating the best alternative is at the heart of rational choice decision making, but it goes hand in hand with the systematic decision process illustrated in Exhibit 7.2.[7] The first step is to identify the problem or recognize an

opportunity. A *problem* is a deviation between the current and the desired situation—the gap between "what is" and "what ought to be." This deviation is a symptom of more fundamental causes that need to be corrected. The "ought to be" refers to goals or performance expectations, which later help to evaluate the selected choice.[8] For instance, if a customer contact centre's goal is to answer incoming client calls within 30 seconds, the problem is the gap between that goal and the actual time the call centre takes to answer most client calls. An *opportunity* is a deviation between current expectations and a potentially better situation that was not previously expected. In other words, an opportunity exists when decision makers discover that some choices may produce better results than current goals or expectations.

The second step involves choosing the best decision process. This is really a meta-decision—deciding how to decide—because it refers to choosing among the different approaches and processes to make the decision.[9] One meta-decision is whether to solve the problem alone or involve others in the process. We'll examine the contingencies of employee involvement in decision making in the last section of this chapter. Another factor in choosing the best decision process is how much time is available to make the decision. A third factor is the degree of decision uncertainty, that is, how difficult it is to estimate outcome probabilities for each alternative. A fourth contingency is whether the problem is routine or novel. Routine problems are *programmed decisions* because the decision maker would have ready-made

EXHIBIT 7.2   Rational Choice Decision Process

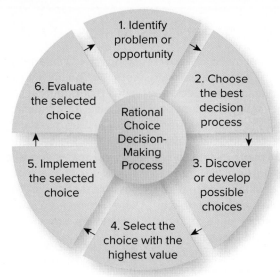

1. Identify problem or opportunity

2. Choose the best decision process

3. Discover or develop possible choices

4. Select the choice with the highest value

5. Implement the selected choice

6. Evaluate the selected choice

Rational Choice Decision-Making Process

alternatives or even solutions learned from the earlier encounters with that problem. In contrast, new or unique problems are *nonprogrammed decisions* because they require the decision maker to work through all steps in the decision model.

The third step in the rational choice decision-making process is to identify and/or develop a list of possible choices. This usually begins by searching for ready-made solutions, such as practices that have worked well on similar problems. If none of the existing solutions is acceptable, then decision makers need to design a custom-made solution or modify an existing one.

The fourth step is to select the best choice by applying the rational choice calculation we described in Exhibit 7.1. To choose the alternative with the greatest expected satisfaction, the decision maker must have information about all possible alternatives and their outcomes. That condition is usually impossible, but the rational choice view of decision making assumes this can be accomplished with ease.

The fifth step in the rational choice decision-making process is to implement the selected alternative. The rational choice view has little to say about this step because it assumes that implementation occurs without any problems. The final step is to evaluate whether the gap has narrowed between "what is" and "what ought to be." Ideally, this information should come from systematic benchmarks so that relevant feedback is objective and easily observed.

PROBLEMS WITH RATIONAL CHOICE DECISION MAKING

The rational choice view seems so logical, yet there are several reasons why it is impossible to apply in reality.[10] Over

the next several pages, we re-examine each step in the rational choice decision-making process, but with more detail about what really happens from the lens of imperfect rationality.

Identifying Problems and Opportunities

LO2

Some sources say that when Albert Einstein was asked how he would save the world in one hour, he replied that most of that time should be spent defining the problem and the rest of that hour solving the problem.[11] Whether Einstein or someone else uttered this advice, it makes the important point that problem identification is not just the first step in decision making; it is arguably the most important step. But problems and opportunities are not clearly labelled objects that appear on our desks. Instead, they are conclusions that we form from ambiguous and conflicting information.[12]

PROBLEMS WITH PROBLEM IDENTIFICATION

Only by forming an accurate understanding of the problem can we move toward a meaningful solution. Unfortunately, the problem identification stage is, itself, filled with problems. Here are five of the most widely recognized concerns.

Solution-Focused Problems

One problem-identification error occurs when decision makers jump to a solution before understanding the problem.[13] This is evident when the problem is described as a veiled

---

Global Connections 7.1

CHOOSING THE BEST DECISION PROCESS AT BOSCH PACKAGING TECHNOLOGY*

To make the best decisions, employees need to know the best decision process for that particular situation. In other words, they need to decide how to decide. German manufacturer Bosch Packaging Technology (BPT) guides its employees through this meta-decision using a matrix that identifies the preferred decision methodology for each type of problem or opportunity.

Some problems, such as deciding how to improve production efficiency, have stable conditions and require fairly simple knowledge and requirements. For these "evident" situations, BPT recommends a decision process that applies lean practices. Lean practices use systematic data collection, testing, and analysis to discover the best ways to improve the current work situation.

For problems that are more complicated and somewhat dynamic or unstable, such as when a client experiences faults with its production technology, Bosch Packaging Technology advocates an agile decision process. Agile practices typically rely on self-directed cross-functional teams to make decisions. BPT teams have diverse knowledge and skills to quickly discover the cause of the problem and implement a customized solution for these types of issues.

Some decisions at Bosch Packaging Technology are highly complex, ambiguous, and novel, such as developing new products and services. In these situations, the

company encourages the design thinking decision process. Design thinking relies on cross-functional, autonomous teams, but employees are more circumspect and reflective about defining the problem or opportunity (whereas the problem is already defined or is quickly determined in other decision processes). BPT's design thinking teams focus on the user experience to gain insight about the problem definition as well as about possible solutions. They also cycle through multiple iterations of prototypes with customer feedback in each cycle to develop the new product or service.

©Hero Images Inc./Alamy Stock Photo

* Based on information at: "The Right Method For Solving The Problem On Hand," Bosch Packaging Technology, accessed January 13, 2020, https://www.boschpackaging.com/company/work-culture.

---

solution, such as: "The problem is that we need more control over our suppliers." This isn't a description of the problem; it is a rephrased statement of a solution to a problem that has little or no diagnosis. The solution-focused mindset recently occurred when the executive who launched Apple's retail stores was subsequently hired as CEO of JCPenney. The executive quickly identified the ailing American retailer's main problem in a way that was actually a veiled solution: It needed to be more like Apple. JCPenney's popular coupons and store sales were abandoned because Apple rarely discounted its products. JCPenney stores were redesigned to look more like Apple stores. The former Apple executive curtly explained that he didn't test these changes because "We didn't test at Apple." Less than two years later, JCPenney's sales had plummeted by one-third and the former Apple executive was out the door.[14]

Why do decision makers fall into the solution-focused problem trap? One reason is that they have been reinforced by

past successes with that solution. When new problems arise, the solution that worked in the past quickly comes to mind before proper problem diagnosis can occur. A second reason is that decision makers are comforted by closure to problems, so they nonconsciously embed a solution in their problem definition. Unfortunately, this solution-focused situation fails to fully diagnose the underlying causes that need to be addressed.

Decisive Leadership

Various studies have found that executives are evaluated by their decisiveness, including how quickly they determine that the situation is a problem, opportunity, or nothing worth their attention.[15] Consequently, many leaders announce problems or opportunities before having a chance to logically assess the situation. The result is often a misguided effort to solve an ill-defined problem by wasting funds on a poorly identified opportunity.

Stakeholder Framing

Employees, suppliers, customers, and other stakeholders present (or hide) information in ways that makes the decision maker see the situation as a problem, opportunity, or steady sailing.[16] Employees point to external factors rather than their own faults as the cause of production delays. Suppliers market their new products as unique opportunities and competitor products as risky choices. Many other stakeholders also frame the situation in ways that decision makers will view as a problem or otherwise. Decision makers fall prey to these constructed realities because they have a need to simplify the daily bombardment of complex and often ambiguous information.

Perceptual Defence

Under some conditions, decision makers either fail to recognize or quickly forget information that threatens the situation. The tendency to engage in perceptual defence (or its variation, called *repressive coping*) is a coping mechanism. It is more likely to occur in decision makers with higher trait anxiety (high neuroticism) and when they have limited options to solve the problem.[17]

Mental Models

Decision makers are victims of their own problem framing due to existing mental models. **Mental models** are knowledge structures that we develop to describe, explain, and predict the world around us.[18] These visual or relational images in our mind of the external world fill in information that we don't immediately see, which fulfils our need to understand and navigate the surrounding environment (see Chapter 3). Many mental images are also prototypes of ideal conditions—they represent models of how things should be. Unfortunately, these mental models can blind us from seeing unique problems or opportunities because they produce a negative evaluation of things that are dissimilar to the mental model. If an idea doesn't fit the existing mental model of how things should work, then it is quickly dismissed as unworkable or undesirable.

mental models Knowledge structures that we develop to describe, explain, and predict the world around us.

IDENTIFYING PROBLEMS AND OPPORTUNITIES MORE EFFECTIVELY

Recognizing problems and opportunities will always be a challenge, but one way to improve the process is by becoming aware of the five problem identification biases just described. For example, by recognizing that mental models restrict a person's perspective of the world, decision makers are more motivated to consider other perspectives of reality. Along with increasing their awareness of problem identification flaws, leaders require considerable willpower to resist the temptation of looking decisive when a more thoughtful examination of the situation is warranted.

A third way to improve problem identification is to create a norm of "divine discontent." Decision makers with this mindset are never satisfied with current conditions, no matter how successful that situation may be, so they more actively search for problems and opportunities.[19] Fourth, employees can minimize problem identification errors by discussing the situation with other people, particularly those with different experiences and backgrounds. It is much easier to discover blind spots in problem identification when listening to how others perceive the situation. Opportunities also become apparent when outsiders explore this information from their different mental models.

Searching for, Evaluating, and Choosing Alternatives

The rational choice view of decision making assumes that decision makers rely on logic to evaluate and choose alternatives. It also assumes that they have well-articulated and agreed-upon organizational goals, that they efficiently and simultaneously process facts about all alternatives and the consequences of those alternatives, and that they choose the alternative with the best possible outcomes.

Nobel Prize–winning organizational scholar Herbert Simon questioned these assumptions a half century ago. He argued that people engage in **bounded rationality** because they process limited and imperfect information and rarely try to select the best choice.[20] Bounded rationality is the most widely known theory questioning the rational choice view, but it is not alone. Other *imperfect rationality* theories identify imperfections in how people form preferences, how they short-circuit the decision-making process, and how their choices are distorted by faulty heuristics and other perceptual biases.[21] Overall, as Exhibit 7.3 illustrates, organizational behaviour theories identify several ways that human decision making differs from rational choice assumptions. Let's look at these differences in terms of goals, information processing, and maximization.

bounded rationality The view that people are bounded in their decision-making capabilities, including access to limited information, limited information processing, and tendency toward satisficing rather than maximizing when making choices.

PROBLEMS WITH GOALS

Goals are a critical component of all decisions because they establish "what ought to be" and, therefore, provide a standard against which each alternative is evaluated. The rational

Global Connections 7.2

MENTAL MODEL MYOPIA ALMOST REJECTED SEINFELD*

One of the most successful sitcoms (situational comedies) in history almost didn't make it to prime time. *Seinfeld* was soundly rejected by executives at Fox network and almost had the same fate at NBC, which aired the pilot episode.

The show's near-miss with success occurred because it was a new form of television comedy, one that was profoundly different from the deeply reinforced mental models that network executives relied on to identify future program gems. Popular sitcoms wove humour into a storyline that often addressed current ethical or social issues, whereas *Seinfeld* was a show about nothing—just humorous dialogue in "moments" of everyday life (such as going to a laundromat or waiting too long for dinner at a restaurant). In the minds of network executives, lead characters in successful sitcoms had emotional attachments or conflicts and displayed occasional heroism. *Seinfeld*'s characters lived separate lives, had minimal emotional relationships, and were hardly heroic.

NBC executive Rick Ludwin is widely credited with saving *Seinfeld* from the dustbin. In his early days, Ludwin had done stand-up comedy and read *Saturday Night Live* scripts, so he recognized the potential of *Seinfeld*'s unique humour. Also, Ludwin was responsible for late-night programming, not sitcoms, so he didn't

rely on the outdated mental models that blinkered sitcom executives regarding what a successful program should look like. Seinfeld scriptwriters Larry David and Jerry Seinfeld also lacked experience in the sitcom industry, which enabled them to produce scripts that forged new territory.

"Larry and Jerry had never written a sitcom, and my department had never developed one," says Rick Ludwin. "We were a good match, because we didn't know what rules weren't supposed to be broken."

©PictureLux/The Hollywood Archive/Alamy Stock Photo

* P. Rosenthal, "NBC Executive Stands Apart by Taking Stands," *Chicago Tribune*, August 21, 2005; L. Mellor, "Seinfeld's Journey from Flop to Acclaimed Hit," *Den of Geek* (London, November 7, 2014), http://www.denofgeek.com (accessed March 6, 2018); S. Austerlitz, "How 'Seinfeld' Revolutionized the Sitcom," *IndieWire* (February 28, 2014), http://www.indiewire.com (accessed March 7, 2018); N. J. Nigro, *Seinfeld FAQ: Everything Left to Know About the Show About Nothing* (Milwaukee: Applause Theatre and Cinema Books, 2015); A. Grant, *Originals: How Non-Conformists Change the World* (New York: Viking, 2016), 44–46.

choice view assumes that organizational goals are clear and agreed upon, yet in reality they are often ambiguous or in conflict with each other.[22] Ambiguous goals make it difficult to know if a particular choice has greater value to the organization. For example, "satisfy customer needs" may refer to providing efficient service, a variety of services, more personalized service, and other possibilities. Conflicting goals also create havoc with rational decision making. When goals conflict, decision makers need to determine which goal gets priority. Unfortunately, they rarely have a guide map to determine which goals take precedence.

PROBLEMS WITH INFORMATION PROCESSING

The rational choice approach assumes that decision makers evaluate all alternatives and all of their features and outcomes

simultaneously using unbiased estimates of valences and outcome probabilities (illustrated earlier in Exhibit 7.1). In reality, people sequentially (not all at the same time) evaluate only a few alternatives and only a handful of characteristics.[23] For example, there are hundreds of smartphone models on the market and dozens of features to consider in each model, yet smartphone purchasers typically pay attention to a small subset of phones and a handful of characteristics or expected outcomes of those products.

Furthermore, purchasers rarely line up all of their limited range of alternatives at the same time to select the best one. Instead, they typically evaluate alternatives sequentially using an **implicit favourite**. An implicit favourite is a preferred alternative that becomes the benchmark

> **implicit favourite** A preferred alternative that the decision maker uses repeatedly as a comparison with other choices.

EXHIBIT 7.3 Rational Choice Assumptions versus Organizational Behaviour Findings about Choosing Alternatives

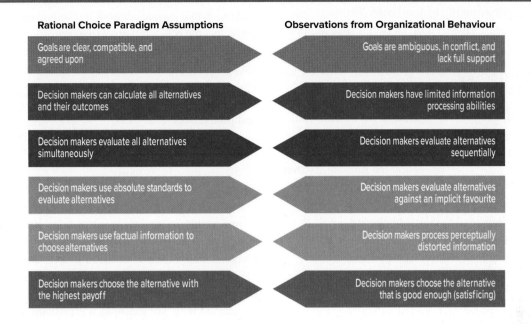

Rational Choice Paradigm Assumptions	Observations from Organizational Behaviour
Goals are clear, compatible, and agreed upon	Goals are ambiguous, in conflict, and lack full support
Decision makers can calculate all alternatives and their outcomes	Decision makers have limited information processing abilities
Decision makers evaluate all alternatives simultaneously	Decision makers evaluate alternatives sequentially
Decision makers use absolute standards to evaluate alternatives	Decision makers evaluate alternatives against an implicit favourite
Decision makers use factual information to choose alternatives	Decision makers process perceptually distorted information
Decision makers choose the alternative with the highest payoff	Decision makers choose the alternative that is good enough (satisficing)

against which other choices are compared. The preferred alternative is called "implicit" because decision makers don't explicitly decide this initial preference and often aren't even aware of their favouritism.[24]

There are several reasons why decision makers follow a sequential evaluation process using an implicit favourite. First, it is often difficult to have all alternatives available at the same time.[25] It is impossible to collect information about every smartphone product all at once, so the most favourable phone found early in your search becomes the implicit favourite when considering phones that you investigate later. Similarly, when filling a job vacancy, some job candidates would have found other employment before the later applicants have applied or been interviewed. Thus, hiring managers evaluate applicants against an implicit favourite (the best candidate interviewed so far).

Second, human beings have a natural preference for comparing two choices rather than systematically evaluating many alternatives at the same time.[26] An implicit favourite assists this process by serving as an anchor comparator for evaluating the other choices. A third reason is that people are cognitive misers. They minimize mental effort by quickly forming a preferred alternative (their implicit favourite), and then looking mainly for evidence that supports the preferred choice. In other words, they engage in **confirmation bias** (see Chapter 3).[27]

confirmation bias The process of screening out information that is contrary to our values and assumptions, and to more readily accept confirming information.

The fourth reason why decision makers compare alternatives sequentially against an implicit favourite is the human need for cognitive consistency and coherence. People want to ensure that their choice is the emotional preference (implicit favourite) as well as the best logical choice. This alignment of rationality with preference and choice occurs most easily through sequential analysis of alternatives against an implicit favourite because decision makers subtly change valences and probabilities. Specifically, they nonconsciously ignore or underweight positive features of alternatives relative to the implicit favourite, and change the importance of factors to support the favourite. If you discover that the camera on the phone you prefer to buy (your implicit favourite) has worse reviews than the camera on another smartphone, you nonconsciously make camera quality less important (at least while making the decision) and discount the accuracy of the reviews about camera quality. Ultimately, you distort valences (importance of camera quality) and probabilities (likelihood that the other phone's camera is superior) so your implicit favourite remains the rational best choice.[28]

Biased Decision Heuristics

The cornerstone of rational choice decision making is to calculate the alternative with the highest expected satisfaction. However, psychologists Amos Tversky and Daniel Kahneman discovered that human beings have built-in *decision heuristics* that automatically distort those calculations. Three of the most widely studied heuristic biases are anchoring and adjustment, availability, and representativeness:[29]

- **Anchoring and adjustment heuristic**. This heuristic states that we are influenced by an initial anchor point and do not sufficiently move away from that point as new information is provided.[30] The anchor point might be an initial offer price, initial opinion of someone, or initial estimated probability that something will occur. This bias is associated with the problem we described a few paragraphs ago, namely that human beings tend to compare alternatives rather than evaluate them purely against objective criteria. Therefore, if someone requests a high initial price for a car we want to buy, we naturally compare—and thereby anchor—our alternative offer against that high initial price.

  > **anchoring and adjustment heuristic** A natural tendency for people to be influenced by an initial anchor point such that they do not sufficiently move away from that point as new information is provided.

- **Availability heuristic**. The availability heuristic is the tendency to estimate the probability of something occurring by how easily we can recall that event. Unfortunately, how easily we recall something is due to several factors, not just how often it occurs (probability).[31] For instance, we easily remember recent events as well as emotional events (such as earthquakes and shark attacks), which causes us to overestimate the probability or frequency of recent or traumatic events.

  > **availability heuristic** A natural tendency to assign higher probabilities to objects or events that are easier to recall from memory, even though ease of recall is also affected by non-probability factors (e.g., emotional response, recent events).

- **Representativeness heuristic**. This heuristic states that we pay more attention to whether something resembles (is representative of) something else than on more precise statistics about its probability.[32] Suppose that one-fifth of the students in your class are in engineering and the others are business majors. Statistically, there is a 20 percent chance that any individual in that class is an engineering student. Yet, if one student looks and acts like a stereotype of an engineer, we tend to believe the person is an engineer even though there is much stronger and more reliable statistical evidence that they are a business major.

  > **representativeness heuristic** A natural tendency to evaluate probabilities of events or objects by the degree to which they resemble (are representative of) other events or objects rather than on objective probability information.

PROBLEMS WITH MAXIMIZATION

One of the main assumptions of rational choice decision making is that people are both motivated and able to identify and select the best alternative (maximization). Yet rather than aiming for maximization, people engage in **satisficing**—they choose the first alternative that exceeds a standard of acceptance for their needs and preferences.[33] In short, they choose an alternative that is "good enough."

> **satisficing** Selecting an alternative that is satisfactory or "good enough," rather than the alternative with the highest value (maximization).

Satisficing is usually necessary because choosing the absolutely best choice (maximization) requires complete and perfect information. This is impossible in reality because information is imperfect, costly, or can't be found at all when the decision is made. Hypothetically, even if decision makers could receive complete and perfect information, they wouldn't have the time or cognitive capacity to input and analyze the mammoth amount of complex data. For example, it is difficult to choose the best possible smartphone because of the large number of choices, the many features to consider for each choice, the numerous consequences of each choice (time to first breakdown, system update limits, etc.), and the ambiguous information about many of those features and outcomes. Under those conditions, maximization leads to a spiral of endless trade-offs among the various choices, which can actually result in worse decisions and less satisfied decision makers.[34]

Studies report that people like to have choices, but deciding from among dozens of alternatives and many outcomes for each alternative is cognitively and emotionally draining. Consequently, decision makers satisfice as a way to minimize cognitive effort.[35] They also reduce cognitive effort by discarding a large selection of alternatives using easily identifiable factors (colour, size, etc.) and by evaluating them using only a handful of possible outcomes (selection criteria).

People who face a large number of alternatives often opt for a decision strategy that is even less cognitively challenging than satisficing: They don't make any decision at all! In one study, grocery store customers saw one of two jam-tasting booths. Thirty percent of consumers who visited the booth displaying six types of jam purchased one of those products. In contrast, only 3 percent of customers who saw the booth displaying 24 types of jam made a purchase. The larger number of choices discouraged them from making any decision. Other studies revealed similar results in decisions about chocolates, term essays, and pension plan investment options.[36]

EVALUATING OPPORTUNITIES

Opportunities are just as important as problems, but the process of acting on an opportunity differs from the process of solving a

©Nerthuz/Shutterstock

People avoid making choices in decisions that have too many alternatives. This is evident when new employees are asked to register for their pension plan and choose one type of investment. More employees delay or avoid pension plan registration when they face dozens of investment options, even though signing up would give them tax benefits, company contributions to that plan, and long-term financial security. Studies have found that employees are significantly more likely to register for the company pension plan when they are given only two or three initial investment options, such as a growth fund, balanced fund, and capital stable investment. After they have signed up, employees are presented with further investment choices for their pension plan.*

* S. Iyengar, *The Art of Choosing* (New York: Hachette, 2010), 194–200; J. Beshears et al., "Simplification and Saving," *Journal of Economic Behavior & Organization* 95 (2013): 130–45.

problem. Decision makers seldom evaluate several alternatives when they find an opportunity; after all, the opportunity *is* the solution, so why look for others! An opportunity is usually experienced as an exciting and rare revelation, so decision makers tend to develop an emotional attachment to the opportunity. Unfortunately, this emotional preference motivates decision makers to apply the opportunity and short-circuit any detailed assessment of its potential benefits. Furthermore, studies indicate that decision makers tend to personalize an opportunity (i.e., it belongs to them) rather than remain impartial evaluators of the opportunity. This ownership mindset makes impersonal analysis of the opportunity even more difficult.[37]

Emotions and Intuition in Decision Making

LO3

EMOTIONS AND MAKING CHOICES

The previous sections of this chapter explained why people are far from perfect at rational decision making. However,

Herbert Simon and other scholars who studied imperfect rationality neglected to mention another problem: The rational choice model completely ignores the effect of emotions in human decision making. Just as both the rational and emotional brain centres alert us to problems, they also influence our choice of alternatives.[38] Emotions affect the evaluation of alternatives in three ways.

Emotions Form Early Preferences

The emotional marker process described earlier in this book (Chapters 3, 4, and 5) shapes our preferences for alternatives before we consciously evaluate them. Our brain very quickly attaches specific emotions to information about each alternative, and our preferred alternative is strongly influenced by those initial emotional markers.[39] Of course, logical analysis also influences which alternative we choose, but it requires strong logical evidence to change our initial preferences (initial emotional markers). Yet even logical analysis depends on emotions to sway our decision. Specifically, neuroscientific evidence says that information produced from logical analysis is tagged with emotional markers, and it is those emotional markers, not logical analysis, that motivate us to choose or avoid a particular alternative. In other words, emotions, not rational logic, energize us to make the preferred choice. In fact, people with damaged emotional brain centres have difficulty making choices.

Emotions Change the Decision Evaluation Process

Moods and specific emotions influence the *process* of evaluating alternatives.[40] For instance, we pay more attention to details when in a negative mood, possibly because a negative mood signals that there is something wrong that requires attention. When in a positive mood, on the other hand, we pay less attention to details and rely on a more programmed decision routine. This phenomenon explains why executive teams in successful companies are often less vigilant about competitors and other environmental threats.[41] Research also suggests that when angry, decision makers rely on stereotypes and other shortcuts to speed up the decision process. Anger also makes them more optimistic about the success of risky alternatives, whereas the emotion of fear tends to make them less optimistic. Overall, emotions shape *how* we evaluate information, not just which choice we select.

Emotions Serve as Information When We Evaluate Alternatives

The third way that emotions influence the evaluation of alternatives is through a process called "emotions as information." This refers to the idea that we listen in on our emotions to acquire guidance when making choices.[42] The emotions-as-information effect is similar to having a temporary improvement in emotional intelligence. Most emotional experiences remain below the level of conscious awareness, but people actively try to be more sensitive to these subtle emotions when making a decision.

When buying a new car, for example, you not only logically evaluate each vehicle's features; you also try to gauge your emotions when visualizing what it would be like to own each of the cars on your list of choices. Even when you have information about each vehicle (purchase price, fuel efficiency, maintenance costs, resale value, etc.), you are swayed by your emotional reaction and actively try to sense that emotional response when thinking about the decision. Everyone pays attention to their emotions to some degree when choosing alternatives. This phenomenon ties directly into our next topic, intuition.

INTUITION AND MAKING CHOICES

Do you get a gut feeling when something isn't quite right? Or perhaps a different emotional experience occurs when you sense an opportunity? These emotional events potentially (but not necessarily) indicate your **intuition**—the ability to know when a problem or opportunity exists and to select the best course of action without conscious reasoning.[43] Some people pay more attention to their gut feelings whereas others are more comfortable with decisions based on logic and data analysis. However, intuition and logical analysis are not opposites and never completely replace each other. Both are always present in human decision making.[44]

> **intuition** The ability to know when a problem or opportunity exists and to select the best course of action without conscious reasoning.

Intuition is both an emotional experience and a rapid nonconscious analytic process. The gut feelings we experience are emotional signals that have enough intensity to make us consciously aware of them. These signals warn us of impending danger or motivate us to take advantage of an opportunity. Some intuition also directs us to preferred choices relative to other alternatives in the situation.

All gut feelings are emotional signals, but not all emotional signals are intuition. Emotional signals are valid intuition when they rely on mental models that reasonably and accurately depict the situation where we sense the problem or opportunity. Intuition involves rapidly comparing our observations with these "templates of the mind." Positive or negative emotions are produced, depending on how well that situation fits our mental model.[45] For example, when chess masters quickly scan a chessboard, they experience emotional signals that the chess configuration poses an opportunity or threat. These emotional signals motivate closer observation to logically confirm the situation and to act on it. Thus, intuition signals that a problem or opportunity exists long before conscious rational analysis has occurred.

However, not all emotional signals are intuition because they are not always based on well-grounded mental models. Instead, we sometimes compare the current situation to more remote templates, which may or may not be relevant. A new employee might feel confident about relations with a supplier, whereas an experienced employee senses potential problems. The difference is that the new employee relies on poorly developed or more remote templates from other experiences that might not fit this situation. Thus, the extent

What is your preferred decision-making style? You can discover your preference for logical or intuitive decision making by locating this self-assessment in Connect.

by the NUMBERS

Intuition versus Data Analysis: Crunch Your Hunch*

78% of 250 senior business leaders in Canada agree or somewhat agree that a business leader must go with their gut and intuition when an important decision needs to be made quickly.

67% of 1,300 CEOs of companies in the 11 largest economies say that within the past three years they have overlooked data-based insights and models because they contradicted their intuition.

33% of 207 C-suite executives in Canada say their decision making is highly data driven (compared to 39% of 1,900 executives globally).

65% of 207 C-suite executives in Canada say their next big decision will likely be based on human judgment (compared to 59% of 1,900 executives globally).

41% of 250 senior business leaders in Canada say they rely too much on intuition and not enough on data and analytics when making decisions (53% said they rely too much on data and analytics).

©Robert Lucian Crusitu/Shutterstock

* "Intuition in the Age of Big Data," Smith School of Business, Queen's University, *Smith Business Insight* (blog), June 21, 2016, https://smith.queensu.ca/insight/content/intuition-in-the-age-of-big-data.php; "Big Decisions™ Global Data and Analytics Survey 2016: Canadian Insights" (Toronto: PricewaterhouseCoopers, July 2016); "Growing Pains: 2018 Global CEO Outlook" (Zurich: KPMG International, May 2018).

to which our gut feelings represent intuition in a specific situation depends on our level of experience in that setting. The key message here is that some emotional signals are not intuition, so gut feelings alone shouldn't guide our decisions.

So far, we have described intuition as an emotional experience (gut feeling) and a process in which we compare the current situation with well-established templates of the mind. Intuition also relies on *action scripts* that speed up our response to pattern matches or mismatches.[46] Action scripts are programmed decisions; they shorten the decision-making process by jumping from problem identification to selection of a solution. Action scripts are also generic, so we need to consciously adapt them to the specific situation.

MAKING CHOICES MORE EFFECTIVELY

It is very difficult to get around the human limitations of making choices, but a few strategies can minimize these problems. One important discovery is that decisions tend to have a higher failure rate when leaders are decisive rather than contemplative about the available options. Of course, decisions can also be ineffective when leaders procrastinate in

decision making, but research indicates that a lack of logical evaluation of alternatives is a greater concern. This recommendation does not suggest that we ignore intuition; rather, it suggests that we use it in combination with careful analysis of relevant information. By systematically assessing alternatives against relevant factors, decision makers minimize the implicit favourite and satisficing problems that occur when they rely on general, subjective judgments. For instance, one recent study of patient flow decisions in Canadian hospitals found that the best choices occurred through systematic discovery and evaluation of alternative interventions. Yet most hospital leaders and committees did the opposite; they selected a myriad of pet projects and a patchwork of multiple alternatives without evaluating or comparing their likely effectiveness.[47]

A second recommendation is to revisit important problems and opportunities at another time so information is reviewed when decision makers are in different moods and have allowed time for their initial emotions to subside. For example, if you sense that your team is feeling too confident when making an important decision, you might decide to have the committee revisit the decision a few days later when its members are thinking more critically.

A related strategy is **scenario planning,** which is a disciplined method for imagining possible futures.[48] It typically involves thinking about what would happen if a significant environmental condition changed and what the organization should do to anticipate and react to such an outcome.

Scenario planning is a useful vehicle for choosing the best solutions under possible scenarios long before they occur, because alternative courses of action are evaluated without the pressure and emotions that occur during real emergencies.

Implementing and Evaluating Decisions

IMPLEMENTING DECISIONS

Implementing decisions is often skipped over in most writing about decision making. Yet leading business writers emphasize that execution—translating decisions into action—is one of the most important and challenging tasks in the decision-making process.[49] Implementing decisions is mainly about organizational change, which we discuss in Chapter 15, but also relates to motivation (Chapter 5), influence processes (Chapter 10), leadership (Chapter 12), and several other themes throughout this book.

EVALUATING DECISIONS

Contrary to the rational choice view, decision makers aren't completely honest with themselves when evaluating the effectiveness of their decisions. Earlier in this chapter, we explained that decision makers engage in *confirmation bias* to support their implicit favourite and to maintain consistency in their preference and decision. This bias continues long after the decision has been made; during the evaluation stage it is also known as *postdecisional justification*.[50] Decision makers ignore or underemphasize negative outcomes of the choice they made and overemphasize new information about its positive features. Postdecisional justification gives people an excessively optimistic evaluation of their decisions, but only until they receive very clear and undeniable information to the contrary.

ESCALATION OF COMMITMENT

Another reason why decision makers don't evaluate their decisions very well is due to **escalation of commitment**—the tendency to repeat an apparently bad decision or allocate more resources to a failing course of action.[51] Why are decision makers led deeper and deeper into failing projects? Several explanations have been identified and discussed over the years, but the four main influences are self-justification effect, self-enhancement effect, prospect theory effect, and sunk costs effect.

Self-Justification Effect

People try to convey a positive public image of themselves. In decision making, this self-justification typically involves appearing to be rational and competent. Decision makers are therefore motivated to demonstrate that their choices will be successful, which includes continuing to support a decision even when it is not having the desired outcomes. In contrast, pulling the plug symbolizes the project's failure and the decision maker's incompetence. This self-justification effect is particularly evident when decision makers are personally identified with the project, have staked their reputations to some extent on the project's success, and have low self-esteem.[52]

Self-Enhancement Effect

People have a natural tendency to feel good about themselves—to feel luckier, more competent, and more successful than average—regarding things that are important to them (see Chapter 3).[53] This **self-enhancement** supports a positive self-concept, but it also increases the risk of escalation of commitment. When presented with evidence that a project is in trouble, self-enhancement biases our interpretation of the information as a temporary aberration from an otherwise positive trend line. And when we eventually realize that the project isn't going as well as planned, we continue to invest in the project

because our self-enhancement overestimates the probability that we can rescue the project. Self-justification and self-enhancement often occur together, but they are different mechanisms. Self-justification is a deliberate attempt to maintain a favourable public image, whereas self-enhancement nonconsciously distorts our perceptions so problems are recognized later, and our probabilities of success are biased so we continue to invest in the losing project.[54]

Prospect Theory Effect

Prospect theory effect is the tendency to experience stronger negative emotions when losing something of value than positive emotions when gaining something of equal value. This is also known as *loss aversion* because we have a stronger motivation to avoid losses than to risk receiving equally valuable gains. The stronger negative valence of a potential loss motivates escalation of commitment because stopping a project is a certain loss, which evokes more negative emotions than the uncertainty of success associated with continuing to fund the project. Given the choice, decision makers choose escalation of commitment, which is the less painful option at the time.[55]

Sunk Costs Effect

People inherently feel motivated to invest more resources in projects that have high sunk costs—the value of resources already invested in the decision.[56] This contrasts with the rational choice view, which states that investing resources should be determined by expected future gains and risk, not by the size of earlier resources invested in the project. A variation of sunk costs is time investment. Time is a resource, so the more time decision makers have devoted to a project, the more motivated they are to continue investing in that project. Finally, sunk costs can take the form of closing costs, that is, the financial or nonfinancial penalties associated with shutting down a project. As with other forms of sunk costs, the higher the closing costs, the more motivated decision makers are to engage in escalation of commitment.

Escalation of commitment is usually framed as poor decision making, but adding more resources to a losing project may be beneficial under some circumstances.[57] Indeed, many breakthroughs have occurred because of the decision maker's persistence and optimism. Continuing with a losing project may be prudent when the cost overruns are small relative to the project cost, the benefits of success are high, and the rewards of a successful project are received quickly. Some experts also suggest that throwing more money into a failing project may be a logical attempt to further understand an ambiguous situation. By adding more resources, the decision maker gains new information about the effectiveness of these funds, which provides more feedback about the project's future success. This strategy is particularly common where the project has high closing costs.

EVALUATING DECISION OUTCOMES MORE EFFECTIVELY

Several strategies have been identified to minimize escalation of commitment and postdecisional justification.[58]

- *Change the decision maker.* Decision evaluation biases are often minimized when those who made the original decision are replaced by those who later evaluate and act on that evaluation. This strategy works best when the decision evaluators have limited alliance with those who made the decision. It minimizes the self-justification effect because the person responsible for evaluating the decision is not connected to the original decision.

- *Create a stop-loss.* Publicly establishing a preset level at which the decision is abandoned or re-evaluated forces the decision maker to abandon the investment if its value falls or cost overruns increase beyond a set level. The problem with this solution is that conditions are often so complex that it is difficult to identify an appropriate point to abandon a project.

- *Seek factual and social feedback.* At some point, even the strongest escalation and confirmation bias effects collapse when the decision maker is faced with systematic and clear feedback about the project's failings. In addition, the decision maker can benefit from ongoing feedback from several (preferably impartial) people. Feedback from others might result in earlier awareness of problems. By relying on advice from several people, the decision maker might also have less psychological attachment to any recommendation to cancel the project.

- *Change the decision maker's mindset.* There is growing evidence that decision makers are less likely to engage in escalation of commitment if they change their mindset regarding the situation. In one recent study, a 15-minute meditation recording reduced escalation of commitment by refocusing the decision maker's attention away from the negative emotions of the project's past financial losses. A second study found that decision makers were more likely to terminate failing projects when they focused on growing the business rather than on maintaining past obligations or preventing losses in past decisions.

Creativity

LO4

As the opening case study to this chapter described, creativity has become a central feature of decision making at Atlantic Lottery Corporation. **Creativity** refers to the development of original ideas that make a socially recognized contribution.[59] It exists when imagining opportunities, such as how a company's expertise might be redirected to untapped markets. Creativity is present when developing alternatives, such as discovering new products or services, or recognizing problems that are not easily apparent from traditional perspectives. Creativity also helps us to develop and choose alternatives by visualizing the future in different ways and figuring out how each choice might be useful or a liability in those scenarios. In short, creativity is valuable throughout the decision-making process.

creativity The development of original ideas that make a socially recognized contribution.

EXHIBIT 7.4   The Creative Process Model

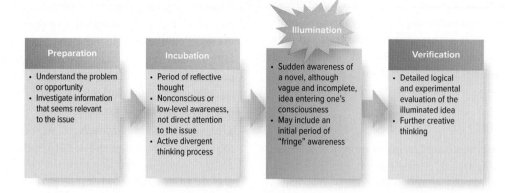

Preparation	Incubation	Illumination	Verification
• Understand the problem or opportunity • Investigate information that seems relevant to the issue	• Period of reflective thought • Nonconscious or low-level awareness, not direct attention to the issue • Active divergent thinking process	• Sudden awareness of a novel, although vague and incomplete, idea entering one's consciousness • May include an initial period of "fringe" awareness	• Detailed logical and experimental evaluation of the illuminated idea • Further creative thinking

THE CREATIVE PROCESS

How does creativity occur? That question has puzzled experts for centuries and has fascinated scientists who saw how creative thinking contributed to their own important discoveries. Notably, more than a century ago, German physicist Hermann von Helmholtz gave a public talk describing the process that led to his innovations (energy physics, instruments for examining eyes, and many others). A few decades later, London School of Economics professor Graham Wallas built on Helmholtz's ideas to construct the four-stage model shown in Exhibit 7.4.[60] To this day, this model is still considered the most elegant representation of the creative process.

The first stage is *preparation*—the process of investigating the problem or opportunity. Preparation involves developing a clear understanding of what you are trying to achieve through a novel solution and then actively studying information seemingly related to the topic. It is a process of developing knowledge and possibly skills about the topic. The second stage, called *incubation,* is the period of reflective thought. We put the problem aside, but our mind is still working on it in the background.[61] The important condition here is to maintain a low-level awareness by frequently revisiting the problem.

divergent thinking Reframing a problem in a unique way and generating different approaches to the issue.

Incubation assists **divergent thinking**—reframing the problem in a unique way and generating different approaches to the issue. Divergent thinking breaks us away from existing mental models so that we can apply concepts or processes from completely different areas of life. This contrasts with *convergent thinking,* which involves calculating the conventionally accepted "right answer" to a logical problem.

The invention of Velcro illustrates how divergent thinking occurs.[62] In the 1940s, Swiss engineer Georges de Mestral had just returned home from a walk with his dog through the countryside when he noticed that his clothing and the dog's fur were covered in burrs. While struggling to remove the barbed seeds, de Mestral engaged in divergent thinking by recognizing that the adhesion used by burrs could be used to attach other things together. It took another dozen years of hard work, but de Mestral eventually perfected the hook-and-loop fastener, which he trademarked as Velcro.

Illumination (also called *insight)* the third stage of creativity, refers to the experience of suddenly becoming aware of a unique idea.[63] Wallas and others also suggest that this stage begins with a "fringe" awareness before the idea fully enters our consciousness. Illumination is often visually depicted as a light bulb, but a better image would be a flash of light or perhaps a briefly flickering candle—these bits of inspiration are fleeting and can be quickly lost if not documented. For this reason, many creative people keep a journal or notebook nearby so they can jot down their ideas before they disappear. Also, flickering ideas don't keep a particular schedule; they might come to you at any time of day or night.

Illumination presents ideas that are usually vague, roughly drawn, and untested. Therefore, the essential final stage of creativity is *verification,* whereby we flesh out the illuminated ideas and

---

How well do you engage in divergent thinking? You can discover the extent to which you have divergent thinking by locating this self-assessment in Connect.

©SFIO CRACHO/Shutterstock

Employees at Halifax-based Bluedrop Training and Simulation engage in divergent thinking to design and develop state-of-the-art training and simulation products. Tushar Sehgal describes one such incident. The Bluedrop technical project manager and a co-worker were shopping at Home Depot when they saw a black pipe coupling product. They soon realized that it could become the hand tracking mechanism they needed for Bluedrop's prototype of the world's first virtual-reality helicopter crew trainer. "It was one of those 'aha' moments," says Sehgal. "We put that around our wrists as a joke and then realized, wait, this is going to work." The employees bought two of them, drilled holes, attached markers, and found out that the item worked nicely. "There [are] many stories like that inspiration coming from random parts and random shopping trips," Sehgal observes.*

*Based on information in: T. Ayres, "Helicopter Simulator Accompanies CH-148 Cyclones," *Halifax Chronicle-Herald,* February 24, 2018, B1.

subject them to systematic and detailed experimentation and evaluation. This stage often calls for further creativity as the ideas evolve into finished products or services. Thus, although verification is labelled the final stage of creativity, it is really the beginning of a long process of creative decision making toward development of an innovative product or service.

CHARACTERISTICS OF CREATIVE PEOPLE

Everyone is creative, but some people have a higher potential for creativity. Four of the main characteristics that give individuals more creative potential are intelligence, persistence, knowledge and experience, and a cluster of personality traits and values representing independent imagination (see Exhibit 7.5).

- *Cognitive and practical intelligence.* Creative people have above-average cognitive intelligence to synthesize and analyze information as well as apply their ideas.[64] They recognize the significance of small bits

of information and are able to connect them in ways that few others can imagine. They also have *practical intelligence*—the capacity to evaluate the potential usefulness of their ideas.

- *Persistence.* Creative people have persistence, which is based on a high need for achievement, a strong motivation from the task itself, and moderate or higher self-esteem. Persistence is vital because people need this motivation to continue working on and investing in a project in spite of failures and advice from others to quit. In fact, people have a general tendency to dismiss or criticize new ideas, so creative people need persistence to withstand these negative social forces.[65]

- *Knowledge and experience.* Creative people require a foundation of knowledge and experience to discover or acquire new knowledge.[66] However, this expertise is a double-edged sword. As people acquire specific knowledge and experience, their mental models about that topic tend to become more rigid. They are less adaptable to new information or rules about that knowledge

EXHIBIT 7.5   Characteristics of Creative People

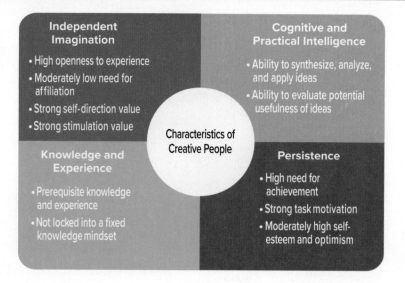

domain. Some writers suggest that expertise also increases "mindless behaviour" because it reduces the tendency to question why things happen.[67] To overcome the limitations of expertise, some corporate leaders like to hire people from other industries and areas of expertise. For instance, when the late Geoffrey Ballard, founder of Burnaby, B.C.–based Ballard Power Systems, hired a chemist to develop a better battery, the chemist protested that he didn't know anything about batteries. Ballard replied: "That's fine. I don't want someone who knows batteries. They know what won't work."[68]

- *Independent imagination.* Creative people possess a cluster of personality traits and values that support an independent imagination: high openness to experience, moderately low need for affiliation, and strong values around self-direction and stimulation.[69] Openness to experience is a Big Five personality dimension representing the extent to which a person is imaginative, curious, sensitive, open-minded, and original (see Chapter 2). Creative people have a moderately low need for affiliation so they are less embarrassed when making mistakes. Self-direction includes the values of creativity and independent thought; stimulation includes the values of excitement and challenge. Together, these values form openness to change—representing the motivation to pursue innovative ways of solving problems (see Chapter 2).

ORGANIZATIONAL CONDITIONS SUPPORTING CREATIVITY

Intelligence, persistence, expertise, and independent imagination represent a person's creative potential, but the extent to which these characteristics produce more creative output depends on how well the work environment supports the creative process.[70] Several job and workplace characteristics have been identified in the literature, and different combinations of situations can equally support creativity; there isn't one best work environment.

One of the most important conditions for creativity is a **learning orientation**.[71] A learning orientation is a set of collective beliefs and norms that encourage employees to question past practices, to learn new ideas, to experiment putting ideas into practice, and to view mistakes as part of the learning process. "My attitude is that a failure should be greeted with an 'Attaboy, attagirl, we've learnt something; move forward, let's innovate with that learning," says Anthony Viel, CEO of Deloitte Canada. "If you don't create that culture, then fear can cripple or stifle innovation within your organization."[72]

> **learning orientation** A set of collective beliefs and norms that encourage people to question past practices, learn new ideas, experiment putting ideas into practice, and view mistakes as part of the learning process.

Do you have a creative personality? You can discover the extent to which you have a disposition for creative thinking by locating this self-assessment in Connect.

Global Connections 7.3

SUPPORTING CREATIVITY FOR EVERYONE AT ESTÉE LAUDER*

Creativity is key to Estée Lauder's success as the global leader in the prestige beauty industry. "To be clear, creativity is at the center of our innovation models," emphasizes Fabrizio Freda, CEO of the New York–based cosmetics and skin care firm. "So while we listen to the consumer and study trends, the majority of our effort is directed at inventing things that don't exist."

Estée Lauder's creative focus begins with the view that creativity is important in every job. "Creativity is about solving problems, and who doesn't solve problems on a daily basis?" asks Mark Polson, Estée Lauder's vice president of creativity and business innovation. "Therefore, everybody by virtue of their innate problem solving skills, is creative."

Along with encouraging every employee to be creative, Estée Lauder supports creativity by nurturing a learning orientation culture. Mark Polson explains that he and other Estée Lauder leaders "do that by creating an environment that doesn't punish failure, but looks to learn from the lessons of failure."

Estée Lauder also supports creativity through training programs and creative activities. For instance, the company hosts design thinking sessions with product developers, engineers, customer-facing employees, and other groups. "We bring them together, put the problem on the table, break them into teams and just let them come up with ideas and put prototypes together. Then we evaluate them, and iterate and do more prototypes," Polson explains.

©TEA/123RF

* J. Anixter, "Mark Polson, Creativity and Estee Lauder—The IX Interview," *Innovation Excellence* (blog), February 16, 2015, https://www.innovationexcellence.com/blog/2015/02/16/mark-polson-creativity-and-estee-lauder-the-ix-interview/; "Estée Lauder Companies: A Home for Creative Talent," *The Business of Fashion,* February 2, 2017; L.R. Rublin, "Shaking Up the Prestige Beauty Business," *Barron's,* June 1, 2018; S. Castellanos, "Estée Lauder Revamps IT, Merging Beauty Business With Innovation," *The Wall Street Journal,* March 20, 2019.

A second contributor to creativity is job design, specifically task significance and autonomy. People are more creative when they believe their work improves the organization or society and when they have the freedom to pursue novel ideas without bureaucratic delays.[73] Creativity is about changing things, and change is possible only when employees have the autonomy and authority to experiment.

Along with a learning orientation and enriched jobs, creativity blossoms through open communication (enabling employees to share ideas and information) and sufficient resources. Organizations also nurture creativity by providing a comfortable degree of job security, which explains why creativity suffers during times of downsizing and corporate restructuring.[74] Some companies also support creativity by designing nontraditional workspaces, such as a unique building design or unconventional office areas.[75] Google is one example. The Internet innovator has funky offices in several countries that include hammocks, slides, brightly painted walls, and privacy spaces that look like gondolas and beehives.

To some degree, creativity also improves with support from leaders and co-workers.[76] Generally, creativity thrives when leaders have an appealing vision of the future and encourage employees to experiment with new ways to achieve that vision (see transformational leadership in Chapter 12). Co-worker support can improve creativity, but a few studies suggest that competition among co-workers improves creativity under some conditions. Similarly, it isn't clear how much pressure should be exerted on employees to produce creative ideas. Extreme time pressures are well-known creativity inhibitors, but lack of pressure doesn't seem to produce the highest creativity, either.

ACTIVITIES THAT ENCOURAGE CREATIVITY

We have described two cornerstones of creativity in organizations: employing people with strong creative potential and providing a work environment that supports creativity. The third cornerstone consists of activities that help employees think more creatively. Four types of creativity-building activities are: redefine the problem, associative play, cross-pollination, and design thinking.

Redefine the Problem

Redefining the problem is a potentially powerful way to unleash creative thinking. One approach is to revisit projects that have been set aside. After a period of neglect, these projects might be seen in new ways.[77] You can also see the problem from different perspectives by asking co-workers unfamiliar with the issue to explore the problem. You state the objectives and give some facts and then let the other person ask questions to further understand the situation. By verbalizing the problem, listening to questions, and hearing what others think, you are more likely to form new perspectives on the issue.[78]

Associative Play

Associative play literally involves playing games or being challenged in unusual ways.[79] One form of associative play is to engage in playful activities, such as completing a treasure hunt in which the clues are ambiguous rhymes. Creative thinking emerges naturally from these playful activities and then carries over to work-related problem solving. A second variation is challenging participants to create something new with a specific purpose (e.g., cleaning cutlery) using existing unrelated products (e.g., blow dryer and electric toothbrush). These activities exercise the mind to break out of traditional mental models about existing products and services.

A third variation of associative play, called *morphological analysis,* involves systematically investigating all combinations of characteristics of a product, service, or event, and then looking at the feasibility of each combination.[80] This exercise encourages people to carefully examine combinations that initially seem nonsensical. For instance, employees at a dairy company might look at all combinations of yogurt-based products by considering the contents (fruit, low fat, etc.), occasion (breakfast, dessert, etc.), target group (children, older adults, etc.), size, and packaging. A novel, yet commercially successful, innovation may emerge from the resulting list.

Cross-Pollination

Cross-pollination occurs when people from different areas of the organization exchange ideas or when new people are brought into an existing team.[81] This may occur by arranging formal social gatherings, encouraging happenstance interactions with people from other work areas or, as a few firms do, asking employees to move their desks every few months to another location with employees who are only acquaintances.

Creative agency Mother is famous for encouraging creativity through cross-pollination at its offices in London, New York, and elsewhere. "Everyone sits together around the same table, and every six weeks, on 'Move Monday,' we all change places," explains Mother's creative director and head of strategy. The company produces a new seating plan where employees are redistributed; most of the London crew sit around a mammoth concrete slab that accommodates more than 100 people. "There's no rules in terms of seniority or discipline, and it means that everybody gets to know each other and ideas can be cross-pollinated."[82] Cross-pollination highlights the fact that creativity rarely occurs alone. Some creative people may be individualistic, but most creative ideas are generated through teams and informal social interaction.

Design Thinking

The opening case study for this chapter described how Atlantic Lotteries Corporation is transforming the way it makes decisions and develops new products by applying design thinking principles and practices. **Design thinking** is a human-centred, solution-focused creative process that applies both intuition and analytical thinking to clarify problems and generate innovative solutions. Contrary to its label, design thinking isn't just for people in design jobs. Rather, it is a tangible scaffolding that guides all employees through the decision-making process using creative thinking, logical analysis, empathy, and intuition.

> **design thinking**
> A human-centred, solution-focused creative process that applies both intuition and analytical thinking to clarify problems and generate innovative solutions.

There are several models and guidelines for design thinking, but one of the most respected frameworks identifies the four rules outlined in Exhibit 7.6 and summarized below:[83]

- *The Human Rule.* Design thinking is a team activity. It depends on collaboration and co-creation among several people with diverse knowledge and experiences, so the issue and its possible solutions are viewed from several angles. Design thinking is also human-centred because designers need to empathize with clients and end users and involve them in the design process.[84] Client involvement facilitates redefinition of the original problem statement (such as the client's briefing) and more dynamic discovery and refinement of potential solutions. As ideas and prototypes develop, clients and end users can provide real-time feedback on the product experience.

- *The Ambiguity Rule.* Creativity and experimentation are possible only when there is ambiguity in the problem and its potential solutions.[85] Therefore, design thinkers preserve ambiguity rather than seek clarity too quickly. Designers do not assume the client's original problem

EXHIBIT 7.6 Four Rules of Design Thinking

Design thinking rule	Description
Human Rule	• Involve several people so the issue and possible solutions are viewed from several angles. • Include clients and end users to enable an iterative process of problem identification and solution development.
Ambiguity Rule	• Preserve ambiguity rather than seek clarity too quickly. • Question and refine the stated problem. • Develop more than one solution to the problem.
Redesign Rule	• Review past solutions to understand how those inventions tried to satisfy human needs. • Use foresight tools to imagine better solutions for the future.
Tangible Rule	• Build several low-cost prototypes to test ideas. • Don't analyze alternatives at a purely conceptual level. • Tolerate failure; embrace a learning orientation.

statement is accurate. Instead, the stated problem is questioned and refined with the client. Design thinkers also avoid the natural temptation to solve the problem too quickly with one solution. Instead, they continually question possible solutions even after one seems likely. They also develop more than one solution to the problem.

• *The Re-Design Rule.* No creative solution is completely original. Therefore, designers review past solutions to understand how well they worked as well as their flaws and limitations. Designers then use foresight tools to imagine better solutions for the future. Environmental scanning, context mapping, and other foresight tools help designers visualize possible futures, such as emerging trends and changes to conditions and rules of the future context.

• *The Tangible Rule.* The design thinking process devotes less time to planning and more time to action. Designers build several low-cost prototypes of their ideas rather than analyze those ideas at a purely conceptual level.[86] Prototypes represent a rich form of communication that does not exist in conceptual planning. One design thinking mantra is "fail fast, fail often," meaning that prototypes are made quickly and frequently along the journey to the final result. This statement also recognizes that design thinking tolerates failure and embraces a learning orientation.

Employee Involvement in Decision Making

LO5

Watson, IBM's cognitive technology platform, received a substantial boost when the company launched Cognitive

Build. This three-month event relied on various forms of employee involvement to determine how Watson's artificial intelligence could assist a myriad of corporate and societal objectives. More than 8,000 teams of IBM employees explored the technology's application for data security, air quality monitoring, anti-bullying, social banking, and other themes. One-third of those teams progressed to Cognitive Build's next stage of a completed proposal with some prototyping. IBM employees each received $2,000 in virtual money through the company's internal funding system to "invest" in one or more projects. In effect, they voted on the best projects. The 50 teams with the most virtual investment dollars were given three weeks to build their prototypes, which were then presented to a panel of experts.[87]

IBM's Cognitive Built challenge applied various forms of *employee involvement*—activities in which employees participate in and influence decisions about their jobs, work units, or organization.[88] Employee involvement exists when employees actually influence decisions to some degree. The distinction is that some situations give employees a voice, yet their ideas and arguments are never actually considered by management or others who control the decisions.

Employee involvement has become a natural process in every organization, but the level of involvement varies with the situation.[89] A low level of involvement occurs when employees are individually asked for specific information but the problem is not described to them. Somewhat higher involvement occurs when the problem is described and employees are asked individually or collectively for information relating to that problem.

Moving further up the involvement scale, the problem is described to employees, who are collectively given

Debating Point: SHOULD ORGANIZATIONS PRACTISE DEMOCRACY?

Most organizational experts recommend some degree of employee involvement, but a few go further by proposing that organizations should operate like democracies rather than hierarchical fiefdoms. Organizational democracy consists of the highest form of involvement, whereby employees have real institutionalized control—either directly or through representation—over organizational decisions. In addition, no one in a democratic enterprise holds higher authority except where such power is explicitly granted by the others (such as through employee election of the company's leaders). Democracy also gives all organizational members protection against arbitrary or unjust decisions (such as protection against being fired without cause).

Some readers might view workplace democracy as an extreme way to run an organization, but advocates point out that it is the principle on which many societies have operated for centuries and most others aspire to. Democratic governance has been established in several high-profile and successful companies, such as Semco SA and W. L. Gore & Associates, as well as many employee-owned firms and worker co-operatives. Legislation in several countries (particularly in continental Europe) requires companies to give employees control over some organizational decisions through works councils or board membership.**

Advocates point out that, as a form of participation, workplace democracy can improve the quality of organizational decisions and employee commitment to those decisions. Indeed, democracy inherently promotes shared leadership (where everyone should be a leader in various ways), which is increasingly recommended for improved decision making and organizational effectiveness. Democratic enterprises might also be more flexible and innovative. Rather than obediently following management's standard operating procedures, employees in democratic organizations have the opportunity—and likely the expectation—to adapt and experiment with new work practices as circumstances change. This form of organization also encourages more organizational learning.***

A final argument is that the democratic enterprise is ethically superior to the traditional hierarchical organization.****

It respects individual rights and dignity, more fully satisfies the standards of ethical conduct, and is more likely than traditional management to adopt the multiple stakeholder approach expected by society. Indeed, some European governments have debated the notion that organizational democracy is a potentially effective way to minimize corporate wrongdoing because it actively monitors top decision makers and continually holds them accountable for their actions.

However, the democratic enterprise model has a number of vocal advocates, but few practitioners. There is somewhat more employee involvement in most organizations today than a few decades ago, but it is still far from the democratic ideal. Most firms operate with the traditional model that management retains control and employees have few rights. There may be reasons for this intransigence. One argument against organizational democracy is that employees have a contractual rather than ownership relationship with the organization. Legally (and possibly morally) they have no right to assume citizenship rights or control over the business. A second consideration is that employees might emphasize their own interests to the detriment of other stakeholders. In contrast, traditional organizations give management an explicit obligation to serve multiple stakeholders to ensure the organization's survival and success.

Another concern is that workplace democracy might dilute accountability. Although moderate levels of employee involvement can improve decision-making quality and commitment, there is a real risk that no one will take responsibility for decisions when everyone has a say in them. In addition, democracy often results in slower decision making, which could lead to a lethargic corporate response to changes in the external environment. Finally, the democratic enterprise model presumes that employees want to control their organizations, but some research suggests that employees prefer a more moderate level of workplace involvement. For this reason (and others noted above), employee-owned companies often maintain a more traditional hierarchical worker–management relationship.*****

* J.R. Foley and M. Polanyi, "Workplace Democracy: Why Bother?," *Economic and Industrial Democracy* 27, no. 1 (2006): 173–91; P.A. Woods and P. Gronn, "Nurturing Democracy," *Educational Management Administration & Leadership* 37, no. 4 (2009): 430–51.

** R. Semler, *The Seven-Day Weekend* (London, UK: Century, 2003); G. de Jong and A. van Witteloostuijn, "Successful Corporate Democracy: Sustainable Cooperation of Capital and Labor in the Dutch Breman Group," *Academy of Management Executive* 18, no. 3 (2004): 54–66.

*** K. Cloke and J. Goldsmith, *The End of Management and the Rise of Organizational Democracy* (San Francisco, CA: Jossey-Bass, 2003); L. Gratton, *The Democratic Enterprise: Liberating Your Enterprise with Freedom, Flexibility, and Commitment* (London, UK: FT Prentice-Hall, 2004).

**** P.E. Slater and W.G. Bennis, "Democracy Is Inevitable," *Harvard Business Review* (1964): 51–59; D. Collins, "The Ethical Superiority and Inevitability of Participatory Management as an Organizational System," *Organization Science* 8, no. 5 (1997): 489–507; W.G. Weber, C. Unterrainer, and B.E. Schmid, "The Influence of Organizational Democracy on Employees' Socio-Moral Climate and Prosocial Behavioral Orientations," *Journal of Organizational Behavior* 30, no. 8 (2009): 1127–49.

***** Collins, D. "The Ethical Superiority and Inevitability of Participatory Management as an Organizational System; R. Bussel, "Business without a Boss": The Columbia Conserve Company and Workers' Control, 1917–1943," *The Business History Review* 71, no. 3 (1997): 417–43; J.D. Russell, M. Dirsmith, and S. Samuel, "Stained Steel: ESOPs, Meta-Power, and the Ironies of Corporate Democracy," *Symbolic Interaction* 27, no. 3 (2004): 383–403.

responsibility for developing recommendations. However, the decision maker is not bound to accept those recommendations. At the highest level of involvement, the entire decision-making process is handed over to employees. They identify the problem, discover alternative solutions, choose the best alternative, and implement that choice. The original decision maker serves only as a facilitator to guide the team's decision process and keep everyone on track.

BENEFITS OF EMPLOYEE INVOLVEMENT

For the past half century, organizational behaviour experts have advised that employee involvement potentially improves decision-making quality and commitment.[90] To begin with, it improves the identification of problems and opportunities. Employees are, in many respects, the sensors of the organization's environment. When the organization's activities misalign with customer expectations, employees are usually the first to know. Employee involvement provides a conduit for organizational leaders to be alerted to such problems. Employee involvement can also potentially improve the number and quality of solutions generated. In a well-managed meeting, team members create synergy by pooling their knowledge to form new alternatives. In other words, several people working together can potentially generate better solutions than the same people working alone.

A third benefit of employee involvement is that, under specific conditions, it improves the evaluation of alternatives. Numerous studies on participative decision making, task conflict, and team dynamics have found that involvement brings out more diverse perspectives, tests ideas, and provides more valuable knowledge, all of which help the decision maker to select the best alternative.[91] A mathematical theorem introduced in 1785 by the Marquis de Condorcet states that the alternative selected by the team's majority is more likely to be correct than is the alternative selected by any team member individually.[92]

©MAD_Production/Shutterstock

Employee involvement has significantly improved environmental sustainability and productivity at Labatt Breweries of Canada. In a typical year, 76 percent of the brewer's employees submit suggestions for workplace improvements through an online questionnaire. Last year, Labatt received 2,700 ideas, 1,603 of which were implemented. Some suggestions have transformed operations. For example, Scott Baldwin, a brewer at Labatt's brewery in London, Ontario, noticed that huge amounts of water were being wasted in the brewing process as well as during beer tank cleaning. Baldwin worked with engineers and others to conserve water in these production activities, saving the brewery 11.4 million litres of water annually. "If it doesn't start with Scott challenging it, then nothing moves," says Alex Martel, general manager of Labatt's London brewery. "These people know their work areas the best."*

* S. Coulter, "Cheers! Innovative Labatt Worker Saves Brewery 15M Litres of Water Annually," *London Free Press,* June 5, 2018; D. Deveau, "Eight Takeaways from Labatt's Successful Employee Engagement Program," *National Post,* June 21, 2018.

Along with improving decision quality, involvement tends to strengthen employee commitment to the decision. Rather than viewing themselves as agents of someone else's decision, those who participate in a decision feel personally responsible for its success. Involvement also has positive effects on employee motivation, satisfaction, and turnover. Furthermore, it increases skill variety, felt autonomy, and task identity, all of which increase job enrichment and, potentially, employee motivation. Participation is also a critical practice in organizational change because employees are more motivated to implement the decision and less likely to resist changes resulting from the decision.[93]

CONTINGENCIES OF EMPLOYEE INVOLVEMENT

If employee involvement is so wonderful, why don't leaders leave all decisions to employees? The answer is that the optimal level of employee involvement depends on the situation. The employee involvement model shown in Exhibit 7.7 lists four contingencies: decision structure, source of decision knowledge, decision commitment, and risk of conflict in the decision process.[94]

- *Decision structure.* At the beginning of this chapter, we learned that some decisions are programmed, whereas others are nonprogrammed. Programmed decisions are less likely to need employee involvement because the solutions are already worked out from past incidents. In other words, the benefits of employee involvement increase with the novelty and complexity of the problem or opportunity.

- *Source of decision knowledge.* Subordinates should be involved in some level of decision making when the leader lacks sufficient knowledge and subordinates have additional information to improve decision quality. In many cases, employees are closer to customers and production activities, so they often know where the company can save money, improve product or service quality, and realize opportunities. This is particularly true for complex decisions where employees are more likely to possess relevant information.

- *Decision commitment.* Participation tends to improve employee commitment to the decision. If employees are unlikely to accept a decision made without their involvement, some level of participation is usually necessary.

- *Risk of conflict.* Two types of conflict undermine the benefits of employee involvement. First, if employee goals and norms conflict with the organization's goals, only a low level of employee involvement is advisable. Second, the degree of involvement depends on whether employees will agree with one another on the preferred solution. If conflict is likely to occur, high involvement (i.e., employees make the decision alone) would be difficult to achieve.

Employee involvement is an important component of the decision-making process. To make the best decisions, we need to involve people who have the most valuable information and who will increase commitment to implement the decision. Employee involvement is a formative stage of team dynamics, so it carries many of the benefits and challenges of working in teams. The next chapter provides a closer look at team dynamics, including processes for making decisions in teams.

EXHIBIT 7.7   Model of Employee Involvement in Decision Making

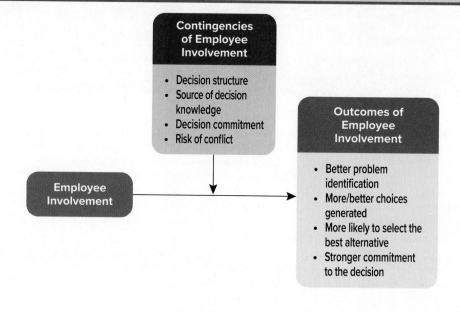

Chapter Summary

LO1

Describe the elements of rational choice decision making.
Decision making is a conscious process of making choices among one or more alternatives with the intention of moving toward some desired state of affairs. Rational choice decision making identifies the best choice based on the valence of numerous outcomes and the probability that those outcomes will occur. It also follows the logical process of identifying problems and opportunities, choosing the best decision style, developing alternative solutions, choosing the best solution, implementing the selected alternative, and evaluating decision outcomes.

LO2

Explain why people don't apply rational choice decision making when identifying problems/opportunities, evaluating/choosing alternatives, and evaluating decision outcomes.
Solution-focused problem identification, decisive leadership, stakeholder framing, perceptual defence, and mental models affect our ability to objectively identify problems and opportunities. We can minimize these challenges by being aware of the human limitations and discussing the situation with colleagues.

Evaluating and choosing alternatives is often challenging because organizational goals are ambiguous or in conflict, human information processing is incomplete and subjective, and people tend to satisfice rather than maximize. Decision makers also short-circuit the evaluation process when faced with an opportunity rather than a problem. People generally make better choices by systematically evaluating alternatives. Scenario planning can improve future decisions without the pressure and emotions that occur during real emergencies.

Confirmation bias and escalation of commitment make it difficult to accurately evaluate decision outcomes. Escalation is mainly caused by the self-justification effect, self-enhancement effect, the prospect theory effect, and sunk costs effect. These problems are minimized by separating decision choosers from decision evaluators, establishing a stop-loss point to abandon the project, seeking out factual information as well as feedback from others, and by refocusing the decision maker's mindset away from the past losses.

LO3

Discuss the roles of emotions and intuition in decision making.
Emotions shape our preferences for alternatives and the process we follow to evaluate alternatives. We also listen in on our emotions for guidance when making decisions. This latter activity relates to intuition—the ability to know when a problem or opportunity exists and to select the best course of action without conscious reasoning. Intuition is both an emotional experience and a rapid nonconscious analytic process that involves both pattern matching and action scripts.

LO4

Describe employee characteristics, workplace conditions, and specific activities that support creativity.
Creativity is the development of original ideas that make a socially recognized contribution. The four creativity stages are preparation, incubation, illumination, and verification. Incubation assists divergent thinking, which involves reframing the problem in a unique way and generating different approaches to the issue.

Four of the main features of creative people are intelligence, persistence, expertise, and independent imagination. Creativity is also strengthened for everyone when the work environment supports a learning orientation, the job has task significance and autonomy, the organization provides a reasonable level of job security, and leaders provide an appealing vision of the future with the right degrees of time pressure and resources. Four types of activities that encourage creativity are redefining the problem, associative play, cross-pollination, and design thinking. Design thinking is a human-centred, solution-focused creative process that applies both intuition and analytical thinking to clarify problems and generate innovative solutions. Four rules guide this process: human rule, ambiguity rule, re-design rule, and tangible rule.

LO5

Describe the benefits of employee involvement and identify four contingencies that affect the optimal level of employee involvement.
Employee involvement refers to situations in which employees participate in and influence decisions about their jobs, work units, or organization. The level of participation may range from an employee providing specific information to the decision maker without knowing the problem or issue, to complete involvement in all phases of the decision process. Employee involvement may lead to better decision quality and commitment, but several contingencies need to be considered, including the decision structure, source of decision knowledge, decision commitment, and risk of conflict.

Key Terms

anchoring and adjustment heuristic
availability heuristic
bounded rationality
confirmation bias
creativity
decision making

design thinking
divergent thinking
escalation of commitment
implicit favourite
intuition
learning orientation

mental models
prospect theory effect
rational choice decision making
representativeness heuristic

satisficing
scenario planning
self-enhancement

Critical Thinking Questions

1. A management consultant is hired by a manufacturing firm to determine the best site for its next production facility. The consultant has had several meetings with the company's senior executives regarding the factors to consider when making the recommendation. Discuss the decision-making problems that might prevent the consultant from choosing the best site location.

2. You have been asked to personally recommend a new travel agency to handle all airfare, accommodation, and related travel needs for your organization of 500 staff. One of your colleagues, who is responsible for the company's economic planning, suggests that the best travel agent could be selected mathematically by inputting the relevant factors for each agency and the weight (importance) of each factor. What decision-making approach is your colleague recommending? Is this recommendation a good idea in this situation? Why or why not?

3. Intuition is both an emotional experience and an unconscious analytic process. One problem, however, is that not all emotions signalling that there is a problem or opportunity represent intuition. Explain how we would know whether our "gut feelings" are intuition, and if not intuition, suggest what might be causing them.

4. A developer received financial backing for a new business financial centre along a derelict section of the waterfront, a few miles from the current downtown area of a large European city. The idea was to build several high-rise structures, attract large tenants to those sites, and have the city extend transportation systems out to the new centre. Over the next decade, the developer believed that others would build in the area, thereby attracting the regional or national offices of many financial institutions. Interest from potential tenants was much lower than initially predicted and the city did not build transportation systems as quickly as expected.

Still, the builder proceeded with the original plans. Only after financial support was curtailed did the developer reconsider the project. Using your knowledge of escalation of commitment, discuss three possible reasons why the developer was motivated to continue with the project.

5. Ancient Book Company has a problem with new book projects. Even when others are aware that a book is far behind schedule and may engender little public interest, acquisitions editors are reluctant to terminate contracts with authors whom they have signed. The result is that editors invest more time with these projects than on more fruitful projects. As a form of escalation of commitment, describe two methods that Ancient Book Company can use to minimize this problem.

6. A recent graduate is offered a job by an employer she admires even before she could start the job search. The student thinks it is an opportunity and jumps on it. Do you think there is an effect of emotions in her decision making?

7. Think of a time when you experienced the creative process. Maybe you woke up with a brilliant (but sketchy and incomplete) idea, or you solved a baffling problem while doing something else. Describe this incident to your class and explain how the experience followed the creative process.

8. Two characteristics of creative people are that they have relevant experience and are persistent in their quest. Does this mean that people with the most experience and the highest need for achievement are the most creative? Explain your answer.

9. Employee involvement applies just as well to the classroom as to the office or factory floor. Explain how student involvement in classroom decisions typically made by the instructor alone might improve decision quality. What potential problems may occur in this process?

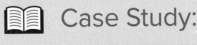

Case Study:
DOGGED BY THE WRONG PROBLEM

by Steven L. McShane, University of Newcastle (Australia)

More than 3 million dogs enter animal shelters each year in the United States, and almost one-third of these have been surrendered by their owners. Until recently, animal shelter employees assumed that the owners didn't want their pets anymore, so they focused their resources on ways to get the surrendered dogs re-adopted with new owners.

Now, animal shelters recognize that they were focused on the wrong problem to some extent. Most owners of surrendered dogs love their pets but believe they are unable to keep them due to financial or family difficulties. "Owner surrenders are not a people problem," explains Lori Weise, founder of Downtown Dog Rescue in Los Angeles. "By and large, they are a poverty problem. These families love their dogs as much as we do, but they are also exceptionally poor." Even when owners surrender their dog due to the pet's behaviour, animal shelter staff have learned that the problem is often the owners' lack of basic training to improve their pet's behaviour.

These discoveries have been a wake-up call for animal shelters. Along with finding new homes for surrendered dogs, shelters now also focus on strategies that enable owners to keep their pets. Downtown Dog Rescue in Los Angeles is a pioneer in applying diverse solutions to minimize the number of dogs surrendered each year to animal shelters. Through donations, the organization provides free dog vaccinations, spay/neutering, medical assistance, pet licences, and other forms of support to help low-income people keep their pets rather than surrender them to shelters.

Until recently, Animal Care Centers (ACC) of New York City also focused solely on getting surrendered dogs to new owners. The municipal agency receives more than 30,000 pets annually at its shelters in five New York City boroughs. Front desk staff members were aware of common themes why owners were surrendering their pets: they couldn't afford veterinary care; they had fallen on hard times and weren't allowed to keep dogs at their new temporary accommodation; the dog had behaviour problems that the owner didn't know how to correct.

Unfortunately, ACC staff receiving the surrendered dogs have many other duties (returning pets to owners, tracing licence tags, etc.). All they could do in most instances was ask the owners the required questions to complete the paperwork. "They were overwhelmed and didn't have time to sit down with clients and have those really in-depth conversations to see if there was anything we could do to help them keep their pet," recalls ACC admissions supervisor Aleah Simpson. It was also an awkward situation because the owners answered the questions and surrendered their pet in ACC's crowded front lobby where many dog-loving clients were listening.

Inspired by the work of Downtown Dog Rescue in Los Angeles, ACC now takes a dramatically different approach to dog surrenders. Instead of answering a few questions asked by busy front desk staff, owners who intend to surrender their dogs are now greeted by trained ACC admission counsellors with impeccable people skills. In a private office, these counsellors listen to the owner's story about why they want or need to surrender their dog. These counsellors are trained by licensed social workers to maintain a nonjudgmental attitude toward the owners and to handle difficult situations. "Once that person (the pet owner) doesn't feel like they're going to be judged in that moment, they might open up and tell you the real situation," says Simpson.

Based on the information from these conversations, ACC counsellors direct some owners to support groups that can provide assistance, such as financial support or temporary lodging for the dog. In other situations, the owners are invited to attend brief training programs where they receive instruction on how to improve the pet's behaviour. The conversations also help counsellors determine which pets are better off with new owners. As new situations arise, ACC staff have found increasingly innovative and customized solutions to enable owners to keep their pet. "Even two years ago, I would think there wouldn't be options for so many of these pet owners and their animals," says Jenny Coffey of the Mayor's Alliance for NYC's Animals.

ACC predicted that over the first 18 months of the program, 150 owners would keep their pets as a result of the counselling program. Instead, this initiative has reduced the intake by more than 90 pets per month. Through New York Community Trust funding, ACC introduced free veterinary and humane care to pets of owners in low-income areas of New York City. Pet surrenders have dropped by 50 percent, on average, in the areas that received this funding.

"It's almost as if a few years back a massive light bulb went off in the animal welfare community," says Matthew Bershadker, CEO of the American Society for the Prevention of Cruelty to Animals (ASPCA), about the industry's reframed mandate. "We stopped thinking about how to get animals out of shelters and we started thinking about how to keep animals from coming into shelters."

Discussion Questions

1. What stage of decision making is mainly discussed in this case about dog surrenders? To what extent and in what ways did the change in that stage of decision making affect later stages of decision making about dog surrenders?

2. How has creativity played a role in the events described in this case study?

Class Exercise:
EMPLOYEE INVOLVEMENT INCIDENTS

Purpose This exercise is designed to help you understand the contingencies of employee involvement.

Instructions (Small or Large Class) Four scenarios are presented in this exercise. Assume you are the manager or person in charge. For each scenario, identify the preferred level of employee involvement from one of the five levels described below. For each scenario, identify and justify what factors led you to choose this level of employee involvement rather than the others. Also, be prepared to discuss what problems might occur with less or more involvement in this case (where possible).

1. *Decide alone.* Use your personal knowledge and insight to complete the entire decision process without conferring with anyone else.

2. *Receive information from individuals.* Ask specific individuals for information. They do not make recommendations and might not even know what the problem is about.

3. *Consult with individuals.* Describe the problem to selected individuals and seek both their information and recommendations. The final decision is made by you, and you may or may not take the advice from others into account.

4. *Consult with the team.* You bring together a team of people (all department staff or a representation of them if the department is large), who are told about the problem and provide their ideas and recommendations. You make the final decision, which may or may not reflect the team's information.

5. *Facilitate the team's decision.* The entire decision-making process is handed over to a team or committee of subordinates. You serve only as a facilitator to guide the decision process and keep everyone on track. The team identifies the problem, discovers alternative solutions, chooses the best alternative, and implements their choice.

For each incident, students or teams should be prepared to answer the following questions:

1. What factors led you to choose this level of employee involvement rather than the others?

2. What problems might occur if less or more involvement occurred in this case (where possible)?

SCENARIO 1: THE PRODUCTIVITY DIVIDEND DECISION

As head of the transmission/distribution group (TD group) in the city's water agency (a government corporation), you have been asked to reduce costs over the next year by a minimum of 3 percent without undermining service. Your department employs about 300 people who are responsible for constructing and maintaining water lines throughout the city. Although you have an engineering background, the work is complex and involves several professions and trades. Even the TD group's first line supervisors (one or two levels below you in the hierarchy) are not fully knowledgeable of all aspects of the business.

You believe that most employees support or at least accept the city's recent mandate to reduce costs (called the "productivity dividend initiative"). The city leaders have stated that this initiative will not result in any layoffs this year. However, the labour union representing most nonmanagement staff in the water agency (including most of your employees) is concerned that the productivity dividend initiative will reduce employment numbers over time and increase employee workloads. Although the TD group is a separate department within the city water agency, it affects most other work units in the agency. It is possible, for example, that ideas that reduce costs in the TD group might increase costs elsewhere. The TD group employees may be unaware of or care about these repercussions because there is limited interaction with or social bonding with employees in the other departments.

SCENARIO 2: THE SUGAR SUBSTITUTE RESEARCH DECISION

You are the head of research and development (R&D) for a major beer company. While working on a new beer product, one of the scientists in your unit seems to have tentatively identified a new chemical compound that has few calories but tastes closer to sugar than current sugar substitutes. The company has no foreseeable need for this product, but it could be patented and licensed to manufacturers in the food industry.

The sugar-substitute discovery is in its preliminary stages and would require considerable time and resources before it would be commercially viable. This means that it would necessarily take some resources away from other projects in the lab. The sugar substitute project is beyond your technical expertise, but some of the R&D lab researchers are familiar with that field of chemistry. It is difficult to determine the amount of research required to further identify and perfect the sugar substitute. You do not know how much demand is expected for this product. Your department has a decision process for funding projects that are behind schedule. However, there are no rules or precedents about funding projects that would be licensed but not used by the organization.

The company's R&D budget is limited, and other scientists in your work group have recently complained that they require more resources and financial support to get their projects completed. Some of these R&D projects hold promise for future beer sales. You believe that most researchers in the R&D unit are committed to ensuring that the company's interests are achieved.

SCENARIO 3: COAST GUARD CUTTER DECISION

You are the captain of a 72-metre Coast Guard cutter with a crew of 16, including officers. Your mission is general at-sea search and rescue. Today at 2:00 a.m., while en route to your home port after a routine 28-day patrol, you received word from the nearest Coast Guard station that a small plane had crashed 100 kilometres offshore. You obtained all the available information concerning the location of the crash, informed your crew of the mission, and set a new course at maximum speed for the scene to commence a search for survivors and wreckage.

You have now been searching for 20 hours. Your search operation has been impaired by increasingly rough seas, and there is evidence of a severe storm building. The atmospherics associated with the deteriorating weather have made communications with the Coast Guard station impossible. A decision must be made shortly about whether to abandon the search and place your vessel on a course that would ride out the storm (thereby protecting the vessel and your crew, but relegating any possible survivors to almost certain death from exposure) or to continue a potentially futile search and the risks it would entail.

Before losing communications, you received an update weather advisory concerning the severity and duration of the storm. Although your crew members are extremely conscientious about their responsibility, you believe that they would be divided on the decision of leaving or staying.

SCENARIO 4: THE SOCIAL MEDIA POLICY DECISION

The Industry Initiatives Agency is a group of 120 professionals responsible for marketing the province as a good place for companies to operate their business or open new operations.

Although you report to the head of the province's ministry of employment and commerce, your agency is semi-autonomous in its policies and practices from the parent department. One of your highest priorities is to recruit and retain young, well-educated, high-potential employees for this growing agency. During a recent recruiting drive at universities and colleges, some potential applicants candidly stated that the provincial government seems out of touch with the younger generation, particularly in their use of technology. A few observed that your agency's website doesn't provide much recruitment information, and they couldn't find the agency's Facebook or Twitter sites.

These comments led to you think about having a social media policy in the Industry Initiatives Agency, and particularly whether or to what degree the agency should allow or possibly even encourage its staff to have work-related Facebook sites, personal blogs, and Twitter sites, and to participate in those sites during work hours. You personally know very little about emerging social media, although many of your direct reports (functional managers and team leaders) have varying degrees of knowledge about them. A few have their own personal Facebook sites and one manager has her own travel blog. Some direct reports are strongly opposed to social media in the workplace, whereas others are very supportive. However, you believe that all of their views are taken in the agency's best interests.

This social media policy decision would be within your mandate; unlike most governments, neither the provincial government nor the employment and commerce ministry has such a policy or restrictions on any policy that is designed by your agency. However, a few specific government departments prohibit Facebook and texting activity during work, and, due to concerns about breaches of confidentiality and employer reputation, do not allow employees to mention work-related matters in any social media. Your decision is to develop a policy specifying whether and, if so, to what degree, agency staff should be allowed and encouraged to engage in social network site activity during work hours.

 Class Exercise:
CREATIVITY BRAINBUSTERS

Purpose This exercise is designed to help students understand the dynamics of creativity and divergent thinking in decision making.

Instructions (Large or small class) The instructor describes the problem, and students are asked to figure out the solution, working alone. When enough time has passed, the instructor may then ask specific students who think they have the solution

to describe (or show using projection technology) their answer. The instructor will review the solutions and discuss the implications of this exercise. In particular, be prepared to discuss what you needed to solve these puzzles and what may have prevented you from solving them more quickly.

1. *Double-circle problem.* Draw two circles, one inside the other, with a single line and with neither circle touching

the other (as shown below). In other words, you must draw both of these circles without lifting your pen (or other writing instrument).

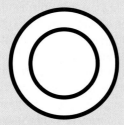

2. *Nine-dot problem.* Below are nine dots. Without lifting your pencil, draw no more than four straight lines that pass through all nine dots.

● ● ●

● ● ●

● ● ●

3. *Nine-dot problem revisited.* Referring to the nine-dot exhibit above, describe how, without lifting your pencil, you could pass a pencil line through all dots with three or fewer straight lines.

4. *Word search.* In the following line of letters, cross out five letters so that the remaining letters, without altering their sequence, spell a familiar English word.

CFRIVEELATETITEVRSE

5. *Burning ropes.* You have two pieces of rope of unequal lengths and a box of matches. In spite of their different lengths, each piece of rope takes one hour to burn; however, parts of each rope burn at unequal speeds. For example, the first half of one piece might burn in 10 minutes. Use these materials to accurately determine when 45 minutes has elapsed.

Self-Assessments for Chapter 7

SELF-ASSESSMENT NAME	DESCRIPTION
What is your preferred decision-making style?	Effective decision making is a critical part of most jobs, particularly in professional and executive positions. But people have different decision-making styles, including how much they rely on facts and logical analysis or emotional responses and gut instinct. This tool assesses your preference for logical or intuitive decision making.
How well do you engage in divergent thinking?	A key feature of creativity is divergent thinking—reframing the problem in a unique way and generating different approaches to the issue. One way to test divergent thinking is by presenting questions or problems in which the answer requires a different approach or perspective from the usual frame of mind. This self-assessment presents a dozen of these questions.
Do you have a creative personality?	Everyone is creative to some extent, but some people have personality traits and personal values that give them higher creative potential. This self-assessment helps you to discover the extent to which you have a creative personality.

CHAPTER 8
Team Dynamics

Each year, teams of undergraduate students compete in the the Bank of Canada Governor's Challenge. Through a video link to Bank of Canada judges, each team presents its analysis of current macroeconomic and financial conditions and recommends monetary policy from that analysis. The judges evaluate not only the quality of each team's economic and financial analysis; they also rate how well the members of each team work together. The team's collaborative performance is assessed both in the presentation and the subsequent question-and-answer session.

Teamwork is an important factor in the Governor's Challenge because teams have become essential in the finance industry. Whether managing invest-

Teamwork has become an integral part of working in the finance industry in Canada and elsewhere.
©Gorodenkoff/Shutterstock

ment funds, providing financial advice to clients, or conducting macroeconomic analysis for central bank policy, teams usually perform better than individual stars working alone.

Executives at RBC Capital Markets identify teamwork as a key reason for their success as Canada's top-ranked investment bank. The company carefully selects job applicants who are "understated and team-oriented." Big-ego Masters of the Universe financiers are not welcome, warns a senior executive. Teamwork is vital because no individual has sufficient expertise to provide the investment bank's complex services. RBC Capital Markets chief executive Derek Neldner gives this example: "If you are going to offer serious coverage to a health care client, you need an analyst who can talk authoritatively on medical devices, an expert on pharmaceuticals, one on biotech and so on."

The shift from individual stars to high-performing teams is very evident at Merrill Lynch Wealth Management. A decade ago, most of the company's 15,000 financial advisors worked alone with their clients. Today, 77 percent of Merrill Lynch's advisors work in teams. These teams offer greater expertise across a broader range of asset classes (stocks, bonds, derivatives, cash management, etc.) as well as expertise across regions of the world.

"It's exceedingly rare that a single individual could deliver everything a client needs today," says Merrill Lynch Wealth Management president Andy Sieg. "When you look at what clients need—comprehensive advice across their financial lives—it very quickly becomes obvious that the only way to deliver that is through a team."[1]

Investment analysts, financial advisors, and others in the finance industry increasingly work in teams rather than alone. In fact, this trend toward teamwork is occurring in many industries. One recent study reports that collaborating with others—whether face-to-face or remotely through technology—now takes up to 80 percent of an employee's time. Another study found that employees are involved in almost twice as many teams than five years ago. By comparison, three decades ago only 20 percent of executives said they worked in teams at all![2]

The importance of teamwork extends to scientific research. A study of almost 20 million research publications reported that the percentage of journal articles written by teams rather than individuals has increased substantially over the past five decades. Team-based articles also had a much higher number of subsequent citations, suggesting that journal articles written by teams are superior to articles written by individuals.[3]

Why are teams becoming so important, and how can organizations improve team effectiveness? We find the answers to these and other questions in this chapter on team dynamics. This chapter begins by defining teams, examining the reasons why organizations rely on teams, and explaining why people join informal groups in organizational settings. A large segment of this chapter examines a model of team effectiveness, which includes team and organizational environment, team design, and team processes (team development, norms, roles, cohesion, trust, and mental models). We then turn our attention to two specific types of teams: self-directed teams and remote teams. The final section of this chapter looks at the challenges and strategies for making better decisions in teams.

Teams and Informal Groups

LO1

Teams are groups of two or more people who interact with and influence each other, are mutually accountable for achieving common goals associated with organizational objectives, and perceive themselves as a social entity within an organization.[4] This definition has a few important components worth repeating. First, all teams exist to fulfil some purpose, such as providing wealth management services, repairing electric power lines, designing a new educational program, or making an important executive decision. Second, team members are held together by their interdependence and need for collaboration to achieve common goals. All teams require some form of communication so that members can coordinate, share information, and develop a common mindset regarding their purpose and objectives. Third, team members influence each other, although some members may be more influential than others regarding the team's goals and activities. Finally, a team exists when its members perceive themselves to be a team. They feel connected to one another through a common interest or purpose.

There are many types of teams in organizations, and each type can be distinguished by three characteristics: team permanence, skill diversity, and authority dispersion (see Exhibit 8.1).[5] Team permanence refers to how long that type of team usually exists. Accounting, marketing, and other departments are usually long-lasting structures, so these teams have high permanence. In contrast, task forces and project teams usually have low permanence because most are formed temporarily to solve a problem, realize an opportunity, or design a product or service.

A second distinguishing characteristic is the team's skill diversity. A team has high skill diversity when its members possess different skills and knowledge, whereas low diversity exists when team members have similar abilities and, therefore, are interchangeable. Most functional departments have

> **teams** Groups of two or more people who interact and influence each other, are mutually accountable for achieving common goals associated with organizational objectives, and perceive themselves as a social entity within an organization.

EXHIBIT 8.1   Team Permanence, Skill Diversity, and Authority Dispersion for Selected Team Types

Team type	Description	Team characteristics
Departmental teams	Teams that consist of employees who have similar or complementary skills and are located in the same unit of a functional structure; usually minimal task interdependence because each person works with clients or with employees in other departments.	*Team permanence:* High—departments continue indefinitely. *Skill diversity:* Low to medium—departments are often organized around common skills (e.g., accounting staff located in the accounting department). *Authority dispersion:* Low—departmental power is usually concentrated in the departmental manager.
Self-directed teams	Teams whose members are organized around work processes that complete an entire piece of work requiring several interdependent tasks and have substantial autonomy over the execution of those tasks (i.e., they usually control inputs, flow, and outputs with little or no supervision).	*Team permanence:* High—teams are usually assigned indefinitely to a specific cluster of production or service activities. *Skill diversity:* Medium to high—members typically perform different tasks requiring diverse skill sets, but cross-training can somewhat reduce skill diversity. *Authority dispersion:* High—team members share power, usually with limited hierarchical authority.
Task forces/project teams	Cross-functional teams whose members are usually drawn from several disciplines to solve a specific problem, realize an opportunity, or design a product or service.	*Team permanence:* Low—teams typically disband on completion of a specific project. *Skill diversity:* Medium to high—members are typically drawn from several functional specializations associated with the complexity of the problem or opportunity. *Authority dispersion:* Medium—teams often have someone with formal authority (project leader), but members also have moderate power due to their expertise and functional representation.

low skill diversity because they organize employees around their common skill sets (e.g., people with accounting expertise are located in the accounting department). In contrast, financial advisory team members have diverse expertise in different asset classes (stocks, bonds, etc.) or economic regions.

Authority dispersion, the third distinguishing characteristic of teams, refers to the degree that decision-making responsibility is distributed throughout the team (high dispersion) or is vested in one or a few members of the team (low dispersion). Departmental teams tend to have low authority dispersion because power is somewhat concentrated in a formal manager. Self-directed teams usually have high authority dispersion because the entire team makes key decisions and hierarchical authority is limited.

INFORMAL GROUPS

This chapter mainly focuses on formal teams, but employees also belong to informal groups. All teams are groups, but many groups do not satisfy our definition of teams. Groups include people assembled together, whether or not they have any interdependence or organizational objective. The friends you meet for lunch are an *informal group,* but they wouldn't be called a team because they have little or no interdependence (each person could just as easily eat lunch alone) and no organizationally mandated purpose. Instead, they exist primarily for the benefit of their members. Although the terms are used interchangeably, *teams* has largely replaced *groups* in the language of business when referring to employees who work together to complete organizational tasks.[6]

Why do informal groups exist? One reason is that human beings are social animals. Our drive to bond is hardwired through evolutionary development, creating a need to belong to informal groups.[7] This is evident by the fact that people invest considerable time and effort forming and maintaining social relationships without any special circumstances or ulterior motives. A second reason why people join informal groups is provided by social identity theory, which states that individuals define themselves by their group affiliations (see Chapter 3). Thus, we join groups—particularly those that are viewed favourably by others and have values similar to our own—because they shape and reinforce our self-concept.[8]

A third reason why informal groups exist is that they accomplish personal objectives that cannot be achieved by individuals working alone. For example, employees will sometimes congregate to support or oppose organizational changes because this collective effort has more power than individuals who try to bring about change alone. These informal groups, called coalitions, are discussed in Chapter 10. A fourth explanation for informal groups is that we are comforted by the mere presence of other people and are therefore motivated to be near them in stressful situations. When in danger, people congregate near each other even though doing so serves no protective purpose. Similarly, employees tend to mingle more often after hearing rumours that the company might be acquired by a competitor. As Chapter 4 explained, this social support minimizes stress by providing emotional and/or informational support to buffer the stress experience.[9]

Informal Groups and Organizational Outcomes

Informal groups are not created to serve corporate objectives, yet they have a profound influence on the organization and its employees. Informal groups potentially minimize employee stress because, as mentioned, group members provide emotional and informational social support. This stress-reducing capability of informal groups improves employee well-being, which potentially increases organizational effectiveness. Informal groups are also the backbone of **social networks**, which are important sources of trust building, information sharing, power, influence, and employee well-being in the workplace.[10] Chapter 10 explains how social networks are a source of influence in organizational settings. Employees with strong informal networks tend to have more power and influence because they receive better information and preferential treatment from others and their talent is more visible to key decision makers.

> **social networks** Social structures of individuals or social units that are connected to each other through one or more forms of interdependence.

Benefits and Limitations of Teams

LO2

Why are teams important at RBC Capital Markets, Merrill Lynch Wealth Management, and so many other organizations around the world? The answer to this question has a long history.[11] Early research on British coal mining in the 1940s, the Japanese economic miracle of the 1970s, and a huge number of investigations since then have revealed that *under the right conditions,* teams make better decisions, develop better products and services, and create a more motivated workforce than do employees working alone.[12] Similarly,

team members can quickly share information and coordinate tasks, whereas these processes are slower and prone to more errors in traditional departments led by supervisors. Teams typically provide superior customer service because they offer clients a greater breadth of knowledge and expertise than do individual "stars" working alone.

Another benefit of teams is that, in many situations, their members are more motivated than when working alone.[13] Teams generate three motivating forces. First, employees have a drive to bond and are motivated to fulfil the goals of groups to which they belong. This felt obligation is particularly strong when the employee's social identity is connected to the team. Second, employees have high accountability to fellow team members, who monitor performance more closely than a traditional supervisor. This accountability is particularly strong when the team's performance depends on the worst performer, such as on an assembly line. Third, each team member creates a moving performance standard for the others. Employees are also motivated to work harder because of apprehension that their performance will be compared to the performance of others. When a few employees complete tasks faster, other team members recognize that they also could work faster, and that they should work faster.

THE CHALLENGES OF TEAMS

Teams are potentially very productive, but they are not always as effective as individuals working alone.[14] The main problem is that teams have additional costs called **process losses**— resources (including time and energy) expended toward team development and maintenance rather than directly toward task performance.[15] Team members need time and effort to develop mutual understanding of their goals, determine the best strategy for accomplishing those goals, negotiate their specific roles, agree on informal rules of conduct, and resolve their disagreements. An employee working alone on a project does not have these internal misunderstandings, divergent viewpoints, disagreements, or coordination problems (at least, not nearly as much as with other people). Teams may be necessary when the work is so complex that it requires knowledge and skills from several people. But when the work can be performed by one person, process losses can make a team much less effective than an individual working alone.

> **process losses** Resources (including time and energy) expended toward team development and maintenance rather than the task.

Process losses tend to increase with the team's diversity and size.[16] Diverse teams offer many benefits, which we describe later in this chapter. However, the wider range of beliefs and values slows the team's development toward an optimally productive work unit. Members of diverse teams

©Guerilla/Alamy Stock Photo

Verafin Inc. thrives on teamwork. The St. John's, Newfoundland, company's 150 employees build and maintain the world's leading cloud-based platform for financial crime management. This is complex and often fast-paced work, which requires dedicated multiskilled project teams, along with impromptu scrum teams that form quickly when urgent problems arise. "We have a great team, we have a singular focus, so it makes every day unique, challenging, but exciting and fun," beams Verafin product specialist Corey Lynch. Jacqueline Rideout, Verafin's director of customer education, is amazed by the incredible power of teamwork. "When a team of people are presented with a problem and all of those creative brilliant minds come together and solve that problem it is inspirational and it makes going to work really, really fun."*

* *Verafin Recruitment Video 2017,* YouTube (St. John's, Nfld: Verafin, December 15, 2017), https://www.youtube.com/watch?v=ubDJB84DbfQ. Some information is also derived from Verafin's website, verafin.com.

spend more time resolving conflicts about the team's purpose, team roles, coordination routines, and so forth. Larger teams have higher process losses because understanding, agreeing with, and synchronizing work with many people is more difficult than with few people. Larger teams also require more time for each member to be meaningfully involved in the team's decisions.

Process losses are also amplified, at least temporarily, when adding new members to an existing team. The new team members consume time and effort figuring out how to work well with other team members. Performance also suffers among existing team members while their attention is diverted from task performance to accommodating and integrating the newcomer. The software industry even has a name for the problems of adding people to a team: **Brooks's law** says that adding more people to a late software project only makes it later![17]

Brooks's law The principle that adding more people to a late software project only makes it later.

Social Loafing

The process losses just described mainly refer to coordination challenges, but teams also suffer from motivational process losses. The best-known motivational process loss is **social loafing,** which occurs when people exert less effort (and usually perform at a lower level) in teams than when working alone.[18]

social loafing The problem that occurs when people exert less effort (and usually perform at a lower level) when working in teams than when working alone.

Social loafing is more pervasive under several conditions.[19] It is more likely to occur when individual performance is hidden or difficult to distinguish from the performance of other team members. Individual performance is less visible in larger rather than smaller teams. It is also hidden when the team produces a single output (e.g., solving a client's problem) rather than separate outputs for each team member (e.g., each member reviews several accounting reports per day). Second, social loafing is more common when the work is boring or the team's overall task has low task significance (see Chapter 6). Third, social loafing is more prevalent among team members with low conscientiousness and low agreeableness personality traits, as well as low collectivist values.

Fourth, social loafing is more widespread when employees lack motivation to help the team achieve its goals. This lack of motivation occurs when individual members have low social identity with the team and the team has low cohesion. Lack of motivation also occurs when employees believe other team members aren't pulling their weight. In other words, social loafers provide only as much effort as they believe others will provide, which is their way of maintaining fairness in work allocation. Employees also exert less effort when they believe they have little control over the team's success, such as when the team is large (their contribution has minimal effect on the team's performance) and when the team is dependent on other members with known performance problems.

By understanding the causes of social loafing, we can identify ways to minimize this problem.[20] Some of the strategies listed below reduce social loafing by making each member's performance more visible. Others increase each member's motivation to perform their tasks and mindfully minimize social loafing within the group.

- *Form smaller teams*—Splitting the team into several smaller groups reduces social loafing because each person's performance becomes more noticeable and important for team performance. "When the group is smaller, there's nowhere to hide," explains Strategic Investments & Holdings principal David Zebro. "You have to pull your weight."[21] Individuals also tend to develop stronger commitment to and identify with smaller than larger teams.
- *Measure individual performance*—Social loafing is minimized when each member's contribution is measured. This is possible when each member can perform parallel tasks, such as serving different customers. But measuring individual performance is difficult to implement when the team produces a single output, such as solving one client's problem.
- *Specialize tasks*—It is easier to measure individual performance when each team member performs a different work activity. For example, rather than pooling their effort for all incoming customer inquiries, each customer service representative might be assigned a particular type of client.

- *Increase job enrichment*—Social loafing is minimized when each team member's job is highly motivating, such as when the work has high task significance or is sufficiently varied and challenging rather than boring.
- *Increase mindfulness of team obligations*—Social loafing can be minimized by alerting team members to this problem and asking them to declare their commitment to the team's performance objectives. This relates to the discussion in Chapter 2 on increasing employee awareness of values and ethics.
- *Select motivated, team-oriented employees*—Employees are less susceptible to social loafing when they identify with the team, have moderate or higher conscientiousness and agreeableness personality traits, and have a fairly high collectivist value orientation. Social loafing is also minimized by selecting team members who are self-motivated, because these people perform their tasks well even when their personal work output is difficult to measure. One recent study reported that teams whose members played team sports had lower levels of social loafing. Team sport members are possibly more collectivist, identify more easily with their teams, are more self-motivated, or have developed greater mindfulness of their obligations to the team.

Overall, teams can be very powerful forces for competitive advantage, or they can be much more trouble than they are worth. To understand when teams are better than individuals working alone, we need to more closely examine the conditions that make teams effective or ineffective. The next few sections of this chapter discuss the model of team effectiveness.

A Model of Team Effectiveness

LO3

Why are some teams effective while others fail? To answer this question, we first need to clarify the meaning of team effectiveness. A team is effective when it benefits the organization and its members and survives long enough to accomplish its mandate.[22] Team effectiveness has three key features. First, teams exist to serve some organizational purpose, so effectiveness is partly measured by the achievement of that objective. Second, a team's effectiveness relies on the satisfaction and well-being of its members. People join groups to fulfil their personal needs, so effectiveness is partly measured

---

 Are you a team player? You can discover your preferences about working in teams by locating this self-assessment in Connect.

by this need fulfilment. Third, team effectiveness includes the ability and motivation of team members to remain together long enough to accomplish the assigned goals. Even teams that exist for only a few days could fall apart, literally (people refuse to join or stay with the team) or cognitively (members become emotionally disengaged from the team).

Over the past half century, researchers have developed several models to identify the features, conditions, and processes that make some teams more effective than others.[23] Exhibit 8.2 integrates the main components of these team effectiveness models. This exhibit is a meta-model because each component (team norms, team cohesion, etc.) includes its own set of theories and models to explain how that component operates. Over the next two sections, we discuss theories for each part of this model.

The organization and team environment refers to the context surrounding the team, such as its physical workspace and organizational leadership. Team design refers to variables that, for the most part, are assigned to the team when it is created and altered throughout its existence. The number of people assigned to the team (team size) and the personal attributes these members bring to the team (team composition) are elements of team design, for example.[24]

Team processes are described in various and sometimes conflicting ways in the literature.[25] In this book, team processes are the cognitive and emotional dynamics of the team that continually change with its development. These processes centre around the team's development and the associated variables of team norms, roles, cohesion, trust, and shared/complementary mental models. Team process variables are sometimes labelled as "emergent states" of the team, but one respected expert has warned that we should focus on team processes rather than the fleeting and continuously evolving team states created by those processes.[26]

ORGANIZATIONAL AND TEAM ENVIRONMENT

The organizational and team environment represents all conditions surrounding the team that influence its effectiveness.[27] Teams thrive where the physical workspace encourages collaborative interaction, information systems support

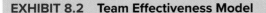

EXHIBIT 8.2   Team Effectiveness Model

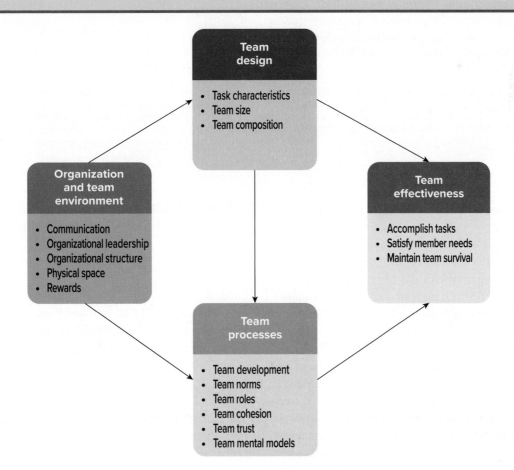

Global Connections 8.1

EUROPEAN FIRMS SUPPORT TEAMWORK WITH OBEYA ROOMS*

Many years ago, Toyota Motor Company discovered that it can speed up new car design by forming a cross-functional team consisting of people from several engineering and related departments, and having those team members meet regularly in an *obeya*—Japanese for "large room."

Companies throughout Europe have recently introduced obeya rooms to improve team performance on complex problems through face-to-face interaction. The obeya room at French automaker PSA Peugeot Citroën is a command central. The walls are plastered with graphs and notes so team members can visualize progress and document key issues. The obeya room at Nike's European Distribution Center in Belgium has been so successful that the sports footwear and apparel company's European information technology group recently built its own obeya space.

ING Bank created obeya rooms in several European countries so operations teams can speed up communication and decision making as the company moves toward a more agile work culture. "This is the heart of ING's transformation," ING chief operating officer Roel Louwhoff says proudly during a tour of ING's obeya room in Amsterdam. "The purpose is simple: having the full overview of the status of all projects and solving issues quickly. . . .You immediately see how everything fits together."

Siemens has introduced obeya rooms throughout Europe to support product development and production process decision making. Siemens quality systems manager Annemarie Kreyenberg noticed that the obeya room at her worksite in Germany has changed the company's culture. "The behaviour of people in this [obeya] room was an excellent reflection of the progress of the cultural change," she observes. "Teams and managers experimented with new behaviours, creating role models and examples for the entire organization."

©Sam Edwards/Getty Images

* F. Mathijssen, "The Story of Nike's Obeya," *Planet Lean*, December 11, 2014; A. Kreyenberg, "The Obeya Room—Tool and Mirror for Culture Change," in *agile42 Connect* (Berlin 2015); F. Parisot, "PSA Généralise Les Réunions Virtuelles (PSA Generalizes Virtual Meetings)," *L'usine Nouvelle*, January 15, 2015; "The Olympian Task of Transforming ING," News release (ING Bank, February 16, 2017); S. Arlt, "Schöne, neue Arbeitswelt (Beautiful, New Working Environment)," *Deutschlandfunk Kultur*, November 7, 2017; M. Korytowska, "Obeya Room in Portfolio Management," *LinkedIn Pulse*, February 11, 2019; J.M. Morgan and J.K. Liker, *Designing the Future: How Ford, Toyota, and Other World-Class Organizations Use Lean Product Development to Drive Innovation and Transform Their Business* (New York: McGraw Hill Professional, 2019), 93–109.

team coordination, organizational leaders instil a culture of teamwork, and the reward system reinforces collaboration rather than competition among team members. Team effectiveness also benefits from an organizational structure that clusters work activities within the team and creates fairly distinct boundaries between the team and other work units.[28]

Verafin Inc., which we featured in the previous section of this chapter, has applied several of these environmental conditions to support its teams. The St. John's, Newfoundland, software company's founders emphasize teamwork as one of four core values. The company also has a team-oriented workplace, including open offices (and no job titles), glass-walled meeting rooms, and casual spaces with massive whiteboards for impromptu scrums. Merrill Lynch Wealth Management, which was described at the beginning of this chapter, also provides a

team-friendly environment through a reward system that motivates financial advisors to work in teams rather than alone.[29]

Team Design Elements

Even in a team-friendly environment, the team's effectiveness will fall short of its potential if the task characteristics, team size, and team composition are poorly designed for the team's objectives and functioning.

TASK CHARACTERISTICS

The case study at the beginning of this chapter reported that investment banks and financial advisory firms have shifted to teams rather than individuals working alone as the preferred work structure. The main reason is the increasing complexity of investments and other services to meet client needs. Complex work requires skills and knowledge beyond one person's abilities. Teams are particularly well suited for complex work that can be divided into more specialized roles, particularly when team members in those specialized roles are able to coordinate frequently with each other.[30]

Task complexity demands teamwork, but teams also function better when the complex work is well-structured rather than ambiguous. Team members on an automobile assembly line have well-structured tasks. They perform the same set of tasks each day (low *task variability* -- see Chapter 6) and the work is predictable enough for well-established procedures (high *task analyzability*). The main benefit of well-structured tasks is that it is easier to coordinate the work among several people.

In contrast, ambiguous and unpredictable tasks are more difficult to coordinate among team members, which leads to higher process losses and errors. Fortunately, teams can still perform these less-structured tasks reasonably well when members are experienced in well-defined broader roles. During surgery, for example, medical team members know generally what to expect of one another even when unique problems arise.[31]

Task Interdependence

Another task-related influence on team effectiveness is **task interdependence**—the extent to which team members must share materials, information, or expertise to perform their jobs.[32] Apart from complete independence, there are three levels of task interdependence, as illustrated in Exhibit 8.3.[33] The lowest level, called *pooled interdependence,* occurs when an employee or work unit shares machinery, technical support, financial support, or other common (pooled) resources, but otherwise operates independently from other employees or work units. A higher level of interdependence occurs when the output of one person or work unit becomes the direct input for another person or unit. This *sequential interdependence* typically occurs on an assembly line because each team member's output is forwarded to the next person on the line for further assembly of the product or service.

Reciprocal interdependence, in which work output is exchanged back and forth among individuals or work units, produces the highest level of interdependence. People who design a new product or service would typically have reciprocal interdependence because their design decisions affect others involved in the design process. Any decision made by the design engineers would influence the work of the manufacturing engineers and purchasing specialists, and vice versa. Employees with reciprocal interdependence should be organized into teams to facilitate coordination in their interwoven relationship.

As a rule, the higher the level of task interdependence, the greater the need to organize people into teams rather

> **task interdependence** The extent to which employees must share materials, information, or expertise with others to perform their jobs.

EXHIBIT 8.3   Levels of Task Interdependence

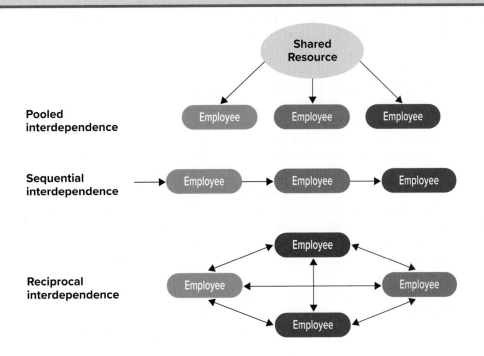

than have them work alone.[34] Higher task interdependence usually requires more intense coordination, and team structures enable better interpersonal communication than when employees work independently from each other or in different departments. High task interdependence also motivates most people to be part of the team and to coordinate with each other. This rule applies when team members have the same task goals, such as serving the same clients or collectively assembling the same product. When team members have different goals (such as serving different clients) but have high interdependence with others to achieve those unique goals, teamwork might create excessive conflict. Under these conditions, the company should try to reduce the level of interdependence or rely on supervision as a buffer or mediator among employees.

TEAM SIZE

What is the ideal size for a team? Online retailer Amazon relies on the "two-pizza team" rule, namely that a team should be small enough to be fed comfortably with two large pizzas. This works out to between five and seven employees. At the other extreme, a few experts suggest that tasks are becoming so complex that many teams need to have more than 100 members.[35] Unfortunately, the former piece of advice (two-pizza teams) is too simplistic, and the latter seems to have lost sight of the meaning and dynamics of real teams.

Teams should be large enough to provide the necessary abilities and viewpoints required for the assigned work, yet small enough to maintain efficient coordination and meaningful involvement of each member.[36] "You need to have a balance between having enough people to do all the things that need to be done, while keeping the team small enough so that it is cohesive and can make decisions effectively and speedily," advises Jim Hassell, board member and until recently Group CEO of BAI Communications, which designs, builds, and operates global telecommunications networks (including mobile and Wi-Fi networks for the Toronto, New York, and Hong Kong public transit systems).[37]

The ideal team size varies with the type of team, the tasks it is expected to perform, and the available forms of coordination (see Chapter 13).[38] Generally, smaller teams (say a half-dozen members) operate more effectively than larger teams because they have less process loss (easier coordination, less conflict, less time to make decisions, etc.). Members of smaller teams also tend to feel more engaged in teamwork because they have more influence on the group's norms and goals and feel more responsible for its successes and failures. Also, members of smaller teams get to know one another better, which improves mutual trust as well as perceived support, help, and assistance from those team members.[39]

Should companies have 100-person teams if the task is highly complex? The answer is that a group this large probably isn't a team, even if management calls it one. A team exists when its members interact and influence one another, are mutually accountable for achieving common goals associated with organizational objectives, and perceive themselves as a social entity within an organization. It is very difficult for everyone in a 100-person work unit to influence one another and perceive themselves as members of the same team. However, such complex tasks can usually be divided into several smaller teams.

TEAM COMPOSITION

Team effectiveness depends on the qualities of the people who are assigned to those teams.[40] To begin with, a team's performance depends on how well its members engage in *taskwork,* that is, task-related behaviours toward the achievement of the team's objectives. Taskwork requires team members who are highly motivated, possess the required abilities, and have clear role perceptions about how and when to perform the assigned work (see MARS model in Chapter 1).

But effective teams demand more than just individuals who perform their own jobs well. They also need members who are motivated, able, and have clear role perceptions about engaging in *teamwork* behaviours.[41] Teamwork behaviours maintain the team's existence and functioning. In other words, the best performing teams have members who are effective at performing their tasks and effective at supporting the team's dynamics. For this reason, RBC Capital Markets and many firms assess job applicants on their teamwork behaviours, not just their taskwork performance.

The most frequently mentioned teamwork behaviours are depicted in the "Five Cs" model illustrated in Exhibit 8.4. Coordinating, communicating, and cooperating are mainly (but not entirely) about supporting team members on their task, whereas comforting and conflict resolving primarily maintain healthy psychological and interpersonal dynamics in the team.[42]

- *Cooperating.* Effective team members are willing and able to work together rather than alone. This includes sharing resources and being sufficiently adaptive or flexible to accommodate the needs and preferences of other team members, such as rescheduling use of machinery so that another team member with a tighter deadline can use it.

- *Coordinating.* Effective team members actively manage the team's work so it is performed efficiently and harmoniously. This includes keeping the team on track and helping to integrate the work performed by different members. To effectively coordinate, team members must know the other team members' work to some extent, not just their own.

EXHIBIT 8.4 **Five Cs of Effective Teamwork Behaviours**

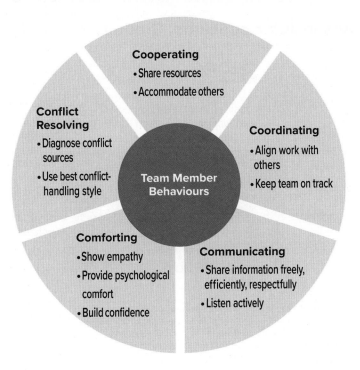

- *Communicating.* Effective team members transmit information freely (rather than reluctantly), efficiently (using the best channel and symbols), and respectfully (minimizing arousal of negative emotions).[43] They also listen actively to co-workers.

- *Comforting.* Effective team members help co-workers to maintain a positive and healthy psychological state. They show empathy, provide psychological comfort, and build co-worker feelings of confidence and self-worth.

- *Conflict resolving.* Conflict is inevitable in social settings, but effective team members have the skills and motivation to resolve disagreements within the group. This involves using appropriate conflict-handling styles as well as diagnostic skills to identify and resolve the structural sources of conflict.

Team Diversity

Diversity, another aspect of team composition, has both advantages and challenges for team effectiveness.[44] One advantage of diverse teams is that people from different backgrounds tend to see a problem or opportunity from different angles. Team members have different mental models, which increases their likelihood of identifying viable solutions to difficult problems. A second advantage is that diverse team members have a broader pool of technical abilities to serve clients or design new products. This explains why RBC

Capital Markets, Merrill Lynch Wealth Management, and most other firms in the finance industry increasingly rely on teams rather than individuals to serve clients.

A third advantage of diverse teams is that they often provide better representation of the team's constituents, such as other departments or clients from similarly diverse backgrounds. This representation not only brings different viewpoints to the decision; it also gives stakeholders a belief that they have a voice in that decision process. As we learned in Chapter 5, voice is an important ingredient in procedural justice, so stakeholders are more likely to believe the team's decision is fair when the team mirrors the surface or deep-level diversity of its constituents.

Team diversity also presents a number of challenges. Employees with diverse backgrounds take longer to become a high-performing team. This occurs partly because people with varied worldviews take longer to reach agreement on team goals, operational procedures, and informal team dynamics (norms, roles, etc.). The team development process is also slower because it takes longer to build trust with co-workers whose personal characteristics, experiences, and beliefs are different from ours.

A related challenge is that diverse teams are susceptible to "faultlines"—hypothetical dividing lines that may split a team into subgroups along gender, ethnic, professional, or other dimensions.[45] These faultlines undermine team effectiveness by reducing the motivation to communicate and

OB by the NUMBERS

Teamwork Behaviours in Job Applicants, Graduates, and Co-workers*

85% of 21,000 students at U.S. colleges and universities consider themselves proficient in teamwork/collaboration.

81% of 25,000 employees in 1,000 companies globally believe they have the right people on their team.

37% of 400 American employers surveyed say that recent college graduates are well prepared at working with others in teams.

67% of managers in 90 large Canadian private sector companies identify collaboration/teamwork skills as most important when evaluating job candidates.

51% of 1,021 hiring managers say that being team-oriented is a top soft skill they assess in job applicants.

©Khakimullin Aleksandr/Shutterstock

** Association of American Colleges & Universities, Falling Short? College Learning and Career Success (Washington, DC: Hart Research Associates, January 20, 2015); "Developing Canada's Future Workforce: A Survey of Large Private-Sector Employers" (Ottawa: Business Council of Canada and Aon Hewitt Inc., March 2016); "Are College Graduates 'Career Ready'?," News Release (Bethlehem, PA: National Association of Colleges and Employers, February 19, 2018); "The 2019 Employee Engagement Report" (Seattle: TINYpulse, February 21, 2019); "Forty Percent of Employers Plan to Hire Full-Time Workers This Year, Forty-Seven Percent Recruiting Part-Time Workers," News Release (Chicago: Career Builder, March 5, 2019).

coordinate with teammates on the other side of the hypothetical divisions. In contrast, members of homogeneous teams experience higher satisfaction, less conflict, and better interpersonal relations. As a result, homogeneous teams tend to be more effective on tasks requiring a high degree of cooperation and coordination, such as emergency response teams.

Team Processes

LO4

The third set of elements in the team effectiveness model, called *team processes,* includes team development, norms, roles, cohesion, trust, and team mental models. As we warned earlier in this chapter, the literature has varied and sometimes confounding definitions of team processes. We define team processes as cognitive and emotional dynamics of the team that continually change with the team's ongoing evolution and development. In other words, this section looks at the continuously evolving collective beliefs, expectations, and feelings of the team as well as how those team dynamics influence team effectiveness.

TEAM DEVELOPMENT

Team development is at the heart of team processes because the other dynamics—shaping norms, roles, cohesion, trust,

and mental models—are embedded in team development. Team members resolve several issues and pass through several stages of development before emerging as an effective work unit. They need to get to know and trust one another, understand and agree on their respective roles, discover appropriate and inappropriate behaviours (norms), develop mutual understanding of the team's objectives and their coordination in that process (team mental models), and develop a strong bond with the team and its members (cohesion).

Numerous team development models have been proposed over the past half century.[46] The model shown in Exhibit 8.5 is the most popular and captures the complexity of the team development processes better than most.[47] The diagram shows teams moving systematically from one stage to the next, while the dashed lines illustrate that teams might—and often do—fall back to an earlier stage of development as new members join or other conditions disrupt the team's maturity.

Forming, the first stage of team development, is a period of testing and orientation in which members learn about one another and evaluate the benefits and costs of continued membership. People tend to be polite, will defer to authority, and try to find out what is expected of them and how they will fit into the team. The *storming* stage is marked by interpersonal conflict as members become more proactive and compete for various team roles. Members try to establish norms of appropriate behaviour and performance standards.

Global Connections 8.2

DIVERSE TEAMS REORGANIZE RIJKSMUSEUM*

The Rijksmuseum in Amsterdam is the world's leading gallery of Dutch art and history. It is also a showcase for the power of diverse teams. Most museums organize their public display areas around paintings, glass, decorative arts, and other specialized collections. In contrast, Rijksmuseum recently reorganized its exhibit areas around century time periods.

"When you organize your own memory, you usually do it by important dates," explains Rijksmuseum general director Taco Dibbits. "We said, well if [Rijkmuseum represents] the country's memory and you organize it by dates you will have a chronological display."

To display diverse objects aesthetically and historically together within each time period, the museum formed cross-functional teams that included representation of staff from the numerous specialized collections. Over 18 months, each working group developed proposals about how the display area for that century should be organized and which objects should be publicly shown.

The process wasn't easy because the curators of each specialization previously had their own distinct section of the museum and worked autonomously from the others. There was also ambiguity about which types of objects should receive priority for each time period. But through their diversity, the teams generated unique ideas and their members gained a fuller understanding and appreciation of co-workers from other specializations.

The proposals submitted by the initial working groups were promising, but they included far too many items for the space available. "Our solution was to basically dissolve the task forces and assemble new ones," says Dibbits. "Their new mission was to create a selection one-third the size of what the first groups had proposed." In addition, the new diverse teams had to provide written justification for inclusion of the objects retained from the first team's list. Dibbits observed that creating the second set of teams with documented justification for their decisions "gave all the specialists a feeling of ownership in the creation of the museum's offerings, even beyond their own area of expertise."

Rijksmuseum continues to form new temporary teams for various initiatives and strategic issues. The teams are typically limited to between five and seven members. "If you have more than seven people, it's difficult to have a fruitful discussion, because by the time everyone gets to have their say, you've lost speed," Dibbits points out. It is also more difficult for employees to remain silent when they are in small teams. One limitation is that small teams don't enable representation from all of the museum's specialist groups. "Ultimately, it's important to communicate from the start that everyone's time on these task forces will come," says Dibbits. "We continue to regularly mix up the people in these groups so that everyone has a chance to participate."

©Danita Delimont/Alamy Stock Photo

* C. Higgins, "Rijksmuseum to Reopen after Dazzling Refurbishment and Rethink," *The Guardian*, April 5, 2013; TEFAF, *TEFAF New York Fall 2016—A Conversation with Taco Dibbits, Director of the Rijksmuseum,* YouTube (New York, 2016), https://www.youtube.com/watch?v=lmzwcp1-IVQ; W. Aghina and A. Webb, "The Rijksmuseum's Agile Process: An Interview with Director Taco Dibbits," *McKinsey Quarterly,* October 2018.

During the *norming* stage, the team develops its first real sense of cohesion as roles are established and a consensus forms around group objectives and common as well as complementary team-based mental models. By the *performing* stage, team members have learned to efficiently coordinate and resolve conflicts. In high-performance teams, members are highly cooperative, have a high level of trust in one another, have functional shared mental models of group objectives and work processes, and identify with the team. Finally, the *adjourning* stage occurs when the team is about to disband. Team members shift their attention away from task orientation to a relationship focus.

This model depicts team development fairly well because it identifies and incorporates the various other team processes that occur over time. It notes that teams become cohesive, develop norms to guide behaviour, assign roles, form team mental models, and develop trust in one another. However, the model is not a perfect representation of team development.[48] It does not show that some teams remain in a particular stage longer than others and does not explain why teams sometimes regress back to earlier stages of development. Perhaps most important, this model does not explain the intricacies of how norms, cohesion, mental models, and other team dynamics evolve (often rapidly) over time. Fortunately, these team processes are explained by separate theories. The remainder of this section describes each of these, beginning with team norms.

TEAM NORMS

Norms are the informal rules and shared expectations that groups establish to regulate the behaviour of their members. Norms apply only to behaviour, not to private thoughts or feelings. Furthermore, norms exist only for behaviours that are important to the team.[49] The team development model in Exhibit 8.5 suggests that team norms develop during the storming stage, likely because conflict often occurs when members try to reach agreement on what

> **norms** The informal rules and shared expectations that groups establish to regulate the behaviour of their members.

behaviour is expected or forbidden. However, it is more accurate to say that norms begin as soon as the team forms and that some norms continue to change over the team's lifespan.

Teams develop norms for a few reasons. First, most norms develop when members associate these behaviours with the team's performance or the well-being of its members. The perceived value of norms motivates members to enact them as well as influence others to do the same.[50] Some norms originate from a critical incident; for instance, a norm of wearing safety glasses emerges after a team member is seriously hurt from not wearing them. Other norms are brought into the team due to experiences that some members have had in previous teams.[51]

Second, team norms develop because they improve predictability and conflict-avoidance in co-worker relations. Newcomers, for instance, try to fit in with the group by actively discovering and behaving consistently with the team's norms. Third, teams develop norms to routinize behaviour with minimal cognitive effort, which improves social order and coordination of each member's activities. This explains why norms often develop regarding seemingly minor issues, such as where people sit in meetings.

An important feature of team norms is that they are enforced.[52] Co-workers display their displeasure if we are absent from work too often or don't have our part of a project

---

EXHIBIT 8.5   Stages of Team Development

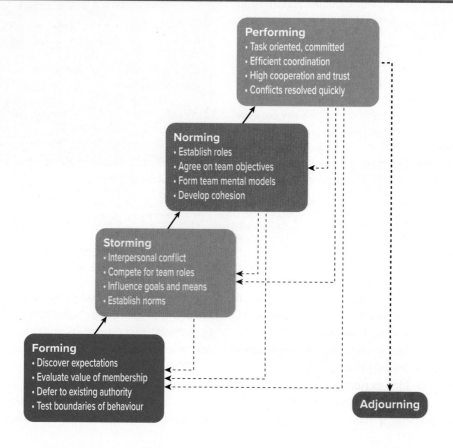

completed on time. Norms are also directly reinforced through praise from high-status members and easier access to valued resources. These forms of peer pressure and reinforcement can occur even when team members work remotely from one another. But team members often conform to prevailing norms without direct reinforcement or punishment because they identify with the group and want to align their behaviour with the team's expectations. The more closely the person's social identity is connected to the group, the more the individual is motivated to obey the team's norms.[53]

Developing and Changing Team Norms

Two of the best ways to establish desired norms in new teams are to select team members whose values and past behaviour are compatible with those norms and to clearly state the norms when those people are assigned to the team. As an example, if organizational leaders want their teams to have strong safety norms, they should hire people who already value safety and clearly state the importance of safety during one of the team's first meetings.

For existing teams, research indicates that leaders have the capacity to remove dysfunctional norms by cautioning team members against these behaviours. They can also introduce desired norms through ongoing coaching of team members.[54] Another suggestion that works sometimes (but not always) is to introduce team-based rewards that counteract dysfunctional norms. Finally, if dysfunctional norms are deeply ingrained and the previous solutions don't work, it may be necessary to disband the group and form a new team whose members have more appropriate norms.

TEAM ROLES

An inherent part of the team development process is assigning and maintaining team roles. A **role** is a set of behaviours that people are expected to perform because they hold specific formal or informal positions in a team and organization.[55] Roles are similar to norms in the sense that they both establish and reinforce expected patterns of behaviour. However, most norms apply to all team members whereas a role typically applies to one or a few specific team members.

role A set of behaviours that people are expected to perform because they hold specific formal or informal positions in a team and organization.

Some team roles are formally assigned to individual members during the team composition aspect of team design. For example, most teams have a leader, who is expected to help clarify task responsibilities, ensure that everyone has an opportunity to present their views in meetings, and so forth. However, many roles are adopted informally during the team development process. Informal roles are shared, but many are eventually associated with specific team members through subtle positioning and negotiation. In many cases, employees are attracted to roles that suit their personality and values. In other cases, team members encourage specific co-workers to take on selected roles.

Several experts have tried to categorize the dozens of team roles that have been proposed over the years.[56] One recent model, shown in Exhibit 8.6, identifies six role categories:

EXHIBIT 8.6 Examples of Team Roles

Role	Description
Organizer	A team member who acts to structure what the team is doing. An Organizer also keeps track of accomplishments and how the team is progressing relative to goals and timelines.
Doer	A team member who willingly takes on work and gets things done. A Doer can be counted on to complete work, meet deadlines, and take on tasks to ensure the team's success. This person should focus on goal accomplishment.
Challenger	A team member who will push the team to explore all aspects of a situation and to consider alternative assumptions, explanations, and solutions. A Challenger often asks "why" and is comfortable debating and critiquing. Think of this role as the team's devil's advocate.
Innovator	A team member who regularly generates new and creative ideas, strategies, and approaches for how the team can handle various situations and challenges. An Innovator often offers original and imaginative suggestions.
Team Builder	A team member who helps establish norms, supports decisions, and maintains a positive work atmosphere within the team. A Team Builder calms members when they are stressed, and motivates them when they are down.
Connector	A team member who helps bridge and connect the team with people, groups, or other stakeholders outside of the team. Think of Connectors as "boundary spanners," who ensure good working relationships between the team and "outsiders."

What team roles do you prefer? You can discover which roles you prefer in meetings and similar team activities by locating this self-assessment in Connect.

organizer, doer, challenger, innovator, team builder, and connector. More broadly, most team roles focus on either task performance (taskwork) or team maintenance (teamwork). Taskwork roles might include coordinating the team, providing constructive critique of the team's plans, and motivating team members when effort is lagging. Teamwork roles might include providing emotional support when the team is frustrated, maintaining harmony among team members, and creating opportunities for social interaction among team members.

TEAM COHESION

Another team process is **team cohesion**, which refers to the degree of attraction people feel toward the team and their motivation to remain members. A team has high cohesion when its members are attracted to the team, take ownership of the team's success, make the team part of their self-concept, are committed to the team's goals or tasks, and feel a collective sense of team pride.[57] Thus, team cohesion is an emotional experience, not just a calculation of whether to stay or leave the team.

team cohesion The degree of attraction people feel toward the team and their motivation to remain members.

Influences on Team Cohesion

Team cohesion increases with team development. Six of the most important influences on team cohesion are described below. Some of these conditions strengthen the individual's identity with the team; others strengthen the individual's belief that team membership will fulfil personal needs.

- *Member similarity.* A well-established research finding is that we are attracted more to co-workers who are similar to us.[58] This similarity-attraction effect occurs because we assume that people are more trustworthy and more likely to accept us if they look and act like us. We also believe that these similar others will create fewer conflicts and violations of our expectations. Thus, teams have higher cohesion or become cohesive more quickly when members are similar to one another. In contrast, high cohesion is more difficult and takes longer for teams with diverse members. This difficulty depends on the form of diversity, however. Teams consisting of people from different job groups seem to get along just as well as teams of people from the same job.[59]

- *Team size.* Smaller teams tend to have more cohesion than larger teams. One reason is that it is easier for a few people to agree on goals and coordinate work activities, so they experience less conflict. Another reason is that members have more influence in smaller teams, so they feel a greater sense of involvement and ownership in the team. However, small teams have less cohesion when they lack enough members to perform the required tasks.

- *Member interaction.* Teams tend to have more cohesion when their members interact with one another fairly regularly. More frequent interaction occurs when team members perform highly interdependent tasks and work in the same physical area or at least communicate remotely through channels with high social presence.

- *Somewhat difficult entry.* Teams tend to have more cohesion when entry to the team is restricted. The more elite the team, the more prestige it confers on its members, and the more they tend to value their membership in the unit. At the same time, research suggests that severe initiations can weaken team cohesion because of the adverse effects of humiliation, even for those who successfully endure the initiation.[60]

- *Team success.* Team cohesion increases with the team's success because people are attracted to groups that fulfil their needs and goals.[61] Furthermore, individuals are more likely to identify with successful teams than with teams that often fail to achieve their goals.

- *External competition and challenges.* Teams tend to have more cohesion when they face external competition or a challenging objective that is important to them. This might include a threat from an external competitor or friendly competition from other teams. Employees value their membership on the team because of its ability to overcome the threat or competition and as a form of social support. However, cohesion can dissipate when external challenges overwhelm the team and threaten its success or viability.[62]

Consequences of Team Cohesion

Teams with higher cohesion tend to perform better than those with low cohesion.[63] In fact, the team's existence depends on a minimal level of cohesion because it motivates team members to remain members and to help the team achieve its objectives. Members of high-cohesion teams spend more time together, share information more frequently, and are

Global Connections 8.3

COMMUNAL MEALS BUILD TEAM COHESION*

When Patrick Mathieu became a firefighter at the Fire Rescue Department in Waterloo, Ontario, he soon learned that communal meals support the team's cohesion and trust. "In the fire service, we pride ourselves on teamwork and unity," says Mathieu. "Eating and cooking is part of our firefighter culture and I have seen the immense team-building benefits that result from a platoon cooking together."

A recent study supports Mathieu's observations. It found that fire stations where the team usually ate together performed better than stations where firefighters ate alone. The higher performance was attributed to better cooperation, trust, and other outcomes of high cohesion.

Mathieu has become a popular chef at his fire station in Waterloo and recently competed in a Canada-wide cooking contest. But the favourite dish among firefighters in his platoon is jalapeño kettle chip fish tacos, partly because everyone is involved in its creation. "With everyone in the kitchen, we talk, laugh, joke and create something special together," he says. "It brings us in for bonding, just like a family dinner."

Mathieu notes that there is one risk of cooking great meals in a fire station. "You make the call for everyone

to come to dinner. Boom—the alarm goes off. Yep, the meal sits and waits until we come back."

©Waterloo firefighter and The FireHouse Chef Cookbook author Patrick Mathieu, @stationhousecco, stationhouse_

* K.M. Kniffin et al., "Eating Together at the Firehouse: How Workplace Commensality Relates to the Performance of Firefighters," *Human Performance* 28, no. 4 (2015): 281–306; J. Hicks, "Ready to Handle the Heat: Waterloo Firefighter a Culinary Contender on Chopped Canada," *Waterloo Regional Record* (Kitchener, Ontario), January 29, 2015, A1; P. Mathieu, "Recipe Rescue: Bond over Meal Prep," *Canadian Firefighter,* April 11, 2016; "How Food Helps Both Firefighters and Families Bond," *CBC News,* December 21, 2017.

more satisfied with one another. They give each other more social support in stressful situations and work to minimize dysfunctional conflict.[64] When conflict does arise, high-cohesion team members tend to resolve their differences swiftly and effectively.

The relationship between team cohesion and team performance depends on two conditions, however. First, team cohesion has less effect on team performance when the team has low task interdependence.[65] High cohesion motivates employees to coordinate and cooperate with other team members. But cooperation and coordination are less critical when the team members don't depend on each other to perform their jobs (i.e., low task interdependence), so the motivational effect of high cohesion is less relevant under those conditions.

Second, the effect of cohesion on team performance depends on whether the team's norms are aligned or conflict with organizational objectives.[66] As Exhibit 8.7 illustrates, teams with high cohesion perform better when their norms support the company's goals, whereas higher cohesion can

potentially reduce team performance when norms conflict with organizational objectives. This effect occurs because cohesion motivates employees to perform at a level more consistent with team norms. If a team's norm tolerates or encourages absenteeism, for example, employees will be more motivated to take unjustified sick leave. If the team's norm discourages absenteeism, employees are more motivated to avoid taking sick leave.

One last comment about team cohesion and performance: A few paragraphs ago, we stated that team performance (success) causes cohesion, whereas we are now saying that team cohesion causes team performance. Both statements are correct. Teams with higher cohesion perform better, and teams with better performance become more cohesive. Which direction is stronger? A major review of past studies reported that in established teams (i.e., typical of teams in most organizations), cohesion has a much stronger effect on team performance than the effect of team performance on team cohesion. Only lab experiments that studied short-lived

---

EXHIBIT 8.7   Effect of Team Cohesion on Task Performance

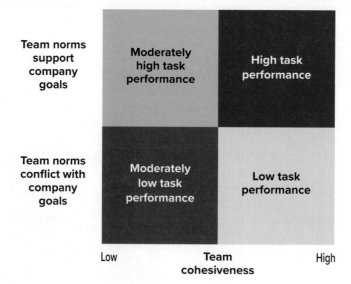

Team norms support company goals

Moderately high task performance | High task performance

Team norms conflict with company goals

Moderately low task performance | Low task performance

Low — **Team cohesiveness** — High

---

student teams found that both directions were equal. Student teams typically have fairly low cohesion due to their brief existence and non-essential purpose to most members.[67]

TEAM TRUST

Any relationship—including the relationship among team members—depends on a certain degree of trust.[68] **Trust**

> **trust** Positive expectations one person has toward another person or group in situations involving risk.

refers to positive expectations one person has toward another person in situations involving risk (see Chapter 4). Trust is ultimately perceptual; we trust others on the basis of our beliefs about their ability, integrity, and benevolence. Trust is also emotional; we experience positive feelings toward those we trust.[69]

Trust is built on three foundations in a hierarchy from lowest to highest: calculus, knowledge, and identification (see Exhibit 8.8).[70] *Calculus-based trust* represents a logical calculation that other team members will act appropriately because they face sanctions if their actions violate reasonable expectations.[71] It offers the lowest potential trust and is easily broken by a violation of expectations. Some scholars suggest that calculus-based trust is not trust at all. Instead, it might be trust in the system rather than in the other person. In any event, calculus-based trust alone cannot sustain a team's relationship because it relies on deterrence.

Knowledge-based trust is based on the predictability of another team member's behaviour. This predictability refers only to "positive expectations"—as the definition of trust

states—because you would not trust someone who tends to engage in harmful or dysfunctional behaviour. Knowledge-based trust includes our confidence in the other person's abilities, such as the confidence that exists when we trust a physician. It also includes perceptions of the other person's reliability and consistency in performing good deeds or enacting their values.[72] Knowledge-based trust offers a higher potential level of trust than calculus-based trust and it is more stable because it develops over time.

Identification-based trust is based on mutual understanding and an emotional bond among team members. It occurs when team members think, feel, and act like one another. High-performance teams exhibit this level of trust because they share the same values and mental models. Identification-based trust is potentially the strongest and most robust of all three types of trust.[73] The individual's self-concept is based partly on membership in the team whose members hold similar values, so any transgressions by other team members are quickly forgiven. People are more reluctant to acknowledge a violation of this high-level trust because it strikes at the heart of their self-concept.

Dynamics of Team Trust

Employees typically join a team with a moderate or high level—not a low level—of trust in their new co-workers.[74] The main explanation why people have high trust (called *swift trust*) at the outset is that they usually believe fellow team members are reasonably competent (knowledge-based trust) and they tend to develop some degree of social identity with the team (identification-based trust). Even when working with strangers, most employees display some level

EXHIBIT 8.8   Three Foundations of Trust in Teams

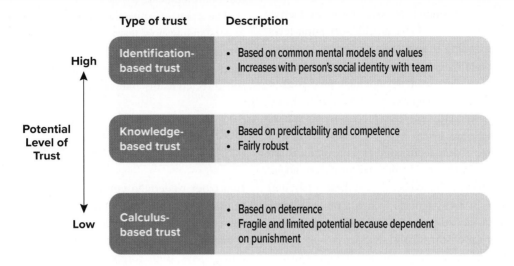

of trust, if only because it supports their self-view of being a good person. However, trust is fragile in new relationships because it is based on assumptions rather than well-established experience.[75] Studies report that trust tends to decrease rather than increase over time. This is unfortunate, because employees become less forgiving and less cooperative toward others as their level of trust decreases, which damages both teamwork and taskwork.

TEAM MENTAL MODELS

Mental models are visual or relational images in our mind that we develop to describe, explain, and predict the world around us (see Chapter 3). Team mental models are cognitive images that team members form about the team's tasks, relationship dynamics, and knowledge repository.[76] Team members have both shared and complementary mental models. As a team matures, its members form shared mental models, meaning that they develop similar images and expectations about the team's objectives, shared values, behaviour norms, and work style, as well as a general picture of how each member participates in the work process.

Complementary mental models are cognitive images held by specific (rather than all) team members but that are compatible with the mental models held by other team members. Each team member has unique images of how the team operates because they have a unique background and are located in different parts of the work process than other team members. For example, engineering team members would view customers somewhat differently from how marketing members of that team view customers. In successful teams, each member's mental model operates in harmony with the unique mental models of other team members.

Shared and complementary mental models enable team members to establish effective coordinating routines.[77] In high-performing teams, each member develops habitual work practices that coordinate almost automatically with the behaviours and expectations of other members. This alignment of mental images and predictions also supports the perception that the group is a functioning social entity with meaningful purpose and performance capabilities.

Team mental models also help team members to know where knowledge is located within the team.[78] Members of cross-functional teams, for instance, have diverse knowledge and skills (production, legal, marketing, technology, etc.) that are collectively applied to achieve the team's objectives. To make better decisions or serve clients well, team members often need to consult with co-workers who possess specific skills and knowledge. This awareness of the team's diverse knowledge repository is therefore a vital part of team mental models.

mental models Knowledge structures that we develop to describe, explain, and predict the world around us.

How trusting are you? You can discover your trust propensity by locating this self-assessment in Connect.

IMPROVING TEAM PROCESSES THROUGH TEAM BUILDING

Teams require time to become cohesive, form productive norms, assign roles, build knowledge and identification-level trust, and form functioning shared and complementary mental models. Team building consists of activities that attempt to speed up or improve these team development processes.[79]

As we have emphasized throughout this section, team development consists of several diverse team processes. Therefore, not surprisingly, there are several types of team building to serve those processes. Some team-building interventions are task-focused. They clarify the team's performance goals, increase the team's motivation to accomplish these goals, and establish a mechanism for systematic feedback on the team's goal performance. A second type of team building focuses on improving the team's problem-solving skills.

A third team building category clarifies and reconstructs each member's perception of their role as well as the role expectations that member has of other team members. Role-definition team building also helps the team to develop shared and complementary mental models, such as how to interact with clients, maintain machinery, and engage in meetings.[80] A fourth—and likely the most popular—type of team building is aimed at helping team members to improve interpersonal relations, such as building trust in each other and becoming a more cohesive team.[81] Popular interventions such as wilderness team activities, paintball wars, and obstacle-course challenges are intended to support these team processes.

Do team building interventions support team development and associated processes? The answer is that all four types of team building are potentially effective, but some interventions work better than others and in some situations more than others.[82] Goal setting tends to be the most successful type of team building, although role clarification and adventure programs (to improve interpersonal relations) are also effective to some extent. Interventions are also more successful when they focus on one rather than multiple team-building objectives.

However, many team-building activities are less successful.[83] One problem is that team building interventions are used as general solutions to ambiguously defined team problems. A better approach is to begin with a sound diagnosis of the team's health and then select team-building interventions that address specific weaknesses. Another problem is that team building is applied as a one-shot medical inoculation that every team should receive when it is formed. In truth, team development is ongoing, so team building should occur at various points during the team's existence. Finally, we must remember that team building occurs on the job, not just on an obstacle course or in a national park. Organizations

should encourage team members to reflect on their work experiences and to experiment with just-in-time learning for team development.

The team effectiveness model is a useful template for understanding how teams work—and don't work—in organizations. With this knowledge in hand, let's investigate two types of teams that have become important in organizations: self-directed teams and remote teams.

Self-Directed Teams

LO5

Buurtzorg Nederland employs almost 15,000 professionals (mostly registered nurses) in more than 1,000 self-directed teams across the Netherlands and other countries. "Self-managing teams have professional freedom with responsibility," says Buurtzorg's website. Each self-directed team consists of up to 12 nurses responsible for between 50 and 60 home-care patients, most of whom are elderly, disabled, or terminally ill. The team members have autonomy to organize the work, make decisions, and build their own caseload of new clients. Performance is measured at the team level, including patient satisfaction, work efficiency, and cost savings. Independent studies report that Buurtzorg's self-directed teams are significantly more cost-efficient than traditional (mostly non-team) services by competitors. Employees also enjoy the team structure. The company has been the top employer in the Netherlands for several consecutive years.[84]

Buurtzorg Nederland is a global model of an organization designed around self-directed teams. **Self-directed teams (SDTs)** are cross-functional groups organized around work processes that complete an entire piece of work requiring several interdependent tasks and have substantial autonomy over the execution of those tasks.[85] This definition captures two distinct features of SDTs. First, these teams complete an entire piece of work requiring several interdependent tasks. Employees within the team are clustered together with minimal interdependence or interaction with people outside the team. The result is a close-knit group of employees who depend on each other to accomplish the team's work objectives. The second distinctive feature of SDTs is that they have substantial autonomy over the execution of their tasks. In particular, these teams plan, organize, and control work activities with little or no direct involvement of a higher-status supervisor.

> **self-directed teams (SDTs)** Cross-functional work groups that are organized around work processes, complete an entire piece of work requiring several interdependent tasks, and have substantial autonomy over the execution of those tasks.

©YASUYOSHI CHIBA/AFP/Getty Images

GE's (General Electric's) aviation plant in Bromont, Quebec, manufactures parts used in the world's most sophisticated aircraft engines for Boeing, Airbus, and other aerospace firms. It is also a world leader in automation and robotics. But you won't find any managers on the plant floor. For the past three decades, the Bromont plant has relied on self-directed teams to get the work done. Production planning, manufacturing process improvements, vacation schedules, and other managerial decisions are determined by the teams themselves. "We say we need x output, and then [production teams] are left to decide, how do they get all that done?" explains a human resources leader at GE Bromont. "That's how a full teaming system works."*

*N. Van Praet, "GE to Modernize Its Aircraft Engine Parts Plant in Quebec," *Globe & Mail,* February 9, 2017; S. Kessler, "GE Has a Version of Self-Management That Is Much like Zappos' Holacracy—and It Works," *Quartz,* June 6, 2017; C. Thatcher, "Smart Factory: GE Aviation," *Skies Magazine,* August 2, 2017.

Self-directed teams are found in several industries. Most of the top-rated manufacturing firms in North America apparently rely on SDTs.[86] Indeed, self-directed teams have become such a popular way to organize employees that many companies don't realize they have them. The popularity of SDTs is consistent with research indicating that they potentially increase both productivity and job satisfaction.[87] For instance, one study found that car dealership service shops that organize employees into SDTs are significantly more profitable than shops where employees work without a team structure. Another study reported that both short- and long-term measures of customer satisfaction increased after street cleaners in a German city were organized into SDTs.

SUCCESS FACTORS FOR SELF-DIRECTED TEAMS

The success of self-directed teams depends on several factors.[88] SDTs should be responsible for an entire work process, such as making an entire product or providing a service. This structure keeps each team sufficiently independent from other teams, yet it demands a relatively high degree of interdependence among employees within the team.[89] SDTs should also have sufficient autonomy to organize and coordinate their work. Autonomy allows them to respond more quickly and effectively to client and stakeholder demands. It also increases intrinsic motivation among team members. Finally, SDTs are more successful when the work site and technology support coordination and communication among team members. Too often, management calls a group of employees a "team," yet the work layout, assembly-line structure, and other technologies isolate the employees from one another.

Remote (Virtual) Teams

Chapter 1 described how remote work—performing work from home or other non-business sites—has become a common arrangement in most organizations. However, the COVID-19 pandemic made remote work more appealing and necessary as a productive way to apply social distancing and self-isolation practices. Most employees work in teams for some or all of their tasks, so the increasing popularity of remote work has produced more remote teams.

Remote teams (also known as *virtual* or *distributed teams*) are teams whose members operate across space, time, and orga-

remote teams Teams whose members operate across space, time, and organizational boundaries and are linked through information technologies to achieve organizational tasks.

nizational boundaries and are linked through information technologies to achieve organizational tasks.[90] Remote teams differ from traditional teams in two ways: (1) one or more members work remotely at least

some of the time rather than always being co-located (working in the same physical area as co-workers), and (2) due to their lack of co-location, members of remote teams depend on information technologies in addition to or instead of face-to-face interaction to communicate and coordinate their work effort.

Teams vary in their degree of remoteness (or *virtuality*). Team remoteness increases with the geographic dispersion of team members, percentage of members who work apart, and percentage of time that members work apart.[91] For example, a team has minimal remoteness when most of its members work in the same physical location most days and only one or two work from home occasionally. High remoteness exists when team members are spread around the world and few members have met the others face to face.

The social distancing and self-isolation requirements in the recent COVID-19 pandemic have made remote teams more commonplace. However, these teams were gaining popularity in organizations long before the recent pandemic. One factor is that an increasing percentage of employees perform knowledge work (rather than physical production work), which enables them to do their job from almost anywhere. Second, information technologies have made it easier than ever to communicate and coordinate remotely with other knowledge workers.[92] A third factor is the increasing

human capital The knowledge, skills, abilities, creative thinking, and other valued resources that employees bring to the organization.

recognition that the organization's competitive advantage is its **human capital**—the knowledge, skills, abilities, creativity, and other valued resources

that employees bring to the organization. Leveraging the potential of human capital typically occurs through teams, many of which have degrees of remoteness because staff members are distributed across several cities and countries.

SUCCESS FACTORS FOR REMOTE TEAMS

Remote teams face all the challenges of traditional teams, as well as the issues arising from time and distance. These

challenges increase with the team's remoteness, particularly when it exists for only a short time.[93] Fortunately, OB research has identified the following strategies to minimize most remote team problems.[94] First, remote team members need to apply the effective team behaviours (the five Cs) described earlier in this chapter. They also require good communication technology skills, self-leadership skills to motivate and guide their behaviour without peers or bosses nearby, and emotional intelligence to decipher the feelings of other team members from text messages and other limited communication media.

Second, remote teams should have a toolkit of communication channels (messaging, online whiteboards, video conferencing, etc.) as well as the freedom to choose the channels that work best for them.[95] This recommendation may seem obvious, but unfortunately senior management tends to impose technology on remote teams—often based on advice from external consultants—and expects team members to use the same communication technology throughout their work. In contrast, research suggests that communication channels gain and lose importance over time, depending on the task and level of trust.

Third, remote teams need plenty of structure. In one review, many of the principles for successful remote teams related mostly to creating these structures, such as clear operational objectives, documented work processes, and agreed-on roles and responsibilities.[96] The final recommendation is that remote team members should meet face-to-face fairly early in the team development process. This idea may seem contradictory to the entire notion of remote teams, but so far, no technology has replaced face-to-face interaction for high-level bonding and mutual understanding.[97]

Team Decision Making

LO6

Self-directed teams, remote teams, and practically all other groups are expected to make decisions. Under specific conditions, teams are more effective than individuals at identifying problems, choosing alternatives, and evaluating their decisions. To leverage these benefits, however, we first need to understand the constraints on effective team decision making. Then, we look at specific team structures that try to overcome these constraints.

CONSTRAINTS ON TEAM DECISION MAKING

Anyone who has spent enough time in the workplace can recite several ways in which teams stumble in decision

Debating Point: ARE REMOTE TEAMS MORE TROUBLE THAN THEY'RE WORTH?

Remote teams were rare before the Internet. Today, they are almost as commonplace as face-to-face teams. To some extent, remote teams have even become "cool." But whether they are stylish or commonplace, remote teams seem to be increasingly necessary for an organization's competitive advantage. In spite of the importance of remote teams, there are a few arguments against them.* Critics don't deny the potential value of creating these teams. Rather, they have added up the negative features and concluded that they outweigh the benefits. A few organizations have even curtailed the extent that employees are allowed to work remotely because of possible problems with their physical absence from the workplace.

One persistent problem is that remote teams lack the richness of face-to-face communication. We'll provide more detail about this important matter in Chapter 9, but no information technology to date offers the same degree of social presence or information richness as communication among people located in the same room.

Another problem is that trust among remote team members is either lower or more fragile compared with co-located team members.** In fact, experts offer one main recommendation to increase trust among remote team

members—have them spend time together as co-located teams.

A third drawback with remote teams is that the farther away people are located, the more they differ in experiences, beliefs, culture, and expectations. These differences can be advantageous for some decisions, of course, but they can also be a curse for team development and performance.

Here's one more reason why companies should think twice before relying on remote teams: People seem to have less influence or control over distant than over co-located co-workers. A team member who stops by your cubicle to ask how your part of the report is coming along has much more effect than an impersonal—or even a flaming—email from afar.

Perhaps that is why surveys reveal less satisfaction with remote team members than co-located team members.*** Surveys report that remote employees believe other team members are less willing to support them and more likely to say bad things behind their back compared to co-located co-workers. Remote workers also receive more complaints than co-located colleagues about working ineffectively (falling behind on projects, missing deadlines, etc.).

* G.R. Berry, "Enhancing Effectiveness on Virtual Teams: Understanding Why Traditional Team Skills Are Insufficient," *The Journal of Business Communication* 48, no. 2 (2011): 186–206; J.H. Dulebohn and J.E. Hoch, "Virtual Teams in Organizations," *Human Resource Management Review* 27, no. 4 (2017): 569–74; S. Mak and S.W.J. Kozlowski, "Virtual Teams: Conceptualization, Integrative Review, and Research Recommendations," in *The Cambridge Handbook of Technology and Employee Behavior,* ed. R.N. Landers, Cambridge Handbooks in Psychology (Cambridge: Cambridge University Press, 2019), 441–79.
** J.V. Hacker et al., "Trust in Virtual Teams: A Multidisciplinary Review and Integration," *Australasian Journal of Information Systems* 23 (2019), https://doi.org/10.3127/ajis.v23i0.1757.
*** *Long-Distance Loathing (Summary and Data),* (Provo, Utah: VitalSmarts, March 2009); "Virtual Reality: Remote Employees Experience More Workplace Politics Than Onsite Teammates," News Release (Provo, Utah: VitalSmarts, November 2, 2017).

making. The four most common problems are time constraints, evaluation apprehension, pressure to conform, and overconfidence.

Time Constraints

Committees keep minutes and waste hours. This popular saying captures the fact that teams take longer than individuals to make decisions.[98] Teams consume time organizing, coordinating, and maintaining relationships (i.e., process losses). Team members require time to build rapport, agree on rules and norms of behaviour in the decision process, and understand one another's ideas.

Another time-related constraint in most team structures is that only one person can speak at a time.[99] This problem, known

as **production blocking**, undermines idea generation in a few ways. First, team members need to listen in on the conversation to find an opportune time to speak

> **production blocking** A time constraint in team decision making due to the procedural requirement that only one person may speak at a time.

up, but this monitoring makes it difficult for them to concentrate on their own ideas. Second, ideas are fleeting, so the longer participants wait to speak, the more likely their flickering ideas will die out. Third, team members might remember their fleeting thoughts by concentrating on them, but this causes them to pay less attention to the conversation. By ignoring what others are saying, team members miss other potentially good ideas.

Global Connections 8.4

MEETUPS STRENGTHEN AUTOMATTIC'S REMOTE TEAMS*

Cesar Abeid lives in London, Ontario, where he leads 15 customer service employees (called happiness engineers) at Automattic. Abeid's team members work well together even though they don't physically work together. In fact, Abeid is the only Automattic employee who lives in London, Ontario.

Automattic, which makes the blogging platform WordPress and other popular site-building products, is a completely distributed organization. It has no physical head office (its mailing address is a UPS postal box in San Francisco) and all of its 1,200 employees work in remote teams from their home locations in 75 countries.

More than 50 Automattic employees live across Canada — from Dawson City, Yukon, to Bedford, Nova Scotia. Even Automattic's executives are distributed. For example, the head of engineering for WordPress VIP lives near Barrie, Ontario.

One key reason for the success of Automattic's distributed teams is that every group meets face-to-face at least twice each year. "Each team will have their own team meetup," usually in the spring or early summer, Abeid explains. "That's a week that we do some work together, but also activities. We hang out at dinners and go out and play, things like that."

Most Automattic employees also have occasional social gatherings with other employees who live in the area. "Toronto is a two-hour drive, and there's a lot of [Automattic] people in that area," says Abeid. "So we'll try to do a yearly Automattic dinner in Toronto for people who are local."

But the most memorable gathering each year is the Grand Meetup, an annual week-long event attended by all Automattic employees. One annual meeting was in Whistler, B.C. The company encourages networking by assigning employees to eat with different co-workers at each meal. A statistical analysis revealed that after attending a recent Grand Meetup, new hires formed strong network ties and current employees expanded their connections with co-workers in other teams around the company.

©ZUMA Press, Inc./Alamy Stock Photo

* O. Staley, "The Creator of WordPress Shares His Secret to Running a Remote Workplace," *Quartz at Work,* May 29, 2018; M. Hollingsworth, "Cesar Abeid, Happiness Team Lead at Automattic," *The Remote Show* (podcast), April 24, 2019, https://weworkremotely.com/the-remote-show-podcast/cesar-abeid-happiness-team-lead-at-automattic. "Work With Us," Automattic (blog), accessed February 7, 2020, https://automattic.com/work-with-us/.

Evaluation Apprehension

Team members are often reluctant to mention ideas that seem silly because they believe (often correctly) that other team members are silently evaluating them.[100] This **evaluation apprehension** is based on the individual's desire to create a favourable public image and need to protect self-esteem. It is most common in meetings attended by people with different levels of status or expertise or when members formally evaluate each other's performance throughout the year. Creative ideas often sound bizarre or illogical when first presented, so evaluation apprehension tends to discourage employees from mentioning them in front of co-workers.

evaluation apprehension
Occurs when individuals are reluctant to mention ideas that seem silly because they believe that others in the decision-making team are silently evaluating them.

Pressure to Conform

Team cohesion leads employees to conform to the team's norms. This control keeps the group organized around common goals, but it may also cause team members to suppress their dissenting opinions, particularly when a strong team norm is related to the issue. When someone does state a point of view that violates the majority opinion, other members might punish the violator or try to persuade them that the opinion is incorrect. Conformity can also be subtle. To some extent, we depend on the opinions that others hold to validate our own views. If co-workers don't agree with us, we begin to question our own opinions even without overt peer pressure.

Overconfidence (Inflated Team Efficacy)

To some degree, teams are more successful when their members have collective confidence in how well they work together and the likely success of their team effort. This **team efficacy** is similar to individual self-efficacy, which we discussed in Chapter 3. High-efficacy teams set more challenging goals and are more motivated to achieve them, both of which increase team performance.

team efficacy The collective belief among team members of the team's capability to successfully complete a task.

Unfortunately, there is a curvilinear relationship between team efficacy and the quality of team decisions (as well as other forms of team performance). In other words, teams make worse decisions when they are overconfident as well as underconfident.[101] Overconfident teams are less vigilant when making decisions, partly because they have more positive than negative emotions and moods during these events. They also engage in less constructive debate and are less likely to seek out or accept information located outside the team, both of which undermine the quality of team decisions.

Why do teams become overconfident? The main reason is a team-level variation of self-enhancement (see Chapter 3). Team members have a natural motivation to believe that the team's capabilities are above average. Overconfidence is more common in highly cohesive teams because self-enhancement occurs for things that are important. By definition, members of cohesive teams value their association with the team. Overconfidence is also stronger when the team has external threats or competition because these adversaries generate "us versus them" differentiation. Team efficacy is further inflated by the mutually reinforcing beliefs of the team. Employees develop a clearer and higher opinion of their team when other team members echo that opinion.

©James Brittain-VIEW/Alamy Stock Photo

Google applied its legendary deep analytics to find out why some teams worked better than others and made better decisions. Google researchers eventually discovered that team composition is less important than the team norm of psychological safety. In other words, teams make better decisions when all team members feel comfortable speaking up and are sensitive to the feelings of their fellow employees. From these results, Google created a checklist urging team leaders to actively listen during meetings, avoid interrupting teammates, rephrase what team members have said, and discourage anyone from being judgmental toward others. "I'm so much more conscious of how I model listening now, or whether I interrupt, or how I encourage everyone to speak," says Sagnik Nandy, who leads one of Google's largest teams.*

* C. Duhigg, *Smarter, Faster, Better: The Secrets of Being Productive in Life and Business* (New York: Random House, 2016), Chap. 2; "Guide: Understand Team Effectiveness," *Re:Work (Google Blog)* (blog), accessed May 3, 2019, https://rework.withgoogle.com/print/guides/5721312655835136/; "How to Foster Psychological Safety on Your Teams" (Google), accessed May 3, 2019, https://docs.google.com/document/d/1PsnDMS2emcPLgMLFAQCXZjO7 C4j2hJ7znOq_g2Zkjgk/export?format=pdf.

IMPROVING DECISION MAKING AND CREATIVITY IN TEAMS

Team decision making is fraught with problems, but there are several ways to minimize these pitfalls. Checks and balances need to be in place to prevent the leader or other individuals from dominating the discussion. The team should also be large enough to possess the collective knowledge to resolve the problem, yet small enough that the team doesn't consume too much time or restrict individual input. Team members should be confident in their decision making but also be wary about being overconfident. This calls for team membership with sufficient diversity as well as team norms that encourage critical thinking.

Another important ingredient for effective team decision making is an environment in which team members have psychological safety.[102] **Psychological safety** is a shared belief that engaging in interpersonal risk-taking will not have adverse consequences. This belief exists when employees are confident that they can constructively disagree with the majority, present weird ideas, or experiment with novel behaviours without fear that co-workers will belittle them or that the company will limit their career progress. Psychological safety requires team norms that encourage employees to respect and value one another, demonstrate interest in one another, be open-minded about and tolerant with co-workers' opinions, and show positive intentions toward one another. Showing positive intentions involves displaying positive emotions and nonthreatening behaviour when discussing different points of view.

psychological safety A shared belief that it is safe to engage in interpersonal risk-taking; specifically, that presenting unusual ideas, constructively disagreeing with the majority, and experimenting with new work behaviours will not result in co-workers posing a threat to one's self-concept, status, or career.

These recommendations improve most types of team-level decisions. OB studies have also identified four team structures that encourage creativity in a team setting: brainstorming, brainwriting, electronic brainstorming, and nominal group technique.

Brainstorming

Brainstorming is a team event in which participants try to think up many ideas for the ultimate objective of generating the most creative ideas.[103] The process was introduced by advertising executive Alex Osborn in 1939 and has four simple rules to maximize the creativity of ideas presented: (1) Speak freely—describe even the craziest ideas; (2) don't criticize others or their ideas; (3) provide as many ideas as possible—the quality of ideas increases with the quantity of ideas; and (4) build on the ideas that others have presented. These rules are supposed to encourage divergent thinking while minimizing evaluation apprehension and other team dynamics problems.[104]

brainstorming A freewheeling, face-to-face meeting where team members aren't allowed to criticize but are encouraged to speak freely, generate as many ideas as possible, and build on the ideas of others.

Brainstorming fell out of favour after numerous lab studies reported that it doesn't produce as many ideas as individuals working alone. Production blocking, evaluation apprehension, and social loafing were identified as the main culprits.[105] These findings are perplexing because some of the most successful creative agencies and product design firms rely on brainstorming to help them in the creative process.[106]

One reason why lab studies differ from real-world experiences is that effective brainstorming requires a skilled facilitator who ensures the rules are followed, encourages everyone to speak up, manages dominant participants, keeps the group focused on the topic, and maintains an efficient flow of ideas. In contrast, lab studies rely on students who have never done brainstorming and whose facilitator is randomly picked from the group. Also, brainstorming asks participants to provide crazy ideas, which requires confident employees in a collaborative learning orientation culture that prioritizes psychological safety. In contrast, most lab studies involve students who barely know one another, are likely highly sensitive to how they are perceived by peers, and probably have limited confidence in their skills for this task. Finally, brainstorming sessions are intended to produce the most creative ideas, whereas most lab studies merely count the number of ideas.[107]

Brainstorming likely improves team creativity, but it does have limitations. First, even with people who are trained and experienced, brainstorming suffers from production blocking. Great thoughts are forgotten while team members listen to one another's ideas, and sparks of insight are forfeited if team members do not listen to one another's ideas. A second problem, called *fixation* or *conformity effect*, is that hearing another person's ideas tends to restrict the variety of ideas that we subsequently think about. In brainstorming, participants are asked to openly describe their ideas, but the first few verbal descriptions might cause participants to limit their thinking to ideas similar to those first suggestions rather than other categories of ideas. On a positive note, however, neuroscience studies report that people think more creatively when exposed to moderately creative ideas generated by other people.[108]

Brainwriting

Brainwriting is a variation of brainstorming that minimizes the problem of production blocking by removing conversation during idea generation.[109] There are many

brainwriting A variation of brainstorming whereby participants write (rather than speak about) and share their ideas.

forms of brainwriting, but they all have the common feature that individuals write down their ideas rather than verbally describe them. In one version, participants write their ideas on cards and place them in the centre of the table. At any time, participants can pick up one or more cards from the centre to spark their thinking or further build (piggyback) on those ideas. In another variation, each person writes one idea on a card, then passes the card to the person on their right. The receiving person writes a new idea on a second card, both cards are sent to the next person, and the process is repeated. The limited research on brainwriting suggests that it produces more and better quality ideas than brainstorming due to the lack of production blocking.

Electronic Brainstorming

Electronic brainstorming is similar to brainwriting but uses digital networks rather than handwritten cards to document and share ideas. After receiving the question or issue, participants enter their ideas using special digital software. The ideas are distributed anonymously to other participants, who are encouraged to piggyback on those ideas. Team members eventually vote electronically on the ideas presented. Face-to-face discussion usually follows. Electronic brainstorming can be quite effective at generating creative ideas with minimal production blocking, evaluation apprehension, or conformity

electronic brainstorming A form of brainwriting that relies on networked computers for submitting and sharing creative ideas.

problems.[110] It can be superior to brainwriting because ideas are generated anonymously and they are viewed by other participants more easily. Despite these numerous advantages, electronic brainstorming is seldom applied because it tends to be too structured and technology-bound.

Nominal Group Technique

Another variation of brainwriting, **nominal group technique**, adds a verbal element to the process.[111] The problem is described, team members silently and independently write down as many solutions as they can, then they describe their solutions to the other team members, usually in a round-robin format. As with brainstorming, there is no criticism or debate, just clarification. Finally, participants silently and independently rank-order or vote on each proposed solution. Nominal group technique has been used in real-world decisions, such as identifying ways to improve tourism in various countries. This method tends to generate more and better-quality ideas than occur in traditional interacting and possibly brainstorming groups. However, production blocking and evaluation apprehension still occur to some extent. Training improves this structured approach to team decision making.[112]

nominal group technique A variation of brainwriting consisting of three stages: participants (1) silently and independently document their ideas, (2) collectively describe these ideas to the other team members without critique, and then (3) silently and independently evaluate the ideas presented.

Chapter Summary

LO1

Define teams and informal groups, and explain why employees join informal groups.

Teams are groups of two or more people who interact and influence one another, are mutually accountable for achieving common goals associated with organizational objectives, and perceive themselves as a social entity within an organization. All teams are groups, because they consist of people who are assembled together. Not all groups are teams, however; some groups do not exist to achieve organizational objectives and members of those groups might not be interdependent.

People join informal groups for four reasons: (1) They have an innate drive to bond, (2) individuals have an inherent need to define themselves to some extent by their group affiliations, (3) some personal goals are accomplished better in groups, and (4) individuals are comforted in stressful situations by the mere presence of other people.

LO2

Discuss the benefits and limitations of teams

Under the right conditions, teams make better decisions, develop better products and services, and create a more motivated workforce than do employees working alone. Teams also coordinate more easily than people working in separate departments. In many situations, employees are more motivated when working in teams than alone. This occurs because the drive to bond motivates team members to fulfil team goals, employees are monitored by and feel accountable to team members, and each team member creates a moving performance standard for the others.

Two limitations of teams are process losses and social loafing. Process losses are resources expended toward team development and maintenance rather than directly toward task performance. These costs increase with the team's diversity and with its size and when adding new members to an existing team. Social loafing occurs when people exert less effort (and usually perform at a lower level) in teams than when working alone. It is more likely to occur under several conditions: (1) Individual performance is hidden or difficult to distinguish from the performance of other team members; (2) the work is boring or has low task significance; (3) the individual team member has low conscientiousness, low agreeableness, and low collectivism; (4) the individual team member has low motivation to help the team achieve its goals, which occurs when the employee doesn't identify with the team, doesn't believe others are pulling their weight, and doesn't believe their effort will affect the team's success.

LO3

Outline the team effectiveness model and discuss how task characteristics, team size, and team composition influence team effectiveness.

Team effectiveness includes the team's ability to achieve its objectives, fulfil the needs of its members, and maintain its survival. The model of team effectiveness considers the team and organizational environment, team design, and team processes. Three team design elements are task characteristics, team size, and team composition. Teams tend to be better suited for situations in which the work is complex yet tasks are well structured and have high task interdependence. Teams should be large enough to perform the work yet small enough for efficient coordination and meaningful involvement. Effective teams are composed of people with the abilities and motivation to perform tasks (taskwork) but who also have the ability and motivation to engage in teamwork—behaviours that support the team's existence and functioning. Team member diversity has advantages and disadvantages for team performance.

LO4

Discuss how the six team processes—team development, norms, roles, cohesion, trust, and mental models—influence team effectiveness.

Several team processes are embedded in team development. Teams develop through the stages of forming, storming, norming, performing, and eventually adjourning. As teams evolve, they develop norms to regulate and guide member behaviour. Norms exist because employees believe these behaviours improve team performance or well-being, because they want predictability and conflict-avoidance in their relations with other team members, and because norms routinize behaviour which improves social order and coordination with minimal cognitive effort.

Team members are assigned or acquire roles—a set of behaviours they are expected to perform. Some roles are assigned in team design; others are informally acquired as a team process. There are numerous team roles, but all generally focus directly either on task performance (taskwork) or on team maintenance (teamwork).

Team cohesion is the degree of attraction people feel toward the team and their motivation to remain members. Cohesion increases with member similarity, smaller team size, higher degree of interaction, somewhat difficult entry, team success, and external challenges. Cohesion increases team performance when the team has high interdependence and its norms are congruent with organizational goals. Trust refers to positive expectations one person has toward another person in situations involving risk. People trust others on the basis of three foundations: calculus, knowledge, and identification.

Team mental models are cognitive images that team members form about the team's tasks, relationship dynamics, and knowledge repository. High-performing teams form shared mental models about their collective objectives, values, norms, work style, and interaction in the work process. Complementary mental models are unique to each team member but are compatible with the mental models held by other team members. Team mental models establish effective coordinating routines and generate perceptions of the team's purpose and performance. They also help team members to quickly know where knowledge is located within the team. Team building consists of activities that attempt to speed up or improve these team development processes.

LO5

Discuss the characteristics and factors required for the success of self-directed teams and remote teams.

Self-directed teams (SDTs) complete an entire piece of work requiring several interdependent tasks, and they have substantial autonomy over the execution of their tasks. Members of remote teams operate across space, time, and organizational boundaries and are linked through information technologies to achieve organizational tasks. Remote teams are more effective when their members apply effective teamwork behaviours, have good communication technology skills, are productive without close supervision (i.e., self-management), and have higher emotional intelligence. The team should have plenty of task structure and freedom to choose the preferred communication channels. Remote team members should also meet face to face fairly early in the team development process.

LO6

Identify four constraints on team decision making and discuss ways to improve decision making and creativity in teams.

Team decisions are impeded by time constraints, evaluation apprehension, conformity to peer pressure, and overconfidence. These concerns can be minimized through a shared belief that engaging in interpersonal risk-taking will not have adverse consequences (psychological safety), checks and balances that prevent anyone from dominating discussion, a team size that is as small as practicable, and wariness about the team's overconfidence. Four structures potentially improve creative decision making in team settings: brainstorming, brainwriting, electronic brainstorming, and nominal group technique.

Key Terms

brainstorming

brainwriting

Brooks's law

electronic brainstorming

evaluation apprehension

human capital

mental models

nominal group technique

norms

process losses

production blocking

psychological safety

remote teams

role

self-directed teams (SDTs)

social loafing

social networks

task interdependence

team cohesion

team efficacy

teams

trust

Critical Thinking Questions

1. Informal groups exist in almost every form of social organization. What types of informal groups exist in your classroom? Why are students motivated to belong to these informal groups?

2. The late management guru Peter Drucker once said: "The now-fashionable team in which everybody works with everybody on everything from the beginning rapidly is becoming a disappointment." Discuss three problems associated with teams.

3. You have been put in charge of a cross-functional task force that will develop enhanced Internet banking services for retail customers. The team includes representatives from marketing, information services, customer service, and accounting, all of whom will move to the same location at headquarters for three months. Describe the behaviours you might observe during each stage of the team's development.

4. You have just been transferred from the Montreal office to the Vancouver office of your company, a national sales organization of electrical products for developers and contractors. In Montreal, team members regularly called customers after a sale to ask whether the products arrived on time and whether they were satisfied. But when you move to the Vancouver office, no one seems to make these follow-up calls. A recently hired co-worker explains that other co-workers discouraged her from making those calls. Later, another co-worker suggests that your follow-up calls are making everyone else look lazy. Give three possible reasons why the norms in Vancouver might be different from those in the Montreal office, even though the customers, products, sales commissions, and other characteristics of the workplace are almost identical.

5. A software engineer in Canada needs to coordinate with four team members in geographically dispersed areas of the world. What team challenges might the team experience and how will they affect the team design elements?

6. You have been assigned to a class project with five other students, none of whom you have met before, and some of whom come from different countries. To what extent would team cohesion improve your team's performance on this project? What actions would you recommend to build team cohesion among student team members in this situation?

7. Suppose that you were put in charge of a remote team whose members are located in different cities around the world. What tactics could you use to build and maintain team trust and performance, as well as minimize the decline in trust and performance that often occurs in teams?

8. You are responsible for convening a major event in which senior officials from several provincial governments will try to come to an agreement on environmental issues. It is well known that some officials take positions to make themselves appear superior, whereas others are highly motivated to solve the environmental problems that cross adjacent provinces. What team decision-making problems are likely to be apparent in this government forum, and what actions can you take to minimize these problems?

9. The chief marketing officer of Sawgrass Widgets wants marketing and sales staff to identify new uses for its products. Which of the four team structures for creative decision making would you recommend? Describe and justify this process to Sawgrass's chief marketing officer.

Case Study:
ARBRECORP LTÉE

by Steven L. McShane, University of Newcastle (Australia), and David Lebeter, Hydro One (Ontario)

ArbreCorp Ltée is a sawmill operation in Quebec that is owned by a major forest products company but operates independently of the parent company. It was built 30 years ago, and completely updated with new machinery five years ago. ArbreCorp receives raw logs from the area for cutting and planing into building-grade lumber, mostly 2-by-4 and 2-by-6 pieces of standard lengths. Higher-grade logs leave ArbreCorp's sawmill department in finished form and are sent directly to the packaging department. The remaining 40 percent of sawmill output are cuts from lower-grade logs, requiring further work by the planing department.

ArbreCorp has one general manager, 16 supervisors and support staff, and 180 unionized employees. The unionized employees are paid an hourly rate specified in the collective agreement, whereas management and support staff are paid a monthly salary. The mill is divided into six operating departments: boom, sawmill, planer, packaging, shipping, and maintenance. The sawmill, boom, and packaging departments operate a morning shift starting at 6:00 a.m. and an afternoon shift starting at 2:00 p.m. Employees in these departments rotate shifts every two weeks. The planer and shipping departments operate only morning shifts. Maintenance employees work the night shift (starting at 10:00 p.m.).

Each department, except for packaging, has a supervisor on every work shift. The planer supervisor is responsible for the packaging department on the morning shift, and the sawmill supervisor is responsible for the packaging department on the afternoon shift. However, the packaging operation is housed in a separate building from the other departments, so supervisors seldom visit the packaging department. This is particularly true for the afternoon shift, because the sawmill supervisor is the furthest distance from the packaging building.

PACKAGING QUALITY

Ninety percent of ArbreCorp's product is sold on the international market through Boismarché Ltée, a large marketing agency. Boismarché represents all forest products mills owned by ArbreCorp's parent company as well as several other clients in the region. The market for building-grade lumber is very price competitive, because there are numerous mills selling a relatively undifferentiated product. However, some differentiation does occur in product packaging and presentation. Buyers will look closely at the packaging when deciding whether to buy from ArbreCorp or another mill.

To encourage its clients to package their products better, Boismarché sponsors a monthly package quality award. The marketing agency samples and rates its clients' packages daily, and the sawmill with the highest score at the end of the month is awarded a framed certificate of excellence. Package quality is a combination of how the lumber is piled (e.g., defects turned in), where the bands and dunnage are placed, how neatly the stencil and seal are applied, the stencil's accuracy, and how neatly and tightly the plastic wrap is attached.

ArbreCorp has won Boismarché's packaging quality award several times over the past five years and received high ratings in the months that it didn't win. However, the mill's ratings have started to decline over the past year or two, and several clients have complained about the appearance of the finished product. A few large customers switched to competitors' lumber, saying that the decision was based on the substandard appearance of ArbreCorp's packaging when it arrived in their lumberyard.

BOTTLENECK IN PACKAGING

The planer and sawmilling departments have significantly increased productivity over the past couple of years. The sawmill operation recently set a new productivity record on a single day. The planer operation has increased productivity to the point where last year it reduced operations to just one (rather than two) shifts per day. These productivity improvements are due to better operator training, fewer machine breakdowns, and better selection of raw logs. (Sawmill cuts from high-quality logs usually do not require planing work.)

Productivity levels in the boom, shipping, and maintenance departments have remained constant. However, the packaging department has recorded decreasing productivity over the past couple of years, with the result that a large backlog of finished product is typically stockpiled outside the packaging building. The morning shift of the packaging department is unable to keep up with the combined production of the sawmill and planer departments, so the unpackaged output is left for the afternoon shift. Unfortunately, the afternoon shift packages even less product than the morning shift, so the backlog continues to build. The backlog adds to ArbreCorp's inventory costs and increases the risk of damaged stock.

ArbreCorp has added Saturday overtime shifts as well as extra hours before and after the regular shifts for the packaging department employees to process this backlog. Last month, the packaging department employed 10 percent of the workforce but accounted for 85 percent of the overtime. This is frustrating to ArbreCorp's management, because time and motion studies recently confirmed that the packaging department is capable of processing all of the daily sawmill and planer production without overtime. With employees earning one and a half times or double their regular pay on overtime, ArbreCorp's cost competitiveness suffers.

Employees and supervisors at ArbreCorp are aware that people in the packaging department tend to extend lunch by 10 minutes and coffee breaks by five minutes. They also typically leave work a few minutes before the end of a shift. This abuse has worsened recently, particularly on the afternoon shift. Employees who are temporarily assigned to the packaging department also seem to participate in this time loss pattern after a few days. Although they are punctual and

productive in other departments, these temporary employees soon adopt the packaging crew's informal schedule when assigned to that department.

Discussion Questions

1. What symptom(s) in this case suggest that something has gone wrong?
2. What are the main causes of these symptoms?
3. What actions should executives take to correct these problems?

Team Exercise:
TEAM TOWER POWER

Purpose This exercise is designed to help you understand team roles, team development, and other issues in the development and maintenance of effective teams.

Materials The instructor will provide enough LEGO® pieces or similar materials for each team to complete the assigned task. All teams should have identical (or very similar) amounts and types of pieces. The instructor will need a measuring tape and stopwatch. Students may use writing materials during the design stage (see Instructions). The instructor will distribute a "Team Objectives Sheet" and "Tower Specifications Effectiveness Sheet" to all teams.

Instructions The instructor will divide the class into teams. Depending on class size and space availability, teams may have between four and seven members, but all should be approximately equal size.

Each team has 20 minutes to design a tower that uses only the materials provided, is freestanding, and provides an optimal return on investment. Team members may wish to draw their tower on paper or a flip chart to facilitate the tower's design. Teams are free to practise building their tower during this stage. Preferably, each team will have a secluded space so

that the design can be created privately. During this stage, each team will complete the Team Objectives Sheet distributed by the instructor. This sheet requires the Tower Specifications Effectiveness Sheet, also distributed by the instructor.

Each team will show the instructor that it has completed its Team Objectives Sheet. Then, with all teams in the same room, the instructor will announce the start of the construction phase. The time allowed for construction will be closely monitored, and the instructor will occasionally call out the time elapsed (particularly if there is no clock in the room).

Each team will advise the instructor as soon as it has completed its tower. The team will write down the time elapsed, as determined by the instructor. The team also may be asked to assist the instructor by counting the number of blocks used and measuring the height of the tower. This information gets added to the Team Objectives Sheet. Then the team calculates its profit.

After presenting the results, the class will discuss the team dynamics elements that contribute to team effectiveness. Team members will discuss their strategy, division of labour (team roles), expertise within the team, and other elements of team dynamics.

Team Exercise:
SURVIVAL ON THE MOON

Purpose This exercise is designed to help you understand the importance and dynamics of team decision making.

Materials All materials are provided below. They include the "Survival on the Moon Scenario" and the "Survival on the Moon Scoring Sheet" for ranking items individually and as a team.

Survival on the Moon Scenario

The year is 2035. You and your crew are travelling toward the Moon in the *Orion* spacecraft. *Orion* is a gumdrop-shaped spacecraft designed to carry people from Earth to the Moon. *Orion* is similar in shape, but larger than the capsules used during the Apollo program. Attached, or docked, to *Orion* is the Lunar Surface Access Module (LSAM), which you alone will use to land on the Moon (other crew members remain onboard the *Orion*).

As your spacecraft enters lunar orbit, you spot the lunar outpost. This outpost has grown, having been built piece by piece during past missions. You are excited to see the outpost. It is located on a crater rim near the lunar south pole, in near-constant sunlight. This location is not far from supplies of water ice that can be found in the cold, permanently shadowed part of the crater.

After transferring into the LSAM and separating from *Orion,* you prepare to descend to the lunar surface. Suddenly, you notice that there is a problem with the thrusters. You land safely, but off course, about 80 kilometres from the lunar outpost. Looking across the charcoal-gray, dusty surface of the Moon, you realize that your survival depends on reaching the outpost, finding a way to protect yourself until someone can reach you, or meeting a rescue party somewhere between your landing site and the outpost.

You know the Moon has basically no atmosphere or magnetosphere to protect you from space radiation. The environment is unlike any found on Earth. The regolith, or lunar soil, is a mixture of materials that includes sharp, glassy particles.

The gravity field on the Moon is only one-sixth as strong as Earth's. More than 80 percent of the Moon is made up of heavily cratered highlands. Temperatures vary widely on the Moon. It can be as cold as −193°C at night at its poles and as hot as 111°C during the day at its equator.

Instructions

Survival will depend on your mode of transportation and ability to navigate. Your basic needs for food, shelter, water, and air must be considered. Your challenge is to choose items that will help you survive.

PART I: INDIVIDUAL DECISION

The scoring sheet below lists 15 items in alphabetical order that are available to you. In the "Your Ranking" column, rank these items from 1 to 15 according to your own beliefs and knowledge about their importance to you and your team (other members of the crew). Place the number 1 in the box beside the most important item and continue ranking the items to number 15, the least important. Be prepared to explain why you gave each item the rank it received and how you plan to use the item to help you survive.

Survival on the Moon Scoring Sheet

Items (alphabetical order)	Your Ranking	Team Ranking	Expert Ranking	Your Score	Team Score
First aid kit: a basic kit with pain medication and medicine for infection					
Food: dehydrated concentrate to which water is added					
Life raft: a self-inflatable flotation device					
Magnetic compass: a tool that uses a magnetic field to determine direction					
Map: document showing the Moon's surface/terrain					
Matches (box of): wooden sticks with sulphur-treated heads					
Oxygen: two 45.5-kilogram tanks					
Parachute: a large piece of silk cloth					
Portable lights: with solar-powered rechargeable batteries					
Radio receiver-transmitter: a solar-powered communication instrument					
Rope: 15 metres of nylon rope					
Signal mirror: a handheld mirror					
Space blanket: a thin sheet of plastic material that is coated with a metallic reflecting layer					

Items (alphabetical order)	Your Ranking	Team Ranking	Expert Ranking	Your Score	Team Score
Space suit repair kit: kit with materials to repair tiny holes in fabric					
Water: one 38-litre container					
TOTAL SCORE: (sum scores within the last two columns)				———— Your score	———— Team score

PART II: TEAM DECISION

After everyone working alone has ranked these 15 items, the instructor will organize students into approximately equal-sized teams. Team members should try to reach a consensus on the rank order of each of these 15 items. Place the number 1 in the box beside the most important item and continue ranking the items to number 15, the least important. Record this ranking of items in the "Team Ranking" column. Your survival depends on the team's ability to agree on the importance of these items, as well as logical explanation of their value and how to use them.

PART III: TOTAL SCORES

After the items have been ranked by teams, your instructor will report how the 15 items were ranked by NASA scientists (experts). Write these rankings in the boxes under the "Expert Ranking" column. Next, calculate the absolute difference (remove the negative sign) between your ranking and the expert's ranking for each of the 15 items and record these scores in the "Your Score" column. Sum these 15 absolute differences to determine your personal total score. Determine your team's score in the same manner using the "Team Score" column. Write these scores and summary statistics into the spaces at the bottom of the scoring sheet for those two columns.

Discussion Questions

1. Did most team members have higher (worse) or lower (better) total scores than the total "team score"? Why did this difference occur?

2. In what situations, if any, would someone's total personal score be very similar to the total team score? Did this occur for anyone on your team? Why?

3. When the team was ranking items, which items had the most difference of opinion regarding the item's importance? Why did this disagreement occur, and how was it resolved by the team?

4. While the team was determining the collective ranking of items, did specific team members take on specific roles, such as leading the discussion, encouraging opinions from quieter members, managing conflict, and so forth? If so, why do you think these people took on these roles?

5. Was your team composed mostly of people you have worked with previously in teams? If so, do you think the discussion was more effective or less effective than when making decisions with people who are new to you? Why?

Source: National Aeronautics and Space Administration

Self-Assessments for Chapter 8

SELF-ASSESSMENT NAME	DESCRIPTION
Are you a team player?	Some people would like to work in teams for almost every aspect of their work, whereas other people would like to keep as far away from teams as possible. Most of us fall somewhere in between. This self-assessment estimates how much you enjoy working in teams.
What team roles do you prefer?	All teams depend on their members to fill various roles. Some roles area assigned through formal jobs, but many team roles are distributed informally. Informal roles are often claimed by team members whose personality and values are compatible with those roles. This assessment identifies the types of roles you prefer in team meetings and activities.
How trusting are you?	Some people have a tendency to trust others, even if they have never met them before, whereas others take a long time to develop a comfortable level of trust. This propensity to trust is due to each individual's personality, values, and socialization experiences. This self-assessment evaluates your general propensity to trust others.

CHAPTER 9
Communicating in Teams and Organizations

LEARNING OBJECTIVES

After reading this chapter, you should be able to:

LO1 Explain why communication is important in organizations, and discuss four influences on effective communication encoding and decoding.

LO2 Compare and contrast the advantages and disadvantages of digital written communication channels, other verbal communication channels, and nonverbal communication.

LO3 Discuss the relevance of synchronicity, social presence, social acceptance, and media richness when choosing the preferred communication channel.

LO4 Discuss various barriers (noise) to effective communication, including cross-cultural and gender-based differences in communication.

LO5 Explain how to get your message across more effectively, and summarize the elements of active listening.

LO6 Describe effective communication strategies in organizational hierarchies, and review the role and relevance of the organizational grapevine.

Stewart Butterfield dislikes email. "It's a real mixed bag and there's a high cognitive tax of going through it and there's an information overload," complains the Canadian entrepreneur who co-founded Slack, the enterprise collaborative platform. Increasingly, corporate leaders agree. Email is being pushed aside as organizations adopt Slack, Microsoft Teams, Workplace from Facebook, and other platforms that integrate a variety of emerging digital communication channels and products.

Norwegian salmon farming company Grieg Seafood replaced email with Workplace from Facebook for its employees in Norway, Shetland, and Canada. "We have a lot of farms on the east coast and west coast of Vancouver Island, so it's quite challenging to keep in touch, so we are hoping that the platform will make it easier for us to reach out to these locations," says Alina Constantin, Vancouver-based HR manager of Grieg Seafood BC.

Slack and other enterprise digital collaborative platforms have become hugely popular communication tools in contemporary organizations, but they also create new issues about how to communicate effectively.
©Noah Berger/AFP/Getty Images

But as enterprise collaborative platforms gain popularity, concerns are also growing about their limitations. One recent study found that Slack users interrupt their work every five minutes, on average, just to check messages. "I found myself compulsively checking Slack even when I had no need to," admits software engineer Alicia Liu. "And as a result, I was in a constant state of distraction."

Also, collaborative platforms rely mainly on multi-channel chat—real-time texting across several threads that assumes employees are always there to respond to messages across those conversation channels. "With Slack, we were more connected than we ever were before," says Dave Teare, founder of Toronto-based AgileBits, which develops 1Password. "[But] being connected doesn't magically enable effective communication . . . . It multiplexed my brain and left me in a constant state of anxiety."

Another concern is that employees switch too slowly from collaborative platform chat messages to more appropriate human-interaction channels when the issues become complex and ambiguous. "When my engineering team has to decide what they want to build in the next two weeks, this is hard to do without meetings," says Octavian Costache, the co-founder and chief technology officer of Stellar Health. "There's so much volume of information [in face-to-face gatherings] . . . I have this image of a giant pipe, so much richness. It couldn't go on Slack."[1]

We are experiencing the most significant and disruptive transformation of organizational communication in our lifetimes. Digital real-time group messaging (chat channels), task-management pages, video conferences, text messaging, document repositories, intranet wikis, and other electronic communication methods barely existed in organizations a decade ago. Indeed, many businesses in Canada and other countries are still struggling with whether—let alone determining how—to incorporate these new ways of interacting in the workplace. Digital communication offers significant potential for information sharing and social bonding. Equally important, employees use these emerging communication channels in their private lives and expect to have them available at work.

Communication refers to the process by which information is transmitted and *understood* between two or more people. We emphasize the word "understood" because communication is effective when the receiver accurately deciphers the sender's message. This chapter begins by discussing the importance of effective communication, outlining the communication process model, and discussing factors that improve communication encoding and decoding. Next, we identify types of communication channels, including digital messaging and social media, followed by factors to consider when choosing a communication medium. This chapter then identifies barriers to effective communication. The latter part of this chapter looks at communication in organizational hierarchies and offers insight about the pervasive organizational grapevine.

communication The process by which information is transmitted and *understood* between two or more people.

The Importance of Communication

LO1

Effective communication is vital to all organizations, so much so that no company could exist without it. The reason? Recall from Chapter 1 that organizations are defined as groups of people who work interdependently toward some purpose. People work interdependently only when they can communicate with one another. Organizations rely on a variety of coordinating mechanisms (see Chapter 13), but frequent, timely, and accurate communication remains the primary means through which employees and work units effectively synchronize their work.[2] Chester Barnard, a telecommunications CEO and a respected pioneer in organizational behaviour theory, made this observation back in 1938: "An organization comes into being when there are persons able to communicate with each other."[3]

Associated with coordinating work, communication is vital for effective decision making. Imagine the challenge of making a decision without any information about the decision context, the alternatives available, the likely outcomes of those options, or the extent to which the decision is achieving its objectives. Communication brings this information from the external environment into the organization and distributes it so employees can solve problems and discover opportunities. For example, airline cockpit crews make much better decisions—and thereby cause far fewer accidents—when the captain encourages the crew to openly share information.[4]

A third function of communication is to change behaviour.[5] When conveying information to others, we are often trying to alter their beliefs, feelings, and ultimately

©Design Pics Inc/Alamy Stock Photo

The Fort McMurray wildfire a few years ago occurred just as the Alberta government began to roll out an integrated first responders communications system. Dozens of fire, police, and emergency medical departments around the region quickly replaced their separate systems with the new (barely tested) technology, which enabled literally every first responder to coordinate and share information much more effectively. This prevented a repeat of the infamous Montana wildfires several years earlier, in which coordination among first responders was severely hampered by separate communication systems. "Without [the unified system], we simply would not have been able to communicate effectively, meaning 90,000 of my neighbours, friends and colleagues [around Fort McMurrray] would not have been able to be successfully evacuated," recalls Brad Grainger, deputy chief of operations of Wood Buffalo Region emergency services.*

* United States Congress Senate Committee on Appropriations Subcommittee on Treasury and General Government, "Northern Border Security: Hearings Before a Subcommittee of the Committee on Appropriations, United States Senate, One Hundred Seventh Congress, First Session, Special Hearing, October 3, 2001, Washington, DC, December 5, 2001, Washington, DC." (U.S. Government Printing Office, 2002); C. Ramsay, "Alberta Takes Steps to Improve Communication between First Responders," *Global News,* June 23, 2016; N. Cordeau-Hilliard, "First Responder Network to Improve Emergency Response," *My McMurray (Radio Fort McMurray),* November 2, 2018; S. Ducatel, "New Radio System Enhances Inter-Agency Communication," *Mountain View Today (Alberta),* January 30, 2019.

their behaviour. This influence process might be passive, such as by merely describing the situation more clearly and fully, or it might be a deliberate attempt to change someone's thoughts and actions. We discuss the topic of persuasion later in this chapter.

A fourth function of communication is to support employee well-being.[6] Communication minimizes stress by conveying knowledge that helps employees better manage their work environment. For instance, research shows that new employees adjust much better to the organization when co-workers communicate subtle nuggets of wisdom, such as how to complete work procedures correctly, find useful resources, handle difficult customers, and avoid office politics. Communication also minimizes stress emotionally; talking with others can be a soothing balm during difficult times. Indeed, people are less susceptible to colds, cardiovascular disease, and other

physical and mental illnesses when they have regular social interaction.[7] In essence, people have an inherent drive to bond, to validate their self-worth, and to maintain their social identity. Communication is the means through which these drives and needs are fulfilled.

A Model of Communication

The model presented in Exhibit 9.1 provides a useful "conduit" metaphor for thinking about the communication process.[8] According to this model, communication flows through one or more channels (also called *media*) between the sender and receiver. The sender forms a message and encodes it into words, gestures, voice intonations, and other symbols or signs. Next, the encoded message is transmitted to the intended receiver through voice, text, nonverbal cues,

EXHIBIT 9.1   The Communication Process Model

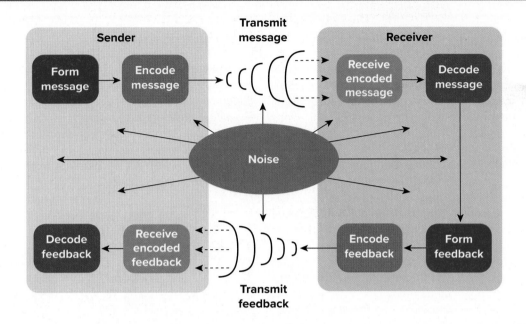

or other channels. The receiver senses the incoming message and decodes it into something meaningful. Ideally, the decoded meaning is what the sender had intended.

In most situations, the sender looks for evidence that the other person has received and understood the transmitted message. This feedback may involve the receiver repeating the message back to the sender or demonstrating awareness of the message indirectly through the receiver's subsequent actions. Notice that feedback repeats the communication process. Intended feedback is encoded, transmitted, received, and decoded from the receiver to the sender of the original message.

This model recognizes that communication is not a free-flowing conduit. Instead, the transmission of meaning from one person to another is hampered by *noise*—the psychological, social, and structural barriers that distort and obscure the sender's intended message. If any part of the communication process is distorted or broken, the sender and receiver will not have a common understanding of the message.

INFLUENCES ON EFFECTIVE ENCODING AND DECODING

According to the communication process model, effective communication depends on the sender's and receiver's ability, motivation, role clarity, and situational support to efficiently and accurately encode and decode information. Four main factors influence the effectiveness of this encoding–decoding process.[9]

Similar Codebooks

The sender and receiver encode and decode more effectively when they have similar "codebooks," which are dictionaries of symbols, language, gestures, idioms, and other tools used to convey information. With similar codebooks, the communication participants assign the same or similar meaning to the transmitted symbols and signs. Communication efficiency also improves because there is less need for redundancy (repeating the message in different ways) and less need for confirmation feedback ("So, you are saying that. . .?").

Sender's Encoding Experience

The encoding–decoding process improves with the sender's experience transmitting a message. The more frequently the sender transmits a specific message, particularly to a similar audience, the more the sender learns which words, symbols, voice intonations, and other features transmit the message more clearly and persuasively to others.

Communication Channel Motivation and Ability

The encoding–decoding process is better when the sender and receiver are skilled and motivated to use the selected communication channel(s).[10] Some people are better at face-to-face conversations, whereas others are more skilled at writing and receiving detailed reports. Even when the sender and receiver are able to communicate using a particular channel, they might misunderstand each other when one or

Global Connections 9.1

ENCODING–DECODING CHALLENGES ACROSS GENERATIONS*

The contemporary workplace is multigenerational. This new reality may be creating problems in the encoding–decoding communication process because each generation has increasingly divergent communication channel preferences, abilities, and even codebooks.

In a recent survey of 14,371 employees across seven countries, 55 percent of Generation Z workers (those born after 1996) said they are happiest using online chat and instant messaging, whereas only 15 percent of Baby Boomers (born 1946 to 1964), 23 percent of Gen Xers (born 1965 to 1980), and 38 percent of Millennials (born 1981 to 1996) are happiest using chat or instant messaging. The overwhelming majority of Baby Boomers (85 percent) prefer face-to-face meetings. In contrast, only half as many Gen Z workers (45 percent) are happiest with in-person meetings. These results are consistent with separate evidence that more than one-third of Baby Boomers never use instant messaging and almost half of them never use social media to communicate with colleagues or clients.

Problems with cross-generational differences in encoding–decoding preferences and abilities are already apparent. In one recent global survey (400 or more respondents per country), 82 percent of Canadian employees and 80 percent of respondents across 33 other countries said that the main difference with working in a multigenerational workplace is communication styles. Furthermore, 31 percent of Canadians (same percentage as the global sample) said they find it difficult to communicate with co-workers who are not from their generation or in their age group.

©Monkey Business Images/Shutterstock

*"Communication Barriers in the Modern Workplace" (London: The Economist Intelligence Unit, March 2018); L. Wright and N. McCullough, "New Survey Explores the Changing Landscape of Teamwork," *Microsoft 365 Blog* (blog), April 19, 2018, https://www.microsoft.com/en-us/microsoft-365/blog/2018/04/19/new-survey-explores-the-changing-landscape-of-teamwork/; "Randstad Workmonitor Q2 2018" (Amsterdam: Randstad Holding nv, June 12, 2018).

both of them dislike using that channel and, consequently, lack the effort to communicate effectively.

Shared Mental Models of the Communication Context

The encoding–decoding process is more successful when the sender and receiver have shared mental models of the communication context. Mental models are internal representations of the external world that allow us to visualize elements of a setting and relationships among those elements (see Chapter 3). A sender and receiver with shared mental models of the communication context have similar images and expectations regarding the location, time, layout, and other contextual features of the information. These shared mental models potentially increase the accuracy of the message content and reduce the need for communication about that context. For example, it is easier for two people to discuss events that occur in a nuclear plant control room if both of them have detailed mental models of the control room.

Notice that shared mental models of the communication context differs from a shared codebook. Codebooks are symbols used to convey message content, whereas mental models are knowledge structures of the communication topic setting.

Communication Channels

LO2

A central feature of the communication model is the channel or medium through which information is transmitted. There are two main types of channels: verbal and nonverbal. Verbal communication uses words, so it includes both spoken and written channels. Nonverbal communication is any part of communication that does not use words. Spoken and written communication are both verbal (i.e., they both use words), but they are quite different from each other and have different communication benefits and limitations, which we discuss later in this section. Also, written communication has traditionally been much slower than spoken communication at transmitting messages, although email, instant messaging, and other digital communication channels have significantly improved written communication efficiency.

DIGITAL WRITTEN COMMUNICATION

In the early 1960s, with funding from the U.S. Department of Defense, university researchers began discussing how to collaborate better by connecting their computers through a network. Their vision of connected computers became a reality in 1969 as the Advanced Research Projects Agency Network (ARPANET). ARPANET initially had only a dozen or so connections and was very expensive and slow by today's standards, but nevertheless it marked the birth of the Internet. Two years later, using that network, a computer engineer sent the first electronic mail (email) message between different computers on a network. By 1973, most communication on ARPANET was through email. ARPANET was mostly restricted to U.S. Department of Defense-funded research centres, so in 1979 two graduate students at Duke University developed a public network system, called Usenet. Usenet allowed people to post information that could be retrieved by anyone else on the network, making it the first public computer-mediated social network.[11]

We have come a long way since the early days of ARPANET and Usenet. Text messaging, online chat, virtual whiteboards, and other digital text-based communication channels barely existed in organizations a dozen years ago, whereas they are increasingly integrated into enterprise communication platforms. Email still dominates the corporate landscape, but its popularity is waning. Employees in almost every age group use email more often than any other communication channel, but chat and text messaging have gained popularity in organizations over the past few years. In fact, Generation Z employees—those in their mid-twenties or younger—already use chat and text messages more than email in the workplace.[12]

As Exhibit 9.2 shows, the average person in a large, continuously monitored sample spent about one hour each work day (18 percent of 5.5 hours of active screen time) communicating via computer. From early 2014 to early 2019, email activity dropped steadily from 75 percent to 56 percent of total computer-mediated communication time. Voice-only communication also dropped (from more than 9 percent to about 3 percent), although some increase in video chat partly offset the voice-only decline. Meanwhile, online chat and instant messaging jumped from 6 percent to 28 percent of total computer-mediated communication over this five-year period.

Why is the preferred type of digital communication changing? One likely explanation is shifting preferences. Younger employees grew up in the era of smartphones, so text messaging, real-time (synchronous) chat, and other emerging digital text-based communication channels are already embedded in their lives. The other likely reason is opportunity. Slack, Microsoft Teams, Workplace from Facebook, Basecamp, and other enterprise collaboration platforms are rapidly being introduced in the workplace. In fact, many of these collaborative communication products didn't exist in

---

EXHIBIT 9.2   Use of Computer-Mediated Communication Channels*

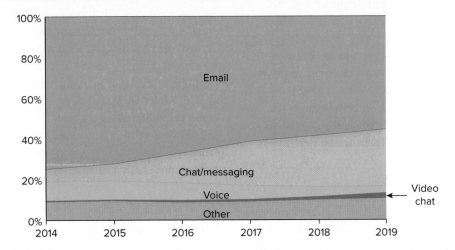

Percentage of total time in computer-mediated communication at work spent actively using each communication channel. Data are for the month of January 2014 to 2019.

* Adapted from information reported in: R. Molla, "The Productivity Pit: How Slack Is Ruining Work," *Vox*, May 1, 2019. Data are from 12,000 RescueTime app users. Data points are from the first month (January) of each year. On average, users actively focused on their screens for 5.5 hours each work day. The data shown here represent the 18 percent (about one hour) of total active screen time spent engaging in communication activity.

2014! These products rely on chat and messaging, not email, as the primary communication channels.

Benefits of Digital Written Communication

Almost all workplaces rely heavily on digital text-based communication in one form or another. Email and text messages are the first choice for coordinating work and transmitting well-defined information. They have become more popular than face-to-face meetings (in-person or remote), voice conversations, and other media. Why? Because digital messages can be written, edited, appended, and transmitted quickly to many people. Most digital written communication is also asynchronous (messages are sent and received at different times), so the dialogue does not require timely coordination. Furthermore, email software and many of the new collaborative communication platforms include search engines, which makes these channels convenient filing cabinets.[13]

Communication patterns changed significantly when email entered the workplace, and these changes will likely continue as other digital written channels become more popular. Specifically, digital written communication reduces face-to-face interactions and telephone calls but increases communication with people further up the hierarchy.[14] Digital channels also reduce social and organizational status differences between sender and receiver, mainly because they provide fewer cues of these differences than is evident in face-to-face interaction. However, status differences still exist to some extent.[15] For instance, one study found that managers signalled their status by replying to emails less quickly and with shorter messages. Text messages can also convey status differences, such as when they are accompanied by an elite signature (e.g., "Sent from my iPhone").

Email and other forms of digital written communication potentially reduce stereotyping and prejudice because age, race, and other features of the participants are unknown or less noticeable.[16] Compared to face-to-face interactions, digital communication channels also give the sender more time to craft diplomatic messages. However, these diplomatic efforts usually occur only when the writer is aware of potential conflict or perceived prejudice. Otherwise, as we discuss next, digital text-based communication has a tendency to generate and amplify conflict and reliance on stereotypes.

Problems with Digital Written Communication

Email, online chat, instant messaging, and other digital written channels dominate organizational communication, but they have several limitations. Here are the top four complaints:

Faulty Communication of Emotions

People consistently and significantly overestimate the degree to which they understand the emotional meaning of digital messages. The problem is that we rely on facial expressions and other nonverbal cues to interpret the emotional meaning of words, whereas digital text-based communication lacks this parallel channel. Senders try to clarify the emotional tone of their messages by using expressive language ("Wonderful to hear from you!"), highlighting phrases in boldface or quotation marks, and inserting graphic faces (emojis and emoticons) representing the desired emotion. Studies suggest that writers are getting better at using these emotion symbols. Even so, emojis do not replace the full complexity of real facial expressions, voice intonation, and hand movements.[17]

Less Politeness and Respectfulness

Digital messages are often less diplomatic than written letters. Indeed, the term *flaming* has entered our language to describe digital messages that communicate hostility and other forms of disrespect. One reason is that digital media are more impersonal (less social presence) than most other communication channels, which reduces the sender's empathy and sensitivity when crafting the message. A second reason is that digital messages can be written and transmitted before the sender's emotions subside. Paper-based messages take longer to prepare and deliver, allowing the sender to reflect more calmly on the content before it is sent. Receivers are also partly to blame because, on average, they infer a less respectful interpretation of the digital message than was intended by the sender.[18] Fortunately, flaming incidents may be in decline as employees improve their skills with digital channels and as more companies establish explicit norms and rules to minimize flaming and cyberbullying.

Inefficient for Ambiguous, Complex, and Novel Situations

Digital messages are incredibly efficient for well-defined situations, such as confirming the location of a meeting or giving basic instructions for a routine activity. But this form of communication can be cumbersome and dysfunctional in ambiguous, complex, and novel situations. As we will describe later in this section, these circumstances require communication channels that transmit a larger volume of information with more rapid feedback. In other words, when the issue gets messy, stop emailing or texting and start talking, preferably face to face.

Contributes to Information Overload

Digital messages contribute to information overload.[19] More than 300 billion business and consumer emails and likely a similar number of text messages are sent and received every day.[20] This glut occurs because these messages are easily created and copied to many people. Text messages are usually much briefer than emails, but they still contribute to information overload because several messages are often transmitted to convey the same information found in fewer emails.

SOCIAL MEDIA COMMUNICATION IN THE WORKPLACE

The emergence of social media is rapidly changing how people exchange information. **Social media** refers to digital (i.e., Internet, intranet, mobile, etc.) communication channels that enable people to collaborate in the creation and exchange of user-generated content. User-generated content exists when audience members (users) are partly or completely responsible for the creation or amendment of the content.[21] Social media is called "social" because user-generated content creation is a reciprocally interactive social process.

social media Digital communication channels that enable people to collaborate in the creation and exchange of user-generated content.

Unlike social media channels, traditional forms of organizational communication "push" information from the content creator (sender) to the audience. For instance, memos, corporate intranet web pages, policy guidelines, company magazines, and video messages from the CEO provide little or no opportunity for recipients to respond, append, revise, or make any other collaborative contribution to the original message. Even email tends to be a one-way exchange, such as when the CEO emails corporate news to employees or an employee notifies co-workers about a meeting.

Most social media activity within organizations initially occurred through Facebook, Twitter, and other public platforms, often without the company's formal approval. These platforms still dominate the workplace, but organizations are quickly introducing the enterprise collaborative platforms described in the opening case study (Slack, Microsoft Teams, etc.). These systems rely heavily on structured chat and instant messaging threads, but they also include shared file space, collaborative document editing, media sharing, group video calls, and shared task scheduling.

Social media exists in many forms. Each social media channel emphasizes specific functions, such as presenting the individual's identity, enabling conversations, sharing information, sensing the presence of others in the virtual space, maintaining relationships, revealing reputation or status, and supporting communities (see Exhibit 9.3).[22] For instance, Facebook has a strong emphasis on maintaining relationships but relatively low emphasis on sharing information or forming communities (groups). Wikis, on the other hand, focus on sharing information or forming communities but have much lower emphasis on presenting the user's identity or reputation.

Several studies conclude that Slack, Microsoft Teams, and other enterprise collaborative platforms improve knowledge sharing and socializing among employees under some conditions.[23] When a major credit card company introduced one of these platforms, its employees became 31 percent better at finding information and 71 percent better at finding the person with the original information. A large-scale study of Twitter tweets reported that this form of communication aided employees in transmitting knowledge, maintaining collegiality among co-workers, and strengthening their professional network. Many social media platforms enable feedback, which potentially gives employees more voice, particularly where management encourages feedback.

EXHIBIT 9.3   Functions of Communicating Through Social Media

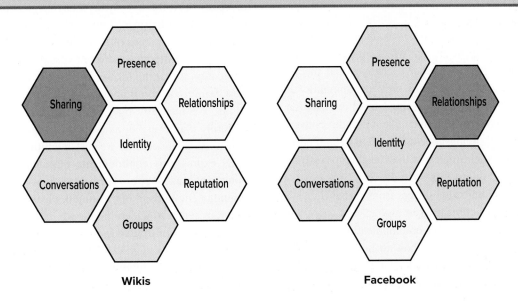

Wikis   Facebook

Global Connections 9.2

BOSCH EMPLOYEES IMPROVE COLLABORATION THROUGH SOCIAL MEDIA*

A few years ago, Robert Bosch GmbH asked hundreds of its employees to describe their image of a future workplace that supports collaboration and idea generation. From this feedback, the German engineering and electronics company introduced Bosch Connect, an enterprise collaboration platform.

Bosch Connect includes several conditions to support collaboration. First, the online communities are self-organizing; employees set them up without seeking permission from management. Second, the communities are transparent, not hidden or restrictive. This means that any Bosch employee can join a community if it is public, or can ask to join if it is moderated. Third, employees are encouraged to ask questions and offer suggestions, even for communities outside their work specialization.

Bosch Connect has significantly boosted productivity and is now part of everyday work for most of the company's 400,000 employees. For example, one team completed a customer localization project in six days using Bosch Connect rather than email, compared to similar projects that took up to four weeks without Bosch Connect (i.e., mainly used email).

Bosch's social media platform is particularly popular among younger employees. "I'm used to chatting electronically with friends and family and using various social media channels to communicate in my private life," says Ee Von Lim, a Bosch accounting manager in Singapore. "Now when I'm collaborating with colleagues, communication is just as intuitive. That makes me more productive—and my work more fun."

©Ahrens + Steinbach Projekte/fotogloria/Newscom

* M. Göhring and K. Perschke, "Internal Community Management @ Bosch," in *KnowTech 2014* (Hanau, Germany: BitKom KnowTech, 2014); R. Roewekamp, "Bosch Bricht Ins Vernetzte Arbeiten Auf (Bosch Launches into Connected Work)," *CIO* (German edition), November 19, 2015; "Boosting Agility on the Job: Bosch Invests in the Workplace of the Future," news release for Robert Bosch GmbH (Stuttgart, Germany: ENP Newswire, June 15, 2015); J. Heinz and A. Kumar, "Enterprise Social Networks—the Nerve-Center of Future Organizations," in *Connect2016* (Orlando, FL: IBM, 2016); P. Tate, "Dialogue: Pioneering an Industrial Revolution at Bosch," *Manufacturing Leadership Journal,* June 2, 2018.

NONVERBAL COMMUNICATION

Nonverbal communication includes facial gestures, voice intonation, physical distance, and even silence.[24] This communication channel is necessary where noise or physical distance prevents effective verbal exchanges and the need for immediate feedback precludes written communication. But even in quiet face-to-face meetings, most information is communicated nonverbally. Rather like a parallel conversation, nonverbal cues signal subtle information to both parties, such as reinforcing their interest in the verbal conversation or demonstrating their relative status in the relationship.[25]

Nonverbal communication differs from verbal (i.e., written and spoken) communication in a couple of ways. First, it is less rule-bound than verbal communication. We receive considerable formal training on how to understand spoken words, but very little on how to understand the nonverbal signals that accompany those words. Consequently, nonverbal cues are generally more ambiguous and susceptible to misinterpretation. At the same time, many facial expressions (such as smiling) are hardwired and universal, thereby providing the only reliable means of communicating across cultures.

The other difference between verbal and nonverbal communication is that the former is typically conscious, whereas most nonverbal communication is automatic and nonconscious. We normally plan the words we say or write, but we rarely plan every blink, smile, or other gesture during a conversation. Indeed, as we just mentioned, many of these facial expressions communicate the same meaning across cultures because they are hardwired, nonconscious responses to human emotions.[26] For example, pleasant emotions cause the brain centre to widen the mouth, whereas negative emotions produce constricted facial expressions (squinting eyes, pursed lips, etc.). Unfortunately, we often transmit messages nonverbally without being aware of this conversation. For example, job applicants don't realize that they engage in the 10 behaviours identified in Exhibit 9.4, yet each of these actions transmits negative nonverbal messages about the applicant's character.

Emotional Contagion

One of the most fascinating aspects of nonverbal communication is **emotional contagion**, which is the automatic process of "catching" or sharing another person's emotions by mimicking that person's facial expressions and other nonverbal behaviour. Technically, human beings have brain receptors that cause them to mirror what they observe. In other words, to some degree our brain causes us to act as though we are the person we are watching.[27]

Consider what happens when you see a co-worker accidentally bang their head against a door frame. Chances are, you wince and put your hand on your own head as if you had hit the door. Similarly, while listening to someone describe a positive event, you tend to smile and exhibit other emotional displays of happiness. While some of our nonverbal communication is planned, emotional contagion represents nonconscious behaviour—we automatically mimic and synchronize our nonverbal behaviours with other people.[28]

Emotional contagion influences communication and social relationships in three ways.[29] First, mimicry provides continuous feedback, communicating that we understand and empathize with the sender. To consider the significance of this, imagine employees remaining expressionless after watching a co-worker bang their head! The lack of parallel behaviour conveys an absence of understanding or caring. A second function is that we experience stronger emotional meaning when we mimic the nonverbal behaviours that represent the emotional experience someone is describing to us. If a co-worker is angry with a client, our tendency to frown and show anger while listening helps us to experience that emotion more fully.

The third function of emotional contagion is to fulfil the drive to bond that we mentioned earlier in this chapter and introduced in Chapter 5. Bonding develops through each person's awareness of a collective sentiment. Emotional

emotional contagion The nonconscious process of "catching" or sharing another person's emotions by mimicking that person's facial expressions and other nonverbal behaviour.

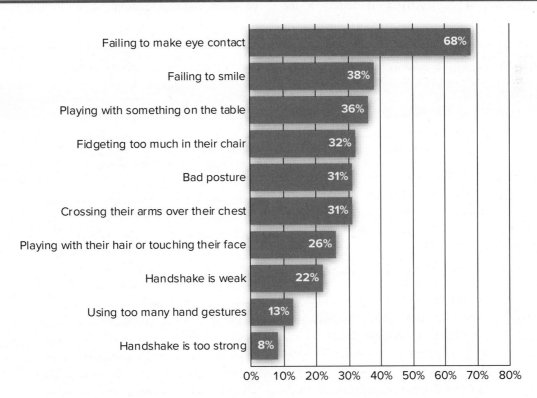

EXHIBIT 9.4 Top 10 Body Language Mistakes in Job Interviews*

Behaviour	Percentage
Failing to make eye contact	68%
Failing to smile	38%
Playing with something on the table	36%
Fidgeting too much in their chair	32%
Bad posture	31%
Crossing their arms over their chest	31%
Playing with their hair or touching their face	26%
Handshake is weak	22%
Using too many hand gestures	13%
Handshake is too strong	8%

Note: Percentage of more than 1,014 human resource and hiring managers surveyed who identified each of these nonverbal behaviours as the biggest body language mistakes made by job candidates during hiring interviews.

* Based on information in: "The Most Unusual Interview Mistakes and Biggest Body Language Mishaps, According to Annual CareerBuilder Survey," News Release (Chicago: CareerBuilder, February 22, 2018).

contagion generates that communal experience because those participating in the communication event witness others sharing the same emotions that they feel. This strengthens relations among team members as well as between leaders and followers by providing evidence of their similarity.

Choosing the Best Communication Channel

LO3

Employees have more communication channels to choose from than ever before, ranging from physical and digital forms of face-to-face interaction to a multitude of ways to transmit written messages. Which communication channel is most appropriate in a particular situation? There are many factors to consider, but the four most important are summarized in Exhibit 9.5 and described in this section.

synchronicity The extent to which the channel requires or allows both sender and receiver to be actively involved in the conversation at the same time (synchronous) or at different times (asynchronous).

SYNCHRONICITY

Communication channels vary in their **synchronicity**, that is, the extent to which they require or allow both sender and receiver to be actively involved in the conversation at the same time.[30] Face-to-face conversations are almost always synchronous, whereas most digital text communication can occur with each party participating at different times (asynchronous). Emails are typically asynchronous because the receiver doesn't need to be around when email messages are sent. Online texting can be asynchronous, but some forms (online chat) are often applied in practice as synchronous conversation.

Synchronous communication is preferred when the information is required quickly (high immediacy) or where the issue is complex and therefore requires the parties to address several related decisions. Asynchronous communication is better when the issue is simple, the issue has low time urgency, getting both parties together at the same time is costly, and/or the receiver would benefit from time to reflect on the message before responding.

SOCIAL PRESENCE

Social presence refers to how much the communication channel creates psychological closeness to others, awareness that there is another human being (or several others) in the conversation, and appreciation

social presence The extent to which a communication channel creates psychological closeness to others, awareness of their humanness, and appreciation of the interpersonal relationship.

EXHIBIT 9.5 Factors in Choosing the Best Communication Channel

Channel choice factor	Description	Depends on...
Synchronicity	The channel requires or allows the sender and receiver to communicate with each other at the same time (synchronous) or at different times (asynchronous).	• Time urgency (immediacy) • Complexity of the topic • Cost of both parties communicating at the same time • Whether receiver should have time to reflect before responding
Social presence	The channel creates psychological closeness to others, awareness of their humanness, and appreciation of the interpersonal relationship.	• Need to empathize with others • Need to influence others
Social acceptance	The channel is approved and supported by others (individuals, teams, organization, or society).	• Organizational, team, and cultural norms • Each party's preferences and skills with the channel • Symbolic meaning of the channel
Media richness	The channel has high data-carrying capacity—the volume and variety of information that can be transmitted during a specific time.	• Situation is nonroutine • Situation is ambiguous

of the interpersonal relationship.[31] Face-to-face interactions almost always have the highest social presence, whereas low social presence would typically occur when uploading a document where anyone in the organization can retrieve it. Social presence is usually stronger in synchronous communication because the receiver's immediate responses to our messages increase the sense of connectedness with that person. Although social presence is affected mostly by specific channel characteristics, message content also plays a role. For example, social presence is higher when the sender's message style is casual rather than formal, and when the message describes personal information about the sender.

A communication channel is valued for its social presence effect when the purpose of the dialogue is to understand and empathize with the other person or group. People are also more willing to listen and help others when there is a degree of interpersonal relationship or feeling of human connectedness. Therefore, channels with high social presence are better when the sender wants to influence the receiver.[32]

SOCIAL ACCEPTANCE

Social acceptance refers to how well the communication channel is approved and supported by co-workers, teams, the organization, and society.[33] One social acceptance factor is the set of norms held by others involved in the communication event. Norms explain why face-to-face meetings are daily events among staff in some firms, whereas video conferences and Twitter tweets are the media of choice in other organizations. National culture also influences preferences for specific communication channels.[34] For instance, Korean employees are less likely than Canadians to email corporate executives because in Korea email is considered insufficiently respectful of the superior's status. Emojis populate more business emails and text messages in China than in Canada, likely because people in China prefer conveying emotions indirectly rather than directly (in words), and because they value the complex, ambiguous, and cute symbolism of emojis.[35]

A second social acceptance factor is the sender's and receiver's preferences for specific communication channels.[36] You may have noticed that some co-workers ignore (or rarely check) voicemail, yet they quickly respond to text messages. These preferences are due to the individual's personality, values, and previous success with some channels more than others.

A third social acceptance factor is the symbolic meaning of a channel.[37] Many years ago, Canadian communications scholar Marshall McLuhan wrote: "The medium is the message." This famous statement has multiple meanings, including the notion that an emerging communication channel (medium) shapes society. However, the statement also highlights the fact that the channel selected communicates a message beyond the content sent through that channel. Some communication channels are viewed as impersonal whereas others are more personal; some are considered professional whereas others are casual; some are seen as "cool" whereas others are old-fashioned. For instance, phone calls and other synchronous communication channels convey a greater sense of urgency than do text messages and other asynchronous channels.

The importance of a channel's symbolic meaning is perhaps most apparent in stories about managers who use emails or text messages to inform employees that they are fired or laid off. In a recent case involving dismissal by text message, Australia's Fair Work Commission warned employers that digital written communication channels are "unnecessarily callous" and therefore (with rare exceptions) should not be used to notify employees of their dismissal. The Commission explained that "termination of employment is a matter of such significance that basic human dignity requires that dismissal be conveyed personally."[38]

MEDIA RICHNESS

In the opening case study for this chapter, Stellar Health co-founder Octavian Costache commented that Slack and similar digital communication platforms are less effective than face-to-face meetings for intense, creative discussions. He specifically noted that digital text messages couldn't provide the volume and richness of information exchange that is possible with in-person meetings. Costache recognizes that communication channels vary in their level of media richness. **Media richness** refers to the channel's data-carrying capacity—the volume and variety of information that can be transmitted during a specific time.[39]

> **media richness** A medium's data-carrying capacity, that is, the volume and variety of information that can be transmitted during a specific time.

Exhibit 9.6 illustrates various communication channels arranged in a hierarchy of richness, with face-to-face interaction at the top and lean data-only reports at the bottom. A communication channel has high richness when it is able to convey multiple cues (such as both verbal and nonverbal information), allows timely feedback from receiver to sender, allows the sender to customize the message to the receiver, and makes use of complex symbols (such as words and phrases with multiple meanings).

Face-to-face communication has very high media richness because it allows us to simultaneously communicate both verbally and nonverbally, to receive feedback almost immediately from the receiver, to quickly adjust our message and style, and to use complex language such as metaphors and idioms (e.g., "spilling the beans"). Rich media tend to be synchronous and have high social presence.

Rich media are better than lean media when the communication situation is nonroutine and ambiguous. Under these

EXHIBIT 9.6 **Media Richness Hierarchy**

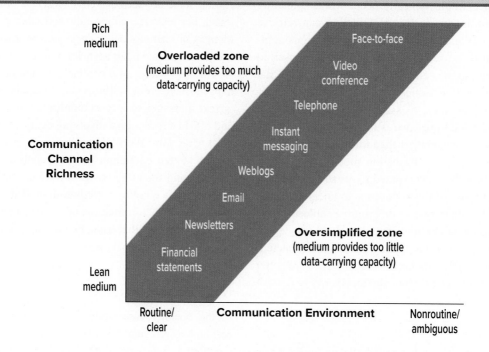

conditions, the sender and receiver need to transmit a large volume of information with immediate feedback so they can understand the situation and agree on the best way to coordinate. For example, department and shift teams in many hospitals have brief stand-up daily huddles during which team members share information and expectations about the day's work.[40] Lean media work well in routine situations because the sender and receiver have shared mental models to understand the situation and determine how to coordinate their work. Using a rich medium—such as holding a special meeting—when the situation is routine and clear would be a waste of time.[41]

Exceptions to Media Richness Theory

Research generally supports media richness theory for traditional channels (face-to-face, written memos, etc.). However, the model doesn't fit reality nearly as well when digital communication channels are studied.[42] Three factors seem to explain why digital channels may have more media richness than the theory proposes:

- *Ability to multi-communicate.* It is usually difficult (as well as rude) to communicate face-to-face with someone while simultaneously transmitting messages to another person using another channel. Most digital communication channels, on the other hand, require less social etiquette and attention, so employees can easily engage in two or more communication events at the same time. In other words, they can multi-communicate.[43] For example, people routinely scan Web pages while talking to

someone on the phone. Employees tap out text messages to a client while listening to a discussion at a large meeting. Research consistently finds that people multitask less efficiently than they assume,[44] but the volume of information transmitted simultaneously through two digital communication channels is sometimes greater than through one high media richness channel.

- *Communication proficiency.* Earlier in this chapter we explained that communication effectiveness is partially determined by the sender's ability and motivation to use the communication channel. People with higher proficiency can "push" more information through the channel, thereby increasing the channel's information flow. Experienced smartphone users, for instance, can whip through messages in a flash, whereas new users struggle to type and retrieve messages. In contrast, the ability to communicate through casual conversation and other natural channels is less varied, because most of us develop good levels of proficiency throughout life and possibly through hardwired evolutionary development.[45]

- *Social presence effects.* Channels with high media richness tend to have more social presence. This improves empathy, but it also sensitizes both parties to their relative status and self-presentation, which can distort or divert attention away from the message.[46] During a personal meeting with the company's CEO, for example, you might concentrate more on your image to the CEO than on what the executive is saying to you. In other

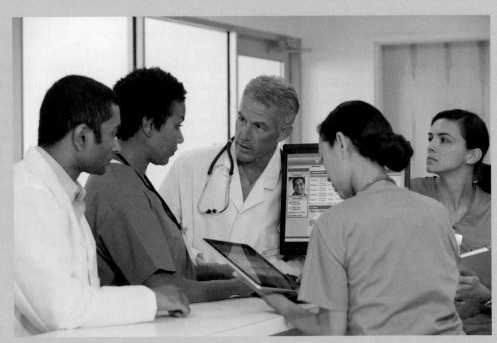

©Ariel Skelley/Blend Images/Getty Images

Patient care is complex, so teams at Toronto's University Health Network (UHN) conduct daily huddles to ensure that staff members directly communicate any potential safety or service quality concerns. These ten-minute, stand-up, face-to-face meetings have high media richness, which enables participants to discuss problems with less risk of misunderstanding. Unresolved issues are escalated to the management and executive team huddles. "The huddles reinforce the message that safety is everyone's job, no matter what their role is," says a manager at UHN's Toronto Rehab. Serious safety events have fallen dramatically at hospitals where huddles and related high-reliability initiatives are introduced.*

* "Daily Unit Safety Huddles Part of Caring Safely Transformation at UHN," Newsroom (Toronto: University Health Network, May 17, 2016); B. Kenefick, "How 10 Minutes a Day Can Sow the Seeds of a Safety Culture," *Hospital News,* November 3, 2016; M. Kaye, "Make No Mistake," *University of Toronto Magazine,* January 3, 2018.

words, the benefits of channels with high media richness may be offset by social presence distractions, whereas lean media have much less social presence to distract or distort the transmitted information.

COMMUNICATION CHANNELS AND PERSUASION

Some communication channels are more effective than others for **persuasion**; that is, using facts, logical arguments, and emotional appeals to change another person's beliefs and attitudes, usually for the purpose of changing behaviour. Studies support the long-held view that spoken communication, particularly face-to-face interaction, is more persuasive than emails, websites, and other forms of written communication. There are three main reasons for this

persuasion The use of facts, logical arguments, and emotional appeals to change another person's beliefs and attitudes, usually for the purpose of changing the person's behaviour.

persuasive effect.[47] First, spoken communication is typically accompanied by nonverbal communication. People are persuaded more when they receive both emotional and logical messages, and the combination of spoken with nonverbal communication provides this dual punch. A lengthy pause, raised voice tone, and (in face-to-face interaction) animated hand gestures can amplify the emotional tone of the message, thereby signalling the vitality of the issue.

A second reason why conversations are more persuasive is that spoken communication offers the sender high-quality immediate feedback about whether the receiver understands and accepts the message (i.e., is being persuaded). This feedback allows the sender to adjust the content and emotional tone of the message more quickly than with written communication. A third reason is that people are persuaded more under conditions of high social presence than low social presence. Listeners have higher motivation to pay attention and consider the sender's ideas in face-to-face conversations (high social presence). In contrast, persuasive communication through a website, email, and other low social presence channels are less effective due to the higher degree of anonymity and psychological distance from the persuader.

Although spoken communication tends to be more persuasive, written communication can also persuade others to some extent. Written messages have the advantage of presenting more technical detail than can occur through conversation. This factual information is valuable when the issue is important to the receiver. Also, people experience a moderate degree of social presence in written communication with friends and co-workers, so those messages can be persuasive when sent and received with close associates.

Communication Barriers (Noise)

LO4

"The greatest barrier to communication is the illusion that it has been achieved." This popular statement was apparently first uttered by American executive Joseph W. Coffman 60 years ago, paraphrasing a similar sentence written a few years earlier by *Fortune* magazine journalist William H. Whyte.[48] It warns that, in spite of the best intentions of sender and receiver to communicate, several barriers (called "noise" earlier in Exhibit 9.1) inhibit the effective exchange of information and its meaning.

PERCEPTIONS

One barrier is that both sender and receiver have imperfect perceptual processes. As receivers, we don't listen as well as senders assume, and our needs and expectations influence what signals get noticed and ignored (see Chapter 3). We aren't any better as senders, either. Some studies suggest that we have difficulty stepping out of our own perspectives and stepping into the perspectives of others, so we overestimate how well other people understand the message we are communicating.[49]

LANGUAGE

Language can be a huge source of communication noise because sender and receiver might not have the same codebook. They might struggle to communicate in a language that neither of them has mastered, or they might come from cultures that assign different meanings for specific words and phrases. The English language (among others) also has built-in ambiguities that cause misunderstandings. Consider the question "Can you close the door?" You might assume the sender is asking whether shutting the door is permitted. However, the question might be asking whether you

are physically able to shut the door, or possibly whether the door is designed such that it can be shut. In fact, this question might not be a question at all; the person could be politely *directing* you to shut the door.[50]

The ambiguity of language isn't always dysfunctional noise, however.[51] At times, leaders purposely use obscure language to reflect the ambiguity of the topic or to avoid unwanted emotional responses produced from more specific words. They might use metaphors to represent an abstract vision of the company's future, or use obtuse phrases such as "rightsizing" and "restructuring" to obscure the underlying message that people would be fired or laid off. Studies report that effective communicators also use more abstract words and symbols when addressing diverse or distant (not well known to the speaker) audiences, because abstraction increases the likelihood that the message is understood across a broader range of listeners.

JARGON

Jargon—specialized words and phrases for specific occupations or groups—potentially improves communication efficiency. However, it is a source of communication noise when transmitted to people who do not possess the jargon codebook. This problem was apparent in one recent study, which reported that physicians used more than two dozen jargon terms, on average, during consultations with parents of children with sleep disorders.[52]

FILTERING

Another source of noise in the communication process is the tendency to filter messages. Filtering may involve deleting or

"You use tech language that I don't understand, so I brought an interpreter."

Jerry King Cartoons

delaying negative information or using less harsh words so the message sounds more favourable.[53] Filtering is less likely to occur when corporate leaders create a "culture of candour." This culture develops when leaders themselves communicate truthfully, seek out diverse sources for information, and protect and reward those who speak openly and truthfully.[54]

INFORMATION OVERLOAD

Start with a daily avalanche of email, then add in text messages, PDF file downloads, cell/mobile phone calls, web pages, hard copy documents, some Twitter tweets, blogs, wikis, and other sources of incoming information. Altogether, you have created a perfect recipe for **information overload**.[55] As Exhibit 9.7 illustrates, information overload occurs whenever the job's information load exceeds the individual's capacity to get through it. Employees have an *information processing capacity*—the amount of information that they are able to process in a fixed unit of time. Meanwhile, jobs have a varying *information load*—the amount of information to be processed per unit of time. Information overload creates noise in the communication system because information gets overlooked or misinterpreted when people can't process it fast enough. The result is poorer-quality decisions as well as higher stress.[56]

information overload A condition in which the volume of information received exceeds the person's capacity to process it.

Information overload problems can be minimized by increasing our information processing capacity, reducing the job's information load, or through a combination of both. Employees can temporarily increase their information processing capacity by reading faster, scanning through documents more efficiently, managing their time use (less wasted time), removing distractions that slow information processing speed, and working longer hours. However, working beyond one's natural capacity is not sustainable for the long term.

Information load can be reduced by buffering, omitting, and summarizing. Buffering involves having incoming communication filtered, usually by an assistant. Omitting occurs when we decide to overlook messages, such as using software rules to redirect emails to folders that we rarely look at. Summarizing involves digesting a condensed version of the complete communication, such as reading an executive summary rather than the full report.

Cross-Cultural and Gender Communication

Globalization and increasing cultural diversity have brought about more cross-cultural communication issues in the workplace.[57] As mentioned in the previous section, language differences can be a significant source of noise in the communication process. Words are easily misunderstood in verbal communication when those involved have a limited vocabulary (such as when two executives need to communicate in a language that neither of them uses regularly). Even

EXHIBIT 9.7 Dynamics of Information Overload

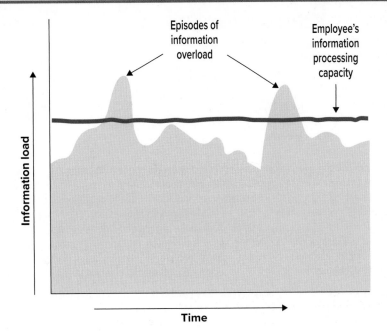

when both are fluent, the sender's accent might distort the usual sound of some words.

Voice intonation is another cross-cultural communication barrier. How loudly, deeply, and quickly people speak varies across cultures, and these voice intonations send secondary messages that have different meaning in each society. Words are also assigned somewhat different meaning across cultures. For example, KPMG staff from the United Kingdom sometimes referred to another person's suggestions as "interesting." They had to clarify to their German colleagues that "interesting" might not be complimenting the idea.[58]

Another cross-cultural dimension of communication is how people interpret conversational gaps (silence) and overlaps. Silence is revered in Japan because it symbolizes respect, indicates that the listener is thoughtfully contemplating what has just been said, and is a way of avoiding overt conflict.[59] Consequently, the informal communication practice in Japan and a few other countries is to let the other person finish speaking and sometimes wait a few seconds before saying anything. In contrast, most people in Canada and similar cultures avoid silence and interpret those incidents as a sign of disagreement.

Conversational overlaps are considered rude in Japan, whereas most people from Brazil and France are more likely to interpret interruptions and overlaps as evidence of the person's interest and involvement in the conversation. Meetings in countries that expect overlapping conversations can seem like a chaotic cacophony to those from other cultures. Aware of these differences, consulting firm Accenture held cross-cultural seminars that helped its Japanese managers to speak up in multinational meetings rather than wait for the silence that never occurs. "I was told I needed to jump into discussions rather than wait until everyone had said what they wanted to say," recalls one of Accenture's Japanese managers.[60]

©Cavan Images/Alamy Stock Photo

Indigenous Canadians communicate with silence much more than do most other Canadians, which can create misunderstanding in business and other relationships. "I really feel that there needs to be more acceptance and more teaching around the act of silence," suggests Roberta Price, an Elder of the Coast Salish peoples in British Columbia. In particular, she advises medical professionals to "just sit in silence and listen very, very carefully . . . when there is huge disconnect between the professional and the patient." A pioneering Canadian study reported how non-Indigenous physicians learned to better understand and practise silence when consulting with Indigenous patients. One physician explains that he sits low to avoid "looming" over the patient and does "not say anything for a long time." Another physician learned about "developing the patience, accepting the pregnant pauses, and the loss, the lack of eye contact."*

* L. Kelly and J.B. Brown, "Listening to Native Patients. Changes in Physicians' Understanding and Behaviour," *Canadian Family Physician* 48 (October 2002): 1645–52; W. Rowland, *Elder Roberta: Welcoming Silence,* Video, Living My Culture (Canadian Virtual Hospice, 2016).

NONVERBAL DIFFERENCES ACROSS CULTURES

Nonverbal communication represents another potential area for misunderstanding across cultures. Many nonconscious or involuntary nonverbal cues (such as smiling) have the same meaning around the world, but deliberate gestures often have different interpretations. For example, most of us shake our head from side to side to say "No," but a variation of head shaking means "I understand" to many people in India. Filipinos raise their eyebrows to give an affirmative answer, yet Arabs interpret this expression (along with clicking one's tongue) as a negative response. Most Canadians maintain eye contact with the speaker to show interest and respect, whereas most Indigenous peoples in Canada learn at an early age to show respect by looking down when an older or more senior person is talking to them.[61]

GENDER DIFFERENCES IN COMMUNICATION

Men and women have similar communication practices, but there are subtle distinctions that can occasionally lead to misunderstanding and conflict (see Exhibit 9.8).[62] One distinction is that men are more likely than women to view conversations as negotiations of relative status and power. They assert their power by directly giving advice to others (e.g., "You should do the following") and using combative language. There is also evidence that men dominate the talk time in conversations with women, as well as interrupt more and adjust their speaking style less than do women.

Men engage in more "report talk," in which the primary function of the conversation is impersonal and efficient information exchange. Women also do report talk, particularly when conversing with men. However, women engage in more "rapport talk"—verbal and nonverbal communication that builds relationships by showing egalitarian, empathetic support, and engagement with the other person.[63] They also subdue their power in the relationship through more deferential communication, including modifiers ("It might be a good idea. . ."), disclaimers ("I'm not certain, but. . ."), and tag questions ("This works, doesn't it?").

Women tend to make more use of indirect requests ("Do you think you should. . ."), apologize more often, and seek advice from others more quickly than do men. Men also use these speech patterns to some extent, but women use them more frequently as well as across communication channels (conversations, text messages, etc.). Research also reports that women are more sensitive than men to nonverbal cues in face-to-face meetings. Together, these conditions can create communication conflicts. Women who describe problems get frustrated that men offer advice rather than rapport, whereas men become frustrated because they can't understand why women don't appreciate their advice.

EXHIBIT 9.8 Gender Differences in Communication

When Men Communicate

1. Report talk—giving advice, assert power
2. Give advice directly
3. Dominant conversation style
4. Apologize less often
5. Less sensitive to nonverbal cues

©Blue Jean Images/Alamy Stock Photo

When Women Communicate

1. Rapport talk—relationship building
2. Give advice indirectly
3. Flexible conversation style
4. Apologize more often
5. More sensitive to nonverbal cues

Improving Interpersonal Communication

LO5

Effective interpersonal communication depends on the sender's ability to get the message across and the receiver's performance as an active listener. In this section, we outline these two essential features of effective interpersonal communication.

GETTING YOUR MESSAGE ACROSS

This chapter began with the statement that effective communication occurs when the other person receives and understands the message. This is more difficult to accomplish than most people believe. To get your message across to the other person, you first need to empathize with the receiver, such as by being sensitive to words that may be ambiguous or trigger the wrong emotional response. Second, be sure that you repeat the message, such as by rephrasing the key points a couple of times. Third, your message competes with other messages and noise, so find a time when the receiver is less likely to be distracted by these other matters. Finally, focus on the problem, not the person, if you have negative information to convey. People stop listening when the information attacks their self-concept. Also, suggest things the listener can do to improve, rather than pointing to the listener as the problem.

ACTIVE LISTENING

Active listening is at least as important as talking. As the Greek philosopher Epictetus wrote almost two millennia ago: "Nature gave us one tongue, but two ears, so we may listen twice as much as we speak."[64] But listening is more than just hearing the other person making sounds; it is a process of actively sensing the sender's signals, evaluating them accurately, and responding appropriately. These three components of active listening—sensing, evaluating, and responding—represent the listener's side of the communication model described at the beginning of this chapter. Listeners receive the sender's signals, decode them as intended, and provide appropriate and timely feedback to the sender. Active listeners constantly cycle through sensing, evaluating, and responding during the conversation and engage in various activities to improve these processes (see Exhibit 9.9).[65]

- *Sensing.* Sensing is the process of receiving signals from the sender and paying attention to them. Active listeners improve sensing in three ways. First, they postpone evaluation by not forming an opinion until the speaker has finished. Second, they avoid interrupting the speaker's conversation. Third, they remain motivated to listen to the speaker.

- *Evaluating.* This component of listening includes understanding the message meaning, evaluating the message, and remembering the message. To improve their evaluation of the conversation, active listeners empathize with the speaker—they try to understand and be sensitive to the speaker's feelings, thoughts, and situation. Evaluation also improves by organizing the speaker's ideas during the communication episode.

- *Responding.* This third component of listening involves providing feedback to the sender, which motivates and directs the speaker's communication. Active listeners accomplish this by maintaining sufficient eye contact and sending back channel signals (e.g., "I see"), both of

---

EXHIBIT 9.9   Active Listening Process and Strategies

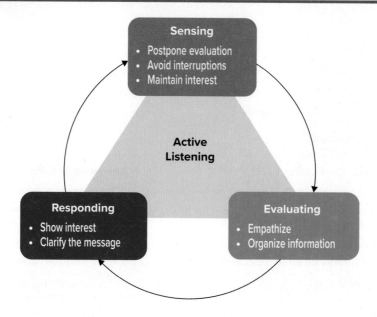

Are you an active listener? You can discover how effectively you practise the skills of active listening by locating this self-assessment in Connect.

which show interest. They also respond by clarifying the message—rephrasing the speaker's ideas at appropriate breaks ("So you're saying that. . . ?").

Improving Communication throughout the Hierarchy

LO6

So far, we have looked at micro-level issues in the communication process, namely, sending and receiving information between two employees or among members of a small team. But in this era where knowledge is a competitive advantage, corporate leaders also need to maintain an open flow of communication up, down, and across the entire organization. In this section, we discuss three organization-wide communication strategies: workspace design, digitally based organizational communication, and direct communication with top management.

WORKSPACE DESIGN

The location and design of hallways, offices, cubicles, and communal areas (cafeterias, elevators) all shape to whom we

 by the NUMBERS

How Well Do Executives Support Organizational Communication?*

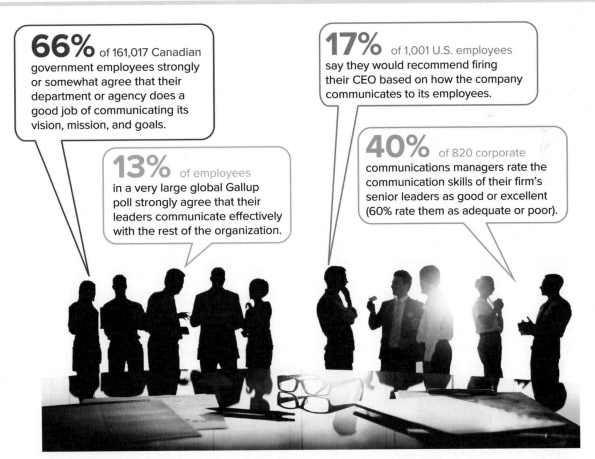

66% of 161,017 Canadian government employees strongly or somewhat agree that their department or agency does a good job of communicating its vision, mission, and goals.

13% of employees in a very large global Gallup poll strongly agree that their leaders communicate effectively with the rest of the organization.

17% of 1,001 U.S. employees say they would recommend firing their CEO based on how the company communicates to its employees.

40% of 820 corporate communications managers rate the communication skills of their firm's senior leaders as good or excellent (60% rate them as adequate or poor).

©Rawpixel.com/Shutterstock

* E. O'Boyle, "American Workplace Changing at a Dizzying Pace," Gallup Workplace, February 15, 2017; "State of the Sector 2019: The Definitive Global Survey of the Internal Communication Profession" (London: Gatehouse, February 2019); "Dynamic Signal Study Finds U.S. Workforce Stressed and Ready to Quit, Compounding Concerns From Tight Labor Market and Possible Economic Downturn," News Release (San Bruno, Calif.: Dynamic Signal, March 20, 2019); "2018 Public Service Employee Survey: Results for the Public Service" (Ottawa: Government of Canada, Treasury Board of Canada Secretariat, 2019).

speak as well as the frequency of that communication.[66] Many organizations have shifted from cubicles to open spaces in the hope that the increased line-of-sight to co-workers will improve information sharing. However, two factors may reverse this trend. First, the COVID-19 pandemic demanded more social distancing to protect the health of employees. Some companies fulfilled this requirement by transferring employees from shared work areas to their own private cubicles. Second, open-space arrangements potentially undermine employee productivity due to noise, distractions, and loss of privacy.[67]

Another workspace strategy is to cloister employees into team spaces, but also encourage sufficient interaction with people from other teams. Pixar Animation Studios constructed its campus in Emeryville, California, with these principles in mind. The buildings encourage communication among team members. At the same time, the campus encourages happenstance interactions with people on other teams. Pixar executives call this the "bathroom effect," because team members must leave their isolated pods to fetch their mail, have lunch, or visit the restroom.[68]

DIGITALLY BASED ORGANIZATIONAL COMMUNICATION

For decades, employees received official company news through hard copy newsletters and magazines. Some firms still use these communication devices, but the traditional company magazine has almost completely been replaced by intranet web pages or PDF format files. The advantage of these *e-zines* is that company news can be prepared and distributed quickly, and with much less damage to the environment.

Even so, employees are increasingly skeptical of information that has been screened and packaged by management. Companies are adapting to this skepticism by introducing social media channels through the emerging enterprise collaborative platforms described earlier in this chapter. Along with enabling task-focused message threads, these systems allow users to generate blogs, shared notices, and other news-oriented sites, most of which also allow feedback comments from readers within the organization. In many instances, company magazines have been replaced by real-time text messages directly from employees where the events occur.[69]

Wikis are another form of organizational communication, particularly where employees need to share structured documentation that continually changes. Wikis are collaborative digital spaces in which anyone in a group can write, edit, or remove material from the site. *Wikipedia,* the popular online encyclopedia, is a massive public example of a wiki. However, employee involvement in corporate wikis has been lower than expected, likely because wiki involvement takes time and the company does not reward or recognize those who provide this time to wiki development.[70]

DIRECT COMMUNICATION WITH TOP MANAGEMENT

Effective organizational communication includes regular interaction directly between senior executives and employees further down the hierarchy. One form of direct communication is through town hall meetings, where executives brief a large gathering of staff on the company's current strategy and developments. Although the communication is mostly from executives to employees, town hall meetings are more personal and credible than video or written channels. Also, these events usually provide some opportunity for employees to ask questions. Another strategy is for senior executives to hold roundtable forums with a small representation of employees, mainly to hear their opinions on various issues.

A less formal approach to direct communication is **management by wandering around (MBWA).** Coined by people at Hewlett-Packard four decades ago, this is the practice of senior executives getting out of their offices and casually chatting with employees on a daily or regular basis. Bob Courteau actively practises MBWA. "Management by wandering around was a big new idea as part of the Hewlett Packard way. . .and I have practised it heavily in my career," says Courteau, who worked at Hewlett Packard early in his career and for the past several years has been CEO of Altus Group, a large Toronto-based commercial real estate services and software company.[71]

> **management by wandering around (MBWA)** A communication practice in which executives get out of their offices and learn from others in the organization through face-to-face dialogue.

Less information is filtered when executives casually and regularly chat directly with employees. These MBWA conversations also help executives acquire a deeper meaning and quicker understanding of internal organizational problems. A third benefit is that employees potentially develop better empathy for decisions made further up the corporate hierarchy.

Communicating through the Grapevine

Organizational leaders may try their best to quickly communicate breaking news to employees through emails, text messages, and other direct formal channels, but employees still rely to some extent on the corporate **grapevine.** The grapevine is an unstructured and informal network founded on social relationships rather than organizational charts or job

> **grapevine** An unstructured and informal communication network founded on social relationships rather than organizational charts or job descriptions.

Global Connections 9.3

ADVICE TO CEOS: LISTEN—ACT—REPEAT*

John Legere has straightforward advice for all leaders. "The most powerful formula for success is three simple steps: 1. Shut up and listen to your customers and employees. 2. Do what they tell you. 3. Repeat."

Legere, who recently stepped down as CEO of T-Mobile US, practises what he preaches. His town hall meetings with employees have become legendary. He constantly tweets with customers and staff alike. And he interacts personally—not just remotely—with the people on the front lines.

"At T-Mobile, we've cut through the layers—and hierarchy—to listen to employees directly every single day," says Legere (centre front in this photo). "I've personally flown over a million miles to visit our call centres and retail stores—because it's so important to cut out all the layers and hear directly from employees."

©Jordan Strauss/AP Images for T-Mobile

* J. Legere, "T-Mobile's CEO on Winning Market Share by Trash-Talking Rivals," *Harvard Business Review,* January-February 2017; J. Legere, "Un-Carrier Is from the Inside Out!," September 26, 2017, https://www.t-mobile.com/news/un-carrier-is-from-the-inside-out; M. Davis, "T-Mobile CEO John Legere Met Employees at Sprint Campus Weeks after Negative Report," *Kansas City Star,* October 5, 2018.

descriptions. What do employees think about the grapevine? Surveys have found that almost all employees use the grapevine, but very few of them prefer this source of information. In one survey, only one-third of employees believe grapevine information is credible. In other words, employees turn to the grapevine when they have few other options.[72]

GRAPEVINE CHARACTERISTICS

Research conducted several decades ago reported that the grapevine transmits information very rapidly in all directions throughout the organization. The typical pattern is a cluster chain, whereby a few people actively transmit information to many others. The grapevine works through informal social networks, so it is more active where employees have similar backgrounds and are able to communicate easily. Many rumours seem to have at least a kernel of truth, possibly because they are transmitted through media-rich communication channels (e.g., face-to-face) and employees are motivated to communicate effectively. Nevertheless, the grapevine distorts information by deleting fine details and exaggerating key points of the story.[73]

Some of these characteristics might still be true, but the grapevine has almost certainly changed as email, text messaging, and other social media practices have replaced the traditional water cooler as sources of gossip. For example,

several Facebook sites are unofficially themed around specific companies, allowing employees and customers to vent their complaints about the organization. Along with altering the speed and network of corporate grapevines, the Internet has expanded these networks around the globe, not just around the next cubicle.[74]

GRAPEVINE BENEFITS AND LIMITATIONS

Should the grapevine be encouraged, tolerated, or quashed? The difficulty in answering this question is that the grapevine has both benefits and limitations.[75] One benefit, as was mentioned earlier, is that employees rely on the grapevine when information is not available through formal channels. It is also the main conduit through which organizational stories and other symbols of the organization's culture are communicated. A third benefit of the grapevine is that this social interaction relieves anxiety, which explains why rumour mills are most active during times of uncertainty.[76] Finally, the grapevine is associated with the drive to bond. Being a recipient of gossip is a sign of inclusion, according to evolutionary psychologists. Trying to quash the grapevine is, in some respects, an attempt to undermine the natural human drive for social interaction.[77]

The grapevine potentially offers these benefits, but it is not a preferred communication medium. Grapevine information is sometimes so distorted that it escalates rather than reduces employee anxiety. Furthermore, employees develop more negative attitudes toward the organization when management is slower than the grapevine in communicating information. What should corporate leaders do with the grapevine? The best advice seems to be to listen to the grapevine as a signal of employee anxiety, then correct the cause of this anxiety. Some companies also listen to the grapevine and step in to correct blatant errors and fabrications. Most important, corporate leaders need to view the grapevine as a competitor, and meet this challenge by directly informing employees of news before it spreads throughout the grapevine.

Debating Point: SHOULD MANAGEMENT USE THE GRAPEVINE TO COMMUNICATE TO EMPLOYEES?

The grapevine has been the curse of management since modern-day organizations were invented. News flows with stealth-like efficiency below the surface, making it difficult to tell where information is travelling, what is being said to whom, or who is responsible for any misinformation. Although employees naturally flock to the grapevine for knowledge and social comfort in difficult times, its messages can be so distorted that they sometimes produce more stress than they alleviate. It is absurd to imagine management trying to systematically transmit important information—or any news whatsoever—through this uncontrollable, quirky communication channel.

But some communication experts are taking a second look at the grapevine, viewing it more as a resource than a nemesis. Their inspiration comes from marketing, where viral and word-of-mouth marketing have become hot topics.* Viral and word-of-mouth marketing occur when information seeded to a few people is transmitted to others based on patterns of friendship. In other words, information is passed along to others at the whim of those who first receive that information. Within organizations, this process is essentially the grapevine at work. Employees transmit information to other people within their sphere of everyday interaction.

The grapevine might seem to transmit information in strange and unreliable ways, but there are two contrary arguments. First, the grapevine channel is becoming more robust and reliable, thanks to social media and other emerging forms of electronic communication. These media have produced a stronger scaffolding than ever before, which potentially makes the grapevine more useful for transmitting information.

The second argument is that the grapevine tends to be more persuasive than traditional communication channels

from management to employees. The grapevine is based on social networks, which we discuss in the next chapter. Social networks are an important source of organizational power because they are built on trust, and trust increases acceptance of information sent through those networks. Consequently, the grapevine tends to be far more persuasive than other communication channels.

The power of the grapevine as a communication tool was illustrated when Novo Nordisk tried to change the image of its regulatory affairs staff.** The European pharmaceutical company made limited progress after a year of using traditional communication channels. "We had posters, meetings, competitions, and everything else you would expect," recalls communication adviser Jakob Wolter. "By the end of it, we'd achieved something—a general awareness among our people—but very little else."

So Novo Nordisk took another route. During the half-yearly gathering of all employees, nine regulatory staff were given wax-sealed confidential envelopes that assigned them to one of three "secret societies." Between conference sessions, these employees met with the managing director, who assigned their manifesto, including a mandate and budget. They were also told to keep their mission secret, saying to inquisitive co-workers, "I can't tell you."

"The [rumour] mill started right there that day," says Wolter. "People were already wondering what on earth was going on." The societies were allowed to recruit more employees, which they did in subsequent months. Many employees throughout Novo Nordisk became intrigued, spreading their opinions and news to others. Meanwhile, empowered to improve their image and work processes, members of the three secret societies introduced several initiatives that brought about improvements.

---

* A. De Bruyn and G.L. Lilien, "A Multi-Stage Model of Word-of-Mouth Influence through Viral Marketing," *International Journal of Research in Marketing* 25, no. 3 (2008): 151–63; J.Y.C. Ho and M. Dempsey, "Viral Marketing: Motivations to Forward Online Content," *Journal of Business Research* 63, no. 9–10 (2010): 1000–06; M. Williams and F. Buttle, "The Eight Pillars of WOM Management: Lessons from a Multiple Case Study," *Australasian Marketing Journal (AMJ)* 19, no. 2 (2011): 85–92.

** K. Dyer, "Changing Perceptions Virally at Novo Nordisk," *Strategic Communication Management* 13, no. 2 (2009): 24–27.

Chapter Summary

LO1

Explain why communication is important in organizations and discuss four influences on effective communication encoding and decoding.

Communication refers to the process by which information is transmitted and *understood* between two or more people. Communication is important for coordinating work, making decisions, changing others' behaviour, and maintaining employee well-being. The communication process involves forming, encoding, and transmitting the intended message to a receiver, who then decodes the message and provides feedback to the sender. Effective communication occurs when the sender's thoughts are transmitted to and understood by the intended receiver. The effectiveness of this process depends on whether the sender and receiver have similar codebooks, the sender's proficiency at encoding that message to the audience, the sender's and receiver's motivation and ability to transmit messages through that particular communication channel, and their common mental models of the communication context.

LO2

Compare and contrast the advantages and disadvantages of digital written communication channels, other verbal communication channels, and nonverbal communication.

The two main types of communication channels are verbal and nonverbal. Email still dominates organizational communication, but other forms of digital written communication (chat, text) are becoming more common because they are preferred by younger employees and recently developed collaborative communication platforms are being adopted in organizations. The main advantages of digital written communication is that it can be written, edited, and transmitted quickly to many people. Most of these channels reduce social and organizational status differences, are asynchronous and, with search functions, are somewhat efficient filing cabinets.

Digital written communication has a number of disadvantages. It is relatively poor at communicating emotions, tends to reduce politeness and respect, and contributes to information overload. It is also inefficient at communicating in ambiguous, complex, and novel situations.

Organizations have recently been installing digital collaborative platforms, most of which emphasize communication channels that encourage interactive conversations and information sharing rather than one-way communication. They are social media—digital communication channels that enable people to collaborate in the creation and exchange of user-generated content. Social media enables reciprocally interactive content, such that senders and receivers become "users" in a community of shared content. Each type of social media serves a unique combination of functions (e.g., enabling conversations, sharing information, maintaining relationships).

Nonverbal communication includes facial gestures, voice intonation, physical distance, and even silence. Unlike verbal communication, nonverbal communication is less rule-bound and is mostly automatic and nonconscious. Some nonverbal communication is automatic through a process called emotional contagion.

LO3

Discuss the relevance of synchronicity, social presence, social acceptance, and media richness when choosing the preferred communication channel.

The most appropriate communication medium depends on several factors. Synchronicity refers to the channel's capacity for the sender and receiver to communicate at the same time (synchronous) or at different times (asynchronous). Synchronous channels are better when the issue is urgent or the topic is complex. Asynchronous channels are better when it is costly for both parties to communicate at the same time or when the receiver should have time to reflect before responding. A channel has high social presence when it creates psychological closeness to the other party and awareness of their humanness. This is valuable when the parties need to empathize with or influence each other. Social acceptance refers to how well the communication medium is approved and supported by others. This acceptance depends on organizational or societal norms, each party's preferences and skills with the channel, and the symbolic meaning of a channel. Media richness refers to a channel's data-carrying capacity. Nonroutine and ambiguous situations require rich media. However, technology-based lean media may be possible where users can multi-communicate, have high proficiency with that technology, and don't have social distractions.

LO4

Discuss various barriers (noise) to effective communication, including cross-cultural and gender-based differences in communication.

Several barriers create noise in the communication process. People misinterpret messages because of misaligned codebooks due to different languages, jargon, and use of ambiguous phrases. Filtering messages and information overload are two other communication barriers. These problems are often amplified in cross-cultural settings where these problems occur along with differences in meaning of nonverbal cues, silence, and conversational overlaps. There are also some communication differences between men and women, such as the tendency for men to exert status and engage in report talk in conversations, and for women to use more rapport talk and to be more sensitive than men to nonverbal cues.

LO5

Explain how to get your message across more effectively, and summarize the elements of active listening.

To get a message across, the sender must learn to empathize with the receiver, repeat the message, choose an appropriate time for the conversation, and be descriptive rather than evaluative. Listening includes sensing, evaluating, and responding. Active listeners support these processes by postponing evaluation, avoiding interruptions, maintaining interest, empathizing, organizing information, showing interest, and clarifying the message.

LO6

Describe effective communication strategies in organizational hierarchies, and review the role and relevance of the organizational grapevine.

Some companies try to encourage communication through workspace design, as well as through digital communication channels. Some executives also meet directly with employees by engaging in management by wandering around (MBWA) and by holding town-hall meetings.

In any organization, employees rely on the grapevine, particularly during times of uncertainty. The grapevine is an unstructured and informal network founded on social relationships rather than organizational charts or job descriptions. Although early research identified several unique features of the grapevine, some of these features may be changing as the Internet plays an increasing role in grapevine communication.

Key Terms

communication
emotional contagion
grapevine
information overload
management by wandering around (MBWA)

media richness
persuasion
social media
social presence
synchronicity

Critical Thinking Questions

1. You have been hired as a consultant to improve communication between engineering and marketing staff in a large high-technology company. Use the communication model and the four ways to improve that process to devise strategies to improve communication effectiveness among employees between these two work units.

2. A consumer goods company holds quarterly meetings involving its three dozen sales managers. These managers are located in several cities and countries, so more than half of them "participate" in the meeting as remote attendees. The one-day meeting has an opening and closing talk by the CEO and vice-president of sales, but most of the day consists of open discussion as well as one small-group session on strategic and operations sales issues. Which digital communication channel(s) would likely work best for involving the remote participants in these sessions? You may assume that more than one digital channel can be used throughout the day and, for some channels, more than one channel may be used at the same time. Your answer should refer to the four factors to consider when choosing the best communication channel (synchronicity, social presence, social acceptance, and media richness).

3. Wikis are collaborative websites where anyone in the group can post, edit, or delete any information. Where might this communication technology be most useful in organizations?

4. Under what conditions, if any, do you think it is appropriate to use email to notify an employee that they have been laid off or fired? Why are text messages and other digital written communication channels usually considered inappropriate for conveying this information?

5. Suppose that you are part of a remote team and must persuade other team members on an important matter (such as switching suppliers or altering the project deadline). Assuming that you cannot visit these people in person, what can you do to maximize your persuasiveness?

6. Under what circumstances should communication messages be somewhat ambiguous? Under what conditions is ambiguous communication dysfunctional?

7. Explain why men and women are sometimes frustrated with each other's communication behaviours.

8. In your opinion, has the introduction of digital written communication (email, instant messages, online chat, etc.) increased or decreased the amount of information flowing through the corporate grapevine? Explain your answer.

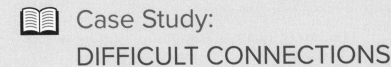

Case Study:
DIFFICULT CONNECTIONS

by Steven L. McShane, University of Newcastle (Australia)

Sophia Reddy is an accountant in her late 20s who works in the downtown Toronto office of Alicamber Ltd., a well-known accounting firm with two dozen offices across Canada. A few days ago, a senior manager in the Toronto office asked her to participate next month in a special project located in Alicamber's main Winnipeg office. The project includes accounting valuation analysis of an insurance firm, and Sophia's specialized knowledge of auditing insurance firms is apparently important for the project team's skill set. She will spend two weeks in Winnipeg working on-site with that team. For two weeks before her visit, as the project gets under way, she will work remotely from Toronto with Thomas Kerbakker, the project leader, and his team members in Winnipeg.

Sophia initially looked forward to her involvement in the Winnipeg project. The brief secondment applies her specialized knowledge, she will meet and learn from colleagues in another city, and working in Winnipeg will be an interesting change from Toronto. Two days after being advised of the assignment by the senior manager in the Toronto office, Sophia had not received any text message from Thomas, so she took the initiative to message him first.

Hi Thomas. Sophia Reddy here. I am excited to join your project. Gr8 to meet the Winnipeg team and learn from each other. Pls text team member list and schedule. Any b/g info you can send this wk would be helpful ☺. Best, Sophia Reddy.

Sophia expected Thomas to reply the same day, preferably within an hour or two after her message was sent. Co-workers in her Toronto office typically texted back within that time frame. But no reply was received by the end of that day. When Sophia checked the next morning, Thomas still hadn't replied. So, she sent the text message a second time. Thomas still had not texted back to her by the end of that day.

Thomas's silence was beginning to irritate and worry Sophia. Either her specialized knowledge for the project wasn't valued, or the project had been delayed, which would throw off her schedule working on other projects with Toronto clients.

On the third morning, with no communication from Thomas, Sophia checked in with the manager who had assigned her to the Winnipeg project. To her surprise, the manager explained that although Thomas has a company-provided smartphone (whose number Sophia had used for the messages she sent), he is one of those near-retirement managers who apparently doesn't do text messages. Staff in the Winnipeg office are aware of this, so they typically speak to him in person or over the phone. The manager acknowledged

that sorting out schedules is important, but also mentioned that the project wouldn't begin for another month.

Armed with this information, Sophia returned to her office to finally make contact with Thomas. She picked up her phone, looked at it for a moment, then slowly set it down again. Sophia visualized an awkward conversation. She had never met Thomas, he is obviously much older than her, and his reluctance or inability to send text messages was a sure sign that the two have considerably divergent ways of thinking. In fact, Sophia wondered whether the entire Winnipeg office does things differently than her colleagues in Toronto. Sophia calls clients when required, but even these conversations are getting rarer in favour of text messages, emails, and on-site visits. As with many people her age, Sophia uses her phone to do almost everything, except make phone calls!

As a compromise, Sophia decided to send Thomas an email. It was a variation of her earlier text message, but with much more formality as well as a subject line, greeting, salutation, and company signature lines. Sophia even changed "Thomas" to "Mr. Kerbakker" in the greeting. She surmised that Thomas would prefer this status-laden introduction, given his age and phobia with text messages. Sophia felt odd writing so formal an email to a co-worker or manager, but Thomas Kerbakker seemed to be the type who would expect this approach.

A few hours later, Sophia received an email reply from Thomas. It consisted of terse comments to each sentence that she had written in her earlier email:

| Hello Mr. Kerbakker:

| I am excited to join the [insurance company] project team
| in Winnipeg.

good

| It will be an excellent opportunity to meet the Winnipeg
| group and learn from each other.

yes it will

| Please send me details of the team members and your
| proposed project scheduling. Any background information
| you can send this week would be helpful.

noted

Thomas

Sophia felt bewildered and dejected as she stared at Thomas's reply. Was he angry with her for some unknown reason? He seemed too busy to welcome her and certainly didn't seem to care whether she was involved in the project. "He didn't even take the trouble to capitalize his words!" Sophia quipped under her breath. Also, Thomas's reply didn't give her confidence that the information she needed would be forthcoming very soon. Sophia increasingly regretted being assigned to this project. "This Winnipeg assignment isn't going to be as enjoyable as I thought," Sophia mumbled to herself.

Discussion Questions

1. Identify one or more symptoms that something has gone wrong here.

2. Analyze the causes of these symptom(s) using one or more communication concepts from this chapter.

3. What do you recommend that Sophia do at this time regarding her interaction with Thomas and the Winnipeg team? Assume that Sophia cannot back out of her assignment to the Winnipeg project.

4. What should Alicamber Ltd. do to minimize these problems in the long run?

Team Exercise:
CROSS-CULTURAL COMMUNICATION GAME

by Steven L. McShane, University of Newcastle (Australia)

Purpose This activity is designed to develop and test your knowledge of cross-cultural differences in communication and etiquette.

Materials The instructor will provide one set of question/answer cards to each pair of teams.

Instructions

Step 1: The class is divided into an even number of teams. Ideally, each team would have three students. (Two- or four-student teams are possible if matched with an equal-sized team.) Each team is then paired with another team and the paired teams (Team "A" and Team "B") are assigned a private space, away from other matched teams.

Step 2: The instructor will hand each pair of teams a stack of cards with the multiple-choice questions face down. These cards have questions and answers about cross-cultural differences in communication and etiquette. No books or other aids are allowed.

Step 3: The exercise begins with a member of Team A picking up one card from the top of the pile and asking the question on that card to the members of Team B. The information given to Team B includes the question and all alternatives listed on the card. Team B has 30 seconds after the question and alternatives have been read to give an answer. Team B earns one point if the correct answer is given. If Team B's answer is incorrect, however, Team A earns that point. Correct answers to each question are indicated on the card and, of course, should not be revealed until the question is correctly answered or time is up. Whether or not Team B answers correctly, it picks up the next card on the pile and reads it to members of Team A. In other words, cards are read alternatively to each team. This procedure is repeated until all of the cards have been read or time has expired. The team receiving the most points wins.

Important note: The textbook provides very little information pertaining to the questions in this exercise. Rather, you must rely on past learning, logic, and luck to win.

Team Exercise:
PRACTISING ACTIVE LISTENING

by Ena Chadha, Schulich School of Business

Purpose This activity illustrates the multi-faceted nature of active listening and the challenges of listening with an open mind to someone who disagrees with you.

Activity Structure This communication exercise takes about 25 minutes, followed by a debrief discussion about the challenges of active listening. Students should begin by finding a partner (preferably someone they do not know) for a two-round communication activity. Pairs should be seated next to each other.

Round 1: The first person should speak for three minutes about a casual, easy-to-relate personal topic (for example, maintaining work/school balance, budgeting, difficulty getting time to exercise, or problems with housemates). The partner should try their best to listen and to refrain from asking questions. After the first person finishes speaking, the second person should take a turn speaking for three minutes about the same or a similar personal topic. Again, the listening person must try their best to listen and abstain from asking questions.

Round 2: After both people have spoken about a personal topic, the instructor will ask them to select a societal topic currently popular in the news (for example, affirmative action, mandatory voting, universal pharmacare). One person should be designated in favour of the topic and the second person designated against the topic (regardless of true beliefs). Ask the first person to speak for three minutes about the points they believe to be in favour of the topic. After the first student finishes speaking, the second student should take a turn speaking for three minutes about the points they believe to be against the topic.

Debrief The instructor will provide specific questions for discussing the important lessons that stem from this activity.

Ena Chadha, LL.B. and LL.M., Sessional Lecturer Schulich School of Business

Self-Assessment for Chapter 9

SELF-ASSESSMENT NAME	DESCRIPTION
Are you an active listener?	Listening is a critical component of communication. But most people put more effort into how well they communicate as a sender than how well they listen as a receiver. Active listening is a skill that can be learned, so the first step is to know which components of active listening require further development. This assessment is designed to assess your strengths and weaknesses on various dimensions of active listening.

CHAPTER 10

Power and Influence in the Workplace

LEARNING OBJECTIVES

After reading this chapter, you should be able to:

LO1 Describe the dependence model of power and describe the five sources of power in organizations.

LO2 Discuss the four contingencies of power.

LO3 Explain how people and work units gain power through social networks.

LO4 Describe eight types of influence tactics, three consequences of influencing others, and three contingencies to consider when choosing an influence tactic.

LO5 Identify the organizational conditions and personal characteristics that support organizational politics, as well as ways to minimize organizational politics.

Jeremy Gutsche is one of the world's leading trend spotters, but he doesn't like to use that word. "Quite simply, the word 'trends' is too broad," says the Canadian entrepreneur, explaining that it can mean anything from next year's fashionable colour to macro-level buying behaviour. "I like to hunt for what I call clusters of inspiration," he offers. "Clustering is the art of identifying insights that are meaningful to your customer. To create clusters, you'll need to collect your observations from trend hunting and filter through the noise."

Whether he is a trend spotter or a cluster hunter, Jeremy Gutsche has developed valuable expertise and a personal brand that generate considerable power for his career success. People who can forecast the future are worth their weight in gold because they help companies cope with environmental uncertainties. This expertise assists leaders in their quest to anticipate the future, which enables them to direct organizational resources toward profitable and sustainable ventures.

Jeremy Gutsche has gained considerable power in his career by developing expertise and a personal brand as a trend hunter.

©Marcel Bieri/EPA/Shutterstock

Gutsche's foray into searching for clusters of inspiration came from his entrepreneurial father. "He used to get me to read hundreds of magazines a month, searching for business ideas and brainstorming what projects we could prototype during the weekend," Gutsche recalls. Gutsche was also influenced during his MBA at Queen's University by a professor who introduced him to the business of "hunting for cool."

Soon after, Gutsche developed a new "trend hunter" website "as a place for people to share business ideas." The website has become phenomenally successful with millions of visitors and 200,000 idea hunters. Gutsche leads a team that dissects this cornucopia of information to identify future trends, including the decline of the luxury market and the rise of "credit crunch couture." He also hosts Future Festivals in several countries, writes bestselling books on the topic, and advises Samsung, Adidas, NASA, and other organizations on future clusters of inspiration.[1]

Power, influence, expertise, personal brand. Although few of us claim to be trend spotters (or cluster hunters), everyone experiences these and other topics on organizational power and influence throughout their careers. In fact, power and influence are inherent in all organizations and in almost every decision and human interaction.

This chapter unfolds as follows: First, we define power and present a basic model depicting the dynamics of power in organizational settings. The chapter then discusses the five bases of power. Next, we look at the contingencies necessary to translate those sources into meaningful power. Our attention then turns to social networks and how they provide power to members through social capital. The latter part of this chapter examines the various types of influence in organizational settings, as well as the contingencies of effective influence strategies. The final section of this chapter looks at situations in which influence becomes organizational politics, as well as ways of minimizing dysfunctional politics.

The Meaning of Power

LO1

Power is the capacity of a person, team, or organization to influence others.[2] There are a few important features of this

> **power** The capacity of a person, team, or organization to influence others.

definition. First, power is not the act of changing someone's attitudes or behaviour; it is only the *potential* to do so. People frequently have power they do not use; they might not even know they have power.

Second, power is based on the target's *perception* that the power holder controls (i.e., possesses, has access to, or regulates) a valuable resource that can help to achieve the target person's goals.[3] An employee might have valuable expertise, yet this power base doesn't translate into actual power because others in the organization don't know about or understand the value of this expertise. At the other extreme, some unscrupulous individuals generate power by convincing others that they control something of value, even though they don't actually control that resource. These people may be perceived as powerful simply because their behaviour

suggests they are not swayed by authority or concerned about abiding by social norms.[4] However, power is not your own perception or feeling of power; it exists only when others believe you have power.

Third, power involves asymmetric (unequal) *dependence* of one party on another party.[5] This dependent relationship is illustrated in Exhibit 10.1. The line from Person B to the goal shows that they believe Person A controls a resource that can help or hinder Person B in achieving that goal. Person A—the dominant power holder in this illustration—might have power over Person B by controlling a desired job assignment, useful information, rewards, or even the privilege of being associated with Person A! For example, if you believe a co-worker has expertise (the resource) that would substantially help you to write a better report (your goal), then that co-worker has some power over you because you value that expertise as a means to achieve your goal. Whatever the resource is, Person B perceives a dependence on Person A (the power holder) to provide the resource so Person B can reach their goal.

Although dependence is a key element of power relationships, we use the phrase "asymmetric dependence" because the less powerful party also has some power—called **countervailing power**—over the more powerful party. In Exhibit 10.1, Person A dominates the power relationship, but Person B has enough countervailing power to keep Person A in the exchange relationship and ensure that person uses their dominant power judiciously. For

> **countervailing power** The capacity of a person, team, or organization to keep a more powerful person or group in the exchange relationship.

example, although managers have power over subordinates in many ways (e.g., controlling job security and preferred work assignments), those employees have countervailing power by possessing skills and knowledge to keep production humming and customers happy, something that management can't accomplish alone.

One other key feature is that all power relationships depend on some minimum level of trust. Trust indicates a level of expectation that the more powerful party will deliver the resource. For example, you trust your employer to give you a paycheque at the end of each pay period. Even those in extremely dependent situations will usually walk away from

---

EXHIBIT 10.1   Dependence in the Power Relationship

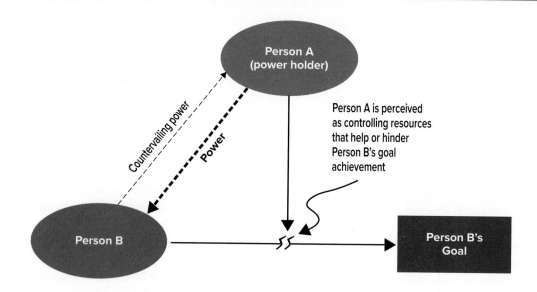

the relationship if they lack a minimum level of trust in the more powerful party.

Let's look at this power dependence model in the employee–manager relationship. You depend on your boss to support your continued employment, satisfactory work arrangements, and other valued resources. At the same time, your manager depends on you to complete required tasks and to work effectively with others in the completion of their work. Managers (and the companies they represent) typically have more power, whereas employees have weaker countervailing power. But sometimes employees do have more power in the employment relationship. The extent that your source of power (such as expertise) actually generates power depends on several factors, such as the employer's awareness of your source of power and how many other employees have that source of power. Finally, trust is an essential ingredient in this relationship. Even with strong power, the employee–manager relationship comes apart when one party no longer sufficiently trusts the other.

The dependence model reveals only the core features of power dynamics between people and work units in organizations. We also need to learn about the specific sources of power and contingencies that support or inhibit those power bases. As Exhibit 10.2 illustrates, power is derived from five sources: legitimate, reward, coercive, expert, and referent. The model also identifies four contingencies of power: the employee's or department's nonsubstitutability, centrality, discretion, and visibility. Over the next few sections of this chapter, we will discuss each of these sources and contingencies of power in the context of organizations.

Sources of Power in Organizations

There are five main sources of power in human interactions.[6] Three of these—legitimate, reward, and coercive—originate mostly (but not completely) from the power holder's formal position or informal role. In other words, the person is granted these sources of power formally by the organization or informally by co-workers. Two other sources of power—expert and referent—originate mainly from the power holder's own characteristics; in other words, people carry these power bases around with them. However, even personal sources of power are not completely within the person because they depend on how others perceive them.

LEGITIMATE POWER

Legitimate power is an agreement among organizational members that people in specific roles can request a set of behaviours from others. This perceived right or obligation originates from formal job descriptions as well as informal rules of conduct. It is the most important source of power in organizational settings, particularly between employees and managers.[7] For example, managers have a legitimate right to tell employees what tasks to perform, whom to work with, what company resources they can use, and so forth. Employees follow the boss's requests because they have agreed to follow a range of requests from

legitimate power An agreement among organizational members that people in certain roles can request certain behaviours of others.

EXHIBIT 10.2   Sources and Contingencies of Power

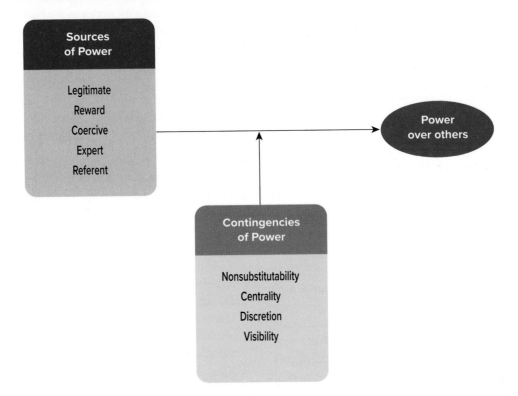

people in positions of higher authority. Employee motivation to comply with these requests occurs separately from the manager's ability to reward or punish employees.

Legitimate power has restrictions; it gives the power holder the right to ask others to perform only a limited range and domain of behaviours, known as the "zone of indifference."[8] Although most employees accept the boss's right to deny them access to Facebook during company time, some might draw the line when the boss asks them to work several hours beyond the regular workday. They either overtly refuse to follow orders or engage in other evasive tactics.

Several factors influence the size of the zone of indifference and, consequently, the magnitude of legitimate power. Highly trusted power holders have a larger zone of indifference. Employees are more willing to abide by the requests of trusted leaders even when those requests are unusual or on the periphery of expected job duties. Some people are more obedient to authority due to their values and personality traits. Specifically, those who value conformity and tradition as well as have high power distance (i.e., they accept an unequal distribution of power) tend to give their bosses a larger zone of indifference. The organization's culture represents another influence on the willingness of employees to follow orders.[9]

Managers are not the only people with legitimate power in organizations. Employees also have legitimate power over their bosses and co-workers through legal and administrative rights as well as informal norms.[10] An organization might give employees the right to request information or training that is required for their job. Laws give employees the right to refuse work in unsafe conditions. More subtle forms of legitimate power also exist. Human beings have a **norm of reciprocity**—a feeling of obligation to help someone who has helped them.[11] If a co-worker previously helped you resolve a difficult problem with a client, that co-worker has power because you feel an obligation to help the co-worker on something of similar value in the future. The norm of reciprocity is a form of legitimate power because it is an informal rule of conduct that we are expected to follow.

> **norm of reciprocity** A felt obligation and social expectation of helping or otherwise giving something of value to someone who has already helped or given something of value to you.

Legitimate Power through Information Control

A particularly potent form of legitimate power occurs where people have the right to control the information that others receive.[12] These information gatekeepers have power in two ways. First, information is a resource, so those who need that information are dependent on the gatekeeper to provide that resource. For example, the maps department of a mining company has incredible power when other departments are dependent on it to deliver maps required for exploration projects.

Second, information gatekeepers gain power by selectively distributing information such that those receiving the information perceive the situation in a specific way.[13] As we learned in the previous chapter on communication, information is often filtered as it flows up the hierarchy, which enables those transmitting the information to frame the situation in a more positive light. This framing allows the information gatekeeper to steer the decision maker toward one decision rather than another.

REWARD POWER

Reward power is derived from the person's ability to control the allocation of rewards valued by others and to remove negative sanctions (i.e., negative reinforcement). Managers have formal authority that gives them power over the distribution of organizational rewards such as pay, promotions, time off, vacation schedules, and work assignments. Employees have reward power over co-workers through organizational citizenship behaviours, such as lending work resources or coaching others. They also have reward power over their bosses through feedback they provide to the company about the boss's leadership.

COERCIVE POWER

Coercive power is the ability to apply punishment. Managers usually have considerable coercive power, ranging from showing disapproval to firing employees. Employees also have coercive power, such as when co-workers use peer pressure to change another employee's behaviour. In fact, one recent study found that hospital employees were more likely to follow prescribed hygienic activity (wash their hands) when faced with peer pressure than when the hospital rewarded this behaviour with a large financial incentive.[14] Nucor is one of many companies that explicitly relies on co-worker coercive power: "If you're not contributing with the team, they certainly will let you know about it," says an executive at the American steelmaker. "The few poor players get weeded out by their peers."[15]

EXPERT POWER

Legitimate, reward, and coercive power originate mostly from an organizational position or role.[16] Expert power, on the other hand, originates mainly from within the power holder. It is an individual's or work unit's capacity to influence others by possessing knowledge or skills valued by others. An important form of expert power is the perceived ability to manage uncertainties in the business environment. Organizations are more effective when they operate in predictable environments, so they value people who can cope with turbulence in consumer trends, societal changes, unstable supply lines, and so forth. Expertise can help companies cope with uncertainty in three ways: through prevention, forecasting, and absorption. These coping strategies are arranged in a hierarchy of importance, with prevention being the most powerful:[17]

- *Prevention.* The most effective strategy is to prevent environmental changes from occurring. For example, financial experts acquire power by preventing the organization from experiencing a cash shortage or defaulting on loans.

- *Forecasting.* The next best strategy is to predict environmental changes or variations. In this respect, Jeremy Gutsche (described at the beginning of this chapter) and other trend spotters have considerable power because they are better than most of us at predicting changes in consumer preferences and other environmental conditions.

- *Absorption.* People and work units also gain power by absorbing or neutralizing the impact of environmental shifts as they occur. An example is the ability of maintenance crews to come to the rescue when machines break down.

REFERENT POWER

People have **referent power** when others identify with them, like them, or otherwise respect them. As with expert power, referent power originates within the power holder. It is largely a function of the person's character and interpersonal skills. Referent power is also associated with **charisma**. Experts have difficulty agreeing on the meaning of charisma. Some describe charisma as a special "gift" or trait within the charismatic person, while others say it is mainly in the eyes of the beholder. It may be best described as a set of self-presentation characteristics and nonverbal communication behaviours (i.e., signalling) that generate interpersonal attraction and referent power over others as well as deference to the charismatic person.[18]

> **referent power** The capacity to influence others on the basis of an identification with and respect for the power holder.
>
> **charisma** A set of self-presentation characteristics and nonverbal communication behaviours (i.e., signalling) that generate interpersonal attraction and referent power over others as well as deference to the charismatic person.

DEFERENCE TO POWER

One of the most troubling observations about power in organizations is the human tendency to mindlessly follow the guidance of people who are charismatic (i.e., have referent power) or claim to have legitimate or expert power. Deferential followers rarely evaluate the appropriateness of the requested behaviour or the powerholder's right to make this request. They don't even investigate whether the powerholder's legitimate authority or expertise is real or incorrectly perceived![19]

Consider this recent example: Before the instructor of an undergraduate course arrived for class, two informally dressed people (a 29-year-old Black male and a 50-year-old White female) entered and set their belongings down at the front of the classroom. Without introduction, one of them said to the students: "I need you to put your cell phones in this box." One of them then walked around the classroom with a box to collect the students' phones. If any student questioned this task, they were authoritatively told "It is important for you to follow instructions and put your phone in the box." The two also said (when asked) that they did not know where the instructor was at that time. Most students cherish their mobile phones, yet an average of 85 percent of students across five small classes surrendered their phones to these strangers without receiving any explanation or assurance! Fortunately, these two people were confederates of the instructor and all phones were returned after the confederates had collected and counted them.[20]

©AP Photo/Chrsitophe Ena

A French television program revealed how far people are willing to follow orders. As a variation of the 1960s experiments conducted by Stanley Milgram, 80 contestants administered electric shocks whenever a volunteer (an actor who didn't receive the shocks at all) answered a question incorrectly. Shocks increased in 20-volt increments, from 20 volts for the first mistake through to 460 volts. Contestants often hesitated after hearing the volunteer screaming for them to stop, yet continued the shocks after the television host reminded them that their job was to apply punishment for wrong answers. Only 16 of the 80 contestants refused to administer the strongest shocks.*

* B. Crumley, "Game of Death: France's Shocking TV Experiment," *Time,* March 17, 2010; M. Portillo, "Would You Torture This Man?," *Sunday Telegraph* (London), March 21, 2010, 22. A recent variation of deference to authority occurred on British television. Four strangers were individually encouraged to assist the head of a (fictitious) charity by impersonating a wealthy would-be donor who died before making the donation, then kicking the supposedly dead body, and later throwing the body off a roof. See H. Mount, "Could You Be Talked into Murder?," *Daily Mail* (London), January 14, 2016, 16.

This example was a small incident in a classroom, but deference to power sometimes has tragic consequences. Not long ago, the Canadian justice system discovered that one of its "star" expert witnesses—a forensic child pathology expert—had provided inaccurate cause of death evaluations in at least 20 cases. A dozen of those cases resulted in wrongful or highly questionable criminal convictions. The pathologist's reputation as a renowned authority was the main reason why his often-weak evidence was accepted without question. "Experts in a courtroom—we give great deference to experts," admits a Canadian defence lawyer familiar with the situation.[21]

Contingencies of Power

LO2

Suppose that you have valuable expertise that can give the organization significant competitive advantage over rivals. Does this expertise mean that you are influential? Not necessarily. As was illustrated earlier in Exhibit 10.2, sources of power generate power only under some conditions. Four important contingencies that affect the degree to which the sources of power are useful are nonsubstitutability, centrality, visibility, and discretion.[22]

NONSUBSTITUTABILITY

Individuals and work units have more power when the resource they offer is nonsubstitutable. If you have expertise that is valuable to the organization and that no other employee can provide, you would be more powerful than if several people in your company possess this valued knowledge. Conversely, power decreases as the number of alternative sources of the resource increases. Substitutability refers not only to other sources that offer the resource; it also refers to substitutions for the resource itself. You might be the only person with specialized knowledge about a topic, but that knowledge becomes substitutable if technology or documented procedures provide similar guidance.

One strategy to increase nonsubstitutability is to control access to the resource. Several professions leverage their expert power by controlling (and limiting) access to the profession and often to the educational programs that train people into that profession. Labour unions also gain more power

©Rawpixel.com/Shutterstock

An important driver of career success is your personal brand—what makes you unique and valuable. "Nurturing and enhancing your professional 'brand' should be up there with performance as top priorities in your career journey," says public relations executive Curtis Sparrer. James Davidson agrees. The Calgary-based leader of the Experienced Talent Acquisition function at PwC Canada has read too many resumés that fail to describe the applicant's distinct and notable attributes (DNA). "If their brand isn't pronounced, I'm afraid they end up in the 'no' pile," Davidson warns. "[Your personal brand is] your unique promise of value; what you can bring to an organization. It needs to be authentic, different, and memorable."*

* L. White, "Go for Gold with a Winning Personal Brand," *24 Hours Vancouver,* February 24, 2014, 12; C. Sparrer, "Establish Your Personal Brand For Workplace Success," *Forbes,* January 7, 2019.

as they represent an increasing percentage of workers in a company or industry. Employees are also less substitutable when they operate special equipment or possess other knowledge that remains undocumented.

A second strategy is to differentiate the resource from the alternatives. Consulting firms sometimes use this tactic. They take skills and knowledge that many competitors can also provide and wrap them into a package (with the latest buzz words, of course) so that it looks like a service that no one else can offer.

Nonsubstitutability through differentiation is also recommended when developing our *personal brand.* Our public image and reputation should be authentic (who we really are and what we can deliver) and valuable to employers. But it also needs to be unique, which leverages the power of nonsubstitutability. "Be unique about something. Be a specialist in something. Be known for something. Drive something," advises Barry Salzberg, the former global CEO of Deloitte Touche Tohmatsu Limited who now teaches at Columbia Business School. "That's very, very important for success in leadership because there are so many highly talented people. What's different about you—that's your personal brand."[23]

CENTRALITY

Centrality refers to the powerholder's importance based on the degree and nature of interdependence with others.[24] Centrality increases with the number of people dependent on you as well as how quickly and severely they are affected by that dependence. Think about your own centrality for a moment: If you decided not to show up for work or school tomorrow, how many people would have difficulty performing their jobs because of your absence? How soon after they arrive at work would these co-workers have to adjust their tasks and work schedule as a result of your absence? If you have high centrality, most people in the organization would be adversely affected by your absence, and they would be affected quickly.

centrality A contingency of power pertaining to the degree and nature of interdependence between the powerholder and others.

VISIBILITY

Jennifer (not her real name) and her team members work from home and other remote locations for most of the workweek. While the British Gas manager enjoys this freedom, she also knows that working remotely can be a career liability due to the lack of visibility. "When I go into the office, where we hot-desk, I have to make an effort to position myself near my boss," says Jennifer. "You need to consciously build relationships when you don't have those water-cooler moments naturally occurring."[25]

Jennifer recognizes that power does not flow to unknown people in the organization. Instead, employees gain power when their talents remain in the forefront of the minds of their boss, co-workers, and others. In other words, power increases with visibility. This visibility can occur, for example, by taking on people-oriented jobs and projects that require frequent interaction with senior executives. Employees also gain visibility by being, quite literally, visible. Jennifer and others strategically locate themselves in more visible work areas, such as those closest to the boss or where other employees frequently pass by.

Professionals often use public symbols as subtle (and not-so-subtle) cues to make their power sources known to others. Some display their educational diplomas and awards on office walls to remind visitors of their expertise. Medical professionals wear white coats with stethoscopes around their necks, which symbolize their legitimate and expert power in hospital settings. Other people play the game of "face time"—spending more time in the office and showing that they are working productively.

DISCRETION

Another important contingency of power in organizations is the freedom to exercise judgment. This discretion involves making decisions without referring to a specific rule or receiving permission from someone else.[26] Employees have more power due to increased discretion when they are given more autonomy over their work (see Chapter 6). In contrast, an employee's discretion to apply their legitimate, reward, and coercive power is often curtailed by rules and higher authorities.[27]

The effect of lack of discretion on power was evident when supervisors at a Tim Hortons restaurant collectively decided to fire an employee for theft after she was caught on camera giving away one free Timbit to the crying toddler of a regular customer. Company policy prohibits giving away free food and store managers usually have the right to fire employees who violate company policies. But the action was so draconian—and quickly caused public outrage—that Tim Hortons central management reversed the employee's termination the next day. The employee accepted work at a nearby Tim Hortons outlet owned by the franchisee.[28]

The Power of Social Networks

LO3

"It's not what you know, but who you know that counts!" This often-heard statement reflects the idea that employees get ahead not just by developing their skills and knowledge, but

Debating Point: HOW MUCH POWER DO CEOS REALLY POSSESS?

It seems reasonable to assume that chief executive officers wield enormous power. They have legitimate power by virtue of their position at the top of the organizational hierarchy. They also have tremendous reward and coercive power because they allocate budgets and other resources. Refusing to go along with the CEO's wishes can be an unfortunate career decision. Some CEOs also gain referent power because their lofty position creates an aura of reverence. Even in this era of equality and low power distance, most employees further down the organization are in awe when the top executive visits.

CEO power is equally apparent through various contingencies. Top executives are almost always visible; some amplify that visibility when they become synonymous with the company's brand.[*] CEOs also have high centrality. Few strategic decisions are put into motion unless the top dog is on board. CEOs are supposed to have replacements-in-waiting (to make them substitutable), yet more than a few don't take enough time to mentor an heir-apparent. Some CEOs create an image of being too unique to be replicated.

It would seem evident that CEOs have considerable power—except that many CEOs and a few experts disagree with that view.[**] New CEOs quickly discover that they no longer have expertise over a specific area of the company or subject matter. Instead, they oversee the entire organization—a domain so broad that CEOs necessarily become jacks-of-all-trades and masters of none. Consequently, the CEO depends on the expertise of others to get things done. CEOs don't even have much knowledge about what goes on in the organization. Reliable sources of information become more guarded when communicating to the top dog; employees further down the hierarchy carefully filter information so the CEO hears more of the good and less of the bad news.

The biggest Achilles' heel for CEO power is that their discretion is much more restricted than most people realize. To begin with, CEOs are rarely at the top of the power pyramid. Instead, they report to the company board, which can reject their proposals and fire them for acting contrary to the board's wishes. The board's power over the CEO is particularly strong when the company has one or two dominant shareholders. But CEOs have been fired by the board even when the CEO is the company's founder! At one time, some CEOs had more power by serving as the board's chair and personally selecting board members. Today, corporate governance rules and laws have curtailed this practice, resulting in more power for the board and less power for the CEO.[***]

The CEO's discretion is also held in check by the power of various groups within the organization. One such group is the CEO's own executive team. These executives constantly monitor their boss because their careers and reputation are affected by the boss's actions, and some of them are eager to fill the top job themselves.[****] Similarly, the actions of hospital CEOs are restricted to some extent by the interests and preferences of physicians associated with the hospital.

One cross-cultural study found that the CEO's discretion is limited in countries where laws offer greater rights to many stakeholders (not just shareholders) and give employees more protection from dismissal. The study also reported that the CEO's discretion is limited in cultures with high uncertainty avoidance, because these social values require executives to take measured rather than bold steps toward change.[*****]

You might think that CEOs have one remaining form of discretion: They can still overrule their vice-presidents. Technically they can, but one group of experts points out that doing so has nasty repercussions. It triggers resentment and sends morale into a tailspin. Worse, this action motivates direct reports to seek out the CEO's involvement much earlier, which overwhelms the CEO's schedule and leaves less time for other priorities. A related observation is that CEOs are the official voice of the organization, so they have much less discretion about what they can say in public or in private conversations.

Finally, though it seems safe to claim that CEOs have high centrality, a few executives see their situation differently. "I am the least important person in this building," claims the CEO of a regional hospital. "This place would run without me for weeks, but the most important groups here are the people taking care of the patients."[******]

* A. Chatterjee and D.C. Hambrick, "It's All About Me: Narcissistic Chief Executive Officers and Their Effects on Company Strategy and Performance," *Administrative Science Quarterly* 52, no. 3 (2007): 351–86.

** M.E. Porter, J.W. Lorsch, and N. Nohria, "Seven Surprises for New CEOs," *Harvard Business Review* 82, no. 10 (2004): 62–72.

*** G. Owen and T. Kirchmaier, "The Changing Role of the Chairman: Impact of Corporate Governance Reform in the United Kingdom 1995–2005," *European Business Organization Law Review (EBOR)* 9, no. 02 (2008): 187–213; M.A. Bliss, "Does CEO Duality Constrain Board Independence? Some Evidence from Audit Pricing," *Accounting & Finance* 51, no. 2 (2011): 361–80.

**** J.G. Combs et al., "The Moderating Effect of CEO Power on the Board Composition–Firm Performance Relationship*," *Journal of Management Studies* 44, no. 8 (2007): 1299–323.

***** C. Crossland and D.C. Hambrick, "Differences in Managerial Discretion across Countries: How Nation-Level Institutions Affect the Degree to Which CEOs Matter," *Strategic Management Journal* 32, no. 8 (2011): 797–819.

****** D. Pressey, "Urbana, Ill.-Area Hospitals Chief Extends Personal Touch," *News-Gazette (Champaign-Urbana, Ill.)*, 18 April 2011.

also by locating themselves within **social networks**—social structures of individuals or social units (e.g., departments, organizations) that are connected to each other through one or more forms of inter-dependence.[29] Some networks are held together due to common interests, such as when employees who exercise over their lunch hours spend more time together. Other networks form around common status, expertise, kinship, or physical proximity. For instance, employees are more likely to form networks with co-workers who have common educational backgrounds and occupational interests.[30]

social networks Social structures of individuals or social units that are connected to each other through one or more forms of interdependence.

Social networks exist everywhere because people have a drive to bond. Cultural norms also seem to influence active network involvement. Social networking may be more of a central life activity in Asian cultures that emphasize *guanxi,* a Chinese term referring to an individual's network of social connections. Guanxi is an expressive activity because being part of a close-knit network of family and friends reinforces one's self-concept. It is also an instrumental activity for receiving favours and opportunities from others. Guanxi is sometimes so pervasive, however, that several experts warn it can undermine the organization's effectiveness.[31]

SOCIAL CAPITAL AND SOURCES OF POWER

Social networks generate power through **social capital**—the knowledge, opportunities, and other resources available to members of a social net-work as well as the mutual support, trust, reciprocity, and coordination that facilitate sharing of those resources.[32] Compared to non-members, members within a social network are more motivated and able to communicate, distribute, or otherwise provide resources within their power to others in that community.

social capital The knowledge, opportunities, and other resources available to members of a social network, along with the mutual support, trust, reciprocity, and coordination that facilitate sharing of those resources.

Social networks potentially enhance and maintain the power of their members through three resources: information, visibility, and referent power. Probably the best-known resource is information from other network members, which improves the individual's expert power.[33] The goodwill of social capital opens communication pipelines among those within the network. Network members receive valuable knowledge more easily and more quickly from fellow network members than do people outside that network.[34] With better information access and timeliness, members have more power because their expertise is a scarce resource; it is not widely available to people outside the network.

Increased visibility is a second contributor to a person's power through social networks. When asked to recommend someone who has a particular expertise, other network members more readily think of you than people outside the network. A third resource from social networks is increased referent power. People tend to gain referent power through networking because members of the network identify with or at least have greater trust in each other. Referent power is also apparent by the fact that reciprocity increases among network members as they become more embedded in the network.[35]

Social networks are often viewed as free spirits, yet they can be orchestrated to some extent through organizational structures and other practices.[36] Whether or not you try to manage social networks, you need to be aware of them. Indeed, people gain power in organizations by knowing what the social networks around them look like.[37]

GAINING POWER THROUGH SOCIAL NETWORKS

How do individuals (and teams and organizations) gain social capital from social networks? To answer this question, we need to consider the number, depth, variety, and centrality of connections that people have in their networks.

Strong Ties, Weak Ties, Many Ties

The volume of information, opportunities, and other social capital that we receive from networks depends on strong ties, weak ties, and many ties. Strong ties are close-knit relationships, which are evident from how often we interact with specific people, how much we share resources with them, and whether we have multiple or single-purpose relationships with them (e.g., friend, co-worker, sports partner). Strong ties are valuable because they offer resources more quickly and usually more plentifully than are available from weak ties (i.e., acquaintances). Strong ties also offer greater social support and greater cooperation for favours and assistance.[38]

Some minimal connection strength is necessary to remain in any social network, but strong connections aren't necessarily the most valuable ties. Instead, having weak ties (i.e., being

 Do you have a guanxi orientation? You can assess how well you nurture interpersonal connections by locating this self-assessment in Connect.

©Lloyd Sutton/Alamy

Operations staff at a global oil and gas company were not using the best available production methods because they didn't share best practices with their peers in other countries or with the company's technical experts. Instead, employees shared information mainly with local co-workers and technical staff who they already knew well. The company's solution was to transfer some field staff to teams in other regions. These transfers eventually formed and strengthened network relationships across borders, which dramatically improved knowledge sharing and social capital. Within a year, productivity increased by 10 percent and costs due to poor quality fell by two-thirds.*

* T. Gibbs, S. Heywood, and L. Weiss, "Organizing for an Emerging World," *McKinsey Quarterly* (2012): 1–11.

merely acquaintances) with people from diverse networks can be equally or more valuable than having only strong ties (i.e., having close friendships) with people in similar networks.[39] Why is this so? Strong ties—our close-knit circle of friends—tend to be similar to us and to each other. Consequently, they provide much of the same information and other resources that we already have or that other strong ties provide.[40] Weak ties, on the other hand, are acquaintances who are different from us and therefore more likely to offer unique opportunities, connections, and other resources not available from our strong ties. Weak ties exist when we serve as a "bridge" across several unrelated networks.

The value of weak ties is most apparent in job hunting and career development.[41] People with diverse networks tend to be more successful job seekers because they have a wider net to catch new job opportunities. In contrast, people who belong to similar overlapping networks tend to receive fewer leads, many of which they already knew about. As careers increasingly require more movement across many organizations and industries, you need to establish connections with people across a diverse range of industries, professions, and other spheres of life.

Finally, our power and social capital increase with many ties—the number of people connected to you in a social network. The more people you know, the more network resources are available to you. Generally, as your social network grows, you have less time and energy to maintain strong ties. However, some people have an amazing capacity to support relatively active and frequent connections to many people. Emerging social media (Twitter, Facebook, LinkedIn, etc.) have further amplified this capacity to maintain numerous connections at a fairly strong level.[42]

Social Network Centrality

Earlier in this chapter, we explained that centrality is an important contingency of power. This contingency also applies to social networks.[43] The more centrally a person (or team or organization) is located in the network, the more social capital and, therefore, more power they acquire. Centrality is one's importance in the network.

Three factors determine your centrality in a social network. One factor is "betweenness," which literally refers to how much you are located between others in the network. In Exhibit 10.3, Person A has high betweenness centrality because they are a gatekeeper who controls the flow of information to and from many other people in the network. Person H has less betweenness, whereas Person F and several other network members in the diagram have no betweenness. The more betweenness you have, the more you control the distribution of information and other resources to people on either side of you.

A second factor in centrality is the number or percentage of connections you have to others in the network (called *degree centrality*). The network resources (information, favours, etc.) available to you increases with the number of people connected to you. The number of connections also increases centrality because you are more visible to other members of the network. Although being a member of a network gives you access to resources in that network, having a direct connection to more people within the network makes that resource sharing more fluid.

A third factor in centrality is the "closeness" of the relationship with others in the network. High closeness refers to strong ties. It is depicted by shorter, more direct, and more efficient paths or connections with others in the network. For example, Person A has fairly high closeness centrality because they have direct paths to most of the network. Also, many of these paths are short, which implies efficient and high quality communication links. Your centrality increases with your closeness to other network members because they are affected more quickly and significantly by you.

One last observation is that Exhibit 10.3 illustrates two clusters of people in the network. The gap between these two clusters is called a **structural hole**.[44] Notice that Person A provides the main bridge across this structural hole (connecting to H and K in the other cluster). This bridging role gives Person A additional power in the network. By bridging this gap, Person A becomes a broker—someone who connects two independent networks and

> **structural hole** An area between two or more dense social network areas that lacks network ties.

EXHIBIT 10.3   Centrality in Social Networks

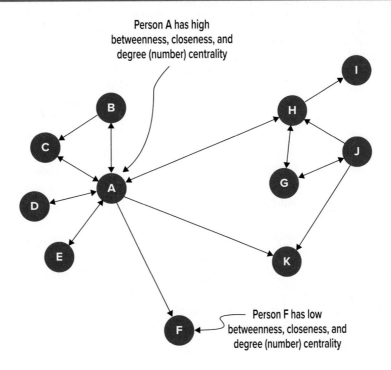

Person A has high betweenness, closeness, and degree (number) centrality

Person F has low betweenness, closeness, and degree (number) centrality

controls information flow between them. Research shows that the more brokering relationships you have, the more likely you are to get early promotions and higher pay.

The Dark Side of Social Networks

Social networks occur naturally in all organizations, yet they can create a formidable barrier to those who are not actively connected to them.[45] Women are often excluded from social networks in male-dominated jobs and industries because people tend to network with others with similar characteristics and backgrounds. These gendered networks can be a liability for women because they limit referrals, knowledge, and other forms of career-enhancing resources that networks provide. Men "are more likely to hear about jobs at the senior levels—and then pass these tips along to their mostly male networks," explains Sharon Ritchey, a former insurance executive and current executive committee member of the United States Golf Association. "This obviously works against women, because men tend to hear earlier and more often about upper-level job leads."[46]

Several years ago, executives at Deloitte Touche Tohmatsu discovered that inaccessibility to powerful social networks partly explained why many junior female employees left the global accounting and consulting firm before reaching partnership level. The organization now relies on mentoring, formal women's network groups, and measurement of career progress to ensure that female staff members have the same career development opportunities as their male colleagues.[47]

Many organizations today try to leverage the power of social networks by supporting several surface-level and deep-level diversity employee groups. For example, more than 11,000 employees at CIBC participate in one or more of the Canadian bank's 10 "people networks." These employee-led groups bring together staff members of similar backgrounds (e.g., Indigenous, LGBTQ, South Asian, etc.) to share informal advice, help career development, and foster client engagement.[48]

Consequences of Power

How does power affect the power holder? The answer depends to some extent on the type of power.[49] When people feel empowered (high self-determination, meaning, competence, and impact), they believe they have power over themselves and freedom from being influenced by others. Empowerment tends to increase motivation, job satisfaction, organizational commitment, and job performance. However,

this feeling of being in control and free from others' authority also increases automatic rather than mindful thinking. In particular, people who feel powerful usually are more likely to rely on stereotypes, have difficulty empathizing, and generally have less accurate perceptions compared with people with less power.[50]

The other type of power is one in which an individual has power *over others,* such as the legitimate, reward, and coercive power that managers have over employees in the workplace. This type of power produces a sense of duty or responsibility for the people over whom the powerholder has authority. Consequently, people who have power over others tend to be more mindful of their actions and engage in less stereotyping. Even when people feel empowered, they can shift their focus from self to others, so the power becomes viewed more as one of social responsibility than enjoyable for its own sake.[51]

Influencing Others

LO4

So far, this chapter has focused on the sources and contingencies of power as well as power derived from social networks. But power is only the *capacity* to influence others. It represents the potential to change someone's attitudes and behaviour. **Influence,** on the other hand, is power in motion. It applies one or more sources of power in an attempt to alter another person's beliefs, feelings, and behaviour.[52] Consequently, the remainder of this chapter looks at how people use power to influence others.

> **influence** Any behaviour that attempts to alter someone's attitudes or behaviour.

Influence tactics are woven throughout the social fabric of all organizations. Influence is central to the definition of leadership. It is an essential process through which people coordinate their efforts and act in concert to achieve organizational objectives. Influence operates down, across, and up the corporate hierarchy. Executives ensure that subordinates complete required tasks. Employees influence co-workers to help them with their job assignments.

TYPES OF INFLUENCE TACTICS

Organizational behaviour researchers have devoted considerable attention to the various types of influence tactics found in organizational settings. They do not agree on a

 What is your approach to influencing co-workers? You can discover the types of influence you might employ and your preference for various tactics by locating this self-assessment on Connect.

Global Connections 10.1

ONTARIO FIRM SYSTEMICALLY SUPPORTS THE "OLD BOYS'" NETWORK*

Some organizations institutionalize the "old boys'" network, which excludes women and limits their career potential. Mississauga-based Systemgroup Consulting was found to be engaging in this systemic practice. The vice-president (V-P) of sales, who had recently joined the information technology services firm, announced various company-paid client relationship events. The V-P's invitations to a "Men's Day" at a local ski club were sent only to male clients and male Systemgroup sales executives. The V-P's invitation referred to massages and Hooters Girls, and included the tag line to bring friends and acquaintances, but cautioned: "just don't bring your wife!"

The company's only female sales executive was not consulted about or invited to the event, was barred from viewing the electronic invitation, and was not informed that some of her male clients were invited (one of her clients, who cautiously hid the invitation from his own staff, showed her the invitation). After learning about the event, she complained to the V-P that it was inappropriate and discriminatory. The V-P apparently replied that the practice was common and that she was the one with the problem.

The female executive then approached the president about her concerns. His written reply stated that the ski club is "family-centric," that the Hooters Girls didn't attend, and that Systemgroup would hold similar events in future if clients are comfortable with them, including a "Ladies type of event" for female clients. He later argued that the event did not disadvantage the female executive, yet also stated that the event was a success because it led to new business leads.

After receiving their Men's Day ski event invitation, two male sales executives also approached the V-P to express their disapproval. One of them refused to participate or involve his clients in the event. The other male sales executive questioned why the event was being held. He also asked the V-P if, hypothetically, the company would support taking clients to strip clubs to build relationships. The vice-president said "absolutely" and

"that is how we are going to do it moving forward." Both executives who complained quit their jobs at Systemgroup soon after, for various reasons.

Almost immediately after complaining about the Men's Day ski event, the female executive was excluded from a meeting involving the V-P and a client in the industry she covered. The V-P's regular one-on-one meetings continued with the male sales executives but not with the female executive. Two months later, the female sales executive was fired, allegedly for poor performance.

An Ontario human rights tribunal ruled that Systemgroup had undermined the female sales executive's "ability to compete on the same playing field as her male peers," and "perpetuated the belief that supporting women sales professionals in interacting with clients is less valuable or important than supporting male sales professionals." The tribunal did not find sufficient evidence of poor performance. Instead, it concluded that her dismissal was retaliation by the company. The V-P who initiated the Men's Day ski event and similar practices had his employment "ended" two years after he was hired and before the case was heard by the tribunal.

©iofoto/Shutterstock

* R. Carey, McConaghie v. Systemgroup Consulting Inc., No. 2012-11560– I (Human Rights Tribunal of Ontario, March 6, 2014).

definitive list, but the most commonly discussed influence tactics are identified in Exhibit 10.4 and described in this section of the chapter.[53] The first five are known as "hard" influence tactics because the influencer applies extrinsic conditions, such as obligations and rewards, to control the other party's behaviour. To varying degrees, hard tactics generate behaviour change through position power (legitimate, reward, and coercion). The latter three tactics—persuasion, impression management, and exchange—are called "soft" tactics because the person being influenced has more autonomy and control over the influence process. Soft tactics rely more on personal sources of power (referent, expert) and appeal to the target person's attitudes and needs.[54]

EXHIBIT 10.4 Types of Influence Tactics in Organizations

Influence tactic	Description
Silent authority	Influencing behaviour through legitimate power without explicitly referring to that power base
Assertiveness	Actively applying legitimate and coercive power by applying pressure or threats
Information control	Explicitly manipulating someone else's access to information for the purpose of changing their attitudes and/or behaviour
Coalition formation	Forming a group that attempts to influence others by pooling the resources and power of its members
Upward appeal	Relying symbolically or in reality on people with higher authority or expertise to support one's position
Persuasion	Using logical arguments, factual evidence, and emotional appeals to convince people of the value of a request
Impression management (including ingratiation)	Actively shaping, through self-presentation and other means, the perceptions and attitudes that others have of us, which includes ingratiation (refers to the influencer's attempt to be more liked by the targeted person or group)
Exchange	Promising benefits or resources in exchange for the target person's compliance

Silent Authority

The silent application of authority occurs when someone complies with a request because of the requester's legitimate power as well as the role expectations of the person receiving the request.[55] Essentially, this is deference to authority, which we discussed earlier in this chapter. It occurs when you comply with your boss's request to complete a particular task. If the task is within your job scope and your boss has the right to make this request, then this influence strategy operates without negotiation, threats, persuasion, or other tactics. Surprisingly, many influence models exclude silent authority, probably because it is so passive and endemic to organizational life. Yet silent authority (deference to authority) is by far the most common form of influence. It is particularly powerful in high power distance cultures.[56] Experts suggest that every organization requires this influence strategy to operate.

Assertiveness

Assertiveness might be called "vocal authority" because it involves actively applying legitimate and coercive power to influence others. This includes persistently reminding the target of their obligations, frequently checking the target's work, confronting the target, and using threats of sanctions to force compliance. Workplace bullying is an extreme form of assertiveness because it involves explicit threats of punishment.

Information Control

Earlier in this chapter we explained that people with centrality in social networks have the power to control information.

This power translates into influence when the power holder selectively distributes information such that it reframes the situation and causes others to change their attitudes and/or behaviour. Controlling information might include withholding information that is more critical or favourable, or distributing information to some people but not to others. For example, one study found that CEOs influence their board of directors by selectively feeding and withholding information.[57]

Coalition Formation

When someone acting alone lacks sufficient power to influence others, they might be able to do so by forming a **coalition** of people who support the proposed change.[58] A coalition is influential in three ways. First, it pools the power and resources of many people, so the coalition potentially has more influence than any number of people operating alone.

> **coalition** A group that attempts to influence people outside the group by pooling the resources and power of its members.

Second, the coalition's mere existence can influence others by symbolizing the legitimacy of the issue. In other words, a coalition creates a sense that the issue deserves attention because it has broad support. Third, a coalition increases the confidence and motivation of its members through social identity theory (see Chapter 3). This motivation occurs because a coalition consists of like-minded people, so its members develop social identity with the group and feel more confident in supporting the coalition's mandate.[59]

Global Connections 10.2

DEADLY CONSEQUENCES OF WORKPLACE BULLYING*

Workplace bullying is a harsh form of influence. Yet, more than half of Canadians say that either they or their co-workers have been victims of this assertiveness. Supervisors engage in more workplace bullying than any other group, yet the outcomes of this influence can be much more severe than compliance with management demands.

Consider the case of Eric Donovan, who worked for 17 years at a not-for-profit organization that operates several group homes and programs for intellectually challenged adults in Prince Edward Island (PEI). Donovan was described as "conscientious and compassionate" to residents and "highly respected" by co-workers. Yet, over several years, he suffered from ongoing harassment and bullying from his supervisor.

Co-workers submitted sworn statements that the supervisor had a reputation for using bullying as a frequent influence tactic. A few former co-workers even testified that they left the organization after experiencing too much of the supervisor's harassment. The supervisor's bullying became more intense after Donovan returned from medical leave due to a back injury he suffered while controlling an aggressive resident.

Donovan discussed the stressful work environment with his wife and family doctor. "Mr. Donovan had significant stress from his relationship with his supervisor at work," Donovan's physician reported. "He often voiced how difficult the relationship was, the sense of being bullied and the resultant stress, anxiety and panic attacks."

Donovan started documenting the bullying incidents. In one of his last entries, he wrote that the relationship with his supervisor "was now so strained that I couldn't work for her." His wife and friends noticed how he looked increasingly unwell. One evening, his wife said:

"You're going on stress leave. You need to get away." Those were her last words to her husband. An hour or two later, Donovan, who didn't have a pre-existing heart condition, suffered cardiac arrest and died a few days later. He was 47 years old.

The PEI Workers Compensation Board initially ruled that Donovan's death was likely due to stress caused by several years of bullying from his supervisor. However, while agreeing that workplace stress caused Donovan's death, the Appeals Tribunal stated that evidence of bullying needs to be more objective than the victim's notes and numerous opinions of co-workers and medical professionals. Meanwhile, the PEI government has passed legislation named after Eric Donovan that provides employees with legal protection against bullying in the workplace.

©Iakov Filimonov/Shutterstock

* S. Pitt, "P.E.I. Widow Awarded Benefits after Husband's Death Linked to Workplace Bullying," *CBC News,* March 30, 2017; J.E. Sleeth, "Fatal Heart Attack May Have Resulted from Years of Workplace Bullying: WCB Ruling," *OHS Canada Magazine,* April 4, 2017; S. Pitt, "Widow Thrilled Her Lobbying Paid off with Anti-Bullying Legislation," *CBC News,* November 9, 2018; "1 in 2 Canadians Have Experienced Bullying in the Workplace," News Release (Toronto: The Forum Poll, November 19, 2018); S. Pitt, "P.E.I. Tribunal Rejects Workplace Bullying Finding, Rules Man's Death Caused by Work Stress," *CBC,* December 2, 2019.

Upward Appeal

Upward appeal involves calling upon higher authority or expertise, or symbolically relying on these sources to support the influencer's position. It occurs when someone says "The boss likely agrees with me on this matter; let's find out!"

> **upward appeal** A type of influence in which someone with higher authority or expertise is relied on in reality or symbolically to support the influencer's position.

Upward appeal also occurs when relying on the authority of the firm's policies or values. By reminding others that your request is consistent with the organization's overarching goals, you are implying support from senior executives without formally involving them.

Persuasion

The influence tactics described so far are called "hard" influence tactics because the persuader attempts to control the other party's behaviour through position power. The three remaining categories—persuasion, impression management, and exchange—are "soft" influence strategies because the person being influenced has more autonomy and control over the influence process. The first of these, **persuasion**, involves the use of facts, logical arguments, and emotional appeals to change another person's beliefs and attitudes, usually for the purpose of changing their behaviour. This is the most widely used and accepted influence strategy in organizations. It is a quality of effective leaders and, in many societies, a noble skill.

> **persuasion** The use of facts, logical arguments, and emotional appeals to change another person's beliefs and attitudes, usually for the purpose of changing the person's behaviour.

The effectiveness of persuasion as an influence tactic depends on characteristics of the persuader, message content, communication channel, and the audience being persuaded (see Exhibit 10.5).[60] People are more persuasive when they are perceived to have expertise and credibility. Persuaders have more credibility when they do not seem to profit from the persuasion attempt, they acknowledge limitations with their position, and they note minor positive features of the alternative choices.

Several characteristics of message content increase your ability to persuade others, particularly when the issue is important to the audience.[61] The speaker's message is more persuasive when it acknowledges several points of view. This increases the speaker's credibility and avoids having the audience feel boxed in by the persuasion attempt. The message should also be limited to a few strong arguments, which are repeated a few times, but not too frequently. The message should use emotional appeals (such as graphically showing the unfortunate consequences of a bad decision), but only in combination with logical arguments and specific recommendations to overcome the threat. Finally, message content is more persuasive when the audience is warned about opposing arguments. This **inoculation effect** causes listeners to generate counterarguments to the anticipated persuasion attempts, which makes the opponent's subsequent persuasion attempts less effective.[62]

> **inoculation effect** A persuasive communication strategy of warning listeners that others will try to influence them in the future and that they should be wary about the opponent's arguments.

Two other considerations when persuading people are the communication channel and characteristics of the audience. Generally, persuasion works best through communication channels with high social presence and media-richness, such as in face-to-face conversations (see Chapter 9). The human presence of face-to-face communication increases the persuader's credibility, and the richness of this channel provides faster feedback that the influence strategy is working. With respect to audience characteristics, it is more difficult to persuade people who have high self-esteem and competence, as well as a self-concept that is strongly tied to the opposing viewpoint.[63]

EXHIBIT 10.5   Elements of Persuasion

Persuasion element	Characteristics of effective persuasion
Persuader characteristics	• Expertise • Credibility • No apparent profit motive • Appears somewhat neutral (acknowledges benefits of the opposing view)
Message content	• Multiple viewpoints (not exclusively supporting the supported option) • Limited to a few strong arguments (not many arguments) • Repeats arguments, but not excessively • Uses emotional appeals in combination with logical arguments • Offers specific solutions to overcome the stated problems • Inoculation effect—audience warned of counterarguments that opposition will present
Communication channel	• Media-rich channels are usually more persuasive
Audience characteristics	Persuasion is LESS effective when the audience: • has higher self-esteem • has higher competence • has a self-concept tied to an opposing position

Impression Management (Including Ingratiation)

The softest of the soft influence tactics is **impression management**—actively shaping the perceptions and attitudes that others have of us.[64] Impression management mostly occurs through self-presentation. Employees routinely engage in pleasant impression management behaviours to satisfy social norms, such as the way they dress and how they behave toward colleagues and customers. People also sometimes craft their public image to depict their importance and expertise, which affects their influence under some circumstances.

impression management
Actively shaping through self-presentation and other means the perceptions and attitudes that others have of us.

As we noted earlier in this chapter, career professionals encourage people to develop a personal "brand"; that is, to form and display an accurate impression of their own distinctive competitive advantage.[65] Impression management plays a role in this brand maintenance, whether in depicting your personality and expertise or in distinctive symbols of your uniqueness (e.g., black shirts, tinted hair, unique signatures). For example, professional services firm PwC Canada suggests: "Make sure your image matches your pitch. You need to dress professionally, but it's okay to show some flair with a bright tie or a unique piece of jewellery."[66]

One sub-category of impression management is *ingratiation*, which is any attempt to increase liking by, or perceived similarity to, some targeted person.[67] Ingratiation includes flattering your boss, demonstrating similar views as your boss (e.g., agreeing with the boss's suggestions), or asking your boss for advice. Ingratiation is one of the more effective influence tactics at boosting a person's career success. However, people who engage in high levels of ingratiation are less (not more) influential and less likely to get promoted because too much ingratiation is viewed as insincere and self-serving.[68]

Exchange

Exchange activities involve the promise of benefits or resources in exchange for the target person's compliance with your request. Negotiation is an integral part of exchange influence activities. For instance, you might negotiate with your boss for a day off in return for working a less-desirable shift at a future date. Exchange also includes applying the norm of reciprocity that we described earlier, such as reminding the target of past benefits or favours, with the expectation that the target will now make up for that debt. The norm of reciprocity also influences others in social networks. Active networkers build up "exchange credits" by helping colleagues in the short term for reciprocal benefits in the long term.

CONSEQUENCES AND CONTINGENCIES OF INFLUENCE TACTICS

Faced with a variety of influence strategies, you are probably asking: Which ones are best? To answer this question, we first need to describe the three ways that people respond to influence: resistance, compliance, or commitment (see Exhibit 10.6).[69] *Resistance* occurs when individuals or work units oppose the behaviour desired by the influencer. At the extreme, they refuse to engage in the behaviour. However, there are degrees of resistance, such as when people do what the powerholder has requested yet maintain their opposition by performing the tasks poorly or continuing to complain about the imposed work.

Compliance occurs when people are extrinsically motivated to implement the influencer's request (see Chapter 5). They perform the requested task for purely instrumental reasons. Compliance usually involves engaging in the behaviour with no more effort than is required. Furthermore, compliance usually stops—employees no longer perform the requested behaviour—when the extrinsic source of motivation is removed. The strongest outcome of influence is *commitment*. This occurs when people identify with the influencer's request and are highly motivated to implement it even when extrinsic sources of motivation are not present.

People usually react more favourably to "soft" tactics than to "hard" tactics. Soft influence tactics rely on personal sources of power (expert and referent power), which tend to build commitment to the influencer's request. In contrast, hard tactics rely on position power (legitimate, reward, and coercion), so they tend to produce compliance or, worse, resistance. Hard tactics also tend to undermine trust, which can hurt future relationships.

The most appropriate influence strategy also depends on a few contingencies.[70] One obvious contingency is the influencer's strongest sources of power. Those with expertise tend to have more influence using persuasion, whereas those with a strong legitimate power base are usually more successful applying silent authority. A second contingency is whether the person being influenced is higher, lower, or at the same level in the organization. As an example, employees may face adverse career consequences by being too assertive with their boss.[71] Meanwhile, supervisors who engage in ingratiation and some other forms of impression management tend to lose the respect of their staff.

Finally, the most appropriate influence tactic depends on personal, organizational, and cultural values.[72] People with a strong power orientation might feel more comfortable using assertiveness, whereas those who value conformity might feel more comfortable with upward appeals. At an organizational level, firms with a competitive culture might encourage

---

EXHIBIT 10.6   **Consequences of Hard and Soft Influence Tactics**

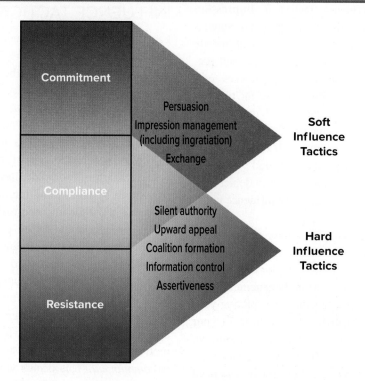

more use of information control and coalition formation, whereas companies with a more collegial culture would likely encourage more influence through persuasion. The preferred influence tactics also vary across societal cultures. Research indicates that ingratiation is much more common among managers in Canada than in Hong Kong. One explanation is that this tactic is incompatible with the more distant roles that managers and employees expect in high power distance cultures.

Organizational Politics

LO5

Organizational politics goes hand in hand with the topics of organizational power and influence. Unfortunately, the meaning of organizational politics is quite muddled. The most widely held view among scholars, which this book adopts, is that **organizational politics** is the use of influence tactics for personal gain at the perceived expense of others and the organization.[73] This definition recognizes that all political behaviours apply one or more influence tactics. However, influence activities are organizational politics only when the perpetrator is apparently motivated by self-interest and the action is likely to have an

> **organizational politics** The use of influence tactics for personal gain at the perceived expense of others and the organization.

adverse effect on others and the organization. Organizational politics is necessarily a perceptual interpretation of events because it is very difficult to know the perpetrator's motives or views on how their actions affect others.

This definition is consistent with the public view that organizational politics is self-serving behaviour. And, although many employees admit that they have engaged in politics to benefit their career advancement, they do not claim it is good for the organization. On the contrary, employees consistently identify "office politics" as one of the top reasons for their work-related stress, suboptimal performance, and motivation to leave the company.[74]

Employees view organizational politics as dysfunctional, yet some scholars and popular press writers claim that it can be beneficial. These "positive politics" sources suggest that "politics is an essential skill in managers who wish to get things done" and that it is "an indispensable component of organizational life."[75]

Can organizational politics be both functional and dysfunctional for organizations? We don't think so.[76] A closer look reveals that the "positive politics" writers seem to be claiming that all influence tactics are political tactics. For example, a frequently cited book defines organizational politics as "power in action, using a range of technique and tactics." Yet *influence* is defined as power in action (as we noted earlier in the chapter). Organizational politics applies influence tactics, but the two concepts aren't the same thing.

by the NUMBERS

How Office Politics Affects Employees*

65% of 3,000 employees say they would be more productive working from home due to minimal office politics compared to an office.

63% of 2,843 professionals identify work politics/colleagues as one of their top five drivers of stress at work.

58% of 763 American employees say they have left jobs, or are considering leaving, because of office politics.

39% of 1,700 employees in India ages 18 to 34 identify office politics as a major barrier to working effectively (second highest barrier, following excessive workload).

25% of 1,000 professional adults identify workplace politics as one of their major career struggles (fourth highest on the list of 10 struggles).

©Elnur/Shutterstock

* Indian Millennials Lack Critical Skills: HBR Ascend Survey," *Hindustan Times,* July 18, 2017; "Your Best Employees Are Leaving, but Is It Personal or Practical?," News Release (Atlanta: Randstad USA, August 28, 2018); J. Howington, "2018 Annual Survey Finds Workers Are More Productive at Home," *FlexJobs Job Search Tips and Blog* (blog), September 9, 2018, https://www.flexjobs.com/blog/post/2018-annual-survey-finds-workers-more-productive-at-home/; Z. Mejia, "These Are the Top 10 Workplace Struggles Employees Face in 2018," *CNBC,* September 19, 2018; P. Petrone, "Stress at Work Report: Who Is Feeling It the Most and How to Combat It," LinkedIn, *The Learning Blog* (blog), accessed February 25, 2020, https://learning.linkedin.com/blog/advancing-your-career/stress-at-work-report--who-is-feeling-it-the-most-and-how-to-com.

Meanwhile, numerous studies have documented the adverse consequences of organizational politics.[77] Employees who observe or experience organizational politics from others have lower job satisfaction, organizational commitment, organizational citizenship, and task performance, as well as higher levels of work-related stress and motivation to leave the organization. "A politically charged work environment can hinder productivity, erode trust, and lead to morale and retention issues," warns Renan Silva, a corporate project management office specialist at Serasa Experian, a credit bureau in São Paulo, Brazil. And because political tactics serve individuals rather than organizations, they potentially divert resources away from the organization's effective functioning and may threaten its survival.

INDIVIDUAL DIFFERENCES IN ORGANIZATIONAL POLITICS

Some people are more likely than others to engage in organizational politics.[78] Employees with a strong need for personalized power seek power for its own sake and try to acquire more power. This contrasts with people with a strong need for socialized power; they seek power as an instrument to accomplish organizationally beneficial objectives.

Individuals with **dark triad** personality characteristics are also more likely to engage in organizational politics (see Chapter 2).[79] These people routinely engage in deceit and malevolently undermine others to maximize their own gains. They believe that using lies, manipulation, exploitation, and other undesirable influence tactics are acceptable ways to achieve their personal goals (*Machiavellianism*). They arrogantly exploit co-workers for personal aggrandizement and take pleasure in others' misfortune (*narcissism*). They are also selfish self-promoters who manipulate others and engage in antisocial, impulsive, and often fraudulent thrill-seeking behaviour without feelings of remorse (*psychopathy*).

> **dark triad** A cluster of three socially undesirable (dark) personality traits: Machiavellianism, narcissism, and psychopathy.

Global Connections 10.3

PLAYING POLITICS WITH THE VACATION SCHEDULE*

The vacation roster is a scarce resource, and resource scarcity brings out the worst office politics. One survey reported that 13 percent of British employees refused to reveal when they would take their vacations so co-workers wouldn't book the same dates. Another 7 percent said they protected their vacation plans by lying to co-workers about those plans. Five percent were even more Machiavellian; they strategically booked vacation dates that scuttled the plans of a disliked co-worker.

"I know this is true," says an employee from Newport, Wales, who was not part of the survey. "I had a colleague who knew my holiday habits and would go in on January the 2nd and book every week that he knew I habitually had for holidays because he knew my wife's holidays were fixed and could not be changed. He didn't really need those days; he did it out of spite."

©pathdoc/Shutterstock

* L. Hull, "Covert War in the Workplace. . .over the Holiday Rota," *Mail Online*, 7 August 2013; "Office Wars: Tis the Season to Be Spiteful," *Officebroker Blog*, 2013, http://www.officebroker.com/blog/.

MINIMIZING ORGANIZATIONAL POLITICS

Organizational experts have identified several conditions that encourage organizational politics. Out of these findings we can identify corresponding strategies to keep political activities to a minimum.[80]

- *Provide sufficient resources.* Organizational politics is triggered by scarce resources in the workplace. When budgets are slashed, people rely on political tactics to safeguard their resources and maintain the status quo. Although it is not easy to maintain or add resources, sometimes this action is less costly than the consequences of organizational politics.

- *Clarify resource allocation rules.* Political tactics are fuelled by ambiguous or complex rules, or the absence of formal rules, because those tactics help people get what they want when decisions lack structural guidelines. Consequently, organizational politics is suppressed when resource allocation decisions are clear and simplified.

- *Apply effective organizational change practices.* Organizational change tends to bring out more organizational politics, mainly because change creates ambiguity and threatens the employee's power and other valued resources. Consequently, leaders need to apply the organizational change strategies that we describe in Chapter 15, particularly through communication, learning, and involvement. Research has found that employees who are kept informed of what is going on in the organization and who are involved in organizational decisions are less likely to engage in organizational politics.

- *Purge political behaviour norms and role models.* Political behaviour is more common in work units and organizations where it is tolerated and reinforced. Some companies seem to nurture self-serving behaviour through reward systems and the role modelling of organizational leaders. To minimize political norms, the organization needs to diagnose and alter systems and role modelling that support self-serving behaviour. They should support organizational values such as altruism and customer-focusing, which oppose political tactics. One of the most important strategies is for leaders to become role models of organizational citizenship rather than symbols of successful organizational politicians.

 How politically charged is your school? You can discover the level of organizational politics in your school by locating this self-assessment in Connect.

Chapter Summary

LO1

Describe the dependence model of power and describe the five sources of power in organizations.

Power is the capacity to influence others. It exists when one party perceives that they are dependent on the other for something of value. However, the dependent person must also have countervailing power—some power over the dominant party—to maintain the relationship, and the parties must have some level of trust.

There are five power bases. Legitimate power is an agreement among organizational members that people in certain roles can request certain behaviours of others. This power has restrictions represented by the target person's zone of indifference. It also includes the norm of reciprocity (a feeling of obligation to help someone who has helped you) as well as control over the flow of information to others. Reward power is derived from the ability to control the allocation of rewards valued by others and to remove negative sanctions. Coercive power is the ability to apply punishment. Expert power is the capacity to influence others by possessing knowledge or skills that they value. An important form of expert power is the (perceived) ability to manage uncertainties in the business environment. People have referent power when others identify with them, like them, or otherwise respect them.

LO2

Discuss the four contingencies of power.

Four contingencies determine whether these power bases translate into real power. Individuals and work units are more powerful when they are nonsubstitutable, that is, there is a lack of alternatives. Employees, work units, and organizations reduce substitutability by controlling tasks, knowledge, and labour; by differentiating themselves from competitors; and by developing a personal brand—a unique combination of knowledge, skills, and experience that are valuable to current or prospective employers.

A second contingency is centrality. Individuals have more power when they have high centrality, which means that many others are quickly affected by the powerholder's actions. The third contingency, visibility, refers to the idea that power increases to the extent that a person's or work unit's valued resources are known to others. Discretion, the fourth contingency of power, refers to the freedom to exercise judgment. Power increases when people have freedom to use their power.

LO3

Explain how people and work units gain power through social networks.

Social networks are social structures of individuals or social units (e.g., departments, organizations) that are connected to each other through one or more forms of interdependence. People receive power in social networks through social capital, which is the knowledge, opportunities, and other resources available to members of a social network, along with the mutual support, trust, reciprocity, and coordination that facilitate sharing of those resources. Three main resources from social networks are information, visibility, and referent power.

Employees gain social capital through their relationship in the social network. Social capital tends to increase with the number of network ties. Strong ties (close-knit relationships) can also increase social capital because these connections offer more resources more quickly. However, having weak ties with people from diverse networks can be more valuable than having strong ties with people in similar networks. Weak ties provide more resources that we do not already possess. Another influence on social capital is the person's centrality in the network. Network centrality is determined in several ways, including the extent to which you are located between others in the network (betweenness), how many direct ties you have (degree), and the closeness of these ties. People also gain power by bridging structural holes—linking two or more clusters of people in a network.

LO4

Describe eight types of influence tactics, three consequences of influencing others, and three contingencies to consider when choosing an influence tactic.

Influence refers to any behaviour that attempts to alter someone's attitudes or behaviour. The most widely studied influence tactics are silent authority, assertiveness, information control, coalition formation, upward appeal, impression management, persuasion, and exchange. "Soft" influence tactics such as friendly persuasion and subtle ingratiation are more acceptable than "hard" tactics such as upward appeal and assertiveness. However, the most appropriate influence tactic also depends on the influencer's power base; whether the person being influenced is higher, lower, or at the same level in the organization; and personal, organizational, and cultural values regarding influence behaviour.

LO5

Identify the organizational conditions and personal characteristics that support organizational politics, as well as ways to minimize organizational politics.

Organizational politics refer to the use of influence tactics for personal gain at the perceived expense of others and the organization. It is more common when ambiguous decisions allocate scarce resources and when the organization tolerates or rewards political behaviour. Individuals with a high need for personal power and strong Machiavellian values have a higher propensity to use political tactics. Organizational politics can be minimized by providing clear rules for resource allocation, establishing a free flow of information, using education and involvement during organizational change, supporting team norms and a corporate culture that discourage dysfunctional politics, and having leaders who role model organizational citizenship rather than political savvy.

Key Terms

centrality

charisma

coalition

countervailing power

dark triad

impression management

influence

inoculation effect

legitimate power

norm of reciprocity

organizational politics

persuasion

power

referent power

social capital

social networks

structural hole

upward appeal

Critical Thinking Questions

1. What role does countervailing power play in the power relationship? Give an example of your own encounter with countervailing power at school or work.

2. Until recently, a mining company's data resided in the department that was responsible for that information. Property data were on the computers in land administration, hydrocarbon data were in the well administration group, maps were found in the map department, and so on. The executive team concluded that this arrangement was dysfunctional, so the CEO announced that all information would be placed on a central server system so it is widely accessible. If someone needs a colour map, for example, they can retrieve it from the central server without going through the map department. Rather than welcome the change, employees in several departments complained, offering numerous arguments why other groups should not have direct access to their data files. Some departments tried to opt out of the centralized server system. Using the model of sources and contingencies of power, explain why some groups opposed the central server model of data access.

3. You have just been hired as a brand manager of toothpaste for a large consumer products company. Your job mainly involves encouraging the advertising and production groups to promote and manufacture your product more effectively. These departments aren't under your direct authority, although company procedures indicate that they must complete certain tasks requested by brand managers. Describe the sources of power you can use to ensure that the advertising and production departments will help you make and sell toothpaste more effectively.

4. Your personal brand is an important form of power for career success. In what ways can you and other students strengthen your personal brands? What sources and contingencies of power are relevant in building a personal brand?

5. Discuss the eight influence tactics described in this chapter in terms of how they are used by students to influence their university instructors. Which influence tactic is applied most often? Which is applied least often, in your opinion? To what extent is each influence tactic considered legitimate behaviour or organizational politics?

6. Consider a situation in which there is only one female member in a team of six, and she is generally excluded from informal gatherings of the team. What kind of influence tactics can she use to address this situation?

7. In the mid-1990s, the CEO of Apple Computer invited the late Steve Jobs (who was not associated with the company at the time) to serve as a special adviser and raise morale among Apple employees and customers. While doing this, Jobs spent more time advising the CEO on how to cut costs, redraw the organization chart, and hire new people. Before long, most of the top people at Apple were Jobs' colleagues, who began to systematically evaluate and weed out teams of Apple employees. While publicly supporting Apple's CEO, Jobs privately criticized him and, in a show of non-confidence, sold 1.5 million shares of Apple stock he had received. This action caught the attention of Apple's board of directors, who soon after decided to replace the CEO with Steve Jobs. The CEO claimed Jobs was a conniving back-stabber who used political tactics to get his way. Others suggest that Apple would be out of business today if he hadn't taken over the company. In your opinion, were Steve Jobs's actions examples of organizational politics? Justify your answer.

8. Successful companies depend on their employees to seek out new information and to share their discoveries and ideas with others in the organization. How does organizational politics interfere with these beneficial activities?

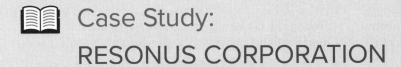

Case Study:
RESONUS CORPORATION

by Steven L. McShane, University of Newcastle (Australia), based on a case written by John A. Seeger.

Frank Choy is normally a quiet person, but his patience has already been worn thin by interdepartmental battles. Choy joined Resonus Corporation, a hearing aid designer and manufacturer, eight months ago as director of engineering. Production of the latest product has been delayed by two months and Choy's engineering services department (ESD)—which prepares final manufacturing specifications—is taking the heat as the main culprit for these delays. Similar delays have been occurring at Resonus for the past few years. The previous engineering director was fired after 18 months; the director before him quit after about the same amount of time.

Bill Hunt, CEO of Resonus for the past 15 years, responded to these problems by urging everyone to remain civil. "I'm sure we can resolve these differences if we just learn to get along better," he said whenever a dispute broke out. Hunt disliked firing anyone, but felt the previous engineering director was too confrontational. "I spent too much time smoothing out arguments when he was here," Hunt thought to himself soon after Choy was hired. "Frank (Choy), on the other hand, seems to fit into our culture of collegiality."

Hunt was groomed by the company's founder and took great pride in preserving the organization's family spirit. He also discouraged bureaucracy, believing that Resonus operated best through informal relationships among its managers. Most Resonus executives were similarly informal, except Jacqui Blanc, the production director, who insisted on strict guidelines. Hunt tolerated Blanc's formal style because soon after joining Resonus five years ago, she discovered and cleaned up fraudulent activity involving two production managers and a few suppliers.

The organizational chart shows that Frank Choy oversees two departments: ESD and research. In reality, "Doc" Kalandry, the research director, informally reports directly to the CEO (Hunt) and has never considered the director of engineering as his boss. Hunt actively supports this informal reporting relationship because of Doc's special status in the organization. "Doc Kalandry is a living genius," Hunt told Choy soon after he joined the firm. "With Doc at the helm of research, this company will continue to lead the field in innovation." Hunt's first job at Resonus was in the research group and Choy suspected that Hunt still favoured that group.

Everyone at Resonus seems to love Doc's successful products, his quirky style, and his over-the-top enthusiasm, but some of Choy's ESD staff are also privately concerned. Says one engineer: "Doc is like a happy puppy when he gets a new product idea. He delights in the discovery, but

also won't let go of it. He also gets Hunt too enthusiastic. But Doc's too optimistic; we've had hundreds of production change orders already this year. If I were in Frank's shoes, I'd put my foot down on all this new development."

Soon after joining Resonus, Choy realized that ESD employees get most of the blame and little of the credit for their work. When production staff find a design fault, they directly contact the research design engineer who developed the technology rather than the ESD group who prepare the specifications. Research engineers willingly work with production because they don't want to let go of their project. "The designers seem to feel they're losing something when one of us (ESD) tries to help," Choy explains.

Meanwhile, production supervisors regularly critique ESD staff whereas they tend to accept explanations from the higher-status research department engineers. "Production routinely complains about every little specification error, many of which are due to design changes made by the research group," says one frustrated ESD technician. "Many of us have more than 15 years' experience in this work. We shouldn't have to prove our ability all the time, but we spend as much time defending ourselves as we do getting the job done."

Choy's latest troubles occurred when Doc excitedly told Hunt about new nano-processor technology that he wanted to install in the forthcoming high-end hearing aid product. As with most of Doc's previous last-minute revisions, Hunt endorsed this change and asked Choy and Blanc (the production director) to show their commitment, even though production was scheduled to begin in less than three weeks. Choy wanted to protest, knowing that his department would have to tackle unexpected incompatibility design errors. Instead, he quietly agreed to Hunt's request to avoid acting like his predecessor and facing similar consequences (getting fired). Blanc curtly stated that her group was ready if Choy's ESD unit could get accurate production specifications ready on time and if the sales director would stop making wild delivery promises to customers.

When Doc's revised design specs arrived more than a week later, Choy's group discovered numerous incompatibilities that had to be corrected. Even though several ESD staff were assigned to 12-hour days on the revisions, the final production specifications weren't ready until a couple of days after the deadline. Production returned these specs two days later, noting a few elements that required revision because they were too costly or difficult to manufacture in their current form. By that time, the production director had to give priority to other jobs and move the new hearing aid product further down the queue. This meant that manufacturing of the new product was delayed by at least two months. The sales director was furious and implied that Frank Choy's incompetence was to blame for this catastrophe.

Discussion Questions

1. What sources and contingencies of power existed among the executives and departments at Resonus?

2. What influence tactics were evident in this case study? Would you define any of these influence activities as organizational politics? Why or why not?

3. Suppose you are a consultant invited to propose a solution to the problems facing this organization's product delays. What would you recommend, particularly regarding power dynamics among the executives and departments?

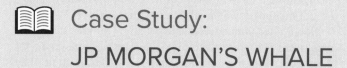 # Case Study:
JP MORGAN'S WHALE

by Steven L. McShane, University of Newcastle (Australia)

JP Morgan Chase & Co. suffered a (USD) $7 billion loss (plus another $1 billion in government fines) from highly speculative investments by a handful of traders in its London office. The ill-fated trades occurred in JP Morgan's chief investment office (CIO), a special unit whose original objective was to use the bank's own money to conservatively hedge against its investment risks. With top management's approval, however, the CIO became an active profit centre by investing in higher risk derivatives. The unit's portfolio tripled over three years to $350 billion (15 percent of JP Morgan's total assets) and apparently generated more than 10 percent of the bank's net income. It had gained senior management's highest respect.

JP Morgan monitored risk compliance among its client-serving trading groups, whereas the CIO traders were under much less scrutiny, possibly because their assets were the bank's money, not clients' money. One U.S. government investigator quipped that supervision of CIO trades "was little more than a rubber stamp." CIO traders reported their results less often than did other groups. Due to the complexity of these products, the CIO traders also had considerable discretion to estimate the size of those gains and losses. One U.S. senator remarked that "the traders seemed to have more responsibility and authority than the higher-up executives."

Bruno Iksil, the lead trader in the CIO group's London operations, had developed a reputation for making bold, but ultimately profitable, bets on whether companies would default on their bond payments. A few years ago, traders nicknamed Iksil the "Caveman" for his aggressive trading style. Later, Iksil became known as "Voldemort" after the powerful Harry Potter villain, because his trades namelessly moved the markets in which he bet. But Iksil's most famous nickname was "the London Whale" because of his mammoth $100 billion credit default bet that ultimately cost the bank $7 billion. Iksil was revered for his trading success and reputation, which likely gave him considerable power to initiate trades that may have otherwise required higher authority.

But Iksil's considerable power couldn't save his oversized credit default position. Hedge funds noticed how his trades distorted the market, so they bet against those trades, which eventually created huge losses rather than profits for JP Morgan. Iksil's trading losses on one day alone were more than a half-billion dollars. "We are dead," Iksil texted to his assistant. "They are going to trash/destroy us. You don't lose $500 million without consequences."

As those losses mounted, Iksil and his assistant avoided scrutiny from head office by underestimating the size of those losses. They distorted or hid information about their trading losses, hoping that this would buy them time to recoup those losses before top management discovered the problem. U.S. government documents indicate that Iksil's boss actively encouraged this practice, even after Iksil eventually refused to continue the charade. When Iksil did eventually refuse to under-report the losses, his boss told him to "leave for the day" so a junior trader could file a lower loss amount.

The losses were revealed only after the bank completed one if its regular reviews. Until then JP Morgan's chief investment officer claimed no knowledge of the problems in the London CIO office. She later complained that "some members of the London team failed to value positions properly" and that they "hid from me important information regarding the true risks of the book." After he was fired, Iksil claimed that CIO's senior management were involved in these trades. "The losses suffered by the CIO were not the actions of one person acting in an unauthorized manner," wrote Iksil in a public letter. "My role was to execute a trading strategy that had been initiated, approved, mandated and monitored by the CIO's senior management."

When JPMorgan's top executives did become aware of Iksil's losses, they apparently delayed informing the board of directors. "JPMorgan's senior management broke a cardinal rule of corporate governance and deprived its board of critical information it needed to fully assess the company's problems," concluded a senior U.S. government official.

Bruno Iksil, his boss, the bank's chief investment officer, and several others have since left the bank.

Discussion Questions

1. What sources and contingencies of power gave Bruno Iksil considerable power in the CIO group at JP Morgan?

2. What influence tactics, if any, were used to hide the financial losses?

3. Was organizational politics evident in the events described in this case? If so, what were the characteristics of those actions that identified them as organizational politics?

Team Exercise:
DECIPHERING THE (SOCIAL) NETWORK

by Steven L. McShane, University of Newcastle (Australia)

Purpose This exercise is designed to help students interpret social network maps, including their implications for organizational effectiveness.

Materials The instructor will distribute several social network diagrams to each student.

Instructions (Smaller classes) The instructor will organize students into teams (typically four to seven people, depending on class size). Teams will examine each social network diagram to answer the following questions:

1. What aspects of this diagram suggest that the network is not operating as effectively as possible?

2. Which people in this network seem to be most powerful? Least powerful? What information or features of the diagram lead you to this conclusion?

3. If you were responsible for this group of people, how would you change this situation to improve their effectiveness?

   After teams have diagnosed each social network map, the class will debrief by hearing each team's assessments and recommendations.

Instructions (Larger classes) This activity is also possible in large classes by projecting each social network diagram on a screen and giving students a minute or two to examine the diagram. The instructor can then ask specific questions to the class, such as pointing to a specific individual in the network and asking whether the individual has high or low power, what level of centrality is apparent, and whether the individual's connections are mainly strong or weak ties. The instructor might also ask which quadrant on the map indicates the most concern and then allow individual students to provide their explanations.

Team Exercise:
MANAGING YOUR BOSS

Purpose This exercise is designed to help students apply influence tactics to real situations, in this case influencing people above them in the hierarchy.

Materials None.

Instructions (For smaller classes only) The instructor will organize students into teams (typically four to seven people, depending on class size). Teams will identify specific strategies to influence people above them in the organizational hierarchy. Teams should consider each of the various influence tactics to determine specific practices that might change the attitudes and behaviour of their bosses. During this team discussion, students should determine which influence tactics are most and least appropriate for managing their bosses. Teams should also consider relevant concepts from other chapters, such as perceptions (Chapter 3), emotions and attitudes (Chapter 4), motivation (Chapter 5), and (if already covered in the course) conflict (Chapter 11).

The class will regroup, and each team will present specific recommendations for influencing people in higher positions.

Self-Assessments for Chapter 10

SELF-ASSESSMENT NAME	DESCRIPTION
Do you have a *guanxi* orientation?	Connections and social networks are important, no matter where you do business around the world. These interpersonal relationships are called *guanxi* in China, where they are very important due to Confucian values and the unique history of that country. This self-assessment estimates the degree to which you display traditional *guanxi* values.
What is your approach to influencing co-workers ?	Working with others in organizations is an ongoing process of coordination and cooperation. Part of that dynamic is changing our attitudes and behaviour as well as motivating others to change their attitudes and behaviour. In other words, everyone engages in influence tactics to get things done. There are many ways to influence other people, some of which work better than others, depending on the situation. Use this tool to assess the types of influence you might employ and your preference for various tactics.
How politically charged is your school?	Every organization has some degree of organizational politics. Depending on behavioural norms and organizational culture, employees in some companies actively use influence tactics to get their own way for personal gain. In other workplaces, employees who engage in organizational politics are quickly reminded to avoid these tactics, or are eventually asked to work somewhere else. Students can usually sense the level of organizational politics at the college where they are taking courses. This tool assesses the level of organizational politics at your school.

CHAPTER 11

Conflict and Negotiation in the Workplace

LEARNING OBJECTIVES

After reading this chapter, you should be able to:

LO1 Define conflict and debate its positive and negative consequences in the workplace.

LO2 Distinguish task conflict from relationship conflict and describe three strategies to minimize relationship conflict during task conflict episodes.

LO3 Diagram the conflict process model and describe six structural sources of conflict in organizations.

LO4 Outline the five conflict-handling styles and discuss the circumstances in which each would be most appropriate.

LO5 Apply the six structural approaches to conflict management and describe the three types of third-party dispute resolution.

LO6 Discuss activities in the negotiation preparation, process, and setting that improve negotiation effectiveness.

On a hot August afternoon, an easyJet flight was taxiing out to the runway at London's Gatwick Airport when an incident delayed its departure to Belfast, Northern Ireland. The problem was neither mechanical nor an external threat. Instead, two cabin crew members had had an irreconcilable disagreement about how to properly unpack and store the water bottles. When notified of the quarrel, the cabin manager advised the employees to try to get along and do their jobs. Unfortunately, the conflict continued, so the cabin manager met with the captain and decided to offload and replace the two squabbling crew members. Facing the frustrated passengers, the captain apologized that the flight would be delayed until two new crew members arrived.

"This is quite incredible," exclaimed a British television presenter who had a front row seat on the flight. "We've all worked with people we don't get on with, right? But this tiff means a one-hour flight is delayed!" The easyJet flight arrived in Belfast 90 minutes late.

Overt conflict is rare among commercial airline crew members, but when these clashes do occur, the consequences can be costly for the airline and inconvenient for passengers.

©RichardBakerFarnborough/Alamy Stock Photo

Overt conflict is infrequent among commercial airline crew members, but when these clashes do occur, the consequences can be costly for the airline and inconvenient for passengers. A few months before the easyJet incident, a Delta Air Lines flight from Los Angeles to Minneapolis made an unscheduled detour to Salt Lake City because two flight attendants got into a nasty argument over work issues. In fact, passengers watched in horror as the two female crew members began physically fighting each other. A third unidentified woman tried to calm down the two combatants but was hit by a wayward fist. The cabin manager notified the captain, who then changed course.

Delta Air Lines later sent an understated letter of apology to passengers, saying: "We expect our flight crew to be nothing but courteous and professional at all times and what you experienced was far from that." The flight arrived 75 minutes late in Minneapolis.

The most recent and arguably most serious airline crew conflict occurred between the captain and her male co-pilot on a Jet Airways flight from London to Mumbai. More than halfway through the nine-hour flight, the visibly upset captain rushed out of the cockpit to the forward galley, complaining to cabin crew that the co-pilot had slapped her during a disagreement over personal matters. The two pilots were reportedly in a relationship and had had less dramatic arguments during earlier flights. The crew tried to comfort the captain but were unable to convince her to return to the cockpit. The co-pilot eventually came out—leaving the cockpit unattended on autopilot mode—and was able to persuade the captain to return with him.

Unfortunately, their disagreement did not abate. Within an hour, the captain left the cockpit a second time, returning only after becoming aware that crew and passengers were feeling increasingly concerned for their safety. Jet Airways initially announced that the pilots had a "misunderstanding" which they "resolved amicably." However, the two were fired a few days later.[1]

These incidents involving flight crew members illustrate that workplace conflict can be very costly, inconvenient, and occasionally dangerous. But as we will learn in this chapter, some forms of conflict are also valuable to organizations. The challenge is to enable beneficial conflict and suppress dysfunctional conflict. We begin this chapter by defining conflict and discussing the age-old question: Is conflict good or bad? Next, we look at the conflict process and examine in detail the main factors that cause or amplify conflict. The five styles of handling conflict are then described, including the contingencies of conflict handling as well as gender and cross-cultural differences. Next, we look at the role of managers and others in third-party conflict resolution. The final section of this chapter reviews key strategies when negotiating conflict resolution.

The Meaning and Consequences of Conflict

LO1

Conflict is a fact of life in organizations. Companies are continuously adapting to their external environment, yet there is no clear road map on what changes are best. Every day, employees disagree on which work objectives should receive priority, which norms they should abide by, and how even minor job tasks should be performed (such as how to properly store water bottles during a flight). These conflict episodes occur because of clashing work goals, divergent personal values and experiences, and a variety of other reasons that we discuss in this chapter.

Conflict is a process in which one party perceives that its interests are being opposed or negatively affected by another party.[2] It occurs when one party obstructs another's goals in some way, or just from one party's perception that the other party is going to do so. Conflict is ultimately based on perceptions; it exists whenever one party *believes* that another might obstruct its efforts, whether or not the other party actually has those intentions.

> **conflict** The process in which one party perceives that its interests are being opposed or negatively affected by another party.

This definition—and the focus of this chapter—is on conflict with others, such as between people on the same team or department, between work units or business divisions, or between the organization and external stakeholders. However, conflict also occurs within each of us (called *intrapersonal conflict*). In earlier chapters, we discussed various intrapersonal conflicts, such as when our behaviour conflicts with our beliefs and values (see Chapter 4 on cognitive dissonance) and when we need to reconcile conflicting goals in decision making, such as providing customer service versus working efficiently (Chapter 7).

IS CONFLICT GOOD OR BAD?

One of the oldest debates in organizational behaviour is whether conflict is good or bad—or, more recently, what forms of conflict are good or bad.[3] The dominant view over most of this time has been that conflict is dysfunctional.[4] This perspective argues that organizations work best through harmonious relations, whereas even moderately low levels of conflict tatter the fabric of workplace relations and sap energy from productive activities.

The "conflict-is-bad" perspective is now considered too simplistic, yet workplace conflict can indeed have negative consequences under some circumstances (see Exhibit 11.1). In fact, by some estimates, dysfunctional workplace conflict costs the Canadian economy several billion dollars in lost productivity each year and consumes an average of almost three hours of work time per employee each week.[5]

Research indicates that some forms or levels of conflict potentially reduce employee performance by consuming otherwise productive time.[6] Conflict threatens personal needs and self-concept, which produces employee stress, reduces job satisfaction, and increases turnover. Stress also reduces performance because it consumes energy and distracts employees from their work. Conflict potentially undermines information sharing, because it reduces employee motivation to ask for, pay attention to, and transmit information with discordant co-workers.[7] Disagreements can also fuel organizational politics and thereby waste resources, such as when employees try to undermine the credibility of their opponents. Conflict among team members may hurt team cohesion and performance. Even when conflict occurs between work units (such as when competing for budget funding), the interdepartmental conflict may lead to conflict and power struggles among employees *within* each work unit.[8]

Benefits of Conflict

In the 1920s, when most organizational scholars viewed conflict as inherently dysfunctional, philosopher and psychologist John Dewey praised its benefits: "Conflict is the gadfly of thought. It stirs us to observation and memory. It instigates to invention. It shocks us out of sheep-like passivity, and sets us at noting and contriving." Three years later, political scientist and management theorist Mary Parker Follett similarly remarked that the "friction" of conflict should be put to use rather than treated as an unwanted consequence of differences.[9] But it wasn't until the 1970s that conflict management experts began to embrace the notion that some level of conflict can be beneficial.[10] They formed an "optimal conflict" perspective, which states that organizations are most effective when employees experience some level of conflict. Organizations are less effective when the intensity of conflict is very low or very high.

What are the benefits of conflict? First, it potentially improves decision making. As Dewey stated, conflict energizes people to debate issues and evaluate alternatives more thoroughly. When employees disagree constructively, they probe and test one another's way of thinking to better understand the underlying issues that need to be addressed. They evaluate the logic of the opposing positions and re-examine each party's basic assumptions about the problem and its possible solution. Conflict also motivates creative thinking to discover novel solutions to the disagreement.[11]

A second potential benefit is that moderate levels of conflict maintain vigilance with the external environment. Through disagreement, employees engage in active thinking, and this often involves ongoing questioning about how the organization can be more closely aligned with its customers, suppliers, and other stakeholders.[12] A third benefit occurs when team members experience conflict with external sources, such as competition with or threats from other teams or organizations. People tend to be more motivated to work together when faced with an external threat, which strengthens cohesion within the team (see Chapter 8). However, as we mentioned a few paragraphs ago, interdepartmental conflict sometimes undermines relations within the department.

EXHIBIT 11.1   Consequences of Workplace Conflict

Negative consequences	Positive consequences
• Lower performance	• Better decision making:
• Higher stress, dissatisfaction, and turnover	○ Tests logic of arguments
• Less information sharing and coordination	○ Questions assumptions
• Increased organizational politics	○ Generates creative thinking
• Wasted resources	• More responsive to changing environment
• Weakened team cohesion (when conflict occurs among team members)	• Stronger team cohesion (when conflict occurs between the team and outside opponents)

The Emerging View: Task and Relationship Conflict

LO2

The "optimal conflict" perspective remains popular and seems to be true in some respects—there is some evidence that any form of conflict becomes dysfunctional beyond some degree of intensity.[13] However, the school of thought most widely accepted today is that there are two dominant types of conflict: task conflict and relationship conflict. These represent two distinct ways that people approach and interact with one another during disagreements.[14]

TASK CONFLICT

Task conflict (also called *constructive conflict*) occurs when people focus their discussion around the issue (i.e., the "task") while showing respect for people involved in that disagreement. This type of conflict keeps the spotlight on the qualities of the ideas presented. With task conflict, participants examine behaviour, ideas, and recommendations in terms of their factual accuracy, logic, and reasonable inferences. The discussion avoids any attention to the competence or power of the people involved. Research indicates that task conflict tends to produce the beneficial outcomes described earlier, particularly better decision making, although there is likely an upper limit to the intensity of any disagreement.[15]

> **task conflict** A type of conflict in which people focus their discussion around the issue (i.e., the "task") in which different viewpoints occur while showing respect for people involved in that disagreement.

We often hear about workplace conflicts caused by "personality clashes." Yet this label typically indicates that someone has oversimplified these interpersonal tiffs in terms of the opponent's personal characteristics (relationship conflict) rather than the task-related events that manifested the disagreement. Suppose an employee describes a disagreement with a co-worker in terms of the latter's reckless personality. The co-worker's behaviours or suggestions may be irritatingly risky. Yet, task-oriented conflict is possible by focusing on what the allegedly reckless employee does (the logic, ethics, and consequences of those actions) and on the logic and factual foundation of that's person's suggestions, not on alleged personal attributes. The point here is that almost all workplace conflicts can be framed as task conflicts, even when some participants try to pin the problem on flaws in the other party's personal characteristics.

RELATIONSHIP CONFLICT

In contrast to task conflict, **relationship conflict** occurs when the discussion focuses on characteristics of participants in the dispute. This type of conflict is evident when employees attack an opposing idea by questioning the competence of those who introduce that position. Rather than identifying logical and factual concerns with someone's suggestion (task conflict), relationship conflict attempts to dismiss the idea by arguing that it was proposed or supported by people who lack expertise, intelligence, credibility, or other traits necessary to make good suggestions.

> **relationship conflict** A type of conflict in which people focus their discussion on qualities of the people in the dispute, rather than on the qualities of the ideas presented regarding a task-related issue.

Relationship conflict also occurs more indirectly when people rely on status or expertise to defend their position ("My recommendation is better because I have the most experience!"). Arguing for an idea by claiming one's own superior talents implies the inferiority of those who present opposing arguments or recommendations. Relationship conflict even occurs when someone is abrasive or assertive to the extent that the behaviour demeans others in the conversation.[16] For example, a manager who bangs a fist on the desk while presenting an argument is demonstrating that the manager has more power and the followers need harsh signals to get their attention.

Relationship conflict is dysfunctional because it threatens the other party's self-esteem (see Chapter 3). It usually triggers defence mechanisms and a competitive orientation between the opponents. It also reduces mutual trust by emphasizing interpersonal differences that weaken any bond that exists between the parties.[17] Relationship conflict escalates more easily than task conflict because the adversaries become less motivated to communicate and share information, making it more difficult for them to discover common ground and ultimately resolve the conflict. Instead, they rely increasingly on distorted perceptions and stereotypes, which tend to reinforce their perceptions of threat.

MINIMIZING RELATIONSHIP CONFLICT DURING TASK CONFLICT

The logical recommendation from our discussion so far is to encourage task conflict and minimize relationship conflict. This sounds good in theory, but separating these two types of conflict isn't easy in practice. Research indicates that we experience some degree of relationship conflict whenever we are engaged in constructive debate.[18] No matter how diplomatically someone questions our ideas and actions, they potentially threaten our self-esteem and our public image, which usually

©Jacob Lund/Shutterstock

Team decision making at Amazon.com is not a casual social gathering. "It is respectful contention and eventually we reach a decision based on the data, but meetings are hotly debated," says a vice president about the meetings he attends at the online retailer. In fact, one of Amazon's principles states that leaders should "respectfully challenge decisions when they disagree, even when doing so is uncomfortable or exhausting." Another Amazon executive explains that "it would certainly be much easier and socially cohesive to just compromise and not debate, but that may lead to the wrong decision." Some observers and employees say that Amazon fuels relationship conflict, not just task conflict. Others counter that relationship conflict is discouraged, pointing out that *respectfully* challenge" means focusing on the problem, not the person. "We debate politely and respectfully, and you are given constructive feedback to course-correct if you are rude or disrespectful," says a middle management engineer.[*]

[*] G. Anders, "Inside Amazon's Idea Machine: How Bezos Decodes Customers," *Forbes,* April 23, 2012; J. Kantor and D. Streitfeld, "Amazon's Bruising, Thrilling Workplace," *The New York Times,* August 16, 2015; N. Ciubotariu, "An Amazonian's Response to 'Inside Amazon: Wrestling Big Ideas in a Bruising Workplace,'" *LinkedIn Pulse,* LinkedIn, August 16, 2015, www.linkedin.com/pulse/amazonians-response-inside-amazon-wrestling-big-ideas-nick-ciubotariu; L. Hook, "Person of the Year: Amazon Web Services' Andy Jassy," *FT.Com (London),* March 17, 2016.

triggers our drive to defend. The stronger the level of debate and the more the issue is tied to our self-view, the more likely that task conflict will evolve into (or mix with) relationship conflict. Fortunately, three conditions potentially minimize the level of relationship conflict that occurs during task conflict episodes.[19]

- *Emotional intelligence.* Relationship conflict is less likely to occur, or is less likely to escalate, when team members have high levels of emotional intelligence, as well as the related attributes of emotional stability personality and trait self-control.[20] Employees with higher emotional intelligence are better able to regulate their emotions during debate, which reduces the risk of escalating perceptions of interpersonal hostility. They are also more likely to view a co-worker's emotional reaction as valuable information about that person's needs and expectations, rather than as a personal attack.

- *Team development.* Team development plays a critical role in suppressing relationship conflict during task

conflict.[21] One explanation is that as teams develop, their members become better at understanding and anticipating one another, which reduces the risk that a co-worker's words or actions will be misinterpreted as a conflict trigger. Newly formed teams (which have less mutual understanding) have more difficulty separating task and relationship conflict, whereas experienced teams (such as senior executive teams) tend to demonstrate a higher capacity to suppress relationship conflict during discussions. A second explanation is that team development produces higher team cohesion, in which employees feel a strong social identity with the group. Members of cohesive teams are motivated to minimize relationship conflict because these episodes threaten the team's stability and the member's future with that group.

- *Norms supporting psychological safety.* Task conflict is less likely to mutate into chronic relationship conflict when the team or broader organization adopts norms that support psychological safety.[22] **Psychological safety** refers to a shared belief that it is safe to engage in interpersonal risk-taking (see Chapter 8). In other words, employees are confident that presenting unusual ideas, constructively disagreeing with the majority, or experimenting with new work behaviours will not cause co-workers to threaten their self-concept, status, or career. Psychological safety flourishes when team and organizational norms encourage employees to respect and value one another, demonstrate interest in one another, be open-minded about and tolerant with co-workers' opinions, and show positive intentions toward one another. Showing positive intentions involves displaying positive emotions and nonthreatening behaviour when discussing different points of view.

> **psychological safety** A shared belief that it is safe to engage in interpersonal risk-taking; specifically, that presenting unusual ideas, constructively disagreeing with the majority, and experimenting with new work behaviours will not result in co-workers posing a threat to one's self-concept, status, or career.

Debating Point: CAN PEOPLE AVOID RELATIONSHIP CONFLICT DURING DISAGREEMENTS?

One of the core ideas in conflict theory is that people can disagree with each other regarding an issue (task conflict) without experiencing negative emotions toward each other (relationship conflict). The most popular book on negotiation makes this point by stating that the parties need to "separate the people from the problem."[*] It advises that the participants need to view themselves as "working side by side, attacking the problem, not each other."

Scholars do recognize that separating task from relationship conflict isn't easy, but they claim it is possible.[**] People with well-developed emotional intelligence can control negative emotional reactions (anger, frustration, hurt, etc.) and can reframe the conflict as a constructive event rather than as a personal attack. Research also suggests that relationship conflict is less likely to occur when the parties understand each other's views, such as in high-performing teams. Psychological safety norms have also been identified as a way to avoid relationship conflict while engaging in task conflict.

The ability to avoid relationship conflict during task conflict sounds promising in theory yet, in practice, it may be a bridge too far. Instead, some degree of relationship conflict may be inevitable. One of the most basic problems is that employees immediately and automatically experience negative emotions when they become aware that co-workers or supervisors disagree with their ideas or behaviour.[***]

Negative emotions aren't just attributed to information in the opposing message; they are also attributed to the source of that message. This occurs because we naturally try to make sense of disruptive conditions, and this includes forming adverse interpretations about why a co-worker has disagreed with our proposal or behaviour. Consequently, relationship conflict seems to form as soon as we become aware that our ideas or actions are being challenged.

Relationship conflict may also be unavoidable because it disrupts the current or expected pattern of behaviour, which produces negative emotions toward those who caused that disruption. People have a natural desire to maintain the status quo.[****] Even those who propose change want to see their ideas flow predictably through to the future without opposition. This effect occurs because people want to believe they control their situation, whereas disagreement reduces perceived control and predictability in the work environment.

Relationship conflict may also be inevitable in any disagreement because all communication has both a relational and substantive function.[*****] This means that when people interact with each other, they not only transmit and receive information (substantive), but also reinforce or strain the fabric of their relationship. Communication is important for one's relatedness needs, so a message that challenges another viewpoint (substantive) also seems to challenge the relationship.

* R. Fisher and W. Ury, *Getting to Yes: Negotiating an Agreement without Giving In* (Random House, 2012). Although few believe task and relationship conflict can be completely separated (Fisher and Ury included), several scholars have developed activities that emphasize the possibility of this separation. For example, see: L. Boyd, M. Gupta, and F. Kuzmits, "The Evaporating Cloud: A Tool for Resolving Workplace Conflict," *International Journal of Conflict Management* 22 (2011): 394–412; C.A. Blair and D.E. Desplaces, "Conflict Management through the Negotiations Canvas, Getting Participants to Understand," *Conflict Resolution Quarterly* 36 (2018): 39–51.

**For a summary of these views, see: T.A. O'Neill et al., "The Structure and Function of Team Conflict State Profiles," *Journal of Management* 44 (2018): 811–36.

*** M.D. Seery et al., "Alone against the Group: A Unanimously Disagreeing Group Leads to Conformity, but Cardiovascular Threat Depends on One's Goals," *Psychophysiology* 53 (2016): 1263–71; A. Hagemeister and J. Volmer, "Do Social Conflicts at Work Affect Employees' Job Satisfaction?: The Moderating Role of Emotion Regulation," *International Journal of Conflict Management* 29 (2017): 213–35.

**** W. Samuelson and R. Zeckhauser, "Status Quo Bias in Decision Making," *Journal of Risk and Uncertainty* 1 (1988): 7–59; D. Proudfoot and A.C. Kay, "System Justification in Organizational Contexts: How a Motivated Preference for the Status Quo Can Affect Organizational Attitudes and Behaviors," *Research in Organizational Behavior* 34 (2014): 173–87; D. De Clercq and I. Belausteguigoitia, "Overcoming the Dark Side of Task Conflict: Buffering Roles of Transformational Leadership, Tenacity, and Passion for Work," *European Management Journal* 35 (2017): 78–90.

***** A.C. Mooney, P.J. Holahan, and A.C. Amason, "Don't Take It Personally: Exploring Cognitive Conflict as a Mediator of Affective Conflict," *Journal of Management Studies* 44 (2007): 733–58; S.J. Beck and J. Keyton, "Perceiving Strategic Meeting Interaction," *Small Group Research* 40 (2009): 223–46; L.R. Weingart et al., "The Directness and Oppositional Intensity of Conflict Expression," *Academy of Management Review* 40 (2015): 235–62.

Conflict Process Model

LO3

Now that we have outlined the history and current knowledge about conflict and its outcomes, let's look at the model of the conflict process, shown in Exhibit 11.2.[23] This model begins with the sources of conflict, which we will describe in the next section. The sources of conflict lead one or both parties to perceive that conflict exists. They become aware that one party's statements and actions interfere with or otherwise threaten their own goals or beliefs. These perceptions produce and interact with emotions experienced about the conflict.

Conflict perceptions usually produce negative emotions, including feelings of stress (emotional strain), anxiety, fear, frustration, and/or anger.[24] However, some people experience positive emotions through cognitive reappraisal of the conflict, such as by perceiving the situation as a positive challenge, an opportunity to learn about other viewpoints, and a relief that nagging concerns about a possible conflict are out in the open and can now be addressed.

Manifest conflict represents each party's decisions and behaviours toward the other. These *conflict episodes* may range from subtle nonverbal communication to warlike aggression. Manifest conflict incidents are influenced by how the other party perceives and reacts emotionally to them.[25] Conflict is also behaviourally revealed by the style each side prefers using to resolve the conflict. Some people tend to avoid the conflict whereas others try to defeat those with opposing views. We discuss different conflict-handling styles later in this chapter.

Exhibit 11.2 shows arrows looping back from manifest conflict to conflict perceptions and emotions. These arrows illustrate that the conflict process is really a series of episodes that potentially cycle into conflict escalation.[26] It doesn't take much to start this conflict cycle—just an inappropriate comment, a misunderstanding, or action that lacks diplomacy. These behaviours cause the other party to perceive that conflict exists.

Even if the first party did not intend to demonstrate conflict, the second party's response may create that perception. Conflict escalation is particularly challenging because any task conflict focus that existed crumbles and relationship conflict takes over. Furthermore, the parties become less motivated to communicate with each other. With less communication, the parties increasingly rely on stereotypes of the opposing group, which amplify differences and further fuel the relationship conflict.

Structural Sources of Conflict in Organizations

The conflict model starts with the sources of conflict. We need to understand these sources to effectively diagnose conflict episodes and subsequently resolve the disagreement or occasionally to generate conflict where it is lacking. The six main conditions that cause conflict in organizational settings are incompatible goals, differentiation, interdependence, scarce resources, ambiguous rules, and communication problems.

INCOMPATIBLE GOALS

Organizations divide work among departments and teams, who divide it further among individuals. Each division of work has associated goals, so employees and departments have different—and often conflicting—work objectives. Goal incompatibility occurs when the goals of one person or department seem to interfere with another person's or department's goals.[27] For example, the production department strives for cost efficiency by scheduling long production runs whereas the sales team emphasizes customer service by delivering the client's product as quickly as possible. If the company runs out of a particular product, the production team would prefer to have clients wait until the next production run. This infuriates sales representatives who would rather change production quickly to satisfy consumer demand.

EXHIBIT 11.2 Model of the Conflict Process

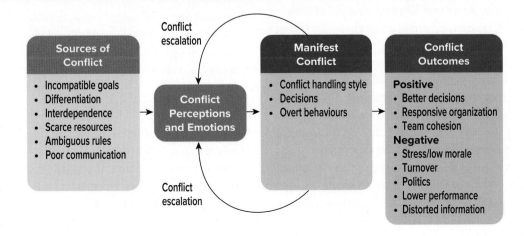

Global Connections 11.1

UBER CONFLICT WITH INCOMPATIBLE GOALS AND DIFFERENTIATION*

Uber developed such a competitive culture that many employees at the ride-sharing service clashed with one another to achieve their own career goals. "It seemed like every manager was fighting their peers and attempting to undermine their direct supervisor so that they could have their direct supervisor's job," complained a former Uber engineer.

Hostilities also occurred across teams due to both incompatible team goals and differentiation. For instance, sources say the San Francisco software engineers working on Uber's self-driving vehicles viewed their robotics hardware co-workers in Pittsburgh as "a bunch of academics with no real-world, product-building experience," whereas the Pittsburgh crew perceived the West Coast engineers as "whiny and ungrateful."

This infighting may have contributed to faulty technology, which was one of several factors in the death of a pedestrian struck by an Uber self-driving vehicle.

©Jeff Swensen/Getty Images

* M. Isaac, "Inside Uber's Aggressive, Unrestrained Workplace Culture," *The New York Times,* February 22, 2017; A. Griswold, "Uber Is Designed so That for One Employee to Get Ahead, Another Must Fail," *Quartz,* February 27, 2017; J. Bort, S. Lee, and N. Behring, "Uber Insiders Describe Infighting and Questionable Decisions before Its Self-Driving Car Killed a Pedestrian," *Business Insider,* November 19, 2018.

DIFFERENTIATION

Another source of conflict is differentiation—differences among people and work units regarding their beliefs, values, and preferences. Differentiation is distinct from goal incompatibility; two people or departments may agree on a common goal (serving customers better) but have different beliefs about how to best achieve that goal (such as by introducing new technology versus employee customer service training). Employees form different beliefs, expectations, and world views due to their childhood socialization, gender, ethnicity, occupation, personal values, and personality.[28] Also, conflict is a perception, so before differences are actually apparent, employees form conflict beliefs based on stereotypes and false expectations about co-workers from different backgrounds.

Generational diversity produces workplace conflict due to differentiation because people across broad age groups tend to have different needs, expectations, and behaviours.[29] This intergenerational differentiation occurs for two reasons. First, each of us is deeply influenced by the unique technological advances (e.g., smartphones versus Sputnik), economic conditions, and other "social forces" we experience growing up and throughout our lives. Second, we tend to have somewhat different needs and priorities at each stage of our career and life, such as a greater

need for skills development during early career, a greater need for job security while raising a family, and a greater need for financial security in retirement toward the end of our career.

Conflict due to differentiation also exists during corporate mergers and acquisitions.[30] Even when people from both companies want the integrated organization to succeed, they fight over the "right way" to do things because of their unique experiences in the separate companies. This form of conflict emerged when CenturyLink acquired Qwest, creating the third largest telecommunications company in the United States. The two companies were headquartered in different parts of the country. "Their languages were different, their food was different, answers were different. We talked fast and interrupted, and they talked slow and were polite," recalls a senior Qwest executive. "If we said up, they said down. If we said yes, they said no. If we said go, they said stop." The result was "unnecessary misunderstandings" as executives tried to integrate the two companies.[31]

INTERDEPENDENCE

All workplace conflict is caused to some extent by task interdependence. Conflict isn't possible between two people or work units that have no mutual involvement or shared resources (i.e., they are independent entities) because they would not have occasion to interfere with one another.

Global Connections 11.2

OPEN OFFICE, HIDDEN CONFLICT*

The social distancing requirements of the COVID-19 pandemic may have halted, at least temporarily, the decade-long movement of employees from cubicles and private offices into open-plan and nonterritorial workspaces. These communal arrangements are now considered high-risk environments for spreading disease. But even before COVID-19, concern was growing that open-plan offices were fuelling workplace conflict, most of which occurs as subtle irritation and resentment among co-workers.

Shared workspace arrangements create higher interdependence among employees regarding the noise, visual movement, territorial privacy, and information privacy of that space. Numerous studies have found that these disturbances and intrusions reduce work concentration and performance, which increases employee stress and conflict with those perceived to be causing the distractions.

"Our open office has absolutely crippled my productivity," concludes a marketing professional in the United States after three years in an open-office arrangement. "I can't hear myself think, I'm starting to feel bitter toward my co-workers, and my anxiety has shot through the roof." One office worker in Toronto observes that the company's move to an open office "led to a very false sense of family and community. We worked together in an open environment, but we were not a team."

In a recent survey of 60,000 Canadian federal government scientists and associated professionals, 79 percent said they had difficulty focusing and concentrating on their work and 62 percent believed their productivity and efficiency got worse after moving to open offices. Only 6 percent said the new open office arrangements improved their productivity.

Conflict may be even more intense in nonterritorial offices because they create ongoing competition over prized locations, such as desks in quieter areas, close to windows, and near strong Wi-Fi. "Each morning in my office is like a grown-up game of musical chairs, with six or so people competing for the last remaining hot desk," complains a British accountant. "Lost productivity spent hunting for somewhere to sit is the least of our concerns. Barely concealed resentment comes to the fore on regular occasions."

To minimize open-office conflict among its 85 employees, a Toronto architectural firm formed an etiquette committee that produced guidelines for appropriate behaviour in communal settings. A Canadian government department produced a similar document for its open-office workers. For example, the booklet warns: "Nail clipping in the open-concept office is not tolerated. Please use the washroom."

©Jacob Lund/Shutterstock

* P. Tomlin, "Hot Desk, Cold Shoulder," *The Guardian,* November 7, 2005; L. Greene, "How Open Offices Are Killing Us," *PsyPost,* August 20, 2016; R.L. Morrison and K.A. Macky, "The Demands and Resources Arising from Shared Office Spaces," *Applied Ergonomics* 60 (April 2017): 103–15; M. Yadav et al., "The Irrelevant Speech Effect in Multi-Talker Environments: Applications to Open-Plan Offices," *The Journal of the Acoustical Society of America* 143, no. 3 (April 2018): 1725; "'It's Not One Size Fits All': Why Open Office Plans Don't Work for Everyone," *Global News,* March 29, 2019; "Fact Sheet: Productivity in Open Workplaces," The Professional Institute of the Public Service of Canada, May 29, 2019, https://pipsc.ca/fact-sheet-productivity-in-open-workplaces; K. Egan, "Ottawa Joins Open Office Revolution; Activity-Based Workplace Model Takes Getting Used To," *Regina Leader Post,* August 19, 2019; W. Immen, "What Happens When Architects Design Their Own Studio?," *Globe & Mail,* November 5, 2019.

Task interdependence exists when employees must share resources or coordinate work activities to perform their jobs (see Chapter 8). Conflict is inherently about relationships because people and work units are affected by others only when they have some level of interdependence.

The probability and intensity of conflict increase with the level of interdependence.[32] Conflict is usually lowest when working with others in a pooled interdependence relationship, such as when sharing a common resource. The potential for conflict is higher in sequential interdependence work relationships, such as an assembly line. The highest risk and intensity of conflict tends to occur in reciprocal interdependence situations. With reciprocal interdependence, employees have high mutual dependence on each other as well as higher centrality. Consequently, relationships with reciprocal interdependence are the most intense because co-workers in reciprocal relationships have the strongest and most immediate risk of interfering with each other's objectives (i.e., high centrality).

SCARCE RESOURCES

Resource scarcity generates conflict because each person or department requiring the same resource necessarily interferes with others who also need that resource to fulfil their goals.[33] Most labour strikes, for instance, occur because there aren't enough financial and other resources for employees and company owners to each receive the outcomes they seek, such as higher pay (employees) and higher investment returns (shareholders). Budget deliberations within organizations also produce conflict because there isn't enough cash flow or debt facility to satisfy the funding aspirations of each work unit. The more resources one group receives, the fewer resources other groups will receive. Fortunately, as we discuss later in this chapter, these interests aren't perfectly opposing in complex negotiations, but limited resources are typically a major source of friction.

AMBIGUOUS RULES

Conflict is more common in work settings where rules are ambiguous, inconsistently enforced, or completely missing.[34] This occurs because uncertainty increases the risk that one party will interfere with the other party's goals. Ambiguity also encourages political tactics and, in some cases, employees enter a free-for-all battle to win decisions in their favour. When clear rules exist, on the other hand, employees know what to expect from each other and have agreed to abide by those rules.

COMMUNICATION PROBLEMS

Conflict often becomes dysfunctional when employees lack the ability or motivation to state their disagreement in a diplomatic, nonconfrontational manner. It is difficult to craft a message that communicates dissent with neither too little nor too much assertiveness.[35] Influenced by their own strong feelings about an issue, employees tend to use emotion-laden language and aggressive nonverbal behaviour when transmitting their concerns. The stronger the emotive language and other signals, the stronger the perception by receivers that the conflict not only exists, but is a high-risk threat. Receivers often reciprocate with a similar response, which further escalates the conflict. Furthermore, aggressive and emotive communication typically fuels relationship conflict and makes it more difficult for the discussants to maintain a task conflict focus.

Poorly crafted communication is a source of conflict, but a lack of communication often amplifies that conflict. Occasionally, lack of communication exists because employees don't have the opportunity to discuss their differences. More often, the quarrel makes the relationship so uncomfortable that the parties actively avoid each other. Unfortunately, less communication can further escalate the conflict because each side increasingly relies on distorted images and stereotypes of the other party. Perceptions are further distorted because people in conflict situations tend to engage in more differentiation with those who are unlike themselves (see Chapter 3). This differentiation creates a more positive and reassuring self-concept and a more negative image of the opponent.[36]

Interpersonal Conflict-Handling Styles

LO4

The six sources of conflict described in the previous section lead to conflict perceptions and emotions which, in turn, motivate people to respond in some way to the conflict. Mary Parker Follett (who argued that conflict can be beneficial) observed almost a century ago that people use a variety of interpersonal conflict-handling styles to address conflict situations. Follett's original list was expanded and refined over the years into the five-category model shown in Exhibit 11.3. This model recognizes that how people respond behaviourally to a conflict situation depends on the relative importance they place on maximizing outcomes for themselves and maximizing outcomes for the other party.[37]

- *Problem solving.* Problem solving tries to find a solution that is beneficial for both parties. This is known as the **win–win orientation** because people using this style believe the resources at stake are expandable rather than fixed if the parties work together to find a creative solution. Information sharing is an important feature of this style because both parties collaborate to identify common ground and potential solutions that satisfy everyone involved.

> **win–win orientation** The belief that conflicting parties will find a mutually beneficial solution to their disagreement.

- *Forcing.* Forcing tries to win the conflict at the other's expense. People who use this style typically have a **win–lose orientation**—they believe the parties are drawing from a fixed pie, so the more one party receives, the less the other party will receive. Consequently, this style relies on "hard" influence tactics (see Chapter 10) to get one's own way. However, forcing is not necessarily aggressiveness or bullying. It includes more moderate degrees of assertiveness,

> **win–lose orientation** The belief that conflicting parties are drawing from a fixed pie, so the more one party receives, the less the other party will receive.

EXHIBIT 11.3   Interpersonal Conflict-Handling Styles*

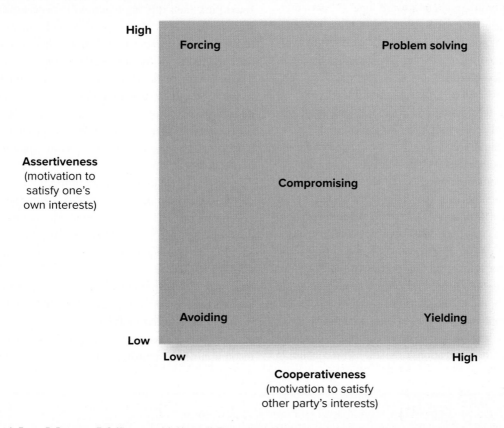

* C. K. W. de Dreu, A. Evers, B. Beersma, E. S. Kluwer, and A. Nauta, "A Theory-based Measure of Conflict Management Strategies in the Workplace," *Journal of Organizational Behavior,* 22 (2001), pp. 645–68. For other variations of this model, see: T. L. Ruble and K. Thomas, "Support For a Two-Dimensional Model of Conflict Behavior," *Organizational Behavior and Human Performance,* 16 (1976), p. 145. R. R. Blake, H. A. Shepard, and J. S. Mouton, *Managing Intergroup Conflict in Industry,* (Houston: Gulf Publishing, 1964); M. A. Rahim, "Toward a theory of managing organizational conflict." *International Journal of Conflict Management* 13, no. 3 (2002): 206–235.

such as speaking up and showing conviction for an idea or request.[38]

- *Avoiding.* Avoiding tries to smooth over or evade conflict situations altogether. A common avoidance strategy is to steer clear of the co-workers associated with the conflict. Another action is to minimize discussion of the sensitive topic when interacting with the other person in the conflict. Although it is situated in the "low–low" sector of the model, avoidance does not necessarily mean that people always have a low concern for both one's own and the other party's interest. Instead, they might be very concerned about one or both party's interests but conclude that avoidance is the best strategy, at least for the short term.[39]

- *Yielding.* Yielding involves giving in completely to the other side's wishes, or at least cooperating with little or no attention to one's own interests. This style involves making unilateral concessions and unconditional promises, as well as offering help with no expectation that the other party needs to reciprocate in the future.

- *Compromising.* Compromising involves actively seeking a middle ground between the interests of the two parties. This involves calculating losses from concessions with equally valued gains, or at least trying to achieve similar levels of how much value each party sacrifices to reach agreement.

What is your preferred conflict-handling style? You can discover your preferred way of handling conflict by locating this self-assessment in Connect.

CHOOSING THE BEST CONFLICT-HANDLING STYLE

Chances are that you gravitate toward one or two conflict-handling styles that match your personality, personal and cultural values, and past experience.[40] You might typically engage in avoiding or yielding because disagreement makes you feel uncomfortable and is contrary to your self-view as someone who likes to get along with everyone. Or perhaps you prefer the forcing and compromising strategies because they reflect your strong need for achievement and to control the situation. However, the best style depends on the situation, so you need to understand and develop the capacity to use each style in the appropriate circumstances.[41]

Exhibit 11.4 summarizes the main contingencies and problems associated with using each conflict-handling style. Problem solving is the preferred conflict-handling style whenever possible. Why? Because this approach offers the highest potential for the conflicting parties to reach a solution that is closest to their needs and goals. Through dialogue and clever thinking, the parties discover a win–win solution. In addition, the problem-solving style tends to improve long-term relationships, reduce stress, and minimize emotional defensiveness and other indications of relationship conflict.[42]

The problem-solving style is not the best conflict-handling style in all situations, however. If the conflict is simple and perfectly opposing (each party wants more of a single fixed pie), then this approach will waste time and increase frustration. It also takes more time and requires a fairly high degree of trust because there is a risk that the other party will take advantage of the information you have openly shared. The problem-solving style can be stressful and difficult when people experience strong feelings of conflict, likely because these negative emotions undermine trust in the other party.[43]

The forcing style is usually inappropriate because a high level of assertiveness tends to generate relationship conflict more quickly or intensely than occurs with other conflict-handling styles. This adverse effect of forcing is conveyed in the old adage: "The more arguments you win, the fewer friends you will have."[44] Even so, a moderate degree of assertiveness may be appropriate where the dispute requires a quick solution or your ideas have a significantly and objectively stronger logical or moral foundation. This conflict-handling style may also be preferred when the other party would take advantage of a more cooperative conflict-handling style.

Avoiding is often ineffective as a conflict-handling style because it produces uncertainty and frustration rather than resolution of the conflict.[45] However, avoiding may be the

---

EXHIBIT 11.4   Conflict-Handling Style Contingencies and Problems

Conflict-handling style	Preferred style when. . .	Problems with this style
Problem solving	• Interests are not perfectly opposing (i.e., not pure win–lose) • Parties have trust, openness, and time to share information • The issues are complex	• Involves sharing information that the other party might use to their advantage
Forcing	• Dispute requires a quick solution • Your position objectively has a much stronger logical or moral foundation • The other party would take advantage of more cooperative strategies	• Highest risk of relationship conflict • May damage long-term relations, reducing future problem-solving success
Avoiding	• Conflict has become too emotionally charged • Parties want to maintain a harmonious relationship • Cost of trying to resolve the conflict outweighs the benefits	• Doesn't usually resolve the conflict • May increase uncertainty and frustration
Yielding	• Issue is much less important to you than to the other party • The value and logic of your position isn't as clear • Parties want to maintain a harmonious relationship • The other party has substantially more power	• Increases other party's expectations in future conflict episodes
Compromising	• Single-issue conflict with opposing interests • Parties lack time or trust for problem solving • Parties want to maintain a harmonious relationship • Parties have equal power	• Suboptimal solution where mutual gains are possible

best short-term strategy when the conflict has become emotionally charged or is so intractable that resolution would be excessively costly in terms of time, effort, and other resources. Avoidance is also one of the preferred cooperative styles in cultures where openly resolving the conflict is a lower priority than maintaining superficial harmony in the relationship (the harmony is *superficial* because the disagreement still exists under the surface).

The yielding style may be appropriate when the other party has substantially more power, the issue is not as important to you as to the other party, and you aren't confident that your position has superior logical or ethical justification.[46] On the other hand, yielding may give the other side unrealistically high expectations and motivate them to seek more from you in the future. In the long run, this style may produce more conflict, not less.

The compromising style may be best where the conflict is simple and perfectly opposing (each party wants more of a single fixed pie). Even if the conflict is sufficiently complex for potential mutual gains, compromising may be necessary when the parties lack time, trust, and openness to apply the problem-solving style. The compromising style is also popular where the parties prioritize harmony in their relationship over personal gains in the dispute.[47] Compromise also tends to occur when both parties have approximately equal power, which prevents one party from gaining advantage over the other. However, many conflicts have the potential for mutual gains, whereas the compromise style settles for a suboptimal solution. Research also suggests that employees are less happy with a compromise agreement under some conditions.

CULTURAL AND GENDER DIFFERENCES IN CONFLICT-HANDLING STYLES

The preferred conflict-handling style varies from one culture to another.[48] For example, people from high collectivist cultures—where people are expected to support and show allegiance to the group—are motivated to maintain harmonious relations and, consequently, are more likely than those from less collectivist cultures to manage disagreements through avoidance or problem solving. However, collectivism motivates harmony *within* the group, not necessarily with people outside the group.[49] Generally, cultural values and norms represent an important contingency when choosing the preferred conflict-handling approach in that culture.

Men and women tend to rely on different conflict-handling styles to some degree.[50] The clearest difference is that men are more likely than women to use the forcing style, whether as managers or nonmanagement employees. Also, women (whether as managers or employees) are more likely than male counterparts to use the avoiding style. Women are

also slightly more likely than men to use problem solving, compromising, and yielding. Overall, except for the male preference for forcing, gender differences in conflict-handling styles are relatively small, but they have a logical foundation. Compared to men, women pay more attention to the relationship between the parties, so their preferred style tries to protect the relationship. This is apparent in less forcing, more avoiding, and slightly more use of compromising, yielding, and problem solving.

Structural Approaches to Conflict Management

LO5

Conflict-handling styles describe how we approach the other party in a conflict situation. But conflict management also involves altering the underlying structural causes of potential conflict. The main structural approaches parallel the sources of conflict discussed earlier. Six structural approaches to minimize dysfunctional conflict are: emphasize superordinate goals, reduce differentiation, improve communication and understanding, reduce interdependence, increase resources, and clarify rules and procedures.

EMPHASIZE SUPERORDINATE GOALS

One of the oldest recommendations for resolving conflict is to increase the parties' commitment to superordinate goals and decrease the importance of the conflicting subordinate goals.[51] **Superordinate goals** are goals that the conflicting employees or departments value and whose attainment requires the joint resources and effort of those parties.[52] These goals are called superordinate because they are higher-order aspirations, such as the organization's strategic objectives, rather than key performance objectives specific to the individual or work unit. Research indicates that the most effective executive teams frame their decisions as superordinate goals that rise above each executive's departmental or divisional goals. Similarly, effective leaders reduce dysfunctional organizational conflict through an inspirational vision that unifies employees and makes them less preoccupied with their subordinate goal differences.[53]

> **superordinate goals** Goals that the conflicting parties value and whose attainment requires the joint resources and effort of those parties.

Suppose that marketing staff want a new product released quickly, whereas engineers want more time to test and add new features. Leaders can potentially reduce this interdepartmental conflict by reminding both groups of the company's mission

Global Connections 11.3

IMPROVING MUTUAL UNDERSTANDING THROUGH LUNCH ROULETTES*

WeWork, the shared workspace company, expanded into Israel and within two years employed more than 100 people in its Tel-Aviv technology group. This rapid growth was exciting for WeWork staff. But as the numbers grew, newcomers increasingly had trouble blending in, informal subgroups were springing up, and some team members had never spoken to one another. The situation might eventually lead to dysfunctional squabbles among employees and their cliques.

"For those that were part of the early team and experienced the close, family-like, relationships of a small group, something started to feel 'off'," recalls software engineer Benny Sitbon. He and a few other early hires began casually thinking of ways to minimize dysfunctional conflict by improving connectedness among staff in their large Tel-Aviv technology group. When someone described "lunch roulette," Sitbon and the others sprang into action.

Lunch roulettes at WeWork's Tel-Aviv technology group are held every second week. Any employee in the technology group can participate (on average, about half of them do). Those who sign up are organized randomly—like a roulette wheel—into lunch groups of three people. To encourage conversation within each trio, Sitbon developed an app in which attendees register for the event and (optionally) briefly state their hobbies and a "talk to me about" category. The app organizes participants a couple of hours before the event and

creates a private space so each luncheon trio can coordinate where to eat and what to order. After several of these events, a survey reported a 66-percent increase in how close employees in the Tel-Aviv technology unit felt to one another.

"Lunch is a great time to talk and get to know one another," says Sitbon. "Although our team is already medium-sized and in hyper-growth, the lunch roulette helps keeping that 'small team' feeling. Not only does this affect our team's happiness, it also improves our collaboration and approachability, and therefore, our efficiency."

©Hero Images/Image Source

* Based on information in: B. Sitbon, "Meet, Eat, Scale, Repeat," *WeWork Technology* (blog), May 29, 2018, https://engineering.wework.com/meet-eat-scale-repeat-b33042383180.

---

to serve customers, or by pointing out that competitors currently threaten sales of the company's existing products. By increasing commitment to corporate-wide goals (customer focus, competitiveness), engineering and marketing employees pay less attention to their competing departmental-level goals, which reduces their perceived conflict with each other.[54]

REDUCE DIFFERENTIATION

Earlier in this chapter, we explained that one of the main sources of workplace conflict is differentiation—differences among people regarding their training, values, beliefs, and experiences. Therefore, reducing differentiation is a logical approach to reducing dysfunctional conflict. As employees develop and recognize more similarities than differences with co-workers in other departments, they increase their

trust in them and are more willing to coordinate activities and resolve their disputes through constructive discussion.[55]

Organizations can reduce differentiation in several ways.[56] One strategy is for employees to have meaningful interaction with people in other groups, such as through temporary assignments to other work units or participation in multidisciplinary projects.[57] A second strategy is to rotate staff to different departments or regions throughout their career. A third strategy is for leaders to build and maintain a strong organizational culture. Employees have shared values and assumptions and a stronger sense of community in a company with a strong culture (see Chapter 14). Each of these strategies creates common experiences or underlying beliefs that increase employee identification with the organization rather than just with a narrow business function, career specialization, or geographic region.

IMPROVE COMMUNICATION AND MUTUAL UNDERSTANDING

A third way to reduce dysfunctional conflict is to give the conflicting parties more opportunities to communicate with and understand each other.[58] These activities don't necessarily reduce differentiation (employees still have divergent beliefs and experiences), but the interaction and discussion may create better awareness of and respect for one another's situation and point of view. This conflict-management strategy can be applied by simply changing physical or reporting arrangements so employees across departments have more occasions to interact with one another. When Telenor, the Norwegian telecommunications company, replaced departmental coffee machines with a few large coffee stations, employees increasingly mingled around these common areas with employees they hadn't previously known.[59] Employees also develop better mutual understanding with people in other departments through lunch-and-learn or poster session gatherings, in which one group summarizes its current projects to co-workers in other groups.

Some companies improve mutual understanding among employees by applying a variation of the Johari Window model (see Chapter 3). In seminars with a trained facilitator, individuals disclose to co-workers information about themselves and their self-perceptions as well as feedback to others about how they are perceived.[60] One excellent example is the full-day intergenerational training program at L'Oréal Canada. The purpose of the session is "to raise awareness of individuals' differing workplace needs as they move through their careers." In one part of the program, for example, employees sit together in their generational cohorts and ask questions to employees in the other cohorts. "Each group is interested and surprised to see what's important to the other group," says a L'Oréal Canada executive who helped develop the seminar.[61]

Where conflicts have escalated, some embattled groups have participated in a deeper version of this process, called *intergroup mirroring*.[62] Led by an external consultant, the conflicting groups separately document their perceptions of: (1) how the group perceives itself, (2) how it perceives the other group, and (3) how the group believes it is perceived by the other group. The "mirroring" stage follows, whereby each group discusses its three sets of perceptions with the other group. The two sides jointly review their relationship problems and establish joint goals and action plans to improve their relationship.

Although communication and mutual understanding can reduce dysfunctional conflict, there are two important warnings. First, these interventions should be applied only where differentiation is not high. If the parties believe they have overwhelming differences, they tend to focus on information during the interaction that reinforces that view.[63] Consequently, dialogue could escalate rather than reduce relationship conflict. The second warning is that people in some cultures are less comfortable with the practice of resolving differences through direct and open dialogue.[64] This approach threatens harmony and loss of face, whereas people in collectivist and high power distance cultures, for example, prefer avoidance, yielding, and compromising to minimize the risk of any manifest conflict.

REDUCE INTERDEPENDENCE

Conflict occurs where people are dependent on one another, so another way to reduce dysfunctional conflict is to minimize the level of interdependence between the parties. Three ways to reduce interdependence among employees and work units are to create buffers, use integrators, and combine jobs.

- *Create buffers.* A buffer is any mechanism that loosens the coupling between two or more people or work units. This decoupling reduces the potential for conflict because the buffer reduces the effect of one party on the other. Building up inventory between people on an assembly line is a buffer, for example, because each employee is less dependent in the short term on the previous person along that line.[65]

- *Use integrators.* Integrators are employees who coordinate the activities of multiple work units toward the completion of a shared task or project.[66] Brand managers, for instance, are responsible for coordinating the efforts of the research, production, advertising, and marketing departments regarding a specific product line. Integrators typically reduce the amount of direct interaction required among these diverse work units. Integrators rarely have direct authority over the departments they integrate, so they must rely on referent power and persuasion to manage conflict and accomplish the work.

- *Combine jobs.* Combining jobs is both a form of job enrichment and a way to reduce task interdependence. Consider a toaster assembly system where one person inserts the heating element, another adds the sides, and so on. By combining these tasks so that each person assembles an entire toaster, the employees now have a pooled rather than sequential form of task interdependence and the likelihood of dysfunctional conflict is reduced.

INCREASE RESOURCES

Resource scarcity is a source of conflict, so increasing the amount of resources available would have the opposite effect.[67] This might not be a feasible strategy for minimizing dysfunctional conflict due to the costs involved. However, these costs need to be compared against the costs of dysfunctional conflict due to the resource scarcity.

CLARIFY RULES AND PROCEDURES

Conflicts that arise from ambiguous rules can be minimized by establishing clear rules and procedures. If two departments are fighting over the use of a new laboratory, a schedule might be established which allocates the lab exclusively to each team at specific times of the day or week.

Third-Party Conflict Resolution

Most of this chapter has focused on people directly involved in a conflict, yet many disputes among employees and departments are resolved with the assistance of a manager, co-worker, or other person outside the dispute. **Third-party conflict resolution** is any attempt by a relatively neutral person to help the parties resolve their differences.[68] There are three main third-party dispute resolution activities: arbitration, inquisition, and mediation. These interventions can be classified by their level of control over the process and control over the decision (see Exhibit 11.5).[69]

third-party conflict resolution
Any attempt by a relatively neutral person to help conflicting parties resolve their differences.

- *Arbitration.* Arbitrators have high control over the final decision, but low control over the process. Executives engage in this strategy by following previously agreed

rules of due process, listening to arguments from the disputing employees, and making a binding decision. Arbitration is applied as the final stage of grievances by unionized employees in many countries, but it is also applied to nonunion conflicts in organizations with formal conflict resolution processes.

- *Inquisition.* Inquisitors control all discussion about the conflict. Like arbitration, the inquisition process has high decision control because it involves choosing the form of conflict resolution. However, it also has high process control because inquisitors choose which information to examine and how to examine it, and they generally decide how the conflict resolution process will be handled.[70]
- *Mediation.* Mediators have high control over the intervention process. In fact, their main purpose is to manage the process and context of interaction between the disputing parties. However, the conflicting parties make the final decision about how to resolve their differences. Thus, mediators have little or no control over the conflict resolution decision.[71]

CHOOSING THE BEST THIRD-PARTY INTERVENTION STRATEGY

Team leaders, executives, and co-workers regularly intervene in workplace disputes. Sometimes they adopt a mediator role; other times they serve as arbitrators. Occasionally, they begin with one approach then switch to another. However, research suggests that managers and other people in positions of authority usually adopt an inquisitional approach

EXHIBIT 11.5   Types of Third-Party Intervention

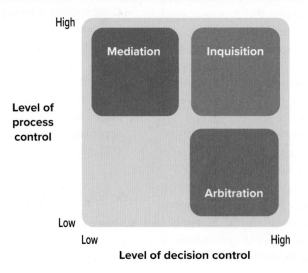

OB by the NUMBERS

Managers as Third-Party Conflict Handlers*

54% of 1,027 employees who recently experienced conflict with a co-worker took the dispute to their supervisor or human resources staff.

47% of 411 New Zealand employees surveyed say that they turn to their manager to help resolve a workplace conflict.

15% is the average percentage of management time that 2,200 U.S. chief financial officers say is "wasted resolving staff personality conflicts."

42% of 1,279 employees surveyed in the U.S. and several other countries say their leader sometimes or never handles workplace conflict effectively.

10% is the average percentage of management time that 270 Canadian chief financial officers say is "wasted resolving staff personality conflicts."

©pathdoc/Shutterstock

*P. Weaver and S. Mitchell, "Lessons for Leaders from the People Who Matter" (Pittsburgh: Development Dimensions International, February 16, 2012); *Conflict in New Zealand Workplaces Study* (Auckland: FairWay Resolution, August 2014); "Clash of the Coworkers (Canada)," News Release (Toronto: Robert Half, March 8, 2017); "Clash Of The Coworkers (U.S.)," News Release (Menlo Park, CA: Accountemps, March 9, 2017); "Co-Worker Conflicts," *Nulab* (blog), October 1, 2019, https://nulab.com/blog/collaboration/co-worker-conflicts/.

whereby they dominate the intervention process as well as make a binding decision.[72] Managers tend to rely on the inquisition approach because it is consistent with the decision-oriented nature of managerial jobs, gives them control over the conflict process and outcome, and tends to resolve disputes efficiently.

However, inquisition is usually the least effective third-party conflict resolution method in organizational settings.[73] One problem is that leaders who take an inquisitional role tend to collect limited information about the problem, so their imposed decision may produce an ineffective solution to the conflict. Another problem is that employees often view inquisitional procedures and outcomes as unfair because they have little control over this approach. In particular, the inquisitional approach potentially violates several procedural justice rules (see Chapter 5).

Which third-party intervention is most appropriate in organizations? The answer partly depends on the situation, such as the type of dispute, the relationship between the manager and employees, and cultural values such as power distance.[74] Also, any third-party approach has more favourable results when it applies the procedural and interactional justice rules described in Chapter 5.[75] Generally, for everyday disagreements between two employees, the mediation approach is usually best because this gives employees more responsibility for resolving their own disputes. The third-party representative merely establishes an appropriate context for conflict resolution. Although not as efficient as other strategies, mediation potentially offers the highest level of employee satisfaction with the conflict process and outcomes.[76] When employees cannot resolve their differences through mediation, arbitration seems to work best because the predetermined rules of evidence and other processes create a higher sense of procedural fairness.[77] Arbitration is also preferred where the organization's goals should take priority over individual goals.

©flairmicro/123RF

Employees at Morning Star Company can't rely on their boss to settle disagreements because there aren't any bosses at the California tomato processing company. Instead, two employees who can't resolve their conflict invite another co-worker to mediate the situation and possibly recommend a solution. If either co-worker in the disagreement still isn't satisfied, then a panel or several co-workers in the affected work setting is established to review and arbitrate the conflict. Almost all disputes are resolved by this stage. But in rare instances, the matter can be brought to the attention of Morning Star's president, who either makes—or designates an arbitrator to make—a binding final decision. "When a panel of peers gets convened, people can see that the process is fair and reasonable," explains Morning Star founder Chris Rufer. "Everyone knows they have recourse."*

* G. Hamel, "First, Let's Fire All the Managers," *Harvard Business Review* 89, no. 12 (2011): 48–60; D. Kirkpatrick, "Self-Management's Success at Morning Star," *T&D,* October 2013, 25–27; "Morning Star: Colleague Principles," The Morning Star Company–About Us, accessed March 14, 2020, http://www.morningstarco.com/about-us/colleague-principles.html.

Resolving Conflict through Negotiation

LO6

Think back through yesterday's events. Maybe you had to reach consensus with other students about what tasks to complete for a team project. Chances are you shared transportation with someone, so you had to agree on the timing of the ride. Then perhaps there was the question of who made dinner. Each of these daily events created potential conflict and, most likely, they were resolved through negotiation.

Negotiation occurs when interdependent parties with divergent beliefs or goals attempt to reach

negotiation The process in which interdependent parties with divergent beliefs or goals attempt to reach agreement on issues that mutually affect them.

agreement on issues that mutually affect them. In other words, people negotiate when they need to work together (mutual dependence), need to reach a consensus on decisions that affect them, and initially don't have identical preferences regarding those decisions.[78] This definition highlights the fact that negotiation skills are vital in organizations and everyday life because they help us achieve our goals, reduce conflict, and build collaborative relationships.[79] In this section, we identify many of the strategies and conditions that effective negotiators consider in organizational and other settings.

DISTRIBUTIVE VERSUS INTEGRATIVE APPROACHES TO NEGOTIATION

Earlier in this chapter, we noted that some conflict-handling styles adopt a win–lose orientation—the view that one party necessarily loses when the other party gains. In negotiations, this is called the *distributive* approach because the negotiator believes those involved in the conflict must distribute portions from a fixed pie. The opposing view is a win–win orientation, known as the *integrative* or *mutual gains* approach to negotiations. This approach exists when negotiators believe the resources at stake are expandable rather than fixed if the parties work creatively together to find a solution.

When do negotiators adopt a distributive or integrative approach to negotiations? The actual situation is a key factor. Distributive negotiation is most common when the parties have only one item to resolve, such as product price or starting salary. Integrative negotiation is more common when multiple issues are open for discussion. Multiple issues provide greater opportunity for mutual gains because each issue or element in the negotiation has different value to each party.

Consider the example of a buyer who wants to pay a low price for several dozen manufactured items from a seller, doesn't need the entire order at once, but does need the payment schedule spread over time due to limited cash flow. The seller would like the buyer to pay a high price, but also values steady production to minimize overtime and layoffs. Through negotiation, the parties learn that spreading out the delivery schedule benefits both of them, and that the buyer would agree to a higher price if payments could be spread out with the delivery schedule.

Negotiators usually begin with a cautiously integrative approach to negotiations, but they switch to a distributive approach when they realize that their interests are perfectly opposing. Another factor is the individual's personality and past experience. Some people have a natural tendency to be competitive and think more distributively whereas others more frequently believe that conflicts can result in mutual gains.

PREPARING TO NEGOTIATE

Preparation is essential for successful negotiations.[80] You can't resolve disagreements unless you know what you want, why you want it, and what power you have to get it. You also need to anticipate the other party for each of these factors.

Develop Goals and Understand Needs

Successful negotiators develop *goals* about what they want to achieve from the exchange. Equally important, they reflect on what *needs* they are trying to fulfil from those goals. The distinction between goals and needs is important because specific needs can be satisfied by different goals. For example, an employee might negotiate for a promotion (a goal), but what the employee really desires is more status and interesting work (underlying needs). Effective negotiators try to understand their own needs and avoid becoming locked into fixed goals. Focusing on needs enables negotiators to actively consider different proposals and opportunities, some of which could fulfil their needs better than their original negotiation goals. Preparation also includes anticipating the other party's goals and their underlying needs, based on available information before negotiation sessions begin.

Negotiators engage in a form of goal setting that identifies the three key positions shown in the bargaining zone model (see Exhibit 11.6).[81] This linear diagram depicts a purely distributive approach to negotiation because it illustrates that one side's gain will be the other's loss. Complex bargaining zone models can depict situations where mutual gains are possible. Also, keep in mind that these positions and other aspects of the negotiation process are ultimately subjective, malleable, and influenced by perceptual distortions.[82]

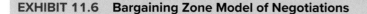

EXHIBIT 11.6   Bargaining Zone Model of Negotiations

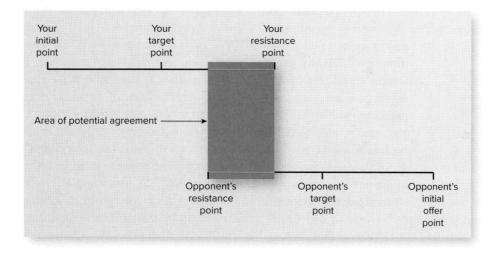

The *initial offer point*—each party's opening offer to the other side—requires careful consideration because it can influence the negotiation outcome. If the initial offer is set higher—but not outrageously higher—than the other party expects, it can anchor the negotiation at a higher point along the range by reframing the other party's perception of what is considered a "high" or "low" demand (see anchoring and adjustment in Chapter 7).[83] In other words, a high initial offer point can potentially move the outcome closer to your target point; it may even cause the other side to lower its resistance point.

Suppose that a prospective employer thinks you would ask no more than $60,000 for an annual salary, but your initial request is for $72,000. This request may change the employer's perception of a high salary to the extent that, after some negotiation activity, the company is comfortable with the final agreement of $65,000. The challenge is to avoid an initial offer that is set so high that the other party breaks off negotiations or becomes highly mistrustful.

The *target point* is your realistic goal or expectation for a final agreement. This position must consider alternative strategies to achieve those objectives and test underlying assumptions about the situation.[84] Negotiators who set high, specific target points usually obtain better outcomes than those with low or vague target points. In this respect, a target point needs to possess the same characteristics as effective goal setting (see Chapter 5). Unfortunately, perceptual distortions cause inexperienced negotiators to form overly optimistic expectations, which can only be averted through careful reflection of the facts.

Know Your BATNA and Power

The *resistance point* in the bargaining zone model is the point beyond which you will make no further concessions and walk away from the negotiations. How do you determine the resistance point? The answer requires thoughtful comparison of how your goals and needs might be achieved through some other means. This comparison is called the **best alternative to a negotiated agreement (BATNA)**.[85] BATNA estimates your power in the negotiation because it represents the estimated cost to you of walking away from the relationship. If sources outside the current negotiation are willing to negotiate with you, then you have a high BATNA because it would cost you very little to walk away from the current negotiation.

best alternative to a negotiated agreement (BATNA) The best outcome you might achieve through some other course of action if you abandon the current negotiation.

Having more than one BATNA to a negotiation increases your power. A common problem, however, is that people tend to overestimate their BATNA.[86] They wrongly believe there are plenty of other ways to achieve their objective rather than through this specific negotiation. Wise advice here is to actively investigate multiple alternatives, not just the current negotiation. For instance, if you are searching for a new job, make specific inquiries at a few organizations. This may give you a more realistic idea of your BATNA, in particular, how much your talents are in demand and what employers are willing to offer for those talents.

Your power in the negotiation depends on the sources and contingencies of power discussed in Chapter 10. For example, you have more power to negotiate a better starting salary and job conditions if you have valued skills that few other people possess (high expertise with low substitutability), the employer knows that you possess these talents (high visibility), and the company will experience costs or lost opportunities fairly quickly if this position is not filled soon (high centrality). Not surprisingly, BATNA tends to be higher for those with favourable sources and contingencies of power, because they would be in demand in the marketplace.

THE NEGOTIATION PROCESS

The negotiation process is a complex human interaction that draws on many topics in this book, including perceptions, attitudes, motivation, decision making, and communication. The most important specific negotiation practices are to gather information, manage concessions, manage time, and build the relationship.

Gather Information

Information is the cornerstone of effective negotiations.[87] It helps you to discover the other party's needs hidden behind their stated offers and negotiation goals. Some types of information reveal the other party's resistance point. Information can also potentially transform distributive negotiations into integrative negotiations by discovering multiple dimensions that weren't previously considered. For example, a simple negotiation over salary may reveal that the employee would prefer more performance-based pay and less fixed salary. Thus, mutual gains may be possible because there is now more than one variable to negotiate. Information is even more important in integrative negotiations, because the parties require knowledge of each other's needs to discover solutions that maximize benefits for both sides.

Information sharing is essential in all negotiations, but it also comes with risks. The information you offer gives the other party more power to leverage a better deal if the opportunity occurs.[88] Skilled negotiators address this dilemma by adopting a cautious problem-solving style at the outset. They begin by sharing information slowly and determining whether the other side will reciprocate. In this way, they try to establish trust with the other party.

©lipik/Shutterstock

Effective negotiators gather information by listening more than talking, as well as by encouraging the other party to reveal more information. "It's not just listening, but it's understanding how to get them to talk more," says former FBI hostage negotiator, Chris Voss. One effective strategy used by the FBI is verbal *mirroring*—repeating back as a question the last few words of what the other person said. If the opponent says "I need to receive your shipment within the next month," you would mirror by asking "I'm sorry, within the next month?" This usually motivates the other person to explain further. "By repeating back what people say, you trigger this mirroring instinct and your counterpart will inevitably elaborate on what was just said and sustain the process of connecting," Voss explains.*

* C. Voss and T. Raz, *Never Split the Difference: Negotiating as If Your Life Depended on It* (Random House, 2016), Chap. 2; C. Clifford, "Ex FBI Negotiator Chris Voss: How to Get What You Want," *CNBC*, October 16, 2017.

Skilled negotiators heed the advice of the late management guru Stephen Covey: "Seek first to understand, then to be understood."[89] They spend most of the negotiation time listening closely to the other party and asking for details. In contrast, inexperienced negotiators mainly talk to the other side about their arguments and justifications. Skilled negotiators draw out more details by presenting open-ended questions, followed by probe questions ("Oh, why is that?"). Nonverbal communication is also observed as an associated source of information during this dialogue.

Skilled negotiators also test how well they understand the other side's facts and position by summarizing the information presented and by asking for clarification on specific points. Furthermore, they gather information by communicating their inner thoughts and feelings about what the other party has said. This practice does not present arguments or proposals. Instead, by reflecting on their own feelings, negotiators encourage the other party to provide further information that will help dissolve concerns ("What you just said

makes me hopeful, but I'm still uncertain about how it would work specifically in our organization.").[90]

Manage Concessions

A concession is one party's revision of a negotiating position so it comes closer to the other party's current position. Successful negotiators actually make fewer concessions and each concession is smaller than those of average negotiators, particularly in distributive negotiations where both parties know the bargaining zone.[91] Even so, the process of making concessions is important to all parties.[92]

Concessions are a form of communication because they signal to the other party the relative importance of each issue being negotiated. Concessions also symbolize each party's motivation to bargain in good faith. In fact, an important feature of negotiations is that each party reciprocates when the other side makes a concession.[93] Ultimately, concessions are necessary for the parties to move toward the area of agreement. Concessions need to be clearly labeled as such and should be accompanied by an expectation that the other party will reciprocate. They should also be offered in instalments because people experience more positive emotions from a few smaller concessions than from one large concession.[94] Generally, the best strategy is to be moderately tough and give just enough concessions to communicate sincerity and motivation to resolve the conflict.

A key objective of concessions is to discover and signal which issues are more and less important to each side. One way to figure out the relative importance of the issues to each party is to make multi-issue offers rather than discuss one issue at a time.[95] You might offer a client a specific price, delivery date, and guarantee period, for example. The other party's counteroffer signals which of the multiple items are more and which are less important to them. Your subsequent concessions similarly signal how important each issue is to your group.

Manage Time

Negotiators make more concessions as the deadline gets closer.[96] This can be a liability if you are under time pressure, or it can be an advantage if the other party alone is under time pressure. Negotiators with more power in the relationship sometimes apply time pressure through an "exploding offer" whereby they give their opponent a very short time to accept their offer.[97] These time-limited offers are frequently found in consumer sales ("On sale today only!") and in some job offers. They produce time pressure, which can motivate the other party to accept the offer and forfeit the opportunity to explore their BATNA. Another time factor is that the more time people have invested in the negotiation, the more committed they become to ensuring an agreement is reached. This commitment increases the tendency to make additional concessions not originally planned so that the negotiations do not fail.

Build the Relationship

Building and maintaining trust is important in all negotiations.[98] In purely distributive negotiation situations, trust keeps the parties focused on the issue rather than personalities, motivates them to return to the bargaining table when negotiations stall, and encourages the parties to engage in future negotiations. Trust is also critical in integrative negotiations because it motivates the parties to share information and actively search for mutual gains.

How do you build trust in negotiations? One approach is to discover common backgrounds and interests, such as places you have lived, favourite hobbies and sports teams, and so forth. If there are substantial differences between the parties (age, gender, etc.), consider including team members that more closely match the backgrounds of the other party. First impressions are also important. Recall from earlier chapters

in this book that people attach emotions to incoming stimuli in a fraction of a second. Therefore, you need to be sensitive to your nonverbal cues, appearance, and initial statements.

Signalling trustworthiness also helps strengthen the relationship. We can do this by demonstrating that we are reliable, will keep our promises, and have shared goals and values with the other party in the negotiation. Trustworthiness also increases by developing a shared understanding of the negotiation process, including its norms and expectations about speed and timing.[99] Finally, relationship building demands emotional intelligence.[100] This includes managing the emotions you display to the other party, particularly avoiding an image of superiority, aggressiveness, or insensitivity. Emotional intelligence also involves managing the other party's emotions. We can use well-placed flattery, humour, and other methods to keep everyone in a good mood and to break unnecessary tension.[101]

THE NEGOTIATION SETTING

The effectiveness of negotiating depends to some extent on the environment in which the negotiations occur. Three key situational factors are location, physical setting, and audience.

Location

It is easier to negotiate on your own turf because you are familiar with the negotiating environment and are able to maintain comfortable routines.[102] Also, there is no need to cope with travel-related stress or depend on others for resources during the negotiation. Of course, you can't walk out of negotiations as easily when the event occurs on your own turf, but this is usually a minor issue. Considering the strategic benefits of home turf, many negotiators agree to neutral territory. Phone calls, videoconferences, email, and other forms of information technology potentially avoid territorial issues, but skilled negotiators usually prefer the media richness and social presence of face-to-face meetings. Frank Lowy, co-founder of retail property giant Westfield Group, says that telephones are "too cold" for negotiating. "From a voice I don't get all the cues I need. I go by touch and feel and I need to see the other person."[103]

Physical Setting

The physical distance between the parties and formality of the setting can influence their orientation toward each other and the disputed issues. So can the seating arrangements. People who sit face to face are more likely to develop a win–lose orientation toward the conflict situation. In contrast, some negotiation groups deliberately intersperse participants around the table to convey a win–win orientation. Others arrange the seating so that both parties face a whiteboard, reflecting the notion that both parties face the same problem or issue.

Global Connections 11.4

REDUCING THE GENDER WAGE GAP THROUGH NEGOTIATION SKILLS*

Susanne Smith (not her real name) was shocked to discover that two male co-workers earned almost double her salary. The web developer worried that confronting her boss about a pay raise would backfire, but she took that chance and was given a 20 percent increase (still well below her male co-workers). Smith had accepted whatever salary was offered when she was hired whereas her male co-workers had negotiated a higher pay deal. "I was like the bargain-basement candidate that didn't bother to negotiate," she says.

Studies report that, compared to men, women are less willing to negotiate, have lower target points, and give more concessions. One recent survey reported that only 31 percent of Canadian female employees tried to negotiate a higher salary in their latest job offer, compared to 40 percent of male employees. The difference was even more striking in the parallel American survey, where 66 percent of men said they tried to negotiate a better pay deal compared to 46 percent of women.

The lack of motivation or skill among women to negotiate better pay doesn't justify the insidious gender pay gap. But some women realize that, until employers become more gender neutral in pay setting, negotiation is one reason why they are paid less than men. "I was annoyed that some of my former employers failed to proactively close the gender pay gap, and was envious of certain men, especially less-qualified colleagues, who knew how to talk their way to the top," complains

a female senior business news writer for a major Canadian newspaper. "But most of all, I was angry at myself for accepting less than I deserved."

Several Canadian organizations have introduced workshops that help women to negotiate more effectively, particularly in male-dominated situations. For instance, the Women's Initiatives for Safer Environments (WISE) sponsors Women on Wheels workshops in Ottawa, which teach female participants minor vehicle repairs and how to negotiate more effectively when buying a vehicle. "Many women felt uncomfortable in that world of negotiation," observes WISE program director Elsy David.

©Morsa/Digital Vision/Getty Images

*I. Caputo, "When It Comes to Negotiating Salaries, Women Face Traps That Men Don't," *Boston Globe,* April 24, 2016, R30; R. Trichur, "Amplify: How I Learned to Negotiate for What I Need and Deserve," *Globe & Mail,* September 28, 2018; "Auto Repair Workshop 1st Stop for Women on Journey from Violence," *CBC News-Radio Morning (Ottawa),* August 25, 2019; "More Than Half Of Workers Negotiated Pay With Last Job Offer, Survey Finds," News Release (Menlo Park, Calif.: Robert Half, February 19, 2020); "Are Canadian Workers Selling Themselves Short? Only One-Third Negotiated Pay With Last Job Offer, Survey Finds," News Release (Toronto: Robert Half, February 18, 2020).

Audience Characteristics

Most negotiators have audiences—anyone with a vested interest in the negotiation outcomes, such as executives, other team members, or the general public. Negotiators tend to act differently when their audience observes the negotiation or has detailed information about the process, compared to situations in which the audience sees only the end results.[104] When the audience has direct surveillance over the proceedings, negotiators tend to be more competitive, less willing to make concessions, and more likely to engage in assertive tactics against the other party. This "hard-line" behaviour shows the audience that the negotiator is working for their interests. With their audience watching, negotiators also have more interest in saving face.

GENDER AND NEGOTIATION

When negotiating, women tend to have poorer economic outcomes than do men.[105] On average, women are less keen to negotiate and less mindful of situations where negotiation can or should occur. When they do negotiate, women often set lower personal target points and are more likely to accept offers just above their resistance points. Men typically set high target points and push to get a deal as close to their target point as possible. Women are also less likely than men to use alternatives to improve their outcomes. One explanation for these differences is that women give higher priority than men to interpersonal relations in the exchange. This is consistent with why there are gender differences in conflict-handling styles, discussed earlier in this chapter. Giving more concessions and even avoiding the negotiation process altogether (accepting the salary offered when hired) are ways that women try to maintain good relations.

Gender differences in negotiation outcomes are not just due to abilities and motivation, however. Women are often treated worse than men by the opposing negotiators.[106] They are also more likely to be deceived by the other party and to receive less generous offers for the same job or product. For instance, men and women in one study visited a used-car lot and asked about the price of one of the cars. The car dealer quoted a lower price to men than to women—for the same car. A second problem is that female negotiators who use effective negotiation tactics—such as making fewer and smaller concessions—are viewed less favourably by the opposing negotiator than when men use these tactics. This reaction likely occurs because some effective negotiation activities violate female stereotypes, so women are viewed as more aggressive than men doing exactly the same thing. The result is that the other negotiator becomes less trustful and engages in more aggressive tactics.

Fortunately, women perform as well as men in negotiations when they receive training and gain experience. Women also negotiate well when the situation signals that negotiation is expected, such as when a job opening states that the salary is negotiable. Another factor that improves negotiation outcomes for women is how well they know the expected bargaining range. For example, women negotiate a better starting salary when they research the salary range for that position. "I was able to come to the table knowing what my value should be because I had done research," says a female executive at a large finance and insurance services company who had reviewed industry salary survey data.[107]

Chapter Summary

LO1

Define conflict and debate its positive and negative consequences in the workplace.

Conflict is the process in which one party perceives that its interests are being opposed or negatively affected by another party. The earliest view of conflict was that it was dysfunctional for organizations. Even today, we recognize that conflict sometimes or to some degree consumes productive time, increases stress and job dissatisfaction, discourages coordination and resource sharing, undermines customer service, fuels organizational politics, and undermines team cohesion. But conflict can also be beneficial. It is known to motivate more active thinking about problems and possible solutions, encourage more active monitoring of the organization in its environment, and improve team cohesion (where the conflict source is external).

LO2

Distinguish task conflict from relationship conflict and describe three strategies to minimize relationship conflict during task conflict episodes.

Task conflict occurs when people focus their discussion around the issue while showing respect for people with other points of view. Relationship conflict exists when people focus their discussion on qualities of the people in the dispute; that is, they view each other, rather than the issue, as the source of conflict. It is apparent when people attack each other's credibility, assert their superior status, and display aggression toward the other party. It is difficult to separate task from relationship conflict. However, three strategies or conditions that minimize relationship conflict during constructive debate are emotional intelligence of the participants, team development, and norms that support psychological safety (a shared belief that it is safe to engage in interpersonal risk-taking).

LO3

Diagram the conflict process model and describe six structural sources of conflict in organizations.

The conflict process model begins with the six structural sources of conflict: incompatible goals, differentiation (different values and beliefs), interdependence, scarce resources, ambiguous rules, and communication problems. These sources lead one or more parties to perceive a conflict and to experience conflict emotions. This produces manifest conflict, such as behaviours toward the other side. The conflict process often escalates through a series of episodes.

LO4

Outline the five conflict-handling styles and discuss the circumstances in which each would be most appropriate.

There are five known conflict-handling styles: problem solving, forcing, avoiding, yielding, and compromising. People who use problem solving have a win–win orientation. Others, particularly forcing, assume a win–lose orientation. In general, people gravitate toward one or two preferred conflict-handling styles that match their personality, personal and cultural values, and past experience.

The best style depends on the situation. Problem solving is best when interests are not perfectly opposing, the parties trust each other, and the issues are complex. Forcing works best when the dispute requires quick action, your position is logically and morally stronger, and the other party would take advantage of a cooperative style. Avoiding is preferred when the conflict has become emotional, there is strong incentive to maintain harmony, or the cost of resolution outweighs the benefits. Yielding works well when the issue is less important to you, the value or logic of your position is less clear, the parties want to maintain harmony, and the other party has substantially more power. Compromising is preferred when there is a single issue (not complex) with opposing interests, the parties are under time pressure, they want to maintain harmony, and they have equal power.

LO5

Apply the six structural approaches to conflict management and describe the three types of third-party dispute resolution.

Conflict can be managed through six structural strategies. One of these is to increase the parties' commitment to superordinate goals— goals that the conflicting employees or departments value and whose attainment requires the joint resources and effort of those parties. Another method is to reduce differentiation between the conflicting parties, such as by temporarily assigning employees to other work units, rotating employees across the organization throughout their career, and building a strong organizational culture. A third method is to improve communication and mutual understanding. This can occur by designing workspaces such that diverse groups coincidentally mingle, engaging in seminars that apply Johari Window principles across groups, and through intergroup mirroring interventions. Fourth, conflict can be minimized by reducing interdependence, such as by creating buffers, using integrators, or combining jobs. The final two structural approaches to conflict management involve increasing resources and clarifying rules and procedures.

Third-party conflict resolution is any attempt by a relatively neutral person to help the parties resolve their differences. The three main forms of third-party dispute resolution are mediation, arbitration, and inquisition. Managers tend to use an inquisition approach, though mediation and arbitration often are more appropriate, depending on the situation.

LO6

Discuss activities in the negotiation preparation, process, and setting that improve negotiation effectiveness.

Negotiation occurs when interdependent parties with divergent beliefs or goals attempt to reach agreement on issues that mutually affect them. Distributive negotiation is most common when the parties have only one item to resolve, such as product price or starting salary. Integrative negotiation is more common when multiple issues are open for discussion. Effective negotiators engage in several preparation activities. These include determining their initial, target, and resistance positions; understanding their needs behind these goals; and knowing their alternatives to the negotiation (BATNA).

During the negotiation process, effective negotiators devote more attention to gathering than giving information. They try to determine the other party's underlying needs rather than just their stated positions. They make fewer and smaller concessions, but use concessions strategically to discover the other party's priorities and to maintain trust. They try to avoid time traps (negotiating under deadlines set by the other side), and they engage in practices to maintain a positive relationship with the other party. Characteristics of the setting—including location, physical setting, and audience characteristics—are also important in successful negotiations.

Key Terms

best alternative to a negotiated agreement (BATNA)
conflict
negotiation
psychological safety
relationship conflict

superordinate goals
task conflict
third-party conflict resolution
win–lose orientation
win–win orientation

Critical Thinking Questions

1. Distinguish task conflict from relationship conflict and explain how to engage in task conflict with minimal levels of relationship conflict.

2. The CEO of Creative Toys Inc. read about cooperation in Japanese companies and vowed to bring this same philosophy to his company. His goal is to avoid all conflict, so that employees will work cooperatively and be happier at Creative Toys. Discuss the merits and limitations of the CEO's policy.

3. Conflict among managers emerged soon after a French company acquired a Swedish firm. The Swedes perceived the French management as hierarchical and arrogant, whereas the French thought the Swedes were naive, cautious, and lacking an achievement orientation. Identify the source(s) of conflict that best explain this

conflict, and describe ways to reduce dysfunctional conflict in this situation.

4. You have just been transferred from one unit of the organization to another unit. On the last day of work in the first unit, your current manager calls your new manager, informing her that you are a tough candidate and that you possess an attitude. The would-be manager calls you, providing you with the information, and expresses apprehension. How would you resolve this conflict?

5. You are a special assistant to the commander-in-chief of a peacekeeping mission to a war-torn part of the world. The unit consists of a few thousand peacekeeping troops from Canada, France, India, and four other countries. The troops will work together for approximately one year. What strategies would you recommend to improve

mutual understanding and minimize conflict among these troops?

6. The chief operating officer (COO) has noticed that production employees in the company's Mexican manufacturing operations are unhappy with some of the production engineering decisions made by engineers in the company's headquarters in Toronto. At the same time, the engineers complain that production employees aren't applying their engineering specifications correctly and don't understand why those specifications were put in place. The COO believes that the best way to resolve this conflict is to have a frank and open discussion between some of the engineers and employees representing the Mexican production crew. This open-dialogue approach worked well recently among managers in the company's Toronto headquarters, so it should work equally well between the engineers and production staff. Based on your knowledge of communication and mutual understanding as a way to resolve conflict, discuss the COO's proposal.

7. Describe the inquisitional approach to resolve disputes between employees or work units. Discuss its

appropriateness in organizational settings, including the suitability of its use with a multigenerational workforce.

8. Jane has just been appointed as purchasing manager of Tacoma Technologies Inc. The previous purchasing manager, who recently retired, was known for his "winner-take-all" approach to suppliers. He continually fought for more discounts and was skeptical about any special deals that suppliers would propose. A few suppliers refused to do business with Tacoma Technologies, but senior management was confident that the former purchasing manager's approach minimized the company's costs. Jane wants to try a more collaborative approach for working with suppliers. Will her approach work? How should she adopt a more collaborative approach in future negotiations with suppliers?

9. Laura is about to renegotiate her job role with her new manager. She has heard through the grapevine that he is a tough negotiator, highly competitive, and unwilling to take others' needs into consideration. She has also heard that even if he gives concessions in the negotiation, he often fails to keep his word. If you were Laura, how would you prepare for this negotiation?

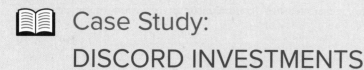

Case Study:
DISCORD INVESTMENTS

by Steven L. McShane, University of Newcastle (Australia)

Discord Investments didn't expect so much conflict when the regional brokerage firm brought in a global information technology (IT) consulting firm to implement a new client/server network. Discord had no plans to outsource its information systems activities, yet the investment firm's own IT employees were worried that they would be replaced or transferred to the consulting firm after the hardware installation was completed. This risk made them somewhat reluctant to provide details about Discord's operations that the consultants needed to do their jobs effectively.

"Why should we tell them what we know and end up losing our jobs or, at best, getting outsourced to some unknown outfit?" Discord's IT employees privately warned each other. The consultants sensed this reluctance, but the Discord employees kept their concerns to themselves.

Scheduling was another source of disagreement between Discord's IT staff and the external consultants. Each week, the consultants flew in from other cities to Discord's offices, typically working 12-hour days, Monday through Thursday, then flew back to their home cities on Friday. Discord's employees lived close to the company's offices and worked Monday to Friday with regular hours, usually 9 to 5 with one or two hours of flexibility around those times. The

consultants raised concerns that the project would be delayed by Discord's IT staff if they did not adjust to the consultants' schedule during the two or three months that the consultants were on-site. The employees complained because the consultants' schedule would mean significant disruption to their usual nonwork life, such as attending evening school events, spending time with family, or participating in sports and other social activities during the week.

Finally, the most serious disagreement broke out regarding who should lead the project— the Discord IT managers or the external consultants? Discord's top executives tried to quell the dispute by giving the leadership role to the consultants, but this decision simply added to the tension. The problem was that Discord's IT people would be responsible for the system long after the external consultants were gone, so they felt somewhat trapped by the consultants' power.

Discussion Questions

1. Identify and explain the main source(s) of conflict in this case.

2. What actions should the organization take immediately and for future consulting interventions to manage the conflict more effectively?

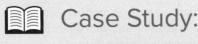

Case Study:
CONFLICT-HANDLING INCIDENTS

by Steven L. McShane, University of Newcastle (Australia)

Purpose This exercise is designed to help you understand the factors to consider when choosing the preferred conflict-handling styles in organizational settings.

Instructions

Step 1: Participants will read each of the three incidents presented below and select the most appropriate response from among the five alternatives for each incident.

Step 2 (Optional): The instructor may ask each student to complete the Conflict-Handling Style Scale (available in Connect if assigned by the instructor) or a similar instrument. This instrument will provide an estimate of your preferred conflict-handling style.

Step 3: As a class, students identify their top two responses from the five provided. They discuss the situational factors they took into account in making those selections.

Step 4 (Optional): Students will compare their responses to the three incidents with their results from the conflict-handling self-assessment. Discussion will focus on the extent to which each person's preferred conflict-handling style influenced their alternatives in this activity, and the implications of this style preference for managing conflict in organizations.

INCIDENT #1

Setting You work as a sonographer for a company that owns a dozen imaging diagnostics clinics in a major city. A sonographer is a medical professional who uses ultrasound medical equipment to create images for medical diagnostics. You are assigned to several clinics, working at each clinic for a few days or a week. You typically rotate across four clinics closest to your home, but occasionally are assigned to one of the company's other eight clinics in the city. Each day, the clinic assigns each of its half-dozen sonographers to a specific consulting room and they receive patients who have been pre-booked by the clinic administrative staff. The company owns more than one brand and model of ultrasound equipment (GE, Toshiba, Siemens, Philips, etc.), so some rooms have different equipment. Each ultrasound machine has similar functions, but staff tend to have more experience with and preferences for one model than for others. Also, some machines are easier to use for some purposes (e.g., scanning, video imaging) or have more modern controls or displays.

On this particular day, you are assigned to a clinic where you have worked only a few times in the past. As you enter your assigned consulting room, you see another sonographer already preparing the equipment for the day's use. The sonographer explains that she decided to use this room because she doesn't like the ultrasound equipment in the room assigned to her. She claims that the clinic rarely assigns her to that other consulting room. She says that you can take the consulting room she was assigned. At that point, she turns away to continue her equipment preparation. You are able to work on the equipment in the other consulting room, although it is not your favourite machine, either. Also, you notice from your appointment sheet that one patient today requires a special type of scan that is much more difficult to complete using the equipment in the other room than in the room to which you were assigned. You barely know the other sonographer. She seemed somewhat presumptuous in casually taking your assigned room, but wasn't aggressive or threatening in her statements. She works frequently at this clinic whereas you are seldom assigned to this clinic. You believe that the clinic management is indifferent regarding who is assigned to each consulting room.

Action Alternatives for Incident #1 Please indicate your first (1) and second (2) choices from among the following alternatives by writing the appropriate number in the space provided.

Action Alternative	Ranking (1st & 2nd)
1. You tell the other sonographer that she must return to her assigned room or trade rooms with another sonographer. If she refuses, you state that you will ask the clinic manager to enforce the room assignment.	_____
2. You politely tell the other sonographer that as a favour to her, you will let her use the consulting room that you were assigned (and she has taken).	_____
3. Given that there is a half hour before the clinic opens, you ask the sonographer to spend a few minutes discussing her needs and preferences to determine if there is some solution on the consulting room or ultrasound equipment that will benefit both of you.	_____
4. You tell the sonographer that she can have the consulting room you were assigned for most of the day, but must swap rooms with you when you have appointments that are much better served by the equipment in this room.	_____
5. Without saying anything, you walk away from the consulting room you were assigned and work in the room assigned to the other sonographer. Later, you make some excuse (such as long driving distance) to the company's central administration to explain why they should not assign you to this clinic in future.	_____

INCIDENT #2

Setting You are district manager responsible for eight salespeople in one region of a national manufacturer and wholesaler of building supplies products. You and fourteen other district sales managers report directly to the company's national sales director, who is located at headquarters in another city. You were promoted to this job almost two years ago and have become increasingly frustrated with the national sales director's ambiguity regarding several key sales management decisions. The director tells district managers that they are empowered to make decisions regarding common sales issues, such as bulk buying deals, addressing customer complaints, and allocating the sales staff training budget. Yet, without warning, the director tends to step in and reverse some of your decisions (and apparently decisions of other district managers). These interventions do not appear to be consistent with any underlying rationale or policy, and the director's explanations for these actions are equally obtuse.

You have learned from others as well as some personal observations that the national sales director sometimes becomes testy when someone disagrees with his views. The director generally treats his district sales managers fairly over the long term, but he can be briefly vindictive if a direct report questions his wisdom. So far, you have only asked the sales director politely to explain why he reversed a few of the decisions. However, this is becoming an important issue to you because the director's actions are making it difficult to make decisions. Also, some direct reports feel less confident about whether your decisions will remain long enough so they can plan their work. You are known for performing your job well, but the sales director does not view your performance any better than that of most other district sales managers.

Action Alternatives for Incident #2 Please indicate your first (1) and second (2) choices from among the following alternatives by writing the appropriate number in the space provided.

Action Alternative	Ranking (1st & 2nd)
1. You decide not to raise this matter with the national sales director because the disagreement is not worth the risk to your career. Instead, you frequently remind your sales staff that your decisions might be reversed by the director.	_____
2. You arrange a meeting with the director and insist that you should have clear decision control over specific district sales decisions. If the director wants to reverse any decision, you explain that he should first speak to you and reach mutual agreement before the decision is reversed.	_____
3. You speak to the director about his tendency to reverse decisions. You suggest that he can reverse decisions on specific matters where a change in decision is less disruptive (such as training budget allocation) but will not interfere with other types of district sales manager decisions (such as addressing customer complaints).	_____
4. You meet with the director to discuss the issue of having decisions reversed. You ask the director to think of ways that would allow you to make decisions without the director feeling the need to reverse some of them.	_____
5. You try to minimize the risk of having your decisions reversed by delaying making decisions that you think are at higher risk of being reversed by the director, even though you eventually need to act on these matters.	_____

INCIDENT #3

Setting You are the manager responsible for operational analysis at a national company that processes citrus fruit into juices, concentrates, oils and essences, pulp cells, and dried fruit. The company has several processing plants and specific measurement metrics are applied to determine their efficiency and effectiveness. The company's executive team increasingly relies on your quarterly report and other analyses you provide to make important decisions regarding future investments, product changes, budgets, and so forth. In fact, your ability to provide timely, high-quality operational performance information has raised your reputation and influence in the organization. Your quarterly reports depend on each production facility to supply you with the raw data identified in a well-developed online reporting system.

As per the established schedule, senior management expects to receive your next quarterly report later this week. However, Ben Estobar, the manager of grapefruit production

at the Florida facility, has not yet submitted key information for you to complete your report. Ben did not reply to your email reminders, so you give him a call. During that conversation, Ben says he is too busy to get the required information within the next couple of days. He explains that his delay for another week or two is due to the busy season for grapefruit processing, even though the data have never been submitted late in the past. You remind Ben that his information is critical to completion of your report, which is vital to senior executive decisions and the company's long-term success. You have a higher position and more seniority in the company than Ben Estobar. Ben is friendly and rarely aggressive in any way, but he has been known to twist facts to make his position look more favourable.

Action Alternatives for Incident #3 Please indicate your first (1) and second (2) choices from among the following alternatives by writing the appropriate number in the space provided.

Action Alternative	Ranking (1st & 2nd)
1. Tell Ben Estobar that you understand his difficult work deadlines, and try to prepare the report by estimating what his data might have been, such as by extrapolating last quarter's numbers.	_____
2. Meet with Ben Estobar and other managers to discover a longer term solution that would almost completely avoid the risk that one or more managers fail to submit the operational data on time.	_____
3. Give Ben Estobar an ultimatum that he must submit the required information by tomorrow afternoon. If he fails to do so, you will ask the chief operating officer (to whom you and Ben Estobar's manager reports) to compel you to provide the operational data this week.	_____
4. Choose a middle ground in which you ask Ben Estobar to send you the most vital information (about half of what is required) and you will use your judgment to fill in the missing information.	_____
5. Ask the senior executive team if they would be willing to have your quarterly report postponed for a week or two, if possible.	_____

 Team Exercise:

KUMQUAT CONFLICT ROLE PLAY

Purpose This exercise is designed to help you understand the dynamics of interpersonal and intergroup conflict, as well as the effectiveness of negotiation strategies in specific conditions.

Materials The instructor will distribute roles for Dr. Rexa, Dr. Chan, and a few observers. Ideally, each negotiation should occur in a private area, away from the other negotiations.

Instructions

Step 1: The instructor will divide the class into an even number of small teams (usually five or six students per team, but larger teams are possible to accommodate larger classes). One student will remove themselves from the team to be an independent observer of that team and the negotiation (e.g., 10 observers if there are 10 teams). One-half of the teams will take the role of Dr. Rexa and the other half will be Dr. Chan.

Step 2: The instructor will describe the activity and read out the statement by Cathal, representative of the farmer's

cooperative that grows the world's only Caismirt Kumquats. The instructor will also state the time frames for preparing the negotiation and the actual negotiation.

Step 3: With teams formed and the instructions read, the instructor will distribute the roles. Members within each team are given a short time (usually 10 minutes), but the instructor may choose another time limit) to learn their roles and decide their negotiating strategy.

Step 4: After reading their roles and discussing strategy, each Dr. Chan team is matched with a Dr. Rexa team and they begin negotiations. Observers will receive observation forms from the instructor, and will watch the paired teams during pre-negotiations and subsequent negotiations.

Step 5: At the end of the exercise, the class will debrief on the negotiations. Observers, negotiators, and the instructor will discuss their observations and experiences and the implications for conflict management and negotiation.

Self-Assessment for Chapter 11

SELF-ASSESSMENT NAME	DESCRIPTION
What is your preferred conflict-handling style?	There are five main conflict-handling styles that people use in response to conflict situations. We are usually most comfortable using one or two of these styles based on our personality, values, self-concept, and past experience. This assessment helps you see what approach you tend to take when dealing with conflict.

CHAPTER 12
Leadership in Organizational Settings

LEARNING OBJECTIVES

After reading this chapter, you should be able to:

LO1 Define leadership and shared leadership.

LO2 Describe the four elements of transformational leadership and explain why they are important for organizational change.

LO3 Compare managerial leadership with transformational leadership, and describe the features of task-oriented, people-oriented, and servant leadership.

LO4 Discuss the elements of path–goal theory and leadership substitutes theory.

LO5 Describe the two components of the implicit leadership perspective.

LO6 Identify eight personal attributes associated with effective leaders and describe authentic leadership.

LO7 Discuss cultural and gender similarities and differences in leadership.

Galvanize may be the sleeping giant among Canada's great technology companies. In less than a decade, CEO Laurie Schultz transformed the Vancouver-headquartered global business from a developer of mature audit software to the leader in cloud-based governance, risk management, and compliance (GRC) software. Equally important, she reshaped the company's culture to one that values employee development and transparency. "We had to disrupt ourselves first in order to get another 30 years of success in our market," says Schultz.

Schultz's leadership has been central to Galvanize's success. In fact, she has been recognized as British Columbia's CEO of the year, EY's entrepreneur of the year, and a WXN Hall of Fame inductee (recognized at least four times as one of Canada's 100 most powerful women). Schultz's leadership combines the vision, communication, and role modelling necessary to transform the organization. She nurtured the vision that

Galvanize CEO Laurie Schultz is recognized as one of Canada's best business leaders due to her vision, role modelling, transparent communication, and personalized support for employees at the Vancouver-based GRC software company.

Photo by Good Side Photo and provided by the Greater Vancouver Board of Trade

Galvanize develops the "operating system of conscious organizations" and that employee development and engagement should be the main drivers of the company's future growth.

Schultz's transformational leadership has a unique personalized touch that builds employee commitment. "Always reject the notion that the C-suite needs to be at arm's length from employees to be effective leaders," Schultz advises. "If you can be accessible by being human and being vulnerable and by leading by example, by being there in the hallways as if you're one of the team, I think you're going to get way more brilliant ideas and you're going to get way more people putting up their hand to take risks."

Furthermore, says Schultz, leaders need to know their personal values and live those values in their decisions and behaviour. This includes "walking away from things when there's a values breach or a values disconnect," she warns. "The message there I would give to folks is: never, ever stay somewhere where you fall out of alignment with values. Life's too short to do that."[1]

The transformation of Galvanize illustrates how Laurie Schultz and other leaders make a difference in an organization's survival and success. This opening case study also highlights specific leadership topics, such as vision, role modelling, and authentic leadership (knowing and living your personal values). Leadership is one of the most researched and discussed topics in the field of organizational behaviour.[2] Google returns a whopping 1.4 billion web pages where *leadership* is mentioned. Google Scholar lists 337,000 journal articles and books with *leader* or *leadership* in the title. Every year over the past five years, Amazon has added an average of 2,500 English language books with *leadership* in the title.

The topic of leadership receives so much attention because we are captivated by the ability of some individuals to influence and motivate beyond normal expectations a large collective of people. This chapter explores leadership from four perspectives: transformational, managerial, implicit, and personal attributes.[3] Although some of these perspectives are currently more popular than others, each helps us to more fully understand the complex topic of leadership. The final section of this chapter looks at cross-cultural and gender issues in organizational leadership. But first, we learn about the meaning of leadership as well as shared leadership.

What Is Leadership?

LO1

Several years ago, dozens of leadership experts from around the world congregated in Calgary to thresh out the meaning of **leadership**. They concluded that leadership is about influencing, motivating, and enabling others to contribute toward the effectiveness and success of the organizations of which they are members.[4] This definition has two key components. First, leaders motivate others through persuasion and other influence tactics. They use their communication skills, rewards, and other resources to energize the collective toward the achievement of challenging objectives. Second, leaders are enablers. They allocate resources, alter work relationships, minimize external disruptions, and establish other work environment changes that make it easier for employees to achieve organizational objectives.

> **leadership** Influencing, motivating, and enabling others to contribute toward the effectiveness and success of the organizations of which they are members.

SHARED LEADERSHIP

Airbus Industrie employs more than 130,000 people from 130 nationalities. The European aerospace company has thousands of managers and executives, yet has adopted the view that every employee should assume a leadership role no matter what position they hold. In fact, the company's recently launched Airbus Leadership University in Toulouse, France, ultimately serves all employees because "Airbus firmly believes that everyone is a leader!"[5]

Airbus Industrie advocates **shared leadership**, which is the view that leadership is a set of roles that everyone performs.[6] Companies are far more effective when everyone assumes leadership responsibilities in various ways and at various times. The formal leader cannot—and should not—try to perform all leadership tasks. Instead, employees lead one another as the occasion arises.

> **shared leadership** The view that leadership is a role, not a position assigned to one person; consequently, people within the team and organization lead each other.

Shared leadership exists when an employee persuades co-workers to try out a new work activity or introduce new technology. It exists when employees help one another through social support or organizational citizenship behaviours. Shared leadership also exists when employees keep one another focused on the task and deadlines. As Sergio Marchionne, the late Canadian-Italian automobile executive, proclaimed several years ago: "We've abandoned the Great Man model of leadership that long characterized Fiat and have created a culture where everyone is expected to lead."[7]

Shared leadership typically supplements formal leadership; that is, employees lead along with the formal

©Fernando Morales/The Globe and Mail/CP Images

At EllisDon, leaders aren't just people in management jobs. The Mississauga-based construction giant believes that leadership extends to every employee in the organization. "Everyone is a leader, everyone is accountable to each other, and everyone is involved in the success of the company as a whole," explains EllisDon CEO Geoff Smith (shown here). "It's a leadership philosophy throughout our company." EllisDon supports shared leadership by setting objectives and then giving employees a high degree of autonomy to achieve them. "Get good people, give them the authority, give them the support, and then get out of their way," Smith advises. "So you create leaders around you."[*]

[*] C. McMorrow, *Entrepreneurs Turn Us On: 20 Years of Recognizing Bright Ideas,* EY Entrepreneur of the year—Ontario 2013, Ernst & Young (October 2013); D. Ovsey, "'Get out of the Way'," *National Post,* 18 February 2014.

manager, rather than as a replacement for that manager. However, W. L. Gore & Associates, Morning Star Company, Valve Corporation, and a few other unique companies rely almost completely on shared leadership because they don't have any formal managers on the organizational chart.[8] In fact, when Gore employees are asked "Are you a leader?" in annual surveys, more than 50 percent of them answer "Yes."

Shared leadership flourishes in organizations where the formal leaders are willing to delegate power and encourage employees to take the initiative and risks without fear of failure (i.e., a learning orientation culture). Shared leadership also calls for a collaborative rather than internally competitive culture because employees succeed in shared leadership roles only when their co-workers support them in these roles. Furthermore, shared leadership lacks formal authority, so it operates best when employees learn to influence others through their enthusiasm, logical analysis, and involvement of co-workers in their idea or vision.

Transformational Leadership Perspective

LO2

Most leadership concepts and practices can be organized into four perspectives: transformational, managerial, implicit, and personal attributes. By far the most popular leadership perspective today—and arguably the most important in the domain of leadership—is transformational leadership. **Transformational leadership** views leaders as change agents. They move the organization or work unit in a new direction that will provide better opportunities and alignment with the external environment.

There are several models of transformational leadership, but four elements

transformational leadership
A leadership perspective that explains how leaders change teams or organizations by creating, communicating, and modelling a vision for the organization or work unit and inspiring employees to strive for that vision.

EXHIBIT 12.1   Elements of Transformational Leadership

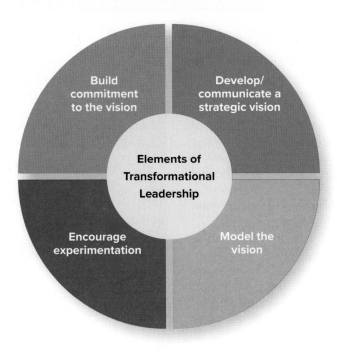

are common throughout most of them and represent the core concepts of this leadership perspective (see Exhibit 12.1).[9] Transformational leaders create, communicate, and model a shared vision for the team or organization. They encourage experimentation so employees discover a better path to the future. Through these and other activities, transformational leaders also build commitment in followers to strive for that vision.

DEVELOP AND COMMUNICATE A STRATEGIC VISION

The heart of transformational leadership is a strategic vision.[10] A vision is a positive representation of a future state that energizes and unifies employees.[11] Sometimes this vision is created by the leader; at other times, it is formed by employees or other stakeholders and then adopted and championed by the formal leader.

The opening case study to this chapter described how Galvanize CEO Laurie Schultz transformed the Vancouver-based GRC software company by developing and communicating a vision of future workplace practices, products, and other changes that will support the organization's long-term term organizational success. In fact, Schultz apparently documented succinctly on a single page her vision of a more sustainable market and revenue stream with a more engaging workplace culture.

An effective strategic vision has several identifiable features.[12] It describes an aspirational future with a higher purpose. This purpose is associated with personal values that directly or indirectly fulfil the needs of multiple stakeholders. A values-based vision is particularly meaningful and appealing to employees, which motivates them to strive for that ideal.

A strategic vision also engages employees because it is a distant goal that is both challenging and abstract. A vision of the future is challenging because it requires substantial change, such as new work practices and belief systems. It is necessarily abstract for two reasons. One reason is that the vision hasn't yet been experienced (at least, not in this company or industry), so it isn't possible to detail exactly what the vision looks like. The other reason is that an abstract description enables the vision to remain stable over time, yet is sufficiently flexible to accommodate operational adjustments in a shifting external environment. As such, a vision describes a broad noble cause related to fulfilling the needs of one or more stakeholder groups.

Another feature of an effective vision is that it is unifying. It is a superordinate objective that bonds employees together and aligns their personal values with the organization's values. In fact, a successful vision is a shared vision because employees collectively define themselves by this aspirational image of the future as part of their identification with the organization.

⬡ Global Connections 12.1

ART PHILLIPS' VISION OF A LIVABLE VANCOUVER*

Vancouver's reputation as one of the world's most livable cities is due in large part to the transformational leadership of the late Art Phillips and other members of his civic party in the early 1970s. "The improvements in quality of life, living downtown, waterfront walks, and protecting neighbourhoods are all the results of Art Phillips' leadership," says Gordon Campbell, who has served as both British Columbia's premier and Vancouver's mayor. Christy Clark, another former B.C. premier, describes Phillips as "a transformational leader who helped make one of Canada's great cities the envy of the world."

Phillips was one of Canada's most successful investment analysts when he was drawn into civic politics by city plans to create an American-style concrete jungle in Vancouver's downtown. "He felt Vancouver was at a crucial turning point, headed in the wrong direction," recalls Carole Taylor, Phillips' wife and a distinguished journalist and politician (also shown in this photo). "Art could see what had to be done to create the future."

"Instead of being dead at night, we wanted the downtown core to be more European, a place to live and enjoy," said Phillips two decades later about this vision of Vancouver's future. "It was all about doing things differently. It was about bringing people in, not

©Bob Olsen/Toronto Star via Getty Images

throwing them out, and making the city a place to enjoy, where people wanted to live." With this vision in mind, Phillips was elected to city council and later became mayor. Over the following years, Phillips and his civic party transformed Vancouver into the enviable urban environment it is today.

* W.G. Hardwick, "Responding to the 1960s: Designing Adaptable Communities in Vancouver," *Environment and Behavior* 26, no. 3 (1994): 338–62; R. Mickleburgh, "Visionary Mayor Art Phillips Remade Vancouver," *The Globe and Mail,* 25 April 2013, S8; J. Lee, "Art Phillips Was "the Best Mayor Vancouver Ever Had": Gordon Campbell," *Vancouver Sun,* 30 March 2013; S. Ip, "Phillips Remembered as 'Visionary Leader'," *Vancouver Province,* 31 March 2013, A12.

Communicate the Vision

The effectiveness of a strategic vision depends on how leaders convey it to followers and other stakeholders.[13] Transformational leaders generate meaning and motivation in followers by relying on symbols, metaphors, stories, and other vehicles that transcend plain language.[14] Metaphors and related communication tools "frame" the vision, meaning that they guide or construct the listener's mental model of the situation.

For example, when David Ossip became CEO of payroll software company Ceridian, he broadened the firm's product offering to human capital management software and relentlessly communicated an inspirational vision for its future. "Our worldwide focus became something more than just paying people correctly," Ossip explains. "At Ceridian, our brand promise is 'Makes Work Life Better'—we believe that our solutions and our people make work life better for employees everywhere, in any role within their organization." The Toronto-based executive travelled to Ceridian offices worldwide to discuss and demonstrate his personal commitment to the company's new vision and values. "Essentially it came down to a lot of communication, a lot of town halls, and a lot of interaction with everyone inside Ceridian, and that's what I did."[15]

Borrowing images from other experiences creates a richer understanding of the abstract vision that generates desired emotions and motivates people to pursue the vision. For instance, when George Cohen, the ebullient CEO of McDonald's Canada, was faced the daunting challenge of opening the first McDonald's restaurants in Russia, he frequently reminded his team members that they were establishing "hamburger diplomacy."[16]

Transformational leaders also convey the vision using verbal and nonverbal communication practices that show humility, sincerity, and a level of passion that reflects their personal belief in the vision and their optimism that employees can succeed. They strengthen team-orientation and employee self-efficacy by referring to the team's strengths and potential. By focusing on shared experiences and the central role of employees in achieving the vision, transformational leaders suppress leader–follower differences, deflect attention from themselves, and avoid any image of superiority over the team.[17]

MODEL THE VISION

Transformational leaders not only talk about a vision; they enact it. They "walk the talk" by stepping outside the executive suite and doing things that symbolize the vision.[18] Leaders model the vision through significant events such as visiting customers, moving their offices closer to (or further from) employees, and holding ceremonies to symbolize significant change. However, they also enact the vision by ensuring that the more routine daily activities—meeting agendas, dress codes, executive schedules—are consistent with the vision and its underlying values.

Modelling legitimizes the vision and demonstrates what it looks like in practice. Modelling the vision also builds employee trust in the leader. The greater the consistency between the leader's words and actions, the more employees will believe in and be willing to follow the leader. "Great leaders walk the talk. They lead by example," observes Mike Perlis, vice-chairman of Forbes Media. "There isn't anything they ask people to do they're not willing to do themselves."[19] Surveys report that "leading by example" is the most important attribute of effective leaders and is one of the most important characteristics of a company's culture.[20]

ENCOURAGE EXPERIMENTATION

Transformational leadership is about change, and central to any change is discovering new behaviours and practices that are better aligned with the desired vision. Transformational leaders support this journey by encouraging employees to question current practices and to experiment with new ways that are potentially more consistent with the vision's future state.[21] In other words, transformational leaders support a **learning orientation** (see Chapter 7). They encourage employees to continuously question the way things are currently done, actively experiment with new ideas and practices, and view reasonable mistakes as a natural part of the learning process.[22]

> **learning orientation** A set of collective beliefs and norms that encourage people to question past practices, learn new ideas, experiment putting ideas into practice, and view mistakes as part of the learning process.

BUILD COMMITMENT TOWARD THE VISION

Transforming a vision into reality requires employee commitment, and transformational leaders build this commitment in several ways.[23] Their words, symbols, and stories build a contagious enthusiasm that energizes people to adopt the vision as their own. Leaders demonstrate a "can do" attitude by enacting and behaving consistently with their vision. This persistence and consistency reflect an image of honesty, trust, and integrity. By encouraging experimentation, leaders involve employees in the change process so it is a collective activity. Leaders also build commitment through rewards, recognition, and celebrations as employees pass milestones along the road to the desired vision.

TRANSFORMATIONAL LEADERSHIP AND CHARISMA

Some experts describe charisma as an essential ingredient of transformational leadership.[24] However, the emerging view, which this book adopts, is that charismatic leadership is distinct from transformational leadership. Several studies and reviews indicate that charisma is not necessarily part of transformational leadership and, in fact, some of its effects on employees may be opposite to the effects of transformational leadership.[25]

Charisma refers to a set of self-presentation characteristics and nonverbal communication behaviours (i.e., signalling) that generate interpersonal attraction and referent power over others as well as follower deference to the charismatic person (see Chapter 10).[26] In contrast, transformational leadership is a set of behaviours that engage followers toward a better future. Charismatic leadership motivates followers directly through the leader's referent power, whereas transformational leadership motivates followers through behaviours that persuade and earn trust. For instance, communicating an inspiring vision is a transformational leadership behaviour that motivates followers to strive for that vision. This motivational effect exists separate from the leader's charismatic appeal.

Being charismatic is not inherently good or bad, but several research studies have concluded that charismatic leaders can produce negative consequences.[27] One concern is that charismatic leadership tends to produce dependent followers because, by definition, followers want to be associated with people who have charisma. Transformational leadership has the opposite effect; it builds follower empowerment, which tends to reduce dependence on the leader.

What are your transformational leadership tendencies? You can discover your level of transformational leadership on each dimension by completing this self-assessment in Connect.

Another concern is that leaders who are charismatic may become intoxicated by this power, which leads to a greater focus on self-interest than on the common good. "Charisma becomes the undoing of leaders," warned Peter Drucker many years ago. "It makes them inflexible, convinced of their own infallibility, unable to change."[28] The late management guru witnessed the destructive effects of charismatic political leaders in Europe a century ago and foresaw that this personal or relational characteristic would create similar problems for organizations. The main point here is that transformational leaders are not necessarily charismatic, and charismatic leaders are not necessarily transformational.

 ## Global Connections 12.2

DID CHARISMATIC LEADERSHIP CAUSE STEINHOFF'S DOWNFALL?*

Board members of Steinhoff International Holdings anxiously waited for CEO Markus Jooste to arrive from Europe with documents supporting the company's unaudited and overdue financial reports. Instead, after hours of delay, Jooste sent a text message saying that he was quitting, seeking legal counsel, and wouldn't attend the board meeting at all. The South African–based company's stock value plummeted by 90 percent with news of its accounting "irregularities." A recent forensic accounting report confirmed the worst: a small group of Steinhoff executives, "led by a senior management executive," had engaged in extensive accounting fraud involving more than (CAD) $10 billion over the previous decade.

Steinhoff's collapse has been attributed to several factors, including overpriced acquisitions, a dual reporting structure, and a board that failed to provide sufficient oversight of management. Another frequently mentioned explanation, however, is that Markus Jooste was a charismatic leader who mesmerized Steinhoff's board, executives, and many external stakeholders. Jooste has been portrayed as a "superhuman businessman," a "ruthlessly ambitious" retail star with "extraordinary dealmaking talent" and "unshakeable confidence." These characteristics were reinforced through his "bold" acquisitions, including Poundland (United Kingdom), Mattress Firm (United States), Freedom (Australia), and Conforama (France).

Jooste cultivated a small cadre of "fiercely loyal insiders who enjoyed social and financial privileges through their close association with Jooste." He was called the "don" of the "Stellenbosch mafia," referring to his tendency to hire executives educated at his alma mater, Stellenbosch University. One South African professor stated that Jooste's "leadership style fostered an institutional culture

©Brenton Geach/Gallo Images/Getty Images

of uncritical subservience and self-censorship" and that "only those subordinates who obsequiously defer to him benefit from his extensive patronage."

Jooste's apparent charisma was even blamed for the board's poor oversight of management. Steinhoff's chairman, who has since resigned, claimed that the accounting fraud "came like a bolt out of the blue." Yet German authorities had been investigating Steinhoff's accounting practices for almost two years and an investment firm (Portsea) had written a scathing report about self-dealing and potentially illegal financial transfers at the company.

A well-known investment analyst summed up the Steinhoff saga with this warning: "You cannot in this day and age have a board full of stooges that rubber-stamp what a charismatic CEO wants to get away with."

* S. Harris, "Is Jooste SA's Top Dealmaker?," *Finweek*, August 25, 2016, 32–34; "The Seagull's Name Was Markus Jooste: Steinhoff And The 'Stellenbosch Mafia,'" *HuffPost UK*, December 12, 2017; R. Henderson, "Steinhoff Sells off Its Luxury Gulfstream Jet to Raise Funds," *Sunday Times (South Africa)*, January 21, 2018; S. Theobald, "Jooste's Obsession with Maintaining Steinhoff Illusion Drove Him to Cross the Line," *Business Day (South Africa)*, March 5, 2018; J. Shapiro, "The 'Murky' Local Origins of Steinhoff's Secret Empire," *Australian Financial Review*, June 15, 2018; "Inside the Steinhoff Saga, One of the Biggest Cases of Corporate Fraud in South African Business History," (Case study written by "Several University of Stellenbosch Business School academics") *CNBC Africa*, June 28, 2018; J.-B. Styan, "The Steinhoff Story That Markus Jooste Left Untold," *Finweek*, September 27, 2018, 34–35; M. Soko, "Book on Steinhoff's Demise Shows Danger of 'Big Men' Business Leaders," *The Conversation*, November 13, 2018; J. Rossouw and J. Styan, "Steinhoff Collapse: A Failure of Corporate Governance," *International Review of Applied Economics* 33, no. 1 (2019): 163–70; PwC, "Overview of Forensic Investigation" (South Africa: Steinhoff International Team Holdings, March 15, 2019).

EVALUATING THE TRANSFORMATIONAL LEADERSHIP PERSPECTIVE

Transformational leaders make a difference.[29] Subordinates are more satisfied and have higher affective organizational commitment under transformational leaders. They also perform their jobs better, engage in more organizational citizenship behaviours, and make better or more creative decisions. One study of Canadian bank branches reported that organizational commitment and financial performance increased where the branch manager completed a transformational leadership training program.[30]

Transformational leadership is currently the most popular leadership perspective, but it faces a number of challenges.[31] One problem is that some models engage in circular logic. They define and measure transformational leadership by its effects on employees (e.g., inspire employees), then (not surprisingly) report that this leadership is effective because it inspires employees. Instead, transformational leadership needs to be defined purely as a set of behaviours that people use to lead others through the change process. A second concern is that some transformational leadership theories combine leader behaviours with the personal characteristics of leaders. For instance, transformational leaders are described as visionary, imaginative, sensitive, and thoughtful, yet these personal characteristics are really predictors of transformational leadership behaviours.[32]

A third concern is that transformational leadership is usually described as a universal concept, that is, it should be applied in all situations. Only a few studies have investigated whether this form of leadership is more valuable in some situations than others.[33] For instance, transformational leadership is probably more appropriate when organizations need to adapt to a rapidly changing external environment than when the environment is stable. Preliminary evidence suggests that the transformational leadership perspective is relevant across cultures. However, there may be specific elements of transformational leadership, such as the way visions are communicated and modelled, that are more appropriate in North America than in other cultures.

Managerial Leadership Perspective

LO3

Leaders don't spend all (or even most) of their time transforming the organization or work unit. They also engage in **managerial leadership**—daily activities that support and guide the performance and well-being of individual employees and the work unit toward current objectives and practices. Leadership experts recognize that leading (transformational leadership) differs from managing (managerial leadership).[34] Although the distinction between these two perspectives remains somewhat fuzzy, each cluster has a reasonably clear set of activities and a strong research foundation.

> **managerial leadership**
> A leadership perspective stating that effective leaders help employees improve their performance and well-being towards current objectives and practices.

One distinction between these two perspectives is that managerial leadership assumes the department's or organization's objectives are stable and aligned with the external environment.[35] It focuses on continuously developing or maintaining the effectiveness of employees and work units toward those established objectives and practices. In contrast, transformational leadership assumes the organization is misaligned with its environment and therefore needs to change its direction. This distinction is captured in the often-cited statement: "Managers are people who do things right and leaders are people who do the right thing."[36] Managers "do things right" by enabling employees to perform established goals more effectively. Leaders "do the right thing" by changing the organization or work unit so its objectives are aligned more closely with the external environment.

A second distinction is that managerial leadership is more micro-focused and concrete, because it relates to the specific performance and well-being objectives of individual employees and the immediate work unit. Transformational leadership is more macro-focused and abstract. It is directed toward an abstract strategic vision for an entire organization, department, or team.

INTERDEPENDENCE OF MANAGERIAL AND TRANSFORMATIONAL LEADERSHIP

Although transformational and managerial leadership are discussed as two leadership perspectives, they are more appropriately viewed as *interdependent* perspectives.[37] In other words, transformational leadership and managerial leadership depend on each other. Transformational leadership identifies, communicates, and builds commitment to a better future for the organization or work unit. But these transformational leadership behaviours are not enough for organizational success. That success also requires managerial leadership to translate the abstract vision into more specific operational behaviours and practices, and to continuously improve employee performance and well-being in the pursuit of that future ideal. Managerial leadership also depends on transformational leadership to set the right direction. Otherwise, managers might produce operational excellence toward goals that are misaligned with the organization's long-term survival.

Senior executives typically engage in more transformational leadership than do middle managers, supervisors, and others further down the hierarchy. This greater emphasis on transformational leadership at higher levels likely occurs because senior leaders are more responsible for the organization's alignment with its environment and because they have more discretion to enable macro-level change. However, managerial and transformational leadership are not embodied in different people or positions in the organization. Every manager needs to apply both transformational and managerial leadership behaviours to varying degrees. Through shared leadership, even front-line employees apply managerial leadership (e.g., helping co-workers through a difficult project) and transformational leadership (e.g., championing more customer-friendly norms in the work unit).

TASK-ORIENTED AND PEOPLE-ORIENTED LEADERSHIP

Managerial leadership research began in the 1940s when several universities launched intensive investigations to answer the question, "What behaviours make leaders effective?" They studied first-line supervisors by asking subordinates to rate their bosses on many behaviours. These independent research teams essentially produced the same two clusters of leadership behaviour from literally thousands of items (Exhibit 12.2).[38]

One cluster, called *task-oriented leadership,* includes behaviours that define and structure work roles. This leadership style includes assigning employees to specific tasks, setting goals and deadlines, clarifying work duties and procedures, defining work procedures, and planning work activities. The other cluster represents *people-oriented leadership.* This leadership style includes behaviours such as listening to employees for their opinions and ideas, creating a pleasant physical work environment, showing interest in staff, complimenting and recognizing employees for their effort, and showing consideration of employee needs.

These early managerial leadership studies tried to find out whether effective managers are more task-oriented or more people-oriented. This proved to be a difficult question to answer because each style has its advantages and disadvantages. In fact, evidence suggests that effective leaders rely on both styles, but in different circumstances.[39] When leaders apply the people-oriented style, their employees tend to have more positive attitudes as well as lower absenteeism, grievances, stress, and turnover. When leaders use task-oriented behaviours, their employees tend to have higher job performance. Not surprisingly, employees generally prefer people-oriented bosses and they form negative attitudes toward bosses who are mostly task-oriented. However, task-oriented leadership is also appreciated to some degree. For example, one Canadian study reported that university students value task-oriented instructors because they provide students with clear objectives and well-prepared lectures that abide by the course objectives.[40]

SERVANT LEADERSHIP

Sylvia Metayer is chief growth officer and member of the senior executive team at SODEXO. Yet the Canadian executive at the Paris-based global food services and facilities management company views her role as serving employees, not the other way around. "I'm learning that to be a CEO is to be a servant," she observes. "My main job is to support our employees, and be a support to our clients and to our consumers." Metayer explains that servant leadership has natural value not just to employees, but also to external stakeholders. "We have a huge onus on ourselves as an organization to understand what it is that makes people thrive in the workplace because we have so many employees, but also because our responsibility to our clients is to create this thriving workplace."[41]

Servant leadership is an extension or variation of people-oriented leadership because it defines leadership as serving others. As Sylvia Metayer stated, servant leaders assist others in

servant leadership The view that leaders serve followers, rather than vice versa; leaders help employees fulfil their needs and are coaches, stewards, and facilitators of employee performance.

EXHIBIT 12.2   Task- and People-Oriented Leadership Styles

Leaders are task-oriented when they...	Leaders are people-oriented when they...
• Assign work and clarify responsibilities	• Show interest in others as people
• Set goals and deadlines	• Listen to employees
• Evaluate and provide feedback on work quality	• Make the workplace more pleasant
• Establish well-defined best-work procedures	• Show appreciation to employees for their performance contribution
• Plan future work activities	• Are considerate of employee needs

©Ruth Bonneville/Winnipeg Free Press

Col. Eric Charron says that he and many other Canadian Forces officers "ultimately aspire to positions of command. Many of us joined to be leaders." But that doesn't mean the commanding officer of Canadian Forces Base Winnipeg and 17 Wing is a task-oriented leader. In fact, he seems to put more emphasis on the people-oriented leadership style. "If we take care of our people—their career aspirations, their professional development, their families. . . I know with the loyalty we have shown them, they will show us the loyalty back and serve the Canadian Armed Forces and our great country Canada to their last breath." Charron's managerial leadership has been favourably observed by others. "I've admired [Col. Charron's] leadership style," says Manitoba politician Stuart Murray. "His style is very open and very inclusive. He's very patient."

*E. Natividad, "New Commander at Winnipeg's 17 Wing," *City News* (Winnipeg, June 28, 2018); D. Speirs, "Commanding a Dream," *Winnipeg Free Press,* December 27, 2019.

their need fulfilment, personal development, and growth.[42] Servant leaders ask, "How can I help you?" rather than expect employees to serve them. They are typically described as selfless, egalitarian, humble, nurturing, empathetic, and ethical coaches. The main objective of servant leadership is to help followers and other stakeholders fulfil their needs and potential, particularly "to become healthier, wiser, freer, more autonomous, more likely themselves to become servants."[43] This description captures three key features of servant leadership:[44]

- *Natural desire or "calling" to serve others.* Servant leaders have a deep commitment to help others in their personal growth for that purpose alone. This commitment is not merely an instrument to achieve company objectives. It is a selfless desire to support others that goes beyond the leader's role obligation.
- *Humble, egalitarian, accepting relationship with followers.* Servant leaders do not view leadership as a position

of power. Rather, they serve without drawing attention to themselves, without evoking superior status, and without being judgmental about others or defensive of criticisms received.

- *Ethical decisions and behaviour.* Servant leaders display sensitivity to and enactment of moral values. They are not swayed by deviant social pressures or expectations. Servant leaders maintain moral integrity by relying on personal values to anchor their decisions and behaviour. In this respect, servant leadership relies heavily on authentic leadership, which we discuss later in this chapter.

Servant leadership was introduced several decades ago and has since had a steady following, particularly among practitioners and religious leaders. Scholarly interest in this topic has bloomed recently, but the concept still faces a number of conceptual hurdles.[45] Although servant leadership writers generally agree on the three features we described here, many have included other characteristics that might confound the concept with its predictors and outcomes. Still, the notion that leaders should be servants has considerable currency and for many centuries has been embedded in the principles of major religions. One study also found that companies have higher performance (return on assets) when their chief executive officer exhibits servant leadership behaviours.[46]

Path–Goal and Leadership Substitutes Theories

LO4

PATH–GOAL LEADERSHIP THEORY

The earliest managerial leadership studies not only identified the task-oriented and people-oriented leadership styles; they also concluded that the best leadership style depends on the situation.[47] In other words, the most appropriate leadership style is contingent on the characteristics of the employee, work setting, leader-follower relationship, and other factors. This "it depends" view is consistent with the contingency anchor of organizational behaviour discussed in Chapter 1.

path–goal leadership theory A leadership theory stating that effective leaders choose the most appropriate leadership style(s), depending on the employee and situation, to influence employee expectations about desired results and their positive outcomes.

Path–goal leadership theory is the dominant model that applies this contingency approach to managerial leadership. The theory states that effective leaders choose one or more leadership styles to influence employee expectations (their preferred path) regarding achievement of desired results (their work-related goals), as well as their perceived satisfaction with those results (outcome valences). Leaders clarify the link between employee behaviours and outcomes, influence the valence of those outcomes, provide a work environment to facilitate goal accomplishment, and so forth.[48] Notice from this description that path–goal theory builds on the expectancy theory of motivation (Chapter 5) and its underlying formula of rational decision making (Chapter 7).[49]

Path–Goal Leadership Styles

Exhibit 12.3 presents the path–goal leadership theory model. It highlights four leadership styles and several contingency factors leading to three indicators of leader effectiveness. The four leadership styles are:[50]

- *Directive.* Directive leadership is the same as task-oriented leadership, described earlier. This leadership style consists of behaviours that provide a psychological structure for subordinates. It includes clarifying performance goals, the means to reach those goals, and the standards against which performance will be judged. Directive leadership also includes judicious use of rewards and disciplinary actions.

- *Supportive.* Supportive leadership is the same as people-oriented leadership, described earlier. This style consists of behaviours that provide psychological support for subordinates. The leader is friendly and approachable, makes the work more pleasant, treats employees with respect, and shows concern for the status, needs, and well-being of employees.

EXHIBIT 12.3   Path–Goal Leadership Theory

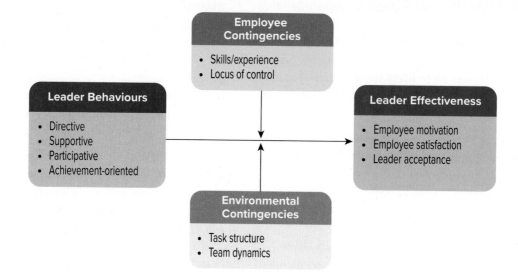

What is your preferred managerial leadership style? You can discover which of the two most commonly studied dimensions of managerial leadership you prefer by completing this self-assessment in Connect.

- *Participative.* Participative leadership consists of behaviours that encourage and facilitate employee involvement in decisions beyond their normal work activities. The leader consults with staff members, asks for their suggestions, and carefully reflects on employee views before making a decision. Participative leadership relates to involving employees in decisions (see Chapter 7).
- *Achievement-oriented.* This leadership style consists of behaviours that encourage employees to reach their peak performance. The leader sets challenging goals, expects employees to perform at their highest level, continuously

seeks improvement in employee performance, and shows a high degree of confidence that employees will assume responsibility and accomplish challenging goals. Achievement-oriented leadership applies goal-setting theory as well as positive expectations in self-fulfilling prophecy.

Path–Goal Theory Contingencies

As a contingency theory, path–goal theory states that each of the four leadership styles will be more effective in some situations than in others. The theory also contends that managers

©mentatdgt/Shutterstock

When asked to describe their favourite boss, employees refer to leadership styles and situations that fit path–goal theory. For example, an experienced community education services worker in Minnesota appreciates her supervisor's participative leadership. "Is he perfect? No. But he listens to others' opinions and always considers them." A junior employee at a pharmaceutical company in London, United Kingdom, praises his boss's supportive style. "She has this magical ability to lead with empathy, compassion, and transparency." And a financial services professional in Illinois says his manager is someone "you would walk on coals for" because of his balance of achievement and supportive leadership. "He pushed you but always had your best interest at heart and wanted you to succeed."[*]

[*] These testimonials are reported in: S. Sahadi, "We Asked CNN Business Readers What Makes a Great Boss. Here's What You Said," *CNN Business,* March 27, 2019.

are able to apply the most appropriate leadership style (or styles) for each situation. Depending on the circumstances, this skill may involve using two or more leadership styles at the same time. The model specifies two sets of situational variables: (1) employee characteristics and (2) characteristics of the employee's work environment. Several employee and workplace contingencies have been studied, but the following four have received the most attention.[51]

- *Skill and experience.* A combination of directive and supportive leadership is best for employees who are (or perceive themselves to be) inexperienced and unskilled.[52] Directive leadership involves providing information about how to accomplish the task, whereas supportive leadership offers support to cope with the uncertainties of unfamiliar work situations. This style is detrimental when employees are skilled and experienced because it introduces too much supervisory control.

- *Locus of control.* People with an internal locus of control believe they have control over their work environment (see Chapter 3). Consequently, these employees prefer participative and achievement-oriented leadership styles and may become frustrated with a directive style. In contrast, people with an external locus of control believe their performance is due more to luck and fate, so they tend to be more satisfied with directive and supportive leadership.

- *Task structure.* Leaders should adopt the directive style when the task is nonroutine, because this style minimizes role ambiguity that tends to occur in complex work situations (particularly for inexperienced employees).[53] The directive style is ineffective when employees have routine and simple tasks because the manager's guidance serves no purpose and may be viewed as unnecessarily micromanaging. Employees in highly routine and simple jobs may require supportive leadership to help them cope with the tedious nature of the work and lack of control over the pace of work. Participative leadership is preferred for employees performing nonroutine tasks because the lack of rules and procedures gives them more discretion to achieve challenging goals. The participative style is ineffective for employees in routine tasks because because they lack discretion over their work.

- *Team dynamics.* Cohesive teams with performance-oriented norms act as a substitute for most leader interventions. High team cohesion substitutes for supportive leadership, whereas performance-oriented team norms substitute for directive and possibly achievement-oriented leadership. Thus, when team cohesion is low, leaders should use the supportive style. Leaders should apply a directive style to counteract team norms that oppose the performance objectives assigned to the team. For

example, the team leader may need to exert authority if team members have developed a norm to "take it easy" rather than get a project completed on time.

Evaluating Path–Goal Theory

Path–goal theory has received more research support than other managerial leadership models. In fact, one study reported that path–goal theory predicts effective leadership better than does transformational leadership.[54] This stronger effect likely exists because managers typically spend more of their time engaging in managerial rather than transformational leadership.[55]

Support for the path–goal model is far from ideal, however. Not all contingencies have research support and a few haven't been investigated at all.[56] Another concern is that path–goal theory assumes effective leaders can change managerial styles to fit the situation. In reality, it takes considerable effort to do so because leaders typically prefer one style that is most consistent with their personality and values. Some experts even suggest that leadership styles are hardwired.[57] In spite of these limitations, path–goal theory remains a relatively robust theory of managerial leadership.

LEADERSHIP SUBSTITUTES THEORY

Path–goal leadership theory recommends changing leadership styles depending on the situation, whereas **leadership substitutes theory** suggests that the situation either limits the leader's ability to influence subordinates or renders a particular leadership style unnecessary. The literature identifies several conditions that possibly substitute for task-oriented or people-oriented leadership (see Exhibit 12.4).

> **leadership substitutes theory** A theory identifying conditions that either limit a leader's ability to influence subordinates or make a particular leadership style unnecessary.

Consistent with path–goal theory, task-oriented leadership is likely less valuable for employees as they gain skill and experience in the job.[58] This leadership style also may be redundant or have less value when performance-based rewards motivate employees to achieve organizational goals, when the work is intrinsically motivating, and when the employee applies self-leadership practices (see Chapter 6).

Under some conditions, teams likely substitute for task-oriented leadership.[59] Team norms that support organizational goals motivate team members to encourage (or pressure) co-workers to perform their tasks and possibly even to develop achievement-oriented performance expectations.[60] Co-workers also engage in organizational citizenship behaviours by instructing less-experienced employees,

EXHIBIT 12.4   Potential Leadership Substitutes

Managerial leadership style	Potential substitutes for that style
Task-oriented	• Performance-based rewards • Employee is skilled and experienced • Guidance from co-workers • Team norms reinforce task objectives • Intrinsically motivating work • Employee applies self-leadership
People-oriented	• Supportive co-workers • Employee is skilled and experienced • Enjoyable work • Employee uses effective stress coping strategies

thereby requiring less task-oriented leadership from the formal manager.

People-oriented leadership may be less valuable when other forms of social support are available (such as supportive team members), when the work itself is enjoyable, and when the employee applies effective coping strategies to minimize stress. Skilled and experienced employees also have higher self-efficacy, which results in less stressful work and therefore less need for people-oriented leadership interaction from the boss.

The leadership substitutes model has intuitive appeal, but the evidence has been mixed. Some studies suggest that a few substitutes do replace the need for task- or people-oriented leadership, but others do not. The difficulties of statistically testing for leadership substitutes may account for some problems. However, a few writers contend that the weak support for substitutes indicates that formal leadership plays a critical role regardless of the situation.[61] Overall, we can conclude that leadership substitutes might reduce the need for managerial leadership behaviours, but they do not completely replace managers in these situations.

Implicit Leadership Perspective

LO5

Research on transformational and managerial leadership has found that leaders do "make a difference"; that is, leaders significantly influence the performance of their departments and organizations. However, a third leadership perspective, called **implicit leadership theory**, explains that followers' perceptions also play a role in a leader's effectiveness. The implicit leadership perspective has two components: leader prototypes and the romance of leadership.[62]

PROTOTYPES OF EFFECTIVE LEADERS

One aspect of implicit leadership theory states that everyone has *leadership prototypes*—preconceived beliefs about the features and behaviours of effective leaders.[63] These prototypes, which develop through socialization within the family and society, shape the follower's expectations and acceptance of others as leaders, and this in turn affects their willingness to remain as a follower. Leadership prototypes not only support a person's role as leader; they also influence follower perceptions of the leader's effectiveness. In other words, a leader is often perceived as more effective when they look like and act consistently with the prototype of a leader.[64]

> **implicit leadership theory**
> A theory stating that people evaluate a leader's effectiveness in terms of how well that person fits preconceived beliefs about the features and behaviours of effective leaders (leadership prototypes), and that people tend to inflate the influence of leaders on organizational events.

This prototype comparison process occurs because people want to trust their leader before they are willing to serve as followers. However, the leader's actual effectiveness usually isn't known for several months or possibly years, so comparing the leader against a prototype is a quick (although faulty) way of estimating the leader's future success.

THE ROMANCE OF LEADERSHIP

Along with relying on implicit prototypes of effective leaders, followers tend to inflate the perceived influence of leaders on the organization's success. This "romance of leadership" effect occurs for two reasons.[65] First, leadership is a useful way for us to simplify life events. It is easier to explain

Do leaders make a difference? You can discover your Romance of Leadership score by completing this self-assessment in Connect.

organizational successes and failures in terms of the leader's ability than by analyzing a complex array of other forces.

The second reason why people inflate their perceptions of the leader's influence over the environment is that people in Canada and many other cultures want to believe that life events are generated more from people than from uncontrollable natural forces.[66] This illusion of control is satisfied by the belief that events result from the rational actions of leaders. In other words, employees feel better believing that leaders make a difference, so they actively look for evidence that this is so.

Fundamental attribution error (see Chapter 3) also explains why followers believe that leaders make a difference. Leaders are often given credit for the company's success because employees do not readily see the external forces that also influence these events. Leaders reinforce this belief by taking credit for organizational successes.[67] "The people at Semco don't look and act like me," explains Ricardo Semler, well-known author, speaker, CEO of Semco Partners, and founder of the Lumiar Schools in Brazil. "They are not yes-men by

any means. . . . [Yet] they credit me with successes that are not my own, and they don't debit me my mistakes."[68]

The implicit leadership perspective highlights the fact that leadership is influenced by followers' perceptions, not only the actual behaviours and formal roles of people calling themselves leaders. Potential leaders must be sensitive to this fact and be aware of follower expectations. Individuals who do not naturally fit leadership prototypes need to provide more direct evidence of their effectiveness as leaders.

Personal Attributes Perspective of Leadership

LO6

Since the beginning of recorded civilization, people have been interested in the personal characteristics that distinguish great leaders from the rest of us.[69] One groundbreaking review in the late 1940s concluded that no valid list of leadership traits could be distilled from previous research.

OB by the NUMBERS

The Leadership Report Card[*]

79% of 181,662 Canadian federal government employees are satisfied with the quality of supervision they receive.

65% of more than 2,000 **American** and United Kingdom full-time employees are confident they could perform their jobs just as well or better without their boss's input.

49% of 2,800 **Americans** who work in an office environment feel that their manager is a good leader.

39% of 400 Canadians who work in an office environment have quit their job due to a bad boss.

38% of 1,019 employees surveyed in India say they could do their boss's job better than their boss.

18% of current managers have the high talent to effectively manage others (based on Gallup's analysis of 2.5 million manager-led teams).

©james weston/Shutterstock

*State of the American Manager: Analytics and Advice for Leaders (Washington, DC: Gallup, March 2015); CareerBuilder, "4 in 10 Indian Employees Believe Their Boss Has Room for Improvement," News Release (Noida, India: CareerMuse, August 6, 2015); "Two in Five Workers in Canada Have Quit Due to a Bad Boss, Survey Reveals," News Release (Toronto: Robert Half, October 8, 2019); "Survey Reveals Cities Where Workers Are Most (And Least) Happy With Bosses," News Release (Menlo Park, Calif.: Robert Half, October 11, 2018); "2019 Public Service Employee Survey Results for the Public Service" (Ottawa: Government of Canada, Treasury Board of Canada Secretariat, January 15, 2020); "The Boss Barometer Report — US 2019," Kimble Applications, accessed March 21, 2020, https://www.kimbleapps.com/resources/boss-barometer-survey-us/; "The Boss Barometer Report — UK 2019," Kimble Applications, accessed March 21, 2020, https://www.kimbleapps.com/resources/boss-barometer-survey-uk/. The Kimble Applications percentage combined the nearly identical statistics from the separate US and UK reports. A third survey on DACH (German-speaking European) employees reported 59 percent for this question, but the sample size was not known.

This conclusion was revised a decade later, suggesting that a few traits are associated with effective leaders.[70] Even so, the initial review caused many scholars to give up their search for the personal characteristics of effective leaders.

EIGHT IMPORTANT LEADERSHIP ATTRIBUTES

Leadership experts have since returned to the notion that effective leaders possess specific personal attributes.[71] Many leadership studies conducted long ago were apparently plagued by methodological problems, lack of theoretical foundation, and inconsistent definitions of leadership. Recent studies have mostly corrected these problems, with the result that several attributes are now consistently identified with effective leadership or leader emergence. Eight important attributes of effective leaders (not in any particular order) are personality, self-concept, leadership motivation, drive, integrity, knowledge of the business, cognitive and practical intelligence, and emotional intelligence (see Exhibit 12.5.)[72]

Personality

Most of the Big Five personality factors (see Chapter 2) are associated with effective leadership.[73] However, the strongest predictors are high levels of extraversion (outgoing, talkative, sociable, and assertive) and conscientiousness (careful, dependable, and self-disciplined). With high extraversion, effective leaders are comfortable having an influential role in social settings. With higher conscientiousness, effective leaders set higher goals for themselves (and others), are organized, and have a strong sense of duty to fulfil work obligations.

Self-Concept

Successful leaders have a complex, internally consistent, and clear self-concept as a leader (see Chapter 3). This "leader identity" also includes a positive self-evaluation, which consists of high self-esteem, high self-efficacy, and an internal locus of control.[74] Many people in leadership positions default to daily managerial leadership and define themselves as managers. Effective leaders, on the other hand, view themselves as both transformational and managerial, and are confident with both of these self-views.[75]

Leadership Motivation

Effective leaders are motivated to lead others. They have a strong need for *socialized power*, meaning that they want power to lead others in accomplishing organizational objectives and similar good deeds. This contrasts with a need for *personalized power*, which is the desire to have power for personal gain or for the thrill one might experience from wielding power over others (see Chapter 5).[76] Leadership

EXHIBIT 12.5 Personal Attributes of Effective Leaders

Leadership attribute	Description
Personality	Effective leaders have higher extraversion (outgoing, talkative, sociable, and assertive) and conscientiousness (careful, dependable, and self-disciplined).
Self-concept	Effective leaders have strong self-beliefs and a positive self-evaluation about their own leadership skills and ability to achieve objectives.
Leadership motivation	Effective leaders have a need for socialized power (not personalized power) to accomplish team or organizational goals.
Drive	Effective leaders have an inner motivation to pursue goals.
Integrity	Effective leaders have strong moral principles, which are demonstrated through truthfulness and consistency of words with deeds.
Knowledge of the business	Effective leaders have tacit and explicit knowledge about the company's environment, enabling them to make more intuitive decisions.
Cognitive and practical intelligence	Effective leaders have above-average cognitive ability to process information (cognitive intelligence) and ability to solve real-world problems by adapting to, shaping, or selecting appropriate environments (practical intelligence).
Emotional intelligence	Effective leaders have the ability to recognize and regulate their own emotions and the emotions of others.

Global Connections 12.3

TRANSFORMATIONAL LEADER CAROLYN MCCALL IDENTIFIES IMPORTANT LEADERSHIP ATTRIBUTES*

Carolyn McCall says she is not a turnaround expert. Yet the chief executive of ITV, the United Kingdom's largest commercial television company, has demonstrated her turnaround skills on more occasions than most leaders. Discount airline easyJet rebounded under her guidance as CEO, and Guardian Media Group also prospered when she led that company in earlier years. McCall is now transforming ITV from a traditional linear broadcaster to the emerging video-on-demand model.

Along with having an inspiring vision, McCall says that successful leaders require several personal attributes. One of these is integrity. "A reputation takes years to build and you can lose it in two seconds," warns McCall, who recently received the British honour of Damehood (the female equivalent of knighthood). "I would rather tell people the truth, even if it's really hard, than avoid the problem."

McCall observes that effective leaders also have the drive to continue under adversity. "You'll get hammered at points in your career and you have to have the resilience to keep going and believe in what you're doing." A third leadership attribute that McCall emphasizes is the need to understand and manage emotions. "Emotional intelligence is important for leadership," she says. "For me, it's about being able to relate to other people and to show you want to nurture that relationship."

©David Levenson/Alamy Stock Photo

McCall also recognizes the importance of knowing yourself and being yourself in leadership roles. "You need to be comfortable with yourself to be confident," she says, warning that "if you change yourself to adapt to that, it's even harder." However, McCall distinguishes pretending to be someone else from adapting your leadership style to the situation. "Of course in different situations you have to have different behaviours. You sometimes have to be a lot more assertive in meetings, but that's a change of tone, not character."

* "Three Leadership Secrets from easyJet Boss Carolyn McCall," *O2 BusinessBlog, O2,* September 19, 2014, http://businessblog.o2.co.uk/three-leadership-secrets-easyjet-boss-carolyn-mccall/; C. Zillman, "easyJet CEO: 'I'm Not a Turnaround Expert,'" *Fortune,* June 15, 2015; L. Roderick, "easyJet CEO Carolyn McCall Explains How Marketers Can Soar," *Marketing Week,* March 9, 2016; K. Magee, "'Women Don't Need to Defeminise, They Need to Be Themselves,' easyJet CEO McCall Says," *Advertising Week,* April 19, 2016; G. Spanier, "ITV's Carolyn McCall: 'We Have Got to Evolve Quickly,'" *Campaign,* February 18, 2019.

---

motivation is also necessary because, even in organizations where managers support one another, they are in contests for positions further up the hierarchy. Effective leaders thrive rather than wither in the face of this competition.[77]

Drive

Related to their high conscientiousness, extraversion, and positive self-evaluation, successful leaders have a moderately high need for achievement (see Chapter 5). This drive represents the inner motivation that leaders possess to pursue their goals and encourage others to move forward with theirs. Drive inspires inquisitiveness, an action orientation, and measured boldness to take the organization or team into uncharted waters.

Integrity

Integrity involves having strong moral principles, which supports the tendency to be truthful and to be consistent in words and deeds. Leaders have a high moral capacity to judge dilemmas using sound values and to act accordingly. Notice that integrity is ultimately based on the leader's values, which provide an anchor for consistency. Several large-scale studies in Canada and globally have reported that integrity and honesty are the most important characteristics of effective leaders.[78]

Knowledge of the Business

Effective leaders understand the business environment in which they operate, including subtle indications of emerging trends. Knowledge of the business also includes a solid grasp of how their organization works effectively.

Cognitive and Practical Intelligence

Leaders have above-average cognitive ability to process enormous amounts of information. Leaders aren't necessarily geniuses; rather, they have a superior ability to analyze a variety of complex alternatives and opportunities. Furthermore, leaders have practical intelligence. This means that they can think through the relevance and application of ideas in real-world settings. Practical intelligence is particularly evident where problems are poorly defined, information is missing, and more than one solution may be plausible.[79]

Emotional Intelligence

Effective leaders have a high level of emotional intelligence.[80] They are able to recognize and regulate emotions in themselves and in other people (see Chapter 4). For example, effective leaders can tell when their conversations are having the intended emotional effect on employees. They are also able to recognize and change their own emotional state to suit the situation, such as feeling optimistic and determined in spite of recent business setbacks.

AUTHENTIC LEADERSHIP

A few paragraphs ago, we said that successful leaders have a complex, internally consistent, and clear self-concept as a leader, and that they have a strong positive self-evaluation. These characteristics lay the foundation for **authentic leadership**, which refers to how well leaders are aware of, feel comfortable with, and act consistently with their values, personality, and self-concept.[81] Authenticity is mainly about knowing yourself and being yourself (see Exhibit 12.6). Leaders learn more about their personality, values, thoughts,

authentic leadership The view that teffective leaders need to be aware of, feel comfortable with, and act consistently with their values, personality, and self-concept.

and habits by reflecting on various situations and personal experiences.

Leaders also improve self-awareness by receiving feedback from trusted people inside and outside the organization. For example, after meetings or interviews, Geoff Molson asks for feedback from employees and other stakeholders who observed him. "I ask how I did, and what I did wrong," says the CEO of Montreal-based Groupe CH (which owns the Montreal Canadiens hockey team). Molson acknowledges that people initially give only positive feedback, but they offer more constructive advice when he asks for specifics. "You learn from getting feedback, and I take that very seriously."[82] Both self-reflection and receptivity to feedback require high levels of emotional intelligence.

As people learn more about themselves, they gain a greater understanding of their inner purpose which, in turn, generates a long-term passion for achieving something worthwhile for the organization or society. Some leadership experts suggest that this inner purpose emerges from a life story, typically initiated by a transformative event or experience earlier in life.[83]

Amiee Chan refers to one such transformative incident many years before she became CEO of Vancouver-based satellite technology company Norsat International Inc. As a co-op engineering student, Chan was given the tedious task of replacing one circuit in each of 400 orange boxes. "When my supervisor noticed I was getting bored, he began describing the purpose of the device, which was a rescue beacon," she recalls. The supervisor then told Chan how one of those beacons had recently saved lives on a family-owned fishing vessel off the Alaska coast. A sudden storm had capsized the boat, but search and rescue teams were able to save the family within a few hours because of the rescue beacon. "This [story] forever stamped into my mind the value of what we do here, and I'm just as passionate about developing communications technology today as I was back then," says Chan.[84]

Authentic leadership is more than self-awareness; it also involves behaving in ways that are consistent with that self-concept rather than pretending to be someone else. It is difficult enough to lead others as your natural self; to lead others while pretending to be someone else is nearly

---

EXHIBIT 12.6 Authentic Leadership

Know yourself	Be yourself
• Engage in self-reflection • Receive feedback from trusted sources • Understand your life story	• Develop your own style • Apply your values • Maintain a positive core self-evaluation

Debating Point: SHOULD LEADERS REALLY BE AUTHENTIC ALL THE TIME?

According to popular business books and several scholarly articles, authentic leadership is one of the core attributes of effective leaders. Authentic leaders know themselves and act in accordance with that self-concept. They live their personal values and find a leadership style that best matches their personality. Furthermore, authentic leaders have a sense of purpose, often developed through a crisis or similar "crucible" event in their lives.

It makes sense that leaders should be authentic. After all, as singer Liza Minnelli has often said, "I would rather be a first-rate version of myself than a second-rate version of anybody else."* In other words, leaders fare better by acting out their natural beliefs and tendencies than by acting like someone else. Furthermore, authenticity results in consistency, which is a foundation of trust. So, by being authentic, leaders are more likely to be trusted by followers.†

But should leaders always be themselves and act consistently with their beliefs and personality? Not necessarily, according to a few experts. The concept of authentic leadership seems to be at odds with well-established research showing that people are evaluated as more effective leaders when they have a high rather than low self-monitoring personality.‡

High "self-monitors" quickly understand their social environment and easily adapt their behaviour to that environment. In other words, high self-monitors change their behaviour to suit what others expect from them. In contrast, low self-monitors behave consistently with their personality and self-concept. They do not change their beliefs, style, or behaviours across social contexts. On the contrary, they feel much more content with high congruence between who they are and what they do, even when their natural style does not fit the situation.

Employees prefer an adaptive (i.e., high self-monitoring) leader because they have preconceived prototypes of how leaders should act (implicit leadership theory, which we discussed earlier in this chapter).§ Authentic leaders are more likely to violate those prototypical expectations and, consequently, to be viewed as less leader-like. The message from this is that leadership is a role that its incumbents are required to perform rather than being free to completely "act naturally." Ironically, while applauding the virtues of authentic leadership, the late leadership expert Warren Bennis acknowledged that "leadership is a performance art." His point was that leaders function best when they act naturally in the leadership role, but the reality of any performance is that people can never be fully themselves.‖

Furthermore, while being yourself is authentic, it may convey an image of inflexibility and insensitivity.¶ This problem was apparent to one management professor and consultant when working recently with a client. The executive's staff followed a work process that was comfortable to the executive but not to many of her employees. When asked to consider adopting a process that was easier for her staff, the executive replied, "Look. This is just how I work." The executive was being authentic, but the inflexibility undermined employee performance and morale.§§

* Liza Minnelli makes this statement to explain why she doesn't perform the songs made famous by her mother, Judy Garland. The earliest versions of this quotation are found in *New Woman* magazine, Vol 8, 1978 and in the 1975 autobiography by Vincente Minnelli, Liza Minnelli's father. The version cited here is from: E. Santosuosso, "Minnelli Brings a Real-Life Concert to Town," *Boston Globe,* 24 September 1992, 61.

† B.J. Avolio et al., "Unlocking the Mask: A Look at the Process by Which Authentic Leaders Impact Follower Attitudes and Behaviors," *Leadership Quarterly* 15 (2004): 801–23.

‡ R.J. Ellis, "Self-Monitoring and Leadership Emergence in Groups," *Personality and Social Psychology Bulletin* 14, no. 4 (1988): 681–93; D.V. Day et al., "Self-Monitoring Personality at Work: A Meta-Analytic Investigation of Construct Validity," *Journal of Applied Psychology* 87, no. 2 (2002): 390–401; I.O. Tueretgen, P. Unsal, and I. Erdem, "The Effects of Sex, Gender Role, and Personality Traits on Leader Emergence— Does Culture Make a Difference?," *Small Group Research* 39, no. 5 (2008): 588–615; D.U. Bryant et al., "The Interaction of Self-Monitoring and Organizational Position on Perceived Effort," *Journal of Managerial Psychology* 26, no. 2 (2011): 138–54.

§ A.G. Bedeian and D.V. Day, "Can Chameleons Lead?," *The Leadership Quarterly* 15, no. 5 (2004): 687–718.

‖ W. Bennis, "We Need Leaders," *Executive Excellence* 27, no. 12 (2010): 4. Also see D. Nyberg and S. Sveningsson, "Paradoxes of Authentic Leadership: Leader Identity Struggles," *Leadership* 10, no. 4 (2014): 437–55.

¶ A.G. Bedeian and D.V. Day, "Can Chameleons Lead?," *The Leadership Quarterly* 15, no. 5 (2004): 687–718.

§§ D. Gruenfeld and L. Zander, "Authentic Leadership Can Be Bad Leadership," *Harvard Business Review Blog,* Harvard Business School, 2011, http://blogs.hbr.org.

impossible. To be themselves, great leaders regulate their decisions and behaviour in several ways. First, they develop their own style and, where appropriate, move into positions where that style is most effective. Although effective leaders adapt their behaviour to the situation to some extent, they invariably understand and rely on decision methods and interpersonal styles that feel most comfortable to them.

Second, effective leaders continually think about and consistently apply their stable hierarchy of personal values to those decisions and behaviours. Leaders face many pressures and temptations, such as achieving short-term share price targets at the cost of long-term profitability. Experts note that authentic leaders demonstrate self-discipline by remaining anchored to their values. Third, leaders maintain consistency around their self-concept by having a strong, positive self-evaluation. They have high self-esteem and self-efficacy as well as an internal locus of control (Chapter 3).

PERSONAL ATTRIBUTES PERSPECTIVE LIMITATIONS AND PRACTICAL IMPLICATIONS

Personality, experience, self-concept, and other individual characteristics potentially contribute to a leader's effectiveness. Still, the personal attributes perspective has a few limitations.[85] First, it assumes that all effective leaders have the same personal characteristics that are equally important in all situations. This is probably a false assumption; leadership is far too complex to have a universal list of traits that apply to every condition. Some attributes might not be important all the time. Second, alternative combinations of attributes may be equally successful; two people with different sets of personal characteristics might be equally good leaders. Third, the personal attributes perspective views leadership as something within a person, yet experts emphasize that leadership is relational. People are effective leaders because of their favourable relationships with followers, not just because they possess specific personal characteristics.[86]

Also remember from our discussion earlier in this chapter that, in the short term, followers tend to define others as effective or ineffective leaders based on their personal characteristics rather than whether the leader actually makes a difference to the organization's success. People who exhibit self-confidence, extraversion, and other traits are called leaders because they fit the widely held prototype of an effective leader. Alternatively, if someone is successful, observers might assign several nonobservable personal characteristics to them, such as intelligence, confidence, and drive. In short, the link between personal characteristics and effective leadership is muddied by several perceptual distortions.

One important final point: The personal attributes perspective of leadership does not necessarily imply that leadership is a talent acquired at birth. On the contrary, attributes indicate only leadership *potential*, not leadership performance. People with these characteristics become effective leaders only after they have developed and mastered the necessary leadership behaviours through experience. However, even those with fewer leadership attributes may become very effective leaders by more fully developing their potential.

Cross-Cultural and Gender Issues in Leadership

LO7

Along with the four perspectives of leadership presented throughout this chapter, cultural values and practices affect what

leaders do. Culture shapes the leader's values and norms, which influence their decisions and actions. Cultural values also shape the expectations that followers have of their leaders. An executive who acts inconsistently with cultural expectations is more likely to be perceived as an ineffective leader. Furthermore, leaders who deviate from those values may experience various forms of influence to get them to conform to the leadership norms and expectations of society. Thus, differences in leadership practices across cultures are partly explained by implicit leadership theory, which was described earlier in this chapter.

A major global research project over the past two decades has found that some features of leadership are universal and some differ across cultures.[83] One leadership category, called *charismatic visionary,* is a universally recognized concept, and middle managers around the world believe it is characteristic of effective leaders. Charismatic visionary represents a cluster of concepts including visionary, inspirational, performance orientation, integrity, and decisiveness.[84] Participative leadership is perceived as characteristic of effective leadership in low power distance cultures but less so in high power distance cultures.[85] In summary, some features of leadership are universal and some differ across cultures.

GENDER AND LEADERSHIP

Studies in work settings have generally found that male and female leaders do not differ in their levels of task-oriented or people-oriented leadership. The main explanation is that real-world jobs require similar behaviour from male and female job incumbents.[86] However, women do adopt a participative leadership style more readily than their male counterparts. One possible reason is that, compared to boys, girls are often raised to be more egalitarian and less status-oriented, which is consistent with being participative. There is also some evidence that, compared to men, women have somewhat better interpersonal skills, and this translates into their relatively greater use of the participative leadership style. A third explanation is that employees are motivated by their own gender stereotypes to expect female leaders to be more participative. Thus, female leaders comply with follower expectations to some extent.

Several studies report that women are rated higher than men on the emerging leadership qualities of coaching, teamwork, and empowering employees.[87] Yet research also suggests that women are evaluated negatively when they try to apply the full range of leadership styles, particularly more directive and autocratic approaches. Thus, ironically, women may be well suited to contemporary leadership roles, yet they often continue to face implicit leadership challenges due to followers' gender stereotypes and prototypes of leaders.[88] Overall, both male and female leaders must be sensitive to the fact that followers have expectations about how leaders should act.

Chapter Summary

LO1

Define leadership and shared leadership.

Leadership is defined as the ability to influence, motivate, and enable others to contribute toward the effectiveness and success of the organizations of which they are members. Leaders use influence to motivate followers and arrange the work environment so they do the job more effectively. Shared leadership views leadership as a role rather than a formal position, so employees throughout the organization act informally as leaders as the occasion arises. These situations include serving as champions for specific ideas or changes as well as filling leadership roles where it is needed.

LO2

Describe the four elements of transformational leadership and explain why they are important for organizational change.

Transformational leadership begins with a strategic vision, which is a positive representation of a future state that energizes and unifies employees. A vision is values-based, a distant goal, abstract, and meaningful to employees. Transformational leaders effectively communicate the vision by framing it around values, showing sincerity and passion toward the vision, and using symbols, metaphors, and other vehicles that contribute richer meaning to the vision. Transformational leaders model the vision (walk the talk) and encourage employees to experiment with new behaviours and practices that are potentially more consistent with the vision's future state. They also build employee commitment to the vision through the above activities as well as by celebrating milestones to the vision. Transformational leaders are not necessarily charismatic, and charismatic leaders do not necessarily apply transformational leadership behaviours.

LO3

Compare managerial leadership with transformational leadership, and describe the features of task-oriented, people-oriented, and servant leadership.

Managerial leadership includes the daily activities that support and guide the performance and well-being of individual employees and the work unit toward current objectives and practices. Transformational and managerial leadership are dependent on each other, but differ in their assumptions of stability versus change and their micro versus macro focus.

Task-oriented behaviours include assigning employees to specific tasks, clarifying their work duties and procedures, ensuring they follow company rules, and pushing them to reach their performance capacity. People-oriented behaviours include showing mutual trust and respect for subordinates, demonstrating a genuine concern for their needs, and having a desire to look out for their welfare.

Servant leadership defines leadership as serving others toward their need fulfilment and personal development and growth. Servant leaders have a natural desire or "calling" to serve others. They maintain a relationship with others that is humble, egalitarian, and accepting. Servant leaders also anchor their decisions and actions in ethical principles and practices.

LO4

Discuss the elements of path–goal theory and leadership substitutes theory.

Path–goal theory of leadership takes the view that effective managerial leadership involves diagnosing the situation and using the most appropriate style for the situation. The core model identifies four leadership styles—directive, supportive, participative, and achievement-oriented—and several contingencies relating to the characteristics of the employee and of the situation. Leadership substitutes theory identifies contingencies that either limit the leader's ability to influence subordinates or make a particular leadership style unnecessary.

LO5

Describe the two components of the implicit leadership perspective.

According to the implicit leadership perspective, people have leadership prototypes, which they use to evaluate the leader's effectiveness. Furthermore, people form a romance of leadership; they want to believe that leaders make a difference, so they engage in fundamental attribution error and other perceptual distortions to support their belief that leaders have an impact.

LO6

Identify eight personal attributes associated with effective leaders and describe authentic leadership.

The personal attributes perspective identifies the characteristics of effective leaders. Recent writing suggests that leaders have specific personality characteristics, positive self-concept, drive, integrity, leadership motivation, knowledge of the business, cognitive and practical intelligence, and emotional intelligence. Authentic leadership refers to how well leaders are aware of, feel comfortable with, and act consistently with their self-concept. Authentic leadership consists mainly of two parts: self-awareness and engaging in behaviour that is consistent with one's self-concept.

LO7

Discuss cultural and gender similarities and differences in leadership.

Cultural values influence the leader's personal values, which in turn influence their leadership practices. Women generally do not differ from men in their degree of people-oriented or task-oriented leadership. However, female leaders more often adopt a participative style. Research also suggests that people evaluate female leaders on the basis of gender stereotypes, which may result in higher or lower ratings.

Key Terms

authentic leadership

implicit leadership theory

leadership

leadership substitutes theory

learning orientation

managerial leadership

path–goal leadership theory

servant leadership

shared leadership

transformational leadership

Critical Thinking Questions

1. Why is it important for top executives to value and support shared leadership?

2. Transformational leadership is the most popular perspective of leadership. However, it is far from perfect. Discuss the limitations of transformational leadership.

3. This chapter distinguished charismatic leadership from transformational leadership. Yet charisma is identified by most employees and managers as a characteristic of effective leaders. Why is charisma commonly related to leadership? In your opinion, are the best leaders charismatic? Why or why not?

4. Consider your favourite teacher. What people-oriented and task-oriented leadership behaviours did they use effectively? In general, do you think students prefer an instructor who is more people-oriented or task-oriented? Explain your preference.

5. Your employees are skilled and experienced customer service representatives who perform nonroutine tasks, such as solving unique customer problems or meeting special needs with the company's equipment. Use path–goal theory to identify the most appropriate leadership style(s) you should use in this situation. Be sure to fully explain your answer, and discuss why other styles are inappropriate.

6. Identify a current political leader (e.g., prime minister, premier, mayor) and their recent accomplishments. Now, using the implicit leadership perspective, think of ways that these accomplishments of the leader may be overstated. In other words, explain why they may be due to factors other than the leader.

7. Find two job advertisements for management or executive positions. What leadership attributes are mentioned in these ads? If you were on the selection panel, what methods would you use to identify these personal attributes in job applicants?

8. How do you think emotional, cognitive, and practical intelligence influence authentic leadership?

9. You hear two people debating the merits of women as leaders. One person claims that women make better leaders than do men because women are more sensitive to their employees' needs and involve them in organizational decisions. The other person counters that although these leadership styles may be increasingly important, most women have trouble gaining acceptance as leaders when they face tough situations in which a more autocratic style is required. Discuss the accuracy of the comments made in this discussion.

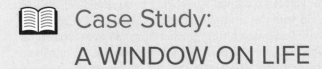

Case Study:
A WINDOW ON LIFE

by Steven L. McShane, University of Newcastle (Australia)

For Gilles LaCroix, there is nothing quite as beautiful as a handcrafted wood-framed window. LaCroix's passion for windows goes back to his youth in St. Jean, Quebec, where he was taught how to make residential windows by an elderly carpenter. He learned about the characteristics of good wood, the preferred tools to use, and how to choose the best glass from local suppliers. LaCroix apprenticed with the carpenter in his small workshop and, when the carpenter retired, was given the opportunity to operate the business himself.

LaCroix hired his own apprentice as he built up business in the local area. His small operation soon expanded as the quality of windows built by LaCroix Industries Ltd. became better known. Within eight years, the company employed nearly 25 people and the business had moved to larger facilities to accommodate the increased demand from southern Quebec. In these early years, LaCroix spent most of his time in the production shop, teaching new apprentices the unique skills that he had mastered and applauding the journeymen for their accomplishments. He often repeated the idea that LaCroix products had to be of the highest quality because they gave families a "window on life."

After 15 years, LaCroix Industries employed over 200 people. A profit-sharing program was introduced to give employees a financial reward for their contribution to the organization's success. Due to the company's expansion, headquarters had to be moved to another area of town, but the founder never lost touch with the workforce. Although new apprentices were now taught entirely by the master carpenters and other craftspeople, LaCroix would still chat with plant and office employees several times each week.

When a second work shift was added, LaCroix would show up during the evening break with coffee and boxes of doughnuts and discuss how the business was doing and how it had become so successful through quality workmanship. Production employees enjoyed the times when he would gather them together to announce new contracts with developers from Montreal and Toronto. After each announcement, LaCroix would thank everyone for making the business a success. They knew that LaCroix quality had become a standard of excellence in window manufacturing across Canada.

It seemed that almost every time he visited, LaCroix would repeat the now well-known phrase that LaCroix products had to be of the highest quality because they provided a window on life to so many families. Employees never grew tired of hearing this from the company founder. However, the phrase gained extra meaning when LaCroix began showing his employees photos of families looking through windows made by LaCroix Industries. At first, LaCroix would personally visit developers and homeowners with a camera in hand. Later, as the "window on life" photos became known by developers and customers, people would send in photos of their own families looking through elegant front windows made by LaCroix Industries. The company's marketing staff began using this idea, as well as LaCroix's famous phrase, in their advertising. After one such marketing campaign, hundreds of photos were sent in by satisfied customers. Production and office employees took time after work to write personal letters of thanks to those who had submitted photos.

As the company's age reached the quarter-century mark, LaCroix, now in his mid-fifties, realized that the organization's success and survival depended on expansion into the United States. After consulting with employees, LaCroix made the difficult decision to sell a majority share to Build-All Products, Inc., a conglomerate with international marketing expertise in building products. As part of the agreement, Build-All brought in a vice-president to oversee production operations while LaCroix spent more time meeting with developers around North America. LaCroix would return to the plant and office at every opportunity, but often this was possible only once a month.

Rather than visiting the production plant, Jan Vlodoski, the new production vice-president, would rarely leave his office in the company's downtown headquarters. Instead, production orders were sent to supervisors by memorandum. Although product quality had been a priority throughout the company's history, less attention had been paid to inventory controls. Vlodoski introduced strict inventory guidelines and outlined procedures on using supplies for each shift. Goals were established for supervisors to meet specific inventory targets. Whereas employees previously could have tossed out several pieces of warped wood, they would now have to justify this action, usually in writing.

Vlodoski also announced new procedures for purchasing production supplies. LaCroix Industries had highly trained purchasing staff who worked closely with senior craftspeople when selecting suppliers, but Vlodoski wanted to bring in Build-All's procedures. The new purchasing methods removed production leaders from the decision process and, in some cases, resulted in trade-offs that LaCroix's employees would not have made earlier. A few employees quit during this time, saying that they did not feel comfortable about producing a window that would not stand the test of time. However, unemployment was high in St. Jean, so most staff members remained with the company.

After one year, inventory expenses had decreased by approximately 10 percent, but the number of defective windows returned by developers and wholesalers had increased markedly. Plant employees had known that the number of defective windows would increase as they had used somewhat lower-quality materials to reduce inventory costs. However, they heard almost no news about the seriousness of the problem until Vlodoski sent a memo to all production staff saying that quality must be maintained. During the latter part of the first year under Vlodoski, a few employees had the opportunity to personally ask LaCroix about the changes and express their concerns. LaCroix apologized, saying due to his travels to new regions he had not heard about the problems, and that he would look into the matter.

Exactly 18 months after Build-All had become majority shareholder of LaCroix Industries, LaCroix called together five of the original staff in the plant. The company founder looked pale and shaken as he said that Build-All's actions were inconsistent with his vision of the company and, for the first time in his career, he did not know what to do. Build-All was not pleased with the arrangement either. Although LaCroix windows still enjoyed a healthy market share and were competitive for the value, the company did not quite provide the minimum 18 percent return on equity that the conglomerate expected. LaCroix asked his long-time companions for advice.

Discussion Questions

1. Identify the symptoms indicating that problems exist at LaCroix Industries, Ltd.

2. Use one or more leadership theories to analyze the underlying causes of the current problems at LaCroix Industries. What other organizational behaviour theories might also help to explain some of the problems?

3. What should Gilles LaCroix do in this situation?

Team Exercise:
LEADERSHIP DIAGNOSTIC ANALYSIS

Purpose To help students learn about the different path-goal leadership styles and when to apply each style.

Instructions

Step 1: Students individually write down two incidents in which someone had been an effective manager or leader over them. The leader and situation might be from work, a sports team, a student work group, or any other setting where leadership might emerge. For example, students might describe how their supervisor in a summer job pushed them to reach higher performance goals than they would have done otherwise. Each incident should state the actual behaviours that the leader used, not just general statements (e.g., "My boss sat down with me and we agreed on specific targets and deadlines, then he said several times over the next few weeks that I was capable of reaching those goals.") Each incident requires only two or three sentences to answer.

Step 2: After everyone has written their two incidents, the instructor will form small groups (typically about four or five

students). Each team will answer the following questions for each incident presented in that team:

Which path–goal theory leadership style(s)—directive, supportive, participative, or achievement-oriented—did the leader apply in this incident?

Ask the person who wrote the incident about the conditions that made this leadership style (or these styles, if more than one was used) appropriate in this situation. The team should list these contingency factors clearly and, where possible, connect them to the contingencies described in path–goal theory. (Note: the team might identify path–goal leadership contingencies that are not described in the book. These, too, should be noted and discussed.)

Step 3: After the teams have diagnosed the incidents, each team will describe to the entire class the most interesting incidents as well as its diagnosis of that incident. Other teams will critique the diagnosis. Any leadership contingencies not mentioned in the textbook should also be presented and discussed.

Self-Assessments for Chapter 12

SELF-ASSESSMENT NAME	DESCRIPTION
What are your transformational leadership tendencies?	Transformational leadership is about leading change toward a better future. This popular leadership perspective includes several dimensions, representing specific sets of behaviours. This instrument estimates your level of transformational leadership and its specific elements.
What is your preferred managerial leadership style?	Managerial leadership refers to behaviours that improve employee performance and well-being in the current situation. These objectives require a variety of managerial leadership styles in different situations. This self-assessment estimates your preferred leadership style on the two most commonly studied dimensions of managerial leadership.
Do leaders make a difference?	People have different views about the extent to which leaders influence the organization's success. Those with a high romance of leadership attribute the causes of organizational events much more to its leaders and much less to the economy, competition, and other factors beyond the leader's short-term control. This self-assessment estimates your romance of leadership score.

CHAPTER 13
Designing Organizational Structures

LEARNING OBJECTIVES
After reading this chapter, you should be able to:

LO1 Describe three types of coordination in organizational structures.

LO2 Discuss the role and effects of span of control, centralization, and formalization, and relate these elements to organic and mechanistic organizational structures.

LO3 Identify and evaluate six types of departmentalization.

LO4 Explain how the external environment, organizational size, technology, and strategy are relevant when designing an organizational structure.

Sobeys Inc. is Canada's second-largest food retailer, but it almost didn't survive its acquisition of Safeway Canada a few years ago. The board of Empire Company Ltd. (Sobeys' parent company) eventually replaced the CEO who led the Safeway acquisition with Michael Medline, previously chief executive of Canadian Tire. A few months after joining the Stellarton, N.S.-based grocery retailer, Medline introduced "Project Sunrise," a three-year initiative to streamline the business and cut annual costs by $500 million.

Redesigning Sobeys' organizational structure was a central feature of Project Sunrise. "The future Sobeys will operate with a simpler, leaner structure, more efficient core processes and tools, and will better leverage its $24-billion national scale," said Medline when the initiative was announced. Along with its numerous store brands— Sobeys, Safeway, IGA, Foodland, FreshCo, Thrifty Foods, Farm Boy, etc.—the company was previously organized around a geographic divisional structure (Quebec, Atlantic, etc.). The result was a large bureaucracy with expensive duplication and convoluted decision making.

"We are a $24-billion retailer and we act more like a number of $5-billion companies," Medline complained soon after his arrival at Sobeys. "We are probably the most difficult company for [suppliers] to do business with, and not because of our people—the structure was holding us back."

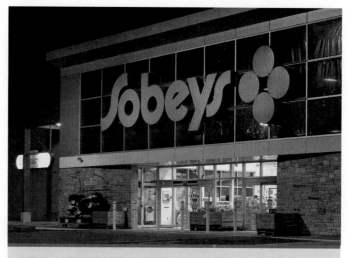

By redesigning its organizational structure, Sobeys recovered from a disastrous acquisition and became a strong competitor among grocery retailers.
©kevin brine/Shutterstock

Project Sunrise transformed Sobeys from a geographic to a functional organizational structure, initially consisting of marketing, finance, human resources, legal, sustainability, and three operations groups. Two operations groups (Full Service and Discount) manage the company's grocery store brands. The third operations group (called Related Businesses) is responsible for pharmacy, wholesale, fuel, liquor, and other non-grocery enterprises. The three operations groups integrate and centralize the former brand and geographic groups, but with substantial staff reductions (800 office staff across Canada were made redundant).

As annual savings approached (and eventually exceeded) Project Sunrise's objective, Medline announced that "resetting the foundation of Sobeys and creating a new organization structure" was almost complete. More recently, in a "shift to offence," he further tweaked the organizational structure by adding two other functional direct reports: an executive responsible for e-commerce and another in charge of innovation & strategy. These senior leadership roles emphasize Sobeys' future priorities around online/delivery shopping and other technological innovations. The company also partnered with a British firm that is building and operating automated customer fulfilment centres for Sobeys online/delivery business.

"We're putting in place the teams, tools, and culture that we need to drive innovation on our business and to win the next generation of grocery retailing," Medline says enthusiastically.[1]

Sobeys' transformation and recovery illustrates how an organization's structure is an important instrument for organizational change. **Organizational structure** refers to the division of labour as well as the patterns of coordination, communication, workflow, and formal power that direct organizational activities. Structure formally dictates the allocation of financial, power, and information resources, as well as what activities receive the most attention. For example, Sobeys' new structure centralizes some decision making and shifts more power from geographic centres to the three types of retail groups. It also refocuses attention and resources around e-commerce and other emerging technologies in the grocery retail business.

> **organizational structure** The division of labour as well as the patterns of coordination, communication, workflow, and formal power that direct organizational activities.

The topic of organizational structure typically conjures up images of an organizational chart. Organizational structure includes these reporting relationships, but it also includes other features that relate to work standards and rules, team dynamics, power relationships, information flow, and job design. As mentioned, the organization's structure is an important instrument in an executive's toolkit for organizational change because it establishes new communication patterns and aligns employee behaviour with the corporate vision. Indeed, one recent global survey of 7,000 business and human resources leaders in 130 countries (including several hundred in Canada) reported that organizational design was their firm's most important trend or priority to improve human capital (leadership and corporate culture were second and third most important, respectively).[2]

This chapter begins by introducing the two fundamental processes in organizational structure: division of labour and coordination. This is followed by a detailed investigation of the four main elements of organizational structure: span of control, centralization, formalization, and departmentalization. The latter part of this chapter examines the contingencies of organizational design, including external environment, organizational size, technology, and strategy.

Division of Labour and Coordination

LO1

All organizational structures include two fundamental requirements: the division of labour into distinct tasks and the coordination of that labour so employees are able to accomplish common goals.[3] Organizations are groups of people who work interdependently toward some purpose. To effectively accomplish this common purpose, most work is divided into manageable chunks, particularly when there are many different tasks required to complete the work. Organizations also introduce various coordinating mechanisms to ensure that everyone is working in concert toward the same objectives.

DIVISION OF LABOUR

Division of labour refers to the subdivision of work into separate jobs assigned to different people. Subdivided work leads to job specialization, because each job now includes a narrow subset of the tasks necessary to complete the product or service. Sobeys divides its employees into hundreds of specific jobs to more effectively transport, stock, and sell food and related merchandise. As companies get larger, horizontal division of labour is usually accompanied by vertical division of labour. Some people are assigned the task of supervising employees, others are responsible for managing those supervisors, and so on.

Why do companies divide the work into several jobs? As we described in Chapter 6, job specialization increases work efficiency.[4] Job incumbents can master their tasks quickly because work cycles are shorter. Less time is wasted changing from one task to another. Training costs are reduced because employees require fewer physical and mental skills to accomplish the assigned work. Finally, job specialization makes it easier to match people with specific aptitudes or skills to the jobs for which they are best suited. It is almost impossible for one person working alone to competitively purchase, transport, store, stock, and sell thousands of grocery products; instead, this enterprise requires hundreds of people with diverse knowledge and skills.

COORDINATING WORK ACTIVITIES

When people divide work among themselves, they require coordinating mechanisms to ensure that everyone works in concert. In fact, the extent to which work can be effectively divided among several people and work units depends on how well the divided work can be coordinated. When an organization divides work beyond its capacity to coordinate that work, individual effort is wasted due to misalignment, duplication, and mistiming of tasks. Coordination also tends to become more expensive and difficult as the division of

labour increases. Therefore, companies specialize jobs only to the point where it isn't too costly or challenging to coordinate the people in those jobs.[5]

Every organization—from the two-person tax accounting business to the largest corporate entity—uses one or more of the following coordinating mechanisms:[6] informal communication, formal hierarchy, and standardization (see Exhibit 13.1). These forms of coordination align the work of staff within the same department as well as across work units. Coordinating mechanisms are also critical when several organizations work together, such as in joint ventures and humanitarian aid programs.[7]

Coordination through Informal Communication

All organizations rely on informal communication as a coordinating mechanism. This process includes sharing information on mutual tasks as well as forming common mental models so that employees synchronize work activities using the same cognitive road map.[8] Informal communication is vital in nonroutine and ambiguous situations because employees need to exchange a large volume of information through face-to-face communication and other media-rich channels. Sobeys relies on coordination through informal communication at each of its stores and warehouses when daily nonroutine and ambiguous situations call for this flexible form of coordination.

Coordination through informal communication is easiest in small firms, but information technologies have further enabled this coordinating mechanism at Sobeys and in other large organizations.[9] Companies employing thousands of people also support informal communication by keeping each production site small. Magna International, the Canadian global auto-parts manufacturer, keeps many

EXHIBIT 13.1 Coordinating Mechanisms in Organizations

Form of coordination	Description	Subtypes/strategies
Informal communication	Sharing information on mutual tasks; forming common mental models to synchronize work activities	• Direct communication • Liaison roles • Integrator roles • Temporary teams
Formal hierarchy	Assigning legitimate power to individuals, who then use this power to direct work processes and allocate resources	• Direct supervision • Formal communication channels
Standardization	Creating routine patterns of behaviour or outpu	• Standardized skills • Standardized processes • Standardized output

Global Connections 13.1

ESA COORDINATES SATELLITE DESIGN THROUGH CONCURRENT ENGINEERING*

More than 2,000 people work at the European Space Agency (ESA), yet the organization relies extensively on informal communication to coordinate the design of satellites and their missions. The government agency forms cross-disciplinary teams that meet in a specially constructed Concurrent Design Facility (CDF) in the Netherlands. This concurrent engineering arrangement is effective because it enables representatives from a dozen interdependent departments to fluidly coordinate through face-to-face interaction.

"Concurrent engineering involves bringing together all necessary experts into a single room to work together in real time," explains Massimo Bandecchi, who founded ESA's Concurrent Design Facility two decades ago. "With all disciplines contributing at the same time and place, we tackle problems from all points of view, to turn a naturally sequential process into something more 'concurrent'."

CDF technical writer Andrew Pickering describes the inefficiency of the sequential process. "Traditional mission design is an 'over-the-fence' type process, where one domain team—mission analysis for instance—starts work based on the initial mission requirements, then throws it over the fence to the next subsystem team, such as propulsion, passing it in turn to the next."

A typical ESA design team consists of two or three dozen people representing numerous disciplines, including propulsion, structures and mechanisms, flight dynamics, electrical systems, thermal control, as well as specialists in technical risk, organization, and cost engineering. The team meets in the CDF for four intense hours twice each week.

"It can be quite draining, but exciting at the same time, because there are always challenges arising," says CDF Study Leader Ilaria Roma. "As a team leader, it's like leading an orchestra, to sustain good communication, guide the process, and keep it moving toward finding solutions."

©Dean Mouhtaropoulos/Getty Images

* M. Bandecchi et al., "The ESA/ESTEC Concurrent Design Facility," in *Proceedings of the 2nd European Systems Engineering Conference* (European Systems Engineering Conference (EuSEC 2000), Munich, 2000), 329–36; "20 Years of ESA's Concurrent Design Facility: An Oral History," News release (Paris: European Space Agency, April 1, 2019); "Where Space Missions Are Born," News release (Paris: European Space Agency, April 1, 2019).

of its plants—including its recently opened paint shop in Hoče, Slovenia—to a maximum size of around 200 employees. Magna's leaders believe that employees have difficulty remembering each other's names in plants that are any larger, a situation that makes informal communication more difficult as a coordinating mechanism.[10]

Some large firms encourage informal communication through *liaison roles.* These employees transmit information between two work units that seldom communicate or coordinate directly with each other. For example, regional managers have liaison roles by coordinating their group's work with the company's activities in other regions. Coordination through informal communication is also possible in larger firms through *integrator roles.* These people coordinate a work process by encouraging employees in each work unit to directly share information and coordinate work activities with each other. Brand managers for luxury perfumes have integrator

roles because they ensure that fragrance developers, bottle designers, advertising creatives, production, and other groups work together to develop the product and brand's image.[11]

Large businesses also encourage coordination through informal communication by organizing employees from several departments into temporary teams. Known as *concurrent engineering,* this cross-disciplinary team-based coordination was pioneered by Toyota almost four decades ago and is now widespread throughout several industries. As design engineers work on product specifications, team members from production engineering, manufacturing, marketing, purchasing, and other departments provide immediate feedback as well as begin their contribution to the process. Without concurrent engineering teams, employees at each stage of product development face the cumbersome task of passing their work "over the wall" to the next department with limited or significantly delayed feedback.[12]

Coordination through Formal Hierarchy

Informal communication is the most flexible form of coordination, but it can become chaotic as the number of employees increases. Consequently, as organizations grow, a second coordinating mechanism gains importance: formal hierarchy.[13] Hierarchy assigns legitimate power to individuals, who then use this power to direct work processes and allocate resources. In other words, work is coordinated through direct supervision—the chain of command. For instance, Sobeys, FreshCo, and other grocery stores have managers and assistant managers who are responsible for ensuring that employees are properly trained, perform their respective tasks, and coordinate effectively with other staff.

A century ago, management scholars applauded the formal hierarchy as the best coordinating mechanism for large organizations. They argued that organizations are most effective when managers exercise their authority and employees receive orders from only one supervisor. The chain of command—in which information flows across work units only through supervisors and managers—was viewed as the backbone of organizational strength.

Although still important, formal hierarchy is much less popular today. One problem, which was minimized to some extent at Sobeys through Project Sunrise, is that hierarchical organizations are not as agile for coordination in complex and novel situations. Formal communication through the chain of command is rarely as fast or accurate as informal communication directly among employees. Another concern with formal hierarchy is that managers are able to closely supervise only a limited number of

 OB **by the NUMBERS**

Coordination through Micromanagement*

18% of 300 Canadian human resource managers say that micromanaging employees has the most negative effect on employee morale (second only to lack of open, honest communication).

59% of 450 American office workers say they have worked for a micromanager.

71% of 889 Koreans say that they have experienced a militaristic (authoritarian, patriarchic, oppressive management) culture at school or work.

39% of 2,000 American employees say that being a micromanager is the worst quality in a boss (most frequent choice, followed by being "overly critical").

31% of 1,525 working Canadians say they have experienced an overbearing micromanager who is constantly hovering and asking for status updates.

©Elnur/Shutterstock

* "Something to Talk About," News Release (Toronto: Accountemps, October 22, 2013); "The Beast in the Corner Office: A Living Nightmare for Many Canadians," News Release (Toronto: Monster Canada, October 28, 2015); "Survey: More Than Half of Employees Have Worked for a Micromanager," news release for Accountemps (Menlo Park, CA: PR Newswire, July 1, 2014); T.K. Ock, "Top-down Corporate Culture Continues to Take Its Toll," *Korea Herald,* July 19, 2016; "Study: The Worst Traits in a Boss," *Comparably* (blog), March 28, 2018, https://www.comparably.com/blog/study-the-worst-traits-in-a-boss/.

employees. As the business grows, the number of supervisors and layers of management must increase, resulting in a costly bureaucracy. A third problem is that today's workforce demands more autonomy over work and more involvement in company decisions. Coordination through formal hierarchy tends to limit employee autonomy and involvement, which increases employee complaints of being micromanaged.

Coordination through Standardization

Standardization, the third means of coordination, involves creating routine patterns of behaviour or output. This coordinating mechanism takes three distinct forms:

- *Standardized processes.* Quality and consistency of a product or service can often be improved by standardizing work activities through job descriptions and procedures.[14] For example, flow charts represent a standardized process. This coordinating mechanism works best when the task is routine (such as mass production) or simple (such as stocking shelves), but it is less effective in nonroutine and complex work such as product design or executive decision making.

- *Standardized outputs.* This form of standardization involves ensuring that individuals and work units have clearly defined goals and output measures (e.g., customer satisfaction, production efficiency). For instance, to coordinate the work of salespeople, companies assign sales targets rather than specific behaviours.

- *Standardized skills.* When work activities are too complex to standardize through processes or outputs, companies often coordinate work effort by extensively training employees or hiring people who have learned precise role behaviours from educational programs. Hospitals, accounting firms, and other organizations that employ professionals rely on coordination through standardized skills. They carefully hire people for their education, training, and past experience so they can perform tasks without continuous supervision, precise job descriptions, or exacting work process guidelines. Training is also a form of standardization through skills. Many companies have in-house training programs where employees learn how to perform tasks consistent with company expectations.

Division of labour and coordination of work represent the two fundamental ingredients of all organizations. But how work is divided, which coordinating mechanisms are emphasized, who makes decisions, and other issues are related to the four elements of organizational structure that we discuss over the next two sections of this chapter.

Elements of Organizational Structure

LO2

Every organizational structure consists of four elements. This section discusses three of them: span of control, centralization, and formalization. The fourth element—departmentalization—is presented in the next section.

SPAN OF CONTROL

Chief executive officers of large corporations are probably much busier today managing their direct reports than they were two or three decades ago. In the 1980s, CEOs of the largest companies had an average of five people (typically vice-presidents) reporting directly to them. By the end of the 1990s, this span of control increased to an average of 6.5 direct reports. Today, CEOs of the largest North American firms have an average of 10 direct reports, double the number a few decades earlier. This increase reflects the fact that most large companies are far more complex today. They operate in many markets, have more variety of products, and employ people with a broader array of technical specialties. Each type of variation demands top-level attention, so CEOs have more vice-presidents than ever before reporting directly to them. In other words, they have a wider span of control.[15]

Span of control (also called *span of management*) refers to the number of people reporting directly to the next level in the hierarchy. A narrow span of control exists when very few people report directly to a manager, whereas a wide span exists when a manager has many direct reports.[16] A century ago, French engineer and management scholar Henri Fayol strongly recommended a relatively narrow span of control, typically no more than 20 employees per supervisor and six supervisors per manager. Fayol championed formal hierarchy as the primary coordinating mechanism, so he believed that supervisors should closely monitor and coach employees. His views were similar to those of Napoleon Bonaparte, who declared that senior military leaders should have no more than five officers directly reporting to them. These prescriptions were based on the belief that managers simply could not monitor and control any more subordinates closely enough.[17]

> **span of control** The number of people directly reporting to the next level in the hierarchy.

Today, we know better. The best-performing manufacturing plants currently have an average of 38 production employees per supervisor (see Exhibit 13.2).[18] What's the secret here? Did Fayol, Napoleon, and others miscalculate the optimal span of control? The answer is that those sympathetic to hierarchical control believed that employees should perform the physical tasks, whereas supervisors

---

EXHIBIT 13.2 **Recommended, Actual, Estimated, and Enforced Spans of Control***

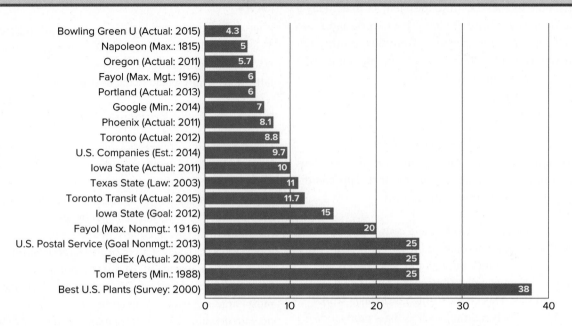

Note: Data represent the average number of direct reports per manager. "Max." is the maximum spans of control recommended by Napoleon Bonaparte and Henri Fayol. "Min." is the minimum span of control applied to teams by Google and recommended by Tom Peters. "Est." is the estimated average span of control across all major U.S. companies, according to consulting firm Deloitte. "Goal" refers to the span of control targets that the U.S. Postal Service and State of Iowa are trying to achieve. (USPS currently exceeds its goal.) The State of Texas number is the span of control mandated by law. The Best U.S. Plants number is the average span of control in American manufacturing facilities identified by *Industry Week* magazine as the most effective. "Actual" refers to the spans of control reported in the cities of Phoenix, Portland, and Toronto, the public service of the U.S. states of Oregon and Iowa, Bowling Green University, the Toronto Transit Commission, and FedEx Corporation in the years indicated. The City of Toronto number excludes firefighters and parks, which have unusually high spans of control. When these units are included, Toronto's span of control is 16.3.

* D. Thompson, "More on the Span of Control Issue," *Statesman Journal Blog* (Oregon), May 16, 2011; Iowa State Legislative Services Agency, *Span of Control,* Fiscal Note, Iowa State (Des Moines: Iowa Legislature, March 10, 2011); Western Management Consultants, *Service Efficiency Study Program Management Span of Control Review Report to the City Manager,* City of Toronto (Toronto: October 31, 2012); United States Postal Service, *Supervisor Workhours and Span of Control: Management Advisory* (Washington, DC: United States Postal Service, April 4, 2013); N. Fish and S. Novick, *FY 2013–14 Budget Subcommittee #1 Final Report,* City of Portland, Oregon (Portland, Oregon: April 8, 2013); E. Schmidt and J. Rosenberg, *How Google Works* (New York: Grand Central, 2014), 42–44; S. Stoll, *Accenture Update: Progress Report through August 31, 2015,* Bowling Green University (Bowling Green, OH: September 18, 2015); WMC Consultants, *Toronto Transit Commission Organizational Review Report,* Toronto Transit Commission (Toronto: July 2015); *The New Organization: Different by Design,* Global Human Capital Trends 2016 (New York: Deloitte University Press, 2016).

and other management personnel should make the decisions and monitor employees to make sure they performed their tasks. In contrast, the best-performing manufacturing operations today rely on self-directed teams, so direct supervision (formal hierarchy) is supplemented with other coordinating mechanisms. Self-directed teams coordinate mainly through informal communication and various forms of standardization (i.e., training and processes), so formal hierarchy plays more of a supporting role.

Managers can often accommodate a wider span of control because staff members are self-managing and coordinate mainly through standardized skills. For instance, nurse managers often have between 25 and 50 direct reports because nurses are professionally trained and have specific protocols to guide most of their work activity.[19]

A second factor influencing the optimal span of control is whether employees perform routine tasks. A wider span

of control is possible when employees perform routine jobs, because they require less direction or advice from supervisors. A narrow span of control is necessary when employees perform novel or complex tasks, because these employees tend to require more supervisory decisions and coaching. This principle is illustrated in a survey of property and casualty insurers. The average span of control in commercial-policy processing departments is around 15 employees per supervisor, whereas the span of control is 6.1 in claims service and 5.5 in commercial underwriting. Staff members in the latter two departments perform more technical work, so they have more novel and complex tasks, which requires more supervisor involvement. Commercial-policy processing, on the other hand, is like production work. Tasks are routine and have few exceptions, so managers have less coordinating to do with each employee.[20]

Vincit California

Vincit California opened offices in California a few years ago and currently employs three dozen people. So far, none of them has a manager. "We stand out for our lack of hierarchy," states Ville Houttu, CEO of the Finland-based company's American subsidiary that creates customized mobile apps for corporate clients. At Vincit, senior employees mentor new hires. Anyone can order supplies and convince co-workers to make workplace changes. "We don't have any managers—employees manage themselves," Houttu explains. "For instance, they don't need to go through an approval process to order something. We don't ask for written reports about what they're working on."*

* S.C. Goulding, "Top Workplaces 2018: How Finnish Culture Opens up Software Development at Vincit," Orange County Register, December 7, 2018; "Inc. Magazine Ranks Vincit among Best Workplaces 2019," News release (Irvine, Calif.: Vincit California, May 17, 2019).

A third influence on span of control is the degree of interdependence among employees within the department or team.[21] Generally, a narrow span of control is necessary for highly interdependent jobs because employees tend to experience more conflict with each other, which requires more of a manager's time to resolve. Also, employees are less clear on their personal work performance in highly interdependent tasks, so supervisors spend more time providing coaching and feedback.

Tall versus Flat Structures

Span of control is interconnected with organizational size (number of employees) and the number of layers in the organizational hierarchy. Consider two companies with the same number of employees. If Company A has a wider span of control (more direct reports per manager) than Company B,

then Company A necessarily has fewer layers of management (i.e., a flatter structure). The reason for this relationship is that a company with a wider span of control has more employees per supervisor, more supervisors for each middle manager, and so on. This larger number of direct reports, compared to a company with a narrower span of control, is possible only by removing layers of management.

The interconnection of span of control, organizational size (number of employees), and number of management layers has important implications. As organizations grow and employ more people, they must widen the span of control, build a taller hierarchy, or both. Most companies end up building taller structures because they rely on direct supervision to some extent as a coordinating mechanism and there are limits to how many people each manager can coordinate.

Unfortunately, building a taller hierarchy (more layers of management) creates problems. One concern is that executives in tall structures tend to receive lower-quality and less timely information. People tend to filter, distort, and simplify information before it is passed to higher levels in the hierarchy because they are motivated to frame the information in a positive light or to summarize it more efficiently. In contrast, information receives less manipulation in flat hierarchies, and is often received much more quickly than in tall hierarchies. "Any new idea condemned to struggle upward through multiple levels of rigidly hierarchical, risk-averse management is an idea that won't see daylight . . . until it's too late," warned Sergio Marchionne, the late Canadian-Italian CEO of Fiat Chrysler Automobiles.[22]

A second problem is that taller structures have higher overhead costs. With more managers per employee, tall hierarchies necessarily have more people administering the company, thereby reducing the percentage of staff who are actually making the product or providing the service. A third issue with tall hierarchies is that employees usually feel less empowered and engaged in their work. Hierarchies are power structures, so more levels of hierarchy tend to draw away power from people at the bottom of that hierarchy. Indeed, the size of the hierarchy itself tends to focus power around managers rather than employees.[23]

These problems have prompted companies to reduce management layers.[24] For example, the Alberta Energy Regulator recently removed dozens of vice-presidents and directors in its new organizational structure "with less hierarchy" that "would help us to become more effective, efficient, and resilient and better support us in delivering on our mandate." Thomson Reuters slashed its hierarchy to a maximum of six layers. The Canadian media conglomerate previously had up to 12 layers between the top executive and front-line staff. Conagra Foods also recently restructured into a flatter organization. CEO Sean Connolly says the packaged food company now has "fewer layers, broader spans of control and the workforce, we believe, is right-sized for speed, empowerment, agility, all the things we need to do."[25]

Although flattening the hierarchy has advantages, this organizational structure change can also produce negative consequences.[26] Critics warn that all companies need managers to translate corporate strategy into coherent daily operations. Delayering widens the span of control, leaving managers with less time to effectively coach employees, resolve conflicts, and make operational decisions within the work unit. Fewer layers also reduce the company's ability to develop managerial skills because there are fewer positions and steps to develop management talent. Promotions are also riskier because they involve a larger jump in responsibility in flatter, compared to taller, hierarchies.

The risks of flattening the organizational hierarchy became apparent at Treehouse a few years ago. The Portland, Oregon, online-education company made headlines by converting all of its managers (except the CEO) to front-line roles. Treehouse's 100 employees would manage themselves. Two years later, the company reversed course. Without managers, employees felt adrift, like "lonely islands with no support," observes Treehouse CEO Ryan Carson. "Humans want that support system and they want to be led, and that's OK." Carson also discovered that the completely flat hierarchy created productivity issues. "Some people weren't pulling their weight and it became clear really, really fast," admits Carson. "When you install management, you get accountability back."[27]

CENTRALIZATION AND DECENTRALIZATION

Centralization means that formal decision-making authority is held by a small group of people, typically those at the top of the organizational hierarchy.

Most organizations begin with centralized structures, as the founder makes most of the decisions and tries to direct the business toward their vision. As organizations grow, however, they diversify and their environments become more complex. Senior executives aren't able to process all the decisions that significantly influence the business. Consequently, larger organizations typically *decentralize;* that is, they disperse decision authority and power throughout the organization.

> **centralization** The degree to which formal decision-making authority is held by a small group of people, typically those at the top of the organizational hierarchy.

The optimal level of centralization or decentralization depends on several contingencies that we will examine later in this chapter. However, different degrees of decentralization can occur simultaneously in different parts of an organization. For instance, 7-Eleven centralizes decisions about information technology and supplier purchasing to improve buying power, increase cost efficiencies, and minimize complexity across the organization. Yet it decentralizes local inventory decisions to store managers because they have the best information about their customers and can respond quickly to local market needs. "We could never predict a busload of football players on a Friday night, but the store manager can," explains a 7-Eleven executive.[28]

FORMALIZATION

Formalization is the degree to which organizations standardize behaviour through rules, procedures, formal training, and related mechanisms.[29] In other words, companies become more formalized as they

> **formalization** The degree to which organizations standardize behaviour through rules, procedures, formal training, and related mechanisms.

©Matthew Horwood/Alamy Stock Photo

Fulfilment by Amazon is well-known—and sometimes infamously identified—for its very high formalization. The warehouse operations for Amazon's third-party sellers relies on standardization of work processes as a coordinating mechanism. Computer algorithms determine how many products employees should pick, move, pack, and store per hour. As soon as one product is picked, the employee's scanner displays the next item with a countdown of the time allowed to find and scan that item. Employees are told to walk at "Amazon pace," which is somewhere between walking and jogging. Bathroom breaks are timed.*

* J. Bloodworth, "I Worked in an Amazon Warehouse," *The Guardian,* September 17, 2018; M. Burin, "When You Click 'Buy Now,' This Is What Happens inside Amazon Australia's Warehouse," *ABC News (Australia),* February 19, 2019; M. Zahn and S. Paget, "'Colony of Hell': 911 Calls From Inside Amazon Warehouses," *The Daily Beast,* March 11, 2019.

increasingly rely on various forms of standardization to coordinate work.

Older companies tend to be more formalized because work activities become routinized, making them easier to document into standardized practices. Larger companies also tend to have more formalization because direct supervision and informal communication among employees do not operate as easily when large numbers of people are involved. External influences, such as government safety legislation and strict accounting rules, also encourage formalization.

Formalization may increase efficiency and compliance, but it can also create problems.[30] Rules and procedures reduce organizational flexibility, so employees follow prescribed behaviours even when the situation clearly calls for a customized response. High levels of formalization tend to undermine creativity. Some work rules become so convoluted that organizational efficiency would decline if they were actually followed as prescribed. Formalization is also a source of job dissatisfaction and work stress. Finally, rules and procedures have been known to take on a life of

their own in some organizations. They become the focus of attention rather than the organization's ultimate objectives of producing a product or service and serving its dominant stakeholders.

MECHANISTIC VERSUS ORGANIC STRUCTURES

We discussed span of control, centralization, and formalization together because they cluster around two broader organizational forms: mechanistic and organic structures (see Exhibit 13.3).[31] A **mechanistic structure** is characterized by a narrow span of control and high degree of formalization and centralization. Mechanistic structures have many rules and procedures, limited decision making at lower levels, tall hierarchies of people in specialized roles, and vertical rather than

mechanistic structure An organizational structure with a narrow span of control and a high degree of formalization and centralization.

EXHIBIT 13.3   **Contrasting Mechanistic and Organic Organizational Structures**

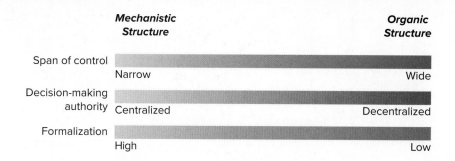

	Mechanistic Structure	*Organic Structure*
Span of control	Narrow	Wide
Decision-making authority	Centralized	Decentralized
Formalization	High	Low

horizontal communication flows. Tasks are rigidly defined and are altered only when sanctioned by higher authorities. Employees at Sobeys grocery stores and warehouses work within a moderately high level of mechanistic structure because decisions are fairly centralized (at least to store managers), job duties are clearly defined, and work activities are guided by established rules and procedures.

Companies with an **organic structure** have the opposite characteristics. They operate with a wide span of control, decentralized decision making, and little formalization. Tasks are fluid, adjusting to new situations and organizational needs. In extremely organic organizations, decision making is decentralized down to teams and individuals, and employees have enough autonomy to adapt their job duties to fit the situation.

> **organic structure** An organizational structure with a wide span of control, little formalization, and decentralized decision making.

As a general rule, mechanistic structures operate better in stable environments because they rely on efficiency and routine behaviours. Organic structures work better in rapidly changing (i.e., dynamic) environments because they are more flexible and responsive to the changes. Organic structures are also more compatible with human capital development (see Chapter 1) because they emphasize information sharing and an empowered workforce rather than hierarchy and status. However, the effectiveness of organic structures depends on how well employees have developed their roles and expertise.[32] Without these conditions, employees are unable to coordinate effectively with each other, resulting in errors and gross inefficiencies.

Forms of Departmentalization

LO3

Span of control, centralization, and formalization are important elements of organizational structure, but most people think about organizational charts when the discussion of organizational structure arises. The organizational chart represents the fourth element in the structuring of organizations, called *departmentalization.* Departmentalization specifies how employees and their activities are grouped together. It is a fundamental strategy for coordinating organizational activities because it influences organizational behaviour in the following ways:[33]

- Departmentalization establishes the chain of command—the system of common supervision among positions and units within the organization. It frames the membership of formal work teams and typically determines which positions and units must share resources. Thus, departmentalization establishes interdependencies among employees and subunits.

- Departmentalization focuses people around common mental models or ways of thinking, such as serving clients, developing products, or supporting a particular skill set. This focus is typically anchored around the common budgets and measures of performance assigned to employees within each departmental unit.

- Departmentalization encourages specific people and work units to coordinate through informal communication. With common supervision and resources, members within each configuration typically work near each other, so they can use frequent and informal interaction to get the work done.

Which organizational structure do you prefer? You can discover which organizational structure is most comfortable for you by completing this self-assessment in Connect.

Courtesy of David Chapman's Ice Cream

Chapman's Ice Cream Limited had a classic simple organizational structure when David and Penny Chapman started their business back in 1973. The couple and four employees performed all the work in a century-old creamery located in the village of Markdale, Ontario. "We did everything," recalls company president Penny Chapman (centre in photo with David at right and son Ashley with several employees). "We made the mixes, built the packages, we worked in cold storage . . . David went out on the road to do sales."

Chapman's grew quickly by offering unique ice cream flavours. The work was eventually divided into more specialized tasks and a functional structure emerged around production, marketing, research, and other departments. Today, Chapman's is Canada's largest independent ice cream manufacturer, employing 700 people and producing more than 200 products on 20 production lines. The company is also a global award winner for innovation in ice cream products.[*]

[*] A. Joseph, "The Cream Always Rises," *Canadian Packaging*, April 2012, 18–22; D. Crosby, "Chapman's Mixes in Some Fun," *Owen Sound Sun Times*, February 26, 2014, C11; "Chapman's Ice Cream Wins Most Innovative Ice Cream Award," news release for Chapman's Ice Cream (Thornbury, ON: Marketwired, October 29, 2015); A. Joseph, "Safety First," *Food In Canada*, October 2018.

There are almost as many organizational charts as there are businesses, but the six most common pure types of departmentalization are simple, functional, divisional, team-based, matrix, and network.

SIMPLE STRUCTURE

A century ago, Sobeys had a *simple structure*.[34] Initially, J.W. Sobey personally sourced from local farmers and delivered meat products to customers around Stellarton, Nova Scotia. A few years later, he opened a store, expanded into vegetables and other produce, and soon hired employees (including his teenage son, Frank Sobey) to serve customers and deliver groceries. Simple structures employ only a few people and typically offer only one distinct product or service. There is minimal hierarchy—usually just employees reporting to the owners. Employees perform broadly defined roles because there are insufficient economies of scale to assign them to specialized jobs. The simple structure is highly flexible and minimizes the walls that form between work units in other structures. However, the simple structure usually depends on the owner's direct supervision to coordinate work activities, so it is very difficult to operate as the company grows and becomes more complex.

FUNCTIONAL STRUCTURE

As organizations grow, they typically shift from a simple structure to a functional structure. Even after they adopt more complex organizational structures that we discuss later, they will have a functional structure at some level of the hierarchy. A **functional structure** organizes employees around specific knowledge or other resources (see Exhibit 13.4). Employees with marketing expertise are grouped into a marketing unit, those with production skills are located in manufacturing, engineers are found in product development, and so on. Organizations with functional structures are typically centralized to coordinate their activities effectively.

functional structure An organizational structure in which employees are organized around specific knowledge or other resources.

EXHIBIT 13.4   A Functional Organizational Structure

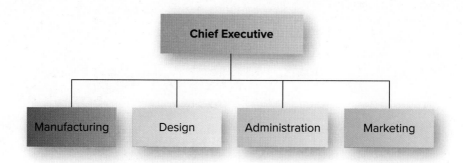

Evaluating the Functional Structure

As the opening case study described, "Project Sunrise" created a functional organizational structure to increase efficiency and improve decision making at Sobeys. A functional structure creates specialized pools of talent that typically serve everyone in the organization. As Sobeys discovered, pooling talent into one group improves economies of scale compared to dispersing functional specialists over different parts of the organization. The functional structure also increases employee identity with the specialization or profession. Direct supervision is easier in functional structures because managers oversee people with common issues and expertise.[35]

The functional structure also has limitations.[36] Grouping employees around their skills tends to focus attention on those skills and related professional needs rather than on the company's product, service, or client needs. Unless people are rotated through several functional units over time, they might not develop a broader understanding of the business. Compared with other structures, the functional structure usually produces more dysfunctional conflict and poorer coordination in serving clients or developing products. These problems occur because employees need to work with co-workers in other departments to complete organizational tasks, yet they have different subgoals and mental models about how to perform the work effectively. Together, these problems require substantial formal controls and coordination when people are organized around functions.

DIVISIONAL STRUCTURE

The **divisional structure** (sometimes called the *multidivisional* or *M-form* structure) groups employees around geographic areas, outputs (products or services), or clients. Exhibit 13.5 illustrates these three variations of divisional structure.[37] The *geographic divisional structure* organizes

employees around distinct regions of the country or world. Exhibit 13.5(a) illustrates the geographic divisional structure adopted by Saputo, the Montreal-based dairy foods company. The *product/service divisional structure* organizes employees around distinct outputs. Exhibit 13.5(b) illustrates the four product divisions at Medtronic, the American medical device company. The *client divisional structure* organizes employees around specific customer groups. Exhibit 13.5(c) illustrates the client-focused divisional structure at Thomson Reuters, the Toronto-based digital information services company.[38]

divisional structure An organizational structure in which employees are organized around geographic areas, outputs (products or services), or clients.

Which form of divisional structure should large organizations adopt? The answer depends mainly on the primary source of environmental diversity or uncertainty.[39] Suppose an organization has one type of product sold to people across the country. If customers have different needs across regions, or if provincial governments impose different regulations on the product, then a geographic structure would be best to be more vigilant of this diversity. On the other hand, if the company sells several types of products across the country and customer preferences and government regulations are similar everywhere, then a product structure would likely work best.

Saputo, the Canadian dairy foods company, is organized mainly around geographic regions, likely because regulations and sales channels vary more by country than by product. Top-level executives at McDonald's are responsible for several functions (marketing, finance, information technology, etc.) as well as two geographic divisions: U.S. and International. The international division of the fast-food chain, led by Canadian executive Ian Borden, is organized into dozens of countries.[40] This geographic organizational structure makes sense because even though it makes the

EXHIBIT 13.5   Three Types of Divisional Structure

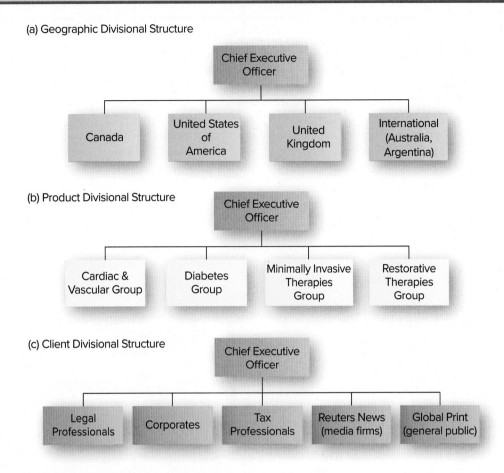

(a) Geographic Divisional Structure

(b) Product Divisional Structure

(c) Client Divisional Structure

Note: Diagram (a) shows the geographic divisions at Saputo; diagram (b) depicts the four product divisions of Medtronic; diagram (c) shows the five client divisions of Thomson Reuters. None of these firms has a pure divisional structure. At all three companies the top executive team also includes the heads of functional units. Medtronic executives reporting to the CEO are responsible for products (shown), geographic areas, or functional responsibilities.

same Big Mac throughout the world, McDonald's has more fish products in Hong Kong and more vegetarian products in India, in line with traditional diets in those countries. Medtronic has numerous country managers to anticipate and respond to cultural differences. However, the American medical devices firm places product groups (cardiac/vascular, diabetes, minimally invasive therapies, and restorative therapies) at the top of its organizational structure, likely because marketing and manufacturing activities vary much more across product divisions than across regions.

Many companies are moving away from structures that organize people around geographic clusters.[41] One reason is that clients can purchase products online and communicate with businesses from almost anywhere in the world, so local representation is becoming less important. Reduced geographic variation is another reason for the shift away from geographic structures; freer trade has reduced government intervention, and consumer preferences for many products and services are becoming more similar (converging) around the world. The third reason is that large companies increasingly have global business customers who demand one global point of purchase, not one in every country or region.

Evaluating the Divisional Structure

The divisional organizational structure is a building-block structure. As the company develops new products, services, or clients, it can sprout new divisions relatively easily. The divisional structure is also outcome-focused. It directs employee attention to customers and products, rather than to their own specialized knowledge.[42]

These advantages are offset by a number of limitations. First, the divisional structure tends to duplicate resources, such as production equipment and engineering or information technology expertise. Also, unless the division is quite

Global Connections 13.2

TOYOTA'S EVOLVING DIVISIONAL STRUCTURE[*]

Toyota Motor Company was fined $1.2 billion by the U.S. government, the largest penalty ever against an automaker, because it "misled regulators, misled customers, and even misstated the facts to Congress," regarding safety issues with its accelerator pedals. The Japanese company's safety processes and reporting procedures in the United States were subsequently monitored for three years. How could one of the largest and most respected automakers in the world get into this situation? A panel of independent experts commissioned by Toyota identified several issues ranging from supplier product quality to business processes. However, its main conclusion was that Toyota's functional organizational structure was inappropriate for the global organization.

Toyota's functional structure created silos around each specialization (sales, engineering, manufacturing), which transmitted information selectively to headquarters in Japan. The result was that most decisions were made by executives in Japan with limited knowledge about practices and problems in specific regions. Based on that review, Toyota added two regional divisions (essentially dividing the world into two groups) to the existing functional structure. "Dealing with our overseas operations on a regional basis, rather than a functional basis, will enable us to conduct decision making on a more comprehensive basis," said Toyota CEO Akio Toyoda when announcing the updated structure.

Toyota recently revised its organizational structure again. Faced with rapid technological change and increasing competition, the automaker announced a massive reorganization that divides the company into several vehicle product groups, such as compact cars and commercial vehicles, as well as functional areas (power train and connected technology). The structure now also includes several leaders representing North America, Europe, Japan, and other geographic regions. "The revisions to our organizational structure are designed, by reducing the number of structural layers, to allow rebirth into a Toyota that is able to reach conclusions more swiftly, make prompt decisions, and take immediate action faster than ever," says Toyoda.

©PA Images/Alamy Stock Photo

* K. Linebaugh, D. Searcey, and N. Shirouzu, "Secretive Culture Led Toyota Astray," *The Wall Street Journal,* February 10, 2010; Toyota North American Quality Advisory Panel, *A Road Forward* (Washington, DC: Toyota North American Quality Advisory Panel, May 23, 2011); J. Muller, "Toyota Admits Misleading Customers; Agrees to $1.2 Billion Criminal Fine," *Forbes,* March 19, 2014; Y. Kubota, "Toyota Plans Organizational Shake-Up," *The Wall Street Journal,* February 29, 2016; "TMC Announces Executive, Organizational, and Personnel Changes," News Release (Toyota City: Toyota Motor Corporation, November 30, 2018).

large, resources are not used as efficiently as they are in functional structures where resources are pooled across the entire organization. The divisional structure also creates silos of knowledge. Expertise is spread across several autonomous business units, which reduces the ability and perhaps motivation of the people in one division to share their knowledge with counterparts in other divisions. In contrast, a functional structure groups experts together, thereby supporting knowledge-sharing within areas of expertise.

Finally, the preferred divisional structure depends on the company's primary source of environmental diversity or uncertainty. This principle seems to be applied easily enough at Saputo and Thomson Reuters, but many global

organizations experience diversity and uncertainty in terms of geography, product, *and* clients. Consequently, some organizations revise their structures back and forth or create complex structures that attempt to give all three dimensions equal status. This muddling generates further complications, because organizational structure decisions shift power and status among executives. If the company switches from a geographic to product structure, people who lead the geographic fiefdoms suddenly get demoted under the product chiefs. In short, leaders of global organizations struggle to find the best divisional structure, often resulting in the departure of some executives and frustration among those who remain.

Global Connections 13.3

BOSCH POWERS AHEAD WITH A TEAM-BASED ORGANIZATIONAL STRUCTURE[*]

Robert Bosch GmbH has been replacing its hierarchical organizational structure with a "podular" design built around teams. "In terms of achieving a flatter organization, for a lot of projects we now work in a "podular" structure," explains Frederic Boumaza, a senior vice-president at the German engineering and technology company. "So, not in a kind of pyramid organization, but by creating teams, or pods, with people from multiple departments with different expertise who can work together on projects much faster."

Bosch's power tools division, for example, replaced a seven-layer hierarchy with cross-functional self-directed teams, each with less than a dozen employees. The home and gardens business unit alone has 54 teams. Most teams are responsible for designing or manufacturing specific products (hedging products, cleaning technology, etc.). However, some teams are assigned support roles, such as engineering services and brand management.

Along with their autonomy to improve the production process, Bosch teams are responsible for providing peer feedback and compensation. The annual performance review conducted by managers has been replaced with ongoing individual development dialogues in which employees discuss their contribution toward team goals. Employees initially rejected the idea of determining each other's pay rates, but this is also occurring in some teams.

Frederic Boumaza points out that the team-based structure enables Bosch to respond more quickly and effectively to changes and customized client requests. "As these teams are mostly independent of any hierarchical constraints, they can connect and act in a much more agile way and really focus on the results." However, Boumaza also warns that leaders need to be more flexible and future-oriented. In addition, leaders "need to work in an agile way, not to be limited by traditional levels of hierarchy, but to accept that, to be fast enough, you have to create expert teams and give them the right levels of autonomy to succeed."

©dpa picture alliance/Alamy Stock Photo

[*] P. Tate, "Pioneering an Industrial Revolution at Bosch," *Manufacturing Leadership Journal,* June 2, 2018; T. Jakob and M.-O. Griesshaber, "How Big Companies Can Survive in the Digital Age: New Models for Culture, Leadership, and Collaboration" (Presentation, Singapore, September 28, 2018); P. Wainewright, "How Bosch Broke Free from Silos to Reorganize as Agile Teams," *Diginomica,* February 7, 2019.

TEAM-BASED STRUCTURE

A **team-based structure** is built around self-directed teams that complete an entire piece of work, such as manufacturing a product or developing an advertising campaign. This type of structure is usually organic. There is a wide span of control because teams operate with minimal supervision. There is no formal leader in its most extreme variation, just someone selected by other team members to help coordinate the work and liaise with top management.

team-based structure An organizational structure built around self-directed teams that complete an entire piece of work.

Team structures are highly decentralized because almost all day-to-day decisions are made by team members rather than someone further up the organizational hierarchy. Many team-based structures also have low formalization because teams are given relatively few rules about how to organize their work. Instead, executives assign quality and quantity output targets and often productivity improvement goals to each team. Teams are then encouraged to use available resources and their own initiative to achieve those objectives.

Team-based structures are usually found within the manufacturing or service operations of larger divisional structures. GE's aircraft engines plants in Bromont, Quebec, and at other locations are organized as team-based structures, but these plants operate within GE's larger divisional structure. A small number of firms apply the team-based structure from top to bottom, including Morning Star Company, W. L. Gore & Associates, and Valve Corporation, where almost all associates work in teams.

EXHIBIT 13.6   Matrix Organizational Structure Similar to Randon S.A.

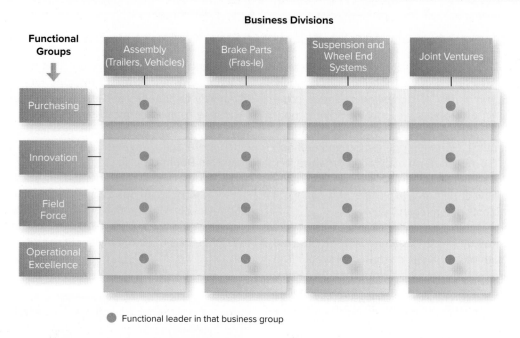

Business Divisions

Functional Groups	Assembly (Trailers, Vehicles)	Brake Parts (Fras-le)	Suspension and Wheel End Systems	Joint Ventures
Purchasing	●	●	●	●
Innovation	●	●	●	●
Field Force	●	●	●	●
Operational Excellence	●	●	●	●

● Functional leader in that business group

Note: This diagram, which is created for illustrative purposes only, is a representation of part of Randon's most recent structure. The complete top-level structure also has non-matrixed functional executives reporting to the CEO or COO. This diagram also assumes a pure matrix structure, in which both product and functional chiefs have equal power. However, it is possible that one of these leader groups will have more authority over the people represented by the dots.

Evaluating the Team-Based Structure

The team-based structure has gained popularity because it tends to be flexible and responsive in turbulent environments.[43] It tends to reduce costs because teams have less reliance on formal hierarchy (direct supervision). A cross-functional team structure improves communication and cooperation across traditional boundaries. With greater autonomy, this structure also allows quicker and more informed decision making.[44] For this reason, some hospitals in Canada and elsewhere have shifted from functional departments to cross-functional teams. Teams composed of nurses, radiologists, anaesthetists, a pharmacology representative, possibly social workers, a rehabilitation therapist, and other specialists communicate and coordinate more efficiently, thereby reducing delays and errors.[45]

The team-based structure also has several limitations. It can be costly to maintain due to the need for ongoing interpersonal skills training. Teamwork potentially takes more time to coordinate than formal hierarchy during the early stages of team development. Employees may experience more stress due to increased ambiguity in their roles. Team leaders also experience more stress due to increased conflict, loss of functional power, and unclear career progression ladders. In addition, team structures suffer from duplication of resources and potential competition (and lack of resource sharing) across teams.[46]

MATRIX STRUCTURE

Randon S.A., one of Brazil's largest private companies, manufactures truck bodies (transport truck trailers), car and truck parts (brake pads, wheel ends, etc.), railcars, and earth-moving vehicles. Although these businesses operated independently, Randon executives felt that they needed to be more responsive to headquarters initiatives on technological innovation, efficiency, and aftermarket business opportunities. Therefore, the company now has a matrix organizational structure that combines the four main business divisions with four functional groups that champion these initiatives. "One of the main gains of the organizational change is to accelerate the growth of operations through the development of new technologies, product innovation, and cost management," says Randon CEO Daniel Randon.[47]

Randon and many other organizations have adopted a **matrix structure**, which overlays two structures (in this case, product divisions with a functional structure) to leverage the benefits of both.[48] Exhibit 13.6 shows a product–functional matrix structure, similar to what Randon has recently introduced. The dots represent the individuals (functional

> **matrix structure** An organizational structure that overlays two structures (such as a geographic divisional and a product structure) in order to leverage the benefits of both.

leaders within each product division) who have two bosses. For example, the head of purchasing in the brake parts division (a company called Fras-le) reports to Randon's head of procurement at headquarters as well as to the head of Fras-le.

A common mistake is to assume that everyone in a matrix organizational structure reports to two bosses. In reality, this particular type of matrix structure has only managers at one level in the organization reporting to two bosses. The executive responsible for innovation at Fras-le (Randon's brake parts business) reports to both the head of Fras-le and to the headquarters leader responsible for innovation. All employees below the innovation leader at Fras-le report to only one manager in the Fras-le operations.

Hennes & Mauritz AB has a matrix organizational structure similar to Randon. Specifically, the Swedish fashion retailer intersects its store brands (H&M, H&M Home, & Other Stories, Monki, Cos, etc.) with almost a dozen functional groups (logistics, production, accounting, human resources, etc.). A related form of matrix organization, particularly among global companies, is the product–geographic structure. One such example is the matrix structure at Shiseido, which has five product groups intersected with six regions. The Japanese cosmetics and personal care firm adopted the product-geographic structure because it needed to assign equal power and attention to regional groups as to its product groups.[49]

Global organizations tend to have complex designs that combine different types of structures, so a "pure" matrix design is relatively uncommon. A pure matrix gives equal power to leaders of both groups (products and regions, for example), whereas in reality companies often give more power to one set of groups while the other set of groups has mostly "dotted line" or advisory authority.

A considerably different form of matrix structure, which can be applied to small or large companies, overlays a functional structure with projects.[50] Bioware adopted this project–functional matrix structure soon after the Edmonton-based electronic games company was born two decades ago. Most Bioware employees have two managers. One manager leads the specific project to which employees are assigned, such as *Star Wars, Mass Effect,* and *Dragon Age;* the other manager is head of the employee's functional specialization, such as art, programming, audio, quality assurance, and design.[51] Employees are assigned permanently to their functional unit but physically work with the temporary project team. When the project nears completion, the functional boss reassigns employees in their functional specialization to another project.

Evaluating the Matrix Structure

The project–functional matrix structure usually makes very good use of resources and expertise, making it ideal for project-based organizations with fluctuating workloads. When properly managed, it improves communication efficiency, project flexibility, and innovation, compared to purely functional or divisional designs. It focuses employees on serving clients or creating products yet keeps people organized around their specialization. The result is that knowledge sharing improves and people are more efficiently assigned to work where they are most needed.

Matrix structures for large organizations are also a logical choice when two different dimensions are equally important (such as regions and products at Shiseido). Structures determine executive power and what should receive priority; the matrix structure works best when the business environment is complex and two different dimensions deserve equal attention and integration. Executives who have worked in a global matrix also say they have more freedom, likely because their two bosses are more advisory and less oriented toward command-and-control leadership.[52]

In spite of these advantages, the matrix structure has several well-known problems.[53] One concern is that it increases conflict among managers who equally share power. Employees working at the matrix level have two bosses and, consequently, two sets of priorities that aren't always aligned with each other. Project leaders might squabble with functional leaders regarding the assignment of specific employees to projects as well as regarding the employee's technical competence. However, successful companies manage this conflict by developing and promoting leaders who can work effectively in matrix structures. "Of course there's potential for friction," says an executive at IBM India. "In fact, one of the prerequisites to attaining a leadership position at IBM is the ability to function in a matrix structure."[54]

Ambiguous accountability is another challenge with matrix structures. In a functional or divisional structure, one manager is responsible for everything, even the most unexpected issues. But in a matrix structure, the unusual problems don't get resolved because neither manager takes ownership of them.[55] Due to this ambiguous accountability, matrix structures have been blamed for corporate ethical misconduct, such as embezzlement at Hana Financial Group in Korea and massive bribery at Siemens AG in Germany. The late technology executive Mark Hurd once warned of this problem: "The more accountable I can make you, the easier it is for you to show you're a great performer," said Hurd. "The more I use a matrix, the easier I make it to blame someone else."[56] The combination of dysfunctional conflict and ambiguous accountability in matrix structures also explains why some employees experience more stress and some managers are less satisfied with their work arrangements.

Debating Point: DO ORGANIZATIONS REALLY NEED TO ADOPT A MATRIX STRUCTURE?*

The matrix organizational structure is gaining in popularity among leaders of large organizations. Multinational firms typically adopt a product–geographic matrix because it potentially balances the importance of the company's core products/services with its geographic diversity. Matrix structures are also gaining popularity in smaller firms, typically as project–functional structures, as leaders try to make their workforce more "agile."

"An agile, matrixed structure can help companies be more nimble, as this approach emphasizes interdisciplinary functionality and enables workers to move from team to team as project needs demand," enthuses consulting firm Gallup. The company claims that matrixed employees are more motivated and focused on the organization's unified mission and vision.

In spite of these potential benefits, matrix organizational structures have a long history of problems that are avoided or minimized through other forms of departmentalization. ABB Group, Proctor & Gamble, Philips, Siemens, and other companies that at one time had boasted their matrix structure have since shifted to divisionalized or functional structures. McLaren Racing is the latest example. The well-known Formula 1 race car organization recently discarded its matrix structure because it undermined decision efficiency and overall coordination. "The current [matrix] structure does not allow certain people to make decisions quickly enough and act as entrepreneurially as I would like," argues McLaren Racing CEO Zak Brown.

The most commonly cited concern is that matrix structures rely on co-management at one or many levels of the organization. The risk is that when employees report to two managers, some degree of responsibility and accountability falls through the cracks. For example, Britain's HM Revenue & Customs (HMRC) lost two computer discs containing confidential details of 25 million child welfare claimants. A review concluded that "[HMRC] is not suited to the so-called 'constructive friction' matrix type organization [that was] in place at the time of the data loss."

A second perennial problem with matrix structures is that they produce unnecessary conflict and organizational politics. Ambiguity is one of the main structural causes of conflict. Matrix structures necessarily produce more ambiguity because joint managers and their employees need to negotiate priorities with each other, whereas single-line authority assigns the decision to one person. Also, no matter how collaborative the culture, managers have a degree of territoriality and inherent competitive tournament mentality that makes it difficult to maintain continuous bipartisanship. In other words, there are limits to how much managers are willing to resolve conflicts through problem solving, yielding, and other supportive actions.

Finally, matrix structures assume that the two dimensions—whether product and geography or project and function—are absolutely equally important. This is rarely true; one group almost always takes priority over other groups at the top of the hierarchy. Yet CEOs take the expedient route of a matrix structure rather than decide through a divisionalized structure that one set of executives (such as product leaders) will be subordinate to another set of executives (such as regional leaders). One CEO candidly described the matrix structure as a "cop-out style of management."

Most organizations with a matrix structure would experience fewer problems with a variation of another structure with a clearer line of accountability. For instance, an organization might have a global footprint, but it should be organized around its diverse product groups if they represent the core focus and competitive advantage. Geographic diversity is still embedded somewhere beneath the top level of the structure, such as under the heads of global sales or manufacturing. Another option is to apply "dotted-line" reporting relationships that clearly identify the executive who leads and the executive with lesser power in the relationship, often with specific statements about where the latter has rights.

* T.J. Peters, "Beyond the Matrix Organization," *Business Horizons* 22, no. 5 (October 1979): 15–27; V. Houlder, "The Merger That Exposed a Taxing Problem for Managers," *Financial Times,* 11 July 2008, 12; K. Poynter, *Review of Information Security at HM Revenue and Customs,* (London: HM Treasury, Government of the United Kingdom, June 2008); "The Multiple Boss Dilemma: Is It Possible to Please More Than One?," *Knowledge@Wharton,* September 2, 2016; B. Johnson and Geal, "The Challenges of Matrix Management," *Training Journal,* October 28, 2016; O. Keogh, "Balancing Bosses in the Matrix Can Be a Daunting Challenge," *The Irish Times,* June 15, 2018; M. Gretton, Z. Haidinger and E. Straw, "Zak Brown: Was Mit 'Matrix-Management' Verkehrt Ist (Zak Brown: What's wrong with "matrix management")," *Motorsport-Total.Com,* July 15, 2018; V. Ratanjee and N. Dvorak, "Mastering Matrix Management in the Age of Agility," *Gallup Workplace,* September 18, 2018.

EXHIBIT 13.7   A Network Organizational Structure

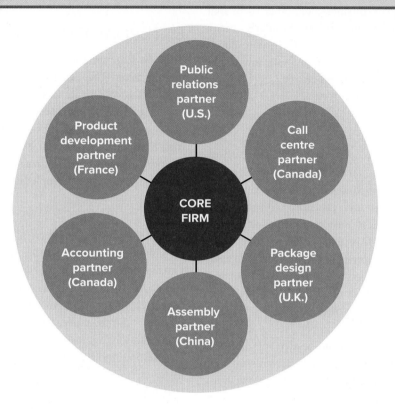

NETWORK STRUCTURE

BMW AG and Daimler AG aren't eager to let you know this, but some of the vehicles manufactured by them with Germanic precision are not constructed by their employees or in Germany. BMW's newest Z4 sports coupe and Daimler's Mercedes G class luxury SUVs are made in Austria by Magna Steyr, a division of Canada's Magna Corporation. For these vehicles, at least, BMW and Daimler Benz are hub organizations that own and market their respective brands, whereas Magna Steyr and other suppliers are spokes around the hub that provide production, engineering, and other services that get the auto firms' luxury products to customers.[57]

BMW, Daimler, and many other organizations are moving toward a **network structure** as they design and build products or serve clients through an alliance of several organizations.[58] As Exhibit 13.7 illustrates, this collaborative structure typically consists of several satellite organizations bee-hived around a hub or core firm. The core firm orchestrates the network process and provides one or two other core competencies, such as marketing or product development. In our example, BMW or Mercedes is the hub that provides

network structure An alliance of several organizations for the purpose of creating a product or serving a client.

design and marketing, whereas other firms perform many other functions. The core firm might be the main contact with customers, but most of the product or service delivery and support activities are farmed out to satellite organizations located anywhere in the world. Extranets (Web-based networks with partners) and other technologies ensure that information flows easily and openly between the core firm and its array of satellites.[59]

One of the main forces pushing toward a network structure is the recognition that an organization has only a few *core competencies.* A core competency is a knowledge base that resides throughout the organization and provides a strategic advantage. As companies discover their core competency, they outsource noncritical tasks to other organizations whose core competency is performing those tasks. For example, the opening case study for this chapter noted that Sobeys recently partnered with a British firm (Ocado) that specializes in automated customer fulfilment centres. The partner firm specializes in building and operating these highly automated facilities, which Sobeys and many other retailers increasingly depend on to provide online purchasing and delivery.[60]

Companies are also more likely to form network structures when technology is changing quickly and production processes are complex or varied.[61] Many firms cannot keep up with the hyperfast changes in information technology, so they have outsourced their entire information system departments to IBM, HP Enterprise Business, and other firms that specialize in information system services. Similarly, many high-technology firms form networks with Toronto-based Celestica and other electronic equipment manufacturers that have expertise in diverse production processes.

Evaluating the Network Structure

Organizational behaviour theorists have long argued that executives should think of their companies metaphorically as plasma-like organisms rather than rigid machines.[62] Network structures come close to the organism metaphor because they offer the flexibility to realign their structure with changing environmental requirements. If customers demand a new product or service, the core firm forms new alliances with other firms offering the appropriate resources. For example, when Magna Steyr's clients need a different type of manufacturing, they aren't saddled with nonessential facilities and resources. Network structures also offer efficiencies because the core firm becomes globally competitive as it shops worldwide for subcontractors with the best people and the best technology at the best price. Indeed, the pressures of global competition have made network structures more vital, and computer-based information technology has made them possible.[63]

A potential disadvantage of network structures is that they expose the core firm to market forces. Other companies may bid up the price for subcontractors, whereas the short-term cost would be lower if the company hired its own employees to perform the same function. A related problem is that there are increased costs of negotiating prices with external providers compared to internal costs with the company's own employees.[64] A third concern is that information technology makes worldwide communication much easier, but it has not yet replaced the degree of control that organizations have when manufacturing, marketing, and other functions are in-house. The core firm can use arm's-length incentives and contract provisions to maintain the subcontractor's quality, but these actions are relatively crude compared with maintaining the quality of work performed by in-house employees.

Contingencies of Organizational Design

LO4

Most organizational behaviour theories and concepts have contingencies: Ideas that work well in one situation might not work as well in another situation. This contingency approach is certainly relevant when choosing the most appropriate organizational structure.[65] In this section, we introduce four contingencies of organizational design: external environment, size, technology, and strategy.

EXTERNAL ENVIRONMENT

The best structure for an organization depends on its external environment. The external environment includes anything outside the organization, including most stakeholders (e.g., clients, suppliers, government), resources (e.g., raw materials, human resources, information, finances), and competitors. Four characteristics of external environments influence the type of organizational structure best suited to a particular situation: dynamism, complexity, diversity, and hostility.[66]

Dynamic versus Stable Environments

Dynamic environments have a high rate of change, leading to unfamiliar situations and a lack of identifiable patterns. Organic structures operate well in dynamic environments. Employees are experienced and coordinate well in teams, which enables the organization to adapt more quickly to changes.[67] For instance, the U.S. Army learned from difficult confrontations against guerrilla insurgents that the battlefield has become too dynamic and complex for its rigid mechanistic structure. It has since evolved into a more organic structure consisting of teams with increased autonomy to accomplish their missions. "We had to tear down familiar organizational structures and rebuild them along completely different lines, swapping our sturdy architecture for organic fluidity, because it was the only way to confront a rising tide of complex threats," says General Stanley McChrystal, who led America's Joint Special Operations Command and NATO forces in the war in Afghanistan. "We became what we called 'a team of teams': a large command that captured at scale the traits of agility normally limited to small teams."[68]

In contrast, stable environments are characterized by regular cycles of activity and steady changes in supply and demand for inputs and outputs. Events are more predictable, enabling the firm to apply rules and procedures. Mechanistic structures are more efficient when the environment is predictable, so they tend to be more profitable than organic structures under these conditions.

Complex versus Simple Environments

Complex environments have many elements, whereas simple environments have few things to monitor. As an example, a major university library operates in a more complex environment than a small-town public library. The university library's clients require several types of services—book borrowing, online full-text databases, research centres, course reserve collections, and so forth. A small-town public library has fewer of these demands placed on it. The more complex the environment, the more decentralized the organization should become.

Global Connections 13.4

THE RISK OF CENTRALIZING AUTHORITY DURING PANDEMICS*

Organizational leaders often make the mistake of temporarily centralizing authority during pandemics, such as during the COVID-19 crisis. Unfortunately, centralization when the external environment becomes hostile can produce worse decisions because headquarters executives have less information than managers on the front lines.

"The temptation in a time of crisis is for leaders to put themselves at the centre of all activity," warns Manley Hopkinson, a leadership consultant and McKinsey advisor who served as an officer in the British Royal Navy during the first Gulf War. "It is vital that a leader resist centralizing control."

Hugo Bague, who was a senior Rio Tinto executive during the Ebola crisis, agrees. "Local teams are often the best positioned to judge the situation on the ground—and their decisions should not be second-guessed." During the Ebola crisis, for instance, Rio Tinto executives in Guinea, West Africa, were given the autonomy to decide whether the expatriates should leave, a decision that would have affected the mining firm's credibility in that country. The local team decided to stay but sent their families home.

Although Rio Tinto's Guinea executives made the decision, senior executives at headquarters monitored the decision process. "We said clearly, whether you stay in Guinea or not is your call," says Bague. "But we want to have a discussion with you to ensure that you've looked at it at every angle."

©Pond Saksit/Shutterstock

* Based on information in: G. Tolub, "Applying Past Leadership Lessons to the Coronavirus Pandemic," *McKinsey & Company,* March 2020.

Decentralization is a logical choice for complex environments because decisions are pushed down to people and subunits with the necessary information to make informed choices.

Diverse versus Integrated Environments

Organizations located in diverse environments have a greater variety of products or services, clients, and regions. In contrast, an integrated environment has only one type of client and product and serves only one geographic area. The more diversified the environment, the more the firm needs to use a divisional structure aligned with that diversity. If it sells a single product around the world, a geographic divisional structure would align best with the firm's geographic diversity, for example. Diverse environments also call for decentralization. By pushing decision making further down the hierarchy, the company can adapt better and more quickly to diverse clients, government requirements, and other circumstances related to that diversity.

Hostile versus Munificent Environments

Firms located in hostile environments face resource scarcity and more competition in the marketplace. These conditions are typically dynamic as well because they reduce the predictability of access to resources and demand for outputs. Organic structures tend to be best in hostile environments. However, when the environment is extremely unfavourable—such as during the COVID-19 pandemic or when there is a severe shortage of raw production materials—organizations tend to temporarily centralize so that decisions can be made more quickly and executives feel more comfortable being in control.[69] Ironically, centralization may result in lower-quality decisions during organizational crises, because top management has less information, particularly when the environment is complex.

ORGANIZATIONAL SIZE

The organizational structures of large organizations differ from those of smaller organizations, for good reason.[70] As the number of employees increases, job specialization increases due to a greater division of labour. The greater division of labour requires more elaborate coordinating mechanisms. Thus, larger firms make greater use of standardization (particularly work processes and outcomes) to coordinate work activities. These coordinating mechanisms create an administrative hierarchy and greater formalization. At one time, growing organizations reduced their reliance on informal communication as a coordinating mechanism. However, emerging information technologies have enabled large firms to coordinate work more through informal communication than was previously possible.[71]

Larger organizations also tend to be more decentralized than are smaller organizations. Executives have neither sufficient time nor expertise to process all the decisions that significantly influence the business as it grows. Therefore, decision-making authority is pushed down to lower levels, where employees are able to make decisions on issues within their narrower range of responsibility.

TECHNOLOGY

Technology is another factor to consider when designing the best organizational structure for the situation.[72] *Technology* refers to the mechanisms or processes an organization relies on to make its products or services. In other words, technology isn't just the equipment used to make something; it also includes how the production process is physically arranged and how the production work is divided among employees.

The two main technological contingencies are task variability and task analyzability, both of which we described as job characteristics in Chapter 6. *Task variability* refers to how predictable the job duties are from one day to the next. In jobs with high variability, employees perform several types of tasks, but they don't know which of those tasks are required from one day to the next. Low variability occurs when the work is highly routine and predictable. *Task analyzability* refers to how much the job can be performed using known procedures and rules. In jobs with high task analyzability, employees have well-defined guidelines to direct them through the work process. In jobs with low task analyzability, employees tackle unique situations with few (if any) guidelines to help them determine the best course of action.

An organic structure should be introduced where employees perform tasks with high variability and low analyzability, such as in a research setting. The reason is that employees face unique situations with little opportunity for repetition. In contrast, a mechanistic structure is preferred where the technology has low variability and high analyzability, such as an assembly line. Assembly work is routine, highly predictable, and has well-established procedures—an ideal situation for a mechanistic structure to operate efficiently.

ORGANIZATIONAL STRATEGY

Organizational strategy refers to the way the organization positions itself in its environment in relation to its stakeholders, given the organization's resources, capabilities, and mission.[73] In other words, strategy represents the decisions and actions applied to achieve the organization's goals. Although size, technology, and environment influence the optimal organizational structure, these contingencies do not necessarily determine structure. Instead, corporate leaders formulate and implement strategies that shape both the characteristics of these contingencies as well as the organization's resulting structure.

> **organizational strategy** The way the organization positions itself in its setting in relation to its stakeholders, given the organization's resources, capabilities, and mission.

This concept is summed up with the simple phrase "structure follows strategy."[74] Organizational leaders decide how large to grow and which technologies to use. They take steps to define and manipulate their environments, rather than let the organization's fate be entirely determined by external influences (see the open systems perspective in Chapter 1). Furthermore, organizational structures don't evolve as a natural response to environmental conditions; they are the outcome of conscious human decisions. Thus, organizational strategy influences both the contingencies of structure and the structure itself.

If a company's strategy is to compete through innovation, a more organic structure would be preferred because it is easier for employees to share knowledge and be creative. If a company chooses a low-cost strategy, a mechanistic structure is preferred because it maximizes production and service efficiency.[75] Overall, it is now apparent that organizational structure is influenced by size, technology, and environment, but the organization's strategy may reshape these elements and loosen their connection to organizational structure.

 Does your job require an organic or mechanistic structure? You can discover which structure is better for your job by completing this self-assessment in Connect.

Chapter Summary

LO1

Describe three types of coordination in organizational structures.

Organizational structure is the division of labour, as well as the patterns of coordination, communication, workflow, and formal power that direct organizational activities. All organizational structures divide labour into distinct tasks and coordinate that labour to accomplish common goals. The primary means of coordination are informal communication, formal hierarchy, and standardization.

LO2

Discuss the role and effects of span of control, centralization, and formalization, and relate these elements to organic and mechanistic organizational structures.

The four basic elements of organizational structure are span of control, centralization, formalization, and departmentalization. The optimal span of control—the number of people directly reporting to the next level in the hierarchy—depends on what coordinating mechanisms are present other than formal hierarchy, whether employees perform routine tasks, and how much interdependence there is among employees within the department.

Centralization occurs when formal decision authority is held by a small group of people, typically senior executives. Many companies decentralize as they become larger and more complex, but some sections of the company may remain centralized while other sections decentralize. Formalization is the degree to which organizations standardize behaviour through rules, procedures, formal training, and related mechanisms. Companies become more formalized as they get older and larger. Formalization tends to reduce organizational flexibility, organizational learning, creativity, and job satisfaction.

Span of control, centralization, and formalization cluster into mechanistic and organic structures. Mechanistic structures are characterized by a narrow span of control and a high degree of formalization and centralization. Companies with an organic structure have the opposite characteristics.

LO3

Identify and evaluate six types of departmentalization.

Departmentalization specifies how employees and their activities are grouped together. It establishes the chain of command, focuses people around common mental models, and encourages coordination through informal communication among people and subunits. A simple structure employs few people, has minimal hierarchy, and typically offers one distinct product or service. A functional structure organizes employees around specific knowledge or other resources. This structure fosters greater specialization and improves direct supervision, but it weakens the focus on serving clients or developing products.

A divisional structure groups employees around geographic areas, clients, or outputs. This structure accommodates growth and focuses employee attention on products or customers rather than tasks. However, this structure also duplicates resources and creates silos of knowledge. Team-based structures are very flat, with low formalization, and organize self-directed teams around work processes rather than functional specialties. The matrix structure combines two structures to leverage the benefits of both types. However, this approach requires more coordination than functional or pure divisional structures, may dilute accountability, and increases conflict. A network structure is an alliance of several organizations for the purpose of creating a product or serving a client.

LO4

Explain how the external environment, organizational size, technology, and strategy are relevant when designing an organizational structure.

The best organizational structure depends on whether the environment is dynamic or stable, complex or simple, diverse or integrated, and hostile or munificent. Another contingency is the organization's size. Larger organizations need to become more decentralized and more formalized. The work unit's technology—including variability of work and analyzability of problems—influences whether it should adopt an organic or mechanistic structure. These contingencies influence but do not necessarily determine structure. Instead, corporate leaders formulate and implement strategies that shape both the characteristics of these contingencies and the organization's resulting structure.

Key Terms

centralization
divisional structure
formalization
functional structure
matrix structure
mechanistic structure

network structure
organic structure
organizational strategy
organizational structure
span of control
team-based structure

Critical Thinking Questions

1. Sobeys' organizational structure was described at the beginning of this chapter. What coordinating mechanism is likely most common in this organization? Describe the extent and form in which the other two types of coordination might be apparent at Sobeys.

2. Think about the business school or other educational group where you are currently attending classes. What is the dominant coordinating mechanism used to guide or control the instructor? Why is this coordinating mechanism used the most here?

3. Administrative theorists concluded many decades ago that the most effective organizations have a narrow span of control. Yet, today's top-performing manufacturing firms have a wide span of control. Why is this possible? Under what circumstances, if any, should manufacturing firms have a narrow span of control?

4. Leaders of large organizations struggle to identify the best level and types of centralization and decentralization. What should companies consider when determining the degree of decentralization?

5. Diversified Technologies Ltd. (DTL) makes four types of products, with each type to be sold to different types of clients. For example, one product is sold exclusively to automobile repair shops, whereas another is used mainly in hospitals. Expectations within each client group are surprisingly similar throughout the world. The company has separate marketing, product design, and manufacturing facilities in Asia, North America, Europe, and South America because, until recently, each jurisdiction had unique regulations governing the production and sales of these products. However, several governments have begun the process of deregulating the products that DTL designs and manufactures, and trade agreements have opened several markets to foreign-made products. Which form of departmentalization might be best for DTL if deregulation and trade agreements occur?

6. Mechanistic and organic structures are two organizational forms. How do the three types of coordination mechanisms operate through these forms?

7. From an employee perspective, what are the advantages and disadvantages of working in a matrix structure?

8. Suppose you have been hired as a consultant to diagnose the environmental characteristics of your college or university. How would you describe the school's external environment? Is the school's existing structure appropriate for this environment?

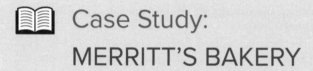

Case Study:
MERRITT'S BAKERY

by Steven L. McShane, University of Newcastle (Australia)

In 1979, Larry Merritt and his wife, Bobbie, bought The Cake Box, a small business located in a tiny 450 square-foot store in Tulsa, Oklahoma. The couple were the only employees. "I would make cakes and Bobbie would come in and decorate them," Larry recalls. Bobbie Merritt was already skilled in decorating cakes, whereas baking was a new occupation for Larry Merritt, who previously worked as a discount store manager. So, Larry spent hours pouring over baking books in the local library and testing recipes through trial-and-error experimentation. "I threw away a lot of ingredients that first year," he recalls.

Sales were initially slow. Then, a doughnut shop around the corner was put up for sale and its owner made it possible for the Merritts to buy that business. They moved to the larger location and changed the company's name to Merritt's Bakery to reflect the broader variety of products sold. The Merritts hired their first two employees, who performed front store sales and service. Over the next decade, Merritt's Bakery's physical space doubled and its revenues increased 13-fold. The company employed 20 people by the time it made its next move.

In 1993, Merritt's Bakery moved to a 6,000 square-foot location across the street. The business became so popular that customers were lining up down the street to buy its fresh-baked goods. "That looks like success to a lot of people, but that was failure," says Bobbie Merritt. The problem was that the couple didn't want to delegate production to employees, but they couldn't produce their baked goods or decorate their carefully crafted cakes fast enough to keep up with demand. "We felt like failures because we had to work those 20 hours (per day)," she reflects.

At some point, the Merritts realized that they had to become business owners and managers rather than bakers. They devised a plan to grow the business and drew up an organizational structure that formalized roles and responsibilities. When a second Merritt's Bakery store opened across town in 2001, each store was assigned a manager, a person in charge of baking production, another in charge of cake decorating and pastries, and someone responsible for sales. A third store opened a few years later. Larry worked on maintaining quality by training bakery staff at each store. "Because it is so difficult to find qualified bakers nowadays, I want to spend more time teaching and developing our products," he said at the time.

Christian Merritt, one of Larry and Bobbie's sons, joined the business in 2000 and has since become head of operations. An engineer by training with experience in the telecommunications industry, Christian soon developed flow charts that describe precise procedures for most work activities, ranging from simple store-front tasks (cashiering) to unusual events such as a power outage. These documents standardized work activities to maintain quality with less reliance on direct supervision. Christian also introduced computer systems to pool information across stores about current inventory levels, which products are selling quickly, and how much demand exists for Merritt's famous custom cakes. The information improved decision making about production, staffing, and purchasing without having to directly contact or manage each store as closely.

In late 2007, Merritt's Bakery's opened a dedicated production centre near the original store and moved all production staff into the building, affectionately called "the Fort." The centralized production facility reduced costs by removing duplication of staff and equipment, provided more consistent quality, and allowed the stores to have more front store space for customers.

Merritt's Bakery refined its training programs, from the initial orientation session to a series of modules on specific skills. For example, front store staff now complete a series of clinics that add up to 20 hours of training. The company also introduced special selection processes so people with the right personality and skills are hired into these jobs. Employees at Merritt's production facility receive decorator training through a graduated program over a longer time. One or two managers at the production site closely coach up to five new hires.

Today, Merritt's Bakery employs more than 80 people, including production managers, store managers, and a marketing director. Two-thirds of the business is in the creation of cakes for birthdays, weddings, and other events, but the company also has three busy and popular stores across Tulsa. "We're just now getting the pieces in place to start to treat Merritt's Bakery like a business, with a lot of parts that we manage from a distance," says Christian Merritt. "We're present but detached; we have our hands in a lot of things, but it's in managing stores instead of operating them."

Discussion Questions

1. How have the division and coordination of labour evolved at Merritt's Bakery from its beginnings to today?

2. Describe how span of control, centralization, and formalization have changed at Merritt's Bakery over the years? Is the company's organizational structure today more mechanistic or organic? Are these three organizational structure elements well-suited to the company in their current form? Why or why not?

3. What form of departmentalization currently exists at Merritt's Bakery? Would you recommend this form of departmentalization to this company? Why or why not?

 Team Exercise:
THE CLUB ED EXERCISE

Purpose This exercise is designed to help you understand the issues to consider when designing organizations at various stages of growth.

Materials Each student team should have several flip chart sheets or other means to draw and show the class several organizational charts.

Instructions Teams receive up to four scenarios, one at a time in chronological sequence. For each scenario, teams are given a fixed time (e.g., 15 minutes) to draw an organizational chart that best suits the firm in that scenario. The first scenario is presented below. The exercise and debriefing require approximately 90 minutes, although fewer scenarios can reduce the time somewhat.

Step 1: Students are placed in teams (typically four or five people).

Step 2: After reading Scenario #1 presented below, each team will design an organizational chart (departmentalization) that is most appropriate for this situation. Students will describe the type of structure drawn and explain why it is most appropriate. The structure should be drawn on a flip chart or using a software program for others to see during later class discussion. The instructor will set a fixed time (e.g., 15 minutes) to complete this task before the next scenario is presented.

Scenario #1: Determined to never suffer another cold Canadian winter, you secured venture capital funding for a new resort business called Club Ed on a small Caribbean island. The resort is under construction and is scheduled to open in less than one year. The resort will employ approximately 75 staff (most employed full-time). Draw an organizational chart that best suits the organization when it opens, and justify your decision.

Step 3: At the end of the time allowed, the instructor will present Scenario #2 and each team will be asked to draw another organizational chart to suit that situation. Again, students will describe the type of structure drawn and explain why it is appropriate.

Step 4: At the end of the time allowed, the instructor will present Scenario #3 and each team will be asked to draw another organizational chart to suit that situation.

Step 5: Depending on the time available, the instructor might present a fourth scenario. The class will gather to present their designs for each scenario. During each presentation, teams should describe the type of structure drawn and explain why it is appropriate.

Self-Assessments for Chapter 13

SELF-ASSESSMENT NAME	DESCRIPTION
Which organizational structure do you prefer?	Personal values influence how comfortable you are working in different organizational structures. You might prefer an organization with clearly defined rules or no rules at all. You might prefer a firm where almost any employee can make important decisions or one in which important decisions are screened by senior executives. This self-assessment estimates which of four organizational structures best fits your needs and expectations.
Does your job require an organic or mechanistic structure?	Different jobs require different types of organizational structures. For some jobs, employees work better in an organic structure. In other jobs, a mechanistic structure helps incumbents perform their work better. Think of the job you currently have or recently held, or even your "job" as a student. This self-assessment estimates whether the type of work you perform is better suited to a mechanistic or organic organizational structure.

CHAPTER 14
Organizational Culture

LEARNING OBJECTIVES

After reading this chapter, you should be able to:

LO1   Describe the elements of organizational culture and discuss the importance of organizational subcultures.

LO2   Describe four categories of artifacts through which corporate culture is deciphered.

LO3   Discuss the importance of organizational culture and the conditions under which organizational culture strength improves organizational performance.

LO4   Compare and contrast four strategies for merging organizational cultures.

LO5   Discuss five strategies for changing and strengthening an organization's culture, including the application of attraction–selection–attrition theory.

LO6   Describe the organizational socialization process and identify strategies to improve that process.

For almost two decades, Microsoft's organizational culture promoted dysfunctional internal competitiveness and organizational politics. This was illustrated in a famous cartoon showing the organizational structure of several technology companies. Microsoft's structure was depicted as three independent hierarchies, each with arms holding handguns pointed at the other two groups. Microsoft also had a "know-it-all" arrogance toward innovation with external partners and aloofness to the needs of non-Windows users.

Microsoft Canada President Kevin Peesker explains that the company's culture is in the process of dramatic transformation under the guidance of CEO Satya Nadella. "Companies that stay relevant are those who are willing to learn and adapt," says Peesker. "Our CEO Satya Nadella talks about being a 'learn-it-all' versus a 'know-it-all' and that is the culture we are trying to create."

Microsoft has transformed its organizational culture to one that embraces internal collaboration and a growth-oriented "learn-it-all" mindset.
©James D Morgan/Shutterstock

Nadella is also shifting the technology firm's culture toward internal cooperation rather than competition. "A core piece to the culture puzzle has been providing Microsoft employees with technology that empowers them to create and collaborate, not only across teams but across offices and time zones,"

Peesker observes. In particular, he notes that the firm's increasingly popular workplace collaboration platform (Microsoft Teams) reflects the company's new cultural mindset to working together rather than against each other.

Microsoft's cultural renaissance has taken time, but Satya Nadella's transformational leadership has played a pivotal role. Immediately after becoming CEO, he asked Microsoft's top executive team to read a popular book on empathetic collaboration. Through internal messages and town hall meetings, Nadella encourages employees to be more empathetic and inclusive, recognize and overcome their personal biases, and work cooperatively with other business units and external partners. He has noticeably modelled those espoused values, but they are also visible in hallway posters and preprinted statements on cafeteria serviettes.

"I believe that culture is not static. It evolves every day based on the behaviours of everyone in the organization," says Nadella. Microsoft's CEO also emphasizes that one of his core responsibilities as a leader is to guide the company's culture. "There is something only a CEO uniquely can do, which is set that tone, which can then capture the soul of the collective. And it's culture."[1]

Microsoft Canada President Kevin Peesker and CEO Satya Nadella not only recognize that organizational culture has a powerful influence on the company's success; they also know that, although challenging, leaders can potentially transform the company's culture through the various targeted strategies that we discuss in this chapter. **Organizational culture** consists of the values and assumptions shared within an organization.[2] It defines what is important and unimportant in the company and, consequently, directs everyone in the organization toward the "right way" of doing things. You might think of organizational culture as the company's DNA—invisible to the naked eye, yet a powerful template that shapes what happens in the workplace.

organizational culture The values and assumptions shared within an organization.

This chapter begins by identifying the elements of organizational culture and then describing how culture is deciphered through artifacts. Next, we examine the relationship between organizational culture and organizational effectiveness, including the effects of cultural strength, fit, and adaptability. Our attention then turns to strategies for merging organizational cultures. The latter part of this chapter examines ways to change and strengthen organizational culture, including a closer look at the related topic of organizational socialization.

Elements of Organizational Culture

LO1

Organizational culture consists of shared values and assumptions. Exhibit 14.1 illustrates how these shared values and assumptions relate to each other and are associated with

artifacts, which are discussed in the next section of this chapter. *Values* are stable, evaluative beliefs that guide our preferences for outcomes or courses of action in a variety of situations (see Chapters 1 and 2).[3] They are conscious perceptions about what is good or bad, right or wrong. In the context of organizational culture, values are discussed as *shared values,* which are values that people within the organization or work unit have in common and place near the top of their hierarchy of values.[4] For example, Microsoft Canada has shifted significantly within the past few years from a culture that values internal competition and status-based superiority to one that prioritizes internal collaboration and a growth (learn-it-all) mindset.

Organizational culture also consists of *shared assumptions*—a deeper element that some experts believe is the essence of corporate culture. Shared assumptions are nonconscious, taken-for-granted perceptions or ideal prototypes of behaviour that are considered the correct way to think and act toward problems and opportunities. Shared assumptions are so deeply ingrained that you probably wouldn't discover them by surveying employees. Only by observing employees, analyzing their decisions, and debriefing them on their actions would these assumptions rise to the surface.

Espoused versus Enacted Values

Most corporate websites have "Careers" web pages for job candidates, and many of these sites proudly list the company's core values. Nature's Path Foods in Richmond, B.C., lists five core values. "We use the acronym PATHS," explains Ratana Stephens, co-founder and chief operating officer of North America's largest certified organic breakfast and snack food company. "'P' for performance-driven, 'A' for always improving, 'T' for team-focused, 'H' for honourable,

EXHIBIT 14.1 Organizational Culture Assumptions, Values, and Artifacts

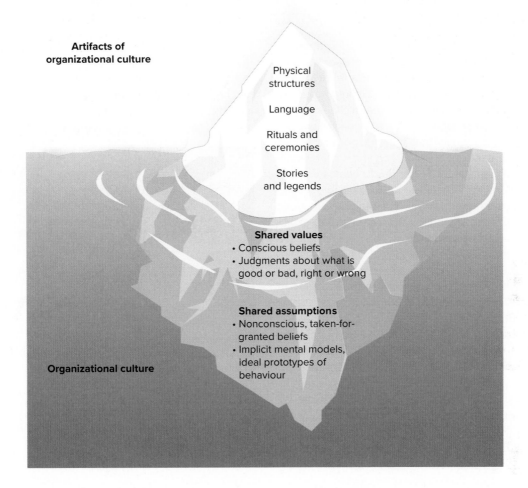

and 'S' for sustainable. We try to find people who have these kinds of values."[5]

Do these values really represent the culture content at Nature's Path Foods? They probably do in this organization, because its culture is well known and deeply entrenched through various artifacts. However, most company websites tend to describe *espoused values*—the values that corporate leaders hope will eventually become the organization's culture, or at least the values they want others to believe guide the organization's decisions and actions.[6] Espoused values are usually socially desirable, so they present a positive public image. Even if top management acts consistently with the espoused values, lower-level employees might not do so. Employees bring diverse personal values to the organization, some of which might conflict with the organization's espoused values. Some companies even describe espoused values that are completely different from their actual culture.[7]

An organization's culture is defined by its *enacted values,* not its espoused values. Values are *enacted* when they

actually guide and influence decisions and behaviour. They are values put into practice. Enacted values are apparent when watching executives and other employees in action, such as where they focus their attention and resources, how they behave toward stakeholders, what decisions they make, and the outcomes of those decisions and behaviour.

CONTENT OF ORGANIZATIONAL CULTURE

Organizations differ in their cultural content, that is, the relative ordering of shared values.[8] Pinterest, the image-focused social media site, has a decidedly collaborative culture that avoids contested debate and other risks of offending co-workers. "We aspire to create a culture where people feel respected and valued," says a Pinterest spokesperson. In contrast, Netflix's culture seems to prioritize individual performance and undertones of internal competitiveness. For instance, the online streaming media provider reminds

Global Connections 14.1

TAKATA'S ESPOUSED VERSUS ENACTED ORGANIZATIONAL VALUES*

For many years, Takata Corporation proudly described the three components of its Takata Way culture: open communication, commitment, and adherence to the fact-based problem-solving principles of San Gen Shugi (principally, investigate what's happening; take a realistic look at your product or service; use facts to arrive at a conclusion).

Yet evidence suggests that these espoused values did not represent the Japanese airbag and seatbelt manufacturer's enacted values. Takata has become infamous for designing dangerous airbags. At least two dozen people have died and hundreds of others have been injured due to flying shrapnel from Takata airbag explosions. These disastrous products can be traced back to a culture that was mostly contrary to what Takata claimed.

Rather than encouraging open communication, Takata's senior management apparently discouraged open debate. And rather than supporting the principles of San Gen Shugi, Takata's leaders actively suppressed fact-based analysis of its products. The company was found guilty of concealing evidence that its airbags had catastrophic safety flaws. An independent panel of experts concluded that "many of the Panel's recommendations require cultural change. Accordingly, Takata must take steps to drive quality into its culture."

The claims against Takata have been so overwhelming that the company entered bankruptcy protection and was sold to a Chinese competitor.

©Franck Robichon/EPA/Shutterstock

* S. Berfield et al., "Sixty Million Car Bombs: Inside Takata's Air Bag Crisis," *Bloomberg*, 2 June 2016; Independent Takata Corporation Quality Assurance Panel, *Ensuring Quality across the Board* (Chicago: February 2016); "Lax Corporate Culture Set up Takata's Fall," *Nikkei Asian Review*, 3 July 2017; H. Tabuchi and N.E. Boudette, "U.S. Charges Takata Officers in Airbag Case," *The New York Times*, 14 January 2017, A1; "Our Aspirations," *About Takata* (Tokyo: Takata Corporation, 2018), http://www.takata.com/en/about/wish.html (accessed 27 March 2018); T. Krisher, T. Krisher, "Takata Recalls 10 Million More Airbags from 14 Automakers Including Subaru, Ford, GM and Toyota," *USA Today*, January 8, 2020.

employees that its managers "hire, develop, and cut smartly" and that "adequate performance gets a generous severance package." Employees say that getting fired is never far from anyone's mind, which seems to fuel organizational politics and undermine collaboration.[9]

How many corporate cultures are there? Several models and measures classify organizational culture into a handful of easy-to-remember categories. One of these, shown in Exhibit 14.2, identifies seven corporate cultures. Another popular model identifies four organizational cultures organized in a two-by-two table representing internal versus external focus and flexibility versus control. Other models organize cultures around a circle with 8 or 12 categories. These circumplex models suggest that some cultures are opposite to others, such as an avoidance culture versus a self-actualization culture, or a power culture versus a collegial culture.[10]

Organizational culture models and surveys are popular with corporate leaders faced with the messy business of diagnosing their company's culture and identifying what kind of culture they want to develop. Unfortunately, the models oversimplify the diversity of cultural values in organizations. There are dozens of individual values, and many more combinations of values, so the number of organizational cultures that these models describe likely falls considerably short of the full set.

The diversity of corporate cultures is evident in a study of espoused values at the top 500 American companies.[11] The study distilled these values down to nine categories. Integrity appeared most often, followed by teamwork, innovation, respect, quality, safety, community, communication, and hard work. But each of these categories encapsulates a large number of specific values. The "respect" category, for instance, includes the specific values of diversity, inclusion, development, empowerment, and dignity. As you can see, there are dozens of espoused values, so there would be an equally long list of enacted values.

Another concern is that organizational culture models and measures typically ignore the shared assumptions aspect of culture. This oversight likely occurs because measuring shared assumptions is even more difficult than measuring shared

EXHIBIT 14.2 **Organizational Culture Profile Dimensions and Characteristics**

Organizational culture dimension	Characteristics of the dimension
Innovation	Experimenting, opportunity seeking, risk taking, few rules, low cautiousness
Stability	Predictability, security, rule-oriented
Respect for people	Fairness, tolerance
Outcome orientation	Action-oriented, high expectations, results-oriented
Attention to detail	Precise, analytic
Team orientation	Collaboration, people-oriented
Aggressiveness	Competitive, low emphasis on social responsibility

values. A third concern is that many organizational culture models and measures incorrectly assume that organizations have a fairly clear, unified culture that is easily decipherable.[12] In reality, an organization's culture is typically blurry and fragmented. Every employee has a somewhat distinct hierarchy of values, so an organization's culture necessarily has noticeable variability. Also, organizations consist of clusters of employees across the organization, and these groups prioritize different values than the company's culture. Thus, many of the popular organizational culture models and measures oversimplify the variety of organizational cultures and falsely presume that organizations can easily be identified within these categories.

ORGANIZATIONAL SUBCULTURES

When discussing organizational culture, we are really referring to the *dominant culture,* that is, the values and assumptions shared most consistently and widely by the organization's members. The dominant culture is usually (but not always) supported by senior management. Cultural values and assumptions can also persist in spite of senior management's desire for another culture.

Organizations are also composed of *subcultures* located throughout their various divisions, geographic regions, and occupational groups.[13] Some subcultures enhance the dominant culture by espousing parallel assumptions and values. Others differ from but do not conflict with the dominant culture. Still others are called *countercultures* because they embrace values or assumptions that directly oppose the organization's dominant culture. It is also possible that some organizations (including some universities, according to one study) consist of subcultures with no decipherable dominant culture at all.[14]

Subcultures, particularly countercultures, may cause conflict and dissension among employees, but they also serve two important functions.[15] First, they maintain the organization's standards of performance and ethical behaviour. Employees who hold countercultural values are an important source of surveillance and critical review of the dominant order. They encourage constructive conflict and more creative thinking about how the organization should interact with its environment. Subcultures potentially support ethical conduct by preventing employees from blindly following one set of values. Subculture members continually question the "obvious" decisions and actions of the majority, thereby making everyone more mindful of the consequences of their actions.

Subcultures serve a second valuable function: they are spawning grounds for emerging values that keep the firm aligned with the evolving needs and expectations of customers, suppliers, communities, and other stakeholders. Companies eventually need to replace their existing dominant values with ones that are more appropriate for the changing environment. Those emerging cultural values and assumptions usually exist in subcultures long before they are ideal for the organization. If subcultures are suppressed, the organization may take longer to discover, develop, and adopt the emerging desired culture.

 Which corporate culture do you prefer? You can discover which of four types of organizational culture you most and least prefer by completing this self-assessment in Connect.

Deciphering Organizational Culture through Artifacts

LO2

Shared values and assumptions are not easily measured through surveys and might not be accurately reflected in the organization's values statements. Instead, as Exhibit 14.1 illustrated earlier, an organization's culture needs to be deciphered through a detailed investigation of artifacts. **Artifacts** are the observable symbols and signs of an organization's culture, such as the way visitors are greeted, the organization's physical layout, and how employees are rewarded.[16] A few experts suggest that artifacts are the essence of organizational culture, whereas most others (including the authors of this book) view artifacts as symbols or indicators of culture. In other words, culture is cognitive (values and assumptions inside people's heads) whereas artifacts are observable manifestations of that culture. Either way, artifacts are important because they represent and reinforce an organization's culture.

artifacts The observable symbols and signs of an organization's culture.

Artifacts provide valuable evidence about a company's culture.[17] An organization's ambiguous and fragmented culture is best understood by observing workplace behaviour, listening to everyday conversations among staff and with customers, studying written documents and emails, viewing physical structures and settings, and interviewing staff about corporate stories. In other words, to truly understand an organization's culture, we need to sample information from a variety of organizational artifacts.

The Mayo Clinic conducted such an assessment. An anthropologist was hired to decipher the medical organization's culture at its headquarters in Minnesota and to identify ways of transferring that culture to its two newer sites in Florida and Arizona. For six weeks, the anthropologist shadowed employees, posed as a patient in waiting rooms, did countless interviews, and accompanied physicians on patient visits. The final report outlined Mayo's dominant culture and how its satellite operations varied from that culture.[18]

In this section, we review four broad categories of artifacts: organizational stories and legends, organizational language, rituals and ceremonies, and physical structures and symbols.

ORGANIZATIONAL STORIES AND LEGENDS

Cirque du Soleil thrives on a culture of creativity and calculated risk. This is apparent in stories detailing how the Montreal-based troupe that combines circus with theatre was started, and how it survived during the lean years. One such story took place soon after the company was formed. Cirque du Soleil was invited to perform at the Los Angeles Arts Festival, but they didn't have enough money to get back home and the festival could not provide funds in advance to cover Cirque du Soleil's costs. Co-founder Guy Laliberté took a gamble by literally emptying the troupe's bank account to transport the performers and equipment one way to California. "I bet everything on that one night [at the Los Angeles Arts Festival]," Laliberté recalls. "If we failed, there was no cash for gas to come home." Fortunately, the gamble paid off. Cirque du Soleil was a huge triumph, which led to more opportunities and successes in the years ahead.[19]

Stories such as Cirque du Soleil's risky business decision permeate strong organizational cultures. Some tales recount heroic deeds, whereas others ridicule past events that deviate from the firm's core values. Organizational stories and legends add human realism to corporate expectations, individual performance standards, and the criteria for getting fired. They also produce emotions, which tend to improve listeners' memory of the lesson within the story.[20] Stories have the greatest effect on communicating corporate culture when they describe real people, are assumed to be true, are known by employees throughout the organization, and convey clear messages about the way things should (or should not) be done.[21]

ORGANIZATIONAL LANGUAGE

The language of the workplace speaks volumes about the company's culture. How employees talk to each other, describe customers, express anger, and greet stakeholders are all verbal symbols of shared values and assumptions. "What we say—and how we say it—can deeply affect a company's culture," advise Tom Kelley and David Kelley, leaders of design firm IDEO.[22]

An organization's culture particularly stands out when employees habitually use customized phrases and labels. For instance, DaVita HealthCare Partners is called the "village" (not the company) and its chief executive is the "mayor" of the village. Employees at the Denver-based provider of kidney care and dialysis services are "teammates" (not employees) who eventually become "citizens" of the village as they "cross the bridge," meaning that they embrace the company's culture. These aren't meaningless slogans. The language symbolizes DaVita's deeply held cultural beliefs that employee well-being and performance depend on the human connection of workplace community that, in turn, translates into superior service to DaVita's patients.[23]

Language also captures less complimentary cultural values. At Goldman Sachs, "elephant trades" are apparently large investment transactions with huge profit potential, so

©Reven T.C. Wurman/Alamy

Galvanize employees often utter the phrase "put the moose on the table," which means talking openly about a known problem or issue that everyone has avoided (i.e., the elephant in the room). "It's a symbolic invitation to have the awkward—but necessary—conversation," says Laurie Schultz, CEO of the Vancouver-based security software company. "We say it all the time. It's a huge, huge, huge part of our culture." As a reminder, Galvanize has stuffed toy moose and moose drawings throughout its offices. Schultz adds: "One thing I've learned is the power of symbols, values, and language when reinforcing a risk-taking culture."*

* F. Stone, "The Conversation: ACL Services Boss Laurie Schultz Knows Fraud When She Sees It," *BC Business,* February 7, 2017; "5 Questions on Culture with Laurie Schultz, CEO, Galvanize," *Business in Vancouver,* January 2020, pp. 30–31.

the investment firm allegedly encourages its salespeople to go "elephant hunting" (seeking out these large trades from clients). A former Goldman Sachs manager reported that some employees at the investment firm also routinely described their clients as "muppets." "My muppet client didn't put me in comp on the trade we just printed," said one salesperson, meaning that the client was a fool because he didn't compare prices, so the salesperson overcharged him. The "muppet" label seems to reveal a culture with a derogatory view of clients. When this language use became public, Goldman Sachs scanned its internal emails for the "muppet" label and warned employees not to use the term.[24]

RITUALS AND CEREMONIES

Rituals are the programmed routines of daily organizational life that dramatize an organization's culture.[25] They include how visitors are greeted, how often senior executives visit subordinates, how people communicate with each other, how much time employees take for lunch, and so forth. Cultural rituals are repetitive, predictable events that have symbolic meaning of underlying cultural values and assumptions. For instance, BMW's fast-paced culture is quite literally apparent in the way employees walk around the German automaker's offices. "When you move through the corridors and hallways of other companies' buildings, people kind of crawl, they walk slowly," observes a BMW executive. "But BMW people tend to move faster."[26] **Ceremonies** are more formal artifacts than rituals. Ceremonies are planned activities conducted specifically for the benefit of an audience.

rituals The programmed routines of daily organizational life that dramatize the organization's culture.

ceremonies Planned displays of organizational culture, conducted specifically for the benefit of an audience.

EXHIBIT 14.3   Workspace Design and Organizational Culture

Collaborative and creative cultures	Controlling and competitive cultures
 ©Robert Daly/Getty Images	 ©Hero Images/Getty Images
• More team space • Informal space • Low/medium enclosure • Flexible environment • Organic layout	• More individual space • More formal than informal space • High/medium enclosure • More fixed environment • More structured, symmetrical layout

This would include publicly rewarding (or punishing) employees or celebrating the launch of a new product or newly won contract.

PHYSICAL STRUCTURES AND SYMBOLS

Winston Churchill once said: "We shape our buildings; thereafter, they shape us."[27] The former British prime minister was reminding us that an organization's culture affects building decisions, but the resulting structure's size, shape, location, and age subsequently reinforce or alter that culture. Physical structures might support a company's emphasis on teamwork, environmental friendliness, hierarchy, or any other set of values.[28]

One such example is Mars, Inc., one of the world's largest food manufacturers (producers of Uncle Ben's rice, Pedigree pet food, Wrigley's gum, etc.). The privately held company's low-profile (some say secretive) culture is evident from its nondescript head offices in most countries. Mars head offices in Canada and the United Kingdom are each buried in one of its manufacturing plants. Only small signs announce the company name; there is even less indication that the corporate chiefs are located there. Its global head office in Virginia could easily be mistaken for an upscale brick warehouse. It has no corporate identification at all, just a "private property" sign. Mars' head office is so low profile, in fact, that locals call it "the Kremlin." The chairman of Nestlé once thought he had arrived at the wrong address when visiting his major competitor.[29]

Even if the building doesn't make much of a statement, there is a treasure trove of physical artifacts inside. Desks, chairs, office layout, and wall hangings (or lack of them) are just a few of the workplace features that might convey cultural meaning.[30] Each physical artifact alone might not say much, but put enough of them together and an image emerges of how they symbolize the organization's culture.

For example, one prominent workspace design and manufacturing company recently identified the workspace features typically found at companies with different organizational cultures. Exhibit 14.3 summarizes the physical space design of collaborative and creative cultures compared to cultures that emphasize efficiency (control) and competition. Collaborative and creative cultures value more teamwork and flexibility, so space design is informal and enables spontaneous group discussion. Controlling and competitive cultures tend to have more structural office arrangements and provide more space for individual work than teamwork.[31]

Is Organizational Culture Important?

LO3

Does a strong organizational culture improve organizational effectiveness? Steve Rhone thinks so: "Culture is the secret ingredient to every great organization: it cannot be copied or easily replicated," advises the president of Weston Forest,

EXHIBIT 14.4   **Potential Benefits and Contingencies of Culture Strength**

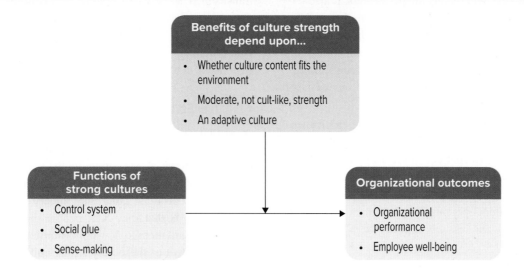

the specialty wood products distributor and re-manufacturer in Mississauga, Ontario. Tony Guzzi agrees. "I am a firm believer that my job is to define the culture we want, model the culture we want, and nourish the culture we want," says the CEO of EMCOR Group, a Fortune 500 company that provides construction, industrial and energy infrastructure, and facilities services. "In the end, the biggest thing you [as CEO] can try to shape is the culture in the organization."[32]

Steve Rhone, Tony Guzzi, and many other leaders believe that an organization's success partly depends on its culture. Several popular-press management books similarly assert that the most successful companies have strong cultures. In fact, one best-selling book, *Built to Last,* suggests that successful companies are "cult-like" (although not actually cults, the authors are careful to point out.)[33] Does OB research support this view that companies are more effective when they have a strong culture? Yes, potentially, but the evidence indicates that the relationship depends on a few conditions.[34]

THE MEANING AND POTENTIAL BENEFITS OF A STRONG CULTURE

Before discussing the contingencies of an effective organizational culture, let's examine the meaning of a "strong" organizational culture and its potential benefits. Culture strength refers to how widely and deeply employees understand and embrace the organization's dominant values and assumptions. In a strong organizational culture, the company's core values are "shared" by most employees across all subunits. Values are "shared" when employees hold a similar

understanding of them and internalize them as part of their personal set of values.

In a strong culture, the company's values and assumptions are also institutionalized through well-established artifacts, which further entrench the culture. In addition, strong cultures tend to be long-lasting; some can be traced back to personal attributes and behaviours of the company's founder. In contrast, companies have weak cultures when the dominant values are held mainly by a few people at the top of the organization, employees lack awareness or agreement on the meaning of those values, the values and assumptions are unstable over time or highly varied across the organization, and the culture is difficult to interpret from artifacts.

Under specific conditions, companies are more effective when they have strong cultures because of the three important functions listed in Exhibit 14.4 and described as follows:

- *Control system.* Organizational culture is a deeply embedded form of social control that guides employee decisions and behaviour.[35] Culture is an automatic pilot, nonconsciously directing employees so their behaviour is consistent with organizational expectations. For this reason, organizational culture is often described as a compass that points everyone in the same direction. "We cannot provide [employees] with a playbook that covers every eventuality, but we can explicitly share a set of values to help them make the best possible choices," says Angela Brown, CEO of Moneris, the Toronto-based market leader in debit and credit card payment systems.[36]

- *Social glue.* Organizational culture is the social glue that bonds people together and makes them feel part of the organizational experience.[37] Employees are motivated to internalize the organization's dominant culture because it fulfils their need for social identity. This social glue attracts new staff and retains top performers. It also becomes the common thread that holds employees together in global organizations. "The values of the company are really the bedrock—the glue which holds the firm together," says Nandan Nilekani, co-founder and non-executive chairman of Infosys, India's second-largest information technology company.[38]

- *Sense-making.* Organizational culture helps employees to make sense of what goes on and why things happen in the company.[39] Corporate culture also makes it easier for them to understand what is expected of them. For instance, research has found that sales employees in companies with stronger organizational cultures have clearer role perceptions and less role-related stress.[40]

CONTINGENCIES OF ORGANIZATIONAL CULTURE AND EFFECTIVENESS

Studies report only a moderately positive relationship between culture strength and organizational effectiveness. The reason for this weak link is that strong cultures improve organizational effectiveness only under specific conditions (see Exhibit 14.4). The three main contingencies are: (1) whether the culture content is aligned with its external environment; (2) whether the culture is moderately strong, not cult-like; and (3) whether the culture incorporates an adaptive culture.

Culture Content Is Aligned with the External Environment

The benefits of a strong culture depend on whether its content—the culture's dominant values and assumptions—is aligned with the external environment. If the culture is congruent with the environment, then employees are more motivated and have clearer role perceptions to practise behaviours that improve the organization's interaction with its environment. But when the culture is misaligned with the environment, a strong culture encourages decisions and behaviours that can undermine the organization's connection with its stakeholders.

Consider Microsoft, which has had a strong culture for many years. As the opening case study explained, until recently, the technology giant's dominant values were noticeably dysfunctional, meaning that they undermined rather than enhanced the organization's capacity to innovate, adapt, and collaborate internally and externally. "Innovation was being replaced by bureaucracy. Teamwork was being replaced by internal politics. We were falling behind," recalls current CEO Satya Nadella. Indeed, experts widely believed that if Microsoft's existing culture continued, the company would be "fading toward irrelevance." Nadella successfully transformed Microsoft's culture by instilling a new set of dominant values around a growth mindset of innovation, information sharing (collaboration), and customer focus— values that are much more aligned with what the technology firm needs to thrive.[41]

Culture Strength Is Not the Level of a Cult

A second contingency is the degree of culture strength. Various experts suggest that companies with very strong cultures—known as corporate "cults"—may be less effective than companies with moderately strong cultures.[42] One reason why corporate cults may undermine organizational effectiveness is that they lock people into mental models, which can blind them to new opportunities and unique problems. The effect of these very strong cultures is that people overlook or incorrectly define subtle misalignments between the organization's activities and the changing environment.

The other reason why very strong cultures may be dysfunctional is that they suppress dissenting subcultures. The challenge for organizational leaders is to maintain not only a strong culture but one that allows subcultural diversity. Subcultures encourage task-oriented conflict, which improves creative thinking and offers some level of ethical vigilance over the dominant culture. In the long run, a subculture's nascent values could become important dominant values as the environment changes. Corporate cults suppress subcultures, thereby undermining these benefits.

Culture Is an Adaptive Culture

A third condition influencing the effect of cultural strength on organizational effectiveness is whether the culture content includes an **adaptive culture**.[43] An adaptive culture embraces change, creativity, open-mindedness, growth, and learning. Organizational leaders across many industries increasingly view an adaptive culture as an important ingredient for the organization's long-term success. Microsoft CEO Satya Nadella particularly emphasized this growth mindset and learning orientation as central ingredients in the technology company's new culture. "The phrase we use to describe our emerging culture is 'growth mindset,'" he says. "It's about every individual, every one of us having that attitude—that mindset—of being able to overcome any constraint, stand up to any challenge, making it possible for us to grow and, thereby, for the company to grow."[44]

adaptive culture An organizational culture in which employees are receptive to change, including the ongoing alignment of the organization to its environment and continuous improvement of internal processes.

Debating Point: IS CORPORATE CULTURE AN OVERUSED PHRASE?

Corporate culture is probably one of the most frequently uttered phrases in organizations these days. That's quite an accomplishment for two words that were rarely paired together prior to 1982.* Executives often say they have crafted the company's culture to attract top talent and better serve clients. Job applicants have made organizational culture one of the top factors in their decision about whether to join a particular company. Journalists routinely blame corporate culture for business failures, deviant activities, and quirky employee conduct.

This chapter offers plenty of arguments supporting the position that organizational culture influences employee decisions and behaviour. A strong culture is a control system that guides employees, often nonconsciously. It is, after all, the "way we do things around here." A strong culture also serves as the company's "social glue," which strengthens cohesion among employees. In other words, employees in strong cultures have similar beliefs and values which, in turn, increases their motivation to follow the corporate herd.

Organizational culture can be a useful concept to explain workplace activities, but some OB experts suggest that the phrase is overused. To begin with, corporate culture is usually presented as a singular thing within the company—one organization with one culture. This presumption of a homogeneous culture—in which every employee understands and embraces the same few dominant values—just doesn't exist. Every organization has a fragmented culture to varying degrees. Furthermore, many employees engage in façades of conformity. They pretend to live the company's values but don't actually do so because they don't believe in them.** Fragmentation and façades suggest that culture

is not an integrated force field that manipulates people like mindless robots. Instead, employees ultimately make decisions based on a variety of influences, not only the organization's values and assumptions.

Another argument that corporate culture is overused as a tool to explain the workplace is that values don't drive behaviour as often as many people believe. Instead, employees turn to their values to guide behaviour only when they are reminded of those values or when the situation produces fairly obvious conflicting or questionable decisions.*** Most of the time, front-line staff perform their jobs without much thought to their values. Their decisions are usually in relation to technical rather than values-based matters. As such, corporate culture has a fairly peripheral role in daily routine work activities.

A third problem is that organizational culture is a blunt instrument for explaining workplace behaviour and for recommending how to change those behaviours. "Fix the culture" is almost meaningless because the problems prompting this advice could be due to any number of artifacts. Furthermore, some problems attributed to a poor corporate culture may be due to more mundane and precise dysfunctions—unintended consequences of poorly designed rewards, ineffective leadership, misaligned corporate strategy, biased information systems, and a host of other conditions.

Rather than blame the company's culture, we should pay more attention to specific systems, structures, behaviours, and attitudes that explain what went wrong. Furthermore, as two experts recently noted, organizational culture is often the outcome of these specific artifacts, not the cause of the problems those artifacts create.****

* The terms "organizational culture" and "corporate culture" were popularized in 1982 in: Deal and Kennedy, *Corporate Cultures;* T.J. Peters and R.H. Waternam, *In Search of Excellence: Lessons from America's Best-Run Companies* (New York: Warner, 1982). However, there are a few early references to an organization's culture, including: N. Margulies, "Organizational Culture and Psychological Growth," *The Journal of Applied Behavioral Science* 5, no. 4 (1969): 491–508; S. Silverzweig and R.F. Allen, "Changing the Corporate Culture," *Sloan Management Review* 17, no. 3 (1976): 33.

** P.F. Hewlin, T.L. Dumas, and M.F. Burnett, "To Thine Own Self Be True? Facades of Conformity, Values Incongruence, and the Moderating Impact of Leader Integrity," *Academy of Management Journal* 60 (2017): 178–99; S.E. Cha et al., "Being Your True Self at Work: Integrating the Fragmented Research on Authenticity in Organizations," *Academy of Management Annals* 13 (2019): 633–71.

*** G.R. Maio and J.M. Olson, "Values as Truisms: Evidence and Implications," *Journal of Personality and Social Psychology* 74, no. 2 (1998): 294–311; S. Arieli, A.M. Grant, and L. Sagiv, "Convincing Yourself to Care about Others: An Intervention for Enhancing Benevolence Values," *Journal of Personality* 82, no. 1 (2014): 15–24; K.M. Sheldon and L.S. Krieger, "Walking the Talk: Value Importance, Value Enactment, and Well-Being," *Motivation and Emotion* 38 (2014): 609–19.

**** J.W. Lorsch and E. McTague, "Culture Is Not the Culprit," *Harvard Business Review* 94, no. 4 (2016): 96–105.

What does an adaptive culture look like? It is one in which employees recognize that the organization's survival and success depends on their ability to discover emerging changes in the external environment and to adapt their own behaviour to those changes. Thus, employees in adaptive cultures adopt an open systems view and take responsibility for

the organization's performance and alignment with the external environment.

In an adaptive culture, receptivity to change extends to internal processes and roles. Employees believe that satisfying stakeholder needs requires continuous improvement of internal work processes. They also recognize the importance

Global Connections 14.2

UBER SHIFTS GEARS TOWARD A MORE ETHICAL CULTURE*

Uber employed more than 5,000 people just six years after the transportation network company was created. To guide employee behaviour in the rapidly expanding organization, co-founder and former CEO Travis Kalanick and another executive penned a list of 14 values representing Uber's "philosophy of work." They were Uber's actual or aspirational culture.

Dressed in a white lab coat, Kalanick introduced the list at a secretive Las Vegas convention with almost all Uber employees in attendance. He explained each value in detail with several slides and a video, then asked specific Uber executives to tell a story that exemplified each value. "When you go through that growth, you have to cement your culture values and talk about them all of the time," said Kalanick after the cultural values were made public.

Kalanick's rationale for articulating the list of 14 values was to maintain Uber's aggressive entrepreneurial spirit. Yet many observers say that several of these values and corresponding leadership role modelling produced a "toxic culture" and a "cultural implosion" that led to lawsuits, employee turnover and dismissals, and government investigations. Uber has faced allegations of sexual harassment, bullying, privacy violations, corporate espionage, anti-competitive activities, and theft of proprietary technology.

Three years after his dramatic corporate culture presentation, Kalanick was replaced as Uber's CEO by outsider Dara Khosrowshahi. One of Khosrowshahi's top priorities was to change the company's culture to one that instilled more ethical conduct and productive behaviour. "The culture and approach that got Uber where it is today is not what will get us to the next level," said Khosrowshahi soon after stepping into the CEO role. "Our values define who we are and how we work, but I had heard from many employees that some of them simply didn't represent the kind of company we want to be."

Uber's original list was developed by two Uber executives alone, whereas Khosrowshahi invited all employees to participate in crafting the new cultural "norms." More than 1,200 staff members worldwide submitted ideas and almost two dozen employee focus group sessions were held. Employees voted on the resulting list of values, which were then distilled down to eight core themes.

Only a few of the original values remained, such as "big bold bets" and "be an owner." Other values were jettisoned because they reinforced some of the unethical activities that got Uber in trouble. Khosrowshahi specifically commented that "toe-stepping" was intended to encourage employees at all levels to share their ideas, "but too often it was used as an excuse for being [a jerk]." Equally important, the new values include the explicit ethical mandate to "do the right thing" whereas nothing similar existed in the original list.

©Vipin Kumar/Hindustan Times/Shutterstock

* R. Parry, "Uber Hosts Top Secret Sin City Extravaganza for 4,800 Employees," *Mail Online,* October 1, 2015; D. Brown, "3 Valuable Lessons From Uber Founder Travis Kalanick's TED Talk," *Inc.,* February 16, 2016; A. Griswold, "Uber Is Designed so That for One Employee to Get Ahead, Another Must Fail," *Quartz,* February 27, 2017; S. Levin, "Uber's Scandals, Blunders and PR Disasters: The Full List," *Guardian,* June 18, 2017; B. Edelman, "Uber Can't Be Fixed—It's Time for Regulators to Shut It Down," *Harvard Business Review,* June 21, 2017; E. Knight, "Uber Pays a $26 Billion Price for Its Toxic Corporate Culture," *Sydney Morning Herald* (Australia), July 1, 2017; B. Stone, *The Upstarts: How Uber, Airbnb, and the Killer Companies of the New Silicon Valley Are Changing the World* (New York: Hachette, 2017); D. Khosrowshahi, "Uber's New Cultural Norms," *Linkedin Blog* (blog), November 7, 2017, https://www.linkedin.com/pulse/ubers-new-cultural-norms-dara-khosrowshahi; S. Bond, "Uber Chief Admits Culture Needs Further Improvement," *Financial Times (London),* October 24, 2018, sec. Companies and Markets; S. Nicholls, "The Uber Story," transcript, *Four Corners* (Sydney: ABC Australia, March 13, 2019).

learning orientation A set of collective beliefs and norms that encourage people to question past practices, learn new ideas, experiment putting ideas into practice, and view mistakes as part of the learning process.

of remaining flexible in their own work roles. The phrase "That's not my job" is typical of nonadaptive cultures. Finally, an adaptive culture has a strong **learning orientation** because being receptive to change necessarily means that the company also supports action-oriented discovery. With a learning orientation, employees welcome new learning opportunities, actively experiment with new ideas and practices, view reasonable mistakes as a natural part of the learning process, and continuously question past practices (see Chapter 7).[45]

ORGANIZATIONAL CULTURE AND BUSINESS ETHICS

An organization's culture influences the ethical conduct of its employees. This makes sense because good behaviour is driven by ethical values, and ethical values become embedded in an organization's dominant culture. For example, AIA Group, Hong Kong's largest life insurance company (by number of policies), has a strong culture focused on "doing the right thing, in the right way, with the right people, and the results will come." This means that employees are expected to think through the ramifications of their actions (right thing) and ensure they always work with integrity and teamwork (right way).[46]

The opposite is equally true. There are numerous instances where an organization's culture has caused unethical conduct. For example, the board of Commonwealth Bank of Australia (CBA) eventually admitted that a dysfunctional corporate culture contributed to serious financial violations that ultimately triggered a national commission on conduct among all of Australia's financial institutions. Government authorities found that CBA financial advisors provided fraudulent or unprofessional advice to clients. Later, CBA traders were charged with "unconscionable conduct and market manipulation" that deliberately moved the interest rate to the bank's advantage. Third, CBA allegedly failed to adequately monitor, intervene, and report to government authorities 53,000 transactions amounting to more than AUD $600 million in possible money laundering. "We've acknowledged there are aspects of our culture where we could improve," said CBA board chair Catherine Livingstone after three years of these events.[47]

Some leaders also try to improve ethical conduct by changing and strengthening the organization's culture around more socially desirable values. This strategy occurred at Barclays Bank PLC, which was found guilty of rigging interest rates a decade ago. After the British bank's most senior executives were

forced out due to the scandal, the new CEO focused on establishing a clear set of ethical values (respect, integrity, service, excellence, stewardship). He then advised all 140,000 Barclays employees that these values should guide their behaviour so Barclays could become a more ethical organization.

"There might be some who don't feel they can fully buy in to an approach which so squarely links performance to the upholding of our values," warned Barclays' CEO. "My message to those people is simple: Barclays is not the place for you. The rules have changed. You won't feel comfortable at Barclays and, to be frank, we won't feel comfortable with you as colleagues."[48] The point here is that culture and ethics go hand-in-hand. To create a more ethical organization, leaders need to instil enacted values that steer employees toward morally correct behaviour.

Merging Organizational Cultures

LO4

Mergers and acquisitions often fail financially when the merging organizations have incompatible cultures.[49] Unless the acquired firm is left to operate independently, companies with clashing cultures tend to undermine employee performance and customer service. Consequently, several studies estimate that only between 30 and 50 percent of corporate acquisitions add value.[50]

Consider one such acquisition by Johnson & Johnson (J&J).[51] The venerable medical devices and consumer products firm has acquired numerous companies over the years, and most of these deals carefully diagnosed the cultural compatibilities of the two firms. But Aileen Stockburger recalls one acquisition that didn't. "We did extremely cursory assessments of the existing organizational cultures," admits the former J&J vice president of mergers and acquisitions. "Based on these assessments, we thought the cultures were very similar. Only later did we learn just how different the cultures were, particularly in terms of decision-making style."

J&J values debate and constructive discussion in the decision process, whereas the acquired firm valued top-down authority. During the integration, executives at the acquired firm felt increasingly uncomfortable and unhappy because their decisions were questioned by others. Most of the acquired firm executives eventually quit and J&J lost considerable value in their business acquisition.

BICULTURAL AUDIT

Organizational leaders can minimize cultural collisions in corporate mergers and fulfil their duty of due diligence by conducting a bicultural audit.[52] A **bicultural audit** diagnoses cultural relations between the companies and determines the extent to which cultural clashes will likely occur. The process begins by identifying cultural differences between the merging companies. This might be done by surveying employees or through an extended series of meetings where executives and staff of both firms discuss how they think through important decisions in their business. From the survey data or meetings, the parties determine which differences between the two firms will result in conflict and which cultural values provide common ground on which to build a cultural foundation in the merged organization. The final stage involves identifying strategies and preparing action plans to bridge the two organizations' cultures.

> **bicultural audit** A process of diagnosing cultural relations between companies and determining the extent to which cultural clashes will likely occur.

STRATEGIES FOR MERGING DIFFERENT ORGANIZATIONAL CULTURES

In some cases, the bicultural audit results in a decision to end merger talks because the two cultures are too different to merge effectively. However, even with substantially different cultures, two companies may form a workable union if they apply the correct plan of action. The four main strategies for merging different corporate cultures are assimilation, deculturation, integration, and separation (see Exhibit 14.5).[53]

Assimilation

Assimilation occurs when employees at the acquired company willingly embrace the cultural values of the acquiring organization. Typically, this strategy works best when the acquired company has a weak culture or is dysfunctional, whereas the acquiring company's culture is strong and aligned with the external environment. The cultural assimilation strategy seldom produces cultural clashes because the acquiring firm's culture is highly respected and the acquired firm's culture is fairly easily altered.

Deculturation

Assimilation is rare. Employees usually resist organizational change, particularly when they are asked to abide by significantly different corporate values. Under these conditions, some acquiring companies apply a *deculturation* strategy by imposing their culture and business practices on the acquired organization. The acquiring firm strips away reward systems and other artifacts that support the old culture. People who cannot adopt the acquiring company's culture often lose their jobs. Deculturation may be necessary when the acquired firm's culture doesn't work, even when employees in the acquired company aren't convinced of this. However, this strategy is difficult to apply effectively because the acquired firm's employees resist the cultural intrusions from the buying firm, thereby delaying or undermining the merger process.

Integration

A third strategy is to combine the cultures of the two firms into one new composite culture that preserves the best features of the previous cultures. Integration is slow and potentially risky because there are many forces preserving the

EXHIBIT 14.5   Strategies for Merging Different Organizational Cultures

Merger strategy	Description	Works best when:
Assimilation	Acquired company embraces acquiring firm's culture.	Acquired firm has a weak culture and acquiring firm's culture is strong and successful.
Deculturation	Acquiring firm imposes its culture on the unwilling acquired firm.	Rarely successful—may be necessary when acquired firm's culture is dysfunctional but its employees aren't yet aware of the problems.
Integration	Merging companies combine the two or more cultures into a new composite culture.	Existing cultures at both firms are relatively weak or have overlapping values and can be improved.
Separation	Merging companies remain distinct entities with minimal exchange of culture or organizational practices.	Firms operate successfully in different businesses requiring different cultures.

Global Connections 14.3

ALASKA AIR'S ACQUISITION OF VIRGIN AMERICA: FROM SEPARATION TO INTEGRATION*

Alaska Air's decision to acquire Virgin America brought audible gasps from customers and investment analysts alike. Both airlines are successful and their routes are complementary, but many observers questioned the cultural fit of a combined airline. "I think of [Virgin America] as a young, hip airline," says one business traveller. "Alaska is more of a friendly aunt."

At first, Alaska Air Group CEO Brad Tilden asserted that both airlines had similar cultures that were focused on employees, customers, and safety. But Tilden's executive team was soon deliberating whether the cultures were sufficiently different that the two airlines should remain separate with their own cultures. Creating a single airline with the best cultural elements of both (integration strategy) would be more cost efficient, but maintaining Alaska and Virgin as distinct operations (separation strategy) might avoid an internal culture clash and retain valued Virgin staff and customers.

Tilden and his executive team eventually chose both cultural merger strategies. For the first two years, Alaska and Virgin remained separate, with their own distinct cultures and practices; but the airlines were then slowly combined into one organization with an integrated culture and a single brand. "Culture has been a real challenge in many mergers, so we're working to do things

differently," explains Ben Minicucci, the Canadian executive who is Alaska Air's president and chief operating officer.

"Alaska Airlines and Virgin America are different airlines, but we believe different works," says Tilden, using the merger's official "different works" catchphrase. Alaska Airlines executives say they want to integrate some of Virgin's "hip culture" in the combined airline. Many Virgin America fans are skeptical, but travel writers are already noticing aspects of Virgin's culture in the new Alaska Airlines.

©AP Photo/Ted S. Warren, File/CP Images

* M. Krupnick, "Virgin America Fans Ask if Alaska Airlines Takeover Will Mean Loss of Cool," *The New York Times,* April 11, 2016; S. Mayerowitz, "Alaska Airlines CEO Says He Might Keep Virgin America Brand," Associated Press, June 15, 2016; H. Martin, "Virgin America Will Disappear into Alaska Airlines in 2019," *Los Angeles Times,* March 22, 2017; L. D. Redman, "The 'New' Alaska Airlines Looks a Lot Like Virgin America," *Condé Nast Traveler,* January 22, 2018.

existing cultures. Still, this strategy should be considered when the companies have relatively weak cultures or when their cultures include several overlapping values. Integration works best when the cultures of both merging companies could be improved, which motivates employees to adopt the best cultural elements of the separate entities. Incorporating the best cultural elements of the original companies symbolizes that employees from both firms have meaningful values for the combined organization. "Find one thing in the organization that was good and use it as a cornerstone for a new culture," advises a respected executive who has led several mergers and acquisitions. "People don't want to work for an organization for years and then be told it's rubbish."[54]

Separation

A separation strategy occurs when the merging companies agree to remain distinct entities with minimal exchange of culture or organizational practices. This strategy is most appropriate when the two merging companies are in unrelated industries, because the most appropriate cultural values tend to differ by industry. Separation is also the preferred approach for the corporate cultures of diversified conglomerates. The cultural separation strategy is rare, however. Executives in acquiring firms usually have difficulty keeping their hands off the acquired firm. According to one estimate, only 15 percent of mergers leave the acquired company as a stand-alone unit.[55]

Changing and Strengthening Organizational Culture

LO5

Is it possible to change an organization's culture? Yes, but doing so isn't easy, the change rarely occurs quickly, and often the culture ends up changing (or replacing) corporate leaders. A few experts argue that an organization's culture "cannot be managed," so attempting to change the company's values and assumptions is a waste of time.[56] This may be an extreme view, but organizational culture experts generally agree that changing an organization's culture is a monumental challenge. At the same time, the external environment changes over time, so organizations eventually need to shift their culture to maintain alignment with the emerging environment.

This section looks at five strategies that have had some success at altering and strengthening corporate cultures. These strategies, illustrated in Exhibit 14.6, are not exhaustive, but each seems to work well in most circumstances.

MODEL DESIRED CULTURE THROUGH ACTIONS OF FOUNDERS AND LEADERS

Whether deliberately or haphazardly, the company's founder usually forms an organization's culture.[57] The founder's personality, values, habits, and critical events all play a role in establishing the firm's core values and assumptions. The founder is often an inspiring visionary who provides a compelling role model for others to follow. In later years, organizational culture is reinforced through stories and legends about the founder that symbolize the core values. "All companies, especially entrepreneurial companies, take the shape of the owner," says Bruce Poon Tip, CEO and founder of Toronto-based G Adventures. For example, he says "we have a culture of winning and a culture of excellence that is driven by me."[58]

Although founders usually establish an organization's culture, subsequent leaders need to actively guide, reinforce, and sometimes alter that culture.[59] This is evident in the opening case study to this chapter. Microsoft needed to replace its dysfunctional culture, which was embedded to some extent by the company's leaders before Satya Nadella became CEO. "It's good to be deliberate about your culture. Because if you're not, it's going to happen either way," warns John Luxford, chief technology officer at Flipside XR, the Winnipeg-based virtual reality animation studio.[60]

The process of leading cultural change is associated with both transformational leadership and authentic leadership (see Chapter 12). In each of those models, leaders base their words and actions on personal values, and those values potentially become a reflection of the organization's values.

EXHIBIT 14.6   Strategies for Changing and Strengthening Organizational Culture

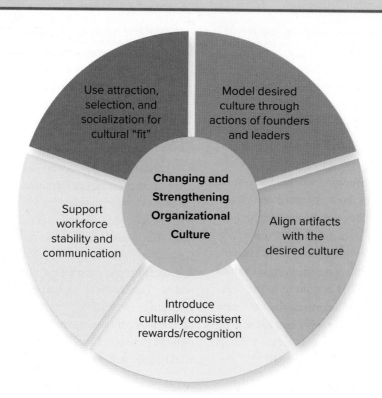

How Well Are Companies Managing Their Culture?*

67% of Canadian employees surveyed say their organization has a "weak" capacity to effectively drive the desired culture.

58% of 812 managers (most in human resources) in the U.K. believe their organization's espoused values generally reflect the actual values practised by management.

40% of 500 Canadian employees say they would decline an offer for the perfect job if the corporate culture wasn't a good fit.

50% of more than 7,000 business leaders across 130 countries say their company is attempting to change its culture.

CORE VALUES

12% of more than 7,000 business leaders across 130 countries believe their company is driving the "right" corporate culture.

©alexmillos/Shutterstock

*D. Lucy et al., The Management Agenda 2016, (West Sussex, UK: Roffey Park, February 2016); Deloitte, Human Capital Trends 2016: Out of Sync?, Deloitte Design Studio (Toronto: 2016); Deloitte University Press, The New Organization: Different by Design, Global Human Capital Trends 2016, (New York: Deloitte University Press, 2016); "Two in Five Canadian Workers Would Pass on Perfect Job If Corporate Culture Was Not a Fit, Survey Finds," News Release (Toronto: Robert Half, November 27, 2018).

For instance, one study found that the preferred conflict-handling style of leaders influences the work unit's or organization's cultural expectations of how employees address conflict situations. Another study reported that work units or companies with strong servant leadership were more likely to have a culture that valued providing service to others.[61]

ALIGN ARTIFACTS WITH THE DESIRED CULTURE

Artifacts represent more than just the visible indicators of a company's culture. They are also mechanisms that keep the culture in place or shift the culture to a new set of values and assumptions.[62] Workplace layout, reporting structures, office rituals, and information systems are some of the various organizational systems and structures. And as we discuss in the next chapter, systems and structures are powerful mechanisms for organizational change because they stabilize and reinforce the desired state of affairs. Corporate cultures are also strengthened through the artifacts of stories and behaviours. According to Max De Pree, the late CEO

of furniture manufacturer Herman Miller Inc., every organization needs "tribal storytellers" to keep the organization's history and culture alive.[63] Leaders play a role by creating memorable events that symbolize the cultural values they want to develop or maintain.

INTRODUCE CULTURALLY CONSISTENT REWARDS AND RECOGNITION

Reward systems and informal recognition practices are artifacts, but they deserve separate discussion because of their formidable capacity to strengthen or reshape an organization's culture.[64] Uber created a new reward system to help replace its "toxic" culture with one that is more compatible with societal expectations. The transportation network company previously had an internally competitive (rank-and-yank) and allegedly biased performance review in which managers rated employees on their best three and worst three performance dimensions, linked to the company's original cultural values. Incoming Uber CEO Dara Khosrowshahi not

©G Adventures

G Adventures, the popular adventure travel company, is a values-driven organization, so it carefully assesses whether job applicants are aligned with the Toronto-based organization's culture. "After a hiring manager wants to move forward with a candidate, we include what is called the 'G Factor' as the last interview," explains Jeremy Brady, G Adventures national sales manager, USA. "This is a culture fit, where we have the candidate [interviewed by] three random employees."

Job applicants in Toronto visit Base Camp (Toronto headquarters) and are interviewed in the "ball pit," the small room shown in this photo filled about one-third of a metre high with plastic balls. The applicant answers several questions randomly chosen by the spin of a large prize wheel on the wall (left side of this photo). The three interviewing employees listen carefully to the applicant's answers to determine whether the applicant's values are compatible with G Adventures' culture. Applicants who fail the G Factor Interview don't get hired, even if they have exceptional skills.*

*M. Baran, "Beards and Ball Pits: Just a Typical Day at G Adventures Base Camp," *Travel Weekly,* November 18, 2015; J. DeLoach, "Jeremy Brady, National Sales Manager, G Adventures," *Travel Research Online* (blog), December 17, 2018, https://www.travelresearchonline.com/blog/index.php/2018/12/jeremy-brady-national-sales-manager-g-adventures/; J. Christoff, "G Adventures Begins Search for 2019 Ambassadors of Change," *TravelPulse,* April 30, 2019; "G Adventures Engineering Culture," Key Values, accessed March 25, 2020, https://www.keyvalues.com/g-adventures.

only threw out the dysfunctional values; he also introduced a new reward system that encourages cooperation, community involvement, and individual development without competing against co-workers. The new personal goal achievement process requires everyone to include one "citizenship goal"(e.g., helping co-workers, volunteering outside the company). "We're shifting the culture very significantly through this process," says an Uber human resources executive.[65]

SUPPORT WORKFORCE STABILITY AND COMMUNICATION

An organization's culture is embedded in the minds of its employees. Organizational stories are rarely written down; rituals and ceremonies do not usually exist in procedure manuals; organizational metaphors are not found in corporate directories. Thus, a strong culture depends on a stable workforce. Workforce stability is important because it takes time for employees to fully understand the organization's culture and how to enact it in their daily work lives. The organization's culture can literally disintegrate during periods of high turnover and precipitous downsizing because the corporate memory leaves with the departing employees. A strong organizational culture also depends on a workplace in which employees regularly interact with one another. Through ongoing communication, everyone in the organization develops shared language, stories, and other artifacts.

USE ATTRACTION, SELECTION, AND SOCIALIZATION FOR CULTURAL FIT

A valuable way to strengthen and possibly change an organization's culture is to recruit and select job applicants whose values are compatible with the culture. This process is explained

attraction–selection–attrition (ASA) theory A theory which states that organizations have a natural tendency to attract, select, and retain people with values and personality characteristics that are consistent with the organization's character, resulting in a more homogeneous organization and a stronger culture.

by **attraction–selection–attrition (ASA) theory.**[66] ASA theory states that organizations have a natural tendency to attract, select, and retain people with values and personality characteristics that are consistent with the organization's character, resulting in a more homogeneous organization and a stronger culture.

- *Attraction.* Job applicants engage in self-selection by avoiding prospective employers whose values seem incompatible with their own values.[67] They look for subtle artifacts during interviews and through public information that communicate the company's culture. Some organizations encourage this self-selection by actively describing their cultures.

- *Selection.* How well the person "fits" in with the company's culture is often a factor in deciding which job applicants to hire.[68] IKEA is a values-driven organization, so it determines how well applicants' personal values are compatible with the global retailer's corporate values as well as how well those applicants are aware of IKEA's values. The idea is that this cultural alignment is good for both the company and the employee. "Be clear of your personal values and connect those with your company values," advises an IKEA human resource manager. "We know that tomorrow's candidates are not necessarily looking for the perfect job; they're looking for the perfect cultural fit."[69]

- *Attrition.* People seek environments that are reasonably congruent with their personal values. They are also motivated to leave environments that are a poor fit. This occurs because person–organization values congruence supports their social identity and minimizes internal role conflict. Even if employees aren't forced out, many quit when values incongruence is sufficiently high.[70] Several companies (Zappos, G Adventures, etc.) will even pay newcomers to quit within the first few weeks of employment if the new employees think their personal values conflict with the company's culture.

Organizational Socialization

LO6

Organizational socialization is the process by which individuals learn the values, expected behaviours, and social knowledge necessary to assume their roles in the organization.[71] It is a valuable set of practices to help companies change and strengthen their organizational culture. Equally important, it helps newcomers adjust to co-workers, work procedures, and other corporate realities. Research indicates that when evidence-based organizational socialization practices are applied, new hires tend to perform better, have higher job satisfaction, and remain longer with the organization.[72]

organizational socialization The process by which individuals learn the values, expected behaviours, and social knowledge necessary to assume their roles in the organization.

Some writers claim that organizational socialization can change employee values to become more aligned with the company's culture. However, personal values are fairly stable beyond early adulthood and therefore are not so easily altered by short-term training and related socialization events. Instead, effective organizational socialization offers newcomers a clearer understanding about the company's values which, in turn, gives them guidelines to more accurately engage in values-consistent behaviours on the job.[73] Better awareness of the company's culture also motivates new hires to reject the job offer or more quickly leave if their personal values are incompatible with the organization's values and assumptions.

LEARNING AND ADJUSTMENT PROCESS

Organizational socialization is a process of both learning and adjustment. It is a learning process because newcomers try to make sense of the company's physical workplace, social dynamics, and strategic and cultural environment. They learn about the organization's performance expectations, power dynamics, corporate culture, company history, and jargon. They also need to form successful and satisfying relationships with other people from whom they can learn the ropes.[74] In other words, effective socialization supports newcomers' *organizational comprehension.* It accelerates development of an accurate cognitive map of the physical, social, strategic, and cultural dynamics of the organization. Ideally, this learning should be distributed over time to minimize information overload.

Organizational socialization is also an adjustment process because individuals need to adapt to their new work environment. They develop new work roles that reconfigure their social identity, adopt new team norms, and practise new behaviours.[75] The adjustment process is fairly rapid for many people, usually occurring within a few months. However, newcomers with diverse work experience seem to adjust better than those with limited previous experience, possibly

Global Connections 14.4

JUNIOR INVESTMENT ANALYSTS EXPERIENCE PSYCHOLOGICAL CONTRACT VIOLATIONS[*]

Steve Wu assumed that his new job as an investment analyst would involve long hours working on prestigious fast-paced deals. The recent university graduate experienced the long hours, but much of the work was drudgery. The reality shock and psychological contract violation motivated Wu to quit just one month before his first year, forfeiting a five-figure bonus. He joined a mobile-gaming startup and is now a product manager at a cloud-based platform for payroll and teamwork.

Chris Martinez also expected long hours at the private equity firm that hired him, but admits the work involved "repetitive, simple work" on spreadsheets, little of which was ever seen by corporate clients. "It's almost expected that an analyst, especially in their first year, is just going to be miserable," says Martinez, who has since quit.

Wu and Martinez are two of the many investment analysts in recent years who concluded that their psychological contracts had been violated. One study reported

that new hires at a dozen investment banks stayed an average of only 17 months, down from 26 months a decade earlier and 30 months two decades ago.

©Tetra Images/Getty Images

[*] K. Tausche, "Wall Street Fights to Keep Young, Restless Analysts," *CNBC*, February 19, 2014; D. Huang and L. Gellman, "Millennial Employees Confound Wall Street," *Wall Street Journal*, April 9, 2016, A1; S. Wu, "Why Happiness Is Overrated," *Medium*, October 5, 2018.

because they have a larger toolkit of knowledge and skills to make the adjustment possible.[76]

PSYCHOLOGICAL CONTRACTS

The **psychological contract** refers to the individual's beliefs about the terms and conditions of a reciprocal exchange agreement between that person and another party (the employer in most work situations). The psychological contract is a perception formed during recruitment and throughout the organizational socialization process about what the employee is entitled to receive and is obliged to offer the employer in return.[77]

Job applicants form perceptions of what the company will offer them by way of career and learning opportunities, job resources, pay and benefits, quality of management, job security, and so forth. They also form perceptions about what the company expects from them, such as hours of work, continuous skill development, and demonstrated loyalty. The psychological contract continues to develop and evolve after job applicants become employees, but they are also continuously testing the employer's fulfilment of that exchange relationship.

> **psychological contract** The individual's beliefs about the terms and conditions of a reciprocal exchange agreement between that person and another party (typically an employer).

Types of Psychological Contracts

Psychological contracts cross the spectrum from transactional to relational.[78] Transactional contracts are primarily short-term economic exchanges. Responsibilities are well defined around a fairly narrow set of obligations that do not change over the life of the contract. People hired in temporary positions and as consultants tend to have more transactional contracts. To some extent, new employees also form transactional contracts until they develop a sense of continuity with the organization.[79]

Relational contracts, on the other hand, are rather like marriages; they are long-term attachments that encompass a broad array of subjective mutual obligations. Employees with a relational psychological contract are more willing to contribute their time and effort without expecting the organization to pay back this debt in the short term. Relational contracts are also dynamic, meaning that the parties tolerate and expect that mutual obligations are not necessarily balanced in the short-run. Not surprisingly, organizational citizenship behaviours are more likely to prevail under relational than transactional psychological contracts. Permanent employees are more likely to believe they have a relational contract.

STAGES OF ORGANIZATIONAL SOCIALIZATION

Organizational socialization is a continuous process, beginning before you submit a job application and continuing throughout your career within the company. However, it is most intense when people move across organizational boundaries, such as when they first join a company or get transferred to an international assignment. Each of these transitions is a process that can be divided into three stages. Our focus here is on the socialization of new employees, so the three stages are called pre-employment socialization, encounter, and role management (see Exhibit 14.7). These stages parallel the individual's transition from outsider to newcomer and then to insider.[80]

Stage 1: Pre-employment Socialization

Think back to the months and weeks before you began working in a new job (or attending a new school). You actively searched for information about the company, formed expectations about working there, and felt some anticipation about fitting into that setting. The pre-employment socialization stage encompasses all the learning and adjustment that occurs before the first day of work. In fact, a large part of the socialization adjustment process occurs during this stage.[81]

The main challenge with pre-employment socialization is that outsiders rely on indirect information about what it is like to work in the organization. This information is often distorted by inherent conflicts that arise during the mating dance between employer and applicant.[82]

- The employer's motivation to attract many high quality job applicants conflicts with the applicant's need to receive complete and accurate information for choosing the best job offer. Many firms describe only positive aspects of the job and company, causing applicants to accept job offers based on misleading expectations about working at that organization.

- The job applicant's motivation to receive job offers conflicts with the employer's need to receive complete and accurate information for choosing the best job applicants. Applicants engage in impression management when seeking employment, motivating them to hide negative information, act out of character, and occasionally embellish information about their past accomplishments. Consequently, the employer chooses applicants that are less qualified or have a poorer cultural fit with the organization.

- Employers are motivated to attract many high-quality job applicants, which conflicts with their need to receive complete and accurate information for choosing the best job applicants. Employers are sometimes reluctant to ask some types of questions to applicants or use potentially valuable selection methods because those information-gathering activities might scare off the best job candidates. As a result, they have a higher risk of forming inaccurate expectations about job candidates and making job offers to people who might not be sufficiently qualified or aligned with the organization's culture.

- Job applicants are motivated to receive job offers, which conflicts with their need to receive complete and accurate information for choosing the best job offer. Applicants avoid asking important questions about the company because they want to convey a favourable image to their prospective employer. For instance, applicants usually don't like to ask about starting salaries and promotion opportunities because it makes them seem greedy or aggressive. Yet, unless the employer provides

EXHIBIT 14.7   Stages of Organizational Socialization

Pre-employment socialization (outsider)	Encounter (newcomer)	Role management (insider)	Socialization outcomes
• Learn about the organization and job • Form employment relationship expectations	• Test expectations against perceived realities	• Strengthen work relationships • Practise new role behaviours • Resolve work–nonwork conflicts	• Higher motivation • Higher loyalty • Higher satisfaction • Lower stress • Lower turnover

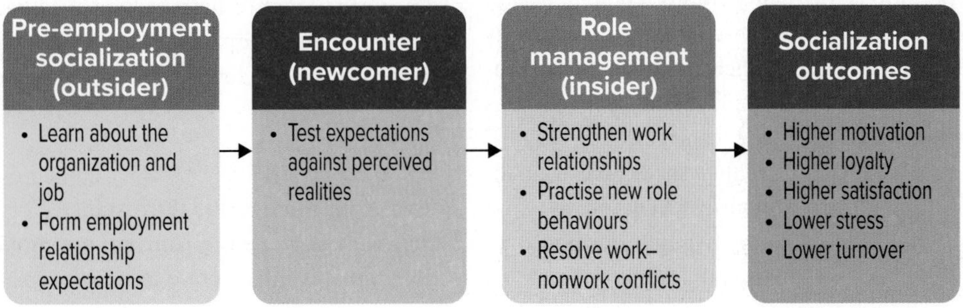

©Clio

Clio, the Burnaby, B.C., cloud-based legal practice management company, has always been led by the belief that successful organizations have a strong organizational culture. For the first few years, the two co-founders applied this principle by personally screening every applicant for cultural fit. As Clio grew (it now employs 400 people across six cities), it introduced more structured forms of selection and socialization. This transition began with Clio employees formally documenting the company's values so everyone—including new hires—would understand them. New hires are "pre-boarded" before their first day of work by having access to Clio's internal communication platform, so they can listen in, ask questions, and make connections with their future co-workers. And as soon as newcomers arrive on the job, they participate in interdepartmental "ride-alongs" and meetings to quickly improve their organizational comprehension.*

*C. Yeh, "How Clio Is Working to Become a Values- Driven Organization," Pulse (LinkedIn, 27 January 2016); D. Deveau, "Creating a Cultural Barometer for Success," *Vancouver Sun,* March 2, 2017; D. Deveau, "Clio's Culture Shifts Into High Gear," *Financial Post,* February 27, 2020.

this information, applicants might fill in the missing details with false assumptions that produce inaccurate job expectations.

Stage 2: Encounter

The first day on the job typically marks the beginning of the encounter stage of organizational socialization. This is the stage in which newcomers test how well their pre-employment expectations fit reality. Many companies fail the test, resulting in **reality shock**—the stress that results when employees perceive discrepancies between their pre-employment expectations and on-the-job reality.[83] Reality shock doesn't necessarily occur on the first day; it might develop over several weeks or even months as newcomers form a better understanding of their new work environment.

Reality shock is common in many organizations.[84] Newcomers sometimes face *unmet expectations* whereby the employer doesn't deliver on its promises, such as failing to provide challenging projects or the resources to get the work done. However, new hires also experience reality shock due to *unrealistic expectations,* which are distorted work expectations formed from the information exchange conflicts described earlier. Whatever the cause, reality shock impedes the learning and adjustment process because the newcomer's energy is directed toward managing the resulting stress.[85]

Stage 3: Role Management

Role management, the third stage of organizational socialization, really begins during pre-employment socialization, but it is most active as employees make the transition

reality shock The stress that results when employees perceive discrepancies between their pre-employment expectations and on-the-job reality.

from newcomers to insiders. They strengthen relationships with co-workers and supervisors, practise new role behaviours, and adopt attitudes and values consistent with their new positions and the organization. Role management also involves resolving the conflicts between work and nonwork activities, including resolving discrepancies between their personal values and those emphasized by the organizational culture.

IMPROVING THE SOCIALIZATION PROCESS

Companies have a tendency to exaggerate positive features of the job and neglect to mention the undesirable elements. Their motivation is to attract as many job applicants as possible, which they assume will improve the selection choices. Unfortunately, this flypaper approach often ends badly. Those hired soon discover that the actual workplace is not as favourable as the employer's marketing hype (i.e., unmet expectations), resulting in reality shock and a broken psychological contract. In contrast, a **realistic job preview (RJP)** offers a balance of positive and negative information about the job and work context.[86] This balanced description of the company and work helps job applicants to decide for themselves whether their skills, needs, and values are compatible with the job and organization.

realistic job preview (RJP) A method of improving organizational socialization in which job applicants are given a balance of positive and negative information about the job and work context.

RJPs scare away some applicants, but they also tend to reduce turnover and increase job performance.[87] This occurs because RJPs help applicants develop more accurate pre-employment expectations, which, in turn, minimize reality shock. RJPs represent a type of vaccination by preparing employees for the more challenging and troublesome aspects of the work context. There is also some evidence that RJPs increase affective organizational commitment. One explanation is that companies providing candid information are easier to trust. Another explanation is that RJPs show respect for the psychological contract and concern for employee welfare.[88]

For example, job applicants get a realistic job preview at HubShout by hearing about both the good and the not-so-good aspects of working at the search engine marketing firm. This balanced view of the company comes from a team—affectionately called the "doom squad"—among the 30 HubShout employees. "We insist that no supervisors or managers be there. We insist they be honest," says HubShout CEO Adam Stetzer. Job applicants apparently appreciate the candid information from the doom squad's realistic job preview. Stetzer points out that the company also benefits. "We're getting better candidates, better fits."[89]

Socialization Agents

Ask new employees what helped them the most to adjust to their jobs and chances are they will mention helpful co-workers, bosses, or maybe even friends who work elsewhere in the organization. The fact is, socialization agents play a central role in this process.[90] Supervisors tend to provide technical information, performance feedback, and information about job duties. They also improve the socialization process by giving newcomers reasonably challenging first assignments, buffering them from excessive demands, helping them form social ties with co-workers, and generating positive emotions around their new work experience.[91]

Co-workers are important socialization agents because they are easily accessible, can answer questions when problems arise, and serve as role models for appropriate behaviour. New employees tend to receive this information and support when co-workers welcome them into the work team. Co-workers also aid the socialization process by being flexible and tolerant in their interactions with new hires.

Organizational socialization is most successful when companies help newcomers strengthen their social bonds with other employees. This can occur casually through immediate involvement with a welcoming team of veteran employees. It also occurs through various social interaction events, particularly where current staff members help newcomers get acquainted with people elsewhere in the organization. For newcomers who work remotely, the best advice is to have them meet co-workers face-to-face within a few months after joining the company. However, distant workers can also build a sense of community through regular video interactions and access to the internal digital communication platform as soon as they accept the job offer.

Social bonding can even occur among the remote newcomers themselves. As an example, U.K.-based company OutreachPete helps new hires to successfully bond together even though it has an almost entirely remote workforce located around the world. "All new workers are put into a separate [Slack] channel together and given instructional materials and initial training tasks to complete," explains Pete McAllister, founder of the SEO link-building company. "You'd be amazed at how it creates an immediate sense of teamwork despite these individuals being spread across the globe."[92]

Chapter Summary

LO1

Describe the elements of organizational culture and discuss the importance of organizational subcultures.

Organizational culture consists of the values and assumptions shared within an organization. Shared assumptions are nonconscious, taken-for-granted perceptions or beliefs that have worked so well in the past that they are considered the correct way to think and act toward problems and opportunities. Values are stable, evaluative beliefs that guide our preferences for outcomes or courses of action in a variety of situations.

Organizations differ in their cultural content, that is, the relative ordering of values. There are several classifications of organizational culture, but they tend to oversimplify the wide variety of cultures and completely ignore the underlying assumptions of culture. Organizations have subcultures as well as the dominant culture. Subcultures maintain the organization's standards of performance and ethical behaviour. They are also the source of emerging values that replace misaligned core values.

LO2

Describe four categories of artifacts through which corporate culture is deciphered.

Artifacts are the observable symbols and signs of an organization's culture. Four broad categories of artifacts include organizational stories and legends, rituals and ceremonies, language, and physical structures and symbols. Understanding an organization's culture requires assessment of many artifacts because they are subtle and often ambiguous.

LO3

Discuss the importance of organizational culture and the conditions under which organizational culture strength improves organizational performance.

Organizational culture has three main functions: it is a form of social control, the "social glue" that bonds people together, and a way to help employees make sense of the workplace. Companies with strong cultures generally perform better than those with weak cultures, but only when the cultural content is compatible with the organization's environment. Also, the culture should not be so strong that it drives out dissenting values, which may form emerging values for the future. Organizations should have an adaptive culture, in which employees support ongoing change in the organization and their own roles.

LO4

Compare and contrast four strategies for merging organizational cultures.

Organizational culture clashes are common in mergers and acquisitions. This problem can be minimized by performing a bicultural audit to diagnose the compatibility of the organizational cultures. The four main strategies for merging different corporate cultures are assimilation, deculturation, integration, and separation.

LO5

Discuss five strategies for changing and strengthening an organization's culture, including the application of attraction–selection–attrition theory.

An organization's culture begins with its founders and leaders, because they use personal values to transform the organization. The founder's activities are later retold as organizational stories. Companies also introduce artifacts as mechanisms to maintain or change the culture. A related strategy is to introduce rewards and recognition practices that are consistent with the desired cultural values. A fourth method to change and strengthen an organization's culture is to support workforce stability and communication. Stability is necessary because culture exists in employees. Communication activities improve sharing of the culture. Finally, companies strengthen and change their culture by attracting and selecting applicants with personal values that fit the company's culture, by encouraging those with misaligned values to leave the company (attrition), and by engaging in organizational socialization—the process by which individuals learn the values, expected behaviours, and social knowledge necessary to assume their roles in the organization.

LO6

Describe the organizational socialization process and identify strategies to improve that process.

Organizational socialization is the process by which individuals learn the values, expected behaviours, and social knowledge necessary to assume their roles in the organization. It is a process of both learning and adjustment. During this process, job applicants and newcomers develop and test their psychological contract—personal beliefs about the terms and conditions of a reciprocal exchange agreement between that person and another party (the employer).

Employees typically pass through three socialization stages: pre-employment, encounter, and role management. To manage the socialization process, organizations should introduce realistic job previews (RJPs) and recognize the value of socialization agents in the process. RJPs give job applicants a realistic balance of positive and negative information about the job and work context. Socialization agents provide information and social support during the socialization process.

Key Terms

adaptive culture

artifacts

attraction-selection-attrition (ASA) theory

bicultural audit

ceremonies

learning orientation

organizational culture

organizational socialization

psychological contract

realistic job preview (RJP)

reality shock

rituals

Critical Thinking Questions

1. Superb Consultants has submitted a proposal to analyze your organization's culture. The proposal states that Superb has developed a revolutionary new survey to tap the company's true culture. The survey takes just 10 minutes to complete, and the consultants say results can be based on a small sample of employees. Discuss the merits and limitations of this proposal.

2. All members of the executive team at Claybuild, a national manufacturer of bricks and related building materials, strongly believe that quality control and efficiency are the two cornerstones of the company's future success. Every Claybuild executive meeting begins by discussing ways to improve product quality and operate more efficiently in the manufacturing process, distribution system, and administrative processes. The company's website proudly describes its dedication to quality and efficiency. The CEO has given speeches to several retail client events on Claybuild's quality–efficiency culture. However, an industry expert suggests that quality and efficiency represent Claybuild's espoused culture, but not so much its enacted culture. What does the industry expert mean by this, and what evidence might suggest that their opinion is correct?

3. The CEO of a manufacturing firm wants everyone to support the organization's dominant culture of lean efficiency and hard work. The CEO has introduced a new reward system to reinforce this culture and personally interviews all professional and managerial applicants to ensure that they bring similar values to the organization. Some employees who criticized these values had their careers sidelined until they left. Two midlevel managers were fired for supporting contrary values, such as work–life integration. Based on your knowledge of organizational subcultures, what are the potential problems the CEO is creating?

4. Identify at least two artifacts you have observed in your department or school from each of the four broad categories: (a) organizational stories and legends, (b) rituals and ceremonies, (c) language, (d) physical structures and symbols.

5. Some people suggest that the most effective organizations have the strongest cultures. What is meant by organizational culture "strength," and what problems might arise in organizations with very strong cultures?

6. "Organizations are more likely to succeed when they have an adaptive culture." What can an organization do to foster an adaptive culture?

7. Senior officers of a city government have assigned you the project of identifying ways to reinforce a new culture of teamwork and collaboration. The senior executives clearly support these values, but they want everyone in the organization to embrace them. Identify four types of activities that would strengthen these cultural values.

8. Suppose you are considering joining one of three accounting firms as your first full-time job in this career. One firm is located only within one large city but has a large portion of the small-business tax and audit business in that city. The second is a national firm with offices across the country, including the city where you intend to work. The third is one of the top three global accounting and professional services firms, and has offices in the city where you intend to work. Only the global firm has a detailed "careers" web page that describes the job expectations, culture, and career development opportunities. The other two firms have minimal information on their websites. All three firms have a standard interview process, including a brief tour of the local offices. All the firms will have booths at a career fair event that you will attend. As a job applicant, what methods and information would you seek out and apply to assess how well the organizational cultures at each of these three accounting firms are compatible with your personal values?

9. Socialization is most intense when people pass through organizational boundaries. One example is your entry into the college or university that you are now attending. What learning and adjustment occurred as you moved from outsider to newcomer to insider as a student?

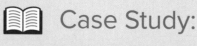

Case Study:
HILLTON'S TRANSFORMATION

by Steven L. McShane, University of Newcastle (Australia)

Twenty years ago, Hillton was a small city (about 70,000 residents) that served as an outer suburb to a large Canadian metropolitan city. Hillton's municipal government treated its employees like family and gave them a great deal of autonomy in their work. Everyone in the organization (including the two labour unions representing employees) implicitly agreed that the leaders and supervisors of the organization should rise through the ranks based on their experience. Few people were ever hired from the outside into middle or senior positions. The rule of employment at Hillton was to learn the job skills, maintain a reasonably good work record, and wait your turn for promotion.

As Hillton's population grew, so did the city's workforce to keep pace with the increasing demand for municipal services. This meant that employees were promoted fairly quickly and were almost assured lifetime employment. Until recently, Hillton had never laid off any employee. The organization's culture could be described as one of entitlement and comfort. Neither the elected city councillors nor the city manager bothered departmental managers about their work. There were few cost controls, because rapid growth placed more emphasis on keeping up with the population expansion. The public became somewhat more critical of the city's poor service, including road construction at inconvenient times and the apparent lack of respect some employees showed toward taxpayers.

During these expansion years, Hillton put most of its money into "outside" (also called "hard") municipal services. These included road building, utility construction and maintenance, fire and police protection, recreational facilities, and land use control. This emphasis occurred because an expanding population demanded more of these services, and most of Hillton's senior people came from the outside services group. For example, Hillton's city manager for many years was a road development engineer. The "inside" workers (taxation, community services, etc.) tended to have less seniority, and their departments were given less priority.

As commuter and road systems developed, Hillton attracted more upwardly mobile professionals into the community. Some infrastructure demands continued, but now these suburban dwellers wanted more of the "soft" services, such as libraries, social activities, and community services. They also began complaining about the way the municipality was being run. By this time, the population had more than tripled, and it was increasingly apparent that the organization needed more corporate planning, information systems, organization development, and cost-control systems. In various

ways, residents voiced their concerns that the municipality was not providing the quality of management that they would expect from a city of its size.

A few years ago, a new mayor and council replaced most of the previous incumbents, mainly on the platform of improving the municipality's management structure. The new council gave the city manager, along with two other senior managers, an early retirement buyout package. Rather than promoting from the lower ranks, council decided to fill all three positions with qualified candidates from large municipal corporations in the region. The following year, several long-term managers left Hillton, and at least half of those positions were filled by people from outside the organization.

In less than two years, Hillton had eight senior or departmental managers hired from other municipalities who played a key role in changing the organization's value system. These eight managers became known (often with negative connotations) as the "professionals." They worked closely with one another to change the way middle- and lower-level managers had operated for many years. They brought in a new computer system and emphasized cost controls where managers previously had complete autonomy. Promotions were increasingly based more on merit than seniority.

The "professionals" frequently announced in meetings and newsletters that municipal employees must provide superlative customer service and that Hillton would become one of the most customer-friendly places for citizens and those who do business with the municipality. To this end, these managers were quick to support the public's increasing demand for more "soft" services, including expanded library services and recreational activities. And when population growth recently flattened out, the city manager and other professionals gained council support to lay off a few of the outside workers due to lack of demand for hard services.

One of the most significant changes was that the "outside" departments no longer held dominant positions in city management. Most of the "professional" managers had worked exclusively in administrative and related inside jobs. Two had Master of Business Administration degrees. This led to some tension between the professional managers and the older outside managers.

Even before the layoffs, managers of outside departments resisted the changes more than others. These managers complained that their employees with the highest seniority were turned down for promotions. They argued for more budget and warned that infrastructure problems would cause liability problems. Informally, these outside managers were supported by the labour union representing outside workers. The union leaders tried to bargain for more job guarantees, whereas the union representing inside workers focused more on improving wages and benefits. Leaders of the outside union made several statements in the local media that the city had "lost its heart" and that the public would suffer from the actions of the new professionals.

Discussion Questions

1. Contrast Hillton's earlier corporate culture with the emerging set of cultural values.

2. Considering the difficulty in changing organizational culture, why does Hillton's management seem to have been successful in this transformation?

3. Identify two other strategies that the city might consider to reinforce the new set of corporate values.

 Team Exercise:
ORGANIZATIONAL CULTURE METAPHORS

by David L. Luechauer, Butler University, and Gary M. Shulman, Miami University

Purpose Both parts of this exercise are designed to help you understand, assess, and interpret organizational culture using metaphors.

PART A: ASSESSING YOUR SCHOOL'S CULTURE

Instructions A metaphor is a figure of speech that contains an implied comparison between a word or phrase that is ordinarily used for one thing but can be applied to another. Metaphors also carry a great deal of hidden meaning—they say a lot about what we think and feel about that object. Therefore, this activity asks you to use several metaphors to define the organizational culture of your university, college, or institute. (Alternatively, the instructor might ask students to assess another organization that most students know about.)

Step 1: The class will be divided into teams of 4 to 6 members.

Step 2: Each team will reach consensus on which words or phrases should be inserted in the blanks of the statements presented below. This information should be recorded on a flip chart or overhead acetate for class presentation. The instructor will provide 15 to 20 minutes for teams to determine which words best describe the college/university's culture.

1. If our school was an animal, it would be a _____ because _____.

2. If our school was a food, it would be _____ because _____.

3. If our school was a place, it would be _____ because _____.

4. If our school was a season, it would be _____ because _____.

5. If our school was a TV show or movie, it would be _____ because _____.

Step 3: The class will listen to each team present the metaphors that it believes symbolize the school's culture. For example, a team that picks winter for a season might mean they are feeling cold or distant about the school and its people.

Step 4: The class will discuss the questions stated below.

Discussion Questions for Part A

1. How easy was it for your group to reach consensus regarding these metaphors? What does that imply about the culture of your school?

2. How do you see these metaphors in action? In other words, what are some critical school behaviours or other artifacts that reveal the presence of your culture?

3. Think of another organization to which you belong (e.g., work, religious congregation). What are its dominant cultural values, how do you see them in action, and how do they affect the effectiveness of that organization?

PART B: ANALYZING AND INTERPRETING CULTURAL METAPHORS

Instructions Previously, you completed a metaphor exercise to describe the corporate culture of your school. That exercise gave you a taste of how to administer such a diagnostic tool and draw inferences from the results generated. This activity builds on that experience and is designed to help refine your ability to analyze such data and make suggestions for improvement. Five work teams (four to seven members, mixed gender in all groups) of an organization completed the metaphor exercise similar to the exercise in which you participated in class (see Part A above). Their responses are shown in the table below. Working in teams, analyze the information in this table and answer these questions:

Discussion Questions for Part B

1. In your opinion, what are the dominant cultural values in this organization? Explain your answer.

2. What are the positive aspects of this type of culture?

3. What are the negative aspects of this type of culture?

4. What is this organization's main business, in your opinion? Explain your answer.

5. These groups all report to one manager. What advice would you give to that person about this unit?

Metaphor Results of Five Teams in an Organization					
Team	Animal	Food	Place	TV Show	Season
1	Rabbit	Big Mac	Casino	*Parks & Recreation*	Spring
2	Horse	Taco	Racetrack	*CSI*	Spring
3	Elephant	Ribs	Circus	*Big Bang Theory*	Summer
4	Eagle	Big Mac	Las Vegas	*Dragons' Den*	Spring
5	Panther	Chinese	New York	*Minds*	Racing

Self-Assessment for Chapter 14

SELF-ASSESSMENT NAME	DESCRIPTION
Which corporate culture do you prefer?	An organization's culture may be very appealing to some people and much less so to others. After all, each of us has a hierarchy of personal values, and that hierarchy may be compatible or incompatible with the company's shared values. This self-assessment identifies the corporate culture that fits most closely with your personal values and assumptions.

CHAPTER 15
Organizational Change

Blueshore Financial relied on communication, involvement, and other organizational change strategies to transform itself from a regular credit union into a successful "financial spa" business on Canada's west coast.

©Blueshore Financial

A dozen or so years ago, the future of North Shore Credit Union was in doubt. "Since our inception in 1941, our regional market transformed from being an outpost for fishing and shipbuilding into one of Canada's wealthiest regions," explains Chris Catliff, CEO of the organization, now called Blueshore Financial. "We needed to provide deeper financial expertise and premium client service." Yet, North Shore Credit Union had remained "little more than a paper-based savings and loan. . . We had no differentiated brand, and the credit union was floundering."

Catliff explained to employees that the organization's survival depended on reinventing itself to better serve its clients through differentiated financial services. "Being fearless in our 180-degree strategic pivot, we rebranded, changed our name and rebuilt BlueShore's branches as Financial Spas, and deepened our advisers' expertise."

A special task force of employees and managers worked with an external consultant to develop the new business model. "They worked in a boardroom for two weeks, fuelled by pizza, the odd beer and a desire to innovate," recalls Catliff, who challenged the team "not to come back until you've reinvented banking." The task force proposed a list of dramatic innovations, including a much narrower focus on wealth-oriented services in a "financial spa" setting, rather like a luxury hotel.

Communication with employees was key to the success of Blueshore's transformation. "The most practical piece of advice I can offer others is to recognize the critical importance of open communication in times of change. Be consistent, repetitive, and authentic," advises Catliff, who has been recognized as one of British Columbia's best CEOs. "Tell them [employees and others] why you are changing and what you hope to gain from the change."

Catliff also emphasizes the power of employee involvement in organizational change. "Ask your staff for their input, actively listen to what they have to say, and show you value their perceptions and opinions. By doing this you will form a relationship based on mutual trust and respect, which will make it easier for you to initiate and integrate change together."

Blueshore's radical transformation took several years and required some difficult adjustments. "The tough part was that some staff didn't like the change, and self-selected out," says Catliff. But the results have exceeded expectations. BlueShore Financial's assets under administration have jumped from $700 million in 2000 to $5 billion today. Blueshore's dozen branches have become leading financial planning centres from Vancouver to Whistler. Blueshore is also consistently rated as one of Canada's best employers.[1]

Blueshore Financial's transformation from a floundering mass market credit union to one of Vancouver's leading financial services firms illustrates many of the strategies and practices necessary to successfully change organizations. Chris Catliff created an urgency for change, actively communicated the change process, and involved employees as partners in the process. Blueshore's transformation took several years and required difficult adjustments. Indeed, most organizational change initiatives are messy, requiring considerable leadership effort and vigilance.

As we will describe throughout this chapter, the challenge of change is not so much in deciding which way to go; the challenge is in the execution of this strategy. When leaders discover the need for change and identify some ideas about the preferred route to a better future, the change process involves navigating around the numerous obstacles and gaining organization-wide support for that change.

This chapter unfolds as follows. We begin by introducing Lewin's model of change and its component parts. This discussion includes sources of resistance to change, ways to minimize this resistance, and ways to stabilize desired behaviours. Next, the chapter examines four approaches to organizational change—action research, appreciative inquiry, large group interventions, and parallel learning structures. The last section of this chapter considers both cross-cultural and ethical issues in organizational change.

Lewin's Force Field Analysis Model

LO1

"I've always believed that when the rate of change inside an institution becomes slower than the rate of change outside, the end is in sight. The only question is when."[2] This statement by the late Jack Welch, former CEO of General Electric, highlights one of the messages throughout this book: Organizations operate as open systems that need to keep pace with ongoing changes in their external environment, such as consumer needs, global competition, technology, community expectations, government (de)regulation, and environmental standards. Successful organizations monitor their environments and take appropriate steps to maintain a compatible fit with new external conditions. Rather than resist change, employees in successful companies embrace change as an integral part of organizational life.

It is easy to see environmental forces pushing companies to change the way they operate. What is more difficult to see is the complex interplay of these forces on individuals, teams, and work units. Social psychologist Kurt Lewin developed a model to describe this process using the metaphor of a force field (see Exhibit 15.1).[3] Although it was developed a half century ago, contemporary reviews of this subject affirm that Lewin's **force field analysis** model remains one of the most widely respected ways of viewing the change process.[4]

> **force field analysis** Kurt Lewin's model of system-wide change that helps change agents diagnose the forces that drive and restrain proposed organizational change.

One side of the force field model represents the *driving forces* that push organizations toward a new state of affairs. These might include new competitors or technologies, evolving client expectations, or a host of other environmental changes. Corporate leaders also produce driving forces even when external forces for change aren't apparent. For instance, even when companies are successful, their leaders urge employees to strive for higher standards or better practices. David Ogilvy, one of the world's most successful advertising executives, stated this view decades ago when describing the culture of his agency: "We have a habit of divine discontent with our performance. It is an antidote to smugness."[5]

The other side of Lewin's model represents the *restraining forces* that maintain the status quo. These restraining forces are commonly called "resistance to change" because they appear to block the change process. Stability occurs when the driving and restraining forces are roughly in equilibrium—that is, they are of approximately equal strength in opposite directions.

Lewin's force field model emphasizes that effective change occurs by **unfreezing** the current situation, moving to a desired condition, and then **refreezing** the system so it remains in the desired state. Unfreezing involves producing disequilibrium between the driving and restraining forces. As we will describe later, this may occur by increasing the driving forces, reducing the restraining forces, or doing a combination of both. Refreezing occurs when the organization's systems and structures are aligned with the desired behaviours. They must support and reinforce the new role patterns and prevent the organization from slipping back into the old way of doing things. In the next two sections of this chapter, we use Lewin's model to understand why change is blocked and how the process can evolve more smoothly.

> **unfreezing** The first part of the organizational change process, in which the change agent produces disequilibrium between the driving and restraining forces.
>
> **refreezing** The latter part of the change process, in which systems and structures are introduced that reinforce and maintain the desired behaviours.

EXHIBIT 15.1   Lewin's Force Field Analysis Model

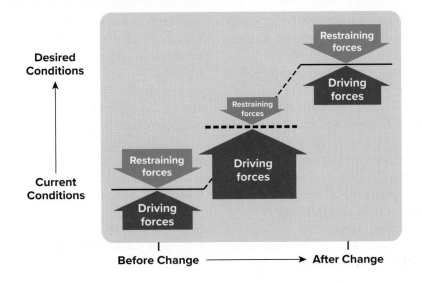

OB by the NUMBERS

The Challenges of Resistance to Change*

55% of Canadian human resources professionals surveyed say that their organization's "capability" is a major barrier to a digital transformation (#1 barrier).

46% of 1,000 nonmanagement white-collar American employees surveyed say they are willing to challenge the status quo (compared with 89% of chief executives).

44% of 1,778 change management professionals surveyed globally say their organization is at or past the point of "change saturation."

34% of more than 2,000 employees surveyed in the U.S. and U.K. say they feel anxiety over new or changing work processes.

28% of 1,512 American employees surveyed say they doubt organizational changes will work as intended or achieve their objectives.

(man) Jacob Wackerhausen/Getty Images, (blocks) Mark Dierker/McGraw Hill Education

*Work and Well-Being Survey, Center for Organizational Excellence (Washington, D.C.: American Psychological Association, May 30, 2017); Addison Group, "Addison Group Survey Finds Nearly Half of Staff Level Employees Don't Feel Confident Their Industry," news release (Chicago: Addison Group, June 5, 2017); D. Meinert, "How to Avoid Common Mistakes in Change Management," *HR Magazine,* February 2018; B. Sanzenbacher, "Why 42% of Workers Are Fed Up and Ready to Bolt," *Wrike Blog,* February 15, 2018, https://www.wrike.com/blog/why-42-of-workers-are-fed-up-and-ready-to-bolt/; "How Operational Inefficiencies Result In Employee Burnout (UK Survey)," *Wrike Blog,* February 22, 2018, https://www.wrike.com/blog/how-operational-inefficiencies-result-in-employee-burn-out-uk-survey/; *The Future of HR: 2019 (Canada)* (Toronto: KPMG Canada, November 29, 2018).

Understanding Resistance to Change

LO2

United Airlines struggled to resolve operational and customer service problems after its merger with Continental Airlines. United executives say the poor results are partly due to the challenges of combining complex reservation and operational systems. But they have also been frustrated by subtle forms of employee resistance to change. Some former Continental employees opposed United Airlines' operational practices, while some veteran United Airlines employees failed to embrace Continental's customer service standards. "You know, the cultural change takes time," explained the former United Airlines CEO who orchestrated the merger. "And people resist change. People are sort of set in their ways."[6]

Executives at United Airlines experienced considerable *resistance to change* following the merger with Continental Airlines. Resistance to change takes many forms, ranging from overt work stoppages to subtle attempts to continue the old ways.[7] A study of Canadian bank employees reported that covert resistance is much more common than overt resistance. Some employees in that study avoided the desired changes by moving into different jobs at the bank. Others continued to perform tasks the old way as long as management didn't notice. Even when employees complied with the planned changes, they showed resistance by performing the new task while letting customers know that they disapproved of these changes forced on them![8]

Most change agents are understandably frustrated by passive or active resistance to their planned change, but resistance is a common and natural human response. As Canadian-born economist John Kenneth Galbraith once quipped, "Faced with the choice between changing one's mind and proving that there is no need to do so, almost everyone gets busy on the proof."[9] Even when people support change, they typically assume that it is others—not themselves—who need to do the changing.

Resistance is a form of conflict, but change agents unfortunately tend to interpret that disagreement as relationship conflict (see Chapter 11). They describe the people who resist as unreasonable, dysfunctional, and irrational reactionaries to a desirable initiative. This viewpoint motivates the change agent to adopt a conflict-oriented response to the resistance which tends to further escalate the conflict. The escalated conflict often generates even stronger resistance to the change initiative.

A more productive approach is to view resistance to change as task conflict. From this perspective, resistance is a signal either that the change agent has not sufficiently prepared employees for change or that the change initiative should be altered or improved.[10] Employees might not feel a sufficiently strong urgency for change, or they might believe the change strategy is ill-conceived. Even if they recognize the need for change and agree with the strategy, employees might resist because they lack confidence to change or believe the change will make them worse off than the current situation. Resistance takes many forms, and change agents need to decipher those different types of resistance to understand their underlying causes.[11]

Resistance is also a form of voice, so giving employees an opportunity to discuss their concerns potentially improves procedural justice (see Chapter 5) as well as decision making (see Chapter 7). By redirecting initial forms of resistance into constructive conversations, change agents can generate a strong feeling of fairness among employees. Furthermore, resistance is motivated behaviour; it potentially engages people to think about the change strategy and process. Change agents can harness that motivational force to ultimately strengthen commitment to the change initiative.

WHY EMPLOYEES RESIST CHANGE

Change management experts have developed a long list of reasons why people resist change.[12] Some people inherently oppose change because of their personality and values.[13] Aside from these dispositional factors, employees typically oppose organizational change because they lack sufficient motivation, ability, role clarity, or situational support to change their attitudes, decisions, and behaviour.[14] In other words, an employee's readiness for change depends on all four elements of the MARS model. These MARS elements are the foundations of the six most commonly cited reasons why people resist change: (1) negative valence of change, (2) fear of the unknown, (3) not-invented-here syndrome,

(4) breaking routines, (5) incongruent team dynamics, and (6) incongruent organizational systems and structures.

Negative Valence of Change

Employees tend to resist change when they believe the new work environment will have more negative than positive outcomes.[15] In other words, they apply (although imperfectly) the rational choice decision-making model (Chapter 7) to estimate whether the change will make them better or worse off (i.e., positive or negative valence). This cost–benefit analysis mainly considers how the change will affect them personally. However, resistance also increases when employees believe the change will do more harm than good to the team, organization, or society.[16]

Fear of the Unknown

Organizational change usually has a degree of uncertainty, and employees tend to assume the worst when they are unsure whether the change will have good or bad outcomes. Uncertainty is also associated with lack of personal control, which is another source of negative emotions. Consequently, the uncertainty inherent in most organizational change is less desirable than the relative certainty of the status quo. This "status quo bias" adds more negative valence to the cost–benefit calculation we described above.[17]

Not-Invented-Here Syndrome

Employees sometimes oppose or even discreetly undermine organizational change initiatives that are initiated by people outside their group. This "not-invented-here" syndrome is most apparent among employees who are usually responsible for the knowledge or initiative.[18] For example, information technology staff are more likely to resist implementing new technology championed by marketing or finance employees. If the IT staff support the change, they are implicitly acknowledging another group's superiority within IT's own area of expertise. To protect their self-worth, some employees deliberately inflate problems with changes they did not initiate, just to "prove" that those ideas were not superior to their own. As one consultant warned, "Unless they're scared enough to listen, they'll never forgive you for being right and for knowing something they don't."[19]

An example of the not-invented-here syndrome occurred several years ago when Goldcorp CEO Rob McEwan decided to post the Canadian mining company's confidential geological data online and offer a generous reward to anyone who

---

 Are you ready for change? You can discover your level of readiness for change by completing this self-assessment in Connect.

©Kristoffer Tripplaar/Alamy Stock Photo

General Motors (GM) has in-sourced almost all of its information technology (IT) work, hired 10,000 IT employees to replace contractors, built new IT innovation centres, and reduced 23 data centres owned by suppliers to just two centres owned by GM. Randy Mott, GM's executive vice president of global information technology, and his executive team faced many logistical challenges throughout the transformation. They were also challenged by resistance from GM line managers, many of whom were concerned that GM's IT staff wouldn't provide the same quality of service that the external contractors had provided. "This supplier is doing a great job for me, so don't mess it up," some managers warned. Line managers' fear of the unknown and perceived negative outcomes about the IT changes led to "some really frank discussions," Mott acknowledges. "In the early days we were fighting the fact that the IT organization's credibility for building and creating and supporting things was not high."[*]

* A. Bongard, "GM CIO Mott Is Confident IT Transformation Making Progress," *automotiveIT International,* June 4, 2014; R. Preston, "General Motors' IT Transformation: Building Downturn-Resistant Profitability," *Forbes,* April 14, 2016; P. High, "After Five Years Of Transformation, GM CIO Randy Mott Has The Company Primed For Innovation," *Forbes,* June 18, 2018.

could help find more gold on the property. The Goldcorp Challenge was a huge success, but the firm's geological staff complained just before the event was launched. "We have real concerns," they told McEwen. "You're going to ask the rest of the world to tell you where we're going to find gold in our mine, and we think they're going to think we're really dumb and that you don't have any confidence in us."[20]

Breaking Routines

People are creatures of habit. They typically resist initiatives that require them to break those automated routines and learn new role patterns. And unless the new patterns of behaviour are strongly supported and reinforced, employees tend to revert to their past routines and habits. "When you are leading for growth, you know you are going to disrupt comfortable routines and ask for new behaviour, new priorities, new skills," says Ray Davis, who transformed Oregon-based Umpqua Bank into one of America's most innovative

financial institutions. "Even when we want to change, and do change, we tend to relax and the rubber band snaps us back into our comfort zones."[21]

Incongruent Team Dynamics

Teams develop and enforce conformity to a set of norms that guide behaviour (see Chapter 8). However, conformity to existing team norms may discourage employees from accepting organizational change. For instance, organizational initiatives to improve customer service may be thwarted by team norms that discourage the extra effort expected to serve customers at this higher standard.

Incongruent Organizational Systems and Structures

Rewards, information systems, patterns of authority, career paths, selection criteria, and other systems and structures are both friends and foes of organizational change. When properly aligned, they reinforce desired behaviours. When misaligned, they pull people back into their old attitudes and behaviour. Even enthusiastic employees lose momentum after failing to overcome the structural confines of the past.

Unfreezing, Changing, and Refreezing

LO3

According to Lewin's force field analysis model, effective change occurs by unfreezing the current situation, moving to a desired condition, and then refreezing the system so it remains in this desired state. Unfreezing occurs when the driving forces are stronger than the restraining forces. This happens by making the driving forces stronger, weakening or removing the restraining forces, or combining both.

The first option is to increase the driving forces, which motivates employees to change through fear or threats (real or contrived). This strategy rarely works, however, because the action of increasing the driving forces alone is usually met with an equal and opposing increase in the restraining forces. A useful metaphor is pushing against the coils of a mattress. The harder corporate leaders push for change, the stronger the restraining forces push back. This antagonism threatens the change effort by producing tension and conflict within the organization.

The second option is to weaken or remove the restraining forces. The problem with this change strategy is that it provides no motivation for change. To some extent, weakening the restraining forces is like clearing a pathway for change. An unobstructed road makes it easier to travel to the destination but does not motivate anyone to go there. The preferred option, therefore, is to both increase the driving forces and reduce or remove the restraining forces. Increasing the driving forces creates an urgency for change, while reducing the restraining forces lessens motivation to oppose the change and removes obstacles such as lack of ability and situational constraints.

CREATING AN URGENCY FOR CHANGE

Organizational change is more likely to succeed when employees develop a sufficiently strong urgency for change.[22] In rare situations, such as the COVID-19 pandemic, the forces for change are widely known and worrisome to most employees. As such, they are motivated (or compliant) to dive into new practices, such as working from home, reducing pay rates, learning new digital communication technology, altering work schedules, wearing protective clothing, and engaging in unusual forms of interaction with co-workers and clients that minimize transmission of disease.

Most of the time, leaders buffer employees from the external environment to such an extent that the prevailing driving forces are hardly felt by anyone below the top executive level. The result is that employees don't understand why they need to change and leaders are surprised when their change initiatives do not have much effect. Consequently, the change process begins by making the external forces for change known to employees and explaining their seriousness for the organization's future. These are the main driving forces in Lewin's model. They push people out of their comfort zone, energizing them to face the risks that change creates.

Some companies fuel the urgency for change by putting employees and managers in direct contact with customers. Dissatisfied customers and other stakeholders represent a compelling driving force for change because the organization's survival typically depends on having customers who are satisfied with the product or service. Personal interaction with customers also provides a human element that further energizes employees to change current behaviour patterns.[23]

Creating an Urgency for Change without External Forces

Exposing employees to external forces can strengthen the urgency for change, but leaders often need to begin the change process before problems come knocking at the company's door. The challenge is greatest when companies are successful in their markets. Studies have found that when the organization is performing well, decision makers become less vigilant about external threats and are more resistant to change. "The biggest risk is that complacency can also come with that success," warns Richard Goyder, former CEO of Wesfarmers, Australia's largest conglomerate. "That complacency may result in risk-aversion, or it may simply show up as a lack of urgency, as people take the foot off the accelerator and just assume that success will come as it always has."[24]

Creating an urgency for change when the organization is the market leader requires plenty of persuasive influence to help employees visualize future competitive threats and environmental shifts. Experts warn, however, that employees may see this strategy as manipulative, which produces cynicism about change and undermines trust in the change agent.[25] Fortunately, the urgency for change doesn't need to originate from problems or threats to the company; this motivation can also develop through the leader's vision of a more appealing future. A future vision of a better organization makes the current situation less appealing. When the vision connects to employees' values and needs, it can be a motivating force for change even when external problems are insignificant.

Slack Technologies, Inc.

Until recently, Slack didn't have any serious competitors. This worried Stewart Butterfield, the Canadian entrepreneur who co-founded the collaborative communication platform. "We don't have any effective competitors," he observed a year before Microsoft Teams and Facebook for Work were launched. "It's handy in one way, but it's also very motivating to have a real competitor." To generate an urgency for change and minimize complacency, Butterfield persuasively warned Slack employees in Vancouver and California of the limited time they had remaining to build an unbeatable product. "It's up to me to instil the message that we have a year, maybe 18 months, before we really have to lock horns with anyone," said Butterfield.[*]

* A. Weckler, "You Don't Have Mail: How Slack Reinvented Chat," *Irish Independent,* January 26, 2017, 6.

Are you tolerant of change? You can discover your level of tolerance for change by completing this self-assessment in Connect.

REDUCING THE RESTRAINING FORCES

Earlier, we used the mattress metaphor to explain that increasing the driving forces alone will not bring about change because employees often push back harder to offset the opposing forces. To minimize this push-back, change agents need to address each of the sources of resistance. Six of the main strategies for minimizing resistance to change are outlined in Exhibit 15.2. Communication, learning, employee involvement, and stress management should be the first priorities for change management.[26] However, negotiation and coercion may be necessary where some people will clearly lose something from the change and in cases where the speed of change is critical.

Communication

Communication is the highest priority and first strategy required for any organizational change. According to one survey, communication (together with involvement) is considered the top strategy for engaging employees in the change process.[27] Communication improves the change process in at least two ways.[28] First, communication generates the urgency for change that we described a few paragraphs ago. Leaders motivate employees to support the change by candidly telling them about the external threats and opportunities that make change so important.

This form of communication was illustrated in the opening case study for this chapter. When the future of North Shore Credit Union (now Blueshore Financial) became apparent, CEO Chris Catliff communicated directly to employees about the problems facing the company and why significant change was urgently needed. "The most practical piece of advice I can offer others is to recognize the critical importance of open communication in times of change," Catliff advises. "Tell them [employees and others] why you are changing and what you hope to gain from the change."[29]

The second way that communication minimizes resistance to change is by illuminating the future and thereby reducing fear of the unknown. The more leaders communicate details

EXHIBIT 15.2 Strategies for Minimizing Resistance to Change

Strategy	Example	When applied	Problems
Communication	Customer complaint letters are shown to employees.	When employees don't feel an urgency for change, don't know how the change will affect them, or resist change due to a fear of the unknown.	Time-consuming and potentially costly.
Learning	Employees learn how to work in teams as company adopts a team-based structure.	When employees need to break old routines and adopt new role patterns.	Time-consuming, potentially costly, and some employees might not be able to learn the new skills.
Employee involvement	Company forms a task force to recommend new customer service practices.	When the change effort needs more employee commitment, some employees need to protect their self-worth, and/or employee ideas would improve decisions about the change strategy.	Very time-consuming. Might lead to conflict and poor decisions if employees' interests are incompatible with organizational needs.
Stress management	Employees attend sessions to discuss their worries about the change.	When communication, training, and involvement do not sufficiently ease employee worries.	Time-consuming and potentially expensive. Some methods may not reduce stress for all employees.
Negotiation	Employees agree to replace strict job categories with multiskilling in return for increased job security.	When employees will clearly lose something of value from the change and would not otherwise support the new conditions. Also necessary when the company must change quickly.	May be expensive, particularly if other employees want to negotiate their support. Also tends to produce compliance but not commitment to the change.
Coercion	Company president tells managers to "get on board" with the change or leave.	When other strategies are ineffective and the company needs to change quickly.	Can lead to more subtle forms of resistance, as well as long-term antagonism with the change agent.

about the vision as well as milestones already achieved, the more easily employees can understand their own roles in that future.

Learning

Learning is an important process in most organizational change initiatives because employees need new knowledge and skills to fit the organization's evolving requirements. Learning not only helps employees perform better following the change; it also increases their readiness for change by strengthening their belief about working successfully in the new situation (called *change self-efficacy).* And when employees develop stronger change self-efficacy, they develop a stronger acceptance of and commitment to the change.[30]

Employee Involvement

Employee involvement is almost essential in the change process, although a low level of involvement may be necessary when the change must occur quickly or employee interests significantly conflict with the organization's needs. The value of involvement is illustrated in the opening case study to this chapter. Blueshore Financial's transformation began

with a task force of employees and executives who generated creative ideas for the North Vancouver credit union's future. As the change proceeded, employees discussed and made suggestions to the executive team about improved operational practices in the emerging financial spa model.

The potential benefits of employee involvement, which were discussed in (Chapter 7), are relevant to organizational change. Rather than being disinterested agents of someone else's decisions, involved employees tend to feel more personal responsibility for successful implementation of the change.[31] This sense of ownership also minimizes the not-invented-here syndrome and fear of the unknown. Furthermore, the work environment is so complex that determining the best direction of the change effort requires ideas and knowledge of many people. Employee involvement is such an important component of organizational change that special initiatives have been developed to allow participation in large groups. These change interventions are described later in the chapter.

Stress Management

Organizational change is a stressful experience for many people because it threatens self-esteem and creates uncertainty

Global Connections 15.1

SUPPORTING CHANGE THROUGH COMMUNICATION AT EE[*]

EE ("Everything Everywhere"), the United Kingdom's largest mobile network, has come a long way over the past decade. It was born out of the merger of French-owned Orange and German-owned T-Mobile, who recently sold EE to BT, the United Kingdom's largest Internet service provider.

Communication has been a key ingredient to successful change throughout EE's turbulent transformation. "During change, employee engagement needs to link heavily to internal communications," advises Linda Kennedy-McCarthy, who was EE's chief change officer during and after the merger. "We used every tool we could to keep our messages consistent and ever-present. We even put up posters in all our toilet cubicles! And we monitored closely whether the roadshow messages were being cascaded effectively."

One important purpose of communicating during EE's transformation was to build an urgency for change. "Senior management may jump up and down about burning platforms, but below the surface everyone could be sitting comfortably," warns Kennedy-McCarthy. "If the front line doesn't understand your message

or—even worse—never hears it, you'll never be able to deliver real, meaningful change."

EE also relied on ongoing communication to maintain momentum and reduce employee fear of the unknown. "You have to help people see that the change is real and that it applies to them," says Kennedy-McCarthy. "And it's your responsibility to make sure they understand how the change will benefit them or how not changing will cost them."

©PA Images/Alamy Stock Photo

* Based on information in: O. Blackwell, "How Employee Engagement Helped To Create EE And Turn It Into The Number One 'Best Big Company To Work For'," *Engage for Success* (blog), May 20, 2018, https://engageforsuccess.org/ee-best-big-company-to-work-for.

about the future.[32] Communication, learning, and employee involvement can reduce some of the stressors.[33] However, research indicates that companies also need to introduce stress management practices to help employees cope with changes.[34] In particular, stress management minimizes resistance by removing some of the negative valence and fear of the unknown about the change process. Stress also saps energy, so minimizing stress potentially increases employee motivation to support the change process.

Negotiation

As long as people resist change, organizational change strategies will require a variety of influence tactics. Negotiation is a form of influence that involves the promise of benefits or resources in exchange for the target person's compliance with the influencer's request. This strategy potentially gains support from those who would otherwise lose out from the change. However, this support usually goes no further than compliance with the change effort. Negotiation rarely produces commitment to change, so negotiation might not be effective in the long term.

Coercion

If all else fails, leaders rely on coercion as part of the change process. Coercion includes a range of assertive influence behaviours (see Chapter 10), such as persistently reminding people of their obligations, frequently monitoring behaviour to ensure compliance, confronting people who do not change, and using threats of punishment (including dismissal) to force compliance.

Replacing or threatening to replace staff who will not support the change is an extreme step, but it is fairly common in major organizational transformations. Several years ago, StandardAero CEO Bob Hamaberg threatened to fire senior managers who opposed his initiative to introduce lean management (methods to improve work efficiency). "You must have senior management commitment," Hamaberg said bluntly at the time. "I had some obstacles. I removed the obstacles." Harsh words and actions, but due to this visionary transformation, StandardAero's Winnipeg location (where the company began) has grown significantly and the company overall has become a world leader in the aircraft engine repair and overhaul business.[35]

Firing people is the least desirable way to change organizations. However, dismissals and other forms of coercion are sometimes necessary when speed is essential and other tactics are ineffective. In particular, it may be necessary to remove executives and other staff who are unwilling or unable to change their existing mental models of the ideal organization. This is also a radical form of "unlearning" the organization's past routines that have become dysfunctional.[36] Even so, coercion is a risky strategy because survivors (employees who do not leave) may have less trust in corporate leaders and engage in more political tactics to protect their own job security.

REFREEZING THE DESIRED CONDITIONS

Unfreezing and changing behaviour won't produce lasting change. People are creatures of habit, so they easily slip back into familiar patterns. Therefore, leaders need to refreeze the new behaviours by realigning organizational systems and team dynamics with the desired changes. The desired patterns of behaviour can be "nailed down" by changing the physical structure and situational conditions. Organizational rewards are also powerful systems that refreeze behaviours.[37] If the change process is supposed to encourage efficiency, then rewards should be realigned to motivate and reinforce efficient behaviour.

Information systems play a complementary role in the change process, particularly as conduits for feedback.[38] Feedback mechanisms help employees learn how well they are moving toward the desired objectives, and they provide a permanent architecture to support the new behaviour patterns in the long term. The adage "What gets measured, gets done" applies here. Employees concentrate on the new priorities when they receive a continuous flow of feedback about how well they are achieving those goals.

 Global Connections 15.2

NEW SYSTEMS AND STRUCTURES REINFORCE CHANGE AT SUPERIOR CABINETS[*]

Superior Cabinets was in serious financial trouble a decade ago, so CEO Scott Hodson (shown here) and his newly hired executive team launched a radical transformation of the Saskatoon-based manufacturer. They refocused the cabinetmaker from a mass production operation to a customer-driven business that continuously reduces wasteful work processes (lean manufacturing). Superior is now highly efficient and profitable. A decade ago, it took 400 people and 16 weeks to produce and install 25 kitchens per day. "Today it takes 250 people and we install it in six weeks, guaranteed," says Hodson.

"The reason we got through it [the transformation] was because our people embraced the change," Hodson explains. Communication, training, and involvement were important. However, the company also introduced several new systems and structures that reinforced and supported the new mindset and employee behaviours. Superior invested in technology that focused information around customers. For instance, customer orders are submitted directly online from Superior's showrooms and the system enables employees to monitor how well customer orders are progressing.

More precise performance standards were introduced with associated visual scorecards that track costs, product quality, on-time delivery, and other key indicators. Production has been reorganized into team-based cells for better coordination among staff. Superior Cabinets employees now participate in a profit-sharing plan so they can benefit financially from the company's success.

©Superior Cabinets

* B. Johnstone, "Superior Cabinets Wins 'Turnaround' Award," *Saskatoon Star-Phoenix*, 24 October 2014, D2; *Superior Cabinets: A Strong Comeback*, (Montreal: Business Development Bank of Canada, 17 June 2015); J. Povhe, "From Dollars to Sense: My Experience as a Lean CFO," *Prairie Manufacturer*, Winter 2016, 14–16; P. Brent, "Working Flat out but Falling Behind," *Globe & Mail*, January 23, 2017; K.M. Koenig, "Superior Cabinets Named Manufacturer of the Year," *Woodworking* 31 (February 2017): 14; K.M. Koenig, "Superior Cabinets Named First Lean Certified Manufacturer in Saskatchewan," *Woodworking Network*, February 13, 2018.

Leadership, Coalitions, and Pilot Projects

LO4

Kurt Lewin's force field analysis model is a useful template to explain the dynamics of organizational change. But it overlooks four other ingredients in effective change processes: leadership, coalitions, social networks, and pilot projects.

TRANSFORMATIONAL LEADERSHIP AND CHANGE

The opening case study to this chapter described how Chris Catliff transformed North Shore Credit Union from a floundering undifferentiated savings and loan business into Blueshore Financial—a highly successful wealth management institution focused on clients with complex and sophisticated financial needs. Catliff and other Blueshore executives were transformational leaders in this change process. They involved employees in developing a vision of the desired future, communicated that vision in ways that were meaningful to staff and other stakeholders, made decisions and acted in ways that were consistent with that vision, and encouraged employees to experiment with ways to align work activities more closely with the vision.[39]

A key element of leading change is a strategic vision.[40] A leader's vision provides a sense of direction and establishes the critical success factors against which the real changes are evaluated. Furthermore, a vision provides an emotional foundation to the change because it links the individual's values and self-concept to the desired change.[41] A strategic vision also minimizes employee fear of the unknown and provides a better understanding of what behaviours employees must learn for the desired future.

COALITIONS, SOCIAL NETWORKS, AND CHANGE

One of the great truths of organizational change is that change agents cannot lead the initiative alone. They need the assistance of several people with a similar degree of commitment to the transformation.[42] Indeed, some research suggests that this group—often called a *guiding coalition*—appears to be the most important factor in the success of public sector organizational renewal programs.[43]

Membership in the guiding coalition extends beyond the executive team. Ideally, it includes a diagonal swath of employees representing different functions and most levels of the organization. The guiding coalition is sometimes formed from a special task force that initially investigates the opportunities for change. Members of the guiding coalition should also be influence leaders; that is, they should be highly respected by peers in their area of the organization.

Social Networks and Viral Change

The change process can be strengthened through social networks, which are structures of people connected to each other through one or more forms of interdependence (see Chapter 10). They have an important role in communication and influence, both of which are key ingredients for organizational change. To some extent, coalition members support the change process by feeding into these networks. But social networks contribute to organizational change whether or not the change process has a formal coalition.

Social networks are not easily controlled, yet some change agents have tapped into social networks to build a groundswell of support for a change initiative. This *viral change* process adopts principles found in word-of-mouth and viral marketing, which occur when information seeded to a few people is transmitted to others through their friendship connections.[44] Within organizations, social networks represent the channels through which news and opinion about change initiatives are transmitted. Participants in that network have relatively high trust, so their opinions are more persuasive than information from more formal channels. Social networks also provide opportunities for behaviour observation—employees observe one another's behaviour and often adopt that behaviour themselves. As key people in the network change their actions, they are copied by others in the network.[45]

PILOT PROJECTS AND DIFFUSION OF CHANGE

Many companies rely on a pilot project, which involves introducing change to one work unit or section of the organization. This cautious approach tests the effectiveness of and employee support for the transformation. Furthermore, a pilot project is more flexible and less risky than a companywide transformation.[46] It is also easier to select organizational groups with high readiness for change, thus increasing the likelihood that the initiative will be successful.

How does change get diffused from the pilot project to other parts of the organization? Using the MARS model as a template (see Chapter 1), Exhibit 15.3 outlines several strategies. First, employees are more likely to adopt the practices of a pilot project when they are motivated to do so.[47] This occurs when they see that the pilot project is successful and people in the pilot project receive recognition and rewards for changing their previous work practices. Diffusion also occurs more successfully when managers support and

Global Connections 15.3

TRAILBLAZING VIRAL CHANGE AT RSA INSURANCE*

RSA Insurance Group launched a flexible benefits package that required employees to pick their preferred benefits options. But instead of just emailing reminders, human resources staff at the U.K. insurance firm relied on a viral change process that more effectively motivated employees to choose their options.

"We used people in the network to communicate what their favourite elements of the proposition were," explains RSA's director of internal communications. Specifically, RSA's HR staff carefully described the flexible benefits plan to 500 "trailblazers"—early adopters of the company's new internal communication platform who had a large following of co-workers. Trailblazers were soon posting their views about the preferred flexible benefits offered. These posts were read by thousands of employees, many of whom would have ignored the email memos from HR.

Trailblazers are not only early adopters of the internal communication platform; they are also role models whose ideas receive considerable attention from other employees. Consequently, the actions of these trailblazers and the information they posted were far more effective at changing employee behaviour (signing up for preferred benefits) than human resources staff would have accomplished through impersonal emails.

©Chris Batson/Alamy Stock Photo

* V. Arnstein, "RSA Group Group Engages Staff with Social Media Network," *Employee Benefits,* September 1, 2015; S. Shah, "Why RSA Insurance Picked BT Global Services over Atos Origin to Host Microsoft Collaboration Products in the Cloud," *Computing,* October 21, 2015.

EXHIBIT 15.3 Strategies for Diffusing Change from a Pilot Project

Motivation
- Widely communicate and celebrate the pilot project's success.
- Reward and recognize pilot project employees as well as those who work at transferring that change to other parts of the organization.
- Ensure that managers support and reinforce the desired behaviours related to the pilot project's success.
- Identify and address potential sources of resistance to change.

Ability
- Give employees the opportunity to interact with and learn from those in the pilot project.
- Reassign or temporarily second some pilot project employees to other work units where they can coach and serve as role models.
- Give employees technical training to implement practices identified in the pilot project.

Role perceptions
- Communicate and teach employees how the pilot project practices are relevant for their own functional areas.
- Ensure that the pilot project is described in a way that is neither too specific nor too general.

Situational factors
- Give staff sufficient time and resources to learn and implement the pilot project practices in their work units.

reinforce the desired behaviours. More generally, change agents need to minimize the sources of resistance to change that we discussed earlier in this chapter.

Second, employees must have the ability—the required skills and knowledge—to adopt the practices introduced in the pilot project. According to innovation diffusion studies, people adopt ideas more readily when they have an opportunity to interact with and learn from others who have already applied the new practices.[48]

Third, pilot projects get diffused when employees have clear role perceptions—that is, when they understand how the practices in a pilot project apply to them even though they are in a completely different functional area. For instance, accounting department employees won't easily recognize how they can adopt lean management practices developed by employees in the production department. The challenge here is for change agents to provide guidance that is not too narrowly defined around the pilot project environment because it might not seem relevant to other areas of the organization. At the same time, the pilot project intervention should not be described too broadly or abstractly to other employees because this makes the information and role model too vague. Finally, employees require supportive situational factors, including the resources and time necessary to adopt the practices demonstrated in the pilot project.

Four Approaches to Organizational Change

LO5

So far, this chapter has examined the dynamics of change that occur every day in organizations. However, organizational change agents and consultants also apply various structured approaches to organizational change. This section introduces four of the leading approaches: action research, appreciative inquiry, large group interventions, and parallel learning structures.

ACTION RESEARCH APPROACH

Along with introducing the force field model, Kurt Lewin recommended an **action research** approach to the change process. The philosophy of action research is that meaningful change is a combination of action orientation (changing attitudes and behaviour) and research orientation (testing theory).[49] On one hand, the change process needs to be action-oriented because the ultimate goal

> **action research** A problem-focused change process that combines action orientation (changing attitudes and behaviour) and research orientation (testing theory through data collection and analysis).

is to improve workplace behaviours and practices. An action orientation involves diagnosing current problems and applying interventions that resolve those problems. On the other hand, the change process is a research study because change agents apply a conceptual framework (such as team dynamics or organizational culture) to a real situation. As with any good research, the change process involves collecting data to diagnose problems more effectively and to systematically evaluate how well the theory works in practice.[50]

Within this dual framework of action and research, the action research approach adopts an open-systems view. It recognizes that organizations have many interdependent parts, so change agents need to anticipate both the intended and the unintended consequences of their interventions. Action research is also a highly participative process because open-systems change requires both the knowledge and the commitment of members within that system. Indeed, employees are essentially co-researchers as well as participants in the intervention. Overall, action research is a data-based, problem-oriented process that diagnoses the need for change, introduces the intervention, and then evaluates and stabilizes the desired changes. The main phases of action research are illustrated in Exhibit 15.4 and described here:[51]

1. *Form client–consultant relationship.* Action research usually assumes that the change agent originates outside the system (such as a consultant), so the process

---

EXHIBIT 15.4   The Action Research Process

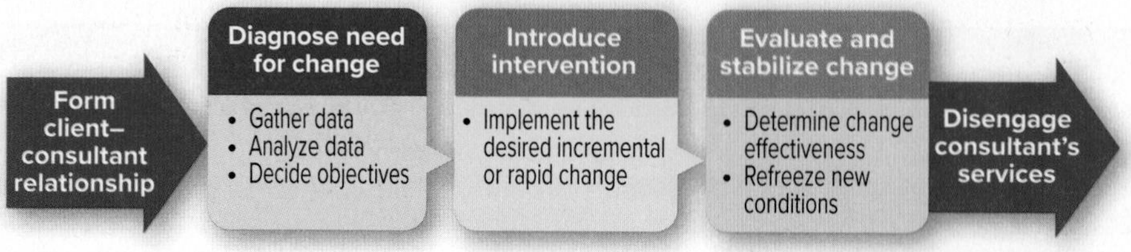

Form client–consultant relationship → **Diagnose need for change**: • Gather data • Analyze data • Decide objectives → **Introduce intervention**: • Implement the desired incremental or rapid change → **Evaluate and stabilize change**: • Determine change effectiveness • Refreeze new conditions → **Disengage consultant's services**

begins by forming the client–consultant relationship. Consultants need to determine the client's readiness for change, including whether people are motivated to participate in the process, are open to meaningful change, and possess the abilities to complete the process.

2. *Diagnose the need for change.* Action research is a problem-oriented activity that carefully diagnoses the problem to determine the appropriate direction for the change effort. Organizational diagnosis relies on systematic analysis of the situation. It involves gathering and analyzing data about an ongoing system, including interviews and surveys of employees and other stakeholders. Organizational diagnosis also involves employees so they improve, understand, and support the appropriate change method, the schedule for the actions involved, and the expected standards of successful change.

3. *Introduce intervention.* This stage in the action research model applies one or more actions to correct the problem. It may include any of the prescriptions mentioned in this book, such as building more effective teams,

managing conflict, building a better organizational structure, or changing the corporate culture. An important issue is how quickly the changes should occur.[52] Some experts recommend *incremental change,* in which the organization fine-tunes the system and takes small steps toward a desired state. Others claim that *rapid change* is often required, in which the system is overhauled decisively and quickly.

4. *Evaluate and stabilize change.* Action research recommends evaluating the effectiveness of the intervention against the standards established in the diagnostic stage. Unfortunately, even when these standards are clearly stated, the effectiveness of an intervention might not be apparent for several years or might be difficult to separate from other factors. If the activity has the desired effect, the change agent and participants need to stabilize the new conditions. This refers to the refreezing process that was described earlier in this chapter. Rewards, information systems, team norms, and other conditions are redesigned so they support the new values and behaviours.

Debating Point: WHAT'S THE BEST SPEED FOR ORGANIZATIONAL CHANGE?

One of the great debates among organizational change experts is how quickly the change should occur. One view is that slow, incremental change is better because it gives employees more time to adjust to the new realities, to keep up with what needs to be learned, and to manage their stress in this process. Incremental change is also preferred because it gives leaders more time to change course if the current direction isn't working as hoped.

In spite of the apparent virtues of incremental change, some experts argue that rapid change is usually a much better choice. They do not claim that change needs to be radical or evenly rapid all of the time. Rather, they suggest that most change initiatives need to be, on average, much quicker than incremental. One argument is that companies operate in such a fast-paced environment that any speed less than "rapid" is risky; an incremental change initiative risks putting organizations further behind their competitors to the point that any change seems futile.

A second argument is that rapid change creates a collective sense of momentum, whereas inertia eventually catches up with incremental change.[*] In other words, employees feel the sense of progress when change occurs quickly. This forward movement generates its own

energy that helps motivate employees toward the future objectives. Incremental change, by comparison, is sluggish and lethargic. A related argument is that any organizational change requires plenty of energy, particularly from the leaders who must continually communicate, role model, coach, and otherwise support and influence employees toward the new state of affairs.[**] This energy is finite, and it is more likely to run out when the change is spread over a long rather than a short period of time.

Third, incremental change doesn't necessarily give employees more time to adjust; instead, it typically gives them more time to dig in their heels! Rapid change, on the other hand, happens at such speed that employees don't have the opportunity to find ways to hold back, retrench, or even think about strategies to oppose the change effort. Finally, though proponents of incremental change point to its benefits for minimizing stress, there is reason to believe that it often has the opposite effect. Changing slowly can feel like a slow train wreck—the more you see it coming, the more painful it feels. Quicker change, particularly when there are support systems to help employees through the process, may be less painful than incremental change.

* D. Miller and P.H. Friesen, "Momentum and Revolution in Organizational Adaptation," *Academy of Management Journal* 23, no. 4 (1980): 591–614; D. Miller and M.-J. Chen, "Sources and Consequences of Competitive Inertia: A Study of the U.S. Airline Industry," *Administrative Science Quarterly* 39, no. 1 (1994): 1–23.
** J. Isern and C. Pung, "Driving Radical Change," *McKinsey Quarterly,* no. 4 (2007): 24–35.

The action research approach has dominated organizational change thinking since it was introduced in the 1940s. However, some experts are concerned that the problem-oriented nature of action research—in which something is wrong that must be fixed—focuses on the negative dynamics of the group or system rather than its positive opportunities and potential. This concern with action research has led to the development of a more positive approach to organizational change, called *appreciative inquiry.*[53]

APPRECIATIVE INQUIRY APPROACH

Appreciative inquiry tries to break out of the problem-solving mindset of traditional change management practices by reframing relationships around the positive and the possible. It searches for organizational (or team) strengths and capabilities and then applies that knowledge for further success and well-being. Appreciative inquiry is therefore deeply grounded in the emerging philosophy of **positive organizational behaviour**, which suggests that focusing on an individual's positive qualities and traits rather than on what is wrong with the person will improve organizational success and personal well-being. In other words, this approach emphasizes building on strengths rather than trying to directly correct problems.[54]

> **appreciative inquiry** An organizational change strategy that directs the group's attention away from its own problems and focuses participants on the group's potential and positive elements.
>
> **positive organizational behaviour** A perspective of organizational behaviour that focuses on building positive qualities and traits within individuals or institutions as opposed to focusing on what is wrong with them.

Appreciative inquiry improves open dialogue by redirecting the group's attention away from its own concerns. This is especially useful when participants are aware of their problems or already suffer from negativity in their relationships. The positive orientation of appreciative inquiry enables groups to overcome these negative tensions and build a more hopeful perspective of their future by focusing on what is possible.[55] This positive approach to change also suggests that change agents should adopt an optimistic view of possibilities, such as seeing a glass half full rather than half empty. Therefore, appreciative inquiry actively frames reality in a way that provides constructive value for future development.

Appreciative inquiry's positive focus is illustrated by the intervention conducted a few years ago at Heidelberg USA. The American arm of the world's largest printing press manufacturer (Heidelberger Druckmaschinen AG) had experienced morale-busting product setbacks as well as downsizing due to an economic recession. To rebuild employee morale and engagement, Heidelberg held a two-day appreciative inquiry summit involving one-third of its staff. Organized into diverse groups from across the organization, participants envisioned what Heidelberg would ideally look like in the future. From these sessions emerged a new vision and greater autonomy for employees to serve customers. "Appreciative inquiry can energize an organization even in tough times because it begins the conversation with possibilities instead of problems," says a senior executive at Heidelberg USA.[56]

Appreciative Inquiry Principles

Appreciative inquiry embraces five principles (see Exhibit 15.5).[57] One of these is the positive principle, which we have just described. A second principle, called the *constructionist principle,* recognizes that the questions we ask and the language we use construct different realities. How questions are stated determines the information we receive, which in turn affects which change intervention we choose. A third principle, called the *simultaneity principle,* states that inquiry and change are simultaneous, not sequential. We begin the change process the moment we ask questions, because the questions themselves influence those who hear and answer those questions. Consequently, change agents need to be mindful of effects that the inquiry has on the direction of the change process.

EXHIBIT 15.5 Five Principles of Appreciative Inquiry

Appreciative inquiry principle	Description
Positive principle	Focusing on positive events and potential produces more positive, effective, and enduring change.
Constructionist principle	How we perceive and understand the change process depends on the questions we ask and language we use throughout that process.
Simultaneity principle	Inquiry and change are simultaneous, not sequential.
Poetic principle	Organizations are open books, so we have choices in how they may be perceived, framed, and described.
Anticipatory principle	People are motivated and guided by the vision they see and believe in for the future.

©Monkey Business Images/Shutterstock

Lewis County General Hospital has adopted appreciative inquiry principles and practices for its long-term strategy development process. "I wanted to focus on what we can do, not on what we can't," says Gerald R. Cayer, CEO of the county-owned medical centre in upstate New York. Instead of focusing on problems, Lewis County General Hospital began with "Discovery and Aspirations" discussion sessions, which reviewed the best practices of rural hospitals around the country. This was followed by the "designing" phase of strategy development. The hospital's appreciative inquiry process involved numerous stakeholders, including hospital administration, employees, labour unions, service providers, the hospital foundation, and community members. "The point is to bring forward great minds, encourage dialogue, and to think about what can make the most sense for the community and for the hospital," Cayer explains.*

* Based on information in: J. Abbass, "Lewis County Hospital Takes a Positive Approach to Planning," *Watertown Daily Times (NY),* February 25, 2019.

A fourth appreciative inquiry principle, called the *poetic principle,* states that organizations are open books, so we have choices in how they may be perceived, framed, and described. The poetic principle encourages change agents to actively frame reality in a way that provides constructive value for future development. The fifth principle, called the *anticipatory principle,* recognizes that people are motivated and guided by an abstract vision of the future that is aligned with their personal values. We noted the importance

of visions earlier in this chapter (change agents) and in our discussion of transformational leadership (Chapter 12).

The Four-D Model of Appreciative Inquiry

Appreciative inquiry follows the "Four-D" process shown in Exhibit 15.6. The model's name refers to its four stages, which begins with *discovery*—identifying the positive elements of the observed events or organization.[58] This might involve documenting positive customer experiences

---

EXHIBIT 15.6   The Four-D Model of Appreciative Inquiry

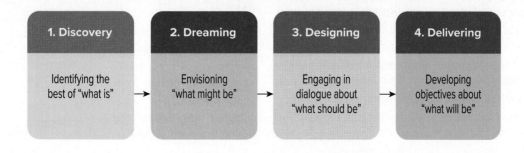

1. Discovery	2. Dreaming	3. Designing	4. Delivering
Identifying the best of "what is"	Envisioning "what might be"	Engaging in dialogue about "what should be"	Developing objectives about "what will be"

elsewhere in the organization. Or it might include interviewing members of another organization to discover its fundamental strengths. As participants discuss their findings, they shift into the *dreaming* stage by envisioning what might be possible in an ideal organization. By pointing out a hypothetical ideal organization or situation, participants feel safer revealing their hopes and aspirations than they would if they were discussing their own organization or predicament.

As participants make their private thoughts public to the group, the process shifts into the third stage, called *designing*. In the designing stage, participants listen with selfless receptivity to each other's models and assumptions and eventually form a collective model for thinking within the team. In effect, they create a common mental model of "what should be." As this model takes shape, group members shift the focus back to their own situation. In the final stage of appreciative inquiry, called *delivering* (also known as *destiny),* participants establish specific objectives and direction for their own organization on the basis of their model of "what will be."

Appreciative inquiry was introduced more than three decades ago, but it gained popularity only within the past dozen years. The City of Cleveland recently held the Cleveland Rising Summit, an appreciative inquiry event in which 600 participants developed numerous ideas to improve the region and clarify aspirations for the next decade. Several dozen health professionals at a Vancouver area hospital were involved in appreciative inquiry sessions to discover how to improve medical practice for dementia patients. A Toronto hospital held an appreciative inquiry retreat to craft a vision for its future. The hospital subsequently developed a program that teaches hospital leaders to embed appreciative principles in their daily interactions with staff. Appreciative inquiry has also been successfully applied across a range of other organizations, including Heidelberg USA, British Broadcasting Corporation, the State of Massachusetts, and several sites in a Canadian urban school district.[59]

Appreciative inquiry has much to offer, but it is not always the best strategy for change and, in fact, has not always been successful. This approach depends on participants' ability to let go of the problem-oriented approach, including the "blame game" of determining who may have been responsible for past failures. It also requires leaders who are willing to accept appreciative inquiry's less-structured process. Another concern is that research has not yet examined the contingencies of this approach.[60] In other words, we don't yet know under what conditions appreciative inquiry is a useful approach to organizational change and under what conditions it is less effective. Overall, appreciative inquiry can be an effective approach to organizational change, but we are still discovering its potential and limitations.

LARGE GROUP INTERVENTION APPROACH

Appreciative inquiry can occur in small teams, but it is often designed to involve a large number of people, such as the hundreds of stakeholders who participated in the recent Cleveland Rising Summit. As such, appreciative inquiry is often identified as one of several large group organizational change interventions. Large group interventions adopt a "whole systems" perspective of the change process.[61] This means that they view organizations as open systems (see Chapter 1) and assume that change will be more successful when many employees and other stakeholders participate.[62] Large group interventions are high-involvement events because participants discuss their experiences, expectations, and ideas with others, typically in small groups within the large collective setting.

Similar to appreciative inquiry, large group interventions adopt a future-oriented positive focus rather than a past-oriented problem focus. *Future search conferences,* for instance, are large group interventions typically held over a few days in which participants identify emerging trends and develop strategies for the organization to realize potential under those future conditions. In addition to this strategy development, large group interventions generate a collective vision or sense-making about the organization and its future. This "meaning-making" process is important for the organization's evolving identity and how participants relate to that identity.

Future search meetings and similar large group change events potentially minimize employee resistance and improve the quality of the change process, but they also have limitations.[63] One problem is that involving so many people invariably limits the opportunity to contribute and increases the risk that a few people will dominate the process. Another concern is that these events focus on finding common ground, and this may prevent the participants from discovering substantive differences that interfere with future progress. A third issue is that these events generate high expectations about an ideal future state that are difficult to satisfy in practice. Employees become even more cynical and resistant to change if they do not see meaningful decisions and actions resulting from these meetings.

PARALLEL LEARNING STRUCTURE APPROACH

Parallel learning structures are highly participative arrangements composed of people from most levels of the organization who follow the action research model to

parallel learning structures
Highly participative arrangements composed of people from most levels of the organization who follow the action research model to produce meaningful organizational change.

©FrameStockFootages/Shutterstock

By applying a parallel learning structure, ENWIN Utilities Ltd. has been able to introduce employee-led innovation without disrupting the Windsor, Ontario, hydro and water services company's regular business operations. While still performing their regular jobs, more than a dozen ENWIN employees (called Catalysts) received design thinking and other problem-solving training, then worked in teams to develop strategies for improving work processes. "We trained the Catalysts in customer-centric design thinking and innovative solutions," explains ENWIN executive Barry Leavitt. "Then it was their job to go out into the company and assess opportunities for change." During the latter part of the year-long program, Catalyst teams pitched their diagnostics and solutions to ENWIN's executive team. Several viable ideas are now in varying stages of implementation and a second intake of Catalysts has begun.*

*T. Campbell, "WEtech Alliance Launches Program to Encourage Innovation by Employees," *The Windsor Star (Ont.),* February 28, 2019; "ENnovation – ENWIN and WEtech Alliance Nurture Innovation," *Perspective,* March 23, 2019; "Class In Session for Second Cohort of ENWIN Innovators," *ENnovation Encore* (blog), May 28, 2019, https://enwin.com/ennovation-encore/.

produce meaningful organizational change. They are social structures developed alongside the formal hierarchy with the purpose of increasing the organization's learning.[64] Ideally, participants in parallel learning structures are sufficiently free from the constraints of the larger organization that they can effectively solve organizational issues.

Royal Dutch/Shell relied on a parallel learning structure to introduce a more customer-focused organization.[65] Rather than try to change the entire organization at once, executives held week-long "retail boot camps" with teams from six countries, consisting of front-line people (such as gas station managers, truck drivers, and marketing professionals). Participants learned about competitive trends in their regions and were taught powerful marketing tools to identify new opportunities. The teams then returned home to study their markets and develop proposals for improvement. Four months later, boot camp teams returned for a second workshop, at which each proposal was critiqued by Royal Dutch/Shell executives. Each team had 60 days to put its ideas into action; then the teams returned for a third workshop to analyze what worked and what didn't. This parallel learning process did much more than introduce new marketing ideas. It created enthusiasm in participants that spread contagiously

to their co-workers, including managers above them, when they returned to their home countries.

Cross-Cultural and Ethical Issues in Organizational Change

LO6

Throughout this chapter, we have emphasized that change is inevitable and often continuous because organizations need to remain aligned with the dynamic external environment. Yet we also need to be aware of cross-cultural and ethical issues with any change process. Many organizational change practices are built around Western cultural assumptions and values, which may differ from and sometimes conflict with assumptions and values in other cultures.[66] One possible cross-cultural limitation is that Western organizational change models, such as Lewin's force field analysis, often assume that change has a beginning and an ending in a logical linear sequence (that is, a straight line from point A to point B). Yet in some cultures change is viewed more as a cyclical phenomenon, such as the earth's revolution around the sun or a pendulum swinging back and forth. Other cultures have an interconnected view of change, whereby one change leads to another (often unplanned) change, which leads to another change, and so forth until the change objective is ultimately achieved in a more circuitous way.

Another cross-cultural issue with some organizational change interventions is the assumption that effective organizational change is necessarily punctuated by tension and overt conflict. Indeed, some change interventions encourage such conflict. But this direct confrontation view is incompatible with cultures that emphasize harmony (see Chapter 11). These cross-cultural differences suggest that a more contingency-oriented perspective is required for organizational change to work effectively in this era of globalization.

Organizational change practices also need to consider ethical issues.[67] One ethical concern is the risk of violating individual privacy rights. The action research model is built on the idea of collecting information from organizational members, yet this asks employees to provide personal information and reveal emotions they would not normally divulge.[68] A second ethical issue is that some change activities potentially increase management's power by inducing compliance and conformity in organizational members. For instance, action research is a system-wide activity that requires employee participation rather than allowing individuals to get involved voluntarily. A third risk is that some organizational change interventions undermine the individual's self-esteem. The unfreezing process requires that participants disconfirm their existing beliefs, sometimes including their own competence at specific tasks or interpersonal relations.

Organizational change is usually more difficult than it initially seems. Yet the dilemma is that most organizations operate in hyperfast environments that demand continuous and rapid adaptation. Organizations survive and gain competitive advantage by mastering the complex dynamics of moving people through the continuous process of change as quickly as the external environment is changing.

Organizational Behaviour: The Journey Continues

More than a century ago, industrialist Andrew Carnegie said, "Take away my people, but leave my factories, and soon grass will grow on the factory floors. Take away my factories, but leave my people, and soon we will have a new and better factory."[69] Carnegie's statement reflects the message woven throughout this textbook: Organizations are not buildings or machinery or financial assets; rather, they consist of people. Organizations are human entities—full of life, sometimes fragile, and always exciting.

Andrew Carnegie
©Everett Historical/Shutterstock

Chapter Summary

LO1

Describe the elements of Lewin's force field analysis model.

Lewin's force field analysis model states that all systems have driving and restraining forces. Change occurs through the process of unfreezing, changing, and refreezing. Unfreezing produces disequilibrium between the driving and restraining forces. Refreezing realigns the organization's systems and structures with the desired behaviours.

LO2

Discuss the reasons why people resist organizational change and how change agents should view this resistance.

Restraining forces are manifested as employee resistance to change. The main reasons why people resist change are the negative valence of change, fear of the unknown, not-invented-here syndrome, breaking routines, incongruent team dynamics, and incongruent organizational systems. Change agents need to view resistance to change as a resource, not an inherent obstacle to change. They should adopt a task conflict rather than relationship conflict approach to resistance. Resistance is a signal that the change agent has not sufficiently strengthened employee readiness for change. It is also seen as a form of voice, so discussion resulting from resistance potentially improves procedural justice.

LO3

Outline six strategies for minimizing resistance to change, and debate ways to effectively create an urgency for change.

Organizational change requires employees to have an urgency for change. This typically occurs by informing them about driving forces in the external environment. Urgency for change also develops by putting employees in direct contact with customers. Leaders often need to create an urgency for change before the external pressures are felt, and this can occur through a vision of a more appealing future.

Resistance to change may be minimized by keeping employees informed about what to expect from the change effort (communicating); teaching employees valuable skills for the desired future (learning); involving them in the change process; helping employees cope with the stress of change; negotiating trade-offs with those who will clearly lose from the change effort; and using coercion (sparingly and as a last resort).

LO4

Discuss how leadership, coalitions, social networks, and pilot projects assist organizational change.

Every successful change requires transformational leaders with an appealing vision of the desired future state. These change agents need the assistance of several people (a guiding coalition) who are located throughout the organization. Change also occurs more informally through social networks. Viral change operates through social networks using influencers.

Many organizational change initiatives begin with a pilot project. The success of the pilot project is then diffused to other parts of the organization. This occurs by applying the MARS model, including motivating employees to adopt the pilot project's methods, training people to know how to adopt these practices, helping to clarify how the pilot can be applied to different areas, and providing time and resources to support this diffusion.

LO5

Describe and compare action research, appreciative inquiry, large group interventions, and parallel learning structures as formal approaches to organizational change.

Action research is a highly participative, open-systems approach to change management that combines an action orientation (changing attitudes and behaviour) with research orientation (testing theory). It is a data-based, problem-oriented process that diagnoses the need for change, introduces the intervention, and then evaluates and stabilizes the desired changes.

Appreciative inquiry embraces the positive organizational behaviour philosophy by focusing participants on the positive and possible. This approach to change also applies the constructionist, simultaneity, poetic, and anticipatory principles. The four stages of appreciative inquiry include discovery, dreaming, designing, and delivering.

Large group interventions are highly participative events that view organizations as open systems (i.e., involve as many employees and other stakeholders as possible), and adopt a future and positive focus of change. Parallel learning structures rely on social structures developed alongside the formal hierarchy with the purpose of increasing the organization's learning. They are highly participative arrangements, comprised of people from most levels of the organization who follow the action research model to produce meaningful organizational change.

LO6

Discuss two cross-cultural and three ethical issues in organizational change.

One significant concern is that organizational change theories developed with a Western cultural orientation potentially conflict with cultural values in some other countries. Also, organizational change practices can raise one or more ethical concerns, including increasing management's power over employees, threatening individual privacy rights, and undermining individual self-esteem.

Key Terms

action research
appreciative inquiry
force field analysis
parallel learning structures

positive organizational behaviour
refreezing
unfreezing

Critical Thinking Questions

1. Chances are that the school you are attending is currently undergoing some sort of change to adapt more closely with its environment. Discuss the external forces that are driving the change. What internal drivers for change also exist?

2. Use Lewin's force field analysis to describe the dynamics of organizational change at Blueshore Financial, the subject of the opening case study for this chapter. That case study provides some information, but think about other forces for and against change beyond the information provided.

3. Employee resistance is a symptom, not a problem, in the change process. What are some of the real problems that may cause employee resistance?

4. Senior management of a large multinational corporation is planning to restructure the organization. Currently, the organization is decentralized around geographic areas, so the executive responsible for each area has considerable autonomy over manufacturing and sales. The new structure will transfer power to the executives responsible for different product groups; the executives responsible for each geographic area will no longer be responsible for manufacturing in their area but will retain control over sales activities. Describe two types of resistance senior management might encounter from this organizational change.

5. Discuss the role of reward systems in organizational change. Specifically, identify where reward systems relate to Lewin's force field model and where they undermine the organizational change process.

6. Web Circuits is a Malaysian-based custom manufacturer for high-technology companies. Senior management wants to introduce lean management practices to reduce production costs and remain competitive. A consultant has recommended that the company start with a pilot project in one department and, when successful, diffuse these practices to other areas of the organization. Discuss the advantages of this recommendation, and identify three ways (other than the pilot project's success) to make diffusion of the change effort more successful.

7. What is the role of formal and informal networks in organizations interested in undergoing change?

8. Suppose that you are vice-president of branch services at the Kelowna Credit Union. You notice that several branches have consistently low customer service ratings even though there are no apparent differences in resources or staff characteristics. Describe an appreciative inquiry process in one of these branches that might help to overcome this problem.

 Case Study:

TRANSACT INSURANCE CORPORATION

by Steven L. McShane, University of Newcastle (Australia) and Terrance J. Bogyo

TransAct Insurance Corporation (TIC) provides automobile insurance in parts of Canada that allow private insurers. Last year, a new CEO was hired by TIC's board of directors to improve the company's competitiveness and customer service. After spending several months assessing the situation, the new CEO introduced a strategic plan to improve TIC's competitive position. He also replaced three vice-presidents. Jim Leon was hired as vice-president of Claims, TIC's largest division with 1,500 employees, 50 claims centre managers, and 5 regional directors.

Jim immediately met with all claims managers and directors, and visited employees at TIC's 50 claims centres. As an outsider, this was a formidable task, but his strong interpersonal skills and uncanny ability to remember names and ideas helped him through the process. Through these visits and discussions, Jim discovered that the claims division had been managed in a relatively authoritarian, top-down manner. He could also see that morale was very low and employee–management relations were guarded. High workloads and isolation (adjusters working in tiny cubicles) were two other common complaints. Several managers acknowledged that the high turnover among claims adjusters was partly due to these conditions.

Following discussions with TIC's CEO, Jim decided to make morale and supervisory leadership his top priority. He initiated a divisional newsletter with a tear-off feedback form for employees to register their comments. He announced an open-door policy in which any Claims Division employee could speak to him directly and confidentially without going first to the immediate supervisor. Jim also fought organizational barriers to initiate a flextime program so that employees could design work schedules around their needs. This program later became a model for other areas of TIC.

One of Jim's most pronounced symbols of change was the "Claims Management Credo" outlining the philosophy that every claims manager would follow. At his first meeting with the complete claims management team, Jim presented a list of what he thought were important philosophies and actions of effective managers. The management group was asked to select and prioritize items from this list. They were told that the resulting list would be the division's management philosophy and all managers would be held accountable for abiding by its principles. Most claims managers were uneasy about this process, but they also understood that the organization was under competitive pressure and that Jim was using this exercise to demonstrate his leadership.

The claims managers developed a list of 10 items, such as encouraging teamwork, fostering a trusting work environment, setting clear and reasonable goals, and so on. The list was circulated to senior management in the organization for their comment and approval, and sent back to all claims managers for their endorsement. Once this was done, a copy of the final document was sent to every claims division employee. Jim also announced plans to follow up with an annual survey to evaluate each claims manager's performance. This concerned the managers, but most of them believed that the credo exercise was a result of Jim's initial enthusiasm and that he would be too busy to introduce a survey after settling into the job.

One year after the credo had been distributed, Jim announced that the first annual survey would be conducted. All claims employees would complete the survey and return it confidentially to the human resources department where the survey results would be compiled for each claims centre manager. The survey asked the extent to which the manager had lived up to each of the 10 items in the credo. Each form also provided space for comments.

Claims centre managers were surprised that a survey would be conducted, but they were even more worried about Jim's statement that the results would be shared with employees. What "results" would employees see? Who would distribute these results? What happens if a manager gets poor ratings from their subordinates? "We'll work out the details later," said Jim in response to these questions. "Even if the survey results aren't great, the information will give us a good baseline for next year's survey."

The claims division survey had a high response rate. In some centres, every employee completed and returned a form. Each report showed the claim centre manager's average score for each of the 10 items as well as how many employees rated the manager at each level of the five-point scale. The reports also included every comment made by employees at that centre.

No one was prepared for the results of the first survey. Most managers received moderate or poor ratings on the 10 items. Very few managers averaged above 3.0 (on a 5-point scale) on more than a couple of items. This suggested that, at best, employees were ambivalent about whether their claims centre manager had abided by the 10 management philosophy items. The comments were even more devastating than the ratings. Comments ranged from mildly disappointed to

extremely critical of their claims manager. Employees also described their long-standing frustration with TIC, high workloads, and isolated working conditions. Several people bluntly stated that they were skeptical about the changes that Jim had promised. "We've heard the promises before, but now we've lost faith," wrote one claims adjuster.

The survey results were sent to each claims manager, the regional director, and employees at the claims centre. Jim instructed managers to discuss the survey data and comments with their regional manager and directly with employees. The claims centre managers were shocked to learn that the reports included individual comments. They had assumed the reports would exclude comments and only show averaged scores for all employees at the centre. Some managers went to their regional director, complaining that revealing the personal comments would ruin their careers. Many directors sympathized, but the results were already available to employees.

When Jim heard about these concerns, he agreed that the results were lower than expected and that the comments should not have been shown to employees. After discussing the situation with his directors, he decided that the discussion meetings between claims managers and their employees should proceed as planned. To delay or withdraw the reports would undermine the credibility and trust that Jim was trying to develop with employees. However, the regional director attended the meeting in each claims centre to minimize direct conflict between the claims centre manager and employees.

Although many of these meetings went smoothly, a few created harsh feelings between managers and their employees. Sources of some comments were easily identified by their content, and this created a few delicate moments in several sessions. A few months after these meetings, two claims centre managers quit and three others asked for transfers back to nonmanagement positions in TIC. Meanwhile, Jim wondered how to manage this process more effectively, particularly since employees expected another survey the following year.

Discussion Questions

1. What symptom(s) exist in this case to suggest that something has gone wrong?

2. What are the main causes of these symptoms?

3. What actions should the company take to correct these problems?

Team Exercise:
STRATEGIC CHANGE INCIDENTS

Purpose This exercise is designed to help you identify strategies for facilitating organizational change in various situations.

Instructions

1. The instructor will place students into teams, and each team will be assigned one or both of the scenarios presented below.

2. Each team will diagnose the scenario to determine the most appropriate set of change management practices. Where appropriate, these practices should (a) create an urgency to change, (b) minimize resistance to change, and (c) refreeze the situation to support the change initiative. Each of these scenarios is based on real events.

3. Each team will present and defend its change management strategy. Class discussion regarding the appropriateness and feasibility of each strategy will occur after all teams assigned the same scenario have presented. The instructor will then describe what the organizations actually did in these situations.

Scenario 1: Greener Telco The chief executive officer of a large telephone company wants its executives to make the organization more environmentally friendly by encouraging employees to reduce waste in the workplace. Government and other stakeholders expect the company to take this action and be publicly successful. Consequently, the CEO wants to significantly reduce paper usage, garbage, and other waste throughout the company's many widespread offices. Unfortunately, a survey indicates that employees do not value environmental objectives and do not know how to "reduce, reuse, recycle." As the executive responsible for this change, you have been asked to develop a strategy that might bring about meaningful behavioural change toward this environmental goal. What would you do?

Scenario 2: Go Forward Airline A major airline had experienced a decade of rough turbulence, including two bouts of bankruptcy protection, 10 managing directors, and morale so low that employees had removed the company's logo from their uniforms because they were embarrassed to let others know where they worked. Service was terrible, and the airplanes rarely arrived or left the terminal on time. This was costing the airline significant amounts of money in passenger layovers. Managers were paralyzed by anxiety; most didn't know how to set strategic goals that actually succeeded. One-fifth of all flights were losing money, and the company overall was near financial collapse (just three months from defaulting on payroll obligations). You and the recently hired CEO must get employees to quickly improve operational efficiency and customer service. What actions would you take to bring about these changes?

Self-Assessments for Chapter 15

SELF-ASSESSMENT NAME	DESCRIPTION
Are you ready for change?	People seldom accept change quickly or easily. They have good reasons for opposing change or don't understand the urgency for change, particularly where it requires them to alter their own behaviour. This self-assessment identifies conditions that are holding back your readiness for a specific change initiative.
Are you tolerant of change?	Some people eagerly seek out novelty and new experiences. Others are keen to maintain the status quo and predictability. No matter how much communication, involvement, and other change management strategies are applied, people in the latter category continue to resist because they have little tolerance of change. This self-assessment estimates your natural tendency to tolerate change.

Additional Cases

Case 1   ARCTIC MINING CONSULTANTS

by Steven L. McShane, University of Newcastle (Australia) and Tim Neale

Tom Parker enjoys working outdoors. At various times in the past, he has worked as a ranch hand, high steel rigger, headstone installer, prospector, and geological field technician. Now 43, Parker is a geological field technician and field coordinator with Arctic Mining Consultants. He has specialized knowledge and experience in all nontechnical aspects of mineral exploration, including claim staking, line cutting and grid installation, soil sampling, prospecting, and trenching. He is responsible for hiring, training, and supervising field assistants for all of Arctic Mining Consultants' programs. Field assistants are paid a fairly low daily wage (no matter how long they work, which may be up to 12 hours) and are provided meals and accommodation. Many of the programs are operated by a project manager who reports to Parker.

Parker sometimes acts as a project manager, as he did on a job that involved staking 15 claims near Eagle Lake, British Columbia. He selected John Talbot, Greg Boyce, and Brian Millar, all of whom had previously worked with Parker, as the field assistants. To stake a claim, the project team marks a line with flagging tape and blazes (ribbons, paint, or other trail markers) along the perimeter of the claim, cutting a claim post every 500 metres (called a "length"). The 15 claims would require almost 100 kilometres of line in total. Parker had budgeted seven days (plus mobilization and demobilization) to complete the job. This meant that each of the four stakers (Parker, Talbot, Boyce, and Millar) would have to complete more than seven lengths each day. The following is a chronology of the project.

DAY 1

The Arctic Mining Consultants' crew assembled in the morning and drove to Eagle Lake, from where they were flown by helicopter to the claim site. On arrival, they set up tents at the edge of the area to be staked, and agreed on a schedule for cooking duties. After supper, they pulled out the maps and discussed the job—how long it would take, the order in which the areas were to be staked, possible helicopter landing spots, and areas that might be more difficult to stake.

Parker pointed out that with only a week to complete the job, everyone would have to average seven and a half lengths per day. "I know that is a lot," he said, "but you've all staked claims before and I'm confident that each of you is capable of it. And it's only for a week. If we get the job done in time, there's a $300 bonus for each of you." Two hours later, Parker and his crew members had developed what seemed to be a workable plan.

DAY 2

Millar completed six lengths, Boyce six lengths, Talbot eight, and Parker eight. Parker was not pleased with Millar's or Boyce's production. However, he didn't make an issue of it, thinking that they would develop their "rhythm" quickly.

DAY 3

Millar completed five and a half lengths, Boyce four, and Talbot seven. Parker, who was nearly twice as old as the other three, completed eight lengths. He also had enough time remaining to walk over and check the quality of stakes that Millar and Boyce had completed, and then walk back to his own area for helicopter pickup back to the tent site.

That night Parker exploded with anger. "I thought I told you that I wanted seven and a half lengths a day!" he shouted at Boyce and Millar. Boyce said that he was slowed down by unusually thick underbrush in his assigned area. Millar said that he had done his best and would try to pick up the pace. Parker did not mention that he had inspected their work. He explained that as far as he was concerned, the field assistants were supposed to finish their assigned area for the day, no matter what.

Talbot, who was sharing a tent with Parker, talked to him later. "I think that you're being a bit hard on them, you know. I know that it has been more by luck than anything else that I've been able to do my quota. Yesterday I only had five lengths done after the first seven hours and there was only an hour before I was supposed to be picked up. Then I hit a patch of really open bush, and was able to do three lengths in 70 minutes. Why don't I take Millar's area tomorrow and he can have mine? Maybe that will help."

"Conditions are the same in all of the areas," replied Parker, rejecting Talbot's suggestion. "Millar just has to try harder."

DAY 4

Millar did seven lengths and Boyce completed six and a half. When they reported their production that evening, Parker grunted uncommunicatively. Parker and Talbot did eight lengths each.

DAY 5

Millar completed six lengths, Boyce six, Talbot seven and a half, and Parker eight. Once again Parker blew up, but he concentrated his diatribe on Millar. "Why don't you do what you say you are going to do? You know that you have to do seven and a half lengths a day. We went over that when we first got here, so why don't you do it? If you aren't willing to do the job then you never should have taken it in the first place!"

Millar replied by saying that he was doing his best, that he hadn't even stopped for lunch, and that he didn't know how he could possibly do any better. Parker launched into him again: "You have got to work harder! If you put enough effort into it, you will get the area done!"

Later Millar commented to Boyce, "I hate getting dumped on all the time! I'd quit if it didn't mean that I'd have to walk 80 kilometres to the highway. And besides, I need the bonus money. Why doesn't he pick on you? You don't get any more done than me; in fact, you usually get less. Maybe if you did a bit more he wouldn't be so bothered about me."

"I only work as hard as I have to," Boyce replied.

DAY 6

Millar raced through breakfast, was the first one to be dropped off by the helicopter, and arranged to be the last one picked up. That evening the production figures were as follows: Millar eight and a quarter lengths, Boyce seven, and Talbot and Parker eight each. Parker remained silent when the field assistants reported their performance for the day.

DAY 7

Millar was again the first out and last in. That night, he collapsed in an exhausted heap at the table, too tired to eat. After a few moments, he announced in an abject tone, "Six lengths. I worked like a dog all day and I only got a lousy six lengths!" Boyce completed five lengths, Talbot seven, and Parker seven and a quarter.

Parker was furious. "That means we have to do a total of 34 lengths tomorrow if we are to finish this job on time!" With his eyes directed at Millar, he added: "Why is it that you never finish the job? Don't you realize that you are part of a team, and that you are letting the rest of the team down? I've been checking your lines and you're doing too much blazing and wasting too much time making picture-perfect claim posts! If you worked smarter, you'd get a lot more done!"

DAY 8

Parker cooked breakfast in the dark. The helicopter dropoffs began as soon as morning light appeared on the horizon. Parker instructed each assistant to complete eight lengths and, if they finished early, to help the others. Parker said that he would finish the other 10 lengths. Helicopter pickups were arranged for one hour before dark.

By noon, after working as hard as he could, Millar had only completed three lengths. "Why bother," he thought to himself, "I'll never be able to do another five lengths before the helicopter comes, and I'll catch the same amount of abuse from Parker for doing six lengths as for seven and a half." So he sat down and had lunch and a rest. "Boyce won't finish his eight lengths either, so even if I did finish mine, I still wouldn't get the bonus. At least I'll get one more day's pay this way."

That night, Parker was livid when Millar reported that he had completed five and a half lengths. Parker had done ten and a quarter lengths, and Talbot had completed eight. Boyce proudly announced that he finished seven and a half lengths, but sheepishly added that Talbot had helped him with some of it. All that remained were the two and a half lengths that Millar had not completed.

The job was finished the next morning and the crew demobilized. Millar has never worked for Arctic Mining Consultants again, despite being offered work several times by Parker. Boyce sometimes does staking for Arctic, and Talbot works full-time with the company.

Case 2   BRIDGING THE TWO WORLDS: THE ORGANIZATIONAL DILEMMA

by William Todorovic, Indiana-Purdue University, Fort Wayne

I had been hired by Aluminum Elements Corp. (AEC), and it was my first day of work. I was 26 years old, and I was now the manager of AEC's customer service group, which looked after customers, logistics, and some of the raw material purchasing. My superior, George, was the vice-president of the company. AEC manufactured most of its products from aluminum, a majority of which were destined for the construction industry.

As I walked around the shop floor, the employees appeared to be concentrating on their jobs, barely noticing me. Management held daily meetings, in which various production issues were discussed. No one from the shop floor was invited to the meeting unless there was a specific problem. Later I also learned that management had separate washrooms, separate lunchrooms, as well as other perks that floor employees did not have. Most of the floor employees felt that management, although polite on the surface, did not really feel they had anything to learn from the floor employees.

John, who worked on the aluminum slitter, a crucial operation required before any other operations could commence, had previously had a number of unpleasant encounters with George. As a result, George usually sent written memos to the floor in order to avoid a direct confrontation with John. Because the directions in the memos were complex, these memos were often more than two pages in length.

One morning, as I was walking around, I noticed that John was very upset. Feeling that perhaps there was something I could do, I approached John and asked him if I could help. He indicated that everything was just fine. From the looks of the situation, and John's body language, I felt that he was willing to talk, but John knew that this was not the way things were done at AEC. Tony, who worked at the machine next to John's, then cursed and said that George was getting on John's back again. John complained that the office guys only cared about schedules, not about the people down on the floor. I just looked at him and then said that I had only begun working at AEC last week, and thought that I could address some of their issues. Tony gave me a strange look, shook his head, and went back to his machine. I could hear him still swearing as I left. Later I realized that most of the office staff were offended by Tony's language.

On the way back to my office, Lesley, a recently hired engineer from Russia, approached me and pointed out that the employees were not accustomed to management talking to them. Management only issued orders and made demands. As we discussed the different perceptions between office and floor staff, we were interrupted by a very loud lunch bell, which startled me. I was happy to join Lesley for lunch, but she asked me why I was not eating in the office lunch room. I replied that if I was going to understand how AEC worked, I had to get to know all the people better. In addition, I realized that this was not how things were done, and wondered about the nature of this apparent division between the management and the floor. In the lunchroom, the other workers were amazed to see me there, commenting that I was just new and had not learned the ropes yet.

After lunch, when I asked George, my supervisor, about his recent confrontation with John, George was surprised that John got upset, and exclaimed, "I just wanted John to know that he did a great job, and as a result, we will be able to ship on time one large order to the West Coast. In fact, I thought I was complimenting him."

Earlier, Lesley had indicated that certain behaviour was expected from management, and therefore from me. I reasoned that I do not think that this behaviour works, and, besides, it is not what I believe or how I care to behave. For the next couple of months, I simply walked around the floor and took every opportunity to talk to the shop floor employees. Often, when the employees related specific information about their workplaces, I felt that it went over my head. Frequently, I had to write down the information and revisit it later. I made a point of listening to them, identifying where they were coming from, and trying to understand them. I needed to keep my mind open to new ideas. Because the shop employees expected me to make requests and demands, I made a point of not doing any of that. Soon enough, the employees became friendly, and started to accept me as one of their own, or at least as a different type of a management person.

During my third month of work, the employees showed me how to improve the scheduling of jobs, especially those on the aluminum slitter. In fact, the greatest contribution was made by John who demonstrated better ways to combine the most common slitting sizes, and reduce waste by retaining some of the "common-sized" material for new orders. Seeing the opportunity, I programmed a spreadsheet to calculate and track inventory. This, in addition to better planning and forecasting, allowed us to reduce our new order turnarounds from four to five weeks to in-by-10 a.m. out-by-5 p.m. on the same day.

By the time I had been employed for four months, I realized that members from other departments were coming to me and asking me to relay messages to the shop employees. When I asked why they were delegating this task to me, they stated that I spoke the same language as the shop employees. Increasingly, I became the messenger for the office-to-floor shop communication.

One morning, George called me into his office and complimented me on the levels of customer service and the improvements that have been achieved. As we talked, I mentioned that we could not have done it without John's help. "He really knows his stuff, and he is good," I said. I suggested that we consider him for some type of a promotion. Also, I hoped that this would be a positive gesture that would improve the communication between the office and shop floor.

George turned and pulled a flyer out of his desk; "Here is a management skills seminar. Do you think we should send John to it?"

"That is a great idea," I exclaimed, "Perhaps it would be good if he were to receive the news from you directly, George." George agreed, and after discussing some other issues, we parted company.

That afternoon, John came into my office, upset and ready to quit. "After all my effort and work, you guys are sending me for training seminars. So, am I not good enough for you?"

Case 3 KEEPING SUZANNE CHALMERS

by Steven L. McShane, University of Newcastle (Australia)

Thomas Chan hung up the telephone and sighed. The vice-president of software engineering at Advanced Photonics Inc. (API) had just spoken to Suzanne Chalmers, who had called to arrange a meeting with Chan later that day. She didn't say what the meeting was about, but Chan almost instinctively knew that Suzanne was going to quit after working at API for the past four years. Chalmers is a software engineer in Internet Protocol (IP), the software that directs fibre-optic light through API's routers. It is very specialized work, and Suzanne is one of API's top talents in that area.

Thomas Chan had been through this before. A valued employee would arrange a private meeting. The meeting would begin with a few pleasantries, then the employee would announce that they wanted to quit. Some employees said they were leaving because of the long hours and stressful deadlines. They said they needed to decompress, get to know their kids again, or whatever. But that wasn't usually the real reason. Almost every organization in this industry was scrambling to keep up with technological advances and the competition. Employees would just leave one stressful job for another one.

Also, many of the people who left API joined a startup company a few months later. These startup firms can be pressure cookers where everyone works 16 hours each day and has to perform a variety of tasks. For example, engineers in these small firms might have to meet customers or work on venture capital proposals rather than focus on specialized tasks related to their knowledge. API now has over 6,000 employees, so it is easier to assign people to work that matches their technical competencies.

No, the problem isn't the stress or long hours, Chan thought. The problem is money—too much money. Most of the people who leave are millionaires. Suzanne Chalmers is one of them. Thanks to generous share options that have sky-rocketed on the stock markets, many employees at API have more money than they can use. Most are under 40 years old,

so it's too early for them to retire. But their financial independence gives them less reason to remain with API.

THE MEETING

The meeting with Suzanne Chalmers took place a few hours after the telephone call. It began like the others, with the initial pleasantries and brief discussion about progress on the latest fibre-optic router project. Then, Suzanne made her well-rehearsed statement: "Thomas, I've really enjoyed working here, but I'm going to leave Advanced Photonics." Suzanne took a breath, then looked at Chan. When he didn't reply after a few seconds, she continued: "I need to take time off. You know, get away to recharge my batteries. The project's nearly done and the team can complete it without me. Well, anyway, I'm thinking of leaving."

Chan spoke in a calm voice. He suggested that Suzanne should take an unpaid leave for two or maybe three months, complete with paid benefits, then return refreshed. Suzanne politely rejected that offer, saying that she needed to get away from work for a while. Thomas then asked Suzanne whether she was unhappy with her work environment—whether she was getting the latest computer technology to do her work and whether there were problems with co-workers. The workplace was fine, Suzanne replied. The job was getting a bit routine, but she had a comfortable workplace with excellent co-workers.

Chan then apologized for the cramped workspace, due mainly to the rapid increase in the number of people hired over the past year. He suggested that if Suzanne took a couple of months off, API would give her special treatment with a larger workspace with a better view of the park behind the campus-like building when she returned. She politely thanked Chan for that offer, but it wasn't what she needed. Besides, it wouldn't be fair to have a large workspace when other team members would be working in smaller quarters.

Chan was running out of tactics, so he tried his last hope: money. He asked whether Suzanne had had higher offers.

Suzanne replied that she regularly received calls from other companies, and some of them offered more money. Most were startup firms that offered a lower salary but higher potential gains in share options. Chan knew from market surveys that Suzanne was already paid well in the industry. He also knew that API couldn't compete on share option potential. Employees working in startup firms sometimes saw their shares increase by five or ten times their initial value, whereas shares at API and other large firms increased more slowly. However, Chan promised Suzanne that he would recommend that she receive a significant raise—maybe 25 percent more—and more share options. Chan added that Chalmers was one of API's most valuable employees and that the company would suffer if she left the firm.

The meeting ended with Chalmers promising to consider Chan's offer of higher pay and share options. Two days later, Chan received her resignation in writing. Five months later, Chan learned that after a few months travelling with her husband, Chalmers joined a startup software firm in the area.

Case 4   NORTHWEST CANADIAN FOREST PRODUCTS LIMITED (REVISED)

by Peter Seidl, British Columbia Institute of Technology

Northwest Canadian Forest Products Ltd. owns and operates five sawmills in British Columbia and Alberta. These mills produce high-quality lumber for use in the manufacture of window frames, doors, and mouldings for markets in the United States and Japan, in addition to lower-quality, commodity-type lumber used in the Canadian construction industry. (The firm's export markets tend to be more demanding and quality-conscious than its domestic markets, but are also more lucrative.) Currently, the president of the company is thinking about the long-term prospects of each of the mills and is paying particular attention to the Jackson Sawmill located in the small town of Jackson, B.C.

This mill was originally built 60 years ago and was last upgraded 20 years ago. The president, June Batna, knows she will soon (in two to three years) have to decide whether or not to invest very substantial sums of money in a new plant and equipment at the Jackson Sawmill. New investment is required in order to keep the mill up-to-date and competitive with similar mills throughout North America. However, the mill has consistently been the poorest performer (in terms of productivity and product quality) in the company over the past 20 years, even though its equipment is of similar age, type, and quality as that found in the other mills.

The president would like to invest the money needed because the alternative to re-investing in Jackson would be to downsize the Jackson Sawmill by reducing production capacity and permanently laying off about half the 200-person workforce. The remaining part of the mill would serve the domestic market only. A new mill would then be built in Alberta in order to serve the more demanding, quality-conscious export markets. A new mill in Alberta would cost somewhat more than the anticipated investment required to modernize the Jackson Sawmill. However, Ms. Batna is willing to seriously consider implementing this alternative because she thinks that the labour relations climate in Alberta is much better than the one found at Jackson.

In fact, she attributes most, if not all, of the problems at Jackson to its poor labour–management relations. During the last round of collective bargaining, there was a strike at all four of the company's B.C. mills. The strike was, however, much more bitter at Jackson than elsewhere. Company buildings suffered minor damage during the strike at the hands of some striking employees. Since then, there have been two separate occasions when the entire workforce walked off the job for a day to protest the firings of two employees who were dismissed for insubordination.

The Jackson Sawmill has the worst safety record of all the company's mills. There is a joint labour–management health and safety committee (as required by law) but it is viewed as a waste of time by both sides. One management member of the safety committee, Des, the production manager and the second highest manager at the mill, has said: "The union guys start each safety committee meeting by complaining about safety but they just can't wait to complain about everything else they can possibly think of. Their whining and complaining is so predictable that I go to every safety meeting ready for a fight on workload and production issues as well as for a fight on safety. Of course, safety is everyone's responsibility but production issues are none of their business. Production is a management responsibility. Plans, budgets, and other management concerns are very definitely not part of the committee's job. Most of what's said at these meetings isn't worth listening to."

The union is also dissatisfied with the functioning of the safety committee. Ivan, the chief union steward who also serves on the committee, observes: "If the safety committee wasn't mandatory by law, management wouldn't even pretend to listen to us. We put forward our safety concerns but management says that we are mixing safety in with workload and production issues. They only want to talk about what they think are safety issues—like serious accidents. Thankfully, we don't have too many of those! But safety is more than just avoiding major accidents. We get far too many 'little accidents' and 'near accidents' here. At least that's what management calls them. They just want us to work faster and faster. We complain and complain at the meetings but they just say 'that's a production issue and this is a safety committee.' They accuse us of trying to run the company when we ask for better equipment. They say we don't understand things like costs and limited budgets. We don't care about their budgets, we've got work issues to talk about and we'll keep speaking out for the crew no matter what. That's what the union is for."

Big Bad John, one of the mill's toughest and most experienced supervisors, describes his job as follows: "The job of supervisor is to keep a close watch on every move the crew makes. If I look away for a second, some guy is going to be doing something wrong—either with the equipment or with the logs. They're always making mistakes. Lots of mistakes! Some of these guys are just plain dumb. And lazy, too! Any chance they can get to steal some company time, they take. They start work late; they take long lunch breaks; they talk too much during their shifts. A minute here, a minute there—it all adds up. The younger guys are the worst. They always want to talk back to me, they can't follow my orders like most of the older guys can. Lousy attitude, that's what they've got."

Des, the production manager, has stated that "the mill has had a problem with worker motivation and attitude for as long as I can remember. But it's slowly getting worse as younger guys are being hired to replace the older, retiring guys. The new workers are better educated than the older ones and because of that they think they can treat their supervisors with disrespect. Don't get me wrong, we get the job done here but it takes a lot of effort on the part of the managers and, especially, the supervisors. The supervisors really earn their pay here. They watch the crew closely and have to put up with a lot of crap from them. Many of the grievances we have are a result of the discipline we have to hand out regarding horseplay, absenteeism, tardiness, careless workmanship, and not reaching production quotas. However, overall, the mill gets the product out the door, but only because we ensure that the crew works hard. Despite grumblings from the crew, we maintain a pretty good pace of work around here."

Vic, the youngest union steward, gives his view of labour–management relations: "The supervisors and the managers, they know it all. They think they're so smart. They treat the guys on the crew like children. Almost everyone on the crew has a high school education. Some even have college backgrounds. Most are raising families. We're not stupid! Sure, some guys come in late and miss a day of work now and then. Who can blame them? The pace of work is exhausting. How can you do a good job when you're tired and rushing all the time?" He adds: "Of course, we're not perfect. We make mistakes just like everyone else does. But nobody ever explains anything to the crew members. The supervisors just watch everyone like hawks and jump all over them, criticize them, and make them feel stupid when they use a piece of equipment the wrong way. We're always so rushed and busy here that the senior crew members don't have much time to explain things to the newer workers, the younger guys. The equipment could be in better shape. That would help."

Des, the production manager, has expressed his views on labour–management relations: "The union just doesn't understand—or even care about—the connection between the poor work ethic, the poor attitude on the part of the crew members here, and the mill's mediocre productivity and product quality. The union and the crew only take their very narrow 'employee view' of how things are done around here. They don't understand the bigger picture. Well, it's very competitive out there. They don't understand what tight budgets, increasing costs, declining quality, missed production targets, and complaining customers mean to a business. They just sit back and complain about our management style. What they don't realize is that their attitude makes our management style necessary. Complaining is easy, no responsibility is needed. Managing, on the other hand, is challenging. And it's especially tough to control this particular crew. We've currently got 40 unresolved grievances—that's a lot of formal complaints for a mill of our size. Some of the union stewards actually go out among the crew and look for grievances just because they're mad they can't run the mill the way they want to. Sometimes I think the stewards want to create grievances where no real problems exist. They want to give us in management headaches."

Vic, a union steward, went on to say: "We've currently got 40 unresolved grievances at different stages of the grievance procedure—I don't have to tell you that's quite a lot for a mill of our size. Some crew members are really mad at management and file a lot of grievances. The grievances are mostly about challenging the discipline management hands out regarding horseplay, absenteeism, tardiness, careless workmanship, and not reaching production quotas. We—the shop stewards—try to calm them down but some guys are really angry about how they're treated. The stewards spend a lot of time trying to settle things outside the formal grievance process, but some of the crew really want the stewards to file grievances and some supervisors don't want to solve things informally. Things are pretty formal around here. It's all such a waste of time and energy. The pay is good but I wouldn't recommend this as a place to work to anyone unless they like being treated like a misbehaving child."

The president of the company has recently informed Digby, the mill's new general manager (he started last month), of the decision she will soon have to make regarding the mill's future. She told Digby that significant improvements in mill productivity and product quality are required if the mill is to receive a substantial investment in new plant and equipment. Without such improvements, the mill would be downsized and about half of the workforce would be permanently laid off. Half the supervisory and managerial personnel would also lose their jobs.

Digby has just telephoned Moe (the president of the local union who does not work at the mill but who is very familiar with developments at the mill) to tell him about the message from the company president. Upon hearing of the potential job losses, Moe was troubled and asked to meet with Digby to discuss the situation. However, Moe was also somewhat skeptical because the previous general manager once told him that some permanent layoffs would occur unless productivity was improved. No layoffs subsequently occurred. Therefore, Moe is uncertain if the company is serious about these potential future layoffs or merely bluffing in order to get the employees to work harder.

Case 5 SIMMONS LABORATORIES

adapted by William Starbuck from a case written by Alex Bavelas

Brandon Newbridge was sitting alone in the conference room of the laboratory. The rest of the group had gone. One of the support staff members had stopped and talked for a while about her husband's coming enrolment in graduate school. Brandon, now alone in the laboratory, slid a little further down in his chair, looking with satisfaction at the results of the first test run of the new photon unit.

He liked to stay after the others had gone. His appointment as project head was still new enough to give him a deep sense of pleasure. His eyes were on the graphs before him, but in his mind, he could hear Dr. William Goh, the project head, saying again, "There's one thing about this place you can bank on. The sky is the limit for anyone who can produce!" Newbridge felt again the tingle of happiness and embarrassment. Well, dammit, he said to himself, he had produced. He wasn't kidding anybody. He had come to the Simmons Laboratories two years ago. During a routine testing of some rejected Clanson components, he had stumbled on the idea of the photon correlator, and the rest just happened. Goh had been enthusiastic: A separate project had been set up for further research and development of the device, and he had been given the job of running it. The whole sequence of events still seemed a little miraculous to Newbridge.

He shrugged out of the reverie and was bent determinedly over the sheets when he heard someone come into the room behind him. He looked up expectantly; Goh often stayed late himself and now and then dropped in for a chat. This always made the day's end especially pleasant for Brandon. But it wasn't Goh. The man who had come in was a stranger. He was tall and thin. He wore steel-rimmed glasses and had a very wide leather belt with a large brass buckle. Lucy, a member of Brandon's team, remarked later that it was the kind of belt the Pilgrims must have worn.

The stranger smiled and introduced himself. "I'm Lester Zapf. Are you Brandon Newbridge?" Brandon said yes, and they shook hands. "Doctor Goh said I might find you in. We were talking about your work, and I'm very much interested in what you are doing." Brandon waved to a chair.

Zapf didn't seem to belong in any of the standard categories of visitors: customer, visiting firefighter, shareholder. Brandon pointed to the sheets on the table. "These are the preliminary results of a test we're running. We have a new gadget by the tail and we're trying to understand it. It's not finished, but I can show you the section we're testing."

He stood up, but Zapf was deep in the graphs. After a moment, he looked up with an odd grin. "These look like plots of a Jennings surface. I've been playing around with some autocorrelation functions of surfaces—you know that stuff." Brandon, who had no idea what he was referring to, grinned back and nodded, and immediately felt uncomfortable. "Let me show you the monster," he said, and led the way to the workroom.

After Zapf left, Newbridge slowly put the graphs away, feeling vaguely annoyed. Then, as if he had made a decision, he quickly locked up and took the long way out so that he would pass Goh's office. But the office was locked. Newbridge wondered whether Goh and Zapf had left together.

The next morning, Newbridge dropped into Goh's office, mentioned that he had talked with Zapf, and asked who he was.

"Sit down for a minute," Goh said. "I want to talk to you about him. What do you think of him?" Newbridge replied truthfully that he thought Zapf was very bright and probably very competent. Goh looked pleased.

"We're taking him on," he said. "He's had a very good background in a number of laboratories, and he seems to have ideas about the problems we're tackling here." Newbridge nodded in agreement, instantly wishing that Zapf would not be placed with him.

"I don't know yet where he will finally land," Goh continued, "but he seems interested in what you are doing. I thought he might spend a little time with you by way of getting started." Newbridge nodded thoughtfully. "If his interest in your work continues, you can add him to your group."

"Well, he seemed to have some good ideas even without knowing exactly what we are doing," Newbridge answered. "I hope he stays; we'd be glad to have him."

Newbridge walked back to the lab with mixed feelings. He told himself that Zapf would be good for the group. He was no dunce; he'd produce. Newbridge thought again of Goh's promise when he had promoted him: "The sky is the limit here for anyone who can produce!" The words seemed to carry the overtones of a threat now.

That day Zapf didn't appear until mid-afternoon. He explained that he had had a long lunch with Goh, discussing his place in the lab. "Yes," said Newbridge, "I talked with Dr. Goh this morning about it, and we both thought you might work with us for a while."

Zapf smiled in the same knowing way that he had smiled when he mentioned the Jennings surfaces. "I'd like to," he said.

Newbridge introduced Zapf to the other members of the lab. Zapf and Link, the group's mathematician, hit it off well and spent the rest of the afternoon discussing a method for analyzing patterns that Link had been worrying over the last month.

It was 6:30 when Newbridge finally left the lab that night. He had waited almost eagerly for the end of the day to come—when they would all be gone and he could sit in the quiet rooms, relax, and think it over. "Think what over?" he asked himself. He didn't know. Shortly after 5 p.m., they had almost all gone except Zapf, and what followed was almost a duel. Newbridge was annoyed that he was being cheated out of his quiet period and finally, resentfully, determined that Zapf should leave first.

Zapf was sitting at the conference table reading, and Newbridge was sitting at his desk in the little glass-enclosed cubby he used during the day when he needed to not be disturbed. Zapf had gotten the last year's progress reports out and was studying them carefully. The time dragged. Newbridge doodled on a pad, the tension growing inside him. What the hell did Zapf think he was going to find in the reports?

Newbridge finally gave up and they left the lab together. Zapf took several of the reports with him to study in the evening. Newbridge asked him if he thought the reports gave a clear picture of the lab's activities.

"They're excellent," Zapf answered with obvious sincerity. "They're not only good reports; what they report is damn good, too!" Newbridge was surprised at the relief he felt and grew almost jovial as he said good night.

Driving home, Newbridge felt more optimistic about Zapf's presence in the lab. He had never fully understood the analysis that Link was attempting. If there was anything wrong with Link's approach, Zapf would probably spot it. "And if I'm any judge," he murmured, "he won't be especially diplomatic about it."

He described Zapf to his wife, who was amused by the broad leather belt and brass buckle.

"It's the kind of belt that Pilgrims must have worn," she laughed.

"I'm not worried about how he holds his pants up," he laughed with her. "I'm afraid that he's the kind that just has to make like a genius twice each day. And that can be pretty rough on the group."

Newbridge had been asleep for several hours when he was jerked awake by the telephone. He realized it had rung several times. He swung off the bed, muttering about damn fools and telephones. It was Zapf. Without any excuses, apparently oblivious of the time, he plunged into an excited recital of how Link's patterning problem could be solved.

Newbridge covered the mouthpiece to answer his wife's stage-whispered "Who is it?"

"It's the genius," replied Newbridge.

Zapf, completely ignoring the fact that it was 2 a.m., went on in a very excited way to explain a completely new approach to certain of the photon lab problems that he had stumbled on while analyzing past experiments. Newbridge managed to put some enthusiasm in his own voice and stood there, half-dazed and very uncomfortable, listening to Zapf talk endlessly about what he had discovered. It was probably not only a new approach but also an analysis that showed the inherent weakness of the previous experiment and how experimentation along that line would certainly have been inconclusive. The following day, Newbridge spent the entire morning with Zapf and Link, the mathematician, the customary morning meeting of Brandon's group having been called off so that Zapf's work of the previous night could be gone over intensively. Zapf was very anxious that this be done, and Newbridge was not too unhappy to call the meeting off for reasons of his own.

For the next several days, Zapf sat in the back office that had been turned over to him and did nothing but read the progress reports of the work that had been done in the last six months. Newbridge caught himself feeling apprehensive about the reaction that Zapf might have to some of his work. He was a little surprised at his own feelings. He had always been proud—although he had put on a convincingly modest face—of the way in which new ground in the study of photon-measuring devices had been broken in his group. Now he wasn't sure, and it seemed to him that Zapf might easily show that the line of research they had been following was unsound or even unimaginative.

The next morning (as was the custom) the members of the lab, including the secretaries, sat around a conference table. Brandon always prided himself on the fact that the work of the lab was guided and evaluated by the group as a whole, and he was fond of repeating that it was not a waste of time to include secretaries in such meetings. Often, what started out as a boring recital of fundamental assumptions to a naive listener, uncovered new ways of regarding these assumptions that would not have occurred to the researcher who had long ago accepted them as a necessary basis for their work.

These group meetings also served Brandon in another sense. He admitted to himself that he would have felt far less secure if he had had to direct the work out of his own mind, so to speak. With the group meeting as the principle of leadership, it was always possible to justify the exploration of blind alleys because of the general educative effect on the team. Zapf was there; Lucy and Martha were there; Link was sitting next to Zapf, their conversation concerning Link's mathematical study apparently continuing from yesterday. The other members, Bob Davenport, Georgia Thurlow, and Arthur Oliver, were waiting quietly.

Newbridge, for reasons that he didn't quite understand, proposed for discussion this morning a problem that all of them had spent a great deal of time on previously with the conclusion that a solution was impossible, that there was no feasible way of treating it in an experimental fashion. When Newbridge proposed the problem, Davenport remarked that there was hardly any use going over it again, that he was satisfied that there was no way of approaching the problem with the equipment and the physical capacities of the lab.

This statement had the effect of a shot of adrenaline on Zapf. He said he would like to know what the problem was in detail and, walking to the blackboard, began setting down the "factors" as various members of the group began discussing the problem and simultaneously listing the reasons why it had been abandoned.

Very early in the description of the problem it was evident that Zapf was going to disagree about the impossibility of attacking it. The group realized this, and finally the descriptive materials and their recounting of the reasoning that had led to its abandonment dwindled away. Zapf began his statement, which, as it proceeded, sounded as if it might well have been prepared the previous night, although Newbridge knew this was impossible. He couldn't help being impressed with the organized and logical way that Zapf was presenting ideas that must have occurred to him only a few minutes before.

Zapf had some things to say, however, which left Newbridge with a mixture of annoyance, irritation, and at the same time, a rather smug feeling of superiority over Zapf in at least one area. Zapf held the opinion that the way that the problem had been analyzed was very typical of group thinking. With an air of sophistication that made it difficult for a listener to dissent, he proceeded to comment on the American emphasis on team ideas, satirically describing the ways in which they led to a "high level of mediocrity."

During this time, Newbridge observed that Link stared studiously at the floor, and he was very conscious of Georgia Thurlow and Bob Davenport's glances toward him at several points of Zapf's little speech. Inwardly, Newbridge couldn't help feeling that this was one point at least in which Zapf was off on the wrong foot. The whole lab, following Goh's lead, talked if not practised the theory of small research teams as the basic organization for effective research. Zapf insisted that the problem could be approached and that he would like to study it for a while himself.

Newbridge ended the morning session by remarking that the meetings would continue and that the very fact that a supposedly insoluble experimental problem was now going to get another chance was an indication of the value of such meetings. Zapf immediately remarked that he was not at all averse to meetings to inform the group about the progress of its members. The point he wanted to make was that creative advances were seldom accomplished in such meetings, that they were made by an individual "living with" a problem closely and continuously, in a rather personal relationship to it.

Newbridge went on to say to Zapf that he was very glad that Zapf had raised these points and that he was sure the group would profit by re-examining the basis on which they had been operating. Newbridge agreed that individual effort was probably the basis for making major advances. He considered the group meetings useful primarily because they kept the group together and they helped the weaker members of the group keep up with the ones who were able to advance more easily and quickly in the analysis of problems.

It was clear as days went by and meetings continued that Zapf came to enjoy them because of the pattern that the meetings assumed. It became typical for Zapf to hold forth, and it was unquestionably clear that he was more brilliant, better prepared on the various subjects that were germane to the problem being studied, and more capable of going ahead than anyone there. Newbridge grew increasingly disturbed as he realized that his leadership of the group had been, in fact, taken over.

Whenever the subject of Zapf was mentioned in occasional meetings with Goh, Newbridge would comment only on the ability and obvious capacity for work that Zapf had. Somehow he never felt that he could mention his own discomforts, not only because they revealed a weakness on his part but also because it was quite clear that Goh himself was considerably impressed with Zapf's work and with the contacts he had outside the photon laboratory.

Newbridge now began to feel that perhaps the intellectual advantages that Zapf had brought to the group did not quite compensate for what he felt were evidences of a breakdown in the cooperative spirit he had seen in the group before Zapf's coming. More and more of the morning meetings were skipped. Zapf's opinion concerning the abilities of others of the group, except for Link, was obviously low. At times during morning meetings or in smaller discussions he had been on the point of rudeness, refusing to pursue an argument when he claimed it was based on another person's ignorance of the facts involved. His impatience with others led him to also make similar remarks to Goh. Newbridge inferred this from a conversation with Goh in which Goh asked whether Davenport and Oliver were going to be continued on; and his failure to mention Link, the mathematician, led Newbridge to feel that this was the result of private conversations between Zapf and Goh.

It was not difficult for Newbridge to make a quite convincing case about whether the brilliance of Zapf was sufficient recompense for initiating this unravelling of the group. He spoke privately with Davenport and Oliver, and it was quite clear that both of them were uncomfortable because of Zapf. Newbridge didn't press the discussion beyond the point of hearing them say that they did feel awkward, and that it was sometimes difficult to understand the arguments Zapf advanced, but often embarrassing to ask him to fill in the basis for his arguments. Newbridge did not interview Link in this manner.

About six months after Zapf's arrival in the photon lab, a meeting was scheduled in which the sponsors of the research would get some idea of the work and its progress. It was customary at these meetings for project heads to present the research being conducted in their groups. The members of each group were invited to other meetings that were held later in the day and open to all, but the special meetings were usually made up only of project heads, the head of the laboratory, and the sponsors.

As the time for the special meeting approached, it seemed to Newbridge that he must avoid the presentation at all costs. He could not trust himself to present the ideas and work that Zapf had advanced because of his apprehension about whether he could present them in sufficient detail and answer such questions about them as might be asked. On the other hand, he did not feel he could ignore these newer lines of work and present only the material that he had done or that had been started before Zapf's arrival. He felt also that it would not be beyond Zapf at all, in his blunt and undiplomatic way—if he were at the meeting, that is—to comment on Newbridge's presentation and reveal his inadequacy. It also seemed quite clear that it would not be easy to keep Zapf from attending the meeting, even though he was not on the administrative level of those invited.

Newbridge found an opportunity to speak to Goh and raised the question. He told Goh that, with the meetings coming up and with the interest in the work and Zapf's contributions to it, Zapf would probably like to come to the meetings; but there was a question of how the others in the group would feel if only Zapf were invited. Goh passed this over very lightly by saying that he didn't think the group would fail to understand Zapf's rather different position and that Zapf certainly should be invited. Newbridge immediately agreed: Zapf should present the work because much of it was work he had done, and this would be a nice way to recognize Zapf's contributions and to reward him, because he was eager to be recognized as a productive member of the lab. Goh agreed, and so the matter was decided.

Zapf's presentation was very successful and in some ways dominated the meeting. He attracted the interest and attention of many of those who had come, and a long discussion followed his presentation. Later in the evening—with the entire laboratory staff present—in the cocktail period before the dinner, a little circle of people formed about Zapf. One of them was Goh himself, and a lively discussion took place concerning the application of Zapf's theory. All of this disturbed Newbridge, and his reaction and behaviour were characteristic. He joined the circle, praised Zapf to Goh and to others, and remarked on the brilliance of the work.

Without consulting anyone, Newbridge began to consider what job opportunities existed elsewhere. After a few weeks he decided to apply for a position at a new laboratory of considerable size that was being organized in a nearby city. Citing Newbridge's training and experience, the new lab invited him for a lengthy interview and, soon after, offered him a project-leader job similar to his current position and with slightly higher salary.

Newbridge immediately accepted the offer and notified Goh by letter, which he mailed on a Friday night to Goh's home. The letter was quite brief, and Goh was stunned. The letter merely said that he had found a better position; that he didn't want to appear at the lab anymore for personal reasons; that he would be glad to come back at a later time to assist if there was any mix-up in the past work; that he felt sure Zapf could supply any leadership that the group required; and that his decision to leave so suddenly was based on personal problems—he hinted at problems of health in his family, specifically his mother and father. All of this was fictitious, of course. Goh took it at face value but still felt that this was very strange behaviour and quite unaccountable, for he had always felt his relationship with Newbridge had been warm and that Newbridge was satisfied and, in fact, quite happy and productive.

Goh was considerably disturbed, because he had already decided to place Zapf in charge of another project that was going to be set up very soon. He had been wondering how to explain this to Newbridge, in view of the obvious help Newbridge was getting from Zapf and the high regard in which he held him. Goh had, indeed, considered the possibility that Newbridge could add to his staff another person with the kind of background and training that had been unique in Zapf and had proved so valuable.

Goh did not make any attempt to meet Newbridge. In a way, he felt aggrieved about the whole thing. Zapf, too, was surprised at the suddenness of Newbridge's departure. When Goh asked Zapf whether he preferred to stay with the photon group instead of the new project for the Air Force, he chose the Air Force project and went on to that job the following week. The photon lab was hard hit. The leadership of the lab was given to Link with the understanding that this would be temporary until someone could come in to take over.

Case 6   TAMARACK INDUSTRIES
by David J. Cherrington, Brigham Young University

Tamarack Industries manufactures motorboats primarily used for water skiing. Students are hired during summer months to fill in for permanent employees on vacation. In past years, students worked alongside permanent employees, but a few staff complained that the students were inexperienced, slow, and arrogant. In general, permanent staff disliked the students' behaviour, such as listening to music with earphones while working. This summer, the company reorganized all permanent employees into three production teams (they usually have four teams, but 25 percent are on holiday at any given time) and assigned the 16 summer students to their own team on the fourth production line.

The supervisor, Dan Jensen, decided to try a different strategy this summer and have all the college students work on the new line. He asked Mark Allen to supervise the new crew because Mark claimed that he knew everything about boats and could perform every job "with my eyes closed." Mark was happy to accept the new job and participated in selecting the student hires. Mark's crew was called "the Geek Team" because all the college students were savvy with computers, unlike most of the permanent employees.

Mark spent many hours training his student team to get the line running at full production. The college students learned quickly, and by the end of June their production rate was up to standard, with an error rate that was only slightly above normal. To simplify the learning process, Dan Jensen assigned the Geek Team long production runs that generally consisted of 30 to 40 identical units. Thus the training period was shortened and errors were reduced. Shorter production runs were assigned to the experienced teams.

By the middle of July, a substantial rivalry had been created between the Geek Team and the older workers. At first, the rivalry was good-natured. But after a few weeks, the older workers became resentful of the remarks made

by the college students. The Geek Team often met its production schedules with time to spare at the end of the day for goofing around. It wasn't uncommon for someone from the Geek Team to go to another line pretending to look for materials just to make demeaning comments. The experienced workers resented having to perform all the shorter production runs and began to retaliate with sabotage. They would sneak over during breaks and hide tools, dent materials, install something crooked, and in other small ways do something that would slow production for the Geek Team.

Dan felt good about his decision to form a separate crew of college students, but when he heard reports of sabotage and rivalry, he became very concerned. Because of complaints from the experienced workers, Dan equalized the production so that all of the crews had similar production runs. The rivalry, however, did not stop. The Geek Team continued to finish early and flaunt their performance in front of the other crews.

One day the Geek Team suspected that one of their assemblies was going to be sabotaged during the lunch break by one of the experienced crews. By skilful deception, they were able to substitute an assembly from the other experienced line for theirs. By the end of the lunch period, the Geek Team was laughing wildly because of their deception, while one experienced crew was very angry with the other one.

Dan Jensen decided that the situation had to be changed and announced that the job assignments between the different crews would be shuffled. The employees were told that when they appeared for work the next morning, the names of the workers assigned to each crew would be posted on the bulletin board. The announcement was not greeted with much enthusiasm, and Mark Allen decided to talk Dan out of his idea. Mark suspected that many of the college students would quit if their team was broken up.

Case 7　THE OUTSTANDING FACULTY AWARD

by David J. Cherrington, Brigham Young University; revised by Steven L. McShane, University of Newcastle (Australia)

I recently served on the Outstanding Faculty Award committee for the College of Business. This award is our college's highest honour for a faculty member, and is bestowed at a special reception ceremony. At the first meeting, our committee discussed the nomination process and decided to follow our traditional practice of inviting nominations from both the faculty and students. During the next month, we received six completed files with supporting documentation. Three of the nominations came from department chairs, two from faculty who recommended their colleagues, and one from a group of 16 graduate students.

At the second meeting, we agreed that we didn't know the six applicants well enough to make a decision that day, so we decided that we would read the applications on our own and rank them. There was no discussion about ranking criteria; I think we assumed that we shared a common definition of the word "outstanding."

During the third meeting, it quickly became apparent that each committee member had a different interpretation of what constitutes an "outstanding" faculty member. The discussion was polite, but we debated the extent to which this was an award for teaching, or research, or service to the college, or scholarly textbook writing, or consulting, or service to society, or some other factor. After three hours, we agreed on five criteria that we would apply to independently rate each candidate using a five-point scale.

When we reconvened the next day, our discussion was much more focused as we tried to achieve a consensus regarding how we judged each candidate on each criterion. After a lengthy discussion, we finally completed the task and averaged the ratings. The top three scores had an average rating (out of a maximum of 25) of 21, 19.5, and 18.75. I assumed the person with the highest total would receive the award. Instead, my colleagues began debating over the relevance of the five criteria that we had agreed on the previous day. Some committee members felt, in hindsight, that the criteria were incorrectly weighted or that other criteria should be considered.

Although they did not actually say this, I sensed that at least two colleagues on the committee wanted the criteria or weights changed because their preferred candidate didn't get the highest score using the existing formula. When we changed the weights in various ways, a different candidate among the top three received the top score. The remaining three candidates received lower ratings every time. Dr. H always received the lowest score, usually around 12 on the 25-point range.

After almost two hours of discussion, the associate dean turned to one committee member and said, "Dolan, I sure would like to see Dr. H in your department receive this honour. He retires next year and this would be a great honour for him and no one has received this honour in your department recently."

Dolan agreed, "Yes, this is Dr. H's last year with us and it would be a great way for him to go out. I'm sure he would feel very honoured by this award."

I sat there, stunned at the suggestion, while Dolan retold how Dr. H had been active in public service, his only real strength on our criteria. I was even more stunned when another committee member, who I think was keen to finish the meeting, said, "Well, I so move" and Dolan seconded it.

The associate dean, who was conducting the meeting, said, "Well, if the rest of you think this is a good idea, all in favour say aye." A few members said "Aye," and, without calling for nays, the associate dean quickly proceeded to explain what we needed to do to advertise the winner and arrange the ceremony.

During my conversations with other committee members over the next two weeks, I learned that everyone—including the two who said "Aye"—were as shocked as I was at our committee's decision. I thought we had made a terrible decision, and I was embarrassed to be a member of the committee. A few weeks later, we were appropriately punished when Dr. H gave a 45-minute acceptance speech that started poorly and got worse.

Case 8　THE REGENCY GRAND HOTEL

by Elizabeth Ho, Gucci Group, under the supervision of Steven L. McShane, University of Newcastle (Australia)

The Regency Grand Hotel is a five-star hotel in Bangkok, Thailand. The hotel was established 15 years ago by a local consortium of investors and has been operated by a Thai general manager throughout this time. The hotel is one of Bangkok's most prestigious hotels and its 700 employees enjoy the prestige of being associated with the hotel. The hotel provides good employee benefits, above-market-rate salary, and job security. In addition, a good year-end bonus amounting to four months' salary is rewarded to employees regardless of the hotel's overall performance during the year.

Recently, the Regency was sold to a large American hotel chain that was very keen to expand its operations into Thailand. When the acquisition was announced, the general manager decided to take early retirement when the hotel changed ownership. The American hotel chain kept all of the Regency employees, although a few were transferred to other positions. John Becker, an American with 10 years of management experience with the hotel chain, was appointed as the new general manager of the Regency Grand Hotel. Becker was selected as the new general manager because of his previous successes in integrating newly acquired hotels in the United States. In most of the previous acquisitions, Becker took over operations with poor profitability and low morale.

Becker is a strong believer in empowerment. He expects employees to go beyond guidelines/standards to consider guest needs on a case–by-case basis. That is, employees must be guest-oriented at all times so as to provide excellent customer service. From his U.S. experience, Becker has found that empowerment increases employee motivation, performance, and job satisfaction, all of which contribute to the hotel's profitability and customer service ratings. Soon after becoming general manager at the Regency Grand, Becker introduced the practice of empowerment so as to replicate the successes that he had achieved back home.

The Regency Grand Hotel has been very profitable since it opened. The employees have always worked according to management's instructions. Their responsibility was to ensure that the instructions from their managers were carried out diligently and conscientiously. Innovation and creativity were discouraged under the previous management. Indeed, employees were punished for their mistakes and discouraged from trying out ideas that had not been approved by management. As a result, employees were afraid to be innovative and to take risks.

Becker met with the Regency's managers and department heads to explain that empowerment would be introduced in the hotel. He told them that employees must be empowered with decision-making authority so that they can use their initiative, creativity, and judgment to satisfy guest needs or handle problems effectively and efficiently. However, he stressed that the more complex issues and decisions were to be referred to superiors, who were to coach and assist rather than provide direct orders. Furthermore, Becker stressed that while mistakes were allowed, repetition of the same mistake more than twice could not be tolerated. He advised his managers and department heads that they should not discuss or consult him on minor issues/problems and decisions. Nevertheless, he told them that they are to discuss important/major issues and decisions with him. He concluded the meeting by asking for feedback. Several managers and department heads told him that they liked the idea and would

support it, while others simply nodded their heads. Becker was pleased with the response, and was eager to have his plan implemented.

In the past, the Regency had emphasized administrative control, resulting in many bureaucratic procedures throughout the organization. For example, the front-counter employees needed to seek approval from their manager before they could upgrade guests to another category of room. The front-counter manager would then have to write and submit a report to the general manager justifying the upgrade. Soon after his meeting with managers, Becker reduced the number of bureaucratic rules at the Regency and allocated more decision-making authority to front-line employees. This action upset those who previously had decision-making power over these issues. As a result, several of these employees left the hotel.

Becker also began spending a large portion of his time observing and interacting with the employees at the front desk, lobby, restaurants, and various departments. This direct interaction with Becker helped many employees to understand what he wanted and expected of them. However, the employees had much difficulty trying to distinguish between a major and minor issue/decision. More often than not, supervisors would reverse employee decisions by stating that they were major issues requiring management approval. Employees who displayed initiative and made good decisions in satisfying the needs of the guests rarely received any positive feedback from their supervisors. Eventually, most of these employees lost confidence in making decisions, and reverted back to relying on their superiors for decision making.

Not long after the implementation of the practice of empowerment, Becker realized that his subordinates were consulting him more frequently than before. Most of them came to him to discuss or consult on minor issues. He had to spend most of his time attending to his subordinates. Soon he began to feel highly frustrated and exhausted, and very often would tell his secretary that "unless the hotel is on fire, don't let anyone disturb me."

Becker thought that the practice of empowerment would benefit the overall performance of the hotel. However, contrary to his expectation, the business and overall performance of the hotel began to deteriorate. There had been an increasing number of guest complaints. In the past, the hotel had minimal guest complaints. Now there were a significant number of formal written complaints every month. Many other guests voiced their dissatisfaction verbally to hotel employees. The number of mistakes made by employees had been on an increase. Becker was very upset when he realized that two of the local newspapers and an overseas newspaper had published negative feedback on the hotel in terms of service standards. He was most distressed when an international travel magazine had voted the hotel as "one of Asia's nightmare hotels."

The stress levels of the employees had been continuously mounting since the introduction of the practice of empowerment. Absenteeism due to illness was increasing at an alarming rate. In addition, the employee turnover rate had reached an all-time high. The good working relationships that were established under the old management had been severely strained. The employees were no longer united and supportive of each other. They were quick to "point fingers" at or to "back stab" one another when mistakes were made and when problems occurred.

Note: This case is based on true events, but the industry and names have been changed.

Case 9   THE SHIPPING INDUSTRY ACCOUNTING TEAM
by Steven L. McShane, University of Newcastle (Australia)

For the past five years, I have been working at McKay, Sanderson, and Smith Associates, a mid-sized accounting firm in Halifax that specializes in commercial accounting and audits. My particular speciality is accounting practices for shipping companies, ranging from small fishing fleets to a couple of the big firms with ships on the St. Lawrence Seaway.

About 18 months ago, McKay, Sanderson, and Smith Associates became part of a large merger involving two other accounting firms across Canada. These firms have offices in Montreal, Ottawa, Toronto, Calgary, and Vancouver. Although the other two accounting firms were much larger than McKay, all three firms agreed to avoid centralizing the business around one office in Toronto. Instead, the new firm—called Goldberg, Choo, and McKay Associates—would rely on teams across the country to "leverage the synergies of our collective knowledge" (an often-cited statement from the managing partner soon after the merger).

The merger began to affect me a year ago when my boss (a senior partner and vice-president of the merger firm) announced that I would be working more closely with three people from the other two firms to become the firm's new shipping industry accounting team. The other "team members" were Rochelle in Montreal, Thomas in Toronto, and Brad in Vancouver. I had met Rochelle briefly at a meeting in Montreal during the merger. I have never met Thomas or Brad, but was informed during the integration meetings that they were shipping accounting professionals at the other firms.

Initially, the shipping "team" activities involved emailing each other about new contracts and prospective clients. Later, we were asked to submit joint monthly reports on accounting statements and issues. Normally, I submitted my own monthly reports that summarize activities involving my own clients. Coordinating the monthly report with three other people took much more time, particularly since different accounting documentation procedures across the three firms were still being resolved. It took numerous emails and a few telephone calls to work out a reasonable monthly report style.

During this aggravating process, it became apparent—to me at least—that this "teams" business was costing me more time than it was worth. Moreover, Brad in Vancouver didn't have a clue as to how to communicate with the rest of us. He rarely replied to emails. Instead, he often used the telephone voicemail system, which resulted in lots of telephone tag. Brad arrives at work at 9 a.m. in Vancouver (and is often late!), which is early afternoon in Halifax. I typically have a flexible work schedule from 7:30 a.m. to 3:30 p.m. so I can chauffeur my kids after school to sports and music lessons. So Brad and I have a window of less than three hours to share information.

The biggest nuisance with the shipping specialist accounting team started two weeks ago when the firm asked the four of us to develop a new strategy for attracting new shipping-firm clients. This new strategic plan is a messy business. Somehow, we have to share our thoughts on various approaches, agree on a new plan, and write a unified submission to the managing partner. Already, the project is taking most of my time just writing and responding to emails, and participating in conference calls (which none of us did much before the team formed).

Thomas and Rochelle have already had two or three "misunderstandings" via email about their different perspectives on delicate matters in the strategic plan. The worst of these disagreements required a conference call with all of us to resolve. Except for the most basic matters, it seems that we can't understand each other, let alone agree on key issues. I have come to the conclusion that I would never want Brad to work in my Halifax office (thank goodness, he's on the other side of the country). While Rochelle and I seem to agree on most points, the overall team can't form a common vision or strategy. I don't know how Rochelle, Thomas, or Brad feel, but I would be quite happy to work somewhere that did not require any of these long-distance team headaches.

Case 10   VERBERG KANSEN N.V.

by Steven L. McShane, University of Newcastle (Australia), based on an earlier case by Steven Palesy and David A. Nadler

Verberg Kansen N.V. (Verkan) is one of the leading European food manufacturers. Headquartered in Amsterdam, the Netherlands, the company manufactures or imports a full range of grocery foods, such as cereals, dairy products, baby foods, and canned foods. Verkan's products are widely respected for their quality, although the product lines are not considered as innovative as those from other large competitors and small start-up boutique-style food manufacturers in the region. The company owns production operations within Europe but also imports a small percentage of its products from outside Europe. It has a well-developed distribution network and warehousing facilities, providing direct delivery of products from the warehouses to food retailers, restaurants, institutions, and other client groups across Europe.

Verkan's baby foods division is a relatively small part of the overall business but, until recently, has provided steady revenue growth with good profit margins. Its baby foods brand is well-known to consumers, and is premium-priced with an overall market share across Europe of approximately 25 percent in a fragmented market of almost a dozen brands. Within the past decade, Verkan expanded sales of several food products, including its full range of baby foods, into Asia. Asian sales of Verkan's baby foods enjoy approximately 15 percent growth per year, compared to 3 or 4 percent growth in recent years for its baby foods in Europe.

The baby foods division was formed more than two decades ago and grew rapidly as it introduced a broad range of foods for the infant market, including strained vegetables, fruits, meats, and combined variations of these foods. Baby food sales growth ranged from 10 and 20 percent per year during the first decade, then growth slowed about 10 years ago. During those early years, the number of different types of infant food products increased tremendously to keep up with increasing demand for a greater number of foods and a greater variety of products. The product line includes foods that are pureed or strained (for babies about 5 months and older) as well as partially strained or chopped (for infants about 10 months and older).

The European market for baby foods has changed considerably in recent years. The growth rate in sales for this market has slowed considerably, which is partly due to decreasing birth rates throughout many European countries. The industry also faces increasing scrutiny from consumers and government regulators regarding product content and food additives, such as food dyes and preservatives. Some online influencers even urge parents to make their own baby food rather than buy products from food manufacturers. Competition in the baby food industry has also increased,

particularly from start-up boutique brands with premium pricing as well as from grocery store private label brands competing on the basis of price. Verkan faces similar competition and consumer challenges in several product groups beyond its baby foods division.

Verkan's senior executive team has been highly concerned about these threats to the company's infant products and, ultimately, the company's financial health. Baby food sales growth barely reached 3 percent in the most recent year, which has resulted in less efficient production and unused warehouse capacity. Verkan's executives have made it a priority to seek out new revenue streams, including innovative alternative markets for the company's products as well as the development of new products.

Verberg Kansen's Organizational Structure

Verkan is organized into six divisions, each of which is led by a vice-president who reports to the chief executive officer (Exhibit 1). Four divisions represent product groups, specifically dairy, cereals, baby, and canned foods. These food groups have somewhat or very distinct customers and marketing practices. A fifth division is responsible for international (mostly Asian) marketing and sales. The sixth division oversees the company's European production operations and warehouse facilities. Also reporting to the CEO are the heads of product research, legal, government relations, and administration.

Each product group is primarily a marketing and sales organization, so most direct reports to the vice-president are sales managers for each of the four European regions. The vice-president's office is responsible for overall market planning, sales promotion, advertising, and sales within that food group, as well as liaison with the company's centralized product research centre.

Exhibit 1 also shows the baby foods group structure beneath the top reporting level. Europe is divided into four regions, so each food group has four regional sales managers. Regions are further divided into several districts. Each district may represent part of a country, or one very large metropolitan area. A food group district manager leads the Verkan sales teams in one district. The food group's sales team is responsible for selling Verkan products to retailers, negotiating shelf space with those customers, addressing delivery issues, and managing promotions developed by the food group's market planning and promotion team.

District managers report to the regional sales manager responsible for that group in a specific area of Europe. The

---

EXHIBIT 1 Partial Organizational Structure of Verberg Kansen (Verkan) N.V.

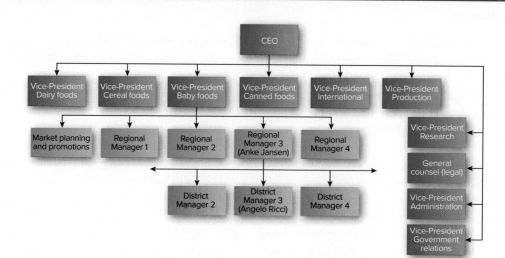

regional sales manager position has been an entry position for graduates of well-regarded MBA programs, who subsequently are promoted to high-level positions within the company. Verkan's current CEO, the vice-presidents of three out of the four food groups, and a few marketing specialists began their careers at Verkan as regional sales managers.

Verberg Kansen's Yearly Sales Plan

Verkan's regional managers focus much of their attention on the yearly sales plan, which includes projections of sales, expenses, and profit. The yearly sales plan consists of the key goals against which the regional managers' performances are measured. The annual sales plan is developed through a multistage process.

In the first stage, the technical market planning team within a food group projects sales for the coming year for that division. Concurrently, regional managers develop sales projections for that food group in their area. These sales manager estimates are typically extrapolations of the previous year's sales figures, adjusting for any expected market changes. The regional managers' projections are submitted to the divisional vice-president and market planning team.

Invariably, the market planning team's projections are higher than the regional manager projections. So, in the second stage, the product group's regional managers negotiate with that food group's market planning team to resolve those differences and agree on a sales plan. Along with stating projected sales volume for the division and each region, the sales plan identifies the division's promotion and advertising budgets, other expenditures, and expected profits.

Next, Verkan's vice-president for each product group communicates formal sales targets to each regional manager. These targets are then cascaded down to the district managers and their sales teams. This information includes both each district's formal sales targets and expense budget for the next financial year.

Each district manager receives a relatively low base salary and a large yearly bonus calculated by their sales team's performance against the sales plan. The district manager also receives a pool of bonus money, the amount of which varies with the district's success compared to the sales plan. The district manager distributes these funds to individual salespeople. Sales staff also receive a relatively low base salary, so the yearly bonus is their major source of income.

Anke Jansen, Southern European Regional Manager, Baby Foods

Anke Jansen is the regional sales manager responsible for baby foods in Southern Europe. Anke completed an MBA program from one of Europe's top universities, majoring in marketing and graduating near the top of her class. Anke's first job following graduation was as an assistant product manager at a large consumer products company. Over her four years employed at that firm, she demonstrated her ability to manage current products and assist the launch of new offerings.

Seeing no opportunities for quick advancement at the consumer products firm, last year Anke accepted the position of regional sales manager at Verkan's baby food group. Her starting salary at Verkan was higher, and she would receive a potentially large bonus based on the baby food group's performance and the entire company's profits. Verkan also offered good career progress opportunities. She learn that many of Verkan's senior executives had started in the regional manager position.

Currently beginning her second year at Verkan, Anke remains eager to perform her job well, particularly working with her eight district managers. She encourages them to identify new markets and other innovations to improve sales of the company's various baby food products.

A Researcher Studies Verberg Kansen

A researcher from a major European business school was recently given permission by Verkan to study the company's operations and management practices. After developing an initial understanding of the company, the researcher decided to more closely study the European sales groups and issues that were being experienced there. One of his earliest interviews was with Anke Jansen, the baby foods regional sales manager for southern Europe, who he visited in her Amsterdam office. After introductions, Anke described the variety of baby food products that Verkan offered the market and how they related to sales in her southern Europe region. After this preliminary discussion, Anke revealed her thoughts and concerns:

"I was hired by Verberg Kansen a little more than a year ago. There has been some growth during that time, but it has been uneven. To some extent, I believe that we are starting to get back on track toward our sales plan. But it has been a much more challenging journey than I ever thought. Our approach to selling baby food is too traditional, too old-school. We need more innovative selling methods and ideas for new markets. Unfortunately, the front-line sales staff—even the district managers—don't seem to be fully on board. Everyone is content to continue their current sales routines just to meet the sales goals. Very few of them have mentioned any new ideas to increase market share and profitability.

Verkan's baby foods is a very mature product line. The vice-president of baby foods recognizes that, as well as our critical need to diversify. In other words, we need to reduce our dependence on a steadily increasing population as the main source of growth. The product development people have some exciting ideas in the works, but it will be a few years of refinement and testing before these products are on the market. Until then, it is up to us in the field to generate new ideas that will boost sales of our existing product line.

I'm sure there must be better ways to market our product—new practices we can apply or clients that *we can serve to boost sales volume and profits for our region and the entire division. It's a known truth that the best ideas come from the field—from our district salespeople. But as I've said, there has been no more than a trickle of suggestions from them. They literally expect the products to continue to sell themselves without any special initiative from front-line sales staff. The districts just think their job is to assist with promotions developed at division headquarters, maintain good relations with our larger customers, and keep the shelves stocked. That's all they have done for years and, in their minds, that's all they need to do for years to come."*

At this juncture of the interview, Anke brought out some sales plan data for the current year in her region, including the sales volumes of the districts and individual salespeople. With a touch of emotion, Anke pointed to data from sales staff in the district covering Northern Italy:

"Look here at Angelo Ricci (pronounced Rik-Chee) and his team in [the northern Italy district]. This illustrates the difficulties I am facing. Our regional and divisional sales growth in baby foods continues to slow down—sales increased by only 3 percent last year across the division! Sales actually contracted from last year in some districts. Yet Angelo's group consistently delivers sales volumes that are 10 percent above the sales plan.

Of course, I've been down to their district office numerous times and spent time talking with Angelo, but he can't seem to explain why they are doing so well. And I can't figure out how they do it, either. Surely they are doing something that would benefit everyone selling Verkan baby foods. Yet whenever I ask Angelo, I get vague answers. He'll often reply: 'Well, my salespeople work very hard to get those sales' or 'Teamwork! Just plain teamwork is why we succeed.' I'm sure there is a reason—maybe a few reasons—beyond these explanations, but I can't seem to get Angelo to open up."

The Researcher Visits Northern Italy

The situation in the Northern Italy district sparked the researcher's curiosity, so he arranged a six-week visit with district manager Angelo Ricci and his team. The researcher was given a letter of introduction from the vice-president of the baby foods division. The letter asked the sales teams to assist the researcher, who was collecting data for a research study that potentially might help the company. The letter emphasized that any information collected by the researcher would be confidential.

During the first week or more, it was evident to the researcher that Angelo Ricci and his district salespeople were suspicious of his visit. But the researcher spent numerous days travelling along the Northern Italian roads with each of the sales staff, visiting a variety of grocery stores and other clients. Slowly, as the researcher gained their trust, the sales staff revealed more of their true feelings about their jobs and the company. (See Exhibit 2 for a listing of Angelo Ricci's Northern Italy sales team members).

Davide Pascutti, the unofficial assistant district manager, gave a heartfelt explanation about why he enjoyed his work as a district salesperson:

"It's the freedom! Really, I'm my own boss in this job most of the time. I couldn't imagine being in an office day in–day out with some supervisor breathing down my neck and checking through all of my work. In sales, you get to drive through the wonderful countryside, colourful city streets, and generally be out in the real world. I'm doing what I like most—talking to people, being out and about, and making the sale."

Raffaele Anzil has worked at Verkan for 30 years, more than anyone else in Angelo Ricci's sales team. Along with discussing his job, he particularly described the unique qualities of the sales group in this district:

"You couldn't ask for a greater bunch of people to work with. Over the years, I've been with a few different teams, and these guys are the best. I've worked with Davide and Angelo for almost 15 years, so I know them well. We are true friends—I wouldn't trade this group for anything. That goes for Angelo, too. He may be the district manager, but Angelo is really one of us. He lets us do our jobs without micromanaging because he knows that we are good at sales. We just continue to do our work as we know best, and that's just fine with Angelo.

What makes these guys special is that they help you out when you need it. I was sick last year, which meant that I couldn't keep up with store checks and other fieldwork for a while. They [the other district salespeople] all took turns covering my territory. We made our plan plus 10 percent, yet didn't report my illness to the company.

I'll tell you, too, that we can be a bit hard on a co-worker who doesn't go along with how we do things around here. One of the young guys, Pietro, joined the team a few years back. My, oh my! He was so fired up about the job! He was going to sell baby food to half the mothers in Italy, personally! It took some, er, gentle coaxing to let Pietro realize that selling at Verkan means that you, uh [hesitates] . . . have to pace yourself and not waste your effort for this firm. Because of his over-eagerness when he got hired, Pietro experienced a few, er, setbacks that slowed him down. Some of his sales orders got lost, a couple of shipments were misdirected, things like that. Yeah, some of the guys were making his life a little bit difficult by creating these mix-ups. But when he finally realized what we were expecting from each other, everyone treated Pietro great and showed him how to work better rather than harder."

The researcher then asked Raffaele about his views on Verkan as a place to work. The salesperson's reply was blunt:

"It doesn't take much brainpower to see that the company is out to screw us [district sales staff]. Up in the

EXHIBIT 2   Northern Italy District Sales Team

Name	Position	Age	Years with Verkan	Education
Angelo Ricci	District sales manager	52	24	Upper secondary school
Davide Pascutti	Salesperson (assistant manager)	50	24	Upper secondary school
Raffaele Anzil	Salesperson	56	30	Upper secondary school
Francesco Orbel	Salesperson	49	18	1 year university
Alessandro Volpe	Salesperson	35	12	2 years university
Mattia Costa	Salesperson	28	4	Laurea (undergrad degree)
Pietro Bianci	Salesperson	30	3	Laurea (undergrad degree)

Netherlands, they are concerned about one thing—the numbers, meeting the plan, no matter what. But it's a no-win situation. Let's say you work hard and meet the plan, and then increase sales so you can earn some decent money. What happens? Head office just raises the sales target next year based on how hard you worked this year! Then, next year, you have to work even harder just to meet the minimum sales quota and make the same money, or more likely less money. It just doesn't pay to bust your ass for this company.

Also, Verkan's people in Amsterdam love paperwork and digital reports. They expect us to file sales reports, call reports, all kinds of reports. If you got online and filled out all of the information that they want, you'd have no time left to do any selling, meeting clients, looking for new accounts, or anything else that a salesperson needs to do to keep ahead of the game."

The researcher soon discovered that Raffaele's views on the company were similar to those held by other Verkan baby food salespeople in Northern Italy. For example, this is what Francesco Orbel said to the researcher as they were driving around Milan meeting clients:

"Have you heard about Verkan's suggestion plan? What a joke! We're supposed to come up with some brilliant ideas about how to increase baby food sales for the company. So, you think up an idea that makes our division a million dollars in profit across the continent. What do they generously give you in return? €3,000, that's all. That's the top figure, €3,000 for your idea. What a joke . . . no, what an insult!

Keep this in mind: we're basically in this for the money. Don't get any fancy ideas that this is a comfortable or glamorous job. It's not! You're out on the road all of the time, staying in mid-standard hotels, and constantly fighting the competition. But these hassles are worth it because I can earn more money than doing any other job available to someone like me. I can live better than most 'professionals' with all their Laurea [completed university degrees].

That's what's so great about Angelo, too. He understands that this is all about making good money. He makes sure that we not only make our plan, but that we get a healthy bonus every year, without fail. And frankly, he is very good at keeping the people in Amsterdam from taking those bonuses away from us. He's not management; he's one of us.

You can see Angelo's commitment to us when the entire district sales team meets. Once every two or three months we all get together, usually in Brescia, Bergamo, or sometimes Verona—someplace small enough that we can get good accommodation at a

decent price. We spend a day going over our sales figures, promotions expenses, and things we noticed about selling. We spend the entire day working on these things in this hotel meeting room. Then everyone goes out and has a fun night on the town, usually drinking. Angelo is one of us. More than a few nights I've had to help carry him back to the hotel."

Almost one month after arriving in Northern Italy, the researcher was invited to attend the team's next meeting, in Brescia. Angelo Ricci drew the researcher aside during the luncheon break and said the following:

"Listen, before we start the afternoon part of the meeting, I need to talk to you about something. The guys trust you enough to let you in on this. You have probably noticed that we have been fairly successful with our sales targets and bonuses. You're right, we have been, and for a good reason.

About three years ago, Francesco made a great discovery. While checking shelf space in one of the stores, he noticed that it wasn't just moms and dads buying our baby food products for their babies. Many customers were elderly people! Well, the others here starting looking more closely in their areas and found the same thing. In fact, a lot of old folks are buying Verkan baby foods for themselves, particularly the chopped and partially strained varieties. We talked with some of them. They like our stuff, but they buy it mainly because they have all kinds of teeth problems so they can't chew food very well.

So, now we have grown a very lucrative trade with a number of the seniors' homes. But to keep it quiet from Amsterdam, we've arranged to sell our products to these seniors residences through supermarkets located nearby where there is a large elderly population. It's a great new market. More to the point: it takes the pressure off us to make plan. In fact, since our discovery, we haven't had to push very hard to keep making plan plus about 10-percent increase in district sales volume.

We've been very careful—and so far quite successful—at keeping Amsterdam from finding out. It would be 'game over' if they knew. They would up our plan, which leaves us no time to sell, to develop new customers, to develop new accounts, to do anything necessary these days to keep our pay at a decent level. This elderly market is our 'cushion.' It adds enough of an annual sales volume increase that we can focus our time on staying on top of our territory. I'm telling you this now because the seniors market is on our agenda this afternoon. Everyone here believes you are OK, so I'm trusting you to keep this to yourself. That letter you showed me when you first showed up said you'd keep everything confidential, right? I hope I'm not making a mistake telling you this."

A week after the Brescia meeting, the researcher bid farewell to Angelo Ricci and his sales team and returned to his university in [another European country]. But on his way back, he arranged a final visit with Anke Jansen in Amsterdam. It was immediately evident that Anke was even more stressed about baby food sales in her region.

"The regional managers met the other day with the VP (vice-president of the baby foods division). Verkan is putting even more pressure on all of us to lift sales. Somehow, I get the sense that my job is on the line. Maybe it's because a couple of my districts are lagging behind most others, but every region has districts that can't make the plan. Even if I'm not fired, the market planning team has made it clear that they will demand a larger sales increase in next year's plan. My future with Verkan doesn't look good unless I can find some way to improve this situation.

What's worse is that I'm getting pressure from both sides. My district managers push back that they are working harder than ever. They claim they have squeezed out all the new sales they can. Even Angelo Ricci objected that he will fall short of the plan if next year's sales targets are increased. Yet his district always seems to pull a rabbit out of their hat and increase sales by an extra 10 percent. I'd love to be a fly on their wall to know what they're really doing there [in the Northern Italy district]."

Case 11   VÊTEMENTS LTÉE

by Steven L. McShane, University of Newcastle (Australia)

Vêtements Ltée is a chain of men's retail clothing stores located throughout the province of Quebec. Two years ago, the company introduced new incentive systems for both store managers and sales employees. Store managers receive a salary with annual merit increases based on store sales above targeted goals, store appearance, store inventory management, customer complaints, and several other performance measures. Some of this information (e.g., store appearance) is gathered during visits by senior management, whereas other information is based on company records (e.g., sales volume).

Sales employees are paid a fixed salary plus a commission based on the percentage of sales credited to that employee over the pay period. The commission represents about 30 percent of a typical paycheque and is intended to encourage employees to actively serve customers and to increase sales volume. Returned merchandise is deducted from commissions, so sales employees are discouraged from selling products that customers do not really want.

Soon after the new incentive systems were introduced, senior management began to receive complaints from store managers regarding the performance of their sales staff. They observed that sales employees tended to stand near the store entrance waiting to "tag" customers as their own. Occasionally, sales staff would argue over "ownership" of the customer. Managers were concerned that this aggressive behaviour intimidated some customers. It also tended to leave some parts of the store unattended by staff.

Many managers were also concerned about inventory duties. Previously, sales staff would share responsibility for restocking inventory and completing inventory reorder forms. Under the new compensation system, however, few employees were willing to do these essential tasks. On several occasions, stores have faced stock shortages because merchandise was not stocked or reorder forms were not completed in a timely manner. Potential sales have suffered from empty shelves when plenty of merchandise was available in the back storeroom or at the warehouse. The company's new automatic inventory system could reduce some of these problems, but employees must still stock shelves and assist in other aspects of inventory management.

Store managers have tried to correct the inventory problem by assigning employees to inventory duty, but this has created resentment among the employees selected. Other managers have threatened sales staff with dismissals if they do not do their share of inventory management. This strategy has been somewhat effective when the manager is in the store, but staff members sneak back onto the floor when the manager is away. It has also hurt staff morale, particularly relations with the store manager.

To reduce the tendency of sales staff to hoard customers at the store entrance, some managers have assigned employees to specific areas of the store. This has also created some resentment among employees stationed in areas with less traffic or lower-priced merchandise. Some staff have openly complained of lower paycheques because they have been placed in a slow area of the store or have been given more than their share of inventory duties.

APPENDIX

Theory Building and Systematic Research Methods

Theory Building

People need to make sense of their world, so they form theories about the way the world operates. A **theory** is a general set of propositions that describes interrelationships among several concepts. We form theories for the purpose of predicting and explaining the world around us.[1] What does a good theory look like? First, it should be stated as clearly and simply as possible so that the concepts can be measured and there is no ambiguity regarding the theory's propositions. Second, the elements of the theory must be logically consistent with each other, because we cannot test anything that doesn't make sense. Third, a good theory provides value to society; it helps people understand their world better than they would without the theory.[2]

theory A general set of propositions that describes interrelationships among several concepts.

Theory building is a continuous process that typically includes the inductive and deductive stages shown in Exhibit A.1.[3] The inductive stage draws on personal experience to form a preliminary theory, whereas the deductive stage uses the scientific method to test the theory.

The inductive stage of theory building involves observing the world around us, identifying a pattern of relationships, and then forming a theory from these personal observations. For example, you might casually notice that new employees want their supervisor to give direction, whereas this leadership style irritates long-service employees. From these observations, you form a theory about the effectiveness of directive leadership. (See Chapter 12 for a discussion of this leadership style.)

Positivism versus Interpretivism

Research requires an interpretation of reality, and researchers tend to perceive reality in one of two ways. A common view, called **positivism**, is that reality exists independent of the perceptions and interpretations of people. It is "out there" to be discovered and tested. Positivism is the foundation for most quantitative research (statistical analysis). It assumes that we can measure variables and those variables have fixed relationships with other variables. For example, the positivist perspective says that we could study whether a supportive style of leadership reduces stress. If we find evidence that it does, then someone else studying leadership and stress would "discover" the same relationship.

positivism A view held in quantitative research in which reality exists independent of the perceptions and interpretations of people.

Interpretivism takes a different view of reality. It suggests that reality comes from shared meaning among people in a particular environment. For example, supportive leadership is a personal interpretation of reality,

interpretivism The view held in many qualitative studies that reality comes from shared meaning among people in a particular environment.

EXHIBIT A.1   Theory Building and Theory Testing

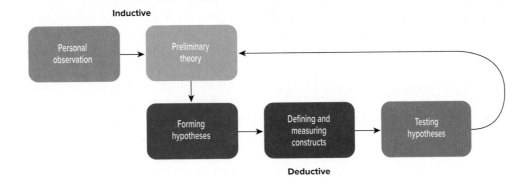

not something that can be measured across time and people. Interpretivists rely mainly on qualitative data, such as observation and nondirective interviews. They particularly listen to the language people use to understand the common meaning that people have toward various events or phenomena. For example, they might argue that you need to experience and observe supportive leadership to effectively study it. Moreover, you can't really predict relationships because the specific situation shapes reality.[4]

Most OB scholars identify themselves somewhere between the extreme views of positivism and interpretivism. Many believe that inductive research should begin with an interpretivist angle. We should consider a new topic with an open mind and search for shared meaning among people in the situation being studied. In other words, researchers should let the participants define reality rather than let the researcher's preconceived notions shape that reality. This process involves gathering qualitative information and letting this information shape their theory.[5] After the theory emerges, researchers shift to the positivist perspective by quantitatively testing relationships in that theory.

Theory Testing: The Deductive Process

Once a theory has been formed, we shift into the deductive stage of theory building. This process includes forming hypotheses, defining and measuring constructs, and testing hypotheses (see Exhibit A.1). **Hypotheses** make empirically testable declarations that certain variables and their corresponding measures are related in a specific way proposed by the theory. For instance, to find support for the directive leadership theory described earlier, we need to form and then test a specific hypothesis from that theory. One such hypothesis might be, "New employees are more satisfied with supervisors who exhibit a directive rather than nondirective leadership style." Hypotheses are indispensable tools of scientific research, because they provide the vital link between the theory and empirical verification.

hypotheses Statements making empirically testable declarations that certain variables and their corresponding measures are related in a specific way proposed by the theory.

DEFINING AND MEASURING CONSTRUCTS

Hypotheses are testable only if we can define and then form measurable indicators of the concepts stated in those hypotheses. Consider the hypothesis in the previous paragraph about new employees and directive leadership. To test this hypothesis, we first need to define the concepts, such as "new employees," "directive leadership," and "supervisor." These are known as **constructs**, because they are abstract ideas constructed by researchers that can be linked to observable information. Organizational behaviour researchers developed the construct called *directive leadership* to help them understand the different effects that leaders have on followers. We can't directly see, taste, or smell directive leadership; instead, we rely on indirect indicators of its existence, such as observing someone giving directions, maintaining clear performance standards, and ensuring that procedures and practices are followed.

constructs Abstract ideas constructed by researchers that can be linked to observable information.

As you can see, defining constructs well is very important because these definitions become the foundation for finding or developing acceptable measures of those constructs. We can't measure directive leadership if we have only a vague idea about what this concept means. The better the construct is defined, the better our chances of finding or developing a good measure of that construct. However, even with a good definition, constructs can be difficult to measure, because the empirical representation must capture several elements in the definition. A measure of directive leadership must be able to identify not only people who give directions, but also those who maintain performance standards and ensure that procedures are followed.

TESTING HYPOTHESES

The third step in the deductive process is to collect data for the empirical measures of the variables. Following our directive leadership example, we might conduct a formal survey in which new employees indicate the behaviour of their supervisors and their attitudes toward their supervisors. Alternatively, we might design an experiment in which people work with someone who applies either a directive or a nondirective leadership style. When the data have been collected, we can use various procedures to statistically test our hypotheses.

A major concern in theory building is that some researchers might inadvertently find support for their theory simply because they use the same information used to form the theory during the inductive stage. Consequently, the deductive stage must collect new data that are completely independent of the data used during the inductive stage. For instance, you might decide to test your theory of directive leadership by studying employees in another organization. Moreover, the inductive process may have relied mainly on personal observation, whereas the deductive process might use survey questionnaires. By studying different samples and using different measurement tools, we minimize the risk of conducting circular research.

Using the Scientific Method

Earlier, we said that the deductive stage of theory building follows the scientific method. The **scientific method** is a systematic, controlled, empirical, and critical investigation of hypothetical propositions about the presumed relationships among natural phenomena.[6] There are several elements to this definition, so let's look at each one. First, scientific research is *systematic and controlled,* because researchers want to rule out all but one explanation for a set of interrelated events. To rule out alternative explanations, we need to control them in some way, such as by keeping them constant or removing them entirely from the environment.

scientific method A set of principles and procedures that help researchers to systematically understand previously unexplained events and conditions.

Second, we say that scientific research is *empirical* because researchers need to use objective reality—or as close as we can get to it—to test a theory. They measure observable elements of the environment, such as what a person says or does, rather than relying on their own subjective opinion to draw conclusions. Moreover, scientific research analyzes these data using acceptable principles of mathematics and logic.

Third, scientific research involves *critical investigation.* This means that the study's hypotheses, data, methods, and results are openly described so that other experts in the field can properly evaluate the research. It also means that scholars are encouraged to critique and build on previous research. The scientific method encourages the refinement and eventually the replacement of a particular theory with one that better suits our understanding of the world.

Grounded Theory: An Alternative Approach

The scientific method dominates the quantitative approach to systematic research, but another approach, called **grounded theory**, dominates research using qualitative methods.[7] Grounded theory is a process of developing knowledge through the constant interplay of data collection, analysis, and theory development. It relies mainly on qualitative methods to form categories and variables, analyze relationships among these concepts, and form a model

grounded theory A process of developing knowledge through the constant interplay of data collection, analysis, and theory development.

based on the observations and analysis. Grounded theory combines the inductive stages of theory development by cycling back and forth between data collection and analysis to converge on a robust explanatory model. This ongoing reciprocal process results in theory that is grounded in the data (thus, the name 'grounded' theory).

Like the scientific method, grounded theory is a systematic and rigorous process of data collection and analysis. It requires specific steps and documentation, and adopts a positivist view by assuming that the results are generalizable to other settings. However, grounded theory also takes an interpretivist view by building categories and variables from the perceived realities of the subjects rather than from an assumed universal truth.[8] It also recognizes that personal biases are not easily removed from the research process.

Selected Issues in Organizational Behaviour Research

There are many issues to consider in theory building, particularly when we use the deductive process to test hypotheses. Some of the more important issues are sampling, causation, and ethical practices in organizational research.

SAMPLING IN ORGANIZATIONAL RESEARCH

When finding out why things happen in organizations, we typically gather information from a few sources and then draw conclusions about the larger population. If we survey several employees and determine that older employees are more loyal to their company, then we would like to generalize this statement to all older employees in our population, not just those whom we surveyed. Scientific inquiry generally requires that researchers engage in **representative sampling**—that is, sampling a population in such a way that we can extrapolate the results of the sample to the larger population.

representative sampling The process of sampling a population in such a way that one can extrapolate the results of that sample to the larger population.

One factor that influences representativeness is whether the sample is selected in an unbiased way from the larger population. Let's suppose that you want to study organizational commitment among employees in your organization. A casual procedure might result in sampling too few employees from the head office and too many located elsewhere in the country. If head office employees actually have higher loyalty than employees located elsewhere, the biased sampling would cause the results to underestimate the true level of loyalty among employees in the company. If you repeat the process again next year but somehow overweight employees from the head office, the results might wrongly suggest that employees have increased their organizational commitment over the past year. In reality, the only change may be the direction of sampling bias.

How do we minimize sampling bias? The answer is to randomly select the sample. A randomly drawn sample gives each member of the population an equal probability of being chosen, so there is less likelihood that a subgroup within that population will dominate the study's results.

The same principle applies to random assignment of subjects to groups in experimental designs. If we want to test the effects of a team development training program, we need to randomly place some employees in the training group and randomly place others in a group that does not receive training. Without this random selection, each group might have different types of employees, so we wouldn't know whether the training explains the differences between the two groups. Moreover, if employees respond differently to the training program, we couldn't be sure that the training program results are representative of the larger population. Of course, random sampling does not necessarily produce a perfectly representative sample, but we do know that it is the best approach to ensure unbiased selection.

The other factor that influences representativeness is sample size. Whenever we select a portion of the population, there will be some error in our estimate of the population values. The larger the sample, the less error will occur in our estimate. Let's suppose that you want to find out how employees in a 500-person firm feel about viewing social media (e.g., Facebook) at work. If you asked 400 of those employees, the information would provide a very good estimate of how the entire workforce in that organization feels. If you survey only 100 employees, the estimate might deviate more from the true population. If you ask only 10 people, the estimate could be quite different from what all 500 employees feel.

Notice that sample size goes hand in hand with random selection. You must have a sufficiently large sample size for the principle of randomization to work effectively. In our example of attitudes toward social media, we would do a poor job of random selection if our sample consisted of only 10 employees from the 500-person organization. The reason is that these 10 people probably wouldn't capture the diversity of employees throughout the organization. In fact, the more diverse the population, the larger the sample size should be, to provide adequate representation through random selection.

CAUSATION IN ORGANIZATIONAL RESEARCH

Theories present notions about relationships among constructs. Often, these propositions suggest a causal relationship,

namely, that one variable has an effect on another variable. When discussing causation, we refer to variables as being independent or dependent. *Independent variables* are the presumed causes of *dependent variables,* which are the presumed effects. In our earlier example of directive leadership, the main independent variable (there might be others) would be the supervisor's directive or nondirective leadership style, because we presume that it causes the dependent variable (satisfaction with supervision).

In laboratory experiments (described later), the independent variable is always manipulated by the experimenter. In our research on directive leadership, we might have subjects (new employees) work with supervisors who exhibit directive or nondirective leadership behaviours. If subjects are more satisfied under the directive leaders, we would be able to infer an association between the independent and dependent variables.

Researchers must satisfy three conditions to provide sufficient evidence of causality between two variables.[9] The first condition of causality is that the variables are empirically associated with each other. An association exists whenever one measure of a variable changes systematically with a measure of another variable. This condition of causality is the easiest to satisfy, because there are several well-known statistical measures of association. A research study might find, for instance, that heterogeneous groups (in which members come from diverse backgrounds) produce more creative solutions to problems. This might be apparent because the measure of creativity (such as number of creative solutions produced within a fixed time) is higher for teams that have a high score on the measure of group heterogeneity. They are statistically associated or correlated with each other.

The second condition of causality is that the independent variable precedes the dependent variable in time. Sometimes, this condition is satisfied through simple logic. In our group heterogeneity example, it doesn't make sense to say that the number of creative solutions caused the group's heterogeneity, because the group's heterogeneity existed before the group produced the creative solutions. In other situations, however, the temporal relationship among variables is less clear. One example is the ongoing debate about job satisfaction and organizational commitment. Do companies develop more loyal employees by increasing their job satisfaction, or do changes in organizational loyalty cause changes in job satisfaction? Simple logic does not answer these questions; instead, researchers must use sophisticated longitudinal studies to build up evidence of a temporal relationship between these two variables.

The third requirement for evidence of a causal relationship is that the statistical association between two variables cannot be explained by a third variable. There are many associations that we quickly dismiss as being causally related.

For example, there is a statistical association between the number of storks in an area and the birth rate in that area. We know that storks don't bring babies, so something else must cause the association between these two variables. The real explanation is that both storks and birth rates have a higher incidence in rural areas.

In other studies, the third variable effect is less apparent. Many years ago, before polio vaccines were available, a study in the United States reported a surprisingly strong association between consumption of a certain soft drink and the incidence of polio. Was polio caused by drinking this pop, or did people with polio have an unusual craving for this beverage? Neither. Both polio and consumption of the pop drink were caused by a third variable: climate. There was a higher incidence of polio in the summer months and in warmer climates, and people drink more liquids in these climates.[10] As you can see from this example, researchers have a difficult time supporting causal inferences, because third variable effects are sometimes difficult to detect.

ETHICS IN ORGANIZATIONAL RESEARCH

Organizational behaviour researchers need to abide by the ethical standards of the society in which the research is conducted. One of the most important ethical considerations is the individual subject's freedom to participate in the study. For example, it is inappropriate to force employees to fill out a questionnaire or attend an experimental intervention for research purposes only. Moreover, researchers have an obligation to tell potential subjects about any possible risks inherent in the study so that participants can make an informed choice about whether to be involved.

Finally, researchers must be careful to protect the privacy of those who participate in the study. This usually includes letting people know when they are being studied as well as guaranteeing that their individual information will remain confidential (unless publication of identities is otherwise granted). Researchers maintain anonymity through careful security of data. The research results usually aggregate data in numbers large enough that they do not reveal the opinions or characteristics of any specific individual. For example, we would report the average absenteeism of employees in a department rather than state the absence rates of each person. When researchers are sharing data with other researchers, it is usually necessary to specially code each case so that individual identities are not known.

Research Design Strategies

So far, we have described how to build a theory, including the specific elements of empirically testing the theory within the standards of scientific inquiry. But what are the different ways to design a research study so that we get the data necessary to achieve our research objectives? There are many strategies, but they mainly fall under three headings: laboratory experiments, field surveys, and observational research.

LABORATORY EXPERIMENTS

A **laboratory experiment** is any research study in which independent variables and variables outside the researcher's main focus of inquiry can be controlled to some extent. Laboratory experiments are usually located outside the everyday work environment, such as in a classroom, simulation lab, or any other artificial setting in which the researcher can manipulate the environment. Organizational behaviour researchers sometimes conduct experiments in the workplace (called *field experiments*) in which the independent variable is manipulated. However, researchers have less control over the effects of extraneous factors in field experiments than they have in laboratory situations.

> **laboratory experiment** Any research study in which independent variables and variables outside the researcher's main focus of inquiry can be controlled to some extent.

Advantages of Laboratory Experiments

There are many advantages of laboratory experiments. By definition, this research method offers a high degree of control over extraneous variables that would otherwise confound the relationships being studied. Suppose we wanted to test the effects of directive leadership on the satisfaction of new employees. One concern might be that employees are influenced by how much leadership is provided, not just the type of leadership style. An experimental design would allow us to control how often the supervisor exhibited this style so that this extraneous variable does not confound the results.

A second advantage of lab studies is that the independent and dependent variables can be developed more precisely than is possible in a field setting. For example, the researcher can ensure that supervisors in a lab study apply specific directive or nondirective behaviours, whereas real-life supervisors would use a more complex mixture of leadership behaviours. By using more precise measures, we are more certain that we are measuring the intended construct. Thus, if new employees are more satisfied with supervisors in the directive leadership condition, we are more confident that the independent variable was directive leadership rather than some other leadership style.

A third benefit of laboratory experiments is that the independent variable can be distributed more evenly among participants. In our directive leadership study, we can ensure that approximately half of the subjects have a directive supervisor, whereas the other half have a nondirective supervisor. In natural settings, we might have trouble finding people who have worked with a nondirective leader and, consequently, we couldn't determine the effects of this condition.

Disadvantages of Laboratory Experiments

With these powerful advantages, you might wonder why laboratory experiments are the least appreciated form of organizational behaviour research.[11] One obvious limitation of this research method is that it lacks realism, and thus the results might be different in the real world. One argument is that laboratory experiment subjects are less involved than their counterparts in an actual work situation. This is sometimes true, although many lab studies have highly motivated participants. Another criticism is that the extraneous variables controlled in the lab setting might produce a different effect of the independent variable on the dependent variables. This might also be true, but remember that the experimental design controls variables in accordance with the theory and its hypotheses. Consequently, this concern is really a critique of the theory, not the lab study.

Finally, there is the well-known problem that participants are aware they are being studied and this causes them to act differently than they normally would. Some participants try to figure out how the researcher wants them to behave and then deliberately try to act that way. Other participants try to upset the experiment by doing just the opposite of what they believe the researcher expects. Still others might act unnaturally simply because they know they are being observed. Fortunately, experimenters are well aware of these potential problems and are usually (although not always) successful at disguising the study's true intent.

FIELD SURVEYS

Field surveys collect and analyze information in a natural environment—an office, a factory, or some other existing location. The researcher takes a snapshot of reality and tries to determine whether elements of that situation (including the attitudes and behaviours of people in that situation) are associated with each other as hypothesized. Everyone does some sort of field research. You might think that people from some provinces are better drivers than others, so you "test" your theory by looking at the way people with out-of-province licence plates drive. Although your methods of data collection might not satisfy scientific standards, this is a form of field research because it takes information from a naturally occurring situation.

field surveys Research design strategies that involve collecting and analyzing information in a natural environment, such as an office, a factory, or other existing location.

Advantages and Disadvantages of Field Surveys

One advantage of field surveys is that the variables often have a more powerful effect than they would in a laboratory experiment. Consider the effect of peer pressure on the behaviour of members within the team. In a natural environment, team members would form very strong cohesive bonds over time, whereas a researcher would have difficulty replicating this level of cohesiveness and corresponding peer pressure in a lab setting.

Another advantage of field surveys is that the researcher can study many variables simultaneously, thereby permitting a fuller test of more complex theories. Ironically, this is also a disadvantage of field surveys because it is difficult for the researcher to contain their scientific inquiry. There is a tendency to shift from deductive hypothesis testing to more inductive exploratory browsing through the data. If these two activities become mixed together, the researcher can lose sight of the strict covenants of scientific inquiry.

The main weakness with field surveys is that it is very difficult to satisfy the conditions for causal conclusions. One reason is that the data are usually collected at one point in time, so the researcher must rely on logic to decide whether the independent variable really preceded the dependent variable. Contrast this with the lab study in which the researcher can usually be confident that the independent variable was applied before the dependent variable occurred. Increasingly, organizational behaviour studies use longitudinal research to provide a better indicator of temporal relations among variables, but this is still not as precise as the lab setting. Another reason why causal analysis is difficult in field surveys is that extraneous variables are not controlled as they are in lab studies. Without this control, there is a higher chance that a third variable might explain the relationship between the hypothesized independent and dependent variables.

OBSERVATIONAL RESEARCH

In their study of brainstorming and creativity, Robert Sutton and Andrew Hargadon observed 24 brainstorming sessions at IDEO, a product design firm in Palo Alto, California. They also attended a dozen "Monday morning meetings," conducted 60 semi-structured interviews with IDEO executives and designers, held hundreds of informal discussions with these people, and read through several dozen magazine articles about the company.[12]

Sutton and Hargadon's use of observational research and other qualitative methods was quite appropriate for their research objective, which was to re-examine the effectiveness of brainstorming beyond the number of ideas generated. Observational research generates a wealth of descriptive accounts about the drama of human existence in organizations. It is a useful vehicle for learning about the complex dynamics of people and their activities, such as brainstorming. (Sutton and Hargadon's study is cited in Chapter 8 on team dynamics.)

Participant observation takes the observation method one step further by having the observer take part in the organization's activities. This experience gives the researcher a fuller understanding of the activities compared to just watching others participate in those activities.

In spite of its intuitive appeal, observational research has a number of weaknesses. The main problem is that the observer is subject to the perceptual screening and organizing biases that we discuss in Chapter 3 of this textbook. There is a tendency to overlook the routine aspects of organizational life, even though they may prove to be the most important data for research purposes. Instead, observers tend to focus on unusual information, such as activities that deviate from what the observer expects. Because observational

research usually records only what the observer notices, valuable information is often lost.

Another concern with the observation method is that the researcher's presence and involvement may influence the people whom they are studying. This can be a problem in short-term observations, but in the long term people tend to return to their usual behaviour patterns. With ongoing observations, such as Sutton and Hargadon's study of brainstorming sessions at IDEO, employees eventually forget that they are being studied.

Finally, observation is usually a qualitative process, so it is more difficult to empirically test hypotheses with the data. Instead, observational research provides rich information for the inductive stages of theory building. It helps us to form ideas about the way things work in organizations. We begin to see relationships that lay the foundation for new perspectives and theory. We must not confuse this inductive process of theory building with the deductive process of theory testing.

Sources

CHAPTER 1

EXHIBIT 1.1 - *Sources:* "The Bloomberg Job Skills Report 2016: What Recruiters Want," *Bloomberg,* February 9, 2016; "Job Outlook 2018" (Bethlehem, PA: National Association of Colleges and Employers, November 2017); Morneau Shepell, "Navigating Change: 2018 Business Council Skills Survey" (Ottawa: Business Council of Canada, April 2018); "AIM Soft Skills Survey 2019" (Sydney: Australian Institute of Management, December 2018).

Case Study - *Sources:* Based on information in: J. Smith, "Top Plant: Mother Parkers: Recipe for Growth," *Plant Engineering* 68, no. 10 (2014): 26–31; "We Listen, We Lead," *Canadian HR Reporter,* October 13, 2016; Canadian HR Reporter, "2016 COS Safety Leader of the Year," YouTube, December 15 2016, https://www.youtube.com/watch?v=ViH3d9B7wOI&t=55s, Video; C. Lotz. Interview: 2016 Canadian Safety Leader of the Year. Michigan: Humantech, Inc. 2016; A. Silliker. Meet the 2016 Safety Leader of the Year. Luxembourg: Thomson Reuters Corporation. 2017; A. Silliker, "Tea Time: Meet the 2016 Safety Leader of the Year," *Canadian Occupational Safety,* December/January 2017, 28–30.

CHAPTER 2

EXHIBIT 2.3 - *Sources:* Adapted from an exhibit found at http://www.16-personality-types.com. Based on data from CPP, Inc., Sunnyvale, CA 94086 from Introduction to Type and Careers by Allen L. Hammer.

EXHIBIT 2.4 - *Sources:* S.H. Schwartz, "Universals in the Content and Structure of Values: Theoretical Advances and Empirical Tests in 20 Countries," *Advances in Experimental Social Psychology* 25 (1992): 1–65; S.H. Schwartz and K. Boehnke, "Evaluating the Structure of Human Values with Confirmatory Factor Analysis," *Journal of Research in Personality* 38, no. 3 (2004): 230–55.

EXHIBIT 2.5 - *Sources:* Individualism and collectivism descriptions and results are from the meta-analysis reported in D. Oyserman, H. M. Coon, and M. Kemmelmeier, "Rethinking Individualism and Collectivism: Evaluation of Theoretical Assumptions and Meta-Analyses," *Psychological Bulletin,* 128 (2002), pp. 3–72. The other information is from G. Hofstede, *Culture's Consequences,* 2d Ed (Thousand Oaks, CA: Sage, 2001).

Case Study - *Sources:* J. Castaldo, "SNC Lavalin's Missing Millions Mess: Is Ben Aissa Responsible?," *Canadian Business,* July 9, 2012; T. McMahon and C. Sorensen, "Boardroom Blunders at SNC-Lavalin," *Macleans,* December 5, 2012, 24; D. Seglins, "SNC-Lavalin International Used Secret Code for 'Bribery' Payments," *CBC News,* May 15, 2013; "SNC-Lavalin Says Former Executive's Illegal Actions Justify Firing," *Macleans,* May 17, 2013; J. Nicol and D. Seglins, "RCMP Moving to Freeze Assets in Widening SNC-Lavalin Probe," *CBC News,* May 23, 2013; B. Hutchinson, "The 'Clandestine World' of SNC's Fallen Star," *National Post* (Toronto), March 19, 2015, FP1; D. Hasselback, "SNC-Lavalin Sues Former Executives over Alleged Kickbacks in Libya," *National Post* (Toronto), 9 April 2015; R. Marowits, "SNC-Lavalin Settles Corruption Case Brought by African Development Bank," *Canadian Press,* October 2, 2015; "SNC-Lavalin Executive Claims He Was Scapegoat in Gadhafi Bribery Scheme," *Global Construction Review* (London), September 14, 2015; R. Marowits, "SNC-Lavalin Still Hoping to Resolve Criminal Charges as Hearing Set for 2018," *Canadian Press,* February 27, 2016; A. Derfel, "Alleged Bribery Behind MUHC Superhospital Contract: Affidavit Suggests Swiss Police Alerted Canadian Officials," *Montreal Gazette,* 10 August 2016.

CHAPTER 3

EXHIBIT 3.6 - *Source:* Based on J. Luft, *Of Human Interaction,* (Palo Alto, CA: National Press Books, 1969)

CHAPTER 4

EXHIBIT 4.1 - *Sources:* Adapted from: J. A. Russell, "Core Affect and the Psychological Construction of Emotion." *Psychological Review* 110, no. 1 (2003): 145–172; M. Yik, J.A. Russell, and J.H. Steiger. "A 12-Point Circumplex Structure of Core Affect." *Emotion* 11, no. 4 (2011): 705–31.

EXHIBIT 4.3 - *Sources:* D. Goleman, "An EI-Based Theory of Performance," in *The Emotionally Intelligent Workplace,* ed. C. Cherniss and D. Goleman (San Francisco: Jossey-Bass, 2001), 28; P. J. Jordan and S. A. Lawrence, "Emotional Intelligence in Teams: Development and Initial Validation of the Short Version of the Workgroup Emotional Intelligence Profile (WEIP-S)," *Journal of Management & Organization* 15 (2009): 452–69.

EXHIBIT 4.5 - *Sources:* J. I. Heskett, W. E. Sasser, and L. A. Schlesinger. *The Service Profit Chain* (New York: Free Press) 1997; A. J. Rucci, S. P. Kirn, and R. T. Quinn. "The Employee-Customer-Profit Chain At Sears." *Harvard Business Review* 76 (1998): 83–97; S. P. Brown and S. K. Lam. "A Meta-Analysis of Relationships Linking Employee Satisfaction to Customer Responses." *Journal of Retailing* 84, no. 3 (2008): 243–255.

EXHIBIT 4.6 - *Source:* Adapted from H. Selye, *The Stress of Life* (New York: McGraw Hill, 1956).

CHAPTER 5

EXHIBIT 5.2 - *Source:* Based on information in P. R. Lawrence and N. Nohria, *Driven: How Human Nature Shapes Our Choices* (San Francisco: Jossey-Bass, 2002).

EXHIBIT 5.3 - *Source:* Based on information in A. H. Maslow, "A Theory of Human Motivation," *Psychological Review* 50 (1943), pp. 370–396.

EXHIBIT 5.6 - *Sources:* Adapted from T. K. Connellan, How to Improve Human Performance (New York: Harper & Row, 1978), p. 50; F. Luthans and R. Kreitner, Organizational Behaviour Modification and Beyond (Glenview, IL: Scott, Foresman, 1985), pp. 85–88.

EXHIBIT 5.10 - *Sources:* Based on information in: G.S. Leventhal, "What Should Be Done with Equity Theory? New Approaches to the Study of Fairness in Social Relationships," in *Social Exchange,* ed. K.J. Gergen, M.S. Greenberg, and R.H. Willis (Boston, MA: Springer US, 1980), 27–55; J.A. Colquitt and J.B. Rodell, "Measuring Justice and Fairness," in *The Oxford Handbook of Justice in the Workplace,* ed. R.S. Cropanzano and M.L. Ambrose (New York: Oxford University Press, 2015), 187–202.

CHAPTER 6

EXHIBIT 6.2 - *Sources:* J.R. Hackman and E.E. Lawler, "Employee Reactions to Job Characteristics," *Journal of Applied Psychology* 55, no. 3 (1971): 259–86; J.R. Hackman and G.R. Oldham, "The Job Diagnostic Survey: An Instrument for the Diagnosis of Jobs and the Evaluation of Job Redesign Projects" (New Haven, Conn.: Dept. of Administrative Sciences, Yale University, May 1974); J.R. Hackman and G.R. Oldham, "Motivation through the Design of Work: Test of a Theory," *Organizational Behavior and Human Performance* 16, no. 2 (1976): 250–79; J. R. Hackman and G. Oldham, *Work Redesign* (Reading, MA: Addison-Wesley, 1980).

Team Exercise - Table 2 - *Source:* Adapted from the Job Diagnostic Survey, developed by J. R. Hackman and G. R. Oldham. The authors have released any copyright ownership of this scale [see J. R. Hackman and G. Oldham, *Work Redesign* (Reading, MA: Addison-Wesley, 1980), p. 275].

CHAPTER 7

EXHIBIT 7.4 - *Source:* Based on G. Wallas, *The Art of Thought* (London: Jonathan Cape, 1926, Chap. 4).

EXHIBIT 7.6 - *Source:* Based on information in C. Meinel and L. Leifer, "Introduction—Design Thinking Is Mainly about Building Innovators," in *Design Thinking Research: Building Innovators,* ed. H. Plattner, C. Meinel, and L. Leifer (Cham, Switzerland: Springer International, 2015), 1–11.

Case Study - *Sources:* J. Falconer, "Unnecessary Surrenders? Fuhgettaboutit!," *Animal Sheltering Magazine,* The Humane Society of the United States, March/April, 2016; T. Wedell-Wedellsborg, "Are You Solving the Right Problems?" *Harvard Business Review,* January/February 2017; A. Torgan, "Keeping People and Their Pets Together," *CNN,* December 18, 2018; L. Lombardi, "Poverty Forces People to Surrender Their Pets. It Doesn't Have to Be This Way," *Talk Poverty,* February 4,

2019; "The New York Community Trust Grants $4.8 Million to Invest in a Fairer, More Equitable New York," News release (New York City: The New York Community Trust, April 8, 2019).

Class Exercise - *Sources:* The Productivity Dividend Decision and The Social Media Policy Decision: © 2013 Steven L. McShane. The Sugar-Substitute Research Decision: © 2002 Steven L. McShane. The Coast Guard Cutter Decision case is adapted from V.H. Vroom and A.G. Jago, *The New Leadership: Managing Participation in Organizations* (Englewood Cliffs, NJ: Prentice Hall, 1988), © 1987 V.H. Vroom and A.G. Jago. Used with permission of the authors.

CHAPTER 8

EXHIBIT 8.4 - *Sources:* Based on information in V. Rousseau, C. Aubé, and A. Savoie, "Teamwork Behaviors: A Review and an Integration of Frameworks," *Small Group Research* 37, no. 5 (2006), 540–70; M.L. Loughry, M.W. Ohland, and D.D. Moore, "Development of a Theory-Based Assessment of Team Member Effectiveness," *Educational and Psychological Measurement* 67, no. 3 (2007), 505–24; E. Salas et al., "Understanding and Improving Teamwork in Organizations: A Scientifically Based Practical Guide," *Human Resource Management* 54, no. 4 (2015): 599–622.

EXHIBIT 8.6 - Adapted from J.E. Mathieu et al., "Team Role Experience and Orientation: A Measure and Tests of Construct Validity," *Group & Organization Management* 40, no. 1 (2015): 6–34.

Team Exercise - *Source:* Several published and online sources describe variations of this exercise, but there is no known origin to this activity.

CHAPTER 9

EXHIBIT 9.3 - *Source:* Based on J.H. Kietzmann, K. Hermkens, I.P. McCarthy, and B.S. Silvestre, "Social Media? Get Serious! Understanding the Functional Building Blocks of Social Media," *Business Horizons* 54, no. 3 (2011): 241–51.

EXHIBIT 9.6 - *Source:* Based on R. L. Daft and R. H. Lengel, "Information Richness: A New Approach to Managerial Behavior and Organization Design," *Research in Organizational Behavior* 6 (1984): 199; R. H. Lengel and R. L. Daft, "The Selection of Communication Media as an Executive Skill," *Academy of Management Executive* 2, no. 3 (August 1988): 226.

CHAPTER 9

Case Study - *Sources:* K. Burne, "Making Waves against 'Whale,'" *The Wall Street Journal,* April 11, 2012, C1; E. Schatzker, C. Harper, and M. Childs, "JPMorgan Said to Transform Treasury to Prop Trading," *Bloomberg,* April 13, 2012; G. Zuckerman, "From 'Caveman' to 'Whale,'" *The Wall Street Journal,* May 17, 2012, C1; E. Flitter and A. Viswanatha, "Ex-JP Morgan Exec Tries to Dodge Harpoon of 'Whale' Losses," *Reuters,* March 15, 2013; R. Sidel, S. Patterson, and J. Eaglesham, "J.P. Morgan Faces a Hard-Line SEC," *The Wall Street Journal,* September 20, 2013, C1; D. Fitzpatrick, J. Eaglesham, and D. Barrett, "Two Charged in 'London Whale' Case," *The Wall Street Journal,* August 15, 2013, C1; "Ex-JP Morgan Boss Blames London Office for £4bn Loss in 'Whale' Scandal," *Mail Online* (London), March 16, 2013; B. Laurence, "Whale Leaves Cracks in Wall St," *Sunday Times* (London), August 18, 2013, 7; M. Cavanagh, *Report of JPMorgan Chase & Co. Management Task Force Regarding 2012 CIO Losses,* JP Morgan Chase & Co (New York: January 16, 2013); J.B. Stewart, "Convictions Prove Elusive in 'London Whale' Trading Case," *The New York Times,* July 17, 2015; L. McNulty and G. Zuckerman, "'London Whale' Breaks Silence," *The Wall Street Journal,* February 23, 2016, C1.

CHAPTER 11

Class Exercise: Conflict Handling Incidents - NOTE: This exercise was inspired by a similar activity in: G.A. Callanan and D.F. Perri, "Teaching Conflict Management Using a Scenario-Based Approach," *Journal of Education for Business* 81 (January/February 2006): 131–39.

Team Exercise: Kumquat Conflict Role Play - This exercise was developed by Steven L. McShane. It is inspired by a similar exercise in D.T. Hall, D.D. Bowen, R.J. Lewicki, and F.S. Hall, *Experiences in Management and*

Organizational Behavior (Chicago: St. Clair Press, 1975). It is also inspired by an incident involving two sisters described in R. Fisher and W. Ury, *Getting to Yes: Negotiating Agreement without Giving In* (New York: Penguin, 1981).

CHAPTER 12

EXHIBIT 12.4 - Based on ideas in S. Kerr and J.M. Jermier, "Substitutes for Leadership: Their Meaning and Measurement," *Organizational Behavior and Human Performance* 22 (December 1978): 375–403; P.M. Podsakoff and S B. MacKenzie, "Kerr and Jermier's Substitutes for Leadership Model: Background, Empirical Assessment, and Suggestions for Future Research," *Leadership Quarterly* 8 (1997): 117–32.

CHAPTER 13

EXHIBIT 13.1 - *Sources:* Based on information in J. Galbraith, *Designing Complex Organizations* (Reading, MA: Addison-Wesley, 1973), pp. 8–19; H. Mintzberg, *The Structuring of Organizations* (Englewood Cliffs, NJ: Prentice Hall, 1979), chap. 1; D. A. Nadler and M. L. Tushman, *Competing by Design: The Power of Organizational Architecture* (New York: Oxford University Press, 1997), Chap. 6.

Case Study - *Sources:* S. Cherry, "Not without Its Merritt's," *Tulsa World,* April 13, 2001, 19; D. Blossom, "Bakery Has Recipe for Success," *Tulsa World,* October 28, 2002, A7; M. Reynolds, "A Difficult Choice Pays Off for Merritt's Bakery," *Modern Baking,* March 2010, 39; "Flour Power," *Tulsa People,* May 2011. Information also was collected from the company's website, www.merrittsbakery.com.

Team Exercise: - Based on C. Harvey and K. Morouney, *Journal of Management Education* 22 (June 1998), pp. 425–29.

CHAPTER 14

EXHIBIT 14.2 - *Source:* Based on information in C. A. O'Reilly III, J. Chatman, and D. F. Caldwell, "People and Organizational Culture: A Profile Comparison Approach to Assessing Person-Organization Fit," *Academy of Management Journal* 34, no. 3 (1991), pp. 487–518.

EXHIBIT 14.3 - *Source:* Based on information in: *How to Create a Successful Organizational Culture: Build It—Literally* (Holland, MI: Haworth Inc., June 2015).

EXHIBIT 14.5 - *Sources:* Based on ideas in A. R. Malekzedeh and A. Nahavandi, "Making Mergers Work by Managing Cultures," *Journal of Business Strategy,* 11 (May–June 1990), pp. 55–57; K. W. Smith, "A Brand-New Culture for the Merged Firm," *Mergers and Acquisitions,* 35 (June 2000), pp. 45–50.

Team Exercise: - *Source:* Adapted from D. L. Luechauer and G. M. Shulman, "Using A Metaphor Exercise To Explore The Principles Of Organizational Culture," *Journal of Management Education* 22 (December 1998), pp. 736-44. *Note:* The television shows listed here are current or recently broadcast programs whose characteristics are similar to the TV shows originally listed by the authors of this activity.

CHAPTER 15

EXHIBIT 15.2 - *Sources:* Adapted from J. P. Kotter and L. A. Schlesinger, "Choosing Strategies for Change," *Harvard Business Review* 57 (1979), pp. 106–114; P. R. Lawrence, "How to Deal with Resistance to Change," *Harvard Business Review,* May–June 1954, pp. 49–57.

EXHIBIT 15.5 - *Sources:* Based on D. L. Cooperrider and D. K. Whitney, Appreciative Inquiry: A Positive Revolution in Change. (San Francisco: Berrett-Koehler, 2005), Chap. 7; D. K. Whitney and A. Trosten-Bloom. The power of appreciative inquiry: A practical guide to positive change. 2nd ed. (San Francisco: Berrett-Koehler Publishers, 2010), Chap. 3.

EXHIBIT 15.6 - *Sources:* Based on F. J. Barrett and D. L. Cooperrider, "Generative Metaphor Intervention: A New Approach for Working with Systems Divided by Conflict and Caught in Defensive Perception," *Journal of Applied Behavioural Science* 26 (1990), p. 229; D. Whitney and C. Schau, "Appreciative Inquiry: An Innovative Process for Organization Change," *Employment Relations Today* 25 (Spring 1998), pp. 11–21; D. L. Cooperrider and D. K. Whitney, Appreciative inquiry: A positive revolution in change. (San Francisco: Berrett-Koehler, 2005), Chap. 3.

Glossary

A

ability The natural aptitudes and learned capabilities required to successfully complete a task.

achievement-nurturing orientation A cross-cultural value describing the degree to which people in a culture emphasize competitive versus cooperative relations with other people.

action research A problem-focused change process that combines action orientation (changing attitudes and behaviour) and research orientation (testing theory through data collection and analysis).

adaptive culture An organizational culture in which employees are receptive to change, including the ongoing alignment of the organization to its environment and continuous improvement of internal processes.

affective organizational commitment An individual's emotional attachment to, involvement in, and identification with an organization.

agreeableness A personality dimension describing people who are trusting, helpful, good-natured, considerate, tolerant, selfless, generous, and flexible.

anchoring and adjustment heuristic A natural tendency for people to be influenced by an initial anchor point such that they do not sufficiently move away from that point as new information is provided.

appreciative inquiry An organizational change strategy that directs the group's attention away from its own problems and focuses participants on the group's potential and positive elements.

artifacts The observable symbols and signs of an organization's culture.

attitudes The cluster of beliefs, assessed feelings, and behavioural intentions towards a person, object, or event (called an *attitude object*).

attraction–selection–attrition (ASA) theory A theory which states that organizations have a natural tendency to attract, select, and retain people with values and personality characteristics that are consistent with the organization's character, resulting in a more homogeneous organization and a stronger culture.

attribution process The perceptual process of deciding whether an observed behaviour or event is caused largely by internal or external factors.

authentic leadership The view that effective leaders need to be aware of, feel comfortable with, and act consistently with their values, personality, and self-concept.

availability heuristic A natural tendency to assign higher probabilities to objects or events that are easier to recall from memory, even though ease of recall is also affected by nonprobability factors (e.g., emotional response, recent events).

B

best alternative to a negotiated agreement (BATNA) The best outcome you might achieve through some other course of action if you abandon the current negotiation.

bicultural audit A process of diagnosing cultural relations between companies and determining the extent to which cultural clashes will likely occur.

bounded rationality The view that people are bounded in their decision-making capabilities, including access to limited information, limited information processing, and tendency toward satisficing rather than maximizing when making choices.

brainstorming A freewheeling, face-to-face meeting where team members aren't allowed to criticize but are encouraged to speak freely, generate as many ideas as possible, and build on the ideas of others.

brainwriting A variation of brainstorming whereby participants write (rather than speak about) and share their ideas.

Brooks's law The principle that adding more people to a late software project only makes it later.

C

categorical thinking Organizing people and objects into preconceived categories that are stored in our long-term memory.

centrality A contingency of power pertaining to the degree and nature of interdependence between the powerholder and others.

centralization The degree to which formal decision-making authority is held by a small group of people, typically those at the top of the organizational hierarchy.

ceremonies Planned displays of organizational culture, conducted specifically for the benefit of an audience.

charisma A set of self-presentation characteristics and nonverbal communication behaviours (i.e., signalling) that generate interpersonal attraction and referent power over others as well as deference to the charismatic person.

coalition A group that attempts to influence people outside the group by pooling the resources and power of its members.

cognitive dissonance An emotional experience caused by a perception that our beliefs, feelings, and behaviour are incongruent with one another.

collectivism A cross-cultural value describing the degree to which people in a culture emphasize duty to groups to which they belong and to group harmony.

communication The process by which information is transmitted and *understood* between two or more people.

confirmation bias The process of screening out information that is contrary to our values and assumptions, and to more readily accept confirming information.

conflict

conflict The process in which one party perceives that its interests are being opposed or negatively affected by another party.

conscientiousness A personality dimension describing people who are organized, dependable, goal-focused, thorough, disciplined, methodical, and industrious.

constructs Abstract ideas constructed by researchers that can be linked to observable information.

contact hypothesis A theory stating that the more we interact with someone, the less prejudiced or perceptually biased we will be against that person.

continuance commitment An individual's calculative attachment to an organization.

corporate social responsibility (CSR) Organizational activities intended to benefit society and the environment beyond the firm's immediate financial interests or legal obligations.

counterproductive work behaviours (CWBs) Voluntary behaviours that have the potential to directly or indirectly harm the organization.

countervailing power The capacity of a person, team, or organization to keep a more powerful person or group in the exchange relationship.

creativity The development of original ideas that make a socially recognized contribution.

D

dark triad A cluster of three socially undesirable (dark) personality traits: Machiavellianism, narcissism, and psychopathy.

decision making The conscious process of making choices among alternatives with the intention of moving toward some desired state of affairs.

deep-level diversity Differences in the psychological characteristics of employees, including personalities, beliefs, values, and attitudes.

design thinking A human-centred, solution-focused creative process that applies both intuition and analytical thinking to clarify problems and generate innovative solutions.

distributive justice The perception that appropriate decision criteria (rules) have been applied to calculate how various benefits and burdens are distributed.

divergent thinking Reframing a problem in a unique way and generating different approaches to the issue.

divisional structure An organizational structure in which employees are organized around geographic areas, outputs (products or services), or clients.

drives Hardwired characteristics of the brain that correct deficiencies or maintain an internal equilibrium by producing emotions to energize individuals.

E

electronic brainstorming A form of brain-writing that relies on networked computers for submitting and sharing creative ideas.

emotional contagion The nonconscious process of "catching" or sharing another person's emotions by mimicking that person's facial expressions and other nonverbal behaviour.

emotional intelligence (EI) A set of abilities to perceive and express emotion, assimilate emotion in thought, understand and reason with emotion, and regulate emotion in oneself and others.

emotional labour The effort, planning, and control needed to express organizationally desired emotions during interpersonal transactions.

emotions Physiological, behavioural, and psychological episodes experienced toward an object, person, or event that create a state of readiness.

empathy A person's understanding of and sensitivity to the feelings, thoughts, and situations of others.

employee engagement A person's emotional and cognitive motivation, particularly a focused, intense, persistent, and purposive effort toward work-related goals.

employee share ownership plans (ESOPs) A reward system that encourages employees to buy company shares.

equity theory A theory explaining how people develop perceptions of fairness in the distribution and exchange of resources.

escalation of commitment The tendency to repeat an apparently bad decision or allocate more resources to a failing course of action.

ethics The study of moral principles or values that determine whether actions are right or wrong and outcomes are good or bad.

evaluation apprehension Occurs when individuals are reluctant to mention ideas that seem silly because they believe that others in the decision-making team are silently evaluating them.

evidence-based management The practice of making decisions and taking actions based on research evidence.

exit-voice-loyalty-neglect (EVLN) model The four ways, as indicated in the name, that employees respond to job dissatisfaction.

expectancy theory A motivation theory based on the idea that work effort is directed toward behaviours that people believe will lead to desired outcomes.

extraversion A personality dimension describing people who are outgoing, talkative, sociable, and assertive.

extrinsic motivation Motivation that occurs when people want to engage in an activity for instrumental reasons, that is, to receive something that is beyond their personal control.

F

false-consensus effect A perceptual error in which we overestimate the extent to which others have beliefs and characteristics similar to our own.

field surveys Research design strategies that involve collecting and analyzing information in a natural environment, such as an office, a factory, or other existing location.

five-factor (Big Five) model The five broad dimensions representing most personality traits: conscientiousness, neuroticism, openness to experience, agreeableness, and extraversion.

force field analysis Kurt Lewin's model of system-wide change that helps change agents diagnose the forces that drive and restrain proposed organizational change.

formalization The degree to which organizations standardize behaviour through rules, procedures, formal training, and related mechanisms.

four-drive theory A motivation theory based on the innate drives to acquire, bond, comprehend, and defend that incorporates both emotions and rationality.

functional structure An organizational structure in which employees are organized around specific knowledge or other resources.

fundamental attribution error The tendency to see the person rather than the situation as the main cause of that person's behaviour.

G

gainsharing plan A team-based reward that calculates bonuses from the work unit's cost savings and productivity improvement.

general adaptation syndrome A model of the stress experience, consisting of three stages: alarm reaction, resistance, and exhaustion.

global mindset An individual's ability to perceive, appreciate, and empathize with people from other cultures, and to process complex cross-cultural information.

goal A cognitive representation of a desired end state that a person is committed to attain.

grapevine An unstructured and informal communication network founded on social relationships rather than organizational charts or job descriptions.

grounded theory A process of developing knowledge through the constant interplay of data collection, analysis, and theory development.

H

halo effect A perceptual error whereby our general impression of a person, usually based on one prominent characteristic, colours our perception of other characteristics of that person.

human capital The knowledge, skills, abilities, creative thinking, and other valued resources that employees bring to the organization.

hypotheses Statements making empirically testable declarations that certain variables and their corresponding measures are related in a specific way proposed by the theory.

I

implicit favourite A preferred alternative that the decision maker uses repeatedly as a comparison with other choices.

implicit leadership theory A theory stating that people evaluate a leader's effectiveness in terms of how well that person fits preconceived beliefs about the features and behaviours of effective leaders (leadership prototypes), and that people tend to inflate the influence of leaders on organizational events.

impression management Actively shaping through self-presentation and other means the perceptions and attitudes that others have of us.

inclusive workplace A workplace that values people of all identities and allows them to be fully themselves while contributing to the organization.

individualism A cross-cultural value describing the degree to which people in a culture emphasize independence and personal uniqueness.

influence Any behaviour that attempts to alter someone's attitudes or behaviour.

information overload A condition in which the volume of information received exceeds the person's capacity to process it.

inoculation effect A persuasive communication strategy of warning listeners that others will try to influence them in the future and that they should be wary about the opponent's arguments.

interactional justice The perception that appropriate rules have been applied in the way the people involved are treated throughout the decision process.

interpretivism The view held in many qualitative studies that reality comes from shared meaning among people in a particular environment.

intrinsic motivation Motivation that occurs when people are fulfilling their needs for competence and autonomy by engaging in the activity itself, rather than from an externally controlled outcome of that activity.

intuition The ability to know when a problem or opportunity exists and to select the best course of action without conscious reasoning.

J

job characteristics model A job design model that relates the motivational properties of jobs to specific personal and organizational consequences of those properties.

job enlargement The practice of increasing the number and variety of related tasks assigned to a job.

job enrichment The practice of giving employees more responsibility for scheduling, coordinating, and planning their own work.

job evaluation Systematically rating the worth of jobs within an organization by measuring their required skill, effort, responsibility, and working conditions.

job satisfaction A person's evaluation of their job and work context.

job specialization The result of division of labour in which work is subdivided into separate jobs assigned to different people.

Johari Window A model of self-awareness and mutual understanding with others that advocates disclosure and feedback to increase our open area and reduce the blind, hidden, and unknown areas.

L

laboratory experiment Any research study in which independent variables and variables outside the researcher's main focus of inquiry can be controlled to some extent.

leadership Influencing, motivating, and enabling others to contribute toward the effectiveness and success of the organizations of which they are members.

leadership substitutes theory A theory identifying conditions that either limit a leader's ability to influence subordinates or make a particular leadership style unnecessary.

learning orientation A set of collective beliefs and norms that encourage people to question past practices, learn new ideas, experiment putting ideas into practice, and view mistakes as part of the learning process.

legitimate power An agreement among organizational members that people in certain roles can request certain behaviours of others.

locus of control A person's general belief about the amount of control they have over personal life events.

M

Machiavellianism A personality trait of people who demonstrate a strong motivation to achieve their own goals at the expense of others, who believe that deceit is a natural and acceptable way to achieve their goals, who take pleasure in outwitting and misleading others using crude influence tactics, and who have a cynical disregard for morality.

management by wandering around (MBWA) A communication practice in which executives get out of their offices and learn from others in the organization through face-to-face dialogue.

managerial leadership A leadership perspective stating that effective leaders help employees improve their performance and well-being towards current objectives and practices.

MARS model A model depicting the four variables—motivation, ability, role perceptions, and situational factors—that directly influence an individual's voluntary behaviour and performance.

Maslow's needs hierarchy theory A motivation theory of needs arranged in a hierarchy, whereby people are motivated to fulfill a higher need as a lower one becomes gratified.

matrix structure An organizational structure that overlays two structures (such as a geographic divisional and a product structure) in order to leverage the benefits of both.

mechanistic structure An organizational structure with a narrow span of control and a high degree of formalization and centralization.

media richness A medium's data-carrying capacity, that is, the volume and variety of information that can be transmitted during a specific time.

mental imagery The process of mentally practising a task and visualizing its successful completion.

mental models Knowledge structures that we develop to describe, explain, and predict the world around us.

mindfulness A person's receptive and impartial attention to and awareness of the present situation as well as to one's own thoughts and emotions in that moment.

moral intensity The degree to which an issue demands the application of ethical principles.

moral sensitivity A person's ability to recognize the presence of an ethical issue and determine its relative importance.

motivation The forces within a person that affect the direction, intensity, and persistence of effort for voluntary behaviour.

Myers-Briggs Type Indicator (MBTI) An instrument designed to measure the elements of Jungian personality theory, particularly preferences regarding perceiving and judging information.

N

narcissism A personality trait of people with a grandiose, obsessive belief in their superiority and entitlement, a propensity to aggressively engage in attention-seeking behaviours, an intense envy of others, and tendency to exhibit arrogance, callousness, and exploitation of others for personal aggrandizement.

need for achievement (nAch) A learned need in which people want to accomplish reasonably challenging goals and desire unambiguous feedback and recognition for their success.

need for affiliation (nAff) A learned need in which people seek approval from others, conform to their wishes and expectations, and avoid conflict and confrontation.

need for power (nPow) A learned need in which people want to control their environment, including people and material resources, to benefit either themselves (personalized power) or others (socialized power).

needs Goal-directed forces that people experience.

negotiation The process in which interdependent parties with divergent beliefs or goals attempt to reach agreement on issues that mutually affect them.

network structure An alliance of several organizations for the purpose of creating a product or serving a client.

neuroticism A personality dimension describing people who tend to be anxious, insecure, self-conscious, depressed, and temperamental.

nominal group technique A variation of brainwriting consisting of three stages: participants (1) silently and independently document their ideas, (2) collectively describe these ideas to the other team members without critique, and then (3) silently and independently evaluate the ideas presented.

norm of reciprocity A felt obligation and social expectation of helping or otherwise giving something of value to someone who has already helped or given something of value to you.

norms The informal rules and shared expectations that groups establish to regulate the behaviour of their members.

O

open systems The view that organizations depend on the external environment for resources, affect that environment through their output, and consist of internal subsystems that transform inputs to outputs.

openness to experience A personality dimension describing people who are imaginative, creative, unconventional, curious, nonconforming, autonomous, and aesthetically perceptive.

organic structure An organizational structure with a wide span of control, little formalization, and decentralized decision making.

organizational behaviour (OB) The study of what people think, feel, and do in and around organizations.

organizational behaviour modification (OB Mod) A theory that explains employee behaviour in terms of the antecedent conditions and consequences of that behaviour.

organizational citizenship behaviours (OCBs) Various forms of cooperation and helpfulness to others that support the organization's social and psychological context.

organizational culture The values and assumptions shared within an organization.

organizational effectiveness The extent to which an organization has a good fit with its external environment, effectively transforms inputs to outputs through human capital, and satisfies the needs of key stakeholders.

organizational politics The use of influence tactics for personal gain at the perceived expense of others and the organization.

organizational socialization The process by which individuals learn the values, expected behaviours, and social knowledge necessary to assume their roles in the organization.

organizational strategy The way the organization positions itself in its setting in relation to its stakeholders, given the organization's resources, capabilities, and mission.

organizational structure The division of labour as well as the patterns of coordination, communication, workflow, and formal power that direct organizational activities.

organizations Groups of people who work interdependently toward some purpose.

P

parallel learning structures Highly participative arrangements composed of people from most levels of the organization who follow the action research model to produce meaningful organizational change.

path–goal leadership theory A leadership theory stating that effective leaders choose the most appropriate leadership style(s), depending on the employee and situation, to influence employee expectations about desired results and their positive outcomes.

perception The process of receiving information about and making sense of our surrounding environment.

personality The relatively enduring pattern of thoughts, emotions, and behaviours that characterize a person, along with the psychological processes behind those characteristics.

persuasion The use of facts, logical arguments, and emotional appeals to change another person's beliefs and attitudes, usually for the purpose of changing the person's behaviour.

positive organizational behaviour A perspective of organizational behaviour that focuses on building positive qualities and traits within individuals or institutions as opposed to focusing on what is wrong with them.

positivism A view held in quantitative research in which reality exists independent of the perceptions and interpretations of people.

power The capacity of a person, team, or organization to influence others.

power distance A cross-cultural value describing the degree to which people in a culture accept unequal distribution of power in a society.

primacy effect A perceptual error in which we quickly form an opinion of people based on the first information we receive about them.

procedural justice The perception that appropriate procedural rules have been applied throughout the decision process.

process losses Resources (including time and energy) expended toward team development and maintenance rather than the task.

production blocking A time constraint in team decision making due to the procedural requirement that only one person may speak at a time.

profit-sharing plan A reward system that pays bonuses to employees on the basis of the previous year's level of corporate profits.

prospect theory effect An innate tendency to feel stronger negative emotion from losing a particular amount than positive emotion from gaining an equal amount.

psychological contract The individual's beliefs about the terms and conditions of a reciprocal exchange agreement between that person and another party (typically an employer).

psychological empowerment A perceptual and emotional state in which people experience more self-determination, meaning, competence, and impact regarding their role in the organization.

psychological safety A shared belief that it is safe to engage in interpersonal risk-taking; specifically, that presenting unusual ideas, constructively disagreeing with the majority, and experimenting with new work behaviours will not result in co-workers posing a threat to one's self-concept, status, or career.

psychopathy A personality trait of people who ruthlessly dominate and manipulate others without empathy or any feelings of remorse or anxiety, use superficial charm, yet are social predators who engage in antisocial, impulsive, and often fraudulent thrill-seeking behaviour.

R

rational choice decision making The process of using pure logic and all available information about all alternatives to choose the alternative with the highest value.

realistic job preview (RJP) A method of improving organizational socialization in which job applicants are given a balance of positive and negative information about the job and work context.

reality shock The stress that results when employees perceive discrepancies between their pre-employment expectations and on-the-job reality.

recency effect A perceptual error in which the most recent information dominates our perception of others.

referent power The capacity to influence others on the basis of an identification with and respect for the power holder.

refreezing The latter part of the change process, in which systems and structures are introduced that reinforce and maintain the desired behaviours.

relationship conflict A type of conflict in which people focus their discussion on qualities of the people in the dispute, rather than on the qualities of the ideas presented regarding a task-related issue.

remote teams Teams whose members operate across space, time, and organizational boundaries and are linked through information technologies to achieve organizational tasks.

representative sampling The process of sampling a population in such a way that one can extrapolate the results of that sample to the larger population.

representativeness heuristic A natural tendency to evaluate probabilities of events or objects by the degree to which they resemble (are representative of) other events or objects rather than on objective probability information.

rituals The programmed routines of daily organizational life that dramatize the organization's culture.

role A set of behaviours that people are expected to perform because they hold specific formal or informal positions in a team and organization.

role perceptions The degree to which a person understands the job duties assigned to or expected of them.

S

satisficing Selecting an alternative that is satisfactory or "good enough," rather than the alternative with the highest value (maximization).

scenario planning A systematic process of thinking about alternative futures and what the organization should do to anticipate and react to those environments.

scientific management The practice of systematically partitioning work into its smallest elements and standardizing tasks to achieve maximum efficiency.

scientific method A set of principles and procedures that help researchers to systematically understand previously unexplained events and conditions.

selective attention The process of attending to some information received by our senses and ignoring other information.

self-concept An individual's self-beliefs and self-evaluations.

self-directed teams (SDTs) Cross-functional work groups that are organized around work processes, complete an entire piece of work requiring several interdependent tasks, and have substantial autonomy over the execution of those tasks.

self-efficacy A person's belief that they have the ability, motivation, correct role perceptions, and favourable situation to complete a task successfully.

self-enhancement A person's inherent motivation to have a positive self-concept (and to have others perceive them favourably), such as being competent, attractive, lucky, ethical, and important.

self-fulfilling prophecy The perceptual process in which our expectations about another person cause that person to act more consistently with those expectations.

self-leadership Specific cognitive and behavioural strategies to achieve personal goals and standards through self-direction and self-motivation.

self-reinforcement Reinforcement that occurs when an employee has control over a reinforcer but doesn't 'take' it until completing a self-set goal.

self-serving bias The tendency to attribute our favourable outcomes to internal factors and our failures to external factors.

self-talk The process of talking to ourselves about our own thoughts or actions.

self-verification A person's inherent motivation to confirm and maintain their existing self-concept.

servant leadership The view that leaders serve followers, rather than vice versa; leaders help employees fulfil their needs and are coaches, stewards, and facilitators of employee performance.

service profit chain model A theory explaining how employees' job satisfaction influences company profitability indirectly through service quality, customer loyalty, and related factors.

share options A reward system that gives employees the right to purchase company shares at a future date at a predetermined price.

shared leadership The view that leadership is a role, not a position assigned to one person; consequently, people within the team and organization lead each other.

skill variety The extent to which employees must use different skills and talents to perform tasks within their jobs.

social capital The knowledge, opportunities, and other resources available to members of a social network, along with the mutual support, trust, reciprocity, and coordination that facilitate sharing of those resources.

social cognitive theory A theory that explains how learning and motivation occur by observing and modelling others as well as by anticipating the consequences of our behaviour.

social identity theory A theory stating that people define themselves by the groups to which they belong or have an emotional attachment.

social loafing The problem that occurs when people exert less effort (and usually perform at a lower level) when working in teams than when working alone.

social media Digital communication channels that enable people to collaborate in the creation and exchange of user-generated content.

social networks Social structures of individuals or social units that are connected to each other through one or more forms of interdependence.

social presence The extent to which a communication channel creates psychological closeness to others, awareness of their humanness, and appreciation of the interpersonal relationship.

span of control The number of people directly reporting to the next level in the hierarchy.

stakeholders Individuals, groups, and other entities that affect, or are affected by, the organization's objectives and actions.

stereotype threat An individual's concern about confirming a negative stereotype about their group.

stereotyping The process of assigning traits to people based on their membership in a social category.

strengths-based coaching An approach to coaching and feedback that focuses on building and leveraging the employee's strengths rather than trying to correct their weaknesses.

stress An adaptive response to a situation that is perceived as challenging or threatening to the person's well-being.

stressors Environmental conditions that place a physical or emotional demand on the person.

structural hole An area between two or more dense social network areas that lacks network ties.

superordinate goals Goals that the conflicting parties value and whose attainment requires the joint resources and effort of those parties.

surface-level diversity The observable demographic or physiological differences in people, such as their race, ethnicity, gender, age, and physical disabilities.

synchronicity The extent to which the channel requires or allows both sender and receiver to be actively involved in the conversation at the same time (synchronous) or at different times (asynchronous).

T

task analyzability The degree to which job duties allow the application of established procedures and rules to guide decisions and behaviour (high analyzability); employee creativity and judgment are necessary to perform jobs with low task analyzability.

task conflict A type of conflict in which people focus their discussion around the issue (i.e., the "task") in which different viewpoints occur while showing respect for people involved in that disagreement.

task identity The degree to which a job requires completion of a whole or an identifiable piece of work.

task interdependence The extent to which employees must share materials, information, or expertise with others to perform their jobs.

task performance The individual's voluntary goal-directed behaviours that contribute to organizational objectives.

task significance The degree to which a job has a substantial impact on the organization and/or larger society.

task variability The degree to which job duties are nonroutine and unpredictable; employees perform diverse tasks from one day to the next because they are faced with unfamiliar and unexpected issues.

team cohesion The degree of attraction people feel toward the team and their motivation to remain members.

team efficacy The collective belief among team members of the team's capability to successfully complete a task.

team-based structure An organizational structure built around self-directed teams that complete an entire piece of work.

teams Groups of two or more people who interact and influence each other, are mutually accountable for achieving common goals associated with organizational objectives, and perceive themselves as a social entity within an organization.

theory A general set of propositions that describes interrelationships among several concepts.

third-party conflict resolution Any attempt by a relatively neutral person to help conflicting parties resolve their differences.

transformational leadership A leadership perspective that explains how leaders change teams or organizations by creating, communicating, and modelling a vision for the organization or work unit and inspiring employees to strive for that vision.

trust Positive expectations one person has toward another person or group in situations involving risk.

U

uncertainty avoidance A cross-cultural value describing the degree to which people in a culture tolerate ambiguity (low uncertainty avoidance) or feel threatened by ambiguity and uncertainty (high uncertainty avoidance).

unfreezing The first part of the organizational change process, in which the change agent produces disequilibrium between the driving and restraining forces.

upward appeal A type of influence in which someone with higher authority or expertise is relied on in reality or symbolically to support the influencer's position.

V

values Relatively stable evaluative beliefs that guide a person's preferences for outcomes or courses of action in a variety of situations.

W

win–lose orientation The belief that conflicting parties are drawing from a fixed pie, so the more one party receives, the less the other party will receive.

win–win orientation The belief that conflicting parties will find a mutually beneficial solution to their disagreement.

work–life integration The extent to which people are effectively engaged in their various work and nonwork roles and have a low degree of role conflict across those life domains.

Endnotes

CHAPTER 1

1. *Working at BlueCat,* YouTube (Toronto, 2016), https://www.youtube.com/watch?v=211aAKu3Q4o; D. O'Neill, "BlueCat Networks Is Leading the Way in Cyber Security," *StartUp HERE Toronto* (blog), February 15, 2018, https://startupheretoronto.com/type/profiles/bluecat-networks-leading-way-cyber-security/; *BlueCat Leadership,* YouTube (Toronto, 2018), https://www.youtube.com/watch?v=sm8OUrNTD5s; *BlueCat Core Values: TRANSPARENCY,* YouTube (Toronto, 2018), https://www.youtube.com/watch?v=pjdVMXK58BY; *BlueCat Core Values: COLLABORATION,* YouTube (Toronto, 2018), https://www.youtube.com/watch?v=Tp2amP2tETk; "Great Place to Work™ Names BlueCat 24th Best Workplace in Canada," BlueCat Networks, April 26, 2019, https://www.bluecatnetworks.com/blog/great-place-to-work-names-bluecat-24th-best-workplace-in-canada/; "2019 Canadian HR Awards Winners Announced," *Human Resources Director,* September 13, 2019.

2. M. Warner, "Organizational Behavior Revisited," *Human Relations* 47 (October 1994): 1151–1166; R. Westwood and S. Clegg, "The Discourse of Organization Studies: Dissensus, Politics, and Paradigms," in *Debating Organization: Point-Counterpoint in Organization Studies,* ed. R. Westwood and S. Clegg (Malden, MA: Blackwood, 2003), 1–42.

3. R.N. Stern and S.R. Barley, "Organizations as Social Systems: Organization Theory's Neglected Mandate," *Administrative Science Quarterly* 41 (1996): 146–62; D. Katz and R.L. Kahn, *The Social Psychology of Organizations* (New York: Wiley, 1966), Chap. 2.

4. P.C. Newman, *Company of Adventurers* (Toronto, ON: Viking, 1985); J. Micklethwait and A. Wooldridge, *The Company: A Short History of a Revolutionary Idea* (New York: Random House, 2003); T. Lawson, "The Nature of the Firm and Peculiarities of the Corporation," *Cambridge Journal of Economics* 39, no. 1 (2015): 1–32.

5. B. Schlender, "The Three Faces of Steve," *Fortune,* 9 November 1998, 96–101.

6. "A Field Is Born," *Harvard Business Review* 86, no. 7/8 (2008): 164; P.R. Lawrence, "The Key Job Design Problem Is Still Taylorism," *Journal of Organizational Behavior* 31, no. 2/3 (2010): 412–21; L.W. Porter and B. Schneider, "What Was, What Is, and What May Be in Op/OB," *Annual Review of Organizational Psychology and Organizational Behavior* 1, no. 1 (2014): 1–21.

7. T. Takala, "Plato on Leadership," *Journal of Business Ethics* 17(1998): 785–98; J.A. Fernandez, "The Gentleman's Code of Confucius: Leadership by Values," *Organizational Dynamics* 33, no. 1 (2004): 21–31; A.M. Blake and J.L. Moseley, "Frederick Winslow Taylor: One Hundred Years of Managerial Insight," *International Journal of Management* 28, no. 4 (2011): 346–53; J.W. Stutje, ed., *Charismatic Leadership and Social Movements: The Revolutionary Power of Ordinary Men and Women,* International Studies in Social History (New York: Berghahn Books, 2012).

8. W.L.M. King, *Industry and Humanity: A Study in the Principles Underlying Industrial Reconstruction* (Toronto, ON: Thomas Allen, 1918); C.D. Wrege, "Solving Mayo's Mystery: The First Complete Account of the Origin of the Hawthorne Studies—the Forgotten Contributions of C. E. Snow and H. Hibarger" (paper presented at the Academy of Management Proceedings, August 1976), 12–16; P. Graham, ed., *Mary Parker Follett: Prophet of Management* (Boston: Harvard Business School Press, 1995); J.H. Smith, "The Enduring Legacy of Elton Mayo," *Human Relations* 51, no. 3 (1998): 221–49; R. Busse and M. Warner, "The Legacy of the Hawthorne Experiments: A Critical Analysis of the Human Relations School of Thought," *History of Economic Ideas* 25, no. 2 (2017): 91–114, https://doi.org/10.19272/201706102004; G.M. Nelson, "Mary Parker Follett – Creativity and Democracy," *Human Service Organizations: Management, Leadership & Governance* 41, no. 2 (2017): 178–85, https://doi.org/10.1080/23303131.2016.1263073.

9. The extent to which OB influences career success depends on course pedagogy as well as the practical value of the OB concepts covered in the course. In fact, OB scholars have an ongoing debate about the practical relevance of OB research. See, for example: J.P. Walsh et al., "On the Relationship between Research and Practice: Debate and Reflections," *Journal of Management Inquiry* 16, no. 2 (2007): 128–54; R. Gulati, "Tent Poles, Tribalism, and Boundary Spanning: The Rigor-Relevance Debate in Management Research," *Academy of Management Journal* 50, no. 4 (2007): 775–82; J. Pearce and L. Huang, "The Decreasing Value of Our Research to Management Education," *Academy of Management Learning & Education* 11, no. 2 (2012): 247–62; J.M. Bartunek and S.L. Rynes, "Academics and Practitioners Are Alike and Unlike: The Paradoxes of Academic–Practitioner Relationships," *Journal of Management* 40, no. 5 (2014): 1181–201; N. Butler, H. Delaney, and S. Spoelstra, "Problematizing 'Relevance' in the Business School: The Case of Leadership Studies," *British Journal of Management* 26, no. 4 (2015): 731–44.

10. The skills identified in these recent surveys are almost identical to those reported in a recent review of more than two dozen surveys on employability skills of higher education graduates. See: M. Osmani et al., "Graduates Employability Skills: A Review of Literature against Market Demand," *Journal of Education for Business* 94, no. 7 (2019): 423–32.

11. G. Loewenstein, "The Psychology of Curiosity: A Review and Reinterpretation," *Psychological Bulletin* 116 (1994): 75–98; C. Kidd and B.Y. Hayden, "The Psychology and Neuroscience of Curiosity," *Neuron* 88 (2015): 449–60; M. Livio, *Why?: What Makes Us Curious* (New York: Simon and Schuster, 2017).

12. R. L. Priem and J. Rosenstein, "Is Organization Theory Obvious to Practitioners? A Test of One Established Theory," *Organization Science* 11, no. 5 (2000): 509–24.

13. R.S. Rubin and E.C. Dierdorff, "How Relevant Is the MBA? Assessing the Alignment of Required Curricula and Required Managerial Competencies," *Academy of Management Learning & Education* 8 (2009): 208–24; Y. Baruch and O. Lavi-Steiner, "The Career Impact of Management Education from an Average-Ranked University: Human Capital Perspective," *Career Development International* 20 (2015): 218–37.

14. M.S. Myers, *Every Employee a Manager* (New York: McGraw Hill, 1970).

15. For example, see: M.A. West et al., "Reducing Patient Mortality in Hospitals: The Role of Human Resource Management," *Journal of Organizational Behavior* 27 (2006): 983–1002; I.S. Fulmer and R.E. Ployhart, " 'Our Most Important Asset': A Multidisciplinary/Multilevel Review of Human Capital Valuation for Research and Practice," *Journal of Management* 40 (2014): 161–92; M.C. Díaz-Fernández, M.R. González-Rodríguez, and B. Simonetti, "Top Management Team's Intellectual Capital and Firm Performance," *European Management Journal* 33 (2015): 322–31; N. Taylor et al., "High Performing Hospitals: A Qualitative Systematic Review of Associated Factors and Practical Strategies for Improvement," *BMC Health Services Research* 15 (2015): 244; S. Hauff, D. Alewell, and N.K. Hansen, "Further Exploring the Links between High-Performance Work Practices and Firm Performance: A Multiple-Mediation Model in the German Context," *German Journal of Human Resource Management* 32 (2018): 5–26.

16. J.T. Comeault and D. Wheeler, "Human Capital–Based Investment Criteria for Total Shareholder Returns," in *Pensions at Work: Socially Responsible Investment of Union-Based Pension Funds,* ed. J. Quarter, I. Carmichael, and S. Ryan (Toronto: University of Toronto Press, 2008); S. Abhayawansa, M. Aleksanyan, and J. Bahtsevanoglou, "The Use of Intellectual Capital Information by Sell-Side Analysts in Company Valuation," *Accounting and Business Research* 45, no. 3 (2015): 279–306; S. Abhayawansa and J. Guthrie, "Drivers and Semantic Properties of Intellectual Capital Information in Sell-Side Analysts' Reports," *Journal of Accounting & Organizational Change* 12, no. 4 (2016): 434–71, https://doi.org/10.1108/JAOC-05-2014-0027. The Canadian investment manager's list is described in: P. Hodson, "5 Qualities to Look for in Stocks," *National Post,* November 15, 2013.

17. S. A. Mohrman, C. B. Gibson, and A. M. Mohrman Jr., "Doing Research That Is Useful to Practice: A Model and Empirical Exploration," *Academy of Management Journal* 44 (2001): 357–75; J. P. Walsh et al., "On the Relationship between Research and Practice," *Journal of Management Inquiry* 16, no. 2 (June 2007): 128–54. Similarly, in 1961, Harvard business professor Fritz Roethlisberger proposed that the field of OB is concerned with human behaviour "from the points of view of both (a) its determination . . . and (b) its improvement." See P. B. Vaill, "F. J. Roethlisberger and the Elusive Phenomena of Organizational Behavior," *Journal of Management Education* 31, no. 3 (2007): 321–38.

18. R. H. Hall, "Effectiveness Theory and Organizational Effectiveness," *Journal of Applied Behavioral Science* 16, no. 4 (1980): 536–45; K. Cameron, "Organizational Effectiveness: Its Demise and Re-Emergence through Positive Organizational

Scholarship," in *Great Minds in Management,* ed. K. G. Smith and M. A. Hitt (New York: Oxford University Press, 2005), 304–30.

19. A.A. Amirkhanyan, H.J. Kim, and K.T. Lambright, "The Performance Puzzle: Understanding the Factors Influencing Alternative Dimensions and Views of Performance," *Journal of Public Administration Research and Theory* 24, no. 1 (2014): 1–34.

20. Chester Barnard gives one of the earliest descriptions of organizations as systems interacting with external environments and that are composed of subsystems. See C. Barnard, *The Functions of the Executive* (Cambridge, MA: Harvard University Press, 1938), esp. Chap. 6. Also see F.E. Kast and J.E. Rosenzweig, "General Systems Theory: Applications for Organization and Management," *Academy of Management Journal* 15, no. 4 (1972): 447–65; P.M. Senge, *The Fifth Discipline: The Art and Practice of the Learning Organization* (New York: Doubleday Currency, 1990); G. Morgan, *Images of Organization,* 2nd ed. (Newbury Park: Sage, 1996); A. de Geus, *The Living Company* (Boston: Harvard Business School Press, 1997).

21. D. Katz and R.L. Kahn, *The Social Psychology of Organizations* (New York: Wiley, 1966), Chap. 2; J. McCann, "Organizational Effectiveness: Changing Concepts for Changing Environments," *Human Resource Planning* 27, no. 1 (2004): 42–50; A.H. Van de Ven, M. Ganco, and C.R. Hinings, "Returning to the Frontier of Contingency Theory of Organizational and Institutional Designs," *Academy of Management Annals* 7, no. 1 (2013): 391–438.

22. K.E. Weick, *The Social Psychology of Organizing* (Reading, MA: Addison-Wesley, 1979); J.L. Claggett and E. Karahanna, "Unpacking the Structure of Coordination Mechanisms and the Role of Relational Coordination in an Era of Digitally Mediated Work Processes," *Academy of Management Review* 43 (2018): 704–22; R.M. Burton and B. Obel, "The Science of Organizational Design: Fit between Structure and Coordination," *Journal of Organization Design* 7, no. 5 (2018).

23. J. Barney, "Firm Resources and Sustained Competitive Advantage," *Journal of Management* 17, no. 1 (1991): 99–120. The scholarly literature has separated human capital from social capital (social networks) and psychological capital (personal cognitive and emotional resources such as hope and optimism). On closer inspection, however, social and psychological capital may be embedded in, or consequences of, human capital. Consequently, the three concepts may be integrated in some ways.

24. J. Combs et al., "How Much Do High-Performance Work Practices Matter? A Meta-Analysis of Their Effects on Organizational Performance," *Personnel Psychology* 59, no. 3 (2006): 501–28; P. Tharenou, A.M. Saks, and C. Moore, "A Review and Critique of Research on Training and Organizational-Level Outcomes," *Human Resource Management Review* 17, no. 3 (2007): 251–73; D.Y. Jeong and M. Choi, "The Impact of High-Performance Work Systems on Firm Performance: The Moderating Effects of the Human Resource Function's Influence," *Journal of Management & Organization* 22, no. 3 (2016): 328–48.

25. J. Camps and R. Luna-Arocas, "A Matter of Learning: How Human Resources Affect Organizational Performance," *British Journal of Management* 23, no. 1 (2012): 1–21; R.R. Kehoe and P.M. Wright, "The Impact of High-Performance Human Resource Practices on Employees' Attitudes and Behaviors," *Journal of Management* 39, no. 2 (2013): 366–91; B. Fabi, R. Lacoursière, and L. Raymond, "Impact of High-Performance Work Systems on Job Satisfaction, Organizational Commitment, and Intention to Quit in Canadian Organizations," *International Journal of Manpower* 36, no. 5 (2015): 772–90.

26. R.E. Freeman, J.S. Harrison, and A.C. Wicks, *Managing for Stakeholders: Survival, Reputation, and Success* (New Haven, CT: Yale University Press, 2007); B.L. Parmar et al., "Stakeholder Theory: The State of the Art," *Academy of Management Annals* 4, no. 1 (2010): 403–45; S. Sachs and E. Rühli, *Stakeholders Matter: A New Paradigm for Strategy in Society* (Cambridge, UK: Cambridge University Press, 2011).

27. A. Santana, "Three Elements of Stakeholder Legitimacy," *Journal of Business Ethics* 105 (2012): 257–65; D. Crilly and P. Sloan, "Autonomy or Control? Organizational Architecture and Corporate Attention to Stakeholders," *Organization Science* 25 (2014): 339–55; M. Hall, Y. Millo, and E. Barman, "Who and What Really Counts? Stakeholder Prioritization and Accounting for Social Value," *Journal of Management Studies* 52 (2015): 907–34; D. Weitzner and Y. Deutsch, "Understanding Motivation and Social Influence in Stakeholder Prioritization," *Organization Studies* 36 (2015): 1337–60.

28. B.M. Meglino and E.C. Ravlin, "Individual Values in Organizations: Concepts, Controversies, and Research," *Journal of Management* 24 (1998): 351–89; S. Hitlin and J.A. Pilavin, "Values: Reviving a Dormant Concept," *Annual Review of Sociology* 30 (2004): 359–93; L. Sagiv et al., "Personal Values in Human Life," *Nature Human Behaviour* 1 (2017): 630–39.

29. M. van Marrewijk, "Concepts and Definitions of CSR and Corporate Sustainability: Between Agency and Communion," *Journal of Business Ethics* 44 (2003): 95–105; H. Aguinis and A. Glavas, "What We Know and Don't Know about Corporate Social Responsibility: A Review and Research Agenda," *Journal of Management* 38 (2012): 932–68; T. Meynhardt and P. Gomez, "Building Blocks for Alternative Four-Dimensional Pyramids of Corporate Social Responsibilities," *Business & Society* 58 (2019): 404–38.

30. A.B. Carroll and K.M. Shabana, "The Business Case for Corporate Social Responsibility: A Review of Concepts, Research and Practice," *International Journal of Management Reviews* 12 (2010): 85–105; J. Kim and J. Kim, "Corporate Sustainability Management and Its Market Benefits," *Sustainability* 10 (2018): 1455; M. Ong et al., "When Corporate Social Responsibility Motivates Employee Citizenship Behavior: The Sensitizing Role of Task Significance," *Organizational Behavior and Human Decision Processes* 144 (2018): 44–59; B. Lis, "Corporate Social Responsibility's Influence on Organizational Attractiveness: An Investigation in the Context of Employer Choice," *Journal of General Management* 43 (2018): 106–14.

31. Most of these anchors are mentioned in: J.D. Thompson, "On Building an Administrative Science," *Administrative Science Quarterly* 1, no. 1 (1956): 102–11.

32. This anchor has a colorful history dating back to critiques of business schools in the 1950s. Soon after, systematic research became a mantra for many respected scholars. See, for example, J.D. Thompson, "On Building an Administrative Science," *Administrative Science Quarterly* 1 (1956): 102–11.

33. J. Pfeffer and R.I. Sutton, *Hard Facts, Dangerous Half-Truths, and Total Nonsense* (Boston, MA: Harvard Business School Press, 2006); D.M. Rousseau and S. McCarthy, "Educating Managers from an Evidence-Based Perspective," *Academy of Management Learning & Education* 6 (2007): 84–101; R.B. Briner and D.M. Rousseau, "Evidence-Based I–O Psychology: Not There Yet," *Industrial and Organizational Psychology* 4 (2011): 3–22.

34. J. Hamet and F. Maurer, "Is Management Research Visible Outside the Academic Community?," *M@n@gement* Vol. 20, no. 5 (2017): 492–516.

35. Pfeffer and Sutton, *Hard Facts, Dangerous Half-Truths, and Total Nonsense* (Boston, MA: Harvard Business School Press, 2006).

36. E. Abrahamson, H. Berkowitz, and H. Dumez, "A More Relevant Approach to Relevance in Management Studies: An Essay on Performativity," *Academy of Management Review* 41, no. 2 (2016): 367–81, https://doi.org/10.5465/amr.2015.0205; J.M. Bartunek and J. McKenzie, eds., *Academic-Practitioner Relationships: Developments, Complexities and Opportunities,* (New York: Routledge, 2017); G. Carton and P. Mouricou, "Is Management Research Relevant? A Systematic Analysis of the Rigor-Relevance Debate in Top-Tier Journals (1994–2013)," *M@n@gement* Vol. 20, no. 2 (2017): 166–203; J. Hamet and S. Michel, "Rigor, Relevance, and the Knowledge 'Market,'" *European Business Review* 30, no. 2 (2018): 183–201, https://doi.org/10.1108/EBR-01-2017-0025.

37. P.H. Kim, R.E. Ployhart, and C.B. Gibson, "Editors' Comments: Is Organizational Behavior Overtheorized?," *Academy of Management Review* 43, no. 4 (October 2018): 541–45, https://doi.org/10.5465/amr.2018.0233.

38. M. N. Zald, "More Fragmentation? Unfinished Business in Linking the Social Sciences and the Humanities," *Administrative Science Quarterly* 41 (1996): 251–61; C. Oswick, P. Fleming, and G. Hanlon, "From Borrowing to Blending: Rethinking the Processes of Organizational Theory Building," *Academy of Management Review* 36 (2011): 318–37; B.M. Staw, "Stumbling Toward a Social Psychology of Organizations: An Autobiographical Look at the Direction of Organizational Research," *Annual Review of Organizational Psychology and Organizational Behavior* 3 (2016): 1–19.

39. D.M. Rousseau and Y. Fried, "Location, Location, Location: Contextualizing Organizational Research*," *Journal of Organizational Behavior* 22, no. 1 (2001): 1–13; C.M. Christensen and M.E. Raynor, "Why Hard-Nosed Executives Should Care About Management Theory," *Harvard Business Review* (2003): 66–74. For excellent critique of the "one best way" approach in early management scholarship, see P.F. Drucker, "Management's New Paradigms," *Forbes* (1998): 152–77.

40. H.L. Tosi and J.W. Slocum Jr., "Contingency Theory: Some Suggested Directions," *Journal of Management* 10 (1984): 9–26.

41. D.M.H. Rousseau, R.J. House, "Meso Organizational Behavior: Avoiding Three Fundamental Biases," in *Trends in Organizational Behavior,* ed. C.L. Cooper and D.M. Rousseau (Chichester, UK: John Wiley & Sons, Inc., 1994), 13–30.

42. B.M. Ferdman, "Paradoxes of Inclusion: Understanding and Managing the Tensions of Diversity and Multiculturalism," *The Journal of Applied Behavioral Science* 53 (2017): 235–63; A.E. Randel et al., "Inclusive Leadership: Realizing Positive Outcomes through Belongingness and Being Valued for Uniqueness," *Human Resource Management Review* 28 (2018): 190–203; L.M. Shore, J.N. Cleveland, and D. Sanchez, "Inclusive Workplaces: A Review and Model," *Human Resource Management Review* 28 (2018): 176–89.

43. D.A. Harrison et al., "Time, Teams, and Task Performance: Changing Effects of Surface- and Deep-Level Diversity on Group Functioning," *Academy of Management Journal* 45, no. 5 (2002): 1029–46; W.J. Casper, J.H. Wayne, and J.G. Manegold, "Who Will We Recruit? Targeting Deep- and Surface-Level Diversity with Human Resource Policy Advertising," *Human Resource Management* 52, no. 3 (2013): 311–32; J.E. Mathieu et al., "A Review and Integration of Team Composition Models: Moving toward a Dynamic and Temporal Framework," *Journal of Management* 40, no. 1 (2014): 130–60.

44. Statistics Canada, "Immigration and Ethnocultural Diversity in Canada," National Household Survey, 2011 (Ottawa, ON: Government of Canada, 2013); Statistics Canada, "Visible Minority (15), Generation Status (4), Age (12) and Sex (3) for the Population in Private Households of Canada, Provinces and Territories, Census Metropolitan Areas and Census Agglomerations, 2016 Census - 25% Sample Data," Data tables, 2016 Census (Ottawa: Statistics Canada, October 25, 2017). The phrase "visible minority" is predominantly used in Canada, and its definition is embedded in the Employment Equity Act. The Employment Equity Act defines visible minorities as "persons, other than Aboriginal peoples, who are non-Caucasian in race or non-white in colour." Statistics Canada states that the visible minority population consists mainly of the following groups: South Asian, Chinese, Black, Filipino, Latin American, Arab, Southeast Asian, West Asian, Korean, and Japanese. See: Statistics Canada, "Visible Minority of Person," Definitions, data sources and methods, April 3, 2019, http://www23.statcan.gc.ca/imdb/p3Var.pl?Function =DEC&Id=45152.

45. J. Qin, N. Muenjohn, and P. Chhetri, "A Review of Diversity Conceptualizations: Variety, Trends, and a Framework," *Human Resource Development Review* 13, no. 2 (2014): 133–57.

46. M.H. Davis, S. Capobianco, and L.A. Kraus, "Gender Differences in Responding to Conflict in the Workplace: Evidence from a Large Sample of Working Adults," *Sex Roles* 63, no. 7 (2010): 500–14; J.L. Locke, *Duels and Duets: Why Men and Women Talk So Differently* (New York: Cambridge University Press, 2011); R. Friesdorf, P. Conway, and B. Gawronski, "Gender Differences in Responses to Moral Dilemmas: A Process Dissociation Analysis," *Personality and Social Psychology Bulletin* 41, no. 5 (2015): 696–713.

47. E. Bolland and C. Lopes, *Generations and Work* (New York: Palgrave Macmillan, 2014); P. Taylor,

The Next America: Boomers, Millennials, and the Looming Generational Showdown (New York: PublicAffairs, 2014); J. Bristow, *Baby Boomers and Generational Conflict* (London: Palgrave Macmillan, 2015).

48. S. Lyons and L. Kuron, "Generational Differences in the Workplace: A Review of the Evidence and Directions for Future Research," *Journal of Organizational Behavior* 35 (2014): S139–57; K.L. Zabel et al., "Generational Differences in Work Ethic: Fact or Fiction?," *Journal of Business and Psychology* 32 (2017): 301–15; J.M. Cucina et al., "Generational Differences in Workplace Attitudes and Job Satisfaction: Lack of Sizable Differences across Cohorts," *Journal of Managerial Psychology* 33 (2018): 246–64; M. Schröder, "Der Generationenmythos (The Generation Myth)," *Kölner Zeitschrift für Soziologie und Sozialpsychologie* 70 (2018): 469–94.

49. M.-E. Roberge and R. van Dick, "Recognizing the Benefits of Diversity: When and How Does Diversity Increase Group Performance?," *Human Resource Management Review* 20, no. 4 (2010): 295–308; M. Singal, "The Business Case for Diversity Management in the Hospitality Industry," *International Journal of Hospitality Management* 40 (2014): 10–19; C.-M. Lu et al., "Effect of Diversity on Human Resource Management and Organizational Performance," *Journal of Business Research* 68, no. 4 (2015): 857–61; Y. Zhang and M.-Y. Huai, "Diverse Work Groups and Employee Performance: The Role of Communication Ties," *Small Group Research* 47, no. 1 (2016): 28–57.

50. Q. Roberson, O. Holmes, and J.L. Perry, "Transforming Research on Diversity and Firm Performance: A Dynamic Capabilities Perspective," *Academy of Management Annals* 11 (2017): 189–216; Y.R.F. Guillaume et al., "Harnessing Demographic Differences in Organizations: What Moderates the Effects of Workplace Diversity?," *Journal of Organizational Behavior* 38 (2017): 276–303; N. Luanglath, M. Ali, and K. Mohannak, "Top Management Team Gender Diversity and Productivity: The Role of Board Gender Diversity," *Equality, Diversity and Inclusion: An International Journal* 38 (2019): 71–86.

51. T. Kochan et al., "The Effects of Diversity on Business Performance: Report of the Diversity Research Network," *Human Resource Management* 42 (2003): 3–21; S.T. Bell et al., "Getting Specific about Demographic Diversity Variable and Team Performance Relationships: A Meta-Analysis," *Journal of Management* 37 (2011): 709–43; S.M.B. Thatcher and P.C. Patel, "Group Faultlines: A Review, Integration, and Guide to Future Research," *Journal of Management* 38 (2012): 969–1009; C. Ozgen et al., "Does Cultural Diversity of Migrant Employees Affect Innovation?," *International Migration Review* 48 (2014): S377–S416; K. Hoisl, M. Gruber, and A. Conti, "R&D Team Diversity and Performance in Hypercompetitive Environments," *Strategic Management Journal* 38 (2017): 1455–77.

52. "The 2016 Deloitte Millennial Survey: Winning over the Next Generation of Leaders" (New York: Deloitte Touche Tohmatsu, January 2016); B.W. Reynolds, "2017 Annual Survey Finds Workers Are More Productive at Home, And More," *FlexJobs* (blog), August 21, 2017, https://www.flexjobs.com/blog/post/ productive-working-remotely-top-companies-hiring/.

53. Jeffrey H. Greenhaus and Lieke L. ten Brummelhuis, "Models and Frameworks Underlying Work–Life Research: Challenges and Opportunities," in *Handbook of Work-Life Integration Among Professionals: Challenges and Opportunities,* ed. D.A. Major and R.J. Burke (Cheltenham, UK: Edward Elgar Publishing, 2013), 14–34; M.J. Sirgy and D.-J. Lee, "Work-Life Balance: An Integrative Review," *Applied Research in Quality of Life* 13 (2018): 229–54.

54. Katie Clarey, "Work-Life Balance? There's No Such Thing," *HR Dive,* December 18, 2018.

55. L.L. ten Brummelhuis and A.B. Bakker, "A Resource Perspective on the Work–Home Interface: The Work–Home Resources Model.," *American Psychologist* 67 (2012): 545–56; L.L. ten Brummelhuis and J.H. Greenhaus, "How Role Jugglers Maintain Relationships at Home and at Work: A Gender Comparison.," *Journal of Applied Psychology* 103 (2018): 1265–82; A. Li, A. Butler, and J. Bagger, "Depletion or Expansion? Understanding the Effects of Support Policy Use on Employee Work and Family Outcomes," *Human Resource Management Journal* 28 (2018): 216–34.

56. S.D. Friedman, *Leading the Life You Want: Skills for Integrating Work and Life* (Boston: Harvard Business Press, 2014); A.M. Foreman et al., "Dogs in the Workplace: A Review of the Benefits and Potential Challenges," *International Journal of Environmental Research and Public Health* 14 (2017); K. Goldin, "Why Meetings On The Move Should Be The New Normal (And How To Ensure They're Productive)," *Forbes,* April 20, 2018; Kris Fannin. "Why Work-Life Integration Is the New Work-Life Balance and How To. . ." *Intelivate* (blog), January 29, 2018. https://www.intelivate.com/ team-strategy/work-life-integration-work-life-balance; K. Lockwood. "Achieving Work-Life Integration In This New World Of Work." *Forbes,* April 18, 2018. Although almost all firms have practices that support work–life integration, many employers implicitly limit the career progress of those who use some of these practices. see: S. Bourdeau, A. Ollier-Malaterre, and N. Houlfort, "Not All Work-Life Policies Are Created Equal: Career Consequences of Using Enabling Versus Enclosing Work-Life Policies," *Academy of Management Review* 44 (2019): 172–93.

57. E.E. Kossek and R.J. Thompson, "Workplace Flexibility: Integrating Employer and Employee Perspectives to Close the Research–Practice Implementation Gap," in *The Oxford Handbook of Work and Family,* ed. T.D. Allen and L.T. Eby (New York: Oxford University Press, 2016), 255–70; M. Beatson, "Megatrends: Flexible Working" (London: Chartered Institute of Personnel and Development, January 15, 2019).

58. T.D. Allen, E. Cho, and L.L. Meier, "Work–Family Boundary Dynamics," *Annual Review of Organizational Psychology and Organizational Behavior* 1 (2014): 99–121; A.R. Koch and C. Binnewies, "Setting a Good Example: Supervisors as Work-Life-Friendly Role Models within the Context of Boundary Management," *Journal of Occupational Health Psychology* 20 (2015): 82–92; Nancy P. Rothbard and Ariane Ollier-Malaterre, "Boundary Management," in *The Oxford Handbook of Work and Family,* ed. T.D. Allen and L.T. Eby (New York: Oxford University Press, 2016), 109–24;

R. Hackwill, "French First to Protect 'the Right to Disconnect'," *EuroNews,* January 2, 2017.

59. T.L. Johns, "The Third Wave of Virtual Work," *Harvard Business Review* 91, no. 1 (2013): 66–73; S. Raghuram et al., "Virtual Work: Bridging Research Clusters," *Academy of Management Annals* 13, no. 1 (2019): 308–41, https://doi.org/10.5465/annals.2017.0020; M. Cassano, "5 Reasons Companies Should Hire Employees Who Work from Home," *Ladders,* October 6, 2019.

60. A. Mann and A. Adkins, "America's Coming Workplace: Home Alone," *Gallup Business Journal,* March 15, 2017; Statistics Canada, "Journey to Work: Key Results from the 2016 Census," The Daily (Ottawa: Statistics Canada, November 29, 2017); "Report: 65% of Employers Think Employees Are More Productive When They Work Remotely," *Indeed Canada Blog* (blog), November 14, 2018, http://blog.indeed.ca/2018/11/14/remote-workers-survey/. One widely cited survey claims that 74 per cent of Canadians work away from the office at least one day a week. Unfortunately, it is unlikely that survey represents the population because it sampled "customers, prospects and business leaders" associated with the survey sponsor, a global firm that rents flexible workspace. See: "IWG Global Workspace Survey: Welcome to Generation Flex, The Employee Power Shift" (Zurich: IWG, March 12, 2019).

61. J. Harter, "How Leaders Are Responding to COVID-19 Workplace Disruption," *Gallup Workplace,* April 7, 2020; J. Fernyhough, "Optus Staff to Work from Home Permanently," *Australian Financial Review,* April 17, 2020.

62. G. Leibowitz, "This CEO Runs a Billion-Dollar Company With No Offices or Email," *Inc,* March 16, 2016; J. Bort, "$1 Billion Startup Automattic Is Closing Its San Francisco Office and Having Everyone Work from Home," *Business Insider,* June 13, 2017; G. Caplan, "Here Come the Frogs (Fully Remote Organizations)," *Medium,* February 13, 2019; J. Pellet, "Real Time with Remote Workers," *Chief Executive,* October 4, 2019. Information about Automattic's workforce in Canada and globally is available on its website. See: https://automattic.com/about/

63. E.J. Hill et al., "Workplace Flexibility, Work Hours, and Work–Life Conflict: Finding an Extra Day or Two," *Journal of Family Psychology* 24, no. 3 (2010): 349–58; M.C. Noonan and J.L. Glass, "The Hard Truth about Telecommuting," *Monthly Labor Review* 135, no. 6 (2012): 38–45; B.H. Martin and R. MacDonnell, "Is Telework Effective for Organizations?," *Management Research Review* 35, no. 7 (2012): 602–16; T.D. Allen, T.D. Golden, and K.M. Shockley, "How Effective Is Telecommuting? Assessing the Status of Our Scientific Findings," *Psychological Science in the Public Interest* 16, no. 2 (2015): 40–68; N. Bloom et al., "Does Working from Home Work? Evidence from a Chinese Experiment," *The Quarterly Journal of Economics* 130, no. 1 (2015): 165–218; R.S. Gajendran, D.A. Harrison, and K. Delaney-Klinger, "Are Telecommuters Remotely Good Citizens? Unpacking Telecommuting's Effects on Performance Via I-Deals and Job Resources," *Personnel Psychology* 68, no. 2 (2015): 353–93. The WestJet quotation is from: R. Marowits, "More Employees Working from Home in Shift to 'Telecommuting,'" *Toronto Star,* 23 May 2016.

64. E.E. Kossek and R.J. Thompson, "Workplace Flexibility: Integrating Employer and Employee

Perspectives to Close the Research–Practice Implementation Gap," in *The Oxford Handbook of Work and Family,* ed. T.D. Allen and L.T. Eby (New York: Oxford University Press, 2016), 255–70; H. Hambly and J. (Donghoon) Lee, "The Rural Telecommuter Surplus in Southwestern Ontario, Canada," *Telecommunications Policy* 43 (2019): 278–86.

65. C.A. Bartel, A. Wrzesniewski, and B.M. Wiesenfeld, "Knowing Where You Stand: Physical Isolation, Perceived Respect, and Organizational Identification among Virtual Employees," *Organization Science* 23, no. 3 (2011): 743–57; E.E. Kossek, R.J. Thompson, and B.A. Lautsch, "Balanced Workplace Flexibility: Avoiding the Traps," *California Management Review* 57, no. 4 (2015): 5–25.

66. T.A. O'Neill, L.A. Hambley, and G.S. Chatellier, "Cyberslacking, Engagement, and Personality in Distributed Work Environments," *Computers in Human Behavior* 40 (2014): 152–60; N.W. Van Yperen, E.F. Rietzschel, and K.M.M. De Jonge, "Blended Working: For Whom It May (Not) Work," *PLoS ONE* 9, no. 7 (2014): e102921; D. Karis, D. Wildman, and A. Mané, "Improving Remote Collaboration with Video Conferencing and Video Portals," *Human–Computer Interaction* 31, no. 1 (2016): 1–58.

67. P. Cappelli and J. Keller, "Classifying Work in the New Economy," *Academy of Management Review* 38 (2013): 575–96; T.S.-C. Poon, "Independent Workers: Growth Trends, Categories, and Employee Relations Implications in the Emerging Gig Economy," *Employee Responsibilities and Rights Journal* 31 (2019): 63–69.

68. S. Mojtehedzadeh, "Temp Agencies on Rise as Province Seeks to Protect Vulnerable Workers," *Toronto Star,* July 15, 2017; World Employment Federation, "Economic Report, 2018" (Brussels, Belgium: World Employment Federation, July 2018); L.F. Katz and A.B. Krueger, "The Rise and Nature of Alternative Work Arrangements in the United States, 1995–2015," *ILR Review* 72, no. 2 (2019): 382–416, https://doi.org/10.1177/0019793918820008.

69. K.M. Kuhn and A. Maleki, "Micro-Entrepreneurs, Dependent Contractors, and Instaserfs: Understanding Online Labor Platform Workforces," *Academy of Management Perspectives* 31, no. 3 (2017): 183–200, https://doi.org/10.5465/amp.2015.0111; UpWork, "New 5th Annual 'Freelancing in America' Study Finds That the U.S. Freelance Workforce, Now 56.7 Million People, Grew 3.7 Million Since 2014," News release (New York: Upwork and Freelancers Union, October 31, 2018); Statistics Canada, "Self-Employed Canadians: Who and Why?," May 28, 2019, https://www150.statcan.gc.ca/n1/pub/71-222-x/71-222-x2019002-eng.htm.

70. M.A. Cherry and A. Aloisi, "'Dependent Contractors' in the Gig Economy: A Comparative Approach," *American University Law Review* 66 (2017): 635–89, https://doi.org/10.2139/ssrn.2847869;

71. M. Banerjee, P.S. Tolbert, and T. DiCiccio, "Friend or Foe? The Effects of Contingent Employees on Standard Employees' Work Attitudes," *The International Journal of Human Resource Management* 23 (2012): 2180–2204; S.L. Fisher and C.E. Connelly, "Lower Cost or Just Lower Value? Modeling the Organizational

Costs and Benefits of Contingent Work," *Academy of Management Discoveries* 3 (2016): 165–86; G.M. Spreitzer, L. Cameron, and L. Garrett, "Alternative Work Arrangements: Two Images of the New World of Work," *Annual Review of Organizational Psychology and Organizational Behavior* 4 (2017): 473–99; C.L. Wilkin, J.P. de Jong, and C. Rubino, "Teaming up with Temps: The Impact of Temporary Workers on Team Social Networks and Effectiveness," *European Journal of Work and Organizational Psychology* 27 (2018): 204–18; E. Selenko et al., "On the Dynamics of Work Identity in Atypical Employment: Setting out a Research Agenda," *European Journal of Work and Organizational Psychology* 27 (2018): 324–34; G. Petriglieri, S.J. Ashford, and A. Wrzesniewski, "Agony and Ecstasy in the Gig Economy: Cultivating Holding Environments for Precarious and Personalized Work Identities," *Administrative Science Quarterly* 64 (2019): 124–70; T.A. Kochan et al., "The Changing Nature of Employee and Labor-Management Relationships," *Annual Review of Organizational Psychology and Organizational Behavior* 6 (2019): 195–219.

72. L.L. Thurstone, "Ability, Motivation, and Speed," *Psychometrika* 2, no. 4 (1937): 249–254; N.R.F. Maier, *Psychology in Industry,* 2nd ed. (Boston, *MA:* Houghton Mifflin Company, 1955); V.H. Vroom, *Work and Motivation* (New York: John Wiley & Sons, Inc., 1964); J.P. Campbell et al., *Managerial Behavior, Performance, and Effectiveness* (New York: McGraw Hill, 1970).

73. R.S. Dalal, D.P. Bhave, and J. Fiset, "Within-Person Variability in Job Performance: A Theoretical Review and Research Agenda," *Journal of Management* 40, no. 5 (2014): 1396–436; S. Aryee et al., "Developing and Leveraging Human Capital Resource to Promote Service Quality: Testing a Theory of Performance," *Journal of Management* 42, no. 2 (2016): 480–99.

74. E.E. Lawler III and L.W. Porter, "Antecedent Attitudes of Effective Managerial Performance," *Organizational Behavior and Human Performance* 2 (1967): 122–42; O.-P. Kauppila, "So, What Am I Supposed to Do? A Multilevel Examination of Role Clarity," *Journal of Management Studies* 51, no. 5 (2014): 737–63.

75. Only a few sources have included all four factors. These include J.P. Campbell and R.D. Pritchard, "Motivation Theory in Industrial and Organizational Psychology," in *Handbook of Industrial and Organizational Psychology,* ed. M.D. Dunnette (Chicago: Rand McNally, 1976), 62–130; T.R. Mitchell, "Motivation: New Directions for Theory, Research, and Practice," *Academy of Man agement Review* 7, no. 1 (1982): 80–88; G.A.J. Churchill et al., "The Determinants of Salesperson Performance: A Meta-Analysis," *Journal of Marketing Research* 22, no. 2 (1985): 103–18; R.E. Plank and D.A. Reid, "The Mediating Role of Sales Behaviors: An Alternative Perspective of Sales Performance and Effectiveness," *Journal of Personal Selling & Sales Management* 14, no. 3 (1994): 43–56. The "MARS" acronym was coined by senior officers in the Singapore Armed Forces during a senior officer program taught by Steve McShane.

76. Technically, the model proposes that situation factors moderate the effects of the three within-person factors. For instance, the effect of employee

motivation on behaviour and performance depends on (is moderated by) the situation.

77. G.P. Latham and C.C. Pinder, "Work Motivation Theory and Research at the Dawn of the Twenty-First Century," *Annual Review of Psychology* 56 (2005): 485–516; G.P. Latham, *Work Motivation: History, Theory, Research, and Practice,* Revised ed. (Thousand Oaks, CA: Sage, 2012), 7.

78. P.R. Sackett et al., "Individual Differences and Their Measurement: A Review of 100 Years of Research," *Journal of Applied Psychology* 102 (2017): 254–73.

79. P. Tharenou, A.M. Saks, and C. Moore, "A Review and Critique of Research on Training and Organizational-Level Outcomes," *Human Resource Management Review* 17, no. 3 (2007): 251–73; Y. Kim and R.E. Ployhart, "The Effects of Staffing and Training on Firm Productivity and Profit Growth before, during, and after the Great Recession," *Journal of Applied Psychology* 99, no. 3 (2014): 361–89; M. Choi and H.J. Yoon, "Training Investment and Organizational Outcomes: A Moderated Mediation Model of Employee Outcomes and Strategic Orientation of the HR Function," *The International Journal of Human Resource Management* 26, no. 20 (2015): 2632–51.

80. BlessingWhite, *Employee Engagement Research Update* (Princeton, NJ: BlessingWhite, January 2013).

81. E.C. Dierdorff, R.S. Rubin, and D.G. Bachrach, "Role Expectations as Antecedents of Citizenship and the Moderating Effects of Work Context," *Journal of Management* 38, no. 2 (2012): 573–98; A. Newman, B. Allen, and Q. Miao, "I Can See Clearly Now: The Moderating Effects of Role Clarity on Subordinate Responses to Ethical Leadership," *Personnel Review* 44, no. 4 (2015): 611–28.

82. W.H. Cooper and M.J. Withey, "The Strong Situation Hypothesis," *Personality and Social Psychology Review* 13 (2009): 62–72; N.A. Bowling et al., "Situational Strength as a Moderator of the Relationship between Job Satisfaction and Job Performance: A Meta-Analytic Examination," *Journal of Business and Psychology* 30 (2015): 89–104; T.A. Judge and C.P. Zapata, "The Person–Situation Debate Revisited: Effect of Situation Strength and Trait Activation on the Validity of the Big Five Personality Traits in Predicting Job Performance," *Academy of Management Journal* 58 (2015): 1149–79; J.F. Rauthmann and R.A. Sherman, "Situation Change: Stability and Change of Situation Variables between and within Persons," *Frontiers in Psychology* 6 (2016), https://doi.org/10.3389/fpsyg.2015.01938.

83. L.H. Peters and E.J. O'Connor, "Situational Constraints and Work Outcomes: The Influences of a Frequently Overlooked Construct," *Academy of Management Review* 5, no. 3 (1980): 391–97; G. Johns, "Commentary: In Praise of Context," *Journal of Organizational Behavior* 22 (2001): 31–42; C.E.J. Härtel and J.M. O'Connor, "Contextualizing Research: Putting Context Back into Organizational Behavior Research," *Journal of Management & Organization* 20, no. 4 (2014): 417–22.

84. R.D. Hackett, "Understanding and Predicting Work Performance in the Canadian Military," *Canadian Journal of Behavioural Science* 34, no. 2 (2002): 131–40; J.P. Campbell and B.M. Wiernik, "The Modeling and Assessment of Work Performance," *Annual Review of Organizational Psychology and Organizational Behavior* 2, no. 1 (2015): 47–74.

85. L. Tay, R. Su, and J. Rounds, "People-Things and Data-Ideas: Bipolar Dimensions?," *Journal of Counseling Psychology* 58, no. 3 (2011): 424–40.

86. M.A. Griffin, A. Neal, and S.K. Parker, "A New Model of Work Role Performance: Positive Behavior in Uncertain and Interdependent Contexts," *Academy of Management Journal* 50, no. 2 (2007): 327–47; A. Charbonnier-Voirin and P. Roussel, "Adaptive Performance: A New Scale to Measure Individual Performance in Organizations," *Canadian Journal of Administrative Sciences* 29, no. 3 (2012): 280–93, https://doi.org/10.1002/cjas.232; S.K. Baard, T.A. Rench, and S.W.J. Kozlowski, "Performance Adaptation: A Theoretical Integration and Review," *Journal of Management* 40, no. 1 (2014): 48–99; D.K. Jundt, M.K. Shoss, and J.L. Huang, "Individual Adaptive Performance in Organizations: A Review," *Journal of Organizational Behavior* 36, no. S1 (2015): S53–S71; J.A. Carpini, S.K. Parker, and M.A. Griffin, "A Look Back and a Leap Forward: A Review and Synthesis of the Individual Work Performance Literature," *Academy of Management Annals* 11, no. 2 (2017): 825–85, https://doi.org/10.5465/annals.2015.0151; S. Park and S. Park, "Employee Adaptive Performance and Its Antecedents: Review and Synthesis," *Human Resource Development Review* 18, no. 3 (September 2019): 294–324, https://doi.org/10.1177/1534484319836315.

87. D.W. Organ, "Organizational Citizenship Behavior: It's Construct Clean-up Time," *Human Performance* 10 (1997): 85–97; J.A. LePine, A. Erez, and D.E. Johnson, "The Nature and Dimensionality of Organizational Citizenship Behavior: A Critical Review and Meta-Analysis," *Journal of Applied Psychology* 87 (2002): 52–65; N.P. Podsakoff et al., "Consequences of Unit-Level Organizational Citizenship Behaviors: A Review and Recommendations for Future Research," *Journal of Organizational Behavior* 35, no. S1 (2014): S87–S119.

88. E.W. Morrison, "Role Definitions and Organizational Citizenship Behavior: The Importance of the Employee's Perspective," *Academy of Management Journal* 37, no. 6 (1994): 1543–67; N. Podsakoff et al., "Individual- and Organizational-Level Consequences of Organizational Citizenship Behaviors: A Meta-Analysis," *Journal of Applied Psychology* 94, no. 1 (2009): 122–41; E.C. Dierdorff, R.S. Rubin, and D.G. Bachrach, "Role Expectations as Antecedents of Citizenship and the Moderating Effects of Work Context," *Journal of Management* 38, no. 2 (2012): 573–598.

89. M. Ozer, "A Moderated Mediation Model of the Relationship between Organizational Citizenship Behaviors and Job Performance," *Journal of Applied Psychology* 96, no. 6 (2011): 1328–36; S.B. Mackenzie, N.P. Podsakoff, and P.M. Podsakoff, "Individual- and Organizational-Level Consequences of Organizational Citizenship Behaviors," in *The Oxford Handbook of Organizational Citizenship Behavior,* ed. P.M. Podsakoff, S.B. MacKenzie, and N.P. Podsakoff (New York: Oxford University Press, 2018).

90. M.C. Bolino, A.C. Klotz, and W.H. Turnley, "The Unintended Consequences of Organizational Citizenship Behaviors for Employees, Teams, and Organizations," in *The Oxford Handbook of Organizational Citizenship Behavior,* ed. P.M. Podsakoff, S.B. Mackenzie, and N.P. Podsakoff (New York: Oxford University Press, 2018), 185–202.

91. M. Rotundo and P. Sackett, "The Relative Importance of Task, Citizenship, and Counterproductive Performance to Global Ratings of Job Performance: A Policy-Capturing Approach," *Journal of Applied Psychology* 87 (2002): 66–80; N.A. Bowling and M.L. Gruys, "Overlooked Issues in the Conceptualization and Measurement of Counterproductive Work Behavior," *Human Resource Management Review* 20, no. 1 (2010): 54–61; B. Marcus et al., "The Structure of Counterproductive Work Behavior: A Review, a Structural Meta-Analysis, and a Primary Study," *Journal of Management* 42, no. 1 (2016): 203–33; R.S. Dalal and N.C. Carpenter, "The Other Side of the Coin?: Similarities and Differences between Organizational Citizenship Behavior and Counterproductive Work Behavior," in *The Oxford Handbook of Organizational Citizenship Behavior,* ed. P.M. Podsakoff, S.B. MacKenzie, and N.P. Podsakoff (New York: Oxford University Press, 2018), 69–90.

92. The relationship between employee turnover and firm performance is actually very low, but this is due to moderators and is stronger for some forms of firm performance. See: J.I. Hancock et al., "Meta-Analytic Review of Employee Turnover as a Predictor of Firm Performance," *Journal of Management* 39, no. 3 (2013): 573–603.

93. T. Mallett, "September 2019 SME Business Outlook Survey Results" (Toronto: Canadian Federation of Independent Business, September 26, 2019); E. McIntosh, "Toronto's Sinai Hospitals Order Staff to Work — Even If They've Travelled Recently," *National Observer,* March 24, 2020; V. Stevenson and J. Montpetit, "With Quebec's Long-Term Care Homes Still Critically Short-Staffed, Premier Asks Ottawa for 1,000 More Soldiers," *CBC News,* April 22, 2020.

94. T.-Y. Park and J. Shaw, "Turnover Rates and Organizational Performance: A Meta-Analysis," *Journal of Applied Psychology* 98, no. 2 (2013): 268–309; J.I. Hancock et al., "Meta-Analytic Review of Employee Turnover as a Predictor of Firm Performance," *Journal of Management* 39, no. 3 (2013): 573–603; J.G. Messersmith et al., "Turnover at the Top: Executive Team Departures and Firm Performance," *Organization Science* 25, no. 3 (2014): 776–93; B.C. Holtom and T.C. Burch, "A Model of Turnover-Based Disruption in Customer Services," *Human Resource Management Review* 26, no. 1 (2016): 25–36.

95. P.S. Goodman and R.S. Atkin, "Effects of Absenteeism on Individuals and Organizations," in *Absenteeism: New Approaches to Understanding, Measuring and Managing Employee Attendance,* ed. P.S. Goodman and R.S. Atkin (San Francisco: Jossey-Bass, 1984), 276–321; D.A. Harrison and J.J. Martocchio, "Time for Absenteeism: A 20-Year Review of Origins, Offshoots, and Outcomes," *Journal of Management* 24, no. 3 (1998): 305–50.

96. Office of National Statistics, "Sickness Absence Falls to the Lowest Rate on Record," News Release (London: Office of National Statistics (UK Government), July 30, 2018); U.S. Bureau of Labor Statistics, "Absences from Work of Employed Full-Time Wage and Salary Workers by Occupation and Industry (2018)," Labor Force Statistics from

the Current Population Survey (Washington, D.C.: U.S. Bureau of Labor Statistics, January 18, 2019); Statistics Canada, "Table: 14-10-0190-01—Work Absence of Full-Time Employees by Geography, Annual," Labour Force Survey (Ottawa: Statistics Canada, October 8, 2019), https://doi.org/10.25318/1410019001-eng.

97. W. Beemsterboer et al., "A Literature Review on Sick Leave Determinants (1984–2004)," *International Journal of Occupational Medicine and Environmental Health* 22, no. 2 (2009): 169–79; C. M. Berry, A. M. Lelchook, and M. A. Clark, "A Meta-Analysis of the Interrelationships between Employee Lateness, Absenteeism, and Turnover: Implications for Models of Withdrawal Behavior," *Journal of Organizational Behavior* 33, no. 5 (2012): 678–99; C. Magee et al., "Workplace Bullying and Absenteeism: The Mediating Roles of Poor Health and Work Engagement," *Human Resource Management Journal* 27, no. 3 (2017): 319–34, https://doi.org/10.1111/1748-8583.12156.

98. G. Johns, "Presenteeism in the Workplace: A Review and Research Agenda," *Journal of Organizational Behavior* 31, no. 4 (2010): 519–42; R. K. Skagen and A.M. Collins, "The Consequences of Sickness Presenteeism on Health and Wellbeing over Time: A Systematic Review," *Social Science & Medicine* 161(2016): 169–77.

99. D. Baker-McClearn et al., "Absence Management and Presenteeism: The Pressures on Employees to Attend Work and the Impact of Attendance on Performance," *Human Resource Management Journal* 20, no. 3 (2010): 311–28; G. Johns, "Attendance Dynamics at Work: The Antecedents and Correlates of Presenteeism, Absenteeism, and Productivity Loss," *Journal of Occupational Health Psychology* 16, no. 4 (2011): 483–500; R. Pohling et al., "Work-Related Factors of Presenteeism: The Mediating Role of Mental and Physical Health," *Journal of Occupational Health Psychology* 21, no. 2 (2016): 220–34.

CHAPTER 2

1. K. Roose, "Ray Dalio Is Building a Baseball Card Collection," *New York Magazine,* June 14, 2012; R. Feloni, "Here's Why the World's Largest Hedge Fund Makes Applicants Take 5 Personality Tests before Sitting through Hours of Intensive Interviews," *Business Insider,* August 16, 2016; R. Feloni, "These Are the Personality Tests You Take to Get a Job at the World's Largest Hedge Fund," *Business Insider,* August 27, 2016; R. Dalio, *Principles: Life and Work* (New York: Simon and Schuster, 2017).

2. The definition presented here is based on: D.C. Funder, *The Personality Puzzle* (New York: W W Norton & Company, 2016); C.S. Carver and M.F. Scheier, *Perspectives on Personality,* 8th ed. (Hoboken, N.J.: Pearson Education, 2017). Both of these books recognize the varied perspectives of and approaches to personality. Several recent articles also recognize and attempt to address this conceptual diversity, such as: D. Cervone and B.R. Little, "Personality Architecture and Dynamics: The New Agenda and What's New about It," *Personality and Individual Differences,* 136 (2019): 12–23, https://doi.org/10.1016/j.paid.2017.07.001; E. Jayawickreme, C.E. Zachry, and W. Fleeson, "Whole Trait Theory: An Integrative Approach to Examining Personality Structure and Process," *Personality and*

Individual Differences, 136 (2019): 2–11, https://doi.org/10.1016/j.paid.2018.06.045.

3. D.P. McAdams, *The Art and Science of Personality Development* (New York: Guildford Press, 2015); J. Anglim and P. O'Connor, "Measurement and Research Using the Big Five, HEXACO, and Narrow Traits: A Primer for Researchers and Practitioners," *Australian Journal of Psychology* 71, no. 1 (2019): 16–25, https://doi.org/10.1111/ajpy.12202.

4. B.W. Roberts and A. Caspi, "Personality Development and the Person-Situation Debate: It's Déjà Vu All over Again," *Psychological Inquiry* 12, no. 2 (2001): 104–109; N.A. Turiano et al., "Personality and Substance Use in Midlife: Conscientiousness as a Moderator and the Effects of Trait Change," *Journal of Research in Personality* 46, no. 3 (2012): 295–305; C.R. Gale et al., "Neuroticism and Extraversion in Youth Predict Mental Wellbeing and Life Satisfaction 40 Years Later," *Journal of Research in Personality* 47, no. 6 (2013): 687–97; M. Pluess and M. Bartley, "Childhood Conscientiousness Predicts the Social Gradient of Smoking in Adulthood: A Life Course Analysis," *Journal of Epidemiology and Community Health* 69, no. 4 (2015): 330–38; M. Blatný et al., "Personality Predictors of Successful Development: Toddler Temperament and Adolescent Personality Traits Predict Well-Being and Career Stability in Middle Adulthood," *PLOS ONE* 10, no. 4 (2015): e0126032.

5. W. Mischel, "Toward an Integrative Science of the Person," *Annual Review of Psychology* 55 (2004): 1–22; W. H. Cooper and M. J. Withey, "The Strong Situation Hypothesis," *Personality and Social Psychology Review* 13, no. 1 (2009): 62–72; T.A. Judge and C.P. Zapata, "The Person–Situation Debate Revisited," *Academy of Management Journal* 58, no. 4 (2015): 1149– 79.

6. T. Vukasović and D. Bratko, "Heritability of Personality: A Meta-Analysis of Behavior Genetic Studies.," *Psychological Bulletin* 141 (2015): 769–85; W. Bleidorn, "What Accounts for Personality Maturation in Early Adulthood?," *Current Directions in Psychological Science* 24 (2015): 245–52; T.J.C. Polderman et al., "Meta-Analysis of the Heritability of Human Traits Based on Fifty Years of Twin Studies," *Nature Genetics* 47 (2015): 702–709; L. Penke and M. Jokela, "The Evolutionary Genetics of Personality Revisited," *Current Opinion in Psychology* 7 (2016): 104–109; M.-T. Lo et al., "Genome-Wide Analyses for Personality Traits Identify Six Genomic Loci and Show Correlations with Psychiatric Disorders," *Nature Genetics* 49 (2017): 152–56.

7. R. Mõttus et al., "Within-Trait Heterogeneity in Age Group Differences in Personality Domains and Facets: Implications for the Development and Coherence of Personality Traits," *PLoS ONE* 10, no. 3 (2015): e0119667; M. Liu and J.L. Huang, "Cross-Cultural Adjustment to the United States: The Role of Contextualized Extraversion Change," *Frontiers in Psychology* 6 (2015), https://doi.org/10.3389/fpsyg.2015.01650; S. Tasselli, M. Kilduff, and B. Landis, "Personality Change: Implications for Organizational Behavior," *Academy of Management Annals* 12 (2018): 467–93; W. Bleidorn, C.J. Hopwood, and R.E. Lucas, "Life Events and Personality Trait Change," *Journal of Personality* 86, (2018): 83–96; P.T. Costa, R.R. McCrae, and C.E. Löckenhoff,

"Personality Across the Life Span," *Annual Review of Psychology* 70 (2019): 423–48.

8. R.F. Baumeister, B.J. Schmeichel, and K.D. Vohs, "Self-Regulation and the Executive Function: The Self as Controlling Agent," in *Social Psychology: Handbook of Basic Principles,* ed. A.W. Kruglanski and E.T. Higgins (New York: Guilford, 2007), 516–39; K. Murdock, K. Oddi, and D. Bridgett, "Cognitive Correlates of Personality: Links between Executive Functioning and the Big Five Personality Traits," *Journal of Individual Differences* 34, no. 2 (2013): 97–104; P. Baggetta and P.A. Alexander, "Conceptualization and Operationalization of Executive Function," *Mind, Brain, and Education* 10, no. 1 (2016): 10–33.

9. J.M. Digman, "Personality Structure: Emergence of the Five-Factor Model," *Annual Review of Psychology* 41 (1990): 417–440; O.P. John and S. Srivastava, "The Big Five Trait Taxonomy: History, Measurement, and Theoretical Perspectives," in *Handbook of Personality: Theory and Research,* ed. L.A. Pervin and O.P. John (New York: Guildford Press, 1999), 102–138; R.R. McCrae, J.F. Gaines, and M.A. Wellington, "The Five-Factor Model in Fact and Fiction," in *Handbook of Psychology,* ed. I.B. Weiner (2012), 65–91.

10. M.R. Barrick and M.K. Mount, "Yes, Personality Matters: Moving on to More Important Matters," *Human Performance* 18 (2005): 359–72; P.R. Sackett and P.T. Walmsley, "Which Personality Attributes Are Most Important in the Workplace?," *Perspectives on Psychological Science* 9 (2014): 538–51; L.M. Penney, E. David, and L.A. Witt, "A Review of Personality and Performance: Identifying Boundaries, Contingencies, and Future Research Directions," *Human Resource Management Review* 21 (2011): 297–310; T. Judge et al., "Hierarchical Representations of the Five-Factor Model of Personality in Predicting Job Performance: Integrating Three Organizing Frameworks with Two Theoretical Perspectives," *Journal of Applied Psychology* 98 (2013): 875–925; J. Huang et al., "Personality and Adaptive Performance at Work: A Meta-Analytic Investigation," *Journal of Applied Psychology* 99 (2014): 162–79.

11. R.D.S. Chiaburu et al., "The Five-Factor Model of Personality Traits and Organizational Citizenship Behaviors: A Meta-Analysis," *Journal of Applied Psychology* 96, no. 6 (2011): 1140–66; D.S. Chiaburu, I.-S. Oh, and S.V. Marinova, "Five-Factor Model of Personality Traits and Organizational Citizenship Behavior: Current Research and Future Directions," in *The Oxford Handbook of Organizational Citizenship Behavior,* ed. P.M. Podsakoff, S.B. Mackenzie, and N.P. Podsakoff (New York: Oxford University Press, 2018), 203–20.

12. R.F. Hurley, "Customer Service Behavior in Retail Settings: A Study of the Effect of Service Provider Personality," *Journal of the Academy of Marketing Science* 26 (1998): 115–27; M.A.G. Peeters et al., "Personality and Team Performance: A Meta-Analysis," *European Journal of Personality* 20 (2006): 377–96; J.L. Huang and A.M. Ryan, "Beyond Personality Traits: A Study of Personality States and Situational Contingencies in Customer Service Jobs," *Personnel Psychology* 64 (2011): 451–88; B.H. Bradley et al., "Team Players and Collective Performance: How Agreeableness Affects Team Performance Over Time," *Small Group Research* 44 (2013): 680–711.

13. A. Neal et al., "Predicting the Form and Direction of Work Role Performance from the Big 5 Model of Personality Traits," *Journal of Organizational Behavior* 33, no. 2 (2012): 175–92.

14. J. L. Huang et al., "Personality and Adaptive Performance at Work," *Journal of Applied Psychology* 99, no. 1 (2014): 162–79.

15. J.B. Lloyd, "Unsubstantiated Beliefs and Values Flaw the Five-Factor Model of Personality," *Journal of Beliefs & Values* 36, no. 2 (2015): 156–64.

16. H. Le et al., "Too Much of a Good Thing: Curvilinear Relationships between Personality Traits and Job Performance," *Journal of Applied Psychology* 96, no. 1 (2011): 113–33; A.M. Grant, "Rethinking the Extraverted Sales Ideal: The Ambivert Advantage," *Psychological Science* 24, no. 6 (2013): 1024–30; G. Blickle et al., "Extraversion and Job Performance: How Context Relevance and Bandwidth Specificity Create a Non-Linear, Positive, and Asymptotic Relationship," *Journal of Vocational Behavior* 87 (2015): 80–88; P.L. Curșeu et al., "Personality Characteristics That Are Valued in Teams: Not Always 'More Is Better'?," *International Journal of Psychology*, 2019, https://doi.org/10.1002/ijop.12511.

17. J. Anglim and P. O'Connor, "Measurement and Research Using the Big Five, HEXACO, and Narrow Traits: A Primer for Researchers and Practitioners," *Australian Journal of Psychology* 71, no. 1 (2019): 16–25, https://doi.org/10.1111/ajpy.12202.

18. N.G. Waller and J.D. Zavala, "Evaluating the Big Five," *Psychological Inquiry* 4, no. 2 (1993): 131–34; S.V. Paunonen and D.N. Jackson, "What Is Beyond the Big Five? Plenty!," *Journal of Personality* 68, no. 5 (2000): 821–35; L.J. Simms, "The Big Seven Model of Personality and Its Relevance to Personality Pathology," *Journal of Personality* 75, no. 1 (February 2007): 65–94.

19. D.L. Paulhus and K.M. Williams, "The Dark Triad of Personality: Narcissism, Machiavellianism, and Psychopathy," *Journal of Research in Personality* 36 (2002): 556–63; J.M. LeBreton, L.K. Shiverdecker, and E.M. Grimaldi, "The Dark Triad and Workplace Behavior," *Annual Review of Organizational Psychology and Organizational Behavior* 5 (2018): 387–414; R. Rogoza and J. Cieciuch, "Dark Triad Traits and Their Structure: An Empirical Approach," *Current Psychology,* March 19, 2018, https://doi.org/10.1007/s12144-018-9834-6; S.M. Spain, "The Dark Side of Personality," in *Leadership, Work, and the Dark Side of Personality,* ed. S.M. Spain (Academic Press, 2019), 41–93. A fourth trait—sadism—has recently been suggested, but it is early days to add this as a dark tetrad to our discussion.

20. D.N. Jones and D.L. Paulhus, "Differentiating the Dark Triad Within the Interpersonal Circumplex," in *Handbook of Interpersonal Psychology,* ed. L.M. Horowitz and S. Strack (Hoboken, NJ, USA: John Wiley & Sons, Inc., 2012), 249–67; A. Book et al., "Unpacking More 'Evil': What Is at the Core of the Dark Tetrad?," *Personality and Individual Differences* 90 (2016): 269–72; M. Moshagen, B.E. Hilbig, and I. Zettler, "The Dark Core of Personality," *Psychological Review* 125 (2018): 656–88; G. Hodson et al., "Is the Dark Triad Common Factor Distinct from Low Honesty-Humility?," *Journal of Research in Personality* 73 (2018): 123–29.

21. R. Christie and F. Geis, *Studies in Machiavellianism* (New York: Academic Press, 1970); S. R. Kessler et al., "Re-Examining Machiavelli: A Three-Dimensional Model of Machiavellianism in the Workplace," *Journal of Applied Social Psychology* 40, no. 8 (2010): 1868–96; E. O'Boyle et al., "A Meta-Analysis of the Dark Triad and Work Behavior: A Social Exchange Perspective," *Journal of Applied Psychology* 97, no. 3 (2012): 557–79.

22. Z. Krizan and O. Johar, "Envy Divides the Two Faces of Narcissism," *Journal of Personality* 80 (2012): 1415–51.

23. C.J. Patrick, "Psychopathy as Masked Pathology," in *Handbook of Psychopathy,* 2nd ed. (New York: The Guilford Press, 2018), 3–21.

24. The quotation is cited in: S.F. Smith and S.O. Lilienfeld, "Psychopathy in the Workplace: The Knowns and Unknowns," *Aggression and Violent Behavior* 18 (2013): 204–18. For research on dark triad and workplace behavior, see: S.F. Smith and S.O. Lilienfeld, "Psychopathy in the Workplace: The Knowns and Unknowns," *Aggression and Violent Behavior* 18 (2013): 204–18; A. Cohen, "Are They among Us? A Conceptual Framework of the Relationship between the Dark Triad Personality and Counterproductive Work Behaviors (CWBs)," *Human Resource Management Review* 26 (2016): 69–85; A. Harrison, J. Summers, and B. Mennecke, "The Effects of the Dark Triad on Unethical Behavior," *Journal of Business Ethics* 153 (2018): 53–77.

25. M.A. Baysinger, K.T. Scherer, and J.M. LeBreton, "Exploring the Disruptive Effects of Psychopathy and Aggression on Group Processes and Group Effectiveness.," *Journal of Applied Psychology* 99 (2014): 48–65; A.G. Nassif, "Heterogeneity and Centrality of 'Dark Personality' within Teams, Shared Leadership, and Team Performance: A Conceptual Moderated-Mediation Model," *Human Resource Management Review* 29 (2019): 100675.

26. H.L. DeShong, D.M. Grant, and S.N. Mullins-Sweatt, "Comparing Models of Counterproductive Workplace Behaviors: The Five-Factor Model and the Dark Triad," *Personality and Individual Differences* 74 (2015): 55–60; J.R. Van Scotter and K.D.D. Roglio, "CEO Bright and Dark Personality: Effects on Ethical Misconduct," *Journal of Business Ethics,* 2018, https://doi.org/10.1007/s10551-018-4061-5.

27. C.R. Boddy, "Corporate Psychopaths, Bullying and Unfair Supervision in the Workplace," *Journal of Business Ethics* 100 (2011): 367–79; S.F. Smith and S.O. Lilienfeld, "Psychopathy in the Workplace: The Knowns and Unknowns," *Aggression and Violent Behavior* 18 (2013): 204–18.

28. D.N. Jones, "Risk in the Face of Retribution: Psychopathic Individuals Persist in Financial Misbehavior among the Dark Triad," *Personality and Individual Differences,* The Dark Triad of Personality, 67 (2014): 109–13; L. ten Brinke, A. Kish, and D. Keltner, "Hedge Fund Managers With Psychopathic Tendencies Make for Worse Investors," *Personality and Social Psychology Bulletin* 44 (2018): 214–23.

29. C.A. O'Reilly et al., "Narcissistic CEOs and Executive Compensation," *The Leadership Quarterly* 25 (2014): 218–31; K.J. Templer, "Dark Personality, Job Performance Ratings, and the Role of Political Skill: An Indication of Why Toxic People May Get Ahead at Work," *Personality and Individual Differences* 124 (2018): 209–14; W. Hart, K. Richardson, and G.K. Tortoriello, "Meet Your Public Relations Team: People with Dark Traits May Help You Manage Your Image," *Personality and Individual Differences* 134 (2018): 164–73; D.K. Marcus, J. Preszler, and V. Zeigler-Hill, "A Network of Dark Personality Traits: What Lies at the Heart of Darkness?," *Journal of Research in Personality* 73 (2018): 56–62.

30. C.G. Jung, *Psychological Types* trans. H.G. Baynes (Princeton, NJ: Princeton University Press, 1971); I.B. Myers, *The Myers-Briggs Type Indicator* (Palo Alto, CA: Consulting Psychologists Press, 1987).

31. J. Michael, "Using the Myers-Briggs Type Indicator as a Tool for Leadership Development? Apply with Caution," *Journal of Leadership & Organizational Studies* 10 (2003): 68–81; R.M. Capraro and M.M. Capraro, "Myers-Briggs Type Indicator Score Reliability across Studies: A Meta-Analytic Reliability Generalization Study," *Educational and Psychological Measurement* 62 (2002): 590–602; B.S. Kuipers et al., "The Influence of Myers-Briggs Type Indicator Profiles on Team Development Processes," *Small Group Research* 40, no. 4 (2009): 436–64; F.W. Brown and M.D. Reilly, "The Myers-Briggs Type Indicator and Transformational Leadership," *Journal of Management Development* 28, no. 10 (2009): 916–32; A. Luse et al., "Personality and Cognitive Style as Predictors of Preference for Working in Virtual Teams," *Computers in Human Behavior* 29, no. 4 (2013): 1825–32.

32. R.B. Kennedy and D.A. Kennedy, "Using the Myers-Briggs Type Indicator in Career Counseling," *Journal of Employment Counseling* 41, no. 1 (2004): 38–44; K.-H. Lee, Y. Choi, and D.J. Stonier, "Evolutionary Algorithm for a Genetic Robot's Personality Based on the Myers-Briggs Type Indicator," *Robotics and Autonomous Systems* 60, no. 7 (2012): 941–61; S.J. Armstrong, E. Cools, and E. Sadler-Smith, "Role of Cognitive Styles in Business and Management: Reviewing 40 Years of Research," *International Journal of Management Reviews* 14, no. 3 (2012): 238–62.

33. J.B. Lloyd, "Unsubstantiated Beliefs and Values Flaw the Five-Factor Model of Personality," *Journal of Beliefs & Values* 36, no. 2 (2015): 156–64.

34. G. Kirbyson, "Manitoba's Top 25 Employers to Be Announced," *Winnipeg Free Press,* 22 November 2014, B7; Assiniboine Credit Union, *2017 Board of Directors Candidate Guide,* (Winnipeg: Assiniboine Credit Union, 20 October 2016), pg.6; "Assiniboine Credit Union Named One of Manitoba's Top Employers for 2019," News Release (Winnipeg: Assiniboine Credit Union, November 28, 2018).

35. B.M. Meglino and E.C. Ravlin, "Individual Values in Organizations: Concepts, Controversies, and Research," *Journal of Management* 24 (1998): 351–89; B.R. Agle and C.B. Caldwell, "Understanding Research on Values in Business," *Business and Society* 38 (1999): 326–87; S. Hitlin and J.A. Pilavin, "Values: Reviving a Dormant Concept," *Annual Review of Sociology* 30 (2004): 359–93; L. Sagiv et al., "Personal Values in Human Life," *Nature Human Behaviour* 1 (2017): 630–39.

36. D. Lubinski, D.B. Schmidt, and C.P. Benbow, "A 20-Year Stability Analysis of the Study of Values for

Intellectually Gifted Individuals from Adolescence to Adulthood," *Journal of Applied Psychology* 81 (1996): 443–451; M. Vecchione et al., "Stability and Change of Basic Personal Values in Early Adulthood: An 8-Year Longitudinal Study," *Journal of Research in Personality* 63 (2016): 111–22; R. Sundberg, "Value Stability and Change in an ISAF Contingent," *Journal of Personality* 84, no. 1 (2016): 91–101, https://doi.org/10.1111/jopy.12142.

37. L. Parks and R.P. Guay, "Personality, Values, and Motivation," *Personality and Individual Differences* 47, no. 7 (2009): 675–84; L. Parks-Leduc, G. Feldman, and A. Bardi, "Personality Traits and Personal Values: A Meta-Analysis," *Personality and Social Psychology Review* 19, no. 1 (2015): 3–29.

38. S.H. Schwartz, "Universals in the Content and Structure of Values: Theoretical Advances and Empirical Tests in 20 Countries," *Advances in Experimental Social Psychology* 25 (1992): 1–65; S.H. Schwartz and K. Boehnke, "Evaluating the Structure of Human Values with Confirmatory Factor Analysis," *Journal of Research in Personality* 38 (2004): 230–55; I. Borg, A. Bardi, and S.H. Schwartz, "Does the Value Circle Exist Within Persons or Only Across Persons?," *Journal of Personality* 85 (2017): 151–62; P.H.P. Hanel, L.F. Litzellachner, and G.R. Maio, "An Empirical Comparison of Human Value Models," *Frontiers in Psychology* 9 (September 25, 2018), https://doi.org/10.3389/fpsyg.2018.01643. Schwartz's model is currently being revised, but the new model is similar in overall design and still requires refinement.

39. N.T. Feather, "Values, Valences, and Choice: The Influence of Values on the Perceived Attractiveness and Choice of Alternatives," *Journal of Personality and Social Psychology* 68 (1995): 1135–51; L. Sagiv, N. Sverdlik, and N. Schwarz, "To Compete or to Cooperate? Values' Impact on Perception and Action in Social Dilemma Games," *European Journal of Social Psychology* 41 (2011): 64–77; S.H. Schwartz and T. Butenko, "Values and Behavior: Validating the Refined Value Theory in Russia," *European Journal of Social Psychology* 44 (2014): 799–813.

40. G.R. Maio et al., "Addressing Discrepancies between Values and Behavior: The Motivating Effect of Reasons," *Journal of Experimental Social Psychology* 37 (2001): 104–17; A. Bardi and S.H. Schwartz, "Values and Behavior: Strength and Structure of Relations," *Personality and Social Psychology Bulletin* 29 (2003): 1207–20; L. Sagiv, N. Sverdlik, and N. Schwarz, "To Compete or to Cooperate? Values' Impact on Perception and Action in Social Dilemma Games," *European Journal of Social Psychology* 41 (2011): 64–77; K.M. Sheldon and L.S. Krieger, "Walking the Talk: Value Importance, Value Enactment, and Well-Being," *Motivation and Emotion* 38 (2014): 609–19.

41. E. Dreezens et al., "The Missing Link: On Strengthening the Relationship between Values and Attitudes," *Basic and Applied Social Psychology* 30, no. 2 (2008): 142–52; S. Arieli, A.M. Grant, and L. Sagiv, "Convincing Yourself to Care About Others: An Intervention for Enhancing Benevolence Values," *Journal of Personality* 82, no. 1 (2014): 15–24.

42. N. Mazar, O. Amir, and D. Ariely, "The Dishonesty of Honest People: A Theory of Self-Concept Maintenance," *Journal of Marketing Research* 45 (December 2008): 633–644.

43. M.L. Verquer, T.A. Beehr, and S.H. Wagner, "A Meta-Analysis of Relations between Person–Organization Fit and Work Attitudes," *Journal of Vocational Behavior* 63 (2003): 473–89; J.W. Westerman and L.A. Cyr, "An Integrative Analysis of Person–Organization Fit Theories," *International Journal of Selection and Assessment* 12, no. 3 (2004): 252–61; J.R. Edwards and D.M. Cable, "The Value of Value Congruence," *Journal of Applied Psychology* 94, no. 3 (2009): 654–77; A.L. Kristof-Brown et al., "Collective Fit Perceptions: A Multilevel Investigation of Person–Group Fit with Individual-Level and Team-Level Outcomes," *Journal of Organizational Behavior* 35, no. 7 (2014): 969–89. We use the phrase "values congruence" (plural, NOT the singular "value congruence") because values operate as a set, not individually. Also, "value" is easily confused with the economic concept of worth of something relative to price.

44. "Honesty and Communication Top Leadership Skills: Nanos," *CBC News,* 20 September 2013; "Leading the Charge: What Do Canadian Workers Look for in Their Leaders," News release (Toronto: Robert Half Management Resources, 22 September 2016); S. Giles, "The Most Important Leadership Competencies, According to Leaders around the World," *Harvard Business Review Digital Articles,* March 2016, 2–6.

45. P.L. Schumann, "A Moral Principles Framework for Human Resource Management Ethics," *Human Resource Management Review* 11(2001): 93– 111; J.A. Boss, *Analyzing Moral Issues,* 6th ed. (New York: McGraw Hill, 2013), Chap. 1; A. Gustafson, "In Defense of a Utilitarian Business Ethic," *Business and Society Review* 118, no. 3 (2013): 325–60.

46. J.C. Tronto, *Moral Boundaries: A Political Argument for an Ethic of Care* (Psychology Press, 1993), Chap. 5; T.F. Hawk, "An Ethic of Care: A Relational Ethic for the Relational Characteristics of Organizations," in *Applying Care Ethics to Business,* ed. M. Hamington and M. Sander-Staudt (Dordrecht: Springer Netherlands, 2011), 3–34, https://doi.org/10.1007/978-90-481-9307-3_1.

47. D. Engster, "Care Ethics and Stakeholder Theory," in *Applying Care Ethics to Business,* ed. M. Hamington and M. Sander-Staudt (Dordrecht: Springer Netherlands, 2011), 93–110; G.J. Lemoine, C.A. Hartnell, and H. Leroy, "Taking Stock of Moral Approaches to Leadership: An Integrative Review of Ethical, Authentic, and Servant Leadership," *Academy of Management Annals* 13 (2018): 148–87; J. Nicholson and E. Kurucz, "Relational Leadership for Sustainability: Building an Ethical Framework from the Moral Theory of 'Ethics of Care,'" *Journal of Business Ethics* 156 (2019): 25–43.

48. For analysis of these predictors of ethical conduct, see: J.J. Kish-Gephart, D.A. Harrison, and L.K. Treviño, "Bad Apples, Bad Cases, and Bad Barrels: Meta-Analytic Evidence About Sources of Unethical Decisions at Work," *Journal of Applied Psychology* 95, no. 1 (2010): 1–31.

49. T.M. Jones, "Ethical Decision Making by Individuals in Organizations: An Issue-Contingent Model," *Academy of Management Review* 16 (1991): 366–95; T. Barnett, "Dimensions of Moral Intensity and Ethical Decision Making: An Empirical Study," *Journal of Applied Social Psychology* 31 (2001): 1038–57; S. Valentine and D. Hollingworth, "Moral Intensity, Issue Importance, and Ethical Reasoning

in Operations Situations," *Journal of Business Ethics* 108 (2012): 509–23; T.T. Moores, H.J. Smith, and M. Limayem, "Putting the Pieces Back Together: Moral Intensity and Its Impact on the Four-Component Model of Morality," *Business and Society Review* 123 (2018): 243–68.

50. K. Weaver, J. Morse, and C. Mitcham, "Ethical Sensitivity in Professional Practice: Concept Analysis," *Journal of Advanced Nursing 62,* no. 5 (2008): 607–18; L.J.T. Pedersen, "See No Evil: Moral Sensitivity in the Formulation of Business Problems," *Business Ethics: A European Review 18,* no. 4 (2009): 335–48. According to one recent neuroscience study, the emotional aspect of moral sensitivity declines and the cognitive aspect increases between early childhood and young adulthood. See: J. Decety, K.J. Michalska, and K.D. Kinzler, "The Contribution of Emotion and Cognition to Moral Sensitivity: A Neurodevelopmental Study," *Cerebral Cortex 22,* no. 1 (2012): 209–20.

51. D. You, Y. Maeda, and M.J. Bebeau, "Gender Differences in Moral Sensitivity: A Meta-Analysis," *Ethics & Behavior* 21, no. 4 (2011): 263–82; A.H. Chan and H. Cheung, "Cultural Dimensions, Ethical Sensitivity, and Corporate Governance," *Journal of Business Ethics* 110, no. 1 (2012): 45–59; J.R. Sparks, "A Social Cognitive Explanation of Situational and Individual Effects on Moral Sensitivity," *Journal of Applied Social Psychology* 45, no. 1 (2015): 45–54; S.J. Reynolds and J.A. Miller, "The Recognition of Moral Issues: Moral Awareness, Moral Sensitivity and Moral Attentiveness," *Current Opinion in Psychology* 6 (2015): 114–17.

52. J. Boegershausen, K. Aquino, and A. Reed II, "Moral Identity," *Current Opinion in Psychology* 6(2015): 162–66.

53. N. Ruedy and M. Schweitzer, "In the Moment: The Effect of Mindfulness on Ethical Decision Making," *Journal of Business Ethics* 95, no. 1 (2010): 73–87.

54. M.H. Bazerman and F. Gino, "Behavioral Ethics: Toward a Deeper Understanding of Moral Judgment and Dishonesty," *Annual Review of Law and Social Science* 8, no. 1 (2012): 85–104; M. Knoll et al., "Examining the Moral Grey Zone: The Role of Moral Disengagement, Authenticity, and Situational Strength in Predicting Unethical Managerial Behavior," *Journal of Applied Social Psychology* 46, no. 1 (2016): 65–78.

55. Ipsos Reid, "Four in Ten (42%) Employed Canadians Have Observed Some Form of Workplace Misconduct," News release (Toronto, ON: Ipsos Reid, 3 July 2013); Ethics & Compliance Initiative, *Global Business Ethics Survey: Measuring Risk and Promoting Workplace Integrity,* (Arlington, VA: Ethics & Compliance Initiative, June 2016).

56. H. Donker, D. Poff, and S. Zahir, "Corporate Values, Codes of Ethics, and Firm Performance: A Look at the Canadian Context," *Journal of Business Ethics* 82, no. 3 (2008): 527–537; L. Preuss, "Codes of Conduct in Organisational Context: From Cascade to Lattice-Work of Codes," *Journal of Business Ethics* 94, no. 4 (2010): 471–487.

57. S.L. Grover, T. Nadisic, and D.L. Patient, "Bringing Together Different Perspectives on Ethical Leadership," *Journal of Change Management* 12 (2012): 377–81; J. Jordan et al., "Someone to Look up To: Executive–Follower

Ethical Reasoning and Perceptions of Ethical Leadership," *Journal of Management* 39 (2013): 660–83; J. Jaeger, "Compliance Culture Depends on Middle Management," *Compliance Week,* February 2014, 47–61. The ethical culture quotation is from: Canadian Centre for Ethics and Corporate Policy, "Business Ethics Faqs," (Toronto, ON: Canadian Centre for Ethics and Corporate Policy, 2019), http://www.ethicscentre.ca/EN/resources/faq.cfm (accessed December 15, 2019).

58. Individual and collectivism information are from the meta-analysis by Oyserman et al., not the earlier findings by Hofstede. See: D. Oyserman, H.M. Coon, and M. Kemmelmeier, "Rethinking Individualism and Collectivism: Evaluation of Theoretical Assumptions and Meta-Analyses," *Psychological Bulletin* 128 (2002): 3–72. Consistent with Oyserman et al., a recent study found high rather than low individualism among Chileans. See: A. Kolstad and S. Horpestad, "Self-Construal in Chile and Norway," *Journal of Cross-Cultural Psychology* 40, no. 2 (March 2009): 275–281.

59. F.S. Niles, "Individualism-Collectivism Revisited," *Cross-Cultural Research* 32 (1998): 315–41; C.P. Earley and C.B. Gibson, "Taking Stock in Our Progress on Individualism-Collectivism: 100 Years of Solidarity and Community," *Journal of Management* 24 (1998): 265–304; C.L. Jackson et al., "Psychological Collectivism: A Measurement Validation and Linkage to Group Member Performance," *Journal of Applied Psychology* 91, no. 4 (2006): 884–99.

60. D. Oyserman, H.M. Coon, and M. Kemmelmeier, "Rethinking Individualism and Collectivism: Evaluation of Theoretical Assumptions and Meta-Analyses," *Psychological Bulletin* 128 (2002): 3–72; H. Vargas and M. Kemmelmeier, "Ethnicity and Contemporary American Culture: A Meta-Analytic Investigation of Horizontal–Vertical Individualism–Collectivism," *Journal of Cross-Cultural Psychology* 44 (2013): 195–222; Y. Kashima, P.G. Bain, and A. Perfors, "The Psychology of Cultural Dynamics: What Is It, What Do We Know, and What Is Yet to Be Known?," *Annual Review of Psychology* 70 (2019): 499–529.

61. M. Voronov and J.A. Singer, "The Myth of Individualism-Collectivism: A Critical Review," *Journal of Social Psychology* 142 (2002): 461–80; Y. Takano and S. Sogon, "Are Japanese More Collectivistic Than Americans?," *Journal of Cross-Cultural Psychology* 39, no. 3 (2008): 237–50; D. Dalsky, "Individuality in Japan and the United States: A Cross-Cultural Priming Experiment," *International Journal of Intercultural Relations* 34, no. 5 (2010): 429–35. Japan scored 46 on individualism in Hofstede's original study, placing it a little below the middle of the range and around the 60th percentile among the countries studied. Recent studies suggest that Japan has become even more individualistic over the past decade. See Y. Ogihara et al., "Are Common Names Becoming Less Common? The Rise in Uniqueness and Individualism in Japan," *Frontiers in Psychology* 6 (2015): 1490.

62. G. Hofstede, *Culture's Consequences: Comparing Values, Behaviors, Institutions, and Organizations across Nations,* 2nd ed. (Thousand Oaks, CA: Sage, 2001).

63. G. Hofstede, *Culture's Consequences: Comparing Values, Behaviors, Institutions, and Organizations across Nations,* 2nd ed. (Thousand Oaks, CA: Sage, 2001). Hofstede used the terms *masculinity* and *femininity* for *achievement* and *nurturing orientation,* respectively. We (along with other writers) have adopted the latter two terms to minimize the sexist labels originally applied these concepts. Achievement orientation is assumed to be opposite of nurturing orientation, but this opposing relationship is far from certain.

64. V. Taras, J. Rowney, and P. Steel, "Half a Century of Measuring Culture: Review of Approaches, Challenges, and Limitations Based on the Analysis of 121 Instruments for Quantifying Culture," *Journal of International Management* 15, no. 4 (2009): 357–373.

65. R.L. Tung and A. Verbeke, "Beyond Hofstede and GLOBE: Improving the Quality of Cross-Cultural Research," *Journal of International Business Studies* 41, no. 8 (2010): 1259–1274.

66. N. Jacob, "Cross-Cultural Investigations: Emerging Concepts," *Journal of Organizational Change Management* 18, no. 5 (2005): 514–528; V. Taras, B.L. Kirkman, and P. Steel, "Examining the Impact of Culture's Consequences: A Three-Decade, Multilevel, Meta-Analytic Review of Hofstede's Cultural Value Dimensions," *Journal of Applied Psychology* 95, no. 3 (2010): 405–439.

67. "Canadian Multiculturalism: An Inclusive Citizenship," *Immigration, Refugees and Citizenship Canada: What We Do: Multiculturalism* (Ottawa: Government of Canada, 19 October 2012) (accessed 26 January 2017).

68. The cultural differences between Quebec and English Canada are reflected in the phrase "two solitudes" by H. McLennan, *Two Solitudes* (Toronto, ON: MacMillan of Canada, 1945). Several studies reveal current differences in beliefs and values between Francophones and Anglophones. See: Z. Wu and D. Baer, "Attitudes toward Family and Gender Roles: A Comparison of English and French Canadian Women," *Journal of Comparative Family Studies* 27 (Autumn 1996): 437–452; J. Massie, "Regional Strategic Subcultures: Canadians and the Use of Force in Afghanistan and Iraq," *Canadian Foreign Policy* 14, no. 2 (2008): 19–48; B. Laplante, "A Matter of Norms: Family Background, Religion, and Generational Change in the Diffusion of First Union Breakdown among French-Speaking Quebeckers," *Demographic Research* 35, no. 27 (2016): 783–812; B. Anderson and D. Coletto, "How Big Are Canadian Regional Differences on Questions of Morality?," (Ottawa: Abacus Data, 10 July 2016), http://abacus-data.ca/how-big-are-canadian-regional-differences-on-questions-of-morality/ (accessed 26 January 2017).

69. M. Major et al., "Meanings of Work and Personal Values of Canadian Anglophone and Francophone Middle Managers," *Canadian Journal of Administrative Sciences* 11 (1994): 251–63; D.A. Hay, "An Investigation into the Swiftness and Intensity of Recent Secularization in Canada: Was Berger Right?," *Sociology of Religion* 75, no. 1 (2014): 136–62; D.A. Hay, "An Investigation into the Swiftness and Intensity of Recent Secularization in Canada: Was Berger Right?," *Sociology of Religion* 75, no. 1 (2014): 136–62.

70. I. Chapman, D. McCaskill, and D. Newhouse, "Management in Contemporary Aboriginal Organizations," *Canadian Journal of Native Studies* 11 (1991): 333–49; T.R. Lituchy et al., "Mohawk

First Nations: Successes and Challenges of Small Business Owners," in *International Handbook of Research on Indigenous Entrepreneurship,* ed. L.-P. Dana and R. Anderson (Cheltenham, UK: Edward Elgar Publishing, 2007), 378–403; D.D. Anderson, "Management Approaches of First Nations Businesses in Saskatchewan" (Doctor of Philosophy, University of Saskatchewan, 2009); K. Medd, "An Application of Hofstede's Values Survey Module with Aboriginal and Non-Aboriginal Governments in Canada" (Doctor of Philosophy, Carleton University, 2011); T. Stonefish, "Discovering the Meaning of Leadership: A First Nations Exploration" (Master of Arts, University of Windsor, 2013); F.M. Main, "Aboriginal Public Servants: Leadership in the British Columbia Public Service" (Master of Public Administration, University of Victoria, 2014); T. Stonefish and C.T. Kwantes, "Values and Acculturation: A Native Canadian Exploration," *International Journal of Intercultural Relations* 61 (November 2017): 63–76, https://doi.org/10.1016/j.ijintrel.2017.09.005.

71. D. McGrane and L. Berdahl, "'Small Worlds' No More: Reconsidering Provincial Political Cultures in Canada," *Regional & Federal Studies* 23, no. 4 (2013): 479–93; M. Héroux-Legault, "Substate Variations in Political Values in Canada," *Regional & Federal Studies* 26, no. 2 (2016): 171–97; M. Adams, "Fire and Ice Revisited: American and Canadian Social Values in the Age of Obama and Harper," *Presentation at the Woodrow Wilson Center* (YouTube, 14 March 2014), https://www.youtube.com/watch?v=sRbwvb9sMmw, Video (accessed 26 January 2017). One of the earliest detailed reports of cultural differences across Canadian regions was written by Bruce Hutchison, *The Unknown Country: Canada and Her People* (Toronto: Longmans, Green & Company, 1942).

72. Angus Reid Institute, *Canadian Values Release Tables to Accompany 'What Makes Us Canadian? A Study of Values, Beliefs, Priorities, and Identity',* (Vancouver: Angus Reid Institute, 3 October 2016). Openness to experience is inferred from Qtn37e and Qtn36. Emotional stability is inferred from Qtn37f. Regional differences in personality in the United States and United Kingdom are reported in: P.J. Rentfrow, "Statewide Differences in Personality: Toward a Psychological Geography of the United States," *American Psychologist* 65, no. 6 (2010): 548–58; K.H. Rogers and D. Wood, "Accuracy of United States Regional Personality Stereotypes," *Journal of Research in Personality* 44, no. 6 (2010): 704–13; P.J. Rentfrow, M. Jokela, and M.E. Lamb, "Regional Personality Differences in Great Britain," *PLOS ONE* 10, no. 3 (2015): e0122245.

73. J.R. Harrington and M.J. Gelfand, "Tightness–Looseness across the 50 United States," *Proceedings of the National Academy of Sciences* 111, no. 22 (2014): 7990–95; M. Motyl et al., "How Ideological Migration Geographically Segregates Groups," *Journal of Experimental Social Psychology* 51 (2014): 1–14; S. Oishi, T. Talhelm, and M. Lee, "Personality and Geography: Introverts Prefer Mountains," *Journal of Research in Personality* 58 (2015): 55–68.

74. M. Adams, *Fire and Ice: The United States, Canada, and the Myth of Converging Values* (Toronto, ON: Penguin Canada, 2004), 142.

75. J. Laxer, *The Border: Canada, the U.S. And Dispatches from the 49th Parallel* (Toronto, ON: Anchor Canada, 2004).

76. M. Adams, *Fire and Ice: The United States, Canada, and the Myth of Converging Values* (Toronto: Penguin Canada, 2004); C. Boucher, "Canada-US Values: Distinct, Inevitably Carbon Copy, or Narcissism of Small Differences?," *Horizons: Policy Research Initiative* 7, no. 1 (June 2004): 42–49; J. Citrin, R. Johnston, and M. Wright, "Do Patriotism and Multiculturalism Collide? Competing Perspectives from Canada and the United States," *Canadian Journal of Political Science* 45, no. 3 (2012): 531–52; R. Dheer et al., "Cultural Regions of Canada and United States," *International Journal of Cross Cultural Management* 14, no. 3 (2014): 343–84; M. Adams, "Fire and Ice Revisited: American and Canadian Social Values in the Age of Obama and Harper," *Presentation at the Woodrow Wilson Center* (YouTube, 14 March 2014), https://www.youtube.com/watch?v=sRbwvb9sMmw, Video (accessed 26 January 2017).

CHAPTER 3

1. "Young Women Working to Change Engineering Stereotypes," News Release (Canberra: Engineers Australia, April 19, 2017); M. Unger, "10 Challenges Facing Women in STEM," *WISE Knowledge Centre* (blog), August 25, 2017; R.C. Barnett and C. Rivers, "We've Studied Gender and STEM for 25 Years. The Science Doesn't Support the Google Memo," *Recode,* August 11, 2017; A. Gouws, "Don't Blame Women for Leaving Fields like Engineering. Blame Bad Attitudes," *The Conversation,* August 24, 2018; "Occupation - National Occupational Classification (NOC) 2016 (693A)," Data Tables, 2016 Census (Ottawa: Statistics Canada, March 28, 2018); "Postsecondary Enrolments, by Registration Status, Institution Type, Status of Student in Canada and Sex" (Ottawa: Statistics Canada, October 22, 2018), https://doi.org/10.25318/3710001801-eng; D. Gray, "The Engineering Mystery: Where Are the Women?," *Globe and Mail,* March 6, 2019, B11; C. Chiang, "Gender Gap Persists in B.C.'s Engineering Sector," *Business in Vancouver,* March 7, 2019; K. Frank, "A Gender Analysis of the Occupational Pathways of STEM Graduates in Canada," Analytical Studies Branch Research Paper Series, Cat: 11F0019M — No. 429 (Ottawa: Statistics Canada, 2019).

2. A.T. Kearney and Your Life, *Tough Choices: The Real Reasons A-Level Students Are Steering Clear of Science and Maths* (London: February 2016).

3. J. Schaubroeck, Y.J. Kim, and A.C. Peng, "The Self-Concept in Organizational Psychology: Clarifying and Differentiating the Constructs," in *International Review of Industrial and Organizational Psychology* (New York: Wiley, 2012): 1–38; J.J. Skowronski and C. Sedikides, "Evolution of Self," in *Encyclopedia of Evolutionary Psychological Science,* ed. T.K. Shackelford and V.A. Weekes-Shackelford (Cham: Springer International Publishing, 2018), 1–10, https://doi.org/10.1007/978-3-319-16999-6_2424-1.

4. V.L. Vignoles, S.J. Schwartz, and K. Luyckx, " Introduction: Toward an Integrative View of Identity," in *Handbook of Identity Theory and Research,* ed. J.S. Schwartz, K. Luyckx, and L.V. Vignoles (New York: Springer New York, 2011), 1–27; L. Gaertner et al., "A Motivational Hierarchy within: Primacy of the Individual Self, Relational Self, or Collective Self?," *Journal of Experimental Social Psychology* 48, no. 5 (2012).

5. E.J. Koch and J.A. Shepperd, "Is Self-Complexity Linked to Better Coping? A Review of the Literature," *Journal of Personality* 72, no. 4 (2004): 727–60; A.R. McConnell, "The Multiple Self-Aspects Framework: Self-Concept Representation and Its Implications," *Personality and Social Psychology Review* 15, no. 1 (2011): 3–27; L.F. Emery, C. Walsh, and E.B. Slotter, "Knowing Who You Are and Adding to It: Reduced Self-Concept Clarity Predicts Reduced Self-Expansion," *Social Psychological and Personality Science* 6, no. 3 (2015): 259–66.

6. C.M. Brown et al., "Between Two Selves: Comparing Global and Local Predictors of Speed of Switching between Self-Aspects," *Self and Identity* 15, no. 1 (2016): 72–89.

7. J.D. Campbell et al., "Self-Concept Clarity: Measurement, Personality Correlates, and Cultural Boundaries," *Journal of Personality and Social Psychology* 70, no. 1 (1996): 141–56.

8. J. Lodi-Smith and B.W. Roberts, "Getting to Know Me: Social Role Experiences and Age Differences in Self-Concept Clarity During Adulthood," *Journal of Personality* 78, no. 5 (2010): 1383–410; H. Adam et al., "The Shortest Path to Oneself Leads around the World: Living Abroad Increases Self-Concept Clarity," *Organizational Behavior and Human Decision Processes* 145 (March 2018): 16–29, https://doi.org/10.1016/j.obhdp.2018.01.002.

9. E.J. Koch and J.A. Shepperd, "Is Self-Complexity Linked to Better Coping? A Review of the Literature," *Journal of Personality* 72, no. 4 (2004): 727–60; A.T. Church et al., "Relating Self-Concept Consistency to Hedonic and Eudaimonic Well-Being in Eight Cultures," *Journal of Cross-Cultural Psychology* 45, no. 5 (2014): 695–712, https://doi.org/10.1177/0022022114527347; A.W. Hanley and E.L. Garland, "Clarity of Mind: Structural Equation Modeling of Associations between Dispositional Mindfulness, Self-Concept Clarity and Psychological Well-Being," *Personality and Individual Differences* 106 (2017): 334–39, https://doi.org/10.1016/j.paid.2016.10.028; M. Parise et al., "Self-Concept Clarity and Psychological Adjustment in Adolescence: The Mediating Role of Emotion Regulation," *Personality and Individual Differences* 138 (2019): 363–65, https://doi.org/10.1016/j.paid.2018.10.023.

10. A.T. Brook, J. Garcia, and M.A. Fleming, "The Effects of Multiple Identities on Psychological Well-Being," *Personality and Social Psychology Bulletin* 34, no. 12 (2008): 1588–600; A.T. Church et al., "Relating Self-Concept Consistency to Hedonic and Eudaimonic Well-Being in Eight Cultures," *Journal of Cross-Cultural Psychology* 45, no. 5 (2014): 695–712.

11. J.D. Campbell, "Self-Esteem and Clarity of the Self-Concept," *Journal of Personality and Social Psychology* 59, no. 3 (1990).

12. S. Hannah et al., "The Psychological and Neurological Bases of Leader Self-Complexity and Effects on Adaptive Decision-Making, " *Journal of Applied Psychology* 98, no. 3 (2013): 393–411; S.J. Creary, B.B. Caza, and L.M. Roberts, "Out of the Box? How Managing a Subordinate's Multiple Identities Affects the Quality of a Manager-Subordinate Relationship, " *Academy of Management Review* 40, no. 4 (2015): 538–62; S.K. Kang and G.V. Bodenhausen, "Multiple Identities in Social Perception and Interaction: Challenges and Opportunities, " *Annual Review of Psychology* 66, no. 1 (2015): 547–74.

13. C. Peus et al., "Authentic Leadership: An Empirical Test of Its Antecedents, Consequences, and Mediating Mechanisms," *Journal of Business Ethics* 107, no. 3 (2012): 331–48; F.O. Walumbwa, M.A. Maidique, and C. Atamanik, "Decision-Making in a Crisis: What Every Leader Needs to Know," *Organizational Dynamics* 43, no. 4 (2014): 284–93; B. Mittal, "Self-Concept Clarity: Exploring Its Role in Consumer Behavior, " *Journal of Economic Psychology* 46 (2015): 98–110.

14. This quotation has been cited since the 1930s, yet we were unable to find it in any of Dewey's writing. The earliest known reference to this quotation is Dale Carnegie's famous self-help book, in which Carnegie attributes this statement to Dewey. See: D. Carnegie, *How to Win Friends and Influence People,* 1st ed. (New York: Simon & Schuster, 1936), 37-38 (First or second page of Chapter 2; page numbers vary in later editions.)

15. C.L. Guenther and M.D. Alicke, "Deconstructing the Better-Than-Average Effect," *Journal of Personality and Social Psychology* 99, no. 5 (2010): 755–70; S. Loughnan et al., "Universal Biases in Self-Perception: Better and More Human Than Average," *British Journal of Social Psychology* 49 (2010): 627–36; D.L. Ferris and C. Sedikides, "Self-Enhancement in Organizations," in *The Self at Work: Fundamental Theory and Research,* ed. D.L. Ferris, R.E. Johnson, and C. Sedikides, 2018, 91–118.

16. D. Dunning, C. Heath, and J.M. Suls, "Flawed Self-Assessment: Implications for Health, Education, and the Workplace," *Psychological Science in the Public Interest* 5, no. 3 (2004): 69–106; D.A. Moore, "Not So above Average after All: When People Believe They Are Worse Than Average and Its Implications for Theories of Bias in Social Comparison," *Organizational Behavior and Human Decision Processes* 102, no. 1 (2007): 42–58. The statistics on student self-perceptions are reported in: J.M. Twenge, W.K. Campbell, and B. Gentile, "Generational Increases in Agentic Self-Evaluations among American College Students, 1966–2009," *Self and Identity* 11, no. 4 (2011): 409–27.

17. D. Gosselin et al., "Comparative Optimism among Drivers: An Intergenerational Portrait," *Accident Analysis & Prevention* 42, no. 2 (2010): 734–40; P.M. Picone, G. Battista Dagnino, and A. Minà, "The Origin of Failure: A Multidisciplinary Appraisal of the Hubris Hypothesis and Proposed Research Agenda," *Academy of Management Perspectives* 28, no. 4 (2014): 447–68; G. Chen, C. Crossland, and S. Luo, "Making the Same Mistake All over Again: CEO Overconfidence and Corporate Resistance to Corrective Feedback," *Strategic Management Journal* 36, no. 10 (2015): 1513–35; M. Dufner et al., "Self-Enhancement and Psychological Adjustment: A Meta-Analytic Review," *Personality and Social Psychology Review* 23, no. 1 (2019): 48–72, https://doi.org/10.1177/1088868318756467.

18. W.B. Swann Jr, "To Be Adored or to Be Known? The Interplay of Self-Enhancement and Self-Verification," in *Foundations of Social Behavior,* ed. R.M. Sorrentino and E.T. Higgins (New York:

Guildford, 1990), 408–48; W.B. Swann Jr, P.J. Rentfrow, and J.S. Guinn, "Self-Verification: The Search for Coherence," in *Handbook of Self and Identity,* ed. M.R. Leary and J. Tagney (New York: Guildford, 2002), 367–83; D.M. Cable and V.S. Kay, "Striving for Self-Verification During Organizational Entry," *Academy of Management Journal* 55, no. 2 (2012): 360–80.

19. A. Meister, A. Sinclair, and K.A. Jehn, "Identities under Scrutiny: How Women Leaders Navigate Feeling Misidentified at Work," *The Leadership Quarterly* 28, no. 5 (2017): 672–90, https://doi.org/10.1016/j.leaqua.2017.01.009.

20. T. Kwang and W.B. Swann, "Do People Embrace Praise Even When They Feel Unworthy? A Review of Critical Tests of Self-Enhancement versus Self-Verification," *Personality and Social Psychology Review* 14, no. 3 (2010): 263–80.; G. S. Preuss and M. D. Alicke, "My Worst Faults and Misdeeds: Self-Criticism and Self-Enhancement Can Co-Exist," *Self and Identity* 16, no. 6 (2017): 645–63.

21. M.R. Leary, "Motivational and Emotional Aspects of the Self," *Annual Review of Psychology* 58, no. 1 (2007): 317–44; A. Meister, K.A. Jehn, and S.M.B. Thatcher, "Feeling Misidentified: The Consequences of Internal Identity Asymmetries for Individuals at Work," *Academy of Management Review* 39, no. 4 (2014): 488–512.

22. We have described three components of core self-evaluation. The remaining component is the personality trait emotional stability, which was described in Chapter 2. However, personality is a behaviour tendency, whereas core self-evaluation includes only "evaluation-focused" variables. There is also recent concern about whether locus of control is part of self-evaluation. See R.E. Johnson, C.C. Rosen, and P.E. Levy, "Getting to the Core of Core Self-Evaluation: A Review and Recommendations," *Journal of Organizational Behavior* 29 (2008): 391–413; C.-H. Chang et al., "Core Self-Evaluations: A Review and Evaluation of the Literature," *Journal of Management* 38, no. 1 (2012): 81–128; R.E. Johnson et al., "Getting to the Core of Locus of Control: Is It an Evaluation of the Self or the Environment?," *Journal of Applied Psychology* 100, no. 5 (2015): 1568–78.

23. W.B. Swann Jr., C. Chang-Schneider, and K.L. McClarty, "Do People's Self-Views Matter?: Self-Concept and Self-Esteem in Everyday Life," *American Psychologist* 62, no. 2 (2007): 84–94; J.L. Pierce, D.G. Gardner, and C. Crowley, "Organization-Based Self-Esteem and Well-Being: Empirical Examination of a Spillover Effect," *European Journal of Work and Organizational Psychology* 25, no. 2 (2016): 181–99

24. A. Bandura, *Self-Efficacy: The Exercise of Control* (New York: W. H. Freeman, 1997); J.B. Vancouver and J.D. Purl, "A Computational Model of Self-Efficacy's Various Effects on Performance: Moving the Debate Forward.," *Journal of Applied Psychology* 102, no. 4 (2017): 599–616, https://doi.org/10.1037/apl0000177.

25. G. Chen, S.M. Gully, and D. Eden, "Validation of a New General Self-Efficacy Scale," *Organizational Research Methods* 4, no. 1 (2001): 62–83.

26. J.B. Rotter, "Generalized Expectancies for Internal versus External Control of Reinforcement," *Psychological Monographs* 80, no. 1 (1966): 1–28;

D.A. Cobb-Clark, "Locus of Control and the Labor Market," *IZA Journal of Labor Economics* 4, no. 1 (February 19, 2015): 1–19, https://doi.org/10.1186/s40172-014-0017-x; B.M. Galvin et al., "Changing the Focus of Locus (of Control): A Targeted Review of the Locus of Control Literature and Agenda for Future Research," *Journal of Organizational Behavior* 39, no. 7 (2018): 820–33, https://doi.org/10.1002/job.2275.

27. T.W.H. Ng, K.L. Sorensen, and L.T. Eby, "Locus of Control at Work: A Meta-Analysis," *Journal of Organizational Behavior* 27 (2006): 1057–87; Q. Wang, N.A. Bowling, and K.J. Eschleman, "A Meta-Analytic Examination of Work and General Locus of Control," *Journal of Applied Psychology* 95, no. 4 (2010): 761–68.

28. G.J. Leonardelli, C.L. Pickett, and M.B. Brewer, "Optimal Distinctiveness Theory: A Framework for Social Identity, Social Cognition, and Intergroup Relations," in *Advances in Experimental Social Psychology,* ed. M.P. Zanna and J.M. Olson (San Diego, CA: Academic Press, 2010), 63–113; M. Ormiston, "Explaining the Link between Objective and Perceived Differences in Groups: The Role of the Belonging and Distinctiveness Motives," *Journal of Applied Psychology* 101, no. 2 (2016): 222–36.

29. We describe relational self-concept as a form of social identity because such connections are inherently social and the dyads are typically members of a collective entity. For example, an employee has a relationship identity with his/her boss, but this is connected to a social identity with the team or department. However, recent discussion suggests that relational self-concept may also be part of personal identity or a separate form of self-concept. See B.E. Ashforth, B.S. Schinoff, and K.M. Rogers, ""I Identify with Her," "I Identify with Him": Unpacking the Dynamics of Personal Identification in Organizations," *Academy of Management Review* 41, no. 1 (2016): 28–60.

30. C. Sedikides and A.P. Gregg, "Portraits of the Self," in *The Sage Handbook of Social Psychology,* ed. M.A. Hogg and J. Cooper (London: Sage, 2003), 110–38; S.A. Haslam and N. Ellemers, "Identity Processes in Organizations," in *Handbook of Identity Theory and Research,* ed. J.S. Schwartz, K. Luyckx, and L.V. Vignoles (New York: Springer New York, 2011), 715–44; M.A. Hogg and M.J. Rinella, "Social Identities and Shared Realities," *Current Opinion in Psychology,* Shared Reality, 23 (October 2018): 6–10, https://doi.org/10.1016/j.copsyc.2017.10.003.

31. M.R. Edwards, "Organizational Identification: A Conceptual and Operational Review," *International Journal of Management Reviews* 7, no. 4 (2005): 207–30; E.S. Lee, T.Y. Park, and B. Koo, "Identifying Organizational Identification as a Basis for Attitudes and Behaviors: A Meta-Analytic Review," *Psychological Bulletin* 141, no. 5 (2015): 1049–80.

32. M.B. Brewer, "The Social Self: On Being the Same and Different at the Same Time," *Personality and Social Psychology Bulletin* 17, no. 5 (1991): 475–82; R. Imhoff and H.-P. Erb, "What Motivates Nonconformity? Uniqueness Seeking Blocks Majority Influence," *Personality and Social Psychology Bulletin* 35, no. 3 (2009): 309–20; K.R. Morrison and S.C. Wheeler, "Nonconformity Defines the Self: The Role of Minority Opinion Status in Self-Concept Clarity," *Personality and*

Social Psychology Bulletin 36, no. 3 (2010): 297–308; M.G. Mayhew, J. Gardner, and N.M. Ashkanasy, "Measuring Individuals' Need for Identification: Scale Development and Validation," *Personality and Individual Differences* 49, no. 5 (2010): 356–61.

33. See, for example: L. Ramarajan, "Past, Present and Future Research on Multiple Identities: Toward an Intrapersonal Network Approach," *The Academy of Management Annals* 8, no. 1 (2014): 589–659; D.L. Ferris, R.E. Johnson, and C. Sedikides, eds., *The Self at Work: Fundamental Theory and Research* (New York: Routledge/Taylor & Francis Group, 2018).

34. E.I. Knudsen, "Fundamental Components of Attention," *Annual Review of Neuroscience* 30, no. 1 (2007): 57–78. For an evolutionary psychology perspective of selective attention and organization, see: L. Cosmides and J. Tooby, "Evolutionary Psychology: New Perspectives on Cognition and Motivation," *Annual Review of Psychology* 64, no. 1 (2013): 201–29.

35. A. Bechara and A.R. Damasio, "The Somatic Marker Hypothesis: A Neural Theory of Economic Decision," *Games and Economic Behavior* 52, no. 2 (2005): 336–72; T.S. Saunders and M.J. Buehner, "The Gut Chooses Faster Than the Mind: A Latency Advantage of Affective over Cognitive Decisions," *Quarterly Journal of Experimental Psychology* 66, no. 2 (2012): 381–88; R. Smith and R. D. Lane, "The Neural Basis of One's Own Conscious and Unconscious Emotional States," *Neuroscience & Biobehavioral Reviews* 57 (2015): 1–29.

36. Plato, *The Republic,* trans. D. Lee (Harmondsworth, UK: Penguin, 1955). For the importance of emotions on memory, see: I. Xenakis, A. Arnellos, and J. Darzentas, "The Functional Role of Emotions in Aesthetic Judgment," *New Ideas in Psychology* 30, no. 2 (2012): 212–26, https://doi.org/10.1016/j.newideapsych.2011.09.003; S. Sheldon and J. Donahue, "More than a Feeling: Emotional Cues Impact the Access and Experience of Autobiographical Memories," *Memory & Cognition* 45, no. 5 (2017): 731–44, https://doi.org/10.3758/s13421-017-0691-6; H.J. Bowen, S.M. Kark, and E.A. Kensinger, "NEVER Forget: Negative Emotional Valence Enhances Recapitulation," *Psychonomic Bulletin & Review* 25, no. 3 (2018): 870–91, https://doi.org/10.3758/s13423-017-1313-9.

37. D.J. Simons and C.F. Chabris, "Gorillas in Our Midst: Sustained Inattentional Blindness for Dynamic Events," *Perception* 28 (1999): 1059–74.

38. R.S. Nickerson, "Confirmation Bias: A Ubiquitous Phenomenon in Many Guises," *Review of General Psychology* 2, no. 2 (1998): 175–220; A.M. Scherer, P.D. Windschitl, and A.R. Smith, "Hope to Be Right: Biased Information Seeking Following Arbitrary and Informed Predictions," *Journal of Experimental Social Psychology* 49, no. 1 (2013): 106–12.

39. Wastell et al., "Identifying Hypothesis Confirmation Behaviors in a Simulated Murder Investigation: Implications for Practice," *Journal of Investigative Psychology and Offender Profiling* 9, no. 2 (2012): 184–98; D.K. Rossmo, "Case Rethinking: A Protocol for Reviewing Criminal Investigations," *Police Practice and Research* 17, no. 3 (2016): 212–28; Government of Canada, "Innocence at Stake: The Need for Continued

Vigilance to Prevent Wrongful Convictions in Canada," Report of the Federal/Provincial/Territorial Heads of Prosecutions Subcommittee on the Prevention of Wrongful Convictions (Ottawa: Department of Justice Canada, April 25, 2019).

40. C.N. Macrae and G.V. Bodenhausen, "Social Cognition: Thinking Categorically about Others," *Annual Review of Psychology* 51 (2000): 93–120; K.A. Quinn and H.E.S. Rosenthal, "Categorizing Others and the Self: How Social Memory Structures Guide Social Perception and Behavior," *Learning and Motivation* 43, no. 4 (2012): 247–58; L.T. Phillips, M. Weisbuch, and N. Ambady, "People Perception: Social Vision of Groups and Consequences for Organizing and Interacting," *Research in Organizational Behavior* 34 (2014): 101–27.

41. S. Avugos et al., "The 'Hot Hand' Reconsidered: A Meta-Analytic Approach," *Psychology of Sport and Exercise* 14, no. 1 (2013): 21–27. For a discussion of cognitive closure and perception, see A. Roets et al., "The Motivated Gatekeeper of Our Minds: New Directions in Need for Closure Theory and Research," in *Advances in Experimental Social Psychology,* ed. M.O. James and P.Z. Mark (San Diego, CA: Academic Press, 2015), 221–83.

42. J. Willis and A. Todorov, "First Impressions: Making Up Your Mind after a 100-Ms Exposure to a Face," *Psychological Science* 17, no. 7 (2006): 592–98; D. Kahneman, *Thinking Fast and Slow* (New York: Farrar, Strauss and Giroux, 2011); A. Todorov, *Face Value: The Irresistible Influence of First Impressions* (Princeton, NJ: Princeton University Press, 2017).

43. P.M. Senge, *The Fifth Discipline: The Art and Practice of the Learning Organization* (New York: Doubleday Currency, 1990), Chap. 10; T.J. Chermack, "Mental Models in Decision Making and Implications for Human Resource Development," *Advances in Developing Human Resources* 5, no. 4 (2003): 408–22; P.N. Johnson-Laird, *Mental Models and Deductive Reasoning,* ed. J.E. Adler and L.J. Rips, Reasoning: Studies of Human Inference and Its Foundations (Cambridge: Cambridge Univ Press, 2008); S. Ross and N. Allen, "Examining the Convergent Validity of Shared Mental Model Measures," *Behavior Research Methods* 44, no. 4 (2012): 1052–62.

44. G.W. Allport, *The Nature of Prejudice* (Reading, MA: Addison-Wesley, 1954); J.C. Brigham, "Ethnic Stereotypes," *Psychological Bulletin* 76, no. 1 (1971): 15–38; D.J. Schneider, *The Psychology of Stereotyping* (New York: Guilford, 2004); S. Kanahara, "A Review of the Definitions of Stereotype and a Proposal for a Progressional Model," *Individual Differences Research* 4, no. 5 (2006): 306–21.

45. L. Jussim, J.T. Crawford, and R.S. Rubinstein, "Stereotype (in)Accuracy in Perceptions of Groups and Individuals," *Current Directions in Psychological Science* 24, no. 6 (2015): 490–97.

46. C.N. Macrae, A.B. Milne, and G.V. Bodenhausen, "Stereotypes as Energy-Saving Devices: A Peek inside the Cognitive Toolbox," *Journal of Personality and Social Psychology* 66 (1994): 37–47; J.W. Sherman et al., "Stereotype Efficiency Reconsidered: Encoding Flexibility under Cognitive Load," *Journal of Personality and Social Psychology* 75 (1998): 589–606; C.K. Soderberg et al., "The Effects of Psychological Distance on

Abstraction: Two Meta-Analyses," *Psychological Bulletin* 141, no. 3 (2015): 525–48, http://dx.doi.org/10.1037/bul0000005.

47. J.C. Turner and S.A. Haslam, "Social Identity, Organizations, and Leadership," in *Groups at Work: Theory and Research,* ed. M.E. Turner (Mahwah, NJ: Lawrence Erlbaum Associates, 2001), 25–65; J. Jetten, R. Spears, and T. Postmes, "Intergroup Distinctiveness and Differentiation: A Meta-Analytic Integration," *Journal of Personality and Social Psychology* 86, no. 6 (2004): 862–79; M.A. Hogg et al., "The Social Identity Perspective: Intergroup Relations, Self-Conception, and Small Groups," *Small Group Research* 35, no. 3 (2004): 246–76; K. Hugenberg and D.F. Sacco, "Social Categorization and Stereotyping: How Social Categorization Biases Person Perception and Face Memory," *Social and Personality Psychology Compass* 2, no. 2 (2008): 1052–72.

48. N. Halevy, G. Bornstein, and L. Sagiv, ""In-Group Love" and "out-Group Hate" as Motives for Individual Participation in Intergroup Conflict: A New Game Paradigm," *Psychological Science* 19, no. 4 (2008): 405–11; T. Yamagishi and N. Mifune, "Social Exchange and Solidarity: In-Group Love or out-Group Hate?," *Evolution and Human Behavior* 30, no. 4 (2009): 229–37; N. Halevy, O. Weisel, and G. Bornstein, "In-Group Love" and "out-Group Hate" in Repeated Interaction between Groups," *Journal of Behavioral Decision Making* 25, no. 2 (2012): 188–95; M. Parker and R. Janoff-Bulman, "Lessons from Morality-Based Social Identity: The Power of Outgroup "Hate," Not Just Ingroup "Love"," *Social Justice Research* 26, no. 1 (2013): 81–96.

49. T. Schmader and W.M. Hall, "Stereotype Threat in School and at Work: Putting Science into Practice," *Policy Insights from the Behavioral and Brain Sciences* 1, no. 1 (2014): 30–37; C.R. Pennington et al., "Twenty Years of Stereotype Threat Research: A Review of Psychological Mediators," *PLoS ONE* 11, no. 1 (2016): e0146487.

50. C.A. Moss-Racusin et al., "Science Faculty's Subtle Gender Biases Favor Male Students," *Proceedings of the National Academy of Sciences* 109, no. 41 (2012): 16474–79.

51. S.T. Fiske, "Stereotyping, Prejudice, and Discrimination," in *Handbook of Social Psychology,* ed. D.T. Gilbert, S.T. Fiske, and G. Lindzey (New York: McGraw Hill, 1998): 357–411; M. Hewstone, M. Rubin, and H. Willis, "Intergroup Bias," *Annual Review of Psychology* 53 (2002): 575–604; C. Stangor, "The Study of Stereotyping, Prejudice, and Discrimination within Social Psychology: A Quick History of Theory and Research," in *Handbook of Prejudice, Stereotyping, and Discrimination,* ed. Todd D. Nelson (New York: Psychology Press, 2016), 1–22.

52. E. Zschirnt and D. Ruedin, "Ethnic Discrimination in Hiring Decisions: A Meta-Analysis of Correspondence Tests 1990–2015," *Journal of Ethnic and Migration Studies* 42, no. 7 (2016): 1115–34; S. Hennekam et al., "Recruitment Discrimination: How Organizations Use Social Power to Circumvent Laws and Regulations," *The International Journal of Human Resource Management* (2019): 1–29.

53. J.A. Bargh and T.L. Chartrand, "The Unbearable Automaticity of Being," *American Psychologist* 54, no. 7 (1999): 462–79; B. Gawronski et al.,

"When 'Just Say No' Is Not Enough: Affirmation versus Negation Training and the Reduction of Automatic Stereotype Activation," *Journal of Experimental Social Psychology* 44 (2008): 370–77; M.D. Burns, M.J. Monteith, and L.R. Parker, "Training Away Bias: The Differential Effects of Counterstereotype Training and Self-Regulation on Stereotype Activation and Application," *Journal of Experimental Social Psychology* 73 (2017): 97–110, https://doi.org/10.1016/j.jesp.2017.06.003; I.R. Johnson, B.M. Kopp, and R.E. Petty, "Just Say No! (And Mean It): Meaningful Negation as a Tool to Modify Automatic Racial Attitudes," *Group Processes & Intergroup Relations* 21, no. 1 (January 1, 2018): 88–110, https://doi.org/10.1177/1368430216647189; G.B. Humiston and E.J. Wamsley, "Unlearning Implicit Social Biases during Sleep: A Failure to Replicate," *PLOS ONE* 14, no. 1 (January 25, 2019): e0211416, https://doi.org/10.1371/journal.pone.0211416.

54. A.M. Rivers et al., "On the Roles of Stereotype Activation and Application in Diminishing Implicit Bias," *Personality and Social Psychology Bulletin* 46 (2020): 349–64.

55. H.H. Kelley, *Attribution in Social Interaction* (Morristown, NJ: General Learning Press, 1971); B.F. Malle, "Attribution Theories: How People Make Sense of Behavior," in *Theories of Social Psychology,* ed. D. Chadee (Chicester, UK: Blackwell Publishing, 2011), 72–95. This "internal-external" or "person-situation" perspective of the attribution process differs somewhat from the original "intentional-unintentional" perspective, which says that we try to understand the deliberate or accidental/involuntary reasons why people engage in behaviours, as well as the reasons for behaviour. Some writers suggest the original perspective is more useful. See: B.F. Malle, "Time to Give up the Dogmas of Attribution: An Alternative Theory of Behavior Explanation," in *Advances in Experimental Social Psychology, Vol 44,* ed. K.M. Olson and M.P. Zanna, *Advances in Experimental Social Psychology* (San Diego: Elsevier Academic Press Inc., 2011), 297–352.

56. H.H. Kelley, "The Processes of Causal Attribution," *American Psychologist* 28 (1973): 107–28.

57. D. Lange and N.T. Washburn, "Understanding Attributions of Corporate Social Irresponsibility," *Academy of Management Review* 37, no. 2 (2012): 300–26. Recent reviews explain that attribution is an incomplete theory for understanding how people determine causation and assign blame. See S.A. Sloman and D. Lagnado, "Causality in Thought," *Annual Review of Psychology* 66, no. 1 (2015): 223–47; M.D. Alicke et al., "Causal Conceptions in Social Explanation and Moral Evaluation: A Historical Tour," *Perspectives on Psychological Science* 10, no. 6 (2015): 790–812.

58. J.M. Crant and T.S. Bateman, "Assignment of Credit and Blame for Performance Outcomes," *Academy of Management Journal* 36 (1993): 7–27; B. Weiner, "Intrapersonal and Interpersonal Theories of Motivation from an Attributional Perspective," *Educational Psychology Review* 12 (2000): 1–14; N. Bacon and P. Blyton, "Worker Responses to Teamworking: Exploring Employee Attributions of Managerial Motives," *International Journal of Human Resource Management* 16, no. 2 (2005): 238–55.

59. D.T. Miller and M. Ross, "Self-Serving Biases in the Attribution of Causality: Fact or Fiction?," *Psychological Bulletin* 82, no. 2 (1975): 213–25; J. Shepperd, W. Malone, and K. Sweeny, "Exploring Causes of the Self-Serving Bias," *Social and Personality Psychology Compass* 2, no. 2 (2008): 895–908.

60. E.W.K. Tsang, "Self-Serving Attributions in Corporate Annual Reports: A Replicated Study," *Journal of Management Studies* 39, no. 1 (2002): 51–65; N.J. Roese and J.M. Olson, "Better, Stronger, Faster: Self-Serving Judgment, Affect Regulation, and the Optimal Vigilance Hypothesis," *Perspectives on Psychological Science* 2, no. 2 (2007): 124–41; R. Hooghiemstra, "East-West Differences in Attributions for Company Performance: A Content Analysis of Japanese and U.S. Corporate Annual Reports," *Journal of Cross-Cultural Psychology* 39, no. 5 (2008): 618–29; M. Franco and H. Haase, "Failure Factors in Small and Medium-Sized Enterprises: Qualitative Study from an Attributional Perspective," *International Entrepreneurship and Management Journal* 6, no. 4 (2010): 503–21.

61. D.T. Gilbert and P.S. Malone, "The Correspondence Bias," *Psychological Bulletin* 117, no. 1 (1995): 21–38.

62. R.E. Nisbett, *The Geography of Thought: How Asians and Westerners Think Differently – and Why* (New York: Free Press, 2003), Chap. 5; S.G. Goto et al., "Cultural Differences in Sensitivity to Social Context: Detecting Affective Incongruity Using the N400," *Social Neuroscience* 8, no. 1 (2012): 63–74; B.F. Malle, "The Actor–Observer Asymmetry in Attribution: A (Surprising) Meta-Analysis," *Psychological Bulletin* 132, no. 6 (2006): 895–919; C.W. Bauman and L.J. Skitka, "Making Attributions for Behaviors: The Prevalence of Correspondence Bias in the General Population," *Basic and Applied Social Psychology* 32, no. 3 (2010): 269–77; I. Scopelliti et al., "Individual Differences in Correspondence Bias: Measurement, Consequences, and Correction of Biased Interpersonal Attributions," *Management Science* 64, no. 4 (2017): 1879–1910, https://doi.org/10.1287/mnsc.2016.2668.

63. Similar models are presented in D. Eden, "Self-Fulfilling Prophecy as a Management Tool: Harnessing Pygmalion," *Academy of Management Review* 9 (1984): 64–73; R.H.G. Field and D. A. Van Seters, "Management by Expectations (Mbe): The Power of Positive Prophecy," *Journal of General Management* 14 (1988): 19–33; D.O. Trouilloud et al., "The Influence of Teacher Expectations on Student Achievement in Physical Education Classes: Pygmalion Revisited," *European Journal of Social Psychology* 32 (2002): 591–607.

64. P. Whiteley, T. Sy, and S.K. Johnson, "Leaders' Conceptions of Followers: Implications for Naturally Occurring Pygmalion Effects," *Leadership Quarterly* 23, no. 5 (2012): 822–34; J. Weaver, J. F. Moses, and M. Snyder, "Self-Fulfilling Prophecies in Ability Settings," *Journal of Social Psychology* 156, no. 2 (2016): 179–89.

65. D. Eden, "Interpersonal Expectations in Organizations," in *Interpersonal Expectations: Theory, Research, and Applications* (Cambridge, UK: Cambridge University Press, 1993), 154–78.

66. K.S. Crawford, E.D. Thomas, and J.J.A. Fink, "Pygmalion at Sea: Improving the Work Effectiveness of Low Performers," *Journal of Applied Behavioral Science* 16 (1980): 482–505; D. Eden, "Pygmalion Goes to Boot Camp: Expectancy, Leadership, and Trainee Performance," *Journal of Applied Psychology* 67 (1982): 194–99; C.M. Rubie-Davies, "Teacher Expectations and Student Self-Perceptions: Exploring Relationships," *Psychology in the Schools* 43, no. 5 (2006): 537–52; P. Whiteley, T. Sy, and S.K. Johnson, "Leaders' Conceptions of Followers: Implications for Naturally Occurring Pygmalion Effects," *Leadership Quarterly* 23, no. 5 (2012): 822–34.

67. S. Madon, L. Jussim, and J. Eccles, "In Search of the Powerful Self-Fulfilling Prophecy," *Journal of Personality and Social Psychology* 72, no. 4 (1997): 791–809; A.E. Smith, L. Jussim, and J. Eccles, "Do Self-Fulfilling Prophecies Accumulate, Dissipate, or Remain Stable over Time?," *Journal of Personality and Social Psychology* 77, no. 3 (1999): 548–65; S. Madon et al., "Self-Fulfilling Prophecies: The Synergistic Accumulative Effect of Parents' Beliefs on Children's Drinking Behavior," *Psychological Science* 15, no. 12 (2005): 837–45.

68. J. Hoffman, "Doctors' Delicate Balance in Keeping Hope Alive," *New York Times,* December 24, 2005, A1, A14; K. Blakely et al., "Optimistic Honesty: Understanding Surgeon and Patient Perspectives on Hopeful Communication in Pancreatic Cancer Care," *HPB* 19 (2017): 611–19. For reviews of positive organizational behavior and associated concepts of positive psychology and psychological capital, see: A. Newman et al., "Psychological Capital: A Review and Synthesis," *Journal of Organizational Behavior* 35, no. S1 (2014): S120–S38; D. S. Dunn, ed. *Positive Psychology: Established and Emerging Issues,* (New York: Routledge, 2018).

69. W.H. Cooper, "Ubiquitous Halo," *Psychological Bulletin* 90 (1981): 218–44; P. Rosenzweig, *The Halo Effect . . . And the Eight Other Business Delusions That Deceive Managers* (New York: Free Press, 2007); J.W. Keeley et al., "Investigating Halo and Ceiling Effects in Student Evaluations of Instruction," *Educational and Psychological Measurement* 73, no. 3 (2013): 440–57.

70. B. Mullen et al., "The False Consensus Effect: A Meta-Analysis of 115 Hypothesis Tests," *Journal of Experimental Social Psychology* 21, no. 3 (1985): 262–83; F.J. Flynn and S.S. Wiltermuth, "Who's with Me? False Consensus, Brokerage, and Ethical Decision Making in Organizations," *Academy of Management Journal* 53, no. 5 (2010): 1074–89; B. Roth and A. Voskort, "Stereotypes and False Consensus: How Financial Professionals Predict Risk Preferences," *Journal of Economic Behavior & Organization* 107, Part B (2014): 553–65.

71. D.D. Steiner and J.S. Rain, "Immediate and Delayed Primacy and Recency Effects in Performance Evaluation," *Journal of Applied Psychology* 74 (1989): 136–42; W. Green, "Impact of the Timing of an Inherited Explanation on Auditors' Analytical Procedures Judgements," *Accounting and Finance* 44 (2004): 369–92; A. Guiral-Contreras, J.A. Gonzalo-Angulo, and W. Rodgers, "Information Content and Recency Effect of the Audit Report in Loan Rating Decisions," *Accounting & Finance* 47, no. 2 (2007): 285–304.

72. E.A. Lind, L. Kray, and L. Thompson, "Primacy Effects in Justice Judgments: Testing Predictions from Fairness Heuristic Theory," *Organizational Behavior and Human Decision Processes* 85 (2001): 189–210; T. Mann and M. Ferguson, "Can We Undo Our First Impressions? The Role of Reinterpretation in Reversing Implicit Evaluations," *Journal of Personality & Social Psychology* 108, no. 6 (2015): 823–49; B.C. Holtz, "From First Impression to Fairness Perception: Investigating the Impact of Initial Trustworthiness Beliefs," *Personnel Psychology* 68, no. 3 (2015): 499–546.

73. D. E. Hogan and M. Mallott, "Changing Racial Prejudice through Diversity Education," *Journal of College Student Development* 46, no. 2 (2005): 115–25; B. Gawronski et al., "When 'Just Say No' Is Not Enough: Affirmation versus Negation Training and the Reduction of Automatic Stereotype Activation," *Journal of Experimental Social Psychology* 44 (2008): 370–77; M. M. Duguid and M. C. Thomas-Hunt, "Condoning Stereotyping? How Awareness of Stereotyping Prevalence Impacts Expression of Stereotypes," *Journal of Applied Psychology* 100, no. 2 (2015): 343–59; F. Dobbin and A. Kalev, "Why Diversity Programs Fail," *Harvard Business Review* 94, no. 7/8 (2016): 52–60; L.M. Leslie, "Diversity Initiative Effectiveness: A Typological Theory of Unintended Consequences," *Academy of Management Review*, October 12, 2018, https://doi.org/10.5465/amr.2017.0087.

74. T.W. Costello and S.S. Zalkind, *Psychology in Administration: A Research Orientation* (Englewood Cliffs, NJ: Prentice Hall, 1963), pp. 45–46; J.M. Kouzes and B.Z. Posner, *The Leadership Challenge,* 4th ed. (San Francisco, CA: Jossey-Bass, 2007), Chap. 3.

75. W. L. Gardner et al., "'Can You See the Real Me?' A Self-Based Model of Authentic Leader and Follower Development," *Leadership Quarterly* 16 (2005): 343–72; C. Peus et al., "Authentic Leadership: An Empirical Test of Its Antecedents, Consequences, and Mediating Mechanisms," *Journal of Business Ethics* 107, no. 3 (2012): 331–48.

76. J.T. Jost et al., "The Existence of Implicit Bias Is Beyond Reasonable Doubt: A Refutation of Ideological and Methodological Objections and Executive Summary of Ten Studies That No Manager Should Ignore," Research in Organizational Behavior 29 (2009): 39–69; A.G. Greenwald et al., "Understanding and Using the Implicit Association Test: III. Meta-Analysis of Predictive Validity," *Journal of Personality and Social Psychology* 97, no. 1 (2009): 17–41; B.A. Nosek et al., "Understanding and Using the Brief Implicit Association Test: Recommended Scoring Procedures," *PLoS ONE* 9, no. 12 (2014): e110938; B. Schiller et al., "Clocking the Social Mind by Identifying Mental Processes in the IAT with Electrical Neuroimaging," *Proceedings of the National Academy of Sciences* 113, no. 10 (2016): 2786–91.

77. "Diversity and Inclusion at CBC/Radio-Canada," accessed November 18, 2019, https://cbc.radio-canada.ca/en/working-with-us/jobs/diversity-inclusion-cbc-rc.

78. J. Luft, *Of Human Interaction* (Palo Alto, CA: National Press, 1969). For a variation of this model, see J. Hall, "Communication Revisited," *California Management Review* 15 (1973): 56–67. For recent discussion of the Johari blind spot, see A.-M.B. Gallrein et al., "You Spy with Your Little Eye:

People Are 'Blind' to Some of the Ways in Which They Are Consensually Seen by Others," *Journal of Research in Personality* 47, no. 5 (2013): 464–71; A.-M.B. Gallrein et al., "I Still Cannot See It—a Replication of Blind Spots in Self-Perception," *Journal of Research in Personality* 60 (2016): 1–7.

79. S. Vazire and M.R. Mehl, "Knowing Me, Knowing You: The Accuracy and Unique Predictive Validity of Self-Ratings and Other-Ratings of Daily Behavior," *Journal of Personality and Social Psychology* 95, no. 5 (2008): 1202–16; D. Leising, A.-M.B. Gallrein, and M. Dufner, "Judging the Behavior of People We Know: Objective Assessment, Confirmation of Preexisting Views, or Both?," *Personality and Social Psychology Bulletin* 40, no. 2 (2014): 153–63. However, there is some evidence that too much self-disclosure has unintended negative consequences for individuals in team settings. see: K.R. Gibson, D. Harari, and J.C. Marr, "When Sharing Hurts: How and Why Self-Disclosing Weakness Undermines the Task-Oriented Relationships of Higher Status Disclosers," *Organizational Behavior and Human Decision Processes* 144 (2018): 25–43.

80. J.D. Vorauer, "Completing the Implicit Association Test Reduces Positive Intergroup Interaction Behavior," *Psychological Science* 23, no. 10 (2012): 1168–75.

81. T.F. Pettigrew and L.R. Tropp, "A Meta-Analytic Test of Intergroup Contact Theory," *Journal of Personality and Social Psychology* 90, no. 5 (2006): 751–83; S.C. Wright, A. Mazziotta, and L.R. Tropp, "Contact and Intergroup Conflict: New Ideas for the Road Ahead," *Journal of Peace Psychology* 23, no. 3 (2017): 317–27, https://doi.org/10.1037/pac0000272; J.F. Dovidio et al., "Reducing Intergroup Bias through Intergroup Contact: Twenty Years of Progress and Future Directions," *Group Processes & Intergroup Relations* 20, no. 5 (2017): 606–20, https://doi.org/10.1177/1368430217712052.

82. The contact hypothesis was first introduced in G.W. Allport, *The Nature of Prejudice* (Reading, MA: Addison-Wesley, 1954), Chap. 16.

83. K. Grimmelt, "People Behind Success of Pulp and Paper Mill," *Peace River Record-Gazette,* 14 September 2010.

84. C.K. Soderberg et al., "The Effects of Psychological Distance on Abstraction: Two Meta-Analyses," *Psychological Bulletin* 141, no. 3 (2015): 525–48, http://dx.doi.org/10.1037/bul0000005.

85. R. Elliott et al., "Empathy," *Psychotherapy* 48, no. 1 (2011): 43–49; J. Zaki, "Empathy: A Motivated Account," *Psychological Bulletin* 140, no. 6 (2014): 1608–47; E. Teding van Berkhout and J. Malouff, "The Efficacy of Empathy Training: A Meta-Analysis of Randomized Controlled Trials," *Journal of Counseling Psychology* 63, no. 1 (2016): 32–41.

86. M. Tarrant, R. Calitri, and D. Weston, "Social Identification Structures the Effects of Perspective Taking," *Psychological Science* 23, no. 9 (2012): 973–78; J.L. Skorinko and S.A. Sinclair, "Perspective Taking Can Increase Stereotyping: The Role of Apparent Stereotype Confirmation," *Journal of Experimental Social Psychology* 49, no. 1 (2013): 10–18.

87. J. Ang, "Q&A: Roselin Lee, Vice President, HR, Shiseido Asia Pacific and Shiseido Travel Retail," *Human Resources,* September 2, 2019; "Shiseido Develops Regional Learning Center to Help Leaders Grow," *SmartBrief,* September 3, 2019, sec. HR People + Strategy.

88. There is no consensus on the meaning of global mindset. The elements identified in this book are common among most of the recent writing on this subject. See, for example: S.J. Black, W.H. Mobley, and E. Weldon, "The Mindset of Global Leaders: Inquisitiveness and Duality," in *Advances in Global Leadership* (JAI, 2006), 181–200; O. Levy et al., "What We Talk About When We Talk About 'Global Mindset': Managerial Cognition in Multinational Corporations," *Journal of International Business Studies* 38, no. 2 (2007): 231–58; S. Beechler and D. Baltzley, "Creating a Global Mindset," *Chief Learning Officer* 7, no. 6 (2008): 40–45; M. Javidan and D. Bowen, "The 'Global Mindset' of Managers: What It Is, Why It Matters, and How to Develop It," *Organizational Dynamics* 42, no. 2 (2013): 145–55.

89. A.K. Gupta and V. Govindarajan, "Cultivating a Global Mindset," *Academy of Management Executive* 16, no. 1 (2002): 116–26.

90. T. Maak, N.M. Pless, and M. Borecká, "Developing Responsible Global Leaders, " *Advances in Global Leadership* 8 (2014): 339–64; P. Caligiuri and C. Thoroughgood, "Developing Responsible Global Leaders through Corporate-Sponsored International Volunteerism Programs," *Organizational Dynamics* 44, no. 2 (2015): 138–45.

CHAPTER 4

1. Z. De Vries, "Quebec City Tracks Their Employees Morale Weekly," *Zac de Vries - Saanich Councillor* (Twitter tweet), May 30, 2019, https://twitter.com/zac4saanich/status/1134191766792540163; N. Murray, "Companies Use Employee Morale Monitoring Tools to Boost Happiness and Performance," *Peninsula News Review (Sidney, B.C.),* June 8, 2019; N. Fearn, "Employee Activism: How Staff Revolts Are Shaking up the IT Recruitment Landscape," *Computer Weekly,* June 27, 2019; "Annual Activity and Corporate Social Responsibility Report: Fiscal Year 2019" (Montreal: CAE Inc., August 7, 2019); "CAE Inc Annual Shareholders Meeting - Final," *Fair Disclosure Wire,* August 14, 2019; M. Hines, "Here's How HR Leaders Are Keeping a Pulse on Remote Teams," *Built In Chicago,* April 7, 2020.

2. Emotions are also cognitive processes. However, we use the narrow definition of *cognition* as a well-used label referring only to reasoning processes. Also, this and other chapters emphasize that emotional and cognitive processes are intertwined. For recent discussion of this in neuroscience, see: L. Pessoa, "Understanding Emotion with Brain Networks," *Current Opinion in Behavioral Sciences,* 19 (2018): 19–25, https://doi.org/10.1016/j.cobeha.2017.09.005.

3. For discussion of emotions in marketing, economics, and sociology, see: W. Kalkhoff, S.R. Thye, and J. Pollock, "Developments in Neurosociology," *Sociology Compass* 10, no. 3 (2016): 242–58, https://doi.org/10.1111/soc4.12355; H. Lin and O. Vartanian, "A Neuroeconomic Framework for Creative Cognition," *Perspectives on Psychological Science* 13, no. 6 (2018): 655–77, https://doi.org/10.1177/1745691618794945; W.M. Lim, "Demystifying Neuromarketing," *Journal of Business Research* 91 (2018): 205–20, https://doi.org/10.1016/j.jbusres.2018.05.036; A. Konovalov and I. Krajbich, "Over a Decade of Neuroeconomics: What Have We Learned?," *Organizational Research Methods* 22, no. 1 (2019): 148–73, https://doi.org/10.1177/1094428116644502. One recent review suggests that organizational behaviour will benefit from the neuroscience of emotion, but there are several methodological issues to address. See: A.I. Jack et al., "Pitfalls in Organizational Neuroscience: A Critical Review and Suggestions for Future Research," *Organizational Research Methods* 22, no. 1 (2019): 421–58, https://doi.org/10.1177/1094428117708857.

4. Although definitions of *emotion* vary, the definition stated here seems to be the most widely accepted. See, for example, N.H. Frijda, "Varieties of Affect: Emotions and Episodes, Moods, and Sentiments," in *The Nature of Emotion: Fundamental Questions,* ed. P. Ekman and R.J. Davidson (New York: Oxford University Press, 1994), 59–67; G. Van Kleef, H. van den Berg, and M. Heerdink, "The Persuasive Power of Emotions: Effects of Emotional Expressions on Attitude Formation and Change," *Journal of Applied Psychology* 100, no. 4 (2015): 1124–42; A. Scarantino, "The Philosophy of Emotions and Its Impact on Affective Science," in *Handbook of Emotions,* ed. L.F. Barrett, M. Lewis, and J.M. Haviland-Jones, 4th ed. (New York: Guilford Press, 2016), 3–47; R. Smith and R.D. Lane, "Unconscious Emotion: A Cognitive Neuroscientific Perspective," *Neuroscience & Biobehavioral Reviews* 69 (2016): 216–38, https://doi.org/10.1016/j.neubiorev.2016.08.013; M. Résibois et al., "The Relation between Rumination and Temporal Features of Emotion Intensity," *Cognition and Emotion* 32, no. 2 (2018): 259–74, https://doi.org/10.1080/02699931.2017.1298993; L.F. Barrett and A.B. Satpute, "Historical Pitfalls and New Directions in the Neuroscience of Emotion," *Neuroscience Letters,* Functional Neuroimaging of the Emotional Brain, 693 (2019): 9–18, https://doi.org/10.1016/j.neulet.2017.07.045.

5. R. Reisenzein, M. Studtmann, and G. Horstmann, "Coherence between Emotion and Facial Expression: Evidence from Laboratory Experiments," *Emotion Review* 5, no. 1 (2013): 16–23; M.D. Lieberman, "Boo! The Consciousness Problem in Emotion," *Cognition and Emotion* 33, no. 1 (2019): 24–30, https://doi.org/10.1080/02699931.2018.1515726.

6. R.B. Zajonc, "Emotions," in *Handbook of Social Psychology,* ed. D.T. Gilbert, S.T. Fiske, and L. Gardner (New York: Oxford University press, 1998), 591–634; P. Winkielman, "Bob Zajonc and the Unconscious Emotion," *Emotion Review* 2, no. 4 (2010): 353–62.

7. A. R. Damasio, *The Feeling of What Happens: Body and Emotion in the Making of Consciousness* (New York: Harcourt Brace, 1999), 286; B.Q. Ford and J.J. Gross, "Emotion Regulation: Why Beliefs Matter," *Canadian Psychology/Psychologie Canadienne* 59, no. 1 (2018): 1–14, https://doi.org/10.1037/cap0000142; K.C. Berridge, "Evolving Concepts of Emotion and Motivation," *Frontiers in Psychology* 9 (2018), https://doi.org/10.3389/fpsyg.2018.01647.

8. R.J. Larson, E. Diener, and R.E. Lucas, "Emotion: Models, Measures, and Differences," in *Emotions in the Workplace* ed. R.G. Lord, R.J. Klimoski,

and R. Kanfer (San Francisco, CA: Jossey-Bass, 2002), 64–113; L.F. Barrett et al., "The Experience of Emotion," *Annual Review of Psychology* 58, no. 1 (2007): 373–403; M. Yik, J.A. Russell, and J.H. Steiger, "A 12-Point Circumplex Structure of Core Affect," *Emotion* 11, no. 4 (2011): 705–31.

9. R.F. Baumeister, E. Bratslavsky, and C. Finkenauer, "Bad Is Stronger Than Good," *Review of General Psychology* 5, no. 4 (2001): 323–70; A. Vaish, T. Grossmann, and A. Woodward, "Not All Emotions Are Created Equal: The Negativity Bias in Social–Emotional Development," *Psychological Bulletin* 134, no. 3 (2008): 383–403; R.H. Fazio et al., "Positive Versus Negative Valence: Asymmetries in Attitude Formation and Generalization as Fundamental Individual Differences," in *Advances in Experimental Social Psychology,* ed. J.M. Olson and M.P. Zanna (Academic Press, 2015), 97–146; K. Bebbington et al., "The Sky Is Falling: Evidence of a Negativity Bias in the Social Transmission of Information, " *Evolution and Human Behavior* 38, no. 1 (2017): 92–101.

10. A.P. Brief, *Attitudes in and around Organizations* (Thousand Oaks, CA: Sage, 1998); A.H. Eagly and S. Chaiken, "The Advantages of an Inclusive Definition of Attitude," *Social Cognition* 25, no. 5 (2007): 582–602; G. Bohner and N. Dickel, "Attitudes and Attitude Change," *Annual Review of Psychology* 62, no. 1 (2011): 391–417. The definition of attitudes is still being debated. First, it is unclear whether an attitude includes emotions (affect), or whether emotions influence an attitude. We take the latter view. Although emotions influence and are closely connected to attitudes, an attitude is best defined as an evaluation of an attitude object. That evaluation is not always conscious, however. Second, a few writers argue that attitudes are formed each time they think about the attitude object, which is contrary to the traditional view that attitudes are fairly stable predispositions toward the attitude object. Third, although less of an issue now, some attitude models refer only to the "feelings" component, whereas we view attitude as a three-component construct (beliefs, feelings, behavioural intentions). For various definitions of attitude and discussion of these variations, see I. Ajzen, "Nature and Operation of Attitudes," *Annual Review of Psychology* 52 (2001): 27–58; D. Albarracín et al., "Attitudes: Introduction and Scope," in *The Handbook of Attitudes,* ed. D. Albarracín, B.T. Johnson, and M.P. Zanna (Mahwah, NJ: Lawrence Erlbaum Associates, 2005), 3–20; W.A. Cunningham and P.D. Zelazo, "Attitudes and Evaluations: A Social Cognitive Neuroscience Perspective," *TRENDS in Cognitive Sciences* 11, no. 3 (2007): 97–104; B. Gawronski, "Editorial: Attitudes Can Be Measured! But What Is an Attitude?," *Social Cognition* 25, no. 5 (2007): 573–81; R.S. Dalal, "Job Attitudes: Cognition and Affect," in *Handbook of Psychology, Second Edition* (John Wiley & Sons, Inc., 2012).

11. Neuroscience has a slightly more complicated distinction in that conscious awareness is "feeling a feeling" whereas "feeling" is a nonconscious sensing of the body state created by emotion, which itself is a nonconscious neural reaction to a stimulus. However, this distinction is not significant for scholars focused on human behaviour rather than brain activity, and the labels collide with popular understanding of "feeling." See: A.R. Damasio,

The Feeling of What Happens: Body and Emotion in the Making of Consciousness (New York, NY: Harcourt Brace and Company, 1999); F. Hansen, "Distinguishing between Feelings and Emotions in Understanding Communication Effects," *Journal of Business Research* 58, no. 10 (2005): 1426–36; T. Bosse, C.M. Jonker, and J. Treur, "Formalisation of Damasio's Theory of Emotion, Feeling and Core Consciousness," *Consciousness and Cognition* 17, no. 1 (2008): 94–113.

12. W.A. Cunningham and P.D. Zelazo, "Attitudes and Evaluations: A Social Cognitive Neuroscience Perspective," *TRENDS in Cognitive Sciences* 11, no. 3 (2007): 97–104; M.D. Lieberman, "Social Cognitive Neuroscience: A Review of Core Processes," *Annual Review of Psychology* 58, no. 1 (2007): 259–89; M. Fenton-O'Creevy et al., "Thinking, Feeling and Deciding: The Influence of Emotions on the Decision Making and Performance of Traders," *Journal of Organizational Behavior* 32 (2011): 1044–61. The dual emotion–cognition processes are likely the same as the implicit–explicit attitude processes reported by several scholars, as well as tacit knowledge structures. See W.J. Becker and R. Cropanzano, "Organizational Neuroscience: The Promise and Prospects of an Emerging Discipline," *Journal of Organizational Behavior* 31, no. 7 (2010): 1055–59; D. Kahneman, *Thinking Fast and Slow* (New York: Farrar, Straus and Giroux, 2011).

13. D. Albarracín, M.S. Chan, and D. Jiang, "Attitudes and Attitude Change: Social and Personality Considerations About Specific and General Patterns of Behavior," in *The Oxford Handbook of Personality and Social Psychology,* ed. K. Deaux and M. Snyder, 2nd ed. (New York: Oxford University Press, 2018), 439–64.

14. S. Orbell, "Intention-Behavior Relations: A Self-Regulation Perspective," in *Contemporary Perspectives on the Psychology of Attitudes,* ed. G. Haddock and G.R. Maio (East Sussex, UK: Psychology Press, 2004), 145–68.

15. H.M. Weiss and R. Cropanzano, "Affective Events Theory: A Theoretical Discussion of the Structure, Causes and Consequences of Affective Experiences at Work," *Research in Organizational Behavior* 18 (1996): 1–74; A. Bechara et al., "Deciding Advantageously before Knowing the Advantageous Strategy," *Science* 275, no. 5304 (1997): 1293–95; B. Russell and J. Eisenberg, "The Role of Cognition and Attitude in Driving Behavior: Elaborating on Affective Events Theory," in *Experiencing and Managing Emotions in the Workplace,* ed. N.M. Ashkanasy, C.E.J. Hartel, and W.J. Zerbe (Bingley, UK: Emerald Group, 2012), 203–24.

16. J.A. Bargh and M.J. Ferguson, "Beyond Behaviorism: On the Automaticity of Higher Mental Processes," *Psychological Bulletin* 126, no. 6 (2000): 925–45; P. Winkielman and K.C. Berridge, "Unconscious Emotion," *Current Directions in Psychological Science* 13, no. 3 (2004): 120–23; A. Moors, "Automaticity: Componential, Causal, and Mechanistic Explanations," *Annual Review of Psychology* 67, no. 1 (2016): 263–87.

17. A.R. Damasio, *Descartes' Error: Emotion, Reason, and the Human Brain* (New York: Putnam Sons, 1994); P. Ekman, "Basic Emotions," in *Handbook of Cognition and Emotion,* ed. T. Dalgleish and M. Power (San Francisco: Jossey-Bass, 1999), 45–60; A. R. Damasio, *The Feeling of What*

Happens: Body and Emotion in the Making of Consciousness (New York: Harcourt Brace and Company, 1999); J.E. LeDoux, "Emotion Circuits in the Brain," *Annual Review of Neuroscience* 23 (2000): 155–84; R. Smith and R.D. Lane, "The Neural Basis of One's Own Conscious and Unconscious Emotional States," *Neuroscience & Biobehavioral Reviews* 57 (2015): 1–29.

18. M.T. Pham, The Logic of Feeling," *Journal of Consumer Psychology* 14, no. 4 (2004): 360–69; N. Schwarz, "Feelings-as-Information Theory," in *Handbook of Theories of Social Psychology,* ed. P. Van Lange, A. Kruglanski, and E.T. Higgins (London: Sage, 2012), 289–308.

19. We have described likely the most common form of emotion–attitude conflict and ambivalence, but other forms exist. See: A.I. Snyder and Z.L. Tormala, "Valence Asymmetries in Attitude Ambivalence," *Journal of Personality and Social Psychology* 112, no. 4 (2017): 555–76, https://doi.org/10.1037/pspa0000075; I.K. Schneider and N. Schwarz, "Mixed Feelings: The Case of Ambivalence," *Current Opinion in Behavioral Sciences, Mixed Emotions,* 15 (2017): 39–45, https://doi.org/10.1016/j.cobeha.2017.05.012; N.B. Rothman and S. Melwani, "Feeling Mixed, Ambivalent, and in Flux: The Social Functions of Emotional Complexity for Leaders," *Academy of Management Review* 42, no. 2 (2017): 259–82, https://doi.org/10.5465/amr.2014.0355.

20. P.C. Nutt, *Why Decisions Fail* (San Francisco, CA: Berrett-Koehler, 2002); S. Finkelstein, *Why Smart Executives Fail* (New York: Viking, 2003); P.C. Nutt, "Search During Decision Making," *European Journal of Operational Research* 160 (2005): 851–76.

21. C.A. Petelczyc et al., "Play at Work: An Integrative Review and Agenda for Future Research," *Journal of Management* 44, no. 1 (2018): 161–90, https://doi.org/10.1177/0149206317731519; S.Y. Kim and D. Lee, "Work–Life Program Participation and Employee Work Attitudes: A Quasi-Experimental Analysis Using Matching Methods," *Review of Public Personnel Administration,* 2019, 0734371X18823250, https://doi.org/10.1177/0734371X18823250; J.W. Michel, M.J. Tews, and D.G. Allen, "Fun in the Workplace: A Review and Expanded Theoretical Perspective," *Human Resource Management Review* 29, no. 1 (2019): 98–110, https://doi.org/10.1016/j.hrmr.2018.03.001.

22. Á. Cain, "8 Incredible Perks Google Offers Its Employees," *Inc.,* November 16, 2017.; B. Nordlo, "Why Zoom Video Communications Built a Team Dedicated to Happiness," Built In Colorado (blog), July 27, 2018, https://www.builtincolorado.com/2018/07/27/spotlight-working-at-zoom-video-communications-culture; Z. Thomas, "Best Big Company to Work For 2019: Fun and Profits at Admiral," *Sunday Times (UK),* February 24, 2019. Admiral Group's awards as best employer are summarized at: https://admiralgroup.co.uk/our-culture/our-awards. The Zoom quotation was retrieved from an employee comment submitted to Glassdoor on June 24, 2019.

23. J. Mesmer-Magnus, D.J. Glew, and C. Viswesvaran, "A Meta-Analysis of Positive Humor in the Workplace," *Journal of Managerial Psychology* 27, no. 2 (2012): 155–90; C. Robert

and M.V.S.P. da, "Conversational Humor and Job Satisfaction at Work: Exploring the Role of Humor Production, Appreciation, and Positive Affect," *HUMOR* 30, no. 4 (2017): 417–438, https://doi.org/10.1515/humor-2017-0034; C. Robert, ed., *The Psychology of Humor at Work: A Psychological Perspective* (London: Routledge, 2017).

24. H.M. Weiss and R. Cropanzano, "Affective Events Theory: A Theoretical Discussion of the Structure, Causes and Consequences of Affective Experiences at Work," *Research in Organizational Behavior* 18 (1996): 1–74.

25. L. Festinger, *A Theory of Cognitive Dissonance* (Evanston, IL: Row, Peterson, 1957); J. Cooper, *Cognitive Dissonance: Fifty Years of a Classic Theory* (London: Sage, 2007); J. Hagège et al., "Suggestion of Self-(in) Coherence Modulates Cognitive Dissonance," *PLOS ONE* 13, no. 8 (August 30, 2018): e0202204, https://doi.org/10.1371/journal.pone.0202204.

26. G.R. Salancik, "Commitment and the Control of Organizational Behavior and Belief," in *New Directions in Organizational Behavior,* ed. B.M. Staw and G.R. Salancik (Chicago: St. Clair, 1977), 1–54; J.M. Jarcho, E.T. Berkman, and M.D. Lieberman, "The Neural Basis of Rationalization: Cognitive Dissonance Reduction during Decision-Making," *Social Cognitive and Affective Neuroscience* 6, no. 4 (2011): 460–67; A. McGrath, "Dealing with Dissonance: A Review of Cognitive Dissonance Reduction," *Social and Personality Psychology Compass* 11, no. 12 (2017): e12362, https://doi.org/10.1111/spc3.12362.

27. T.A. Judge, E.A. Locke, and C.C. Durham, "The Dispositional Causes of Job Satisfaction: A Core Evaluations Approach," *Research in Organizational Behavior* 19 (1997): 151–88; T.W.H. Ng and K.L. Sorensen, "Dispositional Affectivity and Work-Related Outcomes: A Meta-Analysis," *Journal of Applied Social Psychology* 39, no. 6 (2009): 1255–87.

28. J. Schaubroeck, D.C. Ganster, and B. Kemmerer, "Does Trait Affect Promote Job Attitude Stability?," *Journal of Organizational Behavior* 17 (1996): 191–96; C. Dormann and D. Zapf, "Job Satisfaction: A Meta-Analysis of Stabilities," *Journal of Organizational Behavior* 22 (2001): 483–504; A.C. Keller and N.K. Semmer, "Changes in Situational and Dispositional Factors as Predictors of Job Satisfaction," *Journal of Vocational Behavior* 83, no. 1 (2013): 88–98.

29. A.S. Wharton, "The Sociology of Emotional Labor," *Annual Review of Sociology* 35 (2009): 147–65; H. Wang, N.C. Hall, and J.L. Taxer, "Antecedents and Consequences of Teachers' Emotional Labor: A Systematic Review and Meta-Analytic Investigation," *Educational Psychology Review,* 2019; A.A. Grandey and G.M. Sayre, "Emotional Labor: Regulating Emotions for a Wage," *Current Directions in Psychological Science* 28 (2019): 131–37.

30. J. A. Morris and D. C. Feldman, "The Dimensions, Antecedents, and Consequences of Emotional Labor," *Academy of Management Review* 21 (1996): 986–1010; J. Li, B.F. Canziani, and C. Barbieri, "Emotional Labor in Hospitality: Positive Affective Displays in Service Encounters," *Tourism and Hospitality Research* 18, no. 2 (2018): 242–53, https://doi.org/10.1177/1467358416637253.

31. A.A. Grandey and R.C. Melloy, "The State of the Heart: Emotional Labor as Emotion Regulation Reviewed and Revised," *Journal of Occupational Health Psychology* 22 (2017): 407–22; H. Wang, N.C. Hall, and J.L. Taxer, "Antecedents and Consequences of Teachers' Emotional Labor: A Systematic Review and Meta-Analytic Investigation," *Educational Psychology Review* 31 (2019): 663–98.

32. D. Matsumoto, S.H. Yoo, and J. Fontaine, "Mapping Expressive Differences around the World," *Journal of Cross-Cultural Psychology* 39, no. 1 (2008): 55–74; B.Q. Ford and I.B. Mauss, "Culture and Emotion Regulation," *Current Opinion in Psychology* 3 (2015): 1–5; N. Gullekson and A. Dumaisnil, "Expanding Horizons on Expatriate Adjustment: A Look at the Role of Emotional Display and Status," *Human Resource Management Review* 26, no. 3 (2016): 260–69, https://doi.org/10.1016/j.hrmr.2016.03.004.

33. F. Trompenaars and C. Hampden-Turner, *Riding the Waves of Culture,* 2nd ed. (New York: McGraw Hill, 1998), Chap. 6. This major survey is two decades old, but recent studies report similar emotional display rules in the cultures reported by Trompenaars and Hampden-Turner. For example, see: Ю. Менджерицкая, М. Ханзен, и Х. Хорц, "Правила выражения эмоций преподавателями российских и немецких университетов (The Rules Of Emotional Display In Lecturers Of Russian And German Universities)," *Российский психологический журнал* 12, no. 4 (2015): 54–77, https://doi.org/10.21702/rpj.2015.4.5; H.C. Hwang et al., "Self-Reported Expression and Experience of Triumph across Four Countries," *Motivation and Emotion* 40, no. 5 (2016): 731–39, https://doi.org/10.1007/s11031-016-9567-5.

34. K. Gander, "Workers in China Wear Masks for a Day so They Don't Have to Deal with Social Stress," *The Independent,* July 16, 2015. Recent studies on cross-cultural emotion display rules and well-being are reported in: S. Huwaë and J. Schaafsma, "Cross-Cultural Differences in Emotion Suppression in Everyday Interactions," *International Journal of Psychology* 53, no. 3 (2018): 176–83; Y. Nam, Y.-H. Kim, and K.K.-P. Tam, "Effects of Emotion Suppression on Life Satisfaction in Americans and Chinese," *Journal of Cross-Cultural Psychology* 49, no. 1 (2018): 149–60.

35. D.P. Bhave and T.M. Glomb, "The Role of Occupational Emotional Labor Requirements on the Surface Acting–Job Satisfaction Relationship," *Journal of Management* 42, no. 3 (2016): 722–41, https://doi.org/10.1177/0149206313498900; T. Huyghebaert et al., "Investigating the Longitudinal Effects of Surface Acting on Managers' Functioning through Psychological Needs," *Journal of Occupational Health Psychology* 23, no. 2 (April 2018): 207–22, https://doi.org/10.1037/ocp0000080.

36. A.A. Grandey and R.C. Melloy, "The State of the Heart: Emotional Labor as Emotion Regulation Reviewed and Revised," *Journal of Occupational Health Psychology* 22 (2017): 407–22. However, recent evidence suggests that deep acting can also be stressful because it requires cognitive effort. Also, faking negative emotions may be less stressful than faking positive emotions. Another recent study concluded that both surface and deep acting are effortful activities, so both produce emotional exhaustion. See: F. Cheung, V.M.C. Lun, and M.W.-L. Cheung, "Emotional Labor and Occupational Well-Being: A Latent Profile Transition Analysis Approach," *Frontiers in Psychology* 9 (2018); A.C. Lennard, B.A. Scott, and R.E. Johnson, "Turning Frowns (and Smiles) Upside down: A Multilevel Examination of Surface Acting Positive and Negative Emotions on Well-Being.," *Journal of Applied Psychology* 104 (2019): 1164–80.

37. S. Côté, I. Hideg, and G.A. van Kleef, "The Consequences of Faking Anger in Negotiations," *Journal of Experimental Social Psychology* 49, no. 3 (2013): 453–63; Y. Zhan, M. Wang, and J. Shi, "Interpersonal Process of Emotional Labor: The Role of Negative and Positive Customer Treatment," *Personnel Psychology* 69, no. 3 (2016): 525–57; K. Picard, M. Cossette, and D. Morin, "Service with a Smile: A Source of Emotional Exhaustion or Performance Incentive in Call-Centre Employees," *Canadian Journal of Administrative Sciences* 35, no. 2 (2018): 214–27, https://doi.org/10.1002/cjas.1413.

38. J.J. Gross, "Emotion Regulation: Current Status and Future Prospects," *Psychological Inquiry* 26 (2015): 1–26; J.M. Diefendorff et al., "Emotion Regulation in the Context of Customer Mistreatment and Felt Affect: An Event-Based Profile Approach.," *Journal of Applied Psychology* 104 (2019): 965–83; J. Yih et al., "Better Together: A Unified Perspective on Appraisal and Emotion Regulation," *Cognition and Emotion* 33 (2019): 41–47.

39. Y. Kivity and J.D. Huppert, "Emotion Regulation in Social Anxiety: A Systematic Investigation and Meta-Analysis Using Self-Report, Subjective, and Event-Related Potentials Measures," *Cognition and Emotion* 33 (2019): 213–30.

40. R. Brockman et al., "Emotion Regulation Strategies in Daily Life: Mindfulness, Cognitive Reappraisal and Emotion Suppression," *Cognitive Behaviour Therapy* 46, no. 2 (2017): 91–113, https://doi.org/10.1080/16506073.2016.1218926.

41. J.D. Kammeyer-Mueller et al., "A Meta-Analytic Structural Model of Dispositonal Affectivity and Emotional Labor," *Personnel Psychology* 66, no. 1 (2013): 47–90; R.H. Humphrey, B.E. Ashforth, and J.M. Diefendorff, "The Bright Side of Emotional Labor," *Journal of Organizational Behavior* 36, no. 6 (2015): 749–69. Deep acting is considered an adaptation of method acting used by professional actors.

42. A.D.H. Monroe and A. English, "Fostering Emotional Intelligence in Medical Training: The SELECT Program," *Virtual Mentor* 15, no. 6 (2013): 509–13; "SELECT Medical Students Will Learn Match Day Results in Downtown Allentown," *LVHN News,* March 19, 2018; F.J. Coleman, "MCOM SELECT Charter Class Member Makes History at LVHN," *USF Health News,* October 17, 2018.

43. This model is an ability-based adaptation of the original mixed model by Goleman et al. Most recent models and measures of emotional intelligence have also adopted a similar four-quadrant model. These studies have adopted a "trait" approach to EI measurement, which might be more accurately described as a self-perceived EI ability approach. See D. Goleman, R. Boyatzis, and A. McKee, *Primal Leadership* (Boston: Harvard Business School Press, 2002), Chap. 3; R.P. Tett and K.E. Fox, "Confirmatory Factor Structure of Trait Emotional Intelligence in Student and Worker Samples," *Personality and Individual Differences* 41 (2006): 1155–68; D.L. Joseph and D.A. Newman,

"Emotional Intelligence: An Integrative Meta-Analysis and Cascading Model," *Journal of Applied Psychology* 95, no. 1 (2010): 54–78; X. Wei, Y. Liu, and N. Allen, "Measuring Team Emotional Intelligence: A Multimethod Comparison," *Group Dynamics: Theory, Research, & Practice* 20, no. 1 (2016): 34–50; K.A. Pekaar et al., "Self- and Other-Focused Emotional Intelligence: Development and Validation of the Rotterdam Emotional Intelligence Scale (REIS)," *Personality and Individual Differences* 120 (2018): 222–33, https://doi.org/10.1016/j.paid.2017.08.045.

44. H.A. Elfenbein and N. Ambady, "Predicting Workplace Outcomes from the Ability to Eavesdrop on Feelings," *Journal of Applied Psychology* 87, no. 5 (2002): 963–71; T. Quarto et al., "Association between Ability Emotional Intelligence and Left Insula during Social Judgment of Facial Emotions," *PLoS ONE* 11, no. 2 (2016): e0148621.

45. For neurological evidence that people with higher EI have higher sensitivity to others' emotions, see W.D.S. Killgore et al., "Emotional Intelligence Correlates with Functional Responses to Dynamic Changes in Facial Trustworthiness," *Social Neuroscience* 8, no. 4 (2013): 334–46.

46. The hierarchical nature of the four EI dimensions is discussed by Goleman, but it is more explicit in the Salovey and Mayer model. See D.R. Caruso and P. Salovey, *The Emotionally Intelligent Manager* (San Francisco: Jossey-Bass, 2004). Aspects of this hierarchy are also incorporated in recent studies. For example, see: K.A. Pekaar et al., "Managing Own and Others' Emotions: A Weekly Diary Study on the Enactment of Emotional Intelligence," *Journal of Vocational Behavior* 109 (2018): 137–51, https://doi.org/10.1016/j.jvb.2018.10.004.

47. S. Côté, "Emotional Intelligence in Organizations," *Annual Review of Organizational Psychology and Organizational Behavior* 1 (2014): 459–88; M. Parke, M.-G. Seo, and E. Sherf, "Regulating and Facilitating: The Role of Emotional Intelligence in Maintaining and Using Positive Affect for Creativity," *Journal of Applied Psychology* 100 (2015): 917–34; D. Delpechitre and L. Beeler, "Faking It: Salesperson Emotional Intelligence's Influence on Emotional Labor Strategies and Customer Outcomes," *Journal of Business & Industrial Marketing* 33 (2017): 53–71; C. Miao, R.H. Humphrey, and S. Qian, "Emotional Intelligence and Authentic Leadership: A Meta-Analysis," *Leadership & Organization Development Journal* 39 (2018): 679–90.

48. D. Joseph et al., "Why Does Self-Reported Emotional Intelligence Predict Job Performance? A Meta-Analytic Investigation of Mixed EI," *Journal of Applied Psychology* 100, no. 2 (2015): 298–342; P. Checa and P. Fernández-Berrocal, "Cognitive Control and Emotional Intelligence: Effect of the Emotional Content of the Task. Brief Reports," *Frontiers in Psychology* 10 (2019), https://doi.org/10.3389/fpsyg.2019.00195.

49. "Emotional Intelligence Undervalued by One in Four Firms," News Release (London: Robert Half, August 16, 2018); "Survey Shows Lack of Emphasis Put on EQ during Hiring Process for One in Five Australian Companies," News Release (Sydney: Robert Half, March 12, 2019).

50. J. Shaw, S. Porter, and L. ten Brinke, "Catching Liars: Training Mental Health and Legal Professionals to Detect High-Stakes Lies," *Journal of Forensic Psychiatry & Psychology* 24, no. 2 (2013): 145–59; L. Winkley, "Teaching Cops Empathy to Deter Use of Force," *San Diego Union-Tribune,* February 12, 2016; S. Hodzic et al., "How Efficient Are Emotional Intelligence Trainings: A Meta-Analysis," *Emotion Review* 10, no. 2 (2018): 138–48, https://doi.org/10.1177/1754073917708613; "Fidelity Canada Hiring Fall 2019 - Student Opportunities in Toronto, CA," LinkedIn, accessed October 17, 2019, https://ca.linkedin.com/jobs/view/fall-2019-student-opportunities-at-fidelity-canada-1326984058.

51. D.A. Harrison, D.A. Newman, and P.L. Roth, "How Important Are Job Attitudes? Meta-Analytic Comparisons of Integrative Behavioral Outcomes and Time Sequences," *Academy of Management Journal* 49, no. 2 (2006): 305–25. One study has concluded that job satisfaction and organizational commitment are so highly correlated that they represent the same construct. See: H. Le et al., "The Problem of Empirical Redundancy of Constructs in Organizational Research: An Empirical Investigation," *Organizational Behavior and Human Decision Processes* 112, no. 2 (2010): 112–25. They are also considered the two central work-related variables in the broader concept of happiness at work. See: C.D. Fisher, "Happiness at Work," *International Journal of Management Reviews* 12, no. 4 (2010): 384–412.

52. E.A. Locke, "The Nature and Causes of Job Satisfaction," in *Handbook of Industrial and Organizational Psychology,* ed. M. Dunnette (Chicago, IL: Rand McNally, 1976), 1297–350; H.M. Weiss, "Deconstructing Job Satisfaction: Separating Evaluations, Beliefs and Affective Experiences," *Human Resource Management Review,* no. 12 (2002): 173–94. Some definitions still include emotion as an element of job satisfaction, whereas the definition presented in this book views emotion as a cause of job satisfaction. Also, this definition views job satisfaction as a "collection of attitudes," not several "facets" of job satisfaction.

53. Ipsos-Reid, "Ipsos-Reid Global Poll Finds Major Differences in Employee Satisfaction around the World," in *Ipsos-Reid News Release* (Toronto, ON: 2001); International Survey Research, *Employee Satisfaction in the World's 10 Largest Economies: Globalization or Diversity?*, International Survey Research (Chicago, IL: 2002); Watson Wyatt Worldwide, "Malaysian Workers More Satisfied with Their Jobs Than Their Companies' Leadership and Supervision Practices," (Kuala Lumpur: Watson Wyatt Worldwide, 2004); Kelly Global Workforce Index, *American Workers Are Happy with Their Jobs and Their Bosses,* Kelly Services (Troy, MI: November 2006).

54. "2018 Public Service Employee Survey: Results for the Public Service" (Ottawa: Government of Canada, Treasury Board of Canada Secretariat, 2019).

55. The problems with measuring attitudes and values across cultures is discussed in: L. Saari and T.A. Judge, "Employee Attitudes and Job Satisfaction " *Human Resource Management* 43, no. 4 (2004): 395–407; A.K. Uskul et al., "How Successful You Have Been in Life Depends on the Response Scale Used: The Role of Cultural Mindsets in Pragmatic Inferences Drawn from Question Format," *Social Cognition* 31, no. 2 (2013): 222–36.

56. For a review of the various job satisfaction outcome theories, see R.S. Dalal, "Job Attitudes: Cognition and Affect," in *Handbook of Psychology, Second Edition,* ed. I.B. Weiner (New York: John Wiley & Sons, 2013), 341–66.

57. D. Farrell, "Exit, Voice, Loyalty, and Neglect as Responses to Job Dissatisfaction: A Multidimensional Scaling Study," *Academy of Management Journal* 26, no. 4 (1983): 596–607; M.J. Withey and W.H. Cooper, "Predicting Exit, Voice, Loyalty, and Neglect," *Administrative Science Quarterly,* no. 34 (1989): 521–39; A.B. Whitford and S.-Y. Lee, "Exit, Voice, and Loyalty with Multiple Exit Options: Evidence from the US Federal Workforce," *Journal of Public Administration Research and Theory* 25, no. 2 (2015): 373–98. For a critique and explanation of historical errors in the EVLN model, see S.L. McShane, "Reconstructing the Meaning and Dimensionality of Voice in the Exit-Voice-Loyalty-Neglect Model," paper presented at the Voice and Loyalty Symposium, Annual Conference of the Administrative Sciences Association of Canada, Organizational Behaviour Division, Halifax, 2008.

58. K. Morrell, J. Loan-Clarke, and A. Wilkinson, "The Role of Shocks in Employee Turnover," *British Journal of Management* 15 (2004): 335–49; M. Zhang, D.D. Fried, and R.W. Griffeth, "A Review of Job Embeddedness: Conceptual, Measurement Issues, and Directions for Future Research," *Human Resource Management Review* 22 (2012): 220–31; P.W. Hom et al., "One Hundred Years of Employee Turnover Theory and Research," *Journal of Applied Psychology* 102 (2017): 530–45; A.L. Rubenstein et al., "Surveying the Forest: A Meta-Analysis, Moderator Investigation, and Future-Oriented Discussion of the Antecedents of Voluntary Employee Turnover," *Personnel Psychology* 71 (2018): 23–65.

59. E.W. Morrison, "Employee Voice and Silence," *Annual Review of Organizational Psychology and Organizational Behavior* 1, no. 1 (2014): 173–97; M.R. Bashshur and B. Oc, "When Voice Matters: A Multilevel Review of the Impact of Voice in Organizations," *Journal of Management* 41, no. 5 (2015): 1530–54; P.K. Mowbray, A. Wilkinson, and H.H.M. Tse, "An Integrative Review of Employee Voice: Identifying a Common Conceptualization and Research Agenda," *International Journal of Management Reviews* 17, no. 3 (2015): 382–400.

60. A.O. Hirschman, *Exit, Voice, and Loyalty: Responses to Decline in Firms, Organizations, and States* (Cambridge, MA: Harvard University Press, 1970); P. John, "Finding Exits and Voices: Albert Hirschman's Contribution to the Study of Public Services," *International Public Management Journal* 20, no. 3 (2017): 512–29, https://doi.org/10.1080/10967494.2016.1141814.

61. J.D. Hibbard, N. Kumar, and L.W. Stern, "Examining the Impact of Destructive Acts in Marketing Channel Relationships," *Journal of Marketing Research* 38 (2001): 45–61; J. Zhou and J.M. George, "When Job Dissatisfaction Leads to Creativity: Encouraging the Expression of Voice," *Academy of Management Journal* 44 (2001): 682–96.

62. M.J. Withey and I.R. Gellatly, "Situational and Dispositional Determinants of Exit, Voice, Loyalty and Neglect," *Proceedings of the Administrative*

Sciences Association of Canada, Organizational Behaviour Division, 1998; R.D. Zimmerman et al., "Who Withdraws? Psychological Individual Differences and Employee Withdrawal Behaviors," *Journal of Applied Psychology* 101 (2016): 498–519; É. Lapointe and C. Vandenberghe, "Examination of the Relationships between Servant Leadership, Organizational Commitment, and Voice and Antisocial Behaviors," *Journal of Business Ethics* 148, (2018): 99–115; M. Zare and C. Flinchbaugh, "Voice, Creativity, and Big Five Personality Traits: A Meta-Analysis," *Human Performance* 32 (2019): 30–51.

63. VV. Venkataramani and S. Tangirala, "When and Why Do Central Employees Speak Up? An Examination of Mediating and Moderating Variables," *Journal of Applied Psychology* 95 (2010): 582–91; M. Weiss et al., "We Can Do It! Inclusive Leader Language Promotes Voice Behavior in Multi-Professional Teams," *The Leadership Quarterly* 29 (2018): 389–402; I. Hussain et al., "The Voice Bystander Effect: How Information Redundancy Inhibits Employee Voice," *Academy of Management Journal* 62 (2019): 828–49.

64. D. P. Schwab and L. L. Cummings, "Theories of Performance and Satisfaction: A Review," *Industrial Relations* 9 (1970), pp. 408–30.

65. D.J. Schleicher, J.D. Watt, and G.J. Greguras, "Reexamining the Job Satisfaction-Performance Relationship: The Complexity of Attitudes," *Journal of Applied Psychology* 89 (2004): 165–77; D. A. Harrison, D. A. Newman, and P. L. Roth, "How Important Are Job Attitudes? Meta-Analytic Comparisons of Integrative Behavioral Outcomes and Time Sequences," *Academy of Management Journal* 49 (2006): 305–25; N.A. Bowling et al., "Situational Strength as a Moderator of the Relationship Between Job Satisfaction and Job Performance: A Meta-Analytic Examination," *Journal of Business and Psychology* 30 (2015): 89–104; T.A. Judge et al., "Job Attitudes, Job Satisfaction, and Job Affect: A Century of Continuity and of Change," *Journal of Applied Psychology* 102 (2017): 356–74; P. Warr and & K. Nielsen, "Wellbeing and Work Performance," In E. Diener, S. Oishi, and L. Tay (Eds.), *Handbook of Well-Being* (Salt Lake City, UT: DEF Publishers, 2018); J. Peiró et al., "The Happy-Productive Worker Model and Beyond: Patterns of Wellbeing and Performance at Work," *International Journal of Environmental Research and Public Health* 16 (2019): 479.

66. However, panel studies suggest that satisfaction has a stronger effect on performance than the other way around. For a summary, see C. D. Fisher, "Happiness at Work," *International Journal of Management Reviews* 12, no. 4 (2010): 384–412.

67. B. Rigney, "How Earls Linked Culture and Strategy to Drive Engagement," *Hootsuite Blog-Social* (blog), October 7, 2015; "Earls Kitchen + Bar Engages Employees Across Restaurants with Google," *Agosto* (blog), accessed March 13, 2019, https://www.agosto.com/case-study/earls-keeps-internal-teams-and-restaurant-customers-happy-with-google-apps/; "Head Office - EarlsWantsYou.Com," accessed October 14, 2019, https://earlswants-syou.com/jobs/head-office.

68. J.I. Heskett, W.E. Sasser, and L.A. Schlesinger, *The Service Profit Chain* (New York: Free Press, 1997); S.P. Brown and S.K. Lam, "A Meta-Analysis of Relationships Linking Employee Satisfaction to Customer Responses," *Journal of Retailing* 84, no. 3 (2008): 243–55; T.J. Gerpott and M. Paukert, "The Relationship between Employee Satisfaction and Customer Satisfaction: A Meta-Analysis (Der Zusammenhang Zwischen Mitarbeiter- Und Kundenzufriedenheit: Eine Metaanalyse)," *Zeitschrift für Personalforschung* 25, no. 1 (2011): 28–54; R.W.Y. Yee, A.C.L. Yeung, and T.C.E. Cheng, "The Service-Profit Chain: An Empirical Analysis in High-Contact Service Industries," *International Journal of Production Economics* 130, no. 2 (2011): 236–45; H. Evanschitzky, F.v. Wangenheim, and N.V. Wünderlich, "Perils of Managing the Service Profit Chain: The Role of Time Lags and Feedback Loops," *Journal of Retailing* 88, no. 3 (2012): 356–66; Y. Hong et al., "Missing Link in the Service Profit Chain: A Meta-Analytic Review of the Antecedents, Consequences, and Moderators of Service Climate," *Journal of Applied Psychology* 98, no. 2 (2013): 237–67.

69. W.-C. Tsai and Y.-M. Huang, "Mechanisms Linking Employee Affective Delivery and Customer Behavioral Intentions," *Journal of Applied Psychology* 87, no. 5 (2002): 1001–08; P. Guenzi and O. Pelloni, "The Impact of Interpersonal Relationships on Customer Satisfaction and Loyalty to the Service Provider," *International Journal Of Service Industry Management* 15, no. 3–4 (2004): 365–84; S.J. Bell, S. Auh, and K. Smalley, "Customer Relationship Dynamics: Service Quality and Customer Loyalty in the Context of Varying Levels of Customer Expertise and Switching Costs," *Journal of the Academy of Marketing Science* 33, no. 2 (2005): 169–83; P.B. Barger and A.A. Grandey, "Service with a Smile and Encounter Satisfaction: Emotional Contagion and Appraisal Mechanisms," *Academy of Management Journal* 49, no. 6 (2006): 1229–38. On the reciprocal effect, see: E. Kim and D.J.Yoon, "Why Does Service with a Smile Make Employees Happy? A Social Interaction Model," *Journal of Applied Psychology* 97, no. 5 (2012): 1059–67.

70. R.T. Mowday, L.W. Porter, and R.M. Steers, *Employee Organization Linkages: The Psychology of Commitment, Absenteeism, and Turnover* (New York: Academic Press, 1982); J.P. Meyer, "Organizational Commitment," *International Review of Industrial and Organizational Psychology* 12 (1997): 175–228. The definition and dimensions of organizational commitment continue to be debated. Some writers even propose that "affective commitment" refers only to one's psychological attachment to and involvement in the organization, whereas "identification" with the organization is a distinct concept further along a continuum of bonds. See: O.N. Solinger, W. van Olffen, and R.A. Roe, "Beyond the Three-Component Model of Organizational Commitment," *Journal of Applied Psychology* 93, no. 1 (2008): 70–83; H.J. Klein, J.C. Molloy, and C.T. Brinsfield, "Reconceptualizing Workplace Commitment to Redress a Stretched Construct: Revisiting Assumptions and Removing Confounds," *Academy of Management Review* 37, no. 1 (2012): 130–51.

71. M. Taing et al., "The Multidimensional Nature of Continuance Commitment: Commitment Owing to Economic Exchanges Versus Lack of Employment Alternatives," *Journal of Business and Psychology* 26, no. 3 (2011): 269–84; C. Vandenberghe and A. Panaccio, "Perceived Sacrifice and Few Alternatives Commitments: The Motivational Underpinnings of Continuance Commitment's Subdimensions," *Journal of Vocational Behavior* 81, no. 1 (2012): 59–72; S. Jaros and R.A. Culpepper, "An Analysis of Meyer and Allen's Continuance Commitment Construct," *Journal of Management & Organization* 20, no. 1 (2014): 79–99, https://doi.org/10.1017/jmo.2014.21.

72. J.P. Meyer and N.M. Parfyonova, "Normative Commitment in the Workplace: A Theoretical Analysis and Re-Conceptualization," *Human Resource Management Review* 20, no. 4 (2010): 283–94, https://doi.org/10.1016/j.hrmr.2009.09.001; S. Jaros, "A Critique of Normative Commitment in Management Research," *Management Research Review* 40, no. 5 (2017): 517–37, https://doi.org/10.1108/MRR-08-2016-0200.

73. J.P. Meyer et al., "Affective, Continuance, and Normative Commitment to the Organization: A Meta-Analysis of Antecedents, Correlates, and Consequences," *Journal of Vocational Behavior* 61 (2002): 20–52; A.S.D. Semedo, A.F.M. Coelho, and N.M.P. Ribeiro, "Effects of Authentic Leadership, Affective Commitment and Job Resourcefulness on Employees' Creativity and Individual Performance," *Leadership & Organization Development Journal* 37, no. 8 (2016): 1038–55, https://doi.org/10.1108/LODJ-02-2015-0029; C. Devece, D. Palacios-Marqués, and M. Pilar Alguacil, "Organizational Commitment and Its Effects on Organizational Citizenship Behavior in a High-Unemployment Environment," *Journal of Business Research, Designing Implementable Innovative Realities,* 69, no. 5 (2016): 1857–61, https://doi.org/10.1016/j.jbusres.2015.10.069; J.C. Wombacher and J. Felfe, "Dual Commitment in the Organization: Effects of the Interplay of Team and Organizational Commitment on Employee Citizenship Behavior, Efficacy Beliefs, and Turnover Intentions," *Journal of Vocational Behavior* 102 (2017): 1–14, https://doi.org/10.1016/j.jvb.2017.05.004; S.L. Blader, S. Patil, and D.J. Packer, "Organizational Identification and Workplace Behavior: More than Meets the Eye," *Research in Organizational Behavior* 37 (2017): 19–34, https://doi.org/10.1016/j.riob.2017.09.001; D. Charbonneau and V.M. Wood, "Antecedents and Outcomes of Unit Cohesion and Affective Commitment to the Army," *Military Psychology* 30, no. 1 (2018): 43–53, https://doi.org/10.1080/08995605.2017.1420974.

74. J.P. Meyer et al., "Organizational Commitment and Job Performance: It's the Nature of the Commitment That Counts," *Journal of Applied Psychology* 74 (1989): 152–56; A.A. Luchak and I.R. Gellatly, "What Kind of Commitment Does a Final-Earnings Pension Plan Elicit?," *Relations Industrielles* 56 (2001): 394–417; Z.X. Chen and A.M. Francesco, "The Relationship between the Three Components of Commitment and Employee Performance in China," *Journal of Vocational Behavior* 62, no. 3 (2003): 490–510; H. Gill et al., "Affective and Continuance Commitment and Their Relations with Deviant Workplace Behaviors in Korea," *Asia Pacific Journal of Management* 28, no. 3 (2011): 595–607. The negative effect on performance might depend on the type of continuance commitment. See M. Taing et al., "The Multidimensional Nature of Continuance Commitment: Commitment Owing to Economic Exchanges versus Lack of Employment

Alternatives," *Journal of Business and Psychology* 26, no. 3 (2011): 269–84.

75. J.E. Finegan, "The Impact of Person and Organizational Values on Organizational Commitment," *Journal of Occupational and Organizational Psychology* 73 (2000): 149–69; K.Y. Kim, R. Eisenberger, and K. Baik, "Perceived Organizational Support and Affective Organizational Commitment: Moderating Influence of Perceived Organizational Competence," *Journal of Organizational Behavior* 37, no. 4 (2016): 558–83, https://doi.org/10.1002/job.2081; J.N. Kurtessis et al., "Perceived Organizational Support: A Meta-Analytic Evaluation of Organizational Support Theory," *Journal of Management* 43, no. 6 (2017): 1854–84, https://doi.org/10.1177/0149206315575554; D. Charbonneau and V.M. Wood, "Antecedents and Outcomes of Unit Cohesion and Affective Commitment to the Army," *Military Psychology* 30, no. 1 (2018): 43–53, https://doi.org/10.1080/08995605.2017.1420974.

76. A.L. Kristof-Brown, R.D. Zimmerman, and E.C. Johnson, "Consequences of Individuals' Fit at Work: A Meta-Analysis of Person-Job, Person-Organization, Person-Group, and Person-Supervisor Fit," *Personnel Psychology* 58, no. 2 (2005): 281–342; M.E. Bergman et al., "An Event-Based Perspective on the Development of Commitment," *Human Resource Management Review* 23, no. 2 (2013): 148–60; C.D. Ditlev-Simonsen, "The Relationship Between Norwegian and Swedish Employees' Perception of Corporate Social Responsibility and Affective Commitment," *Business & Society* 54, no. 2 (2015): 229–53, https://doi.org/10.1177/0007650312439534; O.A.U. Byza et al., "When Leaders and Followers Match: The Impact of Objective Value Congruence, Value Extremity, and Empowerment on Employee Commitment and Job Satisfaction," *Journal of Business Ethics* 158 (2019): 1097–1112, https://doi.org/10.1007/s10551-017-3748-3.

77. D.M. Rousseau et al., "Not So Different after All: A Cross-Discipline View of Trust," *Academy of Management Review* 23 (1998): 393–404.

78. D.K. Datta et al., "Causes and Effects of Employee Downsizing: A Review and Synthesis," *Journal of Management* 36, no. 1 (2010): 281–348; R. van Dick, F. Drzensky, and M. Heinz, "Goodbye or Identify: Detrimental Effects of Downsizing on Identification and Survivor Performance," *Frontiers in Psychology* 7 (2016), https://doi.org/10.3389/fpsyg.2016.00771.

79. C. Leighton and S.L. McShane, "Being 'in the Know': Introducing Organisational Comprehension and Its Nomological Net" (paper presented at the ANZAM Annual Conference, Brisbane, Australia, 8 August 2016). For similar concepts on information acquisition, see: P. Bordia et al., "Uncertainty During Organizational Change: Types, Consequences, and Management Strategies," *Journal of Business and Psychology* 18, no. 4 (2004): 507–32; H.D. Cooper-Thomas and N. Anderson, "Organizational Socialization: A Field Study into Socialization Success and Rate," *International Journal of Selection and Assessment* 13, no. 2 (2005): 116–28; T.N. Bauer, "Newcomer Adjustment During Organizational Socialization: A Meta-Analytic Review of Antecedents, Outcomes, and Methods," *Journal of Applied Psychology* 92, no. 3 (2007): 707–21.

80. T.S. Heffner and J.R. Rentsch, "Organizational Commitment and Social Interaction: A Multiple Constituencies Approach," *Journal of Vocational Behavior* 59 (2001): 471–90.

81. M. Mayhew et al., "A Study of the Antecedents and Consequences of Psychological Ownership in Organizational Settings," *The Journal of Social Psychology* 147 (2007): 477–500; T.-S. Han, H.-H. Chiang, and A. Chang, "Employee Participation in Decision Making, Psychological Ownership and Knowledge Sharing: Mediating Role of Organizational Commitment in Taiwanese High-Tech Organizations," *The International Journal of Human Resource Management* 21 (2010): 2218–33; D. Gallie et al., "The Implications of Direct Participation for Organisational Commitment, Job Satisfaction and Affective Psychological Well-Being: A Longitudinal Analysis," *Industrial Relations Journal* 48 (2017): 174–91.

82. J.C. Quick et al., *Preventive Stress Management in Organizations* (Washington, DC: American Psychological Association, 1997), pp. 3–4; A.L. Dougall and A. Baum, "Stress, Coping, and Immune Function," in *Handbook of Psychology,* ed. M. Gallagher and R.J. Nelson (Hoboken, NJ: John Wiley & Sons, Inc., 2003), 441–55. There are at least three schools of thought regarding the meaning of stress, and some reviews of the stress literature describe these schools without pointing to any one as the preferred definition. One reviewer concluded that the stress concept is so broad that it should be considered an umbrella concept, capturing a broad array of phenomena and providing a simple term for the public to use. See T.A. Day, "Defining Stress as a Prelude to Mapping Its Neurocircuitry: No Help from Allostasis," *Progress in Neuro-Psychopharmacology and Biological Psychiatry* 29, no. 8 (2005): 1195–200; D.C. Ganster and C.C. Rosen, "Work Stress and Employee Health: A Multidisciplinary Review," *Journal of Management* 39, no. 5 (2013): 1085–122.

83. The cognitive appraisal view is described in: R.S. Lazarus, *Stress and Emotion: A New Synthesis* (New York: Springer Publishing, 2006). In contrast, recent neuroscience studies and reviews indicate a dissociation between a person's subjective feeling of stress and their autonomic physiological responses (i.e., release of stress hormones into the blood stream). In other words, people respond physiologically to stressful situations even when they do not consciously feel stressed. See: J. Campbell and U. Ehlert, "Acute Psychosocial Stress: Does the Emotional Stress Response Correspond with Physiological Responses?," *Psychoneuroendocrinology* 37, no. 8 (2012): 1111–34; N. Ali et al., "Suppressing the Endocrine and Autonomic Stress Systems Does Not Impact the Emotional Stress Experience after Psychosocial Stress," *Psychoneuroendocrinology* 78 (2017): 125–30.

84. M.G. González-Morales and P. Neves, "When Stressors Make You Work: Mechanisms Linking Challenge Stressors to Performance," *Work & Stress* 29, no. 3 (2015): 213–29; M.B. Hargrove, W.S. Becker, and D.F. Hargrove, "The HRD Eustress Model: Generating Positive Stress with Challenging Work," *Human Resource Development Review* 14, no. 3 (2015): 279–98.

85. For the history of the word stress, see: R.M.K. Keil, "Coping and Stress: A Conceptual Analysis," *Journal of Advanced Nursing* 45, no. 6 (2004): 659–65. On the general adaptation syndrome, including recent debate about its relevance to sports exercise, see: H. Selye, *Stress without Distress* (Philadelphia: J.B. Lippincott, 1974); S.L. Buckner et al., "The General Adaptation Syndrome: Potential Misapplications to Resistance Exercise," *Journal of Science and Medicine in Sport* 20 (2017): 1015–17; A.J. Cunanan et al., "The General Adaptation Syndrome: A Foundation for the Concept of Periodization," *Sports Medicine* 48 (2018): 787–97.

86. K. Hasselberg et al., "Self-Reported Stressors among Patients with Exhaustion Disorder: An Exploratory Study of Patient Records," *BMC Psychiatry* 14 (2014): 1–10; I.H. Jonsdottir et al., "Working Memory and Attention Are Still Impaired after Three Years in Patients with Stress-Related Exhaustion," *Scandinavian Journal of Psychology* 58 (2017): 504–9; I. Savic, A. Perski, and W. Osika, "MRI Shows That Exhaustion Syndrome Due to Chronic Occupational Stress Is Associated with Partially Reversible Cerebral Changes," *Cerebral Cortex* 28 (2018): 894–906.

87. A. Rosengren et al., "Association of Psychosocial Risk Factors with Risk of Acute Myocardial Infarction in 11119 Cases and 13648 Controls from 52 Countries (the Interheart Study): Case-Control Study," *The Lancet* 364, no. 9438 (2004): 953–62; D.C. Ganster and C.C. Rosen, "Work Stress and Employee Health: A Multidisciplinary Review," *Journal of Management* 39, no. 5 (2013): 1085–122; J. Goh, J. Pfeffer, and S.A. Zenios, "The Relationship between Workplace Stressors and Mortality and Health Costs in the United States," *Management Science* 62, no. 2 (2016): 608–28; C. Johansen et al., "Stress and Cancer," in *The Handbook of Stress and Health,* ed. C.L. Cooper and J.C. Quick (John Wiley & Sons, Ltd, 2017), 125–34.

88. M. Lauzier, S. Melancon, and K. Cote, "The Effect Of Stress Seen On Absenteeism And Presenteeism Behavior: The Mediating Role Of Health," *Canadian Journal of Behavioural Science* 49 (2017): 221–30; B. Schmidt et al., "A Comparison of Job Stress Models: Associations With Employee Well-Being, Absenteeism, Presenteeism, and Resulting Costs," *Journal of Occupational and Environmental Medicine* 61 (2019): 535–44.

89. G.M. Alarcon, "A Meta-Analysis of Burnout with Job Demands, Resources, and Attitudes," *Journal of Vocational Behavior* 79, no. 2 (2011): 549–62; C. Maslach and M.P. Leiter, "Understanding Burnout," in *The Handbook of Stress and Health,* ed. C.L. Cooper and J.C. Quick (John Wiley & Sons, Ltd, 2017), 36–56.

90. C.L. Cooper and J. Marshall, "Occupational Sources of Stress: A Review of the Literature Relating to Coronary Heart Disease and Mental Ill Health," in *From Stress to Wellbeing Volume 1: The Theory and Research on Occupational Stress and Wellbeing,* ed. C.L. Cooper (London: Palgrave Macmillan UK, 2013), 3–23.

91. C.C. Rosen et al., "Occupational Stressors and Job Performance: An Updated Review and Recommendations," in *New Developments in Theoretical and Conceptual Approaches to Job Stress, Research in Occupational Stress and Well-Being* (Emerald Group Publishing Limited, 2010),

1–60; A.E. Nixon et al., "Can Work Make You Sick? A Meta-Analysis of the Relationships between Job Stressors and Physical Symptoms," *Work & Stress* 25, no. 1 (2011): 1–22.

92. A.E. Nixon et al., "Can Work Make You Sick? A Meta-Analysis of the Relationships between Job Stressors and Physical Symptoms," *Work & Stress* 25, no. 1 (2011): 1–22; S. Pindek and P.E. Spector, "Organizational Constraints: A Meta-Analysis of a Major Stressor," *Work & Stress* 30, no. 1 (2016): 7–25.

93. P. McDonald, "Workplace Sexual Harassment 30 Years On: A Review of the Literature," *International Journal of Management Reviews* 14 (2012): 1–17; B. Verkuil, S. Atasayi, and M.L. Molendijk, "Workplace Bullying and Mental Health: A Meta-Analysis on Cross-Sectional and Longitudinal Data," *PLOS ONE* 10, no. 8 (2015): e0135225, https://doi.org/10.1371/journal.pone.0135225; J.D. Mackey et al., "Abusive Supervision: A Meta-Analysis and Empirical Review," *Journal of Management* 43 (2017): 1940–65.

94. "Let's Slow Down!," *The Royal Bank of Canada Monthly Letter,* September 1949.

95. N.A. Bowling et al., "A Meta-Analytic Examination of the Potential Correlates and Consequences of Workload," *Work & Stress* 29, no. 2 (2015): 95–113.

96. R. Drago, D. Black, and M. Wooden, *The Persistence of Long Work Hours,* Melbourne Institute Working Paper Series, Melbourne Institute of Applied Economic and Social Research, University of Melbourne, August 2005; L. Golden, "A Brief History of Long Work Time and the Contemporary Sources of Overwork," *Journal of Business Ethics* 84, no. S2 (2009): 217–27; M. Tarafdar, E.B. Pullins, and T.S. Ragu-Nathan, "Technostress: Negative Effect on Performance and Possible Mitigations," *Information Systems Journal* 25, no. 2 (2015): 103–32; E. Reid, "Embracing, Passing, Revealing, and the Ideal Worker Image: How People Navigate Expected and Experienced Professional Identities," *Organization Science* 26, no. 4 (2015): 997–1017; *The Work Martyr's Cautionary Tale: How the Millennial Experience Will Define America's Vacation Culture,* (Washington: Project: Time Off, 17 August 2016).

97. R. Karasek and T. Theorell, *Healthy Work: Stress, Productivity, and the Reconstruction of Working Life* (New York: Basic Books, 1990); M. Lavigne-Robichaud et al., "Job Strain and the Prevalence of Uncontrolled Hypertension among White-Collar Workers," *Hypertension Research* 42 (2019): 1616–23.

98. M.K. Holton, A.E. Barry, and J.D. Chaney, "Employee Stress Management: An Examination of Adaptive and Maladaptive Coping Strategies on Employee Health," *Work* 53 (2016): 299–305.

99. M. Zuckerman and M. Gagne, "The Cope Revised: Proposing a 5-Factor Model of Coping Strategies," *Journal of Research in Personality* 37 (2003): 169–204; S. Folkman and J.T. Moskowitz, "Coping: Pitfalls and Promise," *Annual Review of Psychology* 55 (2004): 745–74; C.A. Thompson et al., "On the Importance of Coping: A Model and New Directions for Research on Work and Family," *Research in Occupational Stress and Well-Being* 6 (2007): 73–113.

100. S.E. Taylor et al., "Psychological Resources, Positive Illusions, and Health," *American Psychologist* 55, no. 1 (2000): 99–109; F. Luthans and C.M. Youssef, "Emerging Positive Organizational Behavior," *Journal of Management* 33, no. 3 (2007): 321–49; P. Steel, J. Schmidt, and J. Shultz, "Refining the Relationship between Personality and Subjective Well-Being," *Psychological Bulletin* 134, no. 1 (2008): 138–61; G. Alarcon, K.J. Eschleman, and N.A. Bowling, "Relationships between Personality Variables and Burnout: A Meta-Analysis," *Work & Stress* 23, no. 3 (2009): 244–63; R. Kotov et al., "Linking 'Big' Personality Traits to Anxiety, Depressive, and Substance Use Disorders: A Meta-Analysis," *Psychological Bulletin* 136, no. 5 (2010): 768–821.

101. G.A. Bonanno, "Loss, Trauma, and Human Resilience: Have We Underestimated the Human Capacity to Thrive after Extremely Aversive Events?," *American Psychologist* 59, no. 1 (2004): 20–28; F. Luthans, C.M. Youssef, and B.J. Avolio, *Psychological Capital: Developing the Human Competitive Edge* (New York: Oxford University Press, 2007).

102. M.A. Clark et al., "All Work and No Play? A Meta-Analytic Examination of the Correlates and Outcomes of Workaholism," *Journal of Management* 42, no. 7 (2016): 1836–73; C.S. Andreassen et al., "The Relationships between Workaholism and Symptoms of Psychiatric Disorders: A Large-Scale Cross-Sectional Study," *PLOS ONE* 11, no. 5 (2016): e0152978.

103. This list is based on various reviews, but stress management interventions have been organized in several ways. See, for example, J. H. Ruotsalainen et al., "Preventing Occupational Stress in Healthcare Workers," *Cochrane Database of Systematic Reviews,* no. 4 (2015); L. E. Tetrick and C. J. Winslow, "Workplace Stress Management Interventions and Health Promotion," *Annual Review of Organizational Psychology and Organizational Behavior* 2 (2015): 583–603; M. Savic et al., "How Do Nurses Cope with Shift Work? A Qualitative Analysis of Open-Ended Responses from a Survey of Nurses.," *International Journal of Environmental Research and Public Health* 16, no. 20 (October 10, 2019), https://doi.org/10.3390/ijerph16203821.

104. S.D. Friedman, *Leading the Life You Want: Skills for Integrating Work and Life* (Boston: Harvard Business Press, 2014); T.D. Allen, E. Cho, and L.L. Meier, "Work–Family Boundary Dynamics," *Annual Review of Organizational Psychology and Organizational Behavior* 1 (2014): 99–121; T.D. Allen, T.D. Golden, and K.M. Shockley, "How Effective Is Telecommuting? Assessing the Status of Our Scientific Findings," *Psychological Science in the Public Interest* 16 (2015): 40–68; E.E. Kossek and R.J. Thompson, "Workplace Flexibility: Integrating Employer and Employee Perspectives to Close the Research–Practice Implementation Gap," in *The Oxford Handbook of Work and Family,* ed. T.D. Allen and L.T. Eby (New York: Oxford University Press, 2016), 255–70; M.J. Sirgy and D.-J. Lee, "Work-Life Balance: An Integrative Review," *Applied Research in Quality of Life* 13 (2018): 229–54; M. Beatson, "Megatrends: Flexible Working" (London: Chartered Institute of Personnel and Development, January 15, 2019).

105. A.E. Carr and T.L.-P. Tang, "Sabbaticals and Employee Motivation: Benefits, Concerns, and Implications," *Journal of Education for Business* 80, no. 3 (2005): 160–64; S. Overman, "Sabbaticals Benefit Companies as Well as Employees," *Employee Benefit News,* 15 April 2006; O.B. Davidson et al., "Sabbatical Leave: Who Gains and How Much?," *Journal of Applied Psychology* 95, no. 5 (2010): 953–64. For discussion of psychological detachment and stress management, see: C. Fritz et al., "Happy, Healthy, and Productive: The Role of Detachment from Work During Nonwork Time," *Journal of Applied Psychology* 95, no. 5 (2010): 977–83.

106. M. Tuckey et al., "Hindrances Are Not Threats: Advancing the Multidimensionality of Work Stress," *Journal of Occupational Health Psychology* 20, no. 2 (2015): 131–47.

107. M.H. Abel, "Humor, Stress, and Coping Strategies," *Humor: International Journal of Humor Research* 15 (2002): 365–81; K. Ebner et al., "Coaching as Stress-Management Intervention: The Mediating Role of Self-Efficacy in a Framework of Self-Management and Coping.," *International Journal of Stress Management* 25 (2018): 209–33.

108. O. Kettunen et al., "Greater Levels of Cardiorespiratory and Muscular Fitness Are Associated with Low Stress and High Mental Resources in Normal but Not Overweight Men," *BMC Public Health* 16, no. 1 (2016): 788; M. Gerber et al., "Fitness Moderates the Relationship between Stress and Cardiovascular Risk Factors," *Medicine & Science in Sports & Exercise* 48, no. 11 (2016): 2075–81.

109. H.O. Dickinson et al., "Relaxation Therapies for the Management of Primary Hypertension in Adults," *Cochrane Database of Systematic Reviews,* no. 1 (2008); O.L. Siu, "Stress Management Techniques in the Workplace," in *Routledge Companion to Wellbeing at Work,* ed. C.L. Cooper and M.P. Leiter (Routledge: 2017), 284–97, https://doi.org/10.4324/9781315665979.ch20.

110. C. Viswesvaran, J.I. Sanchez, and J. Fisher, "The Role of Social Support in the Process of Work Stress: A Meta-Analysis," *Journal of Vocational Behavior* 54, no. 2 (1999): 314–34; S.E. Taylor et al., "Biobehavioral Responses to Stress in Females: Tend-and-Befriend, Not Fight-or-Flight," *Psychological Review* 107, no. 3 (2000): 411–29; A. Beehr, N.A. Bowling, and M.M. Bennett, "Occupational Stress and Failures of Social Support: When Helping Hurts," *Journal of Occupational Health Psychology* 15, no. 1 (2010): 45–59; B.A. Scott et al., "A Daily Investigation of the Role of Manager Empathy on Employee Well-Being," *Organizational Behavior and Human Decision Processes* 113, no. 2 (2010): 127–40; S.Y. Shin and S.G. Lee, "Effects of Hospital Workers? Friendship Networks on Job Stress," *PLoS ONE* 11, no. 2 (2016): e0149428.

CHAPTER 5

1. D. Morris, "2017: The Year Performance Reviews Get The Axe," Adobe Conversations-Perspectives (blog), January 11, 2017, https://theblog.adobe.com/2017-the-year-performance-reviews-get-the-axe; V. Galt, "Time to Retire the Employee Ranking System?," *The Globe and Mail,* March 11, 2017; Canada NewsWire, "The New Performance Review: Shorter and More Frequent, Survey Says" (Toronto: OfficeTeam, December 12, 2018).

2. C.C. Pinder, *Work Motivation in Organizational Behavior* (Upper Saddle River, NJ: Prentice-Hall, 1998); R.M. Steers, R.T. Mowday, and D.L. Shapiro, "The Future of Work Motivation Theory," *Academy of Management Review* 29 (2004): 379–87.

3. W.H. Macey and B. Schneider, "The Meaning of Employee Engagement," *Industrial and Organizational Psychology* 1 (2008): 3–30; A.M. Saks and J.A. Gruman, "What Do We Really Know about Employee Engagement?," *Human Resource Development Quarterly* 25, no. 2 (2014): 155–82; J.L. Whittington *et al.*, *Enhancing Employee Engagement: An Evidence-Based Approach* (New York: Palgrave Macmillan, 2017), Chap. 1.

4. D. Macleod and N. Clarke, *Engaging for Success: Enhancing Performance through Employee Engagement* (London: UK Government, Department for Business Innovation and Skills, July 2009); C. Bailey *et al.*, *Evaluating the Evidence on Employee Engagement and Its Potential Benefits to NHS Staff: A Narrative Synthesis of the Literature*, Health Services and Delivery Research Vol. 3, Issue 26 (London: NHS National Institute for Health Research, 2015). The outcomes of employee engagement are confounded by the various ways the concept has been studied, but most perspectives of engagement tend to predict meaningful outcomes. See: A.M. Saks, "Translating Employee Engagement Research into Practice," *Organizational Dynamics* 46, no. 2 (2017): 76–86.

5. "2018 Trends in Global Employee Engagement" (Deerfield, Ill.: Aon Hewitt, March 6, 2018); C. Hall and C. Comeau, "Employee Engagement: Driving Engagement From the Middle" (Ottawa: Conference Board of Canada, September 2018); J. Hartell, "Employee Engagement on the Rise in the U.S." (Washington, DC: Gallup, Inc., August 26, 2018).

6. The confusing array of definitions about drives and needs has been the subject of criticism for a half century. See, for example, R.S. Peters, "Motives and Motivation," *Philosophy* 31 (1956): 117–30; H. Cantril, "Sentio, Ergo Sum: 'Motivation' Reconsidered," *Journal of Psychology* 65, no. 1 (1967): 91–107; G.R. Salancik and J. Pfeffer, "An Examination of Need-Satisfaction Models of Job Attitudes," *Administrative Science Quarterly* 22, no. 3 (1977): 427–456. For a recent effort to condense 162 human "motives" into a small set, see: J.R. Talevich et al., "Toward a Comprehensive Taxonomy of Human Motives," *PLOS ONE* 12, no. 2 (2017): e0172279.

7. D.W. Pfaff, *Drive: Neurobiological and Molecular Mechanisms of Sexual Motivation* (Cambridge, MA: MIT Press, 1999); A. Blasi, "Emotions and Moral Motivation," *Journal for the Theory of Social Behaviour* 29 (1999): 1–19; K.C. Berridge, "Motivation Concepts in Behavioral Neuroscience," *Physiology & Behavior* 81 (2004): 179–209; D. Scheffer and H. Heckhausen, "Trait Theories of Motivation," in *Motivation and Action,* ed. J. Heckhausen and H. Heckhausen (Cham: Springer International Publishing, 2018), 67–112. We distinguish drives from emotions, but future research may find that the two concepts are not so different as is stated here. Woodworth is credited with either coining or popularizing the term *drives* in the context of human motivation. His classic book is certainly the first source to discuss the concept in detail. See R.S. Woodworth, *Dynamic Psychology* (New York: Columbia University Press, 1918).

8. P.R. Lawrence and N. Nohria, *Driven: How Human Nature Shapes Our Choices* (San Francisco: Jossey-Bass, 2002); N. Nohria, B. Groysberg, and L.-E. Lee, "Employee Motivation: A Powerful New Model," *Harvard Business Review* (2008): 78–84; P. Lawrence and M. Pirson, "Economistic and Humanistic Narratives of Leadership in the Age of Globality: Toward a Renewed Darwinian Theory of Leadership," *Journal of Business Ethics* 128 (2015): 383–394.

9. S.G. Barsade and D.E. Gibson, "Why Does Affect Matter in Organizations?," *Academy of Management Perspectives* 21 (2007): 36–59; K.C. Berridge, "Evolving Concepts of Emotion and Motivation," *Frontiers in Psychology* 9 (2018), https://doi.org/10.3389/fpsyg.2018.01647; E. Harmon-Jones, "On Motivational Influences, Moving beyond Valence, and Integrating Dimensional and Discrete Views of Emotion," *Cognition and Emotion* 33 (2019): 101–8.

10. A.R. Damasio, *The Feeling of What Happens: Body and Emotion in the Making of Consciousness* (New York: Harcourt Brace & Company, 1999), p. 286.

11. B. Monin, D.A. Pizarro, and J.S. Beer, "Deciding Versus Reacting: Conceptions of Moral Judgment and the Reason–Affect Debate," *Review of General Psychology* 11 (2007): 99–111; S.H. Schwartz et al., "Refining the Theory of Basic Individual Values," *Journal of Personality and Social Psychology* 103 (2012): 663–88; M. Driver, "Motivation and Identity: A Psychoanalytic Perspective on the Turn to Identity in Motivation Research," *Human Relations* 70 (2017): 617–37.

12. P.R. Lawrence and N. Nohria, *Driven: How Human Nature Shapes Our Choices* (San Francisco: Jossey-Bass, 2002); N. Nohria, B. Groysberg, and L.-E. Lee, "Employee Motivation: A Powerful New Model," *Harvard Business Review* (2008): 78–84; P. Lawrence and M. Pirson, "Economistic and Humanistic Narratives of Leadership in the Age of Globality: Toward a Renewed Darwinian Theory of Leadership," *Journal of Business Ethics* 128 (2015): 383–394.

13. The drive to acquire is likely associated with research on getting ahead, desire for competence, the selfish gene, and desire for social distinction. See R.H. Frank, *Choosing the Right Pond: Human Behavior and the Quest for Status* (New York: Oxford University Press, 1985); L. Gaertner et al., "The 'I,' the 'We,' and the 'When': A Meta-Analysis of Motivational Primacy in Self-Definition," *Journal of Personality and Social Psychology* 83 (2002): 574–91; J. Hogan and B. Holland, "Using Theory to Evaluate Personality and Job-Performance Relations: A Socioanalytic Perspective," *Journal of Applied Psychology* 88 (2003): 100–12; R. Dawkins, *The Selfish Gene,* 30th Anniversary Ed. (Oxford, UK: Oxford University Press, 2006); M.R. Leary, "Motivational and Emotional Aspects of the Self," *Annual Review of Psychology* 58 (2007): 317–44; F. Martela and T.J.J. Riekki, "Autonomy, Competence, Relatedness, and Beneficence: A Multicultural Comparison of the Four Pathways to Meaningful Work," *Frontiers in Psychology* 9 (2018), https://doi.org/10.3389/fpsyg.2018.01157.

14. R.E. Baumeister and M.R. Leary, "The Need to Belong: Desire for Interpersonal Attachments as a Fundamental Human Motivation," *Psychological Bulletin* 117 (1995): 497–529.

15. G. Loewenstein, "The Psychology of Curiosity: A Review and Reinterpretation," *Psychological Bulletin* 116 (1994): 75–98; J. Litman, "Curiosity and the Pleasures of Learning: Wanting and Liking New Information," *Cognition and Emotion* 19 (2005): 793–814; C. Kidd and B.Y. Hayden, "The Psychology and Neuroscience of Curiosity," *Neuron* 88 (2015): 449–60.

16. N. Nohria, B. Groysberg, and L.-E. Lee, "Employee Motivation: A Powerful New Model," *Harvard Business Review,* August 2008, 78–84; F. Beyer et al., "Hit or Run: Exploring Aggressive and Avoidant Reactions to Interpersonal Provocation Using a Novel Fight-or-Escape Paradigm (FOE)," *Frontiers in Behavioral Neuroscience* 11 (2017), https://doi.org/10.3389/fnbeh.2017.00190.

17. A.R. Damasio, *Descartes' Error: Emotion, Reason, and the Human Brain* (New York: Putnam's Sons, 1994); J.E. LeDoux, "Emotion Circuits in the Brain," *Annual Review of Neuroscience* 23 (2000): 155–184; M. Reimann and A. Bechara, "The Somatic Marker Framework as a Neurological Theory of Decision-Making: Review, Conceptual Comparisons, and Future Neuroeconomics Research," *Journal of Economic Psychology* 31 (2010): 767–776; P. Winkielman, K. Berridge, and S. Sher, "Emotion, Consciousness, and Social Behavior," in *The Oxford Handbook of Social Neuroscience,* ed. J. Decety and J.T. Cacioppo (Oxford University Press, 2011), 195–211; T. Poppa and A. Bechara, "The Somatic Marker Hypothesis: Revisiting the Role of the 'Body-Loop' in Decision-Making," *Current Opinion in Behavioral Sciences* 19 (2018): 61–66.

18. P.R. Lawrence and N. Nohria, *Driven: How Human Nature Shapes Our Choices* (San Francisco: Jossey-Bass, 2002), 145–47; R.F. Baumeister, E.J. Masicampo, and K.D. Vohs, "Do Conscious Thoughts Cause Behavior?," *Annual Review of Psychology* 62 (2011): 331–61.

19. P.R. Lawrence and N. Nohria, *Driven: How Human Nature Shapes Our Choices* (San Francisco: Jossey-Bass, 2002), Chap. 11.

20. For recent discussion on the benefits and risks of work practices that encourage employee competition, see: A. Sapegina and A. Weibel, "The Good, the Not So Bad, and the Ugly of Competitive Human Resource Practices: A Multidisciplinary Conceptual Framework," *Group & Organization Management* 42 (2017): 707–47.

21. An increasing number of scholarly publications have incorporated four-drive theory in their writing in recent years. For recent examples, see: R.C. Wood et al., "Evolutionary Neuroscience and Motivation in Organizations," in *Organizational Neuroscience,* eds D.A. Waldman and P.A. Balthazard, *Monographs in Leadership and Management* (Emerald Group Publishing Limited, 2015), 143–67; C. Abraham et al., "Explaining the Unexpected and Continued Use of an Information System with the Help of Evolved Evolutionary Mechanisms," *Journal of the Association for Information Science and Technology* 67, no. 1 (2016): 212–31, https://doi.org/10.1002/asi.23344; M.T. Lee and R.L. Raschke, "Understanding Employee Motivation and Organizational Performance: Arguments for a Set-Theoretic Approach," *Journal of Innovation & Knowledge* 1, no. 3 (2016): 162–69. https://doi.org/10.1016/j.jik.2016.01.004; B. Torgler, "Can

Tax Compliance Research Profit from Biology?," *Review of Behavioral Economics* 3, no. 1 (2016): 113–44. https://doi/10.1561/105.00000045; M.T. Lee, R.L. Raschke, and R.S. Louis, "Exploiting Organizational Culture: Configurations for Value through Knowledge Worker's Motivation," *Journal of Business Research* 69, no. 11 (2016): 5442–47. https://doi.org/10.1016/j.jbusres.2016.04.152; D. Scheffer and H. Heckhausen, "Trait Theories of Motivation," in *Motivation and Action*, ed. J. Heckhausen and H. Heckhausen (Cham: Springer International Publishing, 2018), 67–112, https://doi.org/10.1007/978-3-319-65094-4_3.

22. A.H. Maslow, "A Theory of Human Motivation," *Psychological Review* 50 (1943): 370–96; A.H. Maslow, *Motivation and Personality* (New York Harper & Row, 1954).

23. Maslow did not diagram his theory as a pyramid. He does not even mention pyramids in his writing on human motivation. Instead, Maslow mostly repeats the term *hierarchy* in describing how human needs (drives) are organized relative to each other. The earliest description of human needs as a pyramid is likely from Chapter 2 ("The Pyramid of Man's Needs") of a 1960 book on conflict by F. Alexander Magoun, a professor of human relations at MIT. Magoun's chapter discusses Maslow's needs hierarchy theory. A recent review also points to a step model of Maslow's model in Keith Davis's human relations book, and of a pyramid model in a 1960 article by Charles McDermid. See: F.A. Magoun, *Cooperation and Conflict in Industry* (New York: Harper, 1960), 20–31; T. Bridgman, S. Cummings, and J. Ballard, "Who Built Maslow's Pyramid? A History of the Creation of Management Studies' Most Famous Symbol and Its Implications for Management Education," *Academy of Management Learning & Education* 18 (2019): 81–98.

24. A.H. Maslow, *Motivation and Personality* (New York Harper & Row, 1954), 2, 97–98.

25. D.T. Hall and K.E. Nougaim, "An Examination of Maslow's Need Hierarchy in an Organizational Setting," *Organizational Behavior and Human Performance* 3, no. 1 (1968): 12; M.A. Wahba and L.G. Bridwell, "Maslow Reconsidered: A Review of Research on the Need Hierarchy Theory," *Organizational Behavior and Human Performance* 15 (1976): 212–40; E.L. Betz, "Two Tests of Maslow's Theory of Need Fulfillment," *Journal of Vocational Behavior* 24, no. 2 (1984): 204–20; P.A. Corning, "Biological Adaptation in Human Societies: A 'Basic Needs' Approach," *Journal of Bioeconomics* 2, no. 1 (2000): 41–86. For a recent proposed revision of the model, see: D.T. Kenrick et al., "Renovating the Pyramid of Needs: Contemporary Extensions Built Upon Ancient Foundations," *Perspectives on Psychological Science* 5, no. 3 (2010): 292–314.

26. L. Parks and R.P. Guay, "Personality, Values, and Motivation," *Personality and Individual Differences* 47 (2009): 675–84; R. Fischer and D. Boer, "Motivational Basis of Personality Traits: A Meta-Analysis of Value-Personality Correlations," *Journal of Personality* 83 (2015): 491–510; L. Parks-Leduc, G. Feldman, and A. Bardi, "Personality Traits and Personal Values: A Meta-Analysis," *Personality and Social Psychology Review* 19 (2015): 3–29. Maslow did acknowledge that the needs hierarchy has a different ordering for some people, but he described these as relatively rare exceptions. See:

A.H. Maslow, "A Theory of Human Motivation," *Psychological Review* 50 (1943): 386–88.

27. B. Verplanken and R.W. Holland, "Motivated Decision Making: Effects of Activation and Self-Centrality of Values on Choices and Behavior," *Journal of Personality and Social Psychology* 82 (2002): 434–47; J. Jin and J. Rounds, "Stability and Change in Work Values: A Meta-Analysis of Longitudinal Studies," *Journal of Vocational Behavior* 80 (2012): 326–39. https://doi.org/10.1016/j.jvb.2011.10.007; C.M. Lechner *et al.,* "The Development of Work Values During the Transition to Adulthood: A Two-Country Study," *Journal of Vocational Behavior* 99(2017): 52–65.

28. K. Dye, A.J. Mills, and T.G. Weatherbee, "Maslow: Man Interrupted — Reading Management Theory in Context," *Management Decision* 43 (2005): 1375–95.

29. A.H. Maslow, "A Preface to Motivation Theory," *Psychosomatic Medicine* 5 (1943): 85–92.

30. S. Kesebir, J. Graham, and S. Oishi, "A Theory of Human Needs Should Be Human-Centered, Not Animal-Centered," *Perspectives on Psychological Science* 5 (2010): 315–19.

31. A.H. Maslow, *Maslow on Management* (New York: John Wiley & Sons, 1998); C. Peterson and N. Park, "What Happened to Self-Actualization?," *Perspectives on Psychological Science* 5, no. 3 (2010): 320–22.

32. M. Gagné and E.L. Deci, "Self-Determination Theory and Work Motivation," *Journal of Organizational Behavior* 26, no. 4 (2005): 331–62; C.P. Cerasoli, J.M. Nicklin, and M.T. Ford, "Intrinsic Motivation and Extrinsic Incentives Jointly Predict Performance: A 40-Year Meta-Analysis," *Psychological Bulletin* 140, no. 4 (2014): 980–1008.

33. M. Gagné and D. Bhave, "Autonomy in the Workplace: An Essential Ingredient to Employee Engagement and Well-Being in Every Culture," in *Human Autonomy in Cross-Cultural Context,* ed. V.I. Chirkov, R.M. Ryan and K.M. Sheldon, *Cross-Cultural Advancements in Positive Psychology* (Dordrecht, Netherlands: Springer Netherlands, 2011), 163–87; E.L. Deci and M.R. Ryan, "The Importance of Universal Psychological Needs for Understanding Motivation in the Workplace," in *The Oxford Handbook of Work Engagement, Motivation, and Self-Determination Theory*, ed. M. Gagne (New York: Oxford University Press, 2014), 13–32. For neuroscience research on intrinsic motivation (particularly need for competence), see: W. Lee and J. Reeve, "Identifying the Neural Substrates of Intrinsic Motivation During Task Performance," *Cognitive, Affective, & Behavioral Neuroscience* 17 (2017): 939–53; S.I. Di Domenico and R.M. Ryan, "The Emerging Neuroscience of Intrinsic Motivation: A New Frontier in Self-Determination Research," *Frontiers in Human Neuroscience* 11 (2017), https://doi.org/10.3389/fnhum.2017.00145.

34. C.P. Cerasoli, J.M. Nicklin, and M.T. Ford, "Intrinsic Motivation and Extrinsic Incentives Jointly Predict Performance: A 40-Year Meta-analysis," *Psychological Bulletin* 140, no. 4 (2014): 980–1008; Y. Garbers and U. Konradt, "The Effect of Financial Incentives on Performance: A Quantitative Review of Individual and Team-Based Financial Incentives," *Journal of Occupational

and Organizational Psychology* 87, no. 1 (2014): 102–37.

35. J. Schroeder and A. Fishbach, "How to Motivate Yourself and Others? Intended and Unintended Consequences," *Research in Organizational Behavior* 35 (2015): 123–41.

36. D.C. McClelland, *The Achieving Society* (New York: Van Nostrand Reinhold, 1961); D. McClelland and D. Burnham, "Power Is Great Motivator," *Harvard Business Review* 54, no. 2 (1976): 100–110; M.G. Köllner and O.C. Schultheiss, "Meta-Analytic Evidence of Low Convergence between Implicit and Explicit Measures of the Needs for Achievement, Affiliation, and Power," *Frontiers in Psychology* 5 (2014), https://doi.org/10.3389/fpsyg.2014.00826.

37. D. C. McClelland, *The Achieving Society* (New York: Van Nostrand Reinhold, 1961).

38. M. Frese and M.M. Gielnik, "The Psychology of Entrepreneurship," *Annual Review of Organizational Psychology and Organizational Behavior* 1, no. 1 (2014): 413–38.

39. S. Leroy et al., "Synchrony Preference: Why Some People Go with the Flow and Some Don't," *Personnel Psychology* 68 (2015): 759–809; M.H. Do and A. Minbashian, "A Meta-Analytic Examination of the Effects of the Agentic and Affiliative Aspects of Extraversion on Leadership Outcomes," *The Leadership Quarterly* 25 (2014): 1040–53; B. Steinmann et al., "Implicit Motives and Leadership Performance Revisited: What Constitutes the Leadership Motive Pattern?," *Motivation and Emotion* 39 (2015): 167–74; B. Steinmann, S.K. Ötting, and G.W. Maier, "Need for Affiliation as a Motivational Add-On for Leadership Behaviors and Managerial Success," *Frontiers in Psychology* 7 (2016), https://doi.org/10.3389/fpsyg.2016.01972.

40. J.C. Magee and C.A. Langner, "How Personalized and Socialized Power Motivation Facilitate Antisocial and Prosocial Decision-Making," *Journal of Research in Personality* 42, no. 6 (2008): 1547–59; D. Rus, D. van Knippenberg, and B. Wisse, "Leader Self-Definition and Leader Self-Serving Behavior," *Leadership Quarterly* 21, no. 3 (2010): 509–29; C. Case and J. Maner, "Divide and Conquer: When and Why Leaders Undermine the Cohesive Fabric of Their Group," *Journal of Personality and Social Psychology* 107, no. 6 (2014): 1033–50.

41. D. Miron and D.C. McClelland, "The Impact of Achievement Motivation Training on Small Business," *California Management Review* 21 (1979): 13–28.

42. Expectancies and valences have a long history in motivation and decision making, dating back to the earliest writing on the economics of utilitarianism. See, for example: W.S. Jevons, *The Theory of Political Economy* (London: MacMillan, 1871), Chaps. 2 and 3. For recent discussion in organizational behavior, see: S. Sun, J.B. Vancouver, and J.M. Weinhardt, "Goal Choices and Planning: Distinct Expectancy and Value Effects in Two Goal Processes," *Organizational Behavior and Human Decision Processes* 125 (2014): 220–33.

43. Expectancy theory of motivation in work settings originated in V.H. Vroom, *Work and Motivation* (New York: Wiley, 1964). The version of expectancy theory presented here was developed by Edward Lawler. Lawler's model provides a clearer presentation of the model's three components. P-to-O expectancy

is similar to "instrumentality" in Vroom's original expectancy theory model. The difference is that instrumentality is a correlation whereas P-to-O expectancy is a probability. See J.P. Campbell et al., *Managerial Behavior, Performance, and Effectiveness* (New York: McGraw Hill, 1970); E.E. Lawler III, *Motivation in Work Organizations* (Monterey, CA: Brooks-Cole, 1973); D.A. Nadler and E.E. Lawler, "Motivation: A Diagnostic Approach," in *Perspectives on Behavior in Organizations*, ed. J.R. Hackman, E.E. Lawler III, and L.W. Porter (New York: McGraw Hill, 1983), 67–78.

44. The earliest economic theorists argued that valence is the the the positive or negative emotion that the decision maker anticipates from an outcome. See: S. L. McShane, "Organisational Decision-Making," in *Contemporary Issues in Management and Organisational Behaviour*, ed. P. Murray, D. Poole, and G. Jones (Sydney: Cengage Learning Australia, 2006), 136–65. The connection between valence and emotion is supported by recent neuroscience studies. See: A. Bechara and A.R. Damasio, "The Somatic Marker Hypothesis: A Neural Theory of Economic Decision," *Games and Economic Behavior* 52 (2005): 336–72; J. Bartol and S. Linquist, "How Do Somatic Markers Feature in Decision Making?," *Emotion Review* 7 (2014): 81–89; J.S. Lerner et al., "Emotion and Decision Making," *Annual Review of Psychology* 66 (2015): 799–823.

45. D.A. Nadler and E.E. Lawler, "Motivation: A Diagnostic Approach," in *Perspectives on Behavior in Organizations*, ed. J.R. Hackman, E.E. Lawler III, and L.W. Porter (New York: McGraw Hill, 1983), 70–73.

46. B. Moses, "Time to Get Serious About Rewarding Employees," *The Globe and Mail*, 28 April 2010, B16.

47. For recent applications of expectancy in diverse settings, see R.L. Purvis, T.J. Zagenczyk, and G.E. McCray, "What's in It for Me? Using Expectancy Theory and Climate to Explain Stakeholder Participation, Its Direction and Intensity," *International Journal of Project Management* 33 (2015): 3–14; E. Shweiki et al., "Applying Expectancy Theory to Residency Training: Proposing Opportunities to Understand Resident Motivation and Enhance Residency Training," *Advances in Medical Education and Practice* 6 (2015): 339–46; K.N. Bauer et al., "Re-Examination of Motivation in Learning Contexts: Meta-Analytically Investigating the Role Type of Motivation Plays in the Prediction of Key Training Outcomes," *Journal of Business and Psychology* 31 (2016): 33–50; R. Meymandpour and P. Pawar, "Study of Expectancy Motivation in IT Developers," *Telecom Business Review* 11 (2018): 6–11.

48. R. Kanfer, M. Frese, and R.E. Johnson, "Motivation Related to Work: A Century of Progress.," *Journal of Applied Psychology* 102, no. 3 (2017): 338–55, https://doi.org/10.1037/apl0000133.

49. This limitation was acknowledged by Victor Vroom, who had introduced expectancy theory in his 1964 book. See G.P. Latham, *Work Motivation: History, Theory, Research, and Practice* (Thousand Oaks, CA: Sage, 2007), 47–48.

50. J.B. Watson, *Behavior: An Introduction to Comparative Psychology* (New York: Henry Holt & Co., 1914).

51. B.F. Skinner, *About Behaviorism* (New York: Alfred A. Knopf, 1974); J. Komaki, T. Coombs, and S. Schepman, "Motivational Implications of Reinforcement Theory," in *Motivation and Leadership at Work*, ed. R.M. Steers, L.W. Porter, and G.A. Bigley (New York: McGraw Hill, 1996), 34–52; R.G. Miltenberger, *Behavior Modification: Principles and Procedures* (Pacific Grove, CA: Brooks/Cole, 1997).

52. T.K. Connellan, *How to Improve Human Performance* (New York: Harper & Row, 1978), pp. 48–57; F. Luthans and R. Kreitner, *Organizational Behavior Modification and Beyond* (Glenview, IL: Scott, Foresman, 1985), pp. 85–88.

53. B.F. Skinner, *Science and Human Behavior* (New York: The Free Press, 1965); Miltenberger, *Behavior Modification: Principles and Procedures*, Chap. 4–6.

54. T.R. Hinkin and C.A. Schriesheim, "'If You Don't Hear from Me You Know You Are Doing Fine,'" *Cornell Hotel & Restaurant Administration Quarterly* 45 (2004): 362–72; T.R. Hinkin and C.A. Schriesheim, "An Examination of 'Nonleadership': From Laissez-Faire Leadership to Leader Reward Omission and Punishment Omission," *Journal of Applied Psychology* 93 (2008): 1234–48.

55. K. Cameron et al., "Effects of Positive Practices on Organizational Effectiveness," *The Journal of Applied Behavioral Science* 47 (2011): 266–308; F. Luthans and C.M. Youssef-Morgan, "Psychological Capital: An Evidence-Based Positive Approach," *Annual Review of Organizational Psychology and Organizational Behavior* 4 (2017): 339–66; A.B. Bakker and M. van Woerkom, "Strengths Use in Organizations: A Positive Approach of Occupational Health.," *Canadian Psychology* 59 (2018): 38–46.

56. L.K. Trevino, "The Social Effects of Punishment in Organizations: A Justice Perspective," *Academy of Management Review* 17 (1992): 647–76; L. Wang and J.K. Murnighan, "The Dynamics of Punishment and Trust," *Journal of Applied Psychology* 102 (2017): 1385–1402; L. Wang et al., "Does Anger Expression Help or Harm Leader Effectiveness? The Role of Competence-Based versus Integrity-Based Violations and Abusive Supervision," *Academy of Management Journal* 61 (2018): 1050–72.

57. G.P. Latham and V.L. Huber, "Schedules of Reinforcement: Lessons from the Past and Issues for the Future," *Journal of Organizational Behavior Management* 13 (1992): 125–49; B.A. Williams, "Challenges to Timing-Based Theories of Operant Behavior," *Behavioural Processes* 62 (2003): 115–23.

58. J. Hamari, "Do Badges Increase User Activity? A Field Experiment on the Effects of Gamification," *Computers in Human Behavior* 71 (2017): 469–78, http://dx.doi.org/10.1016/j.chb.2015.03.036; M.T. Cardador, G.B. Northcraft, and J. Whicker, "A Theory of Work Gamification: Something Old, Something New, Something Borrowed, Something Cool?," *Human Resource Management Review* 27 (June 2017): 353–65, https://doi.org/10.1016/j.hrmr.2016.09.014; R.N. Landers et al., "Gamification Science, Its History and Future: Definitions and a Research Agenda," *Simulation & Gaming* 49, no. 3 (2018): 315–37, https://doi.org/10.1177/1046878118774385; M.B. Armstrong and R.N. Landers, "Gamification of Employee Training and Development," *International Journal*

of *Training and Development* 22, no. 2 (2018): 162–69, https://doi.org/10.1111/ijtd.12124.

59. J.A. Bargh and M.J. Ferguson, "Beyond Behaviorism: On the Automaticity of Higher Mental Processes," *Psychological Bulletin* 126, no. 6 (2000): 925–45. Some writers argue that behaviourists long ago accepted the relevance of cognitive processes in behaviour modification. See I. Kirsch et al., "The Role of Cognition in Classical and Operant Conditioning," *Journal of Clinical Psychology* 60, no. 4 (2004): 369–92.

60. A. Bandura, *Social Foundations of Thought and Action: A Social Cognitive Theory* (Englewood Cliffs, N.J: Prentice Hall, 1986); A. Bandura, "Social Cognitive Theory of Self-Regulation," *Organizational Behavior and Human Decision Processes* 50, no. 2 (1991): 248–87; A. Bandura, "Social Cognitive Theory: An Agentic Perspective," *Annual Review of Psychology* 52, no. 1 (2001): 1–26.

61. M.E. Schnake, "Vicarious Punishment in a Work Setting," *Journal of Applied Psychology* 71 (1986): 343–45; Trevino, "The Social Effects of Punishment in Organizations: A Justice Perspective; J. Malouff et al., "Effects of Vicarious Punishment: A Meta-Analysis," *Journal of General Psychology* 136, no. 3 (2009): 271–86.

62. A. Pescuric and W.C. Byham, "The New Look of Behavior Modeling," *Training & Development* 50 (1996): 24–30; P.J. Taylor, D.F. Russ-Eft, and D.W.L. Chan, "A Meta-Analytic Review of Behavior Modeling Training," *Journal of Applied Psychology* 90 (2005): 692–709; C.G. Myers and D.S. DeRue, "Agency in Vicarious Learning at Work," in *Autonomous Learning in the Workplace*, ed. J.E. Ellingson and R.A. Noe, (New York: Routledge, 2017), 15–37.

63. A. Bandura, "Self-Reinforcement: Theoretical and Methodological Considerations," *Behaviorism* 4 (1976): 135–55; J.B. Vancouver and D.V. Day, "Industrial and Organisation Research on Self-Regulation: From Constructs to Applications," *Applied Psychology: An International Journal* 54 (2005): 155–85; A. Neal, T. Ballard, and J.B. Vancouver, "Dynamic Self-Regulation and Multiple-Goal Pursuit," *Annual Review of Organizational Psychology and Organizational Behavior* 4 (2017): 401–23.

64. M. Milyavskaya and K.M. Werner, "Goal Pursuit: Current State of Affairs and Directions for Future Research," *Canadian Psychology* 59 (May 2018): 163–75.

65. E.A. Locke and G.P. Latham, *A Theory of Goal Setting and Task Performance* (Englewood Cliffs, NJ: Prentice Hall, 1990); G. Latham, G. Seijts, and J. Slocum, "The Goal Setting and Goal Orientation Labyrinth: Effective Ways for Increasing Employee Performance," *Organizational Dynamics* 45 (2016): 271–77.

66. The SMARTER goal-setting model is an extension of the earlier SMART model. SMARTER apparently originated from British sports psychology writing around the mid-1990s, such as: P. Butler, *Performance Profiling* (Leeds, UK: The National Coaching Foundation, 1996), 36. There are several variations of the SMARTER goal-setting model; "achievable" is sometimes "acceptable," "reviewed" is sometimes "recorded," and "exciting" is sometimes "ethical." For a summary of variations of meanings within the SMARTER acronym, see: G. Brown, C. Leonard, and M. Arthur-Kelly, "Writing

SMARTER Goals for Professional Learning and Improving Classroom Practices," *Reflective Practice* 17 (2016): 621–35.

67. For debate on the value and limitations of measurement, see: J.M. Henshaw, *Does Measurement Measure Up? How Numbers Reveal and Conceal the Truth* (Baltimore, Maryland: Johns Hopkins Press, 2006).

68. A.C. Crossley, C. Cooper, and T. Wernsing, "Making Things Happen through Challenging Goals: Leader Proactivity, Trust, and Business-Unit Performance," *Journal of Applied Psychology* 98 (2013): 540–49; A. Kruglanski et al., "The Rocky Road from Attitudes to Behaviors: Charting the Goal Systemic Course of Actions," *Psychological Review* 122 (2015): 598–620; K.M. Roose and W.L. Williams, "An Evaluation of the Effects of Very Difficult Goals," *Journal of Organizational Behavior Management* 38 (2018): 18–48.

69. Z. Zhang and M. Jia, "How Can Companies Decrease the Disruptive Effects of Stretch Goals? The Moderating Role of Interpersonal—and Informational—Justice Climates," *Human Relations* 66, no. 7 (2013): 993–1020; L.D. Ordóñez and D.T. Welsh, "Immoral Goals: How Goal Setting May Lead to Unethical Behavior," *Current Opinion in Psychology* 6 (2015): 93–96.

70. E.A. Locke and G.P. Latham, *A Theory of Goal Setting and Task Performance* (Englewood Cliffs, NJ: Prentice Hall, 1990), Chap. 6 and 7; H. Klein, J.T. Cooper, and C.A. Monahan, "Goal Commitment," in *New Developments in Goal Setting and Task Performance,* ed. E.A. Locke and G.P. Latham (London: Taylor and Francis, 2012), 65–89.

71. M. London, E.M. Mone, and J.C. Scott, "Performance Management and Assessment: Methods for Improved Rater Accuracy and Employee Goal Setting," *Human Resource Management* 43, no. 4 (2004): 319–36; G.P. Latham and C.C. Pinder, "Work Motivation Theory and Research at the Dawn of the Twenty-First Century," *Annual Review of Psychology* 56 (2005): 485–516.

72. G.P. Latham, *Work Motivation: History, Theory, Research, and Practice* (Thousand Oaks, CA: Sage, 2007), 198–203; A. Baker et al., "Feedback and Organizations: Feedback Is Good, Feedback-Friendly Culture Is Better," *Canadian Psychology* 54, no. 4 (2013): 260–68.

73. F. Anseel et al., "How Are We Doing after 30 Years? A Meta-Analytic Review of the Antecedents and Outcomes of Feedback-Seeking Behavior," *Journal of Management* 41 (2015): 318–48; M. London, *The Power of Feedback: Giving, Seeking, and Using Feedback for Performance Improvement* (New York: Routledge, 2015); B. Kuvaas, R. Buch and A. Dysvik, "Constructive Supervisor Feedback Is Not Sufficient: Immediacy and Frequency Is Essential," *Human Resource Management* 56 (2017): 519–31.

74. H.H. Meyer, E. Kay and J.R.P. French Jr, "Split Roles in Performance Appraisal," *Harvard Business Review* 43 (1965): 123–29; S. Adler *et al.,* "Getting Rid of Performance Ratings: Genius or Folly? A Debate," *Industrial and Organizational Psychology* 9 (2016): 219–52; A.S. DeNisi and K.R. Murphy, "Performance Appraisal and Performance Management: 100 Years of Progress?," *Journal of Applied Psychology* 102 (2017): 421–33.

75. "Management People: Getting to Know You," *Retail Jeweller,* 27 March 2012; G. Johnson, "Tea Nicola Gives Finance 'a Boost of Benevolence' with WealthBar," *Globe & Mail,* October 28, 2019.

76. M. Buckingham, *Go Put Your Strengths to Work* (New York: Free Press, 2007); A.L. Clancy and J. Binkert, "Appreciative Coaching: Pathway to Flourishing," in *Excellence in Coaching: The Industry Guide,* ed. J. Passmore (London: Kogan Page, 2010), 147–56; H. Aguinis, R.K. Gottfredson, and H. Joo, "Delivering Effective Performance Feedback: The Strengths-Based Approach," *Business Horizons* 55 (2012): 105–11; A.B. Bakker and M. van Woerkom, "Strengths Use in Organizations: A Positive Approach of Occupational Health," *Canadian Psychology* 59 (2018): 38–46. While still encouraging a positive approach to coaching and feedback, some writers believe that negative feedback is also necessary. See, for example: A. Castiello D'Antonio, "Coaching Psychology and Positive Psychology in Work and Organizational Psychology.," *The Psychologist-Manager Journal* 21 (May 2018): 130–50.

77. A.N. Kluger and D. Nir, "The Feedforward Interview," *Human Resource Management Review* 20 (2010): 235–46; H. Aguinis, R.K. Gottfredson, and H. Joo, "Delivering Effective Performance Feedback: The Strengths-Based Approach," *Business Horizons* 55 (2012): 105–11; B. Kuvaas, R. Buch, and A. Dysvik, "Constructive Supervisor Feedback Is Not Sufficient: Immediacy and Frequency Is Essential," *Human Resource Management* 56 (2017): 519–31; J.V. Wingerden and J.V. der Stoep, "The Motivational Potential of Meaningful Work: Relationships with Strengths Use, Work Engagement, and Performance," *PLOS ONE* 13, no. 6 (June 13, 2018): e0197599, https://doi.org/10.1371/journal.pone.0197599.

78. H.H. Meyer, "A Solution to the Performance Appraisal Feedback Enigma," *Academy of Management Executive* 5, no. 1 (1991): 68–76.

79. A. Terracciano, P.T. Costa and R.R. McCrae, "Personality Plasticity after Age 30," *Personality and Social Psychology Bulletin* 32 (2006): 999–1009; R. Mittus et al., "Within-Trait Heterogeneity in Age Group Differences in Personality Domains and Facets: Implications for the Development and Coherence of Personality Traits," *PLoS ONE* 10, no. 3 (2015): e0119667; L. H. Schultz et al., "Vocational Interests across 20 Years of Adulthood: Stability, Change, and the Role of Work Experiences," *Journal of Research in Personality* 71 (2017): 46–56.

80. J.W. Smither, M. London, and R.R. Reilly, "Does Performance Improve Following Multisource Feedback? A Theoretical Model, Meta-Analysis, and Review of Empirical Findings," *Personnel Psychology* 58, no. 1 (2005): 33–66; L.E. Atwater, J.F. Brett, and A.C. Charles, "Multisource Feedback: Lessons Learned and Implications for Practice," *Human Resource Management* 46, no. 2 (2007): 285–307; M.C. Campion, E.D. Campion, and M.A. Campion, "Improvements in Performance Management through the Use of 360 Feedback," *Industrial and Organizational Psychology* 8, no. 1 (2015): 85–93.

81. S.J. Ashford and G.B. Northcraft, "Conveying More (or Less) Than We Realize: The Role of Impression Management in Feedback Seeking," *Organizational Behavior and Human Decision Processes* 53 (1992): 310–34; J.R. Williams et al.,

"Increasing Feedback Seeking in Public Contexts: It Takes Two (or More) to Tango," *Journal of Applied Psychology* 84 (1999): 969–76.

82. J.B. Miner, "The Rated Importance, Scientific Validity, and Practical Usefulness of Organizational Behavior Theories: A Quantitative Review," *Academy of Management Learning and Education* 2 (2003): 250–68; S. Asmus et al., "The Impact of Goal-Setting on Worker Performance - Empirical Evidence from a Real-Effort Production Experiment," *Procedia CIRP,* 12th Global Conference on Sustainable Manufacturing – Emerging Potentials, 26 (January 2015): 127–32.

83. P.M. Wright, "Goal Setting and Monetary Incentives: Motivational Tools That Can Work Too Well," *Compensation and Benefits Review* 26 (1994): 41–49; S. Kerr and D. LePelley, "Stretch Goals: Risks, Possibilities, and Best Practices," in *New Developments in Goal Setting and Task Performance,* ed. E.A. Locke and G.P. Latham (London: Taylor and Francis, 2012), 21–32; L.D. Ordóñez and D.T. Welsh, "Immoral Goals: How Goal Setting May Lead to Unethical Behavior," *Current Opinion in Psychology* 6 (2015): 93–96.

84. G.P. Latham, *Work Motivation: History, Theory, Research, and Practice* (Thousand Oaks, CA: Sage, 2007), 188.

85. J. Norman, "Four in 10 U.S. Workers Think They Are Underpaid," *Gallup.Com,* August 28, 2018; "Money Matters: Survey Finds Canadian Workers Are Scrutinizing Salaries; "Are You Underpaid? Survey Released With Robert Half 2019 Salary Guides Finds 46 Percent Of Workers Feel Shortchanged," News Release (Menlo Park, Calif.: Robert Half, August 28, 2018); "Feelings Split on Pay Satisfaction," News Release (Toronto: Robert Half, August 28, 2019).

86. The most widely studied types in organizational behavior are distributive, procedural, and interactional justice, the latter of which includes two subsets (informational and interpersonal). However, other writers have identified completely different typologies, such as legalistic, retributive, and restorative justice. See, for example: G.D. Paul and L.L. Putnam, "Emergent Paradigms of Organizational Justice," in *Transforming Conflict through Communication in Personal, Family, and Working Relationships,* ed. P.M. Kellett and T. Matyók, Peace and Conflict Studies (Lanham: Lexington Books, 2016), 271–92. For a detailed discussion and critique of the development of the justice domain, see: D.E. Rupp et al., "A Critical Analysis of the Conceptualization and Measurement of Organizational Justice: Is It Time for Reassessment?," *Academy of Management Annals* 11 (2017): 919–59.

87. R. Cropanzano, J.F. Kirk, and M. Fortin, "How Do We Know When We Are Treated Fairly? Justice Rules and Fairness Judgments," *Research in Personnel and Human Resources Management* 33 (2015): 279–350; J.A. Colquitt and J.B. Rodell, "Measuring Justice and Fairness," in *The Oxford Handbook of Justice in the Workplace,* ed. R.S. Cropanzano and M.L. Ambrose (New York: Oxford University Press, 2015), 187–202.

88. M. Deutsch, "Equity, Equality, and Need: What Determines Which Value Will Be Used as the Basis of Distributive Justice?," *Journal of Social Issues* 31, no. 3 (1975): 137–49; D.A. Morand and K.K.

Merriman, "Equality Theory" as a Counterbalance to Equity Theory in Human Resource Management," *Journal of Business Ethics* 111, no. 1 (2012): 133–44; T. Reeskens and W. van Oorschot, "Equity, Equality, or Need? A Study of Popular Preferences for Welfare Redistribution Principles across 24 European Countries," *Journal of European Public Policy* 20, no. 8 (2013): 1174–95.

89. J.S. Adams, "Toward an Understanding of Inequity," *Journal of Abnormal and Social Psychology* 67 (1963): 422–36; P.H. Siegel, M. Schraeder, and R. Morrison, "A Taxonomy of Equity Factors," *Journal of Applied Social Psychology* 38 (2008): 61–75; R. Cropanzana, D.E. Bowen, and S.W. Gilliland, "The Management of Organizational Justice," *Academy of Management Perspectives* 21 (2007): 34–48; D.E. Rupp et al., "A Critical Analysis of the Conceptualization and Measurement of Organizational Justice: Is It Time for Reassessment?," *Academy of Management Annals* 11 (2017): 919–59.

90. C.T. Kulik and M.L. Ambrose, "Personal and Situational Determinants of Referent Choice," *Academy of Management Review* 17 (1992): 212–37; J. Shin and Y.W. Sohn, "Effects of Employees' Social Comparison Behaviors on Distributive Justice Perception and Job Satisfaction," *Social Behavior and Personality* 43, no. 7 (2015): 1071–83; C.M. Sterling and G. Labianca, "Costly Comparisons: Managing Envy in the Workplace," *Organizational Dynamics* 44, no. 4 (2015): 296–305.

91. T.P. Summers and A.S. DeNisi, "In Search of Adams' Other: Reexamination of Referents Used in the Evaluation of Pay," *Human Relations* 43 (1990): 497–511.

92. The emotive dynamics of feelings of inequity are studied in A.W. Cappelen et al., "Equity Theory and Fair Inequality: A Neuroeconomic Study," *Proceedings of the National Academy of Sciences* 111, no. 43 (2014): 15368–72.

93. Y. Cohen-Charash and P.E. Spector, "The Role of Justice in Organizations: A Meta-Analysis," *Organizational Behavior and Human Decision Processes* 86 (2001): 278–321; B. Walker and R.T. Hamilton, "Employee–Employer Grievances: A Review," *International Journal of Management Reviews* 13, no. 1 (2011): 40–58; R. Cropanzana and C. Moliner, "Hazards of Justice: Egocentric Bias, Moral Judgments, and Revenge-Seeking," in *Deviant and Criminal Behavior in the Workplace,* ed. S.M. Elias (New York: New York University Press, 2013), 155–77; B.C. Holtz and C.M. Harold, "Interpersonal Justice and Deviance: The Moderating Effects of Interpersonal Justice Values and Justice Orientation," *Journal of Management* 39, no. 2 (2013): 339–65; C.L. Wilkin and C.E. Connelly, "Green with Envy and Nerves of Steel: Moderated Mediation between Distributive Justice and Theft," *Personality and Individual Differences* 72 (2015): 160–64.

94. Canadian Press, "Pierre Berton, Canadian Cultural Icon, Enjoyed Long and Colourful Career," *Times Colonist (Victoria, B.C.),* 30 November 2004.

95. J. Fizel, A.C. Krautman, and L. Hadley, "Equity and Arbitration in Major League Baseball," *Managerial and Decision Economics* 23, no. 7 (2002): 427–35; M. Ezzamel and R. Watson, "Pay Comparability across and within UK Boards: An Empirical Analysis of the Cash Pay Awards to CEOs

and Other Board Members," *Journal of Management Studies* 39, no. 2 (2002): 207–32.

96. D.R. Bobocel and L. Gosse, "Procedural Justice: A Historical Review and Critical Analysis," in *Oxford Handbook of Justice in the Workplace,* ed. R.S. Cropanzano and M.L. Ambrose (New York: Oxford University Press, 2015), 51–88; Robert J. Bies, "Interactional Justice: Looking Backward, Looking Forward," in *The Oxford Handbook of Justice in the Workplace,* ed. R. Cropanzano and M.L. Ambrose, Oxford Library of Psychology (New York: Oxford University Press, 2015), 89–107.

97. J. Greenberg and E.A. Lind, "The Pursuit of Organizational Justice: From Conceptualization to Implication to Application," in *Industrial and Organizational Psychology: Linking Theory with Practice* ed. C.L. Cooper and E.A. Locke (London: Blackwell, 2000), 72–108; C.B. Goldberg, M.A. Clark, and A.B. Henley, "Speaking Up: A Conceptual Model of Voice Responses Following the Unfair Treatment of Others in Non-Union Settings," *Human Resource Management* 50, no. 1 (2011): 75–94; M.R. Bashshur, "When Voice Matters: A Multilevel Review of the Impact of Voice in Organizations," *Journal of Management* 41, no. 5 (2015): 1530–54.

98. Robert J. Bies, "Interactional Justice: Looking Backward, Looking Forward," in *The Oxford Handbook of Justice in the Workplace,* ed. R. Cropanzano and M.L. Ambrose, Oxford Library of Psychology (New York: Oxford University Press, 2015), 89–107; R. Cropanzano, J.F. Kirk, and M. Fortin, "How Do We Know When We Are Treated Fairly? Justice Rules and Fairness Judgments," *Research in Personnel and Human Resources Management* 33 (2015): 279–350.

99. J.S. Michel, K. Newness, and K. Duniewicz, "How Abusive Supervision Affects Workplace Deviance: A Moderated-Mediation Examination of Aggressiveness and Work-Related Negative Affect," *Journal of Business and Psychology* 31 (2016): 1–22; J.K. Oh and C.I.C. Farh, "An Emotional Process Theory of How Subordinates Appraise, Experience, and Respond to Abusive Supervision Over Time," *Academy of Management Review* 42 (2017): 207–32.

100. D.T. Miller, "Disrespect and the Experience of Injustice," *Annual Review of Psychology* 52 (2001): 527–53; R. Vermunt and H. Steensma, "Procedural Justice," in *Handbook of Social Justice Theory and Research,* ed. C. Sabbagh and M. Schmitt (New York, NY: Springer New York, 2016), 219–36; K.A. DeCelles and K. Aquino, "Dark Knights: When and Why an Employee Becomes a Workplace Vigilante," *Academy of Management Review,* February 15, 2019, https://doi.org/10.5465/amr.2017.0300.

101. M.L. Ambrose, M.A. Seabright, and M. Schminke, "Sabotage in the Workplace: The Role of Organizational Injustice," *Organizational Behavior and Human Decision Processes* 89, no. 1 (2002): 947–65.

CHAPTER 6

1. C. Cancialosi, "Embrace A Culture Of Self-Leadership To Stay Agile As You Scale," *Forbes,* June 13, 2017; "3 Steps To Enable Change," *LinkedIn Blog* (blog), February 16, 2017, https://www.linkedin.com/pulse/3-steps-enable-change-cathy-thorpe; T. Rubin, "5 Reasons You Want to

Work at Nurse Next Door," *Nurse Next Door Senior Care Services* (blog), November 21, 2019, https://www.nursenextdoor.com/blog/5-reasons-you-want-to-work-at-nurse-next-door/; C. Weiner, "Empower Those Around You, to 'Slow Down To Do More', with Cathy Thorpe of Nurse Next Door," *Authority Magazine (Medium),* December 5, 2019.

2. M.C. Bloom and G.T. Milkovich, "Issues in Managerial Compensation Research," in *Trends in Organizational Behavior,* ed. C.L. Cooper and D.M. Rousseau (Chicester, UK: John Wiley & Sons, Inc., 1996), 23–47. For an excellent review of the history of money, see: N. Ferguson, *The Ascent of Money: A Financial History of the World* (New York: Penguin, 2008).

3. A. Furnham, *The New Psychology of Money* (East Sussex, UK: Routledge, 2014), Chap. 5.

4. S. Jia et al., "Attitude toward Money Modulates Outcome Processing: An ERP Study," *Social Neuroscience* 8, no. 1 (2012): 43–51; R.L. Capa and R. Custers, "Conscious and Unconscious Influences of Money: Two Sides of the Same Coin?," in *The Psychological Science of Money,* ed. E. Bijleveld and H. Aarts (New York: Springer, 2014), 73–91; C.R. Leana and J. Meuris, "Living to Work and Working to Live: Income as a Driver of Organizational Behavior," *Academy of Management Annals* 9, no. 1 (2015): 55–95.

5. D.W. Krueger, "Money, Success, and Success Phobia," in *The Last Taboo: Money as Symbol and Reality in Psychotherapy and Psychoanalysis,* ed. D.W. Krueger (New York: Brunner/Mazel, 1986), 3–16.

6. P.F. Wernimont and S. Fitzpatrick, "The Meaning of Money," *Journal of Applied Psychology* 56, no. 3 (1972): 218–26; T.R. Mitchell and A.E. Mickel, "The Meaning of Money: An Individual-Difference Perspective," *Academy of Management Review* (1999): 568–78; S.E.G. Lea and P. Webley, "Money: Metaphors and Motives," in *The Psychological Science of Money,* ed. E. Bijleveld and H. Aarts (New York: Springer, 2014), 21–35; J.M. Beus and D.S. Whitman, "Almighty Dollar or Root of All Evil? Testing the Effects of Money on Workplace Behavior," *Journal of Management* 43 (2017): 2147–67, https://doi.org/10.1177/0149206314565241; N. Tang et al., "Monetary Wisdom: How Do Investors Use Love of Money to Frame Stock Volatility and Enhance Stock Happiness?," *Journal of Happiness Studies* 19 (2018): 1831–62, https://doi.org/10.1007/s10902-017-9890-x.

7. R. Lynn, *The Secret of the Miracle Economy* (London: SAE, 1991); G. Ridinger and M. McBride, "Money Affects Theory of Mind Differently by Gender," *PLoS ONE* 10, no. 12 (2015): e0143973; A. Furnham, S. Stumm, and M. Fenton-O'Creevy, "Sex Differences in Money Pathology in the General Population," *Social Indicators Research* 123, no. 3 (2015): 701–11.

8. A. Furnham, B.D. Kirkcaldy, and R. Lynn, "National Attitudes to Competitiveness, Money, and Work among Young People: First, Second, and Third World Differences," *Human Relations* 47 (1994): 119–32; G. Dell'Orto and K.O. Doyle, "Poveri Ma Belli: Meanings of Money in Italy and in Switzerland," *American Behavioral Scientist* 45, no. 2 (2001): 257–71; T.L.-P. Tang, A. Furnham, and G.M.-T. Davis, "A Cross-Cultural Comparison of the Money Ethic, the Protestant Work Ethic, and

Job Satisfaction: Taiwan, the USA, and the UK," *International Journal of Organization Theory and Behavior* 6, no. 2 (2003): 175–94; R. Luna-Arocas and T.L.-P. Tang, "Are You Satisfied With Your Pay When You Compare? It Depends on Your Love of Money, Pay Comparison Standards, and Culture," *Journal of Business Ethics* 128, no. 2 (2015): 279–89, https://doi.org/10.1007/s10551-014-2100-4.

9. A.E. Mickel and L.A. Barron, "Getting 'More Bang for the Buck': Symbolic Value of Monetary Rewards in Organizations," *Journal of Management Inquiry* 17, no. 4 (2008): 329–38; C.P. Cerasoli, J.M. Nicklin, and M.T. Ford, "Intrinsic Motivation and Extrinsic Incentives Jointly Predict Performance: A 40-Year Meta-Analysis," *Psychological Bulletin* 140, no. 4 (2014): 980–1008; J.D. Shaw and N. Gupta, "Let the Evidence Speak Again! Financial Incentives Are More Effective Than We Thought," *Human Resource Management Journal* 25, no. 3 (2015): 281–93.

10. J.S. Mill, *Utilitarianism,* Seventh ed. (London, UK: Longmans, Green, and Co., 1879; repr., Project Gutenberg EBook), Chap. 4.

11. "Conditions of Employment," *Working at PSI* (Villigen, Switzerland: Paul Scherrer Institut, 2016), www.psi.ch/pa/employment-conditions (accessed April 18, 2016).

12. K. Gilbert, "Promises and Practices: Job Evaluation and Equal Pay Forty Years On!," *Industrial Relations Journal* 43, no. 2 (2012): 137–51; M. Armstrong and D. Brown, "Job Evaluation Versus Market Pricing: Competing or Combining Methods of Pay Determination?," *Compensation & Benefits Review* 49, no. 3 (2017): 153–60, https://doi.org/10.1177/0886368718765827; M. Armstrong, *Armstrong's Job Evaluation Handbook: A Guide to Achieving Fairness and Transparency in Pay and Reward* (London: Kogan Page Publishers, 2018).

13. R. McNabb and K. Whitfield, "Job Evaluation and High Performance Work Practices: Compatible or Conflictual?," *Journal of Management Studies* 38 (2001): 293–312; P.K. Sandberg, "Intertwining Gender Inequalities and Gender-Neutral Legitimacy in Job Evaluation and Performance-Related Pay," *Gender, Work & Organization* 24, no. 2 (2017): 156–70, https://doi.org/10.1111/gwao.12156.

14. P.K. Zingheim and J.R. Schuster, "Competencies and Rewards: Substance or Just Style?," *Compensation Benefits Review* 35, no. 5 (2003): 40–44; K. Kim et al., "Rewarding Self-Initiated Expatriates: A Skills-Based Approach," *Thunderbird International Business Review* 60, no. 1 (2018): 89–104, https://doi.org/10.1002/tie.21832.

15. L. Brown, B. George, and C. Mehaffey-Kultgen, "The Development of a Competency Model and Its Implementation in a Power Utility Cooperative: An Action Research Study," *Industrial and Commercial Training* 50, no. 3 (2018): 123–35, https://doi.org/10.1108/ICT-11-2017-0087.

16. A. Mitra, N. Gupta, and J.D. Shaw, "A Comparative Examination of Traditional and Skill-Based Pay Plans," *Journal of Managerial Psychology* 26, no. 4 (2011): 278–96. The High Liner Foods example is cited in: M. Mayer, "Maintaining a Seafood Savviness Like No Other," *Refrigerated & Frozen Foods* 23, no. 12 (2013): 30, 34, 36, 38.

17. E.C. Dierdorff and E.A. Surface, "If You Pay for Skills, Will They Learn? Skill Change and Maintenance under a Skill-Based Pay System,"

Journal of Management 34, no. 4 (2008): 721–43; M. Díaz-Fernández, A. López-Cabrales, and R. Valle-Cabrera, "In Search of Demanded Competencies: Designing Superior Compensation Systems," *The International Journal of Human Resource Management* 24, no. 3 (2013): 643–66.

18. P.K. Zingheim and J.R. Schuster, "Competencies and Rewards: Substance or Just Style?," *Compensation Benefits Review* 35, no. 5 (2003): 1–15.; F. Giancola, "Skill-Based Pay—Issues for Consideration," *Benefits & Compensation Digest* 44, no. 5 (2007): 1–15.

19. E.B. Peach and D.A. Wren, "Pay for Performance from Antiquity to the 1950s," *Journal of Organizational Behavior Management* 12 (1992): 5–26; R.M. Adams, "Shepherds at Umma in the Third Dynasty of Ur: Interlocutors with a World Beyond the Scribal Field of Ordered Vision," *Journal of the Economic and Social History of the Orient* 49, no. 2 (2006): 133–69; P. Kriwaczek, *Babylon: Mesopotamia, and the Birth of Civilization* (London: Atlantic Books, 2010), pg.142.

20. J. Zhai, "2018 Compensation Best Practices Report: Canadian Edition," *PayScale* (blog), June 27, 2018, https://www.payscale.com/compensation-today/2018/06/2018-compensation-best-practices-canadian-edition; P. Reeburgh, "How Much Money Should a Housekeeper Be Paid per Room at a Motel?" *Quora,* October 29, 2018.

21. N. Byrnes and M. Arndt, "The Art of Motivation," *BusinessWeek,* 1 May 2006, 56; M. Bolch, "Rewarding the Team," *HRMagazine,* February 2007, 91–93; J. McGregor, "Nucor's CEO Is Stepping Aside, but Its Culture Likely Won't," *Washington Post,* 20 November 2012.

22. L.R. Gomez-Mejia, T.M. Welbourne, and R.M. Wiseman, "The Role of Risk Sharing and Risk Taking under Gainsharing," *Academy of Management Review* 25 (2000): 492–507; R.W.D. Zondo, "The Impact of Gainsharing in the Automotive Parts Manufacturing Industry of South Africa," *South African Journal of Economic and Management Sciences* 21, no. 1 (2018): 8, https://doi.org/10.4102/sajems.v21i1.1773; A.M. Benson and S. Sajjadiani, "Are Bonus Pools Driven by Their Incentive Effects? Evidence from Fluctuations in Gainsharing Incentives," *ILR Review* 71, no. 3 (2018): 567–99, https://doi.org/10.1177/0019793917726066.

23. "Collective Agreement between Local 378, Canadian Office and Professional Employees Union and British Columbia Hydro and Power Authority Powertech Labs Inc.," Collective Agreement (Burnaby BC, April 1, 2014); S. Hopkins, J. Surpin, and A. Stanowski, "Lessons Learned from Implementation of Gainsharing," *Healthcare Financial Management* 69, no. 3 (2015): 78–83; A. Scott, L. Tjosvold, and D. Chojecki, "Gainsharing and Shared Savings Strategies in the Healthcare Setting: Evidence for Effectiveness" (Edmonton: Institute of Health Economics, November 18, 2016); A.A. Anoushiravani and R.M. Nunley, "Gainsharing Strategies, Physician Champions, Getting Physician Buy In," *The Journal of Arthroplasty* 32, no. 6 (2017): 1723–27, https://doi.org/10.1016/j.arth.2017.02.011.

24. L. Leyne, "Province, BCGEU Ink Novel Deal for 5 Years," *Victoria Times-Colonist,* 4 December 2013, A1; P. Lambert, "Digging Deep for

Organizational Innovation," *McKinsey Quarterly,* April 2018; "Robust B.C. Economy Results in Pay Raise for Public Sector Workers," *Vancouver Sun,* November 8, 2018.

25. T. Grant, "How One Company Levels the Pay Slope of Executives and Workers," *Globe and Mail,* 16 November 2013, B6; V. Lu, "Leonard Lee, Founder of Lee Valley Tools, Was the Ultimate Craftsman," *Toronto Star,* 16 July 2016; "Bonuses Increase by 13 per Cent at Hydro-Québec, Reach $29.3 Million," *Montreal Gazette,* April 19, 2019.

26. S.H. Wagner, C.P. Parkers, and N.D. Christiansen, "Employees That Think and Act Like Owners: Effects of Ownership Beliefs and Behaviors on Organizational Effectiveness," *Personnel Psychology* 56, no. 4 (2003): 847–71; P. Walsh, M. Peck, and I. Zugasti, "Why the U.S. Needs More Worker-Owned Companies," *Harvard Business Review,* August 8, 2018.

27. R. Meng et al., "Do ESOPs Enhance Firm Performance? Evidence from China's Reform Experiment," *Journal of Banking & Finance* 35, no. 6 (2011): 1541–51; H. Fang, J.R. Nofsinger, and J. Quan, "The Effects of Employee Stock Option Plans on Operating Performance in Chinese Firms," *Journal of Banking & Finance* 54 (2015): 141–59; N.-C. Liu, M.-Y. Chen, and M.-L. Wang, "The Effects of Non-Expensed Employee Stock Bonus on Firm Performance: Evidence from Taiwanese High-Tech Firms," *British Journal of Industrial Relations* 54, no. 1 (2016): 30–54; D. Kruse, "Does Employee Ownership Improve Performance?," *IZA World of Labor,* December 2016, https://doi.org/10.15185/izawol.311.

28. T. Kato, J. Ho Lee, and J.-S. Ryu, "The Productivity Effects of Profit Sharing, Employee Ownership, Stock Option and Team Incentive Plans: Evidence from Korean Panel Data," in *Advances in the Economic Analysis of Participatory & Labor-Managed Firms,* vol. 11, (Emerald, 2010), 111–35; C. Lucifora and F. Origo, "Performance-Related Pay and Firm Productivity: Evidence from a Reform in the Structure of Collective Bargaining," *ILR Review* 68, no. 3 (2015): 606–32, https://doi.org/10.1177/0019793915570876.

29. A. Pendleton and A. Robinson, "Employee Share Ownership and Human Capital Development: Complementarity in Theory and Practice," *Economic and Industrial Democracy* 32, no. 3 (2011): 439–57; G. Loris, "Why Do Firms Adopt Employee Share Ownership? Bundling ESO and Direct Involvement for Developing Human Capital Investments," *Employee Relations* 37, no. 3 (2015): 296–313. However, one recent study in Finland reported that group-level incentives have a stronger effect than individual incentives on organizational productivity. See: T. Kato and A. Kauhanen, "Performance Pay and Enterprise Productivity: The Details Matter," *Journal of Participation and Employee Ownership* 1 (2018): 61–73, https://doi.org/10.1108/JPEO-03-2018-0013.

30. W.C. Hammer, "How to Ruin Motivation with Pay," *Compensation Review* 7, no. 3 (1975): 17–27; A. Kohn, *Punished by Rewards* (Boston: Houghton Mifflin, 1993); M. Beer and M.D. Cannon, "Promise and Peril of Implementing Pay-for-Performance," *Human Resource Management* 43, no. 1 (2004): 3–48; D. Ariely et al., "Large Stakes and Big Mistakes," *Review of Economic Studies* 76, no. 2

(2009): 451–69; C.B. Cadsby, F. Song, and F. Tapon, "The Impact of Risk-Aversion and Stress on the Incentive Effect of Performance-Pay," in *Experiments in Organizational Economics,* vol. 19 (Emerald Group Publishing Limited, 2016), 189–227.

31. S.Y. Sung, J.N. Choi, and S.-C. Kang, "Incentive Pay and Firm Performance: Moderating Roles of Procedural Justice Climate and Environmental Turbulence," *Human Resource Management,* November 20, 2015; J.D. Shaw and N. Gupta, "Let the Evidence Speak Again! Financial Incentives Are More Effective Than We Thought," *Human Resource Management Journal* 25, no. 3 (2015): 281–93; A.J. Nyberg et al., "Collective Pay for Performance: A Cross-Disciplinary Review and Meta-Analysis," *Journal of Management* 44, no. 6 (2018): 2433–72, https://doi.org/10.1177/0149206318770732.

32. J.M. Jones, *Talent Town Hall: A Presentation to OESA,* Towers Watson (New York: 25 October 2012); Towers Watson, *Highlights from the EMEA Region,* Global Workforce Study, Towers Watson (London: 26 April 2013); J. Paterson, "20% of Employers Link Pay to Performance," *Benefits Canada,* 5 February 2016.

33. J. Han, K. Bartol, and S. Kim, "Tightening up the Performance-Pay Linkage: Roles of Contingent Reward Leadership and Profit-Sharing in the Cross-Level Influence of Individual Pay-for-Performance," *Journal of Applied Psychology* 100, no. 2 (2015): 417–30; S.Y. Sung, J.N. Choi, and S.-C. Kang, "Incentive Pay and Firm Performance: Moderating Roles of Procedural Justice Climate and Environmental Turbulence," *Human Resource Management* 56, no. 2 (2017): 287–305, https://doi.org/10.1002/hrm.21765.

34. "United Rentals Inc at Evercore ISI Industrial Conference—Final," *Fair Disclosure Wire* (Linthicum, MD), March 3, 2015.

35. J.S. DeMatteo, L.T. Eby, and E. Sundstrom, "Team-Based Rewards: Current Empirical Evidence and Directions for Future Research," *Research in Organizational Behavior* 20 (1998): 141–83; A.J. Nyberg et al., "Collective Pay for Performance: A Cross-Disciplinary Review and Meta-Analysis," *Journal of Management* 44, no. 6 (2018): 2433–72, https://doi.org/10.1177/0149206318770732.

36. B. Moses, "Time to Get Serious About Rewarding Employees," *The Globe and Mail,* 28 April 2010, B16.

37. "Dream Teams," *Human Resources Professional* (1994): 17–19.

38. S. Kerr, "On the Folly of Rewarding A, While Hoping for B," *Academy of Management Journal* 18 (1975): 769–83; M.E. Davis, "Pay Matters: The Piece Rate and Health in the Developing World," *Annals of Global Health* 82, no. 5 (2016): 858–865.e6, https://doi.org/10.1016/j.aogh.2016.05.005; A.P. Bartel, "Multitasking at Work: Do Firms Get What They Pay For?," *IZA World of Labor,* May 2017, https://doi.org/10.15185/izawol.362; A. Sapegina and A. Weibel, "The Good, the Not So Bad, and the Ugly of Competitive Human Resource Practices: A Multidisciplinary Conceptual Framework," *Group & Organization Management* 42, no. 5 (2017): 707–47, https://doi.org/10.1177/1059601117730238.

39. G.T. Milkovich, J.M. Newman, and C. Milkovich, *Compensation,* 5th ed. (Homewood, IL: Irwin, 1996), 315.

40. M.A. Campion et al., "Work Redesign: Eight Obstacles and Opportunities," *Human Resource Management* 44, no. 4 (2005): 367–90; S.-J. Cullinane et al., "Job Design under Lean Manufacturing and Its Impact on Employee Outcomes," *Organizational Psychology Review* 3, no. 1 (2013): 41–61.

41. A. Shinnar et al., "Survey of Ergonomic Features of Supermarket Cash Registers," *International Journal of Industrial Ergonomics* 34, no. 6 (2004): 535–41; V. O'Connell, "Stores Count Seconds to Trim Labor Costs," *Wall Street Journal,* November 13, 2008; A. Kihlstedt and G.M. Hägg, "Checkout Cashier Work and Counter Design—Video Movement Analysis, Musculoskeletal Disorders and Customer Interaction," *International Journal of Industrial Ergonomics* 41, no. 3 (2011): 201–07; "One Checkout Item Every Three Seconds," *Mail Online* (London), July 8, 2012. Average scanning times vary considerably with the scanning technology, product standardization, and ergonomic design of the cashier station.

42. S. Leroy, "Why Is It So Hard to Do My Work? The Challenge of Attention Residue When Switching between Work Tasks," *Organizational Behavior and Human Decision Processes* 109 (2009): 168–81; S. Leroy and T.M. Glomb, "Tasks Interrupted: How Anticipating Time Pressure on Resumption of an Interrupted Task Causes Attention Residue and Low Performance on Interrupting Tasks and How a 'Ready-to-Resume' Plan Mitigates the Effects," *Organization Science* 29 (2018): 380–97.

43. H. Fayol, *General and Industrial Management,* trans. C. Storrs (London, UK: Pitman, 1949); E.E. Lawler III, *Motivation in Work Organizations* (Monterey, CA: Brooks/Cole, 1973), Chap. 7; M.A. Campion, "Ability Requirement Implications of Job Design: An Interdisciplinary Perspective," *Personnel Psychology* 42 (1989): 1–24.

44. A. Smith, *An Inquiry into the Nature and Causes of the Wealth of Nations,* 1st ed., 2 vols. (London: W. Strahan and T. Cadell, 1776), pp. 6–7. Although Smith's general premise is true in most cases, the estimates he provided were speculated, not empirically tested. He even suggested that the 10 pin makers couldn't complete one pin per day, but he also stipulated that is "without any of them having been educated to this peculiar business."

45. F.W. Taylor, *The Principles of Scientific Management* (New York: Harper & Row, 1911); R. Kanigel, *The One Best Way: Frederick Winslow Taylor and the Enigma of Efficiency* (New York: Viking, 1997); M. Derksen, "Turning Men into Machines? Scientific Management, Industrial Psychology, and the 'Human Factor,'" *Journal of the History of the Behavioral Sciences* 50, no. 2 (2014): 148–65.

46. W.F. Dowling, "Job Redesign on the Assembly Line: Farewell to Blue-Collar Blues?," *Organizational Dynamics* (1973): 51–67; J.A. Häusser et al., "Experimental Evidence for the Effects of Task Repetitiveness on Mental Strain and Objective Work Performance," *Journal of Organizational Behavior* 35 (2014): 705–21; E.A.J. van Hooft and M.L.M. van Hooff, "The State of Boredom: Frustrating or Depressing?," *Motivation and Emotion* 42 (2018): 931–46; W. Han et al., "Assessing the Brain 'on the Line': An Ecologically-Valid Assessment of the Impact of Repetitive Assembly Line Work on Hemodynamic Response and Fine Motor Control Using FNIRS," *Brain and Cognition* 136 (2019): 103613, https://doi.org/10.1016/j.bandc.2019.103613.

47. R. Moorhead, "Lawyer Specialization–Managing the Professional Paradox," *Law & Policy* 32, no. 2 (2010): 226–59.

48. J.R. Hackman and E.E. Lawler, "Employee Reactions to Job Characteristics," *Journal of Applied Psychology* 55, no. 3 (1971): 259–86; J.R. Hackman and G.R. Oldham, "The Job Diagnostic Survey: An Instrument for the Diagnosis of Jobs and the Evaluation of Job Redesign Projects" (New Haven, Conn.: Dept. of Administrative Sciences, Yale University, May 1974); J.R. Hackman and G.R. Oldham, "Motivation through the Design of Work: Test of a Theory," *Organizational Behavior and Human Performance* 16, no. 2 (1976): 250–79; J. R. Hackman and G. Oldham, *Work Redesign* (Reading, MA: Addison-Wesley, 1980).

49. R.W. Buell, T. Kim, and C.-J. Tsay, "Creating Reciprocal Value Through Operational Transparency," *Management Science* 63 (2017): 1673–95; R.W. Buell, "Operational Transparency," *Harvard Business Review* 97(March-April 2019): 102–13.

50. Based on information in: D.M. Cable, *Alive at Work: The Neuroscience of Helping Your People Love What They Do* (Boston: Harvard Business Review Press, 2018), Chap. 9.

51. M. Gagné and D. Bhave, "Autonomy in the Workplace: An Essential Ingredient to Employee Engagement and Well-Being in Every Culture," in *Human Autonomy in Cross-Cultural Context,* ed. V.I. Chirkov, R.M. Ryan, and K.M. Sheldon (Springer Netherlands, 2011), 163–87; E.L. Deci and M.R. Ryan, "The Importance of Universal Psychological Needs for Understanding Motivation in the Workplace," in *The Oxford Handbook of Work Engagement, Motivation, and Self-Determination Theory,* ed. M. Gagne (New York: Oxford University Press, 2014), 13–32. S.I. Di Domenico and R.M. Ryan, "The Emerging Neuroscience of Intrinsic Motivation: A New Frontier in Self-Determination Research," *Frontiers in Human Neuroscience* 11 (2017), https://doi.org/10.3389/fnhum.2017.00145.

52. Maslow introduced or popularized the notion of "growth" to human motivation, and his writing suggests that it is the same as self-actualization. However, a few others suggest that "growth need strength" in the Hackman/Oldham model is a permanent (trait) characteristic. see: A.H. Maslow, *Motivation and Personality* (New York: Harper & Row, 1954); J.B. Miner, *Organizational Behavior: Integrated Theory Development and the Role of the Unconscious,* vol. 6 (Armonk, N.Y.: M.E. Sharpe, 2011), 32-33.

65. R.B. Tiegs, L.E. Tetrick, and Y. Fried, "Growth Need Strength and Context Satisfactions as Moderators of the Relations of the Job Characteristics Model," *Journal of Management* 18, no. 3 (1992): 575–93; J.E. Champoux, "A Multivariate Test of the Job Characteristics Theory of Work Motivation," *Journal of Organizational Behavior* 12, no. 5 (1991): 431–46.

54. G.R. Oldham and J.R. Hackman, "Not What It Was and Not What It Will Be: The Future of Job Design Research," *Journal of Organizational*

Behavior 31, no. 2–3 (2010): 463–79; A.M. Grant, Y. Fried, and T. Juillerat, "Work Matters: Job Design in Classic and Contemporary Perspectives," in *APA Handbook of Industrial and Organizational Psychology,* ed. S. Zedeck (Washington, DC: American Psychological Association, 2011), 417–53. A very early version of the job characteristics model included social interaction but was later excluded.

55. C. Perrow, "A Framework for the Comparative Analysis of Organizations," *American Sociological Review* 32 (1967): 194–208; R.L. Daft and N.B. Macintosh, "A Tentative Exploration into the Amount and Equivocality of Information Processing in Organizational Work Units," *Administrative Science Quarterly* 26 (1981): 207–24. Job analyzability and variability are embedded in "job complexity," but the latter is a much broader concept that has suffered from many diverse interpretations. See P. Liu and Z. Li, "Task Complexity: A Review and Conceptualization Framework," *International Journal of Industrial Ergonomics* 42 (2012): 553–68; S.Y. Sung, A. Antefelt, and J.N. Choi, "Dual Effects of Job Complexity on Proactive and Responsive Creativity: Moderating Role of Employee Ambiguity Tolerance," *Group & Organization Management* 42 (2017): 388–418.

56. M.M. Coşgel and T.J. Miceli, "Job Rotation: Cost, Benefits, and Stylized Facts," *Journal of Institutional and Theoretical Economics* 155 (1999): 301–20; D. Rissén et al., "Psychophysiological Stress Reactions, Trapezius Muscle Activity, and Neck and Shoulder Pain among Female Cashiers before and after Introduction of Job Rotation," *Work & Stress* 16, no. 2 (2002): 127–37; S. Gallagher et al., "Job Rotation as a Technique for the Control of MSDs: A Fatigue Failure Perspective," *Proceedings of the Human Factors and Ergonomics Society Annual Meeting* 61 (September 1, 2017): 993–94; R.S. Padula et al., "Job Rotation Designed to Prevent Musculoskeletal Disorders and Control Risk in Manufacturing Industries: A Systematic Review," *Applied Ergonomics* 58 (2017): 386–97; S. Grochowski, "Aldergrove Packaging Plant Gets Major Safety Nod," *Aldergrove Star (B.C.),* October 24, 2019.

57. G. Jones, "Anything but Burnt Out," *Smart Business Cleveland,* March 2013, 24.

58. Job enlargement, as defined here, refers to "horizontal job enlargement/loading" which involves increasing the number and variety of related tasks assigned to an employee. This differs from "vertical job enlargement/loading" which assigns not only more tasks but also more autonomy and responsibility to the employee performing those tasks. The latter is now considered a form of job enrichment. For early research on job enlargement, see: C. Argyris, *Personality and Organization: The Conflict between System and the Individual* (New York: Harper, 1957), 177–81; K.H. Chung and M.F. Ross, "Differences in Motivational Properties between Job Enlargement and Job Enrichment," *Academy of Management Review* 2, no. 1 (1977): 113–22.

59. M.D. Kilbridge, "Reduced Costs Through Job Enlargement: A Case," *The Journal of Business* 33, no. 4 (1960): 357–62; L.E. Davis, "The Design of Jobs," *Industrial Relations* 6, no. 1 (1966): 21–45; W.E. Reif and P.P. Schoderbek, "Job Enlargement: Antidote to Apathy," *Human Resource Management* 5, no. 1 (1966): 16-23. Recent job enlargement studies are mainly between-person correlational analyses, whereas early research more richly studied temporal attitude and behavioural changes from job enlargement interventions. Some recent studies that investigate job enlargement include: J.A. Häusser et al., "Experimental Evidence for the Effects of Task Repetitiveness on Mental Strain and Objective Work Performance," *Journal of Organizational Behavior* 35, no. 5 (2014): 705–21, https://doi.org/10.1002/job.1920; F. Fraccaroli et al., "Who Benefits from More Tasks? Older versus Younger Workers," *Journal of Managerial Psychology* 29, no. 5 (2014): 508–23, https://doi.org/10.1108/JMP-12-2012-0381; D. Berdicchia, G. Masino, and F. Nicolli, "Job Enlargement, Job Crafting and the Moderating Role of Self-Competence," *Journal of Managerial Psychology* 31, no. 2 (2016): 318–30, https://doi.org/10.1108/JMP-01-2014-0019.

60. M.A. Campion and C.L. McClelland, "Follow-Up and Extension of the Interdisciplinary Costs and Benefits of Enlarged Jobs," *Journal of Applied Psychology* 78 (1993): 339–51; N.G. Dodd and D.C. Ganster, "The Interactive Effects of Variety, Autonomy, and Feedback on Attitudes and Performance," *Journal of Organizational Behavior* 17 (1996): 329–47.

61. J.R. Hackman et al., "A New Strategy for Job Enrichment," *California Management Review* 17, no. 4 (1975): 57–71; R.W. Griffin, *Task Design: An Integrative Approach* (Glenview, IL: Scott Foresman, 1982).

62. E. Frauenheim, "Making the Call for Themselves," *Workforce Management,* August 2010, 16; D. Pierson, "Why Dollar Shave Club Invests in Unscripted Customer Service," *Los Angeles Times,* September 26, 2015.

63. P.E. Spector and S.M. Jex, "Relations of Job Characteristics from Multiple Data Sources with Employee Affect, Absence, Turnover Intentions, and Health," *Journal of Applied Psychology* 76 (1991): 46–53; P. Osterman, "How Common Is Workplace Transformation and Who Adopts It?," *Industrial and Labor Relations Review* 47 (1994): 173–88; R. Saavedra and S.K. Kwun, "Affective States in Job Characteristics Theory," *Journal of Organizational Behavior* 21 (2000): 131–46.

73. J.R. Hackman and G. Oldham, *Work Redesign* (Reading, MA: Addison-Wesley, 1980), 137–38.

65. This definition is based mostly on G.M. Spreitzer and R.E. Quinn, *A Company of Leaders: Five Disciplines for Unleashing the Power in Your Workforce* (San Francisco, CA: Jossey-Bass, 2001). Also see: R. Forrester, "Empowerment: Rejuvenating a Potent Idea," *Academy of Management Executive* 14 (2000): 67–80; S.T. Menon, "Employee Empowerment: An Integrative Psychological Approach," *Applied Psychology: An International Review* 50 (2001): 153–80.

66. Psychological and structural empowerment have separate origins but studies have shown that the structural conditions predict psychological empowerment. Our approach is to define empowerment as a psychological state and to view "structural empowerment" as various antecedents of empowerment. see: M.T. Maynard, L.L. Gilson, and J.E. Mathieu, "Empowerment—Fad or Fab? A Multilevel Review of the Past Two Decades of Research," *Journal of Management* 38, no. 4 (2012): 1231–81, https://doi.org/10.1177/0149206312438773; S.E. Abel and M.W. Hand, "Exploring, Defining, and Illustrating a Concept: Structural and Psychological Empowerment in the Workplace," *Nursing Forum* 53, no. 4 (2018): 579–84, https://doi.org/10.1111/nuf.12289.

67. Y. Melhem, "The Antecedents of Customer-Contact Employees' Empowerment," *Employee Relations* 26, no. 1/2 (2004): 72–93; M.T. Maynard, L.L. Gilson, and J.E. Mathieu, "Empowerment—Fad or Fab? A Multilevel Review of the Past Two Decades of Research," *Journal of Management* 38, no. 4 (2012): 1231–81.

68. X. Zhang and K.M. Bartol, "Linking Empowering Leadership and Employee Creativity: The Influence of Psychological Empowerment, Intrinsic Motivation, and Creative Process Engagement," *Academy of Management Journal* 53, no. 1 (2010): 107–28; S. Pentareddy and L. Suganthi, "Building Affective Commitment through Job Characteristics, Leadership and Empowerment," *Journal of Management & Organization* 21, no. 03 (2015): 307–20.

69. P.N. Sharma and B.L. Kirkman, "Leveraging Leaders: A Literature Review and Future Lines of Inquiry for Empowering Leadership Research," *Group & Organization Management* 40, no. 2 (2015): 193–237; D.M. Sumpter, C.B. Gibson, and C. Porath, "Act Expediently, with Autonomy: Vicarious Learning, Empowered Behaviors, and Performance," *Journal of Business and Psychology* 32, no. 2 (2017): 131–45, https://doi.org/10.1007/s10869-016-9440-2; M. Leyer, A. Richter, and M. Steinhüser, "'Power to the Workers': Empowering Shop Floor Workers with Worker-Centric Digital Designs," *International Journal of Operations & Production Management* 39, no. 1 (2018): 24–42, https://doi.org/10.1108/IJOPM-05-2017-0294.

70. Gazzoli, M. Hancer, and Y. Park, "The Role and Effect of Job Satisfaction and Empowerment on Customers' Perception of Service Quality: A Study in the Restaurant Industry," *Journal of Hospitality & Tourism Research* 34, no. 1 (2010): 56–77; K. BeomCheol, L. Erwin, and M. Simon, "Consequences of Empowerment among Restaurant Servers: Helping Behaviors and Average Check Size," *Management Decision* 51, no. 4 (2013): 781–94.

71. W. Ke and P. Zhang, "Effects of Empowerment on Performance in Open-Source Software Projects," *IEEE Transactions on Engineering Management* 58, no. 2 (2011): 334–46; H. Fock et al., "Moderation Effects of Power Distance on the Relationship between Types of Empowerment and Employee Satisfaction," *Journal of Cross-Cultural Psychology* 44, no. 2 (2013): 281–98; M.M. Tuuli et al., "Individual-Level Antecedents of Psychological Empowerment," *Journal of Management in Engineering* 31, no. 2 (2015): 04014036.

72. "Bosses Love Team Workers," *Lancashire Evening Post (U.K.),* 25 May 2006; O. Keogh, "'Our Biggest Asset Is Not Code. It's People'," *Irish Times,* 3 June 2016, 7.

73. C.C. Manz, "Self-Leadership: Toward an Expanded Theory of Self-Influence Processes in Organizations," *Academy of Management Review* 11 (1986): 585–600; G.L. Stewart, S.H. Courtright, and C.C. Manz, "Self-Leadership: A Multilevel Review," *Journal of Management* 37, no. 1 (2011): 185–222; C.C. Manz, "Taking the Self-Leadership High Road: Smooth Surface or Potholes Ahead?," *Academy of Management Perspectives* 29, no. 1 (2015): 132–51; C.P. Neck, C.C. Manz, and J.D.

Houghton, *Self-Leadership: The Definitive Guide to Personal Excellence* (Thousand Oaks, Calif.: SAGE Publications, 2019).

74. C.C. Manz, "Self-Leadership: Toward an Expanded Theory of Self-Influence Processes in Organizations," *Academy of Management Review* 11 (1986): 585–600; C.C. Manz and C. Neck, *Mastering Self-Leadership*, 3rd ed. (Upper Saddle River, NJ: Prentice Hall, 2004); C.P. Neck and J.D. Houghton, "Two Decades of Self-Leadership Theory and Research," *Journal of Managerial Psychology* 21, no. 4 (2006): 270–95.

75. O.J. Strickland and M. Galimba, "Managing Time: The Effects of Personal Goal Setting on Resource Allocation Strategy and Task Performance," *Journal of Psychology* 135 (2001): 357–67.

76. R.M. Duncan and J.A. Cheyne, "Incidence and Functions of Self-Reported Private Speech in Young Adults: A Self-Verbalization Questionnaire," *Canadian Journal of Behavioral Science* 31 (1999): 133–36.

77. A. Hatzigeorgiadis et al., "Mechanisms Underlying the Self-Talk–Performance Relationship: The Effects of Motivational Self-Talk on Self-Confidence and Anxiety," *Psychology of Sport and Exercise* 10 (2009): 186–92; S.G. Rogelberg et al., "The Executive Mind: Leader Self-Talk, Effectiveness and Strain," *Journal of Managerial Psychology* 28, no. 1–2 (2013): 183–201; A.T. Latinjak et al., "Speaking Clearly . . . 10 Years on: The Case for an Integrative Perspective of Self-Talk in Sport," *Sport, Exercise, and Performance Psychology* 8, no. 4 (2019): 353–67, https://doi.org/10.1037/spy0000160.

78. Mental imagery has recently become an important instrument in therapies to correct maladaptive behavior. See: J. Pearson et al., "Mental Imagery: Functional Mechanisms and Clinical Applications," *Trends in Cognitive Sciences* 19, no. 10 (2015): 590–602, https://doi.org/10.1016/j.tics.2015.08.003; S.E. Blackwell, "Mental Imagery: From Basic Research to Clinical Practice.," *Journal of Psychotherapy Integration*, January 22, 2018, https://doi.org/10.1037/int0000108.

79. J.E. Driscoll, C. Copper, and A. Moran, "Does Mental Practice Enhance Performance?," *Journal of Applied Psychology* 79 (1994): 481–92; C.P. Neck, G.L. Stewart, and C.C. Manz, "Thought Self-Leadership as a Framework for Enhancing the Performance of Performance Appraisers," *Journal of Applied Behavioral Science* 31 (1995): 278–302. Some research separates mental imagery from mental practice, whereas most studies combine both into one concept.

80. C. O'Donnell et al., "The Role of Mental Imagery in Mood Amplification: An Investigation across Subclinical Features of Bipolar Disorders," *Cortex* 105 (2018): 104–17, https://doi.org/10.1016/j.cortex.2017.08.010; F. Renner et al., "Mental Imagery as a 'Motivational Amplifier' to Promote Activities," *Behaviour Research and Therapy* 114 (2019): 51–59, https://doi.org/10.1016/j.brat.2019.02.002.

81. A. Joyce, "Office Perks: Re-Energize to Get through the Blahs," *Washington Post*, 28 August 2005, F05.

82. A. Wrzesniewski and J.E. Dutton, "Crafting a Job: Revisioning Employees as Active Crafters of Their Work," *Academy of Management Review* 26(2001): 179–201; H.J. Gordon et al., "Individual Job Redesign: Job Crafting Interventions in Healthcare," *Journal of Vocational Behavior* 104 (2018): 98–114, https://doi.org/10.1016/j.jvb.2017.07.002; A. Lazazzara, M. Tims, and D. de Gennaro, "The Process of Reinventing a Job: A Meta–Synthesis of Qualitative Job Crafting Research," *Journal of Vocational Behavior* (2019) https://doi.org/10.1016/j.jvb.2019.01.001.

83. B. Harkin et al., "Does Monitoring Goal Progress Promote Goal Attainment? A Meta-Analysis of the Experimental Evidence," *Psychological Bulletin* 142, no. 2 (2016): 198–229.

84. M.I. Bopp, S.J. Glynn, and R.A. Henning, *Self-Management of Performance Feedback During Computer-Based Work by Individuals and Two- Person Work Teams*, Paper presented at the APANIOSH conference, (March 1999).

85. M. Inzlicht, B.D. Bartholow, and J.B. Hirsh, "Emotional Foundations of Cognitive Control," *Trends in Cognitive Sciences* 19, no. 3 (2015): 126–32; A.L. Duckworth, T.S. Gendler, and J.J. Gross, "Situational Strategies for Self-Control," *Perspectives on Psychological Science* 11, no. 1 (2016): 35–55.

86. L. Morin and G. Latham, "The Effect of Mental Practice and Goal Setting as a Transfer of Training Intervention on Supervisors' Self-Efficacy and Communication Skills: An Exploratory Study," *Applied Psychology: An International Review* 49 (2000): 566–78; J.S. Hickman and E.S. Geller, "A Safety Self-Management Intervention for Mining Operations," *Journal of Safety Research* 34 (2003): 299–308; N.G. Panagopoulos and J. Ogilvie, "Can Salespeople Lead Themselves? Thought Self-Leadership Strategies and Their Influence on Sales Performance," *Industrial Marketing Management* 47 (2015): 190–203; G. Lucke and M. Furtner, "Soldiers Lead Themselves to More Success: A Self-Leadership Intervention Study," *Military Psychology* 27, no. 5 (2015): 311–24.

87. J. Ho and P.L. Nesbit, "Self-Leadership in a Chinese Context: Work Outcomes and the Moderating Role of Job Autonomy," *Group & Organization Management* 39, no. 4 (2014): 389–415; J.D. Houghton, A. Carnes, and C.N. Ellison, "A Cross-Cultural Examination of Self-Leadership: Testing for Measurement Invariance across Four Cultures," *Journal of Leadership & Organizational Studies* 21, no. 4 (2014): 414–30.

88. J. Bauman, "The Gold Medal Mind," *Psychology Today* 33 (2000): 62–69; R.A. Hamilton, D. Scott, and M.P. MacDougall, "Assessing the Effectiveness of Self-Talk Interventions on Endurance Performance," *Journal of Applied Sport Psychology* 19, no. 2 (2007): 226–39. J.L. Van Raalte, A. Vincent, and B.W. Brewer, "Self-Talk: Review and Sport-Specific Model," *Psychology of Sport and Exercise* 22 (January 1, 2016): 139–48, https://doi.org/10.1016/j.psychsport.2015.08.004.

89. J. Houghton et al., "The Relationship between Self-Leadership and Personality: A Comparison of Hierarchical Factor Structures," *Journal of Managerial Psychology* 19, no. 4 (2004): 427–41; R.W. Renn, D.G. Allen, and T.M. Huning, "Empirical Examination of the Individual-Level Personality-Based Theory of Self-Management Failure," *Journal of Organizational Behavior* 32, no. 1 (2011): 25–43.

90. J.D. Houghton and S.K. Yoho, "Toward a Contingency Model of Leadership and Psychological Empowerment: When Should Self-Leadership Be Encouraged?," *Journal of Leadership & Organizational Studies* 11, no. 4 (2005): 65–83; J.D. Houghton and D.L. Jinkerson, "Constructive Thought Strategies and Job Satisfaction: A Preliminary Examination," *Journal of Business and Psychology* 22 (2007): 45–53.

CHAPTER 7

1. C. Letson, "How Atlantic Lottery Corporation Thinks Like a Startup," *Huddle Today,* July 19, 2016; I. Montgomery, "Jean Marc Landry, Director of Customer Innovation, Atlantic Lottery," *Medium,* August 15, 2016; B. LaFleur, "Julie LeBlanc Steeves: Are We There Yet? Atlantic Lottery's Innovation Catalyst Journey," *La Fleur's Lottery World* (blog and video), July 18, 2017, https://lafleurs.com/video/conference/2017/07/18/julie-leblanc-steeves-are-we-there-yet-atlantic-lotterys-innovation-catalyst-journey/; "Atlantic Lottery Corporation Hits the Jackpot in Halifax's Innovation District," *Halifax Chronicle-Herald,* February 16, 2019; D. Chafe and S. Gough, "Atlantic Business Magazine's 2019 Top 50 CEOs," *Atlantic Business Magazine,* May 12, 2019.

2. F.A. Shull Jr., A.L. Delbecq, and L.L. Cummings, *Organizational Decision Making* (New York: McGraw Hill, 1970), p. 31.

3. Harvard Business School, *Decision Making: 5 Steps to Better Results* (Cambridge, MA: Harvard Business School Press 2006), Chap. 1; D. Baltzly, "Stoicism" (*Stanford Encyclopedia of Philosophy,* 2008), http://plato.stanford.edu/entries/stoicism/ (accessed March 30, 2008); I. Pownall, *Effective Management Decision Making* (Holstebro, DK: Ventus Publishing, 2012), Chap. 1; C.P. Webel, *The Politics of Rationality: Reason through Occidental History* (New York: Routledge, 2014), Chaps. 1 and 3.

4. J.G. March and H.A. Simon, *Organizations* (New York: Wiley, 1958); K. Manktelow, *Thinking and Reasoning: An Introduction to the Psychology of Reason, Judgment and Decision Making* (Hoboken, NJ: Taylor & Francis, 2012), Chap. 8; F. Lieder and T.L. Griffiths, "Strategy Selection as Rational Metareasoning," *Psychological Review* 124 (2017): 762–94; R.G. O'Connell et al., "Bridging Neural and Computational Viewpoints on Perceptual Decision-Making," *Trends in Neurosciences* 41 (2018): 838–52.

5. This example differs from the game theory model in classic economic theory. In classic economic theory, the "outcomes" are alternatives, so the probabilities must add up to 1.0. For example, if there is a 30 percent probability that your company will choose supplier A, then there is necessarily a 70 percent chance that the company will choose supplier B (if those are the only choices). The current example is the classic expectancy-valence model, which calculates each alternative's composite valence from a set of criteria (outcomes) associated with all alternatives. These probabilities do not add up to 1.0 because they refer to entities that are not perfectly correlated (e.g., both suppliers might have a high probability of offering low prices).

6. These criteria are commonly used in supplier selection modelling. See, for example, H. Karimi and A. Rezaeinia, "Supplier Selection Using

Revised Multi-Segment Goal Programming Model," *International Journal of Advanced Manufacturing Technology* 70, no. 5/8 (2014): 1227–34.

7. This model is adapted from several sources, including H.A. Simon, *The New Science of Management Decision* (New York: Harper & Row, 1960); H. Mintzberg, D. Raisinghani, and A. Théorét, "The Structure of 'Unstructured' Decision Processes," *Administrative Science Quarterly* 21 (1976): 246–75; W.C. Wedley and R.H.G. Field, "A Predecision Support System," *Academy of Management Review* 9 (1984): 696–703.

8. P.F. Drucker, *The Practice of Management* (New York: Harper & Brothers, 1954), 353–57; B.M. Bass, *Organizational Decision Making* (Homewood, IL: Irwin, 1983), Chap. 3; H.E. Posen et al., "Renewing Research on Problemistic Search—A Review and Research Agenda," *Academy of Management Annals* 12 (2017): 208–51.

9. J.G. March and H.A. Simon, *Organizations* (New York: John Wiley & Sons, 1958), Chap. 7; L.R. Beach and T.R. Mitchell, "A Contingency Model for the Selection of Decision Strategies," *Academy of Management Review* 3 (1978): 439–49; I.L. Janis, *Crucial Decisions* (New York: Free Press, 1989), 35–37; W. Zhongtuo, "Meta-Decision Making: Concepts and Paradigm," *Systematic Practice and Action Research* 13, no. 1 (2000): 111–15; Y.-L. Boureau, P. Sokol-Hessner, and N.D. Daw, "Deciding How To Decide: Self-Control and Meta-Decision Making," *Trends in Cognitive Sciences* 19, no. 11 (2015): 700–710, https://doi.org/10.1016/j.tics.2015.08.013; F. Lieder and T.L. Griffiths, "Strategy Selection as Rational Metareasoning," *Psychological Review* 124, no. 6 (2017): 762–94, https://doi.org/10.1037/rev0000075.

10. J. de Jonge, *Rethinking Rational Choice Theory: A Companion on Rational and Moral Action* (Basingstoke: Palgrave Macmillan, 2011).

11. There are a few variations of this quotation, and no direct evidence that Einstein actually offered this advice. Among the earliest citations is a similar quotation allegedly uttered by the head of industrial engineering at Yale University in the 1940s or 1950s. See: R.E. Finley and H.R. Ziobro, eds., *The Manufacturing Man and His Job* (New York: American Management Association, 1966), 18; "I Would Spend 55 Minutes Defining the Problem and Then Five Minutes Solving It—Quote Investigator," May 22, 2014, accessed April 17, 2019, https://quoteinvestigator.com/2014/05/22/solve/.

12. M.A. Roberto, *Know What You Don't Know: How Great Leaders Prevent Problems before They Happen* (Saddle River, NJ: Wharton School Publishing, 2009); M. Meckler and K. Boal, "Decision Errors, Organizational Iatrogenesis and Errors of the 7th Kind," *Academy of Management Perspectives*, October 15, 2018, https://doi.org/10.5465/amp.2017.0144.

13. N.P. Repenning, D. Kieffer, and T. Astor, "The Most Underrated Skill in Management," *MIT Sloan Management Review* 58, no. 3 (2017): 39–48; G. Bhardwaj et al., "Alleviating the Plunging-In Bias, Elevating Strategic Problem-Solving," *Academy of Management Learning & Education* 17 (2018): 279–301.

14. E. Glazer, J.S. Lublin, and D. Mattioli, "Penney Backfires on Ackman," *The Wall Street Journal,* April 10, 2013; D. Mattiolo, "For Penney's

Heralded Boss, the Sine Is Off the Apple," *Wall Street Journal,* February 25, 2013, A1; N. Tichy, *Succession: Mastering the Make-or-Break Process of Leadership Transition* (New York: Portfolio/Penguin, 2014), Chap. 7.

15. P.C. Nutt, *Why Decisions Fail* (San Francisco: Berrett-Koehler, 2002); S. Finkelstein, *Why Smart Executives Fail* (New York: Viking, 2003); G. Bhardwaj et al., "Alleviating the Plunging-In Bias, Elevating Strategic Problem-Solving," *Academy of Management Learning & Education* 17, no. 3 (2018): 279–301, https://doi.org/10.5465/amle.2017.0168.

16. P.C. Nutt, "Framing Strategic Decisions," *Organization Science* 9 (1998): 195–216; S. Kaplan, "Framing Contests: Strategy Making Under Uncertainty," *Organization Science* 19 (2008): 729–52.

17. L.B. Myers, "The Importance of the Repressive Coping Style: Findings from 30 Years of Research," *Anxiety, Stress & Coping* 23, no. 1 (2010): 3–17; C. MacLeod, "Anxiety-Linked Attentional Bias: Backward Glances and Future Glimpses," *Cognition and Emotion* 33, no. 1 (2019): 139–45, https://doi.org/10.1080/02699931.2018.1551190; J. Weinberger and V. Stoycheva, *The Unconscious: Theory, Research, and Clinical Implications* (Guilford Publications, 2020), Chap. 5.

18. M.S. Gary and R.E. Wood, "Mental Models, Decision Rules, and Performance Heterogeneity," *Strategic Management Journal* 32 (2011): 569–94.

19. Various sources suggest that the phrase "divine discontent" may have originated with unspecified writing by either of the poets John Milton (1608–1674) or Alexander Pope (1688–1744). Alternatively, it may have been inspired later based on John Stuart Mill's famous quotation in *Utilitarianism* (1863): "It is better to be a human being dissatisfied than a pig satisfied; better to be Socrates dissatisfied than a fool satisfied." Divine discontent became a particularly popular phrase for a couple of decades from the 1890s. It appeared in various books (e.g., Robert Bury, *The Symposium of Plato,* 1909, xlii) as well as in articles in a wide array of magazines and newspapers, including *The Athenaeum Journal* (1896), *Punch Magazine* (1894), *Edinburgh Review* (1900), and frequently in *The Independent* (New York).

20. H.A. Simon, *Administrative Behavior,* 2nd ed. (New York: Free Press, 1957); H.A. Simon, "Rational Decision Making in Business Organizations," *American Economic Review* 69 (1979): 493–513; M. Cristofaro, "Herbert Simon's Bounded Rationality: Its Historical Evolution in Management and Cross-Fertilizing Contribution," *Journal of Management History* 23 (2017): 170–90.

21. Here are a few of the prominent studies among the dozens that demonstrate imperfect rationality in decision making: E. Witte, N. Joost, and A.L. Thimm, "Field Research on Complex Decision-Making Processes—The Phase Theorem," *International Studies of Management & Organization* 2 (1972): 156–82; H. Mintzberg, D. Raisinghani, and A. Théorêt, "The Structure of 'Unstructured' Decision Processes," *Administrative Science Quarterly* 21 (1976): 246–75; T. Gilovich, D. Griffin, and D. Kahneman, *Heuristics and Biases: The Psychology of Intuitive Judgment* (Cambridge: Cambridge University Press, 2002); S.

Finkelstein, *Why Smart Executives Fail: And What You Can Learn from Their Mistakes* (New York: Penguin, 2004).

22. M.D. Cohen, J.G. March, and J.P. Olsen, "A Garbage Can Model of Organizational Choice," *Administrative Science Quarterly* 17 (1972): 1–25; R.A. Ferrer, E. Orehek, and L.S. Padgett, "Goal Conflict When Making Decisions for Others," *Journal of Experimental Social Psychology* 78 (2018): 93–103.

23. H. A. Simon, *Administrative Behavior,* 2nd ed. (New York: Free Press, 1957), xxv, 80–84.

24. Recent studies refer to implicit favourite as "pre-decision information distortion" and the "coherence effect," but these theories are essentially implicit favourite bias. P.O. Soelberg, "Unprogrammed Decision Making," *Industrial Management Review* 8 (1967): 19–29; K.H. Ehrhart and J.C. Ziegert, "Why Are Individuals Attracted to Organizations?," *Journal of Management* 31 (2005): 901–19; J.E. Russo, "The Predecisional Distortion of Information," in *Neuroeconomics, Judgment, and Decision Making,* ed. E.A. Wilhelms and V.F. Reyna, *Frontiers of Cognitive Psychology* (New York: Psychology Press, 2015), 91–110.

25. S. Sacchi and M. Burigo, "Strategies in the Information Search Process: Interaction among Task Structure, Knowledge, and Source," *Journal of General Psychology* 135 (2008): 252–70.

26. Milton Rokeach famously stated, "Life is ipsa-tive, because decisions in everyday life are inherently and phenomenologically ipsative decisions." *Ipsative* is a process of comparing (usually two) things side-by-side. M. Rokeach, "Inducing Changes and Stability in Belief Systems and Personality Structures," *Journal of Social Issues* 41 (1985): 153–71.

27. R.S. Nickerson, "Confirmation Bias: A Ubiquitous Phenomenon in Many Guises," *Review of General Psychology* 2, no. 2 (1998): 175–220; O. Svenson, I. Salo, and T. Lindholm, "Post-Decision Consolidation and Distortion of Facts," *Judgment and Decision Making* 4, no. 5 (2009): 397–407; A.M. Scherer, P.D. Windschitl, and A.R. Smith, "Hope to Be Right: Biased Information Seeking Following Arbitrary and Informed Predictions," *Journal of Experimental Social Psychology* 49, no. 1 (2013): 106–12.

28. A. L. Brownstein, "Biased Predecision Processing," *Psychological Bulletin* 129 (2003): 545–68; M. Nurek, O. Kostopoulou, and Y. Hagmayer, "Predecisional Information Distortion in Physicians' Diagnostic Judgments: Strengthening a Leading Hypothesis or Weakening Its Competitor?," *Judgment and Decision Making* 9 (2014): 572–85; D. Simon, D. Stenstrom, and S. Read, "The Coherence Effect: Blending Cold and Hot Cognitions," *Journal of Personality & Social Psychology* 109 (2015): 369–94; M. L. DeKay, "Predecisional Information Distortion and the Self-Fulfilling Prophecy of Early Preferences in Choice," *Current Directions in Psychological Science* 24 (2015): 405–11.

29. T. Gilovich, D. Griffin, and D. Kahneman, *Heuristics and Biases: The Psychology of Intuitive Judgment* (Cambridge: Cambridge University Press, 2002); D. Kahneman, "Maps of Bounded Rationality: Psychology for Behavioral Economics," *American Economic Review* 93

(2003): 1449–75; J.S. Blumenthal-Barby and H. Krieger, "Cognitive Biases and Heuristics in Medical Decision Making: A Critical Review Using a Systematic Search Strategy," *Medical Decision Making* 35 (2015): 539–57; M. Richie and S.A. Josephson, "Quantifying Heuristic Bias: Anchoring, Availability, and Representativeness," *Teaching and Learning in Medicine* 30 (2018): 67–75.

30. A. Tversky and D. Kahneman, "Judgment under Uncertainty: Heuristics and Biases," *Science* 185 (1974): 1124–31; I. Ritov, "Anchoring in Simulated Competitive Market Negotiation," *Organizational Behavior and Human Decision Processes* 67 (1996): 16; J.D. Jasper and S.D. Christman, "A Neuropsychological Dimension for Anchoring Effects," *Journal of Behavioral Decision Making* 18 (2005): 343–69; M.H. Jung, H. Perfecto, and L.D. Nelson, "Anchoring in Payment: Evaluating a Judgmental Heuristic in Field Experimental Settings," *Journal of Marketing Research* 53 (2016): 354–68.

31. A. Tversky and D. Kahneman, "Availability: A Heuristic for Judging Frequency and Probability," *Cognitive Psychology* 5 (1973): 207–32; A. Kudryavtsev, "The Availability Heuristic and Reversals Following Large Stock Price Changes," *Journal of Behavioral Finance* 19 (2018): 159–76.

32. D. Kahneman and A. Tversky, "Subjective Probability: A Judgment of Representativeness," *Cognitive Psychology* 3, no. 3 (1972): 430; S.S. Kulkarni et al., "Defining the Representativeness Heuristic in Trauma Triage: A Retrospective Observational Cohort Study," *PLOS ONE* 14, no. 2 (February 8, 2019): e0212201, https://doi.org/10.1371/journal.pone.0212201.

33. H.A. Simon, "Rational Choice and the Structure of Environments," *Psychological Review* 63 (1956): 129–38; B. Schwartz, "On The Meaning And Measurement Of Maximization," *Judgment and Decision Making* 11 (2016): 126–46.

34. K. Jain, J.N. Bearden, and A. Filipowicz, "Do Maximizers Predict Better Than Satisficers?," *Journal of Behavioral Decision Making* 26, no. 1 (2013): 41–50; W. Mao, "When One Desires Too Much of a Good Thing: The Compromise Effect under Maximizing Tendencies," *Journal of Consumer Psychology* 26, no. 1 (2016): 66–80.

35. S. Botti and S.S. Iyengar, "The Dark Side of Choice: When Choice Impairs Social Welfare," *Journal of Public Policy and Marketing* 25, no. 1 (2006): 24–38; K.D. Vohs et al., "Making Choices Impairs Subsequent Self-Control: A Limited-Resource Account of Decision Making, Self-Regulation, and Active Initiative," *Journal of Personality and Social Psychology* 94, no. 5 (2008): 883–98.

36. S. Iyengar, *The Art of Choosing* (New York: Hachette, 2010), 177–95; A. Chernev, U. Böckenholt, and J. Goodman, "Choice Overload: A Conceptual Review and Meta-Analysis," *Journal of Consumer Psychology* 25 (2015): 333–58.

37. P.C. Nutt, "Search During Decision Making," *European Journal of Operational Research* 160 (2005): 851–76; M.S. Wood, A. McKelvie, and J.M. Haynie, "Making It Personal: Opportunity Individuation and the Shaping of Opportunity Beliefs," *Journal of Business Venturing* 29 (2014): 252–72; Y. Chandra, "A Time-Based Process Model of International Entrepreneurial Opportunity Evaluation," *Journal of International Business Studies* 48 (2017): 423–51.

38. P. Winkielman et al., "Affective Influence on Judgments and Decisions: Moving Towards Core Mechanisms," *Review of General Psychology* 11 (2007): 179–92; J.S. Lerner et al., "Emotion and Decision Making," *Annual Review of Psychology* 66 (2015): 799–823; G. Loewenstein, T. O'Donoghue, and S. Bhatia, "Modeling the Interplay between Affect and Deliberation," *Decision* 2 (2015): 55–81; C.A. Trujillo, "The Complementary Role of Affect-Based and Cognitive Heuristics to Make Decisions under Conditions of Ambivalence and Complexity," *PLOS ONE* 13, no. 11 (November 9, 2018): e0206724, https://doi.org/10.1371/journal.pone.0206724.

39. A. Bechara and A.R. Damasio, "The Somatic Marker Hypothesis: A Neural Theory of Economic Decision," *Games and Economic Behavior* 52 (2005): 336–72; T.S. Saunders and M.J. Buehner, "The Gut Chooses Faster Than the Mind: A Latency Advantage of Affective over Cognitive Decisions," *Quarterly Journal of Experimental Psychology* 66 (2013): 381–88; A. Moors, "Automaticity: Componential, Causal, and Mechanistic Explanations," *Annual Review of Psychology* 67 (2016): 263–87; T. Poppa and A. Bechara, "The Somatic Marker Hypothesis: Revisiting the Role of the 'Body-Loop' in Decision-Making," *Current Opinion in Behavioral Sciences* 19 (2018): 61–66.

40. J.P. Forgas and A.S. Koch, "Mood Effects on Cognition," in *Handbook of Cognition and Emotion,* ed. M.D. Robinson, E.R. Watkins, and E. Harmon-Jones (New York: Guilford, 2013), 231–51; J.M. George and E. Dane, "Affect, Emotion, and Decision Making," *Organizational Behavior and Human Decision Processes,* 136 (2016): 47–55; A. Prinz, V. Bergmann, and J. Wittwer, "Happy but Overconfident: Positive Affect Leads to Inaccurate Metacomprehension," *Cognition and Emotion* 33 (2019): 606–15.

41. D. Miller, *The Icarus Paradox* (New York: HarperBusiness, 1990); D. Miller, "What Happens after Success: The Perils of Excellence," *Journal of Management Studies* 31, no. 3 (1994): 325–68; A.C. Amason and A.C. Mooney, "The Icarus Paradox Revisited: How Strong Performance Sows the Seeds of Dysfunction in Future Strategic Decision-Making," *Strategic Organization* 6, no. 4 (2008): 407–34.

42. M.T. Pham, "The Logic of Feeling," *Journal of Consumer Psychology* 14 (2004): 360–69; N. Schwarz, "Feelings-as-Information Theory," in *Handbook of Theories of Social Psychology,* ed. P. Van Lange, A. Kruglanski, and E.T. Higgins (London: Sage, 2012), 289–308; A.I. Tiba, "Feelings-As-Embodied Information: Studying the Role of Feelings As Images in Emotional Disorders," *Frontiers in Psychology* 9 (2018), https://doi.org/10.3389/fpsyg.2018.00186.

43. O. Behling and N.L. Eckel, "Making Sense out of Intuition," *Academy of Management Executive* 5 (1991): 46–54; R.M. Hogarth, "Intuition: A Challenge for Psychological Research on Decision Making," *Psychological Inquiry* 21 (2010): 338–53; S. Epstein, "Demystifying Intuition: What It Is, What It Does, and How It Does It," *Psychological Inquiry* 21 (2010): 295–312; G.P. Hodgkinson and E. Sadler-Smith, "The Dynamics of Intuition and Analysis in Managerial and Organizational Decision Making," *Academy of Management Perspectives* 32 (2018): 473–92.

44. L. Sjöberg, "Intuitive vs. Analytical Decision Making: Which Is Preferred?" *Scandinavian Journal of Management* 19 (2003): 17–29; K. Hamilton, S.-I. Shih, and S. Mohammed, "The Development and Validation of the Rational and Intuitive Decision Styles Scale," *Journal of Personality Assessment* 98 (2016): 523–35; Y. Wang et al., "Meta-Analytic Investigations of the Relation Between Intuition and Analysis," *Journal of Behavioral Decision Making* 30 (2017): 15–25.

45. W.G. Chase and H.A. Simon, "Perception in Chess," *Cognitive Psychology* 4, no. 1 (1973): 55–81; G. Klein, *Intuition at Work* (New York: Currency/Doubleday, 2003); E. Dane, K.W. Rockmann, and M.G. Pratt, "When Should I Trust My Gut? Linking Domain Expertise to Intuitive Decision-Making Effectiveness," *Organizational Behavior and Human Decision Processes* 119, no. 2 (2012): 187–94; A. Linhares and D.M. Chada, "What Is the Nature of the Mind's Pattern-Recognition Process?," *New Ideas in Psychology* 31, no. 2 (2013): 108–21.

46. G. Klein, *Intuition at Work* (New York: Currency/Doubleday, 2003), 12–13, 16–17; G. Kefalidou, D. Golightly, and S. Sharples, "Identifying Rail Asset Maintenance Processes: A Human-Centric and Sensemaking Approach," *Cognition, Technology & Work* 20 (2018): 73–92.

47. Nutt, "Search During Decision Making," *European Journal of Operational Research* 160(3) (2005): 851–876; P.C. Nutt, "Investigating the Success of Decision Making Processes," *Journal of Management Studies* 45, no. 2 (2008): 425–55; S.A. Kreindler, "Planning without Action and Action without Planning? Examining a Regional Health System's Efforts to Improve Patient Flow, 1998–2013," *The International Journal of Health Planning and Management* 33, no. 1 (2018): e333–43, https://doi.org/10.1002/hpm.2481.

48. R. Bradfield et al., "The Origins and Evolution of Scenario Techniques in Long Range Business Planning," *Futures* 37 (2005): 795–812; T.J. Chermack, *Scenario Planning in Organizations* (San Francisco: Berrett-Koehler, 2011); G. Bowman, "The Practice of Scenario Planning: An Analysis of Inter- and Intra-Organizational Strategizing," *British Journal of Management* 27 (2016): 77–96; J.J. Oliver and E. Parrett, "Managing Uncertainty: Harnessing the Power of Scenario Planning," *Strategic Direction* 33 (2016): 5–6.

49. J. Pfeffer and R.I. Sutton, "Knowing 'What' to Do Is Not Enough: Turning Knowledge into Action," *California Management Review* 42, no. 1 (1999): 83–108; R. Charan, C. Burke, and L. Bossidy, *Execution: The Discipline of Getting Things Done* (New York: Crown Business, 2002); S.A. Kreindler, "What If Implementation Is Not the Problem? Exploring the Missing Links between Knowledge and Action," *The International Journal of Health Planning and Management* 31 (2016): 208–26.

50. C.A. O'Reilly and D.F. Caldwell, "The Commitment and Job Tenure of New Employees: Some Evidence of Postdecisional Justification," *Administrative Science Quarterly* 26 (1981): 597–616; S.W.S. Lee and N. Schwarz, "Washing Away Postdecisional Dissonance," *Science* 328, no. 5979 (May 7, 2010): 709–709; J. De Fine Licht et al., "When Does Transparency Generate Legitimacy? Experimenting on a Context-Bound Relationship:

When Does Transparency Generate Legitimacy?," *Governance* 27 (2014): 111–34.

51. B.M. Staw and J. Ross, "Behavior in Escalation Situations: Antecedents, Prototypes, and Solutions," *Research in Organizational Behavior* 9 (1987): 39–78; D.J. Sleesman et al., "Cleaning up the Big Muddy: A Meta-Analytic Review of the Determinants of Escalation of Commitment," *Academy of Management Journal* 55 (2012): 541–62; D.J. Sleesman et al., "Putting Escalation of Commitment in Context: A Multilevel Review and Analysis," *Academy of Management Annals* 12 (2018): 178–207.

52. B.M. Staw, "Knee-Deep in the Big Muddy: A Study of Escalating Commitment to a Chosen Course of Action," *Organizational Behavior and Human Performance* 16 (1976): 27–44; D. Steinkühler, M.D. Mahlendorf, and M. Brettel, "How Self-Justification Indirectly Drives Escalation of Commitment—a Motivational Perspective," *Schmalenbach Business Review: ZFBF* 66 (2014): 191–222; E.A. Lofquist and R. Lines, "Keeping Promises: A Process Study of Escalating Commitment Leading to Organizational Change Collapse," *The Journal of Applied Behavioral Science* 53 (2017): 417–45.

53. S. Loughnan et al., "Universal Biases in Self-Perception: Better and More Human Than Average," *British Journal of Social Psychology* 49 (2010): 627–36; D.L. Ferris and C. Sedikides, "Self-Enhancement in Organizations," in *The Self at Work: Fundamental Theory and Research,* ed. D.L. Ferris, R.E. Johnson, and C. Sedikides (New York: Routledge, 2018), 91–118.

54. M. Keil, G. Depledge, and A. Rai, "Escalation: The Role of Problem Recognition and Cognitive Bias," *Decision Sciences* 38 (2007): 391–421; R. Ronay et al., "Pride before the Fall: (Over) Confidence Predicts Escalation of Public Commitment," *Journal of Experimental Social Psychology* 69 (2017): 13–22.

55. G. Whyte, "Escalating Commitment in Individual and Group Decision Making: A Prospect Theory Approach," *Organizational Behavior and Human Decision Processes* 54 (1993): 430–55; D. Kahneman and J. Renshon, "Hawkish Biases," in *American Foreign Policy and the Politics of Fear: Threat Inflation since 9/11,* ed. T. Thrall and J. Cramer (New York: Routledge, 2009), 79–96.

56. D. J. Sleesman et al., "Cleaning up the Big Muddy: A Meta-Analytic Review of the Determinants of Escalation of Commitment," *Academy of Management Journal* 55 (2012): 541–62; B.M. Sweis et al., "Sensitivity to 'Sunk Costs' in Mice, Rats, and Humans," *Science* 361, no. 6398 (July 13, 2018): 178–81.

57. J.D. Bragger et al., "When Success Breeds Failure: History, Hysteresis, and Delayed Exit Decisions," *Journal of Applied Psychology* 88, no. 1 (2003): 6–14; H. Drummond, "Escalation of Commitment: When to Stay the Course?," *The Academy of Management Perspectives* 28, no. 4 (2014): 430–46.

58. I. Simonson and B.M. Staw, "De-Escalation Strategies: A Comparison of Techniques for Reducing Commitment to Losing Courses of Action," *Journal of Applied Psychology* 77 (1992): 419–26; M. Keil and D. Robey, "Turning around Troubled Software Projects: An Exploratory Study

of the Deescalation of Commitment to Failing Courses of Action," *Journal of Management Information Systems* 15 (1999): 63–87; D.C. Molden and C.M. Hui, "Promoting De-Escalation of Commitment: A Regulatory-Focus Perspective on Sunk Costs," *Psychological Science* 22 (2011): 8–12; A.C. Hafenbrack, Z. Kinias, and S.G. Barsade, "Debiasing the Mind Through Meditation: Mindfulness and the Sunk-Cost Bias," *Psychological Science* 25 (2014): 369–76; K.R. Sarangee et al., "De-Escalation Mechanisms in High-Technology Product Innovation," *Journal of Product Innovation Management* 31 (2014): 1023–38; D.V. Chulkov and J.M. Barron, "Turnover in Top Management and De-Escalation of Commitment," *Applied Economics* 51 (2019): 2534–51.

59. M.I. Stein, "Creativity and Culture," *Journal of Psychology* 36 (1953): 311–22; M.A. Runco and G.J. Jaeger, "The Standard Definition of Creativity," *Creativity Research Journal* 24, no. 1 (2012): 92–96.

60. G. Wallas, *The Art of Thought* (London, UK: Jonathan Cape, 1926). For recent applications of Wallas's classic model, see T. Kristensen, "The Physical Context of Creativity," *Creativity and Innovation Management* 13, no. 2 (2004): 89–96; U.-E. Haner, "Spaces for Creativity and Innovation in Two Established Organizations," *Creativity and Innovation Management* 14, no. 3 (2005): 288–98.

61. R.S. Nickerson, "Enhancing Creativity," in *Handbook of Creativity* ed. R.J. Sternberg (New York: Cambridge University Press, 1999), 392–430.

62. E. Oakes, *Notable Scientists: A to Z of STS Scientists* (New York: Facts on File, 2002), pp. 207–09.

63. R.J. Sternberg and J.E. Davidson, *The Nature of Insight* (Cambridge, MA: MIT Press, 1995); W. Shen et al., "Feeling the Insight: Uncovering Somatic Markers of the 'Aha' Experience," *Applied Psychophysiology and Biofeedback* 43 (2018): 13–21.

64. R.J. Sternberg and L.A. O'Hara, "Creativity and Intelligence," in *Handbook of Creativity,* ed. R.J. Sternberg (New York: Cambridge University Press, 1999), 251–72; S. Taggar, "Individual Creativity and Group Ability to Utilize Individual Creative Resources: A Multilevel Model," *Academy of Management Journal* 45 (2002): 315–30; R.J. Sternberg, "Successful Intelligence: A Model for Testing Intelligence beyond IQ Tests," *European Journal of Education and Psychology* 8 (2015): 76–84.

65. G.J. Feist, "The Influence of Personality on Artistic and Scientific Creativity," in *Handbook of Creativity,* ed. R.J. Sternberg (New York: Cambridge University Press, 1999), 273–96; T. Åstebro, S.A. Jeffrey, and G.K. Adomdza, "Inventor Perseverance after Being Told to Quit: The Role of Cognitive Biases," *Journal of Behavioral Decision Making* 20 (2007): 253–72; J.S. Mueller, S. Melwani, and J.A. Goncalo, "The Bias against Creativity: Why People Desire but Reject Creative Ideas," *Psychological Science* 23, no. 1 (2012): 13–17.

66. R.W. Weisberg, "Creativity and Knowledge: A Challenge to Theories," in *Handbook of Creativity,* ed. R.J. Sternberg (New York: Cambridge University Press, 1999), 226–50.

67. R.I. Sutton, *Weird Ideas That Work* (New York: Free Press, 2002), pp. 53–54, 121; E. Dane, "Reconsidering the Trade-Off between Expertise

and Flexibility: A Cognitive Entrenchment Perspective," *Academy of Management Review* 35 (2010): 579–603.

68. T. Koppell, *Powering the Future* (New York: Wiley, 1999), p. 15.

69. Feist, "The Influence of Personality on Artistic and Scientific Creativity; C.E. Shalley, J. Zhou, and G.R. Oldham, "The Effects of Personal and Contextual Characteristics on Creativity: Where Should We Go from Here?," *Journal of Management* 30, no. 6 (2004): 933–58; S.J. Dollinger, K.K. Urban, and T.A. James, "Creativity and Openness to Experience: Validation of Two Creative Product Measures," *Creativity Research Journal* 16, no. 1 (2004): 35–47; T.S. Schweizer, "The Psychology of Novelty-Seeking, Creativity and Innovation: Neurocognitive Aspects within a Work-Psychological Perspective," *Creativity and Innovation Management* 15, no. 2 (2006): 164–72; S. Acar and M.A. Runco, "Creative Abilities: Divergent Thinking," in *Handbook of Organizational Creativity,* ed. M. Mumford (Waltham, MA: Academic Press, 2012), 115–39.

70. C.E. Shalley, J. Zhou, and G.R. Oldham, "The Effects of Personal and Contextual Characteristics on Creativity: Where Should We Go from Here?," *Journal of Management* 30 (2004): 933–58; S.T. Hunter, K.E. Bedell, and M.D. Mumford, "Climate for Creativity: A Quantitative Review," *Creativity Research Journal* 19 (2007): 69–90; N. Anderson, K. Potočnik, and J. Zhou, "Innovation and Creativity in Organizations: A State-of-the-Science Review, Prospective Commentary, and Guiding Framework," *Journal of Management* 40 (2014): 1297–1333.

71. Learning orientation has multiple meanings. This definition and discussion refers to the market-ing-based concept associated with organizational learning. It differs from "learning goal orientation." See, for example: W.E. Baker and J.M. Sinkula, "The Synergistic Effect of Market Orientation and Learning Orientation on Organizational Performance," *Journal of the Academy of Marketing Science* 27 (1999): 411–27; O. Pesämaa et al., "How a Learning Orientation Affects Drivers of Innovativeness and Performance in Service Delivery," *Journal of Engineering and Technology Management* 30 (2013): 169–87; J.C. Real, J.L. Roldán, and A. Leal, "From Entrepreneurial Orientation and Learning Orientation to Business Performance: Analysing the Mediating Role of Organizational Learning and the Moderating Effects of Organizational Size," *British Journal of Management* 25 (2014): 186–208.

72. "Staying Ahead with Innovation," *Canadian HR Reporter* 32, no. 12 (December 2019): 21–23.

73. A. Cummings and G.R. Oldham, "Enhancing Creativity: Managing Work Contexts for the High Potential Employee:," *California Management Review* 40 (Fall 1997): 22-38; F. Coelho and M. Augusto, "Job Characteristics and the Creativity of Frontline Service Employees," *Journal of Service Research* 13 (2010): 426–38; G. Hirst et al., "How Does Bureaucracy Impact Individual Creativity? A Cross-Level Investigation of Team Contextual Influences on Goal Orientation–Creativity Relationships," *Academy of Management Journal* 54 (2011): 624–41; W. Zhang et al., "Exploring the Effects of Job Autonomy on Engagement and Creativity: The Moderating Role of Performance

Pressure and Learning Goal Orientation," *Journal of Business and Psychology* 32 (2017): 235–51.

74. T.M. Amabile, "Changes in the Work Environment for Creativity During Downsizing," *Academy of Management Journal* 42 (1999): 630–40.

75. J. Moultrie et al., "Innovation Spaces: Towards a Framework for Understanding the Role of the Physical Environment in Innovation," *Creativity & Innovation Management* 16, no. 1 (2007): 53–65.

76. C.E. Shalley, J. Zhou, and G.R. Oldham, "The Effects of Personal and Contextual Characteristics on Creativity: Where Should We Go from Here?," *Journal of Management* 30 (2004): 933–58; S. Powell, "The Management and Consumption of Organisational Creativity," *Journal of Consumer Marketing* 25 (2008): 158–66; D.J. Hughes et al., "Leadership, Creativity, and Innovation: A Critical Review and Practical Recommendations," *Leadership Quarterly* 29 (2018): 549–69.

77. A. Hiam, "Obstacles to Creativity - and How You Can Remove Them," *Futurist* 32 (1998): 30–34.

78. M.A. West, *Developing Creativity in Organizations* (Leicester, UK: BPS Books, 1997), pp. 33–35.

79. S. Brown, *Play: How It Shapes the Brain, Opens the Imagination, and Invigorates the Soul* (New York: Avery, 2009); C. Mainemelis and D.D. Dionysiou, "Play, Flow, and Timelessness," in *The Oxford Handbook of Creativity, Innovation, and Entrepreneurship*, ed. C. Shalley, M. Hitt, and J. Zhou (New York: Oxford University Press, 2015), 121–40; C.A. Petelczyc et al., "Play at Work: An Integrative Review and Agenda for Future Research," *Journal of Management* 44 (2018): 161–90.

80. T. Ritchey, *Wicked Problems—Social Messes: Decision Support Modelling with Morphological Analysis, Risk, Governance and Society* (Berlin: Springer-Verlag, 2011); S. Seidenstricker and C. Linder, "A Morphological Analysis-Based Creativity Approach to Identify and Develop Ideas for BMI: A Case Study of a High-Tech Manufacturing Company," *International Journal of Entrepreneurship and Innovation Management* 18, no. 5–6 (2014): 409–24.

81. A. Hargadon and R.I. Sutton, "Building an Innovation Factory," *Harvard Business Review* 78 (2000): 157–66; T. Kelley, *The Art of Innovation* (New York: Currency Doubleday, 2001), pp. 158–62; P.F. Skilton and K.J. Dooley, "The Effects of Repeat Collaboration on Creative Abrasion," *Academy of Management Review* 35, no. 1 (2010): 118–34.

82. M. Burton, "Open Plan, Open Mind," *Director* (2005): 68–72; S. Pathak, "On the Inside at Mother New York, Where Rotating Desks Are the Norm," *Digiday,* November 6, 2015; I. Davies, "Iconic Ads, Communal Working and Fierce Independence: We Meet the Team at Mother London," *Lecture In Progress,* March 13, 2018, https://lectureinprogress.com/journal/mother-london.

83. C. Meinel and L. Leifer, "Introduction—Design Thinking Is Mainly about Building Innovators," in *Design Thinking Research: Building Innovators,* ed. H. Plattner, C. Meinel, and L. Leifer (Cham, Switzerland: Springer International, 2015), 1–11.

84. E. Köppen and C. Meinel, "Empathy Via Design Thinking: Creation of Sense and Knowledge," in *Design Thinking Research: Building Innovators,*

ed. H. Plattner, C. Meinel, and L. Leifer (Cham, Switzerland: Springer International, 2015), 15–28; K.D. Elsbach and I. Stigliani, "Design Thinking and Organizational Culture: A Review and Framework for Future Research," *Journal of Management* 44 (2018): 2274–2306.

85. R. Glen et al., "Teaching Design Thinking in Business Schools," *The International Journal of Management Education* 13 (2015): 182–92; L. Carlgren, I. Rauth, and M. Elmquist, "Framing Design Thinking: The Concept in Idea and Enactment," *Creativity and Innovation Management* 25 (2016): 38–57; K.D. Elsbach and I. Stigliani, "Design Thinking and Organizational Culture: A Review and Framework for Future Research," *Journal of Management* 44 (2018): 2274–2306.

86. J. Kolko, "Design Thinking Comes of Age," *Harvard Business Review* 93, no. 9 (2015): 66–71; C. Vetterli et al., "How Deutsche Bank's IT Division Used Design Thinking to Achieve Customer Proximity," *MIS Quarterly Executive* 15 (2016): 37–53; D. Henriksen, C. Richardson, and R. Mehta, "Design Thinking: A Creative Approach to Educational Problems of Practice," *Thinking Skills and Creativity* 26 (2017): 140–53.

87. V. van de Vliet, "How to Become a True Cognitive Enterprise," *Inspire Beyond Today's Technology* (Amsterdam: IBM, 2016), https://www.ibm.com/systems/be/inspire/ibm-cognitive-build (accessed 9 March 2018); "Internal Communications Interview with IBM," podcast in *csuite podcast* (Audere Communications, 12 December 2016); "Cognitive Build Hits World of Watson," *Medium,* October 28, 2016; "Best in Internal Communications 2017," *PR Week,* March 17, 2017.

88. C.D. Zatzick and R.D. Iverson, "Putting Employee Involvement in Context: A Cross-Level Model Examining Job Satisfaction and Absenteeism in High-Involvement Work Systems," *The International Journal of Human Resource Management* 22 (2011): 3462–76; R. Markey and K. Townsend, "Contemporary Trends in Employee Involvement and Participation," *Journal of Industrial Relations* 55 (2013): 475–87; M. Marchington, "Analysing the Forces Shaping Employee Involvement and Participation (EIP) at Organisation Level in Liberal Market Economies (LMEs)," *Human Resource Management Journal* 25 (2015): 1–18.

89. V.H. Vroom and A.G. Jago, *The New Leadership: Managing Participation in Organizations* (Englewood Cliffs, NJ: Prentice Hill, 1988).

90. Some of the early OB writing on employee involvement includes C. Argyris, *Personality and Organization* (New York: Harper & Row, 1957); D. McGregor, *The Human Side of Enterprise* (New York: McGraw Hill, 1960); R. Likert, *New Patterns of Management* (New York: McGraw Hill, 1961).

91. R.J. Ely and D.A. Thomas, "Cultural Diversity at Work: The Effects of Diversity Perspectives on Work Group Processes and Outcomes," *Administrative Science Quarterly* 46 (2001): 229–73; E. Mannix and M.A. Neale, "What Differences Make a Difference?: The Promise and Reality of Diverse Teams in Organizations," *Psychological Science in the Public Interest* 6, no. 2 (2005): 31–55.

92. D. Berend and J. Paroush, "When Is Condorcet's Jury Theorem Valid?," *Social Choice and Welfare* 15, no. 4 (1998): 481–88.

93. K.T. Dirks, L.L. Cummings, and J.L. Pierce, "Psychological Ownership in Organizations: Conditions under Which Individuals Promote and Resist Change," *Research in Organizational Change and Development,* no. 9 (1996): 1–23; J.P. Walsh and S.-F. Tseng, "The Effects of Job Characteristics on Active Effort at Work," *Work & Occupations,* no. 25 (1998): 74–96; B. Scott-Ladd and V. Marshall, "Participation in Decision Making: A Matter of Context?," *Leadership & Organization Development Journal* 25, no. 8 (2004): 646–62.

94. V.H. Vroom and A.G. Jago, *The New Leadership: Managing Participation in Organizations* (Englewood Cliffs, NJ: Prentice Hall, 1988).

CHAPTER 8

1. "The Governor's Challenge: Participant Guidelines" (Ottawa: Bank of Canada, September 2017); S. Garmhausen, "Why Teams Dominate at the Top Financial Advisors," *Barron's,* April 19, 2019; A. Willis, "Why RBC Is Becoming the New England Patriots of Bay Street," *Globe & Mail,* April 24, 2019; "Canada's Best Investment Bank 2019: RBC Capital Markets," *Euromoney,* July 10, 2019.

2. "Trends: Are Many Meetings a Waste of Time? Study Says So," news release (MeetingsNet, November 1, 1998); R. Cross, R. Rebele, and A. Grant, "Collaborative Overload," *Harvard Business Review,* Jan-Feb 2016, 74–79; L. Wright and N. McCullough, "New Survey Explores the Changing Landscape of Teamwork," *Microsoft 365 Blog* (blog), April 19, 2018, https://www.microsoft.com/en-us/microsoft-365/blog/2018/04/19/new-survey-explores-the-changing-landscape-of-teamwork/.

3. S. Wuchty, B.F. Jones, and B. Uzzi, "The Increasing Dominance of Teams in Production of Knowledge," *Science* 316 (2007): 1036–39. For a detailed analysis of teamwork in scientific research, see N.J. Cooke and M.L. Hilton, *Enhancing the Effectiveness of Team Science,* Committee on the Science of Team Science; Board on Behavioral, Cognitive, and Sensory Sciences; Division of Behavioral and Social Sciences and Education; National Research Council (Washington, DC: National Academies Press, 2015).

4. M.E. Shaw, *Group Dynamics,* 3rd ed. (New York: McGraw Hill, 1981), 8; E. Sundstrom, "The Challenges of Supporting Work Team Effectiveness," in *Supporting Work Team Effectiveness* ed. E. Sundstrom and Associates (San Francisco, CA: Jossey-Bass, 1999), 6–9; L.E. Benishek and E.H. Lazzara, "Teams in a New Era: Some Considerations and Implications," *Frontiers in Psychology* 10 (2019), https://doi.org/10.3389/fpsyg.2019.01006. Even though a distinct social entity, a team's boundaries (who is and who is not a member) may be fuzzier than previously assumed. See: M. Mortensen and M.R. Haas, "Perspective—Rethinking Teams: From Bounded Membership to Dynamic Participation," *Organization Science* 29 (2018): 341–55.

5. J.R. Hollenbeck, B. Beersma, and M.E. Schouten, "Beyond Team Types and Taxonomies: A Dimensional Scaling Conceptualization for Team Description," *Academy of Management Review* 37, no. 1 (2012): 82–106. This article uses the term *skill differentiation,* whereas we use *skill diversity* which

is a more common label to describe variations among team members; skill differences represent a form of deep-level diversity. The original article also uses the label *authority differentiation,* whereas we believe that *authority dispersion* is more consistent with similar language on power in organizations, such as in decentralization of organizational structures.

6. R.A. Guzzo and M.W. Dickson, "Teams in Organizations: Recent Research on Performance and Effectiveness," *Annual Review of Psychology* 47 (1996): 307–38; L.R. Offerman and R.K. Spiros, "The Science and Practice of Team Development: Improving the Link," *Academy of Management Journal* 44 (2001): 376–92.

7. J.R. Spoor and J.R. Kelly, "The Evolutionary Significance of Affect in Groups: Communication and Group Bonding," *Group Processes & Intergroup Relations* 7 (2004): 398–412; W.S. Jansen et al., "Inclusion: Conceptualization and Measurement," *European Journal of Social Psychology* 44 (2014): 370–85.

8. S.A. Haslam and N. Ellemers, "Identity Processes in Organizations," in *Handbook of Identity Theory and Research,* ed. J.S. Schwartz, K. Luyckx, and L.V. Vignoles (New York: Springer New York, 2011), 715–44; R. Spears, "Group Identities: The Social Identity Perspective," in *Handbook of Identity Theory and Research,* ed. S.J. Schwartz, K. Luyckx, and V.L. Vignoles (New York: Springer New York, 2011), 201–24; S.K. Kang and G.V. Bodenhausen, "Multiple Identities in Social Perception and Interaction: Challenges and Opportunities," *Annual Review of Psychology* 66 (2015): 547–74.

9. S. Schacter, *The Psychology of Affiliation* (Stanford, CA: Stanford University Press, 1959), 12–19; S. Cohen, "The Pittsburgh Common Cold Studies: Psychosocial Predictors of Susceptibility to Respiratory Infectious Illness," *International Journal of Behavioral Medicine* 12, no. 3 (2005): 123–31; S.Y. Shin and S.G. Lee, "Effects of Hospital Workers' Friendship Networks on Job Stress," *PLoS ONE* 11, no. 2 (2016): e0149428.

10. R. Cross and R.J. Thomas, *Driving Results through Social Networks: How Top Organizations Leverage Networks for Performance and Growth* (San Francisco, CA: Jossey-Bass, 2009); R. McDermott and D. Archibald, "Harnessing Your Staff's Informal Networks," *Harvard Business Review* 88, no. 3 (2010): 82–89; J.R. Methot, E.H. Rosado-Solomon, and D.G. Allen, "The Network Architecture of Human Capital: A Relational Identity Perspective," *Academy of Management Review* 43 (2018): 723–48.

11. M. Moldaschl and W. Weber, "The 'Three Waves' of Industrial Group Work: Historical Reflections on Current Research on Group Work," *Human Relations* 51 (1998): 347–88. Several popular books in the 1980s encouraged teamwork, based on the Japanese economic miracle. These books include W. Ouchi, *Theory Z: How American Management Can Meet the Japanese Challenge* (Reading, MA: Addison-Wesley, 1981); R.T. Pascale and A.G. Athos, *Art of Japanese Management* (New York: Simon and Schuster, 1982).

12. C.R. Emery and L.D. Fredenhall, "The Effect of Teams on Firm Profitability and Customer Satisfaction," *Journal of Service Research* 4 (2002): 217–29; J.R. Hackman, *Collaborative Intelligence: Using Teams to Solve Hard Problems* (San Francisco: Berrett-Koehler Publishers, 2011); E. Salas, D.L. Reyes, and S.H. McDaniel, "The Science of Teamwork: Progress, Reflections, and the Road Ahead.," *American Psychologist* 73 (2018): 593–600.

13. R.E. Baumeister and M.R. Leary, "The Need to Belong: Desire for Interpersonal Attachments as a Fundamental Human Motivation," *Psychological Bulletin* 117 (1995): 497–529; J.M. Feinberg and J.R. Aiello, "Social Facilitation: A Test of Competing Theories," *Journal of Applied Social Psychology* 36, no. 5 (2006): 1087–109; A.M. Grant, "Relational Job Design and the Motivation to Make a Prosocial Difference," *Academy of Management Review* 32, no. 2 (2007): 393–417; N.L. Kerr and D.H. Seok, "'. . . with a Little Help from My Friends': Friendship, Effort Norms, and Group Motivation Gain," *Journal of Managerial Psychology* 26, no. 3 (2011): 205–18; D. Herbst and A. Mas, "Peer Effects on Worker Output in the Laboratory Generalize to the Field," *Science* 350, no. 6260 (2015): 545–49.

14. E.A. Locke et al, "The Importance of the Individual in an Age of Groupism," in *Groups at Work: Theory and Research* ed. M.E. Turner (Mahwah, NJ: Lawrence Erbaum Associates, 2001), 501–28; N.J. Allen and T.D. Hecht, "The 'Romance of Teams': Toward an Understanding of Its Psychological Underpinnings and Implications," *Journal of Occupational and Organizational Psychology* 77 (2004): 439–61.

15. I.D. Steiner, *Group Process and Productivity* (New York: Academic Press, 1972); S. Coyle, K. Conboy, and T. Acton, "Group Process Losses in Agile Software Development Decision Making," *International Journal of Intelligent Information Technologies* 9, no. 2 (2013): 38–53; K. Srikanth, S. Harvey, and R. Peterson, "A Dynamic Perspective on Diverse Teams: Moving from the Dual-Process Model to a Dynamic Coordination-Based Model of Diverse Team Performance," *Academy of Management Annals* 10 (2016): 453–93.

16. G.K. Stahl et al., "Unraveling the Effects of Cultural Diversity in Teams: A Meta-Analysis of Research on Multicultural Work Groups," *Journal of International Business Studies* 41 (2010): 690–709; M.W. McCarter and R.M. Sheremeta, "You Can't Put Old Wine in New Bottles: The Effect of Newcomers on Coordination in Groups," *PLoS ONE* 8, no. 1 (2013): e55058.

17. F.P. Brooks, ed. *The Mythical Man-Month: Essays on Software Engineering,* Second ed. (Reading, MA: Addison-Wesley, 1995); B.R. Staats, K.L. Milkman, and C.R. Fox, "The Team Scaling Fallacy: Underestimating the Declining Efficiency of Larger Teams," *Organizational Behavior and Human Decision Processes* 118, no. 2 (2012): 132–42; T. van Balen and M. Tarakci, "Never Change a Winning Team?," ssRN Scholarly Paper (Rochester, NY: Social Science Research Network, May 4, 2017).

18. S.J. Karau and K.D. Williams, "Social Loafing: A Meta-Analytic Review and Theoretical Integration," *Journal of Personality and Social Psychology* 65 (1993): 681–706; R.C. Liden et al., "Social Loafing: A Field Investigation," *Journal of Management* 30 (2004): 285–304; L.L. Chidambaram, "Is out of Sight, out of Mind? An Empirical Study of Social Loafing in Technology-Supported Groups," *Information Systems Research* 16, no. 2 (2005): 149 –68; U.-C. Klehe and N. Anderson, "The Moderating Influence of Personality and Culture on Social Loafing in Typical Versus Maximum Performance Situations," *International Journal of Selection and Assessment* 15, no. 2 (2007): 250–62.

19. B. Latane, K. Williams, and S. Harkins, "Many Hands Make Light the Work: The Causes and Consequences of Social Loafing," *Journal of Personality & Social Psychology* 37 (1979): 822–32; U.-C. Klehe and N. Anderson, "The Moderating Influence of Personality and Culture on Social Loafing in Typical versus Maximum Performance Situations," *International Journal of Selection and Assessment* 15 (2007): 250–62; R. B. Lount and S. L. Wilk, "Working Harder or Hardly Working? Posting Performance Eliminates Social Loafing and Promotes Social Laboring in Workgroups," *Management Science* 60 (2014): 1098–106; M. C. Schippers, "Social Loafing Tendencies and Team Performance: The Compensating Effect of Agreeableness and Conscientiousness," *Academy of Management Learning & Education* 13 (2014): 62–81; B. Meyer, C. C. Schermuly, and S. Kauffeld, "That's Not My Place: The Interacting Effects of Faultlines, Subgroup Size, and Social Competence on Social Loafing Behaviour in Work Groups," *European Journal of Work and Organizational Psychology* 25 (2016): 31–49.

20. C. Lam, "The Role of Communication and Cohesion in Reducing Social Loafing in Group Projects," *Business and Professional Communication Quarterly* 78 (2015): 454–75; S.H. Czyż et al., "Participation in Team Sports Can Eliminate the Effect of Social Loafing," *Perceptual and Motor Skills* 123 (2016): 754–68; V. Peñarroja, V. Orengo, and A. Zornoza, "Reducing Perceived Social Loafing in Virtual Teams: The Effect of Team Feedback with Guided Reflexivity," *Journal of Applied Social Psychology* 47 (2017): 424–35; I. Fronza and X. Wang, "Towards an Approach to Prevent Social Loafing in Software Development Teams," in *11th ACM/IEEE International Symposium on Empirical Software Engineering and Measurement (Esem 2017)* (New York: IEEE, 2017), 241–46; A.A. Curcio and M.A. Lynch, "Addressing Social Loafing on Faculty Committees," *Journal of Legal Education* 67 (2017): 242–62.

21. J.R. Engen, "Tough as Nails," *Bank Director,* July 2009, 24.

22. E. Sundstrom, K.P. De Meuse, and D. Futrell, "Work Teams: Applications and Effectiveness," *American Psychologist,* Organizational Psychology, 45, no. 2 (1990): 120–33; J.R. Hackman et al., "Team Effectiveness in Theory and in Practice," in *Industrial and Organizational Psychology: Linking Theory with Practice,* ed. C.L. Cooper and E.A. Locke (Oxford, UK: Blackwell, 2000), 109–29. Recent literature has focused mainly on the first two functions, but team survival is also an important outcome. See: J.E. Mathieu et al., "Embracing Complexity: Reviewing the Past Decade of Team Effectiveness Research," *Annual Review of Organizational Psychology and Organizational Behavior* 6 (2019): 17–46.

23. P.S. Goodman, E.C. Ravlin, and L. Argote, "Current Thinking About Groups: Setting the Stage for New Ideas," in *Designing Effective Work Groups,* ed. P.S. Goodman and and Associates (San

Francisco: Jossey-Bass, 1986); M.A. Marks, J.E. Mathieu, and S.J. Zaccaro, "A Temporally Based Framework and Taxonomy of Team Processes," *Academy of Management Review* 26, no. 3 (2001): 356–76;E. Salas, D.L. Reyes, and S.H. McDaniel, "The Science of Teamwork: Progress, Reflections, and the Road Ahead.," *American Psychologist* 73, no. 4 (2018): 593–600, https://doi.org/10.1037/amp0000334; J.E. Mathieu et al., "Embracing Complexity: Reviewing the Past Decade of Team Effectiveness Research," *Annual Review of Organizational Psychology and Organizational Behavior* 6, no. 1 (2019): 17–46, https://doi.org/10.1146/annurev-orgpsych-012218-015106.

24. M. Kouchaki et al., "The Treatment of the Relationship between Groups and Their Environments: A Review and Critical Examination of Common Assumptions in Research," *Group & Organization Management* 37, no. 2 (2012): 171–203.

25. Several writers describe "team processes" as team activities in the transformation of input resources to outputs. However, this defines the team's involvement in the production process, whereas earlier scholars emphasized "team processes" that explain the team's continuously evolving characteristics (norms, cohesion, etc.). Indeed, much recent writing unwittingly applies both definitions. See: M.A. Marks, J.E. Mathieu, and S.J. Zaccaro, "A Temporally Based Framework and Taxonomy of Team Processes," *The Academy of Management Review* 26, no. 3 (2001): 356–76, https://doi.org/10.2307/259182; S.W.J. Kozlowski and B.S. Bell, "Work Groups and Teams in Organizations," in *Handbook of Psychology: Industrial and Organizational Psychology,* ed. N.W. Schmitt, S. Highhouse, and I.B. Weiner, 2nd ed., vol. 12 (Hoboken, NJ,: John Wiley & Sons Inc, 2013), 412–69; L.E. Benishek and E.H. Lazzara, "Teams in a New Era: Some Considerations and Implications," *Frontiers in Psychology* 10 (2019), https://doi.org/10.3389/fpsyg.2019.01006.

26. McGrath recommended that team models and studies should focus on team processes rather than the snapshot "series of states" that emerge from those processes. He explained that the processes generating team states are logically more important for understanding team dynamics. Unfortunately, recent writers on teams have neglected that advice. See: J.E. McGrath, "Studying Groups at Work: Ten Critical Needs for Theory and Practice," in *Designing Effective Work Groups,* ed. P.S. Goodman and and Associates (San Francisco: Jossey-Bass, 1986), 362–92.

27. G.R. Bushe and A.L. Johnson, "Contextual and Internal Variables Affecting Task Group Outcomes in Organizations," *Group & Organization Studies* 14, no. 4 (1989): 462–82; M. Kouchaki et al., "The Treatment of the Relationship between Groups and Their Environments: A Review and Critical Examination of Common Assumptions in Research," *Group & Organization Management* 37, no. 2 (2012): 171–203; T. Driskell, E. Salas, and J.E. Driskell, "Teams in Extreme Environments: Alterations in Team Development and Teamwork," *Human Resource Management Review,* 28, no. 4 (2018): 434–49, https://doi.org/10.1016/j.hrmr.2017.01.002.

28. E. Sundstrom, "The Challenges of Supporting Work Team Effectiveness," in *Supporting Work Team Effectiveness* ed. E. Sundstrom and Associates (San Francisco, CA: Jossey-Bass, 1999), 6–9; G.L. Stewart, "A Meta-Analytic Review of Relationships between Team Design Features and Team Performance," *Journal of Management* 32, no. 1 (2006): 29–54; J.E. Mathieu, L. D'Innocenzo, and M.R. Kukenberge, "Contextual Issues in Project Performance: A Multilevel Perspective," in *The Psychology and Management of Project Teams: An Interdisciplinary Perspective,* ed. B. Hobbs, E.K. Kelloway, and F. Chiocchio (New York: Oxford University Press, 2015), 101–36; F. Schölmerich, C.C. Schermuly, and J. Deller, "How Leaders' Diversity Beliefs Alter the Impact of Faultlines on Team Functioning," *Small Group Research* 47, no. 2 (2016): 177–206; S.A. Conroy and N. Gupta, "Team Pay-for-Performance: The Devil Is in the Details," *Group & Organization Management* 41, no. 1 (2016): 32–65.

29. G. Peyton, "Let There Be Light," *Atlantic Business,* July 5, 2018; B. Kelly, "Merrill Lynch to Focus Team Pay on Digital, Online Areas," *InvestmentNews,* November 6, 2018.

30. J.E. Mathieu et al., "Embracing Complexity: Reviewing the Past Decade of Team Effectiveness Research," *Annual Review of Organizational Psychology and Organizational Behavior* 6 (2019): 17–46.

31. M.A. Campion, E.M. Papper, and G.J. Medsker, "Relations between Work Team Characteristics and Effectiveness: A Replication and Extension," *Personnel Psychology* 49 (1996): 429–52; N. Sivasubramaniam, S.J. Liebowitz, and C.L. Lackman, "Determinants of New Product Development Team Performance: A Meta-Analytic Review," *Journal of Product Innovation Management* 29, no. 5 (2012): 803–20; M.A. Valentine and A.C. Edmondson, "Team Scaffolds: How Mesolevel Structures Enable Role-Based Coordination in Temporary Groups," *Organization Science* 26, no. 2 (2015): 405–22.

32. G. Van der Vegt and E. Van de Vliert, "Intragroup Interdependence and Effectiveness: Review and Proposed Directions for Theory and Practice," *Journal of Managerial Psychology* 17, no. 1/2 (2002): 50–67; R. Wageman, "The Meaning of Interdependence," in *Groups at Work: Theory and Research* ed. M.E. Turner (Mahwah, NJ: Lawrence Erlbaum Associates, 2001), 197–217; M.R. Barrick et al., "The Moderating Role of Top Management Team Interdependence: Implications for Real Teams and Working Groups," *Academy of Management Journal* 50, no. 3 (2007): 544–57; S.H. Courtright et al., "Structural Interdependence in Teams: An Integrative Framework and Meta-Analysis.," *Journal of Applied Psychology* 100, no. 6 (2015): 1825–46.

33. J.D. Thompson, *Organizations in Action* (New York: McGraw Hill, 1967), 54–55; F.M. Barbibi and G. Masino, *J.D. Thompson's Organizations In Action 50Th Anniversary: A Reflection* (Bologna. Italy: TAO Digital Library, 2017), Chap. 1. A slight variation of Thompson's model is also applied to understand interdependence in multi-team systems. See: R. Rico et al., "Structural Influences upon Coordination and Performance in Multiteam Systems," *Human Resource Management Review* 28 (2018): 332–46.

34. J.D. Thompson, *Organizations in Action* (New York: McGraw Hill, 1967), 55–59.

35. L. Gratton and T.J. Erickson, "Ways to Build Collaborative Teams," *Harvard Business Review* (2007): 100–09; B. Stone, *The Everything Store: Jeff Bezos and the Age of Amazon* (New York: Random House, 2013), 203–05.

36. J.R. Hackman, *Leading Teams: Setting the Stage for Great Performances* (Boston: Harvard Business Review Press, 2002), 116–22; C. Aube, V. Rousseau, and S. Tremblay, "Team Size and Quality of Group Experience: The More the Merrier?," *Group Dynamics: Theory Research and Practice* 15, no. 4 (2011): 357–75; J.S. Mueller, "Why Individuals in Larger Teams Perform Worse," *Organizational Behavior and Human Decision Processes* 117, no. 1 (2012): 111–24; Y.-N. Lee, J.P. Walsh, and J. Wang, "Creativity in Scientific Teams: Unpacking Novelty and Impact," *Research Policy* 44, no. 3 (2015): 684–97.

37. J. O'Toole, "The Power of Many: Building a High-Performance Management Team," *ceoforum.com.au* (2003).

38. S.W.J. Kozlowski and B.S. Bell, "Work Groups and Teams in Organizations," in *Handbook of Psychology: Industrial and Organizational Psychology,* ed. N.W. Schmitt, S. Highhouse, and I.B. Weiner, 2nd ed., vol. 12 (Hoboken, NJ,: John Wiley & Sons Inc, 2013), 412–69.

39. J.S. Mueller, "Why Individuals in Larger Teams Perform Worse," *Organizational Behavior and Human Decision Processes* 117, no. 1 (2012): 111–24.

40. J.E. Mathieu et al., "A Review and Integration of Team Composition Models: Moving toward a Dynamic and Temporal Framework," *Journal of Management* 40, no. 1 (2014): 130–60; N.J. Allen and T. O'Neill, "Team Composition and Performance: Considering the Project-Team Challenge," in *The Psychology and Management of Project Teams: An Interdisciplinary Perspective,* ed. B. Hobbs, E.K. Kelloway, and F. Chiocchio (New York: Oxford University Press, 2015), 301–28.

41. Taskwork and teamwork have varied definitions in the literature (e.g. behaviours versus competencies; individual- versus team-level phenomena). Our definition, which refers to individual-level behaviours focused on task performance versus team maintenance, is similar to the conceptualizations by Eduardo Salas and his colleagues, as well as to Lewin's seminal ideas about locomotion versus maintenance in groups. See, for example: J.E. Driskell, E. Salas, and T. Driskell, "Foundations of Teamwork and Collaboration," *American Psychologist* 73, no. 4 (2018): 334–48; E. Salas et al., "Can Teamwork Promote Safety in Organizations?," *Annual Review of Organizational Psychology and Organizational Behavior* 7 (2020): 283–313.

42. F.P. Morgeson, M.H. Reider, and M.A. Campion, "Selecting Individuals in Team Settings: The Importance of Social Skills, Personality Characteristics, and Teamwork Knowledge," *Personnel Psychology* 58, no. 3 (2005): 583–611; V. Rousseau, C. Aubé, and A. Savoie, "Teamwork Behaviors: A Review and an Integration of Frameworks," *Small Group Research* 37, no. 5 (2006): 540–70; M.L. Loughry, M.W. Ohland, and D.D. Moore, "Development of a Theory-Based Assessment of Team Member Effectiveness," *Educational and Psychological Measurement* 67, no. 3 (2007): 505–24; E. Salas et al., "Understanding and Improving Teamwork in Organizations: A Scientifically Based Practical Guide," *Human Resource Management* 54, no. 4 (2015): 599–622.

43. S. McComb et al., "The Five Ws of Team Communication," *Industrial Management* 54, no. 5 (2012): 10–13.

44. D. van Knippenberg, C.K.W. De Dreu, and A.C. Homan, "Work Group Diversity and Group Performance: An Integrative Model and Research Agenda," *Journal of Applied Psychology* 89, no. 6 (2004): 1008–22; E. Mannix and M.A. Neale, "What Differences Make a Difference?: The Promise and Reality of Diverse Teams in Organizations," *Psychological Science in the Public Interest* 6, no. 2 (2005): 31–55; L.M. Shore et al., "Inclusion and Diversity in Work Groups: A Review and Model for Future Research," *Journal of Management* 37, no. 4 (2011): 1262–89; S.K. Horwitz, "Functional Diversity in Project Teams: Working across Boundaries," in *The Psychology and Management of Project Teams: An Interdisciplinary Perspective,* ed. B. Hobbs, E.K. Kelloway, and F. Chiocchio (New York: Oxford University Press, 2015), 329–63.

45. D.C. Lau and J.K. Murnighan, "Interactions within Groups and Subgroups: The Effects of Demographic Faultlines," *Academy of Management Journal* 48, no. 4 (2005): 645–59; S.M.B. Thatcher and P.C. Patel, "Group Faultlines: A Review, Integration, and Guide to Future Research," *Journal of Management* 38, no. 4 (2012): 969–1009; M. Shemla et al., "A Review of Perceived Diversity in Teams: Does How Members Perceive Their Team's Composition Affect Team Processes and Outcomes?," *Journal of Organizational Behavior* 37 (2016): S89–S106.

46. Some of the better-known team development models over the years have been: W.G. Bennis and H.A. Shepard, "A Theory of Group Development," *Human Relations* 9, no. 4 (1956): 415–37; S.R. Kaplan and M. Roman, "Phases of Development in an Adult Therapy Group," *International Journal of Group Psychotherapy* 13, no. 1 (1963): 10–26; A.P. Hare, "Theories of Group Development and Categories for Interaction Analysis," *Small Group Behavior* 4, no. 3 (1973): 259–304; A.P. Beck, "A Study of Group Phase Development and Emergent Leadership," *Group* 5, no. 4 (1981): 48–54; C.J.G. Gersick, "Time and Transition in Work Teams: Toward a New Model of Group Development," *Academy of Management Journal* 31, no. 1 (1988): 9–41.

47. B.W. Tuckman and M.A.C. Jensen, "Stages of Small-Group Development Revisited," *Group and Organization Studies* 2 (1977): 419–42; B.W. Tuckman, "Developmental Sequence in Small Groups," *Group Facilitation* (2001): 66–81; D.A. Bonebright, "40 Years of Storming: A Historical Review of Tuckman's Model of Small Group Development," *Human Resource Development International* 13, no. 1 (2010): 111–20.

48. G.R. Bushe and G.H. Coetzer, "Group Development and Team Effectiveness: Using Cognitive Representations to Measure Group Development and Predict Task Performance and Group Viability," *Journal of Applied Behavioral Science* 43, no. 2 (2007): 184–212; D.A. Bonebright, "40 Years of Storming: A Historical Review of Tuckman's Model of Small Group Development," *Human Resource Development International* 13, no. 1 (2010): 111–20.

49. D.C. Feldman, "The Development and Enforcement of Group Norms," *Academy of Management Review* 9 (1984): 47–53; E. Fehr and U. Fischbacher, "Social Norms and Human Cooperation," *Trends in Cognitive Sciences* 8, no. 4 (2004): 185–90; B.A. De Jong, K.M. Bijlsma-Frankema, and L.B. Cardinal, "Stronger Than the Sum of Its Parts? The Performance Implications of Peer Control Combinations in Teams," *Organization Science* 25 (2014): 1703–21.

50. J.M. Nolan, "Social Norms and Their Enforcement," in *The Oxford Handbook of Social Influence,* ed. S.G. Harkins, K.D. Williams, and J. Burger (New York: Oxford University Press, 2015); A. Diekmann and W. Przepiorka, "'Take One for the Team!' Individual Heterogeneity and the Emergence of Latent Norms in a Volunteer's Dilemma," *Social Forces* 94 (2016): 1309–33.

51. K.-D. Opp, "How Do Norms Emerge? An Outline of a Theory," *Mind & Society* 2, no. 1 (2001): 101–28.

52. J.M. Nolan, "Social Norms and Their Enforcement," in *The Oxford Handbook of Social Influence,* ed. S.G. Harkins, K.D. Williams, and J. Burger (New York: Oxford University Press, 2015); B. Manata, "The Structural Effects of Team Density and Normative Standards on Team Member Performance," *Human Communication Research* 45 (2019): 309–33.

53. N. Ellemers and F. Rink, "Identity in Work Groups: The Beneficial and Detrimental Consequences of Multiple Identities and Group Norms for Collaboration and Group Performance," *Advances in Group Processes* 22 (2005): 1–41. For research on norm development and reinforcement in virtual teams, see K. Moser and C. Axtell, "The Role of Norms in Virtual Work: A Review and Agenda for Future Research," *Journal of Personnel Psychology* 12, no. 1 (2013): 1–6.

54. S. Taggar and R. Ellis, "The Role of Leaders in Shaping Formal Team Norms," *Leadership Quarterly* 18, no. 2 (2007): 105–20; B.A. De Jong, K.M. Bijlsma-Frankema, and L.B. Cardinal, "Stronger Than the Sum of Its Parts? The Performance Implications of Peer Control Combinations in Teams," *Organization Science* 25, no. 6 (2014): 1703–21; A. Lieberman, K.E. Duke, and O. Amir, "How Incentive Framing Can Harness the Power of Social Norms," *Organizational Behavior and Human Decision Processes* 151 (2019): 118–31, https://doi.org/10.1016/j.obhdp.2018.12.001.

55. A.P. Hare, "Types of Roles in Small Groups: A Bit of History and a Current Perspective," *Small Group Research* 25 (1994): 443–48; A. Aritzeta, S. Swailes, and B. Senior, "Belbin's Team Role Model: Development, Validity and Applications for Team Building," *Journal of Management Studies* 44, no. 1 (2007): 96–118.

56. A.P. Hare, "Types of Roles in Small Groups: A Bit of History and a Current Perspective," *Small Group Research* 25 (1994): 443–48; A. Aritzeta, S. Swailes, and B. Senior, "Belbin's Team Role Model: Development, Validity and Applications for Team Building," *Journal of Management Studies* 44, no. 1 (2007): 96–118; J.E. Mathieu et al., "Team Role Experience and Orientation: A Measure and Tests of Construct Validity," *Group & Organization Management* 40 (2015): 6–34; N. Lehmann-Willenbrock, S.J. Beck, and S. Kauffeld, "Emergent Team Roles in Organizational Meetings: Identifying Communication Patterns Via Cluster Analysis," *Communication Studies* 67 (2016): 37–57; T. Driskell et al., "Team Roles: A Review and Integration," *Small Group Research* 48 (2017): 482–511.

57. D.J. Beal et al., "Cohesion and Performance in Groups: A Meta-Analytic Clarification of Construct Relations," *Journal of Applied Psychology* 88, no. 6 (2003): 989–1004; S.W.J. Kozlowski and D.R. Ilgen, "Enhancing the Effectiveness of Work Groups and Teams," *Psychological Science in the Public Interest* 7 (3)(2006): 77–124; C. Lee, J.-L. Farh, and Z.-J. Chen, "Promoting Group Potency in Project Teams: The Importance of Group Identification," *Journal of Organizational Behavior* 32, no. 8 (2011): 1147–62.

58. R.M. Montoya, R.S. Horton, and J. Kirchner, "Is Actual Similarity Necessary for Attraction? A Meta-Analysis of Actual and Perceived Similarity," *Journal of Social and Personal Relationships* 25, no. 6 (2008): 889–922; M.T. Rivera, s.B. Soderstrom, and B. Uzzi, "Dynamics of Dyads in Social Networks: Assortative, Relational, and Proximity Mechanisms," *Annual Review of Sociology* 36 (2010): 91–115.

59. van Knippenberg, De Dreu, and Homan, "Work Group Diversity and Group Performance; K.A. Jehn, G.B. Northcraft, and M.A. Neale, "Why Differences Make a Difference: A Field Study of Diversity, Conflict, and Performance in Workgroups," *Administrative Science Quarterly* 44, no. 4 (1999): 741–63. For evidence that diversity/similarity does not always influence cohesion, see S.S. Webber and L.M. Donahue, "Impact of Highly and Less Job-Related Diversity on Work Group Cohesion and Performance: A Meta-Analysis," *Journal of Management* 27, no. 2 (2001): 141–62.

60. E. Aronson and J. Mills, "The Effects of Severity of Initiation on Liking for a Group," *Journal of Abnormal and Social Psychology* 59 (1959): 177–81; J.E. Hautaluoma and R.S. Enge, "Early Socialization into a Work Group: Severity of Initiations Revisited," *Journal of Social Behavior & Personality* 6 (1991): 725–48.

61. B. Mullen and C. Copper, "The Relation between Group Cohesiveness and Performance: An Integration," *Psychological Bulletin* 115 (1994): 210–27; C.J. Fullagar and D.O. Egleston, "Norming and Performing: Using Microworlds to Understand the Relationship between Team Cohesiveness and Performance," *Journal of Applied Social Psychology* 38, no. 10 (2008): 2574–93.

62. M. Rempel and R.J. Fisher, "Perceived Threat, Cohesion, and Group Problem Solving in Intergroup Conflict," *International Journal of Conflict Management* 8 (1997): 216–34; M.E. Turner and T. Horvitz, "The Dilemma of Threat: Group Effectiveness and Ineffectiveness under Adversity," in *Groups at Work: Theory and Research* ed. M.E. Turner (Mahwah, NJ: Lawrence Erlbaum Associates, 2001), 445–70.

63. A.V. Carron et al., "Cohesion and Performance in Sport: A Meta-Analysis," *Journal of Sport and Exercise Psychology* 24 (2002): 168–88; D.J. Beal et al., "Cohesion and Performance in Groups: A Meta-Analytic Clarification of Construct Relations," *Journal of Applied Psychology* 88, no. 6 (2003): 989–1004; S.M. Gully, D.J. Devine, and D.J. Whitney, "A Meta-Analysis of Cohesion and Performance: Effects of Level of Analysis and Task Interdependence," *Small Group Research* 43, no. 6 (2012): 702–25.

64. W. Piper et al., "Cohesion as a Basic Bond in Groups," *Human Relations* 36 (1983): 93–108; S.Y. Shin and S.G. Lee, "Effects of Hospital Workers? Friendship Networks on Job Stress," *PLoS ONE* 11, no. 2 (2016): e0149428.

65. S.M. Gully, D.J. Devine, and D.J. Whitney, "A Meta-Analysis of Cohesion and Performance: Effects of Level of Analysis and Task Interdependence," *Small Group Research* 43, no. 6 (2012): 702–25.

66. C. Langfred, "Is Group Cohesiveness a Double-Edged Sword? An Investigation of the Effects of Cohesiveness on Performance," *Small Group Research* 29 (1998): 124–43; K.L. Gammage, A.V. Carron, and P.A. Estabrooks, "Team Cohesion and Individual Productivity: The Influence of the Norm for Productivity and the Identifiability of Individual Effort," *Small Group Research* 32 (2001): 3–18. Concerns about existing research on cohesion–performance are discussed in M. Casey-Campbell and M.L. Martens, "Sticking It All Together: A Critical Assessment of the Group Cohesion–Performance Literature," *International Journal of Management Reviews* 11, no. 2 (2009): 223–46.

67. J. Mathieu et al., "Modeling Reciprocal Team Cohesion-Performance Relationships, as Impacted by Shared Leadership and Members' Competence," *Journal of Applied Psychology* 100, no. 3 (2015): 713–34.

68. D.M. Rousseau et al., "Not So Different after All: A Cross-Discipline View of Trust," *Academy of Management Review* 23 (1998): 393–404; I. Yang, "What Makes an Effective Team? The Role of Trust (Dis)Confirmation in Team Development," *European Management Journal* 32 (2014): 858–69; A.C. Costa, C.A. Fulmer, and N.R. Anderson, "Trust in Work Teams: An Integrative Review, Multilevel Model, and Future Directions," *Journal of Organizational Behavior* 39 (2018): 169–84.

69. D.J. McAllister, "Affect- and Cognition-Based Trust as Foundations for Interpersonal Cooperation in Organizations," *Academy of Management Journal* 38, no. 1 (1995): 24–59; M. Williams, "In Whom We Trust: Group Membership as an Affective Context for Trust Development," *Academy of Management Review* 26, no. 3 (2001): 377–96; M. Pirson and D. Malhotra, "Foundations of Organizational Trust: What Matters to Different Stakeholders?," *Organization Science* 22, no. 4 (2011): 1087–104.

70. R.J. Lewicki, E.C. Tomlinson, and N. Gillespie, "Models of Interpersonal Trust Development: Theoretical Approaches, Empirical Evidence, and Future Directions," *Journal of Management* 32, no. 6 (2006): 991–1022.

71. R.J. Lewicki, E.C. Tomlinson, and N. Gillespie, "Models of Interpersonal Trust Development: Theoretical Approaches, Empirical Evidence, and Future Directions," *Journal of Management* 32 (2006): 991–1022; N. Zhao et al., "The Impact of Traditionality/Modernity on Identification- and Calculus-Based Trust," *International Journal of Psychology* 54 (2019): 237–46.

72. E.M. Whitener et al., "Managers as Initiators of Trust: An Exchange Relationship Framework for Understanding Managerial Trustworthy Behavior," *Academy of Management Review* 23 (1998): 513–30; T. Simons et al., "How Leader Alignment of Words and Deeds Affects Followers: A Meta-Analysis of Behavioral Integrity Research," *Journal of Business Ethics* 132 (2015): 831–44.

73. H. Akrout and M.F. Diallo, "Fundamental Transformations of Trust and Its Drivers: A Multi-Stage Approach of Business-to-Business Relationships," *Industrial Marketing Management* 66 (2017): 159–71; A.C. Costa, C.A. Fulmer, and N.R. Anderson, "Trust in Work Teams: An Integrative Review, Multilevel Model, and Future Directions," *Journal of Organizational Behavior* 39 (2018): 169–84.

74. C.B. Crisp and S.L. Jarvenpaa, "Swift Trust in Global Virtual Teams: Trusting Beliefs and Normative Actions," *Journal of Personnel Psychology* 12 (2013): 45–56; O. Schilke and L. Huang, "Worthy of Swift Trust? How Brief Interpersonal Contact Affects Trust Accuracy," *Journal of Applied Psychology* 103 (2018): 1181–97.

75. K.T. Dirks and D.L. Ferrin, "The Role of Trust in Organizations," *Organization Science* 12 (2004): 450–67; I. Yang, "What Makes an Effective Team? The Role of Trust (Dis)Confirmation in Team Development," *European Management Journal* 32 (2014): 858–69.

76. L.A. DeChurch and J.R. Mesmer-Magnus, "The Cognitive Underpinnings of Effective Teamwork: A Meta-Analysis," *Journal of Applied Psychology* 95 (2010): 32–53; C. Aubé, V. Rousseau, and S. Tremblay, "Perceived Shared Understanding in Teams: The Motivational Effect of Being 'on the Same Page,'" *British Journal of Psychology* 106 (2015): 468–86; J.M. Schmidtke and A. Cummings, "The Effects of Virtualness on Teamwork Behavioral Components: The Role of Shared Mental Models," *Human Resource Management Review* 27 (2017): 660–77.

77. R. Rico, M. Sánchez-Manzanares, and C. Gibson, "Team Implicit Coordination Processes: A Team Knowledge-Based Approach," *Academy of Management Review* 33 (2008): 163–84; J.C. Gorman, "Team Coordination and Dynamics: Two Central Issues," *Current Directions in Psychological Science* 23 (2014): 355–60; J. Schmutz et al., "Effective Coordination in Medical Emergency Teams: The Moderating Role of Task Type," *European Journal of Work and Organizational Psychology* 24 (2015): 761–76.

78. L. Argote, B.L. Aven, and J. Kush, "The Effects of Communication Networks and Turnover on Transactive Memory and Group Performance," *Organization Science* 29 (2018): 191–206.

79. C.A. Beatty and B.A. Barker, *Building Smart Teams: Roadmap to High Performance* (Thousand Oaks, CA: Sage, 2004); W.G. Dyer, J.H. Dyer, and W.G. Dyer, *Team Building: Proven Strategies for Improving Team Performance,* 5th ed. (San Francisco: Jossey-Bass, 2013); C.N. Lacerenza et al., "Team Development Interventions: Evidence-Based Approaches for Improving Teamwork.," *American Psychologist* 73, no. 4 (2018): 517–31, https://doi.org/10.1037/amp0000295.

80. J. Langan-Fox and J. Anglim, "Mental Models, Team Mental Models, and Performance: Process, Development, and Future Directions," *Human Factors and Ergonomics in Manufacturing* 14 (2004): 331–52; J.E. Mathieu et al., "Scaling the Quality of Teammates' Mental Models: Equifinality and Normative Comparisons," *Journal of Organizational Behavior* 26 (2005): 37–56.

81. D.R. Seibold and R.A. Meyers, "Interventions in Groups: Methods for Facilitating Team Development," in *Research Methods for Studying Groups and Teams: A Guide to Approaches, Tools, and Technologies,* ed. A. Hollingshead and M.S. Poole (New York: Routledge, 2012), 418–41; A. Hämmelmann and R. van Dick, "Building the Team: Effect on the Individual—an Evaluation of Team Building Interventions (Entwickeln Im Team—Effekte FüR Den Einzelnen: Eine Evaluation Von Teamentwicklungsmaßnahmen)," *Gruppendynamik und Organisationsberatung* 44, no. 2 (2013): 221–38.

82. L.J. Martin, A.V. Carron, and S.M. Burke, "Team Building Interventions in Sport: A Meta-Analysis," *Sport & Exercise Psychology Journal* 5, no. 2 (2009): 3–18; C. Klein et al., "Does Team Building Work?," *Small Group Research* 40, no. 2 (2009): 181–222; I. Nadler, P.M. Sanderson, and H.G. Liley, "The Accuracy of Clinical Assessments as a Measure for Teamwork Effectiveness," *Simulation in Healthcare* 6, no. 5 (2011): 260–68; Y.J. Yi, "Effects of Team-Building on Communication and Teamwork among Nursing Students," *International Nursing Review* 63, no. 1 (2016): 33–40; C.N. Lacerenza et al., "Team Development Interventions: Evidence-Based Approaches for Improving Teamwork.," *American Psychologist* 73 (2018): 517–31.

83. R.W. Woodman and J.J. Sherwood, "The Role of Team Development in Organizational Effectiveness: A Critical Review," *Psychological Bulletin* 88 (1980): 166–86; C.J. Miller et al., "A Systematic Review of Team-Building Interventions in Non-Acute Healthcare Settings," *BMC Health Services Research* 18, no. 1 (2018): 146, https://doi.org/10.1186/s12913-018-2961-9.

84. K. Monsen and J. deBlok, "Buurtzorg Nederland," *American Journal of Nursing* 113, no. 8 (2013): 55–59; J.D. Blok, "Neighbourhood Scheme Transforms Services," *Primary Health Care* 25, no. 2 (2015); B. Gray, D.O. Sarnak, and J. Burgers, *Home Care by Self-Governing Nursing Teams: The Netherlands' Buurtzorg Model,* The Commonwealth Fund (New York: May 29, 2015); "The Buurtzorg Model—Buurtzorg International," *Buurtzorg—About Us,* accessed May 2, 2019, https://www.buurtzorg.com/about-us/buurtzorgmodel/; L. Gill, "Buurtzorg and the Power of Self-Managed Teams of Nurses," Episode 26, *Leadermorphosis,* December 17, 2018, accessed May 2, 2019, http://leadermorphosis.co/ep-26-buurtzorg-and-the-power-of-self-managed-teams-of-nurses.

85. Mohrman, Cohen, and Mohrman Jr., *Designing Team-Based Organizations: New Forms for Knowledge Work;* D.E. Yeatts and C. Hyten, *High- Performing Self-Managed Work Teams: A Comparison of Theory and Practice* (Thousand Oaks, CA: Sage, 1998); E.E. Lawler, *Organizing for High Performance* (San Francisco, CA: Jossey-Bass, 2001); R.J. Torraco, "Work Design Theory: A Review and Critique with Implications for Human Resource Development," *Human Resource Development Quarterly* 16, no. 1 (2005): 85–109.

86. P. Panchak, "Production Workers Can Be Your Competitive Edge," *Industry Week,* October 2004, 11; S.K. Muthusamy, J.V. Wheeler, and B.L. Simmons, "Self-Managing Work Teams: Enhancing Organizational Innovativeness," *Organization Development Journal* 23, no. 3 (2005): 53–66.

87. A. Krause and H. Dunckel, "Work Design and Customer Satisfaction: Effects of the Implementation of Semi-Autonomous Group Work on Customer Satisfaction Considering Employee Satisfaction and Group Performance (translated abstract)," *Zeitschrift für Arbeits-und Organisationspsychologie* 47, no. 4 (2003): 182–93; G.L. Stewart, S.H. Courtright, and M.R. Barrick, "Peer-Based Control in Self-Managing Teams: Linking Rational and Normative Influence with Individual and Group Performance," *Journal of Applied Psychology* 97 (2012): 435–47; E.E.M. Maurits et al., "Home-Care Nursing Staff in Self-Directed Teams Are More Satisfied with Their Job and Feel They Have More Autonomy over Patient Care: A Nationwide Survey," *Journal of Advanced Nursing* 73 (2017): 2430–40.

88. J.L. Cordery et al., "The Impact of Autonomy and Task Uncertainty on Team Performance: A Longitudinal Field Study," *Journal of Organizational Behavior* 31 (2010): 240–58; N.C. Magpili and P. Pazos, "Self-Managing Team Performance: A Systematic Review of Multilevel Input Factors," *Small Group Research* 49 (2018): 3–33; M. Renkema, T. Bondarouk, and A. Bos-Nehles, "Transformation to Self-Managing Teams: Lessons Learned: A Look at Current Trends and Data," *Strategic HR Review* 17 (2018): 81–84.

89. E. Ulich and W.G. Weber, "Dimensions, Criteria, and Evaluation of Work Group Autonomy," in *Handbook of Work Group Psychology* ed. M.A. West (Chichester, UK: John Wiley & Sons, Inc., 1996), 247–82.

90. J. Lipnack and J. Stamps, *Virtual Teams: People Working across Boundaries with Technology* (New York: Wiley, 2001); J.H. Dulebohn and J.E. Hoch, "Virtual Teams in Organizations," *Human Resource Management Review* 27 (2017): 569–74. Some suggest that remote teams differ slightly from distributed teams, where the latter have no physical base location. However, we group them together because they overlap in terms of OB concepts and practices.

91. L. Schweitzer and L. Duxbury, "Conceptualizing and Measuring the Virtuality of Teams," *Information Systems Journal* 20, no. 3 (2010): 267–95; M.K. Foster et al., "Rethinking Virtuality and Its Impact on Teams," *Small Group Research* 46, no. 3 (2015): 267–99; J.M. Schaubroeck and A. Yu, "When Does Virtuality Help or Hinder Teams? Core Team Characteristics as Contingency Factors," *Human Resource Management Review* 27 (2017): 635–47.

92. L.L. Gilson et al., "Virtual Teams Research: 10 Years, 10 Themes, and 10 Opportunities," *Journal of Management* 41, no. 5 (2015): 1313–37.

93. L. Cordery and C. Soo, "Overcoming Impediments to Virtual Team Effectiveness," *Human Factors and Ergonomics in Manufacturing & Service Industries* 18, no. 5 (2008): 487–500; A. Ortiz de Guinea, J. Webster, and D.S. Staples, "A Meta-Analysis of the Consequences of Virtualness on Team Functioning," *Information & Management* 49, no. 6 (2012): 301–08; T.A. O'Neill, L.A. Hambley, and G.S. Chatellier, "Cyberslacking, Engagement, and Personality in Distributed Work Environments," *Computers in Human Behavior* 40 (2014): 152–60.

94. L.L. Martins and M.C. Schilpzand, "Global Virtual Teams: Key Developments, Research Gaps, and Future Directions," *Research in Personnel and Human Resources Management* 30 (2011): 1–72; S. Krumm et al., "What Does It Take to Be a Virtual Team Player? The Knowledge, Skills, Abilities, and Other Characteristics Required in Virtual Teams," *Human Performance* 29, no. 2 (2016): 123–42; J.L. Gibbs, A. Sivunen, and M. Boyraz, "Investigating the Impacts of Team Type and Design on Virtual Team Processes," *Human Resource Management Review* 27 (2017): 590–603.

95. S.L. Marlow, C.N. Lacerenza, and E. Salas, "Communication in Virtual Teams: A Conceptual Framework and Research Agenda," *Human Resource Management Review* 27 (2017): 575–89; L. Handke et al., "Teams, Time, and Technology: Variations of Media Use Over Project Phases," *Small Group Research* 50 (2019): 266–305.

96. G.G. Harwood, "Design Principles for Successful Virtual Teams," in *The Handbook of High-Performance Virtual Teams: A Toolkit for Collaborating across Boundaries,* ed. J. Nemiro and M.M. Beyerlein (San Francisco, CA: Jossey-Bass, 2008), 59–84. Also see: H. Duckworth, "How TRW Automotive Helps Global Virtual Teams Perform at the Top of Their Game," *Global Business and Organizational Excellence* 28, no. 1 (2008): 6–16; L. Dubé and D. Robey, "Surviving the Paradoxes of Virtual Teamwork," *Information Systems Journal* 19, no. 1 (2009): 3–30.

97. L. Dubé and D. Robey, "Surviving the Paradoxes of Virtual Teamwork," *Information Systems Journal,* (2008).

98. V.H. Vroom and A.G. Jago, *The New Leadership* (Englewood Cliffs, NJ: Prentice Hall, 1988), 28–29.

99. M. Diehl and W. Stroebe, "Productivity Loss in Idea-Generating Groups: Tracking Down the Blocking Effects," *Journal of Personality and Social Psychology* 61 (1991): 392–403; W. Stroebe, B.A. Nijstad, and E.F. Rietzschel, "Beyond Productivity Loss in Brainstorming Groups: The Evolution of a Question," in *Advances in Experimental Social Psychology,* ed. P.Z. Mark and M.O. James (Academic Press, 2010), 157–203; D.D. Henningsen and M.L.M. Henningsen, "Generating Ideas About the Uses of Brainstorming: Reconsidering the Losses and Gains of Brainstorming Groups Relative to Nominal Groups," *Southern Communication Journal* 78 (2013): 42–55.

100. P. Bordia, B.E. Irmer, and D. Abusah, "Differences in Sharing Knowledge Interpersonally and via Databases: The Role of Evaluation Apprehension and Perceived Benefits," *European Journal of Work and Organizational Psychology* 15, no. 3 (2006): 262–80; L. McGrath, "When Pairing Reduces Scaring: The Effect Of Dyadic Ideation On Evaluation Apprehension," *International Journal of Innovation Management* 19, no. 04 (2015): 1550039.

101. D. Miller, *The Icarus Paradox: How Exceptional Companies Bring About Their Own Downfall* (New York: HarperBusiness, 1990); G. Whyte, "Recasting Janis's Groupthink Model: The Key Role of Collective Efficacy in Decision Fiascoes," *Organizational Behavior and Human Decision Processes* 73, no. 2–3 (1998): 185–209; K. Tasa and G. Whyte, "Collective Efficacy and Vigilant Problem Solving in Group Decision Making: A Non-Linear Model," *Organizational Behavior and Human Decision Processes* 96, no. 2 (2005): 119–29; T.L. Rapp et al., "The Role of Team Goal Monitoring in the Curvilinear Relationship between Team Efficacy and Team Performance.," *Journal of Applied Psychology* 99 (2014): 976–87; W.-W. Park, M.S. Kim, and S.M. Gully, "Effect of Cohesion on the Curvilinear Relationship Between Team Efficacy and Performance," *Small Group Research* 48 (2017): 455–81.

102. A.C. Edmondson and Z. Lei, "Psychological Safety: The History, Renaissance, and Future of an Interpersonal Construct," *Annual Review of Organizational Psychology and Organizational Behavior* 1 (2014): 23–43; A. Newman, R. Donohue, and N. Eva, "Psychological Safety: A Systematic Review of the Literature," *Human Resource Management Review* 27 (2017): 521–35.

103. The term *brainstorm* dates back to a New York murder trial in February 1907, during which an alienist (psychiatrist) gave expert testimony that the accused had a "brain storm," which he described as a form of temporary insanity. But by the mid-1920s, a brainstorm was associated with creative thinking. For example, *Popular Science* magazine's lead article in April 1926 described innovative camera operators, one of whom received a film award for a brainstorm of filming while strapped to a windmill. Advertising executive Alex Osborn (the *O* in BBDO, the largest creative agency owned by Omnicom) first described the brainstorming process in the little-known 1942 booklet *How to Think Up* (p. 29). Osborn gave a fuller description of the brainstorming process in his popular 1948 (*Your Creative Power*) and 1953 (*Applied Imagination*) books. See A.F. Osborn, *How to Think Up* (New York: McGraw Hill, 1942), Chap. 4; A.F. Osborn, *Your Creative Power* (New York: Scribner's Sons, 1948); A.F. Osborn, *Applied Imagination* (New York: Scribner's Sons, 1953).

104. The term "brainstorm" dates back to a New York murder case in 1907 as one expert's reference to temporary insanity. By the mid-1920s, the meaning of a brainstorm had shifted markedly to a state of creative thinking. Advertising executive Alex Osborn (the *O* in BBDO, a global advertising agency) first described the brainstorming process in the little-known 1942 booklet *How to Think Up* (p. 29). Osborn gave a fuller description of the brainstorming process in his popular 1948 (Your Creative Power) and 1953 (Applied Imagination) books. See: A.F. Osborn, *How to Think Up* (New York: McGraw Hill, 1942), Chap. 4; A.F. Osborn, *Your Creative Power* (New York: Charles Scribner's Sons, 1948); A.F. Osborn, *Applied Imagination* (New York: Charles Scribner's Sons, 1953).

105. B. Mullen, C. Johnson, and E. Salas, "Productivity Loss in Brainstorming Groups: A Meta-Analytic Integration," *Basic and Applied Psychology* 12 (1991): 2–23.

106. R.I. Sutton and A. Hargadon, "Brainstorming Groups in Context: Effectiveness in a Product Design Firm," *Administrative Science Quarterly* 41(1996): 685–718; T. Kelley, *The Art of Innovation* (New York: Currency Doubleday, 2001); T. Kelley, *The Ten Faces of Innovation* (New York: Doubleday, 2005); A.B. Hargadon and B.A. Bechky, "When Collections of Creatives Become Creative Collectives: A Field Study of Problem Solving at Work," *Organization Science* 17, no. 4 (2006): 484–500; K. Sawyer, *Group Genius: The Creative Power of Collaboration* (New York: Basic Books, 2007). However, brainstorming researchers now suggest that brainstorming can be quite effective when

specific conditions are put in place. See: P.B. Paulus and J.B. Kenworthy, "Effective Brainstorming," in *The Oxford Handbook of Group Creativity and Innovation,* ed. P.B. Paulus and B.A. Nijstad (New York: Oxford University Press, 2019), 287–306.

107. J. Baruah and P.B. Paulus, "Effects of Training on Idea Generation in Groups," *Small Group Research* 39, no. 5 (2008): 523–41; N.W. Kohn, P.B. Paulus, and Y.H. Choi, "Building on the Ideas of Others: An Examination of the Idea Combination Process," *Journal of Experimental Social Psychology* 47(2011): 554–61. Recent studies provide evidence that brainstorming is effective in conditions closer to real-world organizations. See: J.M. Levine et al., "Group Brainstorming: When Regulatory Nonfit Enhances Performance," *Group Processes & Intergroup Relations* 19, no. 2 (2016): 257–71, https://doi.org/10.1177/1368430215577226; K.J. Levine, K.B. Heuett, and K.M. Reno, "Re-Operationalizing Established Groups in Brainstorming: Validating Osborn's Claims," *The Journal of Creative Behavior* 51, no. 3 (2017): 252–62, https://doi.org/10.1002/jocb.122.

108. N.W. Kohn and S.M. Smith, "Collaborative Fixation: Effects of Others' Ideas on Brainstorming," *Applied Cognitive Psychology* 25, no. 3 (2011): 359–71; A. Fink et al., "Stimulating Creativity Via the Exposure to Other People's Ideas," *Human Brain Mapping* 33, no. 11 (2012): 2603–10.

109. P.A. Heslin, "Better Than Brainstorming? Potential Contextual Boundary Conditions to Brainwriting for Idea Generation in Organizations," *Journal of Occupational and Organizational Psychology* 82, no. 1 (2009): 129–45; N. Michinov, "Is Electronic Brainstorming or Brainwriting the Best Way to Improve Creative Performance in Groups? An Overlooked Comparison of Two Idea-Generation Techniques," *Journal of Applied Social Psychology* 42 (2012): E222–E243; M. Litcanu et al., "Brain-Writing Vs. Brainstorming Case Study For Power Engineering Education," *Procedia - Social and Behavioral Sciences* 191 (2015): 387–90.

110. R.B. Gallupe, L.M. Bastianutti, and W.H. Cooper, "Unblocking Brainstorms," *Journal of Applied Psychology* 76 (1991): 137–42; W.H. Cooper et al., "Some Liberating Effects of Anonymous Electronic Brainstorming," *Small Group Research* 29, no. 2 (1998): 147–78; J. Baruah and P.B. Paulus, "The Role of Time and Category Relatedness in Electronic Brainstorming," *Small Group Research* 47 (2016): 333–42; H. Al-Samarraie and S. Hurmuzan, "A Review of Brainstorming Techniques in Higher Education," *Thinking Skills and Creativity* 27 (2018): 78–91.

111. A.L. Delbecq, A.H. Van de Ven, and D.H. Gustafson, *Group Techniques for Program Planning: A Guide to Nominal Group and Delphi Processes* (Middleton, Wis: Green Briar Press, 1986).

112. S. Frankel, "NGT + MDS: An Adaptation of the Nominal Group Technique for Ill-Structured Problems," *Journal of Applied Behavioral Science* 23 (1987): 543–51; H. Barki and A. Pinsonneault, "Small Group Brainstorming and Idea Quality: Is Electronic Brainstorming the Most Effective Approach?," *Small Group Research* 32, no. 2 (2001): 158–205; P. P. Lago et al., "Structuring Group Decision Making in a Web-Based Environment by Using the Nominal Group Technique," *Computers & Industrial Engineering* 52, no. 2 (2007): 277–95; D.M. Spencer,

"Facilitating Public Participation in Tourism Planning on American Indian Reservations: A Case Study Involving the Nominal Group Technique," *Tourism Management* 31, no. 5 (2011): 684–90.

CHAPTER 9

1. V. Heffernan, "Meet Is Murder," *New York Times,* February 28, 2016, 28; D. Teare, "Curing Our Slack Addiction," AgileBits Blog, April 19, 2016, https://blog.agilebits.com/2016/04/19/curing-our-slack-addiction/; J. Titcomb, "Slack's Stewart Butterfield: 'We'll Never Kill Email,'" *The Telegraph (UK),* May 6, 2017; J. Dujay, "Enterprise Social Media Gains Traction with Facebook Launch," *Canadian HR Reporter,* November 13, 2017; A. Liu, "Death By a Thousand Pings: The Hidden Side of Using Slack," Medium (blog), March 20, 2018, https://medium.com/counter-intuition/the-hidden-side-of-using-slack-2443d9b66f8a; "New Study Shows Grim Reality of Communication Overload at Work," News release (Seattle: RescueTime, July 11, 2018); R. Molla, "The Productivity Pit: How Slack Is Ruining Work," *Vox,* May 1, 2019.

2. A.H. Van de Ven, A.L. Delbecq, and R. Koenig, Jr., "Determinants of Coordination Modes within Organizations," *American Sociological Review* 41, no. 2 (1976): 322–38; J.H. Gittell, R. Seidner, and J. Wimbush, "A Relational Model of How High-Performance Work Systems Work," *Organization Science* 21, no. 2 (2010): 490–506; R. Foy et al., "Meta-Analysis: Effect of Interactive Communication between Collaborating Primary Care Physicians and Specialists," *Annals of Internal Medicine* 152, no. 4 (2010): 247–58.

3. C. Barnard, *The Functions of the Executive* (Cambridge, MA: Harvard University Press, 1938), pg. 82. Barnard's entire statement also refers to the other features of organizations that we describe in Chapter 1, namely that (a) people are willing to contribute their effort to the organization and (b) they have a common purpose.

4. J. O'Toole and W. Bennis, "What's Needed Next: A Culture of Candor," *Harvard Business Review* 87, no. 6 (2009): 54–61.

5. W.J.L. Elving, "The Role of Communication in Organisational Change," *Corporate Communications* 10, no. 2 (2005): 129–38; P.M. Leonardi, T.B. Neeley, and E.M. Gerber, "How Managers Use Multiple Media: Discrepant Events, Power, and Timing in Redundant Communication," *Organization Science* 23, no. 1 (2012): 98–117; D.A. Tucker, P. Yeow, and G.T. Viki, "Communicating During Organizational Change Using Social Accounts: The Importance of Ideological Accounts," *Management Communication Quarterly* 27, no. 2 (2013): 184–209.

6. R.E. Baumeister and M.R. Leary, "The Need to Belong: Desire for Interpersonal Attachments as a Fundamental Human Motivation," *Psychological Bulletin* 117 (1995): 497–529; K.H. Greenaway et al., "Social Identities Promote Well-Being Because They Satisfy Global Psychological Needs," *European Journal of Social Psychology* 46 (2016): 294–307; N. Steverink et al., "The Associations of Different Social Needs with Psychological Strengths and Subjective Well-Being: An Empirical Investigation Based on Social Production Function Theory," *Journal of Happiness Studies* 21 (2020): 799–824.

7. S. Cohen, "The Pittsburgh Common Cold Studies: Psychosocial Predictors of Susceptibility to Respiratory Infectious Illness," *International Journal of Behavioral Medicine* 12, no. 3 (2005): 123–31; B. A. Scott et al., "A Daily Investigation of the Role of Manager Empathy on Employee Well-Being," *Organizational Behavior and Human Decision Processes* 113, no. 2 (2010): 127–40; S. Y. Shin and S. G. Lee, "Effects of Hospital Workers' Friendship Networks on Job Stress," *PLoS ONE* 11, no. 2 (2016): e0149428.

8. C.E. Shannon and W. Weaver, *The Mathematical Theory of Communication* (Urbana, Il: University of Illinois Press, 1949); R.M. Krauss and S.R. Fussell, "Social Psychological Models of Interpersonal Communication," in *Social Psychology: Handbook of Basic Principles,* ed. E.T. Higgins and A. Kruglanski (New York: Guilford Press, 1996), 655–701.

9. J.R. Carlson and R.W. Zmud, "Channel Expansion Theory and the Experiential Nature of Media Richness Perceptions," *Academy of Management Journal* 42 (1999): 153–70.

10. Y. van den Boer et al., "Towards a Model of Source and Channel Choices in Business-to-Government Service Interactions: A Structural Equation Modeling Approach," *Government Information Quarterly* 34 (2017): 434–56; R. McColl and M. Michelotti, "Sorry, Could You Repeat the Question? Exploring Video-Interview Recruitment Practice in HRM," *Human Resource Management Journal* 29 (2019): 637–56.

11. M. Hauben and R. Hauben, "Netizens: On the History and Impact of Usenet and the Internet," *First Monday* 3, no. 8 (1998); J. Abbate, *Inventing the Internet* (Cambridge, MA: MIT Press, 1999); B.M. Leiner et al., *Brief History of the Internet* (Reston, VA: Internet. Society, October 15, 2012).

12. "Email Statistics Report, 2019-2023" (Palo Alto, CA: The Radicati Group, February 2019); "Communication Barriers in the Modern Workplace" (London: The Economist Intelligence Unit, March 2018); L. Wright and N. McCullough, "New Survey Explores the Changing Landscape of Teamwork," *Microsoft 365 Blog* (blog), April 19, 2018, https://www.microsoft.com/en-us/microsoft-365/blog/2018/04/19/new-survey-explores-the-changing-landscape-of-teamwork/.

13. N.B. Ducheneaut and L.A. Watts, "In Search of Coherence: A Review of E-Mail Research," *Human–Computer Interaction* 20, no. 1–2 (2005): 11–48; R.S. Mano and G.S. Mesch, "E-Mail Characteristics, Work Performance and Distress," *Computers in Human Behavior* 26, no. 1 (2010): 61–69.

14. W. Lucas, "Effects of E-mail on the Organization," *European Management Journal* 16 (1998): 18–30; D.A. Owens, M.A. Neale, and R.I. Sutton, "Technologies of Status Management Status Dynamics in E-Mail Communications," *Research on Managing Groups and Teams* 3 (2000): 205–30; G. de La Rupelle, C. Guthrie, and M. Kalika, "La relation entre l'intensité perçue d'utilisation de la messagerie électronique et la qualité de la relation hiérarchique," *Relations Industrielles* 70 (2015): 157–85; C. M. Brotheridge, D. J. Neufeld, and B. Dyck, "Communicating Virtually in a Global Organization," *Journal of Managerial Psychology* 30 (2015): 909–24.

15. N. Panteli, "Richness, Power Cues and Email Text," *Information & Management* 40 (2002): 75–86; C. T. Carr and C. Stefaniak, "Sent from My iPhone: The Medium and Message as Cues of Sender Professionalism in Mobile Telephony," *Journal of Applied Communication Research* 40 (2012): 403–24; D. C. DeAndrea, "Advancing Warranting Theory," *Communication Theory* 24 (2014): 186–204; C. M. Brotheridge, D. J. Neufeld, and B. Dyck, "Communicating Virtually in a Global Organization," *Journal of Managerial Psychology* 30 (2015): 909–24.

16. N. Epley and J. Kruger, "When What You Type Isn't What They Read: The Perseverance of Stereotypes and Expectancies over E-Mail," *Journal of Experimental Social Psychology* 41, no. 4 (2005): 414–22; J.B. Walther et al., "Computer-Mediated Communication and the Reduction of Prejudice: A Controlled Longitudinal Field Experiment among Jews and Arabs in Israel," *Computers in Human Behavior* 52 (2015): 550–58.

17. K. Byron, "Carrying Too Heavy a Load? The Communication and Miscommunication of Emotion by Email," *Academy of Management Review* 33 (2008): 309–27; M.A. Riordan and L.A. Trichtinger, "Overconfidence at the Keyboard: Confidence and Accuracy in Interpreting Affect in E-Mail Exchanges," *Human Communication Research* 43 (2017): 1–24; K. Lohmann, S.S. Pyka, and C. Zanger, "The Effects of Smileys on Receivers' Emotions," *Journal of Consumer Marketing* 34 (2017): 489–95; C. Laubert and J. Parlamis, "Are You Angry (Happy, Sad) or Aren't You? Emotion Detection Difficulty in Email Negotiation," *Group Decision and Negotiation* 28 (2019): 377–413.

18. H. Lee, "Behavioral Strategies for Dealing with Flaming in an Online Forum," *The Sociological Quarterly* 46 (2005): 385–403; A.K. Turnage, "Email Flaming Behaviors and Organizational Conflict," *Journal of Computer-Mediated Communication* 13 (2007): 43–59; K. Byron, "Carrying Too Heavy a Load? The Communication and Miscommunication of Emotion by Email," *Academy of Management Review* 33 (2008): 309–27.

19. N. Sobotta and M. Hummel, "A Capacity Perspective on E-Mail Overload: How E-Mail Use Contributes to Information Overload" (paper presented at the 2015 48th Hawaii International Conference on System Sciences, January 5–8, 2015), 692–701; S. Drössler et al., "Informationsüberflutung durch digitale Medien am Arbeitsplatz (Information overload by digital media at the workplace. Systematic review of qualitative studies)," *Zentralblatt für Arbeitsmedizin, Arbeitsschutz und Ergonomie (*Central Journal for Occupational Medicine, Occupational Safety and Ergonomics) 68 (2018): 77–88.

20. "Email Statistics Report, 2019-2023" (Palo Alto, CA: The Radicati Group, February 2019). The daily number of text messages globally could be as much as 300 billion. This is estimated from statistics on Apple iMessages, Whatapp messages, and a recent estimate of 26 billion daily messages in the U.S. in 2018. See "How Many Texts Do People Send Every Day (2018)?," November 2018, https://www.textrequest.com/blog/how-many-texts-people-send-per-day/.

21. Social media definitions in the literature tend to be obtuse, varied, and in many cases, elusive. Our definition is based on two of the more widely cited sources: A.M. Kaplan and M. Haenlein, "Users of the World, Unite! The Challenges and Opportunities of Social Media," *Business Horizons* 53 (2010): 59–68; C.T. Carr and R.A. Hayes, "Social Media: Defining, Developing, and Divining," *Atlantic Journal of Communication* 23 (2015): 46–65.

22. J.H. Kietzmann et al., "Social Media? Get Serious! Understanding the Functional Building Blocks of Social Media," *Business Horizons* 54 (2011): 241–51; J.W. Treem and P.M. Leonardi, "Social Media Use in Organizations: Exploring the Affordances of Visibility, Editability, Persistence, and Association," *Communication Yearbook* 36 (2012): 143–89; C.V. Baccarella et al., "Social Media? It's Serious! Understanding the Dark Side of Social Media," *European Management Journal* 36 (2018): 431–38.

23. W. van Zoonen, T.G.L.A. van der Meer, and J.W.M. Verhoeven, "Employees Work-Related Social-Media Use: His Master's Voice," *Public Relations Review* 40 (2014): 850–52; G. Martin, E. Parry, and P. Flowers, "Do Social Media Enhance Constructive Employee Voice All of the Time or Just Some of the Time?," *Human Resource Management Journal* 25 (2015): 541–62; W. van Zoonen, J.W.M. Verhoeven, and R. Vliegenthart, "How Employees Use Twitter to Talk about Work: A Typology of Work-Related Tweets," *Computers in Human Behavior* 55, Part A (2016): 329–39; P. Leonardi and T. Neeley, "What Managers Need to Know About Social Tools," *Harvard Business Review,* Nov-Dec, 2017.

24. S. Bonaccio et al., "Nonverbal Behavior and Communication in the Workplace: A Review and an Agenda for Research," *Journal of Management* 42 (2016): 1044–74.

25. L.Z. Tiedens and A.R. Fragale, "Power Moves: Complementarity in Dominant and Submissive Nonverbal Behavior," *Journal of Personality and Social Psychology* 84, no. 3 (2003): 558–68.

26. P. Ekman and E. Rosenberg, *What the Face Reveals: Basic and Applied Studies of Spontaneous Expression Using the Facial Action Coding System* (Oxford, England: Oxford University Press, 1997); P. Winkielman and K.C. Berridge, "Unconscious Emotion," *Current Directions in Psychological Science* 13, no. 3 (2004): 120–23.

27. W.J. Becker and R. Cropanzano, "Organizational Neuroscience: The Promise and Prospects of an Emerging Discipline," *Journal of Organizational Behavior* 31 (2010): 1055–59; S.G. Barsade, C.G.V. Coutifaris, and J. Pillemer, "Emotional Contagion in Organizational Life," *Research in Organizational Behavior* 38 (2018): 137–51.

28. M. Sonnby-Borgstrom, P. Jonsson, and O. Svensson, "Emotional Empathy as Related to Mimicry Reactions at Different Levels of Information Processing," *Journal of Nonverbal Behavior* 27 (2003): 3–23; V. Vijayalakshmi and S. Bhattacharyya, "Emotional Contagion and Its Relevance to Individual Behavior and Organizational Processes: A Position Paper," *Journal of Business and Psychology* 27 (2012): 363–74. However, emotional contagion is not universally automatic. It may depend on social relations between the parties. See: M. Wróbel and K.K. Imbir, "Broadening the Perspective on Emotional Contagion and Emotional Mimicry: The Correction Hypothesis," *Perspectives on Psychological Science* 14 (2019): 437–51.

29. T.L. Chartrand and J.L. Lakin, "The Antecedents and Consequences of Human Behavioral Mimicry," *Annual Review of Psychology* 64 (2013): 285–308; E. Prochazkova and M.E. Kret, "Connecting Minds and Sharing Emotions through Mimicry: A Neurocognitive Model of Emotional Contagion," *Neuroscience & Biobehavioral Reviews* 80 (2017): 99–114.

30. A.R. Dennis, R.M. Fuller, and J.S. Valacich, "Media, Tasks, and Communication Processes: A Theory of Media Synchronicity," *MIS Quarterly* 32 (2008): 575–600; S. Taipale, "Synchronicity Matters: Defining the Characteristics of Digital Generations," *Information, Communication & Society* 19 (2016): 80–94; I. Geiger and C. Laubert, "Situational Strategic versus Personal Influences on Negotiation Medium Choice: Media Synchronicity Theory and Affect for Communication Channel," *International Journal of Conflict Management* 29 (2018): 398–423.

31. R.E. Rice, "Media Appropriateness: Using Social Presence Theory to Compare Traditional and New Organizational Media," *Human Communication Research* 19 (1993): 451–84; D. Gooch and L. Watts, "The Impact of Social Presence on Feelings of Closeness in Personal Relationships," *Interacting with Computers* 27 (2015): 661–74; C.S. Oh, J.N. Bailenson, and G. Welch, "A Systematic Review of Social Presence: Definition, Antecedents, and Implications," *Frontiers in Robotics and AI* (October 15, 2018), https://doi.org/10.3389/frobt.2018.00114.

32. N. Walter, K. Ortbach, and B. Niehaves, "Designing Electronic Feedback—Analyzing the Effects of Social Presence on Perceived Feedback Usefulness," *International Journal of Human-Computer Studies* 76 (2015): 1–11; S.C. Srivastava and S. Chandra, "Social Presence in Virtual World Collaboration: An Uncertainty Reduction Perspective Using a Mixed Methods Approach," *MIS Quarterly* 42 (2018): 779–803.

33. J. Fulk, "Social Construction of Communication Technology," *Academy of Management Journal* 36 (1993): 921–50; J.W. Turner et al., "Exploring the Dominant Media: How Does Media Use Reflect Organizational Norms and Affect Performance?," *Journal of Business Communication* 43 (2006): 220–50; J.B. Bayer, S.W. Campbell, and R. Ling, "Connection Cues: Activating the Norms and Habits of Social Connectedness," *Communication Theory* 26 (2016): 128–49.

34. Z. Lee and Y. Lee, "Emailing the Boss: Cultural Implications of Media Choice," *IEEE Transactions on Professional Communication* 52, no. 1 (2009): 61–74; D. Holtbrügge, A. Weldon, and H. Rogers, "Cultural Determinants of Email Communication Styles," *International Journal of Cross Cultural Management* 13, no. 1 (2013): 89–110.

35. "Emojis Gain Hearts, Business in Shy Chinese," *Xinhua News Agency,* August 18, 2016; J. D'Onfro, "13 Rules Regarding Proper Email Etiquette from Around the World," *Mental Floss,* February 20, 2017; Z. Zhang, "WeChat's Exclusive Emojis Express Emotions Western Apps Cannot," *Quartz,* July 19, 2018; O. Surcouf, "Korean Apps Conquer Asia with Cute Emojis," *Asia Times,* March 16, 2019.

36. R.C. King, "Media Appropriateness: Effects of Experience on Communication Media Choice," *Decision Sciences* 28 (1997): 877–910; A. Oeldorf-Hirsch and K.L. Nowak, "There Is Something I

Need to Tell You: Balancing Appropriateness and Efficiency in Modality Choice for Interpersonal Disclosures," *Communication Studies* 69 (2018): 125–44.

37. K.K. Stephens, A.K. Barrett, and M.J. Mahometa, "Organizational Communication in Emergencies: Using Multiple Channels and Sources to Combat Noise and Capture Attention," *Human Communication Research* 39 (2013): 230–51; J. Eden and A.E. Veksler, "Relational Maintenance in the Digital Age: Implicit Rules and Multiple Modalities," *Communication Quarterly* 64 (2016): 119–44. Marshall McLuhan's treatise on the medium is the message is found in: M. McLuhan, *Understanding Media: The Extensions of Man* (New York: McGraw Hill, 1964).

38. Kurt Wallace v AFS Security 24/7 Pty Ltd, No. 4292 (Fair Work Commission (Australia) June 28, 2019).

39. R.L. Daft and R.H. Lengel, "Information Richness: A New Approach to Managerial Behavior and Organization Design," *Research in Organizational Behavior* 6 (1984): 191–233; R.H. Lengel and R.L. Daft, "The Selection of Communication Media as an Executive Skill," *Academy of Management Executive* 2 (1988): 225–32.

40. H. Rodriguez et al., "Huddle Up!: The Adoption and Use of Structured Team Communication for VA Medical Home Implementation," *Health Care Management Review* 40 (2015): 286–99; R. W. Quinn and J. S. Bunderson, "Could We Huddle on This Project? Participant Learning in Newsroom Conversations," *Journal of Management* 42 (2016): 386–418.

41. R.E. Rice, "Task Analyzability, Use of New Media, and Effectiveness: A Multi-Site Exploration of Media Richness," *Organization Science* 3 (1992): 475–500; V.W. Kupritz and E. Cowell, "Productive Management Communication: Online and Face-to-Face," *Journal of Business Communication* 48 (2011): 54–82.

42. R.F. Otondo et al., "The Complexity of Richness: Media, Message, and Communication Outcomes," *Information & Management* 45, no. 1 (2008): 21–30.

43. N.L. Reinsch Jr., J.W. Turner, and C.H. Tinsley, "Multicommunicating: A Practice Whose Time Has Come?," *Academy of Management Review* 33 (2008): 391–403; A.F. Cameron and J. Webster, "Multicommunicating: Juggling Multiple Conversations in the Workplace," *Information Systems Research* 24 (2013): 352–71; N.L. Reinsch and J.W. Turner, "Multicommunicator Aspirational Stress, Suggestions for Teaching and Research, and Other Insights After 10 Years of Multicommunication Research," *Journal of Business and Technical Communication* 33 (2019): 141–71.

44. S. Xu, Z. Wang, and P. David, "Media Multitasking and Well-Being of University Students," *Computers in Human Behavior* 55, Part A (2016): 242–50; A.-F. Cameron et al., "Multicommunicating in Meetings: Effects of Locus, Topic Relatedness, and Meeting Medium," *Management Communication Quarterly* 32 (2018): 303–36.

45. J.R. Carlson and R.W. Zmud, "Channel Expansion Theory and the Experiential Nature of Media Richness Perceptions," *Academy of Management Journal* 42 (1999): 153–70; N. Kock, "Media Naturalness Theory: Human Evolution

and Behaviour towards Electronic Communication Technologies," in *Applied Evolutionary Psychology*, ed. S.C. Roberts (Oxford, UK: Oxford University Press, 2012), 381–98; I. Blau, O. Weiser, and Y. Eshet-Alkalai, "How Do Medium Naturalness and Personality Traits Shape Academic Achievement and Perceived Learning? An Experimental Study of Face-to-Face and Synchronous E-Learning," *Research in Learning Technology* 25 (2017), https://doi.org/10.25304/rlt.v25.1974.

46. L.P. Robert and A.R. Dennis, "Paradox of Richness: A Cognitive Model of Media Choice," *IEEE Transactions on Professional Communication* 48 (2005): 10–21; C. Belletier et al., "Choking under Monitoring Pressure: Being Watched by the Experimenter Reduces Executive Attention," *Psychonomic Bulletin & Review* 22 (2015): 1410–16; C. Belletier, A. Normand, and P. Huguet, "Social-Facilitation-and-Impairment Effects: From Motivation to Cognition and the Social Brain," *Current Directions in Psychological Science* 28 (2019): 260–65.

47. E.V. Wilson, "Perceived Effectiveness of Interpersonal Persuasion Strategies in Computer-Mediated Communication," *Computers in Human Behavior* 19, no. 5 (2003): 537–52; K. Sassenberg, M. Boos, and S. Rabung, "Attitude Change in Face-to-Face and Computer-Mediated Communication: Private Self-Awareness Ad Mediator and Moderator," *European Journal of Social Psychology* 35 (2005): 361–74; P. Di Blasio and L. Milani, "Computer-Mediated Communication and Persuasion: Peripheral vs. Central Route to Opinion Shift," *Computers in Human Behavior* 24, no. 3 (2008): 798–815.

48. Most sources incorrectly attribute this famous quotation (usually with "accomplished" rather than "achieved") to the Irish playwright and social critic George Bernard Shaw. To the best of our knowledge, it was first uttered in the late 1950s by Joe Coffman, president of Tecnifax Corporation (which made visual education technology). Coffman held patents for specialized slide transparencies and related apparatus on overhead projectors. Given the company's products, Coffman was also an enthusiast of visual and interpersonal communication. Twice each year at its head office in Holyoke, Massachusetts, Tecnifax held international seminars on communication practices. This quotation was originally published in a 1960 article summarizing a public health conference, during which one of the speakers credited Coffman as the originator of this quotation. There is one more twist to the origins of this quotation. Coffman may have adapted it from the following passage in William H. Whyte's 1950 *Fortune* magazine article on communication, which became one of *Fortune*'s most-read articles: "The great enemy of communication, we find, is the illusion of it." See W. H. Whyte, "Is Anybody Listening," *Fortune,* September 1950, 77–83, 167–78; "Web of Mutual Anticipations: Conference Report," *Public Health Reports* 75, no. 10 (1960): 927–32; D. M. Davis, *A Biased Biography: Mine*(Lincoln, NE: iUniverse, 2004); "The Biggest Problem in Communication Is the Illusion That It Has Taken Place," *Quote Investigator,* August 31, 2014, http://quoteinvestigator.com/2014/08/31/illusion/.

49. J.W. Bang and D. Rahnev, "Stimulus Expectation Alters Decision Criterion but Not Sensory Signal in Perceptual Decision Making,"

Scientific Reports 7, no. 1 (December 6, 2017): 1–12; M.M. Roghanizad and V.K. Bohns, "Ask in Person: You're Less Persuasive than You Think over Email," *Journal of Experimental Social Psychology* 69 (March 2017): 223–26; A. Tapal, Y. Yeshurun, and B. Eitam, "Relevance-Based Processing: Little Role for Task-Relevant Expectations," *Psychonomic Bulletin & Review* 26 (2019): 1426–32.

50. R.M. Krauss, "The Psychology of Verbal Communication," in *International Encyclopedia of the Social and Behavioral Sciences,* ed. N. Smelser and P. Baltes (London, CA: Elsevier, 2002), 16161–16165.

51. A.M. Carton, C. Murphy, and J.R. Clark, "A (Blurry) Vision of the Future: How Leader Rhetoric about Ultimate Goals Influences Performance," *Academy of Management Journal* 57 (2014): 1544–70; P.D. Joshi et al., "Communicating with Distant Others: The Functional Use of Abstraction," *Social Psychological and Personality Science* 7 (2016): 37–44. Ambiguous language by politicians also increases with with the diversity of constituents. See: C. Chapp et al., "Going Vague: Ambiguity and Avoidance in Online Political Messaging," *Social Science Computer Review* 37 (2019): 591–610.

52. A.R. Links et al., "Surgeon Use of Medical Jargon with Parents in the Outpatient Setting," *Patient Education and Counseling* 102 (2019): 1111–18.

53. C.E. Connelly et al., "Knowledge Hiding in Organizations," *Journal of Organizational Behavior* 33 (2012): 64–88.

54. J. O'Toole and W. Bennis, "What's Needed Next: A Culture of Candor," *Harvard Business Review,* (2009).

55. T.W. Jackson and P. Farzaneh, "Theory-Based Model of Factors Affecting Information Overload," *International Journal of Information Management* 32, no. 6 (2012): 523–32; S. Drössler et al., "Informationsüberflutung durch digitale Medien am Arbeitsplatz (Information overload by digital media at the workplace. Systematic review of qualitative studies)," *Zentralblatt für Arbeitsmedizin, Arbeitsschutz und Ergonomie (*Central Journal for Occupational Medicine, Occupational Safety and Ergonomics) 68, no. 2 (2018): 77–88, https://doi.org/10.1007/s40664-018-0267-8.

56. A. Edmunds and A. Morris, "The Problem of Information Overload in Business Organisations: A Review of the Literature," *International Journal of Information Management* 20 (2000): 17–28;C.-Y. Li, "Why Do Online Consumers Experience Information Overload? An Extension of Communication Theory," *Journal of Information Science* 43, no. 6 (2017): 835–51, https://doi.org/10.1177/0165551516670096.

57. A.-W. Harzing, K. Köster, and U. Magner, "Babel in Business: The Language Barrier and Its Solutions in the HQ-Subsidiary Relationship," *Journal of World Business* 46 (2011): 279–87; N. Aichhorn and J. Puck, "Bridging the Language Gap in Multinational Companies: Language Strategies and the Notion of Company-Speak," *Journal of World Business* 52 (2017): 386–403; D.E. Welch and L.S. Welch, "Developing Multilingual Capacity: A Challenge for the Multinational Enterprise," *Journal of Management* 44 (2018): 854–69.

58. D. Woodruff, "Crossing Culture Divide Early Clears Merger Paths," *Asian Wall Street Journal,* 28

May 2001, 9; "Differentstrokes," *Personnel Today,* 25 November 2008, 190.

59. D. C. Barnlund, *Communication Styles of Japanese and Americans: Images and Realities* (Belmont, CA: Wadsworth, 1988); H. Yamada, *American and Japanese Business Discourse: A Comparison of Interaction Styles* (Norwood, NJ: Ablex, 1992), chap. 2; T. Hasegawa and W. B. Gudykunst, "Silence in Japan and the United States," *Journal of Cross-Cultural Psychology* 29 (1998): 668–84; M. Fujio, "Silence during Intercultural Communication: A Case Study," *Corporate Communications* 9 (2004): 331–39.

60. Adapted from: M. Nakamoto, "Cross-Cultural Conversations," *Financial Times (London),* 12 January 2012, 16.

61. H. Blagg, "A Just Measure of Shame?," *British Journal of Criminology* 37 (1997): 481–501; R. E. Axtell, *Gestures: The Do's and Taboos of Body Language around the World,* rev. ed. (New York: Wiley, 1998); A. McCarthy et al., "Cultural Display Rules Drive Eye Gaze During Thinking," *Journal of Cross-Cultural Psychology* 37 (2006): 717–22; H. Akechi et al., "Attention to Eye Contact in the West and East: Autonomic Responses and Evaluative Ratings," *PLOS ONE* 8, no. 3 (March 13, 2013): e59312; H. Yamada, O.R. Kelm, and D.A. Victor, *The 7 Keys to Communicating in Japan: An Intercultural Approach* (Georgetown University Press, 2017), pp. 163-65.

62. D. Tannen, *You Just Don't Understand: Men and Women in Conversation* (New York: Ballantine Books, 1990); J.L. Locke, *Duels and Duets: Why Men and Women Talk So Differently* (Cambridge, UK: Cambridge University Press, 2011); M.R. Atai and F. Chahkandi, "Democracy in Computer-Mediated Communication: Gender, Communicative Style, and Amount of Participation in Professional Listservs," *Computers in Human Behavior* 28, no. 3 (2012): 881–88; A.B. Hancock and B.A. Rubin, "Influence of Communication Partner's Gender on Language," *Journal of Language and Social Psychology* 34, no. 1 (2015): 46–64.

63. A. Mulac et al., "'Uh-Huh. What's That All About?' Differing Interpretations of Conversational Backchannels and Questions as Sources of Miscommunication across Gender Boundaries," *Communication Research* 25 (1998): 641–68; C. Leaper and R.D. Robnett, "Women Are More Likely Than Men to Use Tentative Language, Aren't They? A Meta-Analysis Testing for Gender Differences and Moderators," *Psychology of Women Quarterly* 35, no. 1 (2011): 129–42; L. Jefferson et al., "Effect of Physicians' Gender on Communication and Consultation Length: A Systematic Review and Meta-Analysis," *Journal of Health Services Research & Policy* 18, no. 4 (2013): 242–48, https://doi.org/10.1177/1355819613486465.

64. This quotation is varied slightly from the original translations by: E. Carter, *All the Works of Epictetus, Which Are Now Extant,* Third ed., 2 vols., vol. 2 (London, UK: J. and F. Rivington, 1768), pg. 333; T.W. Higginson, *The Works of Epictetus* (Boston, MA: Little, Brown, and Company, 1866), pg. 428.

65. L.B. Comer and T. Drollinger, "Active Empathetic Listening and Selling Success: A Conceptual Framework," *Journal of Personal Selling & Sales Management* 19 (1999): 15–29; T. Drollinger, L.B. Comer, and P.T. Warrington,

"Development and Validation of the Active Empathetic Listening Scale," *Psychology and Marketing* 23, no. 2 (2006): 161–80; P. JungKun et al., "The Role of Listening in E-Contact Center Customer Relationship Management," *Journal of Services Marketing* 29, no. 1 (2015): 49–58.

66. T.J. Allen, "Architecture and Communication among Product Development Engineers," *California Management Review* 49, no. 2 (2007): 23–41; M.C. Davis, D.J. Leach, and C.W. Clegg, "The Physical Environment of the Office: Contemporary and Emerging Issues," in *International Review of Industrial and Organizational Psychology 2011* (Wiley, 2011), 193–237; J. Kim and R. de Dear, "Workspace Satisfaction: The Privacy-Communication Trade-Off in Open-Plan Offices," *Journal of Environmental Psychology* 36 (2013): 18–26.

67. A. Seddigh et al., "The Association between Office Design and Performance on Demanding Cognitive Tasks," *Journal of Environmental Psychology* 42 (2015): 172–81; M. Yadav et al., "The Irrelevant Speech Effect in Multi-Talker Environments: Applications to Open-Plan Offices," *The Journal of the Acoustical Society of America* 143, no. 3 (2018): 1725; K. Chan, "Cubicle Comeback? Pandemic Will Reshape Office Life for Good," *Chicago Tribune,* May 12, 2020.

68. S.P. Means, "Playing at Pixar," *Salt Lake Tribune (Utah),* 30 May 2003, D1; G. Whipp, "Swimming against the Tide," *Daily News of Los Angeles,* 30 May 2003, U6.

69. C.J. Turco, "A New Era of Corporate Conversation," *MIT Sloan Management Review* 58, no. 1 (Fall 2016): 11–12.

70. M.L. Yeo and O. Arazy, "What Makes Corporate Wikis Work? Wiki Affordances and Their Suitability for Corporate Knowledge Work," in *Design Science Research in Information Systems. Advances in Theory and Practice,* ed. K. Peffers, M. Rothenberger, and B. Kuechler, vol. 7286 (Berlin, Heidelberg: Springer Berlin Heidelberg, 2012), 174–90, https://doi.org/10.1007/978-3-642-29863-9_14; H. Hasan and C.C. Pfaff, "An Activity-Theory Analysis of Corporate Wikis," *Information Technology & People* 25 (2012): 423–37; E. Bolisani and E. Scarso, "Factors Affecting the Use of Wiki to Manage Knowledge in a Small Company," *Journal of Knowledge Management* 20 (2016): 423–43.

71. S.-L. Tan, "Altus Group's Bob Courteau Manages by Wandering Around," *Australian Financial Review,* March 7, 2019.

72. R. Rousos, "Trust in Leaders Lacking at Utility," *The Ledger (Lakeland, Fl)* 29 July 2003, B1; B. Whitworth and B. Riccomini, "Management Communication: Unlocking Higher Employee Performance," *Communication World,* Mar–Apr 2005, 18–21.

73. K. Davis, "Management Communication and the Grapevine," *Harvard Business Review* 31 (1953): 43–49; W.L. Davis and J.R. O'Connor, "Serial Transmission of Information: A Study of the Grapevine," *Journal of Applied Communication Research* 5 (1977): 61–72.

74. G. Dalziel, *Rumor and Communication in Asia in the Internet Age* (New York: Routledge, 2013); K.L. Robinson and P.D. Thelen, "What Makes the Grapevine So Effective? An Employee Perspective on Employee- Organization Communication and

Peer-to-Peer Communication," *Public Relations Journal* 12, no. 2 (2018).

75. S.R. Clegg and A. van Iterson, "Dishing the Dirt: Gossiping in Organizations," *Culture and Organization* 15 (2009): 275–89; C. Mills, "Experiencing Gossip: The Foundations for a Theory of Embedded Organizational Gossip," *Group & Organization Management* 35 (2010): 213–40; T.J. Grosser et al., "Hearing It through the Grapevine: Positive and Negative Workplace Gossip," *Organizational Dynamics* 41 (2012): 52–61.

76. R.L. Rosnow, "Inside Rumor: A Personal Journey," *American Psychologist* 46 (1991): 484–96; P. Bordia et al., "Management Are Aliens!: Rumors and Stress during Organizational Change," *Group & Organization Management* 31 (2006): 601–21; K. Smet et al., "The Explanatory Role of Rumours in the Reciprocal Relationship between Organizational Change Communication and Job Insecurity: A within-Person Approach," *European Journal of Work and Organizational Psychology* 25 (2016): 631–44.

77. N. Nicholson, "Evolutionary Psychology: Toward a New View of Human Nature and Organizational Society," *Human Relations* 50 (1997): 1053–78; E.K. Foster, "Research on Gossip: Taxonomy, Methods, and Future Directions," *Review of General Psychology* 8, no. 2 (2004): 78–99; B. Beersma and G.A. Van Kleef, "Why People Gossip: An Empirical Analysis of Social Motives, Antecedents, and Consequences," *Journal of Applied Social Psychology* 42, no. 11 (2012): 2640–70.

CHAPTER 10

1. R. Spence, "Seven 'Patterns of Opportunity' as Seen in the Crystal Ball of Change," *Financial Post (Toronto),* October 18, 2017; A. Gopinath, "Trend Hunter Helps You Identify the Next Big Thing," *The Edge (Malaysia),* July 2, 2018; "Interview with Jeremy Gutsche," *Media Planet-Careers and Education* (blog), September 2018, http://www.careersandeducation.ca/inspiration/interview-with-jeremy-gutsche.

2. J.R.P. French and B. Raven, "The Bases of Social Power," in *Studies in Social Power,* ed. D. Cartwright (Ann Arbor, Mich: University of Michigan Press, 1959), 150–67; A.D. Galinsky et al., "Power and Perspectives Not Taken," *Psychological Science* 17, no. 12 (2006): 1068–74. Also see: H. Mintzberg, *Power in and around Organizations* (Englewood Cliffs, NJ: Prentice Hall, 1983), Chap. 1; J. Pfeffer, *Managing with Power* (Boston, MA: Harvard Business University Press, 1992), pp. 17, 30; A. Guinote and T.K. Vescio, "Introduction: Power in Social Psychology," in *The Social Psychology of Power,* ed. A. Guinote and T.K. Vescio (New York: Guilford Press, 2010), 1–18.

3. R.A. Dahl, "The Concept of Power," *Behavioral Science* 2 (1957): 201–18; R.M. Emerson, "Power-Dependence Relations," *American Sociological Review* 27 (1962): 31–41; A.M. Pettigrew, *The Politics of Organizational Decision-Making* (London, UK: Tavistock, 1973).

4. G.A. van Kleef et al., "The Social Dynamics of Breaking the Rules: Antecedents and Consequences of Norm-Violating Behavior," *Current Opinion in Psychology* 6 (2015): 25–31.

5. J. Pfeffer and G.R. Salancik, *The External Control of Organizations* (New York: Harper & Row,

1978), 52–54; K. Cowan, A.K. Paswan, and E. Van Steenburg, "When Inter-Firm Relationship Benefits Mitigate Power Asymmetry," *Industrial Marketing Management* 48 (2015): 140–48.

6. J.R. French and B. Raven, "The Bases of Social Power," in *Studies in Social Power,* ed. D. Cartwright (Ann Arbor: University of Michigan Press, 1959), 150–67; P.M. Podsakoff and C. Schreisheim, "Field Studies of French and Raven's Bases of Power: Critique, Analysis, and Suggestions for Future Research," *Psychological Bulletin* 97 (1985): 387–411; P.P. Carson and K.D. Carson, "Social Power Bases: A Meta-Analytic Examination of Interrelationships and Outcomes," *Journal of Applied Social Psychology* 23 (1993): 1150–69. Most alternative models of power bases parallel French and Raven's list. See P. Heinemann, *Power Bases and Informational Influence Strategies: A Behavioral Study on the Use of Management Accounting Information* (Wiesbaden, Germany: Deutscher Universitäts-Verlag, 2008). Raven subsequently proposed information power as a sixth source of power. We present information power as forms of legitimate and expert power rather than as a distinct sixth power base.

7. Legitimate power and expert power are also consistently the strongest source of power that coaches have over players in sports. See P. Rylander, "Coaches' Bases of Power: Developing Some Initial Knowledge of Athletes' Compliance with Coaches in Team Sports," *Journal of Applied Sport Psychology* 27, no. 1 (2015): 110–21.

8. C. Barnard, *The Function of the Executive* (Cambridge, MA: Harvard University Press, 1938), 167–70; B.J. Tepper, "What Do Managers Do When Subordinates Just Say, 'No'?: An Analysis of Incidents Involving Refusal to Perform Downward Requests," in *Power and Influence in Organizations,* ed. L.L. Neider and C.A. Schreisheim (Charlotte, NC: IAP/Information Age Publishing, 2006), 1–20.

9. A.I. Shahin and P.L. Wright, "Leadership in the Context of Culture: An Egyptian Perspective," *Leadership & Organization Development Journal* 25, no. 5/6 (2004): 499–511; Y.J. Huo et al., "Leadership and the Management of Conflicts in Diverse Groups: Why Acknowledging Versus Neglecting Subgroup Identity Matters," *European Journal of Social Psychology* 35, no. 2 (2005): 237–54.

10. B.H. Raven, "Kurt Lewin Address: Influence, Power, Religion, and the Mechanisms of Social Control," *Journal of Social Issues* 55 (1999): 161–86.

11. A.W. Gouldner, "The Norm of Reciprocity: A Preliminary Statement," *American Sociological Review* 25 (1960): 161–78.

12. G. Yukl and C.M. Falbe, "Importance of Different Power Sources in Downward and Lateral Relations," *Journal of Applied Psychology* 76 (1991): 416–23; B.H. Raven, "Kurt Lewin Address: Influence, Power, Religion, and the Mechanisms of Social Control," *Journal of Social Issues* vol. 55, Issue 1 (1999):161–186.

13. A.M. Pettigrew, "Information Control as a Power Resource," *Sociology* 6, no. 2 (1972): 187–204; P.L. Dawes, D.Y. Lee, and G.R. Dowling, "Information Control and Influence in Emergent Buying Centers," *Journal of Marketing* 62, no. 3 (1998): 55–68; J. Webster et al., "Beyond Knowledge Sharing: Withholding Knowledge at Work," *Research in Personnel and Human Resources Management* 27 (2008): 1–37; C.E. Connelly et al., "Knowledge Hiding in Organizations," *Journal of Organizational Behavior* 33, no. 1 (2012): 64–88.

14. S.L. Robinson, J. O'Reilly, and W. Wang, "Invisible at Work: An Integrated Model of Workplace Ostracism," *Journal of Management* 39 (2013): 203–31; S. Gallani, "Incentives Don't Help People Change, but Peer Pressure Does," *Harvard Business Review,* March 23, 2017.

15. M. Bolch, "Rewarding the Team," *HR Magazine,* February 2007, 91–93.

16. J.M. Peiro and J.L. Melia, "Formal and Informal Interpersonal Power in Organisations: Testing a Bifactorial Model of Power in Role-Sets," *Applied Psychology* 52, no. 1 (2003): 14–35.

17. C.R. Hinings et al., "Structural Conditions of Intraorganizational Power," *Administrative Science Quarterly* 19 (1974): 22–44. Also see: C.S. Saunders, "The Strategic Contingency Theory of Power: Multiple Perspectives," *The Journal of Management Studies* 27 (1990): 1–21.

18. W.H. Friedland, "For a Sociological Concept of Charisma," *Social Forces* 43, no. 1 (1964): 18–26; K. Miyahara, "Charisma: From Weber to Contemporary Sociology," *Sociological Inquiry* 53, no. 4 (1983): 368–88; J.D. Kudisch and M.L. Poteet, "Expert Power, Referent Power, and Charisma: Toward the Resolution of a Theoretical Debate," *Journal of Business & Psychology* 10 (1995): 177– 95; K.O. Tskhay, R. Zhu, and N.O. Rule, "Perceptions of Charisma from Thin Slices of Behavior Predict Leadership Prototypicality Judgments," *Leadership Quarterly,* 28 (2017): 555–62. One recent review analyzes various definitions and concludes that charisma "is values-based, symbolic, and emotion-laden leader signaling." Although a useful development, even this definition may miss the mark somewhat because all interactions generate emotions, and people can be charismatic by their mere presence (signalling) without conversation and therefore perhaps without values-based interaction. See: J. Antonakis et al., "Charisma: An Ill-Defined and Ill-Measured Gift," *Annual Review of Organizational Psychology and Organizational Behavior* 3 (2016): 293–319.

19. R.B. Cialdini and N.J. Goldstein, "Social Influence: Compliance and Conformity," *Annual Review of Psychology* 55 (2004): 591–621.

20. S.D. Farley, D.H. Carson, and T.J. Pope, "'I Would Never Fall for That': The Use of an Illegitimate Authority to Teach Social Psychological Principles," *Teaching of Psychology* 46, no. 2 (2019): 146–52.

21. C. Perkel, "It's Not CSI," *Canadian Press,* November 10, 2007; "Dr. Charles Smith: The Man behind the Public Inquiry," *CBC News*(Toronto), August 10, 2010; J. Chipman, *Death in the Family* (Toronto: Doubleday Canada, 2017). The broader problem of judicial deference to medical experts is discussed in: C. Foster, "The Dangers Of Deferring To Doctors | Practical Ethics," *Oxford University-Practical Ethics* (blog), July 30, 2018, http://blog.practicalethics.ox.ac.uk/2018/07/the-dangers-of-deferring-to-doctors/.

22. D.J. Hickson et al., "A Strategic Contingencies' Theory of Intraorganizational Power," *Administrative Science Quarterly* 16 (1971): 216–27; Hinings et al., "Structural Conditions of Intraorganizational Power; R.M. Kanter, "Power Failure in Management Circuits," *Harvard Business Review* (1979): 65–75.

23. A. Bryant, "The Right Job? It's Much Like the Right Spouse," *The New York Times,* May 22, 2011, 2.

24. Hickson et al., "A Strategic Contingencies' Theory of Intraorganizational Power," pp. 219–21; J.D. Hackman, "Power and Centrality in the Allocation of Resources in Colleges and Universities," *Administrative Science Quarterly* 30 (1985): 61–77; D.J. Brass and M.E. Burkhardt, "Potential Power and Power Use: An Investigation of Structure and Behavior," *Academy of Management Journal* 36 (1993): 441–70.

25. M. Kennett, "Remote Control," *Management Today,* 1 March 2011, 46.

26. A. Caza, "Typology of the Eight Domains of Discretion in Organizations," *Journal of Management Studies* 49, no. 1 (2012): 144–77.

27. B.E. Ashforth, "The Experience of Powerlessness in Organizations," *Organizational Behavior and Human Decision Processes* 43 (1989): 207–42; D.B. Wangrow, D.J. Schepker, and V.L. Barker, "Managerial Discretion: An Empirical Review and Focus on Future Research Directions," *Journal of Management* 41, no. 1 (2015): 99–135.

28. "Woman Fired for Giving 16-Cent Treat to Toddler," *Reuters,* May 9, 2008; C. Rush, "Rehired Timbit Mom Needs the Dough," *Toronto Star,* May 9, 2008.

29. S. Wasserman and K. Faust, *Social Network Analysis: Methods and Applications* (Cambridge, UK: Cambridge University Press, 1994), Chap. 1; D. Brass et al., "Taking Stock of Networks and Organizations: A Multilevel Perspective," *Academy of Management Journal* vol. 47 no. 6 (December, 2004).

30. M. Grossetti, "Where Do Social Relations Come From?: A Study of Personal Networks in the Toulouse Area of France," *Social Networks* 27, no. 4 (2005): 289–300.

31. R.J. Taormina and J.H. Gao, "A Research Model for Guanxi Behavior: Antecedents, Measures, and Outcomes of Chinese Social Networking," *Social Science Research* 39, no. 6 (2010): 1195–212; J. Barbalet, "Guanxi, Tie Strength, and Network Attributes," *American Behavioral Scientist* 59, no. 8 (2015): 1038–50; X.-A. Zhang, N. Li, and T.B. Harris, "Putting Non-Work Ties to Work: The Case of Guanxi in Supervisor–Subordinate Relationships," *Leadership Quarterly* 26, no. 1 (2015): 37–54. For problems with guanxi, see W.R. Vanhonacker, "When Good Guanxi Turns Bad," *Harvard Business Review* 82, no. 4 (2004): 18–19; F. Yang, "Guanxi Human Resource Management Practices as a Double-Edged Sword: The Moderating Role of Political Skill," *Asia Pacific Journal of Human Resources* 52, no. 4 (2014): 496–510.

32. A. Portes, "Social Capital: Its Origins and Applications in Modern Society," *Annual Review of Sociology* 24 (1998): 1–24; P.S. Adler and S.W. Kwon, "Social Capital: Prospects for a New Concept," *Academy of Management Review* 27, no. 1 (2002): 17–40; R. Lee, "Social Capital and Business and Management: Setting a Research Agenda," *International Journal of Management Reviews* 11, no. 3 (2009): 247–73.

33. R.F. Chisholm, *Developing Network Organizations: Learning from Practice and Theory*

(Reading MA: Addison Wesley Longman, 1998); W.S. Chow and L.S. Chan, "Social Network, Social Trust and Shared Goals in Organizational Knowledge Sharing," *Information & Management* 45, no. 7 (2008): 458–65.

34. R.S. Burt, *Structural Holes: The Social Structure of Competition* (Cambridge, MA: Harvard University Press, 1992).

35. M.T. Rivera, S.B. Soderstrom, and B. IUzzi, "Dynamics of Dyads in Social Networks: Assortative, Relational, and Proximity Mechanisms," *Annual Review of Sociology* 36 (2010): 91–115.

36. R. Cross and R.J. Thomas, *Driving Results through Social Networks: How Top Organizations Leverage Networks for Performance and Growth* (San Francisco, CA: Jossey-Bass, 2009); R. McDermott and D. Archibald, "Harnessing Your Staff's Informal Networks," *Harvard Business Review* 88, no. 3 (2010): 82–89.

37. M. Kilduff and D. Krackhardt, *Interpersonal Networks in Organizations: Cognition, Personality, Dynamics, and Culture* (New York: Cambridge University Press, 2008).

38. D.J. Brass et al., "Taking Stock of Networks and Organizations: A Multilevel Perspective," *Academy of Management Journal* 47, no. 6 (2004): 795–817; D. Melamed and B. Simpson, "Strong Ties Promote the Evolution of Cooperation in Dynamic Networks," *Social Networks* 45 (2016): 32–44.

39. M.S. Granovetter, "The Strength of Weak Ties," *American Journal of Sociology* 78 (1973): 1360–80; B. Erickson, "Social Networks," in *The Blackwell Companion to Sociology,* ed. J.R. Blau (Malden, MA: Blackwell Publishing, 2004), 314–26.

40. B. Uzzi and S. Dunlap, "How to Build Your Network," *Harvard Business Review* 83, no. 12 (2005): 53–60.

41. Y. Zenou, "A Dynamic Model of Weak and Strong Ties in the Labor Market," *Journal of Labor Economics* 33, no. 4 (2015): 891–932; C. Gubbins and T. Garavan, "Social Capital Effects on the Career and Development Outcomes of HR Professionals," *Human Resource Management* 55, no. 2 (March 2016): 241–60.

42. C.C. Su and N.K. Chan, "Predicting Social Capital on Facebook: The Implications of Use Intensity, Perceived Content Desirability, and Facebook-Enabled Communication Practices," *Computers in Human Behavior* 72 (2017): 259–68.

43. C. Phelps, R. Heidl, and A. Wadhwa, "Knowledge, Networks, and Knowledge Networks: A Review and Research Agenda," *Journal of Management* 38, no. 4 (2012): 1115–66.

44. R. S. Burt, *Structural Holes: The Social Structure of Competition,* (Cambridge, MA: Harvard University Press, 1995).

45. B.R. Ragins and E. Sundstrom, "Gender and Power in Organizations: A Longitudinal Perspective," *Psychological Bulletin* 105 (1989): 51–88; S. McDonald et al., "Frontiers of Sociological Research on Networks, Work, and Inequality," in *Networks, Work and Inequality,* ed. S. McDonald, *Research in the Sociology of Work* (Emerald Group Publishing Limited, 2013), 1–41.

46. S. Ritchey, "The Biggest Mistake Women Make When Networking," *Fortune,* February 1, 2016.

47. D.M. McCracken, "Winning the Talent War for Women: Sometimes It Takes a Revolution," *Harvard Business Review* (2000): 159–67.

48. "Inclusion and Diversity at CIBC—Our Team," Canadian Imperial Bank of Commerce Website, accessed February 23, 2020, https://www.cibc.com/en/about-cibc/corporate-profile/inclusion-and-diversity/team.html.

49. J. Lammers, J. I. Stoker, and D. A. Stapel, "Differentiating Social and Personal Power: Opposite Effects on Stereotyping, but Parallel Effects on Behavioral Approach Tendencies," *Psychological Science* 20, no. 12 (2009): 1543–49.

50. J. Lammers et al., "Power and Morality," *Current Opinion in Psychology* 6 (2015): 15–19.

51. A.D. Galinsky et al., "Acceleration with Steering: The Synergistic Benefits of Combining Power and Perspective-Taking," *Social Psychological and Personality Science* 5, no. 6 (2014): 627–35.

52. S. Lee et al., "How Do I Get My Way? A Meta-Analytic Review of Research on Influence Tactics," *The Leadership Quarterly* 28 (2017): 210–28.

53. D. Kipnis, S.M. Schmidt, and I. Wilkinson, "Intraorganizational Influence Tactics: Explorations in Getting One's Way," *Journal of Applied Psychology* 65 (1980): 440–52; G. Yukl, "Power and the Interpersonal Influence of Leaders," in *Power and Interdependence in Organizations,* ed. D. Tjosvold and B. Wisse (New York: Cambridge University Press, 2009), 207–23. A recent review includes these influence tactics but divides some of them into narrower sub-categories. See: S. Lee et al., "How Do I Get My Way? A Meta-Analytic Review of Research on Influence Tactics," *The Leadership Quarterly* 28 (2017): 210–28.

54. B. van Knippenberg, R. van Eijbergen, and H. Wilke, "The Use of Hard and Soft Influence Tactics in Cooperative Task Groups:," *Group Processes & Intergroup Relations* 2 (1999): 231–44.

55. R.B. Cialdini and N.J. Goldstein, "Social Influence: Compliance and Conformity," *Annual Review of Psychology* 55, (2004): 591–621; A. Bourgoin, N. Bencherki, and S. Faraj, "'And Who Are You?': A Performative Perspective on Authority in Organizations," *Academy of Management Journal,* July 25, 2019.

56. The most widely applied model or power excludes silent authority. Its closest category is "legitimating tactics," which is an active attempt to demonstrate one's right to the request based on rules or contracts. See: G. Yukl, C.F. Seifert, and C. Chavez, "Validation of the Extended Influence Behavior Questionnaire," *The Leadership Quarterly* 19 (2008): 609–21. Several studies identify the importance of silent authority in high power distance cultures. For example, see: Y. Zhai, "Values of Deference to Authority in Japan and China," *International Journal of Comparative Sociology* 58, no. 2 (April 2017): 120–39.

57. S. Maitlis, "Taking It from the Top: How CEOs Influence (and Fail to Influence) Their Boards," *Organization Studies* 25, no. 8 (2004): 1275–311. This type of influence is a form of manipulation. See P. Fleming and A. Spicer, "Power in Management and Organization Science," *Academy of Management Annals* 8, no. 1 (2014): 237–98.

58. J.K. Murnighan, "Organizational Coalition Formation: Process, Consequences and Dominant

Coalitions," BEBR faculty working paper, 1985; W.B. Stevenson, J.L. Pearce, and L.W. Porter, "The Concept of 'Coalition' in Organization Theory and Research," *Academy of Management Review* 10, no. 2 (1985): 256–68; F. Liu, O. Dedehayir, and B. Katzy, "Coalition Formation during Technology Adoption," *Behaviour & Information Technology* 34, no. 12 (2015): 1186–99.

59. A.T. Cobb, "Toward the Study of Organizational Coalitions: Participant Concerns and Activities in a Simulated Organizational Setting," *Human Relations* 44 (1991): 1057–79; E.A. Mannix, "Organizations as Resource Dilemmas: The Effects of Power Balance on Coalition Formation in Small Groups," *Organizational Behavior and Human Decision Processes* 55 (1993): 1–22; K. Rangus and M. Černe, "The Impact of Leadership Influence Tactics and Employee Openness toward Others on Innovation Performance: Leadership Influence Tactics and Employee Openness," *R&D Management* 49, no. 2 (2019): 168–79.

60. A.P. Brief, *Attitudes in and around Organizations*(Thousand Oaks, CA: Sage, 1998), 69–84; D.J. O'Keefe, *Persuasion: Theory and Research* (Thousand Oaks, CA: Sage, 2002); R.H. Gass and J.S. Seiter, *Persuasion: Social Influence and Compliance Gaining,* 5th ed. (New York: Routledge, 2014); J.T. Cacioppo, S. Cacioppo, and R.E. Petty, "The Neuroscience of Persuasion: A Review with an Emphasis on Issues and Opportunities," *Social Neuroscience* 13, no. 2 (2018): 129–72.

61. These and other features of message content in persuasion are detailed in: R. Petty and J. Cacioppo, *Attitudes and Persuasion: Classic and Contemporary Approaches* (Dubuque, Iowa: W.C. Brown, 1981); O'Keefe, *Persuasion: Theory and Research,* Chap. 9; G. Van Kleef, H. van den Berg, and M. Heerdink, "The Persuasive Power of Emotions: Effects of Emotional Expressions on Attitude Formation and Change," *Journal of Applied Psychology* 100 (2015): 1124–42; E. Falk and C. Scholz, "Persuasion, Influence, and Value: Perspectives from Communication and Social Neuroscience," *Annual Review of Psychology* 69 (2018): 329–56; D. Albarracin and S. Shavitt, "Attitudes and Attitude Change," *Annual Review of Psychology* 69 (2018): 299–327.

62. J.A. Banas and S.A. Rains, "A Meta-Analysis of Research on Inoculation Theory," *Communication Monographs* 77, no. 3 (2010): 281–311; B. Ivanov et al., "Beyond Simple Inoculation: Examining the Persuasive Value of Inoculation for Audiences with Initially Neutral or Opposing Attitudes," *Western Journal of Communication* 81, no. 1 (2017): 105–26.

63. Y. Lim and R.J. Lee-Won, "When Retweets Persuade: The Persuasive Effects of Dialogic Retweeting and the Role of Social Presence in Organizations' Twitter-Based Communication," *Telematics and Informatics* 34, no. 5 (2017): 422–33; P. Briñol and R.E. Petty, "The Impact of Individual Differences on Attitudes and Attitude Change," in *The Oxford Handbook of Personality and Social Psychology,* ed. D. Albarracín and B. Johnson, 2nd ed., vol. 1 (New York: Oxford University Press, 2019), 520–56.

64. M. Bolino, D. Long, and W. Turnley, "Impression Management in Organizations: Critical Questions, Answers, and Areas for Future

Research," *Annual Review of Organizational Psychology and Organizational Behavior* 3 (2016): 377–406.

65. T. Peters, "The Brand Called You," *Fast Company,* August 1997; C. Johnson, *Platform: The Art and Science of Personal Branding* (New York: Penguin Random House, 2019); L.A. King, *Just Do You: Authenticity, Leadership, and Your Personal Brand* (Toronto: Ingenium Books, 2019).

66. *Building Your Brand: Personal Brand Week.* PricewaterhouseCoopers Canada. Retrieved from: http://www.pwc.com/ca/en/campus-recruiting/publications/pwc-personal-brand-week-e-book-2012-03-en.pdf.

67. D. Strutton and L.E. Pelton, "Effects of Ingratiation on Lateral Relationship Quality within Sales Team Settings," *Journal of Business Research* 43 (1998): 1–12; R. Vonk, "Self-Serving Interpretations of Flattery: Why Ingratiation Works," *Journal of Personality and Social Psychology* 82 (2002): 515–26.

68. D. Strutton, L. E. Pelton, and J. F. Tanner, "Shall We Gather in the Garden: The Effect of Ingratiatory Behaviors on Buyer Trust in Salespeople," *Industrial Marketing Management* 25 (1996): 151–62; J. O'Neil, "An Investigation of the Sources of Influence of Corporate Public Relations Practitioners," *Public Relations Review* 29 (2003): 159–69; C. A. Higgins, T. A. Judge, and G. R. Ferris, "Influence Tactics and Work Outcomes: A Meta-Analysis," *Journal of Organizational Behavior* 24 (2003): 90–106.

69. C.M. Falbe and G. Yukl, "Consequences for Managers of Using Single Influence Tactics and Combinations of Tactics," *Academy of Management Journal* 35 (1992): 638–52.

70. G. Yukl and J. Tracey, "Consequences of Influence Tactics Used with Subordinates, Peers, and the Boss," *Journal of Applied Psychology* 77, no. 4 (1992): 525–35; B. Oc and M.R. Bashshur, "Followership, Leadership and Social Influence," *Leadership Quarterly* 24, no. 6 (2013): 919–34; M.B. Wadsworth and A.L. Blanchard, "Influence Tactics in Virtual Teams," *Computers in Human Behavior* 44 (2015): 386–93.

71. C.-J. Su, "An Examination of the Usage and Impact of Upward Influence Tactics by Workers in the Hospitality Sector of Taiwan: Expanding the Framework of Rao, Schmidt, and Murray (1995)," *Canadian Journal of Administrative Sciences* 27, no. 4 (2010): 306–19.

72. P.P. Fu et al., "The Impact of Societal Cultural Values and Individual Social Beliefs on the Perceived Effectiveness of Managerial Influence Strategies: A Meso Approach," *Journal of International Business Studies* 35, no. 4 (2004): 284–305; A.N. Smith et al., "Gendered Influence: A Gender Role Perspective on the Use and Effectiveness of Influence Tactics," *Journal of Management* 39, no. 5 (2013): 1156–83; C.C. Lewis and J. Ryan, "Age and Influence Tactics: A Life-Stage Development Theory Perspective," *The International Journal of Human Resource Management* 25, no. 15 (2014): 2146–58.

73. A. Drory and T. Romm, "The Definition of Organizational Politics: A Review," *Human Relations* 43, no. 11 (1990): 1133–54; C.C. Rosen and P.E. Levy, "Stresses, Swaps, and Skill: An Investigation of the Psychological Dynamics That Relate Work Politics to Employee Performance," *Human Performance* 26, no. 1 (2013): 44–65; A. Bedi and A. Schat, "Perceptions of Organizational Politics: A Meta-Analysis of Its Attitudinal, Health, and Behavioural Consequences," *Canadian Psychology* 54 (2013): 246–59.

74. Surveys of employees consistently identify organizational politics as self-serving behaviour that is dysfunctional for employee well-being and performance. See, for example: "Sloppy Worker Wake-Up Call: Sweating The Small Stuff Matters," News Release (Menlo Park, Calif.: Accountemps, January 10, 2017)' "Indian Millennials Lack Critical Skills: HBR Ascend Survey," *Hindustan Times,* July 18, 2017; Z. Mejia, "These Are the Top 10 Workplace Struggles Employees Face in 2018," *CNBC,* September 19, 2018; "New DDI Research: 57 Percent of Employees Quit Because of Their Boss," News Release (Pittsburgh: Development Dimensions International, December 9, 2019).

75. D. Buchanan and R. Badham, *Power, Politics, and Organizational Change: Winning the Turf Game* (SAGE, 2008); W.A. Hochwarter, "The Positive Side of Politics," In G.R. Ferris and D.C. Treadway (Eds.), *Politics in Organizations: Theory and Research Considerations,* (New York: Routledge, 2012), 27–66 at 33; "How to Play Office Politics the Smart Way," *BBC,* August 14, 2015; E.M. Landells and S.L. Albrecht, "Positive Politics, Negative Politics, and Engagement: Psychological Safety, Meaningfulness, and Availability as 'Black Box' Explanatory Mechanisms," in *Research in Occupational Stress and Well-Being,* ed. C.C. Rosen and P.L. Perrewé, vol. 15 (Emerald Publishing Limited, 2017), 33–49, https://doi.org/10.1108/S1479-355520170000015004.

76. D.L. Madison et al., "Organizational Politics: An Exploration of Managers' Perceptions," *Human Relations* 33, no. 2 (1980): 79–100; P. Kumar and R. Ghadially, "Organizational Politics and Its Effects on Members of Organizations," *Human Relations* 42, no. 4 (1989): 305–14; D. Buchanan and R. Badham, *Power, Politics, and Organizational Change: Winning the Turf Game* (SAGE, 2008), pg. 11; E.M. Landells and S.L. Albrecht, "Positive Politics, Negative Politics, and Engagement: Psychological Safety, Meaningfulness, and Availability as 'Black Box' Explanatory Mechanisms," in *Research in Occupational Stress and Well-Being,* ed. C.C. Rosen and P.L. Perrewé, vol. 15 (Emerald Publishing Limited, 2017), 33–49; E.M. Landells and S.L. Albrecht, "The Positives and Negatives of Organizational Politics: A Qualitative Study," *Journal of Business and Psychology* 32 (2017): 41–58.

77. E. Vigoda, "Stress-Related Aftermaths to Workplace Politics," *Journal of Organizational Behavior* 23, no. 5 (August 2002), 571–91; C.H. Chang, C.C. Rosen, and P.E. Levy, "The Relationship between Perceptions of Organizational Politics and Employee Attitudes, Strain, and Behavior: A Meta-Analytic Examination," *Academy of Management Journal* 52, no. 4 (2009): 779–801; A. Bedi and A. Schat, "Perceptions of Organizational Politics: A Meta-Analysis of Its Attitudinal, Health, and Behavioural Consequences," *Canadian Psychology* 54 (2013): 246–59. The quotation is from M. Landry, "Navigating the Political Minefield," *PM Network,* March 2013, 38–43.

78. L.W. Porter, R.W. Allen, and H.L. Angle, "The Politics of Upward Influence in Organizations," *Research in Organizational Behavior* 3 (1981): 120–22; R.J. House, "Power and Personality in Complex Organizations," *Research in Organizational Behavior* 10 (1988): 305–57.

79. E. O'Boyle et al., "A Meta-Analysis of the Dark Triad and Work Behavior: A Social Exchange Perspective," *Journal of Applied Psychology* 97, no. 3 (2012): 557–79; A. Harrison, J. Summers, and B. Mennecke, "The Effects of the Dark Triad on Unethical Behavior," *Journal of Business Ethics* 153, no. 1 (2018): 53–77; M. Moshagen, B.E. Hilbig, and I. Zettler, "The Dark Core of Personality," *Psychological Review* 125, no. 5 (2018): 656–88; S.M. Spain, "The Dark Side of Personality," in *Leadership, Work, and the Dark Side of Personality,* ed. S.M. Spain (Academic Press, 2019), 41–93.

80. C. Hardy, *Strategies for Retrenchment and Turnaround: The Politics of Survival* (Berlin: Walter de Gruyter, 1990), Chap. 14; G.R. Ferris et al., "Perceptions of Organizational Politics: Prediction, Stress-Related Implications, and Outcomes," *Human Relations* 49 (1996): 233–63; M.C. Andrews and K.M. Kacmar, "Discriminating among Organizational Politics, Justice, and Support," *Journal of Organizational Behavior* 22 (2001): 347–66.

CHAPTER 11

1. S. Hradecky, "Incident: Delta B752 near Salt Lake City on Jan 22nd 2016, Unruly Crew," *The Aviation Herald,* January 28, 2016; T. Harlow, "Delta Flight Attendants Scrap, Stir up Turbulence," *Star Tribune* (Minneapolis), February 2, 2016, B3; J. Shammas, "EasyJet Flight from Gatwick Delayed after 'Unbelievable Fight between Staff,'" *The Mirror* (UK), August 24, 2016; E. Kerr, "Passengers 'aghast' at Easyjet Crew Spat," *BBC News,* August 25, 2016; R. Flood, "EasyJet Flight Delayed by Fighting Crew in Bizarre Row 'over Bottled Water,'" *Sunday Express* (UK), August 25, 2016; S. Francis, "EasyJet Flight 'Delayed for an Hour after Crew Members Fight over Water Bottles,'" *Daily Mail* (UK), August 25, 2016; S. Sinha, "Jet Grounds Two Senior Pilots for Fighting in Cockpit of London-Mumbai Flight," *The Times of India,* January 3, 2018; M. Bartiromo, "Jet Airways Fires Pilots Who Fought on Flight, Left Cockpit Unattended," *Fox News,* January 5, 2018.

2. J.A. Wall and R.R. Callister, "Conflict and Its Management," *Journal of Management* 21 (1995): 515–58; M.A. Rahim, *Managing Conflict in Organizations,* 4th ed. (New Brunswick, NJ: Transaction, 2011), 15–17; D. Tjosvold, A.S.H. Wong, and N.Y.F. Chen, "Constructively Managing Conflicts in Organizations," *Annual Review of Organizational Psychology and Organizational Behavior* 1, no. 1 (2014): 545–68.

3. J.A. Litterer, "Conflict in Organization: A Re-Examination," *Academy of Management Journal* 9, no. 3 (September 1966): 178–86; M.A. Rahim, *Managing Conflict in Organizations,* 4th ed. (New Brunswick, NJ: Transaction, 2011), Chap. 1.

4. L. Urwick, *The Elements of Administration,* 2nd ed. (London: Pitman, 1947); H.L. Sheppard and S. Chase, "The Social and Historical Philosophy of Elton Mayo [with Comment]," *The Antioch Review* 10, no. 3 (1950): 396–406; C. Argyris, "The Individual and Organization: Some Problems

of Mutual Adjustment," *Administrative Science Quarterly* 2, no. 1 (1957): 1–24; K.E. Boulding, "Organization and Conflict," *Conflict Resolution* 1, no. 2 (1957): 122–34; R.R. Blake, H.A. Shepard, and J.S. Mouton, *Managing Intergroup Conflict in Industry* (Houston: Gulf, 1964).

5. *Workplace Conflict and How Businesses Can Harness It to Thrive,* CPP Global Human Capital Report (Mountain View, CA: CPP, Inc., July 2008); F.R.C. de Wit, L.L. Greer, and K.A. Jehn, "The Paradox of Intragroup Conflict: A Meta-Analysis," *Journal of Applied Psychology* 97, no. 2 (2012): 360–90; L.L. Meier et al., "Relationship and Task Conflict at Work: Interactive Short-Term Effects on Angry Mood and Somatic Complaints," *Journal of Occupational Health Psychology* 18, (2013): 144–56; N.L. Jimmieson, M.K. Tucker, and J.L. Campbell, "Task Conflict Leads to Relationship Conflict When Employees Are Low in Trait Self-Control: Implications for Employee Strain," *Personality and Individual Differences* 113 (2017): 209–18; A. Robertson, "How Best to Manage Workplace Conflict," *Douglas Magazine (Victoria, BC),* October 10, 2017.

6. C.K.W. De Dreu and L.R. Weingart, "A Contingency Theory of Task Conflict and Performance in Groups and Organizational Teams," in *International Handbook of Organizational Teamwork and Cooperative Working,* ed. M.A. West, D. Tjosvold, and K.G. Smith (Chichester, UK: Wiley, 2003), 151–66; S. Rispens, "Benefits and Detrimental Effects of Conflict," in *Handbook of Conflict Management Research,* ed. O.B. Ayoko, N.M. Ashkanasy, and K.A. Jehn (Cheltenham, UK: Edward Elgar, 2014), 19–32; D. De Clercq and I. Belausteguigoitia, "Overcoming the Dark Side of Task Conflict: Buffering Roles of Transformational Leadership, Tenacity, and Passion for Work," *European Management Journal* 35, no. 1 (February 2017): 78–90.

7. Meng, J. Fulk, and Y.C. Yuan, "The Roles and Interplay of Intragroup Conflict and Team Emotion Management on Information Seeking Behaviors in Team Contexts," *Communication Research* 42, no. 5 (July 2015): 675–700; M.-H. Tsai and C. Bendersky, "The Pursuit of Information Sharing: Expressing Task Conflicts as Debates vs. Disagreements Increases Perceived Receptivity to Dissenting Opinions in Groups," *Organization Science* 27, no. 1 (December 2015): 141–56.

8. L.L. Greer, L. Van Bunderen, and S. Yu, "The Dysfunctions of Power in Teams: A Review and Emergent Conflict Perspective," *Research in Organizational Behavior* 37 (2017): 103–24; L. van Bunderen, L.L. Greer, and D. van Knippenberg, "When Interteam Conflict Spirals into Intrateam Power Struggles: The Pivotal Role of Team Power Structures," *Academy of Management Journal* 61, no. 3 (2018): 1100–30.

9. J. Dewey, *Human Nature and Conduct: An Introduction to Social Psychology* (New York: Holt, 1922), 300; M.P. Follett, "Constructive Conflict," in *Dynamic Administration: The Collected Papers of Mary Parker Follett,* ed. H.C. Metcalf and L. Urwick (Bath, UK: Management Publications Trust, 1941), 30–49.

10. Although the 1970s marked a point when the benefits of conflict became widely acknowledged, a few earlier writers had also expressed this view. See

L.A. Coser, *The Functions of Social Conflict* (New York: Free Press, 1956); J.A. Litterer, "Conflict in Organization: A Re-Examination," *Academy of Management Journal* 9 (1966): 178–86; H. Assael, "Constructive Role of Interorganizational Conflict," *Administrative Science Quarterly* 14 (1969): 573–82.

11. P.J. Carnevale, "Creativity in the Outcomes of Conflict," in *The Handbook of Conflict Resolution: Theory and Practice,* ed. M. Deutsch, P.T. Coleman, and E.C. Marcus (San Francisco: Jossey-Bass, 2006), 414–35; T.A. O'Neill, N.J. Allen, and S.E. Hastings, "Examining the 'Pros' and 'Cons' of Team Conflict: A Team-Level Meta-Analysis of Task, Relationship, and Process Conflict," *Human Performance* 26 (2013): 236–60; X.-Y. Xie, W.-L. Wang, and K. Luan, "It Is Not What We Have, but How We Use It: Re-exploring the Relationship between Task Conflict and Team Innovation from the Resource-Based View," *Group Processes & Intergroup Relations* 17 (2014): 240–51, P. Petrou, A.B. Bakker, and K. Bezemer, "Creativity under Task Conflict: The Role of Proactively Increasing Job Resources," *Journal of Occupational and Organizational Psychology* 92 (2019): 305–29.

12. K.M. Eisenhardt, J.L. Kahwajy, and L.J. Bourgeois III, "Conflict and Strategic Choice: How Top Management Teams Disagree," *California Management Review* 39 (1997): 42–62; T. Greitemeyer et al., "Information Sampling and Group Decision Making: The Effects of an Advocacy Decision Procedure and Task Experience," *Journal of Experimental Psychology: Applied* 12, no. 1 (2006): 31–42; U. Klocke, "How to Improve Decision Making in Small Groups: Effects of Dissent and Training Interventions," *Small Group Research* 38, no. 3 (2007): 437–68.

13. C.K.W. De Dreu, "When Too Little or Too Much Hurts: Evidence for a Curvilinear Relationship Between Task Conflict and Innovation in Teams," *Journal of Management* 32 (2006): 83–107; J.L. Farh, C. Lee, and C.I.C. Farh, "Task Conflict and Team Creativity: A Question of How Much and When," *Journal of Applied Psychology* 95 (2010): 1173–80; G. Todorova, J.B. Bear, and L.R. Weingart, "Can Conflict Be Energizing? A Study of Task Conflict, Positive Emotions, and Job Satisfaction," *Journal of Applied Psychology* 99 (2014): 451–67; L.R. Weingart et al., "The Directness and Oppositional Intensity of Conflict Expression," *Academy of Management Review* 40 (2015): 235–62.

14. This book adopts the long-standing perspective (Fisher & Ury, Tjosvold, etc.) that all conflict can be framed as either (or degrees of) task and relation-ship conflict. For example employees who refer to a conflict as a "personality clash" have attributed the conflict to problems with the other party's personal characteristics (relationship conflict). Yet others frame the same situation as task conflict by attribut-ing the disagreement to different beliefs and feelings about the issue that need to be understood and ana-lyzed logically. This "framing" perspective contrasts with the view by some writers that task and relation-ship (and process and status) conflict are somehow fundamental sources of conflict. This latter per-spective has inherent problems, partly because the research relied on the subjects to analyze and label the sources of conflict. For literature on the meaning of conflict types, see: A.C. Amason, "Distinguishing

the Effects of Functional and Dysfunctional Conflict on Strategic Decision Making: Resolving a Paradox for Top Management Teams," *Academy of Management Journal* 39 (1996): 123–48; R. Fisher and W. Ury, *Getting to Yes: Negotiating an Agreement without Giving In* (Random House, 2012); K.A. Jehn, "Types of Conflict: The History and Future of Conflict Definitions and Typologies," in *Handbook of Conflict Management Research,* ed. O.B. Ayoko, N.M. Ashkanasy, and K.A. Jehn (Cheltenham, UK: Edward Elgar, 2014), 3–18; D. Tjosvold, A.S.H. Wong, and N.Y.F. Chen, "Constructively Managing Conflicts in Organizations," *Annual Review of Organizational Psychology and Organizational Behavior* 1 (2014): 545–68; T.A. O'Neill et al., "The Structure and Function of Team Conflict State Profiles," *Journal of Management* 44, no. 2 (February 2018): 811–36. One recent review reaffirms the preference of study-ing conflict in terms of how it is framed (expressed) rather than arbitrarily categorized. See: L.R. Weingart et al., "The Directness and Oppositional Intensity of Conflict Expression," *Academy of Management Review* 40 (2015): 235–62.

15. F.R.C. de Wit, L.L. Greer, and K.A. Jehn, "The Paradox of Intragroup Conflict: A Meta-Analysis," *Journal of Applied Psychology* 97 (2012): 360–90. Earlier meta-analyses reported either nonsignificant or somewhat negative correlations between task conflict and team outcomes. However, the recent meta-analysis and other writers point to several methodological problems with conflict research that explain the mixed findings. For a review, see M.L. Loughry and A.C. Amason, "Why Won't Task Conflict Cooperate? Deciphering Stubborn Results," *International Journal of Conflict Management* 25 (2014): 333–58.

16. J.M. Leon-Perez et al., "The Relationship between Interpersonal Conflict and Workplace Bullying," *Journal of Managerial Psychology* 30 (2015): 250–63; K.A. Graham et al., "Too Many Cooks in the Kitchen: The Effects of Dominance Incompatibility on Relationship Conflict and Subsequent Abusive Supervision," *Leadership Quarterly* 30 (2019): 351–64.

17. R.S. Lau and A.T. Cobb, "Understanding the Connections between Relationship Conflict and Performance: The Intervening Roles of Trust and Exchange," *Journal of Organizational Behavior* 31, no. 6 (2010): 898–917.

18. C.K.W. De Dreu and L.R. Weingart, "Task Versus Relationship Conflict, Team Performance, and Team Member Satisfaction: A Meta-Analysis," *Journal of Applied Psychology* 88 (August 2003): 587–60; A.C. Mooney, P.J. Holahan, and A.C. Amason, "Don't Take It Personally: Exploring Cognitive Conflict as a Mediator of Affective Conflict," *Journal of Management Studies* 44, no. 5 (2007): 733–75; K. Choi and B. Cho, "Competing Hypotheses Analyses of the Associations between Group Task Conflict and Group Relationship Conflict," *Journal of Organizational Behavior* 32, no. 8 (2011): 1106–1126.

19. J.X. Yang and K.W. Mossholder, "Decoupling Task and Relationship Conflict: The Role of Intergroup Emotional Processing," *Journal of Organizational Behavior* 25 (2004): 589–60; B.H. Bradley et al., "Ready to Rumble: How Team Personality Composition and Task Conflict Interact to Improve Performance," *Journal of Applied*

Psychology 98, no. 2 (2013): 385–39; B.H. Bradley et al., "Reaping the Benefits of Task Conflict in Teams: The Critical Role of Team Psychological Safety Climate," *Journal of Applied Psychology* 97, no. 1 (2012): 151–158.

20. P.L. Curseu, S. Boros, and L.A.G. Oerlemans, "Task and Relationship Conflict in Short-Term and Long-Term Groups: The Critical Role of Emotion Regulation," *International Journal of Conflict Management* 23 (2012): 97–107; A. Schlaerth, N. Ensari, and J. Christian, "A Meta-Analytical Review of the Relationship between Emotional Intelligence and Leaders' Constructive Conflict Management," *Group Processes & Intergroup Relations* 16 (2013): 126–36; N.L. Jimmieson, M.K. Tucker, and J.L. Campbell, "Task Conflict Leads to Relationship Conflict When Employees Are Low in Trait Self-Control: Implications for Employee Strain," *Personality and Individual Differences* 113 (2017): 209–18; H.R. Flores, X. Jiang, and C.C. Manz, "Intra-Team Conflict: The Moderating Effect of Emotional Self-Leadership," *International Journal of Conflict Management* 29 (2018): 424–44.

21. F.R.C. de Wit, L.L. Greer, and K.A. Jehn, "The Paradox of Intragroup Conflict: A Meta-Analysis," *Journal of Applied Psychology* 97, no. 2 (March 2012): 360–90; S.E. Humphrey et al., "Team Conflict Dynamics: Implications of a Dyadic View of Conflict for Team Performance," *Organizational Behavior and Human Decision Processes* 142 (2017): 58–70; T.A. O'Neill and M.J.W. McLarnon, "Optimizing Team Conflict Dynamics for High Performance Teamwork," *Human Resource Management Review* 28 (2018): 378–94.

22. A.C. Edmondson and Z. Lei, "Psychological Safety: The History, Renaissance, and Future of an Interpersonal Construct," *Annual Review of Organizational Psychology and Organizational Behavior* 1 (2014): 23–43; D. Tjosvold, A.S.H. Wong, and N.Y.F. Chen, "Constructively Managing Conflicts in Organizations," *Annual Review of Organizational Psychology and Organizational Behavior* 1 (2014): 545–68; A. Newman, R. Donohue, and N. Eva, "Psychological Safety: A Systematic Review of the Literature," *Human Resource Management Review* 27 (2017): 521–35.

23. L. Pondy, "Organizational Conflict: Concepts and Models," *Administrative Science Quarterly* 2 (1967): 296–320; K.W. Thomas, "Conflict and Negotiation Processes in Organizations," in *Handbook of Industrial and Organizational Psychology,* ed. M.D. Dunnette and L.M. Hough (Palo Alto, CA: Consulting Psychologists Press, 1992), 651–718.

24. E. Halperin, "Emotion, Emotion Regulation, and Conflict Resolution," *Emotion Review* 6 (2014): 68–76; G. Todorova, J.B. Bear, and L.R. Weingart, "Can Conflict Be Energizing? A Study of Task Conflict, Positive Emotions, and Job Satisfaction.," *Journal of Applied Psychology* 99 (2014): 451–67; S. Čehajić-Clancy et al., "Social-Psychological Interventions for Intergroup Reconciliation: An Emotion Regulation Perspective," *Psychological Inquiry* 27 (2016): 73–88; M. Caldara et al., "A Study of the Triggers of Conflict and Emotional Reactions," *Games* 8 (2017): 21; G.A. van Kleef and S. Côté, "Emotional Dynamics in Conflict and Negotiation: Individual, Dyadic, and Group Processes," *Annual Review of Organizational*

Psychology and Organizational Behavior 5 (2018): 437–64.

25. E. Halperin, "Emotion, Emotion Regulation, and Conflict Resolution," *Emotion Review* 6 (2014): 68–76; D. Motro, T. Kugler, and T. Connolly, "Back to the Basics: How Feelings of Anger Affect Cooperation," *International Journal of Conflict Management* 27 (2016): 523–46; J. Folger, M.S. Poole, and R.K. Stutman, *Working through Conflict: Strategies for Relationships, Groups, and Organizations,* 7th ed. (Oxon, UK: Routledge, 2016), Chap. 2.

26. G.E. Martin and T.J. Bergman, "The Dynamics of Behavioral Response to Conflict in the Workplace," *Journal of Occupational & Organizational Psychology* 69 (1996): 377–87; K.A. Kennedy and E. Pronin, "When Disagreement Gets Ugly: Perceptions of Bias and the Escalation of Conflict," *Personality and Social Psychology Bulletin* 34 (2008): 833–48; L.F. Smyth, "Escalation and Mindfulness," *Negotiation Journal* 28 (2012): 45–72.

27. R.E. Walton and J.M. Dutton, "The Management of Conflict: A Model and Review," *Administrative Science Quarterly* 14 (1969): 73–8; S.M. Schmidt and T.A. Kochan, "Conflict: Toward Conceptual Clarity," *Administrative Science Quarterly* 17, no. 3 (Sept. 1972): 359–370.

28. K.A. Jehn, C. Chadwick, and S.M.B. Thatcher, "To Agree or Not to Agree: The Effects of Value Congruence, Individual Demographic Dissimilarity, and Conflict on Workgroup Outcomes," *International Journal of Conflict Management* 8 (1997): 287–305; A.N. Garman, D.C. Leach, and N. Spector, "Worldviews in Collision: Conflict and Collaboration across Professional Lines," *Journal of Organizational Behavior* 27 (2006): 829–49; L.L. Greer et al., "Why and When Hierarchy Impacts Team Effectiveness: A Meta-Analytic Integration," *Journal of Applied Psychology* 103 (2018): 591–613; X. "Paul" Zhang et al., "One World, Two Realities: Perception Differences between Software Developers and Testers," *Journal of Computer Information Systems* 58 (2018): 385–94.

29. D.R. Hillman, "Understanding Multigenerational Work-Value Conflict Resolution," *Journal of Workplace Behavioral Health* 29 (2014): 240–57; S. Lyons and L. Kuron, "Generational Differences in the Workplace: A Review of the Evidence and Directions for Future Research," *Journal of Organizational Behavior* 35 (2014): S139–57; M.J. Urick et al., "Understanding and Managing Intergenerational Conflict: An Examination of Influences and Strategies," *Work, Aging and Retirement* 3 (2017): 166–85.

30. R.M. Sarala, "The Impact of Cultural Differences and Acculturation Factors on Post-Acquisition Conflict," *Scandinavian Journal of Management* 26 (2010): 38–56; J. Joseph, "Managing Change after the Merger: The Value of Pre-Merger Ingroup Identities," *Journal of Organizational Change Management* 27 (2014): 430–48; H.E. Yildiz, "'Us vs. Them' or 'Us over Them'? On the Roles of Similarity and Status in M&As," *International Business Review* 25 (2016): 51–65. Differentiation conflict in mergers is similar to differentiation conflict between people and work units across national cultures. See, for example: J. Brett, "Intercultural Challenges in Managing

Workplace Conflict—A Call for Research," *Cross Cultural & Strategic Management* 25, no. 1 (2018): 32–52.

31. T. Taylor, "Change Is an Inevitable Part of Life," *Denver Business Journal Online,* 8 October 2012.

32. P.C. Earley and G.B. Northcraft, "Goal Setting, Resource Interdependence, and Conflict Management," in *Managing Conflict: An Interdisciplinary Approach,* ed. M.A. Rahim (New York: Praeger, 1989), 161–70; K. Jehn, "A Multimethod Examination of the Benefits and Detriments of Intragroup Conflict," *Administrative Science Quarterly* 40 (1995): 245–82; P.T. Coleman et al., "Navigating Conflict and Power at Work: The Effects of Power and Interdependence Asymmetries on Conflict in Organizations," *Journal of Applied Social Psychology* 43 (2013): 1963–83.

33. J.G. March and H.A. Simon, *Organizations* (New York: John Wiley & Sons, 1958), 126.

34. Some scholars suggest that ambiguous rules may be the rule violator's opportunistic interpretation of rules that others believe are clear. For a discussion of the conditions under which conflict results from ambiguous or inconsistently enforced rules, see: A.W. Martin et al., "Against the Rules: Synthesizing Types and Processes of Bureaucratic Rule-Breaking," *Academy of Management Review* 38 (2013): 550–74.

35. L.R. Weingart et al., "The Directness and Oppositional Intensity of Conflict Expression," *Academy of Management Review* 40 (2015): 235–62; D. Ames, A. Lee, and A. Wazlawek, "Interpersonal Assertiveness: Inside the Balancing Act," *Social and Personality Psychology Compass* 11 (2017): e12317; C. Samba, D. Van Knippenberg, and C.C. Miller, "The Impact of Strategic Dissent on Organizational Outcomes: A Meta-Analytic Integration," *Strategic Management Journal* 39 (2018): 379–402.

36. M. Hewstone, M. Rubin, and H. Willis, "Intergroup Bias," *Annual Review of Psychology* 53 (2002): 575–604; T. Yamagishi and N. Mifune, "Social Exchange and Solidarity: In-Group Love or Out-Group Hate?," *Evolution and Human Behavior* 30 (2009): 229–37; N. Halevy, O. Weisel, and G. Bornstein, "'In-Group Love' and 'Out-Group Hate' in Repeated Interaction between Groups," *Journal of Behavioral Decision Making* 25 (2012): 188–95; O. Weisel and R. Böhm, "'Ingroup Love' and 'Outgroup Hate' in Intergroup Conflict between Natural Groups," *Journal of Experimental Social Psychology* 60 (2015): 110–20.

37. M.P. Follett, "Constructive Conflict," in *Dynamic Administration: The Collected Papers of Mary Parker Follett,* ed. H.C. Metcalf and L. Urwick, (Bath, UK: Management Publications Trust, 1941), 30–49; R.R. Blake, H.A. Shepard, and J.S. Mouton, *Managing Intergroup Conflict in Industry* (Houston: Gulf Publishing, 1964); T. Ruble and K. Thomas, "Support for a Two-Dimensional Model of Conflict Behavior," *Organizational Behavior and Human Performance* 16 (1976): 143–55; C.K.W. De Dreu et al., "A Theory-Based Measure of Conflict Management Strategies in the Workplace," *Journal of Organizational Behavior* 22 (2001): 645–68; D. Tjosvold, A.S.H. Wong, and N.Y.F. Chen, "Constructively Managing Conflicts in Organizations," *Annual Review of Organizational Psychology and Organizational Behavior* 1 (2014): 545–68; K.E. Johnson and J.A. Hall, "Validity of

Self-Reported Conflict Handling Preferences and the Role of Self-Enhancement," *International Journal of Conflict Management* 29 (2018): 543–63.

38. D. Ames, A. Lee, and A. Wazlawek, "Interpersonal Assertiveness: Inside the Balancing Act," *Social and Personality Psychology Compass* 11, no. 6 (2017): e12317.

39. Q. Wang, E.L. Fink, and D.A. Cai, "The Effect of Conflict Goals on Avoidance Strategies: What Does Not Communicating Communicate?," *Human Communication Research* 38, no. 2 (2012): 222–252.

40. Several studies have identified personal characteristics that predict a person's preferred conflict style. For example, see P.J. Moberg, "Linking Conflict Strategy to the Five-Factor Model: Theoretical and Empirical Foundations," *International Journal of Conflict Management* 12 (2001): 47–68; J.E. Barbuto Jr., K.A. Phipps, and Y. Xu, "Testing Relationships between Personality, Conflict Styles and Effectiveness," *International Journal of Conflict Management* 21 (2010): 434–47; M. Gunkel, C. Schlaegel, and V. Taras, "Cultural Values, Emotional Intelligence, and Conflict Handling Styles: A Global Study," *Journal of World Business* 51 (2016): 568–85; L. Parmer, "Relationships between Philosophical Values and Conflict Management Styles," *International Journal of Conflict Management* 29 (2017): 236–52.

41. D.W. Johnson et al., "Effects of Cooperative, Competitive, and Individualistic Goal Structures on Achievement: A Meta-Analysis," *Psychological Bulletin* 89 (1981): 47–62; G.A. Callanan, C.D. Benzing, and D.F. Perri, "Choice of Conflict-Handling Strategy: A Matter of Context," *Journal of Psychology* 140 (2006): 269–88; T.J. Hargrave and A.H. Van de Ven, "Integrating Dialectical and Paradox Perspectives on Managing Contradictions in Organizations," *Organization Studies* 38 (2017): 319–39.

42. X.M. Song, J. Xile, and B. Dyer, "Antecedents and Consequences of Marketing Managers' Conflict-Handling Behaviors," *Journal of Marketing* 64 (2000): 50–66; L.A. DeChurch, K.L. Hamilton, and C. Haas, "Effects of Conflict Management Strategies on Perceptions of Intragroup Conflict," *Group Dynamics* 11 (2007): 66–78; D.G. Oore, M.P. Leiter, and D.E. LeBlanc, "Individual and Organizational Factors Promoting Successful Responses to Workplace Conflict," *Canadian Psychology* 56 (2015): 301–10.

43. G.A. Chung-Yan and C. Moeller, "The Psychosocial Costs of Conflict Management Styles," *International Journal of Conflict Management* 21, no. 4 (2010): 382–399.

44. Several variations of this quotation have appeared over the past century. The field of marketing has an even older version of this quotation— "Win an argument and lose a sale (or customer)." Marketing textbooks and trade publications cited it in the 1890s. Dale Carnegie popularized the idea behind the notion that winning arguments loses friends. The entire first chapter of Part 3 in his best-selling book *How to Win Friends and Influence People* (1936) is devoted to this topic: "You Can't Win an Argument." The version of the quotation cited here is published in E. Knowles, *Little Oxford Dictionary of Proverbs* (Oxford, UK: Oxford University Press, 2009), 21.

45. A. Chunyan Peng and D. Tjosvold, "Social Face Concerns and Conflict Avoidance of Chinese Employees with Their Western or Chinese Managers," *Human Relations* 64 (2011): 1031–50; J.B. Bear, L.R. Weingart, and G. Todorova, "Gender and the Emotional Experience of Relationship Conflict: The Differential Effectiveness of Avoidant Conflict Management," *Negotiation and Conflict Management Research* 7 (2014): 213–31; I. Yang, "Perceived Conflict Avoidance by Managers and Its Consequences on Subordinates' Attitudes," *Business Ethics: A European Review* 24 (2015): 282–96; Z.-X. Zhang and X. Wei, "Superficial Harmony and Conflict Avoidance Resulting from Negative Anticipation in the Workplace," *Management and Organization Review* 13 (2017): 795–820.

46. A. Ergeneli, S.M. Camgoz, and P.B. Karapinar, "The Relationship between Self-Efficacy and Conflict-Handling Styles in Terms of Relative Authority Positions of the Two Parties," *Social Behavior & Personality: An International Journal* 38, no. 1 (2010): 13–28.

47. K. Leung et al., "Harmony and Conflict: A Cross-Cultural Investigation in China and Australia," *Journal of Cross-Cultural Psychology* 42 (2011): 795–816; W.-F. Lin et al., "We Can Make It Better: 'We' Moderates the Relationship Between a Compromising Style in Interpersonal Conflict and Well-Being," *Journal of Happiness Studies* 17 (2016): 41–57.

48. C.H. Tinsley, "How Negotiators Get to Yes: Predicting the Constellation of Strategies Used across Cultures to Negotiate Conflict," *Journal of Applied Psychology* 86 (2001): 583–93; M. Gunkel, C. Schlaegel, and V. Taras, "Cultural Values, Emotional Intelligence, and Conflict Handling Styles: A Global Study," *Journal of World Business* 51 (2016): 568–85.

49. F.P. Brew and D.R. Cairns, "Styles of Managing Interpersonal Workplace Conflict in Relation to Status and Face Concern: A Study with Anglos and Chinese," *International Journal of Conflict Management* 15 (2004): 27–57; A. C-Y. Peng and D. Tjosvold, "Social Face Concerns and Conflict Avoidance of Chinese Employees with Their Western or Chinese Managers," *Human Relations* 64 (2011): 1031–50; X. Li, V. Worm, and P. Xie, "Towards an Integrative Framework of Conflict-Handling Behaviour: Integrating Western and Chinese Perspectives," *Asia Pacific Business Review* 24 (2018): 22–36; J. Brett, "Intercultural Challenges in Managing Workplace Conflict—A Call for Research," *Cross Cultural & Strategic Management* 25 (2018): 32–52.

50. J.L. Holt and C.J. DeVore, "Culture, Gender, Organizational Role, and Styles of Conflict Resolution: A Meta-Analysis," *International Journal of Intercultural Relations* 29 (2005): 165–96; M. Davis, S. Capobianco, and L. Kraus, "Gender Differences in Responding to Conflict in the Workplace: Evidence from a Large Sample of Working Adults," *Sex Roles* 63 (2010): 500–14; B.M. Gayle, R.W. Preiss, and M. Allen, "Where Are We Now? A Meta-Analytic Review of Sex Difference Expectations for Conflict Management Strategy Selection," in *Managing Interpersonal Conflict: Advances through Meta-Analysis,* ed. N.A. Burrell, et al. (New York: Routledge, 2014), 226–47.

51. K. Lewin, *Resolving Social Conflicts* (New York: Harper, 1948).

52. M. Sherif, "Superordinate Goals in the Reduction of Intergroup Conflict," *The American Journal of Sociology* 63, no. 4 (1958): 349–356; J.D. Hunger and L.W. Stern, "An Assessment of the Functionality of the Superordinate Goal in Reducing Conflict," *Academy of Management Journal* 19, no. 4 (1976): 591–605.

53. K.M. Eisenhardt, J.L. Kahwajy, and L.J. Bourgeois III, "How Management Teams Can Have a Good Fight," *Harvard Business Review* (July/August 1997): 77–85; O. Doucet, J. Poitras, and D. Chenevert, "The Impacts of Leadership on Workplace Conflicts," *International Journal of Conflict Management* 20 (2009): 340–54; J. DiBenigno, "Anchored Personalization in Managing Goal Conflict between Professional Groups: The Case of U.S. Army Mental Health Care," *Administrative Science Quarterly* 63 (2018): 526–69.

54. R.S. Lau and A.T. Cobb, "Understanding the Connections between Relationship Conflict and Performance: The Intervening Roles of Trust and Exchange," *Journal of Organizational Behavior* 31 (2010): 898–917; D.E. Rast, M.A. Hogg, and D. van Knippenberg, "Intergroup Leadership Across Distinct Subgroups and Identities," *Personality and Social Psychology Bulletin* 44 (2018): 1090–103; R. Harush, A. Lisak, and E. Glikson, "The Bright Side of Social Categorization: The Role of Global Identity in Reducing Relational Conflict in Multicultural Distributed Teams," *Cross Cultural & Strategic Management* 25 (2018): 134–56.

55. M.-G. Seo and N.S. Hill, "Understanding the Human Side of Merger and Acquisition: An Integrative Framework," *The Journal of Applied Behavioral Science* 41 (2005): 422–43; H.E. Yildiz, "'Us vs. Them' or 'Us over Them'? On the Roles of Similarity and Status in M&As," *International Business Review* 25, Part A (2016): 51–65; F. Du and K. Xu, "The Path to Independence: Board Cohesion, Cognitive Conflict, and Information Sharing," *Journal of Management Accounting Research* 30 (2018): 31–54.

56. J. Sanchez-Burks, C.-Y. Cheng, and F. Lee, "Taking Advantage of Differences: Increasing Team Innovation through Identity Integration," in *Diversity and Groups,* vol. 11, *Research on Managing Groups and Teams* 11 (Emerald Group Publishing Limited, 2008), 55–73; A.M. Carton and B.A. Tewfik, "Perspective—A New Look at Conflict Management in Work Groups," *Organization Science* 27 (2016): 1125–41; H. Rubinstein, "The Importance of Multiple Perspectives," in *Applying Behavioural Science to the Private Sector: Decoding What People Say and What They Do,* ed. H. Rubinstein (Cham: Springer International Publishing, 2018), 89–106; T. Wei and J. Clegg, "Effect of Organizational Identity Change on Integration Approaches in Acquisitions: Role of Organizational Dominance," *British Journal of Management* 29 (2018): 337–55.

57. J. DiBenigno, "Anchored Personalization in Managing Goal Conflict between Professional Groups: The Case of U.S. Army Mental Health Care," *Administrative Science Quarterly* 63 (2018): 526–69.

58. J.F. Dovidio et al., "Reducing Intergroup Bias through Intergroup Contact: Twenty Years of Progress and Future Directions," *Group Processes & Intergroup Relations* 20 (2017): 606–20; R. Böhm, H. Rusch, and J. Baron, "The Psychology of Intergroup Conflict: A Review of Theories and Measures," *Journal of Economic Behavior & Organization,* 2018, in press.

59. B. Waber, J. Magnolfi, and G. Lindsay, "Workspaces That Move People," *Harvard Business Review* 92, no. 10 (October 2014): 68–77, 121.

60. J. Luft, *Of Human Interaction* (Palo Alto, CA: National Press, 1969); E.H. Schein, "Reactions, Reflections, Rejoinders, and a Challenge," *The Journal of Applied Behavioral Science* 45 (2009): 141–58; L. Shamoa-Nir, "The Window Becomes a Mirror: The Use of the Johari Window Model to Evaluate Stereotypes in Intergroup Dialogue in Israel," *Israel Affairs* 23 (2017): 727–46.

61. D. Nebenzahl, "Managing the Generation Gap," *Montreal Gazette,* February 28, 2009, G1; "L'Oréal Canada Considers Inter-Generational Teams a Strength," *National Post,* May 13, 2013; R. Yerema and K. Leung, "L'Oréal Canada: Recognized As One Of Canada's Top 100 Employers (2020) And Montreal's Top Employers (2020)," November 21, 2019, https://reviews.canadastop100.com/top-employer-loreal

62. R.R. Blake and J.S. Mouton, "Reactions to Intergroup Competition under Win-Lose Conditions," *Management Science* 7 (1961): 420–35; R.R. Blake and J.S. Mouton, *Solving Costly Organizational Conflicts,* 1st ed, (San Francisco: Jossey-Bass Publishers, 1984), Chapter 6; M.L. Marks, "Merger Management HR's Way," *HRMagazine* 36, no. 5 (May 1991): 60; G. Gemmill and M. Elmes, "Mirror, Mask, and Shadow: Psychodynamic Aspects of Intergroup Relations," *Journal of Management Inquiry* 2 (1993): 43–51. Along with the intervention described here, "intergroup mirroring" refers to the associated interpersonal phenomenon of empathizing with similar others and distancing or differentiating with non-similar others. See: M. Hřebíčková et al., "We Are the Opposite of You! Mirroring of National, Regional and Ethnic Stereotypes," *Journal of Social Psychology* 157 (2017): 703–19; J.T. Krautheim et al., "Intergroup Empathy: Enhanced Neural Resonance for Ingroup Facial Emotion in a Shared Neural Production-Perception Network," *NeuroImage* 194 (2019): 182–90.

63. A.-K. Newheiser and J.F. Dovidio, "Individual Differences and Intergroup Bias: Divergent Dynamics Associated with Prejudice and Stereotyping," *Personality and Individual Differences* 53 (2012): 70–74; L. Cosmides and J. Tooby, "Evolutionary Psychology: New Perspectives on Cognition and Motivation," *Annual Review of Psychology* 64 (2013): 201–29.

64. M.A. Von Glinow, D.L. Shapiro, and J.M. Brett, "Can We Talk, and Should We? Managing Emotional Conflict in Multicultural Teams," *Academy of Management Review* 29 (2004): 578–92; X. Li, V. Worm, and P. Xie, "Towards an Integrative Framework of Conflict-Handling Behaviour: Integrating Western and Chinese Perspectives," *Asia Pacific Business Review* 24 (2018): 22–36.

65. J.R. Galbraith, *Organization Design* (Addison-Wesley Pub. Co., 1977), 132.

66. P.R. Lawrence and J.W. Lorsch, "New Management Job: The Integrator," *Harvard Business Review,* December 1967, 142–51; J.R. Galbraith, *Organization Design* (Addison-Wesley Pub. Co., 1977), 152–58; R. Cappetta and P. Cillo, "Managing Integrators Where Integration Matters: Insights from Symbolic Industries," *The International Journal of Human Resource Management* 19 (2008): 2235–51.

67. J.G. March and H.A. Simon, *Organizations* (New York: John Wiley & Sons, 1958), 126.

68. A.R. Elangovan, "The Manager as the Third Party: Deciding How to Intervene in Employee Disputes," in *Negotiation: Readings, Exercises, and Cases,* ed. R.J. Lewicki, J.A. Litterer, and D. Saunders, 5th Ed. (New York: McGraw Hill, 2007), 473–84; D.E. Conlon et al., "Third Party Interventions across Cultures: No 'One Best Choice,'" in *Research in Personnel and Human Resources Management* (Greenwich, CT: JAI, 2007), 309–49. A broader variation of third-party conflict resolution is peacemaking. See: X. Zhang et al., "Peacemaking at the Workplace: A Systematic Review," *Negotiation and Conflict Management Research* 11 (2018): 204–24.

69. J.W. Thibaut and L. Walker, *Procedural Justice: A Psychological Analysis* (Hillsdale, N.J.: L. Erlbaum Associates, 1975); B.H. Sheppard, "Managers as Inquisitors: Lessons from the Law," in *Bargaining inside Organizations,* ed. M.H. Bazerman and R.J. Lewicki (Beverly Hills, CA: Sage, 1983).

70. D.J. Bussel, "A Third Way: Examiners as Inquisitors," *American Bankruptcy Law Journal* 90 (2016): 59–127.

71. J.A. Wall and T.C. Dunne, "Mediation Research: A Current Review," *Negotiation Journal* 28 (2012): 217–44; K. Bollen and M. Euwema, "Workplace Mediation: An Underdeveloped Research Area," *Negotiation Journal* 29 (2013): 329–53. Some researchers suggest that there are several forms of mediation, not all of which have high process and low decision control. See: D.L. Shapiro and E.N. Sherf, "The Role of Conflict in Managing Justice," in *The Oxford Handbook of Justice in the Workplace,* ed. R. Cropanzano and M.L. Ambrose (New York: Oxford University Press, 2015), 443–60.

72. B.H. Sheppard, "Managers as Inquisitors: Lessons from the Law," in *Bargaining inside Organizations,* ed. M.H. Bazerman and R.J. Lewicki (Beverly Hills, CA: Sage, 1983). Even in cultures that support managerial mediation, managers slip easily into inquisition and arbitration approaches where conflict has escalated. See M.K. Kozan, C. Ergin, and K. Varoglu, "Bases of Power and Conflict Intervention Strategy: A Study on Turkish Managers," *International Journal of Conflict Management* 25 (2014): 38–60.

73. R. Karambayya and J.M. Brett, "Managers Handling Disputes: Third Party Roles and Perceptions of Fairness," *Academy of Management Journal* 32 (1989): 687–704; B.M. Goldman et al., "The Role of Third Parties/Mediation in Managing Conflict in Organizations," in *The Psychology of Conflict and Conflict Management in Organizations,* ed. C.K.W. De Dreu and M.J. Gelfand (New York: Lawrence Erlbaum Associates, 2008): 291-319.

74. A.R. Elangovan, "Managerial Intervention in Organizational Disputes: Testing a Prescriptive Model of Strategy Selection," *International Journal of Conflict Management* 4 (1998): 301–33; P.S. Nugent, "Managing Conflict: Third-Party Interventions for Managers," *Academy Of Management Executive* 16, no. 1 (February 2002): 139–154.

75. K. Bollen, H. Ittner, and M.C. Euwema, "Mediating Hierarchical Labor Conflicts: Procedural Justice Makes a Difference—For Subordinates," *Group Decision and Negotiation* 21 (2012):

621–36; R. Nesbit, T. Nabatchi, and L.B. Bingham, "Employees, Supervisors, and Workplace Mediation: Experiences of Justice and Settlement," *Review of Public Personnel Administration* 32 (2012): 260–87.

76. J.P. Meyer, J.M. Gemmell, and P.G. Irving, "Evaluating the Management of Interpersonal Conflict in Organizations: A Factor-Analytic Study of Outcome Criteria," *Canadian Journal of Administrative Sciences* 14 (1997): 1–13; L.B. Bingham, "Employment Dispute Resolution: The Case for Mediation," *Conflict Resolution Quarterly* 22, no. 1–2 (2004): 145–17; M. Hyde et al., "Workplace Conflict Resolution and the Health of Employees in the Swedish and Finnish Units of an Industrial Company," *Social Science & Medicine* 63, no. 8 (2006): 2218–2227.

77. W.H. Ross and D.E. Conlon, "Hybrid Forms of Third-Party Dispute Resolution: Theoretical Implications of Combining Mediation and Arbitration," *Academy of Management Review* 25, no. 2 (2000): 416–42; W.H. Ross, C. Brantmeier, and T. Ciriacks, "The Impact of Hybrid Dispute-Resolution Procedures on Constituent Fairness Judgments," *Journal of Applied Social Psychology* 32, no. 6 (Jun 2002): 1151–1188.

78. L.L. Thompson, J. Wang, and B.C. Gunia, "Negotiation," *Annual Review of Psychology* 61 (2010): 491–515; B. O'Neill, "International Negotiation: Some Conceptual Developments," *Annual Review of Political Science* 21 (2018): 515–33.

79. R.J. Lewicki, et al., *Essentials of Negotiation,* 4th Canadian Edition. (Toronto: McGraw Hill Canada, 2020).

80. Several models of negotiations have been developed. Preparation (also called planning) is a key part of these models in organizational settings. See, for example: D. Jang, H.A. Elfenbein, and W.P. Bottom, "More than a Phase: Form and Features of a General Theory of Negotiation," *Academy of Management Annals* 12, no. 1 (2018): 318–56.

81. R. Stagner and H. Rosen, *Psychology of Union—Management Relations* (Belmont, CA: Wadsworth, 1965), pp. 95–96, 108–11; R.E. Walton and R.B. McKersie, *A Behavioral Theory of Labor Negotiations: An Analysis of a Social Interaction System* (New York: McGraw Hill, 1965), pp. 41–4; L. Thompson, *The Mind and Heart of the Negotiator* (Upper Saddle River, NJ: Prentice-Hall, 1998), Chap. 2.

82. A. Caputo, "A Literature Review of Cognitive Biases in Negotiation Processes," *International Journal of Conflict Management* 24 (2013): 374–98; A.B.V. Zant and L.J. Kray, "Negotiation and Conflict Resolution: A Behavioral Decision Research Perspective," in *The Wiley Blackwell Handbook of Judgment and Decision Making,* ed. G. Keren, and G. Wu (John Wiley & Sons, Ltd, 2015), 828–48; M. Schaerer, D.D. Loschelder, and R.I. Swaab, "Bargaining Zone Distortion in Negotiations: The Elusive Power of Multiple Alternatives," *Organizational Behavior and Human Decision Processes* 137 (2016): 156–71.

83. A. Tversky and D. Kahneman, "Judgment under Uncertainty: Heuristics and Biases," *Science* 185, no. 4157 (1974): 1124–31; J.D. Jasper and S.D. Christman, "A Neuropsychological Dimension for Anchoring Effects," *Journal of Behavioral Decision Making* 18 (2005): 343–69.

84. S. Doctoroff, "Reengineering Negotiations," *Sloan Management Review* 39 (1998): 63–71; D.C.

Zetik and A.F. Stuhlmacher, "Goal Setting and Negotiation Performance: A Meta-Analysis," *Group Processes & Intergroup Relations* 5 (2002): 35–52.

85. L.L. Thompson, J. Wang, and B.C. Gunia, "Negotiation," *Annual Review of Psychology* 61 (2010): 491–515. Some negotiation experts warn that BATNA is often misunderstood and that "no deal option" may be a better way of viewing such situations. see: J.K. Sebenius, "BATNAs in Negotiation: Common Errors and Three Kinds of 'No,'" *Negotiation Journal* 33 (2017): 89–99.

86. R.L. Pinkley et al., "The Power of Phantom Alternatives in Negotiation: How What Could Be Haunts What Is," *Organizational Behavior and Human Decision Processes* 151 (2019): 34–48.

87. L.L. Thompson, "Information Exchange in Negotiation," *Journal of Experimental Social Psychology* 27 (1991): 161–79; R. Fells, *Effective Negotiation: From Research to Results,* 2nd ed. (Melbourne: Cambridge University Press, 2012), Chap. 6.

88. J.M. Brett, "Managing Organizational Conflict," *Professional Psychology: Research and Practice* 15 (1984): 664–78. For recent research on cautious information exchange among skilled negotiators, see R. Fells et al., "Unraveling Business Negotiations Using Practitioner Data," *Negotiation and Conflict Management Research* 8 (2015): 119–36.

89. S.R. Covey, *The 7 Habits of Highly Effective People* (New York: Free Press, 1989), pp. 235–260. Covey's statement was likely inspired by a prayer that first appeared in France in 1912 and was translated to English in the 1930s, part of which says: "Grant that I may not so much seek. . . To be understood as to understand." see: https://en.wikipedia.org/wiki/Prayer_of_Saint_Francis

90. N. Rackham and J. Carlisle, "The Effective Negotiator—Part I: The Behaviour of Successful Negotiators," *Journal of European Industrial Training* 2, no. 6 (1978): 6–11.

91. A.R. Herrman and M. Allen, "Hardline Versus Softline Bargaining Strategies: A Meta-Analytic Review," in *Managing Interpersonal Conflict: Advances through Meta-Analysis,* ed. N.A. Burrell, et al. (New York: Routledge, 2014), 213–25; J. Hüffmeier et al., "Being Tough or Being Nice? A Meta-Analysis on the Impact of Hard- and Softline Strategies in Distributive Negotiations," *Journal of Management* 40 (2014): 866–92.

92. S. Kwon and L.R. Weingart, "Unilateral Concessions from the Other Party: Concession Behavior, Attributions, and Negotiation Judgments," *Journal of Applied Psychology* 89 (2004): 263–78; R. Fells, *Effective Negotiation* (Cambridge, UK: Cambridge University Press, 2012), Chap. 8.

93. C. Thuderoz, "Why Do We Respond to a Concession with Another Concession? Reciprocity and Compromise," *Negotiation Journal* 33, no. 1 (2017): 71–83.

94. D. Malhotra, "The Fine Art of Making Concessions," *Negotiation* (2006): 3–5.

95. R.J. Lewicki et al., *Negotiation,* 4th ed. (New York: McGraw Hill/Irwin, 2003), 95; M. Olekalns and P.L. Smith, "Testing the Relationships among Negotiators' Motivational Orientations, Strategy Choices, and Outcomes," *Journal of Experimental Social Psychology* 39, no. 2 (2003): 101–17.

96. A.F. Stuhlmacher, T.L. Gillespie, and M.V. Champagne, "The Impact of Time Pressure in Negotiation: A Meta-Analysis," *International Journal of Conflict Management* 9 (1998): 97–116; C.K.W. De Dreu, "Time Pressure and Closing of the Mind in Negotiation," *Organizational Behavior and Human Decision Processes* 91 (2003): 280–95; P.J. Carnevale, "Strategic Time in Negotiation," *Current Opinion in Psychology,* 26 (2019): 106–12.

97. As with other forms of time pressure, exploding offers have complex consequences for negotiations. Those who apply these offers can be worse off in the negotiation under some circumstances. See N. Lau et al., "Exploding Offers Can Blow up in More Than One Way," *Decision Analysis* 11, no. 3 (2014): 171–88; W. Güth and M.G. Kocher, "More Than Thirty Years of Ultimatum Bargaining Experiments: Motives, Variations, and a Survey of the Recent Literature," *Journal of Economic Behavior & Organization* 108 (2014): 396–409.

98. M. Olekalns and P.L. Smith, "Moments in Time: Metacognition, Trust, and Outcomes in Dyadic Negotiations," *Personality and Social Psychology Bulletin* 31 (2005): 1696–1707.

99. D.W. Choi, "Shared Metacognition in Integrative Negotiation," *International Journal of Conflict Management* 21 (2010): 309–333.

100. J.M. Brett et al., "Sticks and Stones: Language, Face, and Online Dispute Resolution," *Academy of Management Journal* 50 (2007): 85–9; D. Pietroni et al., "Emotions as Strategic Information: Effects of Other's Emotional Expressions on Fixed-Pie Perception, Demands, and Integrative Behavior in Negotiation," *Journal of Experimental Social Psychology* 44 (2008): 1444–145; D. Druckman and M. Olekalns, "Emotions in Negotiation," *Group Decision and Negotiation* 17 (2008): 1–11; M.J. Boland and W.H. Ross, "Emotional Intelligence and Dispute Mediation in Escalating and De-Escalating Situations," *Journal of Applied Social Psychology* 40 (2010): 3059–3105.

101. P.J. Carnevale and A.M. Isen, "The Influence of Positive Affect and Visual Access on the Discovery of Integrative Solutions in Bilateral Negotiation," *Organizational Behavior and Human Decision Processes* 37 (1986): 1–13; L. Thompson, *The Mind and Heart of the Negotiator*(Upper Saddle River, NJ: Prentice-Hall, 1998), Chap. 2.

102. J.W. Salacuse and J.Z. Rubin, "Your Place or Mine? Site Location and Negotiation," *Negotiation Journal* 6 (1990): 5–10; G. Brown and M. Baer, "Location in Negotiation: Is There a Home Field Advantage?," *Organizational Behavior and Human Decision Processes* 114 (2011): 190–200.

103. J. Margo, "The Persuaders," *Boss Magazine,* December 29, 2000, 38. For a full discussion of the advantages and disadvantages of face-to-face and alternative negotiation situations, see M.H. Bazerman et al., "Negotiation," *Annual Review of Psychology* 51 (2000): 279–314.

104. R. Lewicki, B. Barry, and D. Saunders, *Negotiation,* 8th ed. (New York, NY: McGraw Hill Education, 2020). Chap. 11.

105. J.A. Kennedy and L.J. Kray, "A Pawn in Someone Else's Game?: The Cognitive, Motivational, and Paradigmatic Barriers to Women's Excelling in Negotiation," *Research in Organizational Behavior* 35 (2015): 3–28; J. Mazei et al., "A Meta-Analysis on Gender Differences in Negotiation Outcomes and Their Moderators," *Psychological Bulletin* 141 (2015): 85–104.

106. I. Ayres and P. Siegelman, "Race and Gender Discrimination in Bargaining for a New Car," *American Economic Review* 83 (1995): 304–21; L.J. Kray, J.A. Kennedy, and A.B. Van Zant, "Not Competent Enough to Know the Difference? Gender Stereotypes about Women's Ease of Being Misled Predict Negotiator Deception," *Organizational Behavior and Human Decision Processes* 125 (2014): 61–72.

107. D. Mahoney, "Risk Manager Pay Survey Reveals Significant Gender Gap," *Business Insurance* 49, no. 26 (2015): 3.

CHAPTER 12

1. F. Stone, "The Conversation: ACL Services Boss Laurie Schultz Knows Fraud When She Sees It," *BCBusiness,* February 7, 2017; L. Schultz, "CEOs Need to Be Invested in Their Employees' Careers," *Globe & Mail,* July 29, 2018; H. Woodin, "2019 BC CEO Awards: Laurie Schultz," *Business in Vancouver,* October 2019; "EY Announces Laurie Schultz, CEO of Galvanize, as a 2019 Entrepreneur of the Year," News Release (Vancouver: Galvanize, October 8, 2019).

2. These statistics were collected in June 2019 using the advanced search features of Google, Google Scholar, and Amazon.

3. Many of these perspectives are summarized in R.N. Kanungo, "Leadership in Organizations: Looking Ahead to the 21st Century," *Canadian Psychology* 39 (1998): 71–82; G.A. Yukl, *Leadership in Organizations,* 8th ed. (Upper Saddle River, NJ: Pearson Education, 2013).

4. R. House, M. Javidan, and P. Dorfman, "Project GLOBE: An Introduction," *Applied Psychology: An International Review* 50 (2001): 489–505; R. House et al., "Understanding Cultures and Implicit Leadership Theories across the Globe: An Introduction to Project GLOBE," *Journal of World Business* 37 (2002): 3–10.

5. "Leadership University," Airbus Industrie, Careers—Working for Airbus, accessed June 9, 2019, https://www.airbus.com/careers/working-for-airbus/leadership-university.html.

6. J.A. Raelin, "We the Leaders: In Order to Form a Leaderful Organization," *Journal of Leadership & Organizational Studies* 12, no. 2 (2005): 18–30; C.L. Pearce, J.A. Conger, and E.A. Locke, "Shared Leadership Theory," *Leadership Quarterly* 19, no. 5 (2008): 622–28; E. Engel Small and J.R. Rentsch, "Shared Leadership in Teams: A Matter of Distribution," *Journal of Personnel Psychology* 9, no. 4 (2010): 203–11.

7. S. Marchionne, "Fiat's Extreme Makeover," *Harvard Business Review* (2008): 45–48.

8. J.A. Raelin, *Creating Leaderful Organizations: How to Bring out Leadership in Everyone* (San Francisco, CA: Berret-Koehler, 2003).

9. Most or all of these elements are included in: W. Bennis and B. Nanus, *Leaders: The Strategies for Taking Charge* (New York: Harper & Row, 1985); N.M. Tichy and M.A. Devanna, *The Transformational Leader* (New York: Wiley, 1986); B.M. Bass and R.E. Riggio, *Transformational Leadership,* 2nd ed. (Mahwah, NJ: Lawrence Erlbaum Associates, 2006); J.M. Kouzes and B.Z.

Posner, *The Leadership Challenge,* 6th ed. (San Francisco: Jossey-Bass, 2017).

10. Strategic collective vision has been identified as a key factor in leadership since Chester Barnard's seminal book in organizational behaviour. see: C. Barnard, *The Functions of the Executive* (Cambridge, MA: Harvard University Press, 1938), pp. 86–89.

11. W. Bennis and B. Nanus, *Leaders: The Strategies for Taking Charge* (New York: Harper & Row, 1985), 27–33, 89; R.E. Quinn, *Building the Bridge as You Walk on It: A Guide for Leading Change* (San Francisco: Jossey-Bass, 2004), Chap. 11; R. Gill, *Theory and Practice of Leadership* (London: Sage, 2011), Chap. 4; D. O'Connell, K. Hickerson, and A. Pillutla, "Organizational Visioning: An Integrative Review," *Group & Organization Management* 36, no. 1 (2011): 103–25.

12. J.M. Strange and M.D. Mumford, "The Origins of Vision: Effects of Reflection, Models, and Analysis," *Leadership Quarterly* 16 (2005): 121–48; S. Kantabutra, "Toward a Behavioral Theory of Vision in Organizational Settings," *Leadership & Organization Development Journal* 30 (2009): 319–37; S.A. Kirkpatrick, "Lead through Vision and Values," in *Handbook of Principles of Organizational Behavior,* ed. E.A. Locke (Chichester, UK: Wiley, 2010), 367–87; R. Ashkenas and B. Manville, "You Don't Have to Be CEO to Be a Visionary Leader," *Harvard Business Review (Online),* April 4, 2019.

13. J.A. Conger and R.N. Kanungo, *Charismatic Leadership in Organizations* (Thousand Oaks, CA: Sage, 1998), 173–83; M. Venus, D. Stam, and D. van Knippenberg, "Leader Emotion as a Catalyst of Effective Leader Communication of Visions, Value-Laden Messages, and Goals," *Organizational Behavior and Human Decision Processes* 122 (2013): 53–68; J. Mayfield, M. Mayfield, and W.C. Sharbrough, "Strategic Vision and Values in Top Leaders' Communications: Motivating Language at a Higher Level," *International Journal of Business Communication* 52 (2015): 97–121.

14. D.A. Waldman, P.A. Balthazard, and S.J. Peterson, "Leadership and Neuroscience: Can We Revolutionize the Way That Inspirational Leaders Are Identified and Developed?," *Academy of Management Perspectives* 25 (2011): 60–74; S. Denning, *The Leader's Guide to Storytelling: Mastering the Art and Discipline of Business Narrative,* rev. ed. (San Francisco: Jossey-Bass, 2011); J.C. Sarros et al., "Leaders and Their Use of Motivating Language," *Leadership & Organization Development Journal* 35 (2014): 226–40; A.M. Carton, C. Murphy, and J.R. Clark, "A (Blurry) Vision of the Future: How Leader Rhetoric About Ultimate Goals Influences Performance," *Academy of Management Journal* 57 (2014): 1544–70.

15. D. Ossip, "Create a Culture of Engagement for Successful Customer Outcomes," *The CEO Forum* 2015, 30–31; R. Reiss, " Interview with David Ossip," *The CEO Forum,* 11 October 2015, 73–76; L. Efron, "How Transformational Leadership Saved This Company: Ceridian's Story," *Forbes,* 6 July 2016.

16. L. Black, "Hamburger Diplomacy," *Report on Business Magazine* August 1988, 30–36.

17. J.E. Baur et al., "More Than One Way to Articulate a Vision: A Configurations Approach to Leader Charismatic Rhetoric and Influence," *Leadership Quarterly* 27, no. 1 (2016): 156–71.

18. D.E. Berlew, "Leadership and Organizational Excitement," *California Management Review* 17, no. 2 (1974): 21–30; W. Bennis and B. Nanus, *Leaders: The Strategies for Taking Charge* (New York: Harper & Row, 1985), 43–55; T. Simons, "Behavioral Integrity: The Perceived Alignment between Managers' Words and Deeds as a Research Focus," *Organization Science* 13, no. 1 (2002): 18–35.

19. S. Kolesnikov-Jessop, "You're the Conductor: Listen to the Music You Can Create with the Group," *New York Times,* April 11, 2016.

20. For a discussion of trust in leadership, see C.S. Burke et al., "Trust in Leadership: A Multi-Level Review and Integration," *Leadership Quarterly* 18, no. 6 (2007): 606–32. The surveys on leading by example are reported in J.C. Maxwell, "People Do What People See," *BusinessWeek,* 19 November 2007, 32; "Who's the Boss of Workplace Culture?," News release (Chelmsford, MA: Kronos, 9 March 2016). One recent study found that leading by doing has a positive correlation with employee productivity and service quality. See: L. Eldor, "Leading by Doing: Does Leading by Example Impact Productivity and Service Quality?," *Academy of Management Journal,* March 26, 2020, amj.2018.0706.

21. B.M. Bass and R.E. Riggio, *Transformational Leadership,* 2nd ed. (Mahwah, NJ: Erlbaum, 2006), 7; J.M. Kouzes and B.Z. Posner, *The Leadership Challenge,* 5th ed. (San Francisco: Jossey-Bass, 2012), Chaps. 6 and 7.

22. W.E. Baker and J.M. Sinkula, "The Synergistic Effect of Market Orientation and Learning Orientation on Organizational Performance," *Academy of Marketing Science Journal* 27, no. 4 (1999): 411–27; Z. Emden, A. Yaprak, and S.T. Cavusgil, "Learning from Experience in International Alliances: Antecedents and Firm Performance Implications," *Journal of Business Research* 58, no. 7 (2005): 883–92.

23. J.M. Kouzes and B.Z. Posner, *The Leadership Challenge,* 6th ed. (San Francisco: Jossey-Bass, 2017).

24. R.J. House, "A 1976 Theory of Charismatic Leadership," in *Leadership: The Cutting Edge,* ed. J.G. Hunt and L.L. Larson (Carbondale, IL.: Southern Illinois University Press, 1977), 189–207; J.A. Conger, "Charismatic Leadership," in *The Sage Handbook of Leadership,* ed. A. Bryman, et al. (London, UK: Sage, 2011), 86–102.

25. J.E. Barbuto Jr., "Taking the Charisma out of Transformational Leadership," *Journal of Social Behavior & Personality* 12 (1997): 689–97; Y.A. Nur, "Charisma and Managerial Leadership: The Gift That Never Was," *Business Horizons* 41 (1998): 19–26; M.D. Mumford and J.R. Van Doorn, "The Leadership of Pragmatism— Reconsidering Franklin in the Age of Charisma," *Leadership Quarterly* 12 (2001): 279–309; A. Fanelli, "Bringing out Charisma: CEO Charisma and External Stakeholders," *The Academy of Management Review* 31 (2006): 1049–61; M.J. Platow et al., "A Special Gift We Bestow on You for Being Representative of Us: Considering Leader Charisma from a Self-Categorization Perspective," *British Journal of Social Psychology* 45 (2006): 303–20.

26. W.H. Friedland, "For a Sociological Concept of Charisma," *Social Forces* 43 (1964): 18–26; K. Miyahara, "Charisma: From Weber to Contemporary Sociology," *Sociological Inquiry* 53 (1983): 368–88; J. Antonakis et al., "Charisma: An Ill-Defined and Ill-Measured Gift," *Annual Review of Organizational Psychology and Organizational Behavior* 3 (2016): 293–319; K.O. Tskhay, R. Zhu, and N.O. Rule, "Perceptions of Charisma from Thin Slices of Behavior Predict Leadership Prototypicality Judgments," *Leadership Quarterly,* 28 (2017): 555–62.

27. B. Shamir et al., "Correlates of Charismatic Leader Behavior in Military Units: Subordinates' Attitudes, Unit Characteristics, and Superiors' Appraisals of Leader Performance," *Academy of Management Journal* 41 (1998): 387–409; R.E. de Vries, R.A. Roe, and T.C.B. Taillieu, "On Charisma and Need for Leadership," *European Journal of Work and Organizational Psychology* 8 (1999): 109–33; R. Khurana, *Searching for a Corporate Savior: The Irrational Quest for Charismatic CEOs* (Princeton, NJ: Princeton University Press, 2002); R.E. de Vries, R.D. Pathak, and A.R. Paquin, "The Paradox of Power Sharing: Participative Charismatic Leaders Have Subordinates with More Instead of Less Need for Leadership," *European Journal of Work and Organizational Psychology* 20 (2010): 779–804. The effect of charismatic leadership on follower dependence was also noted earlier by U.S. government leader John Gardner. See J.W. Gardner, *On Leadership* (New York: Free Press, 1990), 34–36.

28. J. Lipman-Blumen, "A Pox on Charisma: Why Connective Leadership and Character Count," in *The Drucker Difference: What the World's Greatest Management Thinker Means to Today's Business Leaders,* ed. C.L. Pearce, J.A. Maciariello, and H. Yamawaki (New York: McGraw Hill, 2010), 149–74.

29. A. Mackey, "The Effect of CEOs on Firm Performance," *Strategic Management Journal* 29, no. 12 (2008): 1357–67. However, one study reported that transformational leadership is less effective than authoritarian (command-control with punishment) leadership in resource scarcity environments. See X. Huang et al., "When Authoritarian Leaders Outperform Transformational Leaders: Firm Performance in a Harsh Economic Environment," *Academy of Management Discoveries* 1, no. 2 (2015): 180–200.

30. J. Barling, T. Weber, and E.K. Kelloway, "Effects of Transformational Leadership Training on Attitudinal and Financial Outcomes: A Field Experiment," *Journal of Applied Psychology* 81 (1996): 827–32.

31. A. Bryman, "Leadership in Organizations," in *Handbook of Organization Studies,* ed. S.R. Clegg, C. Hardy, and W.R. Nord (Thousand Oaks, CA: Sage, 1996), 276–92; D. van Knippenberg and S.B. Sitkin, "A Critical Assessment of Charismatic— Transformational Leadership Research: Back to the Drawing Board?," *Academy of Management Annals* 7, no. 1 (2013): 1–60.

32. G. Yukl and J.W. Michel, "A Critical Assessment of Research on Effective Leadership Behavior," in *Advances in Authentic and Ethical Leadership,* ed. L.L. Neider and C.A. Schriesheim (Charlotte, NC: Information Age, 2014), 209–30.

33. B.S. Pawar and K.K. Eastman, "The Nature and Implications of Contextual Influences on Transformational Leadership: A Conceptual Examination," *Academy of Management Review*

22 (1997): 80–109; C.P. Egri and S. Herman, "Leadership in the North American Environmental Sector: Values, Leadership Styles, and Contexts of Environmental Leaders and Their Organizations," *Academy of Management Journal* 43, no. 4 (2000): 571–604.

34. A. Zaleznik, "Managers and Leaders: Are They Different?," *Harvard Business Review* 55, no. 3 (1977): 67–78; J.P. Kotter, *A Force for Change: How Leadership Differs from Management* (New York: Free Press, 1990); E.A. Locke, *The Essence of Leadership* (New York: Lexington Books, 1991); G. Yukl and R. Lepsinger, "Why Integrating the Leading and Managing Roles Is Essential for Organizational Effectiveness," *Organizational Dynamics* 34, no. 4 (2005): 361–75; D.V. Simonet and R.P. Tett, "Five Perspectives on the Leadership–Management Relationship: A Competency-Based Evaluation and Integration," *Journal of Leadership & Organizational Studies* 20, no. 2 (2013): 199–213.

35. R.J. House and R.N. Aditya, "The Social Scientific Study of Leadership: Quo Vadis?," *Journal of Management* 23, no. 3 (1997): 409–73.

36. W. Bennis and B. Nanus, *Leaders: The Strategies for Taking Charge* (New York: Harper & Row, 1985), 20. Peter Drucker is also widely cited as the source of this quotation. The closest passage we could find, however, is in the first two pages of *The Effective Executive* (1966) where Drucker states that effective executives "get the right things done." On the next page, he states that manual workers need only efficiency, "that is, the ability to do things right rather than the ability to get the right things done." See P.F. Drucker, *The Effective Executive* (New York: Harper Business, 1966), 1–2.

37. G. Yukl and R. Lepsinger, "Why Integrating the Leading and Managing Roles Is Essential for Organizational Effectiveness," *Organizational Dynamics* 34 (2005): 361–75. One critique of leadership theories suggests that scholars need to further clarify the distinction, if any exists, between leading and managing. See S.T. Hannah et al., "Debunking the False Dichotomy of Leadership Idealism and Pragmatism: Critical Evaluation and Support of Newer Genre Leadership Theories," *Journal of Organizational Behavior* 35 (2014): 598–621.

38. E.A. Fleishman, "The Description of Supervisory Behavior," *Journal of Applied Psychology* 37, no. 1 (1953): 1–6. For discussion on methodological problems with the development of these people vs task-oriented leadership constructs, see: C.A. Schriesheim, R.J. House, and S. Kerr, "Leader Initiating Structure: A Reconciliation of Discrepant Research Results and Some Empirical Tests," *Organizational Behavior and Human Performance* 15, no. 2 (1976): 297–321; L. Tracy, "Consideration and Initiating Structure: Are They Basic Dimensions of Leader Behavior?," *Social Behavior and Personality* 15, no. 1 (1987): 21–33.

39. A.K. Korman, "Consideration, Initiating Structure, and Organizational Criteria—a Review," *Personnel Psychology* 19 (1966): 349–62; E.A. Fleishman, "Twenty Years of Consideration and Structure," in *Current Developments in the Study of Leadership,* ed. E.A. Fleishman and J.C. Hunt (Carbondale: Southern Illinois University Press, 1973), 1–40; T.A. Judge, R.F. Piccolo, and R. Ilies, "The Forgotten Ones?: The Validity of Consideration and Initiating Structure in Leadership

Research," *Journal of Applied Psychology* 89 (2004): 36–51; D.S. DeRue et al., "Trait and Behavioral Theories of Leadership: An Integration and Meta-Analytic Test of Their Relative Validity," *Personnel Psychology* 64 (2011): 7–52; G.A. Yukl, *Leadership in Organizations,* 8th ed. (Upper Saddle River, NJ: Pearson Education, 2013), 62–75.

40. V.V. Baba, "Serendipity in Leadership: Initiating Structure and Consideration in the Classroom," *Human Relations* 42 (1989): 509–25.

41. B. Hassell, "What Do Today's Workforce Trends Mean for Business, Leadership?," *Chief Learning Officer,* March 20, 2017.

42. S.J. Peterson, B.M. Galvin, and D. Lange, "CEO Servant Leadership: Exploring Executive Characteristics and Firm Performance," *Personnel Psychology* 65, no. 3 (2012): 565–96.

43. R.K. Greenleaf, *Servant Leadership: A Journey into the Nature of Legitimate Power & Greatness*(Mahwah, NJ: Paulist Press, 1977; repr., 2002), 27.

44. S. Sendjaya, J.C. Sarros, and J.C. Santora, "Defining and Measuring Servant Leadership Behaviour in Organizations," *Journal of Management Studies* 45 (2008): 402–24; R.C. Liden et al., "Servant Leadership: Development of a Multidimensional Measure and Multi-Level Assessment," *Leadership Quarterly* 19 (2008): 161–77; D. van Dierendonck, "Servant Leadership: A Review and Synthesis," *Journal of Management* 37 (2011): 1228–61; R. VanMeter et al., "In Search of Clarity on Servant Leadership: Domain Specification and Reconceptualization," *AMS Review* 6 (2016): 59–78.

45. R. VanMeter et al., "In Search of Clarity on Servant Leadership: Domain Specification and Reconceptualization," *AMS Review* 6 (2016): 59–78.

46. S.J. Peterson, B.M. Galvin, and D. Lange, "CEO Servant Leadership: Exploring Executive Characteristics and Firm Performance," *Personnel Psychology* 65, no. 3 (2012): 565–96.

47. S. Kerr et al., "Towards a Contingency Theory of Leadership Based Upon the Consideration and Initiating Structure Literature," *Organizational Behavior and Human Performance* 12 (1974): 62–82; L.L. Larson, J.G. Hunt, and R.N. Osbom, "The Great Hi—Hi Leader Behavior Myth: A Lesson from Occam's Razor," *Academy of Management Journal* 19 (1976): 628–41.

48. R.J. House, "A Path Goal Theory of Leader Effectiveness," *Administrative Science Quarterly* 16 (1971): 321–39; M.G. Evans, "Extensions of a Path-Goal Theory of Motivation," *Journal of Applied Psychology* 59 (1974): 172–78; R.J. House and T.R. Mitchell, "Path-Goal Theory of Leadership," *Journal of Contemporary Business* (1974): 81–97; M.G. Evans, "Path Goal Theory of Leadership," in *Leadership,* ed. L.L. Neider and C.A. Schriesheim (Greenwich, CT: Information Age Publishing, 2002), 115–38.

49. For a thorough study of how expectancy theory of motivation relates to leadership, see R.G. Isaac, W.J. Zerbe, and D.C. Pitt, "Leadership and Motivation: The Effective Application of Expectancy Theory," *Journal of Managerial Issues* 13 (2001): 212–26.

50. R.J. House, "Path-Goal Theory of Leadership: Lessons, Legacy, and a Reformulated Theory," *The Leadership Quarterly* 7 (1996): 323–52.

51. J. Indvik, "Path-Goal Theory of Leadership: A Meta-Analysis," *Academy of Management Proceedings* (1986): 189–92; J.C. Wofford and L.Z. Liska, "Path-Goal Theories of Leadership: A Meta-Analysis," *Journal of Management* 19 (1993): 857–76.

52. J.D. Houghton and S.K. Yoho, "Toward a Contingency Model of Leadership and Psychological Empowerment: When Should Self-Leadership Be Encouraged?," *Journal of Leadership & Organizational Studies* 11 (2005): 65–83.

53. R.T. Keller, "A Test of the Path-Goal Theory of Leadership with Need for Clarity as a Moderator in Research and Development Organizations," *Journal of Applied Psychology* 74 (1989): 208–12.

54. R.P. Vecchio, J.E. Justin, and C.L. Pearce, "The Utility of Transactional and Transformational Leadership for Predicting Performance and Satisfaction within a Path-Goal Theory Framework," *Journal of Occupational and Organizational Psychology* 81 (2008): 71–82.

55. B. Carroll and L. Levy, "Defaulting to Management: Leadership Defined by What It Is Not," *Organization* 15 (2008): 75–96; I. Holmberg and M. Tyrstrup, "Well Then— What Now? An Everyday Approach to Managerial Leadership," *Leadership* 6 (2010): 353–72.

56. C.A. Schriesheim and L.L. Neider, "Path-Goal Leadership Theory: The Long and Winding Road," *Leadership Quarterly* 7 (1996): 317–21.

57. N. Nicholson, *Executive Instinct*(New York: Crown, 2000); T. A. Judge, R. F. Piccolo, and R. Ilies, "The Forgotten Ones?: The Validity of Consideration and Initiating Structure in Leadership Research," *Journal of Applied Psychology* 89, no. 1 (2004): 36–51; T. A. Judge, R. F. Piccolo, and T. Kosalka, "The Bright and Dark Sides of Leader Traits: A Review and Theoretical Extension of the Leader Trait Paradigm," *Leadership Quarterly* 20 (2009): 855–75. One pioneering managerial leadership expect specifically argued that managers cannot easily switch leadership styles. See: F.E. Fiedler, "Engineer the Job to Fit the Manager," *Harvard Business Review* 43, no. 5 (1965): 115–22.

58. This observation has also been made by C.A. Schriesheim, "Substitutes-for-Leadership Theory: Development and Basic Concepts," *Leadership Quarterly* 8 (1997): 103–08.

59. D.F. Elloy and A. Randolph, "The Effect of Superleader Behavior on Autonomous Work Groups in a Government Operated Railway Service," *Public Personnel Management* 26 (1997): 257–72; C.C. Manz and H. Sims Jr., *The New SuperLeadership: Leading Others to Lead Themselves* (San Francisco, CA: Berrett-Koehler, 2001).

60. M.L. Loughry, "Coworkers Are Watching: Performance Implications of Peer Monitoring," *Academy of Management Proceedings* (2002): O1–O6.

61. P.M. Podsakoff and S.B. MacKenzie, "Kerr and Jermier's Substitutes for Leadership Model: Background, Empirical Assessment, and Suggestions for Future Research," *Leadership Quarterly* 8 (1997): 117–32; S.D. Dionne et al., "Neutralizing Substitutes for Leadership Theory: Leadership Effects and Common-Source Bias," *Journal Of Applied Psychology* 87 (2002): 454–64; J.R. Villa et al., "Problems with Detecting Moderators in Leadership Research Using

Moderated Multiple Regression," *Leadership Quarterly* 14 (2003): 3–23; S.D. Dionne et al., "Substitutes for Leadership, or Not," *Leadership Quarterly* 16 (2005): 169–93.

62. J.R. Meindl, "On Leadership: An Alternative to the Conventional Wisdom," *Research in Organizational Behavior* 12 (1990): 159–203; L.R. Offermann, J.J.K. Kennedy, and P.W. Wirtz, "Implicit Leadership Theories: Content, Structure, and Generalizability," *Leadership Quarterly* 5, no. 1 (1994): 43–58; R.J. Hall and R.G. Lord, "Multi-Level Information Processing Explanations of Followers' Leadership Perceptions," *Leadership Quarterly* 6 (1995): 265–87; O. Epitropaki and R. Martin, "Implicit Leadership Theories in Applied Settings: Factor Structure, Generalizability, and Stability over Time," *Journal of Applied Psychology* 89, no. 2 (2004): 293–310. For a broader discussion of the social construction of leadership, see: G.T. Fairhurst and D. Grant, "The Social Construction of Leadership: A Sailing Guide," *Management Communication Quarterly* 24, no. 2 (2010): 171–210.

63. R.G. Lord et al., "Contextual Constraints on Prototype Generation and Their Multilevel Consequences for Leadership Perceptions," *Leadership Quarterly* 12, no. 3 (2001): 311–38; K.A. Scott and D.J. Brown, "Female First, Leader Second? Gender Bias in the Encoding of Leadership Behavior," *Organizational Behavior and Human Decision Processes* 101 (2006): 230–42; S.J. Shondrick, J.E. Dinh, and R.G. Lord, "Developments in Implicit Leadership Theory and Cognitive Science: Applications to Improving Measurement and Understanding Alternatives to Hierarchical Leadership," *Leadership Quarterly* 21, no. 6 (2010): 959–78.

64. S.F. Cronshaw and R.G. Lord, "Effects of Categorization, Attribution, and Encoding Processes on Leadership Perceptions," *Journal of Applied Psychology* 72 (1987): 97–106; J.L. Nye and D.R. Forsyth, "The Effects of Prototype-Based Biases on Leadership Appraisals: A Test of Leadership Categorization Theory," *Small Group Research* 22 (1991): 360–79.

65. MJ.R. Meindl, "On Leadership: An Alternative to the Conventional Wisdom," *Research in Organizational Behavior* 12 (1990): 163; B. Schyns, J.R. Meindl, and M.A. Croon, "The Romance of Leadership Scale: Cross-Cultural Testing and Refinement," *Leadership* 3, no. 1 (2007): 29–46; J. Felfe and L.E. Petersen, "Romance of Leadership and Management Decision Making," *European Journal of Work and Organizational Psychology* 16, no. 1 (2007): 1–24.

66. J. Pfeffer, "The Ambiguity of Leadership," *Academy of Management Review* 2 (1977): 102–12.

67. R. Weber et al., "The Illusion of Leadership: Misattribution of Cause in Coordination Games," *Organization Science* 12, no. 5 (2001): 582–98; N. Ensari and S.E. Murphy, "Cross-Cultural Variations in Leadership Perceptions and Attribution of Charisma to the Leader," *Organizational Behavior and Human Decision Processes* 92 (2003): 52–66; M.L.A. Hayward, V.P. Rindova, and T.G. Pollock, "Believing One's Own Press: The Causes and Consequences of CEO Celebrity," *Strategic Management Journal* 25, no. 7 (2004): 637–53.

68. L.M. Fisher, "Ricardo Semler Won't Take Control," *strategy + business,* no. 41 (2005): 1–11.

69. The history of the personal attributes perspective of leadership, as well as more recent research on this topic, is nicely summarized in S.J. Zaccaro, C. Kemp, and P. Bader, "Leader Traits and Attributes," in *The Nature of Leadership,* ed. J. Antonakis, A.T. Cianciolo, and R.J. Sternberg (Thousand Oaks, CA: Sage, 2004), 101–24.

70. R.M. Stogdill, *Handbook of Leadership* (New York: The Free Press, 1974), Chap. 5.

71. J. Intagliata, D. Ulrich, and N. Smallwood, "Leveraging Leadership Competencies to Produce Leadership Brand: Creating Distinctiveness by Focusing on Strategy and Results," *Human Resources Planning* 23, no. 4 (2000): 12–23; J.A. Conger and D.A. Ready, "Rethinking Leadership Competencies," *Leader to Leader* (2004): 41–47; S.J. Zaccaro, C. Kemp, and P. Bader, "Leader Traits and Attributes," in *The Nature of Leadership,* ed. J. Antonakis, A.T. Cianciolo, and R.J. Sternberg (Thousand Oaks, CA: Sage, 2004), 101–24. For a recent discussion on leadership traits and evolutionary psychology, see: T.A. Judge, R.F. Piccolo, and T. Kosalka, "The Bright and Dark Sides of Leader Traits: A Review and Theoretical Extension of the Leader Trait Paradigm," *Leadership Quarterly* 20(2009): 855–75.

72. This list is based on S.A. Kirkpatrick and E.A. Locke, "Leadership: Do Traits Matter?," *Academy of Management Executive* 5 (1991): 48–60; S.J. Zaccaro, C. Kemp, and P. Bader, "Leader Traits and Attributes," in *The Nature of Leadership,* ed. J. Antonakis, A.T. Cianciolo, and R.J. Sternberg (Thousand Oaks, CA: Sage, 2004), 101–24; G.A. Yukl, *Leadership in Organizations,* 8th ed. (Upper Saddle River, NJ: Pearson Education, 2013), Chap. 6.

73. T.A. Judge et al., "Personality and Leadership: A Qualitative and Quantitative Review," *Journal Of Applied Psychology* 87, no. 4 (2002): 765–80; D.S. Derue et al., "Trait and Behavioral Theories of Leadership: An Integration and Meta-Analytic Test of Their Relative Validity," *Personnel Psychology* 64, no. 1 (2011): 7–52; A. Deinert et al., "Transformational Leadership Sub-Dimensions and Their Link to Leaders' Personality and Performance," *Leadership Quarterly* 26, no. 6 (2015): 1095–120; A.D. Parr, S.T. Lanza, and P. Bernthal, "Personality Profiles of Effective Leadership Performance in Assessment Centers," *Human Performance* 29, no. 2 (2016): 143–57.

74. D.V. Day, M.M. Harrison, and S.M. Halpin, *An Integrative Approach to Leader Development: Connecting Adult Development, Identity, and Expertise* (New York: Routledge, 2009); D.S. DeRue and S.J. Ashford, "Who Will Lead and Who Will Follow? A Social Process of Leadership Identity Construction in Organizations," *Academy of Management Review* 35, no. 4 (2010): 627–47; H. Ibarra et al., "Leadership and Identity: An Examination of Three Theories and New Research Directions," in *The Oxford Handbook of Leadership and Organizations,* ed. D.V. Day (New York: Oxford University Press, 2014), 285–301; L. Guillén, M. Mayo, and K. Korotov, "Is Leadership a Part of Me? A Leader Identity Approach to Understanding the Motivation to Lead," *Leadership Quarterly* 26, no. 5 (2015): 802–20.

75. B. Carroll and L. Levy, "Defaulting to Management: Leadership Defined by What It Is Not," *Organization* 15, no. 1 (2008): 75–96.

76. One recent study suggests that leaders retain their power by undermining followers' power. See

C. Case and J. Maner, "Divide and Conquer: When and Why Leaders Undermine the Cohesive Fabric of Their Group," *Journal of Personality and Social Psychology* 107, no. 6 (2014): 1033–50.

77. J.B. Miner, "Twenty Years of Research on Role Motivation Theory of Managerial Effectiveness," *Personnel Psychology* 31 (1978): 739–60; C.J. Vinkenburg et al., "Arena: A Critical Conceptual Framework of Top Management Selection," *Group & Organization Management* 39, no. 1 (2014): 33–68; B.L. Connelly et al., "Tournament Theory: Thirty Years of Contests and Competitions," *Journal of Management* 40, no. 1 (2014): 16–47; Y. Baruch and Y. Vardi, "A Fresh Look at the Dark Side of Contemporary Careers: Toward a Realistic Discourse," *British Journal of Management* 27, no. 2 (2016): 355–72.

78. "Managing in an Era of Mistrust: Maritz Poll Reveals Employees Lack Trust in Their Workplace," News release for Maritz Research (St. Louis: Business Wire, 14 April 2010); Willis Towers Watson, *Under Pressure to Remain Relevant, Employers Look to Modernize the Employee Value Proposition,* (London: Willis Towers Watson, 9 September 2016). For surveys on the importance of leader integrity, see: J.M. Kouzes and B.Z. Posner, *The Leadership Challenge,* 5th ed. (San Francisco: Jossey-Bass, 2012), Chap. 2; "Honesty and Communication Top Leadership Skills: Nanos," *CBC News,* 20 September 2013; "Leading the Charge: What Do Canadian Workers Look for in Their Leaders," News release (Toronto: Robert Half Management Resources, 22 September 2016); S. Giles, "The Most Important Leadership Competencies, According to Leaders around the World," *Harvard Business Review Digital Articles,* March 2016, 2–6.

79. J. Hedlund et al., "Identifying and Assessing Tacit Knowledge: Understanding the Practical Intelligence of Military Leaders," *Leadership Quarterly* 14, no. 2 (2003): 117–40; R.J. Sternberg, "A Systems Model of Leadership: WICS," *American Psychologist* 62, no. 1 (2007): 34–42.

80. J.M. George, "Emotions and Leadership: The Role of Emotional Intelligence," *Human Relations* 53 (2000): 1027–55; D. Goleman, R. Boyatzis, and A. McKee, *Primal Leaders* (Boston: Harvard Business School Press, 2002); R.G. Lord and R.J. Hall, "Identity, Deep Structure and the Development of Leadership Skill," *Leadership Quarterly* 16, no. 4 (2005): 591–615; C. Skinner and P. Spurgeon, "Valuing Empathy and Emotional Intelligence in Health Leadership: A Study of Empathy, Leadership Behaviour and Outcome Effectiveness," *Health Services Management Research* 18, no. 1 (2005): 1–12.

81. B. George, *Authentic Leadership* (San Francisco, CA: Jossey-Bass, 2004); W.L. Gardner et al., "'Can You See the Real Me?' A Self-Based Model of Authentic Leader and Follower Development," *Leadership Quarterly* 16 (2005): 343–72; B. George, *True North* (San Francisco, CA: Jossey-Bass, 2007), Chap. 4; M.E. Palanski and F.J. Yammarino, "Integrity and Leadership: Clearing the Conceptual Confusion," *European Management Journal* 25, no. 3 (2007): 171–84; F.O. Walumbwa et al., "Authentic Leadership: Development and Validation of a Theory-Based Measure," *Journal of Management* 34, no. 1 (2008): 89–126.

82. K. Moore, "The Ladder: You Need to Be Humble, You Need to Allow Others to Lead," *Globe & Mail,* 18 July 2016, B7.

83. W.G. Bennis and R.J. Thomas, "Crucibles of Leadership," *Harvard Business Review* 80, no. 9 (2002): 39–45; R.J. Thomas, *Crucibles of Leadership: How to Learn from Experience to Become a Great Leader* (Boston, MA: Harvard Business Press, 2008).

84. "Woman in Orbit," *Taste of Life Magazine,* December 2012, 46–49; "Executive Spotlight: Amiee Chan," *SatMagazine,* March 2013.

85. R. Jacobs, "Using Human Resource Functions to Enhance Emotional Intelligence," in *The Emotionally Intelligent Workplace* ed. C. Cherniss and D. Goleman (San Francisco, CA: Jossey-Bass, 2001), 161–63; Conger and Ready, "Rethinking Leadership Competencies."

86. R.G. Lord and D.J. Brown, *Leadership Processes and Self-Identity: A Follower-Centered Approach to Leadership* (Mahwah, NJ: Lawrence Erlbaum Associates, 2004); R. Bolden and J. Gosling, "Leadership Competencies: Time to Change the Tune?," *Leadership* 2, no. 2 (2006): 147–63.

87. Six of the Project GLOBE clusters are described in a special issue of the *Journal of World Business,* 37 (2000). For an overview of Project GLOBE, see House, Javidan, and Dorfman, "Project GLOBE: An Introduction; House et al., "Understanding Cultures and Implicit Leadership Theories across the Globe: An Introduction to Project GLOBE."

88. J.C. Jesiuno, "Latin Europe Cluster: From South to North," *Journal of World Business* 37 (2002): 88. Another GLOBE study, of Iranian managers, also reported that "charismatic visionary" stands out as a primary leadership dimension. See A. Dastmalchian, M. Javidan, and K. Alam, "Effective Leadership and Culture in Iran: An Empirical Study," *Applied Psychology: An International Review* 50 (2001): 532–58.

89. D.N. Den Hartog et al., "Culture Specific and Cross-Cultural Generalizable Implicit Leadership Theories: Are Attributes of Charismatic/Transformational Leadership Universally Endorsed?," *Leadership Quarterly* 10 (1999): 219–56; F.C. Brodbeck and e. al., "Cultural Variation of Leadership Prototypes across 22 European Countries," *Journal of Occupational and Organizational Psychology* 73 (2000): 1–29; E. Szabo and e. al., "The Europe Cluster: Where Employees Have a Voice," *Journal of World Business* 37 (2002): 55–68.

90. G.N. Powell, "One More Time: Do Female and Male Managers Differ?," *Academy of Management Executive* 4 (1990): 68–75; M.L. van Engen and T.M. Willemsen, "Sex and Leadership Styles: A Meta-Analysis of Research Published in the 1990s," *Psychological Reports* 94, no. 1 (2004): 3–18.

91. A.H. Eagly, M.C. Johannesen-Schmidt, and M.L. van Engen, "Transformational, Transactional, and Laissez-Faire Leadership Styles: A Meta-Analysis Comparing Women and Men," *Psychological Bulletin* 129 (2003): 569–91; S. Paustian-Underdahl, L. Walker, and D. Woehr, "Gender and Perceptions of Leadership Effectiveness: A Meta-Analysis of Contextual Moderators," *Journal of Applied Psychology* 99, no. 6 (2014): 1129–45.

92. A.H. Eagly, S.J. Karau, and M.G. Makhijani, "Gender and the Effectiveness of Leaders: A Meta-Analysis," *Psychological Bulletin* 117 (1995): 125–45; M.E. Heilman et al., "Penalties for Success: Reactions to Women Who Succeed at Male Gender-Typed Tasks," *Journal of Applied Psychology* 89, no. 3 (2004): 416–27; A.H. Eagly, "Achieving Relational Authenticity in Leadership: Does Gender Matter?," *Leadership Quarterly* 16, no. 3 (2005): 459–74; A.J. Anderson et al., "The Effectiveness of Three Strategies to Reduce the Influence of Bias in Evaluations of Female Leaders," *Journal of Applied Social Psychology* 45, no. 9 (2015): 522–39.

CHAPTER 13

1. "Empire Launches Major Transformation Initiative to Simplify Its Business, Unlock National Scale and Significantly Reduce Costs," News Release (Stellarton, N.S.: Empire Company Ltd., May 4, 2017); H. Shaw, "Beleaguered Sobeys Owner Announces Sweeping Overhaul Aimed at $500 Million in Annual Savings," *Financial Post,* May 4, 2017; D. Paddon, "Sobeys to Axe 800 Office Jobs across Canada in Reorganization of Grocery Business," *Financial Post,* November 24, 2017; "Empire Hones Executive Structure for Shift to Offense," News Release (Stellarton, N.S.: Empire Company Ltd., May 16, 2019); K. Laird, "Empire CEO Says Innovation Is the Future," *Canadian Grocer,* July 5, 2019; R. Redman, "Sobeys CEO Michael Medline Calls Ocado Online Grocery Platform 'Game-Changing,'" *Supermarket News,* December 16, 2019.

2. S. Ranson, R. Hinings, and R. Greenwood, "The Structuring of Organizational Structure," *Administrative Science Quarterly* 25 (1980): 1–14; J.-E. Johanson, "Intraorganizational Influence," *Management Communication Quarterly* 13 (2000): 393–435; K. Walsh, "Interpreting the Impact of Culture on Structure," *Journal of Applied Behavioral Science* 40, no. 3 (2004): 302–22. The recent survey is reported in: J. Bersin et al., "The New Organization: Different by Design," in *Global Human Capital Trends 2016* (Westlake, TX: Deloitte University Press, 2016), 1–14.

3. H. Mintzberg, *The Structuring of Organizations* (Englewood Cliffs, NJ: Prentice Hall, 1979), 2–3.

4. E.E. Lawler III, *Motivation in Work Organizations* (Monterey, CA: Brooks/Cole, 1973); M.A. Campion, "Ability Requirement Implications of Job Design: An Interdisciplinary Perspective," *Personnel Psychology* 42 (1989): 1–24.

5. G.S. Becker and K.M. Murphy, "The Division-of-Labor, Coordination Costs and Knowledge," *Quarterly Journal of Economics* 107, no. 4 (1992): 1137–60; L. Borghans and B. Weel, "The Division of Labour, Worker Organisation, and Technological Change," *The Economic Journal* 116, no. 509 (2006): F45–F72.

6. Mintzberg, *The Structuring of Organizations* Chap. 1; D.A. Nadler and M.L. Tushman, *Competing by Design: The Power of Organizational Architecture* (New York: Oxford University Press, 1997), Chap. 6; J.R. Galbraith, *Designing Organizations: An Executive Guide to Strategy, Structure, and Process* (San Francisco, CA: Jossey-Bass, 2002), Chap. 4.

7. J. Stephenson, Jr., "Making Humanitarian Relief Networks More Effective: Operational Coordination, Trust and Sense Making," *Disasters* 29, no. 4 (2005): 337.

8. A. Willem, M. Buelens, and H. Scarbrough, "The Role of Inter-Unit Coordination Mechanisms in Knowledge Sharing: A Case Study of a British MNC," *Journal of Information Science* 32, no. 6 (2006): 539–61; R.R. Gulati, "Silo Busting," *Harvard Business Review* 85, no. 5 (2007): 98–108.

9. L. Borghans and B. Weel, "The Division of Labour, Worker Organisation, and Technological Change," *The Economic Journal* 116, no. 509 (2006): F45–F72.

10. T. Van Alphen, "Magna in Overdrive," *Toronto Star,* July 24, 2006; "Production at Magna Paint Shop Finally under Way," News release (Hoče, Slovenia: Magna Steyr, March 19, 2019).

11. J.R. Galbraith, *Designing Organizations: An Executive Guide to Strategy, Structure, and Process* (San Francisco, CA: Jossey-Bass, 2002), 66–72; D. Aaker, *Spanning Silos: The New CMO Imperative* (Cambridge, MA: Harvard Business Press, 2008), 95–96; A. Pike, *Brands and Branding Geographies* (Cheltenham, UK: Edward Elgar, 2011), 133.

12. S.M. Sapuan, M.R. Osman, and Y. Nukman, "State of the Art of the Concurrent Engineering Technique in the Automotive Industry," *Journal of Engineering Design* 17, no. 2 (2006): 143–57; D.M. Anderson, *Design for Manufacturing: How to Use Concurrent Engineering to Rapidly Develop Low-Cost, High-Quality Products for Lean Management* (Boca Raton, FL: CRC Press/Taylor & Francis, 2014), Chap. 2.

13. A.H. Van De Ven, A.L. Delbecq, and R.J. Koenig Jr., "Determinants of Coordination Modes within Organizations," *American Sociological Review* 41, no. 2 (1976): 322–38.

14. Y.-M. Hsieh and A. Tien-Hsieh, "Enhancement of Service Quality with Job Standardisation," *Service Industries Journal* 21 (2001): 147–66.

15. M. Guadalupe, J. Wulf, and H. Li, "The Rise of the Functional Manager: Changes Afoot in the C-Suite," *European Business Review* (2012);M. Guadalupe, H. Li, and J. Wulf, "Who Lives in the C-Suite? Organizational Structure and the Division of Labor in Top Management," *Management Science* 60, no. 4 (2014): 824–44.

16. B. Davison, "Management Span of Control: How Wide Is Too Wide?," *Journal of Business Strategy* 24, no. 4 (2003): 22–29; N.A. Theobald and S. Nicholson-Crotty, "The Many Faces of Span of Control: Organizational Structure across Multiple Goals," *Administration Society* 36, no. 6 (2005): 648–60; R.M. Meyer, "Span of Management: Concept Analysis," *Journal of Advanced Nursing* 63, no. 1 (2008): 104–12.

17. D.D. Van Fleet and A.G. Bedeian, "A History of the Span of Management," *Academy of Management Review* 2 (1977): 356–72; H. Fayol, *General and Industrial Management,* trans. C. Storrs (London, UK: Pitman, 1949); D.A. Wren, A.G. Bedeian, and J.D. Breeze, "The Foundations of Henri Fayol's Administrative Theory " *Management Decision* 40, no. 9 (2002): 906–18.

18. D. Drickhamer, "Lessons from the Leading Edge," *Industry Week,* 21 February 2000, 23–26.

19. For examples of nurse manager span of control, see: D. Jones et al., "Nurse Manager Scope and Span of Control: An Objective Business and Measurement Model" (AONE 45th Annual Conference, Denver, 2013); R.O. Sherman, "Span of Control in Nurse Leader Roles," *Emerging Nurse Leader* (blog), June 27, 2013, https://www.emergingrnleader.com/

span-of-control-in-nurse-leader-roles/; J.M. Kendall, "Nurse Manager Span of Control and the Impact on Employee Engagement," DNP Projects (University of Kentucky, 2018), https://uknowledge.uky.edu/dnp_etds/185.

20. J. Greenwald, "Ward Compares the Best with the Rest," *Business Insurance,* August 26, 2002, 16. One recent article also emphasized that claims managers require a narrow span of control. See M.T. Murdock, "Getting Claim Costs under Control: Improve Your Loss Ratio Using These Proven Fundamentals," *Claims Journal,* March 1, 2016.

21. J.H. Gittell, "Supervisory Span, Relational Coordination and Flight Departure Performance: A Reassessment of Postbureaucracy Theory," *Organization Science* 12, no. 4 (2001): 468–83.

22. S. Marchionne, "Navigating the New Automotive Epoch," *Vital Speeches of the Day* (2010): 134–37.

23. T.D. Wall, J.L. Cordery, and C.W. Clegg, "Empowerment, Performance, and Operational Uncertainty: A Theoretical Integration," *Applied Psychology: An International Review* 51 (2002): 146–69.

24. J. Morris, J. Hassard, and L. McCann, "New Organizational Forms, Human Resource Management and Structural Convergence? A Study of Japanese Organizations," *Organization Studies* 27, no. 10 (2006): 1485–511.

25. Conagra Foods, "Conagra Brands Investor Day," news release (Chicago: CQ FD Disclosure, October 18, 2016); J. Tashea, "With Significant Changes, Thomson Reuters Wants to Be Closer to Its Customers," *ABA Journal,* May 15, 2019; G. Morgan, "AER Lays off Dozens of Senior Staff as Board and Alberta Government Review Embattled Regulator," *Calgary Herald,* January 22, 2020.

26. Q.N. Huy, "In Praise of Middle Managers," *Harvard Business Review* 79 (2001): 72–79; C.R. Littler, R. Wiesner, and R. Dunford, "The Dynamics of Delayering: Changing Management Structures in Three Countries," *Journal of Management Studies* 40, no. 2 (2003): 225–56; H.J. Leavitt, *Top Down: Why Hierarchies Are Here to Stay and How to Manage Them More Effectively* (Cambridge: Harvard Business School Press, 2005); L. McCann, J. Morris, and J. Hassard, "Normalized Intensity: The New Labour Process of Middle Management," *Journal of Management Studies* 45, no. 2 (2008): 343–71; "Why Middle Managers May Be the Most Important People in Your Company," *Knowledge @ Wharton,* May 25, 2011.

27. M. Rogoway, "Portland Startup Treehouse Eliminates the Boss, Tells Workers to Manage Themselves," *The Oregonian,* December 20, 2013; M. Rogoway, "No-Boss Office Brings Back the Boss: 'We Were Naive,'" *The Oregonian,* June 18, 2016.

28. The variations of decentralization within a company are discussed in: G. Masada, "To Centralize or Decentralize?," *Optimize,* May 2005, 58–61. The 7-Eleven example is described in: J.G. Kelley, "Slurpees and Sausages: 7-Eleven Holds School," *Richmond (Va.) Times-Dispatch,* 12 March 2004, C1; S. Marling, "The 24-Hour Supply Chain," *InformationWeek,* 26 January 2004, 43.

29. H. Mintzberg, *The Structuring of Organizations,* (Pearson: 1978): Chap. 5.

30. W. Dessein and T. Santos, "Adaptive Organizations," *Journal of Political Economy*

114, no. 5 (2006): 956–95; A.A.M. Nasurdin et al., "Organizational Structure and Organizational Climate as Potential Predictors of Job Stress: Evidence from Malaysia," *International Journal of Commerce and Management* 16, no. 2 (2006): 116–29; C.-J. Chen and J.-W. Huang, "How Organizational Climate and Structure Affect Knowledge Management— the Social Interaction Perspective," *International Journal of Information Management* 27, no. 2 (2007): 104–18.

31. T. Burns and G. Stalker, *The Management of Innovation* (London, UK: Tavistock, 1961).

32. W.D. Sine, H. Mitsuhashi, and D.A. Kirsch, "Revisiting Burns and Stalker: Formal Structure and New Venture Performance in Emerging Economic Sectors," *Academy of Management Journal* 49, no. 1 (2006): 121–32.

33. Mintzberg, *The Structuring of Organizations:* 106.

34. Mintzberg, *The Structuring of Organizations* Chap. 17; R.M. Burton, B. Obel, and G. DeSanctis, *Organizational Design: A Step-by-Step Approach,* 2nd ed. (Cambridge, UK: Cambridge University Press, 2011), 61–63. Sobeys early days are described in: M. Haynes, "Inside Sobeys' Cross-Country Journey," *Strategy,* Summer 2017; "Sobeys' 110th Anniversary," 2017, http://www.sobeys110.com/en/timeline/.

35. J.R. Galbraith, *Designing Organizations: An Executive Guide to Strategy, Structure, and Process* (San Francisco: Jossey-Bass, 2002), 23–25; R.M. Burton, B. Obel, and G. DeSanctis, *Organizational Design: A Step-by-Step Approach,* 2nd ed. (Cambridge, UK: Cambridge University Press, 2011), 63–65.

36. E.E. Lawler III, *Rewarding Excellence: Pay Strategies for the New Economy* (San Francisco, CA: Jossey-Bass, 2000), 31–34.

37. The evolutionary development of the divisional structure is described in: J.R. Galbraith, "The Evolution of Enterprise Organization Designs," *Journal of Organization Design* 1, no. 2 (2012): 1–13.

38. These structures were identified from corporate Web sites and annual reports. These organizations typically rely on a mixture of other structures, so the charts shown have been adapted for learning purposes.

39. M. Goold and A. Campbell, "Do You Have a Well-Designed Organization," *Harvard Business Review* 80 (2002): 117–24. Others have added factors such as economies of scale and what resources need to be controlled to most. See: G. Kesler and A. Kates, *Leading Organization Design: How to Make Organization Design Decisions to Drive the Results You Want* (San Francisco, CA: Jossey-Bass, 2011), Chap. 3.

40. "5 Things to Know About Ian Borden," News Release (Chicago: McDonald's Corporation, December 10, 2019).

41. J.R. Galbraith, "Structuring Global Organizations," in *Tomorrow's Organization* ed. S.A. Mohrman, et al. (San Francisco, CA: Jossey-Bass, 1998), 103–29; C. Homburg, J.P. Workman Jr., and O. Jensen, "Fundamental Changes in Marketing Organization: The Movement toward a Customer-Focused Organizational Structure," *Academy of Marketing Science. Journal* 28 (2000): 459–78; T.H. Davenport, J.G. Harris, and A.K. Kohli, "How Do They Know Their Customers So Well?," *Sloan Management Review* 42 (2001): 63–73;

J.R. Galbraith, "Organizing to Deliver Solutions," *Organizational Dynamics* 31 (2002): 194–207.

42. R.M. Burton, B. Obel, and G. DeSanctis, *Organizational Design: A Step-by-Step Approach,* 2nd ed. (Cambridge, UK: Cambridge University Press, 2011), 65–68.

43. J.R. Galbraith, E.E. Lawler III, and Associates, *Organizing for the Future: The New Logic for Managing Complex Organizations* (San Francisco, CA: Jossey-Bass, 1993); R. Bettis and M. Hitt, "The New Competitive Landscape," *Strategic Management Journal* 16 (1995): 7–19.

44. P.C. Ensign, "Interdependence, Coordination, and Structure in Complex Organizations: Implications for Organization Design," *Mid-Atlantic Journal of Business* 34 (1998): 5–22.

45. M.M. Fanning, "A Circular Organization Chart Promotes a Hospital-Wide Focus on Teams," *Hospital & Health Services Administration* 42 (1997): 243–54; B. Cougot et al., "Impact at Two Years of an Intervention on Empowerment among Medical Care Teams: Study Protocol of a Randomised Controlled Trial in a Large French University Hospital," *BMC Health Services Research* 19, no. 1 (2019): 1–13; N. Wellman et al., "Beyond the Pyramid: Alternative Formal Hierarchical Structures and Team Performance," *Academy of Management Journal* 63 (2020): 997–1027.

46. R. Cross, "Looking before You Leap: Assessing the Jump to Teams in Knowledge-Based Work," *Business Horizons* 43, no. 5 (2000): 29–36; M. Fenton-O'Creevy, "Employee Involvement and the Middle Manager: Saboteur or Scapegoat?," *Human Resource Management Journal* 11 (2001): 24–40; C. Douglas and W.L. Gardner, "Transition to Self-Directed Work Teams: Implications of Transition Time and Self-Monitoring for Managers' Use of Influence Tactics," *Journal of Organizational Behavior* 25 (2004): 47–65; G. Garda, K. Lindstrom, and M. Dallnera, "Towards a Learning Organization: The Introduction of a Client-Centered Team-Based Organization in Administrative Surveying Work," *Applied Ergonomics* 34 (2003): 97–105.

47. "Randon Companies announce change in organizational structure," News Release (Caxias do Sul, Brazil: Randon S.A., February 3, 2020).

48. S.M. Davis and P.R. Lawrence, *Matrix* (Reading, Mass: Addison-Wesley, 1977); J.R. Galbraith, *Designing Matrix Organizations That Actually Work* (San Francisco, CA: Jossey-Bass, 2009).

49. "Corporate Governance Report 2018" (Stockholm: H&M Hennes & Mauritz AB, April 15, 2019); "Annual Report 2018 Digest" (Tokyo: Shiseido Company, Limited, October 11, 2019).

50. R.C. Ford and W.A. Randolph, "Cross-Functional Structures: A Review and Integration of Matrix Organization and Project Management," *Journal of Management* 18 (1992): 267–94.

51. R. Muzyka and G. Zeschuk, "Managing Multiple Projects," *Game Developer,* March 2003, 34–42.

52. J.X.J. Qiu and L. Donaldson, "Stopford and Wells Were Right! MNC Matrix Structures Do Fit a 'High-High' Strategy," *Management International Review (MIR)* 52, no. 5 (2012): 671–89; D. Ganguly and M. Mitra, "Survive the Matrix," *Economic Times (Mumbai, India),* 29 March 2013.

53. G. Calabrese, "Communication and Co-Operation in Product Development: A Case

Study of a European Car Producer," *R & D Management* 27 (1997): 239–52; T. Sy and L.S. D'Annunzio, "Challenges and Strategies of Matrix Organizations: Top-Level and Mid-Level Managers' Perspectives," *Human Resource Planning* 28, no. 1 (2005): 39–48; J. Wolf and W.G. Egelhoff, "An Empirical Evaluation of Conflict in MNC Matrix Structure Firms," *International Business Review* 22, no. 3 (2013): 591–601.

54. D. Ganguly, "Matrix Evolutions," *Economic Times (Mumbai, India),* 18 February 2012.

55. Nadler and Tushman, *Competing by Design,* Chap. 6; M. Goold and A. Campbell, "Structured Networks: Towards the Well-Designed Matrix," *Long Range Planning* 36, no. 5 (2003): 427–39.

56. D. Ciampa and M. Watkins, "Rx for New CEOs," *Chief Executive,* January 2008.

57. M. Beecham, "Magna Steyr President on Launching Products Smarter and Quicker—Q&A," *Just-Auto Global News,* March 16, 2016; M. Panait, "Magna Steyr Celebrates 300,000th Mercedes-Benz G-Class Produced Since 1978," *AutoEvolution,* July 19, 2017; A. Padeanu, "2019 BMW Z4 Production Starts In Austria," *Motor1,* November 8, 2018; A. Karr, "First 2020 Toyota Supra Rolls Off Magna Steyr Assembly Lines," *Motor1,* March 25, 2019.

58. R.F. Miles and C.C. Snow, "The New Network Firm: A Spherical Structure Built on a Human Investment Philosophy," *Organizational Dynamics* 23, no. 4 (1995): 5–18; C. Baldwin and K. Clark, "Managing in an Age of Modularity," *Harvard Business Review* 75 (1997): 84–93.

59. J. Hagel III and M. Singer, "Unbundling the Corporation," *Harvard Business Review* 77 (1999): 133–41; R. Hacki and J. Lighton, "The Future of the Networked Company," *McKinsey Quarterly* 3 (2001): 26–39.

60. R. Redman, "Sobeys CEO Michael Medline Calls Ocado Online Grocery Platform 'Game-Changing,'" *Supermarket News,* December 16, 2019.

61. M.A. Schilling and H.K. Steensma, "The Use of Modular Organizational Forms: An Industry-Level Analysis," *Academy of Management Journal* 44 (2001): 1149–68.

62. G. Morgan, *Images of Organization,* Second ed. (Newbury Park: Sage, 1996); G. Morgan, *Imagin-I-Zation: New Mindsets for Seeing, Organizing and Managing* (Thousand Oaks, CA: Sage, 1997).

63. H. Chesbrough and D.J. Teece, "When Is Virtual Virtuous? Organizing for Innovation," *Harvard Business Review* 74, no. 1 (1996): 65–73; P.M.J. Christie and R. Levary, "Virtual Corporations: Recipe for Success," *Industrial Management* 40 (1998): 7–11.

64. The lower transaction costs of employee relationships versus market exchange relationships was explained almost a century ago in: R.H. Coase, "The Nature of the Firm," *Economica* 4, no. 16 (1937): 386–405.

65. L. Donaldson, *The Contingency Theory of Organizations* (Thousand Oaks, CA: Sage, 2001); J. Birkenshaw, R. Nobel, and J. Ridderstråle, "Knowledge as a Contingency Variable: Do the Characteristics of Knowledge Predict Organizational Structure?," *Organization Science* 13, no. 3 (2002): 274–89.

66. P. R. Lawrence and J. W. Lorsch, *Organization and Environment*(Homewood, IL: Irwin, 1967); H. Mintzberg, *The Structuring of Organizations*(Englewood Cliffs, NJ: Prentice Hall, 1979), chap. 15.

67. T. Burns and G. Stalker, *The Management of Innovation* (London: Tavistock, 1961); P.R. Lawrence and J.W. Lorsch, *Organization and Environment*(Homewood, IL: Irwin, 1967).

68. G.S. McChrystal et al., *Team of Teams: New Rules of Engagement for a Complex World* (New York: Penguin, 2015); R. Feloni, "Retired 4-Star Gen. Stanley McChrystal Explains How the Realisation the US Was Losing the Iraq War in 2004 Led to the Transformation of Special Operations," *Business Insider,* January 4, 2019.

69. H. Mintzberg, *The Structuring of Organizations* (Englewood Cliffs, NJ: Prentice Hall, 1979), 282.

70. D.S. Pugh and C.R. Hinings, *Organizational Structure: Extensions and Replications* (Farnborough, UK: Lexington Books, 1976); H. Mintzberg, *The Structuring of Organizations*(Englewood Cliffs, NJ: Prentice Hall, 1979), Chap. 13.

71. G. Hertel, S. Geister, and U. Konradt, "Managing Virtual Teams: A Review of Current Empirical Research," *Human Resource Management Review* 15 (2005): 69–95; J.R. Galbraith, *Designing Matrix Organizations That Actually Work*(San Francisco, CA: Jossey-Bass, 2009), 52–55.

72. C. Perrow, "A Framework for the Comparative Analysis of Organizations," *American Sociological Review* 32 (1967): 194–208; D. Gerwin, "The Comparative Analysis of Structure and Technology: A Critical Appraisal," *Academy of Management Review* 4, no. 1 (1979): 41–51; C.C. Miller et al., "Understanding Technology-Structure Relationships: Theory Development and Meta-Analytic Theory Testing," *Academy of Management Journal* 34, no. 2 (1991): 370–99.

73. R.H. Kilmann, *Beyond the Quick Fix* (San Francisco, CA: Jossey-Bass, 1984), p. 38.

74. A.D. Chandler, *Strategy and Structure* (Cambridge, MA: MIT Press, 1962).

75. D. Miller, "Configurations of Strategy and Structure," *Strategic Management Journal* 7 (1986): 233–49.

CHAPTER 14

1. M. Weinberger, "How Microsoft CEO Satya Nadella Did What Steve Ballmer and Bill Gates Couldn't," *Business Insider,* January 31, 2016; H. McCracken, "Satya Nadella Rewrites Microsoft's Code," *Fast Company,* September 18, 2017; H. McCracken, "Transforming Culture at Microsoft: Satya Nadella Sets a New Tone," *InTheBlack,* June 1, 2018; A.E. Jackson, "Why Joining Microsoft Canada May Be The Best Career Move You'll Ever Make," *Glassdoor Blog* (blog), December 5, 2018, https://www.glassdoor.com/blog/microsoft-bptw19/; A. Carr and D. Bass, "The Nadellaissance," *Bloomberg Businessweek,* no. 4613 (May 6, 2019): 36–41; E. Douglas, "Microsoft President Reveals What a 'successful CHRO' Looks Like," *Human Resources Director (Canada),* October 18, 2019.

2. A. Williams, P. Dobson, and M. Walters, *Changing Culture: New Organizational Approaches* (London, UK: Institute of Personnel Management, 1989); E.H. Schein, "What Is Culture?," in *Reframing Organizational Culture,* ed. P.J. Frost, et al. (Newbury Park, CA: Sage, 1991), 243–53.

3. B.M. Meglino and E.C. Ravlin, "Individual Values in Organizations: Concepts, Controversies, and Research," *Journal of Management* 24, no.

3 (1998): 351–89; B.R. Agle and C.B. Caldwell, "Understanding Research on Values in Business," *Business and Society* 38, no. 3 (1999): 326–87; S. Hitlin and J.A. Pilavin, "Values: Reviving a Dormant Concept," *Annual Review of Sociology* 30 (2004): 359–93.

4. N.M. Ashkanasy, "The Case for Culture," in *Debating Organization,* ed. R. Westwood and S. Clegg (Malden, MA: Blackwell, 2003), 300–10.

5. B. Bouw, "Ratana Stephens: 'People Are My Strength and My Weakness,'" *Globe & Mail,* November 7, 2016; "Careers," Nature's Path, accessed March 28, 2020, https://www.naturespath.com/en-ca/careers/.

6. B. Kabanoff and J. Daly, "Espoused Values in Organisations," *Australian Journal of Management* 27 (2002): 89–104; H. Bourne and M. Jenkins, "Organizational Values: A Dynamic Perspective," *Organization Studies* 34, no. 4 (2013): 495–514. Bourne and Jenkins note that organizational values may also be attributed and aspirational.

7. At least one study suggests that espoused values have a positive influence on organizational performance by motivating employees (emotional contagion), signalling desired behaviours, and enhancing public reputation. However, in many firms studied, these espoused values may also have been enacted values. See: K. Jonsen et al., "Evaluating Espoused Values: Does Articulating Values Pay Off?," *European Management Journal* 33, no. 5 (2015): 332–40.

8. C. Ostroff, A.J. Kinicki, and R.S. Muhammad, "Organizational Culture and Climate," in *Handbook of Psychology,* 2nd ed. (John Wiley & Sons, Inc., 2012), 643–76.

9. R. Hastings and P. McCord, *Netflix Culture: Freedom and Responsibility* (Los Gatos, CA: Netflix, August 2009); R. Hastings, *Culture at Netflix* (Los Gatos, CA: Netflix, 21 June 2017), https://jobs.netflix.com/culture (accessed 11 July 2017); S. Ramachandran and J. Flint, "At Netflix, Radical Transparency and Blunt Firings Unsettle the Ranks," *Wall Street Journal,* October 25, 2018; B. Murphy Jr., "You Don't Just Get Fired at Netflix," *Inc,* October 27, 2018; S. Rodriguez, "Pinterest: Overly 'Nice' Culture Has Hurt Growth, Ex-Employees Say," *CNBC News,* April 10, 2019; R. Hastings and E. Meyer, *No Rules Rules: Netflix and the Culture of Reinvention* (New York: Penguin Random House, 2020).

10. C.A. O'Reilly III, J. Chatman, and D.F. Caldwell, "People and Organizational Culture: A Profile Comparison Approach to Assessing Person–Organization Fit," *Academy of Management Journal* 34 (1991): 487–516; J.J. van Muijen, "Organizational Culture," in *A Handbook of Work and Organizational Psychology: Organizational Psychology,* ed. P.J.D. Drenth, H. Thierry, and C.J. de Wolff (East Sussex, UK: Psychology Press, 1998), 113–32; P.A. Balthazard, R.A. Cooke, and R.E. Potter, "Dysfunctional Culture, Dysfunctional Organization: Capturing the Behavioral Norms That Form Organizational Culture and Drive Performance," *Journal of Managerial Psychology* 21, no. 8 (2006): 709–32; C. Helfrich et al., "Assessing an Organizational Culture Instrument Based on the Competing Values Framework: Exploratory and Confirmatory Factor Analyses," *Implementation Science* 2, no. 1 (2007): 13. For

reviews of organizational culture survey instruments, see T. Scott et al., "The Quantitative Measurement of Organizational Culture in Health Care: A Review of the Available Instruments," *Health Services Research* 38, no. 3 (2003): 923–45; D.E. Leidner and T. Kayworth, "A Review of Culture in Information Systems Research: Toward a Theory of Information Technology Culture Conflict," *MIS Quarterly* 30, no. 2 (2006): 357–99; S. Scott-Findlay and C.A. Estabrooks, "Mapping the Organizational Culture Research in Nursing: A Literature Review," *Journal of Advanced Nursing* 56, no. 5 (2006): 498–513.

11. L. Guiso, P. Sapienza, and L. Zingales, "The Value of Corporate Culture," *Journal of Financial Economics* 117, no. 1 (2015): 60–76.

12. J. Martin, P.J. Frost, and O.A. O'Neill, "Organizational Culture: Beyond Struggles for Intellectual Dominance," in *Handbook of Organization Studies,* ed. S. Clegg, et al. (London, UK: Sage, 2006), 725–53; N.E. Fenton and S. Inglis, "A Critical Perspective on Organizational Values," *Nonprofit Management and Leadership* 17, no. 3 (2007): 335–47; K. Haukelid, "Theories of (Safety) Culture Revisited—an Anthropological Approach," *Safety Science* 46, no. 3 (2008): 413–26.

13. G. Hofstede, "Identifying Organizational Subcultures: An Empirical Approach," *Journal of Management Studies* 35, no. 1 (1990): 1–12; J. Martin and C. Siehl, "Organizational Culture and Counterculture: An Uneasy Symbiosis," *Organizational Dynamics* (1983): 52–64; E. Ogbonna and L.C. Harris, "Organisational Culture in the Age of the Internet: An Exploratory Study," *New Technology, Work and Employment* 21, no. 2 (2006): 162–75.

14. H. Silver, "Does a University Have a Culture?," *Studies in Higher Education* 28, no. 2 (2003): 157–69.

15. A. Sinclair, "Approaches to Organizational Culture and Ethics," *Journal of Business Ethics* 12 (1993); T.E. Deal and A.A. Kennedy, *The New Corporate Cultures* (Cambridge, MA: Perseus Books, 1999), Chap. 10; A. Boisnier and J. Chatman, "The Role of Subcultures in Agile Organizations," in *Leading and Managing People in Dynamic Organizations,* ed. R. Petersen and E. Mannix (Mahwah, NJ: Lawrence Erlbaum Associates, 2003), 87–112; C. Morrill, M.N. Zald, and H. Rao, "Covert Political Conflict in Organizations: Challenges from Below," *Annual Review of Sociology* 29, no. 1 (2003): 391–415.

16. J.S. Ott, *The Organizational Culture Perspective* (Pacific Grove, CA: Brooks/Cole, 1989), Chap. 2; J.S. Pederson and J.S. Sorensen, *Organizational Cultures in Theory and Practice* (Aldershot, England: Gower, 1989), pp. 27–29; M.O. Jones, *Studying Organizational Symbolism: What, How, Why?* (Thousand Oaks, CA: Sage, 1996).

17. A. Furnham and B. Gunter, "Corporate Culture: Definition, Diagnosis, and Change," *International Review of Industrial and Organizational Psychology* 8 (1993): 233–61; E.H. Schein, "Organizational Culture," *American Psychologist* (1990): 109–19; E.H. Schein, *The Corporate Culture Survival Guide* (San Francisco, CA: Jossey-Bass, 1999), Chap. 4.

18. M. Doehrman, "Anthropologists—Deep in the Corporate Bush," *Daily Record (Kansas City, MO),* 19 July 2005, 1.

19. R. Ouzounian, "Cirque's Dream Factory," *Toronto Star,* 1 August 2004; M. Miller, "The Acrobat," *Forbes,* 15 March 2004, 100–03.

20. T.E. Deal and A.A. Kennedy, *Corporate Cultures* (Reading, MA: Addison-Wesley, 1982), chap. 5; C.J. Boudens, "The Story of Work: A Narrative Analysis of Workplace Emotion," *Organization Studies* 26, no. 9 (2005): 1285–306; S. Denning, *The Leader's Guide to Storytelling* (San Francisco, CA: Jossey-Bass, 2005).

21. A.L. Wilkins, "Organizational Stories as Symbols Which Control the Organization," in *Organizational Symbolism,* ed. L.R. Pondy, et al. (Greenwich, CT: JAI Press, 1984), 81–92; R. Zemke, "Storytelling: Back to a Basic," *Training* 27 (1990): 44–50; J.C. Meyer, "Tell Me a Story: Eliciting Organizational Values from Narratives," *Communication Quarterly* 43 (1995): 210–24; W. Swap et al., "Using Mentoring and Storytelling to Transfer Knowledge in the Workplace," *Journal of Management Information Systems* 18 (2001): 95–114.

22. T. Kelley and D. Kelley, *Creative Confidence: Unleashing the Creative Potential within Us All* (New York: Random House, 2013), 198.

23. J. Mossman, "Employee-Friendly Workplace Culture a Key to Company Success," *Denver Post,* April 21, 2013; Darden MBA, "'Community First, Company Second': Javier Rodriguez, DaVita Kidney Care" (YouTube, November 18, 2015), www.youtube.com/watch?v=sdTYtXSEIFQ (accessed June 15, 2016); Stanford Graduate School of Business, "DaVita CEO Kent Thiry on Building a Signature Company Culture" (YouTube, November 23, 2015), www.youtube.com/watch?v=9CN85CFllME (accessed June 15, 2016); D. Hoerman, "Inside DaVita's Corporate Culture: 'A Community First And A Company Second,'" *Chief Executive,* August 10, 2018.

24. G. Smith, *Why I Left Goldman Sachs: A Wall Street Story* (New York: Grand Central Publishing, 2012); R. Blackden, "Goldman Sachs in Hunt for 'Muppet' Email," *The Telegraph,* 22 March 2012; B. Tuttle, "16 Amazing Facts About the Muppets That'll Make You Laugh, Cry & Sing Along," *Money,* 22 September 2015. Goldman Sachs apparently found the word *muppets* in 0.3% of all emails over the previous year or two, but almost all of those messages referred to a staff outing to watch the latest muppet film. The word *muppet* is apparently widely used today by investors (when being gullible about investment advice) and others in the investment community.

25. A.C.T. Smith and B. Stewart, "Organizational Rituals: Features, Functions and Mechanisms," *International Journal of Management Reviews* 13 (2011): 113–33.

26. "The Ultimate Chairman," *Business Times Singapore,* September 3, 2005.

27. Churchill apparently made this statement on October 28, 1943 in the British House of Commons, when London, damaged by bombings in World War II, was about to be rebuilt.

28. G. Turner and J. Myerson, *New Workspace New Culture: Office Design as a Catalyst for Change* (Aldershot, UK: Gower, 1998); J.C. McElroy and P.C. Morrow, "Employee Reactions to Office Redesign: A Naturally Occurring Quasi-Field Experiment in a Multi-Generational Setting," *Human Relations* 63 (2010): 609–36; T.J. Kallio, K.-M. Kallio, and A.J. Blomberg, "Physical Space, Culture and Organisational Creativity—A Longitudinal Study," *Facilities* 33 (2015): 389–411;

S. Zerella, K. von Treuer, and S.L. Albrecht, "The Influence of Office Layout Features on Employee Perception of Organizational Culture," *Journal of Environmental Psychology* 54 (2017): 1–10.

29. A. Clark, "Life in Mars," *The Guardian (London),* 3 May 2008; D.A. Kaplan, "Mars Incorporated: A Pretty Sweet Place to Work," *Fortune,* 17 January 2013. Also based on a virtual Google street view tour of Mars' head offices in Maclean Virginia, Slough UK, and Bolton, Ontario.

30. K.D. Elsbach and B.A. Bechky, "It's More Than a Desk: Working Smarter through Leveraged Office Design," *California Management Review* 49, no. 2 (2007): 80–101.

31. *How to Create a Successful Organizational Culture: Build It—Literally* (Holland, MI: Haworth Inc., June 2015).

32. G. Forsythe, K. Kuhla, and D. Rice, "The CEO's Role in Shaping an Organization's Culture," *Chief Executive,* February 6, 2018; "Weston Forest Receives Canada's Most Admired Corporate Cultures Award," *Wood Business (Canadian Forest Industries Magazine),* December 2, 2019.

33. J.C. Collins and J.I. Porras, *Built to Last: Successful Habits of Visionary Companies* (London, UK: Century, 1994); T.E. Deal and A.A. Kennedy, *The New Corporate Cultures* (Cambridge, MA: Perseus Books, 1999); R. Barrett, *The Values-Driven Organization,* 2nd ed. (New York: Routledge, 2017); J.M. Kouzes and B.Z. Posner, *The Leadership Challenge,* Sixth ed. (Hoboken, N.J.: John Wiley & Sons, 2017), Chap. 3.

34. C. Siehl and J. Martin, "Organizational Culture: A Key to Financial Performance?," in *Organizational Climate and Culture,* ed. B. Schneider (San Francisco, CA: Jossey-Bass, 1990), 241–81; G.G. Gordon and N. DiTomasco, "Predicting Corporate Performance from Organizational Culture," *Journal of Management Studies* 29 (1992): 783–98; J.P. Kotter and J.L. Heskett, *Corporate Culture and Performance* (New York: Free Press, 1992); C.P.M. Wilderom, U. Glunk, and R. Maslowski, "Organizational Culture as a Predictor of Organizational Performance," in *Handbook of Organizational Culture and Climate,* ed. N.M. Ashkanasy, C.P.M. Wilderom, and M.F. Peterson (Thousand Oaks, CA: Sage, 2000), 193–210; A. Carmeli and A. Tishler, "The Relationships between Intangible Organizational Elements and Organizational Performance," *Strategic Management Journal* 25 (2004): 1257–78; S. Teerikangas and P. Very, "The Culture-Performance Relationship in M&A: From Yes/No to How," *British Journal of Management* 17, no. S1 (2006): S31–S48.

35. Y. Wiener, "Forms of Value Systems: A Focus on Organizational Effectiveness and Cultural Change and Maintenance," *Academy of Management Review* 13, no. 4 (1988): 534–45; J.A. Chatman and S.E. Cha, "Leading by Leveraging Culture," *California Management Review* 45 (2003): 20–34; M. Alvesson, *Understanding Organizational Culture,* 2nd ed. (London, UK: Sage, 2013).

36. A.A. Brown, "How to Create a Values Framework and Make It Work," *Financial Post,* August 9, 2018.

37. B. Ashforth and F. Mael, "Social Identity Theory and the Organization," *Academy of Management Review* 14 (1989): 20–39; M. Alvesson,

Understanding Organizational Culture, 2nd ed. (London: Sage, 2013).

38. Heidrick and Struggles, *Leadership Challenges Emerge as Asia Pacific Companies Go Global,* Heidrick and Struggles (Melbourne: August 2008).

39. M.R. Louis, "Surprise and Sensemaking: What Newcomers Experience in Entering Unfamiliar Organizational Settings," *Administrative Science Quarterly* 25 (1980): 226–51; S.G. Harris, "Organizational Culture and Individual Sensemaking: A Schema-Based Perspective," *Organization Science* 5 (1994): 309–21.

40. J.W. Barnes et al., "The Role of Culture Strength in Shaping Sales Force Outcomes," *Journal of Personal Selling & Sales Management* 26, no. 3 (2006): 255–70.

41. H. McCracken, "Satya Nadella Rewrites Microsoft's Code," *Fast Company,* September 18, 2017; H. Ibarra, A. Rattan, and A. Johnston, "Microsoft: Instilling a Growth Mindset," *London Business School Review* 29, no. 3 (October 2018): 50–53.

42. C.A. O'Reilly III and J.A. Chatman, "Culture as Social Control: Corporations, Cults, and Commitment," *Research in Organizational Behavior* 18 (1996): 157–200; B. Spector and H. Lane, "Exploring the Distinctions between a High Performance Culture and a Cult," *Strategy & Leadership* 35 (2007): 18–24. Organizational cults are closely associated with high organizational identification, which has several known dysfunctional outcomes for companies and individuals. See: S. Conroy et al., "Where There Is Light, There Is Dark: A Review of the Detrimental Outcomes of High Organizational Identification," *Journal of Organizational Behavior* 38 (2017): 184–203.

43. J.P. Kotter and J.L. Heskett, *Corporate Culture and Performance* (New York: Free Press, 1992), Chap. 4; B.M. Bass and R.E. Riggio, *Transformational Leadership,* 2nd ed. (New York: Routledge, 2006), Chap. 7; D.P. Costanza et al., "The Effect of Adaptive Organizational Culture on Long-Term Survival," *Journal of Business and Psychology* (2015): 1–21.

44. H. Ibarra, A. Rattan, and A. Johnston, "Microsoft: Instilling a Growth Mindset," *London Business School Review* 29, no. 3 (October 2018): 50–53; S. Nadella, G. Shaw, and J.T. Nichols, *Hit Refresh: The Quest to Rediscover Microsoft's Soul and Imagine a Better Future for Everyone,* Updated edition (New York: Harper Business, 2019), pp. 93–94.

45. W.E. Baker and J.M. Sinkula, "The Synergistic Effect of Market Orientation and Learning Orientation on Organizational Performance," *Academy of Marketing Science Journal* 27, no. 4 (1999): 411–27; O. Pesämaa et al., "How a Learning Orientation Affects Drivers of Innovativeness and Performance in Service Delivery," *Journal of Engineering and Technology Management* 30 (2013): 169–87; J.C. Real, J.L. Roldán, and A. Leal, "From Entrepreneurial Orientation and Learning Orientation to Business Performance: Analysing the Mediating Role of Organizational Learning and the Moderating Effects of Organizational Size," *British Journal of Management* 25 (2014): 186–208.

46. *AIA Code of Conduct* (Hong Kong: AIA Group Limited, April 30, 2015); K. Whitehead, "Case Study: AIA, Hong Kong," *People Management Asia,* January 21, 2016, 10–11.

47. A. Ferguson and C. Vedelago, "Targets, Bonuses, Trips—Inside the CBA Boiler Room," *Sydney Morning Herald,* 22 June 2013; T. Boyd, "CBA's Unfortunate Pattern of Poor Cultural Behaviour," *Australian Financial Review,* 4 August 2017; P. Williams, "How Criminal Gangs Ran Rings around Commonwealth Bank Culture," *The Australian,* 14 September 2017; J. Frost, "ASIC Hits CBA with BBSW Rate-Rigging Allegations," *Australian Financial Review,* 30 January 2018; S. Letts, "Banks Inquiry: APRA to Focus on CBA Culture and Pay in Studying Its 'Fall from Grace'," *ABC News (Australia),* 1 February 2018; P. Durkin, "ASIC Expands Bank Bill Swap Rate-Rigging Case against Commonwealth Bank," *Australian Financial Review,* 26 February 2018.

48. "Antony Jenkins to Staff: Adopt New Values or Leave Barclays," *The Telegraph (London),* 17 January 2013. Also, original email to Barclays employees distributed in January 2013.

49. M.L. Marks, "Adding Cultural Fit to Your Diligence Checklist," *Mergers & Acquisitions* 34, no. 3 (1999): 14–20; Schein, *The Corporate Culture Survival Guide* Chap. 8; Teerikangas and Very, "The Culture-Performance Relationship in M&A: From Yes/No to How; G.K. Stahl and A. Voigt, "Do Cultural Differences Matter in Mergers and Acquisitions? A Tentative Model and Examination," *Organization Science* 19, no. 1 (2008): 160–76.

50. J.P. Daly et al., "The Effects of Initial Differences in Firms' Espoused Values on Their Postmerger Performance," *Journal of Applied Behavioral Science* 40, no. 3 (2004): 323–43; C. Cook and D. Spitzer, *World Class Transactions,* KPMG (London, UK: 2001); J. Krug, *Mergers and Acquisitions: Turmoil in Top Management Teams* (Williston, VT: Business Expert Press, 2009).

51. J. Chao et al., "The Role of Leadership in Merger Integration," *McKinsey Quarterly,* July 2018; O. Engert et al., "Organizational Culture in Mergers: Addressing the Unseen Forces," *McKinsey & Company,* March 2019.

52. C.A. Schorg, C.A. Raiborn, and M.F. Massoud, "Using a 'Cultural Audit' to Pick M&A Winners," *Journal of Corporate Accounting & Finance* (2004): 47–55; W. Locke, "Higher Education Mergers: Integrating Organisational Cultures and Developing Appropriate Management Styles," *Higher Education Quarterly* 61, no. 1 (2007): 83–102.

53. A.R. Malekazedeh and A. Nahavandi, "Making Mergers Work by Managing Cultures," *Journal of Business Strategy* (1990): 55–57; K.W. Smith, "A Brand-New Culture for the Merged Firm," *Mergers and Acquisitions* 35 (2000): 45–50.

54. A. Hyland, "Howzat? Wesfarmers and Boral Chairman Bob Every on Career and Overcoming Adversity," *Australian Financial Review,* July 6, 2015.

55. Hewitt Associates, "Mergers and Acquisitions May Be Driven by Business Strategy—but Often Stumble over People and Culture Issues" (Lincolnshire, IL: PR Newswire, 1998).

56. J. Martin, "Can Organizational Culture Be Managed?," in *Organizational Culture,* ed. P.J. Frost, et al. (Beverly Hills, CA: Sage, 1985), 95–98.

57. E.H. Schein, "The Role of the Founder in Creating Organizational Culture," *Organizational Dynamics* 12, no. 1 (1983): 13–28; A.S. Tsui et al., "Unpacking the Relationship between CEO Leadership Behavior and Organizational Culture,"

Leadership Quarterly 17 (2006): 113–37; Y. Berson, S. Oreg, and T. Dvir, "CEO Values, Organizational Culture and Firm Outcomes," *Journal of Organizational Behavior* 29, no. 5 (2008): 615–33; B. Schneider, M.G. Ehrhart, and W.H. Macey, "Organizational Climate and Culture," *Annual Review of Psychology* 64, no. 1 (2013): 361–88.

58. J. Pachner, "The Gospel According to Bruce," *Profit,* 7 October 2011; " A Travel Guru's Guide to Good Leadership," *National Post (Toronto),* 17 June 2013, FP6.

59. Y. Berson, S. Oreg, and T. Dvir, "CEO Values, Organizational Culture and Firm Outcomes," *Journal of Organizational Behavior* 29, no. 5 (2008): 615–33; A.S. Klein, J. Wallis, and R.A. Cooke, "The Impact of Leadership Styles on Organizational Culture and Firm Effectiveness: An Empirical Study," *Journal of Management & Organization* 19 (2013): 241–54; D.V. Day, M.A. Griffin, and K.R. Louw, "The Climate and Culture of Leadership in Organizations," in *The Oxford Handbook of Organizational Climate and Culture,* ed. B. Schneider and K.M. Barbera (New York: Oxford University Press, 2014), 101–17.

60. J. Botelho-Urbanski, "Good Job!," *Winnipeg Free Press,* November 25, 2017.

61. M.J. Gelfand et al., "Conflict Cultures in Organizations: How Leaders Shape Conflict Cultures and Their Organizational-Level Consequences," *Journal of Applied Psychology* 97, no. 6 (2012): 1131–47; R.C. Liden et al., "Servant Leadership and Serving Culture: Influence on Individual and Unit Performance," *Academy of Management Journal* 57, no. 5 (2014): 1434–52.

62. J.C. McElroy and P.C. Morrow, "Employee Reactions to Office Redesign: A Naturally Occurring Quasi-Field Experiment in a Multi-Generational Setting," *Human Relations* 63 (2010): 609–36; S.J. Hogan and L.V. Coote, "Organizational Culture, Innovation, and Performance: A Test of Schein's Model," *Journal of Business Research* 67 (2014): 1609–21; S. Zerella, K. von Treuer, and S.L. Albrecht, "The Influence of Office Layout Features on Employee Perception of Organizational Culture," *Journal of Environmental Psychology* 54 (2017): 1–10.

63. M. De Pree, *Leadership Is an Art* (East Lansing, MI: Michigan State University Press, 1987).

64. J. Kerr and J.W. Slocum Jr., "Managing Corporate Culture through Reward Systems," *Academy of Management Executive* 1 (1987): 99–107; J.M. Higgins et al., "Using Cultural Artifacts to Change and Perpetuate Strategy," *Journal of Change Management* 6, no. 4 (2006): 397–415; H. Hofstetter and I. Harpaz, "Declared Versus Actual Organizational Culture as Indicated by an Organization's Performance Appraisal," *International Journal of Human Resource Management* (2011): 1–22.

65. A. Griswold, "Uber Is Designed so That for One Employee to Get Ahead, Another Must Fail," *Quartz,* February 27, 2017; M.R. Dickey, "Inside Uber's New Approach to Employee Performance Reviews," *TechCrunch,* August 1, 2017.

66. B. Schneider, "The People Make the Place," *Personnel Psychology* 40, no. 3 (1987): 437–53; B. Schneider et al., "Personality and Organizations: A Test of the Homogeneity of Personality Hypothesis," *Journal of Applied Psychology* 83, no. 3 (1998):

462–70; T.R. Giberson, C.J. Resick, and M.W. Dickson, "Embedding Leader Characteristics: An Examination of Homogeneity of Personality and Values in Organizations," *Journal of Applied Psychology* 90, no. 5 (2005): 1002–10.

67. T.A. Judge and D.M. Cable, "Applicant Personality, Organizational Culture, and Organization Attraction," *Personnel Psychology* 50, no. 2 (1997): 359–94; D.S. Chapman et al., "Applicant Attraction to Organizations and Job Choice: A Meta-Analytic Review of the Correlates of Recruiting Outcomes," *Journal of Applied Psychology* 90, no. 5 (2005): 928–44; A.L. Kristof-Brown, R.D. Zimmerman, and E.C. Johnson, "Consequences of Individuals' Fit at Work: A Meta-Analysis of Person–Job, Person–Organization, Person–Group, and Person–Supervisor Fit," *Personnel Psychology* 58, no. 2 (2005): 281–342; C. Hu, H.-C. Su, and C.-I.B. Chen, "The Effect of Person–Organization Fit Feedback Via Recruitment Web Sites on Applicant Attraction," *Computers in Human Behavior* 23, no. 5 (2007): 2509–23.

68. A. Kristof-Brown, "Perceived Applicant Fit: Distinguishing between Recruiters' Perceptions of Person–Job and Person–Organization Fit," *Personnel Psychology* 53, no. 3 (2000): 643–71; A.E.M. Van Vianen, "Person–Organization Fit: The Match between Newcomers' and Recruiters' Preferences for Organizational Cultures," *Personnel Psychology* 53 (2000): 113–49.

69. E. Keating, "'Leadership Is Not Genetics': How Ikea Australia's National Talent Manager D'neale Prosser Puts Authentic Leadership into Practice," *SmartCompany,* March 8, 2018; "'We Believe That Your Values Are More Important than Your CV,'" *Human Resources Director Australia,* April 11, 2018.

70. D.M. Cable and J.R. Edwards, "Complementary and Supplementary Fit: A Theoretical and Empirical Integration," *Journal of Applied Psychology* 89, no. 5 (2004): 822–34.

71. J. Van Maanen, "Breaking In: Socialization to Work," in *Handbook of Work, Organization, and Society,* ed. R. Dubin (Chicago, IL: Rand McNally, 1976).

72. D.G. Allen, "Do Organizational Socialization Tactics Influence Newcomer Embeddedness and Turnover?," *Journal of Management* 32, no. 2 (2006): 237–56; A.M. Saks, K.L. Uggerslev, and N.E. Fassina, "Socialization Tactics and Newcomer Adjustment: A Meta-Analytic Review and Test of a Model," *Journal of Vocational Behavior* 70, no. 3 (2007): 413–46.

73. S.L. McShane, G. O'Neill, and T. Travaglione, "Managing Employee Values in Values-Driven Organizations: Contradiction, Façade, and Illusions" (paper presented at the 21st Annual ANZAM Conference, Sydney, Australia, December 2007); S.L. McShane, G. O'Neill, and T. Travaglione, "Rethinking the Values-Driven Organization Process: From Values Engineering to Behavioral Domain Training," in *Academy of Management 2008 Annual Meeting* (Anaheim, CA: 2008).

74. G.T. Chao et al., "Organizational Socialization: Its Content and Consequences," *Journal of Applied Psychology* 79 (1994): 450–63; H.D. Cooper-Thomas and N. Anderson, "Organizational Socialization: A Field Study into Socialization Success and Rate," *International Journal of Selection and Assessment* 13, no. 2 (2005): 116–28.

75. N. Nicholson, "A Theory of Work Role Transitions," *Administrative Science Quarterly* 29 (1984): 172–91; A. Elfering et al., "First Years in Job: A Three-Wave Analysis of Work Experiences," *Journal of Vocational Behavior* 70, no. 1 (2007): 97–115; B.E. Ashforth, D.M. Sluss, and A.M. Saks, "Socialization Tactics, Proactive Behavior, and Newcomer Learning: Integrating Socialization Models," *Journal of Vocational Behavior* 70, no. 3 (2007): 447–62; T.N. Bauer, "Newcomer Adjustment During Organizational Socialization: A Meta-Analytic Review of Antecedents, Outcomes, and Methods," *Journal of Applied Psychology* 92, no. 3 (2007): 707–21.

76. J.M. Beyer and D.R. Hannah, "Building on the Past: Enacting Established Personal Identities in a New Work Setting," *Organization Science* 13 (2002): 636–52; H.D.C. Thomas and N. Anderson, "Newcomer Adjustment: The Relationship between Organizational Socialization Tactics, Information Acquisition and Attitudes," *Journal of Occupational and Organizational Psychology* 75 (2002): 423–37.

77. S.L. Robinson and E. Wolfe Morrison, "The Development of Psychological Contract Breach and Violation: A Longitudinal Study," *Journal of Organizational Behavior* 21 (2000): 525–46; K.J. McInnis, J.P. Meyer, and S. Feldman, "Psychological Contracts and Their Implications for Commitment: A Feature-Based Approach," *Journal of Vocational Behavior* 74 (2009): 165–80; C.-M. Alcover et al., "Understanding the Changing Nature of Psychological Contracts in 21st Century Organizations: A Multiple-Foci Exchange Relationships Approach and Proposed Framework," *Organizational Psychology Review* 7 (2017): 4–35.

78. S.L. Robinson and D.M. Rousseau, "Violating the Psychological Contract: Not the Exception but the Norm," *Journal of Organizational Behavior* 15 (1994): 245–59; E.W. Morrison and S.L. Robinson, "When Employees Feel Betrayed: A Model of How Psychological Contract Violation Develops," *Academy of Management Review* 22 (1997): 226–56; S.D. Montes and P.G. Irving, "Disentangling the Effects of Promised and Delivered Inducements: Relational and Transactional Contract Elements and the Mediating Role of Trust," *Journal of Applied Psychology* 93, no. 6 (2008): 1367–81.

79. S. Persson and D. Wasieleski, "The Seasons of the Psychological Contract: Overcoming the Silent Transformations of the Employer–Employee Relationship," *Human Resource Management Review* 25, no. 4 (2015): 368–83.

80. L.W. Porter, E.E. Lawler III, and J.R. Hackman, *Behavior in Organizations* (New York: McGraw Hill, 1975), pp. 163–67; Van Maanen, "Breaking In: Socialization to Work," pp. 67–130; D.C. Feldman, "The Multiple Socialization of Organization Members," *Academy of Management Review* 6 (1981): 309–18.

81. B.E. Ashforth and A.M. Saks, "Socialization Tactics: Longitudinal Effects on Newcomer Adjustment," *Academy of Management Journal* 39 (1996): 149–78; J.D. Kammeyer-Mueller and C.R. Wanberg, "Unwrapping the Organizational Entry Process: Disentangling Multiple Antecedents and Their Pathways to Adjustment," *Journal of Applied Psychology* 88 (2003): 779–94.

82. L. W. Porter, E. E. Lawler III, and J. R. Hackman, *Behavior in Organizations* (New York: McGraw Hill, 1975), chap. 5

83. M.R. Louis, "Surprise and Sensemaking: What Newcomers Experience in Entering Unfamiliar Organizational Settings," *Administrative Science Quarterly* 25 (1980): 226–51.

84. S.L. Robinson and D.M. Rousseau, "Violating the Psychological Contract: Not the Exception but the Norm," *Journal of Organizational Behavior* 15 (1994): 245–59.

85. D.L. Nelson, "Organizational Socialization: A Stress Perspective," *Journal of Occupational Behavior* 8 (1987): 311–24; A. Elfering et al., "First Years in Job: A Three-Wave Analysis of Work Experiences," *Journal of Vocational Behavior* 70 (2007): 97–115; C.-M. Alcover et al., "Understanding the Changing Nature of Psychological Contracts in 21st Century Organizations: A Multiple-Foci Exchange Relationships Approach and Proposed Framework," *Organizational Psychology Review* 7, no. 1 (2017): 4–35.

86. J.P. Wanous, *Organizational Entry* (Reading, MA: Addison-Wesley, 1992); J.A. Breaugh and M. Starke, "Research on Employee Recruitment: So Many Studies, So Many Remaining Questions," *Journal of Management* 26 (2000): 405–34.

87. J.M. Phillips, "Effects of Realistic Job Previews on Multiple Organizational Outcomes: A Meta-Analysis," *Academy of Management Journal* 41 (1998): 673–90.

88. Y. Ganzach et al., "Social Exchange and Organizational Commitment: Decision-Making Training for Job Choice as an Alternative to the Realistic Job Preview," *Personnel Psychology* 55 (2002): 613–37.

89. J. Rosenberg, "Companies Transform Cultures as They Compete for Staffers," *AP News,* December 19, 2018.

90. C. Ostroff and S.W.J. Koslowski, "Organizational Socialization as a Learning Process: The Role of Information Acquisition," *Personnel Psychology* 45 (1992): 849–74; H.D. Cooper-Thomas and N. Anderson, "Organizational Socialization: A Field Study into Socialization Success and Rate," *International Journal of Selection and Assessment* 13, no. 2 (2005): 116–28; S. Nifadkar and T. Bauer, "Breach of Belongingness: Newcomer Relationship Conflict, Information, and Task-Related Outcomes during Organizational Socialization," *Journal of Applied Psychology* 101, no. 1 (2016): 1–13.

91. S. Nifadkar, A.S. Tsui, and B.E. Ashforth, "The Way You Make Me Feel and Behave: Supervisor-Triggered Newcomer Affect and Approach-Avoidance Behavior," *Academy of Management Journal* 55, no. 5 (2012): 1146–68.

92. N. Davies, "5 Secrets Of Onboarding 100% Remote Workers Revealed By Hiring Experts And Leaders," *Forbes,* November 6, 2019.

CHAPTER 15

1. "Case Study: Blueshore Financial and Its Epic Brand Transformation" (Seattle, Wash.: Weber Marketing Group, March 2014); J. O'Kane, "Should Bank Branches Be More Like Spas? This Man Thinks So," *Globe & Mail,* April 12, 2016; T. Wanless, "Credit Union Evolves to Meet Needs of Its Affluent Members," *Vancouver Sun,* July 4, 2016, N6; "BlueShore Financial's Chris Catliff Honoured with BC CEO Award," News Release (North Vancouver: BlueShore Financial, October

11, 2017); "BlueShore Financial Named One of Canada's Best Employers for Nine Consecutive Years," News Release (North Vancouver: BlueShore Financial, September 17, 2019); C. Catliff, "Strategies for Developing Your Inner Intrapreneur," *Globe & Mail,* November 8, 2019; Jostle, "Culture Hero Series: Chris Catliff, BlueShore Financial," *The Jostle Blog* (blog), accessed April 3, 2020, https://blog.jostle.me/blog/culture-hero-series-chris-catliff-north-shore-credit-union/.

2. J. Welch, *Jack: Straight from the Heart* (New York: Warner Business books, 2001), pg. 432.

3. K. Lewin, *Field Theory in Social Science* (New York: Harper & Row, 1951).

4. D. Coghlan and T. Brannick, "Kurt Lewin: The 'Practical Theorist' for the 21st Century," *Irish Journal of Management* 24, no. 2 (2003): 31–37; B. Burnes, "Kurt Lewin and the Planned Approach to Change: A Re-Appraisal," *Journal of Management Studies* 41, no. 6 (2004): 977–1002.

5. M. Young, *Ogilvy on Advertising in the Digital Age* (London: Goodman Books, 2017), pg. 267. For details about the likely origins of "divine discontent," see the annotation/reference near the end of the "Identifying Problems and Opportunities" section in Chapter 7 (Decision Making and Creativity) of this book.

6. J. Mouawad, "Largest Airline Has Bigger Troubles," *International Herald Tribune,* November 30, 2012, 14; M. Mecham, "Not Yet United," *Overhaul & Maintenance,* April 2012, 46; M. Brownell, "Here's Why United Was Just Named America's Worst Airline," *Daily Finance,* June 18, 2013; D. Bennett, "United's Quest to Be Less Awful," *Bloomberg Businessweek,* January 14, 2016.

7. Some experts suggest that resistance to change should be restated in a more positive way by its opposite: readiness for change. See: M. Choi and W.E.A. Ruona, "Individual Readiness for Organizational Change and Its Implications for Human Resource and Organization Development," *Human Resource Development Review* 10, no. 1 (2011): 46–73.

8. S. Chreim, "Postscript to Change: Survivors' Retrospective Views of Organizational Changes," *Personnel Review* 35, no. 3 (2006): 315–35.

9. J.K. Galbraith, *Economics, Peace, and Laughter* (Boston, MA: Houghton Mifflin, 1971), pg. 50.

10. E.B. Dent and S.G. Goldberg, "Challenging 'Resistance to Change,'" *Journal of Applied Behavioral Science* 35 (1999): 25–41; D.B. Fedor, S. Caldwell, and D.M. Herold, "The Effects of Organizational Changes on Employee Commitment: A Multilevel Investigation," *Personnel Psychology* 59, no. 1 (2006): 1–29.

11. B.J. Tepper et al., "Subordinates' Resistance and Managers' Evaluations of Subordinates' Performance," *Journal of Management* 32, no. 2 (2006): 185–209; J.D. Ford, L.W. Ford, and A. D'Amelio, "Resistance to Change: The Rest of the Story," *Academy of Management Review* 33, no. 2 (2008): 362–77.

12. D.A. Nadler, "The Effective Management of Organizational Change," in *Handbook of Organizational Behavior,* ed. J.W. Lorsch (Englewood Cliffs, NJ: Prentice Hall, 1987), 358–69; R. Maurer, *Beyond the Wall of Resistance: Unconventional Strategies to Build Support for Change*(Austin, TX: Bard Books, 1996); P. Strebel,

"Why Do Employees Resist Change?," *Harvard Business Review* (1996): 86–92; D.A. Nadler, *Champions of Change*(San Francisco: Jossey-Bass, 1998).

13. S. Oreg et al., "Dispositional Resistance to Change: Measurement Equivalence and the Link to Personal Values across 17 Nations," *Journal of Applied Psychology* 93, no. 4 (2008): 935–44.

14. R.R. Sharma, *Change Management: Concepts and Applications* (New Delhi: Tata McGraw Hill, 2007), Chap. 4; I. Cinite, L.E. Duxbury, and C. Higgins, "Measurement of Perceived Organizational Readiness for Change in the Public Sector," *British Journal of Management* 20, no. 2 (2009): 265–77; A.A. Armenakis and S.G. Harris, "Reflections: Our Journey in Organizational Change Research and Practice," *Journal of Change Management* 9, no. 2 (2009): 127–42; S. Jaros, "Commitment to Organizational Change: A Critical Review," *Journal of Change Management* 10, no. 1 (2010): 79–108.

15. D.T. Holt et al., "Readiness for Organizational Change: The Systematic Development of a Scale," *Journal of Applied Behavioral Science* 43, no. 2 (2007): 232–55; G. Bohner and N. Dickel, "Attitudes and Attitude Change," *Annual Review of Psychology* 62, no. 1 (2011): 391–417; A.M. García-Cabrera and F. García-Barba Hernández, "Differentiating the Three Components of Resistance to Change: The Moderating Effect of Organization-Based Self-Esteem on the Employee Involvement-Resistance Relation," *Human Resource Development Quarterly* 25, no. 4 (2014): 441–69.

16. R. de la Sablonnière et al., "Profound Organizational Change, Psychological Distress and Burnout Symptoms: The Mediator Role of Collective Relative Deprivation," *Group Processes & Intergroup Relations* 15, no. 6 (2012): 776–90.

17. W. Samuelson and R. Zeckhauser, "Status Quo Bias in Decision Making," *Journal of Risk and Uncertainty* 1 (1988): 7–59; D. Proudfoot and A.C. Kay, "System Justification in Organizational Contexts: How a Motivated Preference for the Status Quo Can Affect Organizational Attitudes and Behaviors," *Research in Organizational Behavior* 34 (2014): 173–87; K. Lee and K. Joshi, "Examining the Use of Status Quo Bias Perspective in IS Research: Need for Re-Conceptualizing and Incorporating Biases," *Information Systems Journal* 27 (2017): 733–52; B.H. Martin, "Unsticking the Status Quo: Strategic Framing Effects on Managerial Mindset, Status Quo Bias and Systematic Resistance to Change," *Management Research Review* 40 (2017): 122–41; S. Nicholson-Crotty, J. Nicholson-Crotty, and S. Webeck, "Are Public Managers More Risk Averse? Framing Effects and Status Quo Bias across the Sectors," *Journal of Behavioral Public Administration* 2 (2019), https://doi.org/10.30636/jbpa.21.3.

18. D. Grosse Kathoefer and J. Leker, "Knowledge Transfer in Academia: An Exploratory Study on the Not-Invented-Here Syndrome," *Journal of Technology Transfer* 37, no. 5 (2012): 658–75; A.L.A. Burcharth, M.P. Knudsen, and H.A. Søndergaard, "Neither Invented nor Shared Here: The Impact and Management of Attitudes for the Adoption of Open Innovation Practices," *Technovation* 34, no. 3 (2014): 149–61.

19. V. Newman, "The Psychology of Managing for Innovation," *KM Review* 9, no. 6 (2007): 10–15.

20. L. Brody and D. Raffa, *Everything I Need to Know About Business. . .I Learned from a Canadian,* 2nd ed. (Mississauga, ON: John Wiley & Sons Canada, 2009), pp. 201–02.

21. R. Davis, *Leading for Growth: How Umpqua Bank Got Cool and Created a Culture of Greatness* (San Francisco, CA: Jossey-Bass, 2007), pg. 40. Ray Davis also famously pointed out that "change is changing," meaning that the nature and type of change continuously evolves, so leaders need to adapt to new futures. See: S. Gotz, "Ray's List (or What I Learned Working for the CEO of the World's Greatest Bank)," *LinkedIn Pulse* (blog), February 9, 2020, https://www.linkedin.com/pulse/rays-list-what-i-learned-working-ceo-worlds-greatest-bank-steve-gotz.

22. J.P. Kotter, *A Sense of Urgency* (Boston: Harvard Business School Press, 2008); S.H. Appelbaum et al., "Back to the Future: Revisiting Kotter's 1996 Change Model," *Journal of Management Development* 31, no. 8 (2012): 764–82.

23. L.D. Goodstein and H.R. Butz, "Customer Value: The Linchpin of Organizational Change," *Organizational Dynamics* 27 (1998): 21–35.

24. D. Miller, *The Icarus Paradox: How Exceptional Companies Bring About Their Own Downfall* (New York: HarperBusiness, 1990); S. Finkelstein, *Why Smart Executives Fail* (New York: Viking, 2003); A.C. Amason and A.C. Mooney, "The Icarus Paradox Revisited: How Strong Performance Sows the Seeds of Dysfunction in Future Strategic Decision-Making," *Strategic Organization* 6, no. 4 (2008): 407–34. Richard Goyder's quotation is from: "Sustaining High Performance (Richard Goyder: Wesfarmers)," *CEOForum,* September 2006.

25. T.F. Cawsey and G. Deszca, *Toolkit for Organizational Change* (Los Angeles, CA: Sage, 2007), p. 104.

26. J.P. Kotter and L.A. Schlesinger, "Choosing Strategies for Change," *Harvard Business Review* (1979): 106–14.

27. M. Meaney and C. Pung, "Creating Organizational Transformations: Mckinsey Global Survey Results," *McKinsey Quarterly,* July 2008, 1–7; A.E. Rafferty, N.L. Jimmieson, and A.A. Armenakis, "Change Readiness: A Multilevel Review," *Journal of Management* 39, no. 1 (2013): 110–35.

28. J.P. Kotter and D.S. Cohen, *The Heart of Change* (Boston, MA: Harvard Business School Press, 2002), pp. 83–98; J. Allen et al., "Uncertainty During Organizational Change: Managing Perceptions through Communication," *Journal of Change Management* 7, no. 2 (2007): 187–210; T.L. Russ, "Communicating Change: A Review and Critical Analysis of Programmatic and Participatory Implementation Approaches," *Journal of Change Management* 8, no. 3 (2008): 199 – 211; M. van den Heuvel et al., "Adapting to Change: The Value of Change Information and Meaning-Making," *Journal of Vocational Behavior* 83, no. 1 (2013): 11–21.

29. Jostle, "Culture Hero Series: Chris Catliff, Blueshore Financial," *The Jostle Blog,* October 30, 2013, http://blog.jostle.me/blog/culture-hero-series-chris-catliff-north-shore-credit-union.

30. D.M. Herold and S.D. Caldwell, "Beyond Change Management: A Multilevel Investigation of Contextual and Personal Influences on Employees' Commitment to Change," *Journal of Applied*

Psychology 92, no. 4 (2007): 942–51; D.T. Holt and J.M. Vardaman, "Toward a Comprehensive Understanding of Readiness for Change: The Case for an Expanded Conceptualization," *Journal of Change Management* 13, no. 1 (2013): 9–18.

31. K.T. Dirks, L.L. Cummings, and J.L. Pierce, "Psychological Ownership in Organizations: Conditions under Which Individuals Promote and Resist Change," *Research in Organizational Change and Development* 9 (1996): 1–23; E.A. Lofquist, "Doomed to Fail: A Case Study of Change Implementation Collapse in the Norwegian Civil Aviation Industry," *Journal of Change Management* 11 (2011): 223–43; L.K. Lewis and T.L. Russ, "Soliciting and Using Input During Organizational Change Initiatives: What Are Practitioners Doing," *Management Communication Quarterly* 26 (2012): 267–94.

32. S.G. Bamberger et al., "Impact of Organisational Change on Mental Health: A Systematic Review," *Occupational and Environmental Medicine* 69, no. 8 (2012): 592–98.

33. N.T. Tan, "Maximising Human Resource Potential in the Midst of Organisational Change," *Singapore Management Review* 27, no. 2 (2005): 25–35; A.E. Rafferty and S.L.D. Restubog, "The Impact of Change Process and Context on Change Reactions and Turnover During a Merger," *Journal of Management* 36, no. 5 (2010): 1309–38.

34. M. McHugh, "The Stress Factor: Another Item for the Change Management Agenda?," *Journal of Organizational Change Management* 10 (1997): 345–62; D. Buchanan, T. Claydon, and M. Doyle, "Organisation Development and Change: The Legacy of the Nineties," *Human Resource Management Journal* 9 (1999): 20–37.

35. T. Wakefield, "No Pain, No Gain," *Canadian Business,* January 1993, 50–54; M. Cash, "New Owner for StandardAero," *Winnipeg Free Press,* 27 May 2015.

36. J.P. Hausknecht and J.A. Holwerda, "When Does Employee Turnover Matter? Dynamic Member Configurations, Productive Capacity, and Collective Performance," *Organization Science* 24, no. 1 (2013): 210–25.

37. E.E. Lawler III, "Pay Can Be a Change Agent," *Compensation & Benefits Management* 16 (2000): 23–26; Kotter and Cohen, *The Heart of Change* pp. 161–77; M.A. Roberto and L.C. Levesque, "The Art of Making Change Initiatives Stick," *MIT Sloan Management Review* 46, no. 4 (2005): 53–60.

38. Goodstein and Butz, "Customer Value: The Linchpin of Organizational Change; R.H. Miles, "Leading Corporate Transformation: Are You up to the Task?," in *The Leader's Change Handbook* ed. J.A. Conger, G.M. Spreitzer, and E.E. Lawler III (San Francisco, CA: Jossey-Bass, 1999), 221–67.

39. R.E. Quinn, *Building the Bridge as You Walk on It: A Guide for Leading Change* (San Francisco: Jossey-Bass, 2004), Chap. 11; S. Oreg and Y. Berson, "Leaders' Impact on Organizational Change: Bridging Theoretical and Methodological Chasms," *Academy of Management Annals* 13 (2019): 272–307.

40. M.S. Cole, S.G. Harris, and J.B. Bernerth, "Exploring the Implications of Vision, Appropriateness, and Execution of Organizational Change," *Leadership & Organization Development Journal* 27, no. 5 (2006): 352–67; S. Kirkpatrick, "Leading through Vision and Values," in *Handbook*

of Principles of Organizational Behavior: Indispensable Knowledge for Evidence-Based Management, ed. E. Locke (Hoboken: Wiley, 2010), 367–87; V. Lundy and P.-P. Morin, "Project Leadership Influences Resistance to Change: The Case of the Canadian Public Service," *Project Management Journal* 44, no. 4 (2013): 45–64.

41. J.P. Kotter and D.S. Cohen, *The Heart of Change* (Boston: Harvard Business School Press, 2002), 61–82; D.S. Cohen and J.P. Kotter, *The Heart of Change Field Guide* (Boston: Harvard Business School Press, 2005).

42. J.P. Kotter, "Leading Change: Why Transformation Efforts Fail," *Harvard Business Review* (1995): 59–67.

43. J.B. Cunningham and S.K. James, "Implementing Change in Public Sector Organizations," *Management Decision* 47, no. 2 (2009): 330.

44. A. De Bruyn and G.L. Lilien, "A Multi-Stage Model of Word-of-Mouth Influence through Viral Marketing," *International Journal of Research in Marketing* 25, no. 3 (2008): 151–63; J.Y.C. Ho and M. Dempsey, "Viral Marketing: Motivations to Forward Online Content," *Journal of Business Research* 63, no. 9–10 (2010): 1000–06; M. Williams and F. Buttle, "The Eight Pillars of Wom Management: Lessons from a Multiple Case Study," *Australasian Marketing Journal (AMJ)* 19, no. 2 (2011): 85–92.

45. L. Herrero, *Homo Imitans* (Beaconsfield Bucks, UK: meetingminds, 2011).

46. M. Beer, R.A. Eisenstat, and B. Spector, *The Critical Path to Corporate Renewal* (Boston, MA: Harvard Business School Press, 1990).

47. Beer, Eisenstat, and Spector, *The Critical Path to Corporate Renewal* Chap. 5; R.E. Walton, "Successful Strategies for Diffusing Work Innovations," *Journal of Contemporary Business* (1977): 1–22; R.E. Walton, *Innovating to Compete: Lessons for Diffusing and Managing Change in the Workplace* (San Francisco, CA: Jossey-Bass, 1987).

48. E.M. Rogers, *Diffusion of Innovations,* Fourth ed. (New York, NY: Free Press, 1995).

49. P. Reason and H. Bradbury, *Handbook of Action Research,* (London, UK: Sage, 2001); Coghlan and Brannick, "Kurt Lewin: The 'Practical Theorist' for the 21st Century; C. Huxham and S. Vangen, "Researching Organizational Practice through Action Research: Case Studies and Design Choices," *Organizational Research Methods* 6 (2003): 383–403.

50. V.J. Marsick and M.A. Gephart, "Action Research: Building the Capacity for Learning and Change," *Human Resource Planning* 26 (2003): 14–18.

51. L. Dickens and K. Watkins, "Action Research: Rethinking Lewin," *Management Learning* 30 (1999): 127–40; J. Heron and P. Reason, "The Practice of Co-Operative Inquiry: Research 'with' Rather Than 'on' People," in *Handbook of Action Research,* ed. P. Reason and H. Bradbury (Thousand Oaks, CA: Sage, 2001), 179–88.

52. D.A. Nadler, "Organizational Frame Bending: Types of Change in the Complex Organization," in *Corporate Transformation: Revitalizing Organizations for a Competitive World,* ed. R.H. Kilmann, T.J. Covin, and a. Associates (San Francisco, CA: Jossey-Bass, 1988), 66–83; K.E. Weick and R.E. Quinn, "Organizational Change and

Development," *Annual Review of Psychology* 50 (1999): 361–86.

53. T.M. Egan and C.M. Lancaster, "Comparing Appreciative Inquiry to Action Research: OD Practitioner Perspectives," *Organization Development Journal* 23, no. 2 (2005): 29–49.

54. N. Turner, J. Barling, and A. Zacharatos, "Positive Psychology at Work," in *Handbook of Positive Psychology,* ed. C.R. Snyder and S. Lopez (Oxford, UK: Oxford University Press, 2002), 715–30; K. Cameron, J.E. Dutton, and R.E. Quinn, eds., *Positive Organizational Scholarship: Foundation of a New Discipline* (San Francisco: Berrett-Koehler, 2003); S.L. Gable and J. Haidt, "What (and Why) Is Positive Psychology?," *Review of General Psychology* 9, (2005): 103–10; M.E.P. Seligman et al., "Positive Psychology Progress: Empirical Validation of Interventions," *American Psychologist* 60 (2005): 410–21. On the origins of appreciative inquiry, see: G.R. Bushe, "Foundations of Appreciative Inquiry: History, Criticism and Potential," *AI Practitioner* 14 (February 2012): 8–20.

55. D.K. Whitney and D.L. Cooperrider, "The Appreciative Inquiry Summit: Overview and Applications," *Employment Relations Today* 25 (1998): 17–28; J.M. Watkins and B.J. Mohr, *Appreciative Inquiry: Change at the Speed of Imagination* (San Francisco, CA: Jossey-Bass, 2001).

56. D. Meinert, "Positive Momentum," *HRMagazine* 58, no. 6 (2013): 68–74.

57. D.L. Cooperrider and D.K. Whitney, *Appreciative Inquiry: A Positive Revolution in Change* (San Francisco, CA: Berrett-Koehler, 2005). Recent writing has extended this list to eight principles. see: D.K. Whitney and A. Trosten-Bloom, *The Power of Appreciative Inquiry: A Practical Guide to Positive Change,* 2nd ed. (San Francisco, CA: Berrett-Koehler Publishers, 2010).

58. F.J. Barrett and D.L. Cooperrider, "Generative Metaphor Intervention: A New Approach for Working with Systems Divided by Conflict and Caught in Defensive Perception," *Journal of Applied Behavioral Science* 26 (1990): 219–39; D.K. Whitney and D.L. Cooperrider, "The Appreciative Inquiry Summit: Overview and Applications," *Employment Relations Today* 25 (1998): 17–28; J.M. Watkins and B.J. Mohr, *Appreciative Inquiry: Change at the Speed of Imagination* (San Francisco: Jossey-Bass, 2001), 15–21.

59. S. Berrisford, "Using Appreciative Inquiry to Drive Change at the BBC," *Strategic Communication Management* 9 (2005):22–25; G.R. Bushe, "A Comparative Case Study of Appreciative Inquiries in One Organization: Implications for Practice," *Review of Research and Social Intervention* 29 (2010): 7–24; "2013-2015 Massachusetts Joint Statewide Three-Year Electric & Gas Energy Efficiency Plan" (State of Massachusetts, July 2, 2012; Z. Pedersen, "Using Appreciative Inquiry to Focus on Positives, Transform Workplace Culture," *Canadian HR Reporter,* 13 August 2012, 10–12; M.K. McCarthy, M.J. McNally, and K. Sabo, "Toronto Western Hospital Positive Leadership Program: Creating a Culture of Excellence," in *National Health Leadership Conference* (Niagara Falls, ON: Canadian College of Health Leaders, 2013); T. Wall, J. Russell, and N. Moore, "Positive Emotion in Workplace Impact: The Case of a Work-Based

Learning Project Utilising Appreciative Inquiry," *Journal of Work-Applied Management* 9, no. 2 (2017): 129–46; L. Hung et al., "Appreciative Inquiry: Bridging Research and Practice in a Hospital Setting," *International Journal of Qualitative Methods* 17, no. 1 (2018): 1–17; A. Scerri, A. Innes, and C. Scerri, "Using Appreciative Inquiry to Implement Person-Centred Dementia Care in Hospital Wards," *Dementia* 18, no. 1 (2019): 190–209; P. Krouse and M. Kilpatrick, "Cleveland Rising Aspires to Greatness, Needs a Way Forward," *Cleveland.Com,* October 31, 2019.

60. G.R. Bushe, "Five Theories of Change Embedded in Appreciative Inquiry" (paper presented at the 18th Annual World Congress of Organization Development, Dublin, Ireland, July 14–18, 1998); T.F. Yaeger, P.F. Sorensen, and U. Bengtsson, "Assessment of the State of Appreciative Inquiry: Past, Present, and Future," *Research in Organizational Change and Development* 15 (2004): 297–319; G.R. Bushe and A.F. Kassam, "When Is Appreciative Inquiry Transformational? A Meta-Case Analysis," *Journal of Applied Behavioral Science* 41 (2005): 161–81.

61. J.M. Bartunek, J. Balogun, and B. Do, "Considering Planned Change Anew: Stretching Large Group Interventions Strategically, Emotionally, and Meaningfully," *Academy of Management Annals* 5, no. 1 (2011): 1–52.

62. M. Weisbord and S. Janoff, *Future Search: An Action Guide to Finding Common Ground in Organizations and Communities* (San Francisco, CA: Berrett-Koehler, 2000); R.M. Lent, M.T. McCormick, and D.S. Pearce, "Combining Future Search and Open Space to Address Special Situations," *Journal of Applied Behavioral Science* 41, no. 1 (2005): 61–69; S. Janoff and M. Weisbord, "Future Search as 'Real-Time' Action Research," *Futures* 38, no. 6 (2006): 716–22.

63. For a critique of future search conferences and similar whole-system events, see A. Oels, "Investigating the Emotional Roller-Coaster Ride: A Case Study-Based Assessment of the Future Search Conference Design," *Systems Research and Behavioral Science* 19 (2002): 347–55; M.F.D. Polanyi, "Communicative Action in Practice: Future Search and the Pursuit of an Open, Critical and Non-Coercive Large-Group Process," *Systems Research and Behavioral Science* 19 (2002): 357–66; A. De Grassi, "Envisioning Futures of African Agriculture: Representation, Power, and Socially Constituted Time," *Progress in Development Studies* 7, no. 2 (2007): 79–98.

64. G.R. Bushe and A.B. Shani, *Parallel Learning Structures* (Reading, MA: Addison-Wesley, 1991); E.M. Van Aken, D.J. Monetta, and D.S. Sink, "Affinity Groups: The Missing Link in Employee Involvement," *Organization Dynamics* 22 (1994): 38–54.

65. D.J. Knight, "Strategy in Practice: Making It Happen," *Strategy & Leadership* 26 (1998): 29–33; R.T. Pascale, "Grassroots Leadership – Royal Dutch/ Shell," *Fast Company,* no. 14 (1998): 110–20; R.T. Pascale, "Leading from a Different Place," in *The Leader's Change Handbook* ed. J.A. Conger, G.M. Spreitzer, and E.E. Lawler III (San Francisco, CA: Jossey-Bass, 1999), 301–20; R. Pascale, M. Millemann, and L. Gioja, *Surfing on the Edge of Chaos* (London, UK: Texere, 2000).

66. T.C. Head and P.F. Sorenson, "Cultural Values and Organizational Development: A Seven-Country Study," *Leadership and Organization Development Journal* 14 (1993): 3–7; R.J. Marshak, "Lewin Meets Confucius: A Review of the OD Model of Change," *Journal of Applied Behavioral Science* 29 (1993): 395–415; C.-M. Lau, "A Culture-Based Perspective of Organization Development Implementation," *Research in Organizational Change and Development* 9 (1996): 49–79; C.M. Lau and H.Y. Ngo, "Organization Development and Firm Performance: A Comparison of Multinational and Local Firms," *Journal Of International Business Studies* 32, no. 1 (2001): 95–114.

67. M. McKendall, "The Tyranny of Change: Organizational Development Revisited," *Journal of Business Ethics* 12 (1993): 93–104; C.M.D. Deaner, "A Model of Organization Development Ethics," *Public Administration Quarterly* 17 (1994): 435–46.

68. G.A. Walter, "Organization Development and Individual Rights," *Journal of Applied Behavioral Science* 20 (1984): 423–39.

69. The source of this often-cited quotation was not found. It does not appear, even in other variations, in the books that Andrew Carnegie wrote (such as *Gospel of Wealth,* 1900; *Empire of Business,* 1902; and *Autobiography,* 1920). However, Carnegie may have stated these words (or similar ones) elsewhere. He gave many speeches and wrote numerous articles, parts of which have been reported by other authors.

APPENDIX

1. F.N. Kerlinger, *Foundations of Behavioral Research* (New York: Holt, Rinehart, & Winston, 1964), 11.

2. J.B. Miner, *Theories of Organizational Behavior* (Hinsdale, IL.: Dryden, 1980), 7–9.

3. Ibid., 6–7.

4. J. Mason, *Qualitative Researching* (London, UK: Sage, 1996).

5. A. Strauss and J. Corbin (eds.), *Grounded Theory in Practice* (London, UK: Sage Publications, 1997); B.G. Glaser and A. Strauss. *The Discovery of Grounded Theory: Strategies for Qualitative Research* (Chicago, IL: Aldine Publishing Co, 1967).

6. Kerlinger, *Foundations of Behavioral Research,* 13.

7. A. Strauss and J. Corbin (eds.), *Grounded Theory in Practice* (London, UK: Sage Publications, 1997); B.G. Glaser and A. Strauss. *The Discovery of Grounded Theory: Strategies for Qualitative Research* (Chicago, IL: Aldine Publishing Co, 1967).

8. W.A. Hall and P. Callery, "Enhancing the Rigor of Grounded Theory: Incorporating Reflexivity and Relationality," *Qualitative Health Research,* 11 (March 2001), 257–72.

9. P. Lazarsfeld, *Survey Design and Analysis* (New York: The Free Press, 1955).

10. This example is cited in D.W. Organ and T.S. Bateman, *Organizational Behavior,* 4th ed. (Homewood, IL.: Irwin, 1991), 42.

11. Ibid., p. 45.

12. R.I. Sutton and A. Hargadon, "Brainstorming Groups in Context: Effectiveness in a Product Design Firm," *Administrative Science Quarterly* 41 (1996), 685–718.

Index